THE VICTORIA HISTORY
OF THE
COUNTIES OF ENGLAND

A HISTORY OF
SUSSEX

VOLUME V

PART I

Oxford University Press, Great Clarendon Street, Oxford OX2 6DP
Oxford New York
Athens Auckland Bangkok Bogota Bombay
Buenos Aires Calcutta Cape Town Dar es Salaam
Delhi Florence Hong Kong Istanbul Karachi
Kuala Lumpur Madras Madrid Melbourne
Mexico City Nairobi Paris Singapore
Taipei Tokyo Toronto Warsaw

and associated companies in
Berlin Ibadan

Published in the United States
by Oxford University Press Inc., New York

British Library Cataloguing in Publication Data
Data available
Library of Congress Cataloging in Publication Data

ISBN 0 19 722781 3

Typeset by Julie Geoghegan
at the Institute of Historical Research
Printed by H Charlesworth &Co Ltd
Huddersfield, England

ARUNDEL: THE CATHEDRAL IN 1966
from the north-west,
with the St. Mary's Gate inn in the foreground

THE VICTORIA HISTORY OF THE COUNTIES OF ENGLAND

EDITED BY C. R. J. CURRIE

THE UNIVERSITY OF LONDON
INSTITUTE OF
HISTORICAL RESEARCH

INSCRIBED TO THE

MEMORY OF HER LATE MAJESTY

QUEEN VICTORIA

WHO GRACIOUSLY GAVE THE TITLE TO

AND ACCEPTED THE DEDICATION

OF THIS HISTORY

A HISTORY OF THE COUNTY OF SUSSEX

EDITED BY T. P. HUDSON

VOLUME V

PART 1

ARUNDEL RAPE
(SOUTH-WESTERN PART)
INCLUDING ARUNDEL

PUBLISHED FOR
THE INSTITUTE OF HISTORICAL RESEARCH
BY
OXFORD UNIVERSITY PRESS
1997

CONTENTS OF VOLUME FIVE, PART ONE

NOTE. Each parish history is divided into sections. The standard sections are Introduction, Manors and Other Estates, Economic History, Local Government, Church, Nonconformity, Education, and Charities for the Poor.

LIST OF ILLUSTRATIONS

For permission to reproduce copyright material grateful acknowledgement is made to His Grace the Duke of Norfolk, K.G., G.C.V.O., C.B., C.B.E., M.C., the British Library, the Royal Commission on the Historical Monuments of England for material from the National Monuments Record, and the West Sussex County Council for material from the West Sussex Record Office. Unattributed photographs dated 1988–90 are by J. M. H. Bevan and plans dated 1996 are by A. P. Baggs.

LIST OF MAPS

The maps were drawn by K. J. Wass from drafts prepared by Ann Hudson and Monica Maloney. That of Arundel, *c.* 1785, is based on contemporary maps chiefly at Arundel castle by kind permission of His Grace the Duke of Norfolk; that of Barnham, *c.* 1762, on W.S.R.O., Goodwood MS. E4996 by courtesy of the Directors of the Goodwood Estate Co. Ltd.; and that of Middleton, 1606, on W.S.R.O., Add. MS. 2027, f. 31, by permission of the West Sussex County Council. The others are based on Ordnance Survey Maps 6" and 1/2,500 (1879 and later edns.); for information since 1912 Ordnance Survey material was used, Crown Copyright reserved.

EDITORIAL NOTE

THE PRESENT volume, the eleventh to be published of the *Victoria History of the County of Sussex*, deals with the south-western part of the rape of Arundel. The revival of the Sussex *V.C.H.* is described in the Editorial Note to Volume VI, Part 1, published in 1980. The arrangement outlined there by which the West Sussex County Council and the University of London collaborate to produce the *History* of the county has remained unaltered, and the present volume is the fourth to be produced by that partnership. Again the University wishes to record its gratitude to the West Sussex County Council for its generosity.

Many people have given help with the compilation of the histories printed below, and they are all offered sincere thanks. For access to the many libraries, record offices, and collections, both public and private, whose resources have been exploited special acknowledgement is made to His Grace the Duke of Norfolk, K.G., G.C.V.O., C.B., C.B.E., M.C., his Archivist (Miss A. P. Taylor), and his Librarian and Assistant Librarian (Dr. J. M. Robinson and Mrs. Ian Rodger), to successive West Sussex County Archivists (Mrs. P. Gill and Mr. R. Childs) and their staff, to the East Sussex County Records Officer (Mr. C. R. Davey) and his staff, to successive West Sussex County Librarians (Mr. R. Huse and Mr. R. Kirk) and their staff, and to the librarians and staff of the libraries of the Chichester Institute of Higher Education and the Sussex Archaeological Society. Documents in the Goodwood estate archives were used by courtesy of the Directors of the Goodwood Estate Co. Ltd. and with acknowledgements to the West Sussex Record Office and the County Archivist. Those who provided material for illustrations and maps are named on pages viii and x; the Royal Commission on the Historical Monuments of England took numerous photographs specially on request. Those whose assistance related to individual parishes are named in the appropriate footnotes; the West Sussex County Council Archaeological Officer (Mr. M. Taylor) and Mr. T. J. McCann of the West Sussex Record Office gave invaluable help on topics which recur throughout the volume. Mr. J. M. H. Bevan, Miss D. Howell-Thomas, Mrs. A. P. Hudson, Mrs. M. G. Maloney, the late Mr. G. Martin, and the Hon. Susan Spens gave voluntary help with a variety of research and editorial tasks during the compilation of the volume and are offered special thanks. Thanks are also due to all those who allowed access to buildings in their ownership or occupation.

A particular debt is owed to the Employment Service for financial and technical support provided since 1994.

The structure and aims of the *Victoria History* as a whole are described in the *General Introduction*, published in 1970, and its *Supplement*, published in 1990.

LIST OF CLASSES OF DOCUMENTS IN THE PUBLIC RECORD OFFICE

USED IN THIS VOLUME WITH THEIR CLASS NUMBERS

Board of Trade	
BT 31	Files of Dissolved Companies
Chancery	Proceedings
C 2	Series I
C 3	Series II
C 43	Rolls Chapel Series
C 52	Cartae Antiquae Rolls
C 53	Charter Rolls
C 54	Close Rolls
C 60	Fine Rolls
C 66	Patent Rolls
C 78	Decree Rolls
	Commissioners for Charitable Uses
C 90	Confirmations and Exonerations of Decrees
C 91	Depositions
C 93	Inquisitions and Decrees
C 131	Extents for Debts
	Inquisitions post mortem
C 132	Series I, Hen. III
C 133	Edw. I
C 134	Edw. II
C 135	Edw. III
C 136	Ric. II
C 138	Hen. V
C 139	Hen. VI
C 142	Series II
C 143	Inquisitions ad quod damnum
Duchy of Lancaster	
DL 25	Deeds, Series L
Exchequer, King's Remembrancer	
E 106	Extents of Alien Priories
E 122	Customs Accounts
E 126	Decrees and Orders, Entry Books, Series IV
E 134	Depositions taken by Commission
E 178	Special Commissions of Inquiry
E 179	Subsidy Rolls, etc.
E 190	Port Books
E 210	Deeds, Series D
Exchequer, Augmentation Office	
E 309	Enrolments of Leases
E 310	Particulars for Leases
E 311	Counterparts or Transcripts of Leases
E 315	Miscellaneous Books
E 328	Deeds, Series BB
Ministry of Education	
ED 7	Public Elementary Schools, Preliminary Statements
ED 49	Endowment Files, Elementary Schools
Home Office	
HO 107	Population Returns, 1841–51
HO 129	Various Censuses, Ecclesiastical Returns
Board of Inland Revenue	
IR 18	Tithe Files
IR 58	Valuation Office Field Books
Justices Itinerant, Assize and Gaol Delivery Justices, etc.	
JUST 1	Eyre Rolls, Assize Rolls, etc.
Auditors of the Land Revenue	
LR 2	Miscellaneous Books
LR 3	Court Rolls
Ministry of Agriculture, Fisheries, and Food	
MAF 68	Agricultural Returns: Parish Summaries
Maps and Plans	
MPHH	Maps, plans, or pictures taken from various classes
MR	Maps, plans, or pictures taken from various classes
Probate	
PROB 5	Probate Inventories, P.C.C.
PROB 11	Registered Copies of Wills proved in P.C.C.
Court of Requests	
REQ 2	Proceedings
Registrar General	
	Population Returns
RG 9	1861
RG 10	1871
RG 11	1881
RG 12	1891
RG 31	Registers of Places of Worship, 1689–1852
Special Collections	
SC 1	Ancient Correspondence
SC 2	Court Rolls
SC 6	Ministers' Accounts
	Rentals and Surveys
SC 11	Rolls
SC 12	Portfolios
State Paper Office	
	State Papers Domestic
SP 12	Eliz. I
SP 14	Jas. I
War Office	
WO 30	Miscellanea: Inns and Alehouses

SELECT LIST OF CLASSES OF DOCUMENTS IN THE WEST SUSSEX RECORD OFFICE

USED IN THIS VOLUME

A.B.A.	Arundel Borough records before 1835
Acc.	Unlisted
Add. MSS.	Additional Manuscripts
BO/AR	Arundel Borough records, 1835–1974
Cap.	Dean and Chapter, Chichester, Records
CC	West Sussex County Council Records, Miscellaneous
CE	Customs and Excise
E	School Records
Ecc. Comm.	Ecclesiastical Commissioners' Records
Ep.	Episcopal Records
Ep. I	Chichester Diocese and Archdeaconry
Ep. I/22–3	Churchwardens' Presentments and Ministers' Articles of Enquiry
Ep. I/25	Glebe Terriers
Ep. I/26	Church Inspection Books
Ep. I/29	Probate Inventories
Ep. VI	Episcopal Estates
F/PD	Fuller Prints and Drawings
HW/AR	Arundel Hospital Records
IR	Inland Revenue Land Valuation Records
LD	Land Drainage Records
LH	Littlehampton Harbour Records
M/PD	Mitford Prints and Drawings
MF	Microfilms
MP	Miscellaneous Papers
NC/B	Nonconformist Records, Baptists
NC/C	Nonconformist Records, Congregationalists
NC/M	Nonconformist Records, Methodists
OH	Oral History Archive
Par.	Parish Records
PD	Prints and Drawings
PH	Photographs
PHA	Petworth House Archives

PM	Printed Maps
POL	Police Records
Q	Quarter Sessions Records
QA	Administration
QAB	Bridges and Roads
QAC	Constabulary
QC	Clerk of the Peace
QCR	Parliamentary Returns
QD	Enrolment, Registration, and Deposit
QDD	Enrolled Deeds, Awards, and Agreements
QDE	Parliamentary Electors, including Land Tax
QDP	Deposited Plans
QDS	Charities
QR	Sessions Rolls
RD/WH	Westhampnett Rural District Council Records
S.A.S. MS. B	Miscellaneous
S.A.S. MS. BA	Montague Archives
S.A.S. MS. C	Miscellaneous
S.A.S. MS. HB	Miscellaneous
S.A.S. MS. OR	Orlebar Archives
S.A.S. MS. RB	Miscellaneous
S.A.S. MS. WH	Wallace Hills Collection
SP	Sale Particulars
SR	Shipping Records
STC	Sussex Testamentary Collection, Chichester Archdeaconry
TD/W	Tithe Maps and Awards
UD/BR	Bognor Regis Urban District Council Records
WDC	West Sussex County Council, Departmental Records, 1889–
WNC	West Sussex County Council Records, 1974–
WOC	West Sussex County Council Records, 1889–1974

LIST OF CLASSES OF DOCUMENTS IN THE ARUNDEL CASTLE ARCHIVES

USED IN THIS VOLUME

A	Accounts
AP	Acts of Parliament, Bills, and Associated Documents
C	Correspondence
D	Deeds
DB	Papers of Duke Bernard (d. 1975)
FA	The Fitzalan Chapel Case
FC	Papers formerly at Few & Co.
H	Maps and Plans
HC	Papers formerly at Holmes, Campbell & Co.
IN	Inventories and Valuations
K	Maps and Plans
LM	Maps and Plans
M	Manorial Documents
MD	Miscellaneous Documents
P	Maps and Plans
PM	Maps and Plans

LIST OF SUSSEX RECORD SOCIETY VOLUMES

USED IN THIS VOLUME

S.R.S. ii	Feet of Fines, 1190–1249
S.R.S. iii	Inquisitions Post Mortem, 1558–83
S.R.S. iv	Miscellaneous Records
S.R.S. v	West Sussex Protestation Returns, 1642
S.R.S. vii	Feet of Fines, 1249–1307
S.R.S. viii, xi	Register of Bishop Robert Rede, 1397–1415
S.R.S. x	Subsidies, 1296–1332
S.R.S. xiv	Inquisitions Post Mortem, 1485 onwards
S.R.S. xvi	Star Chamber Proceedings, 1485–1558
S.R.S. xix–xx	Feet of Fines, 1509–1833
S.R.S. xxiii	Feet of Fines, 1307–1509
S.R.S. xxviii	Apprentices and Masters, 1710–52
S.R.S. xxix	Muniments of H. C. Lane
S.R.S. xxxi	Custumals of Manors of Bishop of Chichester
S.R.S. xxxiii	Inquisitions Post Mortem
S.R.S. xxxvi	Chantry Records
S.R.S. xl	Lewes Priory Chartulary, ii
S.R.S. xli–xliii, xlv	Wills up to 1560
S.R.S. xlvi	Chichester Cathedral Chartulary
S.R.S. xlix	Churchwardens' Presentments, 17th century
S.R.S. li	Deputations of Gamekeepers
S.R.S. lii	Acts of Dean and Chapter of Chichester, 1472–1544
S.R.S. liv	Quarter Sessions Order Book, 1642–9
S.R.S. lv	Petworth Manor Ministers' Accounts, 1347–53
S.R.S. lvi	Lay Subsidy Rolls, 1524–5
S.R.S. lvii	Custumals of Manors of Archbishop of Canterbury
S.R.S. lviii	Acts of Dean and Chapter of Chichester, 1545–1642
S.R.S. lix	Boxgrove Priory Chartulary
S.R.S. lx	Laughton, Willingdon and Goring Manor Custumals
S.R.S. lxiv	Rye Shipping Records, 1566–90
S.R.S. lxvi	Catalogue of Maps, ii
S.R.S. lxvii	Estate Surveys of FitzAlan Earls of Arundel
S.R.S. lxxii	Printed Maps, 1575–1900
S.R.S. lxxiii	Correspondence of Dukes of Richmond and Newcastle, 1724–50
S.R.S. lxxiv	Coroners' Inquests, 1485–1558
S.R.S. lxxv	Religious Census, 1851
S.R.S. lxxviii	Chichester Diocesan Surveys, 1686 and 1724
Suss. Views (S.R.S.)	*Sussex Views selected from the Burrell Collections*, ed. W. H. Godfrey and L. F. Salzman (Lewes, 1951)

NOTE ON ABBREVIATIONS

Among the abbreviations and short titles used the following may require elucidation:

A.C.M.	Arundel Castle Manuscripts
A Visit to Arundel Cast. (1851)	*A Visit to Arundel Castle* (Arundel and London, 1851)
Abbrev. Plac. (Rec. Com.)	*Placitorum in Domo Capitulari Westmonasteriensi asservatorum Abbreviatio*, ed. G. Rose and W. Illingworth (Record Commission, 1811)
acct.	account
Acts & Ords. of Interr. ed. Firth & Rait	*Acts and Ordinances of the Interregnum, 1642–1660*, ed. C. H. Firth and R. S. Rait (3 vols., 1911)
Acts of P.C.	*Acts of the Privy Council of England* (H.M.S.O., 1890–1964)
Add. Ch., MS.	Additional Charter, Manuscript
Alum. Cantab. to 1751; 1752–1900	*Alumni Cantabrigienses, a Biographical List ... to 1900*, comp. J. Venn and J. A. Venn, *Part 1, to 1751; Part 2, 1752–1900* (10 vols., Cambridge, 1922–54)
Alum. Oxon. 1500–1714; 1715–1886	*Alumni Oxonienses, 1500–1714*, ed. J. Foster (4 vols.); *1715–1886* (4 vols.) (Oxford, 1888–92)
Ann.	*Annual*
Antiq.	*Antiquities, Antiquaries*
Arch.	*Archaeological, Archaeology, Archaeologia*
Armada Surv. ed. Lower	*A Survey of the Coast of Sussex, made in 1587*, ed. M. A. Lower (Lewes, 1870)
Arundel Cast. Archives	*Arundel Castle Archives*, ed. F. W. Steer (4 vols., Chichester, 1968–80)
Arundel Rds.	*The Arundel Roads: Report of the Appeal tried at the West Sussex Quarter Sessions* (Brighton, 1851)
B.L.	British Library (used in references to documents transferred from the British Museum). Add. MSS. 5670–5711 and 39326–39546 are notes and transcripts made by or for, respectively, Sir William Burrell (d. 1796) and E. H. W. Dunkin (d. 1915)
bd.	board
bdle.	bundle
Beauties of Eng. and Wales, Suss.	*The Beauties of England and Wales*, vol. xiv, by F. Shoberl, [part 3], Sussex (1813)
Berry, *Suss. Geneal.* annot. Comber	W. Berry, *Pedigrees of the Families in the County of Sussex* (1830; copy in W.S.R.O., annotated by J. Comber)
Bk. of Fees	*The Book of Fees* (3 vols., H.M.S.O., 1920–31)
bp(ric).	bishop(ric)
Breads's Guide Worthing (1865)	*The Library (Breads) Guide and Handbook to Worthing* (1865)
Budgen, *Suss. Map* (1724)	R. Budgen, *An Actual Survey of the County of Sussex* (1724)
Burke, *Land. Gent.*	J. Burke and others, *Landed Gentry*
C.I.H.E.	Chichester Institute of Higher Education
C.J.	*Journals of the House of Commons*
C.K.S.	Centre for Kentish Studies
Cal. Assize Rec. Suss. Eliz. I; Jas. I	*Calendar of Assize Records, Sussex Indictments, Elizabeth I; James I*, ed. J. S. Cockburn (H.M.S.O., 1975)
Cal. Chart. R.	*Calendar of the Charter Rolls preserved in the Public Record Office* (H.M.S.O., 1903–27)
Cal. Close	*Calendar of the Close Rolls preserved in the Public Record Office* (H.M.S.O., 1892–1963)
Cal. Cttee. for Compounding	*Calendar of the Proceedings of the Committee for Compounding, etc.* (H.M.S.O., 1889–92)
Cal. Doc. France, ed. Round	*Calendar of Documents preserved in France, illustrative of the History of Great Britain and Ireland*, ed. J. H. Round (H.M.S.O., 1899)
Cal. Fine R.	*Calendar of the Fine Rolls preserved in the Public Record Office* (H.M.S.O., 1911–62)

Cal. Inq. Misc.	*Calendar of Inquisitions Miscellaneous (Chancery) preserved in the Public Record Office* (H.M.S.O., 1916–68)
Cal. Inq. p.m.	*Calendar of Inquisitions post mortem preserved in the Public Record Office* (H.M.S.O., 1904–)
Cal. Inq. p.m. Hen. VII	*Calendar of Inquisitions post mortem, Henry VII* (H.M.S.O., 1898–1955)
Cal. Pat.	*Calendar of the Patent Rolls preserved in the Public Record Office* (H.M.S.O., 1891–1982)
Cal. S.P. Dom.	*Calendar of State Papers, Domestic Series* (H.M.S.O., 1856–1972)
Cal. Treas. Bks.	*Calendar of Treasury Books* (H.M.S.O., 1904–69)
Camd. Soc.	Camden Society
Camden, *Brit.*	W. Camden, *Britannia*
Cant. & York Soc.	Canterbury and York Society
Caplan, 'Outline of Nonconf. in Suss.'	N. Caplan, 'An Outline of the Origins and Development of Nonconformity in Sussex 1603–1803' (TS. in Dr. Williams's Library, London, and in S.A.S. library)
Caraccioli, *Arundel*	[C. Caraccioli], *The Antiquities of Arundel* (1766)
Cartland, *Arundel*	*Arundel: a Picture of the Past*, comp. J. Cartland (Chichester, 1978)
Cat. Anct. D.	*A Descriptive Catalogue of Ancient Deeds in the Public Record Office* (H.M.S.O., 1890–1915)
Cath. Rec. Soc.	Catholic Record Society
Char. Com.	Charity Commission
Char. Don.	*Charitable Donations*
Chich. Acta (Cant. & York Soc.)	*The Acta of the Bishops of Chichester, 1075–1207*, ed. H. Mayr-Harting (Canterbury and York Society, 1964)
Chich. Dioc. Kal.	*Chichester Diocesan Kalendar*
Chich. Dioc. Regy.	Chichester Diocesan Registry
Chron.	*Chronicle(s)*
chwdn.	churchwarden
Close R.	*Close Rolls of the Reign of Henry III preserved in the Public Record Office* (H.M.S.O., 1902–75)
Colvin, *Biog. Dict. Brit. Architects*	H. Colvin, *A Biographical Dictionary of British Architects 1600–1840* (1978)
Colvin, *Biog. Dict. Eng. Architects*	H. M. Colvin, *A Biographical Dictionary of English Architects 1660–1840* (1954)
Com.	Commission, common
Complete Peerage	G. E. C[okayne] and others, *The Complete Peerage* ... (2nd edn., 13 vols., 1910–59)
Cong. Yr. Bk.	*Congregational Year Book*
corp.	corporation
Crockford	*Crockford's Clerical Directory*
ct.	court
Cur. Reg. R.	*Curia Regis Rolls preserved in the Public Record Office* (H.M.S.O., 1922–91)
D. & C.	Dean and Chapter
D.N.B.	*Dictionary of National Biography*
Dallaway, *Hist. W. Suss.* Dallaway & Cartwright, *Hist. W. Suss.*	J. Dallaway and E. Cartwright, *A History of the Western Division of the County of Sussex* (2 vols., 1815–32)
Dally, *Bognor* (1828)	[R. Dally], *The Bognor, Arundel and Littlehampton Guide* (Chichester, 1828)
Dioc.	Diocesan, Diocese
Dir.	*Directory*
dist.	district
Dugdale, *Mon.*	W. Dugdale, *Monasticon Anglicanum*, ed. J. Caley and others (6 vols., 1817–30)
E.H.R.	*English Historical Review*
E.S.R.O.	East Sussex Record Office
Educ. Enq. Abstract	*Education Enquiry Abstract*, H.C. 62 (1835), xli
Educ. List 21	*Board of Education, List 21* (H.M.S.O.)

Educ. of Poor Digest	*Digest of Returns to the Select Committee on the Education of the Poor*, H.C. 224 (1819), ix (2)
Elphick, *Bells*	G. P. Elphick, *Sussex Bells and Belfries* (Chichester, 1970)
Elwes & Robinson, *W. Suss.*	D. G. C. Elwes and C. J. Robinson, *A History of the Castles, Mansions, and Manors of Western Sussex* (1876)
Emden, *Biog. Reg. Univ. Camb. to 1500*	A. B. Emden, *A Biographical Register of the University of Cambridge to 1500* (Cambridge, 1963)
Emden, *Biog. Reg. Univ. Oxf. to 1500*	A. B. Emden, *A Biographical Register of the University of Oxford to A.D. 1500* (3 vols., Oxford, 1957–9)
Eng. P.N. Elements (E.P.N.S.)	A. H. Smith, *English Place-Name Elements* (English Place-Name Society, vols. xxv–xxvi, 1956)
Eustace, *Arundel*	G. W. Eustace, *Arundel: Borough and Castle* (1922)
Evans, *Worthing* (1805, 1814)	J. Evans, *Picture of Worthing* (1805; 2nd edn., 2 vols., Worthing, 1814)
Excursions through Suss. (1822)	*Excursions through Sussex, illustrated with Engravings* (publ. Longman & Co., 1822)
Feud. Aids	*Inquisitions and Assessments relating to Feudal Aids preserved in the Public Record Office* (H.M.S.O., 1899–1920)
1st Rep. Com. Mun. Corp.	*First Report of the Royal Commission on Municipal Corporations*, H.C. 116, Appendix II (1835), xxiv
G.E.C. *Baronetage*	G. E. C[okayne], *Complete Baronetage* (6 vols., 1900–9)
G.R.O.	General Register Office
Gardner, *Suss. Map* (1778–83)	T. Yeakell and W. Gardner, *An Actual Topographical Survey of the County of Sussex* (1778–83)
Gardner, *Suss. Map* (1795)	W. Gardner, T. Yeakell, and T. Gream, *A Topographical Map of the County of Sussex* ... (1795)
Gent. Mag.	*The Gentleman's Magazine* (1731–1867)
Geog.	*Geographical, Geography*
Geol. Surv.	Geological Survey
Goodliffe, *Littlehampton* (1903)	W. Goodliffe, *Littlehampton and Arundel, with their Surroundings* (Littlehampton, Arundel, and London, 1903)
Greenwood, *Suss. Map* (1825)	C. and J. Greenwood, *Map of the County of Sussex* ... (1825)
H.B.M.C.	Historic Buildings and Monuments Commission
H.C.	House of Commons
H.L.R.O.	House of Lords Record Office
H.M.S.O.	Her (His) Majesty's Stationery Office
High Stream of Arundel	*A Description of the High Stream of Arundel*, ed. J. Fowler (Littlehampton, 1929)
Hillier, *Arundel* (1847, 1851)	G. Hillier, *A Day at Arundel* (Arundel, 1847; 2nd edn., London, 1851)
Hist.	Historical, History
Hist. MSS. Com.	Historical Manuscripts Commission
Horsfield, *Hist. Suss.*	T. W. Horsfield, *The History, Antiquities, and Topography of the County of Sussex* (2 vols., Lewes, 1835)
hosp.	hospital
hund.	hundred
Ind.	*Industrial, Industry*
Inq. Non. (Rec. Com.)	*Nonarum Inquisitiones in Curia Scaccarii*, ed. G. Vanderzee (Record Commission, 1807)
Jesse, *Agric. of Suss.*	R. H. B. Jesse, *A Survey of the Agriculture of Sussex* (Royal Agricultural Society of England, 1960)
Jnl.	*Journal*
Kelly's Dir. Suss.	*The Post Office Directory of the Six Home Counties; The Post Office Directory of Sussex; Kelly's Directory of Sussex*
Kimpton, *Arundel* (*c.* 1890, 1893, 1897, 1903)	*Kimpton's Popular Guide to Arundel* (Arundel, *c.* 1890; 1893; 1897; 1903)
L. & I. Soc.	*List and Index Society* series
L. & P. Hen. VIII	*Letters and Papers, Foreign and Domestic, of the Reign of Henry VIII* (H.M.S.O., 1864–1932)

L.G.B. Prov. Order(s) Conf. Act	Local Government Board Provisional Order(s) Confirmation Act
L.J.	*Journals of the House of Lords*
Lamb. Pal. Libr.	Lambeth Palace Library
Le Neve, *Fasti, ... Chich.*	J. Le Neve, *Fasti Ecclesiae Anglicanae, ... Chichester Diocese*, ed. J. M. Horn
Lewis, *Topog. Dict. Eng.*	S. Lewis, *A Topographical Dictionary of England*
Lond. Gaz.	*London Gazette*
Lower, *Hist. Suss.*	M. A. Lower, *A Compendious History of Sussex* (2 vols., Lewes, 1870)
M.A.F.F., agric. statistics, 1975	Ministry of Agriculture, Fisheries, and Food, parish summaries of statistics for 1975
Magna Britannia	[T. Cox], *Magna Britannia Antiqua & Nova* (6 vols., 1730)
man.	manor, manorial
Mins. Educ. Cttee. 1854–5	*Minutes of the Education Committee of the Privy Council, 1854–5* [1926], H.C. (1854–5), xlii
mkt.	market
mon.	monument(al)
MS., MSS.	Manuscript, Manuscripts
Mus.	Museum
N.M.R.	National Monuments Record
N.R.A. Man. Doc. Reg.	National Register of Archives, Manorial Documents Register
Nairn & Pevsner, *Suss.*	I. Nairn and N. Pevsner, *The Buildings of England: Sussex* (1965)
Nat. Soc. *Inquiry, 1846–7*, Suss.	*Result of the Returns to the General Inquiry made by the National Society ... 1846–7* (1849)
Norden, *Suss. Map* (1595)	J. Norden, *Map of Sussex* (1595)
O.E.D.	*Oxford English Dictionary*
O.S. (Nat. Grid)	Ordnance Survey (National Grid)
Oxf.	Oxford
P.N. Suss. (E.P.N.S.)	*The Place-Names of Sussex*, ed. A. Mawer and F. M. Stenton (English Place-Name Society, vols. vi-vii, 1929–30)
P.R.O.	Public Record Office
Parl.	Parliament(ary)
Pat. R.	*Patent Rolls of the Reign of Henry III preserved in the Public Record Office* (H.M.S.O., 1901–3)
Petch, 'Arundel Coll.'	R. B. K. Petch, 'The Organisation of a College of Secular Priests as illustrated by the Records of the College of Holy Trinity, Arundel 1380–1544' (London University M.A. thesis, 1942)
Pigot, *Nat. Com. Dir.* (1832–4)	*Pigot and Co.'s National London and Provincial Commercial Directory for 1832–3–4*
Pipe R.	*Pipe Rolls*
Pla.	Place
Plac. de Quo Warr. (Rec. Com.)	*Placita de Quo Warranto ... in Curia Receptae Scaccarii Westm. asservata*, ed. W. Illingworth and J. Caley (Record Commission, 1818)
Plans of Arundel Cast.	*Plans Elevations and Particular Measurements of Arundel Castle in Sussex*, ed. F. W. Steer (Arundel, 1976)
Poor Law Abstract, 1818	*Abstract of Returns to Orders of the House of Commons relative to Assessments for the Relief of the Poor*, H.C. 82 (1818), xix
Priv. Act	Private Act
Proc.	*Proceedings*
Public Elem. Schs. 1875–6, 1907	*Public Elementary Schools 1875–6*, H.C. 133 (1875), lix; *1907* [Cd. 3901], H.C. (1908), lxxxiv
rec.	record(s)
Red Bk. Exch. (Rolls Ser.)	*The Red Book of the Exchequer*, ed. H. Hall (3 vols., Rolls Series, 1896)
Reg.	*Register*
Reg. Regum Anglo-Norm.	*Regesta Regum Anglo-Normannorum 1066–1154*, ed. H. W. C. Davis and others (4 vols., 1913–69)
Rep. Com. Eccl. Revenues	*Report of the Commissioners appointed ... to inquire into the Ecclesiastical Revenues of England and Wales* [67], H.C. (1835), xxii

Rep. Com. on Children and Women in Agric.	*First Report of the Commissioners on the Employment of Children, Young Persons, and Women in Agriculture*, Appendix part II [4068–I], H.C. (1867–8), xvii
Rep. Educ. Cttee. 1859–60, 1865–6, 1871–2, 1878–9, 1885–6, 1893–4	*Report of the Education Committee of the Privy Council*, 1859–60, H.C. (1859–Sess. 1), xxi; *1865–6* [3666], H.C. (1866), xxvii; *1871–2* [C. 601], H.C. (1872), xxii; *1878–9* [C. 2342–I], H.C. (1878–9), xxiii; *1885–6* [C. 4849–I], H.C. (1886), xxiv; *1893–4* [C. 7437–I], H.C. (1894), xxix
Res.	Research
Return of Non-Provided Schs.	*Return of Non-Provided Schools*, H.C. 178 (1906), lxxxviii
Rev.	*Review, Revue*
Rom.	Roman
Rot. Cur. Reg. (Rec. Com.)	*Rotuli Curiae Regis. Rolls and Records of the Court held before the King's Justiciars or Justices, 6 Richard I–1 John*, ed. F. Palgrave (2 vols., Record Commission, 1835)
Rot. Hund. (Rec. Com.)	*Rotuli Hundredorum temp. Hen. III & Edw. I in Turri Londinensi, et in Curia Receptae Scaccarii Westm. asservati*, ed. W. Illingworth and J. Caley (2 vols., Record Commission, 1812–18)
Rot. Litt. Claus. (Rec. Com.)	*Rotuli Litterarum Clausarum in Turri Londinensi asservati, 1204–27*, ed. T. D. Hardy (2 vols., Record Commission, 1833–44)
Rot. Litt. Pat. (Rec. Com.)	*Rotuli Litterarum Patentium in Turri Londinensi asservati, 1201–16*, ed. T. D. Hardy (Record Commission, 1835)
Rot. Parl.	*Rotuli Parliamentorum* ... (6 vols., [1783])
S.A.C.	*Sussex Archaeological Collections* (1848–)
S.A.S.	Sussex Archaeological Society
S.C.M.	*Sussex County Magazine* (1926–56)
S.I.A.S.	Sussex Industrial Archaeology Society
S.M.R.	Sites and Monuments Record
S.N.Q.	*Sussex Notes and Queries* (1926–71)
S.R.S.	*Sussex Record Society* series (1902–)
Schs. Inquiry Com.	*Report of Schools Inquiry Commission* [3966], H.C. (1867–8), xxviii
Schs. Parl. Grants, 1900–1	*Schools in Receipt of Parliamentary Grants, 1900–1* [Cd. 703], H.C. (1901), lv
ser.	series
Soc.	Social, Society
Spec.	Special
Surr.	Surrey
surv.	survey
Suss. Fam. Historian	*Sussex Family Historian* (1973–)
Suss. in 20th Cent.	*Sussex in the 20th Century* (publ. W. T. Pike & Co., Brighton, 1910)
Suss. Ind. Arch. (1972)	*Sussex Industrial Archaeology, a Field Guide*, comp. J. Hoare and J. Upton (Sussex Industrial Archaeology Study Group, 1972)
Suss. Ind. Arch. (1985)	*Sussex Industrial Archaeology, a Field Guide*, ed. B. Austen and others (Chichester, 1985)
Suss. Ind. Hist.	*Sussex Industrial History* (Journal of the Sussex Industrial Archaeology Study Group, later Society, 1970/1–)
Suss. Poor Law Rec.	*Sussex Poor Law Records*, ed. J. M. Coleman (Chichester, 1960)
Tax. Eccl. (Rec. Com.)	*Taxatio Ecclesiastica Angliae et Walliae auctoritate P. Nicholai IV* circa *A.D. 1291*, ed. S. Ayscough and J. Caley (Record Commission, 1802)
Tierney, *Arundel*	M. A. Tierney, *The History and Antiquities of the Castle and Town of Arundel* (2 vols., 1834)
TS.	Typescript
Univ. Brit. Dir.	*The Universal British Directory of Trade, Commerce, and Manufacture*, ed. P. Barfoot and J. Wilkes (5 vols., 1791–8)
V.C.H.	*Victoria County History*
Valor Eccl. (Rec. Com.)	*Valor Ecclesiasticus temp. Henr. VIII auctoritate regia institutus*, ed. J. Caley and J. Hunter (Record Commission, 1810–34)
Visit.	*Visitation*
Visitors' Guide to Arundel (1868)	*Visitors' Guide to Arundel Castle, Church, &c., &c.* (Arundel, 1868)

NOTE ON ABBREVIATIONS

W.S.R.O.	West Sussex Record Office
W. Suss. C.C.	West Sussex County Council
W. Suss. Gaz.	*West Sussex Gazette*
White, *Geol. of Brighton and Worthing*	H. J. O. White, *Memoirs of the Geological Survey. The Geology of the Country near Brighton and Worthing* (H.M.S.O., 1924)
Wright, *Arundel* (1817)	C. Wright, *The Antiquities and Description of Arundel Castle* (Brighton and London, 1817)
Wright, *Arundel* (1818)	C. Wright, *The History and Description of Arundel Castle* (1818)
Young, *Agric. of Suss.*	A. Young, *General View of the Agriculture of the County of Sussex* (1813, reprinted 1970)

V.C.H. SUSSEX: KEY TO VOLUMES

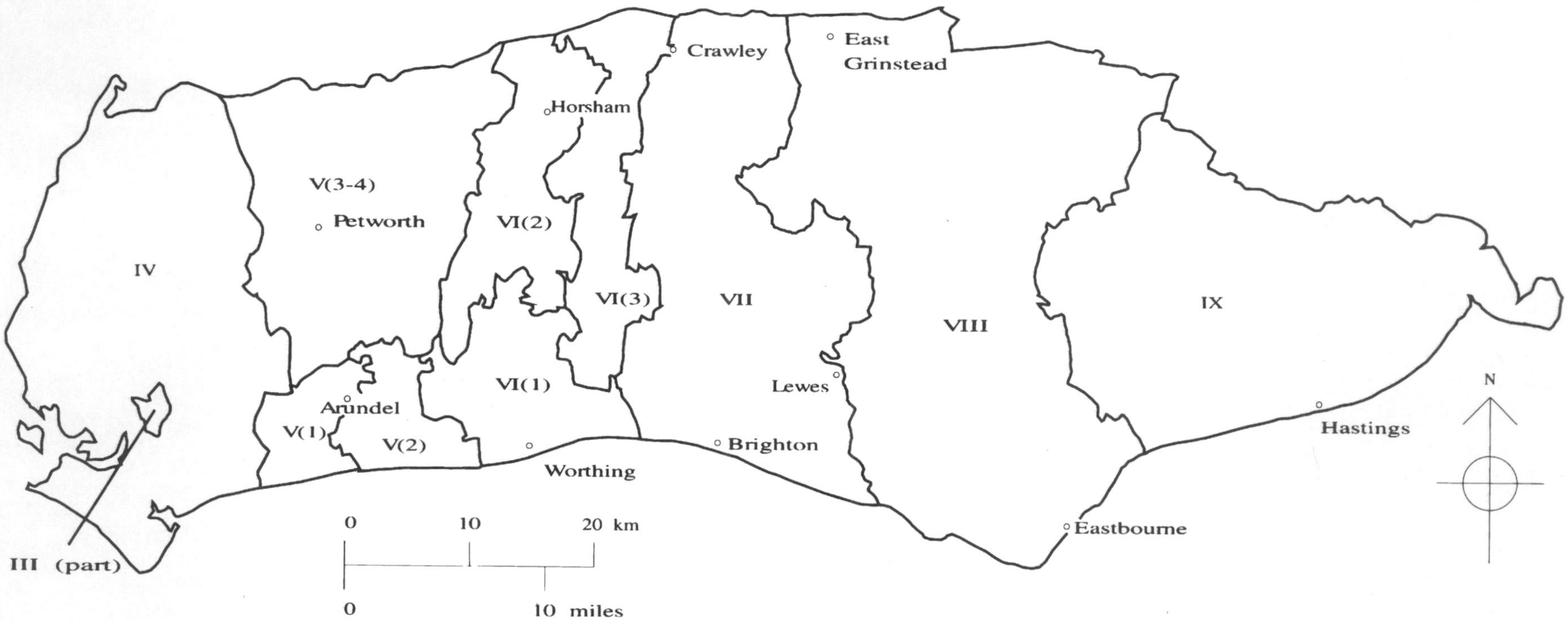

PREVIOUSLY PUBLISHED VOLUMES
I & II General Volumes
III Romano-British Sussex and Chichester City
IV Chichester Rape
VI(1-3) Bramber Rape
VII Lewes Rape
IX Hastings Rape

VOLUMES IN PROGRESS OR
TO BE STARTED
V(2-4) Arundel Rape
VIII Pevensey Rape

ARUNDEL RAPE

The rapes of Arundel and Chichester were originally one, called in the late 11th century either Arundel rape or, more often, the rape of earl Roger (de Montgomery).[1] The division into two was made in the mid 13th century: at the eyre of 1248 the hundreds of the two rapes were not separately listed, but by 1262 those of Chichester rape were listed under the heading 'bailiwick of Chichester'; the name rape of Chichester occurs in 1275.[2] The honor of Arundel, however, continued undivided, no honor of Chichester being known.[3] An honor of Petworth was mentioned as subordinate from 1181[4] and an honor of Halnaker from *c.* 1205; at the latter date the honor of Petworth supplied 22½ of the 84½ fees at which the honor of Arundel was assessed and the honor of Halnaker 12.[5] Fees in Hampshire and Warwickshire were also held of the honor.[6] The descent that follows is of the rape rather than of the honor which included it.

The rape of Arundel was granted to Roger de Montgomery *c.* 1067;[7] he may be considered the first earl of Arundel. At his death in 1094 he was succeeded by his son Hugh, who at his death without issue in 1098 was followed by his elder brother Robert of Bellême, earl of Shrewsbury. For his part in the rebellion of 1101–2 against Henry I Robert forfeited the rape to the Crown.[8] At the king's death in 1135 it passed as dower to his widow Adelize.[9] She afterwards married William d'Aubigny, who then or later became earl of Arundel; in 1139 they were living at Arundel castle. Though a partisan of King Stephen (d. 1154),[10] William was confirmed in the rape by Henry II *c.* 1155.[11]

At his death in 1176 William's heir was his son William, also earl of Arundel, but the rape was retained by the Crown[12] until in 1190 it was returned to him by Richard I.[13] Between 1179 and 1187 or later Walter de Coutances, bishop of Lincoln and afterwards archbishop of Rouen, had the keeping.[14] William was succeeded in 1193 by his son William (d. 1221), a favourite of King John.[15] The younger William seems not to have had the rape since, though he apparently paid to receive it in 1195,[16] it was being accounted for between 1194 and 1202 by William of St. Mary Church,[17] and in 1209 was part of the dower of Queen Berengaria (d. after 1230), widow of Richard I, though then withheld by King John.[18] In 1216 the earl of Arundel joined the future Louis VIII of France during the latter's invasion of England, but after John's death he submitted to Henry III, who ordered his forfeited possessions to be restored.[19]

William's son, another William, died without issue in 1224; during the minority of his brother and heir Hugh[20] the rape was in the keeping of Hubert de Burgh in

1 *V.C.H. Suss.* i. 351 n. 1, 421.
2 Ibid. iv. 1–2.
3 e.g. *Feud. Aids*, vi. 520.
4 *Pipe R.* 1181 (P.R.S. xxx), 146; *Chanc. R.* 1196 (P.R.S. N.S. vii), 83; cf. Tierney, *Arundel*, i. 23–4.
5 *V.C.H. Suss.* i. 491; cf. ibid. iv. 143; *S.R.S.* lxvii. 103.
6 W. Farrer, *Honors and Kts.' Fees*, iii. 3–4; *Pipe R.* 1187 (P.R.S. xxxvii), 201; *Cal. Inq. p.m.* i, p. 279; cf. *S.R.S.* lxvii. 92.
7 *Trans. Royal Hist. Soc.* 5th ser. xiii. 1–2.
8 *Complete Peerage*, s.vv. Arundel, Shrewsbury.
9 Sanders, *Eng. Baronies*, 2.
10 *Complete Peerage*, s.v. Arundel; below, Arundel, castle (institutional hist.).
11 *Cal. Chart. R.* 1327–41, 257, inspecting earlier charts.
12 *Complete Peerage*, s.v. Arundel.
13 P.R.O., C 52/22, no. 29; *Pipe R.* 1190 (P.R.S. N.S. i), 129.
14 *Pipe R.* 1179 (P.R.S. xxviii), 38; 1183 (P.R.S. xxxii), 107; 1187 (P.R.S. xxxvii), 109.
15 *Complete Peerage*, s.v. Arundel.
16 *Pipe R.* 1195 (P.R.S. N.S. vi), 238.
17 Ibid. 1194 (P.R.S. N.S. v), 230; 1198 (P.R.S. N.S. ix), 225; 1202 (P.R.S. N.S. xv), 140.
18 *Cal. Papal Reg.* i. 33; *D.N.B.*
19 *Complete Peerage*, s.v. Arundel.
20 Ibid.

1227[21] and apparently of Peter de Rivaux in 1232–3.[22] In 1234 Hugh received the rape while still a minor,[23] and at his death without issue in 1243 it passed to his nephew John FitzAlan,[24] then in the king's wardship, Geoffrey of Langley and Henry le Breton being granted the keeping.[25] John was in opposition to the king in the 1250s, but was reconciled in 1261 and fought on the royalist side at the battle of Lewes in 1264.[26] At his death in 1267 his heir was his son John (d. 1272); during the minority of the younger John's son Richard[27] successive keepers of the rape were Robert Aguillon between 1272 and 1274,[28] William of Hever in 1274,[29] Henry of Newbury in 1278,[30] Emery de Chanceus *c.* 1279,[31] John's widow Isabel in 1280,[32] and her kinsman Edmund Mortimer in 1282.[33]

Richard FitzAlan had seisin of his lands in 1287, and was apparently created earl of Arundel in 1289; at his death in 1302 he was succeeded by his son Edmund,[34] the custody of the rape being granted during minority to Amadeus, count of Savoy.[35] Edmund later fought first against, then for, Edward II, until after his capture by the party of Queen Isabel he was executed and attainted in 1326.[36] The rape was granted in the same year[37] to Edmund of Woodstock, earl of Kent, the king's brother,[38] and confirmed to him in 1327 by Edward III.[39] After his execution and attainder in 1330[40] it was restored in the following year to Richard FitzAlan, earl of Arundel.[41] Richard, a soldier, sailor, and diplomat,[42] invested much of his considerable wealth in Sussex property, especially in Arundel rape. By 1373, three years before his death, he had made over his Sussex estates to his son Richard,[43] the greatest landowner in the county in his time,[44] who was executed and attainted in 1397 for treason committed in 1386.[45]

The rape was granted later in 1397, at first during pleasure and afterwards in tail male, to John Holand, earl of Huntingdon and subsequently duke of Exeter; in 1399, however, after Holand's disgrace,[46] the lands formerly of Richard FitzAlan, earl of Arundel, were restored, with his title, to his son Thomas.[47] Thomas died without issue in 1415, and the rape passed under a settlement of 1347–8 to his cousin John d'Arundel, earl of Arundel (d. 1421),[48] Thomas's widow Beatrice retaining dower until her death in 1439.[49]

John's son and heir, another John d'Arundel, known as 'the English Achilles', died in 1435 in France of wounds received in battle;[50] in 1433 he had proved in Parliament, against the counter-claim of his cousin John Mowbray, duke of Norfolk, that the title of earl of Arundel should descend with Arundel castle.[51] John's son Humphrey died in 1438 while a minor; his uncle and heir William

21 *Cal. Chart. R.* 1226–57, 57.
22 *Close R.* 1231–4, 167; *Cal. Lib.* 1226–40, 205.
23 *Cal. Pat.* 1232–47, 57.
24 Ibid. 408; *Complete Peerage*, s.v. Arundel.
25 *Cal. Pat.* 1266–72, 722; *Cal. Lib.* 1240–5, 276.
26 Tierney, *Arundel*, i. 196–9.
27 *Complete Peerage*, s.v. Arundel; *Cal. Inq. p.m.* i, pp. 278–9.
28 *Close R.* 1268–72, 504; *Cal. Close*, 1272–9, 34, 85.
29 *Cal. Fine R.* 1272–1307, 33.
30 *Cal. Pat.* 1272–81, 275.
31 Ibid. 374; cf. *Cal. Fine R.* 1272–1307, 109.
32 *Cal. Pat.* 1272–81, 374.
33 Ibid. 1281–92, 32; cf. *Complete Peerage*, s.v. Arundel.
34 *Complete Peerage*, s.v. Arundel; *Cal. Inq. p.m.* iv, pp. 50–1.
35 *Cal. Pat.* 1301–7, 46.
36 *Complete Peerage*, s.v. Arundel.
37 *Cal. Close*, 1323–7, 622.
38 *Complete Peerage*, s.vv. Arundel, Kent.
39 *Cal. Chart. R.* 1327–41, 4.
40 *Complete Peerage*, s.v. Arundel; *Cal. Inq. p.m.* vii, pp. 222, 226–7.
41 *Cal. Close*, 1330–3, 293; *Cal. Chart. R.* 1327–41, 257–8. The life interest granted during 1330 to Queen Isabel was evidently rescinded: *Cal. Pat.* 1327–30, 519; 1330–4, 12.
42 Tierney, *Arundel*, i. 225–40.
43 M. Aston, *Thos. Arundel*, 16–17; *S.A.C.* xci. 33.
44 A. Goodman, *Loyal Conspiracy*, 108.
45 Tierney, *Arundel*, i. 246–7, 253, 257–9, 261–3.
46 *Cal. Pat.* 1396–9, 176, 360; *Complete Peerage*, s.vv. Arundel, Exeter.
47 *Cal. Pat.* 1399–1401, 134; *Complete Peerage*, s.v. Arundel.
48 *Complete Peerage*, s.v. Arundel; P.R.O., C 138/59, no. 51, m. 14; *S.R.S.* xxiii, pp. 123–4.
49 *Cal. Fine R.* 1413–22, 165; *Complete Peerage*, s.v. Arundel.
50 *Complete Peerage*, s.v. Arundel; Tierney, *Arundel*, i. 303; P.R.O., C 139/71, no. 37, m. 32.
51 *Complete Peerage*, i. 231 n.; Tierney, *Arundel*, i. 102; *Rot. Parl.* iv. 441–3.

FitzAlan, earl of Arundel,[52] survived various changes of allegiance during the political upheavals of the mid 15th century[53] and died in 1487. William's son Thomas (d. 1524) was succeeded in the direct line by William (d. 1544) and Henry (d. 1580);[54] the latter, a partisan first of Mary I and then of Elizabeth I, was later imprisoned for complicity in the duke of Norfolk's plan to marry Mary, Queen of Scots.[55]

In 1570 the reversion of Henry's Sussex lands was settled on his daughter Jane and her husband John Lumley, Lord Lumley. Jane died without issue in 1576.[56] Lumley had been dealing with property in Arundel rape in the 1560s[57] and continued to do so in the 1570s,[58] but in 1580 conveyed his interest in the rape to Philip Howard, earl of Arundel, Henry's grandson by his younger daughter Mary.[59] Philip was imprisoned in the Tower as a Roman Catholic in 1585 and attainted for high treason in 1589. At his death in 1595 he was succeeded by his son Thomas, who was restored to his honours and estates in 1604 and created earl of Norfolk in 1644. The greatest English art connoisseur of his day, he lived the last part of his life abroad, dying in Padua in 1646.[60] Meanwhile, an Act of 1627 had annexed certain estates, later known as the parliamentary estates, to descend with the title of earl of Arundel.[61]

Thomas's son and heir Henry Frederick, a zealous Royalist, was fined £6,000 by Parliament in 1648, but allowed to compound for his estates; Thomas's widow Alathea (d. 1654),[62] however, had Arundel castle and rents belonging to it, apparently as dower, in 1651.[63] At Henry Frederick's death in 1652 the rape passed to his son Thomas, a lunatic from 1653, who was restored to the dukedom of Norfolk in 1660, dying, also in Padua, in 1677.[64] Thereafter the rape passed successively, with the dukedom, to Thomas's brother Henry (d. 1684), Henry's son Henry (d. 1701), and the younger Henry's nephew Thomas (d. 1732), who was succeeded by his brother Edward (d. 1777), a former Jacobite. Edward's cousin and heir Charles Howard (d. 1786) left as heir his son, another Charles;[65] he began the expansion of the Sussex estates of the family,[66] greatly reduced since the Middle Ages, but which by 1873 comprised nearly 20,000 a.[67] and in 1975 *c.* 16,000 a.[68]

At his death in 1815 the rape passed to his cousin Bernard Edward Howard (d. 1842), who was succeeded in the direct line by Henry Charles (d. 1856), Henry Granville (d. 1860), who had changed his surname in 1842 to Fitzalan-Howard, Henry (d. 1917),[69] and Bernard Marmaduke (d. 1975), from whom the dukedom passed to a cousin,[70] Miles Francis Fitzalan-Howard. The entail of the 1627 Act was broken by an Act of 1957,[71] which enabled the Fitzalan-Howard estates in

52 *Complete Peerage*, s.v. Arundel; P.R.O., C 139/88, no. 50, m. 19.
53 Tierney, *Arundel*, i. 304–5, 307–8.
54 *Complete Peerage*, s.v. Arundel.
55 Tierney, *Arundel*, i. 331, 334, 338, 342–3; cf. Hist. MSS. Com. 9, *Salisbury*, i, p. 458.
56 *S.R.S.* xix. 9–10; *Lavington Estate Archives*, ed. F. W. Steer, pp. 21–2; *Complete Peerage*, i. 253; viii. 276–8.
57 A.C.M., MD 535, ff. 5–6; B.L. Add. MS. 39347, f. 164v.; *Cal. Pat.* 1560–3, 582; 1566–9, pp. 101, 301; *S.R.S.* iii, pp. 83–4.
58 e.g. W.S.R.O., A.B.A., F2/3; *Lavington Estate Archives*, p. 22; *Cal. Pat.* 1572–5, p. 538. Cf. the fact that contemporary accts. and other rec. for Arundel rape are or were among the Lumley MSS.: Sandbeck Park, Rotherham, Lumley MSS. (TS. cat.); Dallaway & Cartwright, *Hist. W. Suss.* ii (1) (1832), 91 n.; *S.R.S.* lxvii, p. xxvii. Mention of a Ld. Lumley's chamber in Arundel cast. in 1580 suggests regular visits there: B.L. Lansd. MS. 30, f. 218.
59 P.R.O., C 66/1258, m. 1; *Complete Peerage*, s.v. Arundel. For Lumley's later construction of a mon. to his wife's ancestors, below, Arundel, church (mons.).
60 *Complete Peerage*, s.v. Arundel; *Arundel Cast. Archives*, ed. F. W. Steer, i, p. 26; D. Howarth, *Ld. Arundel and His Circle*, *passim*.
61 3 Chas. I, c. 4 (Priv. Act); 26 & 27 Vic. c. 7 (Private).
62 *Complete Peerage*, s.v. Arundel.
63 *Cal. Cttee. for Money*, iii. 1258.
64 *Complete Peerage*, s.v. Arundel; *S.R.S.* xiv, p. 8.
65 *Complete Peerage*, s.v. Norf.; H. A. Wyndham, *A Fam. Hist. 1688–1837*, 241–2; Eustace, *Arundel*, 267.
66 Camden, *Brit.* (1806), i. 287; J. M. Robinson, *Dukes of Norf.* (1982), 177, 194; Dallaway & Cartwright, *Hist. W. Suss.* ii (1) (1832), 84 n., 218–19, 221, 240.
67 *Return of Owners of Land* [C. 1097], Suss. p. 22, H.C. (1874), lxxii (2).
68 *Country Life*, 3 July 1980, p. 6.
69 *Complete Peerage*, s.v. Norf.
70 *The Times*, 1 Feb. 1975.
71 Ibid. 26 June 1957; 5 & 6 Eliz. II, c. 1 (Personal).

Sussex to be divided between the new duke's family and that of his predecessor. In 1988 the 'Arundel estate', settled on the duke's eldest son Lord Arundel, included Park farm, Arundel park, and land in Burpham and North and South Stoke, while the 'Norfolk estate' of Duke Bernard's widow and daughters comprised land in Angmering and further east.[72]

The Norman sheriff presumably held a court.[73] An honor court was apparently mentioned in 1225;[74] in 1272 and later it was held every three weeks.[75] Richard FitzAlan, earl of Arundel (d. 1376), under colour of a grant made in 1337 of the right to hold the sheriff's tourn,[76] was said in 1376 to have set up a new three-weekly court called a shire court at Arundel, which dealt with business formerly transacted at the shire court in Chichester.[77] In the mid 15th century Richard's descendants held 'the court of the liberty of Arundel called Shirecourt', presumably the same.[78] There are court records for the honor court for the years 1473–6, 1499–1574, 1749–76, and 1795–6.[79]

The court dealt with a case concerning land in Poling in 1225[80] and with the sale of a felon's goods in 1275.[81] Pleas of assault, affray, debt, trespass, and detinue were heard between the mid 15th century and the 16th, when the honor court had become fused with the Arundel borough court; most cases in the mid 16th century seem to have related to Arundel town.[82]

The lord's loss of control over the honor court to the borough corporation was lamented by a ducal servant in the early 18th century.[83] By the later 18th century, however, the court was again being held every three weeks, and in 1776 it had jurisdiction over debts under £2.[84] It was still held in 1796.[85]

A sheriff's tourn called Nomansland was mentioned between the early 13th century and the 18th;[86] it served the whole honor *c.* 1209[87] and later,[88] but in the 18th century leet jurisdiction was claimed over most of the county.[89] In 1361 the court was held at a site in Rotherbridge hundred,[90] presumably the place called Nomansland gate on the South Downs near the boundary between Arundel and Chichester rapes.[91] Later there was apparently a court house on the downs near Madehurst, at the spot where the court was held under a tree in the 18th century.[92] The right to hold the tourn belonged to the earls of Arundel from 1337,[93] and in the later 16th century to Lord Abergavenny and others.[94] A post-mortem inquisition was apparently held at it in 1331.[95] There are rolls of the tourn for the years 1542, 1562, 1564–7, 1587, 1592, and 1594.[96] In the later 16th century and in the 18th[97] it was held twice a year. Business at the earlier date included the oversight of rights of way, and of the repair of pounds, ditches, bridges, and fences;

72 Inf. from the duke of Norf.'s librarian, Dr. J. M. Robinson.

73 *V.C.H. Suss.* iii. 96 n.

74 *Cur. Reg. R.* xii, p. 212; cf. P.R.O., SC 6/1117/13, rot. 2d.

75 *Cal. Inq. p.m.* i, p. 279; ii, p. 28; xv, p. 80; xvii, p. 171; A.C.M., A 1403, 1407; ibid. M 10, 24.

76 *Cal. Chart. R.* 1327–41, 402.

77 *Rot. Parl.* ii. 348; *V.C.H. Suss.* iii. 95–6; Goodman, *Loyal Conspiracy*, 110.

78 P.R.O., C 139/71, no. 37, m. 32; C 139/88, no. 50, m. 19.

79 A.C.M., M 10–20, 24–5, 27–9, 38–9, 46–52, 271.

80 *Cur. Reg. R.* xii, pp. 212–13.

81 P.R.O., SC 6/1019/22, rot. 1.

82 e.g. A.C.M., A 1403, 1407; ibid. M 10–20, 24; 271, f. [18v.].

83 Ibid. MD 821; below, Arundel, boro. govt. (cts.).

84 A.C.M., M 38; B.L. Add. MS. 5687, f. 28; *Cat. of Horsham Mus. MSS.* ed. S. Freeth and others, p. 29. For the corp.'s contemporary revival of boro. ct. as a separate entity, below, Arundel, boro. govt. (cts.).

85 A.C.M., M 39.

86 e.g. Tierney, *Arundel*, i. 20–1; *Plac. de Quo Warr.* (Rec. Com.), 759; *S.R.S.* xlvi, p. 1.

87 *S.R.S.* lxvii. 104.

88 *Cal. Chart. R.* 1327–41, 402.

89 A.C.M., MD 495, f. [58v.]; 821.

90 *Cal. Fine R.* 1356–68, 160.

91 *P.N. Suss.* (E.P.N.S.), i. 77–8; *250 Yrs. of Mapmaking in Suss.* ed. H. Margary, pl. 26.

92 A.C.M., MD 495, f. [58v.]; 821.

93 *Cal. Chart. R.* 1327–41, 402; cf. P.R.O., SC 6/1120/1.

94 B.L. Add. MS. 5701, f. 145.

95 *Cal. Inq. p.m.* vii, p. 226.

96 A.C.M., MD 2344–8; E.S.R.O., DYK 1121, m. 36; 1123, mm. 26–7; W.S.R.O., PHA 6683, f. 11.

97 A.C.M., MD 821.

two cases of assault on headboroughs in the execution of their duty were heard in the 1560s.

A forest court called the court of wood pleas or woodplayt, which had previously been held yearly, was held every three weeks in 1275, when inhabitants of Avisford hundred complained of its injustice.[98] In 1301, because of poor administration, the income was only 10*s.* a year.[99] An alternative name in 1435 was woodcourt.[1]

Robert FitzTetbald (d. 1087), a prominent under-tenant of earl Roger, was sheriff of the rape in 1086.[2] A bailiff of the honor, evidently also of the rape, was mentioned from 1225,[3] and plural bailiffs occasionally from 1351 or earlier.[4] Holders of the office in the later 16th century included John Apsley[5] and Thomas Lewknor.[6] In the mid 17th century a deputy bailiff,[7] and in 1701 two under-bailiffs,[8] were recorded. The last known bailiff was appointed in 1816.[9] Stewards of the rape were mentioned at various dates between the 13th century and the early 18th.[10] A beadle was recorded in 1275[11] and a receiver between the 14th century and the 16th.[12] A chief forester was mentioned between 1275 and the mid 15th century;[13] in 1435 his jurisdiction covered all the earl of Arundel's forests, woods, and parks in Sussex and Surrey.[14] Leather searchers and sealers were appointed by 1563 to serve both for the rape and for Arundel borough.[15]

A water bailiff appointed in the 15th century had jurisdiction over the Arun from Arundel bridge to Stopham bridge;[16] William Barttelot of Stopham held the office in 1576–7,[17] and Henry Howard-Molyneux-Howard, a relation of the duke of Norfolk, in 1792.[18] The rights and duties of the office were codified *c.* 1637.[19] In 1792 the water bailiff additionally collected harbour dues at Littlehampton.[20]

The office of honor coroner existed by 1567[21] but had lapsed by the early 18th century.[22]

Right to wreck along most of the coastline of the rape belonged to the lord *c.* 1209 and later.[23] In 1275 the Crown as lord had the assize of bread and of ale in each hundred, together with gallows. The rape steward was then attempting to assert his own authority against that of the sheriff: he insisted that 'private' business could not be treated at the tourn in his absence, and also imprisoned felons and accepted fines for their release, on one occasion intercepting a robbery suspect being taken to the gaol at Guildford.[24]

In 1337 the king granted to Richard FitzAlan, earl of Arundel (d. 1376), and his heirs return of all writs and of summonses of the exchequer in Arundel rape.[25] At

98 *S.A.C.* lxxxiv. 68–9; cf. P.R.O., SC 6/1019/22, rot. 1.
99 *S.R.S.* lxvii. 2.
1 P.R.O., C 139/71, no. 37, m. 32; cf. *S.R.S.* lxvii. 93.
2 *V.C.H. Suss.* i. 378; J. A. Green, *Eng. Sheriffs to 1154*, 81.
3 *Cur. Reg. R.* xii, p. 213; *S.A.C.* xxiv. 292; *S.R.S.* lxxiv, p. 53; A.C.M., A 1874.
4 *Cal. Close*, 1272–9, 85; *Cal. Fine R.* 1347–56, 310; 1356–68, 160–1.
5 *Cal. Assize Rec. Suss. Eliz. I*, pp. 1, 50; *S.R.S.* lxxiv, pp. 60, 62.
6 P.R.O., SC 6/Eliz. I/2213, mm. 8–9; Sandbeck Park, Rotherham, Lumley MS. EMA/1/5; *Cal. Assize Rec. Suss. Eliz. I*, pp. 69–152, *passim.*
7 *S.R.S.* liv. 80, 117.
8 *Arundel Cast. Archives*, ed. F. W. Steer, ii, p. 111.
9 W.S.R.O., S.A.S. MS. WH 380 (TS. cat.).
10 *S.R.S.* xl. 66; *S.A.C.* lxxxiv. 69; lxxxix. 159; *Cal. Pat.* 1327–30, 504.
11 *S.A.C.* lxxxiv. 70.
12 Ibid. xci. 34; *S.R.S.* lv. 83; *Cal. Pat.* 1429–36, 464; Sandbeck Park, Rotherham, Lumley MS. EMA/1/5.
13 P.R.O., SC 6/1019/22, rot. 1, m. 3; *Plac. de Quo Warr.* (Rec. Com.), 752; *Cal. Pat.* 1436–41, 63; *Cal. Inq. p.m.* iv, p. 51; *Lavington Estate Archives*, ed. F. W. Steer, p. 20; *S.R.S.* lxvii. 104, 115.
14 *Cal. Pat.* 1429–36, 464.
15 Below, Arundel, boro. govt. (officers).
16 *Cal. Pat.* 1436–41, 32; cf. A.C.M., A 1874.
17 Sandbeck Park, Rotherham, Lumley MS. EMA/1/5.
18 W.S.R.O., QDA/5/W 1.
19 *High Stream of Arundel*, 45–9, 57–62.
20 W.S.R.O., QDA/5/W 1.
21 *Suss. Coroners' Inquests, 1558–1603*, ed. R. Hunnisett, p. 10; cf. *Cal. Pat.* 1572–5, p. 430; 1578–80, p. 137; P.R.O., SC 6/Eliz. I/2213, mm. 8–9.
22 A.C.M., MD 821.
23 Tierney, *Arundel*, i. 21; *S.R.S.* xlvi, p. 220; lxvii. 2, 105; *Cal. Inq. Misc.* i, p. 384; *Abbrev. Plac.* (Rec. Com.), 201; A.C.M., A 339, Arundel surv. 1702, f. 1v.; P.R.O., JUST 1/924, rot. 65d.; below, Avisford Hund.
24 *S.A.C.* lxxxiv. 68–9.
25 *Cal. Chart. R.* 1327–41, 387; *Abbrev. Rot. Orig.* (Rec. Com.), ii. 111, 120. For an example of a return of writ, P.R.O., C 131/50, no. 1.

the confirmation of the grant in 1554 further franchises were added in the hundreds of Avisford, West Easwrith, and Poling only: the estreats and precepts of the eyre justices for pleas of the Crown, common pleas and pleas of the forest, and those of other justices, and attachments of pleas of the Crown and of others; the goods of convicted felons, heretics, and traitors, waifs and strays, deodands, treasure trove, and free warren and free chase.[26] In 1570 those franchises were claimed in all five hundreds of the rape.[27] Goods belonging to murderers and suicides were taken between the 1550s and 70s and deodands in the 1570s.[28] The right to appoint a coroner was also enjoyed by 1567.[29]

Fines from the court of king's bench and post fines under the green wax were still received in the later 17th century and early 18th. At the latter period the dukes of Norfolk still claimed, in addition to the franchises granted or confirmed in 1554, the right to appoint a clerk of the market and all fines and forfeitures at the sessions and assizes; through failure to attend the latter, however, the income had been usurped by the officers of the Crown. The income under the green wax was then *c.* £15 a year, but was said once to have been over £100.[30] The collection of most of the monies was farmed in 1700 and later.[31] Deodands were still taken in the 1780s,[32] and post fines under the green wax and fines from the court of common pleas and from the sessions were still received in the early 19th century.[33] As late as the 1930s the duke of Norfolk claimed the foreshore and right to wreck within Arundel rape.[34]

From the mid 13th century the rape consisted of five hundreds or half-hundreds: Avisford, Bury, West Easwrith, Poling and Rotherbridge.[35] In 1086 Avisford was called Binsted and Poling Risberge.[36] West Easwrith was the section of Easwrith hundred in Arundel rape, the rest being in Bramber rape; it was called a half-hundred in 1296, but thereafter a hundred.[37] Bury hundred was called a half-hundred in 1296 and 1302[38] but not apparently after that. The fact that Arundel and Chichester rapes had only 12 hundreds between them, while each of the other rapes had more than ten, presumably reflects their having once been a single rape.[39]

26 *Cal. Pat.* 1553–4, 69–70.

27 A.C.M., MD 535, f. 6v.

28 *S.R.S.* lxxiv, pp. 53, 60, 62; P.R.O., SC 6/Eliz. I/ 2213, mm. 8–9; Sandbeck Park, Rotherham, Lumley MS. EMA/1/5.

29 Above.

30 *Arundel Cast. Archives*, i, p. 169; A.C.M., A 118, pp. 38–40; 1282–8; ibid. MD 505, loose sheet between ff. [9v.] and [10]; 821; 2353.

31 *Arundel Cast. Archives*, i, p. 169; *Cat. of Horsham Mus. MSS.* p. 124; A.C.M., MD 1262, f. 6.

32 A.C.M., A 444.

33 Ibid. 480–1, 1289–1305, 1364.

34 *Arundel Cast. Archives*, ii, p. 49; iii, p. 80; cf. ibid. ii, p. 46.

35 *V.C.H. Suss.* iv. 2; *S.R.S.* x. 68–81.

36 *V.C.H. Suss.* i. 538.

37 *S.A.C.* xcviii. 38; *S.R.S.* x. 74, 146, 259.

38 *Cal. Inq. p.m.* iv, p. 51; *S.R.S.* x. 72.

39 Above.

ARUNDEL RAPE

(South-western Part)

THE south-western part of Arundel rape, the hundred of Avisford, lies west of the river Arun, partly on the dip slope of the South Downs but mostly on the coastal plain. The river formerly made a wide estuary, while other inlets rendered Yapton, Climping, and Ford a peninsula and Felpham and Middleton perhaps once an island. The valleys were gradually reclaimed from the early Middle Ages. Both the river Arun and other watercourses were followed by parish boundaries, the Ryebank rife separating several parishes and a former detached part of a parish, and south-flowing streams dividing Walberton from Binsted and Eastergate from Barnham. Much land was lost to the sea in historic times along the whole coastal frontage, and erosion and inland flooding remained problems in the late 20th century.

The area has been densely settled from an early period. The configuration of parish boundaries may suggest the existence of larger pre-medieval jurisdictional and tenurial units: Barnham, Eastergate, and Yapton appear to go together, Binsted and Tortington with Walberton, and Ford with most of Climping, while the Ryebank rife may have been the northern boundary of a unit including Felpham, Middleton, Cudlow (in Climping), and the detached parts of Littlehampton within Climping. Many parishes in the Middle Ages had more than one nucleated settlement, and two villages, Barnham and Walberton, show evidence of a planned layout. Many settlements later shrank or disappeared altogether through the movement of population or sea erosion.

The only town in the hundred, Arundel, perhaps originated as a late Anglo-Saxon *burh* in succession to Burpham nearby. After the Norman Conquest, in the shadow of its castle, it was the head of a feudal honor which included Chichester rape as well as Arundel. The town remained small, but partly because of self-consciously antiquarian rebuilding in the 19th and 20th centuries became one of the county's chief tourist attractions.

The 19th and 20th centuries have seen a great growth in population in the rest of the area. Felpham and Middleton developed as seaside resorts and places for residence and retirement, especially during the 20th century, when both were joined physically to Bognor Regis. The opening of Barnham station in 1864 led by the early 20th century to much building in Eastergate. Walberton and Yapton villages also greatly expanded in the later 20th century. After 1964 the area of the 'five villages', including Barnham, Eastergate, Walberton, and Yapton,[1] was characterized by a mixture of countryside and suburbia; much land was given over to market gardens, farm shops, riding stables, and paddocks. Other leisure activities, which included a marina at Ford, centred on roadside or riverside inns and tea gardens, and on two hotels in former country houses, Bailiffscourt in Climping and Avisford House in Walberton.

Both arable and brookland pasture in the area have long been highly regarded. Arable was dominant in the mid 14th century and early 19th, but in the later 19th and 20th centuries pasture increased to supply growing urban populations with milk and meat. Most open fields were inclosed early by agreement, but Eastergate

[1] Char. Com. files, for the Five-village soc. founded in that yr.; the 5th village is Aldingbourne.

and Walberton commons remained uninclosed until the late 18th century. The northern part of the area carries much woodland, and parkland, especially in the north, has been an important land use since medieval times.

The Eocene and later deposits of the coastal plain supported brick- and tilemaking from the 14th century,[2] and after the later 19th the favourable climate led to a great expansion in market gardening, especially in the 'five villages' area, to serve local towns, London, and places further afield. The sea provided much employment, both in fishing and in maritime trade, with small harbours or landing places at Felpham, Middleton, and Cudlow (in Climping). The port of Arundel had commercial links with various parts of the Continent, but declined in the 19th century in favour of Littlehampton at the mouth of the Arun. Arundel's other economic activity before the 19th century related chiefly to its agricultural hinterland or to the port.

In the early 20th century an aircraft factory at Middleton and an airfield at Ford were constructed to take advantage of the flat terrain. The site of Ford airfield in 1996 accommodated two industrial estates, and there were also small rural business estates in other places as well as an industrial estate in Arundel. In the 19th and early 20th centuries many residents in the area worked for the great landed proprietors, but by the later 20th century large numbers travelled daily to work elsewhere, especially in London and the coastal towns.

Arundel's medieval markets and fairs were eclipsed after 1882 by Barnham market in Eastergate near the railway junction, but the later revival of road transport helped cause the closure of Barnham market itself.

Some parishes in Avisford hundred had only a single manor, while in others, notably Yapton, the manorial structure was more complex. In the Middle Ages much property belonged to religious houses, among them Sées abbey (Orne), Tortington and Boxgrove priories, and Arundel priory and college. The extensive estates of the earls of Arundel and dukes of Norfolk are mentioned above.[3] Other important landowners in the area were the St. John and Poynings families in the Middle Ages and the Edmundses in the 16th and 17th centuries. Parts of the area belonged at different periods to the estates centred on Goodwood House near Chichester, Slindon House, and Dale Park in Madehurst. Christ's Hospital in London had lands at Ford and Climping in the 18th and 19th centuries which eventually comprised most of those two parishes, while shorter-lived great estates in the 19th and 20th belonged to the owners of Walberton House and Avisford House in Walberton and Bailiffscourt in Climping. Distinctive estate cottages mark the extent of the Christ's Hospital and Arundel castle estates.

A possibly pre-Conquest minster church at Arundel was succeeded in the later Middle Ages by a group of religious houses in and around the town. A remarkable proportion of churches in Avisford hundred were dedicated to St. Mary. Two medieval parishes ceased to exist and were incorporated in Climping by the 16th century; both their churches have disappeared, as has the medieval church of Middleton because of coastal erosion. There were medieval chapels of ease in Felpham and Yapton, long disused.

Nonconformists, especially Presbyterians, were prominent in Arundel in the mid 17th century. Dissent was further encouraged by Anglican stagnation during the 18th, when many incumbents did not reside and several parishes were without

[2] Below, Binsted, econ. hist.

[3] Above, Arundel Rape.

glebe houses. Anglicanism revived during the 19th century. All the churches underwent restoration between *c.* 1850 and 1900, though at Binsted and at Middleton, where a new site was found further inland, the potential congregations hardly justified the work. New clergy houses were provided after *c.* 1840 at Barnham, Binsted, Eastergate, Felpham, and Yapton. After the mid 19th century there was a striking growth in Roman Catholicism in and around Arundel.

The Roman road from Chichester to Brighton passed through the northern part of the hundred, and in the Middle Ages was succeeded by the great road from Southampton to Canterbury which used the lowest bridging point on the river Arun at Arundel.[4] Some north–south routes evidently linked manors near the coast with outlying holdings in the Weald, but there was no reliable north–south route in the Arun valley until the arrival of the railway in the mid 19th century. The road from Chichester via Eastergate to Climping was important in the Middle Ages and later, but other road communication in the south part of Avisford hundred was poor. No coast road was ever provided, and direct communication between Bognor and Littlehampton only became possible from the 1820s.

The river Arun was used by passenger as well as commercial transport, with a wharf at Ford besides the port at Arundel; there may also have been coastal passenger routes, and the beach itself could be used by horses and wagons, even the Arun estuary being fordable at low tide. New east–west routes through the area were provided in the 19th century first by the Portsmouth–Arundel canal and then by the Brighton–Portsmouth railway.

4 Cf. *V.C.H. Suss.* vi (1), 203.

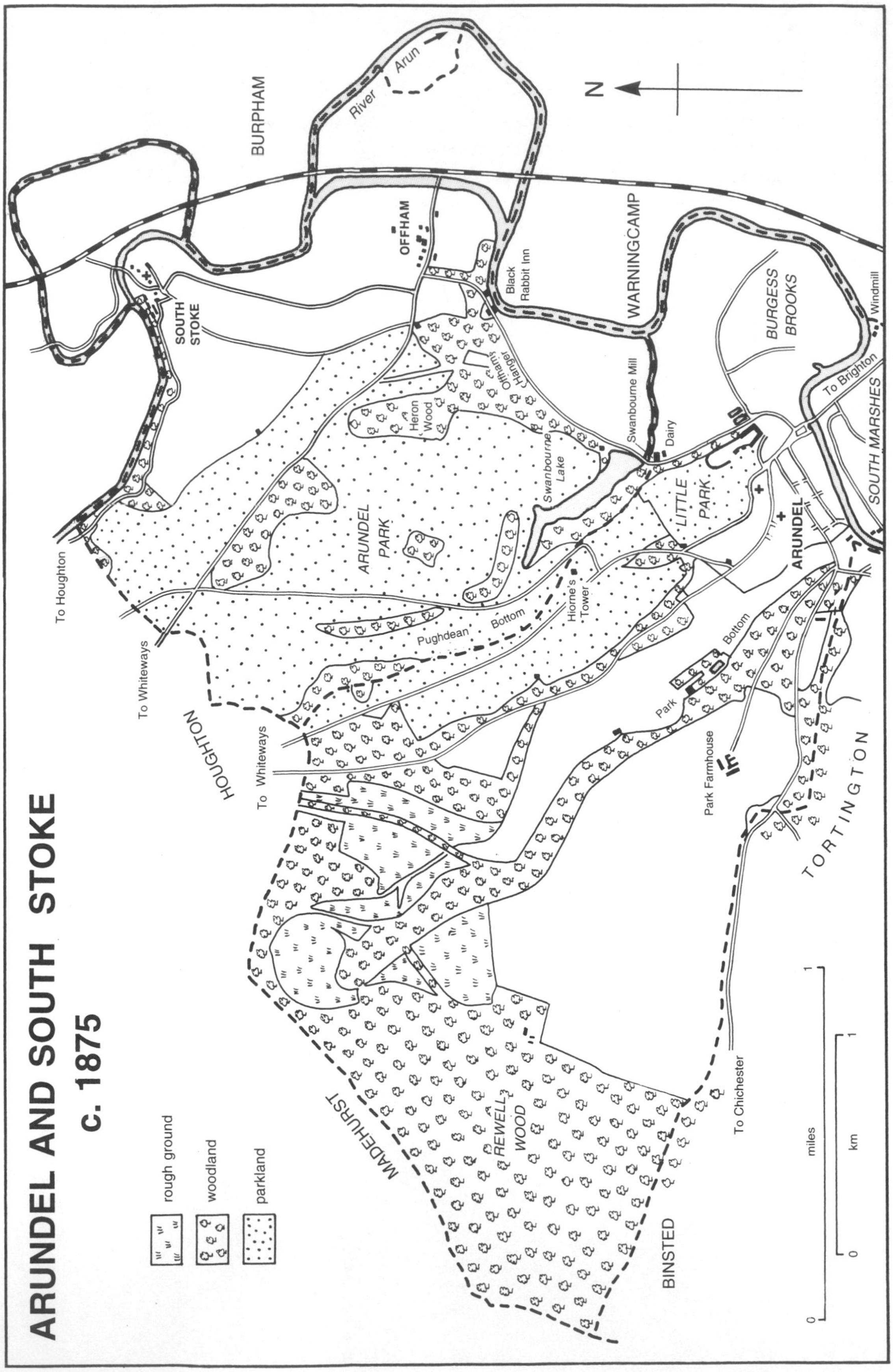
ARUNDEL AND SOUTH STOKE
c. 1875
rough ground
woodland
parkland
N
BURPHAM
River Arun
OFFHAM
Black Rabbit Inn
WARNINGCAMP
BURGESS BROOKS
Windmill
To Brighton
SOUTH MARSHES
SOUTH STOKE
Offham Hanger
Heron Wood
Swanbourne Mill
Dairy
Swanbourne Lake
ARUNDEL PARK
LITTLE PARK
ARUNDEL
To Houghton
To Whiteways
HOUGHTON
Pughdean Bottom
Hiorne's Tower
Park Bottom
Park Farmhouse
TORTINGTON
To Whiteways
MADEHURST
REWELL WOOD
BINSTED
To Chichester
0 miles 1
0 km 1

ARUNDEL

THE former borough of Arundel,[1] dominated by its castle and 19th-century Roman Catholic church, later cathedral, lies *c.* 3 miles (5 km.) from Littlehampton, at the lowest point where the river Arun could be bridged.

The borough and civil parish were co-extensive in the early 19th century[2] and possibly earlier.[3] In 1881 they consisted of 1,969 a. including water. In 1902 they were enlarged on the south side by the addition of the north-east corner of Tortington (*c.* 85 a.), together with a strip of waste land belonging to the same parish north of Chichester Road. In 1911 and 1971 Arundel had 2,054 a. (831 ha.).[4] Most of the rest of the ancient parish of Tortington was transferred to Arundel in 1985.[5] The present article deals broadly with Arundel parish as constituted before the last named date.[6]

The parish in past centuries included arable north-west of the town, since converted to other uses, together with downland pasture in the same area; riverside meadow in the south and east; and forest and parkland, the latter afterwards converted to agriculture, on the shallower soil of the west and north-west.[7] In the east the boundary followed a meander of the river Arun, evidently to include the meadow later known as the burgess brooks. The south-eastern boundary, including other meadow called the south marshes, also follows a watercourse which, however, *pace* Allcroft, apparently never was the main course of the river.[8] Part of the western boundary follows a linear earthwork, possibly prehistoric,[9] which also served as the boundary of Rewell wood west of the medieval Great park. In 1605 part of that boundary was disputed between Arundel and Madehurst.[10]

The parish lies largely on chalk, overlain in the south-west by brickearth, valley gravel, and Reading Beds clay, and in the river valley and in Park bottom west of the town by alluvium.[11] North and west of the town the ground rises on the dip slope of the South Downs to between 100 and 125 metres (328 and 410 ft.), giving fine views of the coastal plain; beyond the north-western boundary it falls sharply away to Fairmile bottom in Madehurst. Park bottom west of the town and Pughdean bottom to the north are valleys in the chalk, in each of which a stream formed a pond. Swanbourne lake in Pughdean bottom, a former mill pond, lies in South Stoke. Park bottom may once have been an inlet of the river Arun, since the town gate at the west end of Maltravers Street was known as the Watergate. In the mid 17th century, when the pond there was called the great pond, it was 17 a. in area.[12] By 1732 it had been drained, forming a close later called the Boggy meads.[13]

The river Arun seems in Roman times to have formed a wide tidal estuary,[14] its Celtic name Trisantona (i.e. Tarrant) perhaps alluding to its proneness to flooding.[15] The depth of alluvium at more than one place near the town is over 30 metres (100 ft.).[16] In the early Middle Ages there may have been more than one channel, as in the river Adur at Bramber,[17] but the often repeated, yet erroneous, statement that the present course of the river past the town was newly cut by the earl of Arundel in the mid 16th century[18] seems to derive from misconstruction of a 17th-century reference to river improvement higher up the valley.[19] The name Tarrant is recorded *c.* 725 and *c.* 1270, but the normal medieval name was apparently the river of Arundel, Arundel river, or the high stream of Arundel.[20] The modern name is recorded from 1577,[21] but the names Arundel river or great river continued to be used later.[22] In the 20th century the Arun was said to be the second fastest flowing river in the country, with a speed of up to seven knots at full flood.[23]

1 This article was written in 1990 and revised in 1995–6. Much help was received from Mrs. Ian Rodger and Dr. J. M. Robinson, Arundel Cast., Mr. F. Penfold, Burpham, and Mr. J. Godfrey, Arundel.

2 *Rep. Parl. Bdries.* H.C. 141–V, p. 63 (1831–2), xl; *1st Rep. Com. Mun. Corp.* 668.

3 Below, boro. govt.

4 *Census*, 1881–1971; *Kelly's Dir. Suss.* (1903); W.S.R.O., WOC/CC 8/6.

5 Arun (Parishes) Order 1985.

6 Cf. below, Tortington, intro.

7 Below, agric.; A.C.M., A 339, Arundel surv. 1702, f. 2.

8 A. H. Allcroft, *Waters of Arun*, 56.

9 S.M.R. 1305.

10 P.R.O., E 134/3 Jas. I East./28, rott. 3–4d., 7–8; cf. A.C.M., MD 775, giving a probably 16th-cent. opinion.

11 Para. based on Geol. Surv. Map 1", drift, sheet 317 (1957 edn.); O.S. Map 1/25,000, SU 80/90 (1981 edn.); TQ 00/10 (1979 edn.).

12 A.C.M., MD 505, f. [5].

13 Ibid. D 6266; ibid. H 1/3.

14 *S.A.C.* cxvii. 66, 68; *S.N.Q.* xi. 142, 145–6; below, communications (rds.).

15 A. L. F. Rivet and C. Smith, *Place Names of Rom. Brit.* 476–7.

16 C. Reid, *Geol. of Country near Chich.* 45; cf. F. H. Edmunds, *Wells and Springs of Suss.* 199; W. Whitaker, *Water Supply of Suss., Suppl.* 205.

17 *V.C.H. Suss.* vi (1), 201.

18 Allcroft, *Waters of Arun*, 58, 141; *S.N.Q.* ix. 175.

19 *High Stream of Arundel*, 21; cf. Caraccioli, *Arundel*, 270; Horsfield, *Hist. Suss.* i. 7.

20 *P.N. Suss.* (E.P.N.S.), i. 3; *Cal. Pat.* 1388–92, 440; 1575–8, p. 520; *Cal. S.P. Dom.* Addenda 1566–79, 68; *High Stream of Arundel*, 11; *Wiston Archives*, i, ed. J. Booker, p. 33; P.R.O., C 133/104, no. 21, m. 2.

21 *P.N. Suss.* (E.P.N.S.), i. 3.

22 *S.R.S.* xxix, p. 10; *S.A.C.* lxxi. 55; Young, *Agric. of Suss.* 351; W.S.R.O., Add. MS. 8697.

23 *W. Suss. Gaz.* 7 Aug. 1986.

The area later called the burgess brooks had been inned by the late 11th or early 12th century, when the burgesses had pasture rights there.[24] Several meadow of 84 a. mentioned in 1272[25] was presumably what later became the south marshes; the hay on 75 a. was said in 1275 to have been destroyed by floods.[26] The 100 a. of meadow belonging to the castle in 1386[27] was evidently the same. River defences in Arundel are perhaps alluded to in the late 14th century,[28] and there are references to inning in the area in the 1540s.[29] The burgess brooks had defences against flooding in 1546[30] and the south marshes apparently in 1570.[31] A particularly destructive flood was recorded in 1509.[32]

In the burgess brooks in the 17th and 18th centuries a river wall, i.e. bank, delimited brookland pasture from strips of land called slips or slipes outside; osiers or reeds grew on the slipes in the earlier 17th century, but by 1761 the land provided good pasture, one slipe having been mowed regularly for *c.* 60 years.[33] An outer bank was constructed to include the slipes, apparently by 1782 and certainly by 1799.[34] Under an Act of 1793 a towpath was made from Arundel to Littlehampton on the west side of the river.[35] Further severe floods were recorded in 1774, in 1809,[36] and later in the 19th century and early 20th, possibly exacerbated by dredging, embanking, and the elimination of meanders above the town, which increased the volume and force of water in the river.[37] The river bank was raised in 1834.[38]

The fishing of the river at Arundel was held in demesne by the lords of the rape from 1086[39] or earlier, often being farmed.[40] The fishing of a weir (*gurgite*), perhaps at Swanbourne, was also mentioned in 1272;[41] in 1421 and presumably earlier the earl of Arundel's fishery extended from the sea as far upstream as Pallingham in Wisborough Green.[42] In the 17th century[43] and again in the mid 19th[44] the lords of the rape acted strenuously to preserve their rights to the river, though in 1658 there was only poor fishing since the river was full of weeds.[45] The Arundel estate still claimed the bed of the river from the sea to Pallingham in 1980, letting fishing rights to local clubs and mooring rights to individuals.[46] Pike and eel were abundant in 1817,[47] but the grey mullet caught between Arundel and the sea had a special reputation for size and flavour from the mid 17th century, being praised by Isaak Walton and Thomas Fuller, and the subject of a rhyme.[48] In the 1650s and 60s mullet were sent both to Arundel House in London and to Henry Howard's house at Albury (Surr.), and in the 18th century and early 19th to London.[49] Large quantities were netted *c.* 1907, but catches afterwards became rarer,[50] though they still occurred in 1991.[51] The name mullet has been used as a sobriquet for natives of the town.

GENERAL HISTORY OF THE TOWN. There are traces of prehistoric settlement, including a field system, in the west end of the parish,[52] and there was possibly a prehistoric earthwork on the site of Arundel castle.[53] A large and luxurious Roman villa, with a hypocaust, mosaic work, and much painted plaster, was built in the 1st century A.D. between the west end of Tarrant Street and the river Arun. Comparable to those at Angmering and elsewhere in Sussex, and accessible both from the river and from the Roman road between Chichester and Brighton, it may be the successor to a pre-Roman nobleman's farm.[54] No later Roman settlement in the parish is known.

There was apparently a minster church at Arundel before the Norman Conquest, suggesting an important Anglo-Saxon settlement, but the entry in Domesday Book is equivocal.[55] Possibly the earthworks north-west of the castle represent a late Saxon *burh* succeeding that at Burpham 1½ miles (2.4 km.) north-east, in the same way that Guildford (Surr.) replaced Eashing.[56] Their site is traversed from north to south by a presumably ancient road; it would have been a likely one for settlement, and there may already have been a small port on the river.[57]

By 1086 Arundel was a town with burgesses.[58] In the Middle Ages it was very much under the domination of the lords of the rape, both economically and in other ways, and also served

24 Below, agric.
25 P.R.O., C 132/42, no. 5, deducing acreage from valuation.
26 Ibid. SC 6/1019/22, rot. 1.
27 *Cal. Inq. p.m.* vi, p. 219.
28 *Cal. Pat.* 1388–92, 440; *Cal. Close,* 1399–1402, 186.
29 *S.N.Q.* xiii. 155.
30 W.S.R.O., A.B.A., A1, f. 257v.
31 A.C.M., MD 535, f. 5.
32 *S.N.Q.* xiii. 154; cf. *Cal. S.P. Dom.* Addenda 1566–79, 68.
33 A.C.M., MD 2510; W.S.R.O., Ep. I/25/1 (1615, 1663).
34 W.S.R.O., A.B.A., F1/13, no. 1; F1/25, no. 11.
35 33 Geo. III, c. 100; W.S.R.O., QDP/W 1.
36 *S.A.C.* lxxi. 37, 52.
37 Ibid. lxiii. 58–9; *W. Suss. Gaz.* 17 Feb. 1983; W.S.R.O., Hawkins Papers 21/7, p. 15; *Arundel Rds.* 46, 50, 54, 58; but cf. ibid. 26.
38 W.S.R.O., A.B.A., F1/1.
39 *V.C.H. Suss.* i. 421.
40 A.C.M., MD 535, f. 4v.; P.R.O., SC 6/1029/22; SC 6/1117/13, rot. 2d.; *Cal. Inq. Misc.* vi, p. 219; *S.R.S.* lxvii. 94.
41 P.R.O., C 132/42, no. 5; cf. ibid. C 133/104, no. 21, m. 2; *Cal. Inq. p.m.* vii, p. 227.
42 P.R.O., C 138/59, no. 51, m. 14.
43 *V.C.H. Suss.* ii. 270; *Arundel Cast. Archives,* ii. 41; A.C.M., A 262, f. [23v.].
44 A.C.M., MD 628.
45 Ibid. A 262, f. [23v.].
46 *Country Life,* 3 July 1980, p. 7.
47 Wright, *Arundel* (1817), 3.
48 *High Stream of Arundel,* 42–3; Allcroft, *Waters of Arun,* 48; Camden, *Brit.* (1789), i. 197; Horsfield, *Hist. Suss.* ii. 122; *S.A.C.* xiii. 232; Hist. MSS. Com. 29, *13th Rep. II, Portland,* ii, pp. 275–6 ('Arundel mullet as they hear. Is the best in England for good cheer, But at 6*d.* the pound 'tis pretty dear').
49 *V.C.H. Suss.* ii. 271; Defoe, *Tour,* ed. Cole, i. 132; Wright, *Arundel* (1817), 3; A.C.M., A 262, ff. [11, 22, 23v.]; 263, acct. 1664.
50 *V.C.H. Suss.* ii. 466; Allcroft, *Waters of Arun,* 48–9.
51 Inf. from Mrs. Rodger.
52 *S.A.C.* lxi. 28 and facing p. 20; cxvii. 257; S.M.R. 1315, 1342, 1382; O.S. Map 1/25,000, SU 80/90 (1981 edn.).
53 Below, defences.
54 P. Drewett, D. Rudling and M. Gardiner, *SE. to AD 1000,* 191, 193; *S.A.S. Newsletter,* xliii. 384–5; *S.A.C.* cxvii. 79.
55 Below, church; *V.C.H. Suss.* i. 421. The derivation of the name is 'horehound dell', the plant being profuse locally: M. Gelling, *Place-Names in Landscape,* 258; *Shoreham Herald,* 4 Aug. 1961; *Surr. Arch. Coll.* xxxvii. 124 n.
56 *A.-S. Towns in Southern Eng.* ed. J. Haslam, 46, 265; cf. ibid. 262, 264; below, defences.
57 Drewett, Rudling and Gardiner, op. cit. 337.
58 *V.C.H. Suss.* i. 421.

as the centre of rape administration. The prosperity of the town in the later 13th century is perhaps shown by the presence of a Jewish community, which may have lived in Mill Lane, later known as Jury Lane.[59] In 1334 Arundel had the third largest assessment to subsidy of any Sussex town outside the Cinque ports.[60] Its development was retarded by two fires, in 1338 and 1344–5, the first of which was claimed to have destroyed at least half the town;[61] as a result, Arundel's assessment to the tax of 1340 was the lowest among Sussex towns outside the Cinque ports.[62] In the later Middle Ages the less regular residence of the earls of Arundel may have acted as a brake on the growth of trade. Another reason for sluggish development at that date is likely to have been the nearness of Chichester, which besides being the centre of a rape and a more important port, was also the seat of the bishop. Arundel was the scene of a rising during the Peasants' Revolt of 1381[63] and of an abortive aristocratic plot against Richard II in 1397.[64]

In 1524 three quarters of the inhabitants owned goods valued at £2 or more; yet Arundel was then only tenth in the ranking of Sussex towns,[65] a position it roughly retained during the 17th and 18th centuries.[66] In 1586 Camden described the town as 'greater in fame than in fact'.[67] By the mid 16th century a close corporation had developed, which in the 17th and 18th centuries was the chief governing body of the town.[68] During the same period the earls of Arundel and their successors the dukes of Norfolk, partly because they only occasionally resided, and partly perhaps as a consequence of the attainder of Philip Howard, earl of Arundel, in 1589, lost much of their control over the town.

In the mid 17th century a Presbyterian party was dominant in Arundel.[69] In 1631 a clergyman, William Lewis, was violently seized and imprisoned on suspicion of drunkenness by the mayor and constable; they were later fined *in absentia* and excommunicated by the court of High Commission.[70] The corporation minute book in the 1640s and 50s uses the expressions 'minister' for vicar, 'Lord's day' for Sunday, and 'ungodly' behaviour, and *c.* 1650 the oath for new burgesses was replaced by a 'faithful promise'.[71] In 1662 the mayor and 11 burgesses, presumably the entire corporation, were dismissed from office for refusal to take the Corporation Act oath.[72] At the view of frankpledge in 1671, however, the Presbyterian faction engineered the election of several Dissenting burgesses and a Dissenting mayor, John Pellett; while the resulting lawsuit was in progress two more Nonconformist mayors were elected.[73] Two burgesses refused the oath of fidelity to William III in 1690.[74]

In the early 18th century visitors to the town described it variously as poor, paltry, and decayed.[75] From the 1720s the dukes of Norfolk began to reside there more often, leading to a gradual revival of Arundel's dependence on the castle. Duke Edward's attempt in 1735 to regain the seigneurial interest in parliamentary elections was abortive, but by the 1770s he had succeeded,[76] and in 1775 he was on good enough terms with the corporation to receive it officially.[77] From 1779 or earlier the dukes presented the corporation annually with a buck for a feast.[78]

Duke Charles (d. 1815) began from the later 18th century to buy property in and around the town on a large scale; the consequent enlargement of the castle grounds, the creation of the new landscaped park north of the town, and the rebuilding of the castle itself gave physical embodiment to the re-establishment of seigneurial dominance. In 1796 the Arundel volunteers were entertained to dinner at the castle,[79] and the corporation's acceptance of a similar invitation in 1810[80] indicates its acquiescence in the new situation. In 1814 the duke founded what was later the Church of England school, setting the pattern for many further acts of largesse by successive dukes.[81] In 1815 the newly refurbished castle was the setting for a fête held to mark the 600th anniversary of the signing of Magna Carta, and which also expressed the dukes' renewed local status. In a deliberate attempt to recreate the town's medieval splendour, carriages as they arrived were saluted by bugles from the parapet of the new castle gateway, suits of armour and weapons were hung from the internal walls as decoration, and dinner was accompanied by martial music, venison being served by two park keepers and the chief forester dressed in Lincoln green; a ball concluded the celebrations.[82]

Meanwhile, the late 18th century and early 19th had seen a considerable boom in the town's trade,[83] evidenced in the grand buildings put up then; it had begun to slow down apparently by

59 *Sel. Pleas of Exch. of Jews* (Selden Soc. xv), 69–70; *Cal. Plea Rolls of Exch. of Jews* (Jewish Hist. Soc. of Eng.), i. 291; M. Adler, *Jews of Medieval Eng.* 308, 351; cf. *Pipe R.* 1197 (P.R.S. N.S. viii), 224; below, growth of town (street names).

60 *S.A.C.* l. 163.

61 *Cal. Close*, 1337–9, 454; 1339–41, 214; *Rot. Parl.* ii. 185–6; *Inq. Non.* (Rec. Com.), 370.

62 *S.A.C.* lxxviii. 212.

63 R. B. Dobson, *Peasants' Revolt of 1381* (1970), 143, 194.

64 *D.N.B.* s.v. Thos. de Beauchamp, earl of Warw. (d. 1401); Dallaway & Cartwright, *Hist. W. Suss.* ii (1) (1832), 103.

65 *S.A.C.* cxiv. 7, 16; *S.R.S.* lvi. 43–4.

66 *S.A.C.* xcvi. 103–4.

67 Camden, *Brit.* (1586), 156.

68 Below, boro. govt.

69 *S.A.C.* cxxviii. 157–75.

70 *Cal. S.P. Dom.* 1635, 49, 203; 1644, 79.

71 W.S.R.O., A.B.A., A1, ff. 50v.–51, 54v., 62; Eustace, *Arundel*, 180.

72 W.S.R.O., A.B.A., M11.

73 Ibid. A.B.A., L3, no. 3; Eustace, *Arundel*, 188–9.

74 W.S.R.O., A.B.A., A1, f. 109v.

75 Defoe, *Tour*, ed. Cole, i. 132; J. Macky, *Journey through Eng.* i (1732), 129; B.L. Add. MS. 5842, f. 125v.

76 Below, parl. representation.

77 *S.A.C.* lxxi. 39.

78 Below, boro. govt. (activity, property, and income).

79 *S.C.M.* iii. 665–6.

80 *S.A.C.* lxxi. 54.

81 Below, soc. and cultural activities; castle grounds; boro. govt. (town halls); church [fabric], (other fittings); educ.; charities for the poor. There seems no evidence for the statement that Duke Thos. (d. 1732) paid half the cost of the new bridge in 1724: Eustace, *Arundel*, 204; below, communications (rds.).

82 A.C.M., DB 68; *Excursions through Suss.* (1822), 157–8; J. M. Robinson, *Dukes of Norf.* (1982), 182–3. For a similar idea at Windsor in 1805, M. Girouard, *Return to Camelot*, 24.

83 Dally, *Bognor* (1828), 191.

the 1830s, with the town's replacement by Littlehampton as the chief port on the river Arun.[84] Labourers from the town took part in the unrest of 1830 with the support of some better-off inhabitants who were reluctant to be enrolled as special constables.[85] In the early 1830s, during the agitation which led to the reform of municipal corporations in 1835, opposition to Arundel's close corporation was fomented by Duke Bernard Edward (d. 1842) through his steward Robert Watkins, who organized a petition on the subject.[86] After the reform Watkins, who was the object of strong personal dislike in the town,[87] attempted to influence elections to the new town council.[88] By then, however, the vast increase of the ducal estates in and around Arundel was beginning to be felt by some as a threat: the duke was thought to have designs on the burgess brooks, and to be planning to develop Littlehampton at Arundel's expense.[89] In 1851 Duke Henry Charles's attempt to close Mill Lane was successfully opposed at quarter sessions.[90]

An important aspect of the town's history in the same period was the growth of tourism. Bishop Pococke in 1754[91] had noted Arundel's 'very pleasant' situation on the side of a hill, and another writer in 1790 praised the view from Lyminster and Burpham, with the 'noble shade of woods and hills' as a backdrop to town and castle.[92] In the late 18th century and early 19th visitors to Brighton and Bognor made summer excursions to Arundel,[93] and *c.* 1832 its environs were said to have many pleasant walks and rides.[94] Like other Sussex towns, it was already becoming a place of residence for retired or moneyed people;[95] sixteen 'private residents' were listed *c.* 1832, including five clergy,[96] and in 1851 many were said to be drawn to live there because of the fine scenery nearby.[97] One visitor in the mid 1830s who was particularly struck was the painter John Constable (d. 1837); he stayed more than once with the brewer George Constable, not a relative, finding the town and its surroundings magnificent: 'the Castle is the cheif ornament ... but all here sinks to insignificance in comparison with the woods, and hills'.[98]

Relations between town and castle improved after the accession of Duke Henry in 1860, an address being presented to him on his majority in 1868 by the town council, and a firework display held in honour of his wedding in 1877.[99] The new rapprochement survived the high feelings engendered by the 'Fitzalan chapel case' of 1879–80 and the building of the new Roman Catholic church shortly before,[1] and was symbolized at the end of the century by the replacement of Mill Lane in 1894, to the town's satisfaction, with the tree-lined Mill Road, and by the duke's election in 1902 as mayor.[2] In 1897 five thousand local children were entertained in Arundel park in celebration of the Diamond Jubilee, the whole town being *en fête*.[3]

Meanwhile, the renewed dominance of the dukes led from the mid 19th century to a bias against change. Duke Bernard Edward (d. 1842) had apparently opposed the idea of a railway in 1837,[4] the first two stations to serve the town were over a mile away, and the direct line when it arrived in the 1860s remained at a distance. As a result, the town's economy continued to be eroded. In 1847 Arundel was said to be quiet except on market and fair days,[5] and in 1874 to have changed little in the previous 25 years.[6] Writers in the early 20th century referred to its 'low pulse' and stationary trade;[7] that period saw the decline of important industries and the extinction of the town's port, market, and fairs.

Duke Henry was particularly concerned to preserve the town's historic character, and medieval styles were used in the later 19th century both in the rebuilding of the castle and in new buildings on the Norfolk estate and elsewhere.[8] The growth of tourism continued. With the advent of the railway Arundel had become a goal of excursionists, for instance members of the Ancient Order of Foresters from Brighton in 1849.[9] In the later 19th century the town's ancient appearance and restful atmosphere attracted increasing numbers.[10] By then many individual visitors too were day excursionists from the lower middle classes, to judge from a contemporary guide book explicitly addressed to the 'toilers and moilers' and 'the fagged clerk, or wearied assistant'.[11] Anglers from London were said to visit Arundel in 1904.[12] By 1934 the chamber of commerce was trying to boost

84 Below, port and river traffic (1800–50).
85 E. J. Hobsbawm and G. Rudé, *Capt. Swing*, 111, 255; W. Albery, *Millennium of Facts in Hist. of Horsham and Suss. 947–1947*, 553.
86 W.S.R.O., A.B.A., M49.
87 Ibid. A.B.A., M50.
88 A.C.M., MD 2036.
89 Ibid. 417, 2036.
90 Below, communications (rds.).
91 *Pococke's Travels*, ii (Camd. Soc. 2nd ser. xliv), 107.
92 *Topographer*, iii (1791), 201, 205; cf. *Worthing Parade*, i (Worthing Art Devel. Scheme), 161; Tierney, *Arundel*, i. 8. Many prints of the view appeared at the time: W.S.R.O., PD 1374; *Beauties of Eng. and Wales, Suss.* facing p. 77; *Excursions through Suss.* (1822), facing p. 150.
93 *European Mag. and Lond. Rev.* xxxvi (1799), 151; Dally, *Bognor* (1828), p. x.
94 Pigot, *Nat. Com. Dir.* (1832–4), 1003; cf. Dally, *Bognor* (1828), 191.
95 Dally, *Bognor* (1828), 191.
96 Pigot, *Nat. Com. Dir.* (1832–4), 1003.
97 *Arundel Rds.* 57. The case against the new rd. to replace Mill Lane rested chiefly on the importance of the scenery, in an early example of the conservationist argument: e.g. ibid. 40–1.
98 *D.N.B.*; *John Constable's Corresp.* iii (Suff. Rec. Soc. viii), 111–12; v (Suff. Rec. Soc. xi), 9, 17, 25, 37; cf. below, mills.
99 *Arundel Cast. Archives*, iii. 71.

1 e.g. A.C.M., MD 2016.
2 Eustace, *Arundel*, 244; below, communications (rds.). 'H. Howard', presumably Lord Hen. Howard-Molyneux-Howard, brother of Duke Bernard Edw. (d. 1842), had been mayor in 1800: ibid. 253.
3 Kimpton, *Arundel* (1897), 5; A.C.M., MD 1716; cf. W.S.R.O., BO/AR 24/1/1, docs. relating to Jubilee celebrations, 1887.
4 A.C.M., MD 417.
5 Hillier, *Arundel* (1847), 14.
6 *Jnl. of Horticulture and Cottage Gdnr.* 1 Jan. 1874, p. 12.
7 E. V. Lucas, *Highways and Byways in Suss.* 69; W.S.R.O., BO/AR 24/2/1, statement to L.G.B. enquiry by J. J. Robinson, 1913.
8 Kimpton, *Arundel* (1893), 4; below, secular bldgs. One of the duke's chief monuments, the new Rom. Cath. ch., was, however, considered by at least one contemporary a serious blot on the town's skyline: *Builder*, 19 Feb. 1876, p. 162.
9 A.C.M., MD 2327; cf. ibid. 2406, newspaper rep. 1860.
10 Kimpton, *Arundel* (1893), 4; below, soc. and cultural activities (inns).
11 Kimpton, *Arundel* (1893), [3].
12 E. V. Lucas, op. cit. 69.

tourism,[13] and by 1953 there was a large car park by the river which could accommodate hundreds of cars and coaches, many other summer visitors coming from Littlehampton by boat.[14] In the 1980s there were large numbers of visitors in the town during much of the year.

The number of 'private residents' listed had risen to 46 by 1874 and 72 by 1895, but declined thereafter.[15] Unlike other Sussex towns, Arundel did not become a centre of large-scale villa settlement in the later 19th century and early 20th, because of the resistance of the Norfolk estate and the unsuitability of the ground for building.[16] After *c.* 1970, however, many newcomers bought houses in the town itself.[17]

Royal visits to Arundel were made by William II in 1097,[18] Henry I in 1101,[19] Stephen in 1139,[20] Henry II *c.* 1182,[21] Richard I perhaps in 1189,[22] and John[23] and Edward I[24] on several occasions. Letters patent of Edward II, Edward III, Richard II, and Henry VII of various dates were given at Arundel.[25] Henry VIII stayed at the castle in 1526, hunting in the park and receiving the nobility and gentry of the district;[26] he was again in Arundel in 1538.[27] Queen Victoria passed through the town twice in 1842 *en route* between Brighton and Portsmouth.[28] In 1846 she made a three-days' visit to the duke of Norfolk; received by the town council at the west end of Maltravers Street, where a triumphal arch was erected near the site of the medieval Watergate, she was taken from there in procession to the castle gates.[29]

POPULATION. Fifty-six persons were assessed to the subsidy in 1296, 53 in 1327, and 34 in 1332.[30] In 1524 there were 79 taxpayers,[31] and 69 men were mustered in 1539.[32] The figure of 400 inhabitants recorded in the Compton census of 1676 seems to represent the total population of the parish, but is suspiciously round.[33] In 1724 there were 188 families,[34] and in 1767 apparently 182 heads of families.[35] The population in 1801 was 1,855; it rose quickly to 2,803 in 1831, then fluctuated between *c.* 2,500 and 3,000 during the rest of the 19th century. A steep drop in the 1850s was followed by a steeper rise in the 1860s, attributed to the influx of building workers on the Roman Catholic church and other buildings. The area of the parish as enlarged in 1902 had 3,059 inhabitants in 1901, 320 of whom lived in the added area. Despite an increase in that area to 464 in 1921, the population of the parish as a whole declined to 2,490 in 1931; a rise in the 1930s and 40s was followed by another fall. In 1991 the parish as further enlarged had 3,039 inhabitants.[36]

THE TOWN AS A COUNTY CENTRE. The county court met at Arundel at least once in the early 14th century[37] and the county coroner *c.* 1330 was an Arundel man.[38] Richard FitzAlan, earl of Arundel (d. 1376), attempted unsuccessfully shortly before his death to subsume the county court into his Arundel honor court.[39] The county coroner sat at Arundel in the 1540s and 1550s on local cases.[40]

The county Vice-Admiralty court was held at Arundel in 1594[41] and a Vice-Admiralty visitation in 1638.[42] In the 1640s the Sussex county committee regularly met in the inns of the town.[43] Quarter sessions were held from 1562 or earlier, most often at Epiphany. Between 1640 and 1690 sessions were held *c.* 10 or 12 times a decade, but thereafter until 1732 with decreasing frequency.[44] The sessions house mentioned in 1638[45] was apparently part of the buildings of Arundel college.[46] A house of correction was ordered to be established at Arundel for the three western rapes in 1650, replacing separate ones at Chichester, Horsham, and Petworth.[47] Quakers from the town were committed there in the 1650s and 60s,[48] but there is no evidence that it functioned after that date and the building, which adjoined the churchyard, is not mentioned after 1702.[49]

MILITARY EVENTS. The castle was the object of a siege in 1102.[50] In 1322 Arundel was wealthy enough to supply two armed footmen for service against the Scots,[51] and in 1588 it was ordered to help bear the cost of a ship to fight

13 *Arundel, the Gem of Suss.* (Arundel, 1934), which it published.
14 R. O. Dunlop, *Ancient Arundel* (Arundel, 1953), 51–3.
15 *Kelly's Dir. Suss.* (1874 and later edns.).
16 W. H. Parker, 'Settlement in Suss. 1840–1940', *Geography*, xxxv. 16, 20.
17 e.g. *New Statesman*, 22 Dec. 1972, p. 941.
18 F. Barlow, *Wm. Rufus*, 369.
19 *Reg. Regum Anglo-Norm.* ii, no. 543.
20 Ibid. iii, no. 679.
21 *Cartae Antiquae*, ii (Pipe R. Soc. N.S. xxxiii), p. 131.
22 *Cal. Doc. France*, ed. Round, pp. 384–5.
23 *V.C.H. Suss.* i. 491–2; *Pipe R.* 17 John (P.R.S. N.S xxxvii), 78 n.; *S.A.C.* ii. 134–5.
24 *Itin. of Edw. I* (L. & I. Soc.), i. 209; ii. 106, 139, 196, 246.
25 *Cal. Pat.* 1321–4, 439–40; 1343–5, 54–5, 110; 1381–5, 433; 1385–9, 497; 1485–94, 257; cf. below, castle (institutional hist.).
26 *L. & P. Hen. VIII*, iv (2), pp. 1058, 1061–2, 1151.
27 Ibid. xiii (2), pp. 87 and n., 533, 536.
28 Eustace, *Arundel*, 237.
29 Ibid. 237–40 and facing p. 238; J. M. Robinson, *Dukes of Norf.* (1982), 199–200.
30 *S.R.S.* x. 81, 134, 226.
31 Ibid. lvi. 43–4.
32 *L. & P. Hen. VIII*, xiv (1), p. 296.
33 *Compton Census*, ed. Whiteman, 144. No protestation return was made in 1642 despite more than one request: *S.R.S.* v. 7, 23.
34 *S.R.S.* lxxviii. 59.
35 W.S.R.O., A.B.A., M22.
36 *Census*, 1801–1991.
37 R. C. Palmer, *County Cts. of Medieval Eng.* 12–13.
38 *Cal. Close*, 1330–3, 12.
39 *V.C.H. Suss.* iii. 95–6; A. Goodman, *Loyal Conspiracy*, 110.
40 *S.R.S.* lxxiv, pp. 32, 58.
41 Hist. MSS. Com. 6, *7th Rep., More Molyneux*, p. 652.
42 W.S.R.O., Ep. I/55/6; Ep. I/88/1, ff. 165–6.
43 A. Fletcher, *County Community in Peace and War*, 325–6.
44 W.S.R.O., TS. list of quarter sess. rolls; Hist. MSS. Com. 9, *Salisbury*, i, p. 269; *S.A.C.* cxviii. 388–9; Fletcher, *County Community*, 135.
45 W.S.R.O., Ep. I/55/6.
46 *Camd. Misc.* xvi (Camd. 3rd ser. lii), Hammond, 33.
47 *S.R.S.* liv, p. xix; Fletcher, *County Community, 167*.
48 *Cal. S.P. Dom.* 1656–7, 230; W. Albery, *Millennium of Facts in Hist. of Horsham and Suss. 947–1947*, 415, 422.
49 W.S.R.O., S.A.S. MS. RB 2 (TS. cat.).
50 Below, castle (institutional hist.).
51 *Cal. Pat.* 1321–4, 131.

ARUNDEL CASTLE AND TOWN IN 1644

the Spanish Armada.[52] In 1589 it was to be a port of embarkation for soldiers going to the help of Henri IV of France,[53] and in 1599 or 1600 to raise soldiers for the defence of the county;[54] 160 soldiers from the rape were ordered in 1626 to be billeted in and around the town.[55] Apparently *c.* 1586,[56] and certainly in 1626,[57] Arundel was one of the towns in the county appointed to be a store for arms and powder.

In December 1642 Sir William Waller, *en route* for Chichester, sent 100 men to capture the castle, which in the absence abroad of the earl of Arundel had been left poorly guarded. The main gate was blown in with a petard, the garrison surprised, and the castle taken.[58] Arundel remained in Parliamentary hands until December 1643, when a detachment from Lord Hopton's garrison at Petersfield under Sir Edward Ford and Col. Joseph Bampfield retook the town for the King as part of a planned three-pronged Royalist advance on London. The castle was put under siege, and three days later, after the arrival of Hopton himself, was surrendered by its garrison.[59] Fortifications were quickly thrown up to improve its defence: a double earthwork near Swanbourne lake, and the south-westwards extension to Park bottom of the northern earthwork of the Little park (the present castle cricket ground). The northern earthwork itself was perhaps strengthened as well.[60] Ford and Bampfield were then left in charge with over 200 foot and a fair number of horse.[61] Claims later made by 38 inhabitants of Arundel for loss and damage sustained during the Royalist capture of the town and castle indicate that they were hotly contested, even allowing for exaggeration: the sums concerned range from £1 to £950, making a total of £3,772.[62]

On 19 December 1643[63] Waller returned from Farnham, camping in the Great park, and the following day after an artillery bombardment he attacked Arundel from both the north-west and south-west. After the northern earthwork of the Little park and its south-westwards extension were gained the town fell, the outer castle gate near the churchyard being also captured, and the Royalists being forced back into the castle itself. Simultaneously another party advanced down Pughdean bottom north of the town and forced the double earthwork near the mill at Swanbourne in order to reach Arundel by way of Mill Lane.[64]

There followed a 17-days' siege of the castle. Parliamentary troops are said to have been quartered in the Fitzalan chapel of the parish church,[65] and cannon were mounted on the tower of the church to fire into the castle, the defendants also being kept awake by setting off alarms. The defendants were ill supplied with provisions, either for themselves or for their stock, some oxen eventually being pushed over the curtain wall for lack of fodder. Meanwhile Waller succeeded in diverting the water supply. Numerous reinforcements arrived to swell the besieging force, while many members of the garrison deserted; an attempt by Hopton to raise the siege was unsuccessful. A sortie from the castle on Christmas day was driven back, and there were other skirmishes. On 6 January 1644 the garrison surrendered, *c.* 1,000 prisoners being taken, including the High Church divine William Chillingworth who had been acting as an engineer.[66] Arundel town had once again suffered during the siege; a visitor arriving there not long afterwards found it depopulated, 'all the windows broken with the great guns', and many of the shops and lower rooms of houses turned into stables by the soldiers.[67]

The castle was immediately strongly fortified by Waller,[68] a permanent garrison and magazine being installed.[69] Capt. William Morley was governor between 1645 and 1652.[70] In 1645 prisoners taken during the 'Clubmen' riots were sent to the castle for safe keeping,[71] and in 1647 the ordnance, arms, and ammunition from the dismantled garrison at Chichester was taken to Arundel, whose establishment in future was to be 100 foot besides officers.[72] In the same year the town's arrears of the county rate for poor relief and the maintenance of maimed soldiers were waived because of the financial burden caused by the presence of the garrison.[73] In 1651 the establishment was reduced to 57 besides the governor,[74] but partly because of the castle's usefulness as a prison[75] Arundel remained a garrison town until 1653, when it was disgarrisoned, 'the walls and works' of the castle were made indefensible, and the keys to the domestic part of the castle returned to 'Mr. Howard', i.e. Henry Howard, brother of the earl of Arundel.[76]

52 *Acts of P.C.* 1588, 61, 66–7.
53 Ibid. 1589–90, 113.
54 *S.A.C.* xi. 170.
55 Ibid. xl. 21.
56 Hist. MSS. Com. 41, *15th Rep. V, Foljambe*, p. 17.
57 *Acts of P.C.* 1626, 76.
58 *S.A.C.* v. 41–2; C. Thomas- Stanford, *Suss. in Great Civil War*, 50–1.
59 *S.A.C.* v. 55–7; Thomas-Stanford, op. cit. 71–3; P. Young and R. Holmes, *Eng. Civil War: a Milit. Hist.* 160–1; for Bampfield, *D.N.B.*
60 Tierney, *Arundel*, i. 61–2, 70.
61 Young and Holmes, op. cit. 161; *S.A.C.* v. 61.
62 W.S.R.O., A.B.A., M9.
63 Following two paras. based mainly on *S.A.C.* ix. 51–3; xix. 118; Tierney, *Arundel*, i. 61–78; W. Freeman, *Arundel Cast. Guide* (*c.* 1972), 40–5; Dallaway & Cartwright, *Hist. W. Suss.* ii (1) (1832), 108–9, 114–15.
64 Hillier, *Arundel* (1847), 37–8, and ibid. (1851), 43, give further details of the capture of the town from an unknown source; cf. *Sieges of Arundel Cast.* ed. G. Hillier (1854) (copy in S.A.S. libr.). Waller's ref. to the bombardment having 'scoured' (i.e. raked) 'a weedy hill in the park on the W. side of the pond' is unclear, since the pond in question was the great pond in Park bottom: Tierney, *Arundel*, i. 61–2; *O.E.D.* s.v. 'scour'; cf. above, intro. J. Rouse, *Beauties and Antiq. of Suss.* i. 294, reads 'woody' for 'weedy'.
65 Tierney, *Arundel*, ii. 619.
66 *Gent. Mag.* lxiv (2), 697; cf. Dallaway, *Hist. W. Suss.* ii (1) (1819), 102 n.
67 Thomas-Stanford, *Suss. in Great Civil War*, 116. For burials of those killed in the fighting, W.S.R.O., Par. 8/1/1/1, f. 56v.; Tierney, *Arundel*, ii. 649–50.
68 *S.A.C.* ix. 53; cf. Thomas- Stanford, op. cit. 259.
69 *Cal. S.P. Dom.* 1644, 26, 500; 1644–5, 541; 1651–2, 524.
70 Ibid. 1651–2, 614, wrongly calling him John; *C.J.* iv. 136; v. 122.
71 Thomas-Stanford, op. cit. 171.
72 *C.J.* v. 103.
73 *S.R.S.* liv. 115.
74 *C.J.* vii. 47.
75 Fletcher, *County Community in Peace and War*, 297–8; *Cal. S.P. Dom.* 1651, 358, 504.
76 *Cal. S.P. Dom.* 1653–4, 191, 256–7, 432.

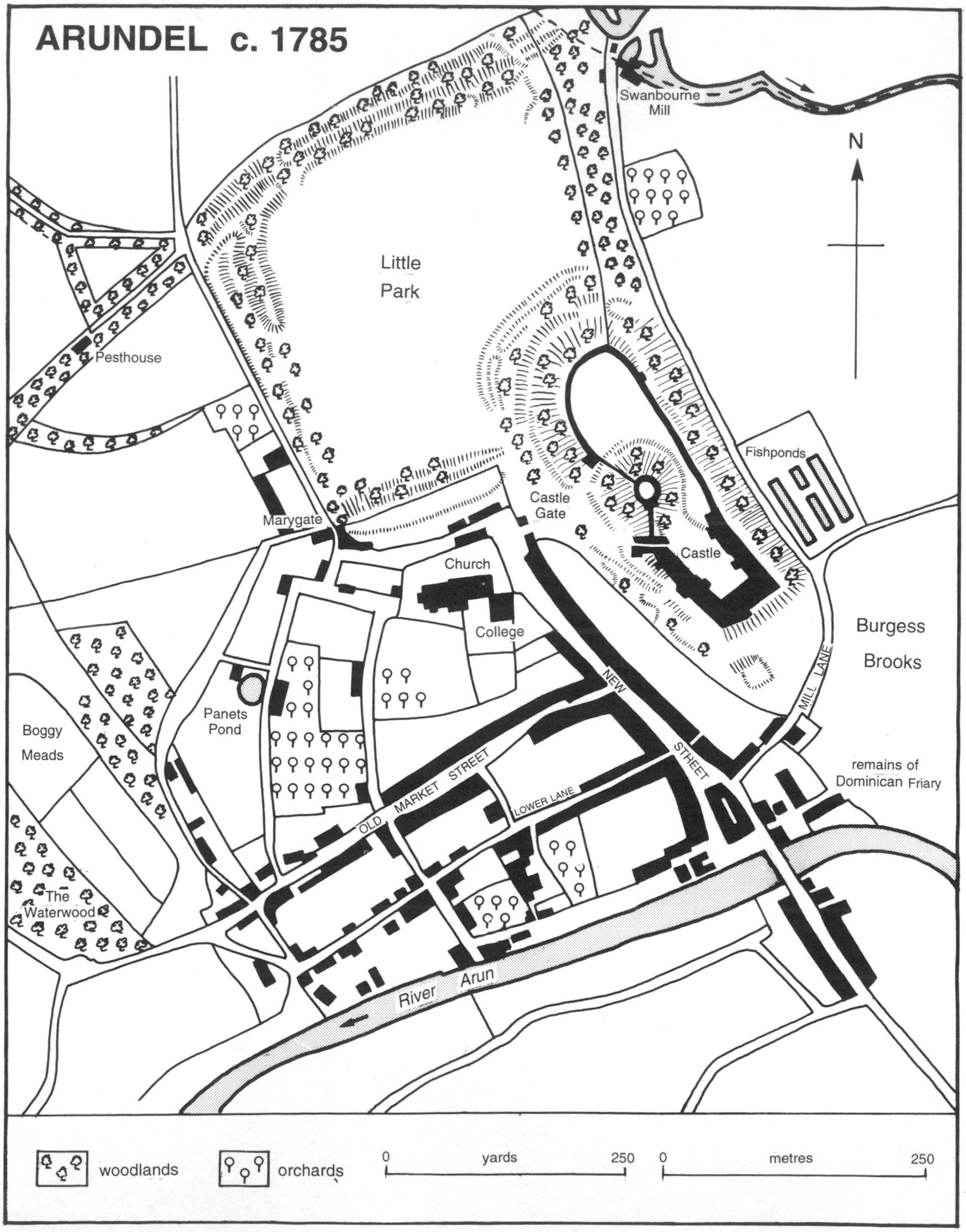
ARUNDEL c. 1785
Swanbourne Mill
N
Little Park
Pesthouse
Fishponds
Marygate
Castle Gate
Castle
Church
College
Burgess Brooks
MILL LANE
NEW STREET
Panets Pond
Boggy Meads
OLD MARKET STREET
LOWER LANE
remains of Dominican Friary
The Waterwood
River Arun
woodlands
orchards
0 yards 250
0 metres 250

Soldiers were stationed at Arundel on at least one occasion in the 18th century to combat smugglers,[77] and in 1778–9 when a French invasion was feared the castle was to be held as an advance post.[78] A corps of volunteer infantry based on the town was formed in 1794 to man guns at the coastal batteries, and was revived in 1803.[79] In the early 19th century barracks were built at Crossbush in Lyminster just east of the town.[80]

GROWTH OF THE TOWN. In 1086 there were at least 4 burgages in the town, besides 13 'haws', or urban properties attached to estates outside it.[81] The Norman town seems to have lain chiefly along the north-west to south-east route the lower part of which was followed in 1995 by High Street, climbing steeply the spur of chalk on which Arundel is built; *c.* 1200 it was described as the street leading to the ferry (*passag'*).[82] Whether or not the earthworks north-west of the castle represent a late Saxon *burh*,[83] there seems to have been early medieval settlement within what was later the Little park (the present castle cricket ground);[84] that may have included the place called Vinhard or Wynyerd (i.e. vineyard), in the south-west corner of which two tenements and gardens were mentioned *c.* 1200.[85] Buildings between the Little park and the top of the modern High Street were demolished in the early 19th century during enlargement of the castle grounds.[86]

Maltravers and Tarrant streets, running west-south-westwards roughly at right angles to High Street, were probably subsidiary streets of the Norman town. Maltravers Street was the road to Chichester, the other chief town of Roger de Montgomery's Sussex lands; its former name Old Market Street[87] is reflected in its wider central section where presumably the market was once held. Tarrant Street ran along the edge of the higher ground to give access to the river frontage. A roughly parallel street north of the church, later called Marygate Street,[88] may also have been part of the Norman town layout, since there were houses along it by *c.* 1200;[89] it was later to form part of the main road to London.[90] On the other side of High Street there was once a road running from the site of the George inn (nos. 30–4) under the south-east front of the castle; it was closed by the duke of Norfolk before 1785.[91]

In 1302 there were 94 burgages.[92] Most evidently lay in High and Maltravers streets, as later; Tarrant Street presumably had little early settlement, since in the 1780s only three entries in the borough rental were for property there.[93] The area enclosed by defences *c.* 1300, however, was considerably larger,[94] evidently comprising much open land: in the 15th century the earl of Arundel's property in the borough included numerous gardens, tofts, and other plots without buildings.[95] Very likely the west end of the town within the defences was former arable belonging to the pre-Conquest settlement, since the only arable later recorded near the town lay north-west of the Marygate.[96]

Mill Lane, leading north-east from the lower end of High Street round the foot of the hill on which the castle stands, may have existed by the later 13th century if its alternative name Jury Lane refers to the Jewish community then living in the town; the modern name occurs in 1379.[97] The low-lying land between Tarrant Street and the river, however, including what was later the market place at the south-east end of High Street, may not at first have been part of the built-up area. Though at the west end of Tarrant Street there was settlement in Roman times and at least one house in the later Middle Ages,[98] nearer the bridge the river may once have been wider, the waterfront, with the common quay, being extended gradually outwards, as in other medieval ports.[99] The area would probably have been liable to flooding and therefore less suited to settlement; no through road was ever constructed along it,[1] and the land by the bridge occupied by the Dominican friary is likely to have been unused before the friars arrived in the mid 13th century.[2] That may also have been the reason why the south-east corner of the town never had defences. The original market area, indeed, seems to have been in Maltravers Street rather than High Street: for much of its length High Street seems too steep for use as a market site, and its alternative name in the later 18th century was New Market Street.[3] Possibly, there-

77 *Cal. Treas. Bks. and Papers*, 1731–4, 622; W. Albery, *Millennium of Facts in Hist. of Horsham and Suss. 947–1947*, 282, 464–5, 473.

78 *V.C.H. Suss.* i. 533.

79 *S.A.C.* cxxii. 166, 168, 172.

80 W.S.R.O., MP 2549, f. 2.

81 *V.C.H. Suss.* i. 421; A. Ballard, *Domesday Boros.* 22; *Domesday Geog. of SE. Eng.* ed. H. Darby and E. Campbell, 470. Byworth and Warningcamp man., presumably representing one of the estates, had tenements in the town later: A.C.M., D 6589–90 (MS. cat.); W.S.R.O., Add. MS. 20572 (TS. cat.); cf. below, this section (street names).

82 W.S.R.O., Par. 8/7/35.

83 Below, defences.

84 Dallaway, *Hist. W. Suss.* ii (1) (1819), 165; Dally, *Bognor* (1828), 214; Tierney, *Arundel*, i. 95; Horsfield, *Hist. Suss.* ii. 128; *A Visit to Arundel Cast.* (1851), 93; Eustace, *Arundel*, 19; W.S.R.O., A.B.A., M52; S.M.R. 1963.

85 W.S.R.O., Par. 8/7/35; for the alternative spelling, P.R.O., SC 6/1019/22, rot. 1.

86 Below, this section.

87 Below, this section (street names).

88 A.C.M., MD 505, f. [1v.].

89 W.S.R.O., Par. 8/7/35.

90 Below, communications (rds.).

91 W.S.R.O., MP 3041 (photocopy of town plan, 1785, in possession of the late Mrs. J. Liardet, née Constable, Warningcamp Ho., in 1989); *S.A.C.* lxxi. 53. For the George inn, below, secular bldgs. A continuation of the line of the street can be traced intermittently W. of High St. as a path between properties in Maltravers and Tarrant sts.; its E. end has been absorbed into no. 59 High St.

92 P.R.O., C 133/104, no. 21, m. 2.

93 A.C.M., A 339, boro. rental, 1784–93.

94 Below, defences.

95 *S.R.S.* lxvii. 115–20.

96 A.C.M., MD 505, ff. [6–8, 16 and v.]. For parallels cf. e.g. Stratford-upon-Avon (Warws.) and Norwich: *Urban Arch. in Brit.* ed. J. Schofield and R. Leech, 57; B. Green and R. M. R. Young, *Norwich, the Growth of a City* (1981), 12. Cf. below, agric.

97 Above, gen. hist. of town; below, this section (street names).

98 Above, gen. hist. of town; *S.A.S. Newsletter*, xliii. 384.

99 H. Clarke, *Arch. of Medieval Eng.* 181–7; *Urban Arch. in Brit.* ed. Schofield and Leech, 192.

1 Despite plans of 1930s: *S.C.M.* xiii. 218.

2 For friary, below, relig. hos.

3 Below, this section (street names).

fore, the open area between the foot of High Street and the bridge developed later as a new or additional market area closer to river transport.

The 38 shops or stalls recorded in 1302[4] perhaps included some in the market place. In the early 15th century property was mentioned there or in the market quarter; the five shops and a 'shamble' lying in Middle or Mid Street[5] presumably belonged to the island of buildings between the market place and the bridge, or to the smaller island north-west of it, comprising the court house and other buildings, which was removed in the mid and later 18th century.[6] By the early 15th century there were at least two buildings on the quay.[7]

In the mid 17th century there were houses north of Maltravers Street in the King Street and Mount Pleasant area.[8] Coxes croft pond, later Panets pond, at the north end of King Street is recorded from 1679.[9] Reference was made in 1703 to the upper end of the town near the Marygate.[10] The junction of Marygate and High streets near the former gate to the castle was known as Castle green in 1636,[11] while College green mentioned in 1796 apparently lay south of the church along the line of what was later London Road.[12] The common quay in 1680 extended between the bridge and a point part of the way down the modern River Road,[13] so that there were unlikely to have been houses along the river there in the mid 17th century as depicted by Hollar.[14]

In the mid 18th century the court house which stood in the market place was demolished by the corporation, the two or three houses adjoining it being pulled down by Sir John Shelley and the duke of Norfolk in or before 1773.[15] In the 1780s[16] High and Maltravers streets still contained most of the town's buildings. High Street, which had the grander and more regular ones, was fully built up on both sides between the market place and the site of the modern castle lodge, and on the east side also north of that, opposite the college and churchyard. Much of Maltravers Street was built up by the same period, though in 1789 the street was described as a hollow way meanly built;[17] both there and in the lesser streets were many stables and other non-domestic buildings, together with much open land, especially north of Maltravers Street, used as gardens, nurseries, and orchards. At the north end of the town, besides houses in Marygate Street, there were buildings west and south-west of the church,[18] including the Parsonage farm buildings.[19] Between Tarrant Street and the river much land was then in industrial or commercial use. Much of the river frontage remained an open quay; there were some warehouses along it, which were joined in 1831 by a corn store near the bridge. Commercial and industrial premises in the area included a shipbuilding yard or yards, timber yards, and presumably the premises of the various merchants mentioned in the 1790s.[20] There were six or eight houses in Mill Lane in 1785.

During the later 18th century and earlier 19th there was much building in the town, reflecting contemporary prosperity. Four builders were listed in the 1790s;[21] in the period 1801–31 the number of houses grew by over half, from 355 to 537, the rate of increase being especially rapid in the decade 1801–11.[22] Maltravers Street during the period established its character, adumbrated in the mid 18th century,[23] as the best residential street and the home of the town's professional men,[24] the houses on its south side enjoying fine views of the Arun valley.

In the same period Duke Charles (d. 1815) began to engross property at the north end of the town[25] in order to enlarge the grounds of the castle and reassert ducal dominance. Nineteen houses in High Street, presumably chiefly on the east side, were demolished between 1800 and 1805,[26] their gardens, which had run up to the castle ditch,[27] being later incorporated in the castle grounds. In 1803 the London road was diverted to run south of the church instead of north;[28] the old castle gate north-east of the churchyard was removed shortly afterwards and a new one built further south on the site of the modern lodge.[29] Six houses in Marygate Street, including four near the Marygate, were taken down in 1805.[30] About the same date two houses remained west of the gate and two to the east,[31] and by 1809 the duke had acquired the gate itself.[32] In 1811 he received the site of the former vicarage nearby in exchange for a new vicarage house in Parson's Hill.[33] The lands thus engrossed were enclosed by a forbidding wall of grey stone from Plymouth[34] along the new London

4 P.R.O., C 133/104, no. 21, m. 2.
5 *S.R.S.* lxvii. 116–20.
6 Below, boro. govt. (town halls).
7 *S.R.S.* lxvii. 118, 120.
8 A.C.M., MD 505, f. [iv.]; for identification of site cf. below, this section.
9 W.S.R.O., A.B.A., P1/16, mentioning Thos. Pannett as an adjacent occupier; ibid. MP 3041 (photocopy of town plan, 1785).
10 Ibid. Par. 8/7/38; cf. ibid. Par. 8/11/7, f. 2v.
11 A.C.M., MD 505, f. [2]; cf. Sandbeck Park, Rotherham, Lumley MS. EMA/1/5.
12 A.C.M., D 1977; cf. *Arundel Cast. Archives*, iv. 47.
13 Below, port and river traffic.
14 W.S.R.O., PD 1367, illus. above, p. 16. For other inaccuracies in Hollar's view, below, relig. hos. (Dominican friary); *Country Life*, 12 July 1990, p. 94; cf. S. Calloway, *Eng. Prints for the Collector*, 23.
15 W.S.R.O., A.B.A., A1, f. 201; Eustace, *Arundel*, 219; below, boro. govt. (town halls).
16 Rest of para. based mainly on A.C.M., D 3210; ibid. MD 2179; W.S.R.O., MP 3041 (photocopy of town plan, 1785), which, however, shows only rateable property.
17 Camden, *Brit.* (1789), i. 197.
18 B.L. Add. MS. 5674, f. 16; W.S.R.O., M/PD 338.
19 A.C.M., MD 2180.
20 *Univ. Brit. Dir.* ii. 56–7; cf. Pigot, *Nat. Com. Dir.* (1832–4), 1003–4; W.S.R.O., TD/W 5; for corn store, below, mkts. and fairs (mkts.).
21 *Univ. Brit. Dir.* ii. 55–6.
22 *Census*, 1801–31.
23 Below, secular bldgs.
24 e.g. Pigot, *Nat. Com. Dir.* (1832–4), 1003–4.
25 A.C.M., D 60–93, 828–52 (MS. cat.); ibid. MD 619, pp. 5, 15, 17, 21, 25, 29, 35, 37, 39, 53, 56, 64.
26 Ibid. MD 619, pp. 42, 52, 65, 67, 69; cf. ibid. pp. 1, 5.
27 Ibid. D 926–40, 3200–3 (MS. cat.); ibid. MD 505, f. [2 and v.]; 2179; *Lavington Estate Archives*, ed. F. W. Steer, p. 29; Dallaway & Cartwright, *Hist. W. Suss.* ii (1) (1832), 211.
28 Below, communications (rds.).
29 A.C.M., MD 619, pp. 52, 67; ibid. PM 107.
30 Ibid. MD 619, p. 65.
31 Ibid. PM 107.
32 *S.A.C.* lxxi. 53.
33 A.C.M., D 610–13; Eustace, *Arundel*, 230–1.
34 Below, this section.

road, though some property within the wall remained for the moment in other hands; seven tenements near the Marygate were bought by Duke Bernard Edward in 1826.[35] Until 1848, moreover, the former north section of High Street remained a right of way to the north door of the church.[36] Further houses on the east side of High Street were bought in 1850,[37] enabling the construction there in 1850–1 of another stone wall, of more picturesque design in castellated style, with a new matching lodge and gateway to the castle.[38]

At the south-east end of the town Duke Charles also bought houses and meadow in Mill Lane with the aim of increasing the castle's privacy on that side;[39] three of the houses were demolished in 1794–5.[40] An attempt to close Mill Lane in 1850, however, was abortive, and its diversion was not achieved until 1894.[41]

The houses demolished for the enlargement of the castle grounds were replaced by new streets at the north-west end of the town. Fifty houses, chiefly let out on building leases, are said to have been put up in that area *c.* 1810,[42] others following.

Between the mid 19th century and the early 20th High and Tarrant streets were the chief shopping streets of the town, Tarrant Street in 1910 having four general stores. Markets and fairs ceased to be held in the streets by the early 20th century. Maltravers Street, meanwhile, remained the best residential street;[43] the Parade on its north side was apparently constructed *c.* 1850[44] and is first mentioned as an address in 1855.[45] New buildings erected at the time, many in medieval styles, are described below;[46] their cumulative effect was to make the town by *c.* 1900 appear much more medieval than it had done a century earlier. The medieval centrepiece proposed for the market place in 1893–4, however, a tall cross with a fountain on a stepped polygonal plinth,[47] was not carried out. The town by *c.* 1900 was also evidently more ducal and more Catholic, the skyline presenting as dominant accents from the later 19th century the enlarged castle and the huge new Roman Catholic church; around the latter was a Catholic enclave containing the various buildings mentioned below, besides a Catholic cemetery.[48] The reduced importance of the borough since its reform in 1835 was clearly expressed by the much less prominent position of the 19th-century town hall by comparison with that of the earlier court house.

Many 19th-century walls survived in 1995, besides those of the castle grounds mentioned above; several are of grey Plymouth stone, for instance in the churchyard, in Parson's Hill, in Surrey Street, and in Mount Pleasant.[49] The raised pavements necessitated by the steepness of the land in several places, for instance at the lower end of King Street and notably in Maltravers Street, are also 19th-century, the latter being datable from the posts of railings along them to the years 1849–50.[50]

Between Tarrant Street and the river houses were built in the mid 19th century and early 20th for artisans, labourers, or mariners.[51] The least salubrious were the *c.* 15 old and dilapidated buildings, some closed at the rear, in a court east of Arun Street, which in 1885 were served by a central open drain and had only two closets between them.[52] Industry and commerce continued in the same area, with timber yards, the premises of builders, stonemasons, and barge builders, coal yards, corn merchants' and other warehouses, and the Eagle brewery, besides numerous wharves, including one owned and occupied by the duke of Norfolk at the west end of the town.[53]

In the 1930s the approach to the town from the south-east was made more open by widening the bridge and removing buildings nearby, especially the burnt-out corn store on the river front.[54] Gardens were laid out on both sides of the bridge at that period.[55]

South of the river there seem likely to have been buildings by the early 13th century; the two messuages in the 'suburb' of Arundel with which Pynham priory in Lyminster was dealing at that date[56] were probably along the causeway, for whose upkeep the priory was responsible. More houses were built there later,[57] presumably by reclamation from adjacent marshland as at Bramber;[58] three or four are mentioned on one occasion in the early 15th century.[59] By 1785 there were 15–20.[60] During the succeeding 50 years industrial firms settled on the south bank of the river; by *c.* 1841 there were a brewery and maltings on opposite sides of the Brighton road, together

35 A.C.M., D 485–503 (MS. cat.).

36 Ibid. HC 162. Negotiations had begun in 1836: ibid. FA 59.

37 Ibid. D 3345–72 (MS. cat.); ibid. HC 163.

38 Below, castle grounds.

39 A.C.M., MD 619, pp. 3, 25, 37, 53, 83, 130.

40 Ibid. p. 42.

41 Below, communications (rds.).

42 Dallaway & Cartwright, *Hist. W. Suss.* ii (1) (1832), 211.

43 *Kelly's Dir. Suss.* (1845 and later edns.); Pike, *Bognor Dir.* (1910–11); below, mkts. and fairs.

44 Date 1849 on railings in street.

45 *Kelly's Dir. Suss.* (1855).

46 Below, secular bldgs.

47 A.C.M., MD 2026; W.S.R.O., BO/AR 53/2.

48 Below, secular bldgs.; public servs.; Rom. Cath.; educ. The town's foreign appearance was first noted by E. V. Lucas, *Highways and Byways in Suss.* 69.

49 Wright, *Arundel* (1818), 25, 66; Tierney, *Arundel*, ii. 715. Of the same stone are the former lodges of Park Ho. SW. of the town: cf. below, secular bldgs. (outside the town). Cf. also below, defences; relig. hos. (coll. bldgs.); *Plans of Arundel Cast.* 16, 19–20, 22–3.

50 The cast-iron posts dated 1819 at the ends of Bakers Arms and Kings Arms hills and in Mount Pleasant are apparently *ex situ*: below, mkts. and fairs (mkts.).

51 O.S. Map 1/2,500, Suss. LXIII. 1 (1877 and later edns.); cf. W.S.R.O., SP 257; ibid. TD/W 5.

52 *12th Ann. Rep. on Combined Sanit. Dist. of W. Suss.* (Worthing, 1886), 154–5 (copy at W.S.R.O., WDC/CL 74/1).

53 *Kelly's Dir. Suss.* (1845 and later edns.); *S.C.M.* xviii. 144; xxvi. 231; Cartland, *Arundel*, 54; P. A. L. Vine, *Lond.'s Lost Route to Sea* (1986), pl. 55; O.S. Map 1/2,500, Suss. LXIII. 1 (1877 and later edns.); A.C.M., D 614–33, sale cat. 1887; W.S.R.O., SP 257; ibid. TD/W 5; cf. Pigot, *Nat. Com. Dir.* (1832–4), 1003–4.

54 Below, communications (rds.); mkts. and fairs (mkts.); *S.A.C.* lxxiv. 250.

55 *Arundel, the Gem of Suss.* (Arundel, 1937), 23.

56 *S.R.S.* ii, p. 14.

57 Turner & Coxe, *Cal. Chart. & R. in Bodl.* 576–8; A.C.M., D 1085.

58 *V.C.H. Suss.* vi (1), 201–2.

59 *S.R.S.* lxvii. 116–17. The location of the places called Snorhull and Paradise in the 14th and 15th cents. is unknown: ibid. 116; B.L. Lansd. Ch. 105 (MS. cal.).

60 W.S.R.O., MP 3041 (photocopy of town plan, 1785).

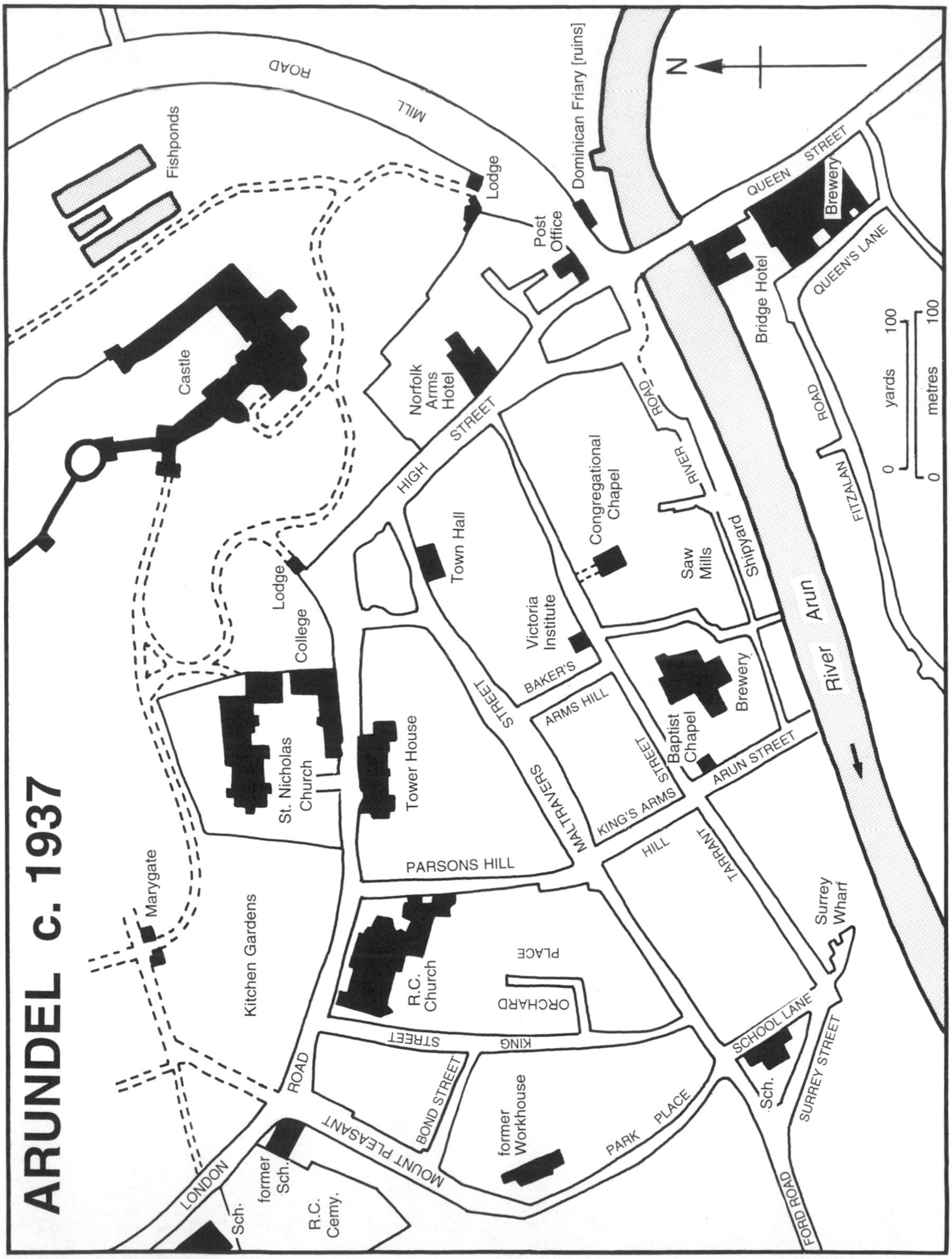
ARUNDEL c. 1937
N
0 yards 100
0 metres 100
MILL ROAD
Fishponds
Castle
Lodge
Dominican Friary [ruins]
Post Office
QUEEN STREET
Brewery
Bridge Hotel
QUEEN'S LANE
Norfolk Arms Hotel
HIGH STREET
RIVER ROAD
Congregational Chapel
Town Hall
Saw Mills
Shipyard
FITZALAN ROAD
River Arun
Lodge
College
Victoria Institute
BAKER'S STREET
ARMS HILL
KING'S ARMS STREET
Baptist Chapel
Brewery
ARUN STREET
St. Nicholas Church
Tower House
MALTRAVERS
PARSONS HILL
HILL
TARRANT
Marygate
Kitchen Gardens
R.C. Church
ORCHARD PLACE
KING STREET
Surrey Wharf
SCHOOL LANE
Sch.
SURREY STREET
BOND STREET
former Workhouse
PARK PLACE
MOUNT PLEASANT
LONDON ROAD
former Sch.
R.C. Cemy.
Sch.
FORD ROAD

with a timber yard, coal yards, and a soap factory to the west.[61] The unsuitability of the adjacent ground for building inhibited southwards expansion, though by *c.* 1875 the advent of the railway had brought a few scattered villas between the bridge and the station, which lay just beyond the Arundel–Lyminster boundary; more were built before 1910,[62] together with six 'co-operative cottages' south of Queen Street.[63] There were a few houses along the river to the south-west by *c.* 1841 in the part of the parish already called the south marshes:[64] by the 1870s there was one terrace, more were built by 1896, and there was further building in the early 20th century in what by the 1930s was called Fitzalan Road;[65] six council houses were put up there in 1935.[66]

Arundel's chief expansion in the early 20th century, however, was south of Chichester Road in what before 1902 was part of Tortington parish. Red or brown brick terrace houses, some belonging to the Norfolk estate, were built in Ford Road and Wood View by 1896 and in Kirdford Road by 1910.[67] The higher-lying land to the west around Torton Hill Road was developed by the town council from *c.* 1913 as an estate chiefly of large detached houses in various styles.[68]

In the mid 20th century High Street continued to be the chief shopping and business street, with smaller shops in Tarrant Street and elsewhere, Tarrant Street after *c.* 1980 having arcades or closes of shops occupying some former commercial or industrial premises. Maltravers Street remained largely in residential or professional use; in 1947 guest houses were apparently becoming common there,[69] but in 1988 even the biggest houses were still mostly in single domestic occupation. Tower House in London Road, on the other hand, was converted into flats in 1984.[70] The River Road area was earmarked after 1945 for light industry,[71] but by 1972 an industrial estate had opened on the south side of the river,[72] and concurrently firms in or near Tarrant Street and River Road began to close or move away. By 1990 only one factory was left there, many former industrial or commercial buildings later being converted as dwellings or replaced by new houses and flats, usually in vernacular styles. Beyond the bridge by the 1980s there were some larger shops in Queen Street. Further houses and bungalows were built after 1945,[73] some being destroyed when Fitzalan Road was cut in two by the town relief road of 1973.

The west end of the town also continued to grow in the mid 20th century. Houses for the Norfolk estate had been erected near the sawmill *c.* 1909,[74] and more were put up near the castle stables in the 1950s and south-west of London Road at about the same date.[75] Between Torton Hill and Chichester roads many dwellings, including some council houses, were built from the 1950s;[76] by 1991 the area south of Chichester Road had become twice as populous as the older part of the town.[77]

STREET NAMES. Of the town's streets *High Street* was so called *c.* 1216;[78] its lower portion may have been the Wide Street mentioned in the early 15th century.[79] Alternative names were High Market Street, recorded from 1658,[80] New Market Street, used in the later 18th century,[81] and possibly Market Street, mentioned in 1570 and later.[82] *Maltravers Street* was apparently Old Chipping (i.e. Market) Street in the early 15th century,[83] and was generally Old Market Street between the 16th and 18th centuries;[84] the modern name has not been found before the 1830s,[85] the old name being occasionally used later.[86] The junction of High Street and Maltravers Street was called Warningcamp corner by 1601,[87] either from property nearby belonging to Byworth and Warningcamp manor,[88] or from the surname of a property owner or tenant.[89]

Tarrant Street was so named in the early 15th century,[90] and from the mid 18th was also the lower lane.[91] *Mill Lane*, the old road to South Stoke, was so called in 1379;[92] its alternative

61 Ibid. TD/W 5; cf. Pigot, *Nat. Com. Dir.* (1832–4), 1003–4. The maltings were there by the early 18th cent. and the brewery by *c.* 1832: W.S.R.O., Par. 8/11/7; Pigot, op. cit. 1003.

62 O.S. Map 1/2,500, Suss. LXIII. 1 (1877 and later edns.).

63 W.S.R.O., BO/AR 12/18; Pike, *Bognor Dir.* (1910–11), 186.

64 A.C.M., Hodskinson surv. 1778, f. 20; W.S.R.O., TD/W 5; Pike, *Bognor Dir.* (1910–11), 191.

65 O.S. Map 1/2,500, Suss. LXIII. 1 (1877 and later edns.); W.S.R.O., BO/AR 16/1/41–2.

66 W.S.R.O., BO/AR 40/1/1; cf. ibid. BO/AR 38/1; 53/10.

67 O.S. Map 6", Suss. LXIII. NW. (1899 and later edns.); A.C.M., MD 950; W.S.R.O., BO/AR 10/7–8; 16/1/17–20; 24/4/20; ibid. Holmes, Campbell & Co. MS. 837 (TS. cat.); *W. Suss. Gaz.* 26 Oct. 1893; Pike, *Bognor Dir.* (1912–13); cf. *Census*, 1881–1901, s.v. Tortington.

68 O.S. Map 6", Suss. LXIII. NW. ([1938] edn.); W.S.R.O., BO/AR 24/2/1, statement to L.G.B. enquiry by J. J. Robinson, 1913, and agreement by L.G.B. to lease of land by Arundel town council, 1913; 24/2/8; Goodliffe, *Littlehampton* [1915], 8; *Arundel, the Gem of Suss.* (Arundel, 1934), 26–7.

69 F. D. Allison, *Little Town of Arundel*, 15.

70 *Financial Times*, 24 Nov. 1984.

71 Below, other trades and inds. (after 1945).

72 *New Statesman*, 22 Dec. 1972, p. 941.

73 O.S. Map 1/2,500, TQ 0006–0106 (1971 edn.).

74 W.S.R.O., BO/AR 16/1/25.

75 Below, castle grounds; local inf.; O.S. Map 1/2,500, TQ 0007–0107 (1971 edn.).

76 O.S. Map 1/25,000, TQ 00 (1959 edn.); TQ 00/10 (1979 edn.).

77 *W. Suss. Gaz.* 31 Jan. 1991.

78 *S.R.S.* lix, pp. 105–6; cf. B.L. Lansd. Ch. 92.

79 *S.R.S.* lxvii. 116.

80 W.S.R.O., A.B.A., P1/29 (TS. cat.); ibid. Add. MSS. 3364, 12938, 15821 (TS. cat.).

81 Ibid. S.A.S. MS. RB 35 (TS. cat.); A.C.M., Hodskinson surv. 1778, f. 3.

82 A.C.M., M 301, pp. [184–5]; ibid. MD 535, f. 5; W.S.R.O., Add. MS. 3012 (TS. cat.).

83 *S.R.S.* lxvii. 116–17.

84 Ibid. xxix, pp. 10–11; xli. 54; A.C.M., MD 535, f. 4; E.S.R.O., SAS/HA 489 (TS. cat.); cf. W.S.R.O., Par. 8/37/16.

85 Pigot, *Nat. Com. Dir.* (1832–4), 1003; cf. A.C.M., D 399–423 (MS. cat.).

86 A.C.M., MD 1104; W.S.R.O., MP 962, list of burgesses, 1865.

87 *S.R.S.* xxix, p. 9; cf. Hillier, *Arundel* (1847), 29; A.C.M., D 283–302 (MS. cat.).

88 A.C.M., D 6589–90 (MS. cat.); *Arundel Cast. Archives*, iii, p. 56. Cf. the tenement in the town called Warningcamp in 1570: ibid. MD 535, f. 3v.

89 *S.R.S.* lxvii. 116.

90 Ibid. 116–18.

91 A.C.M., Hodskinson surv. 1778, f. 3; W.S.R.O., A.B.A., J1, f. 2.

92 A.C.M., D 1158; cf. W.S.R.O., Cap. I/15/1.

name Jury Lane, recorded from 1570,[93] may allude to a medieval Jewish quarter.[94] The junction of Mill Lane and High Street was called Lasseter's corner by 1851,[95] after the watchmaker whose shop was there.[96]

Other streets in the town have also had multiple names. *King Street*, recorded from 1636,[97] may have been the Kings Lane mentioned in 1525 and later;[98] in 1785 it was Panets Pond Lane,[99] and it may have been Punetts Lane recorded in 1574.[1] *Parson's Hill*, so called by the 1870s,[2] was previously Ibbetsons Lane, commemorating a property occupier of that surname;[3] it was also Farmers Lane in 1785[4] and Parsonage Hill in 1879.[5] The street which marks the western edge of the town, formerly known as Whitings dyke,[6] was called Poorhouse Hill or Lane in the late 18th century and later;[7] by 1875 its lower part was *Park Place*[8] and by 1889 apparently its upper part *Mount Pleasant*.[9] *School Lane* was apparently Pottmans Ware Lane in 1636.[10] *London Road* was so called by the 1830s,[11] but was alternatively New Road in 1874–5.[12] The central part of *River Road* was called the Shipyard in 1660 and later.[13] *Bakers Arms Hill* was Short Lane in 1785[14] and Baker Hill in 1874–5;[15] *Brewery Hill* was Brewhouse Hill in 1872[16] and evidently the Short Lane mentioned in 1805.[17] The road beyond the bridge was described as Arundel causeway in 1660,[18] and later as the causeway between Arundel and Lyminster.[19] Its west part was Bridge Street or *Queen Street* in 1830,[20] and the east part Brighton Road *c.* 1832[21] and *Station Road* by 1896.[22]

Lost or unidentified streets were Potente Street (recorded 1311),[23] Dede, Dide, or Dyde Street (early 15th century),[24] Jennet Lane (1570 and later),[25] Mincing Lane south of Tarrant Street (1686),[26] and Puttock's Hill north of Tarrant Street (1875).[27] Postern Lane near Hermitage Lane (recorded 1615 and later) and Slutters Lane nearby (1636) evidently lay beyond the Marygate.[28]

RURAL SETTLEMENT. Outside the town there was never much settlement in the Middle Ages or later, apart from the water mill at Swanbourne,[29] replaced in the mid 19th century by the castle dairy, windmills and a malthouse by the river in the 19th and 20th centuries, and lodges in the successive parks of the parish. At the conversion of the Great park into a farm in the mid 18th century a farmhouse was built in Park bottom. Apparently at the end of the century it was replaced by Park House, which was demolished after 1824;[30] a flint terrace of estate cottages was put up on its site before *c.* 1841[31] and survived in 1986. The farmhouse moved in the later 18th century to the modern Park Farmhouse further west. A row of what were apparently farm cottages, called Rooks buildings, was put up south of Chichester Road by 1842;[32] one single-storeyed cottage survived in 1986. Further cottages east and west of Park Farmhouse were built later in the 19th century.

SECULAR BUILDINGS. Surviving late medieval secular buildings in High Street are nos. 37–41 (the former Crown inn), including a range parallel with the street much altered later,[33] and no. 71 (Sefton House), a Wealden house with a small hall. On the corner of High Street and Maltravers Street was a big medieval house jettied on both frontages which was demolished in the later 19th century.[34] No. 8 Maltravers Street nearby is part of a late medieval three-bayed hall house with crown-post roof, while no. 79 at the west end of the same street has evidence of a crown-post roof mostly destroyed. There was a late medieval house at the west end of Tarrant Street on part of the site of the Roman villa,[35] and a timber-framed house, apparently jettied and perhaps medieval, facing the west front of the church.[36]

There are many 16th- and 17th-century houses in the town. No. 51 High Street has late 16th-century timber-framed ranges along High and Tarrant streets; the angle between was filled in the earlier 17th century by a new block whose ground-floor room has an elaborately moulded

93 A.C.M., MD 535, f. 3; 1532; W.S.R.O., A.B.A., F4/1, no. 1; A.B.A., P1/22 (TS. cat.).
94 Above, gen. hist. of town.
95 *Arundel Rds.* 19.
96 Below, other trades and inds. (1800–1945).
97 A.C.M., MD 505, f. [1v.]; W.S.R.O., Par. 8/37/16.
98 *S.R.S.* xli. 54; A.C.M., D 864–81 (MS. cat.); ibid. MD 535, f. 3v.; W.S.R.O., Add. MS. 15767; ibid. Ep. I/25/1 (1615). 'King St. Lane' is recorded in 18th cent.: A.C.M., D 734–44 (MS. cat.).
99 W.S.R.O., MP 3041 (photocopy of town plan, 1785).
1 Bodl. MS. Rawl. B. 318, p. 174.
2 O.S. Map 1/2,500, Suss. LXIII. 1 (1877 edn.).
3 A.C.M., D 610–13, deed, 1811; for the site cf. below, church.
4 W.S.R.O., MP 3041 (photocopy of town plan, 1785).
5 42 & 43 Vic. c. 8 (Private).
6 W.S.R.O., Ep. I/25/1 (1615, 1663), the latter transcr. at Tierney, *Arundel*, ii. 654; *S.R.S.* xxix, p. 10; Hillier, *Arundel* (1847), 68.
7 A.C.M., Hodskinson surv. 1778, f. 3; E.S.R.O., SAS/E 294 (TS. cat.); inf. from Mr. F. Penfold, Burpham.
8 O.S. Map 1/2,500, Suss. LXIII. 1 (1877 edn.).
9 A.C.M., D 30–59 (MS. cat.); cf. Pike, *Bognor Dir.* (1910–11), 189.
10 A.C.M., MD 505, f. [3v.]; for location of meadow called the Bedds bounding lane on W., ibid. f. [5]; ibid. Hodskinson surv. 1778, ff. 9, 12.
11 Pigot, *Nat. Com. Dir.* (1832–4), 1004.
12 O.S. Map 1/2,500, Suss. LXIII. 1 (1877 edn.).
13 Ibid.; *S.A.C.* xxxix. 87; Pigot, *Nat. Com. Dir.* (1832–4), 1004; A.C.M., MD 1104, 2179; W.S.R.O., MP 962, list of burgesses, 1865; ibid. SP 257, 1106.
14 W.S.R.O., MP 3041 (photocopy of town plan, 1785).
15 O.S. Map 1/2,500, Suss. LXIII. 1 (1877 edn.).
16 W.S.R.O., Add. MS. 13826 (TS. cat.).
17 Ibid. 25823 (TS. cat.).
18 *S.A.C.* xxxix. 87; cf. *S.R.S.* xxix, p. 12.
19 *Wiston Archives*, i, ed. J. Booker, p. 6.
20 W.S.R.O., Par. 8/37/16; cf. A.C.M., MD 1104.
21 Pigot, *Nat. Com. Dir.* (1832–4), 1004.
22 O.S. Map 1/2,500, Suss. LXIII. 1 (1897 edn.).
23 Bodl. MS. Chart. Suss. a. 2, no. 61.
24 *S.R.S.* lxvii. 115, 117–19.
25 A.C.M., MD 535, f. 4; W.S.R.O., Add. MS. 15767.
26 *S.R.S.* xxix, p. 12.
27 W.S.R.O., SP 257.
28 Ibid. Ep. I/25/1 (1615, 1663); A.C.M., MD 505, ff. [7v.–8]; below, relig. hos. (hospitals); communications (rds.).
29 Mill and ho. illus. at *Victorian Countryside*, ed. G. E. Mingay, i, pl. 26.
30 Below, secular bldgs. (outside the town).
31 W.S.R.O., TD/W 5.
32 A.C.M., LM 15; O.S. Map 6", Suss. LXIII (1879 edn.).
33 For traces of mural painting found there, *W. Suss. Gaz.* 7 Nov. 1963.
34 Cartland, *Arundel*, 23.
35 *S.A.S. Newsletter*, xliii. 384.
36 W.S.R.O., M/PD 338.

plaster ceiling; both that room and the one above retain much original panelling. No. 26 High Street is a notable house of *c.* 1600 with panelling of early 17th-century style, apparently *ex situ*, in one back room; there is identical panelling in the front room of no. 33 High Street, which is jettied. No. 12 High Street was perhaps also originally jettied, as was a large house now demolished on the east side of the street opposite Maltravers Street.[37] In the island of buildings between the market place and the river the low no. 25 High Street on the west side, of timber framing with brick nogging, is 17th-century or earlier, while nos. 17 and 19 on the north side, of the late 17th century, are faced with painted brick. A hip-roofed and timber-framed 16th- or 17th-century house with a large chimneystack stood beside the bridge until the early 20th century.[38]

Sixteenth- or 17th-century houses in Maltravers Street include the timber-framed Little House on the corner of Bakers Arms Hill and the low adjacent brick terrace; two substantial 17th-century or earlier buildings east of no. 14[39] were destroyed in the later 19th century. In Tarrant Street surviving timber-framed houses of the period include the low nos. 13 and 15, faced partly in weatherboarding and partly in painted brick, and no. 21, which is jettied.[40] A timber-framed, hip-roofed house on the south side of the street demolished *c.* 1900 was 17th-century or earlier,[41] while the Quaker meeting house on the corner of Tarrant and Arun streets, demolished in 1867, was a tall range, apparently flint- or rubble-faced, with a doorway of 16th-century character.[42]

A much larger demolished building apparently of the 16th or early 17th century was the house called Nineveh at the east end of Tarrant Street.[43] It was roughly square in plan, faced with flint with stone dressings and stone mullioned windows, and had a massive brick chimneystack. The street frontage was probably occupied from the first by shops, for the two entrances in the early 19th century were a brick arched side doorway in Gothic style and a large porch on the south or river front, both then leading to a large hall which contained a staircase with big newel posts and elaborately carved balusters. There were four or five other rooms on the ground floor, besides cellars in the sloping ground. The chief room seems to have been upstairs; it had moulded oak panelling, two bay windows, and a large open fireplace containing a chimneypiece of Sussex marble with a carved wooden overmantel. The builder of the house is unknown; despite the presence in it of allusions to the heraldry of the earls of Arundel, it seems less likely to have belonged to them than to be the town house of some other important local family. The name Nineveh is recorded, as 'Ninivy', from 1718 and may be a cryptic biblical reference to the house's size.[44] In 1718 part at least of the building was the Star inn, but by the early 19th century it was in multiple occupation as dwellings and workshops. The building was demolished after 1833,[45] part of the site being later occupied by the Congregational chapel.

Two 17th-century timber-framed houses remain in Queen Street south of the bridge: the low no. 10, faced with red brick, and no. 20, which lies back from the street and is rendered. The White Hart inn, also in Queen Street, demolished in the later 19th century, was an apparently jettied building of the 16th century or earlier.[46]

During the early and mid 18th century several houses in the town were refronted in brick, for instance nos. 37–41 and 71 High Street and nos. 8 and 79 Maltravers Street; the encroachment on the street which often accompanied refronting was opposed in vain by the corporation in 1766.[47] New houses were also built during the period. The former George inn, nos. 30–4 High Street, which incorporates an earlier brick chimneystack at its north end, is a three-storeyed red brick building with rusticated brick quoins, Venetian windows, and some 18th-century internal fittings. It seems likely to have had a central archway to the inn yard, later converted to the shop front of no. 32; the shop fronts of nos. 30 and 34 are late 18th- and early 19th-century respectively. The back range of nos. 55–7 High Street is a three-storeyed red brick structure of mid 18th-century date with an original staircase, while no. 61, also of three storeys, the residence in the 1780s of the lawyer Edward Carleton,[48] has a simple 18th-century staircase and late 18th-century decoration in some rooms. In the island of buildings between the market place and the river are two three-storeyed houses of the mid or late 18th century: no. 1 High Street facing the river, of red brick formerly stuccoed, and no. 11 on the east side, of whitewashed brick.

In Maltravers Street nos. 14 and 16 are basically early 18th-century and mid or late 18th-century respectively. Three other mid 18th-century houses in the same street are grander. No. 51, the residence in the 1780s of the timber merchant John Bull,[49] is a detached three-bayed house with a red and grey brick front, the central bay being pedimented; it has some original internal fittings, and was enlarged at the back in the early 19th century. There is a contemporary detached coach house and stable in Kings Arms Hill. No. 26, the house of John Shaft, grocer and tallow chandler, in the 1780s[50] which became the vicarage in the mid 20th century, has an impressive brick front with original two-storeyed canted bay windows and a later porch.[51] The interior is fitted to a high standard with plaster cornices

37 Ibid. PH 1467, f. 130; Cartland, *Arundel*, 11.

38 Cartland, *Arundel*, 33–4.

39 W.S.R.O., PH 1467, f. 131, illus. at Eustace, *Arundel*, facing p. 185.

40 Below, pl. facing p. 26.

41 Cartland, *Arundel*, 47.

42 Ibid. 46; *W. Suss. Gaz.* 14 Nov. 1867.

43 Para. based mainly on *S.A.C.* xx. 184–93. The ho. is not identifiable on Hollar's view of Arundel of 1644: W.S.R.O., PD 1367, illus. above, p. 16.

44 A.C.M., A 339, [affidavit], 1718; cf. Jonah, iii. 3.

45 W.S.R.O., Add. MS. 15674.

46 Cartland, *Arundel*, 40, wrongly giving King St.

47 W.S.R.O., A.B.A., M28.

48 Ibid. A.B.A., M32; ibid. MP 3041 (photocopy of town plan, 1785).

49 Ibid. A.B.A., M32; ibid. MP 3041.

50 Ibid. A.B.A., J1, f. 123v.; A.B.A., M32; ibid. MP 3041; *Univ. Brit. Dir.* ii. 57.

51 Below, pl. facing p. 26.

and much original joinery; the staircase has original carved tread ends, but its newel posts and fret in Chinese Chippendale style do not match them, and were apparently brought from elsewhere. A contemporary coach house and stable adjoin. Nos. 50–4 Maltravers Street, the residence in the 1780s of the coal merchant George Lane,[52] comprise a mid or late 18th-century building of two and a half storeys and three bays, which was enlarged in the early 19th century at the sides and rear, with overarched Venetian windows in the side bays. The side façade of the west wing has a Portland stone depressed-arched doorway with 'Gibbsian' rusticated quoins, and two Portland stone key-stones; the type of stone is unusual for Arundel, and they may be fragments from the early 18th-century work at the castle, removed during rebuilding *c.* 1800.

In minor streets, no. 2 Bakers Arms Hill, of the early 18th century, has a façade with elaborately moulded brick window cornices surprising in such a small building, while no. 24 River Road, of grey brick with red brick dressings and rubbed brick voussoirs, is very lavish for its position. There are also 18th-century brick or flint houses and cottages in less important areas of the town: Arun Street, Park Place and Mount Pleasant on the west edge, and Queen Street south of the river; in Park Place is an 18th- or early 19th-century coach house possibly for a house in Maltravers Street.

Many large red brick houses in the town of the late 18th and early 19th centuries share common features: a weak cornice formed by a single course of brick modillions, a terrace plan with toplit staircase across the building between front and rear rooms, and a slim unbroken baluster rail, usually of mahogany.

The grandest are in Maltravers Street.[53] No. 13 (Duff House) at the east end, is a three-bayed, two-storeyed building, originally detached; a brick on the rear façade has a date in the 1780s, when the merchant Joseph Coote lived there.[54] There is 18th-century decoration on the first floor, but the ground floor was refitted *c.* 1815, when the two main rooms were interconnected by double doors. No. 15, of three much taller storeys, was built on to no. 13 apparently in the 1790s;[55] a dining room with a low coved ceiling and other 'Soanian' decoration was added on the west side *c.* 1825, and the porch is 20th-century.[56] There is a contemporary stable and coach house adjoining, and the garden preserves its original extent downhill to Tarrant Street. Further west nos. 53–61 form a continuous terrace of two or three storeys with a basement. Nos. 55–7, which externally seem a single house, were built *c.* 1780 for two members of the Digance family, both merchants.[57] No. 55 has a good front room on the first floor and a large back room on the ground floor with a fine Adam-style entablature and a boarded dado with elaborate top moulding; a new wide entrance hall was added on the east in the early 19th century, the old hall being thrown into the front room. Nos. 59–61 are also a pair: no. 59, the smaller, has a big first-floor front room with fine late 18th-century decoration including an Adam-style entablature, while no. 61 has a very large first-floor room across its whole frontage and a fine square staircase hall with pyramidal skylight.[58]

Nos. 45–9 and 49A Maltravers Street, also on the south side, are an early 19th-century[59] stuccoed terrace of three storeys and basement with a prominent continuous cornice; nos. 49 and 49A were refitted internally in the mid or late 19th century, when a two-storeyed tiled iron veranda and bow windows were added at the back. No. 18 Maltravers Street on the north side is also stuccoed, with a segmentally bowed window on the ground floor; built between 1833 and 1847, it occupies the site of one of Arundel's theatres.[60]

The tall front range of nos. 55–7 High Street, of the late 18th century, is of local yellow brick with stone dressings; in the 1780s it was the residence of the mercer, later banker, Charles Bushby.[61] Almost opposite, the imposing red brick Norfolk Arms hotel was built by the duke of Norfolk between 1782 and 1785,[62] its most striking feature being the large-scale lettering of its name added in the early 19th century over the central archway to the yard. The early 19th-century no. 67 High Street has various internal fittings brought from elsewhere, including a coffered ceiling in Italian 16th-century style.

Tarrant Street between 1785 and 1788 acquired at its western end a group of mainly three-storeyed red brick houses;[63] no. 42 has a fine porch, while no. 54 has an original coach house and stable on the west, and a business office added later between with a separate entrance. New buildings built elsewhere in the town in the early 19th century were generally humbler. At the north-west end there are plain two-storeyed terraces mostly of flint or beach pebbles with brick dressings, some whitewashed, in King and Bond streets, Orchard Place, and Mount Pleasant. Other contemporary terraces of cottages are nos. 8–18 Arun Street, of galletted flint with yellow brick dressings, nos. 7–25 Surrey Street, of Plymouth stone[64] with yellow brick dressings and dated 1821, and the mid 19th-century stuccoed nos. 74–84 Maltravers Street.[65]

Some 19th-century public buildings in the town were in classical style: the Bridge hotel in Queen Street,[66] the corn store on the town quay,[67] and the Victoria institute in Tarrant

52 W.S.R.O., MP 3041; below, other trades and inds. (1500–1800).

53 Below, pl. facing p. 27.

54 W.S.R.O., MP 3041; *Univ. Brit. Dir.* ii. 56.

55 Unlike no. 13, it is not shown on W.S.R.O., MP 3041 (photocopy of town plan, 1785).

56 H.B.M.C. hist. bldgs. list.

57 W.S.R.O., Add. MS. 20622 (TS. cat.); ibid. MP 3041; *Univ. Brit. Dir.* ii. 56.

58 The 4 hos. are apparently depicted at B.L. Add. MS. 5674, f. 9, of 1789.

59 Tierney, *Arundel*, ii. 672; for site of custom ho., below, this section.

60 Below, soc. and cultural activities.

61 W.S.R.O., A.B.A., M32; ibid. MP 3041; *Univ. Brit. Dir.* ii. 57.

62 A.C.M., MD 19.

63 They are not shown on W.S.R.O., MP 3041 (photocopy of town plan, 1785), but appear on a map of 1788: A.C.M., LM 10.

64 Cf. above, growth of town.

65 The last named terrace does not appear on W.S.R.O., TD/W 5 of *c.* 1841, but is shown on O.S. Map 1/2,500, Suss. LXIII. 1 (1877 edn.).

66 Cartland, *Arundel*, 37.

67 Ibid. 99.

The former *West Sussex Gazette* office in High Street in the late 19th century

The 18th-century vicarage in Maltravers Street

No. 21 Tarrant Street

ARUNDEL

Nos. 40–4 Maltravers Street,
designed by J. A. Hansom, with the Parade on the right

Nos. 55–61 Maltravers Street, on the south side

ARUNDEL

Street, built in the 1840s or 50s as the Arundel savings bank,[68] which has 'Egyptian'-style window surrounds. The Swan hotel was rebuilt in the mid 19th century in Italianate style. By far the more common style for new buildings in the town after that period was revived medieval or Tudor. Two earlier examples were Tower House in London Road built *c.* 1795[69] and the new town hall in Maltravers Street of 1834–5.[70] Tower House is a pair of tall semidetached villas of yellow stock brick with ashlar dressings, asymmetrical in plan with a polygonal stone tower at the east end. Its castellated Gothic style, which can be compared to that of the contemporary work on the castle and was evidently meant to match it, seems to have been due to the duke of Norfolk, and was dubbed by a visitor in 1803 the 'Arundelian order of architecture'. Further examples in the town alluded to then and later[71] evidently included the restored Marygate and college buildings, and buildings in the castle grounds and park. The town hall, designed by Robert Abraham,[72] is in a gloomy Norman style, evidently also intended to pay homage to the castle, and echoed in the same architect's Congregational chapel in Tarrant Street and in the contemporary pumping house at Swanbourne lake.[73]

Medieval- or Tudor-style buildings put up between the mid 19th century and the earlier 20th are more picturesque. A pair of Norfolk estate cottages in Maltravers Street of 1849 are in Tudor style, in red and grey brick with decorated bargeboards; the brick and stone façade of no. 38, the former custom house, is similar.[74] Nos. 40–4 Maltravers Street of *c.* 1883, designed by J. A. Hansom,[75] are also of red brick and stone with a prominent first-floor corner statue in a niche of Duke Henry's patron saint, the Emperor Henry II. Also perhaps by Hansom, and with some half-timbering, are nos. 66–70 Maltravers Street, at the west end, and a building on the corner of Maltravers and High streets, whose first floor is jettied on both frontages like that of its medieval predecessor.

The north-west part of the town, largely belonging to the Norfolk estate, acquired several comparable buildings from the 1860s, notably Hansom's French Gothic Roman Catholic church of 1869–73 and its attached presbytery. The Catholic boys' school, later St. Mary's hall, on the corner of London Road and Mount Pleasant, is also by Hansom, and has a prominent corner statue under a canopy of the Virgin and Child.[76] In Bond Street is a terrace of red brick and sandstone estate cottages dated 1868, enlivened by projecting porches and dormer windows with bargeboards, and raised on a brick platform. Other Tudor-style estate cottages of *c.* 1870 in London Road also have tall chimneystacks.

Four striking buildings in historical styles were put up at the lower end of the town in the 1890s and early 1900s. Nos. 18–20 High Street, dated 1890, is of red brick and stone with flushwork and diaper patterning, one of its six gables carrying a stone anvil emblematic of the ironmonger's shop below. Lloyds Bank next door, built before 1893,[77] is in Norman Shavian half-timbered style with tall chimneys, a dormer window, and another prominent gable. The post office building of *c.* 1895, by the Norfolk estate architect W. Heveningham,[78] with a red brick ground floor and half-timbered, many-gabled upper floor, acts as a frontispiece to the town when approached from the south-east, leading the eye up to the castle on the skyline. Still more picturesque are the new offices of the *West Sussex Gazette* built in 1899–1900 to the designs of Wheeler and Lodge of London, and then described as probably 'the most artistic newspaper office ... in England'.[79] The elaborately detailed façade of three storeys with a gable uses glass, pebbledash, and limestone ashlar as well as brick and timber, and the south side is crowned by six attached chimneys of hexagonal plan. The printing works of 1906 at the rear, with an ornate façade on Tarrant Street, is by the same firm of architects.[80]

OUTSIDE THE TOWN. Park House or Arundel Park,[81] in Park bottom west of the town, may have existed by the mid 1790s. The home of Lord Henry Howard-Molyneux-Howard (d. 1824), brother of Duke Bernard Edward (d. 1842),[82] it was of nine bays and two storeys;[83] it was demolished after his death.[84] The grounds of the house included an oblong lake and specimen trees.[85] A pair of stone lodges on Chichester Road, built by 1804,[86] survived in 1995.

Park Farmhouse further west is chiefly late 18th- or early 19th-century, with a three-bayed classical west front of knapped flint with yellow brick dressings; the building is otherwise mostly of flint rubble. A chimneystack, together with some window frames and a stone moulding on the east front, perhaps re-used, survive from an earlier building, which was presumably a lodge in the park; some internal doorcases, however, seem grander than would be expected in a lodge, and may be 18th-century work from the castle, removed at its remodelling in the later 18th century or early 19th. The north front, in contrast

68 Below, professions.

69 A.C.M., D 1977; illus. at *Connoisseur*, Mar. 1978, p. 165.

70 Below, boro. govt. (town halls).

71 *Gent. Mag.* lxxiii (1), 130; *Excursions through Suss.* (1822), 35; cf. below, castle (cast. fabric).

72 W.S.R.O., BO/AR 53/1.

73 Below, protestant nonconf. (Presbyterians and Independents); public servs.

74 A.C.M., uncat. archit. drawings, plan of boro. 1849; W.S.R.O., SP 257.

75 Nairn & Pevsner, *Suss.* 95 n.; A.C.M., uncat. archit. drawings; pl. opposite.

76 Below, educ.; pl. facing p. 91. A plan of 1882 by Hansom's firm for a picturesque row of 10 almshos. on the N. side of London Rd. opposite the Rom. Cath. ch. was not carried out: A.C.M., MD 1928.

77 Kimpton, *Arundel* (1893), 5; cf. W.S.R.O., BO/AR 16/1/13.

78 A.C.M., uncat. archit. drawings, 1893–4; Kimpton, *Arundel* (1897), 4.

79 F. V. Wright, *100 Yrs. of W. Suss. Gaz. 1853–1953*, 28, 30; cf. Goodliffe, *Littlehampton* (1903), 71.

80 W.S.R.O., BO/AR 16/1/58.

81 Wright, *Arundel* (1817), 31; *D.N.B.* s.v. Edw. Long.

82 *Univ. Brit. Dir.* ii. 56; Wright, *Arundel* (1818), 155, 161; Burke, *Peerage* (1956), 1623.

83 Cartland, *Arundel*, 126.

84 e.g. W.S.R.O., TD/W 5.

85 Ibid.; Cartland, *Arundel*, 126; Wright, *Arundel* (1818), 161.

86 A.C.M., PM 17.

to the west, is in asymmetrical Gothic style with a two-storeyed stone bay window apparently intended as an 'eyecatcher'; the front is not 16th-century[87] and may have been designed by Duke Charles (d. 1815).[88] Model farm buildings were added to the east in the mid 19th century, including a large flint barn dated 1837 and a piggery built in 1845.[89] There is also an octagonal horse gin.

DEFENCES. As the first defensible site inland from the Arun estuary Arundel is likely to have had fortifications of some sort from an early period. Part of a curved earthwork which survives north-west of the north bailey of the castle may represent a fortification preceding that, perhaps prehistoric in date.

The Little park (the present castle cricket ground) north-west of the castle is bounded on its north, west, and south sides by linear earthworks. That on the north, of impressive size, was continued south-westwards in the mid 17th century on a much slighter scale;[90] the earthwork as a whole, therefore, cannot be a prehistoric attempt to defend the chalk promontory on which the town lies, as suggested by Tierney.[91]

The Little park earthworks may have been constructed to contain the putative late Anglo-Saxon *burh*,[92] an idea perhaps corroborated by Saxo-Norman pottery found in the northern earthwork.[93] The south part of the western earthwork is missing, possibly through 19th-century landscaping of the castle grounds, while the lack of an eastern earthwork may be due to the steepness of the cliff at that point.[94] The southern earthwork seems to have been re-used as part of the later medieval town defences.[95] At the point where the northern earthwork is cut by the apparently early track descending the downs, the lower portion of which is followed by High Street,[96] are the remains of a chalk rubble and Caen stone gateway seemingly built in the late 11th century or early 12th,[97] but perhaps succeeding an earlier one. The gate was apparently the Red gate mentioned in 1570,[98] since the London road to the north was called Red Lane.[99] It still stood in part in 1851[1] but was afterwards grassed over.

The Norman town, which seems to have lain chiefly along the track mentioned both inside and outside the Little park,[2] probably had no defences until the late 13th century, the north gateway being then perhaps used less for defence than for collecting tolls. In 1295 a 10-years' grant of murage was obtained for the town by the earl of Arundel.[3] The line of defences created was apparently new and excluded the Little park, the north-westwards continuation of High Street being diverted. Starting from what was apparently a new gate[4] by the outer ditch of the north bailey of the castle the circuit ran west to a second gate, the Marygate, built across the new London road; the earthwork between the two gates may be the re-used southern defence of the putative Anglo-Saxon *burh*, turned to face outwards instead of inwards, and provided with a ditch on the north side which survived in 1995. From the Marygate the line of the new defences ran south-west, first within the modern castle grounds, and then down Mount Pleasant, Park Place, and School Lane, where a natural cliff was scarped back.[5] Mount Pleasant was known by 1615 as Whitings dyke,[6] possibly from a personal name. A section of earthwork was said to be still visible by the St. Mary's Gate inn in London Road in 1851.[7] At the point where the circuit crossed Maltravers Street was a third gate called the Marshgate or Watergate.[8]

The medieval defences seem only ever to have been of earth, as also happened in some larger medieval towns.[9] It is notable that they protected only the north and west sides of the town. The south side would have been defended by the river, though nothing is known of any gate on the bridge. The sector between the bridge and the castle was undefended, the terrain perhaps making it unnecessary. References to 'the new ditch' in or near Tarrant Street in the early 15th century[10] may suggest either that the south end of the western line of defence was not completed until then, or that it was extended at that date nearer the river.

It is not clear which gate was referred to in 1321, when packing service was owed at Ham manor in Angmering 'beyond the gate of Arundel'.[11] The Marygate probably existed in 1343, when a chapel, apparently dedicated to St. Mary, was said to have been newly founded at the north gate of the town.[12] The name Marygate was in

87 *Pace* H.B.M.C. hist. bldgs. list.

88 Cf. above, this section; below, castle (cast. fabric).

89 J. M. Robinson, *Georgian Model Fms.* 114.

90 Below, this section.

91 Tierney, *Arundel*, i. 30–1; cf. *V.C.H. Suss.* i. 467–8; Eustace, *Arundel*, 18.

92 Above, gen. hist. of town; for site and layout cf. *A.-S. Towns in Southern Eng.* ed. J. Haslam, 264–5; P. Drewett, D. Rudling and M. Gardiner, *SE. to AD 1000*, 323, 326. The *burhs* at Wallingford (Berks.) and Wareham (Dors.) have comparable earthworks: *A.-S. Towns in Southern Eng.* 76; *Medieval Arch.* xiv. 85–6; *S.A.C.* cxxx. 137.

93 *S.A.C.* cxxx. 135, 139. Since its layout is unrelated to the cast. the Little park area is less likely to have been created as an outer bailey of it, e.g. for sheltering troops: cf. *Urban Arch. in Brit.* ed. J. Schofield and R. Leech, 130; Dallaway, *Hist. W. Suss.* ii (1) (1819), 165.

94 Cf. Wareham: *Medieval Arch.* xiv. 85.

95 Below, this section.

96 Below, communications (rds.).

97 *S.A.C.* cxxx. 130–9.

98 A.C.M., MD 535, f. 5v. Bogherwerth gate, associated with the site at Eustace, *Arundel*, 18 n., was a gate of the Great park: below, woods and parks.

99 Below, communications (rds.).

1 *A Visit to Arundel Cast.* (1851), 93–4; cf. Dallaway, *Hist. W. Suss.* ii (1) (1819), 165; Tierney, *Arundel*, i. 95; Eustace, *Arundel*, 18; A.C.M., LM 18; ibid. MD 2592; W.S.R.O., A.B.A., M52.

2 Above, growth of town.

3 *Cal. Pat.* 1292–1301, 137.

4 B.L. Add. MS. 5674, f. 27; Tierney, *Arundel*, ii. 712.

5 Eustace, *Arundel*, 19.

6 W.S.R.O., Ep. I/25/1 (1615); *S.R.S.* xxix, p. 10; Hillier, *Arundel* (1847), 68.

7 Hillier, *Arundel* (1851), 23.

8 Below, this section; Ogilby, *Britannia* (1675), 8.

9 e.g. Sandwich (Kent) or Grimsby and Boston (Lincs.): H. L. Turner, *Town Defences in Eng. and Wales*, 163–4; *Plans and Topog. of Medieval Towns in Eng. and Wales*, ed. M. W. Barley, 60.

10 *S.R.S.* lxvii. 117.

11 Ibid. lx. 71.

12 *Cal. Pat.* 1343–5, 121; cf. *S.R.S.* xlvi, p. 311.

use by the early 15th century.[13] The medieval building is said to have been of ashlar masonry. Besides the chapel over the archway, which had a two-light cusped window and was reached by an external flight of steps, there was a room each side on the ground floor.[14] Part of the gate at least had apparently been converted into a dwelling by 1636,[15] and the structure was certainly used as dwellings later.[16] Only the side piers of the gate next to the north bailey ditch remained in 1781,[17] and only the ivy-covered stump of its east pier, of flint and stone, by 1989. The Marshgate or Watergate is recorded only between 1615[18] and 1712[19] and had been demolished by 1785.[20] A postern gate near the Marygate is indicated by the road name Postern Lane recorded in the area in the early 17th century.[21]

The town defences were strengthened in December 1643 by Ralph Hopton, Lord Hopton, after his capture of the town for Charles I.[22] A south-westwards continuation of the northern earthwork of the Little park down to Park bottom prevented access from the west; the portion of Hopton's work which survives on either side of London Road and which was later known as Roads ditch, possibly from a personal name,[23] is distinguished from the northern earthwork of the park by its much slighter scale.[24] At the same time the latter was apparently heightened and its ditch deepened. Hopton also threw up a double earthwork north of the town near Swanbourne lake in order to cut off a possible approach by way of Mill Lane under the east side of the castle. That seems to be the ditch and banks of which there are traces on the steep hill between the lake and the north-east corner of the Little park.[25] When Sir William Waller returned to retake the town for Parliament soon afterwards he broke through both lines of defence, those on the west withstanding his assault for two hours.[26] The circular mounds at each end of the northern earthwork of the Little park[27] may be gun emplacements created thereafter to command the castle.

After Waller's capture of the town and castle in January 1644 the fortifications of the town may again have been strengthened. In 1653, however, the castle was slighted,[28] and six years later the town defences were ordered to be 'thoroughly' demolished.[29]

The Marygate may have been damaged in the Civil War, for lead was removed from the roof, apparently by the mayor, before 1652.[30] The upper storey survived in the 1720s,[31] but by 1780 the arch had been taken down as dangerous to users of the London road,[32] apparently the chief means of approach to the town by land.[33] By 1809 the duke of Norfolk had acquired the remains of the gate[34] and before 1815 he restored it in medieval style.[35] Part of the original structure remains on the south side west of the archway, but the present building is mostly 19th-century and later; it is of flint with sandstone dressings, including some flushwork, and has battlements and machicolations on both faces. The portion of wall west of the gate was built of Plymouth rock shortly before 1817.[36] The gate was again restored in the early 20th century, when an external staircase to the upper floor was built on the south side.[37] The ceiling of the upstairs room has four massive oak timbers with 16th-century-style heraldic decoration which partly relates to the FitzAlan family.[38] Evidently too large and too much weathered to have been part of an interior decorative ensemble, they may be timbers from a drawbridge.[39]

The landscaping of the castle grounds in the early 19th century apparently included major alterations to the Little park earthworks, which in 1819 had been said to be still complete.[40] The bank east of the Marygate was levelled and turned into two terraces apparently by 1825,[41] while its east end seems to have been pushed into the ditch to give a link and a level vista to the park from the section of the grounds nearer the castle. The south part of the park's western earthwork may have been removed at the same date.

RELIGIOUS HOUSES. Arundel was the site of seven medieval religious houses; five at least were under the patronage of successive lords of the rape, as were two others nearby, Pynham priory in Lyminster and Tortington priory.[42]

The histories of the apparently pre-Conquest minster church, the Norman priory, and the college which succeeded it in the later 14th century are treated below.[43]

COLLEGE BUILDINGS. The buildings of the college perhaps occupied the same site as those of

13 *S.R.S.* xli. 370; lxvii. 116.
14 B.L. Add. MS. 5674, f. 13, illus. at *Suss. Views* (S.R.S.), 9; ibid. Lansd. MS. 918, f. 38; Tierney, *Arundel*, ii. 712.
15 A.C.M., MD 505, f. [iv.].
16 *Gent. Mag.* lxiii (2), 786.
17 B.L. Add. MS. 5674, f. 27; cf. A.C.M., MD 2592; Tierney, *Arundel*, ii. 712.
18 W.S.R.O., Ep. I/25/1 (1615); cf. *Glynde Pla. Archives*, ed. R. F. Dell, p. 132.
19 W.S.R.O., A.B.A., P1/24 (TS. cat.); cf. *S.R.S.* xxix, p. 13.
20 W.S.R.O., MP 3041 (photocopy of town plan, 1785).
21 A.C.M., MD 505, f. [7v.].
22 Above, milit. events; cf. Wareham (Dors.): *Medieval Arch.* iii. 123.
23 W.S.R.O., A.B.A., F1/1, f. 2v.; Hillier, *Arundel* (1847), 68; ibid. (1851), 23.
24 The low cliff along the NE. side of Park bottom, marked by the O.S. as a rampart, is apparently natural: O.S. Map 1/2,500, TQ 0007–0107 (1971 edn.).
25 Cf. Wright, *Arundel* (1818), 66; Eustace, *Arundel*, 18.
26 W. Freeman, *Arundel Cast. Guide* (*c.* 1972), 40.
27 Eustace, *Arundel*, 18.
28 Above, milit. events.
29 *Cal. S.P. Dom.* 1659–60, 173.
30 W.S.R.O., Par. 8/12/2, f. 7; for John Albery as mayor, Eustace, *Arundel*, 251.
31 B.L. Lansd. MS. 918, f. 38.
32 Ibid. Add. MS. 5674, f. 13; *Gent. Mag.* lxiii (2), 786.
33 Cf. Ogilby, *Britannia* (1675), 8; *Gardener's Mag.* v (1829), 585.
34 *S.A.C.* lxxi. 53.
35 Horsfield, *Hist. Suss.* ii. 132.
36 Wright, *Arundel* (1817), 39; illus. at W.S.R.O., F/PD 457, f. 13.
37 A.C.M., uncat. archit. drawings; the steps are not shown at ibid. MD 799, f. 37, of the mid or late 19th cent.
38 W.S.R.O., MP 2898.
39 Cf. Wright, *Arundel* (1817), 38.
40 Dallaway, *Hist. W. Suss.* ii (1) (1819), 165.
41 J. Rouse, *Beauties and Antiq. of Suss.* i. 292.
42 *V.C.H. Suss.* ii. 80, 82–3, 97, 108, 119; *S.R.S.* xli. 55.
43 Below, church.

the priory, and are architecturally *en suite* with the new parish church of the same date. The Fitzalan chapel of the parish church formed the college's north side, and there were two-storeyed east, south and west ranges; the east range lies beyond the east end of the Fitzalan chapel, and the outer wall of the west range is aligned with the east wall of the south transept of the church. The entrance gateway was apparently at the south-west corner,[44] on the same site as the present 19th-century entrance, and the master's house is said to have been in the north-east corner, a small gallery giving access to the Fitzalan chapel behind its high altar.[45] There was a cloister along the northern section of the east range and also along the wall of the Fitzalan chapel;[46] part survived in 1989.

Since the area enclosed by the three ranges and the chapel is very large, it may originally have been divided into separate north and south courtyards, as at the slightly earlier college at Cobham (Kent).[47] If so, the northern courtyard may have had a cloister all round, and the hall mentioned in 1382[48] may have lain in the cross range between the courtyards, as at Cobham. A chapter house was mentioned in 1401.[49] It is not clear whether there was a college graveyard separate from the parish churchyard.

In 1644 the east and south ranges of the college were depicted as complete.[50] A visitor in 1635 had mentioned the cloister and gardens, and 'a fair long building' nearby, perhaps the hall, in which quarter sessions were then held, and at the end of which was a low round tower of stone with a conical top, apparently a former calefactory.[51] At that time part of the buildings at least was let, presumably as a dwelling.[52] The college was apparently damaged during the Civil War, for stone and timber were removed from it for re-use elsewhere in 1657–8.[53] Repairs were carried out between 1659 and 1664[54] and *c.* 1678.[55] In the mid 18th century the buildings were described by two separate visitors as merely remains,[56] and in 1780 the east and west ranges seem to have survived in parts of their outer walls only.[57] There were some structures inside the shell of the south range in 1788.[58]

The north-east corner of the quadrangle, on the other hand, had been rebuilt or restored during the 18th century as a residence for the duke of Norfolk's agent.[59] In the 1780s that building consisted of a west range running north–south, with a canted bay under its north gable, and an east range running east–west with an 18th-century porch on the north side.[60] Between 1804[61] and 1815[62] the building was rebuilt in Gothic style and about that time it housed a private school.[63]

In the late 18th or early 19th century, apparently by 1797,[64] Duke Charles (d. 1815) restored the south range of the college, its west end becoming a Roman Catholic chapel, with the chaplain's residence and other dwellings further east;[65] a terrace was constructed on the south side above the new London road. Some contemporary fittings remained in that range in 1989. The late 18th- or early 19th-century work was in grey Plymouth stone,[66] in contrast to the flint and stone with sandstone dressings of the original work; the walls were crenellated, a practice continued in later 19th- and 20th-century alterations.[67] In 1834 the external walls of the unrestored east and west ranges retained many, if not most, of their original trefoil-headed windows.[68] The Catholic chapel was lengthened westwards in 1865, but ceased to be used after the new Catholic church was opened in 1873.[69]

By 1842 part of the east range was used as a laundry for the castle,[70] as later.[71] In the 1850s the south-east corner of the college was converted into a convent,[72] as it remained until the 1950s.[73] At the same period the appearance of the north side of the courtyard was spoilt by the building of the funerary chapel of Duke Henry Granville (d. 1860), which projects from the south side of the Fitzalan chapel. Between the mid 1870s[74] and the 1890s[75] the west part of the south range and a new west range were used for a girls' and infants' school; a girls' club occupied part of those premises in 1899, and they were added to the convent in 1903–4, when further alterations and repairs were carried out.[76] The 19th-century west range was later removed, leaving the west wall to stand alone.

Between *c.* 1961 and 1974 the college buildings were used as a children's home with 30 inmates, and after 1976 the south range and part of the east range were converted as an old people's home and the north-east corner was divided into flats for the elderly, both run by the Order of

44 Cf. B.L. Add. MS. 5674, f. 24 (view looking E.).
45 Tierney, *Arundel*, ii. 599, 614.
46 Cf. *Camd. Misc.* xvi (Camd. 3rd ser. lii), Hammond, 32; A.C.M., A 263, acct. 1663.
47 *Arch. Cantiana*, lxxix. 113–14 and facing p. 110.
48 Tierney, *Arundel*, ii. 600 n.
49 *S.R.S.* viii. 78.
50 W.S.R.O., PD 1367, illus. above, p. 16.
51 *Camd. Misc.* xvi (Camd. 3rd ser. lii), Hammond, 33; cf. A.C.M., MD 505, f. [1].
52 A.C.M., MD 505, f. [1]; W.S.R.O., A.B.A., F2/14, f. [3]; *Clough and Butler Archives*, ed. J. Booker, p. 21. Cf. the name College Ho.: A.C.M., MD 505, f. [1].
53 A.C.M., A 262, ff. [7, 27].
54 Ibid. 262, f. [38v.]; 263, accts. 1663–4.
55 Ibid. 1757.
56 B.L. Add. MS. 15776, f. 232; *Pococke's Travels*, ii (Camd. Soc. 2nd ser. xliv), 107.
57 B.L. Add. MS. 5674, ff. 23–4; for the E. range cf. Dallaway, *Hist. W. Suss.* ii (1) (1819), 166.
58 A.C.M., LM 10.
59 Ibid. Hodskinson surv. 1778, f. 8; Tierney, *Arundel*, ii. 614; *Univ. Brit. Dir.* ii. 56.
60 B.L. Add. MS. 5674, f. 16.
61 Ibid. 36389, f. 71v.
62 Horsfield, *Hist. Suss.* ii. 131.
63 A.C.M., PM 107; cf. *Kelly's Dir. Suss.* (1845, 1852).
64 G. Anstruther, *Seminary Priests*, iv. 312; cf. *Gent. Mag.* lxxiii (1), 131.
65 Tierney, *Arundel*, ii. 613–14; Wright, *Arundel* (1817), 13; A.C.M., MD 2592.
66 Wright, *Arundel* (1818), 25.
67 The restored S. range is shown at Dallaway, *Hist. W. Suss.* ii (1) (1819), 166.
68 Tierney, *Arundel*, ii. 613.
69 Below, Rom. Cath.
70 A.C.M., FA 95, f. 7.
71 e.g. Kimpton, *Arundel* (1893), 19; A.C.M., MD 2592; ibid. uncat. archit. drawings, plan of convent, 1895; W.S.R.O., BO/AR 16/1/24.
72 A.C.M., uncat. archit. drawings.
73 Below, Rom. Cath.
74 O.S. Map 1/2,500, Suss. LXIII. 1 (1877 edn.).
75 A.C.M., uncat. archit. drawings, plan of convent, 1895.
76 Ibid. uncat. archit. drawings, plans of convent; W.S.R.O., BO/AR 16/1/24.

Malta Homes Trust.[77] The former Catholic chapel was converted in 1976–7 for use as a theatre,[78] the early 19th-century west gallery and flat ceiling in Gothic style remaining, the former *ex situ*.

DOMINICAN FRIARY. The Dominican friary founded in Arundel by 1253[79] has been said since 1834, on the basis of oral tradition, to have occupied a site on the east or west corner of Maltravers Street and Parson's Hill;[80] Hollar's view of Arundel of 1644 shows a church apparently there with a tower and low spire like those of the parish church.[81]

Hollar's view of the town, however, is untrustworthy in other details,[82] and it is more likely that the second church in it was added simply for artistic effect. It is clear from other evidence that the friary occupied the buildings beside the bridge hitherto identified with Holy Trinity hospital (the Maison Dieu). In 1619–20 reference was made to the building of a pier or jetty at the north side of the bridge next to the Friars,[83] and two drawings of the buildings by Grimm are captioned 'the friary chapel'.[84] A body was said to have been washed ashore at 'Fryers' within the borough in 1543,[85] which corroborates a riverside site, as does mention of a boathouse beside the friary in the late 14th century.[86] A close next to the former friary in the 16th or 17th century was called Friars meadow.[87]

Further, though the buildings of the 'Maison Dieu' themselves lack dating evidence, except for a possibly 14th-century doorway in the demolished west range,[88] finds made during partial excavation of the site in the 1960s included 13th- and early 14th-century material.[89] The prominent site by the bridge, the port, and the market would be much more appropriate to a preaching order than to a hospital. Moreover, the scale of the buildings is not incommensurate with the friary, which though it was poor by 1402[90] and remained so at the Dissolution, when there were only five inmates, had earlier had perhaps 20 or 22.[91] In the mid 19th century interments were said to be still traceable in what was presumed to be a former cemetery nearby.[92]

The buildings of the friary, formerly known as the Maison Dieu, may have consisted of north, south, and west ranges round a courtyard;[93] no east range is known, and the east side of the courtyard may have been open. In the 17th century part of the site at least was apparently let as a dwelling, and repairs were mentioned in 1659.[94] The two-storeyed south range, which survived in 1995 between Mill Road and the river, had been gutted by 1780, when only its east wall, with a large window, survived above ground-floor level. At that date it was used as a timber yard,[95] as it continued to be in the mid 19th century.[96] The range is of flint and clunch with sandstone dressings, the north wall showing evidence of a cloister on its north face. The west range, also of two storeys, may have been the dormitory;[97] an arched doorway in its west wall was possibly 14th-century,[98] and there was a large three-light window in the north wall of its upper storey.[99] By 1780 the range had become a malthouse,[1] as it remained in 1851;[2] most of it was destroyed apparently in the later 19th century,[3] and what remained of the north wall collapsed in a gale in 1965.[4] The north range was apparently already in ruins by 1780;[5] part, also of flint and clunch with stone dressings, survived in 1995 behind the post office in High Street. The north range evidently contained the church, which in 1382 had both a high and a low altar.[6] Traces of a gateway between the south and west ranges are said to have been visible in 1834.[7] The surviving remains were consolidated and restored in the 1990s.[8]

HOSPITALS. The hospital of St. James for female lepers recorded between 1182 and 1301[9] was occupied by a hermit by 1435.[10] Its site was north-west of the town towards Park bottom near the pale of the Great park,[11] where ruins of the hermitage were visible in 1636[12] and where fields called the Hermitage or Armitage remained in 1776.[13] Foundations were said to be discernible in 1834[14] and medieval tiles and pottery were found there in the early 20th century.[15]

Since 1793 the site of Holy Trinity hospital (the Maison Dieu) founded in 1395 has been assumed to occupy the remains of buildings by the bridge;[16] but for reasons stated above those

77 Archives of Dioc. of Arundel and Brighton, Bishop's Ho., Hove, Arundel par. file; *W. Suss. Gaz.* 20 Apr. 1978; *Country Life*, 3 July 1980, p. 7; inf. from Mrs. Ian Rodger and Dr. J. M. Robinson, Arundel Cast.

78 *W. Suss. Gaz.* 22 July 1976; 9 Feb. 1978.

79 For its hist., *V.C.H. Suss.* ii. 93–4; Tierney, *Arundel*, ii. 672–5.

80 Tierney, op. cit. 675; Eustace, *Arundel*, 51; *W. Suss. Gaz.* 9 July 1987. For site of custom ho. mentioned, above, secular bldgs.

81 W.S.R.O., PD 1367, illus. above, p. 16.

82 Above, growth of town; secular bldgs. [Nineveh]; *Country Life*, 12 July 1990, pp. 94–5.

83 W.S.R.O., A.B.A., F2/1, f. 9.

84 B.L. Add. MS. 5674, f. 14.

85 *S.R.S.* lxxiv, p. 34.

86 A.C.M., uncat. late 14th-cent. acct. roll (Suss. box 3, no. 1).

87 W.S.R.O., PHA 1407, f. 56v.

88 Below, this section.

89 *S.A.C.* cvii. 73–4.

90 *Cal. Papal Reg.* iv. 352.

91 *V.C.H. Suss.* ii. 93–4.

92 Hillier, *Arundel* (1851), 61.

93 Cf. plan at *S.A.C.* cvii. 71.

94 A.C.M., A 262, f. [38v.], naming the friary ho.; ibid. MD 505, f. [3]; W.S.R.O., A.B.A., F2/14, f. [2].

95 B.L. Add. MS. 5674, f. 14; A.C.M., Hodskinson surv. 1778, f. 4.

96 A.C.M., H 2/44; cf. W.S.R.O., PD 2245, illus. below, pl. facing p. 74.

97 *Country Life*, 12 July 1990, p. 95.

98 B.L. Add. MS. 5674, f. 15, illus. at *Suss. Views* (S.R.S.), 12; W.S.R.O., PD 2245, illus. below, pl. facing p. 74.

99 Cartland, *Arundel*, 32.

1 B.L. Add. MS. 5674, f. 15.

2 Hillier, *Arundel* (1851), 61; cf. Tierney, *Arundel*, ii. 671; W.S.R.O., TD/W 5.

3 O.S. Map 1/2,500, Suss. LXIII. 1 (1877 edn.); Cartland, *Arundel*, 32.

4 *S.A.C.* cvii. 72.

5 B.L. Add. MS. 5674, f. 15; cf. W.S.R.O., MP 3041 (photocopy of town plan, 1785); Cartland, *Arundel*, 32.

6 *S.R.S.* xli. 56.

7 Tierney, *Arundel*, ii. 663.

8 *W. Suss. Gaz.* 25 Oct. 1990; 18 May 1995.

9 *Pipe R.* 1182 (P.R.S. xxxi), 91; *Chanc. R.* 1196 (P.R.S. N.S. vii), 200; *Cal. Inq. p.m.* i, p. 279; *S.R.S.* lxvii. 2.

10 P.R.O., C 139/71, no. 37, m. 32; cf. Tierney, *Arundel*, ii. 679.

11 P.R.O., SC 6/1019/22, rot. 1.

12 A.C.M., MD 505, ff. [7v., 16].

13 Ibid. H 1/30.

14 Tierney, *Arundel*, ii. 680.

15 *S.A.C.* lxiii. 24.

16 *Gent. Mag.* lxiii (2), 1165; for its hist., *V.C.H. Suss.* ii. 97–8.

buildings rightly belong to the Dominican friary. The hospital, which was to have chapel, refectory, and dormitory,[17] was founded under the aegis of the college,[18] and could be expected to be near it and secluded, rather than half a mile away and in a prominent, public, and noisy position. Further, one of the tasks enjoined on the aged or infirm inmates was weeding the churchyard walks,[19] a difficulty if it involved climbing the length of High Street. The most likely site for the hospital is north-west of the church, where an almshouse was said to stand in 1636,[20] and where a visitor in the 1720s mentioned an 'old priory' in the process of being demolished, stone from it being used to build the new bridge.[21] The northern part of the west wall of the churchyard together with the westwards continuation of its north wall seem in their lower courses to belong to that building; they are of flint and stone, with windows and doorways of 14th- or 15th-century character,[22] and closely match the contemporary church and college in style. Within the castle car park which they partly enclose numerous human bones were excavated in the early 19th century,[23] perhaps from the chapel of the hospital.

The hospital of St. John the Baptist mentioned in 1269[24] has not been located, and no more is heard of it.

COMMUNICATIONS.[25] ROADS. The Roman road from Chichester to Brighton passed through the south end of the parish, apparently crossing the river Arun by a ferry between the sites of the gasworks and the railway station.[26] High Street seems to be part of another early route, running from the crest of the downs, through what later became first the Little park and afterwards the castle cricket ground, to a higher river crossing on or near the site of the modern bridge. The route later followed by Mill Lane along the west side of the river valley north of the bridge may also be early.

In the Middle Ages[27] and later[28] Arundel lay on the main road between Chichester and Lewes, part of the great route between Southampton and Canterbury. The section between Chichester and Arundel was especially important while the rapes of Arundel and Chichester were still undivided;[29] east of Arundel the road used the drier downland country via Findon and Steyning. The downland road to Steyning remained important in later times, providing an alternative route to Horsham in 1771[30] and to London in 1775.[31] The road from Arundel to Shoreham, the modern A 27, was mentioned *c.* 1215[32] and also remained important,[33] though never turnpiked.[34] South and south-east of Park Farm the gradient was apparently eased in the late 18th century or early 19th by a cutting and embankment which survived in 1986. Canada Road, south of Chichester Road, was cut *c.* 1813 to replace part of it[35] but never did so; it was called Green Lane in 1910.[36]

A causeway across the valley existed at a date before 1151, when Adelize, wife of William d'Aubigny, earl of Arundel, founded Pynham priory in Lyminster with the duty of maintaining it; the alternative name of the priory was *de Calceto* ('of the causeway'). The priory's exemption from tax in the 1340s seems to have been granted in order not to prejudice that work.[37] It is not clear whether the main channel or channels of the river were bridged by the mid 12th century as well; the description of High Street in the later 12th or early 13th century as the road leading to the ferry (*apud passag'*) suggests not.[38] A bridge existed, however, by 1263.[39] Bridge and causeway are mentioned together in 1454,[40] and implicitly in 1568, when the bridge was described as an ancient one of timber, of great height and length.[41] The borough authorities were concerned with repair by the mid 15th century,[42] and in the early 16th income was also received from bequests.[43]

After the Dissolution the borough assumed Pynham priory's responsibility for the bridge,[44] perhaps including the rest of the causeway, and between the 16th century and the 19th the mayor generally had the additional title of bridgewarden.[45] The profits of the burgess brooks, however, were retained by the corporation for its own use.[46] The cost of bridge repair was met partly by local collections until 1568, when the corporation received licence to raise money for the purpose by the export, duty free, of 400 qr. wheat a year for five years.[47] Further collections were made *c.* 1593[48] and in 1610[49] from parishes in western Sussex, and in the early 1640s in the town and its immediate vicinity, 100 loads of

17 Tierney, *Arundel*, ii. 665.
18 *V.C.H. Suss.* ii. 97–8.
19 Ibid. 98.
20 A.C.M., MD 505, f. [1v.].
21 B.L. Lansd. MS. 918, f. 23, perhaps the source of the idea that the friary bldgs. were so used: e.g. Tierney, *Arundel*, ii. 670.
22 Illus. at *Country Life*, 12 July 1990, p. 94.
23 Wright, *Arundel* (1817), 39; Tierney, *Arundel*, ii. 677.
24 B.L. Lansd. Ch. 92.
25 For river communications, below, port and river traffic.
26 I. D. Margary, *Rom. Rds. in Brit.* (1967), 75–6; *S.N.Q.* xi. 142, 145–6.
27 *S.A.C.* lxxii. 182; *V.C.H. Suss.* i. 492; *Itin. of Edw. I* (L. & I. Soc.), i. 209; ii. 106, 139, 196–7, 246.
28 *Cal. S.P. Dom.* Addenda 1566–79, 68; *S.A.C.* lii. 41; cix. 21; J. Macky, *Journey through Eng.* i (1732), 128–9.
29 Above, Arundel Rape.
30 *S.A.C.* lii. 41.
31 Ibid. lxxi. 38.
32 *S.R.S.* lix, p. 85.
33 e.g. ibid. lxviii. 285, 288; Budgen, *Suss. Map* (1724); Young, *Agric. of Suss.* 416.
34 Despite plans of 1770: *S.A.C.* lxxi. 26.
35 A.C.M., K 2/64, ff. [13, 15v.]; ibid. LM 15.
36 O.S. Map 1/2,500, Suss. LXIII. 1 (1912 edn.).
37 *V.C.H. Suss.* ii. 80.
38 W.S.R.O., Par. 8/7/35. The word bridge used in another doc. may merely mean causeway: *Cat. Anct. D.* v, A 11537; cf. *V.C.H. Suss.* vi (1), 203.
39 P.R.O., JUST 1/912A, rot. 44; cf. *S.R.S.* lvii. 12.
40 Bodl. MS. Chart. Suss. a. 2, no. 72.
41 *Cal. S.P. Dom.* Addenda 1566–79, 68.
42 Bodl. MS. Chart. Suss. a. 2, no. 72.
43 *S.R.S.* xli. 48.
44 Dallaway, *Hist. W. Suss.* ii (1) (1819), 182; Tierney, *Arundel*, ii. 716–17; W.S.R.O., QAB/3/W 1, pp. 1–2; below, boro. govt. (activity, property, and income).
45 Tierney, *Arundel*, ii. 716.
46 Below, boro. govt.
47 *Cal. Pat.* 1566–9, p. 169; *Cal. S.P. Dom.* Addenda 1566–79, 68.
48 W.S.R.O., A.B.A., F2/5–6.
49 Ibid. A.B.A., F2/1, f. 8.

timber being supplied by the earl of Arundel.[50] Money was still apparently sometimes collected in the early 19th century.[51]

Meanwhile, an application to quarter sessions in 1592 for a rate to be levied for the purpose on the three western rapes was refused,[52] and in the early 1640s the corporation was forbidden to levy a bridge rate within the borough.[53] As a *quid pro quo* Arundel was exempted in the 18th and 19th centuries, and perhaps earlier too, from the general rate for bridge repair within the rape, and from rates for the repair of other individual bridges in the county.[54] In 1679, nevertheless,[55] the corporation did levy a bridge rate, and in the early 19th century the poor rate met most of the cost of repair, the sum received in 1802 being £68.[56] Two additional items of income between the later 16th century and the early 20th[57] were the annuity of £2 devised in 1592 by Thomas Taylor, a former mayor, from the Crown house in High Street, presumably the Crown inn,[58] and the rent of a storehouse by the quay devised in the following year by another former mayor, Edmund Shephard.[59]

The bridge was depicted in 1644 as of wooden trestle construction.[60] It was replaced in 1724 by a new stone bridge of three arches, paid for by a relation of one of the town's M.P.s.[61] Portland stone was used for repairs in 1784 and 1805, and the crown of the bridge was levelled in 1785.[62] In 1825 the inhabitants resolved to widen the bridge to cater for the increased traffic caused by the growth of nearby coastal resorts.[63] The work, which included levelling the approaches and adding a paved footpath on each side supported on brackets, was carried out in 1831 using surplus funds of the Arundel savings bank which the mayor and bridgewarden William Holmes later had to repay.[64]

In 1896 repairs were being financed from the town rates and a Local Government Board loan.[65] The unfairness of a small town's having to maintain a bridge for the benefit of traffic generated by much larger, and faster growing, places was finally recognized in 1900, when the new West Sussex county council agreed to pay £150, three fifths of the estimated cost of the bridge's improvement;[66] the county council, however, did not take over permanent responsibility for the bridge until 1930.[67] A new, wider, three-arched bridge of reinforced concrete faced with sandstone was built in 1935, inscriptions of 1724 and 1831 being reset in it.[68]

A ferry at an unknown site was maintained by the corporation in 1609.[69]

A relief road for east–west traffic, first planned in the late 1930s,[70] was opened in 1973[71] across the marshes south of the town; a north-westwards continuation beside Park bottom bypassed the town for London traffic too. A new bypass road further south was being planned in 1995.

The medieval road to London, as indicated above, originally passed through what was later first the Little park and afterwards the castle cricket ground. It seems to have been diverted westwards round the Little park when the latter was created apparently *c.* 1300, passing through the new line of defences by way of the Marygate. North of the town the road was known as Red Lane by 1636.[72] In 1675 the London road was depicted via Billingshurst,[73] but in the 18th century an alternative route ran through Petworth.[74] In the later 18th century the Arundel–London road was said to be very good.[75]

In 1757 the London road in the parish was made a turnpike, as part of a route via Bury to Guildford;[76] the work authorized had not been completed by 1778,[77] however, and in 1799 the trustees were absolved from repairing the section of road between Arundel and Newbridge in Wisborough Green.[78] The London road within the parish was afterwards diverted in two stages during the creation of the new landscaped park. In 1793 the duke of Norfolk was authorized to close the northern section and replace it by a new road already built from the north-west corner of the Little park by way of a new lodge, the Green Doors lodge, to Whiteways in Houghton on the crest of the downs.[79] The southern section was replaced in 1803 by a second new road,[80] planned from 1796,[81] which led from near the top of High Street round the south side of the church and college to a point beyond the Green Doors lodge. The two new sections of road were turnpiked between 1803 and 1881.[82] The southern part of the old road, however, remained open in

50 Ibid. A.B.A., F2/1, f. 17 and v.; A.B.A., F2/15; ibid. QAB/3/W 1, p. 1; Tierney, *Arundel*, ii. 719.

51 Tierney, *Arundel*, ii. 717.

52 Ibid. ii. 718; *Acts of P.C.* 1591–2, 171–2.

53 Tierney, *Arundel*, ii. 719; W.S.R.O., A.B.A., F2/14.

54 W.S.R.O., QAB/2/W 12–13.

55 Ibid. A.B.A., F2/1, f. 18.

56 Tierney, *Arundel*, ii. 718; *1st Rep. Com. Mun. Corp.* 672; W.S.R.O., A.B.A., F2/2.

57 W.S.R.O., A.B.A., F2/1–2, *passim*.

58 Ibid. A.B.A., P1/2; for Taylor as mayor, Eustace, *Arundel*, 250.

59 Eustace, *Arundel*, 133, 250; W.S.R.O., A.B.A., F2/1, f. 8.

60 W.S.R.O., PD 1367, illus. above, p. 16; cf. Ogilby, *Britannia* (1675), 8.

61 B.L. Lansd. MS. 918, f. 22v., naming Ld. Scarbro., whereas Tierney, *Arundel*, ii. 720, has the Hon. Jas. Lumley; cf. *Hist. Parl., Commons*, 1715–54, i. 332. The duke of Norf.'s contribution mentioned by Tierney was probably only the supply of stone: Dallaway & Cartwright, *Hist. W. Suss.* ii (1) (1832), 210; above, relig. hos. (hospitals).

62 W.S.R.O., A.B.A., F1/16, nos. 7, 11; A.B.A., F2/23, no. 9.

63 Ibid. Par. 8/13/2.

64 Ibid. A.B.A., M46; ibid. Add. MS. 16006; A.C.M., MD 416; Tierney, *Arundel*, ii. 720; *S.N.Q.* xvii. 211; illus. at Cartland, *Arundel*, 34.

65 W.S.R.O., BO/AR 24/4/17, f. 10; ibid. CC 61, papers relating to Arundel bridge.

66 Ibid. BO/AR 24/4/15; ibid. CC 61, county surveyor's rep. 1901; A.C.M., MD 421.

67 *S.N.Q.* ix. 177.

68 Ibid. xvii. 211; *S.C.M.* xi. 654; W.S.R.O., CC 323; cf. *W. Suss. Gaz.* 22 Jan. 1970.

69 W.S.R.O., A.B.A., F2/8.

70 *W. Suss. Gaz.* 8 Oct. 1987; *S.C.M.* xiii. 218.

71 *Brighton Evening Argus*, 2 Oct. 1973.

72 A.C.M., MD 505, f. [6]; cf. ibid. 2180; W.S.R.O., Add. MS. 8697; ibid. MP 962, list of burgesses, 1865. For Little park, below, woods and parks.

73 Ogilby, *Britannia* (1675), 8.

74 Budgen, *Suss. Map* (1724); *S.A.C.* lxxi. 29, 42.

75 Young, *Agric. of Suss.* 416.

76 30 Geo. II, c. 60.

77 18 Geo. III, c. 110.

78 39 Geo. III, c. 34 (Local and Personal).

79 W.S.R.O., QR/W 601, mm. 42–5. For lodge, below, woods and parks (modern park).

80 43 Geo. III, c. 67 (Local and Personal); A.C.M., MD 2478; ibid. PM 114.

81 A.C.M., D 1977; ibid. MD 2470.

82 43 Geo. III, c. 67 (Local and Personal); 37 & 38 Vic. c. 95.

1829, when a visitor complained that the entrance through the Marygate was one of the worst town approaches in Britain.[83] The line of the medieval road was followed by a track in 1995.

Two minor roads branched off from the old London road north of the Little park. Pughdean Lane to the north-east, recorded from 1615,[84] led to Houghton by way of Pughdean bottom above Swanbourne lake.[85] On the west side Hermitage Lane, so called in 1636,[86] led to the site of the former leper hospital near Park bottom.[87] Both roads survived in the 1770s[88] but were later absorbed into the new landscaped park created after 1786. Hermitage Lane was still traceable in 1834[89] but afterwards disappeared. The line of Pughdean Lane was marked in 1922 by a double row of old trees 400 ft. (122 metres) south of Hiorne's tower;[90] in 1988 it was followed in part by a bank.

A road to Madehurst was mentioned in 1158.[91] The track leading to Slindon along the south-west side of Rewell wood is presumably ancient, since it is followed in part by the parish boundary;[92] in 1817, however, it was overgrown and evidently ceasing to be used.[93] Queens Lane and Fitzalan Road on the east side of the river led to the windmill south of the town[94] but were unnamed until the 20th century.[95]

The street names of the town are discussed above.[96] Surrey Street joining the western ends of Tarrant and Maltravers streets was cut *c.* 1783 by the parish surveyors of highways across land belonging to the duke of Norfolk.[97] The New Cut between the eastern ends of Maltravers Street and London Road, so named *c.* 1875,[98] was made *c.* 1805.[99] Mill Lane, the old road northwards to Swanbourne mill and South Stoke along the edge of the river valley, was proposed for closure by the duke of Norfolk in 1850, since conversations, including offensive language, could be heard from it within the castle; a new road was to replace it across the marshes up to ⅓ mile (535 metres) east of the town. The proposal was rejected on appeal to quarter sessions by the brewer George Constable.[1] Mill Lane was eventually closed to traffic in 1894, when the wide, tree-lined Mill Road was opened, nearer the town than the replacement road of 1850.[2] The line of Mill Lane through the castle grounds could still be traced in 1987.

CARRIERS. A carrier of Arundel was presented apparently for Sunday drinking in Binsted in 1626.[3] There was a carrier to London in 1657[4] and there were two in 1681;[5] probate inventories survive for three others between 1690 and 1734.[6] In the mid 1790s a carter's wagon arrived from London twice weekly.[7] By the early 1830s there were carriers to London and Portsmouth four days a week, to Chichester, Brighton, and Bognor two days a week, and to Littlehampton daily.[8] The London carrier no longer operated in 1852, when a 'railway carrier' at the Norfolk Arms hotel was first mentioned, the service continuing until 1938 or later. By 1866 Chichester and Brighton were the only distant places to be served by carriers; the service to Brighton ceased by 1874, and that to Chichester after 1913.[9] In 1900 carriers plied between Arundel and several nearby villages at least weekly.[10]

COACHES AND BUSES. An Arundel coach ran to London apparently by way of Lewes in 1791;[11] in the mid 1790s there were coaches to London and back three times a week.[12] A short-lived service via Horsham was running in 1809,[13] and in 1812 the London coach went by way of Petworth.[14] About 1818 R. W. Walker of Michelgrove house in Clapham set up a rival daily coach via Dorking.[15] In the early 1830s there were six London coaches a week in winter and nine in summer;[16] in the 1840s the journey apparently took four hours.[17] Brighton and Portsmouth were served three times weekly in the mid 1790s;[18] there was a daily service to Brighton in 1812[19] and to Portsmouth by 1817.[20] A coach to Salisbury and Bath ran via Chichester in 1809.[21] In the early 1830s there were six coaches a week to Southampton and three to Bath and Bristol.[22] London, Southampton, and Portsmouth could all still be reached daily by coach in 1845, but all coach services to and from the town ceased soon afterwards. From 1847 or earlier horse omnibuses of the railway company met each train at successive stations serving Arundel. Motor buses plied to Worthing, Brighton, Littlehampton, and Pulborough in 1907; in 1927 there

83 *Gardener's Mag.* v (1829), 585.
84 W.S.R.O., Ep. I/25/1 (1615).
85 Ibid. Ep. I/25/1 (1635); *Arundel Rds.* facing p. [3].
86 A.C.M., MD 505, f. [7].
87 W.S.R.O., Ep. I/25/1 (1635); for hosp., above, relig. hos. (hospitals).
88 A.C.M., H 1/30; *250 Yrs. of Mapmaking in Suss.* ed. H. Margary, pl. 14.
89 Tierney, *Arundel*, ii. 680.
90 *S.A.C.* lxiii. 24.
91 W.S.R.O., Par. 8/6/5, f. 3.
92 Cf. A.C.M., H 1/3.
93 Ibid. FC 148.
94 *250 Yrs. of Mapmaking in Suss.* pl. 19; below, mills.
95 Above, growth of town; O.S. Map 1/2,500, Suss. LXIII. 1 (1912, 1937 edns.); cf. Pike, *Bognor Dir.* (1912–13), 198.
96 Above, growth of town (street names).
97 A.C.M., D 3212, p. 8; W.S.R.O., QR/W 562, mm. 10, 12.
98 O.S. Map 1/2,500, Suss. LXIII. 1 (1877 edn.).
99 A.C.M., MD 619, pp. 50, 52, 69.
1 *Arundel Rds. passim.*
2 *W. Suss. Gaz.* 9 Aug. 1894; Goodliffe, *Littlehampton* (1903), 70; illus. at Cartland, *Arundel*, 113.
3 *S.R.S.* xlix. 125.
4 A.C.M., A 262, f. [6]; cf. ibid. 263, acct. 1662.
5 J. Greenwood, *Posts of Suss., Chich. Branch* (priv. print. 1973), 105.
6 W.S.R.O., Ep. I/29/8/195, 234, 284.
7 *Univ. Brit. Dir.* ii. 57.
8 Pigot, *Nat. Com. Dir.* (1832–4), 1004.
9 *Kelly's Dir. Suss.* (1852 and later edns.); Cartland, *Arundel*, 22; W.S.R.O., MP 123, f. 23.
10 *Arundel Yr.-Bk. for 1900* (publ. A. W. Lapworth, Arundel), [7].
11 *S.C.M.* xvii. 256; cf. Hillier, *Arundel* (1847), 67.
12 *Univ. Brit. Dir.* ii. 57.
13 *S.A.C.* lxxi. 52.
14 *Letters of John Hawkins and Sam. and Dan. Lysons, 1812–1830*, ed. F. W. Steer, pp. 1, 3.
15 Wright, *Arundel* (1818), 8; W.S.R.O., PHA 110, printed corresp. relating to coach.
16 Pigot, *Nat. Com. Dir.* (1832–4), 1004.
17 Hillier, *Arundel* (1847), 67.
18 *Univ. Brit. Dir.* ii. 57.
19 *Letters of Hawkins and Lysons*, ed. Steer, p. 5.
20 Wright, *Arundel* (1817), 140.
21 *S.A.C.* lxxi. 53.
22 Pigot, *Nat. Com. Dir.* (1832–4), 1004.

were frequent services to Chichester and Horsham.[23] An express motor coach to London ran daily in 1934.[24] In 1992 there were regular buses to Littlehampton, Worthing, and Brighton, and less regular ones to Bognor Regis and elsewhere. A bus station near the bridge on the corner of River Road was built in 1954 and demolished before 1981.[25]

RAILWAYS. The railway line from Worthing to Lyminster, with a station at Lyminster called Arundel and Littlehampton, was opened in 1846, and the line from Lyminster to Chichester later in the same year, with a station at Ford originally called Arundel. A plan of 1837 to bring the railway closer to Arundel had apparently been opposed by the duke of Norfolk. The present Mid Sussex line from Hardham junction to Ford was opened in 1863, with a new station, at first called New Arundel and later Arundel, also in Lyminster parish. It was electrified in 1938.[26] Facilities for goods traffic at Arundel were withdrawn in 1963.[27]

SOCIAL AND CULTURAL ACTIVITIES.

A theatre was built *c.* 1792 by the manager Henry Thornton.[28] A performance is recorded in 1801,[29] and Thomas Trotter's company played there several times in the early 19th century.[30] In 1807 Thornton built on the site later occupied by no. 18 Maltravers Street a new theatre under the duke of Norfolk's patronage; the opening performances by Master Betty were said to have drawn 'all the families of rank and taste' within 20 miles. The building was modelled on the Theatre Royal, Drury Lane, and was of brick.[31] Occasional performances took place between the 1810s and the early 1830s, *She Stoops to Conquer* being played in 1827, but the theatre seems to have fallen out of use *c.* 1835 and was pulled down soon afterwards.[32] What may have been its side walls could be seen in 1988 flanking the garden of no. 18 Maltravers Street, the seating having presumably been in the slope of the hill.[33]

In the mid 19th century the town hall was sometimes used as a theatre, again under the duke's patronage.[34] During the mid 1970s the Arundel players performed in Slindon village hall for lack of a suitable hall in Arundel, but in 1976–7 part of the former college buildings south of the church was converted as the Priory playhouse.[35]

The dramatic and musical entertainment advertised in 1797 probably took place in the theatre.[36] In 1835 there was said to be no public hall in the town, the big room over the entrance of the Norfolk Arms hotel being used instead for meetings,[37] as it was later for at least one concert.[38] After *c.* 1835 the new town hall was another venue for concerts, balls, and other public events.[39] A 'harmonic society' was mentioned *c.* 1840.[40] The Arundel town brass band flourished between the 1860s and 1890s, regularly playing in the market place and in the castle grounds during the summer, and touring several times in France; the Blackman family which ran it[41] were involved in other aspects of Arundel's musical life over three generations: the church choir from the later 19th century, a dance band, and a concert party which performed over a wide hinterland in the 20th century.[42]

About 1900 the church choristers gave an annual Christmas concert at the town hall.[43] Plans to build a church hall at the corner of Maltravers Street and Park Place, which could also serve for concerts and other entertainments, were canvassed from 1910, but the site was sold *c.* 1951.[44] In 1990 premises used for meetings and entertainment by groups in the town included St. Mary's hall in London Road and the premises of the Wildfowl and Wetlands Trust in South Stoke. An Arundel and District music, later choral, society was formed in 1912 and survived in 1992 as the Arun choral society.[45]

A historical pageant was held in 1923 in aid of West Sussex hospitals in the grounds of the castle.[46] An annual summer arts festival was started in 1977, with concerts, open-air plays, and other events.[47]

A lecture on astronomy was held in 1830, apparently at the theatre.[48] Besides libraries recorded below, there were various circulating libraries in the town in the 19th century, including one kept by a printer and one by the Arundel library society;[49] there were also lending libraries at the Independent Sunday school in 1833 and the National school in 1879.[50] In 1851, nevertheless, George MacDonald, the minister of the Independent chapel, regretted that at Arundel he could have no society and no books of any

23 Hillier, *Arundel* (1847), 8–9; *Kelly's Dir. Suss.* (1845 and later edns.); cf. below, this section (rlys.).
24 *Arundel, the Gem of Suss.* (Arundel, 1934), inside front cover.
25 *W. Suss. Gaz.* 2 July 1981.
26 *Southern Region Rec.* comp. R. H. Clark, 51–2, 62, 64, 74; A.C.M., MD 417.
27 C. R. Clinker, *Reg. of Closed Stations*, ii (1964), 4.
28 *Suss. Wkly. Advertiser*, 23 April 1792; *Theatre Notebk.* xii. 60.
29 *S.A.C.* lxxi. 47.
30 M. T. Odell, *More About Old Theatre, Worthing*, 25.
31 *Hants Telegraph and Suss. Chronicle*, 12 Dec. 1807; for site, *S.A.C.* lxxi. 50, 52; cf. W.S.R.O., MP 3041 (photocopy of town plan, 1785).
32 Odell, op. cit. 26–7; Wright, *Arundel* (1818), 26; A.C.M., MD 2389; W.S.R.O., MP 1172.
33 The theatre bldg. depicted at W.S.R.O., MP 1172, however, is apparently no. 5 Maltravers St.; cf. A.C.M., D 579–86, TS. cal. of deeds.
34 Odell, op. cit. 26; cf. W.S.R.O., POL AB/16/1 (Oct. 1876).
35 *W. Suss. Gaz.* 22 July 1976; 9 Feb. 1978.
36 W.S.R.O., MP 962, poster, 1797.
37 *1st Rep. Com. Mun. Corp.* 668; below, this section (inns).
38 W.S.R.O., MP 962, poster, 1854.
39 Ibid. Par. 8/7/26; Hillier, *Arundel* (1847), 29; below, this section.
40 *Rep. of Standing Cttee. for Relief of Necessitous Poor in Arundel* (Arundel, 1841) (copy at A.C.M., MD 787).
41 *S.C.M.* xviii. 317, 319; *W. Suss. Gaz.* 7 Sept. 1865.
42 *S.C.M.* xxv. 396–7; *W. Suss. Gaz.* 7 June 1973.
43 W.S.R.O., Par. 8/7/24.
44 Ibid. BO/AR 16/1/35; ibid. Par. 8/10/1; Par. 8/15/1–2.
45 *W. Suss. Gaz.* 24 Sept. 1992; *Arundel Cast. Archives*, ii. 77; local inf.
46 W.S.R.O., BO/AR 24/1/7–8; Cartland, *Arundel*, 96.
47 *W. Suss. Gaz.* 3 Mar. 1983; *Country Life*, 19 Sept. 1985, p. 816; local inf.
48 W.S.R.O., MP 1172.
49 Hillier, *Arundel* (1847), advertisment at end; *Visitors' Guide to Arundel* (1868), [32]; Worthing Ref. Libr., Arundel cuttings file, bookplates of White's circulating libr. and Arundel libr. soc.
50 *Educ. Enq. Abstract*, 962; A.C.M., MD 2016.

kind except his own.[51] A branch of the county council library service was opened at no. 51 Maltravers Street by *c.* 1960,[52] later moving to the former National school in Surrey Street.

Three inhabitants subscribed jointly to a London newspaper in 1778.[53] *Mitchell's Monthly Advertiser and West Sussex Market and Railway Intelligencer*, of independent outlook, was founded at premises in High Street in 1853 by the printer T. H. Mitchell, with his son W. W. Mitchell, later mayor, as editor and publisher. It was soon renamed the *West Sussex Advertiser*, and from the following year appeared weekly as the *West Sussex Advertiser and South Coast Journal*, later the *West Sussex Gazette and County Advertiser*. Despite the smallness of the town in the 19th and 20th centuries, the paper claimed in 1903 to have the largest circulation of any provincial newspaper in southern England.[54] In 1995 it remained one of the two chief West Sussex newspapers, but though its offices were still in Arundel it was no longer printed there, ownership having passed to Portsmouth and Sunderland Newspapers.[55] A rival paper, *The News (Littlehampton and Arundel), Local Guide, District Reporter and Visitors' Journal*, was published in both towns between 1869 and 1880 or later.[56]

A society for mutual improvement was formed in 1835, whose 30 members, all churchgoers, subscribed 2*d.* a week. Lectures were given on scientific subjects and on church history, and there was a small library. The society still flourished in the 1920s.[57] An Anglican working men's club was founded by the Revd. George Arbuthnot in 1876; it occupied two rooms of a house in Mill Lane, where there were a library, open for five hours each evening, and a lecture room. Coffee was provided, and cards and billiards were played. Membership rose to over 90, but the club closed after Arbuthnot's departure in 1879. Other 'improving' societies founded by him were a coal club, a boot and shoe club, and a children's savings bank.[58] A Roman Catholic working men's club existed by 1878; in 1895, when it had over 100 members, it was in Park Place and in 1903 it was known as St. Philip's club. By 1907 there were a library, a billiard room, and a gymnasium. The club closed in the 1930s.[59] A Catholic girls' club occupied part of the former college courtyard in 1899.[60]

The Arundel co-operative industrial and provident society had 287 members in 1892. Besides stores in Tarrant Street, it ran a shoe club, a coal club, and a free library, all open for an hour each evening.[61] The Victoria institute in Tarrant Street, occupying the former savings bank premises, was opened *c.* 1897; in 1900 the duke of Norfolk was president and the mayor vice-president. There were a reading room, a library also used for classes and meetings, and a ladies' room; billiards, bagatelle, and other games were played. By 1907 there were *c.* 160 members. The institute survived in 1991 in a slightly altered form.[62]

The Norfolk centre in Mill Road, a day centre for the elderly, was given to the town in 1967 by the duke of Norfolk.[63]

A conservation society, later called the Arundel Society, was founded in 1965[64] and flourished in 1995. A prosecuting society founded in 1796 survived in 1988 as a dining club.[65]

A programme of cinema films, perhaps open to the public, was given at the castle in 1923.[66] The Arun cinema in Queen Street, with an 'Art Deco' façade, opened in 1939;[67] it closed in 1959[68] and was replaced by a garage.

An Arundel museum society was formed *c.* 1963, and a local history museum, run by the town council with the society's advice, was started in the town hall basement in 1964, when it was open two afternoons a week in summer.[69] In 1977 it moved to no. 61 High Street, leased from Arun district council,[70] and by 1995 its opening hours were much longer. Other museums which reflected Arundel's growth as a tourist centre in the 1970s and 80s were the 'museum of curiosity', formerly in Bramber, which flourished between 1974 and *c.* 1986,[71] and a toy museum opened in 1978.[72]

SPORT. Bowls was apparently played in Arundel in 1565.[73] A square bowling green had been laid out on a mount south of the south-east front of the castle by 1737;[74] it was restored *c.* 1990.

An Arundel cricket team existed in 1702,[75] but where it played is not known. The modern cricket ground south of Park Farmhouse was in use by *c.* 1875.[76] The Arundel cricket club mentioned in 1877[77] still used the ground in 1980, when it claimed to have existed since *c.* 1775.[78] A boys' cricket club was set up in the 1870s, apparently in connexion with the National school.[79] Another ground south-east of Park Farmhouse was used from *c.* 1896[80] by the Catholic St. Philip's cricket club, which apparently survived in the 1930s.[81] A third ground was

51 W. Raeper, *Geo. MacDonald*, 84.
52 *Littlehampton, Arundel and Dist. Dir.* (*c.* 1960), 26.
53 *S.A.C.* lxxi. 42.
54 F. V. Wright, *100 Yrs. of W. Suss. Gaz. 1853–1953*, 1, 3–4, 6, 18, 20, 22; Kimpton, *Arundel* (1903), p. x.
55 *W. Suss. Gaz.* 1 June 1978.
56 W.S.R.O., Par. 126/7/3.
57 A.C.M., MD 2326; inf. from Mr. F. Penfold, Burpham.
58 A.C.M., MD 2016; W.S.R.O., Par. 8/7/21–2.
59 *Kelly's Dir. Suss.* (1878 and later edns.).
60 A.C.M., uncat. archit. drawings, plan of Servite convent, 1899.
61 W.S.R.O., Add. MS. 21088; *Kelly's Dir. Suss.* (1895).
62 W.S.R.O., MP 3689; *Kelly's Dir. Suss.* (1903 and later edns.); *Arundel Yr.-Bk. for 1900* (publ. A. W. Lapworth, Arundel), [5]; inf. from Mr. J. Godfrey, Arundel.
63 *W. Suss. Gaz.* 16 Feb. 1967.
64 Ibid. 15 July 1965.
65 *S.C.M.* ix. 198–9; xx. 80–1; inf. from Mrs. A. W. Dales, Church Fmho., Lyminster.
66 A.C.M., MD 1153.
67 *Norf. Arms hotel prospectus* (*c.* 1950), 8 (copy in B.L., class mark 010368 q. 8); W.S.R.O., BO/AR 16/1/190.
68 *W. Suss. Gaz.* 3 Sept. 1959.
69 Ibid. 7, 14 Feb. 1963; 30 July 1964.
70 Ibid. 2 May 1985.
71 Ibid. 20 Feb. 1986.
72 *Suss. Life*, Jan. 1986, p. 9.
73 A.C.M., M 18.
74 W.S.R.O., PD 14, illus. below, p. 40; cf. A.C.M., H 1/19; B.L. Add. MS. 5674, f. 29.
75 *S.A.C.* cxiv. 122; cf. H. F. and A. P. Squire, *Henfield Cricket*, 49.
76 O.S. Map 6", Suss. LXIII (1879 edn.).
77 W.S.R.O., POL AB/16/1 (Apr. 1877).
78 *Country Life*, 3 July 1980, p. 8.
79 A.C.M., MD 2016.
80 O.S. Map 6", Suss. LXIII. NW. (1899 edn.).
81 Ibid. (1938 edn.); Pike, *Bognor Dir.* (1910–11), 181; inf. from Mr. J. Seller, Park Fm.

created in the former Little park north-west of the castle in 1895; Duke Bernard (d. 1975) played there during most of his life, and the Arundel castle cricket club was still under the patronage of his widow in 1995.[82] Visiting national touring teams often played a game there after 1956.[83] In the mid 1980s there were over 40 games a year at the ground.[84] An indoor cricket school was opened there in 1991.[85]

Annual race meetings called Arundel races were held in July or August between 1838 and 1843;[86] the course used may have been on Park farm, where races were apparently held in 1876.[87] A summer regatta took place on the river in the years before 1914.[88]

In 1859 open-air swimming baths between Ford Road and the river south of the gasworks in Tortington were opened at the joint expense of the town council, the duke of Norfolk, and Lord Edward Howard, M.P.; they consisted of two long pools side by side for segregated swimming. They were closed in the late 1940s as a health risk[89] and by 1991 the site had been built over. A new open-air swimming pool was opened in 1960 on a site in Queen Street given by the duke of Norfolk;[90] it survived in 1995.

A football club formed in 1889 and originally playing on a pitch in Arundel park[91] still flourished in 1994, and there was a rifle club between 1910 and 1938.[92] A sports field was opened in 1912 in Mill Road with facilities for tennis and croquet;[93] by 1938 there were also a putting and a bowling green.[94] Other sports clubs in the 20th century were a riding club in 1938[95] and an archery club started *c.* 1963.[96] There was a recreation ground in Fitzalan Road between 1946 and 1991[97] and another in Canada Road in 1986.

INNS. There were at least four inns in the town in 1570,[98] and thereafter apparently always at least two.[99] In 1642 there was also a 'wine cellar',[1] presumably a wine shop. After Arundel became a garrison town in 1644 the number of inns seems to have greatly increased: in 1645 there were 30 alehouses, of which 20 were not licensed.[2] The inns of the town could supply 26 guest beds and stabling for 50 horses in 1686.[3] High Street as the chief commercial street seems to have had the highest concentration: at one time there may have been three adjacent to each other on the east side,[4] and on another occasion the same on the west.[5] In 1785 there were at least 11 licensed premises in the town,[6] and in the early 1830s three commercial inns and nine taverns or public houses.[7] In 1874, besides 12 inns, there were eight beer retailers, of whom six were in or near Tarrant Street.[8] The number of licensed premises in the town *c.* 1910 was 17;[9] it had fallen by 1938 to 13.[10]

The two chief inns by the mid 18th century were the George on the east side of High Street and the Crown on the west; the George at least had apparently existed in 1570.[11] The Arundel rape sewers commissioners met at the George in 1714;[12] in the 1770s it was the centre for the duke of Norfolk's party at elections.[13] It was bought by Duke Charles (d. 1815), then earl of Surrey, in 1784 or 1785,[14] and ceased to be an inn apparently by 1809[15] and certainly by *c.* 1832.[16] The Crown in the 1770s was the election centre for the Shelley party.[17] In 1817 it was fitted up to accommodate families,[18] but its chief clientèle in the 19th century until its closure *c.* 1875 was commercial.[19] It was a coaching stop by 1817.[20]

The duke of Norfolk built a large hotel, the Norfolk Arms, between 1782 and 1785,[21] the landlord of the George later moving there.[22] In the late 18th century and earlier 19th the turnover of tenants was high, but a farm was attached to the lease by 1818 to make it more attractive.[23] In 1799 fashionable visitors from Brighton stayed there.[24] A rear entrance in Mill Lane led to the stables and coach house.[25] The Norfolk Arms was the chief coaching inn of the town in the early 19th century,[26] and from the 1850s it offered a railway carrier and omnibus service.[27] A billiard room was added *c.* 1890, and in 1893

82 M. Marshall, *Cricket at the Cast.* 9, 170–1, 180; O.S. Map 6", LXIII. NW. (1899 edn.).
83 W.S.R.O., MP 3117.
84 T. Heald, *Character of Cricket*, 105.
85 *W. Suss. Gaz.* 1, 8 Aug. 1991.
86 A.C.M., MD 1888.
87 W.S.R.O., POL AB/16/1 (Dec. 1876).
88 Cartland, *Arundel*, 76–7.
89 Eustace, *Arundel*, 242; *Brighton Evening Argus*, 1 Sept. 1959; O.S. Map 6", Suss. LXIII. NW. (1899 edn.).
90 *W. Suss. Gaz.* 22 Oct. 1959; 4 Aug. 1960.
91 Ibid. 20 July, 26 Oct. 1989.
92 Pike, *Bognor Dir.* (1910–11), 182; *Kelly's Dir. Suss.* (1918 and later edns.).
93 *W. Suss. Gaz.* 19 June 1975.
94 *Arundel, the Gem of Suss.* (Arundel, 1934), 42; W.S.R.O., BO/AR 16/1/181.
95 *Kelly's Dir. Suss.* (1938).
96 *W. Suss. Gaz.* 4 July 1963.
97 O.S. Maps 6", Suss. LXIII. NW. (1952 edn.); 1/2,500, TQ 0006–0106 (1980 edn.); local inf.
98 A.C.M., MD 535, f. 3 and v.
99 e.g. ibid. A 262, f. [36]; 1240; ibid. M 301, pp. [343–5]; W.S.R.O., A.B.A., F2/14, ff. [1v., 2v.].
1 W.S.R.O., A.B.A., F2/14, f. [1v.].
2 *S.R.S.* liv. 70–1; A. Fletcher, *County Community in Peace and War*, 154.
3 P.R.O., WO 30/48, f. 182.
4 A.C.M., D 926–40, deed, 1670.
5 Ibid. 671–87, deed, 1755.
6 W.S.R.O., MP 3041 (photocopy of town plan, 1785), omitting the Red Lion and the Norf. Arms hotel: cf. below, this section.
7 Pigot, *Nat. Com. Dir.* (1832–4), 1004.
8 *Kelly's Dir. Suss.* (1874).
9 Pike, *Bognor Dir.* (1910–11).
10 *Kelly's Dir. Suss.* (1938).
11 A.C.M., MD 535, f. 3; cf. ibid. 505, f. [2v.]; *S.A.C.* xvi. 67; *S.R.S.* xxxiii, p. 55; above, communications (rds.).
12 A.C.M., MD 724, f. [13].
13 *S.A.C.* lxxi. 28; below, parl. representation.
14 A.C.M., MD 619, p. 3; 1532.
15 *S.A.C.* lxxi. 53.
16 Pigot, *Nat. Com. Dir.* (1832–4), 1004. For the bldg., above, secular bldgs.
17 *S.A.C.* lxxi. 28, 30.
18 Wright, *Arundel* (1817), 140.
19 Pigot, *Nat. Com. Dir.* (1832–4), 1004; W.S.R.O., Par. 8/9/10, no. 1044; *W. Suss. Gaz.* 18 Nov. 1875.
20 Wright, *Arundel* (1817), 140; cf. Pigot, *Nat. Com. Dir.* (1832–4), 1004; W.S.R.O., Par. 8/9/10, no. 1044.
21 A.C.M., MD 19; Tierney, *Arundel*, i. 81 n.
22 A.C.M., MD 1532; W.S.R.O., MP 3041 (photocopy of town plan, 1785); *Univ. Brit. Dir.* ii. 56.
23 Evans, *Worthing* (1814), ii. 76; Wright, *Arundel* (1818), 7.
24 *European Mag. and Lond. Rev.* xxxvi (1799), 151.
25 A.C.M., H 2/44; W.S.R.O., MP 3041.
26 Pigot, *Nat. Com. Dir.* (1832–4), 1004; cf. *Kelly's Dir. Suss.* (1845).
27 *Kelly's Dir. Suss.* (1852 and later edns.).

the hotel claimed to serve commercial travellers, tourists, and families.[28] The room over the entrance archway which from the early 19th century hosted public meetings and other events[29] could accommodate 150 people at dinner in 1903.[30] The hotel still belonged to the Norfolk estate in 1980.[31]

A second hotel, put up apparently shortly before 1814, was the Bridge in Queen Street, a long two-storeyed brick building[32] on the site of an earlier inn.[33] One coach and one carrier called there in the early 1830s.[34] Between the 1850s and 1870s the hotel housed the town's excise office.[35] In 1893 there were a large dining room, a billiard room, and a veranda and balcony overlooking the river; fishing and boating were offered to patrons in 1903.[36] The hotel collapsed when its foundations were undermined by the reconstruction of the bridge in the 1930s;[37] a new building, of red brick with a river terrace and tea garden, was put up in 1935[38] and demolished in 1988.

Other inns in High Street which survived in 1990 were the Red Lion, perhaps recorded from 1658,[39] and the Swan, previously the Ship, recorded from 1759[40] and rebuilt in the mid 19th century. Between the early 1830s and the 1850s the Swan was the chief place of call for carriers;[41] both inns catered for cyclists in the later 19th century or earlier 20th.[42] The St. Mary's Gate or Marygate inn in London Road, built in the early 19th century,[43] replaced the Bell or Blue Bell inn by the Marygate itself which the duke of Norfolk had bought in 1795 or 1796 for demolition;[44] the new inn had a bowling green in the mid 19th century.[45] Other former inns or beerhouses in the town include the Wheatsheaf in Maltravers Street, previously the Sundial (fl. 1785;[46] closed *c.* 1932);[47] the Victory in King Street (apparently built shortly before 1829;[48] closed 1974);[49] the Gardeners Arms in Mill Lane (fl. *c.* 1841–50);[50] and the Jolly Sailor in River Road, which evidently served mariners (fl. 1910; closed *c.* 1933).[51]

CASTLE. INSTITUTIONAL HISTORY. Some fortification seems likely to have existed on the site of Arundel castle before 1066, though the entry in Domesday Book is equivocal.[52] The present building was begun by Roger de Montgomery probably *c.* 1067, descending thereafter with the rape[53] except as noted below. Much medieval work survives, but additions made in the 16th and 18th centuries have largely been removed or concealed; in 1995 the castle owed its appearance chiefly to the last of three building campaigns of the period 1791–1909.

In 1102 the castle was fortified against the king by Robert of Bellême, enduring a three-months' siege until Robert surrendered it *in absentia*.[54] The empress Maud on her arrival in England in 1139 stayed at the castle under the protection of William d'Aubigny, earl of Arundel, and his wife Adelize, but the threatened siege was averted when she was given safe conduct to Bristol.[55] Henry II stayed at Arundel *c.* 1182 and presumably at other times,[56] and Richard I perhaps in 1189.[57] William's grandson and namesake, also earl of Arundel (d. 1221), paid to have the castle in 1198.[58]

After the rape was granted to Hugh d'Aubigny, earl of Arundel (d. 1243), during his minority, the castle was retained by the Crown, Hugh Sanzaver having the keeping in 1235.[59] It was restored to the earl, however, by 1240.[60] John FitzAlan (d. 1267) may have surrendered it to the Crown in 1265 as a pledge of good faith.[61] During the minority of his grandson Richard it was in the custody of John de Wauton in 1275–6 and Ralph of Sandwich in 1276,[62] and at other times of those mentioned elsewhere as keepers of the rape.[63]

Richard FitzAlan, earl of Arundel (d. 1302), was living at the castle in 1292.[64] During the minority of his heir the Crown retained it when the custody of the rape was granted out in 1302.[65] In 1330, after the execution of Edmund, earl of Kent, the keeper of the castle was required to pay to his widow Margaret maintenance for herself and her children as long as she continued to live there.[66] In 1336 the castle was ordered to be safely guarded and provided with armed men.[67] Richard FitzAlan, earl of Arundel (d. 1376), was living there in the 1340s and 50s[68] and his

28 Kimpton, *Arundel* (1893), back cover.
29 *S.A.C.* lxxi. 51; above, this section.
30 Goodliffe, *Littlehampton* (1903), p. xxiv.
31 *Country Life*, 3 July 1980, p. 7.
32 Evans, *Worthing* (1814), i. 161; illus. at Cartland, *Arundel*, 37.
33 W.S.R.O., MP 3041 (photocopy of town plan, 1785).
34 Pigot, *Nat. Com. Dir.* (1832–4), 1004.
35 *Kelly's Dir. Suss.* (1852 and later edns.).
36 Kimpton, *Arundel* (1893), inside back cover; Goodliffe, *Littlehampton* (1903), p. iv.
37 Cartland, *Arundel*, 36, 38–9.
38 W.S.R.O., BO/AR 16/1/139; ibid. SP 1086.
39 A.C.M., A 262, f. [36]; ibid. D 671; cf. W.S.R.O., Add. MS. 20560 (TS. cat.).
40 W.S.R.O., MP 3041 (photocopy of town plan, 1785); 3045.
41 Pigot, *Nat. Com. Dir.* (1832–4), 1004; *Kelly's Dir. Suss.* (1845 and later edns.).
42 Kimpton, *Arundel* (1893), p. vi; ibid. (1903), p. xvii.
43 Above, frontispiece; cf. Pigot, *Nat. Com. Dir.* (1832–4), 1004.
44 A.C.M., D 60–93 (MS. cat.); ibid. MD 619, p. 25; W.S.R.O., MP 3045.
45 W.S.R.O., TD/W 5; A.C.M., uncat. archit. drawings, plan of part of cast. grounds, 1856.
46 W.S.R.O., MP 3041; cf. ibid. TD/W 5; A.C.M., FC 435.
47 *Kelly's Dir. Suss.* (1930, 1934).
48 W.S.R.O., Add. MS. 26436 (TS. cat.).
49 *W. Suss. Gaz.* 10 Oct. 1974.
50 A.C.M., H 2/44; W.S.R.O., TD/W 5.
51 Pike, *Bognor Dir.* (1910–11), 191; W.S.R.O., BO/AR 16/1/123.
52 Above, defences; *V.C.H.* i. 385. No evidence for any Roman structures has been found: e.g. *S.N.Q.* ii. 60. *Country Life*, 5–19 Dec. 1914, has many good illuss. of the bldgs.
53 Above, Arundel Rape. The cast. is mentioned in 1071: D. J. C. King, *Castellarium Anglicanum*, ii. 469.
54 *Eccl. Hist. of Orderic Vitalis*, ed. M. Chibnall, vi. 21, 23; Tierney, *Arundel*, i. 56.
55 *Eccl. Hist. of Orderic Vitalis*, ed. Chibnall, vi. 534 n. 3; Tierney, *Arundel*, i. 56–8; cf. Dallaway, *Hist. W. Suss.* ii (1) (1819), 96.
56 *Cartae Antiquae*, ii (Pipe R. Soc. N.S. xxxiii), 131; cf. *Pipe R.* 1173 (P.R.S. xix), 26; below, this section (cast. fabric).
57 *Cal. Doc. France*, ed. Round, pp. 384–5.
58 *Pipe R.* 1198 (P.R.S. N.S. ix), 93.
59 *Ex. e Rot. Fin.* (Rec. Com.), i. 250; *Cal. Pat.* 1232–47, 104.
60 *Cal. Papal Reg.* i. 189.
61 *Cal. Pat.* 1258–66, 420.
62 *Cal. Fine R.* 1272–1307, 57, 76.
63 e.g. *Close R.* 1268–72, 499 (Rob. de Aguillon); *Cal. Close*, 1272–9, 85 (the same); above, Arundel Rape.
64 *S.R.S.* xlvi, p. 282.
65 *Cal. Pat.* 1301–7, 46.
66 *Cal. Close*, 1330–3, 14.
67 Ibid. 1333–7, 679.
68 *List of Anct. Corresp.* (L. & I. xv), pp. 607, 624, 650, 842–3.

son and namesake (d. 1397) in the 1380s; the king and queen and members of the nobility were present at Arundel in 1384 at the marriage of the younger Richard's daughter.[69] Later earls still lived at the castle in the 15th and 16th centuries;[70] Henry VIII visited William FitzAlan, earl of Arundel (d. 1544), in 1526 and 1538.[71] The castle was in Crown hands in 1586.[72]

In the early 17th century the castle was not often inhabited;[73] its Civil War vicissitudes are described elsewhere.[74] Thomas Howard, duke of Norfolk (d. 1732), lived there at least sometimes,[75] and his successors continued to use the castle as an occasional residence during the 18th century,[76] though their chief country house was then at Worksop (Notts.).[77] Charles Howard, duke of Norfolk (d. 1815), who rebuilt much of the castle, was said in 1805 to live there a great part of the time.[78] From *c.* 1832 it was the dukes' regular residence[79] until 1961.[80] In the 1950s and 60s Queen Elizabeth II stayed there in alternate years for Goodwood races.[81] Duke Bernard Marmaduke's proposal of 1957 that the castle should be settled on the nation as the official residence of the Earl Marshal was rejected by Parliament,[82] and his later wish that it should pass to the National Trust was not achieved; instead a private trust was set up after his death in 1975.[83] Only occasional residential use was made of the building after 1961[84] until the early 1990s when Duke Miles's son Lord Arundel and his family made it their chief home.

Castle guard service was exacted from tenants of lands in the rape in the 13th century.[85] The part of the castle called the Percies' hall in 1279 was perhaps for the accommodation of the Percy lords of Petworth, who owed the service of 22½ knights.[86]

Jocelin of Louvain, brother of Queen Adelize, was castellan of Arundel *c.* 1160.[87] A constable was recorded between 1244 and 1589, some holders of the office being known by name.[88] In 1435, when the post was for life, the salary was £10 a year.[89] In 1589 the post was held with that of keeper of the Little park.[90] A castle porter received 2*s.* a day in 1244, when two watchmen were paid 3*d.* a day,[91] but his successor in 1302 had £2 5*s.* 6*d.* a year.[92] In 1275 a second keeper had responsibility for the north bailey.[93] The office of porter was evidently honorific by 1576–7 when it was held by a gentleman.[94] Lieut. Hammond on his visit in 1635 was entertained by 'the keepers of the castle' and mentioned lodgings in the gatehouse belonging to the constable, the warder, and the porter.[95]

A steward was mentioned in the late 12th or early 13th century[96] and in the 16th.[97] There was presumably usually a chaplain, and in 1300 there were more than one.[98] In the 1210s the chaplain received 10*s.* a year;[99] between then and *c.* 1300 the sum came from the farm of Chichester,[1] and in 1301 there was income from Swanbourne mill.[2] Other officers were an usher of the chamber recorded in 1487,[3] a treasurer, a comptroller,[4] and a yeoman of the wardrobe in 1580,[5] and a marshal of the household in 1465.[6]

The castle was used as a prison between 1232–3 and 1306; it was delivered regularly from 1275–6. In the late 1270s suspects taken within the honor of Arundel had to be imprisoned at Arundel instead of being sent to the county gaol at Guildford;[7] in 1275 the steward of the rape was accepting fines to release some.[8] During most of the 14th century the prison seems not to have been needed since there was another at Chichester,[9] but in 1381 it was brought into temporary use to accommodate prisoners taken during the Peasants' Revolt. Prisoners were sent there on three other occasions between 1397[10] and 1405,[11] but no more is heard of the prison except for an equivocal reference of 1577–8 to money spent on its repair.[12]

The castle could be visited by tourists in the mid and later 18th century,[13] and has generally

69 *S.R.S.* xlvi, p. 263; A. Goodman, *Loyal Conspiracy*, 11.

70 e.g. *Haughmond Cartulary*, ed. U. Rees, p. 94; *Cal. S.P. Dom.* 1547–80, 153; *Jnl. of Brit. Studies*, xiii (2), 19–23; *Ven. Phil. Howard, Earl of Arundel* (Cath. Rec. Soc. xxi), 387; cf. ibid. 36.

71 *L. & P. Hen. VIII*, iv (2), pp. 1058, 1061–2; xiii (2), p. 533.

72 *Acts of P.C.* 1586–7, 271.

73 J. M. Robinson, *Arundel Cast. Guide* (1994), 17; *Cal. S.P. Dom.* Addenda 1625–49, 505.

74 Above, milit. events.

75 A.C.M., A 339, Arundel surv. 1702, f. 2; B.L. Lansd. MS. 918, ff. 22v.–23.

76 B.L. Add. MS. 15776, f. 230; *Horace Walpole's Corresp. with Geo. Montagu*, ed. W. S. Lewis and R. S. Brown, i. 96; *Arundel Cast. Archives*, ii. 138–9; *Cat. of Earl Marshal's Papers at Arundel Cast.* ed. F. W. Steer, p. 64; *S.A.C.* lii. 71–2; lxxi. 38–9, 42; *Country Life*, 10 Feb. 1983, p. 333.

77 J. M. Robinson, *Dukes of Norf.* (1982), 152, 160; P. Leach, *Jas. Paine*, 29.

78 Below, this section (cast. fabric); Evans, *Worthing* (1805), 100.

79 Pigot, *Nat. Com. Dir.* (1832–4), 1003; (1839), 653; *Kelly's Dir. Suss.* (1845 and later edns.); Robinson, *Dukes of Norf.* (1982), 195.

80 Below, woods and parks (modern park).

81 J. M. Robinson, *Latest Country Hos.* 33.

82 *Country Life*, 21 Feb. 1957, p. 322; *The Times*, 26 June 1957; A.C.M., AP 89.

83 *Country Life*, 3 July 1980, p. 6.

84 Robinson, *Latest Country Hos.* 131; *The Times*, 24 Jan. 1983.

85 Elwes & Robinson, *W. Suss.* 240, 249; *Cal. Inq. p.m.* i, p. 279; *S.R.S.* lxvii. 105.

86 Ibid. 91; Tierney, *Arundel*, i. 54; cf. B.L. Lansd. MS. 30, f. 219 and v.

87 *S.R.S.* xl. 79; *Arch. Jnl.* xxii. 154.

88 *Cal. Lib.* 1240–5, 276; *Cal. Pat.* 1401–5, 286; *Cal. Close*, 1330–3, 27; *S.R.S.* xli. 42; P.R.O., E 178/1906, f. 1v.

89 *Cal. Pat.* 1429–36, 464.

90 P.R.O., E 178/1906, f. 1v.

91 *Cal. Lib.* 1240–5, 276.

92 *Cal. Inq. p.m.* iv, p. 51. For a later porter, *S.R.S.* xi. 279.

93 P.R.O., SC 6/1019/22, rot. 1, m. 3.

94 Sandbeck Park, Rotherham, Lumley MS. EMA/1/5.

95 *Camd. Misc.* xvi (Camd. 3rd ser. lii), Hammond, 30–1.

96 W.S.R.O., Par. 8/7/35.

97 P.R.O., E 315/101, f. 55; Eustace, *Arundel*, 118.

98 *Cal. Inq. p.m.* iii, p. 462.

99 *Pipe R.* 1210 (P.R.S. N.S. xxvi), 86; 1214 (P.R.S. N.S. xxxv), 163.

1 *Bk. of Fees*, i. 73; *Rot. Litt. Claus.* (Rec. Com.), ii. 168; *Cal. Inq. p.m.* iii, p. 462.

2 *S.R.S.* lxvii. 2.

3 Ibid. xli. 42 (*hostiarius camere*).

4 Eustace, *Arundel*, 118; cf. *S.R.S.* xlv. 426.

5 B.L. Lansd. MS. 30, f. 217v.

6 *S.A.C.* lxxvi. 69.

7 Ibid. xcvii. 73; *Close R.* 1259–61, 48; *Cal. Chart. R.* 1257–1300, 214; *Plac. de Quo Warr.* (Rec. Com.), 752.

8 *S.A.C.* lxxxiv. 69.

9 Ibid. xcvii. 76.

10 Ibid. 78.

11 *Cal. Pat.* 1401–5, 286; *S.R.S.* viii. 44.

12 P.R.O., SC 6/Eliz. I/2213, mm. 8–9, which may not relate to Arundel.

13 *Horace Walpole's Corresp. with Geo. Montagu*, ed. W. S. Lewis and R. S. Brown, i. 96; *Pococke's Travels*, ii (Camd. Soc. 2nd ser. xliv), 108; *S.C.M.* xxv. 573; xxviii. 226.

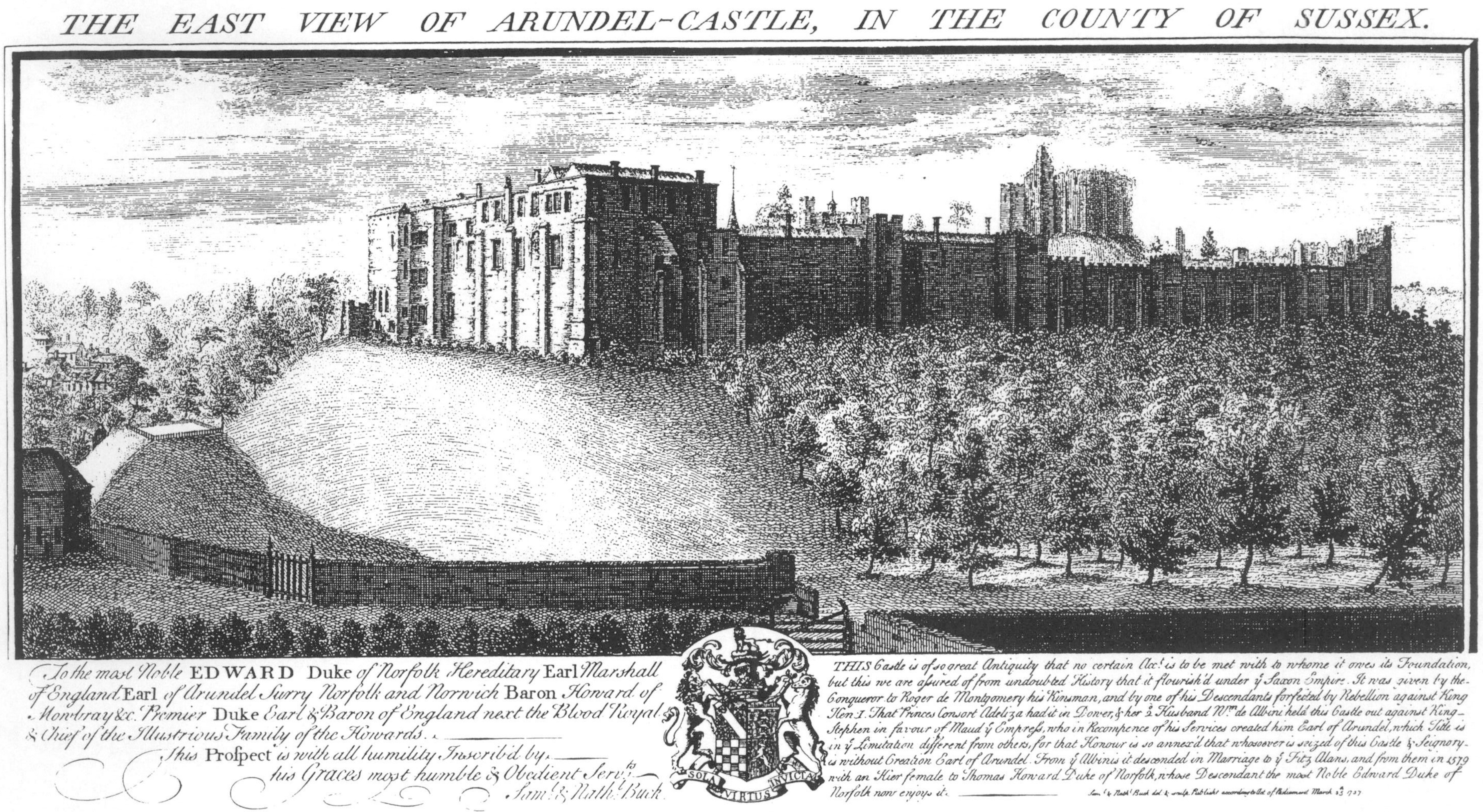
THE EAST VIEW OF ARUNDEL-CASTLE, IN THE COUNTY OF SUSSEX.
To the most Noble EDWARD Duke of Norfolk Hereditary Earl Marshall of England Earl of Arundel Surry Norfolk and Norwich Baron Howard of Mowbray &c. Premier Duke Earl & Baron of England next the Blood Royal & Chief of the Illustrious Family of the Howards.
This Prospect is with all humility Inscrib'd by his Graces most humble & Obedient Serv.ts Sam.l & Nath.l Buck
SOLA VIRTUS INVICTA
THIS Castle is of so great Antiquity that no certain Acc.t is to be met with to whome it owes its Foundation, but this we are assured of from undoubted History that it flourish'd under y.e Saxon Empire. It was given by the Conqueror to Roger de Montgomery his Kinsman, and by one of his Descendants forfeited by Rebellion against King Hen. I. That Princes Consort Adeliza had it in Dower, & her 2.d Husband W.m de Albini held this Castle out against King Stephen in favour of Maud y.e Empress, who in Recompence of his Services created him Earl of Arundel, which Title is in y.e Limitation different from others, for that Honour is so annex'd that whosoever is seized of this Castle & Seignory is without Creation Earl of Arundel. From y.e Albinis it descended in Marriage to y.e Fitz Alans, and from them in 1579 with an Heir female to Thomas Howard Duke of Norfolk, whose Descendant the most Noble Edward Duke of Norfolk now enjoys it.

Arundel Castle from the east in 1737

been open for public inspection since *c.* 1800; in 1817 visitors were said to come from all over Britain.[14] The keep and gatehouse were open 'constantly' in 1802,[15] but from 1805 until *c.* 1900 apparently usually twice a week.[16] By 1814[17] if not before[18] some interiors too were shown weekly; they could still be seen in the 1840s,[19] when the castle was described as one of the most superb 'show houses' in the country.[20] In the early 20th century the keep was generally open once a week in summer,[21] and the state rooms were also open between 1913 and 1934 at least,[22] as they were in the later 20th century. By 1929 the barons' hall was sometimes used for charitable entertainments,[23] and the castle has continued to be made available for a variety of events.

CASTLE FABRIC. The earthworks of the early Norman castle are very similar to those of the contemporary, though larger, royal castle at Windsor.[24] At the centre is a circular motte, to north-west and south-east of which are baileys[25] abutting the edge of the river cliff on the east side, but having deep ditches to west and north which must always have been dry. The motte in 1994 was *c.* 100 ft. (30 metres) high from the bottom of the western ditch; the southern section of that ditch was evidently once more prominent, since properties on the eastern side of High Street were formerly described as extending up to it.[26] The total dimensions of the castle are *c.* 950 ft. (290 metres) by *c.* 250 ft. (76 metres). It is not clear whether both baileys were constructed at the same time as the motte[27] nor how, or if, they were originally divided from each other on its east side. A ditch on the east and south sides of the motte survived in the later 18th century,[28] but was afterwards filled in.

Presumably wooden palisades surmounted the earthworks at first, and there would have been timber buildings in the bailey or baileys and a timber keep on the motte. The earliest surviving stone building is the lower two storeys of the gatehouse, south of the motte, which may be late 11th-century; built of large blocks of Pulborough stone, it has a round-arched entrance of one order.

The castle was in royal hands 1102–35 and 1176–90. Payment for work on it is recorded in 1130.[29] A larger programme of work is evidenced in the 1170s and 80s, when Henry II may have intended to attach it permanently to the Crown. Payments were then made for building a wall; for flooring a tower; and for work on the chapel and on the king's chamber, which had a garden in front.[30]

The surviving 12th-century work in the keep and in a residential block in the south-east corner of the south bailey was previously connected with those payments,[31] but has recently been suggested[32] to have been carried out in the 1140s by William d'Aubigny, earl of Arundel (d. 1176). The keep was enclosed by a thick wall of Caen and Quarr abbey stones, with pilaster buttresses, and a doorway, later blocked, in its south-east side whose elaborate decoration, including a double chevron moulding, can be paralleled by work of that date at Castle Hedingham (Essex).[33] Only corbels and mural fireplaces remain of the two-storeyed internal buildings; in the centre of the courtyard is a later undercroft with a ribbed vault, presumably for storage. The residential block of flint and stone in the south-east corner of the south bailey has in its south-eastern external wall two blocked two-light windows apparently of *c.* 1160–70 and four original buttresses;[34] in the basement at the east corner is a long barrel-vaulted room lined with clunch, with two round-headed windows and a buttress in its inner wall which originally would have faced into the bailey.[35] The range had apparently been extended south-westwards by 1275;[36] in 1580 it had various chambers including Lord Lumley's chamber and the king's chamber,[37] perhaps the room mentioned in the later 12th century. The east corner of the range was higher than the rest,[38] and in the later 18th century was called the high building.[39]

At the north end of the north bailey is a short length of curved foundation outside the curtain wall which seems also to date from about the 1140s: in its battered plinth and in the stone of which it is built it matches the keep, while its round plan parallels that of a tower at New

14 Wright, *Arundel* (1817), 20.

15 *European Mag. and Lond. Rev.* xlii (1802), 374.

16 Evans, *Worthing* (1805), 110; ibid. (1814), i. 182; *Illus. Lond. News*, 20 Sept. 1845, p. 180; *A Visit to Arundel Cast.* (1851), p. v; *Kelly's Dir. Suss.* (1855 and later edns.); Kimpton, *Arundel* (1893), front cover.

17 Evans, *Worthing* (1814), i. 166–7, 181; cf. Wright, *Arundel* (1817), 20.

18 *European Mag. and Lond. Rev.* xlii (1802), 374.

19 *Illus. Lond. News*, 20 Sept. 1845, p. 180; Hillier, *Arundel* (1847), 44–50; W.S.R.O., Add. MS. 29745 ([Aug.] 1841); cf. Clwyd R.O., Glynne ch. notes, cii. 48–9.

20 *Illus. Lond. News*, 20 Sept. 1845, p. 181.

21 Goodliffe, *Littlehampton* (1903), 71; ibid. (1909), [6]; *Kelly's Dir. Suss.* (1922 and later edns.).

22 *Arundel Cast.* comp. Gwendolen, duchess of Norf. (1913); *Arundel, the Gem of Suss.* (Arundel, 1934), 32; J. M. Robinson, *Arundel Cast. Guide* [1980s], 24; *S.C.M.* iii. 282.

23 *S.C.M.* iii. 282; cf. *W. Suss. Gaz.* 13 Nov. 1986; *New Statesman*, 22 Dec. 1972, p. 941.

24 *Hist. King's Works*, ed. Colvin, i. 24 n.

25 Here called N. and S. baileys for ease of reference.

26 Above, growth of town; Dallaway & Cartwright, *Hist. W. Suss.* ii (1) (1832), 211; *Lavington Estate Archives*, ed. F. W. Steer, p. 29; B.L. Add. MS. 5674, f. 28; cf. O.S. Map 1/2,500, Suss. LXIII. 1 (1877 edn.); *Camd. Misc.* xvi (Camd. 3rd ser. lii), Hammond, 31.

27 e.g. *Hist. King's Works*, ed. Colvin, i. 24 n.; *E.H.R.* xix. 213.

28 B.L. Add. MS. 5674, ff. 27–8; Dallaway, *Hist. W. Suss.* ii (1) (1819), facing p. 92.

29 *Pipe R.* 1130 (H.M.S.O. facsimile), 42.

30 Ibid. 1171 (P.R.S. xvi), 135; 1179 (P.R.S. xxviii), 39; 1182 (P.R.S. xxxi), 91; 1183 (P.R.S. xxxii), 107; 1187 (P.R.S. xxxvii), 107, 109; 1188 (P.R.S. xxxviii), 185; *Hist. King's Works*, ed. Colvin, ii. 554.

31 *E.H.R.* xix. 213; *Hist. King's Works*, ed. Colvin, ii. 554.

32 By Mr. P. Curnow, formerly of Eng. Heritage, and the late Prof. R. Allen Brown.

33 Inf. from Mr. Curnow.

34 *Country Life*, 19 Dec. 1914, p. 818; *Plans of Arundel Cast.* 3.

35 J. M. Robinson, *Arundel Cast. Guide* (1994), 6–7; below, pl. facing p. 43.

36 Below, this section.

37 B.L. Lansd. MS. 30, f. 218 and v.

38 e.g. W.S.R.O., PD 1367, illus. above, p. 16; *Plans of Arundel Cast.* 3 and frontispiece.

39 *Plans of Arundel Cast.* 4, 23. Some 12th-cent. fragments of carved stone survived in the so-called sacristy of the Fitzalan chapel at the par. ch. in 1991; 3 are illus. at *Connoisseur*, Mar. 1978, p. 155.

Buckenham (Norf.) built at that period by William d'Aubigny, earl of Arundel (d. 1176).[40] It may represent a secondary keep built to dominate the north bailey before the curtain wall was built. The curtain wall itself seems likely to be the wall mentioned in the 1180s; it had a wall walk and regularly spaced rectangular towers and was originally quite thin[41] though later increased to a thickness of *c.* 10 ft. (3 metres). The Bevis tower[42] north-west of the keep, built to defend the weak point formed by its ditch, was possibly originally open-backed and seems to have been a postern from the first; it was rebuilt in the late 13th century or early 14th, its top storey being again altered in the 16th. At least two of the other three towers in the north bailey, all of which were much altered later, were also originally open-backed,[43] as perhaps was the tower in the south bailey south-east of the keep.[44]

In the late 12th century a tower was built on older footings above the well on the south side of the keep and a new south entrance to the keep was made from the wall walk; the tower's two-light windows with shouldered heads are late 13th-century insertions. The tower was presumably the 'high tower' used as a treasury in 1376.[45] About 1300 the Norman gatehouse was heightened, the new work having sandstone dressings; the two-light shouldered-headed window motif appears there too. At the same date a barbican, of knapped flint with sandstone dressings, was built outside the gatehouse; its upper floors each have a hall, garderobe, and two small chambers, while the basement contains what seem to have been prisons.[46]

A freestanding hall range was built on the south-west side of the south bailey in the 13th century; it had a projecting porch with a room above. The hall seems to have been substantially remodelled in the late 14th or 15th century,[47] perhaps to the design of Henry Yeveley,[48] with a timber roof compared by one writer with those of Westminster Hall and Eltham Palace,[49] and an apparently later open louvre or turret on top. A 'great chamber' apparently to the south-east and two other chambers apparently to the north-west were mentioned in 1580.[50] During the 16th century there was building between the hall and the western curtain wall, where a vaulted undercroft, perhaps a cellar leading off the screens passage, survived in 1988.[51] Kitchens and other offices lay between the hall and the gatehouse in 1635.[52] It was in the great hall in 1549 that Henry FitzAlan, earl of Arundel (d. 1580), heard complaints deriving from a peasants' uprising, refreshment being provided both in the hall and in the south bailey.[53]

A chapel existed by 1183,[54] and by 1275 there were two, dedicated respectively to St. Martin and St. George.[55] Since St. Martin was also the dedication of Sées abbey (Orne), which was patronized by Roger de Montgomery (d. 1094), the former chapel may have been founded in the late 11th century.[56] It is said to have been in the keep.[57] One or other chapel in 1275 presumably occupied the site on the first floor of the south-east range of the south bailey, at its south-west end, which it still had in the later 18th century.[58] In 1345 it was proposed to endow three chaplains in the castle, and in 1355 a college of priests and clerks, to serve the family of the earl of Arundel.[59] In 1375, when the second proposal was repeated, six priests and three choristers were to live in a new tower in the north bailey called the Beaumont tower and buildings adjoining it;[60] the college beside the parish church was later founded instead.[61] The castle chapel was presumably still used in 1517,[62] but its description as 'the old chapel' and the absence of chapel furniture in it in 1580[63] indicate that it no longer was by then.

In 1526 the castle was said to be in great decay.[64] During the 16th century a range of buildings was put up on the north-east side of the south bailey; the work was apparently done in at least two builds, perhaps partly *c.* 1574 when work was going on at the castle.[65] Fragments of decorative stonework from the buildings of the college are said to have been found in the range when it was demolished in the early 19th century.[66] The north-east range had a projecting two-storeyed porch of flint and stone chequerwork, and contained a first-floor gallery *c.* 120 ft. (37 metres) long, together with several apartments;[67] in 1635 and later there was also a dining room there.[68] A battlemented and two-storeyed

40 Inf. from Mr. Curnow.
41 Ibid.
42 So named, from Arundel's mythical hero, by 1780: B.L. Add. MS. 5674, f. 25. The name was also used to describe keep in 1636 and barbican in early 19th cent.: A.C.M., MD 505, f. [1]; Dallaway, *Hist. W. Suss.* ii (1) (1819), 92 n.; Tierney, *Arundel*, i. 39; cf. B.L. Lansd. MS. 918, f. 23.
43 B.L. Add. MS. 5674, f. 28, shows one in its orig. form.
44 Illus. at *Plans of Arundel Cast.* frontispiece.
45 *S.A.C.* xci. 34.
46 Hillier, *Arundel* (1851), 20.
47 *Plans of Arundel Cast.* frontispiece; Dallaway, *Hist. W. Suss.* ii (1) (1819), 94; Tierney, *Arundel*, i. 51; J. Harris, *Artist and Country Ho.* no. 364*b*, illus. opposite; W.S.R.O., PD 1367, illus. above, p. 16.
48 J. Harvey, *Eng. Medieval Architects*, 365.
49 Dallaway, op. cit. 94.
50 B.L. Lansd. MS. 30, ff. 217v., 220.
51 Cf. *Plans of Arundel Cast.* 15; Dallaway, *Hist. W. Suss.* ii (1) (1819), 94.
52 *Camd. Misc.* xvi (Camd. 3rd ser. lii), Hammond, 30.
53 *Jnl. of Brit. Studies*, xiii (2), 21–3.
54 *Pipe R.* 1183 (P.R.S. xxxii), 107; cf. ibid. 1205 (P.R.S. N.S. xix), 109; above, this section (institutional hist.).
55 *Cal. Pat.* 1272–81, 80, 82.
56 *V.C.H. Suss.* i. 376. Tierney's statement that it was mentioned in Domesday bk., however, is based on a misconstruction of a ref. to the abbey: ibid. i. 421; Tierney, *Arundel*, ii. 591.
57 e.g. Dallaway, *Hist. W. Suss.* ii (1) (1819), 92; Tierney, *Arundel*, i. 49; *V.C.H. Suss.* ii. 338.
58 Below, this section; cf. B.L. Lansd. MS. 30, f. 218.
59 *Cal. Papal Reg.* iii. 188, 573. *Pace* Tierney, *Arundel*, ii. 592–4, that did not happen: *V.C.H. Suss.* ii. 108.
60 *V.C.H. Suss.* ii. 108; Lamb. Pal. Libr., Reg. Sudbury, f. 93; cf. *Cal. Pat.* 1374–7, 129; 1377–81, 402. The tower is not identified; B.L. Lansd. MS. 30, f. 219v., mentions it after NE. range of S. bailey, but Tierney's gloss as keep does not occur in original doc.: Tierney, *Arundel*, ii. 732.
61 Below, church.
62 *Archaeologia*, lxi. 82.
63 B.L. Lansd. MS. 30, f. 218.
64 *L. & P. Hen. VIII*, iv (2), pp. 1061–2.
65 Sandbeck Park, Rotherham, Lumley MS. EMA/1/4.
66 Dallaway, *Hist. W. Suss.* ii (1) (1819), 93; but see Tierney, *Arundel*, i. 53.
67 *Camd. Misc.* xvi (Camd. 3rd ser. lii), Hammond, 31; *Plans of Arundel Cast.* 18–19 and frontispiece; A.C.M., MD 946; pl. opposite.
68 *Camd. Misc.* xvi (Camd. 3rd ser. lii), Hammond, 30; *Plans of Arundel Cast.* 18; A.C.M., PM 113.

The south bailey in the mid 18th century,
showing the ruins of the medieval great hall on the left
and 16th-century work on the right

Benediction in the south bailey *c.* 1900

ARUNDEL CASTLE

Rebuilding the castle in the late 19th century

The Norman undercroft in the south-east range of the south bailey

ARUNDEL CASTLE

range of red brick with stone dressings, depicted as closing the south bailey on its north-west side in the early 18th century,[69] seems also to have been 16th-century. Apparently containing service rooms, it was separated from the north-east range by a gateway. The south bailey was thus surrounded by buildings,[70] in contrast to the uninhabited north bailey. A small part of the north-west range of the south bailey survived in the early 1780s[71] but was demolished soon afterwards.[72]

The Arundel estate Act of 1627 settled £100 a year after the deaths of Thomas Howard, earl of Arundel (d. 1646), and his wife (d. 1654) for the repair of the castle and the Fitzalan chapel of the parish church.[73] The keep was in poor preservation in 1635, but at the same date the hall, described as 'somewhat ruinous', was being repaired.[74] The defences too must have been restored, since in 1643–4 they were able to withstand a 17-day siege. The siege caused damage,[75] but the defences were made good, and some repairs to the residential buildings were carried out by the Parliamentary governor in 1644 for his own occupation.[76] In 1653 when the castle ceased to be garrisoned the keys of the 'house' were ordered to be delivered to 'Mr. Howard',[77] evidently Henry Howard, later duke of Norfolk (d. 1684).[78] The order given at the same date to demolish the fortifications of the castle seems to have been obeyed only so far as to render it indefensible.[79] Glazing and other repairs were carried out in 1656–7 and 1665; in 1664 the bridge leading into the castle, evidently that through the medieval gatehouse, was rebuilt.[80] By 1658 Lady Anne Howard, wife of Henry Howard, was in residence,[81] but between that date and 1664 building materials, including lead and timber from the old dining room, were taken from the castle to Henry Howard's house at Albury (Surr.).[82] About 1678 the hall roof was repaired.[83] Other parts of the buildings remained in ruins in the 18th century,[84] notably the keep;[85] the barbican still had only a temporary roof in 1834.[86]

In 1702 the duke and his agent each had an apartment in the north-east range of the south bailey, though separated by two rooms without a roof; the agent's apartment was apparently at the north-west end.[87] Repairs to the castle on a larger scale were begun in or before the early 1720s[88] by Duke Thomas (d. 1732). A sequence of rooms described by Horace Walpole in 1749 as an 'indifferent apartment'[89] was created in the south-east range of the south bailey with views over the river valley, and corridors were added on the side of the range facing the bailey, fronted by an eight-bayed, three-storeyed brick façade in classical style with two rusticated doorways.[90] The main entrance to the castle remained in the north-east range, the new rooms being reached by means of a staircase and the 16th-century long gallery.[91] Sash windows were inserted on the south-east external front either then or later in the century, together with some in the north-east range.[92] It was perhaps about the 1720s that designs were commissioned from James Gibbs for a complete rebuilding of the castle which was not carried out.[93]

The castle chapel was used as a chapel in 1746;[94] later in the 18th century Catholics from the town attended as well as the duke's household.[95] The room seems to have been redecorated in the 1760s to the design of James Paine with a coved ceiling and an Ionic pedimented altarpiece containing a 'Nativity' by Gennari from James II's chapel at Whitehall Palace; in the later 18th century there were three steps to the sanctuary and a north-west gallery or tribune. Paine may have done other decorative work at the castle.[96] The north-east range was said in the later 18th century to have recently been repaired.[97] At that time the residential part of the castle was the upper floors of the north-east and south-east ranges of the south bailey; there were offices below, including the laundry and dairy at the north-west end of the north-east range, while the upper part of the gatehouse housed servants' rooms and a dovecot.[98]

Duke Charles (d. 1786) apparently intended to restore the castle, securing by an Act of 1783 up to £5,000 for the purpose from the renewal fines on leases on the family estate off the Strand in London.[99] His son and namesake (d. 1815) began

69 Arundel Cast., early 18th-cent. painting of S. bailey looking NW.

70 Cf. *Camd. Misc.* xvi (Camd. 3rd ser. lii), Hammond, 30.

71 B.L. Add. MSS. 5674, f. 30, printed at *Suss. Views* (S.R.S.), 10; 5677, f. 76; W.S.R.O., PD 804.

72 It does not appear in Dallaway, *Hist. W. Suss.* ii (1) (1819), facing p. 92, of 1789; cf. S.A.S. libr., prints and drawings 368. The cast. as it was in 1580 is described in an inv. at B.L. Lansd. MS. 30, ff. 217v.–220, inaccurately transcr. at Tierney, *Arundel*, ii. 729–33; Dallaway, *Hist. W. Suss.* ii (1) (1819), 98.

73 3 Chas. I, c. 4 (Priv. Act); *Complete Peerage*, s.v. Arundel.

74 *Camd. Misc.* xvi (Camd. 3rd ser. lii), Hammond, 30–1.

75 e.g. Dallaway, *Hist. W. Suss.* ii (1) (1819), 93; Wright, *Arundel* (1818), 32; Tierney, *Arundel*, i. 50; above, milit. events. Hollar's view of Arundel dated 1644 fails to show the damage: W.S.R.O., PD 1367, illus. above, p. 16.

76 *L.J.* vii. 25–6, 39–40; C. Thomas-Stanford, *Suss. in Great Civil War*, 259.

77 *Cal. S.P. Dom.* 1653–4, 256; above, milit. events.

78 Since he lived at Albury (Surr.): *D.N.B.*; cf. below, this section. Thos. Howard, earl of Arundel and later duke of Norf. (d. 1677), the then owner of cast., was a lunatic: above, Arundel Rape.

79 *Cal. S.P. Dom.* 1653–4, 191, 256–7.

80 A.C.M., A 262, f. [7]; 263, acct. 1664[–5].

81 Ibid. 262, f. [21]; cf. below, woods and parks (Great park).

82 A.C.M., A 262, ff. [21v.–22, 27]; 263, acct. 1664[–5].

83 Ibid. 1757, f. [39v.].

84 Ibid. 339, Arundel surv. 1702, f. 2; B.L. Add. MS. 15776, f. 230; ibid. Lansd. MS. 918, f. 22v.; *Plans of Arundel Cast.* 6–7.

85 B.L. Add. MS. 5674, ff. 26, 30.

86 Tierney, *Arundel*, i. 40.

87 A.C.M., A 339, Arundel surv. 1702, f. 2; cf. ibid. MD 946; *Arundel Cast. Archives*, iv, p. 85; *Plans of Arundel Cast.* 5, 22.

88 B.L. Lansd. MS. 918, ff. 22v.–23.

89 *Horace Walpole's Corresp. with Geo. Montagu*, ed. W. S. Lewis and R. S. Brown, i. 98.

90 *Plans of Arundel Cast.* 4, 19–20, 22, and frontispiece; Tierney, *Arundel*, i. 82; B.L. Add. MSS. 5674, f. 29; 15776, f. 231. Two classical fireplaces from the rms. are illus. at A.C.M., MD 961.

91 *Plans of Arundel Cast.* 18–20.

92 Ibid. 3 and frontispiece; B.L. Add. MS. 5687, f. 27v.

93 T. Friedman, *Jas. Gibbs*, 324.

94 A.C.M., IN 42; cf. ibid. 6–7.

95 Below, Rom. Cath.

96 P. Leach, *Jas. Paine*, 29, 172–3; *Plans of Arundel Cast.* 4, 20–2; J. M. Robinson, *Dukes of Norf.* (1982), 160; P. Bagni, *Benedetto Gennari* ([Padua], 1986), p. 106; A.C.M., MD 18; ceiling illus. at *Illus. Lond. News*, 5 Dec. 1846, p. 360.

97 *Plans of Arundel Cast.* 15.

98 Ibid. *passim*; Dallaway, *Hist. W. Suss.* ii (1) (1819), facing p. 92.

99 Tierney, *Arundel*, i. 80–1; 23 Geo. III, c. 29 (Priv. Act).

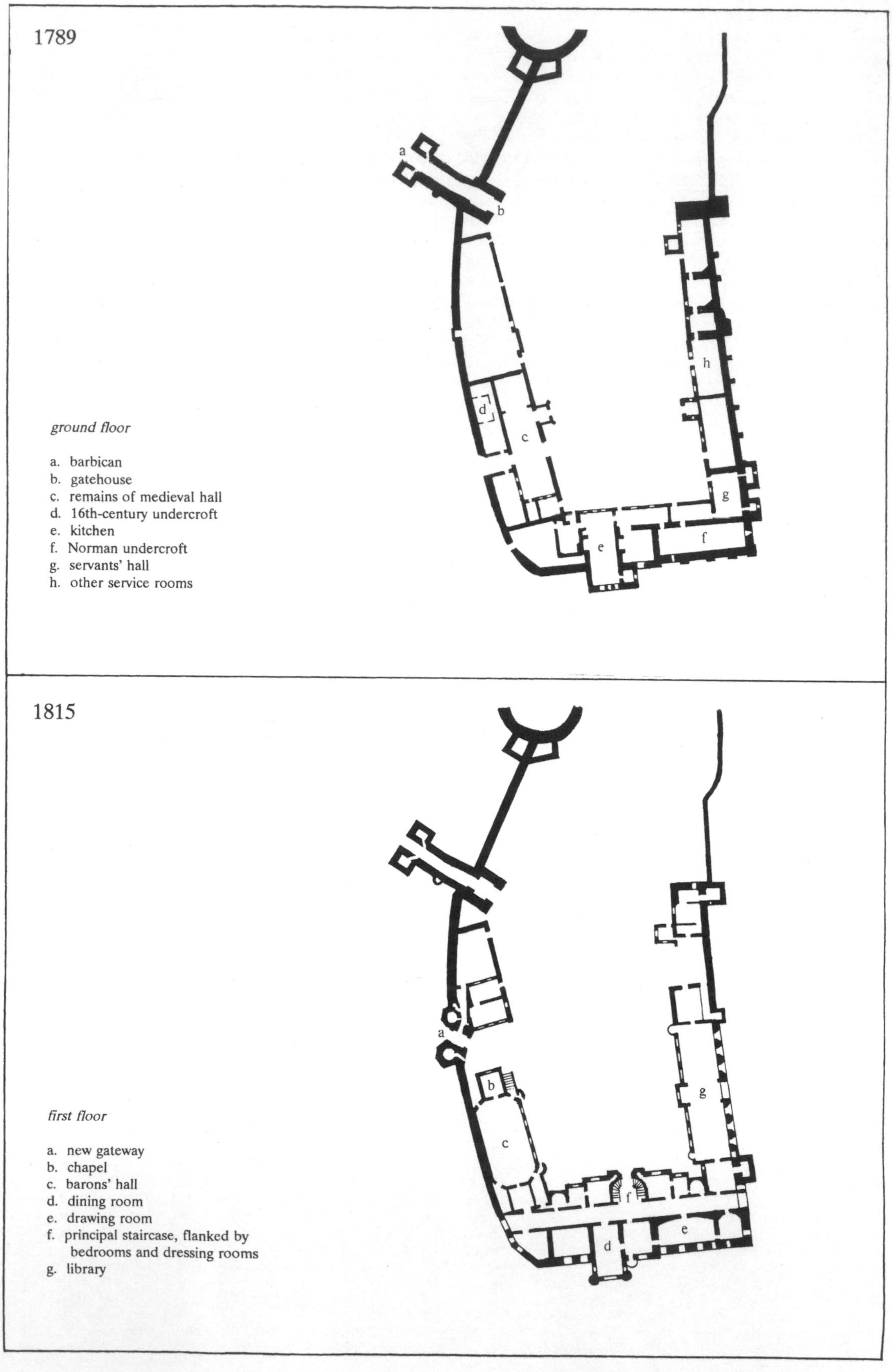
1789
a
b
d
c
h
g
e
f
ground floor
a. barbican
b. gatehouse
c. remains of medieval hall
d. 16th-century undercroft
e. kitchen
f. Norman undercroft
g. servants' hall
h. other service rooms
1815
a
b
c
g
f
d
e
first floor
a. new gateway
b. chapel
c. barons' hall
d. dining room
e. drawing room
f. principal staircase, flanked by bedrooms and dressing rooms
g. library

ARUNDEL CASTLE IN 1789 AND 1815

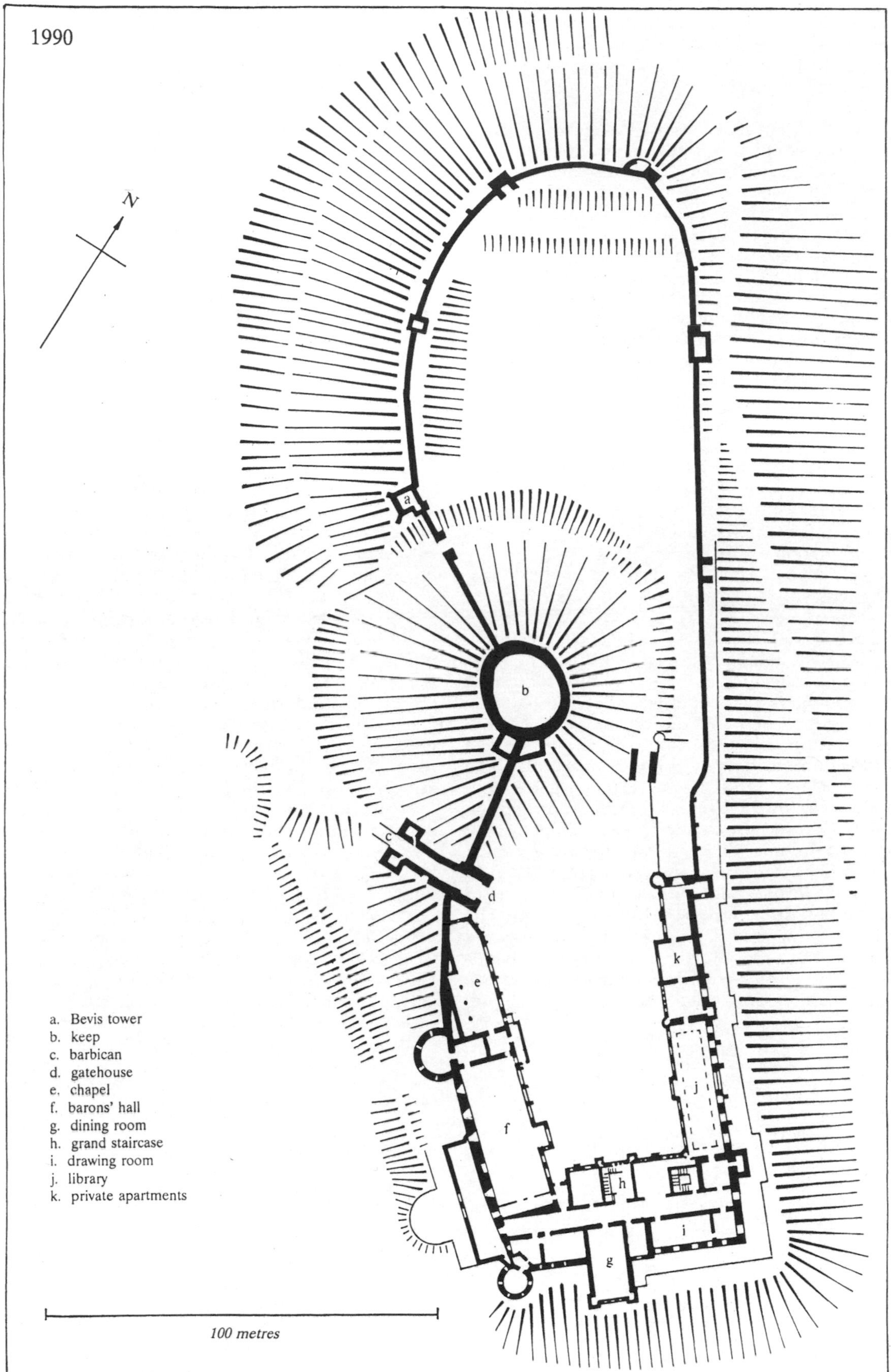

ARUNDEL CASTLE IN 1990

the reconstruction of the residential buildings on a large scale soon after his succession in 1786; it was still in progress at his death. The work was extremely lavish; by 1797 £200,000 is said to have been spent[1] and by 1816 an estimated £600,000.[2]

The first plan of the duke's architect Francis Hiorne[3] was apparently to restore the medieval gatehouse and keep and to link them to new castellated buildings to be built in the north bailey, clearing the south bailey completely to give a prospect over the Arun valley. After Hiorne's death in 1789 the duke decided to rebuild on more conventional lines and to be his own architect,[4] using as executants workers from his Cumberland estate whom he sent to London to train under leading architects and sculptors; one of them, James Teasdale, described himself as an architect in 1806.[5] In style the new work was to conform to the medieval buildings, and brown Whitby stone was chosen for much of it to match the medieval stonework in colour.[6] Duke Charles's work is paralleled in the mid 18th-century alterations at Warwick castle[7] and in the early 19th-century rebuilding of Windsor castle,[8] but by contrast was intended to express anti-monarchist, libertarian ideas.

Work began in 1791 or 1792[9] on heightening the medieval tower at the south-east corner of the south bailey. During the 1790s the rest of the south-east range was extensively restored, the old walls being preserved. A new kitchen was built on the ground floor by 1800. On the first floor the medieval chapel was replaced between 1796 and 1801 by a dining room projecting beyond the south-east front, with a richly carved Gothic music gallery at its north-west end.[10] The room was lit by a 20-ft. (6-metre) high painted-glass Gothic window by Francis Eginton representing Solomon entertaining the Queen of Sheba, the figure of Solomon being a portrait of the duke.[11] The 18th-century rooms were partly refitted in a similar Gothic style.[12] The great drawing room was apparently complete by 1799,[13] and the duke's sitting room by 1805.[14] The drawing room in 1815 was lined with crimson velvet.[15] The 18th-century corridors giving access to the rooms in the south-east range were preserved, but had to be chiefly end-lit, as the north-west front of the range was advanced a further 24 ft. (7 metres) into the bailey to accommodate bedrooms for the duke's family.[16] A double-return staircase rising through two floors, with a Gothic balustrade, was built by 1799; it was separated from the first-floor corridor by five stone arches, alternately semicircular and pointed, with Norman mouldings.[17] The symmetrical front of the range towards the bailey was built between 1795 and 1800 of Bath and Portland stones with a large Norman entrance archway;[18] flanking the staircase window above it were larger than life-size Coade stone figures of Liberty and Hospitality made in 1798 and perhaps designed by John Bacon the elder.[19] The rest of the south-east front towards the valley was reconstructed before 1804, the 18th-century sash windows being replaced by Gothic ones including tall lancets in the first-floor rooms; twin turrets flanking the projecting dining room provided another vertical accent.[20]

In 1801[21] work began on the north-east range of the south bailey. On the ground floor a rib-vaulted Norman-style undercroft with a Norman archway at each end[22] gave access from the bailey to a terrace outside. On the first floor was created an aisled and galleried library *c.* 120 ft. (37 metres) long in Perpendicular style, with decorative details taken from particular medieval buildings; it was near completion in 1805 and finished by 1814.[23] The symmetrical façade of the library towards the bailey was Norman in style on the ground floor and 15th-century Gothic above; in the centre was a square projecting entrance tower with an oriel window.[24] North-west of the library a room called the Alfred saloon had been added by 1814,[25] being fronted towards the bailey over a three-bayed arcade by a huge Coade stone bas-relief of King Alfred instituting trial by jury on Salisbury plain which was sculpted in 1797;[26] the room itself was unfinished in 1834. Beyond it the north-west end of the 16th-century range survived in 1876.[27]

The remains of the medieval hall on the south-west side of the south bailey,[28] occupied in the 18th century as stables and coach house with an entrance through the curtain wall, were cleared

1 *Gent. Mag.* lxvii (2), 883.
2 Wright, *Arundel* (1818), 39–40; cf. ibid. (1817), 19.
3 Para. based mainly on Dallaway, *Hist. W. Suss.* ii (1) (1819), 161–2 and facing p. 92; Colvin, *Biog. Dict. Brit. Architects*, 418, 819; *Connoisseur*, Mar. 1978, pp. 163, 165, 171.
4 *European Mag. and Lond. Rev.* xxxvi (1799), 302; *Beauties of Eng. and Wales, Suss.* 82; cf. Wright, *Arundel* (1818), 62; *Country Life*, 30 June 1983, p. 1796.
5 *Gent. Mag.* lxxxvi (2), 32.
6 *Beauties of Eng. and Wales, Suss.* 80.
7 *V.C.H. Warws.* viii. 462.
8 D. Linstrum, *Sir Jeffry Wyattville*, 166, 252; M. Girouard, *Return to Camelot*, 24.
9 Para. based mainly on Tierney, *Arundel*, i. 82–3; Dallaway, *Hist. W. Suss.* ii (1) (1819), 94, 162; *Gent. Mag.* lxiv (2), 697 and facing p. 694; lxx (2), 786.
10 *S.C.M.* x. 753; Wright, *Arundel* (1817), 22; illus. at W.S.R.O., PD 2207; *Illus. Lond. News*, 5 Dec. 1846, p. 360.
11 Wright, *Arundel* (1818), 54–5 and facing p. 49.
12 *European Mag. and Lond. Rev.* xlii (1802), 373; *Connoisseur*, Mar. 1978, pp. 167–8.
13 *European Mag. and Lond. Rev.* xxxvi (1799), 302; illus. at *Illus. Lond. News*, 5 Dec. 1846, p. 360.
14 Evans, *Worthing* (1805), 101.
15 A.C.M., MD 1354.
16 Wright, *Arundel* (1818), 62–4.
17 *European Mag. and Lond. Rev.* xxxvi (1799), 302; *Illus. Lond. News*, 5 Dec. 1846, pp. 356, 361; *Connoisseur*, Mar. 1978, p. 168; *Country Life*, 7 July 1983, p. 49.
18 A.C.M., MD 1354; illus. at W.S.R.O., PD 1843; *Country Life*, 7 July 1983, p. 47.
19 W.S.R.O., PD 1843; Wright, *Arundel* (1818), 42; *S.A.C.* cxxvi. 182.
20 B.L. King's Maps XLII. 12c; *Beauties of Eng. and Wales, Suss.* facing p. 77; Elwes & Robinson, *W. Suss.* facing p. 21; *Country Life*, 7 July 1983, p. 46.
21 Para. based mainly on Tierney, *Arundel*, i. 83; Dallaway, *Hist. W. Suss.* ii (1) (1819), 162–3 and facing p. 164; *Connoisseur*, Mar. 1978, pp. 162, 165–8, 170.
22 *Illus. Lond. News*, 20 Sept. 1845, p. 181.
23 Evans, *Worthing* (1805), 107; ibid. (1814), i. 165.
24 *Illus. Lond. News*, 20 Sept. 1845, p. 181.
25 Evans, *Worthing* (1814), i. 166.
26 Wright, *Arundel* (1818), 42–3; *S.A.C.* cxxvi. 181–2; illus. at *Country Life*, 7 July 1983, p. 47.
27 Elwes & Robinson, *W. Suss.* 20; cf. *Gent. Mag.* lxxiii (1), 130; Wright, *Arundel* (1818), 33; Tierney, *Arundel*, i. 54–5.
28 Para. based mainly on Tierney, *Arundel*, i. 79–80, 84–7; Dallaway, *Hist. W. Suss.* ii (1) (1819), 94, 163–4, and facing pp. 92, 164; *Plans of Arundel Cast.* 7, 15, 32.

away in 1806. Work began in the same year on a battlemented 'barons' hall' 70 ft. (21 metres) long, an early example of such a full-blown medieval revival.[29] The room, dedicated to 'Liberty championed by the barons in the reign of King John',[30] was on the first floor, above a Norman arcade fronting the bailey which also carried a paved walk to give access; its outer wall was the medieval curtain wall. In style it was 14th-century, and the elaborate roof of Spanish chestnut was inspired distantly by surviving medieval roofs; the plan, however, an elongated octagon, and the marble chimneypiece were far from medieval.[31] At the south-east end of the room was a musicians' gallery. The opposite end wall had a large painted-glass window by Joseph Backler representing the signing of Magna Carta, but only eight of the 12 projected side windows by Eginton showing ancestors of the duke were completed;[32] the figures were described in 1834 by the painter Constable as resembling 'drunk bargemen dressed up as crusaders'.[33] The room was nearly ready for roofing in 1814,[34] but could be fitted up only temporarily in 1815 for the fête to celebrate the sixth centenary of the signing of Magna Carta.[35] It had still not been completed in 1834 despite a provision in Duke Charles's will,[36] and was not used at Queen Victoria's visit in 1846.[37]

North-west of the barons' hall[38] a small new chapel in 15th-century style was in progress in 1806[39] and complete externally by 1814, with pinnacled buttresses and Perpendicular tracery.[40] The interior was finished by 1825[41] and the chapel was in use in 1845.[42] Beyond it a new gateway had been begun in 1809 to give a less constricted access to the south bailey than that provided by the medieval gatehouse, which in the later 18th century was considered low, crooked, and gloomy.[43] Intended to be 88 ft. (27 metres) high, and with a low four-centred arch, machicolations, and tall flanking hexagonal turrets, it had reached only 68 ft. (21 metres) before work ceased. In 1834 it had a temporary covering of wood, and it was still unfinished in 1851.[44] The first-floor corridor of the south-east range was continued along the south-west range by a paved promenade on the curtain wall *c.* 250 ft. (76 metres) long, which extended through the new gateway to the medieval gatehouse and gave fine views over the coast. Between the new gateway and the old gatehouse remains of one-storeyed medieval buildings still stood in 1856.[45]

Duke Charles's state rooms all had fittings of dark mahogany with carving of very high quality;[46] the surviving library is an example.[47] The gloomy effect was criticized after his death, as were the low proportions of the interiors and the lack of overall coherence in the design. In particular, Loudon in 1829 considered the south bailey lacked dignity because of its irregular shape, the poor design of its elevations, and the drop in level between the new gateway and the entrance to the south-east range.[48]

Little seems to have been done to the castle by Duke Bernard Edward (succ. 1815; d. 1842), but much refurbishment was carried out shortly before Queen Victoria's visit in 1846 by the firm of Morant, a royal suite of six rooms being created on the second floor of the south-east range.[49] About 1849 the Bevis tower was restored by William Burn, who also made unexecuted designs for further work between 1848 and 1853.[50] The King Alfred bas-relief in the south bailey was perhaps removed *c.* 1853.[51]

In 1859[52] Duke Henry Granville (d. 1860) began a programme of new building to the designs of M. E. Hadfield of Sheffield in a simpler and more massive Gothic style than that of Duke Charles, stone from Whitby again being used. The early 19th-century chapel and the unfinished gateway to the south bailey were demolished, and a new flint and stone gateway was built in 14th-century style. A grand staircase led thence to the barons' hall, forming a more direct entrance to the state rooms, while to the north-west, reached by an antechapel over the gateway, was a new five-bayed chapel, also in 14th-century style, above a ground-floor crypt. The chapel was to accommodate 200 persons seated, with a separate entrance for Catholics from the town. The crypt was nearly complete in 1861 and the shell of the building was finished by 1868;[53] in 1876 the chapel had a dedication to St. George.[54] In 1887 it was described as white, lofty, and very cold; it was not then in use, Duke Charles's dining room having reverted to its former use as a private chapel,[55] and the town congregation using the new church

29 Girouard, *Return to Camelot*, 297 n. 16.
30 *Gent. Mag.* lxxxvi (2), 32.
31 Wright, *Arundel* (1818), 41, 53; *Connoisseur*, Mar. 1978, pp. 162, 167; A.C.M., MD 799, no. 45; W.S.R.O., PD 1843.
32 Wright, *Arundel* (1817), 25–8.
33 *John Constable's Corresp.* iii (Suff. Rec. Soc. viii), 111.
34 Evans, *Worthing* (1814), i. 165.
35 A.C.M., MD 1354.
36 *Complete Peerage*, ix. 634 n.
37 *Illus. Lond. News*, 5 Dec. 1846, p. 361.
38 Para. based mainly on Dallaway, *Hist. W. Suss.* ii (1) (1819), 165 and facing pp. 90, 164; Tierney, *Arundel*, i. 84, 88.
39 A.C.M., MD 2306.
40 Evans, *Worthing* (1814), i. 166; *Connoisseur*, Mar. 1978, p. 162.
41 J. Rouse, *Beauties and Antiq. of Suss.* i. 322.
42 *Kelly's Dir. Suss.* (1845).
43 *Plans of Arundel Cast.* 15.
44 *A Visit to Arundel Cast.* (1851), 61.
45 A.C.M., MD 2592, drawing of SW. range, 1856; cf. S.A.S. libr., Sharpe drawings, no. 14A; B.L. Add. MS. 5674, f. 30, printed at *Suss. Views* (S.R.S.), 10.
46 *Gent. Mag.* lxx (2), 786; *European Mag. and Lond. Rev.* xxxvi (1799), 302; Wright, *Arundel* (1817), 25; Tierney, *Arundel*, i. 83; *S.C.M.* x. 753.
47 Illus. at *Connoisseur*, Mar. 1978, pp. 166–7.
48 Tierney, *Arundel*, i. 83, 89–90; *Creevey Papers*, ed. H. Maxwell, ii. 162; *Creevey*, ed. J. Gore, 289; *Gardener's Mag.* v (1829), 585–6.
49 *Illus. Lond. News*, 5 Dec. 1846, pp. 360, 362.
50 Colvin, *Biog. Dict. Brit. Architects*, 166; *A Visit to Arundel Cast.* (1851), 72; *Cat. of Drawings Colln. of R.I.B.A., B*, p. 121; A.C.M., MD 2021.
51 A.C.M., uncat. archit. drawings, drawings for billiard rm. 1853.
52 Para. based mainly on *Connoisseur*, Mar. 1978, pp. 170, 172; *Plans of Arundel Cast.* 32; A.C.M., MD 909, plan of cast. 1864; 2021, photos. of drawings of chapel; 2042–3, 2592; ibid. uncat. archit. drawings; W.S.R.O., PH 403; 696, f. 11.
53 *Visitors' Guide to Arundel* (1868), 18.
54 *Builder*, 19 Feb. 1876, p. 162; cf. *Miscellanea*, xiv (Cath. Rec. Soc. xxvii), 94, 96.
55 *Illus. Lond. News*, 9 Apr. 1887, p. 429, stating that the chapel then contained Duke Hen. Granville's marble effigy.

opened in 1873. The great Magna Carta window from the barons' hall was removed before 1866.[56]

A much larger programme of new work[57] was carried out by Duke Henry (d. 1917) between 1875 and 1909, almost all to the designs of the herald C. A. Buckler in 13th-century style, and using grey Somerset limestone in large part.[58] Like his father's work that of Duke Henry was austere and scholarly, the opposite of Duke Charles's; in place of Republican sympathies it expressed authority and tradition, much use being made of heraldic decoration. It parallels the contemporary work of the marquess of Bute at Cardiff castle and Mount Stuart (Bute),[59] and contains notable decorative work, including sculpture by Thomas Earp and stained glass by Hardman and Co. Part of the cost was met by sales of land in Sheffield.[60]

The state rooms in the south-east range[61] were reconstructed between the mid 1870s and *c.* 1900. Work was going on on the drawing room between 1875 and 1877. The dining room was rebuilt and extended further south-eastwards during the 1890s; it is of stone, with tall transverse arches and a timber minstrels' gallery. Duke Charles's main staircase was replaced in the early 1890s by a high, vaulted one of stone and Derbyshire marble which, however, went only between the first and second floors, small side stairs connecting with the ground floor. The side walls of the staircase carry statues, including the patron saints of the duke and duchess. At about the same time the first-floor corridor was rebuilt in stone with a ribbed vault. The south-east front overlooking the Arun valley was partly altered between 1879 and 1882,[62] and further reworked during the 1890s, when the new dining room was flanked by square turrets battered at the base. The façade of the range towards the south bailey was refaced in the early 1890s, acquiring a slightly projecting central tower.

A new kitchen and other offices[63] were built in the south-west wing between 1879 and 1882, the tall kitchen projecting beyond the medieval curtain wall. The rest of the south-west wing was completely rebuilt during the 1890s in a mixture of flint and ashlar. Hadfield's gateway and chapel were pulled down, the entrance to the bailey was re-routed through the medieval barbican and gatehouse, following the suggestion of Tierney,[64] and a new ground-floor chapel was built in 13th-century style. Of stone and Purbeck marble with stone vaulting and carving by Earp, it has an apse, two liturgical north aisles, a west gallery, and stained glass by Hardman and Co. The early 19th-century barons' hall still apparently stood in 1891, when it was the setting for the sale of 18th- and early 19th-century fixtures and fittings, including the Coade stone statues of Liberty and Hospitality made in 1798.[65] Its huge successor, with a hammerbeam roof and two end galleries, was finished by 1896 when the Sussex Archaeological Society lunched there,[66] but decorative features, including more stained glass by Hardman and Co., were still being added in 1899.[67] The new entrance to the state rooms, made *c.* 1894,[68] was through an unobtrusive ground-floor doorway between hall and chapel leading into a low vaulted undercroft, thence up a staircase, and so through the barons' hall. Externally the south-west range was articulated by two tall round towers of ashlar, also of the 1890s, which are battered at the base.

Between 1879 and 1882 the north-east range[69] was continued north-westwards by a billiard room, breakfast room, and boudoir *en suite* with the library, other private apartments being created above and below. A new ground-floor entrance to those rooms was provided from the bailey. The boudoir, large, white, and with a heavy timber ceiling, was described in 1887 as 'not like an ordinary boudoir'.[70] The façade of the range towards the bailey was closed to the north-west by a tall octagonal turret containing stairs to Duchess Flora's terrace garden, created at first-floor level to the north-west and linked to the north bailey garden.[71] The medieval tower at the north-east angle of the boudoir was restored and heightened as a vertical accent in the castle's silhouette. The entire length of the façade to the bailey was refaced. Alone of the major early 19th-century interiors the library was not destroyed, though its classical white marble chimneypieces were replaced *c.* 1897–1900 by Gothic ones contrived in recesses like chantry chapels in the thickness of the medieval curtain wall.[72] The private apartments on the second floor, of the 1890s and early 1900s, have internal timber-framing more domestic in character than the new rooms below.

The castle was entirely lit by electricity in 1897.[73] Many other contemporary services were similarly advanced, including service lifts, central heating, and the fire-fighting system.[74]

Duke Henry also set about restoring the ruined medieval parts of the castle, making them visually part of the modern house as they had not been before. In the early 19th century the remains of the keep had been covered in ivy both outside and in,[75] and from *c.* 1800 or before it was the haunt of several large horned owls;[76] in 1802 there were also an eagle and other foreign

56 *N. & Q.* 3rd ser. x. 341.
57 Para. based mainly on *Connoisseur*, Mar. 1978, pp. 172–85; J. M. Robinson, *Arundel Cast. Guide* (1994), 45–54. Cf. above, pl. facing p. 43.
58 A.C.M., MD 574.
59 J. M. Crook, *Wm. Burges*, 260–89.
60 A.C.M., A 2158.
61 Para. based mainly on *Connoisseur*, Mar. 1978, pp. 173–7; A.C.M., MD 2022, 2232; ibid. uncat. archit. drawings.
62 *Bldg. News*, 31 Mar. 1882, p. 386.
63 Para. based mainly on ibid.; *Connoisseur*, Mar. 1978, pp. 174–7, 179–81, 184–5; A.C.M., MD 574, 2022; ibid. uncat. archit. drawings.
64 Tierney, *Arundel*, i. 88–9.
65 A.C.M., MD 961.
66 *S.A.C.* lxxxv. 37.
67 A.C.M., MD 22, 2023.
68 Ibid. 21, Buckler to duke, 5 Feb. 1894.
69 Para. based mainly on *Connoisseur*, Mar. 1978, pp. 167, 174, 179, 182; *Bldg. News*, 31 Mar. 1882, p. 386 and pl.; A.C.M., MD 574, 2022; ibid. uncat. archit. drawings.
70 *Illus. Lond. News*, 9 Apr. 1887, p. 429.
71 Cf. below, castle grounds.
72 A.C.M., MD 2232.
73 Kimpton, *Arundel* (1897), 5; cf. A.C.M., MD 2159.
74 J. M. Robinson, *Arundel Cast. Guide* (1994), 46–7, 49, 52–3.
75 *S.C.M.* x. 753; Wright, *Arundel* (1817), 17; *Illus. Lond. News*, 20 Sept. 1845, p. 180; Cartland, *Arundel*, 102.
76 *S.C.M.* x. 753; Wright, *Arundel* (1818), 36–8; *Illus. Lond. News*, 5 Dec. 1846, p. 357.

birds.[77] The owls remained until 1868 or later.[78] The medieval gatehouse and barbican were also ivy-covered in the mid 19th century.[79] The keep was cleared of ivy in 1875, the walls being carefully restored.[80] Before 1876 the ground level under the gatehouse, which by the 18th century[81] had risen *c.* 3 ft. (1 metre), was lowered to bring the entrance back into use;[82] the medieval doors, adjusted to the 18th-century level, remained *c.* 3 ft. shorter in 1991. The restoration of the curtain wall and towers in the north bailey was being considered in the 1880s,[83] but little was done before 1901, when Buckler advocated using the surviving section next to the keep as a model.[84] The Bevis tower was restored in 1901–2, a new top storey being added.[85] At the top of the north bailey an oratory was created in the thickness of the curtain wall. The wall walk was complete by 1907.[86] Meanwhile the keep was fully but conservatively restored in 1905–6 under John Morley of Cambridge.[87] An external gateway to the north bailey had apparently been made south-east of the Bevis tower in the early 19th century;[88] it was replaced before 1909 by a new one, the moat being deepened to its original level at that point and crossed by a picturesque bridge. At the same time a gate was built between the two baileys.[89] The Coade stone lion and horse which flank the north bailey drawbridge were brought from the old New Shoreham suspension bridge at its demolition in the 1920s.[90]

Duke Henry's restoration left the castle's silhouette much more striking than before, especially when seen from the river valley to the east. The south bailey elevations, however, were little better co-ordinated, being still too varied in rooflines, floor levels, and fenestration, while the concealment of the entrance was both confusing and denied a potential focus for the design.

The castle was again extensively restored and repaired after 1975.[91] The late 19th-century private rooms in the north-east range were restored in the 1990s for permanent occupation by the family of the duke of Norfolk's eldest son Lord Arundel.[92]

CASTLE GROUNDS. A garden in the castle was mentioned between 1187, when it was in front of the king's chamber,[93] and the later 16th century.[94] In the late 13th century and early 14th there was also a garden outside, apparently in the Little park.[95] The old kitchen garden used as an orchard in the 1630s was evidently nearby, since it lay at the castle gate next to Castle green,[96] in an area described either as the outer court of the castle[97] or as part of the Little park.[98] There were apple, pear, plum, and filbert trees there in 1635.[99] A fishpond apparently in Park bottom was mentioned in 1275.[1] The surviving fishponds below the castle to the east may also be medieval. They seem to have been in use in 1636, when a 'new kitchen garden' lay near them.[2] A dovecot of unknown site was mentioned in 1576–7.[3]

In the 1630s the north bailey of the castle was used as a garden.[4] A formal layout may have existed in 1706;[5] then or later a spiral path, still visible in 1987, was made on the north side of the motte. In the later 18th century the north bailey contained the kitchen garden as well as the flower garden,[6] and had three stepped terraces at its north end[7] which also remained in 1987. An apricot tree planted in the mid 18th century covered *c.* 1,000 sq. ft. (93 sq. metres) of the curtain wall in the 1830s, producing large quantities of fruit, chiefly for tarts. Five large standard fig trees then also bore good crops.[8]

In the early 19th century or perhaps earlier the kitchen garden was moved elsewhere,[9] and by 1835 the north bailey had been laid out in an early revival of the formal parterre with flowers, shrubs, and a central fountain.[10] The outer face of the north bailey earthwork near the Bevis tower was thickly planted with shrubs and trees by 1825,[11] as the motte had been earlier.[12] In 1874 there were laurels and bays among the

77 *European Mag. and Lond. Rev.* xlii (1802), 374.

78 *N. & Q.* 3rd ser. v. 513; *Visitors' Guide to Arundel* (1868), 9.

79 Wright, *Arundel* (1818), 36; B.L. Add. MS. 42023, f. 5.

80 *W. Suss. Gaz.* 18 Nov. 1875.

81 B.L. Add. MS. 5674, f. 30, printed at *Suss. Views* (S.R.S.), 10; J. Harris, *Artist and Country Ho.* no. 364*b*, illus. above, pl. facing p. 42; cf. A.C.M., MD 2592, drawing of SW. range.

82 *Builder*, 19 Feb. 1876, p. 161.

83 A.C.M., uncat. archit. drawings.

84 Ibid. MD 2022.

85 Ibid. 22; *Connoisseur*, Mar. 1978, pp. 182, 185.

86 *Suss. Historical, Biographical, and Pictorial* (publ. A. North, 1907), s.v. duke of Norf.; cf. A.C.M., uncat. archit. drawings.

87 *Country Life*, 12 Dec. 1914, pp. 784–5; Goodliffe, *Littlehampton* (1909), 79; A.C.M., MD 22, 2024.

88 J. Rouse, *Beauties and Antiq. of Suss.* ii. 107; probably the 'new gateway' mentioned at *Jnl. of Horticulture and Cottage Gdnr.* 1 Jan. 1874, p. 12. It is not shown at *Plans of Arundel Cast.* 6, nor at Dallaway, *Hist. W. Suss.* ii (1) (1819), facing pp. 92, 164.

89 Goodliffe, *Littlehampton* (1909), 79–80; A.C.M., MD 949, 2025; ibid. uncat. archit. drawings.

90 Inf. from Dr. J. M. Robinson, Arundel Cast.

91 *Country Life*, 3 July 1980, p. 6.

92 Ibid. 3 Dec. 1992, pp. 72–6.

93 *Pipe R.* 1187 (P.R.S. xxxvii), 107; cf. P.R.O., C 132/42, no. 5; ibid. SC 6/1029/22, m. 1.

94 P.R.O., E 178/1906, f. 1v.; W.S.R.O., MP 1768.

95 P.R.O., C 133/104, no. 21, m. 2; C 135/24, m. 29; ibid. SC 6/1019/22, rot. 1, mentioning the gdn. 'de Wynyerd'. For name Wynyerd, above, growth of town.

96 A.C.M., MD 505, f. [2]; for Castle green, above, growth of town.

97 B.L. Add. MS. 5674, f. 25; P.R.O., E 178/1906, f. 1.

98 A.C.M., MD 535, f. 5; *Lavington Estate Archives*, ed. F. W. Steer, p. 29.

99 *Camd. Misc.* xvi (Camd. 3rd ser. lii), Hammond, 31.

1 P.R.O., SC 6/1019/22, rot. 1; the site was near bdry. of Great park: cf. below, woods and parks.

2 A.C.M., MD 505, f. [10]; cf. ibid. Hodskinson surv. 1778, f. 6.

3 Sandbeck Park, Rotherham, Lumley MS. EMA/1/5.

4 *Camd. Misc.* xvi (Camd. 3rd ser. lii), Hammond, 30–1; A.C.M., MD 505, f. [1].

5 A.C.M., A 283, pp. 5, 25.

6 Horsfield, *Hist. Suss.* ii. 128; cf. B.L. Add. MS. 15776, f. 231.

7 A.C.M., LM 10.

8 Ibid. MD 2278; Dallaway & Cartwright, *Hist. W. Suss.* ii (1) (1832), 101; *Gardener's Mag.* v (1829), 587.

9 Below, this section.

10 Horsfield, *Hist. Suss.* ii. 128; Eustace, *Arundel*, facing p. 226; *Connoisseur*, Mar. 1978, pp. 165, 182. It is not clear what W. A. Nesfield's contribution was there: ibid. 171 n. 7; *D.N.B.*

11 J. Rouse, *Beauties and Antiq. of Suss.* i. 296–7; ii, pl. 107.

12 B.L. Add. MS. 5674, f. 30, printed at *Suss. Views* (S.R.S.), 10; cf. *A Visit to Arundel Cast.* (1851), 62.

bedding plants in the north bailey, fruit trees and ivy along the curtain wall, and pampas grass on the terraces. The parterre was removed between 1885[13] and 1900; at the latter date there were four lawns with topiary bushes.[14] In 1902 Gertrude Jekyll made designs for eight large beds bordering a central lawn;[15] the single lawn had been created by 1914[16] and remained in the late 20th century, when the area was known as the tiltyard. There was a swimming pool in the lawn between the late 1930s and 1976,[17] and in 1987 the lawn was flanked by shrubs, topiary trees, and palm trees. Both sides of the motte were still planted with yews in 1914,[18] but they were later removed.

After his succession in 1815 Duke Bernard Edward[19] set about improving the surroundings of the newly restored castle to gain more privacy; in the same way as earlier at Warwick castle,[20] that was achieved partly at the town's expense. Houses at the north end of High Street opposite the churchyard were engrossed in the later 18th century and earlier 19th and demolished;[21] their plots, together with the site of the 'outer court' mentioned above, were laid out before 1817 with lawns, shrubberies, and plantations.[22] By the mid 19th century there was a conservatory on the lawn east of the churchyard, which had gone by 1896.[23]

The original approach to the castle had evidently been through the Little park, curving towards the medieval barbican and gatehouse.[24] In 1785 there was a gate in High Street near the north-east corner of the churchyard,[25] but with the closure of the upper part of High Street it was replaced by a 'commonplace brick cottage' on the site of the present High Street lodge, a drive being laid out from there to Duke Charles's new south bailey gateway.[26] In the mid 19th century further houses on the east side of High Street were demolished opposite Maltravers Street and the new London road, their plots also being thrown into the castle grounds.[27] The part of the castle's western ditch along the south bailey was then apparently removed.[28] A new lodge in Gothic style, and matching castellated stretches of wall to south and west of it, were built of grey Purbeck limestone in 1850–1 to the design of William Burn.[29] The entrance drive acquired at the same time low flanking embattled parapets.[30] By the mid 19th century the closure of Marygate Street and of the right of way from the top of the present High Street to the north door of the church[31] had enabled the medieval town wall earthwork east of the Marygate to be laid out in two terraces. By then, too, the Fitzalan chapel of the church had come to seem like a proprietary chapel, almost a garden ornament. Some specimen trees from the mid 19th century remained in the area in 1996.[32]

To the north-east and south-east the castle precinct was bounded in the early 19th century by Mill Lane. There had been a wall along the lane in the later 18th century[33] and perhaps earlier,[34] with a gate by the later 18th century[35] which in the mid 19th was called the bowling green gate.[36] The bowling green in the grounds south of the castle is mentioned elsewhere;[37] in the later 18th century there was also a gazebo nearby.[38]

Duke Henry Charles in 1850 attempted to enlarge the grounds eastwards by replacing Mill Lane with a new road further from the town.[39] That would have included, besides the earlier fishponds, the new dairy built in 1844–5 to the design of Robert Abraham on the site of Swanbourne water mill. Of flint in Tudor style, it was octagonal in plan with a wooden veranda and crowning lantern. Adjoining, and in the same style, were cowsheds and a dairyman's residence, together with a reading room for Duchess Charlotte opening on a terrace walk with an ornamental garden below.[40] There was also a kitchen garden nearby in 1874.[41] In 1893 the dairy supplied butter, milk, and cream daily to the family even when in London; the surplus milk was given to the poor.[42] The building was open for public inspection between 1849 and 1934.[43] In 1980 and later it was let to the Wildfowl Trust.[44]

The Little park north-west of the castle[45] was considered as part of the pleasure grounds in the mid and later 19th century,[46] the easternmost

13 *Jnl. of Horticulture and Cottage Gdnr.* 1 Jan. 1874, pp. 12–13; 8 Oct. 1885, p. 317.
14 *Gardeners' Mag.* 24 Mar. 1900, suppl. p. iii.
15 A.C.M., MD 22.
16 *Country Life*, 5 Dec. 1914, p. 752.
17 Inf. from Dr. J. M. Robinson and Mr. R. Puttock, Arundel Cast.
18 *Country Life*, 5 Dec. 1914, pp. 752, 754; 12 Dec. 1914, p. 788.
19 *Creevey Papers*, ed. H. Maxwell, ii. 162; Tierney, *Arundel*, i. 95.
20 *V.C.H. Warws.* viii. 432, 463–4.
21 Above, growth of town.
22 Wright, *Arundel* (1817), 30; cf. W.S.R.O., TD/W 5.
23 A.C.M., MD 2592, plan of cast. grounds; O.S. Maps 1/2,500, Suss. LXIII. 1 (1877 edn.); 6", Suss. LXIII. NW. (1899 edn.); site visible as parch marks in 1989.
24 Cf. A.C.M., LM 18.
25 W.S.R.O., MP 3041 (photocopy of town plan, 1785); cf. A.C.M., PM 107.
26 Hillier, *Arundel* (1847), 32; Dallaway, *Hist. W. Suss.* ii (1) (1819), facing p. 90; W.S.R.O., TD/W 5.
27 Above, growth of town; A.C.M., MD 2592, plan of cast. grounds.
28 Above, castle (cast. fabric); O.S. Map 1/2,500, Suss. LXIII. 1 (1877 edn.), showing remains.
29 A.C.M., uncat. archit. drawings; *Cat. of Drawings Colln. of R.I.B.A., B*, p. 121; for the stone, *A Visit to Arundel Cast.* (1851), 92; Goodliffe, *Littlehampton* (1903), 71–2.
30 Illus. at W.S.R.O., PH 403.
31 Above, growth of town.
32 Cf. *Jnl. of Horticulture and Cottage Gdnr.* 1 Jan. 1874, p. 12. Thick planting of grounds in later 19th cent. illus. at A.C.M., MD 799.
33 J. Harris, *Artist and Country Ho.* no. 364*a*, now dated 1783: inf. from Dr. J. M. Robinson, Arundel Cast.
34 A.C.M., uncat. late 14th-cent. acct. roll (Suss. box 3, no. 1).
35 Harris, op. cit. no. 364*a*; B.L. Add. MS. 5674, f. 29.
36 A.C.M., MD 2592, plan of cast. grounds.
37 Above, soc. and cultural activities (sport).
38 Harris, op. cit. no. 364*a*.
39 Above, communications (rds.).
40 A.C.M., A 1939; ibid. uncat. archit. drawings; W.S.R.O., F/PD 202, f. 5; *Illus. Lond. News*, 5 Dec. 1846, pp. 357–8; Cartland, *Arundel*, 114–16.
41 *Jnl. of Horticulture and Cottage Gdnr.* 1 Jan. 1874, p. 12; cf. ibid. 8 Oct. 1885, p. 319.
42 Kimpton, *Arundel* (1893), 28.
43 Ibid. (1897), 6; *Kelly's Dir. Suss.* (1855 and later edns.); A.C.M., MD 2327.
44 *Country Life*, 3 July 1980, p. 8; *W. Suss. Gaz.* 27 Apr. 1989.
45 For Little park, below, woods and parks.
46 e.g. A.C.M., MD 2592, plan of cast. grounds; *Jnl. of Horticulture and Cottage Gdnr.* 8 Oct. 1885, pp. 317–19.

section of the medieval town wall earthwork apparently being removed to give access and a vista to it. Beyond the park to the east the slopes of the river cliff were laid out with paths during the 19th century, one of which led from the north bailey to the dairy.[47]

After the replacement of Mill Lane by Mill Road in 1894 the boundary of the castle grounds was extended eastwards to the latter, where a new lodge, more convenient for the railway station, was built *c.* 1896 to the design of C. A. Buckler.[48] A new entrance drive led by a serpentine route to the medieval barbican, by then again in use, and the previous entrance drive was landscaped away.

The lack of an overall plan for the castle grounds, which Loudon had criticized in 1829,[49] was still evident in 1989, when in addition the Little park was no longer directly accessible from them and the eastern slopes below the castle had become overgrown and largely impassable. A major programme of redesign began soon afterwards. The lie of the land still meant, however, as Tierney had noted in 1834,[50] that the residential parts of the castle had no outlook over either the gardens or the park.

During the 19th and 20th centuries the closure of the old London road through the Marygate[51] made possible a further expansion of the castle precincts west and north-west of the church. The site of the Maison Dieu west of the churchyard may have been a kitchen garden by *c.* 1800 if its high red brick walls are partly 18th-century, as they seem. By 1815[52] it had become the chief kitchen garden for the castle. In the early 19th century there was a 'garden house' there[53] and by 1841, when there were hothouses and pine pits, figs and wall fruit were also grown.[54] Two iron-framed hothouses and two span-roofed houses were erected by the firm of Jones and Clark, later Henry Hope Ltd., in 1853–4;[55] one of the former survived in 1996. There were other glasshouses in the area by the 1870s, when fruit grown included peaches, grapes, figs, cherries, pineapples, and strawberries.[56] The garden gates were made in 1937 as a wedding present for Duke Bernard (d. 1975). After 1975[57] the area ceased to be used as a kitchen garden, part becoming a visitors' car park and part a tea garden.

By the early 19th century[58] the stables and coach house had been moved from the south bailey of the castle[59] to a site north of the Marygate. Further north, the present stable courtyard was then a farmyard,[60] with a 'deer house', either for hanging venison or for housing deer in winter, at its south-east corner; the building, which survived in part in 1988, was of knapped flint with stone dressings in the same Gothic style as Duke Charles's work at the castle. West of the farmyard in the early 19th century lay the estate timber yard and carpenter's shop, later the estate building yard.[61] A large domed ice house was constructed east of the old London road opposite the deer house at about that date.

By the mid 19th century the former stable area had become an orchard, the stables moving to their later site,[62] where the old farm buildings were replaced. A red brick and stone drill hall was put up near the building yard in the later 19th century;[63] it was converted to cottages in 1946–7.[64] The stable courtyard housed the estate fire engine in 1942,[65] but the coach house was converted to cottages *c.* 1947,[66] vehicles later being kept in the former castle electricity station,[67] of red brick and half-timbering, which had been built west of the kitchen garden *c.* 1894.[68] By 1970 the stable yard accommodated racehorses.[69] Ten bungalows for stable staff were built nearby in the 1950s.[70] Meanwhile the estate building yard had expanded to the north-west, where a steam sawmill was built by 1875, a railway joining the two sites.[71] After *c.* 1983 the old building yard became the estate office; the sawmill, however, remained in use.

The Marygate lodge on the old London road north of the stable courtyard was built *c.* 1853–5 to the design of William Burn.[72]

By 1874 the kitchen garden had expanded westwards beyond the London road; the new area, which was reached by a tunnel, sloped southwards, suiting early crops,[73] and was said to be the chief vegetable garden for the castle in 1885, when it also supplied flowers for the high altar of the Catholic church.[74] It ceased to be used in the mid 20th century.[75]

WOODS AND PARKS. Arundel parish lay within the forest or chase of Arundel, which extended from the river Arun almost to the

47 Royal Archives, Windsor Cast., Queen Victoria's jnl. 1–4 Dec. 1846; *Jnl. of Horticulture and Cottage Gdnr.* 1 Jan. 1874, p. 12; 8 Oct. 1885, p. 319; *Gardeners' Mag.* 24 Mar. 1900, suppl. p. vi.

48 A.C.M., uncat. archit. drawings.

49 *Gardener's Mag.* v (1829), 586–8.

50 Tierney, *Arundel*, i. 95.

51 Above, communications (rds.).

52 A.C.M., LM 18; cf. Wright, *Arundel* (1817), 39; ibid. (1818), 66–7.

53 A.C.M., PM 107.

54 W.S.R.O., Add. MS. 29745; ibid. TD/W 5; cf. A.C.M., uncat. archit. drawings, plans of kitchen gdn. area, 1852, 1855.

55 Order bks. of Messrs. Jones and Clark, formerly in possession of Crittall-Hope Ltd. (ref. from Dr. Robinson); A.C.M., uncat. archit. drawings, plans of hothos. 1853, and plan of kitchen gdn. area, 1855.

56 O.S. Map 1/2,500, Suss. LXIII. 1 (1877 edn.); *Jnl. of Horticulture and Cottage Gdnr.* 1 Jan. 1874, pp. 12, 14.

57 Inf. from Dr. Robinson. Kitchen gdn. *c.* 1973 illus. at F. W. Steer, *Cathedral Ch. of Our Lady and St. Phil., Arundel*, frontispiece.

58 Para. mainly based on A.C.M., LM 18; ibid. PM 107.

59 Cf. above, castle (cast. fabric).

60 Cf. below, agric.

61 e.g. A.C.M., MD 2592, plan of cast. grounds; W.S.R.O., BO/AR 16/1/152.

62 A.C.M., MD 2592, plan of cast. grounds; cf. W.S.R.O., BO/AR 16/1/152; O.S. Map 1/2,500, Suss. LXIII. 1 (1877 edn.).

63 Cf. A.C.M., uncat. archit. drawings, plans for drill hall, 1886.

64 W.S.R.O., BO/AR 16/1/251.

65 Ibid. BO/AR 16/1/152.

66 Ibid. BO/AR 16/1/278.

67 Inf. from Dr. Robinson.

68 Below, public servs.

69 O.S. Map 1/2,500, TQ 0007–0107 (1971 edn.).

70 Inf. from Dr. Robinson.

71 O.S. Map 1/2,500, Suss. LXIII. 1 (1877 edn.).

72 A.C.M., MD 1901; 2592, plan of cast. grounds; ibid. uncat. archit. drawings; *Cat. of Drawings Colln. of R.I.B.A.*, *B*, p. 121.

73 *Jnl. of Horticulture and Cottage Gdnr.* 1 Jan. 1874, p. 12; cf. O.S. Map 1/2,500, Suss. LXIII. 1 (1912 edn.).

74 *Jnl. of Horticulture and Cottage Gdnr.* 8 Oct. 1885, p. 319.

75 O.S. Maps 6", Suss. LXIII. NW. (1952 edn.); 1/2,500, TQ 0007–0107 (1971, 1979 edns.).

Hampshire border and from the coast to the north side of the South Downs.[76] There were two medieval parks in the parish, the Great park in the west, which later became Park farm, and a home park called the Little park, which in 1995 was the castle cricket ground. The modern landscaped park north of the town was created in the late 18th and early 19th centuries, and extends into South Stoke and Houghton.

GREAT PARK. The Great park was apparently made by Roger de Montgomery (d. 1094), since a hide formerly of Tortington was included in it between 1066 and 1086.[77] It was not adjacent to the castle, but occupied less fertile land in the west part of the parish.[78]

In 1275 the north and south boundaries of the Great park seem to have been roughly those of the ancient parish; on the east side the pale ran above Park bottom to the east, and on the west side west of the modern Park Farmhouse.[79] The park was said to contain 450 a. in 1589.[80] In 1570 the pale was said to be three miles round,[81] but by the earlier 17th century its eastern side seems to have been removed.[82] The park was apparently enlarged before 1636, when its total area was given as 845 a. (342 ha.), including 216 a. called the new ground; a distinction was then made between the 494 a. south-west of Park bottom and the 117 a. north-east of it.[83] In 1661 the park was said to have 823 a.[84] and in the 18th century between 823 a. and 960 a.[85] Much of the pale was destroyed during or after the siege of the town in 1643–4.[86] Repairs were carried out in and after 1657,[87] though in 1675 only the south side and the southern parts of the east and west sides seem still to have existed.[88] Traces of the bank survived on the south side in 1996 near the beginning of the track leading from the Chichester–Arundel road to Slindon.[89]

The main gate to the park, at the south-east corner, may have been called Parkgate in the early 15th century.[90] Two other gates besides were mentioned in 1275.[91] The gate in or near Park bottom by the leper hospital was presumably the same as the Hermitage gate of 1661; the 'gate of Bogherwerth', evidently on the north side, was perhaps replaced by Sherwood gate mentioned in 1661. Other gates recorded in the 17th century were 'Boyers', presumably Bowyers, gate[92] on the south-east; Slindon gate, a 'postern gate', and 'Glastis' gate on the south-west (the first two perhaps the same); and Betts gate on the south, possibly replacing the 'stile (*scaleram*) of Tortington' mentioned in 1275.[93] Yewtree gate on the north-west side was mentioned *c.* 1875.[94] In 1275 there were two deerleaps on the east side and two or more on the west.

Oak timber was mentioned in the park in 1244[95] and 1280, beech between 1280[96] and 1722,[97] and maple in 1661.[98] In 1570 the park was said to be 'indifferently well wooded'[99] but in the earlier 17th century it seems to have been chiefly woodland,[1] though much timber was cut down in 1644, partly to repair the castle and partly to remove possible cover for an advancing enemy.[2] Both underwood and wind-fallen wood were apparently sold in 1275,[3] and wood in both the Great and Little parks in 1525–6.[4] In the mid 17th century 110 a. in the south-west part of the Great park were managed as coppice for sale, as the Waterwood (29 a.) in the south-east may also have been.[5] In 1702 a wood in the Great park belonged to a Mr. Fugar, presumably the shipwright Joseph Fugar.[6]

Sherwood plain in the north-west and Crossham lawn in the south-west, both mentioned in 1661,[7] and East and West Waterwood plain mentioned in 1772[8] were perhaps survivals of medieval 'lawns' or areas of open grassland. There were at least 28 a. of meadow in 1272,[9] perhaps in Park bottom, where Pond mead was mentioned in 1732,[10] or on the south side, where meadow land in 'Parkwysse' was mentioned in 1275[11] and Rooks mead, producing hay, in 1658.[12]

Deer are recorded in the Great park in the later 13th century;[13] in 1301 the earl of Arundel could take five bucks and seven does a year.[14] Henry VIII enjoyed hunting there in 1526.[15] In 1570 there were 300 or 400 fallow deer and *c.* 24 red deer;[16] 'stately herds of deer' were seen by a visitor in 1635.[17] About 500 deer were said to have been killed by the Parliamentary soldiers in 1644.[18] The herd was replenished in or before

76 *S.R.S.* lxvii. 92–3, 105–6; Tierney, *Arundel*, i. 25–6; *Cal. Inq. Misc.* i, pp. 155, 384; *Goodwood Estate Archives*, i, ed. F. W. Steer and J. Venables, pp. 38, 153; Hist. MSS. Com. 8, *9th Rep. I, D. & C., St. Paul's*, p. 41; A.C.M., PM 193; cf. ibid. MD 535, f. 6v.

77 *V.C.H. Suss.* i. 431.

78 A.C.M., A 339, Arundel surv. 1702, f. 2. For descent of park, below, manor and other estates.

79 P.R.O., SC 6/1019/22, rot. 1.

80 Ibid. E 178/1906, f. 1.

81 A.C.M., MD 535, f. 6v.

82 Ibid. PM 193; but cf. ibid. MD 505, ff. [7v., 16].

83 Ibid. MD 505, f. [5].

84 Ibid. PM 87.

85 Ibid. D 6266; ibid. H 1/3; W.S.R.O., Par. 8/6/8.

86 *L.J.* vi. 592.

87 A.C.M., A 262, ff. [8, 38]; 263, acct. 1664.

88 W.S.R.O., PM 12.

89 Cf. A.C.M., FC 148; S.M.R. 1323.

90 *S.R.S.* lxvii. 118; A.C.M., MD 719, f. [2], describing the Waterwood at SE. corner in 1722 as seriously damaged by the 'ways leading to the park'. For Waterwood, below, this section.

91 Rest of para. based mainly on A.C.M., PM 87, 193; P.R.O., SC 6/1019/22, rot. 1.

92 Cf. below, this section.

93 'Crossham stile', depicted in early 17th cent., was presumably the same: A.C.M., PM 193; cf. ibid. FC 399, map of Tortington, 1724.

94 O.S. Map 6", Suss. XLIX (1880 edn.).

95 *Close R.* 1242–7, 174.

96 *Cal. Close*, 1279–88, 15; cf. W.S.R.O., A.B.A., F2/11.

97 A.C.M., MD 719, f. [2].

98 Ibid. A 263, acct. 1661.

99 Ibid. MD 535, f. 6v.

1 Ibid. PM 193.

2 *L.J.* vi. 592, 693; vii. 25–6, 39–40; cf. A.C.M., PM 87.

3 P.R.O., SC 6/1019/22, rot. 1.

4 A.C.M., A 241, rot. 12d.

5 Ibid. PM 87; cf. ibid. A 263, acct. 1663.

6 Ibid. A 339, Arundel surv. 1702, f. 2v.; below, timber trades.

7 A.C.M., PM 87.

8 Ibid. H 1/3. The former was divided between Middle and Lower plain *c.* 1841: W.S.R.O., TD/W 5.

9 P.R.O., C 132/42, no. 5.

10 A.C.M., D 6266.

11 P.R.O., SC 6/1019/22, rot. 1.

12 A.C.M., A 262, f. [21]; for location, below, Tortington, intro.

13 *Cal. Close*, 1272–9, 291.

14 *S.R.S.* lxvii. 2.

15 *L. & P. Hen. VIII*, iv (2), p. 1058.

16 A.C.M., MD 535, f. 6v.

17 *Camd. Misc.* xvi (Camd. 3rd ser. lii), Hammond, 33.

18 Hist. MSS. Com. 5, *6th Rep., H.L.* p. 25.

1659 from Cowdray park near Midhurst.[19] In 1657 there was a deer house in the park,[20] either for hanging venison or for housing animals in winter.

Pannage for swine was mentioned between the later 12th century and 1589; in 1525–6 the income from the Great and Little parks together was £8 2*s.* 8*d.*[21] There was both winter and summer pasture for cattle in 1275,[22] and in 1525–6 the agistment of the two parks produced £1 4*s.* 6*d.*[23] Cattle were still kept in 1658, when Lady Anne Howard, wife of Henry Howard of Albury (Surr.), later duke of Norfolk, had a dairy apparently in the Great park; at about the same date her husband's horses seem also to have grazed there.[24] There were rabbits in the park in 1644,[25] and in 1702, when they were spoiling the trees.[26] An eyrie of sparrowhawks in the park was destroyed by bustards before 1272.[27]

A keeper was mentioned in 1244,[28] and a parker, who rendered annually for his bailiwick a silver cup worth 13*s.* 4*d.*, in 1272.[29] A ranger in the early 15th century was apparently responsible also for the Little park.[30] By 1576 the office of keeper of the Great park had become honorific and was held by a gentleman.[31]

A keeper's lodge was mentioned in 1570,[32] and in the early 17th century occupied a roughly central site in the park.[33] In 1636 it had adjacent yards and gardens.[34] It was repaired in the later 1650s,[35] perhaps after Civil war damage. Another lodge called Bowyers lodge in 1636 perhaps lay in the south-east.[36] There was a lodge in the north part of the park besides in 1732.[37]

A fishpond apparently within the park was mentioned in 1275.[38] It was perhaps the same as the great pond of 17 a. which in 1636 lay in Park bottom near the south-east corner of the park.[39] Fish from the pond were sold in 1662.[40]

In 1702 the Great park was let. A rabbit warren was felt to be the most suitable use because of the poor soil,[41] but in 1732 the duke of Norfolk leased the land to Abraham Ibbotson for 11 years for conversion to a farm.[42] A large area was arable in 1772, when sheep were kept as well; there was a barn on the site of the modern Park Farmhouse. The closes in 1778 were large. In 1772 there were still 190 a. of woodland in the former park including the Waterwood; East Sherwood rough and Red Lane rough in the north; and Cricket Hill wood in the east.[43] Part of the north end of the former park remained rough ground in the 1870s,[44] and in 1986 was open grassland with some large spreading beeches and yews of parkland type.

THE REWELL. The area called the Rewell west of the Great park formed a separate bailiwick[45] or 'walk'[46] of Arundel forest. In the mid 16th century it extended into Madehurst,[47] and in 1570 it was said to be *c.* 20 miles round;[48] the total area was given as 335 a. in 1636[49] and *c.* 380 a. in the late 19th century.[50] It is not clear whether the linear earthwork which is followed by both its western boundary and that of the parish is medieval or earlier.[51] The Rewell had its own ranger in the early 15th century[52] and its own keeper or forester in the 1570s,[53] but in 1589 the keeper was also keeper of the Great park.[54] No record of a separate keeper has been found after 1605.[55] A keeper's lodge stood roughly in the centre of the Rewell in the early 17th century.[56]

In the Middle Ages the Rewell apparently had both woods and open pasture.[57] Common pasture rights were mentioned in 1302.[58] There is no medieval evidence that the Rewell was commonable by all the inhabitants of an area of the county like the Wealden commons of the lathes of Kent,[59] though the pasturing of pigs there in 1587 by two men of Angmering and Amberley suggests it.[60] Enclosures of oblong shape whose earthworks survived in the late 20th century seem likely to be medieval pastoral enclosures.[61] Deer were kept at the Rewell in 1331[62] and in the 17th century,[63] and pannage for pigs brought in £10 9*s.* 6*d.* in 1525–6.[64] Sheep, cattle, and horses were all pastured there *c.* 1600.[65]

By 1636 the Rewell contained 245 a. of woods and only 90 a. of pasture, called the Plain;[66] it remained mostly woodland thereafter.[67] There

19 A.C.M., A 262, f. [38]. 20 Ibid. f. [8].
21 *Pipe R.* 1178 (P.R.S. xxvii), 55; Dugdale, *Mon.* ii (1661), 144; *S.R.S.* lxvii. 2; A.C.M., A 241, rot. 12d.; P.R.O., C 132/42, no. 5; ibid. E 178/1906, f. 1.
22 P.R.O., SC 6/1019/22, rot. 1.
23 A.C.M., A 241, rot. 12d.
24 Ibid. 262, ff. [6v., 21].
25 *S.R.S.* liv. 61, presumably referring to Great park.
26 A.C.M., A 339, Arundel surv. 1702, f. 2v.
27 *Cal. Inq. Misc.* i, p. 137. 28 *Cal. Lib.* 1240–5, 276.
29 P.R.O., C 132/42, no. 5. 30 *S.R.S.* lxvii. 115.
31 Sandbeck Park, Rotherham, Lumley MS. EMA/1/5.
32 A.C.M., MD 535, f. 6v. 33 Ibid. PM 193.
34 Ibid. MD 505, f. [5]; cf. W.S.R.O., Ep. I/29/8/92.
35 A.C.M., A 262, ff. [7v., 38]; cf. ibid. A 263, acct. 1661.
36 Ibid. MD 505, f. [5]; cf. Bowyers gate: above, this section. 37 A.C.M., D 6266.
38 P.R.O., SC 6/1019/22, rot. 1.
39 A.C.M., MD 505, f. [5]; *L.J.* vii. 26; cf. above, intro.
40 A.C.M., A 263, acct. 1663.
41 Ibid. A 339, Arundel surv. 1702, f. 2.
42 Ibid. D 6266, incl. husbandry covenants.
43 Ibid. H 1/3; Gardner, *Suss. Map* (1778–83); cf. O.S. Map 6", Suss. XLIX–L, LXIII (1879–80 edn.).
44 O.S. Map 6", Suss. XLIX (1880 edn.).
45 A.C.M., A 241, rot. 12d.; P.R.O., SC 6/Eliz. I/2214, rot. 52.
46 A.C.M., MD 535, f. 6v.; 719, f. [iv.]; P.R.O., E 178/1906, f. 1v. The name perhaps means 'rough nook of land': *P.N. Staffs.* (E.P.N.S.), i. 136; cf. *P.N. Suss.* (E.P.N.S.), i. 137.
47 *Cal. Assize Rec. Suss. Eliz. I*, pp. 36, 207; cf. P.R.O., E 134/3 Jas. I East./28, rott. 3–4.
48 A.C.M., MD 535, f. 6v.
49 Ibid. MD 505, f. [5]. 50 Ibid. H 1/7.
51 S.M.R. 1305, 1308; cf. above, intro.
52 *S.R.S.* lxvii. 115.
53 A.C.M., MD 535, f. 6v.; Sandbeck Park, Rotherham, Lumley MS. EMA/1/5. 54 P.R.O., E 178/1906, f. 1v.
55 Ibid. E 134/3 Jas. I East./28.
56 A.C.M., PM 193; cf. ibid. 87.
57 e.g. P.R.O., C 132/42, no. 5.
58 Ibid. C 133/104, no. 21, m. 2.
59 K. P. Witney, *Jutish Forest, passim.*
60 *Cal. Assize Rec. Suss. Eliz. I*, p. 207; cf. P.R.O., SC 2/205/55, f. 12; above, Avisford Hund.; below, Tortington, econ. hist. (agric.). 61 S.M.R. 1306, 1308.
62 *Cal. Inq. p.m.* vii, p. 227.
63 A.C.M., A 262, f. [11]; P.R.O., E 134/3 Jas. I East./28, rot. 4d.
64 A.C.M., A 241, rot. 12d.; cf. *Cal. Assize Rec. Suss. Eliz. I*, p. 36.
65 P.R.O., E 134/3 Jas. I East./28, rot. 4d.
66 A.C.M., MD 505, f. [5].
67 e.g. ibid. A 339, Arundel surv. 1702, f. 2v.; W.S.R.O., TD/W 5; O.S. Map 6", Suss. XLIX (1880 and later edns.); *250 Yrs. of Mapmaking in Suss.* ed. H. Margary, pls. 5, 14, 26.

was mixed coppice with standard trees, chiefly birch and oak, in the early 18th century, when timber there was apparently sold to the shipbuilder George Moore.[68] By 1772 the area had been laid out with the diagonal rides to facilitate shooting[69] which remained in 1991. In 1929 the south-facing slopes were thickly clad with hazel and sweet chestnut.[70] By 1981 Rewell wood, comprising 288 a. in Arundel, Binsted, and Houghton, was let to the Forestry Commission;[71] beech, sweet chestnut, and conifers grew there in 1987.

Other woods in the parish included the earl's wood called Moselee in 1158,[72] which has not been located but may be the same as the wood of Arundel mentioned in the 1270s,[73] and the hangers on the cliff above the river Arun: Park or Little park hanger mentioned from 1636 and Castle hanger mentioned from 1702.[74]

LITTLE PARK. The Little park north-west of the castle seems to include the area called Wynyard (i.e. vineyard) in 1158,[75] which in 1275 was partly a garden and partly pasture.[76] The modern name is recorded from 1301, when deer were being kept there.[77] In 1570 there were *c.* 30 fallow deer and two or three red deer. A keeper was recorded at the same date,[78] and pannage for swine was taken during the 16th century.[79] The park had 26 a. in 1636;[80] the 120 a. mentioned in 1589 presumably included land adjacent to the castle considered part of the park at that period.[81] Part at least of the pale survived in 1615 and perhaps later.[82] The park was let in 1641,[83] but was in hand in the early 18th century[84] and presumably always thereafter.[85] In the 18th century it seems generally to have been used as a home paddock for the castle,[86] but there were apparently deer there *c.* 1750.[87] A hay crop was taken in 1711.[88]

Only a small part of the Little park was wooded in 1570,[89] but beech trees grew there in 1625.[90] After *c.* 1815 the park was incorporated into the enlarged pleasure grounds of the castle.[91] In the mid and later 19th century it apparently contained an arboretum,[92] and in 1874 it was bordered on all sides by shrubs, with oak, elm, lime, hawthorn, and spruce outside.[93] The surrounding earthworks had already been overgrown with trees, notably elm and beech, by 1828, making a striking backcloth to the church and castle as seen from Crossbush in Lyminster.[94] The trees were thinned after storm damage in 1989–90. Meanwhile, the central area of the park had been levelled in 1895 to create the castle cricket ground.[95]

THE MODERN PARK. The rebuilding of the castle after 1786 required a setting worthy of it and, as earlier at Warwick[96] and Petworth,[97] a large new park was created beyond the Little park to the north, on the site of arable, sheepdown, and a rabbit warren in South Stoke parish.[98] Much land had been emparked by 1789,[99] and by the mid 1790s, after the first diversion of the London road in 1793, the park contained several hundred acres.[1] By the 1810s a wall with lodges had been built to enclose over 1,100 a., which could contain 1,000 head of deer.[2] The area was not greatly increased thereafter.[3] There were at least two keepers in 1815.[4] Extensive planting had begun by 1814, clumps of trees, notably beech, alternating with open lawns from which there were wide views of the coast. Pughdean bottom, the valley above Swanbourne lake, was particularly remarked on in 1819 for the contrast of old woods on its west slope with new terraced plantations to the east.[5] Besides beech in 1900 there were elm, ash, oak, maple, and various coniferous trees in the park.[6] Many trees had reached maturity by 1987, when much damage was sustained in a great storm. Large-scale replanting, mainly with beech, was undertaken later to restore the original appearance of the park.

In the early 1890s there were between 600 and 1,000 fallow deer, many nearly white in colour, and 30 red deer which chiefly lived in the remoter and more wooded parts of the park. Other animals kept at the same date were Indian or Brahmin cattle, Cashmere goats, llamas, and South American ostriches.[7] Both red and fallow deer could be seen in 1939, together with dark-

68 A.C.M., A 339, Arundel surv. 1702, ff. 2v., 5v.; ibid. MD 719, f. [2]; W.S.R.O., Par. 8/6/8; cf. below, timber trades.

69 A.C.M., H 1/3.

70 E. C. Curwen, *Prehist. Suss.* 137.

71 Inf. from Mr. J. D. Cameron, Forestry Com. (1981).

72 W.S.R.O., Par. 8/6/5, f. 3.

73 *Abbrev. Rot. Orig.* (Rec. Com.), i. 32–3; *Cal. Fine R.* 1272–1307, 109.

74 A.C.M., A 339, Arundel surv. 1702, f. 2; ibid. MD 505, f. [1]; 719, ff. [2v.–3]; W.S.R.O., Par. 8/6/8.

75 W.S.R.O., Par. 8/6/5, f. 3v.; cf. above, growth of town; below, agric.

76 P.R.O., SC 6/1019/22, rot. 1; SC 6/1029/22.

77 *S.R.S.* lxvii. 2.

78 A.C.M., MD 535, f. 6v.

79 Ibid. A 241, rot. 12d.; P.R.O., E 178/1906, f. 1.

80 A.C.M., MD 505, f. [1].

81 P.R.O., E 178/1906, f. 1; above, castle grounds.

82 W.S.R.O., Ep. I/25/1 (1615, 1663).

83 A.C.M., A 1351.

84 Ibid. 339, Arundel surv. 1702, f. 3; W.S.R.O., Par. 8/6/8.

85 e.g. A.C.M., H 1/19; ibid. MD 2180; W.S.R.O., TD/W 5.

86 e.g. A.C.M., Hodskinson surv. 1778, f. 6; ibid. MD 2180.

87 *Topographer*, iii (1791), 202.

88 A.C.M., A 284, p. 16. The park keeper mentioned in the par. in 1767 was presumably of the Little park since Great park was then disparked: *Returns of Papists, 1767* (Cath. Rec. Soc.), ii. 145.

89 A.C.M., MD 535, f. 6v.

90 W.S.R.O., A.B.A., F2/11.

91 Above, castle grounds.

92 A.C.M., MD 2592, plan of cast. grounds; *Jnl. of Horticulture and Cottage Gdnr.* 8 Oct. 1885, p. 319.

93 *Jnl. of Horticulture and Cottage Gdnr.* 1 Jan. 1874, p. 12.

94 Dally, *Bognor* (1828), 214; Tierney, *Arundel*, i. 8, 96.

95 Above, soc. and cultural activities.

96 *V.C.H. Warws.* viii. 470–3; cf. ibid. 419, 468.

97 *Apollo*, May 1977, pp. 337–8.

98 Dallaway, *Hist. W. Suss.* ii (1) (1819), 166; below, agric.; S. Stoke, intro.

99 A.C.M., MD 2469, particulars of vicarage; 2534.

1 *Univ. Brit. Dir.* ii. 55; *Gent. Mag.* lxiv (2), 697; Gardner, *Suss. Map* (1795); above, communications (rds.).

2 Evans, *Worthing* (1814), ii. 103; Dallaway, *Hist. W. Suss.* ii (1) (1819), 166; cf. Greenwood, *Suss. Map* (1825).

3 W.S.R.O., TD/W 5; O.S. Map 6", Suss. L (1879 and later edns.).

4 A.C.M., DB 68.

5 Evans, *Worthing* (1814), ii. 103; Dallaway, *Hist. W. Suss.* ii (1) (1819), 166; *Worthing Parade*, i (Worthing Art Devel. Scheme), 163.

6 *Gardeners' Mag.* 24 Mar. 1900, suppl. p. vi.

7 J. Whitaker, *Deer-Parks and Paddocks of Eng.* 151; Kimpton, *Arundel* (1893), 26. *V.C.H. Suss.* ii. 306 gives over 200 red deer in 1907.

coloured Japanese deer and a few muntjak, but only the red deer remained after the Second World War until their dispersal in 1959.[8] Some roe deer lived around the castle earthworks in the 1980s.[9]

The new park was evidently open to the public in 1805,[10] as it always seems to have been since except for a short time after 1842.[11] After the arrival of the railway in 1846 it became a popular object of excursions from the coastal resorts, from Portsmouth, and from London.[12] Since the mid 19th century numerous fêtes and similar events have been held there,[13] and it was the setting for free entertainments given by Duke Henry (d. 1917) to local people to celebrate Queen Victoria's two Jubilees and the Coronation of 1911.[14] Between *c.* 1890 and 1934 summer training camps were held there for volunteers and other army units.[15] During the Second World War gallops were laid out in the park for training racehorses.[16]

A three-storeyed Gothic banqueting house of triangular plan with polygonal corner turrets was built near the old London road *c.* 1787. Known from the name of its architect as Hiorne's tower,[17] it is of flint and stone chequerwork, and remarkably correct in detail for its date. Its site on the brow of the hill yields fine coastal views and stamps the park as belonging to a castle. The embattled terrace round it was laid out apparently between 1860 and 1879.[18] For some years before *c.* 1960 the tower housed estate workers.[19] Nearby stands a Greek altar found at the museum at Sebastopol in 1855.[20]

In 1814 there were said also to be Gothic temples and other ornamental buildings in the park, including one called the Ladies' bower.[21] Another called Mount Pleasant was covered in ivy in 1817.[22] None survived in 1990. A Gothic-style lodge in flint and stone called the Green Doors lodge was built on the line of the new London road of 1793, perhaps to the design of Duke Charles (d. 1815), and survived in 1989, the second diversion of the London road in 1803 having brought it within the park.[23] Butler's lodge, leading into the new park from the town, existed in the early 19th century[24] and was later enlarged; it had its present name by 1851.[25] There are other lodges in South Stoke and Houghton parishes.

Arundel Park house was built for the duke of Norfolk between 1958 and 1962 as a smaller, more private house *c.* ½ mile (800 metres) north-west of the castle. Designed by the Hon. Claud Phillimore, it is in early 19th-century classical style with canted wings, and has wide views of the coast.[26] Duke Bernard and his family lived there from 1961,[27] and in 1995 it was still the home of his widow. Six pieces of classical sculpture from the collection of Thomas Howard, earl of Arundel (d. 1646), stood outside the entrance in 1996.[28]

MANOR AND OTHER ESTATES. The manor or borough of *ARUNDEL* generally descended with the rape.[29] In 1253 it was wrongly said to have been ancient demesne.[30]

The descent of the *CASTLE* is given elsewhere.[31] The *GREAT* and *LITTLE PARKS* and Rewell wood also descended with the rape.[32]

The *BURGESS BROOKS*, comprising 80–100 a. in the bend of the river Arun east of the town, were also once part of the demesne lands of the lords of Arundel, but the borough was leasing them by the 1270s, and after the mid 16th century its estate became a freehold. In 1902 the lands were exchanged by the town council to the duke of Norfolk for land in Tortington.[33] Meanwhile much other marshland had remained in demesne.[34]

Arundel priory had lands in the parish in 1230,[35] which in 1291 were rented at 19*s.* 6*d.*[36] More land was acquired in 1353.[37] The priory's property passed in the later 14th century to Arundel college,[38] whose holdings were further augmented in 1391.[39] In 1535 the college had rents and farms in Arundel worth £4 1*s.* 11*d.*[40] At the Dissolution its lands passed to Henry FitzAlan, earl of Arundel (d. 1580).[41]

Holy Trinity hospital (the Maison Dieu) owned lands in the parish from 1395,[42] which at

8 G. K. Whitehead, *Deer of G.B. and Ireland*, 91–2, 277, 378; E. C. Curwen, *Prehist. Suss.* 137; Cartland, *Arundel*, 107.

9 Inf. from Dr. J. M. Robinson and Mrs. Ian Rodger, Arundel Cast.

10 Evans, *Worthing* (1805), 110.

11 Ibid. (1814), ii. 102–4; *Kelly's Dir. Suss.* (1874); J. M. Robinson, *Dukes of Norf.* (1982), 196; Kimpton, *Arundel* (1897), 6; *Country Life*, 3 July 1980, p. 6.

12 e.g. *Arundel Cast. Archives*, ii. 198; *Gardeners' Mag.* 24 Mar. 1900, suppl. p. vi; A.C.M., MD 2406.

13 e.g. A.C.M., MD 2406; Jesse, *Agric. of Suss.* 119.

14 A.C.M., MD 1716; W.S.R.O., BO/AR 24/1/1, docs. relating to Jubilee celebrations, 1887; 24/1/4; *Worthing Gaz.* 30 June 1897; Cartland, *Arundel*, 60, 62.

15 *Rec. of Royal Suss. Regiment*, ed. A. Readman, pp. 22, 163–71, 175–83; *Ellis's Popular Guide Arundel* (Arundel, pre 1893), 24 (copy in C.I.H.E. libr.); Cartland, *Arundel*, 80–2; W.S.R.O., PH 8183–4.

16 J. M. Robinson, *Latest Country Hos.* 129.

17 Colvin, *Biog. Dict. Brit. Architects*, 419.

18 W.S.R.O., F/PD 204, f. 12; ibid. PD 813.

19 *Country Life*, 3 July 1980, p. 7.

20 *S.C.M.* xxix. 452.

21 Evans, *Worthing* (1814), ii. 103–4.

22 Wright, *Arundel* (1817), 30.

23 A.C.M., LM 18; above, secular bldgs.; communications (rds.); for the name, O.S. Map 1/25,000, TQ 00/10 (1979 edn.).

24 A.C.M., PM 107.

25 *Arundel Rds.* facing p. [3].

26 J. M. Robinson, *Latest Country Hos.* 127–9, 198.

27 *Worthing Gaz.* 23 May 1962.

28 *Trans. Lond. and Mdx. Arch. Soc.* xxvi. 248; inf. from Mrs. Rodger.

29 e.g. *V.C.H. Suss.* i. 421; *Pipe R.* 1179 (P.R.S. xxviii), 38; *Cal. Inq. p.m.* i, p. 278; vii, p. 226; *S.R.S.* xix. 9–10; lxvii. 2, 115; 3 Chas. I, c. 4 (Priv. Act); 26 & 27 Vic. c. 7 (Private). In 1610 it was called the man. *of* the boro.: P.R.O., C 142/314, no. 150.

30 *Close R.* 1251–3, 337; cf. ibid. 1259–61, 99.

31 Above, castle (institutional hist.).

32 e.g. *Cal. Chart. R.* 1257–1300, 187; *Cal. Inq. Misc.* vi, p. 222; A.C.M., H 1/3; ibid. MD 535, f. 6v.; P.R.O., C 132/42, no. 5; W.S.R.O., TD/W 5; 3 Chas. I, c. 4 (Priv. Act); but cf. e.g. *Pipe R.* 1198 (P.R.S. N.S. ix), 227.

33 Below, agric.; boro. govt.; W.S.R.O., BO/AR 10/5.

34 Below, agric.

35 *Close R.* 1227–31, 403; cf. W.S.R.O., Par. 8/7/35.

36 *Tax. Eccl.* (Rec. Com.), 139.

37 *Cal. Pat.* 1350–4, 399.

38 Below, church.

39 *S.A.C.* xlvi, p. 226, from P.R.O., C 143/410, no. 22.

40 *Valor Eccl.* (Rec. Com.), i. 313.

41 *L. & P. Hen. VIII*, xix (2), p. 475.

42 *Cal. Pat.* 1391–6, 562; *Valor Eccl.* (Rec. Com.), i. 315.

the Dissolution were granted to Sir Richard Lee.[43]

Pynham priory in Lyminster had lands in Arundel, including two houses probably on the causeway south-east of the bridge in 1201, land under the castle on its east side about the same date, and a shop and a house on the quay in the early 15th century.[44] In 1526 they passed with the priory to Cardinal Wolsey's college at Oxford.[45] Between the later 16th century and the mid 18th or later property formerly of the priory descended with Calceto manor in Lyminster in the family of Browne, viscounts Montague.[46]

Tortington priory had lands in Arundel by 1291,[47] which in the early 15th century included at least three tenements and a store in the market place.[48] In the 1530s the total rental was £2 6*s.* 7*d.*[49]

Other religious institutions holding lands in the parish were Boxgrove priory (including a plot in High Street *c.* 1216),[50] Durford abbey in Rogate,[51] the Knights Templar[52] and the Knights Hospitaller,[53] the dean and chapter of Chichester cathedral (including property in Mill Lane),[54] and St. Mary's hospital in Chichester.[55] Lyminster priory had property in the town and outside,[56] part of which later belonged to Eton college.[57]

Arundel church had tithes worth £1 4*s.* in 1086.[58] In 1341 the *RECTORY* estate included a house and garden, 32 a. of land, and 2 a. of meadow, together with rents worth £1 6*s.* and tithes of meadow, mills, and fish;[59] in 1374 its annual value was said to be £5.[60] It remained distinct from the other former lands of the priory after the priory's replacement by Arundel college, but at the Dissolution passed like those to the earl of Arundel,[61] descending afterwards with the rape. The estate was let in 1535[62] and later.[63] By 1636 the rectory had come to comprise 137 a., chiexy arable and downland, north-west of the town and 28 a. in Tortington.[64] In the later 18th century the rectory lands were nearly 300 a. in area, mostly north-west of the town, and were divided into two farms called Parsonage and Rooks farms.[65] The lands north-west of the town were afterwards thrown into the new park. At the commutation of tithes *c.* 1841 the duke of Norfolk as impropriator received £160 tithe rent charge.[66]

The rector's house mentioned in 1324–5[67] may have been on the same site as the parsonage house described as south of the churchyard in 1636.[68] In 1778 the two portions of the rectory farm each had a house south-west of the church on either side of Parson's Hill.[69] One of them at least seems to have survived in 1818,[70] but is not heard of again.

In 1772 the Great park and Rewell wood alone were estimated at 1,210 a., virtually two thirds of the parish.[71] With the enlargement of the castle grounds and the creation of the new park,[72] by *c.* 1841 the duke of Norfolk owned nearly the whole parish, the only other estate over 20 a. in area being the burgess brooks.[73] Three areas of the town besides the castle precincts were largely in his ownership by the mid 19th century: the eastern side of High Street, the upper part of the town, and the southern frontage of the river Arun;[74] in 1910 perhaps a third of the town's buildings belonged to him.[75] The ducal estate was further increased by the purchase of the burgess brooks in 1902.[76] All the rural land was still owned by either the Norfolk or the Arundel estate in 1995,[77] but after the Second World War much urban property was sold: *c.* 120 houses in the north-west part of the town *c.* 1947, and miscellaneous property, especially in High Street, in 1950. Many sales were to long-term tenants at low prices.[78] In 1980 the Arundel estate owned little commercial property in Arundel.[79]

AGRICULTURE. In common with other parishes in the Arun valley, land use in Arundel during the Middle Ages was divided between meadow beside the river, arable on the lower slopes of the downs, and some rough pasture on the highest land. The west part with its poorer soil supported parkland and woods.[80]

43 *L. & P. Hen. VIII*, xxi (1), p. 570.
44 *S.A.C.* xi. 96–8; *S.R.S.* ii, p. 14; lxvii. 118; *Cat. Anct. D.* v, A 11537; for first named cf. above, growth of town.
45 *L. & P. Hen. VIII*, iv (1), p. 849.
46 *S.R.S.* xxxiii, p. 34; *Cowdray Archives*, ed. A. Dibben, i, p. 19; A.C.M., A 339, Thos. Morrell to Mr. Ellis, 1745; ibid. D 6410–16 (MS. cat.); ibid. MD 505, ff. [2, 6v., 7v., 10].
47 *Tax. Eccl.* (Rec. Com.), 139; cf. *Cal. Pat.* 1340–3, 575.
48 *S.R.S.* lxvii. 118.
49 P.R.O., SC 6/Hen. VIII/3674, rot. 10; cf. ibid. LR 2/198, f. 62v.
50 *Valor Eccl.* (Rec. Com.), i. 306; *S.R.S.* lix, pp. 75, 85, 105–6, 195; cf. ibid. xxxiii, p. 55.
51 *Chich. Acta* (Cant. & York Soc.), p. 166.
52 *Pipe R.* 1187 (P.R.S. xxxvii), 109.
53 B.L. Add. Ch. 7208 (MS. cal.); *Cal. Pat.* 1547–8, 143–4. The property of the Hospitallers apparently descended with Poling man. in later 16th cent.: ibid. 1566–9, p. 44; 1572–5, p. 398.
54 *S.R.S.* xlvi, p. 86; lviii, p. 147; A.C.M., MD 535, f. 4; W.S.R.O., Cap. I/15/1; Cap. I/16/1, ff. 55–6.
55 *Valor Eccl.* (Rec. Com.), i. 304; *Cal. Pat.* 1580–2, p. 171.
56 Eton Coll. Libr. MS. 56/32, 85 (TS. cat.); *S.A.C.* xlvi, p. 226.
57 W.S.R.O., Add. MS. 14313, f. 33v.; ibid. TD/W 5.
58 *V.C.H. Suss.* i. 421.
59 *Inq. Non.* (Rec. Com.), 370; cf. P.R.O., E 106/8/19, rot. 18.
60 *Cal. Inq. Misc.* iii, p. 351.
61 *L. & P. Hen. VIII*, xix (2), p. 475.
62 *Valor Eccl.* (Rec. Com.), i. 313.
63 A.C.M., Hodskinson surv. 1778, ff. 13, 15; ibid. MD 535, f. 5v.; P.R.O., E 178/1906, f. 1; Sandbeck Park, Rotherham, Lumley MS. EMA/1/5.
64 A.C.M., MD 505, f. [16 and v.]; cf. W.S.R.O., A.B.A., F2/14, f. [1].
65 A.C.M., H 1/30; ibid. Hodskinson surv. 1778, ff. [i], 12–16.
66 W.S.R.O., TD/W 5.
67 P.R.O., E 106/8/19, rot. 18.
68 A.C.M., MD 505, f. [16].
69 Ibid. Hodskinson surv. 1778, ff. 3, 14, 16.
70 Wright, *Arundel* (1818), 32, 66.
71 A.C.M., H 1/3. Urban property of the duke in 1778 is shown at ibid. Hodskinson surv. 1778, ff. 3–4, 7–10.
72 Above, castle grounds; woods and parks (modern park).
73 W.S.R.O., TD/W 5; cf. A.C.M., P 5/37, no. 1; 26 & 27 Vic. c. 7 (Private).
74 A.C.M., H 2/6.
75 W.S.R.O., IR 6, *passim*.
76 Above, this section; below, boro. govt. (after 1835).
77 Inf. from Dr. J. M. Robinson, Arundel Cast. For the div. between the two, above, Arundel Rape.
78 W.S.R.O., SP 95; *W. Suss. Gaz.* 4 Dec. 1947; *Suss. Daily News*, 17 Feb. 1950; *S.C.M.* xxiv. 168; *New Statesman*, 22 Dec. 1972, p. 941.
79 *Country Life*, 3 July 1980, p. 7.
80 Above, woods and parks.

Open fields mentioned in 1269[81] presumably included the Portfield recorded from 1401[82] and the Limefield and apparently the Mary field in the 17th. The Limefield lay north of the Little park[83] and the Mary field perhaps near the Marygate;[84] Portfield from its name was presumably also close to the town.[85] All three fields seem to have been inclosed by 1636. In that year there was arable beyond the Marygate on both sides of the old London road, the largest holding being Parsonage farm.[86] Possibly the west part of the town, which seems to represent later medieval development, had replaced other arable, as apparently happened, for instance, at Lichfield (Staffs.) and Stratford-upon-Avon (Warws.).[87]

The 80–100 a. later known as the burgess brooks, which lay east of the town in a meander of the river,[88] were common pasture from an early period. Pasture rights there were granted to the burgesses by William d'Aubigny, earl of Arundel (d. 1176), or his son or grandson of the same name; in the later 12th century Pynham priory in Lyminster received the right to put 14 cows and 2 bulls there.[89]

There was also much demesne meadow in the parish in the Middle Ages. The 84 a. belonging to the earl of Arundel in 1272[90] perhaps included the 75 a. of which the hay was destroyed by flooding in 1275;[91] at the same period there were 28 a. of meadow belonging to the earl in the Great park.[92] By 1302 there were 120 a. in all.[93] Other meadow was in small parcels belonging to local religious houses and to manors further afield. Of the former Arundel priory had 5 a. in 1324–5,[94] the Dominican friary apparently 2 a. in 1324,[95] St. James's leper hospital an unspecified amount in 1339–40,[96] the college a 'marsh' in the early 16th century,[97] Pynham priory in Lyminster 1 a. or more *c.* 1230,[98] and Tortington priory 22 a. in the 14th century.[99] Of manors further afield Cudlow in Climping had 10 a. in 1279–80,[1] Preston Millers in East Preston 4 a. in 1321,[2] Petworth at least 18 a. and Heyshott perhaps 2 a. in 1352–3,[3] Halnaker in Boxgrove 19 a. in 1347,[4] and Westbourne and Stansted an unnamed amount in 1331.[5] The St. Owen family of Clapham had 11 a. in 1402[6] and a Lurgashall man an unspecified amount in 1454.[7] In addition, the rectory estate had 2 a. in 1341.[8] The meadow belonging to the college[9] and to Petworth and Heyshott manors lay along Mill Lane east of the castle.[10] In the mid 14th century the hay crop belonging to Petworth, Heyshott, and Westbourne and Stansted manors was sold.[11]

Rough pasture was provided in the Middle Ages by the Great park[12] and by downland north of the open fields along the old London road. In 1636, perhaps because of assarting to replace fields lost to the westwards expansion of the town, there were only 23 a. of downland there, which lay open to the downland of neighbouring parishes.[13] Parsonage farm had common rights on the down in 1570,[14] but no other reference to such rights has been found.

There was apparently a vineyard in what later became the Little park in the 12th century,[15] and apples were grown in the parish in 1276–7.[16] In the mid 14th century sheep seem to have been unimportant compared with arable.[17] Pigs were kept in 1400–1.[18]

The two chief farms in the parish in the later Middle Ages were the demesne farms of the earls of Arundel and of the rector. The former had 158 a. in 1301 and 174 a. in the early 15th century.[19] The location of its medieval buildings and of the two barns mentioned in 1435 is unknown.[20] Tenants of Prinsted manor and of an unidentified estate owed mowing service there in 1301.[21] The medieval buildings of the rectory farm presumably lay south-west of the church, as later;[22] in 1400–1 the farm had income from the sale of corn and the agistment of pigs on the stubble in autumn.[23] There were tenants of the priory,[24] later college,[25] and rectory[26] estates and of Petworth[27] and apparently South Stoke[28] manors at least in the Middle Ages; many *servi* and *coloni* of the priory, including presumably some in Arundel, died in the Black Death.[29]

By the mid 16th century the burgess brooks had ceased to be common pasture, and between

81 B.L. Lansd. Ch. 92; cf. *S.R.S.* xli. 48; xlv. 253; lxvii. 117–18.
82 A.C.M., A 338; ibid. D 6410–16 (MS. cat.); P.R.O., E 210/9671 (TS. cat.); *S.R.S.* lxxiv, p. 34.
83 W.S.R.O., Ep. I/25/1 (1615).
84 *Glynde Pla. Archives*, ed. R. F. Dell, p. 132.
85 Cf. Portfield in Chich.: *A.-S. Towns in Southern Eng.* ed. J. Haslam, 325.
86 A.C.M., MD 505, ff. [6–8v., 16 and v.].
87 *Urban Arch. in Brit.* ed. J. Schofield and R. Leech, 56.
88 A.C.M., H 2/40; W.S.R.O., A.B.A., M25; A.B.A., P4/1.
89 Dugdale, *Mon.* ii (1661), 143–4.
90 P.R.O., C 132/45, no. 5, deducing acreage from valuation given.
91 Ibid. SC 6/1019/22, rot. 1.
92 Ibid. C 132/42, no. 5.
93 Ibid. C 133/104, no. 21, m. 2.
94 Ibid. E 106/8/19, rot. 18.
95 *Cal. Pat.* 1321–4, 407.
96 B.L. Lansd. Ch. 110.
97 *Valor Eccl.* (Rec. Com.), i. 313; cf. A.C.M., MD 535, f. 5; W.S.R.O., A.B.A., F2/14.
98 *Cat. Anct. D.* v, A 11537.
99 *Cal. Close,* 1419–22, 33.
1 *S.R.S.* vii, pp. 118–19; cf. *Cal. Chart. R.* 1257–1300, 58.
2 *S.R.S.* lx. 64.
3 Ibid. lv. 65, 87; cf. ibid. iii, p. 159.
4 *Cal. Inq. p.m.* ix, p. 38; cf. ibid. vii, p. 184; viii, p. 50.
5 Ibid. vii, p. 226.
6 Ibid. xviii, p. 217.
7 *S.R.S.* xli. 45.
8 *Inq. Non.* (Rec. Com.), 370.
9 *L. & P. Hen. VIII*, xix (2), p. 475.
10 W.S.R.O., PHA 1407, f. 56v.; *S.R.S.* iii, p. 159.
11 *S.R.S.* lv. 3, 36, 46, 87; *Cal. Inq. p.m.* vii, p. 226.
12 Above, woods and parks.
13 A.C.M., MD 505, f. [16v.].
14 Ibid. 535, f. 5v.
15 W.S.R.O., Par. 8/6/5, f. 3v.; Par. 8/7/35; cf. above, woods and parks (Little park); *V.C.H. Warws.* viii. 433, 473. For other early medieval urban vineyards, *Plans and Topog. of Medieval Towns in Eng. and Wales*, ed. M. W. Barley, 81.
16 P.R.O., SC 6/1029/22.
17 *Inq. Non.* (Rec. Com.), 370.
18 A.C.M., A 338.
19 *S.R.S.* lxvii. 2, 115.
20 P.R.O., C 139/71, no. 37, m. 32; but cf. below, this section.
21 *S.R.S.* lxvii. 24.
22 A.C.M., Hodskinson surv. 1778, ff. 13–16; cf. ibid. MD 505, f. [16].
23 Ibid. A 338; for identification of estate cf. ibid. 342.
24 P.R.O., E 106/8/19, rot. 18; W.S.R.O., Par. 8/7/35.
25 *Valor Eccl.* (Rec. Com.), i. 313.
26 *Inq. Non.* (Rec. Com.), 370; A.C.M., A 342.
27 *S.R.S.* lv. 31, 62.
28 Ibid. xxiii, p. 143.
29 Ibid. xlvi, p. 291.

that period and the early 19th century they were managed by the close corporation virtually for its exclusive benefit.[30] Between 1646 and 1758 a meeting to regulate the use both of the brooks and of the slipes, or extra strips of land outside the original river wall,[31] was generally held in the spring. A brookwarden was appointed for day-to-day management from the mid 16th century or earlier, assisted by a cowherd who in 1686 fetched the burgesses' cows for milking twice a day. The burgess brooks were chiefly used during the period as pasture for cattle and horses. The number of cattle each burgess could put there during the season was usually 6 or 7 in the brooks and between 2 and 7 in the slipes. By 1643 the mayor had *ex officio* a double share, and by 1647 the exclusive use of one slipe. The season ran from the spring to late December, but from 1653 animals were to be removed after Michaelmas if the land was flooded. Oxen and steers over two years old were prohibited in 1646, and uncastrated horses in 1727, when horses could not be replaced by substitutes until they had been there for six days. In 1653 also the mayor and senior burgesses were required to put a 'sufficient' bull into the brooks before mid May. During the 17th century part of the land was set aside each year for hay; the area in 1653 was 32 a. Between *c.* 1694 and the mid 18th century, however, hay seems never to have been grown.[32]

Only burgesses could normally enjoy pasture rights, subletting unwanted leazes only to other burgesses.[33] An exception was made in 1646, provided other burgesses had had first refusal. By 1615 the vicar had 6 bullock leazes in the brooks, perhaps in lieu of tithes;[34] in 1724 he also enjoyed 2 leazes in the slipes,[35] but by 1834 he had ceased to claim any of his entitlement.[36] In 1663 twin brookwardens were allowed to let up to 30 leazes and a slipe, dividing the proceeds among the mayor and burgesses;[37] eight leazes were similarly let in 1727. Sometimes leazes were granted for special reasons: to the attorney Thomas Peckham for life in 1675 in gratitude for help over litigation, and to two burgesses in 1736 who in exchange were to pay for a Michaelmas feast. Both the brookwarden and the cowherd had leazes as part of their wages. For some years before 1780 non-burgesses' horses could be put into the brooks for a small sum, a fact which was claimed by some inhabitants in 1835 as evidence of lost common rights.[38]

In 1758 all the brooks and slipes except the mayor's slipe were let to three burgesses for 21 years in parcels of 18 a., 24 a., and 42 a.; the burgesses in general evidently received the rent.[39] In 1780 the brooks were divided instead into 52 shares and distributed by ballot among the 13 burgesses on 21-year leases at reserved rents, the mayor receiving all the slipes.[40] During the early 19th century[41] some land was let to burgesses and some to non-burgesses; each new burgess could take a lease on election, a non-burgess tenant if necessary being removed. Leases were still of 21 years in 1819.[42] Land let to non-burgesses was put out to tender, presumably at the market rate.[43] Burgesses, however, seem to have paid less, since they often sublet at rents considerably higher. After the reform of the corporation in 1835, the brooks were let at more realistic rents,[44] by tender in 1855 if not before.[45] There were 15 tenants *c.* 1841.[46]

Individual landowners continued to have several meadow in the 16th century and later. In 1570 the earl of Arundel had 30 a. called the Castle meadows and 160 a. called the Great marsh, both let;[47] the Great marsh seems to have been or to have included what were later known as the south marshes south of the town beyond the river.[48] In 1589 the earl's meadow was said to have been recently improved.[49] In 1778 the duke of Norfolk retained much meadow in hand, both in the south marshes and east of the castle; some was attached to farms elsewhere, for instance 16 a. to Park farm.[50] Part at least of the meadow of the medieval Petworth manor still belonged to the Petworth estate in the 18th century.[51]

There were tenants of Tortington[52] and apparently Lyminster[53] manors in the 16th and 17th centuries. The two chief farms in that period remained the demesne farm attached to the castle, and the rectory farm, which after the Dissolution also descended with the rape.[54] The former included land north-west of the Marygate in 1636,[55] its buildings in the early 19th century and perhaps earlier occupying the site of the modern racing stables nearby.[56] The rectory farm was let on a 40-year lease in 1570,[57] and in 1636, besides land in Tortington, had 137 a. in the parish, of which 98 a. lay north-west of the Marygate.[58] By 1776 the two farms had been amalgamated as one holding of *c.* 300 a., but in 1778 there were again two farms, both let.[59] By 1795 the land north-west of the Marygate had been thrown into the new landscaped park.[60]

In 1732 the former Great park of 823 a. was

30 Para. based mainly on W.S.R.O., A.B.A., A1. The apparent description of the brooks as com. meadows in 1777 was in error: W.S.R.O., MP 124, f. [5].
31 A.C.M., MD 2510.
32 Cf. ibid.
33 Para. based mainly on W.S.R.O., A.B.A., A1.
34 Ibid. Ep. I/25/1 (1615); cf. Tierney, *Arundel*, ii. 655.
35 *S.R.S.* lxxviii. 59.
36 Tierney, *Arundel*, ii. 656; cf. ibid. 709.
37 W.S.R.O., A.B.A., M12.
38 *1st Rep. Com. Mun. Corp.* 673.
39 W.S.R.O., A.B.A., M25.
40 Ibid. A.B.A., A1, ff. 207v.–209v.; A.C.M., H 2/40.
41 Rest of para. based mainly on *1st Rep. Com. Mun. Corp.* 673.
42 Dallaway, *Hist. W. Suss.* ii (1) (1819), 179.
43 Cf. A.C.M., MD 1099; W.S.R.O., A.B.A., F3/44.
44 *Lond. Gaz.* 27 May 1836, pp. 954–5; 31 May 1836, p. 974.
45 W.S.R.O., MP 962, notice inviting tenders, 1855.
46 Ibid. TD/W 5.
47 A.C.M., MD 535, ff. 4v.–5; cf. ibid. 505, f. [10 and v.].
48 Ibid. Hodskinson surv. 1778, f. 20.
49 P.R.O., E 178/1906, f. 1v.
50 A.C.M., Hodskinson surv. 1778, ff. 6, 18, 20; cf. ibid. PM 86.
51 Ibid. D 853–63 (MS. cat.); cf. W.S.R.O., PHA 477, f. [6]; 500; 1407, f. 56v.
52 *Cal. Pat.* 1547–8, 213; Bodl. MS. Rawl. B. 318, p. 174; P.R.O., LR 2/197, ff. 80, 82 and v.; ibid. SC 12/22/85, ff. 1–2.
53 *S.R.S.* xix. 287.
54 Above, manor.
55 A.C.M., MD 505, ff. [6–8v.].
56 Ibid. PM 107. Wright, *Arundel* (1817), 39, apparently refers to them, in terms implying antiquity. For contemporary invs. of the farm, A.C.M., IN 43–9.
57 A.C.M., MD 535, f. 5v.
58 Ibid. MD 505, ff. [8v., 16 and v.].
59 Ibid. H 1/30; ibid. Hodskinson surv. 1778, ff. [i], 13–16.
60 Gardner, *Suss. Map* (1795).

leased by the duke of Norfolk to Abraham Ibbotson for conversion to a farm, with covenants against ploughing more than 200 a. in any year and for manuring and adequately fencing any arable closes created.[61] The conversion for both arable and pasture had been carried out by 1746.[62] The farm was let again in 1778,[63] but at other times in the later 18th century was in hand.[64] In the early 1760s it seems to have been chiefly involved in sheep rearing.[65] The original farmhouse was in Park bottom, with a barn at the site of the later Park Farmhouse.[66]

Elizabeth Scutt (d. *c.* 1776), with 128 sheep and farming at least 107 a. at her death, was apparently tenant of Parsonage farm. Large farmers recorded in 17th- and 18th-century probate inventories whose lands have not been identified include John Pellatt (d. *c.* 1660), who had over 100 sheep and farmed at least 73 a., John Tompson (d. *c.* 1707) who had 120 sheep and farmed at least 112 a., and the 'victualler' Anthony Weeden (d. *c.* 1715), with over 303 sheep and farming at least 51 a.[67]

Apart from the victualler mentioned, tradesmen in the town during the period can only rarely be shown to have had agricultural interests greater than the keeping of a few animals:[68] a miller in 1629 had animals but apparently no crops, a tanner in 1712 nineteen cattle, and a butcher in 1734 ten sheep. Cattle, poultry, and pigs were widely kept during the 17th and 18th centuries. Wheat and barley were then jointly the most important crops, oats, peas, and tares also being grown. More rarely mentioned were hemp in 1665, seeds, including clover, in 1727 and later, turnips in the 1760s, buckwheat in 1776, and hops in 1570 and later;[69] in 1720 one farmer had 1,600 hop poles at his death. A cider mill was recorded in 1776. A vineyard belonging to the duke of Norfolk existed by 1763, when the wine produced was compared to (presumably white) Burgundy;[70] its site was on the east side of Park bottom. It may still have been used in 1804.[71]

Most farming land between the later 18th century and the later 20th belonged to the castle estate; there was only one farmer outside the estate in 1799[72] and only one non-ducal holding over 20 a. in area *c.* 1841. The largest farm, Park farm, which had 474 a. *c.* 1841,[73] 577 a. *c.* 1910,[74] and 370 a. in 1989,[75] was kept in hand as the home farm apparently throughout the 19th century,[76] but after *c.* 1918 was tenanted, from 1927 or earlier by members of the Seller family from Devon.[77] Only 7 per cent of the population was chiefly employed in agriculture in 1801, and only 29 families in 1821. In 1831 there were 43 agricultural labourers.[78] In 1985 fourteen inhabitants were farmers or farm workers.[79] In 1990 the holding called Meadowcroft, on the Causeway, had 400 a.[80]

In 1801 corn was said to be abundant,[81] and during the 19th century there were 300–330 a. under crops. On Park farm rough ground was being reclaimed, presumably for arable, in 1816–17;[82] three planned farmyards were laid out east of the farmhouse by *c.* 1841,[83] including a flint barn 110 ft. (34 metres) long built in 1837.[84] During the same period between *c.* 700 a. and 850 a. were pasture and meadow, apart from parkland; in 1875 all but 100 a. of the pasture was permanent. Sheep were the chief livestock: 1,076 were returned in 1801 and 818 in 1875. Park farm had a flock of 345 in 1816, which was soon afterwards increased.[85] In 1801 there were also 240 pigs. The proportion of pasture increased after *c.* 1875. Two dairy farmers were mentioned in 1881.[86] In 1909, of the area returned, there was nearly four times as much pasture as arable, including 389 a. of hay; more than half the arable at the same date raised oats, turnips, and swedes, evidently for feed. There was a dairy farm of 43 a. in 1904.[87]

In 1934[88] Home and Mill farms, both on the Causeway, were dairy farms supplying Dare and Co.'s dairy in Arundel.[89] Home farm was succeeded by Meadowcroft, which in 1990 had land in the south marshes.[90] Cricket Hill farm, *c.* 70 a. in 1989, was also a dairy farm before 1962. Dairying and beef production were major enterprises on Park farm after 1922, but dairying ceased there in 1989.[91] Brookland in the Arun valley continued to be attached to farms elsewhere, for instance to Park farm in the 1920s or 30s. The horses of town tradesmen are said to have been kept in the south marshes in the early 20th century.[92] Dairying was succeeded in the parish after the mid 20th century by livestock raising: in 1989 three of the farms mentioned were raising stock, Cricket Hill farm beef cattle and Park farm chiefly lambs. In 1985 holdings based in the parish returned 258 cattle and 1,559 sheep.[93]

Much watercress was grown in 1874 in the

61 A.C.M., D 6266.

62 Ibid. A 438.

63 Ibid. Hodskinson surv. 1778, f. 18.

64 Ibid. A 438–9, 441–3.

65 Ibid. A 439, 441; cf. ibid. H 1/3.

66 Ibid. H 1/3; cf. ibid. Hodskinson surv. 1778, ff. 17–18.

67 W.S.R.O., Ep. I/29/8. For Eliz. Scutt cf. A.C.M., Hodskinson surv. 1778, f. 15; for Pellatt, *S.A.C.* xxxix. 87.

68 Para. based mainly on A.C.M., A 438–9, 441; W.S.R.O., Ep. I/29/8.

69 A.C.M., MD 535, f. 4v.; W.S.R.O., Par. 8/11/7, f. 1.

70 *Archaeologia*, i (1770), 332; *Suss. Hist.* i (5), 11.

71 A.C.M., H 1/3; ibid. PM 17.

72 *S.A.C.* lxxi. 46.

73 W.S.R.O., TD/W 5.

74 Ibid. IR 6, f. 14.

75 Inf. from the farmer, Mr. J. Seller.

76 A.C.M., A 1394; Pigot, *Nat. Com. Dir.* (1839), 654; *Kelly's Dir. Suss.* (1862 and later edns.); Pike, *Bognor Dir.* (1910–11), 190.

77 *Kelly's Dir. Suss.* (1918 and later edns.); inf. from Mr. Seller and from Mr. F. Penfold, Burpham.

78 *Census*, 1801–31.

79 M.A.F.F., agric. statistics, 1985.

80 Inf. from the farmer, Mr. J. A. Harriott.

81 Para. based mainly on E.S.R.O., LCG/3/EW 1, f. [43v.]; P.R.O., MAF 68/433, 2371; W.S.R.O., TD/W 5; *L. & I. Soc.* cxcv. 30, 38.

82 A.C.M., A 1394.

83 W.S.R.O., TD/W 5.

84 Date on bldg.

85 A.C.M., A 1394; ibid. IN 43–9, inv. of Park fm., 1816.

86 P.R.O., RG 11/1121, ff. 7v., 41.

87 A.C.M., MD 2003.

88 Para. based mainly on inf. from Mr. Seller, Mr. Harriott, Mr. Penfold, and Mr. P. W. Knight, Arundel Estate Fms.

89 *Arundel, the Gem of Suss.* (Arundel, 1934), 3.

90 Inf. from Mr. P. Simmons, Madehurst; cf. O.S. Map 1/10,000, TQ 00 NW. (1976 edn.).

91 W.S.R.O., MP 3785, f. 56.

92 *W. Suss. Gaz.* 7 June 1973.

93 M.A.F.F., agric. statistics, 1985.

Arun valley,[94] presumably beside Mill Lane where further beds were made shortly before 1890.[95] There were also beds in Park bottom between that date and the 1970s.[96] Allotment gardens had been laid out on the south side of the river by 1896,[97] and others south of Chichester Road by 1900.[98] In the 1970s they had been replaced by other sites in London and Fitzalan roads.[99]

There was market-garden land east of Ford Road in the mid 19th century.[1] In 1985 there were a general horticultural holding and one chiefly growing fruit.[2]

A vineyard on Cricket hill north-west of the town produced white wine in the 1970s and 80s.[3]

MILLS. A water mill at Arundel in 1066 returned the large sum of 40*s.* a year; in 1086 it could grind 10 bushels (*modia*) of corn, 10 bushels of mixed grain (*grosse annone*), and 4 bushels of unspecified grain.[4] Its site was presumably at Swanbourne, north of the town, where an important mill was recorded between 1272[5] and the mid 19th century. Twelfth- and 13th-century references to mills at Arundel are probably also to Swanbourne mill; references to two or more mills on the same occasion[6] are presumably either to plural pairs of stones on that site or to small Norse-type mills in sequence. A miller was recorded in or before 1199.[7] The mill was at farm in 1232–3,[8] and in 1272 was held on a life tenancy.[9] In 1340 mill tithes in the parish brought in £3.[10] The mill remained in hand in 1386 and later,[11] the income from it supporting the priory and the leper hospital of St. James in 1272[12] and the castle chaplain in 1301.[13]

In a lease of 1560 the lord reserved the right to build a fulling mill at Swanbourne, presumably to replace one which he held of the corporation on an unknown site;[14] it is not clear whether that at Swanbourne was built. The Horne family leased Swanbourne mill from the dukes of Norfolk in the 18th century and earlier 19th, for a time in partnership with the Gorhams;[15] John Horne was described as miller and baker in 1787.[16] Corn from Michelgrove in Clapham was brought there in 1768–9.[17] The mill was depicted by John Constable in his last painting in 1837, when it was a large timber-framed structure.[18] It was demolished in the early 1840s.[19] Shortly before 1987 the elliptical masonry mill pond, fed by the overflow from Swanbourne lake, was converted into a trout farm.[20]

It is not clear whether the stream in Park bottom west of the town ever drove a mill. What seems to be a reference to it in 1635 may in fact allude to Swanbourne mill.[21] Reference to the 'water mill of Arundel', evidently that at Swanbourne, in 1615[22] suggests there was no second water mill then, and in 1801 there was only one in the parish.[23]

A windmill belonging to the earl of Arundel recorded from 1272[24] may have been the mill called 'Tollelone' in 1331.[25] It perhaps stood east of the old London road near the site of Hiorne's tower in the modern Arundel park, where a Windmill field was recorded in 1776.[26] Remains of two circular mounds could be seen there in 1851.[27]

Arundel's two other windmills had sites on the river bank for ease of transport. The mill at Portreeve's acre south-east of the town existed by 1724.[28] A new mill was built after 1768.[29] By the mid 19th century the site was used for making cement.[30] In 1864 the mill was moved to an adjacent site;[31] it ceased to be used between 1875 and 1896.[32] The tower windmill in the south marshes was built in 1830;[33] the Bartlett family were tenants by *c.* 1841, and also had a corn merchant's business in the town between 1845 and 1922. About 1841 there was a wharf beside the mill.[34] The mill ceased working after damage in a gale in 1915;[35] it was derelict in 1937[36] and in the 1940s was converted into a dwelling.[37]

A steam mill near the river Arun existed in 1824.[38] In 1882 Charles Bartlett had the same or

94 *Jnl. of Horticulture and Cottage Gdnr.* 1 Jan. 1874, p. 12.

95 *17th Ann. Rep. on Combined Sanit. Dist. of W. Suss.* (Littlehampton, 1891), 87 (copy at W.S.R.O., WDC/CL 74/1).

96 A.C.M., MD 2243; O.S. Maps 6", Suss. LXIII. NW. (1899 and later edns.); 1/2,500, TQ 0007–0107 (1971, 1979 edns.).

97 O.S. Map 1/2,500, Suss. LXIII. 1 (1897 edn.).

98 A.C.M., MD 2037; cf. O.S. Map 1/2,500, Suss. LXIII. 1 (1912 edn.).

99 O.S. Maps 1/2,500, TQ 0007–0107 (1971 edn.); 1/10,000, TQ 00 NW. (1976 edn.).

1 Ibid. 6", Suss. LXIII (1879); W.S.R.O., TD/W 128.

2 M.A.F.F., agric. statistics, 1985.

3 Inf. from Mr. Penfold.

4 *V.C.H. Suss.* i. 421.

5 *Cal. Inq. p.m.* i, p. 279.

6 *Pipe R.* 1130 (H.M.S.O. facsimile), 42; 1179 (P.R.S. xxviii), 38; 1199 (P.R.S. N.S. x), 274; P.R.O., SC 6/1117/13, rot. 2d.; *S.R.S.* lxvii. 2.

7 *S.R.S.* xlvi, p. 86.

8 P.R.O., SC 6/1117/13, rot. 2d.

9 Ibid. C 132/42, no. 5.

10 *Inq. Non.* (Rec. Com.), 370.

11 *Cal. Inq. Misc.* vi, p. 219; below, this section.

12 *Cal. Inq. p.m.* i, p. 279.

13 *S.R.S.* lxvii. 2.

14 A.C.M., MD 535, ff. 4v., 5v.

15 Ibid. D 6272 (MS. cat.); ibid. Hodskinson surv. 1778, f. 8; *S.A.C.* lv. 85; lxxi. 13.

16 *Wiston Archives*, i, ed. J. Booker, p. 132.

17 *S.A.C.* lxxi. 13, 23.

18 G. Reynolds, *Cat. of Constable Colln.* pp. 219–20 and pl. 274; *Victorian Countryside*, ed. G. E. Mingay, i, pl. 26.

19 W.S.R.O., TD/W 5; *Illus. Lond. News*, 5 Dec. 1846, p. 357.

20 *S.I.A.S. Newletter*, N.S. lv. 2.

21 *Camd. Misc.* xvi (Camd. 3rd ser. lii), Hammond, 31.

22 W.S.R.O., Ep. I/25/1 (1615).

23 E.S.R.O., LCG/3/EW 1, f. [44].

24 P.R.O., C 132/42, no. 5; *S.R.S.* lxvii. 2.

25 *Cal. Inq. p.m.* vii, p. 226.

26 A.C.M., H 1/30. The mill was apparently not that mentioned in Waller's acct. of siege of Arundel in 1643–4, *pace* Hillier, *Arundel* (1851), 75; cf. above, milit. events.

27 Hillier, *Arundel* (1851), 75.

28 Budgen, *Suss. Map* (1724); cf. B.L. Lansd. MS. 918, f. 39.

29 W.S.R.O., Wiston MS. 100; depicted at B.L. Add. MS. 5674, f. 9; cf. A.C.M., PM 2.

30 A.C.M., MD 831; below, other trades and inds. (1800–1945).

31 *W. Suss. Gaz.* 15 Dec. 1864.

32 O.S. Map 6", Suss. LXIII (1879, 1899 edns.); cf. W.S.R.O., SP 1041.

33 M. Brunnarius, *Windmills of Suss.* 72–3 and pl. 70; below, pl. facing p. 75.

34 W.S.R.O., TD/W 5; *Kelly's Dir. Suss.* (1845 and later edns.); Pike, *Bognor Dir.* (1910–11), 186, 191.

35 Brunnarius, *Windmills*, 73.

36 *S.C.M.* xi. 739.

37 Inf. from Mr. F. Penfold, Burpham; cf. *W. Suss. Gaz.* 7 June 1973.

38 A.C.M., D 164–81, deed, 1824.

another north of River Road behind the Swan inn; it was still operating in 1907.[39]

MARKETS AND FAIRS. MARKETS. A market at Arundel evidently existed from the time the place became urban, and certainly by 1086, when the earl's sheriff took market dues (*theoloneum*) from men living outside the honor.[40] The lord's income from tolls was £1 4*s.* 8*d.* in 1276–7.[41] By 1288 if not earlier there were two markets, on Monday and Thursday,[42] the former later moving to Saturday. The corporation was leasing the tolls from the earl by the early 15th century at £3 12*s.* a year;[43] as a result, in 1586 and later it was able to claim the markets as the property of the town.[44]

Reference to a 'measure of Arundel' by which beans were weighed in the later 12th century[45] suggests that the market had more than local importance. Cases of forestalling and regrating were presented in the later Middle Ages.[46] In 1568 Arundel market was described as among the chief corn markets in the county.[47] By the later 17th century the Thursday market had become the main one, the smaller Saturday market being for provisions only.[48] The Thursday market remained important in 1766, when much corn was exported,[49] and in the mid 1790s its annual turnover of corn was worth more than £30,000.[50] The Saturday market in 1766 was said to have been long disused,[51] but it was held again by 1788.[52] The market hinterland in the Middle Ages included Chichester, West Tarring,[53] and Amberley;[54] it also took in the environs of Petworth in 1623[55] and later,[56] and perhaps Hambledon (Hants) in 1588.[57] By the 1630s, however, corn from the neighbourhood was being taken to Surrey markets to supply London.[58]

The Thursday market moved before 1805 to Wednesday,[59] and *c.* 1819 to Tuesday.[60] In 1831 it was chiefly for corn, with a large fortnightly cattle market.[61] The Saturday market is not heard of after 1855.[62] A corn store was built by public subscription on the town quay north-west of the bridge in 1831, the corporation letting the land to trustees for 99 years; thereafter the corn market was held by sample. No market tolls were taken in 1835, but charges for the use of hurdles brought the town *c.* £12 a year net.[63] By 1845 market day had changed again to Monday, and by 1862 the market, for cattle and corn, was held fortnightly; it was then said to be well attended, thanks to the nearness of Brighton, Worthing, and Bognor.[64] An annual Christmas fatstock show was held in early December by 1844.[65] The tolls on cattle were let at tender by the town council in 1855.[66] The town council still owned the market in 1891, when cattle, pigs, and sheep were sold but only in a small way.[67] The market had presumably begun to decline after the opening in 1882 of Barnham market, which was better served by the railway.[68] It ceased by 1903,[69] though in 1907 the annual agricultural show was still being held.[70] The corn store was in commercial use from 1909 or earlier until its destruction by fire in 1930.[71]

The market place mentioned in 1438[72] was presumably the wider lower end of High Street, though the original site of the market may have been elsewhere.[73] A 'market house' was mentioned in the 1690s.[74] Nearby were the butchers' shambles first mentioned in 1617[75] and probably the same as the 'oaken shops' which the corporation held of the earl of Arundel in 1570.[76] The shambles were rebuilt on a different site in the market place in 1772.[77] In the early 1830s there were two, one let to a butcher at a yearly rent and the other used by the public without charge.[78] The shambles were removed in 1834.[79]

The pig market was near the Swan inn in 1829.[80] In the later 19th century cattle were sold in the market place, sheep further up High Street,[81] and poultry near the river. Pigs and sheep are also said to have been sold in the 19th century in Maltravers Street,[82] where the annual fatstock show was apparently held.[83] Iron posts in the market place with rings for tethering cattle[84] were moved after the cessation of the market to Kings Arms Hill, Bakers Arms Hill, and Mount Pleasant, where some, dated 1819,

39 Ibid. HC 7; W.S.R.O., Add. MS. 13827 (TS. cat.); ibid. BO/AR 16/1/197; *Kelly's Dir. Suss.* (1882 and later edns.); illus. at Cartland, *Arundel*, 26.

40 *V.C.H. Suss.* i. 379, 421; for Rob. FitzTetbald, above, Arundel Rape.

41 P.R.O., SC 6/1029/22.

42 Ibid. JUST 1/924, rot. 65d. Tierney, *Arundel*, ii. 696 n., citing the doc., mistakenly says Sat.

43 *S.R.S.* lxvii. 115; cf. A.C.M., MD 495, f. [64v.]; 535, f. 4.

44 Eustace, *Arundel*, 125; W.S.R.O., A.B.A., M28, printed at ibid. 217–18.

45 *S.R.S.* lix, p. 45.

46 Tierney, *Arundel*, ii. 694; A.C.M., M 23.

47 *Cal. Pat.* 1566–9, p. 169.

48 Ogilby, *Britannia* (1675), 8.

49 Caraccioli, *Arundel*, 4.

50 *Univ. Brit. Dir.* ii. 55.

51 Caraccioli, *Arundel*, 4.

52 *S.C.M.* xx. 311.

53 *Plac. de Quo Warr.* (Rec. Com.), 751.

54 *S.R.S.* xxxi. 61; cf. *Arundel Rds.* 36.

55 *S.R.S.* xlix. 73.

56 *S.C.M.* xx. 311.

57 *Cal. Assize Rec. Suss. Eliz. I*, p. 214.

58 *Cal. S.P. Dom.* 1631–3, 257.

59 Evans, *Worthing* (1805), 99.

60 *1st Rep. Com. Mun. Corp.* 673; cf. A.C.M., MD 1099.

61 Lewis, *Topog. Dict. Eng.* (1831).

62 *Kelly's Dir. Suss.* (1855).

63 W.S.R.O., A.B.A., A1, f. 228; A.B.A., F1/1 (1831); Dallaway & Cartwright, *Hist. W. Suss.* ii (1) (1832), 211; *1st Rep. Com. Mun. Corp.* 673.

64 *Kelly's Dir. Suss.* (1845 and later edns.).

65 A.C.M., MD 1258; cf. W.S.R.O., MP 461; ibid. POL AB/16/1 (4 Dec. 1876).

66 W.S.R.O., MP 962, notice inviting tenders, 1855.

67 *Rep. Com. Mkt. Rights* [C. 6268–VI], p. 276, H.C. (1890–1), xxxix.

68 Below, Eastergate, econ. hist. (fair and mkts.).

69 *Kelly's Dir. Suss.* (1903).

70 *V.C.H. Suss.* ii. 290.

71 Goodliffe, *Littlehampton* (1909), 69; Cartland, *Arundel*, 98–9; J. Godfrey, *Arundel and Arun Valley in Old Photos.* 69.

72 *S.R.S.* iv. 210.

73 Above, growth of town.

74 A.C.M., A 339; cf. below, boro. govt. (town halls).

75 E.S.R.O., SAS/C 30 (TS. cat.); cf. W.S.R.O., A.B.A., P1/5, 28.

76 A.C.M., MD 495, ff. [10v., 64v.].

77 W.S.R.O., A.B.A., F1/5, nos. 2–3; A.B.A., P1/41.

78 *1st Rep. Com. Mun. Corp.* 673.

79 W.S.R.O., A.B.A., F1/1.

80 A.C.M., FC 435; cf. *Arundel Rds.* 36.

81 Cartland, *Arundel*, 1; below, pl. facing p. 90.

82 W.S.R.O., MP 461.

83 *W. Suss. Gaz.* 24 May 1956.

84 Illus. at Cartland, *Arundel*, 1.

survived in 1996. The hurdles for the sheep pens were kept in a building in Mill Lane in 1850[85] and later in a building in Queen Street next to the bridge.[86] The fish market was said in 1675 apparently once to have been at the west end of Maltravers Street.[87] Later it was evidently on the town quay near the bridge; two stone tables from which fish was sold stood between the corn store and the bridge in the early 20th century.[88] In 1995 they survived beside the friary in Mill Road.

FAIRS. Richard FitzAlan, earl of Arundel, in 1285 was granted, or confirmed in, two three-day fairs at the feasts of the Finding of the Cross (3 May) and St. Nicholas (6 December);[89] another on 14 September (the Exaltation of the Cross) was mentioned in 1288.[90] Fair tolls were still taken by the lord's officers in the 15th and 16th centuries.[91] By 1586 a fourth fair was being held on 10 August, but only the December fair then lasted longer than one day.[92] All four fairs survived in 1784, their dates modified by the change in the calendar; the May fair then specialized in cattle and pigs, the August one in pigs, cattle, and sheep, the September one in sheep and cattle, and the December one in cattle and pedlary.[93] In that year a Chailey man bought Welsh heifers at the December fair while returning from Chichester.[94]

By the mid 1790s the August fair was very little patronized;[95] it seems to have ceased soon afterwards.[96] The other three fairs were said to be chiefly for cattle and pedlary in 1831, but attendance had greatly declined since the establishment of the fortnightly cattle market.[97] After 1845 they were chiefly for pedlary.[98] Only the May and September fairs remained in 1888,[99] ceasing shortly after 1907.[1] The September fair in the mid 1880s was unpopular with many in the town, since it produced little toll income and was frequented by gypsies, with music and 'sports'.[2]

The fairs were held in the market place in the early 20th century[3] and presumably earlier.

PORT AND RIVER TRAFFIC. MEDIEVAL.

There was perhaps a port at Arundel before 1066, since by 1086 the church had a dedication to St. Nicholas, the patron saint of sailors. At the latter date Roger de Montgomery received income from both the port (*portum aque*) and ship dues (*consuetudinem navium*).[4] William II disembarked at Arundel in 1097[5] and the empress Maud in 1139,[6] and the town remained a passenger port for Normandy in the early 13th century.[7] Medieval Rouen pottery found in excavations in the town had probably been imported there,[8] and Caen stone was evidently landed[9] as at other Sussex ports. The port was also involved in coastwise trade, sending to Dover castle in 1326 provisions brought from Chichester by road.[10] Flints for building were brought downstream by barge in the late 14th century.[11] Statistics relating to medieval trade were usually included in those of Chichester port,[12] but goods passing through the port of Arundel, first so called, were listed separately in 1497–8: exports, besides timber and wood, were grain, cattle, horses, cloth, tanned calfskins, and tallow, while imports included salt, apples, hops, salt fish, nuts, wine, oil, soap, tar, glass, nails, canvas, paper, brass, paving tiles, and painted cloth.[13] The quay mentioned from the early 15th century[14] was evidently below the bridge, as the common,[15] town,[16] or mayor's quay[17] was later, and was presumably at least as long then as in 1680, when it stretched part of the way down what was later River Road.[18]

1500–1800. By 1563 the corporation had acquired the right to take 'wharfage' and 'quayage' from vessels using the port.[19] In 1643 and later it claimed 'petty customs' on a variety of goods to pay for maintaining the town quay, besides dues on coal, salt, and grain, payable to the mayor.[20] It is not certain, however, whether the latter were actually received before the early 19th century,[21] since payment was resisted on several occasions between 1681 and 1769.[22] The right to take tolls implies control of the quay, which is also shown by the corporation's paying for repairs to it from *c.* 1600;[23] a claim to ownership was specifically made by *c.* 1700.[24] A 'pier', i.e. a jetty, was built upstream of the bridge on the town side in 1619–20.[25] In 1680

85 A.C.M., H 2/44; cf. W.S.R.O., A.B.A., F4/2, nos. 3, 4, 8.
86 Cartland, *Arundel*, 35.
87 Ogilby, *Britannia* (1675), 8.
88 *Lapworth & Son's Popular Arundel Hist. and Guide* (Arundel, 1915), 45; W.S.R.O., PH 1895, f. 25.
89 P.R.O., C 53/73, m. 7.
90 Ibid. JUST 1/924, rot. 65d.
91 A.C.M., M 23, 41; 271, f. [18]; ibid. MD 535, f. 4v.
92 Eustace, *Arundel*, 125.
93 G. A. Walpoole, *New Brit. Traveller* (1784), 51.
94 *S.A.C.* cxiv. 80.
95 *Univ. Brit. Dir.* ii. 55.
96 e.g. Lewis, *Topog. Dict. Eng.* (1831); Pigot, *Nat. Com. Dir.* (1832–4), 1003; though *Kelly's Dir. Suss.* (1855) still lists it.
97 Lewis, *Topog. Dict. Eng.* (1831).
98 *Kelly's Dir. Suss.* (1845 and later edns.).
99 *Rep. Com. Mkt. Rights* [C. 5550], p. 207, H.C. (1888), liii.
1 *Kelly's Dir. Suss.* (1907, 1913).
2 *W. Suss. Gaz.* 3 Oct. 1985; 2 Oct. 1986; 1 Oct. 1987.
3 Ibid. 24 May 1956.
4 *V.C.H. Suss.* i. 421; cf. below, church [fabric]. The expression 'between the boro. and the port' for the source of the sum received in 1086 has been wrongly taken to mean that the port was at Ford: A. H. Allcroft, *Waters of Arun*, 60, 75–9; below, Ford, econ. hist.
5 F. Barlow, *Wm. Rufus*, 369.
6 *Gesta Stephani*, ed. K. R. Potter, 58.
7 *Close R.* 1231–4, 563.
8 *S.A.C.* cxviii. 124.
9 e.g. above, castle (cast. fabric).
10 *S.A.C.* lxxii. 172–3.
11 A.C.M., uncat. late 14th-cent. acct. roll (Suss. box 3, no. 1).
12 e.g. E. M. Carus-Wilson and O. Coleman, *Eng.'s Export Trade, 1275–1547*, 7.
13 W.S.R.O., MP 9, ff. 31–42, using P.R.O., E 122/35/11; for timber and wood, below, timber trades. The port presumably included other landing places, as later: below, this section.
14 *S.R.S.* lxvii. 118, 120.
15 e.g. W.S.R.O., A.B.A., A1, f. 179v.
16 e.g. ibid. A.B.A., F1/2 (1761); ibid. TD/W 5.
17 e.g. ibid. S.A.S. MS. RB 32 (TS. cat.).
18 P.R.O., E 178/6501, m. 4; cf. below, pl. facing p. 75.
19 W.S.R.O., A.B.A., F2/1, ff. 1v., 2, 4; cf. ibid. A.B.A., A1, f. 255.
20 Ibid. A.B.A., M8.
21 Below, this section (1800–50).
22 W.S.R.O., A.B.A., A1, ff. 100, 175, 198v.
23 Ibid. A.B.A., A1, ff. 109, 115, 132v.; A.B.A., F1/1 (1757, 1816); A.B.A., F1/2 (1761); A.B.A., F1/5, no. 3; A.B.A., F2/1, f. 5; A.B.A., F2/16.
24 Ibid. A.B.A., A1, f. 120; cf. ibid. ff. 175, 179v.
25 Ibid. A.B.A., F2/1, f. 9; *O.E.D.* s.v. pier; for the site cf. above, relig. hos. (Dominican friary).

the quay was *c.* 270 ft. (82 metres) long by 20 ft. (6 metres) deep,[26] but from 1728 a section of it was let.[27] The leaving of timber or other heavy goods on the quay for longer than six days was prohibited in 1647 and later, both for the damage it caused and for its hindrance to other users. Stone, ore, sand, and gravel in 1647 were to be left at a subsidiary quay on the south bank of the river[28] maintained by the parish surveyors of highways.[29]

Commodities passing through the port in the late 16th century and early 17th are indicated in the record of royal customs collected, though no distinction is made between Arundel and the neighbouring places, including Littlehampton, then counted as part of the port for customs purposes; the port was generally then described as Arundel with Littlehampton.[30] In 1680 its area was defined as extending from the west end of Middleton to the east end of Heene, and inland as far as Arundel town, the town quay being the legal quay for foreign trade then and presumably earlier.[31] The most frequent exports during the period, besides timber and wood, were grain and iron. Grain went to London, to south-coast ports including Newport (I.W.), and to Limerick and Waterford in Ireland,[32] Middelburg (Netherlands), and Lisbon. A Southampton merchant was shipping wheat overseas from Arundel in the earlier 16th century,[33] and the port was used to victual Calais in 1552.[34] Iron was sent to Portsmouth, Yarmouth (Norf.), London, Poole (Dors.), and Plymouth, and to Middelburg and Flushing (Netherlands).[35] Other goods exported during the period were cloth (to Normandy and Ireland), clothing (to Ireland), skins and glovers' chippings (to Dover, Normandy, the Low Countries, and Portugal), ashes and reddle (to Normandy), grindstones (to Portsmouth), English glass (to London, Poole,[36] and King's Lynn (Norf.)),[37] and wool and hops to 'Apsome', i.e. Topsham (Devon).[38]

Some goods were sent to other English ports for reshipping in larger vessels, for instance wheat to Portsmouth to be sent to Lisbon in 1619–20,[39] wheat and 'wooden stuff' to Chichester in 1629–30 for reshipping in a Dutch ship, and reddle to West Cowes (I.W.) in the same year en route for Flushing.[40] The port was also evidently involved in coastwise distribution of imported goods, for instance Burgundy glass to Dartmouth (Devon) and Weymouth (Dors.) in 1590–1,[41] and 'aquavitye' (presumably brandy) to Topsham in 1640–1.[42]

Between 1650 and 1750 grain continued to be sent to London, the West country, Ireland, and elsewhere abroad.[43] By the later 17th century, however, Arundel's grain exports were much less important than those of Shoreham or Chichester,[44] and from 1710 about a fifth went to Chichester for milling.[45] Provisions were shipped to Portsmouth and Chatham *c.* 1666.[46] Other exports in the later 17th century included hops, shipped coastwise,[47] and 60 swans sent as a present to France by Lord Montague in 1678;[48] in the late 17th or early 18th century red ochre, perhaps from Graffham or Chidham, was sent to London.[49] The general foreign trade of the port had declined by that time. It was much less than that of either Chichester or Shoreham,[50] and accounted for less than one in ten cargoes between 1663 and 1688;[51] just over half was with the area of Normandy between the Seine and the Somme, and the rest with the Low Countries.[52] In the 1730s, nevertheless, goods were still being exported as far as Spain and Portugal.[53]

Imports from London in the late 16th century and early 17th[54] included grocery wares, white salt and bay salt, hops, fish, coal, iron,[55] soap, lead, stone pots, sails, and anchors, and luxury goods such as tobacco pipes, cut glass, and French wine. Foreign goods were brought from other English ports besides: raisins and spices from Poole, figs from Poole and perhaps Plymouth, and wine, vinegar, and bay salt from Southampton. Spanish wool, salt, corks, and 'aquavita', however, came direct from Cadiz, onions from Middelburg, salt, hops, fish, dressed flax, muskets, and covered stone pots from Flushing, and canvas, white paper, and drinking glasses[56] from Normandy. Among other named English ports Yarmouth[57] and apparently King's Lynn[58] supplied grain, Sunderland coal, Newcastle coal and grindstones, Rye, Newhaven, and Pevensey cast iron,[59] Southampton butter, cheese, and shop wares, Plymouth sheepskins and perhaps lead, and Dartmouth fish, kersies, and train oil. Imports

26 P.R.O., E 178/6501, m. 4.
27 W.S.R.O., A.B.A., P1/29, 31, 35, 37.
28 Ibid. A.B.A., A1, ff. 56v.–57, 120.
29 Ibid. Par. 8/12/2, f. 7.
30 Para. based mainly on ibid. MP 9, using customs rec. and port bks. 1553–1604; sample port bks. 1608–41: P.R.O., E 190/755/18; E 190/758/13; E 190/760/11; E 190/763/9; E 190/764/16; E 190/767/32; *S.R.S.* lxiv, *passim.* For timber and wood, below, timber trades; for wrought iron cf. *V.C.H. Suss.* ii. 248.
31 P.R.O., E 178/6501, m. 4; cf. *Cal. Treas. Bks. and Papers,* 1731–4, 299. The legal quay was greatly reduced in area in 1831: P.R.O., E 178/7005; W.S.R.O., A.B.A., A1, f. 228.
32 Cf. *Cal. Pat.* 1557–8, 66.
33 *S.R.S.* xvi. 69.
34 *Acts of P.C.* 1552–4, 24; cf. *L. & P. Hen. VIII,* xvii, p. 324.
35 *S.N.Q.* ix. 107.
36 G. H. Kenyon, *Glass Ind. of Weald,* 113.
37 N. J. Williams, *Maritime Trade of E. Anglian Ports,* 179.
38 For identification, *P.N. Devon* (E.P.N.S.), ii. 454; inf. from Mr. P. Cornford, Univ. of Exeter.
39 P.R.O., E 190/758/13, f. 3; cf. *Cal. S.P. Dom.* 1651, 548.
40 P.R.O., E 190/763/9, f. 2.
41 W.S.R.O., MP 9, ff. 119–20, using P.R.O., E 190/746/9.
42 P.R.O., E 190/767/32, f. 3.
43 J. H. Andrews, 'Geog. Aspects of Maritime Trade of Kent and Suss. 1650–1750' (Lond. Univ. Ph.D. thesis, 1954), 196, 198 n., and facing ff. 191, 196, 198–9; *Cal. S.P. Dom.* 1651, 548.
44 Andrews, op. cit. facing f. 186.
45 *S.A.C.* xcii. 102.
46 *Cal. S.P. Dom.* 1666–7, 425.
47 Andrews, op. cit. facing f. 213.
48 *Cal. Treas. Bks.* 1676–9, 933.
49 Andrews, op. cit. 278–9.
50 Ibid. 51.
51 Ibid. 60.
52 Ibid. facing f. 336.
53 W.S.R.O., LH 10/1/1.
54 Para. based mainly on ibid. MP 9, using customs rec. and port bks. 1553–1604; sample port bks. 1608–41: P.R.O., E 190/755/18; E 190/758/13; E 190/760/11; E 190/763/9; E 190/764/16; E 190/767/32.
55 Cf. H. Cleere and D. Crossley, *Iron Ind. of Weald* (1995), 348.
56 Kenyon, *Glass Ind.* 113.
57 Williams, *Maritime Trade,* 160.
58 P.R.O., C 43/8/108.
59 Cf. *S.A.C.* cxvi. 43.

of unnamed provenance included woolcards, black thread, plaster of Paris, gum Arabic, and Dutch cheese.

Between 1650 and 1750 imports continued to include coal,[60] cast iron,[61] salt, of which over nine tenths between 1650 and 1688 came from south-west Europe,[62] and wine;[63] pipe clay was also imported.[64] Total cargoes of coal and wine were considerably less than at Shoreham and Chichester;[65] between 1702 and 1704 four Arundel ships were engaged in the Newcastle coal trade in comparison with 33 from Hastings and 56 from Brighton.[66] General cargoes were brought from London and Southampton, as earlier, and also from Portsmouth.[67] In the earlier 18th century Dorset stone was imported in large quantities.[68]

River traffic above the town between the 16th century and the 18th, besides timber, included lead from the castle taken by barge in 1658 to Pallingham in Wisborough Green en route for Albury (Surr.).[69] Bargemen were recorded in the parish in 1571 and in the 18th century.[70] In the later 17th century and earlier 18th some small tradesmen and farmers of the parish kept barges on the river.[71] The port still catered for passenger traffic in the same period, for instance Catholic priests passing between England and the Continent in the late 16th century.[72] Soldiers for Calais were embarked in 1542.[73]

In the late 16th century most ships using the port were not from Arundel itself,[74] though four Arundel ships were mentioned in 1590–1 and five in 1622–3. London merchants often used the port in the late 16th century and early 17th.[75] Besides places already mentioned, ships or boats belonging to the following are recorded between 1497 and 1591: Felpham, Worthing, Shoreham, and Brighton; Portsmouth, Emsworth, and Gosport (Hants); Sandwich and Gillingham (Kent); Dieppe and St. Valéry (Seine Maritime); Bruges; and Ostend and Sluis (Netherlands). Most ships belonging to the port in the 16th and 17th centuries were of 30 tons or less, though a naval ship of 90 tons was mentioned in 1522[76] and a 100-ton coastwise trader in 1572.[77] In 1701 the port had ten ships, with a total tonnage of 465 tons and with 32 men; Brighton at the same date had 77 ships, Hastings 35, and Chichester 18, though Rye, Newhaven, and Shoreham had fewer than Arundel.[78] In the later 17th century and earlier 18th some parishioners owned ship shares: a baker an unspecified share in 1677, and two other men eighth shares in 1682 and 1720, on the first occasion in a Brighton vessel.[79]

The estuary of the river Arun at Littlehampton was said in 1589 to be in a very bad state.[80] Thanks to improvements in the 17th century[81] vessels of 100 tons could reach Arundel in 1675,[82] and a ship of 300–400 tons was built there in the late 17th century or early 18th.[83] It does not seem, however, that ships of that size regularly used the port; in the 1730s and 40s most recorded were of less than 40 tons.[84] By 1698 the estuary was again beginning to be obstructed by the formation of a delta[85] and of a shingle bar; the bar was dangerous to cross, and in the early 18th century some ships had to load or unload outside it.[86] A new channel was cut, with piers to preserve it, under a harbour Act of 1733 which made the mayor of Arundel and the senior burgess for the time being two of the commissioners; the river navigation was also subsequently improved.[87] Despite an immediate improvement in trade,[88] in the later 18th century the harbour deteriorated again until the passing of a second Act in 1793, under which the piers were extended and groynes constructed, and a towpath made to Arundel.[89] The customs officers of the port sometimes lived at Littlehampton in the late 17th century and early 18th,[90] and the custom house was moved there for a time in the 1710s until protests from inhabitants of Arundel forced its return.[91] By the later 18th century Littlehampton's rivalry was becoming more serious; in 1793 several merchants and shipowners trading there petitioned against the new Bill on the ground that though their dues would finance the making of the towpath their own vessels were too large for them to use it.[92]

1800–50. The improvements carried out after 1793 made possible Arundel's period of greatest prosperity as a port, between that date and *c.* 1830. Arundel residents dominated the harbour commission in 1811, supplying 48 of the 74

60 Andrews, 'Geog. Aspects of Maritime Trade', facing ff. 288–9, 308.
61 Ibid. 262.
62 Ibid. 298 and facing ff. 296, 298.
63 Ibid. facing f. 313.
64 Ibid. facing f. 300.
65 Ibid. facing ff. 288–9, 313.
66 *S.N.Q.* xiv. 48.
67 Andrews, op. cit. 310 and facing ff. 307, 311.
68 Ibid. facing f. 301.
69 A.C.M., A 262, ff. [21v.–22]; for timber, below, timber trades.
70 W.S.R.O., A.B.A., L5, bdle. 1, no. 23; A.B.A., M22; ibid. Ep. I/23/1, ff. 58v.–59; *Univ. Brit. Dir.* ii. 56.
71 W.S.R.O., Ep. I/29/8/155, 183, 230.
72 P.R.O., SP 12/164, f. 95; *Studies in Suss. Ch. Hist.* ed. M. Kitch, 109; *Cal. S.P. Dom.* 1581–90, 124, 137–8; 1591–4, 388–9; cf. ibid. 1654, 199–200.
73 *L. & P. Hen. VIII*, xvii, p. 324; cf. *V.C.H. Suss.* i. 519.
74 Para. based mainly on W.S.R.O., MP 9, using customs rec. and port bks. 1553–1604; sample port bks. 1608–41: P.R.O., E 190/755/18; E 190/758/13; E 190/760/11; E 190/763/9; E 190/764/16; E 190/767/32.
75 Cf. *Cal. Assize Rec. Suss. Eliz. I*, p. 153; *Acts of P.C.* 1629–30, p. 296.
76 *L. & P. Hen. VIII*, iii (2), pp. 1045, 1396.
77 *V.C.H. Suss.* ii. 151.
78 Andrews, 'Geog. Aspects of Maritime Trade', f. 50.
79 W.S.R.O., Ep. I/29/8/152, 169, 250, 254.
80 Hist. MSS. Com. 23, *12th Rep. I, Cowper*, p. 12.
81 *High Stream of Arundel*, 27; W. B. Prichard, *Treatise on Harbours*, i (1844), 50–1; A.C.M., A 262, ff. [38v., 95]; 263, acct. 1661.
82 Ogilby, *Britannia* (1675), 8.
83 *C.J.* xxii. 73.
84 W.S.R.O., LH 10/1/1; cf. B.L. Add. MS. 15776, f. 230; Andrews, 'Geog. Aspects of Marit. Trade', facing f. 61.
85 B.L. Sloane MS. 3233, ff. 14–15.
86 *C.J.* xxii. 55, 73; Andrews, op. cit. 58–9.
87 6 Geo. II, c. 12; J. H. Farrant, *Harbours of Suss. 1700–1914* (Brighton, 1976), 13.
88 *Cal. Treas. Bks. and Papers*, 1742–5, 215.
89 33 Geo. III, c. 100; 6 Geo. IV, c. 170 (Local and Personal); Prichard, *Harbours*, i. 54–5.
90 e.g. *Cal. Treas. Bks.* 1685–9, 730; 1689–92, 924; 1714–15, 619; 1716, 534; *Cal. Treas. Bks. and Papers*, 1735–8, 149.
91 *Cal. Treas. Bks.* 1714, 40; 1716, 383; cf. A.C.M., A 1240.
92 J. H. Farrant, *Mid-Victorian Littlehampton*, 2.

commissioners to Littlehampton's five, while the introduction of a property qualification for commissioners in 1825 further favoured the established interests of the town. A proposal to build a bridge at Littlehampton was defeated, chiefly by Arundel merchants and shipowners, in 1822,[93] and plans to move the custom house to Littlehampton were successfully resisted at least twice between 1834 and 1848.[94] The presence of the custom house led to Arundel's becoming a bonding port in 1817, despite the greater convenience of Littlehampton.[95] Ships of 200 or 300 tons could reach the town on spring tides in the 1830s,[96] and by *c.* 1841 the landing area on the south bank of the river had four docks, including the bonding dock and another for landing coal.[97]

The expansion of the Arun navigation after 1785, with the completion of the Wey and Arun canal in 1816,[98] greatly increased Arundel's hinterland; already by the 1790s there was a service of cargo boats to London.[99] Thirteen boats were listed in the parish in 1801, when five persons aged between 15 and 60 were willing to act as boatmen or bargemen in the event of a French invasion. In 1803 there were 15 boats, all but three undecked, with a total tonnage of 266 tons; in addition, two Arundel boats were listed at Wisborough Green.[1] John Boxold the timber merchant was a bargemaster or barge owner *c.* 1815 and in 1832.[2] The firm of Seward and Co., called the Arundel Barge or Lighter Co. and by various other names, started a regular service to London with three barges from a wharf near the town quay *c.* 1820. By 1823 the firm had 10 barges, and in 1830 seven, of which five had been built at Arundel.[3] About 1832 it offered a twice-weekly service to London, Chichester, Midhurst, and Petworth, and perhaps to Portsmouth.[4]

The long-term trend, however, was for deep-sea shipping to unload at Littlehampton, and already by 1824 four times as much seagoing shipping used Littlehampton as Arundel;[5] in 1831 Littlehampton could be described as a considerable port,[6] and the inevitable transfer of the custom house was achieved in 1864.[7] The opening of local railway lines from the 1840s meanwhile reduced the use of the inland navigations; by 1852 the Arundel–London barge service was only weekly, and it ceased apparently soon after 1855.[8]

Exports from Arundel[9] between the 1820s and 1840s included ships' provisions, grain, and flour, of which the two last named in 1849 went to the West country, Liverpool, and Ireland. Imports were by then much more significant;[10] besides timber[11] they were chiefly grain, in 1849 from Ireland and the Netherlands, and coal and culm from Newcastle and from Scotland. In 1831 fruit ships from the Mediterranean were said to reach Arundel twice in the season.[12] Wine and oilcake were brought from France in 1849. Other imports at the same period were brandy, apples, eggs, dairy products, pork, bacon, and tar.

The town quay was rebuilt by the corporation in 1813 and added to in 1825.[13] In 1835 the corporation was said to take dues on all goods landed there at the rates listed in 1643, but the sum raised was not more than £3–4 a year, which the mayor received. At the same date the mayor also took dues from all coal, culm, and salt cargoes landed, usually at a money commutation; their average annual value between 1830 and 1832 was £6 11*s.* 1*d.*[14] In 1902 quay dues brought the borough less than £10 a year.[15] Besides wharves belonging to various businesses on both sides of the river, there was a private quay belonging to the duke of Norfolk at the west end of Tarrant Street *c.* 1841.[16] New steps from the town quay to the river were constructed *c.* 1936[17] and survived in 1989.

The river continued to be used for passenger traffic in the early 19th century, for instance by John Tompkins the sometime mayor, going to Littlehampton with the duke of Norfolk in 1803 in connexion with a building project,[18] or by George MacDonald the Independent minister, leaving the town in 1853 with his family and all their goods, since he could not afford a carriage.[19]

AFTER 1850. With the removal of the custom house, the arrival of the railway in the 1840s, and the growth of Littlehampton's port, accommodating larger ships, the port at Arundel began to decline. In 1863 vessels drawing up to 14 ft. could reach it.[20] By 1886 only *c.* 20 ships a year reached the town, almost all of the coastwise trade.[21] In the early 20th century most were towed by paddle tug.[22] Coal, especially for the gasworks, and salt were still imported at that

93 Ibid.
94 A.C.M., MD 417, 1004; W.S.R.O., Goodwood MS. 644, rep. 1834.
95 Tierney, *Arundel*, ii. 721; *Rep. Parl. Bdries.* H.C. 141–V, p. 64 (1831–2), xl.
96 W.S.R.O., Add. MS. 15674; Tierney, *Arundel*, ii. 721; Dallaway & Cartwright, *Hist. W. Suss.* ii (1) (1832), 210; cf. Dallaway, *Hist. W. Suss.* i (1) (1815), p. cxlviii.
97 W.S.R.O., TD/W 5; P. A. L. Vine, *Lond.'s Lost Route to Sea* (1986), pl. 54.
98 Vine, op. cit. 26 sqq., 64–5; Farrant, *Harbours of Suss.* 13.
99 *Univ. Brit. Dir.* i. 520; cf. *S.A.C.* lxiii. 57 n.
1 E.S.R.O., LCG/3/EW 1, ff. [46, 90v.–91].
2 W.S.R.O., Add. MS. 2615 (TS. cat.); ibid. CE 1/1/1, f. 65; ibid. Par. 8/37/16.
3 Vine, *Lond.'s Lost Route*, 119, 121, 262; M. Bouquet, *South Eastern Sail*, 86; *S.A.C.* civ. 119; A.C.M., D 3059–72 (MS. cat.); W.S.R.O., CE 1/1/1, ff. 42–3, 53, 55–6.
4 Pigot, *Nat. Com. Dir.* (1832–4), 1004; cf. Vine, op. cit. 119.
5 Farrant, *Mid-Victorian Littlehampton*, 2.
6 Lewis, *Topog. Dict. Eng.* (1831), s.v. Hampton.
7 Farrant, *Harbours of Suss.* 35.
8 *Kelly's Dir. Suss.* (1852 and later edns.).
9 Para. based mainly on Tierney, *Arundel*, ii. 721–2; Dallaway & Cartwright, *Hist. W. Suss.* ii (1) (1832), 210; *1st Rep. Com. Mun. Corp.* 675; Lewis, *Topog. Dict. Eng.* (1849).
10 Cf. *Suss. Ind. Hist.* xv. 9.
11 Below, timber trades.
12 Lewis, *Topog. Dict. Eng.* (1831).
13 W.S.R.O., A.B.A., F1/1 (1813, 1825).
14 *1st Rep. Com. Mun. Corp.* 674; cf. W.S.R.O., A.B.A., M8.
15 W.S.R.O., BO/AR 24/4/17, f. 9.
16 Ibid. TD/W 5; Vine, *Lond.'s Lost Route to Sea*, pl. 54.
17 W.S.R.O., BO/AR 53/12.
18 *S.A.C.* lxxi. 48.
19 W. Raeper, *Geo. MacDonald*, 98.
20 Farrant, *Mid-Victorian Littlehampton*, 3.
21 *12th Ann. Rep. on Combined Sanit. Dist. of W. Suss.* (Worthing, 1886), 155 (copy at W.S.R.O., WDC/CL 74/1); cf. *Census*, 1901, listing only 1 vessel at the port; ibid. 1881–91, 1911, listing none. For a contemporary view of the port, Vine, op. cit. pl. 55, illus. below, facing p. 75.
22 *W. Suss. Gaz.* 9 Dec. 1965; Cartland, *Arundel*, 138.

period, besides timber,[23] and fishing vessels continued to unload their catches on the town quay.[24] Vessels of 300–400 tons could still reach the port in 1904 using the tide.[25] South Wales coal as well as timber was still being sent up river from Arundel into Surrey in the mid 19th century,[26] but by 1886, when the town's chief traffic was in barges taking timber, coal, and building materials inland from Littlehampton, river transport could no longer reach beyond Petworth, Midhurst, and Newbridge in Wisborough Green. Fifteen or twenty barges then plied the river.[27] In the late 19th century riverside farmers went to Arundel market and elsewhere by barge.[28] Chalk and lime were still barged downstream from the Amberley chalkpits in the early 20th century.[29]

By 1910 trade on the river was said to be practically extinct;[30] the last steamer came to the town in or shortly before 1914 and the last sailing vessel *c.* 1917.[31] The opening of the swing bridge at Littlehampton in 1908[32] was an impediment, and after the construction of the fixed railway bridge at Ford in 1938[33] masted craft could no longer reach the town. With the decline of the port the two most westerly of three docks on the south bank of the river had silted up by 1875, and the remaining one by 1896.[34] The town quay and the other wharves along the river were gradually disused during the 20th century.[35]

The firm of Buller, boat proprietor, was started in the late 19th century as Edward Slaughter, later Buller and Slaughter. It was based at first at the General Abercrombie inn in Queen Street[36] and was hiring pleasure boats by 1903,[37] as it continued to do in 1990.

TIMBER TRADES. In the late 14th century timber was brought from Pulborough by river.[38] Wealden timber and wood were among the chief exports mentioned in the record of royal customs collected at Arundel port between the later 15th century and the mid 17th.[39] Carriage downstream to Arundel was eased after *c.* 1560 by the earl of Arundel's improvement of the river for that purpose between Stopham bridge and Pallingham quay in Wisborough Green.[40] Cargoes, including planks and various kinds of boards, went to London,[41] Yarmouth (Norf.),[42] and various south-coast ports in England, and to Dieppe and the Low Countries abroad. During the same period ships' masts were imported from London.

Between 1650 and 1750 Arundel was perhaps the chief timber exporting port in south-east England. Large cargoes were sent towards London, especially to the naval dockyards, and to Portsmouth, in the later 17th century, particularly during the wars of the 1650s and 60s.[43] During the quarter century of war after 1694 the trade reached its greatest peak, *c.* 40 cargoes of timber a year being exported; the average was 40 loads and the largest 90. In that period Plymouth dockyard too was supplied.[44] In the 1720s timber shipped from Arundel was considered the best and largest brought to the dockyards by sea from anywhere in England.[45] Timber and bark were also exported to Ireland and timber to Poole in the early 18th century. Already by the same date there was a small import trade in Norwegian deals.[46]

By the early 19th century exports of timber and bark were much less significant,[47] though timber continued to be supplied to the naval dockyards[48] and in 1849 was sent to the West country, Liverpool, and Ireland.[49] At the same period Baltic timber and deals were imported, together with masts, spars, and oars.[50] In the mid 19th century timber was still being sent up river from Arundel into Surrey,[51] but by 1886 barges belonging to the town were instead taking timber inland from Littlehampton.[52]

The Arundel man to whom a Kirdford man agreed to deliver 2,000 oak barrel boards and 2,000 hogshead boards in 1584[53] was presumably a timber merchant. Christopher Coles, who in 1668 had much timber in the river Arun awaiting transport to the naval dockyards,[54] was evidently another; he may still have been involved in the trade in 1685.[55] There was a timber merchant in

23 *W. Suss. Gaz.* 9 Dec. 1965; 7 June 1973; Cartland, *Arundel*, 127–8; inf. from Mr. G. Campbell, former clerk to Littlehampton harbour bd.; W.S.R.O., PH 1007, 1251, 1254. For timber, below, timber trades.

24 *W. Suss. Gaz.* 7 June 1973.

25 *Bradshaw's Canals and Navig. Rivers of Eng. and Wales* (1904), 44, 46.

26 Vine, *Lond.'s Lost Route*, 121.

27 *12th Ann. Rep. on Combined Sanit. Dist. of W. Suss.* (Worthing, 1886), 155.

28 *S.A.C.* lxiii. 57.

29 Inf. from Mrs. Ian Rodger, Arundel, and Mr. F. Penfold, Burpham.

30 Pike, *Bognor Dir.* (1910–11), 167.

31 *W. Suss. Gaz.* 9 Dec. 1965.

32 *S.N.Q.* xvii. 210.

33 Below, Tortington, intro.

34 O.S. Map 1/2,500, Suss. LXIII. 1 (1877, 1897 edns.).

35 Cf. ibid. (1912 edn.); *W. Suss. Gaz.* 9 Dec. 1965.

36 *Kelly's Dir. Suss.* (1899 and later edns.).

37 Kimpton, *Arundel* (1903), p. iv.

38 A.C.M., uncat. late 14th-cent. acct. roll (Suss. box 3, no. 1).

39 Rest of para. based mainly on W.S.R.O., MP 9, using customs rec. and port bks. 1497–1604; sample port bks. 1608–41: P.R.O., E 190/755/18; E 190/758/13; E 190/760/11; E 190/763/9; E 190/764/16; E 190/767/32; *S.N.Q.* ix. 108; *V.C.H. Suss.* ii. 233. For interpretation of statistics, above, port and river traffic.

40 *High Stream of Arundel*, 21.

41 Cf. Hist. MSS. Com. 23, *12th Rep. I, Cowper*, p. 12.

42 Cf. N. J. Williams, *Maritime Trade of E. Anglian Ports*, 100, 172.

43 J. H. Andrews, 'Geog. Aspects of Maritime Trade of Kent and Suss. 1650–1750' (Lond. Univ. Ph.D. thesis, 1954), 252–3 and facing f. 245; *Cal. S.P. Dom.* 1651, 507; 1653–4, 515; 1654, 560; 1668–9, 354.

44 Andrews, op. cit. 253; W.S.R.O., A.B.A., M14; Defoe, *Tour*, ed. Cole, i. 132.

45 Defoe, *Tour*, ed. Cole, i. 132.

46 Andrews, op. cit. 254 and facing f. 302; W.S.R.O., A.B.A., M14.

47 Tierney, *Arundel*, ii. 722.

48 *Fisher's New Brighton Guide* (1804), 74 (copy in Worthing Ref. Libr.); Wright, *Arundel* (1817), 3.

49 Lewis, *Topog. Dict. Eng.* (1849).

50 Ibid.; Tierney, *Arundel*, ii. 721–2; Dallaway & Cartwright, *Hist. W. Suss.* ii (1) (1832), 210; *1st Rep. Com. Mun. Corp.* 675.

51 P. A. L. Vine, *Lond.'s Lost Route to Sea* (1986), 121.

52 *12th Ann. Rep. on Combined Sanit. Dist. of W. Suss.* (Worthing, 1886), 155 (copy at W.S.R.O., WDC/CL 74/1).

53 *Lavington Estate Archives*, ed. F. W. Steer, p. 109.

54 *Cal. S.P. Dom.* 1667–8, 202–3, 489; 1673, 277.

55 *Cal. Treas. Bks.* 1685–9, 322, naming Chas. Coles; cf. below, this section [shipbldg.].

1700,[56] and between the mid 18th century[57] and the mid 20th there seems always to have been at least one in the parish.[58] About 1832 there were four.[59] One of those, Thomas Fry, evidently leased the remains of the south range of the friary by the bridge,[60] which had been a timber yard in the late 18th century and continued to be so used *c.* 1850.[61] Another, the firm of Samuel Evershed and Co., had premises on the south side of the river,[62] where Fry also had a yard by *c.* 1841.[63]

After *c.* 1850 two firms remained.[64] The former shipbuilding site in River Road called the Nineveh shipyard[65] was occupied from 1862 or earlier by the firm of Edward Fry, apparently Thomas's successor since in 1887 it was claimed to be over 75 years old.[66] Later occupants of the site were G. H. Bulbeck (fl. 1892–1902),[67] Brown and Creese (1907–12),[68] described as English, foreign, and bentwood merchants, Louis Blackman Ltd. (1913–22), which also dealt in both English and foreign timber, Lowden Bros. (1927–30), the Arundel Timber and Sawmills Co. (1934–8), and H. D. Sinclair (1941).[69] South of the river Marshall and Fry, later Fry and Son or William Fry, dealt in timber in the 1850s and foreign timber in the 60s and 70s.[70] By 1910 the two businesses were in the same ownership.[71] There was still a timber yard on the south bank of the river in 1952.[72]

The timber trade at the port and the relatively well wooded surroundings of the town supplied occasional specialized trades before the 19th century like those of sawyer,[73] maker of spade handles,[74] joiner,[75] and cabinet maker.[76] There were two chairmakers, four cabinet makers, and a clog maker in the 1830s.[77]

The chief business using timber between the 16th and 18th centuries, however, was shipbuilding, which may have been carried on in 1401, when the town was ordered, together with Lewes, to build a balinger or light sea-going vessel.[78] The borough seems to have been responsible for building one or two other ships in 1579.[79] At least two shipwrights and a 'ship carpenter' were mentioned in the early 17th century,[80] but in 1665 it was claimed, admittedly in response to a request for impressment, that there were no shipwrights in the town.[81] Several ships were said in 1675 to have been built recently at Arundel,[82] a 60–ton hoy was built for the timber trade by Charles Coles in 1684,[83] and in the 1690s two advice, i.e. dispatch, boats, each of 152 tons, for the navy.[84] Joseph Fugar worked as a shipwright between 1682 and 1702,[85] negotiating for timber from Shipley in 1695.[86] A ship of between 300 and 400 tons was built in the late 17th century or early 18th.[87] At least one timber merchant was also a shipbuilder, George Moore,[88] whose shipyard mentioned in 1705[89] may have been on the site of the later shipyard in River Road.[90] Two other shipwrights were recorded in 1720 and 1721, one of whom had come from Portsmouth,[91] and a shipbuilder in 1767.[92] In 1728 Arundel was said to be eminent for the building of hoys and ketches.[93]

In the late 18th century and early 19th the firm of Briggs and Crookenden built merchant barges; in 1804 it consisted of a master and two apprentices.[94] A 20–ton merchant ship was built at Arundel in 1818,[95] but of 13 other craft built there between 1795 and 1848 five and probably at least three more were barges.[96] Two firms of barge builders were recorded between the 1830s and 1850s[97] and there were three shipwrights and an apprentice in 1851.[98] There was a boat builder in 1938,[99] and a firm of boat builders had premises in Ford Road in 1970.[1]

By 1874 the timber firm of Thomas Fry in River Road had a steam sawmill;[2] in 1887 there was also a millwright's shop.[3] There were sawmills south of the river by 1910, which had gone by 1937.[4] In the 1930s *c.* 40 people were employed at the sawmills in River Road, which used timber from the Norfolk, Dale Park, and Petworth estates.

56 *Arundel Cast. Archives*, ii, p. 20.
57 Ibid. iv, p. 86; cf. W.S.R.O., A.B.A., M32.
58 e.g. A.C.M., M 900; *Wiston Archives*, i, ed. J. Booker, p. 131; *Arundel Rds.* 34–5; W.S.R.O., CE 1/1/1, f. 65; ibid. Par. 8/37/16.
59 Pigot, *Nat. Com. Dir.* (1832–4), 1004.
60 W.S.R.O., TD/W 5.
61 Above, relig. hos. (Dominican friary); below, pl. facing p. 74.
62 Cf. *Kelly's Dir. Suss.* (1845).
63 W.S.R.O., TD/W 5.
64 Para. based mainly on *Kelly's Dir. Suss.* (1852 and later edns.).
65 Name recorded from 1948: W.S.R.O., BO/AR 16/1/269; cf. *W. Suss. Gaz.* 16 May 1974; above, secular bldgs. For shipbldg., below, this section.
66 A.C.M., D 614–33, sale cat. 1887.
67 Cf. *Goodwood Estate Archives*, i, ed. F. W. Steer and J. Venables, p. 202; W.S.R.O., BO/AR 24/4/16.
68 Cf. W.S.R.O., SP 1057.
69 Ibid. BO/AR 16/1/221.
70 Cf. 9 & 10 Vic. c. 37 (Private); *Arundel Rds.* 34.
71 Pike, *Bognor Dir.* (1910–11), 190–1; *W. Suss. Gaz.* 19 June 1975.
72 *S.C.M.* xxvi. 231.
73 e.g. *Cal. Assize Rec. Suss. Eliz. I*, p. 427; *Returns of Papists, 1767* (Cath. Rec. Soc.), ii. 145; W.S.R.O., A.B.A., B1/25; ibid. Ep. I/29/8/289.
74 W.S.R.O., Add. MS. 316 (TS. cat.).
75 e.g. ibid. A.B.A., B1/15–16; A.B.A., M22, list of inhabitants, 1767; ibid. Ep. I/29/8/19, 68.
76 *Univ. Brit. Dir.* ii. 57.
77 Pigot, *Nat. Com. Dir.* (1832–4), 1003–4.
78 *Cal. Close*, 1399–1402, 239; *O.E.D.*
79 W.S.R.O., A.B.A., F2/3.
80 Ibid. A.B.A., B1/17, 28; A.B.A., B2/3; *S.R.S.* xxix, p. 10; cf. ibid. xlix. 23; *Cal. S.P. Dom.* Addenda 1660–85, 264.
81 *Cal. S.P. Dom.* 1665–6, 118.
82 Ogilby, *Britannia* (1675), 8.
83 *Cal. Treas. Bks.* 1685–9, 322.
84 *V.C.H. Suss.* ii. 166; *O.E.D.*
85 W.S.R.O., Ep. I/55/247; *Goodwood Estate Archives*, i, ed. Steer and Venables, p. 195; *S.R.S.* xxix, p. 159.
86 *Wiston Archives*, i, ed. J. Booker, p. 298.
87 *C.J.* xxii. 73.
88 *Arundel Cast. Archives*, ii. 20.
89 W.S.R.O., Par. 8/11/7, f. 1; cf. ibid. Add. MS. 15818B (TS. cat.).
90 Cf. above, growth of town (street names).
91 *S.R.S.* xxviii. 9; W.S.R.O., Par. 8/32/1/2, no. 48.
92 *Returns of Papists, 1767* (Cath. Rec. Soc.), ii. 145; cf. [P. Phillips], *Diary kept in Excursion to Littlehampton* (1780), i. 39.
93 *S.A.C.* xi. 181.
94 *Univ. Brit. Dir.* ii. 56; *Further Papers and Accts. respecting Ships of War, etc.* H.C. 193, p. 485 (1805), viii; E.S.R.O., SAS/HA 489–90 (TS. cat.).
95 W.S.R.O., SR 96 (TS. cat.).
96 Ibid. CE 1/1/1, ff. 15, 23, 28, 37, 42–3, 53, 55–6, 65, 78, 111, 121; CE 1/1/2, f. 38; for Jas. Soulter, Slater, or Slaughter cf. Pigot, *Nat. Com. Dir.* (1832–4), 1004; *Kelly's Dir. Suss.* (1852, 1862).
97 Pigot, *Nat. Com. Dir.* (1832–4), 1004; ibid. (1839), 654; *Kelly's Dir. Suss.* (1845 and later edns.).
98 P.R.O., HO 107/1651, ff. 560v., 562v., 580.
99 *Kelly's Dir. Suss.* (1938).
1 O.S. Map 1/2,500, TQ 0006–0106 (1971 edn.).
2 *Kelly's Dir. Suss.* (1874).
3 A.C.M., D 614–33, sale cat. 1887.
4 O.S. Map 1/2,500, Suss. LXIII. 1 (1912, 1937 edns.).

Much dressed timber was supplied to the building trade and some to yacht builders in Littlehampton, but more specialized products were also sent to various parts of England.[5] Joinery was made there besides.[6] In or soon after 1941[7] the premises were sold to Alfred Lockhart Ltd. of Brentford (Mdx.), which had Admiralty contracts; the firm closed at some time between 1948 and 1957, the former sawmill chimney remaining until 1985.[8]

About 1832 there were four carpenters in the town, besides a wheelwright.[9] Three firms of coach builders are recorded in the 19th century and early 20th,[10] and the timber merchants Brown and Creese (fl. 1907–12) also made carriages and wagons.[11] The firm of Abel Peirce and Sons in Surrey Street, which flourished between 1874 and 1956 as both wheelwrights and blacksmiths, also built farm carts and repaired vehicles.[12] In the 19th century there were two organ builders in the town[13] and in 1985 a furniture repairer on the industrial estate.[14]

There was a wood reeve on the Norfolk estate in the 19th and early 20th centuries.[15] The estate had its own timber department by the early 19th century, occupying a courtyard west of the modern racing stables between that date[16] and its closure in the 1980s. A steam sawmill was built further north by the 1870s, when it was connected with the courtyard by a railway.[17] The sawmill was rebuilt in the mid 20th century. In 1980 7 people were employed in the estate forestry department and 7 in the building department, besides 2 sawyers at the sawmill. A wood-turning business in Park bottom founded by Duke Bernard before 1970 had by then become a commercial enterprise;[18] in 1989, as Singleton Joinery, it employed 24 people making doors.[19]

OTHER TRADES AND INDUSTRIES. MEDIEVAL. Twelve cloth merchants and at least 19 wine merchants were presented for sales contrary to the assize between 1248 and 1288.[20] Wool merchants were mentioned in 1296 and later,[21] and there were at least six merchants dealing in unspecified goods in 1340–1.[22] Trading links with Amiens (Somme) or St. Omer (Pas de Calais) may be indicated in 1305,[23] and there were links with London in the 15th century.[24] In 1436 three Netherlands merchants and one from Saxony were living in the town.[25] There was at least one Jew in Arundel in 1197[26] and a Jewish community in the mid 13th century; in 1272, however, when they were taxed at the same rate as those of Chichester, the Jews of Arundel were said to have only some empty houses.[27] Thirteenth- and 14th-century surnames suggest the presence in the town, besides the usual tradesmen, of a ropemaker, a dyer, a soap maker, a locksmith, and at least one fisherman.[28] There was possibly a cutler in the mid 14th century[29] and certainly in the early 15th.[30] Goldsmiths are recorded between 1288 and 1364.[31]

1500–1800. Between the 16th century and the later 18th the many parishioners described simply as merchants[32] presumably dealt in general merchandise, both import and export. The continuing foreign trading links shown by traffic at the port are corroborated by the presence of nine aliens in the town in 1524,[33] while the burgess who was living in Denmark between 1574 and 1580[34] was possibly there on business. The timber trade is discussed above.[35] Corn merchants were mentioned in 1574[36] and in the mid 17th century when George Taylor (d. *c.* 1669) traded in malt and was sending grain to Ireland.[37] A 'winer' and three vintners were recorded between 1570 and 1724,[38] and a wine merchant who was also a shipbuilder in 1780.[39] About 1670 several 'considerable' merchants are said to have lived in the town.[40] George Lane was a coal merchant between 1759 and 1771,[41] and Daniel Digance (fl. 1783) perhaps another.[42] In the 1790s there were 3 wine merchants and 2 wool merchants, besides 5 others dealing in unspecified goods.[43]

Numerous mercers, grocers, and shopkeepers were also recorded between the 16th and 18th centuries.[44] There were two mercers in 1546[45] and

5 *W. Suss. Gaz.* 16 May 1974; 2 May 1985.
6 *Kelly's Dir. Suss.* (1934, 1938); cf. W.S.R.O., BO/AR 16/1/221, 235.
7 Cf. above, this section.
8 *W. Suss. Gaz.* 2 May 1985; W.S.R.O., BO/AR 16/1/269.
9 Pigot, *Nat. Com. Dir.* (1832–4), 1003–4.
10 Ibid. (1839), 654; *Kelly's Dir. Suss.* (1845 and later edns.).
11 W.S.R.O., SP 1057.
12 *W. Suss. Gaz.* 7 June 1973.
13 *Kelly's Dir. Suss.* (1845 and later edns.).
14 *Ind. in W. Suss.* (W. Suss. C.C. 1985), [50].
15 *Kelly's Dir. Suss.* (1887 and later edns.); *Arundel Rds.* 37.
16 A.C.M., PM 107; cf. W.S.R.O. TD/W 5.
17 O.S. Map 1/2,500, Suss. LXIII. 1 (1877 edn.).
18 Ibid. TQ 0007–0107 (1971 edn.); *Country Life*, 3 July 1980, p. 8; inf. from Mr. F. Penfold, Burpham.
19 *W. Suss. Gaz.* 20 July 1989.
20 P.R.O., JUST 1/909A, rot. 22d.; JUST 1/912A, rot. 45; JUST 1/917, rot. 22; JUST 1/924, rot. 65d.
21 *S.N.Q.* iv. 69, 162; *S.A.C.* lxxii. 165; lxxviii. 218.
22 P.R.O., E 179/189/19; *Inq. Non.* (Rec. Com.), 370.
23 *Cal. Fine R.* 1272–1307, 519–20.
24 *Cal. Pat.* 1416–22, 96; 1446–52, 197; 1467–77, p. 224; *Cal. Close*, 1485–1500, p. 34; cf. ibid. 1500–9, pp. 121–2.
25 *Cal. Pat.* 1429–36, 545; one may have been the Nic. 'Ducheman' mentioned at *S.R.S.* xxiii, p. 249.
26 *Pipe R.* 1197 (P.R.S. N.S. viii), 224.
27 *Sel. Pleas of Exch. of Jews* (Selden Soc. xv), 69–70; cf. above, growth of town (street names).
28 *S.R.S.* x. 81, 134; B.L. Lansd. Ch. 86, 105 (MS. cal.); cf. *Inq. Non.* (Rec. Com.), 370.
29 *S.R.S.* xxiii, p. 158; *Inq. Non.* (Rec. Com.), 370.
30 *S.R.S.* lxvii. 116.
31 Ibid. vii, p. 157; x. 134; xxiii, p. 156; P.R.O., JUST 1/924, rot. 43d.; cf. B.L. Lansd. Ch. 86 (MS. cal.).
32 e.g. *Cal. Pat.* 1553–4, 442; *S.R.S.* lviii, p. 61; *Wiston Archives*, i, ed. J. Booker, pp. 6, 132; *Arundel Cast. Archives*, iii, p. 22; W.S.R.O., A.B.A., B1/7; A.B.A., B2/12; A.B.A., M32.
33 *S.R.S.* lvi. 43–4.
34 W.S.R.O., A.B.A., A1, f. 22.
35 Above, timber trades.
36 Hist. MSS. Com. 31, *13th Rep. IV, Rye Corp.* p. 37.
37 *Cal. S.P. Dom.* 1651, 548; 1651–2, 549, 592; W.S.R.O., Ep. I/29/8/122.
38 W.S.R.O., Ep. I/29/8/1, 10, 39, 262; cf. *Cal. Treas. Bks.* 1702, 206.
39 [P. Phillips], *Diary kept in Excursion to Littlehampton* (1780), i. 39.
40 *C.J.* xxii. 73.
41 W.S.R.O., MP 3045.
42 Ibid. Add. MS. 20618 (TS. cat.); *Univ. Brit. Dir.* ii. 56.
43 *Univ. Brit. Dir.* ii. 56–7.
44 e.g. *Cal. Assize Rec. Suss. Eliz. I*, p. 88; W.S.R.O., A.B.A., M32; ibid. Add. MS. 29765 (TS. cat.); ibid. Ep. I/29/8/6, 9, 274, 287.
45 *Lavington Estate Archives*, ed. F. W. Steer, p. 63.

a woollen draper between 1594 and 1603.[46] In the late 17th century there were several mercers in the town[47] including William Nye (d. *c.* 1674), who dealt in clothing and grocery ware, and Thomas Watersfield (d. *c.* 1683), who sold woollen and hosiery ware, linen, and haberdashery. Thomas Horne, grocer (d. *c.* 1719), and Henry Newman, shopkeeper (d. *c.* 1720), sold cloth, provisions, household vessels, and miscellaneous goods.[48]

Others involved in the clothing trades between the 16th and late 18th centuries included two hempdressers, a shearman,[49] two hatters,[50] a sergemaker,[51] a staymaker, a feltmaker,[52] and a mantua maker.[53] There was a fuller in 1555.[54] Members of the Older family were tanners between 1602 and 1669,[55] and members of the Booker family worked in various leather trades between the mid 17th century and the mid 18th.[56] There were fellmongers in 1706 and later.[57] Tallow chandlers recorded during the same period included Robert Sotcher (d. *c.* 1701), who had three furnaces and traded in candles, cotton, soap, and matches,[58] and members of the Pecknell,[59] Shaft,[60] and Elliott families.[61]

Besides brewing, malting was widely carried on.[62] There were malthouses in 1705 and later[63] in Queen Street, where an apparently 18th-century oast kiln survived in 1985.[64] The west range of the friary by the bridge was used as a malthouse by 1780.[65]

Representatives of the metal trades included an armourer,[66] a 'mettleman',[67] cutlers,[68] a gunsmith,[69] plumbers,[70] and a locksmith.[71] A bellfounder from Reading settled in Arundel in 1712 before moving to London.[72] Richard Harman (d. *c.* 1719) evidently worked as both brazier and joiner, and was perhaps succeeded in his business by Richard Gillham (d. *c.* 1738) who, though described as an ironmonger, also sold brazier's, cutler's, and pewterer's goods, and at his death had stock in the joiner's and cabinet maker's trades.[73] Thomas Withers, ironmonger (fl. 1775),[74] was perhaps related to a cutler of the same surname mentioned in 1674.[75]

Other specialized trades in the 17th and 18th centuries were those of glazier,[76] bookseller,[77] clockmaker,[78] pipemaker,[79] wig maker,[80] and stationer.[81] A tobacconist *c.* 1705 also sold paper, stockings, and brandy.[82] There was a gingerbread baker *c.* 1730.[83] Two or more members of the Spencer family were basket makers between 1693 and *c.* 1800.[84] Though only two fishing boats were listed at Arundel in 1565, and four in 1581,[85] mariners were often recorded between the mid 16th century and the early 19th,[86] as later,[87] and two fishermen were mentioned in 1709[88] and 1740.[89]

Some indication of Arundel's trading hinterland is perhaps given by settlement certificates of the period 1674–1822: 29 migrants were from other Sussex towns, 14 from towns in Hampshire, 89 from elsewhere in Sussex, chiefly places nearby but including more distant villages such as Amberley and Findon with good road communication, and 15 from rural Hampshire, from Surrey, and from London.[90]

In the mid 1790s tradesmen in the town, apart from those mentioned elsewhere,[91] included: 4 bakers, 5 butchers, a milk seller, 5 grocers, and a brewer; 7 shoemakers, 2 curriers and leather cutters, and 2 saddlers; 4 tailors, 2 staymakers, 2 milliners, one or more drapers, a hat maker, and a breeches maker; 4 builders, 2 bricklayers, a carpenter, 3 stonemasons, and 4 plumbers and glaziers; 4 blacksmiths, 4 ironmongers, and a brazier; four or more mercers and 3 shopkeepers; a basket maker; a seedsman; 2 gardeners; 4 hairdressers; a stationer; 2 auctioneers; 2 watchmakers; and a dealer in silver goods.[92]

1800–1945. Numerous merchants were recorded in the 19th and 20th centuries; *c.* 1832, besides

46 Ibid. pp. 86, 101; Eustace, *Arundel*, 255; W.S.R.O., Add. MS. 15681 (TS. cat.).
47 E.S.R.O., SAS/C 40 (TS. cat.); W.S.R.O., A.B.A., L3, no. 19, f. 20; A.B.A., P1/10; ibid. Add. MSS. 12938, 15818A–B, 15821 (TS. cat.); *S.R.S.* xxix, pp. 2–3, 12, 166; *Danny Archives*, ed. J. Wooldridge, p. 87.
48 W.S.R.O., Ep. I/29/8/144, 172, 249, 254; cf. ibid. Ep. I/29/8/287.
49 Ibid. A.B.A., B1/21, 24, 27.
50 *Greatham Archives*, ed. A. Dibben, p. xiv; *S.R.S.* xxviii. 127.
51 *Wiston Archives*, i, ed. J. Booker, p. 262.
52 W.S.R.O., Par. 8/32/1/2, nos. 70, 124.
53 *S.R.S.* xxviii. 157.
54 Ibid. xli. 41.
55 A.C.M., A 263, rental, 1657; E.S.R.O., SAS/K 106 (TS. cat.); W.S.R.O., A.B.A., B1/3, 29; A.B.A., F2/14, f. [3v.]; ibid. Add. MS. 15689 (TS. cat.); P.R.O., E 134/17 Chas. II Trin./3, rot. 3.
56 W.S.R.O., A.B.A., B4/5 (TS. cat.); ibid. Add. MS. 15771 (TS. cat.); ibid. S.A.S. MS. HB 167 (TS. cat.); S.A.S. MS. RB 7 (TS. cat.).
57 *S.R.S.* xxviii. 39, 141; A.C.M., D 1124–8 (MS. cat.); W.S.R.O., Ep. I/29/8/227; cf. ibid. Ep. I/29/8/188.
58 W.S.R.O., Ep. I/29/8/221.
59 Ibid. Add. MSS. 15743, 35555 (TS. cat.); *S.R.S.* xxviii. 144, 147, 213.
60 W.S.R.O., A.B.A., J1, ff. 123v.–125; A.B.A., M32.
61 Ibid. A.B.A., L3, no. 19, f. 47; ibid. Add. MSS. 17012; 35556–7 (TS. cat.); cf. *Univ. Brit. Dir.* ii. 56.
62 e.g. W.S.R.O., Ep. I/29/8/157, 183, 228, 232, 250.
63 Ibid. Par. 8/11/7, f. 1; below, this section (1800–1945).
64 *Suss. Ind. Arch.* (1985), p. 7.
65 *S.A.C.* cvii. 67.
66 *Cal. Assize Rec. Suss. Eliz. I*, p. 325.
67 W.S.R.O., A.B.A., B1/8.
68 Ibid. A.B.A., B2/2; A.B.A., L3, no. 19, f. 46; *Cal. Assize Rec. Suss. Eliz. I*, p. 99; *Jas. I*, p. 102.
69 W.S.R.O., Ep. I/29/8/235.
70 Ibid. S.A.S. MS. RB 35 (TS. cat.); *Wiston Archives*, ii, ed. S. Freeth, p. 43.
71 W.S.R.O., Par. 8/32/1/2, no. 28.
72 Ibid. no. 32; *S.A.C.* lvi. 202.
73 W.S.R.O., Ep. I/29/8/251, 294.
74 Ibid. A.B.A., M32; *Univ. Brit. Dir.* ii. 57.
75 W.S.R.O., A.B.A., L3, no. 19, f. 46; cf. *S.R.S.* xxviii. 13.
76 e.g. W.S.R.O., A.B.A., B1/11; A.B.A., M32; ibid. Ep. I/29/8/161, 270.
77 Ibid. Add. MS. 44822 (TS. cat.); *S.R.S.* xxix, p. 12.
78 A.C.M., A 1240; W.S.R.O., Ep. I/29/8/247.
79 W.S.R.O., Ep. I/29/8/268; *S.A.C.* cx. 39.
80 W.S.R.O., A.B.A., L5, bdle. 1, no. 23, f. 3; ibid. Add. MS. 15743 (TS. cat.); ibid. Par. 8/32/1/2, no. 56; *S.R.S.* xxviii. 26, 57.
81 W.S.R.O., A.B.A., M32.
82 Ibid. Ep. I/29/8/226; cf. *Goodwood Estate Archives*, i, ed. F. W. Steer and J. Venables, p. 158.
83 W.S.R.O., Ep. I/29/8/275.
84 Ibid. A.B.A., P1/25; ibid. Add. MSS. 29748–9, 29753, 29763–4, 29766 (TS. cat.); *Goodwood Estate Archives*, i, p. 147.
85 *V.C.H. Suss.* ii. 145; vi (1), 163.
86 e.g. *S.R.S.* xli. 41; *Cal. Pat.* 1569–72, p. 483; *Univ. Brit. Dir.* ii. 56–7; E.S.R.O.,SAS/E 306 (TS. cat.); W.S.R.O., Add. MSS. 2615, 15819 (TS. cat.); ibid. Ep. I/55/229 (TS. cat.).
87 Above, port and river traffic; *Kelly's Dir. Suss.* (1862 and later edns.).
88 W.S.R.O., Ep. I/29/8/230.
89 Ibid. A.B.A., L5, bdle. 1, no. 23, f. 3.
90 Ibid. Par. 8/32/1/2.
91 e.g. above, mills; port and river traffic; timber trades.
92 *Univ. Brit. Dir.* ii. 56–7.

those in the timber trade, there were 5 coal merchants, 4 corn merchants, and 3 wine merchants.[93] Most merchants dealt in more than one kind of goods. The wine merchants Shaft and Co. (fl. 1820–72) also dealt in coal in the 1850s and 60s.[94] The corn merchant's and miller's business of the Bartlett family (fl. *c.* 1841–1922) diversified in the later 19th century into animal feed, artificial manure, and coal.[95] Most timber merchants in the 19th century also dealt in coal, Evershed and Co. also in slate in 1845, and Marshall and Fry, later Fry and Son or William Fry, in slate in the 1860s and 70s[96] and in tiles and chimney pots *c.* 1890.[97] The building firm of John Peckham Henly,[98] later Charles Henly, also traded in lime and coal in the 1860s and 70s and by the 1880s had become coal merchants solely, while the stone mason's business of William Smart, later Alfred Smart (fl. *c.* 1832–78), also dealt in slate, Pulborough stone, and fire bricks and tiles.[99]

In the same period Arundel supplied a large range of other goods and services. The other chief building firm in the 19th century was that of Arthur Burrell (fl. 1887), who in 1893 was also described as painter, glazier, plumber, and sanitary engineer.[1] The carpenter's firm of Charles Sparks in Tarrant Street was dealing in furniture in 1852, later taking on the businesses of auctioneer, house and estate agent, cabinet maker, upholsterer, house decorator, and undertaker,[2] and from *c.* 1877 occupying a large brick building in Tarrant Street of six bays and three storeys.[3] Both firms also had premises in Littlehampton.[4] A gas and water engineer was mentioned in 1912.[5] Other more specialized trades and services not found in the town before the 19th century included those of confectioner recorded in 1814,[6] fruiterer, tea dealer, and chemist and druggist in the 1830s,[7] marine store dealer and fishmonger in the 1850s, horse dealer in 1874,[8] and taxidermist and ornithological painter before 1893.[9] There were a steam laundry in 1912,[10] a firm of radio dealers and a haulage contractor by 1938,[11] and a riding school in Fitzalan Road in the late 1930s.[12]

A circulating library in the early 19th century also sold books and stationery wares, besides drugs, china, glass, tea, and coffee.[13] In the 1830s there were two printers; one then also sold books, fancy stationery, and music, and later newspapers.[14] T. Mitchell was a bookseller and stationer in 1830[15] and a printer by 1842.[16] His son from 1853 published what became the *West Sussex Gazette*,[17] and as a result printing could be described in 1884 as one of Arundel's two chief industries, the other being brewing.[18] Mitchell's remained jobbing printers *c.* 1980, but by then the *Gazette* was printed outside the town.[19] Other stationers, booksellers, and newsagents in Arundel in the later 19th century and the 20th included a Catholic bookseller, later a Catholic repository, from 1882.[20] Other indications of middle-class culture in the mid 19th century were the presence of music teachers and a piano tuner.[21]

The growth of tourism during the 19th century brought souvenir shops and tea and refreshment rooms. A 'fancy repository' selling photographic views existed by 1868.[22] Others later in the 19th century and early 20th sold 'view china' and other 'view goods', postcards, and guide books to town and castle.[23] In 1910 there were five such businesses.[24] Tea and coffee rooms near the castle existed by 1897;[25] in 1910 there were five tea or refreshment rooms and a dining room[26] and by 1938 seven tea or refreshment rooms and two guest houses.[27]

Long-lived retail businesses in the 19th and 20th centuries were those of Osborne, baker, in King Street (fl. 1856–1962),[28] and Lasseter, watchmaker and later jeweller, recorded *c.* 1832[29] and still existing in 1990. The Arundel Co-operative Stores opened by 1874, and the International Tea Co.'s Stores, also in Tarrant Street, by 1895. Both survived in 1938.[30] In 1910 there were also two other general stores.[31]

Fellmongering, brewing, and the manufacture of candles and soap continued in the 19th century and early 20th.

A fellmonger and glover had premises in Mill Lane in the mid 19th century,[32] but the trade is not heard of later.

93 Pigot, *Nat. Com. Dir.* (1832–4), 1004; above, timber trades.

94 W.S.R.O., Add. MSS. 13820, 15673 (TS. cat.); *Kelly's Dir. Suss.* (1852 and later edns.); *Arundel Rds.* 34.

95 *Kelly's Dir. Suss.* (1845 and later edns.); Cartland, *Arundel*, 11; W.S.R.O., MP 3152, p. 43; above, mills.

96 Pigot, *Nat. Com. Dir.* (1832–4), 1004; *Kelly's Dir. Suss.* (1845 and later edns.).

97 Kimpton, *Arundel* (*c.* 1890), p. iv.

98 *Petworth Ho. Archives*, ii, ed. A. McCann, p. 36; cf. *Univ. Brit. Dir.* ii. 56.

99 Pigot, *Nat. Com. Dir.* (1832–4), 1004; (1839), 654; *Kelly's Dir. Suss.* (1845 and later edns.).

1 *Kelly's Dir. Suss.* (1887 and later edns.); Kimpton, *Arundel* (1893), p. xiv.

2 *Kelly's Dir. Suss.* (1852 and later edns.).

3 [J. Forlong], *Around Historic Suss.* 17.

4 e.g. *Kelly's Dir. Suss.* (1895).

5 W.S.R.O., SP 1056.

6 Ibid. Ep. I/17/44, f. 117.

7 Pigot, *Nat. Com. Dir.* (1832–4), 1004.

8 *Kelly's Dir. Suss.* (1855, 1874).

9 *Ellis's Popular Guide Arundel* (Arundel, pre 1893), title page (copy in C.I.H.E. libr.); the bk. is the source for Kimpton, *Arundel* (1893).

10 W.S.R.O., BO/AR 16/1/39.

11 *Kelly's Dir. Suss.* (1938).

12 Ibid.; W.S.R.O., BO/AR 16/1/214.

13 Worthing Ref. Libr., Arundel cuttings file, bookplate of White's circulating libr.

14 Pigot, *Nat. Com. Dir.* (1832–4), 1003; A.C.M., MD 2326; W.S.R.O., Par. 8/9/10, nos. 970, 1106.

15 W.S.R.O., Par. 8/9/10, no. 662.

16 A.C.M., MD 2237; cf. W.S.R.O., Par. 8/9/10, no. 1125.

17 F. V. Wright, *100 Yrs. of W. Suss. Gaz. 1853–1953*, 1.

18 W.S.R.O., Ep. I/22A/1 (1884).

19 Inf. from Mrs. Ian Rodger, Arundel; *W. Suss. Gaz.* 1 June 1978.

20 *Kelly's Dir. Suss.* (1882 and later edns.).

21 e.g. ibid. (1845, 1866); W.S.R.O., Add. MS. 11351 (TS. cat.).

22 *Visitors' Guide to Arundel* (1868), [32].

23 Kimpton, *Arundel* (1893), inside front cover; Goodliffe, *Littlehampton* (1903), p. xxiv.

24 Pike, *Bognor Dir.* (1910–11), 186–7, 192.

25 Kimpton, *Arundel* (1897), p. x.

26 Pike, *Bognor Dir.* (1910–11), 186–7, 189, 192.

27 *Kelly's Dir. Suss.* (1938).

28 *W. Suss. Gaz.* 7 May 1987.

29 Pigot, *Nat. Com. Dir.* (1832–4), 1004.

30 *Kelly's Dir. Suss.* (1874 and later edns.); *Arundel, the Gem of Suss.* (Arundel, 1934), 50; W.S.R.O., Add. MS. 21088 (TS. cat.).

31 Pike, *Bognor Dir.* (1910–11), 192.

32 Pigot, *Nat. Com. Dir.* (1832–4), 1004; *Kelly's Dir. Suss.* (1845).

The two chief breweries in the 19th and 20th centuries, which together employed 25 people in 1851,[33] were the Eagle brewery in Tarrant Street and the Swallow brewery in Queen Street.[34] The Eagle brewery, so called by 1839,[35] had been Wise's brewery in 1829, when it had tied houses in Arundel, Littlehampton, and elsewhere.[36] About 1832 it was bought by Robert Watkins, the duke of Norfolk's agent, to be run by him in opposition to the brewery of George Constable, the duke's rival in parliamentary elections in the town.[37] By 1839 it was again tenanted,[38] and *c.* 1841 the malthouses in Queen Street and in the west range of the friary belonged to it.[39] In 1872 it had 22 tied houses.[40] By 1882 the brewery had passed to the firm of Lambert and Co., later Lambert and Norris, which in 1935 was taken over by Friary, Holroyd and Healy of Guildford; it had ceased production by 1938, when the premises were used as a depot.[41]

The Swallow brewery, so called by *c.* 1841, belonged to George Constable *c.* 1832. By *c.* 1841, when there were six tied houses in the town, it had malthouses at the west end of Tarrant Street and in the south marshes south of the town.[42] In 1851, when Constable lived next door to the brewery, he owned property at Arundel said to be worth £7,000 or £8,000.[43] In 1921 the firm, by then known as Constable and Sons, amalgamated with Henty's of Chichester to form Henty and Constable Ltd.[44] The brewery buildings had been demolished by 1937.[45]

Of two firms of tallow chandlers that existed in the later 18th century, that of Christopher Elliott (d. 1798 × 1806), later Thomas Elliott and Jabez Shotter, remained in 1818.[46] Between the 1830s and the 1850s three other firms were recorded.[47] That of William Evershed, tallow chandler and soap manufacturer, existed by 1817[48] and had premises on the south bank of the river *c.* 1841.[49] In the 1830s and 40s the business also included limeburning.[50] It remained in the family until closure in 1903,[51] also dealing in soda and salt in the 1860s and 70s.[52]

The chief representative of the metal trades in the 19th century was the firm of Penfolds,[53] which began from Charles Penfold's partnership with the ironmonger, brazier, and oil dealer John Wimble in 1833.[54] Penfold was making agricultural implements by 1835,[55] and was described as a locksmith and whitesmith in 1839[56] and a brass founder in 1855.[57] The business moved to Tortington *c.* 1871, afterwards being known as Tortington ironworks.[58] Thirteen men and three boys were employed in that year. The firm continued to make agricultural implements, and by *c.* 1878 it hired out machinery and did steam threshing and ploughing by contract.[59] Bone crushing and paint crushing were carried on in the later 19th century.[60] After 1918 Penfolds briefly engaged in the motor trade, with a showroom in Tarrant Street, and from the 1930s the firm dealt in garden machinery. Branches were opened in Pulborough by 1886, in Sidlesham in the 1950s, and later at Golden Cross near Hailsham. At the firm's closure in 1987 it was trading solely in farm and garden machinery.[61] During the mid 20th century there had been *c.* 50 staff in the ironworks and on contract work.[62]

Thomas Fry, described as ironmonger, brazier, tinman, locksmith, and bellhanger in 1840[63] and as oil and colour merchant in 1845, also made agricultural implements in the 1860s and 70s. There was a millwright and machinist in 1855.[64] The ironmongery business of Alfred Pain, in existence by 1893,[65] survived in 1994; by 1927, as well as fitting gas and water installations, it dealt in china, glass, and earthenware, and had branches in Barnham and Pulborough.[66] There were still at least five blacksmiths in the town in the early 20th century.[67]

At the same date there was at least one firm of motor engineers which had grown out of a coach builder's business,[68] and two businesses making cycles. There was a garage at the Norfolk hotel by 1910.[69] Several firms of motor engineers were recorded in the 1920s and 30s; one, G. W. Hare, later Hare and Sons, had the Norfolk hotel

33 P.R.O., HO 107/1651, ff. 544, 552v.; cf. Lewis, *Topog. Dict. Eng.* (1849).
34 For other breweries, e.g. *Arundel Cast. Archives*, iv, p. 58; *Kelly's Dir. Suss.* (1855). There were 5 maltsters *c.* 1832 including the 2 chief brewers: Pigot, *Nat. Com. Dir.* (1832–4), 1003–4.
35 W.S.R.O., Add. MSS. 25816–54 (TS. cat.).
36 A.C.M., FC 435; cf. W.S.R.O., MP 3041 (photocopy of town plan, 1785).
37 W.S.R.O., A.B.A., M49; ibid. Add. MSS. 956 (TS. cat.); 22641; for Constable's brewery, below, this section.
38 Pigot, *Nat. Com. Dir.* (1839), 653.
39 W.S.R.O., TD/W 5; cf. below, pl. facing p. 74.
40 W.S.R.O., SP 79.
41 Ibid. Add. MSS. 25816–54 (TS. cat.); *Kelly's Dir. Suss.* (1882 and later edns.).
42 Pigot, *Nat. Com. Dir.* (1832–4), 1003; W.S.R.O., TD/W 5; cf. Pike, *Bognor Dir.* (1910–11), 191.
43 *Arundel Rds.* 25, 53.
44 *V.C.H. Suss.* ii. 263; *S.I.A.S. Newsletter*, N.S. xvii. 10.
45 W.S.R.O., BO/AR 16/1/237; O.S. Map 1/2,500, Suss. LXIII. 1 (1937 edn.).
46 W.S.R.O., A.B.A., J1, f. 123v.; ibid. Add. MS. 17012; ibid. Holmes, Campbell & Co. MS. 575 (TS. cat.).
47 Ibid. Par. 8/9/10, no. 1008; ibid. TD/W 5, no. 628; Pigot, *Nat. Com. Dir.* (1832–4), 1004; *Kelly's Dir. Suss.* (1845 and later edns.).
48 W.S.R.O., Add. MS. 3013 (TS. cat.); cf. ibid. 13308–9 (TS. cat.).
49 Ibid. TD/W 5.
50 Pigot, *Nat. Com. Dir.* (1832–4), 1004; *Kelly's Dir. Suss.* (1845).
51 *W. Suss. Gaz.* 18 Sept. 1980.
52 *Kelly's Dir. Suss.* (1862 and later edns.).
53 Para. based mainly on [F. Penfold], *Penfolds of Arundel* (Arundel, 1983); *Kelly's Dir. Suss.* (1845 and later edns.); Pike, *Dir. SW. Suss.* (1886–7), 86.
54 Cf. Pigot, *Nat. Com. Dir.* (1832–4), 1004; W.S.R.O., Par. 8/9/10, nos. 567, 631.
55 W.S.R.O., Par. 8/9/10, no. 983.
56 Pigot, *Nat. Com. Dir.* (1839), 654.
57 *Kelly's Dir. Suss.* (1855).
58 Cf. O.S. Map 6", Suss. LXIII. NW. (1899 edn.).
59 Cf. P. Jerrome and J. Newdick, *Old and New, Teasing and True*, 34.
60 *W. Suss. Gaz.* 7 June 1973.
61 Ibid. 7 May 1987.
62 Ibid. 13 June 1991.
63 W.S.R.O., Par. 8/9/10, no. 975.
64 *Kelly's Dir. Suss.* (1845 and later edns.).
65 Kimpton, *Arundel* (1893), p. xix.
66 W.S.R.O., Par. 8/7/26, billhead, 1927.
67 Inf. from Mr. F. Penfold, Burpham. Cf. O.S. Map 1/2,500, Suss. LXIII. 1 (1912 edn.); *W. Suss. Gaz.* 7 June 1973; Cartland, *Arundel*, 26; Pike, *Bognor Dir.* (1910–11), 185, 190, 192.
68 W.S.R.O., SP 1055, 1061, 1064; Cartland, *Arundel*, 25; Pike, *Bognor Dir.* (1910–11), 186; *Kelly's Dir. Suss.* (1918 and later edns.); cf. above, timber trades.
69 Pike, *Bognor Dir.* (1910–11), 186, 192.

garage and a car hire business based there. There were other garages in the town by the 1930s.[70]

A cement works east of Queen Street was working between *c.* 1830[71] and 1887 using river transport; at the latter date the business also included that of builder, brick- and tilemaker, and mason.[72] Several firms made mineral waters during the 19th century.[73] In 1929 the former corn store by the bridge was a factory making self-adjusting deck chairs and other light home and garden furniture;[74] it was burnt down in the following year and not rebuilt.[75]

In the rural part of the parish there is evidence of glass- and brickmaking. The place names Glastis gate and Glasshouse gate field west of Park Farmhouse, recorded in 1661 and 1772 respectively, suggest a glassmaking site of which no other record has been found.[76] Two or more brick kilns existed in 1732,[77] and between 1768 and 1781 at least there was a Norfolk estate brickyard west of Park Farmhouse on the north side of the Chichester–Arundel road; though it was chiefly for estate consumption, bricks and tiles were also sold to others.[78] Bricks were made apparently near the cement works east of Queen Street between 1846 and 1887.[79] Charcoal burning was carried on in Arundel park, perhaps within the parish, in the early 20th century[80] and in Rewell wood in the 1970s.[81]

In the 19th and early 20th centuries the Norfolk estate employed many people, including at different times a steward, a clerk of works, an agent, keepers, a stud groom, a foreman of bricklayers, a 'castle warder', and an electrical engineer;[82] in 1851 there were 36 gardeners.[83] The economic importance of the estate to the town grew as the estate itself increased in size, and as other trades and industries declined.[84]

AFTER 1945. After the Second World War the River Road area was earmarked, with local authority encouragement, for light industry.[85] Hago Products Ltd. took over the site of the former sawmills in 1957, producing sheet metal and wire goods until closure after 1985.[86] The only industrial use in the town north of the river in 1988 was a factory near the new road bridge which made statues. By 1972 there was an industrial estate on the south bank of the river.[87] In 1985–6 businesses there included those of coal merchant, motor engineer, stone mason, sailmaker, metal sprayer, and precision engineer, besides a plant hire firm, and a firm making electronic equipment[88] founded in 1977, which had a staff of 30 in 1987.[89]

In 1963 Arundel's specialized shops served a wide hinterland,[90] and there were three private art galleries in 1969.[91] Among businesses in the town in 1986–7 were 3 bookshops, a map and print seller, several antique shops, an art dealer, several estate agents, 2 delicatessens, specialized shops selling glass, lingerie, walking sticks, and chocolates, a staff recruitment agency, and numerous cafés and restaurants. Larger businesses at the same date were in Queen Street: a supermarket and a shop selling bedroom furniture, together with a garage. In 1990 many shops in the centre of the town served tourists and other visitors, though Tarrant Street, especially at its west end, still had several small shops catering for residents. General shops in Ford and Jarvis roads served the built-up area south of Chichester Road.

Already by 1951 there were 233 male and 71 female residents in the borough who worked elsewhere, chiefly nearby, while 269 males and 77 females working in the town lived elsewhere.[92] Especially after *c.* 1970 many residents were either retired or travelled daily to work in larger towns, particularly London.

The largest number of jobs in the parish in the 1980s was provided by the castle estate and related activities. Duke Bernard's racing stables had been transferred to Arundel during the Second World War from Michelgrove in Clapham, using gallops in the park.[93] In the 1980s 100–200 horses were kept there, and with a staff of 80–100 the stables were the largest individual employer.[94] The castle estate in 1980 employed 23 people in and around the town, excluding the castle itself and the estate office, which was managed by agents; besides those in the timber trades there were four in the game department, two farmworkers, and a mechanic.[95] In addition there was a trout fishery at Park bottom. By 1987 the former mill pond at Swanbourne was being used for breeding the fish.[96]

Pheasants had been reared from the early 20th century.[97] A riding centre on the west edge of the town started in 1960 and still flourished in 1990.[98]

70 *Kelly's Dir. Suss.* (1922 and later edns.).
71 Pigot, *Nat. Com. Dir.* (1832–4), 1004; W.S.R.O., Par. 8/37/16; ibid. TD/W 5.
72 *Kelly's Dir. Suss.* (1845 and later edns.).
73 Ibid. (1862 and later edns.); Kimpton, *Arundel* (1893), p. xii; W.S.R.O., Par. 8/9/10, no. 1005.
74 *S.C.M.* iii. 262, 340–1.
75 Cartland, *Arundel*, 98–9.
76 G. H. Kenyon, *Glass Ind. of Weald*, 212; A.C.M., PM 87; ibid. H 1/3.
77 A.C.M., MD 6266; cf. W.S.R.O., A.B.A., M22, list of inhabitants, 1747.
78 A.C.M., A 442, 444; ibid. H 1/3.
79 9 & 10 Vic. c. 37 (Private); *Kelly's Dir. Suss.* (1887).
80 *Victorian and Edwardian Suss. from Old Photos.* ed. J. S. Gray, 111; *S.C.M.* xii. 602.
81 Inf. from Mrs. Ian Rodger, Arundel.
82 Pigot, *Nat. Com. Dir.* (1839), 654; *Kelly's Dir. Suss.* (1845 and later edns.); *Arundel Rds.* 38; cf. above, timber trades.
83 P.R.O., HO 107/1651, f. 529.
84 The working of the estate during the period is described at W.S.R.O., MP 3200.
85 F. D. Allison, *Little Town of Arundel*, 9.
86 *W. Suss. Gaz.* 2 May 1985.
87 *New Statesman*, 22 Dec. 1972, p. 941.
88 *Ind. in W. Suss.* (W. Suss. C.C., 1985), [50].
89 *W. Suss. Gaz.* 23 July 1987.
90 Ibid. 15 Dec. 1988; cf. *Suss. Trade Guide* (1962) (copy at C.I.H.E. libr.).
91 *Worthing Herald*, 19 Dec. 1969.
92 *Census*, 1951.
93 J. M. Robinson, *Latest Country Hos.* 129; *W. Suss. Gaz.* 14 May 1987; cf. *V.C.H. Suss.* vi (1), 16; O.S. Map 1/25,000, TQ 00/10 (1979 edn.).
94 *Country Life*, 3 July 1980, p. 8; *Suss. Life*, Jan. 1986, p. 8; *W. Suss. Gaz.* 29 May 1986; 14 May 1987; local inf.
95 *Country Life*, 3 July 1980, p. 8; above, timber trades.
96 *W. Suss. Gaz.* 28 May 1987; cf. O.S. Map 1/2,500, TQ 0007–0107 (1979 edn.).
97 O.S. Map 6", XLIX. SE. (1914 edn.); SU 90 NE. (1961 edn.).
98 *W. Suss. Gaz.* 6 June 1990.

PROFESSIONS. A summoner was apparently mentioned in the late 13th century.[99]

Customs officers lived in the town from the late 16th century.[1] By *c.* 1832 the custom house was in Maltravers Street, with four officers;[2] there were six in 1845, but only one in 1862.[3] Officers of the excise, later of the inland revenue, lived at Arundel between the late 18th century and the early 20th; in 1852 and later they were based at the Bridge hotel.[4]

Several apothecaries were recorded in the 17th and 18th centuries,[5] William Manestie in 1611 also practising as a surgeon.[6] Other surgeons were mentioned in 1646 and later,[7] among them a woman in 1690,[8] and there was a midwife in 1613.[9] By the later 18th century there seem usually to have been two surgeons in the town[10] and *c.* 1832 there were six.[11] Medical families in Arundel were the Collinses in the 18th century[12] and the Byasses in the late 18th and 19th.[13] There was a vet by *c.* 1832[14] and a dentist *c.* 1910.[15] In 1938 there were 2 surgeons, both also physicians, 2 dentists, 2 midwives, 2 vets, and an optician.[16] A doctor's surgery which existed in Torton Hill Road by 1990 served the whole town. A chiropodist practised in Arundel in 1991.

Attorneys are recorded from 1730[17] and there seem usually to have been at least two by the later 18th century.[18] There were five solicitors *c.* 1832 and four in 1874.[19] The firm of Holmes, Campbell & Co., which still existed in 1988, had its origins in the attorney James Holmes (fl. in the 1790s); by 1938, as Holmes, Beldam and Co., it was the only firm in the town, though another was represented on certain days.[20] There were two other solicitors' firms in 1987.

There were two banks in Arundel in the mid 1790s, both drawing on London banks: those of Charles Bushby and Sons, and Shaft, Robinson, Shaft and Co., which was open eight hours a day.[21] The banker Thomas Bushby was also collector of customs in 1805.[22] Various banks are recorded in the town in the early 19th century[23] including one founded in 1805 by William Olliver, John Tompkins, and others, which occupied a building opposite the Swan inn.[24] That building belonged *c.* 1841 to Olliver, Edwin Henty, and Edward Upperton,[25] later Henty and Co.;[26] the bank was known as the Arundel Old Bank[27] and was taken over in the 1890s by Capital and Counties Bank Ltd., later part of Lloyds Bank.[28] The firm of Hopkins, Drewitt, and Wyatt (fl. 1831)[29] was taken over before 1845 by the London and County Banking Co.,[30] later part of the National Westminster Bank. Both banks remained in 1994. The Arundel Savings Bank, founded in 1818 as the Arundel Provident Bank for the benefit of 'industrious labourers, servants, mechanics and others',[31] was at the National school by 1839, when it was open for an hour a week;[32] by 1852 it had moved to a new building in Tarrant Street, later the Victoria institute.[33] It closed in 1896.[34]

There was a surveyor in the town *c.* 1775.[35] The surveyor James Teasdale[36] also worked as an architect for the duke of Norfolk in the early 19th century.[37] Other surveyors were recorded between the 1830s and 1850s,[38] and an actuary in 1853.[39] Another architect was mentioned in 1855 and there was a civil engineer in 1862. In 1930 there were an architect and a firm of accountants,[40] and in 1990 two architectural firms and three firms of accountants.

BOROUGH GOVERNMENT. Arundel was a borough in 1086[41] and was separately repre-

99 *Cal. Close*, 1279–88, 427; *S.R.S.* x. 81. The surname Chancellor, however, recorded in early 14th cent., seems likely to be a nickname: ibid. 134, 226; R. McKinley, *Surnames of Suss.* 237.

1 *Acts of P.C.* 1571–5, 85; *Cal. Treas. Bks.* 1679–1718, *passim*; *Cal. Treas. Bks. and Papers*, 1729–45, *passim*; *S.A.C.* xvi. 40; lxxi. 33; *Univ. Brit. Dir.* ii. 56; W.S.R.O., A.B.A., M32; ibid. Add. MS. 2612 (TS. cat.).

2 Pigot, *Nat. Com. Dir.* (1832–4), 1004.

3 *Kelly's Dir. Suss.* (1845, 1862).

4 Ibid. (1852 and later edns.); Pike, *Bognor Dir.* (1910–11), 179; *S.C.M.* ix. 102; E.S.R.O., SAS/HA 492 (TS. cat.).

5 e.g. *Goodwood Estate Archives*, i, ed. F. W. Steer and J. Venables, p. 101; *Danny Archives*, ed. J. Wooldridge, p. 52; *S.R.S.* xxviii. 208; *S.A.C.* lxix. 152; W.S.R.O., Add. MS. 35555 (TS. cat.); ibid. S.A.S. MS. WH 85 (TS. cat.).

6 W.S.R.O., Ep. I/17/13, f. 176v.

7 Ibid. A.B.A., B3/2 (TS. cat.); A.B.A., L3, no. 19, f. 33; ibid. Ep. I/29/8/166, 168; *Goodwood Estate Archives*, i, p. 158.

8 W.S.R.O., Ep. I/66/3.

9 Ibid. Ep. I/17/14, f. 30v. For medical men not otherwise specified, ibid. Ep. VI/56/34/1; ibid. STC III/F, f. 62v.; A.C.M., A 1240; C. Thomas-Stanford, *Suss. in Great Civil War*, 106.

10 W.S.R.O., A.B.A., M32; *Univ. Brit. Dir.* ii. 56.

11 Pigot, *Nat. Com. Dir.* (1832–4), 1004.

12 *S.R.S.* xxviii. 208; *Danny Archives*, p. 52; W.S.R.O., Add. MS. 35555 (TS. cat.); ibid. MP 124, f. [1].

13 *Univ. Brit. Dir.* ii. 56; Pigot, *Nat. Com. Dir.* (1832–4), 1004; *Kelly's Dir. Suss.* (1874); W.S.R.O., Add. MS. 13308 (TS. cat.); ibid. Par. 8/37/9; ibid. S.A.S. MS. RB 57 (TS. cat.).

14 Pigot, *Nat. Com. Dir.* (1832–4), 1004; cf. *Kelly's Dir. Suss.* (1845 and later edns.).

15 Pike, *Bognor Dir.* (1910–11), 188.

16 *Kelly's Dir. Suss.* (1938).

17 *S.R.S.* xxviii. 31, 212.

18 W.S.R.O., A.B.A., M32; *Univ. Brit. Dir.* ii. 56.

19 Pigot, *Nat. Com. Dir.* (1832–4), 1003; *Kelly's Dir. Suss.* (1874).

20 *Univ. Brit. Dir.* ii. 56; cf. Pigot, *Nat. Com. Dir.* (1832–4), 1003; *Kelly's Dir. Suss.* (1852 and later edns.).

21 *Univ. Brit. Dir.* ii. 57, reading Bushley.

22 Evans, *Worthing* (1805), 82.

23 *S.A.C.* lxxi. 48; *I am, my dear Sir*, ed. F. W. Steer, 5; Wright, *Arundel* (1818), 26; G. L. Grant, *Standard Cat. of Provincial Banks and Banknotes*, 5; W.S.R.O., S.A.S. MS. RB 43 (TS. cat.).

24 *S.A.C.* lxxi. 48.

25 W.S.R.O., TD/W 5; cf. Pigot, *Nat. Com. Dir.* (1832–4), 1003.

26 *Kelly's Dir. Suss.* (1874).

27 e.g. *Arundel Cast. Archives*, iv, p. 115; W.S.R.O., SP 1049.

28 *Kelly's Dir. Suss.* (1895, 1899).

29 W.S.R.O., Par. 8/9/10, no. 718; cf. Pigot, *Nat. Com. Dir.* (1832–4), 1003.

30 *Kelly's Dir. Suss.* (1845 and later edns.); cf. *Arundel Rds.* 54.

31 A.C.M., MD 2650; W.S.R.O., QDS/4/1/W 4.

32 Pigot, *Nat. Com. Dir.* (1839), 653.

33 *Kelly's Dir. Suss.* (1852 and later edns.); cf. A.C.M., H 2/24.

34 W.S.R.O., MP 3545.

35 *S.R.S.* lxvi. 19.

36 Ibid. 171, 173; *Arundel Cast. Archives*, iv, p. 52.

37 Above, castle (cast. fabric).

38 Pigot, *Nat. Com. Dir.* (1832–4), 1004; *Arundel Cast. Archives*, i, pp. 51–5.

39 W.S.R.O., Holmes, Campbell & Co. MS. 588 (TS. cat.).

40 *Kelly's Dir. Suss.* (1855, 1862, 1930).

41 *V.C.H. Suss.* i. 421.

sented by 12 jurors at the eyre of 1248.[42] There were 94 burgesses in 1302,[43] and in 1720 seventy properties paid quit rent to the lord; by then, however, they were no longer called burgages.[44]

References to the borough or the burgesses dealing directly with the Crown in the later 12th century indicate the beginnings of urban independence.[45] In 1288, however, the burgesses claimed no privileges except through the earl of Arundel and his predecessors,[46] and the town never broke completely free from the lord before the 19th century. By the mid 13th century there was a coroner and soon afterwards a mayor.[47] By 1276–7 'the men of the vill' were paying 13*s.* 4*d.* a year rent to the lord for the burgess brooks,[48] as the town continued to do later.[49] In the early 15th century the town was leasing from the lord both the market tolls, at £3 12*s.*, and the pound.[50] Port dues, formerly the lord's, were being taken by 1563,[51] and the perquisites apparently of the borough court by 1579.[52] In 1641[53] and perhaps long before the town was collecting the burgage rents on the lord's behalf. A composite payment of £6 0*s.* 2½*d.* including the farms of the market tolls, the brooks, and the pound was paid to the lord between 1657 and *c.* 1950.[54]

Already by 1454 the mayor and a small group of burgesses were acting as the government of the borough.[55] That inner group was perhaps originally elected by the inhabitants in general at the annual view of frankpledge, a custom twice at least re-established in the mid 17th century.[56] Apparently by *c.* 1539, however,[57] and certainly from 1554, a close corporation consisting of the mayor and *c.* 12 burgesses co-opted new members itself, like similar bodies at Lewes and elsewhere; the title burgess was thereafter restricted to them.[58] The close form of government continued, with the exceptions mentioned, until the reform of the borough in 1835. In 1554 co-option apparently had to be unanimous, as it certainly did after 1695;[59] in 1586 and 1835,[60] however, it required only a majority of the corporation, on the former occasion including all the 'senior' burgesses, i.e. former mayors. From 1539 the mayor and burgesses kept their own minute book and by 1568 they were managing a borough fund, called in 1579 the burgess chest.[61] Corporate status seems first to have been claimed by them in 1586;[62] though there was never a charter, exemplifications of two judgments of 1586 and 1677 functioned in place of one.[63] There was a common seal by 1569.

In 1562 and 1582 two nominees of the earl of Arundel were accepted as burgesses,[64] but the duke of Norfolk's attempt to revive the custom of seigneurial nomination in 1735 was successfully resisted.[65] Financial barriers to recruitment to the corporation were from the mid 16th century the introduction of entry fines,[66] and by the mid 17th the requirement to pay for a dinner for the existing burgesses and their wives.[67] Besides having extensive privileges in the burgess brooks,[68] members of the corporation could use the borough seal on reasonable request.[69] Widows of burgesses could enjoy their late husbands' perquisites.[70] In 1789 one burgess sold his burgess rights to another.[71] Members of the corporation were disciplined where appropriate by fines or by the withdrawal of privileges, especially in the brooks,[72] and could be expelled for non-residence,[73] misbehaviour,[74] or refusal to hold office;[75] after 1580, however, non-residence could be licensed,[76] and in 1835 one burgess had been absent for ten years.[77] A burgess resigned through old age in 1796.[78]

Loyalty to the corporation was enjoined *c.* 1539,[79] and to create an *esprit de corps* burgesses were encouraged from *c.* 1650 to resolve mutual differences among themselves rather than through the courts.[80] From 1637 secrecy was urged about the deliberations[81] of what was then beginning to be described as the 'company' or 'society'.[82] To defend the rights and privileges of the corporation burgesses were required from 1643 to contribute equally to the cost of

42 P.R.O., JUST 1/909A, rot. 22d.
43 Ibid. C 133/104, no. 21, m. 2.
44 A.C.M., A 1240.
45 *Pipe R.* 1180 (P.R.S. xxix), 31; 1187 (P.R.S. xxxvii), 113; 1195 (P.R.S. N.S. vi), 242; *Rot. Lib.* (Rec. Com.), 95. Cf. refs. to 'the coroner with the whole township' in 1278 and 'the bailiffs, lawful men and community' of Arundel in 1338: *S.A.C.* lxi. 89; *Cal. Close*, 1337–9, 527.
46 P.R.O., JUST 1/924, rot. 65.
47 Below, this section (officers).
48 P.R.O., SC 6/1029/22.
49 *S.R.S.* lxvii. 120; A.C.M., MD 495, f. [64v.]; 535, f. 4; W.S.R.O., A.B.A., F2/3.
50 *S.R.S.* lxvii. 115, 120, using the word 'community'.
51 Above, port and river traffic (1500–1800).
52 W.S.R.O., A.B.A., F2/3. The corp. later seems to have lost them: in 1650 a former petition to the earl for profits of ct. was produced possibly to prove title: ibid. A.B.A., F2/1, f. 18.
53 A.C.M., A 1351, f. [1v.]; cf. ibid. 263, rental, 1657.
54 Ibid. 263, rental, 1657, and particular of Arundel estate, 1733; W.S.R.O., A.B.A., M28; ibid. BO/AR 24/4/30; *1st Rep. Com. Mun. Corp.* 668.
55 Bodl. MS. Chart. Suss. a. 2, no. 72.
56 *S.A.C.* cxxviii. 157–75; Eustace, *Arundel*, 183, 188, 190; W.S.R.O., A.B.A., A1, f. 91v.; A.B.A., L3, no. 3; A.B.A., L3, no. 18, f. 24.
57 Rest of para. based mainly on W.S.R.O., A.B.A., A1.
58 A. Fletcher, *County Community in Peace and War*, 234; *S.A.C.* cxix. 157–9, 170; cxxi. 95.
59 Cf. *S.A.C.* lxxi. 35.
60 *1st Rep. Com. Mun. Corp.* 670.
61 W.S.R.O., A.B.A., F2/3; cf. ibid. A.B.A., A1, f. 54; below, this section (activity, property, and income).
62 Eustace, *Arundel*, 124.
63 W.S.R.O., A.B.A., I1–2. The former is mostly transcr. at Eustace, *Arundel*, 122–6; for an omission on p. 125 cf. Tierney, *Arundel*, ii. 698. The corp. apparently intended to obtain a charter in 1645: W.S.R.O., A.B.A., A1, f. 54.
64 W.S.R.O., A.B.A., A1, ff. 17v., 22v.
65 Ibid. A.B.A., M21.
66 Below, this section (activity, property, and income).
67 W.S.R.O., A.B.A., A1, ff. 52, 62.
68 Above, agric.
69 W.S.R.O., A.B.A., A1, f. 19.
70 Ibid. ff. 14, 30v. The woman described as a burgess in 1572 was presumably a widow: ibid. f. 19v.; cf. ibid. ff. 8, 31.
71 W.S.R.O., A.B.A., M35. For Thos. Coote, *Univ. Brit. Dir.* ii. 56.
72 W.S.R.O., A.B.A., A1, *passim.*
73 Ibid. ff. 25, 44v., 147v., 203v.; cf. ibid. f. 26.
74 Ibid. ff. 20, 23v., 25, 50v., 206, 224, 254.
75 Ibid. ff. 50v., 94.
76 Ibid. f. 22; cf. ibid. ff. 27v., 148v.
77 *1st Rep. Com. Mun. Corp.* 671.
78 W.S.R.O., A.B.A., A1, ff. 215v., 216v.
79 Ibid. ff. 8v.–9.
80 Ibid. f. 62.
81 Ibid. f. 41; cf. ibid. ff. 62, 71v., 101.
82 W.S.R.O., A.B.A., A1, ff. 60, 62, 94; A.B.A., F2/3.

Arundel: the ruins of the Dominican friary from the south-west *c.* 1800,
with the castle in the background

Tortington: the ruins of the priory from the south

RELIGIOUS HOUSES

The windmill beside the river Arun south of the town *c.* 1900

The port in the late 19th century,
showing the corn store by the bridge

necessary litigation; reference at that date to the possibility of an action over the burgess brooks[83] suggests that the burgesses felt their control of them was in some sense a usurpation. Reverence and respect for the mayor and senior burgesses were enjoined in 1637,[84] and ten years later a livery of black cloth gowns faced with black velvet was introduced, like that of the aldermen of Chichester.[85] In 1664, and evidently earlier, burgesses had to wear gowns to accompany the mayor to Sunday morning service.[86] Regulations about burgesses' conduct were codified *c.* 1650.[87]

The personnel of the corporation has not been analysed in detail, but it is clear that in the late 18th century and early 19th it comprised the richer tradesmen and professional men of the town,[88] who were often related:[89] the 13 burgesses in the mid 1790s included two Shafts, two Cootes, two Bushbys, and one member of the Holmes family.[90] In the early 19th century the corporation was united in politics and religion, no Dissenters being included.[91] The corporation's adherence to maintaining its rights extended to its refusal in 1797–8 to allow inspection or copying of its documents when ordered by the central courts,[92] and to its co-operating only under protest with the Municipal Corporations commission's investigations in the early 1830s, which it regarded as illegal and 'an intrusion on the rights of Englishmen'.[93]

COURTS. A borough court is mentioned from 1288.[94] There are court rolls or draft court rolls for 1361–2, 1387–8, 1473–4, various years between 1536 and 1574,[95] 1706, and 1753–1835.[96] The court was originally the lord's, but by 1579 the perquisites were apparently leased by the burgesses,[97] who in 1586 claimed the court as theirs.[98] The mayor presided by the 15th century.[99]

The court was held in theory every three weeks,[1] but by the mid 16th century the frequency was no longer observed.[2] In the mid 14th century and later the court dealt with pleas of debt, trespass, and detinue, held the assize of bread and of ale, and heard cases of assault.[3] By the later 15th century it had become fused with the three-weekly honor court.[4] In the mid 16th century nuisances were dealt with and cases of affray were heard.[5] By 1586, however, the assize of bread and of ale had ceased to be held at the court, whose business was restricted to cases of debt under 40*s.*,[6] as it continued to be during the 17th century; in 1649 that role was said to be a very useful one.[7] In 1645 the court was ordered to be held at least every six weeks,[8] but by 1706 all business seems to have ceased.[9]

The court was revived by the corporation apparently in 1753, with a similar scope of business to that it had had in the Middle Ages, and seemingly in opposition to the lord's view of frankpledge.[10] As well as the assize of bread and of ale and the regulation of street nuisances, it dealt with matters of public order, for instance expelling vagrants and beggars[11] and enforcing Sunday observance.[12] In an attempt to re-establish the court as the chief organ for borough government officers were sometimes fined for non-attendance.[13] Until 1786 the court was held *c.* 10 or 12 times a decade, but between 1786 and 1801 an attempt was made to reintroduce three-weekly holding. Attendance was often thin, however, and the court does not seem to have been effective in dealing with the many small debt cases brought to it during that time; the last was heard in 1800. Between 1801 and the reform of the borough in 1835 the court was generally held between two and four times a year with very little business.[14]

Evidently in order to encourage attendance at the borough court, the mayor from 1619 had to give a dinner after each session to the burgesses, the steward, and the borough officers.[15] The dinner continued to be held three times a year in the early 19th century although the court was then effectively defunct.[16]

The view of frankpledge, on the other hand, was always the lord's court; first recorded in 1288,[17] it was held by his steward.[18] The mayor always attended, though his role in 1835 was unclear.[19] There are court rolls or draft court rolls for *c.* 1361, 1387, various years between 1536 and 1573, 1696,[20] 1722–40,[21] 1763–1806,[22]

83 Ibid. A.B.A., A1, f. 48; cf. ibid. ff. 80v., 100, 143v., 175, 187, 198v.–199.

84 Ibid. f. 41; cf. ibid. f. 62.

85 Ibid. f. 57.

86 W.S.R.O., A.B.A., A1, f. 85v.; cf. ibid. A.B.A., M13.

87 Ibid. A.B.A., A1, f. 62.

88 Ibid. ff. 196–234v. (elections of burgesses, 1760–1832).

89 *1st Rep. Com. Mun. Corp.* 670.

90 *Univ. Brit. Dir.* ii. 56, reading Bushley; for the Holmeses cf. Eustace, *Arundel*, 253.

91 *1st Rep. Com. Mun. Corp.* 670.

92 W.S.R.O., A.B.A., A1, f. 217v.; A.B.A., F1/23, no. 6.

93 *1st Rep. Com. Mun. Corp.* 667. The corp. also refused Tierney access to its rec.: Tierney, *Arundel*, i, pp. vii–viii; ii. 717 n.

94 P.R.O., JUST 1/924, rot. 65. It was apparently the ct. called 'husteng' mentioned in 1397: *Cal. Inq. Misc.* vi, p. 218.

95 A.C.M., M 8–20, 24; 28, rot. 1; 271, ff. [13, 16v., 17v., 18v.–19v., 29].

96 W.S.R.O., A.B.A., J1; A.B.A., L5, bdle. 2, nos. 1–2.

97 Ibid. A.B.A., F2/3.

98 Eustace, *Arundel*, 125. Cf. the fact that ct. rolls before 1574 are at Arundel cast. and those after 1706 among the rec. of the boro.

99 A.C.M., A 340; cf. Eustace, *Arundel*, 130; Caraccioli, *Arundel*, 2; *1st Rep. Com. Mun. Corp.* 671.

1 e.g. A.C.M., M 8, 24; Eustace, *Arundel*, 125.

2 e.g. A.C.M., M 13, 16–17.

3 e.g. ibid. 8–10, 24.

4 Ibid. 24; cf. ibid. 10–20; above, Arundel Rape.

5 e.g. A.C.M., M 10–12, 17.

6 Eustace, *Arundel*, 125; Tierney, *Arundel*, ii. 698. The claim that the constables were elected there at that date is wrong: cf. below, this section.

7 W.S.R.O., A.B.A., A1, ff. 60, 124.

8 Ibid. f. 53.

9 W.S.R.O., A.B.A., L5, bdle. 2, nos. 1–2.

10 Para. based mainly on ibid. A.B.A., J1; for the view, below, this section.

11 e.g. W.S.R.O., A.B.A., J1, ff. 68, 84, 157.

12 Ibid. ff. 31v., 58, 222.

13 e.g. ibid. ff. 2, 28, 88, 192, 261v.

14 Cf. *1st Rep. Com. Mun. Corp.* 672. The ct. was again revived in 1839: below, this section (after 1835).

15 W.S.R.O., A.B.A., A1, ff. 35, 60, 108, 124.

16 A.C.M., MD 1099; *1st Rep. Com. Mun. Corp.* 671.

17 P.R.O., JUST 1/924, rot. 65d.

18 A.C.M., M 900; B.L. Add. MS. 5687, f. 28; W.S.R.O., A.B.A., L4, no. 7; A.B.A., M20.

19 *1st Rep. Com. Mun. Corp.* 668.

20 A.C.M., A 339, mins. of view, 1696; ibid. M 8–20; 28, rot. 1; 45; 271, f. [13].

21 W.S.R.O., A.B.A., L5, bdle. 2, nos. 3–21.

22 A.C.M., A 339, mins. of view, 1763; ibid. M 900.

and 1813–35.[23] The fact that those for 1722–40 are among the borough records rather than those of the lord may indicate that the corporation had a share in its control at that time.

The view was held annually, and by the mid 14th century elected the borough officers including the bailiffs and the mayor.[24] From 1536 it was often held with the borough court. Attendance was said to average 50 in 1835.[25] In 1542 pleas of debt were heard,[26] and in 1573 and later street nuisances were presented. By the 1720s the view had replaced the borough court as the place for holding the assize of bread, and in 1730 it heard a case of forestalling the market.[27] After 1763 it was less effective than the revived borough court in dealing with the same sort of business, and in 1777 the jurors complained that the lord's steward's failure to impose fines for nuisances made their presentments there of little use. The view continued to present street nuisances after 1785 as if the improvement commissioners did not exist.[28]

A feast for the inhabitants in general which had customarily been given after the view by the retiring mayor was ordered to be abolished in 1619 because of the trouble and expense it caused;[29] the order was repeated in 1649 and later, with the threat of a fine on any mayor who held it in future, though that did not prevent it happening, sometimes accompanied by riots and tumult. The custom may have arisen as compensation for the loss of some right, since in 1657 the burgesses agreed to defend any suit brought on account of its neglect.[30] The feast is not recorded after 1736.[31] In 1835 the inhabitants were said at one time to have received 2*s.* in lieu of it.[32] By 1649 a dinner to replace it was given for the steward and the jury;[33] other inhabitants were invited besides by 1773, and in 1789 some of those not invited received a 'treat', apparently in money.[34]

A fair court was held by the lord at least between 1407 and 1536; tolls and other profits were taken there, and presentments made by the aletasters of breaches of the assize and regrating at the fairs.[35]

The court baron of which there are court rolls for 1680 and 1687 dealt only with conveyances of burgage tenements,[36] and seems to represent an attempt by the lord to resume control of the borough property. It may not have met after 1687, for in 1776 it was said to have long ceased.[37]

By the mid 16th century the corporation was holding its own meetings whose minutes are recorded in the corporation book;[38] one such meeting in 1643 was described erroneously as a court. They were sometimes held in the mayor's house,[39] but on at least three occasions in the late 18th century and early 19th at inns.[40] The meetings had no regular frequency, except that between 1646 and 1758 one was held almost every spring to settle the management of the burgess brooks for the summer. Other business discussed related chiefly to maintaining the dignity and privileges of the corporation, but licences for settling in the town and for opening shops were granted in 1563 and 1593.[41]

OFFICERS. The bailiffs mentioned from 1254[42] were evidently the lord's officers; they were elected at the view by 1361.[43] The existence by 1255 of a borough coroner,[44] acting for the lord and also elected by the burgesses,[45] shows the town's independence by that date from the county. The office had apparently never been formally granted, but it was successfully claimed in 1288 as immemorial.[46] In 1361 the coroner's jurisdiction included the environs of Batworth park in Lyminster outside the borough.[47] The last reference found to a coroner is of 1611.[48]

By the late 13th century there was also a mayor: Richard Dodding, borough coroner 1271–9 (d. by 1288), had the title at an unknown date,[49] and John Alexander in 1311–12.[50] The mayor was elected yearly at the view,[51] perhaps originally by all the inhabitants, but by the 18th century only by those who paid scot and lot.[52] In 1361 the inhabitants named two candidates of whom one was chosen, presumably by the lord's steward.[53] By 1588 the two names were supplied by a jury of 24 returned by the retiring mayor;[54] in 1735 and perhaps earlier the jury included all the burgesses.[55] Though the corporation was foiled in its attempt to elect the mayor itself in 1587,[56] it was able nevertheless to influence later elections either by treating[57] or by packing the

23 W.S.R.O., Holmes, Campbell & Co. MSS., ct. leet bk. 1813–35.

24 A.C.M., M 8, m. 1; 9, m. 1; cf. B.L. Add. MS. 5687, f. 28; *1st Rep. Com. Mun. Corp.* 668.

25 *1st Rep. Com. Mun. Corp.* 670.

26 A.C.M., M 45.

27 Ibid. A 339, mins. of view, 1696, 1763; ibid. M 20; W.S.R.O., A.B.A., L5, bdle. 2, nos. 3–21.

28 A.C.M., A 339, mins. of view, 1763; ibid. M 900; W.S.R.O., Holmes, Campbell & Co. MSS., ct. leet bk. 1813–35.

29 W.S.R.O., A.B.A., A1, ff. 35, 60.

30 Ibid. ff. 60, 71v., 113, 124.

31 Ibid. f. 164.

32 *1st Rep. Com. Mun. Corp.* 674. Free entertainment was also provided by the corp. on special occasions after 1736, e.g. to celebrate victories in 1759 or the downfall of Napoleon in 1814: W.S.R.O., A.B.A., F1/1, ff. 8, 69.

33 W.S.R.O., A.B.A., A1, f. 60; cf. ibid. f. 124; *1st Rep. Com. Mun. Corp.* 671.

34 W.S.R.O., A.B.A., M36; *S.A.C.* lxxi. 36; Tierney, *Arundel*, ii. 706.

35 A.C.M., A 340; ibid. M 23, 41–4; 271, f. [18].

36 Ibid. M 301, pp. [184–6, 343–7].

37 B.L. Add. MS. 5687, f. 28.

38 Para. based mainly on corp. bk.: W.S.R.O., A.B.A., A1. Cf. the Lewes town bk.: *S.R.S.* xlviii, pp. xviii–xx.

39 Eustace, *Arundel*, 202, citing W.S.R.O., A.B.A., M13; *S.A.C.* lxxi. 53; A.C.M., MD 1099.

40 *S.A.C.* lxxi. 32, 39, 41, 50.

41 W.S.R.O., A.B.A., F2/1, ff. 1 and v., 2v.

42 *Cal. Pat.* 1247–58, 368.

43 A.C.M., M 8, m. 1.

44 *S.A.C.* xcviii. 68.

45 A.C.M., M 10, 20; P.R.O., JUST 1/924, rot. 65.

46 *S.A.C.* xcviii. 45; P.R.O., JUST 1/924, rot. 65.

47 *S.A.C.* xcv. 47–8. It is not clear why a case concerning Amersham (Bucks.) came before the Arundel coroner in 1391: ibid. xcvi. 26–7.

48 *Cal. Assize Rec. Suss. Jas. I*, p. 38; cf. ibid. *Eliz. I*, *passim*; *S.R.S.* lxxiv, p. xxxvi.

49 *S.A.C.* xxxv. 89; xcviii. 68; Bodl. MS. Chart. Suss. a. 2, no. 41.

50 *S.A.C.* xi. 98.

51 e.g. A.C.M., M 8, m. 1; *1st Rep. Com. Mun. Corp.* 670.

52 Caraccioli, *Arundel*, 2; W.S.R.O., A.B.A., M28.

53 A.C.M., M 8, m. 1.

54 Eustace, *Arundel*, 129; cf. W.S.R.O., A.B.A., L4, no. 7.

55 Eustace, *Arundel*, 206; cf. ibid. 129.

56 Ibid. 128–30.

57 *S.A.C.* lxxi. 35–6, 40; *1st Rep. Com. Mun. Corp.* 670.

jury.[58] By 1690 burgesses were put forward for the mayoralty in rotation.[59]

The small size of the corporation meant that many mayors served more than once, though rarely in successive years. Between 1578 and 1835 *c.* 50 men served only once as against *c.* 70 more often, 2 serving six times and at least 1 seven times.[60] By the early 19th century the mayor could live outside the town within a three-mile radius.[61]

To encourage acceptance of the office, which bore heavy expenses,[62] burgesses who had not held it were penalized after 1569,[63] while from 1549 mayors received financial privileges: extra pasture rights in the brooks,[64] an allowance in money of £30 from 1635[65] and £100 by 1820,[66] the rents of four butchers' shambles and a shop from 1645, and river dues. The expenses of the office were nevertheless said in 1835 to exceed its income by £30.[67]

Other officers of the borough were 2 under-bailiffs, 2 constables, and 2 aletasters, all elected by the view in the later 14th century.[68] A bailiff is only twice recorded after the 16th century, and under-bailiffs not at all.[69] By 1563 there were leather searchers and sealers, usually two, whose jurisdiction included the whole rape as well as the borough. The constables in 1835 were supplied in rotation from among the inhabitants, but could serve through substitutes at the mayor's discretion for a fine of £5.[70] The aletasters had evidently lost much of their importance by the later 18th century, when they often failed to appear at the borough court to make presentments.[71] The office of leather searcher and sealer was obsolete by 1835.[72]

By the early 16th century there were also two portreeves.[73] As their name indicates, they collected the market tolls, paying the farm to the lord.[74] They also regulated weights and measures,[75] eventually supplanting the aletasters. One portreeve was elected at the view in 1782,[76] but the portreeves may earlier have been chosen by the burgesses, as the brookwarden was.[77] In 1767 one was a burgess and the other a non-burgess.[78] The office could be served by deputy in 1782.[79] By 1835 the portreeves kept the market tolls for themselves after payment of the farm; the profit then amounted to *c.* £26.[80] A clerk of the market was elected besides at the view in the 1790s.[81]

A part-time town clerk was mentioned from 1751. In the early 19th century he received no fee.[82]

The brookwarden and sergeants at mace, later sometimes called the mayor's sergeants,[83] were functioning by the mid 16th century;[84] both were under the direction of the close corporation rather than the borough courts.[85] The brookwarden was appointed annually at the burgesses' meeting by 1643,[86] and the sergeants by the mayor in 1835[87] and perhaps earlier.[88] There was usually only one brookwarden, but in 1663 and sometimes later there were two.[89] Besides managing the brooks, the brookwarden was a general executive officer and treasurer for the corporation, dealing with business of all kinds.[90] By 1546 there was a cowherd to assist him;[91] in the mid 17th century he himself chose the cowherd, who had to be a poor man.[92] Both officers received pasture rights in the brooks for their services.[93]

The sergeants' duties *c.* 1650, besides waiting on the mayor, included managing the pound, setting a watch, keeping the weights and measures, putting out the butchers' stalls on market and fair days and collecting the tolls, cleaning the court house, and taking fines and amercements at the borough court. The junior sergeant was also the town crier.[94] In the mid 18th century the sergeants also collected tolls from vessels unloading in the port.[95] They received wages, of £1 a year each in 1614[96] and £4 in the early 19th century,[97] together with a livery,[98] a third of the fines and amercements at courts, and a fee for use of the town seal.[99] In the early 19th century their wages were paid by the mayor.[1]

ACTIVITY, PROPERTY, AND INCOME. The chief functions of borough government in the Middle Ages, for example controlling the trade of the town and managing the markets and fairs, are

58 *1st Rep. Com. Mun. Corp.* 669; W.S.R.O., A.B.A., A1, f. 117; cf. ibid. f. 28.
59 W.S.R.O., A.B.A., A1, f. 111; cf. ibid. A.B.A., M30; *1st Rep. Com. Mun. Corp.* 670. In 1690 and later an unelected candidate could stand again in the 2 succeeding yrs., though the jury often rejected him: W.S.R.O., A.B.A., A1, f. 111; *1st Rep. Com. Mun. Corp.* 670.
60 Eustace, *Arundel*, 250–3, omitting yrs. 1583, 1634.
61 *1st Rep. Com. Mun. Corp.* 670.
62 W.S.R.O., A.B.A., A1, f. 58v.
63 Ibid. ff. 19, 62; cf. ibid. f. 58v.
64 e.g. ibid. ff. 49, 64, 152, 256v.
65 Ibid. f. 39v.
66 W.S.R.O., A.B.A., F1/1, f. 75; *1st Rep. Com. Mun. Corp.* 671.
67 W.S.R.O., A.B.A., A1, f. 53; *1st Rep. Com. Mun. Corp.* 671.
68 A.C.M., M 8, m. 1; 9, m. 1.
69 Ibid. A 263, rental, 1657; Eustace, *Arundel*, 208; cf. P.R.O., E 178/1906; *Lavington Estate Archives*, ed. F. W. Steer, p. 29.
70 A.C.M., M 17; W.S.R.O., A.B.A., J1; *1st Rep. Com. Mun. Corp.* 668.
71 W.S.R.O., A.B.A., J1; cf. *1st Rep. Com. Mun. Corp.* 668.
72 *1st Rep. Com. Mun. Corp.* 668.
73 A.C.M., A 235, m. 1; cf. W.S.R.O., A.B.A., A1, f. 8.
74 Eustace, *Arundel*, 125; A.C.M., MD 535, f. 4.
75 W.S.R.O., A.B.A., F2/1, f. 6; A.B.A., M28; *S.A.C.* lxxi. 53; *1st Rep. Com. Mun. Corp.* 668.
76 W.S.R.O., A.B.A., M34.
77 Below, this section. The claim that portreeves were elected at boro. ct. in 1586 has not been substantiated: Eustace, *Arundel*, 125.
78 W.S.R.O., A.B.A., M28.
79 Ibid. A.B.A., M34.
80 *1st Rep. Com. Mun. Corp.* 668.
81 A.C.M., M 900.
82 W.S.R.O., A.B.A., A1, f. 186v.; A.B.A., F1/23, no. 6; ibid. MP 962, notice of letting land in burgess brooks, 1834; *1st Rep. Com. Mun. Corp.* 671.
83 e.g. W.S.R.O., A.B.A., A1, f. 175; cf. Eustace, *Arundel*, 130, 208.
84 W.S.R.O., A.B.A., A1, ff. 8, 19; cf. Eustace, *Arundel*, 125.
85 e.g. W.S.R.O., A.B.A., A1, *passim*; A.B.A., M28.
86 Ibid. A.B.A., A1, f. 48v.
87 *1st Rep. Com. Mun. Corp.* 671.
88 The claim made in 1586 that they were elected at boro. ct. has not been substantiated: Eustace, *Arundel*, 125.
89 W.S.R.O., A.B.A., A1, ff. 92, 94v., 164; A.B.A., M12.
90 e.g. ibid. A.B.A., A1, ff. 57, 115, 132v., 152, 157; A.B.A., F1/1; A.B.A., F3/1–26; A.B.A., M12; A.B.A., P1/7 (TS. cat.).
91 Ibid. A.B.A., A1, f. 257v.
92 Ibid. ff. 56, 64, 68v.
93 e.g. ibid. ff. 68v., 81v., 152.
94 Ibid. f. 61v.
95 Ibid. ff. 175, 198v.
96 Ibid. f. 33; cf. ibid. f. 61v.
97 W.S.R.O., A.B.A., F1/1, f. 73; *1st Rep. Com. Mun. Corp.* 671.
98 W.S.R.O., A.B.A., A1, ff. 19, 61v.–62; *1st Rep. Com. Mun. Corp.* 671; *S.A.C.* lxxi. 54.
99 W.S.R.O., A.B.A., A1, f. 61v.
1 Tierney, *Arundel*, ii. 706 n.; *1st Rep. Com. Mun. Corp.* 671.

alluded to above.[2] The borough was probably also responsible for the town's defences, though it seems to have been the parish authorities who looked after the Marygate in 1652.[3] Concern for the town's trade led the borough to take an interest in the bridge by 1454, when a collection was made for its repair.[4]

New functions were assumed by the corporation from the 16th century. After the dissolution of Pynham priory it became solely responsible for the bridge, the mayor having the additional title of bridgewarden.[5] From the later 16th century it controlled port activity and maintained the town quay,[6] while at the same period it was restricting settlement in the town and licensing shops.[7]

The corporation's activity in poor relief is discussed below.[8] On at least two occasions in the early 17th century the mayor acted as trustee for the property of minors.[9] At the same period the corporation clearly had some responsibility for church repair, a bequest for which in 1610 was to be administered by the mayor and churchwardens together, with the consent of a majority of the senior burgesses.[10]

Other miscellaneous activity by the corporation in the 17th century included managing charitable endowments,[11] which it attempted to rationalize in 1655,[12] and paying towards poor children's schooling.[13] Both then and later it was responsible for preserving public order, including Sunday observance.[14] During the early 18th century it was less active, but an interest in town planning was shown in the middle of the century by the clearing of the old court house site in High Street and by an abortive attempt to control street encroachments.[15] After 1785, however, such matters were the responsibility of the improvement commissioners.[16] On two occasions during the French wars of the late 18th century and early 19th the mayor issued regulations about the size and weight of loaves.[17]

A very large proportion of the corporation's business between the 16th century and 1835, however, concerned the defence of its rights and privileges.[18] Feasting, too, became an important activity by the later 18th century. In addition to the feasts mentioned above, the annual provision of a buck by the duke of Norfolk from 1779 or earlier, evidently as a form of electoral treating, was the excuse for a new feast, for burgesses only, which was held each August at the Norfolk Arms hotel.[19] By 1818, when *c.* 20 guests might attend as well, the cost to the corporation was £25–£28 a year.[20] The feast was discontinued because of expense in 1831.[21]

In the early 19th century, perhaps in anticipation of reform, the corporation began to spend more on projects of public utility, after 1818 applying the surplus of its common fund for the benefit of the town.[22] In 1831 it leased land near the bridge to build a corn store for the sale of corn by sample, subscribing £100 towards the cost.[23] The corporation also subscribed to the macadamizing of High Street in 1834[24] and paid for 24 street lamps in 1825.[25] Its earlier interest in the poor law was continued by the provision of Christmas doles of beef in 1817 and by subscriptions to poor relief in 1824 and 1830.[26] It also paid at the same period for the 'ladies' corporation seats' and a new sergeants' pew in the church, and for prayer books for corporation use and for hymn books, and it subscribed to the newly erected organ in 1818.[27] Other subscriptions were to the Arundel rape volunteers in 1803, the free school, the Chichester infirmary, and the building or repair of Hardham causeway and of the Storrington to Balls hut turnpike road, both of which improved northwards communication from the town.[28] In the same spirit subscriptions were taken out against the proposed bridges at Littlehampton and New Shoreham, which seemed likely to divert trade.[29] In 1832 the corporation was preparing measures against a threatened cholera outbreak.[30]

Partly because few parishioners lived outside the town, and partly because by 1776 at least[31] the borough's jurisdiction was claimed to include the whole parish, the corporation strongly influenced parish government in general as well as poor-law administration. By the mid 17th century each parochial office was by custom divided equally between burgesses and non-burgesses;[32] the election of non-burgesses as the two overseers in 1673 was ordered not to become a precedent.[33] By 1769 the corporation's nominee as overseer was usually the preceding mayor,[34] and later its nomination for churchwarden apparently went in rotation among the burgesses.[35] Inevitably one man sometimes held a borough and a parish office together, for instance *c.* 1663 when the mayor was also a churchwarden,[36] or in 1683 when both churchwardens were also borough

2 Cf. Tierney, *Arundel*, ii. 693–5.
3 W.S.R.O., Par. 8/12/2, f. 7; but cf. *S.A.C.* lxxi. 53.
4 Bodl. MS. Chart. Suss. a. 2, no. 72.
5 Above, communications (rds.); Tierney, *Arundel*, ii. 716; *1st Rep. Com. Mun. Corp.* 672.
6 Above, port and river traffic (1500–1800).
7 W.S.R.O., A.B.A., F2/1, ff. 1 and v., 2v.; cf. ibid. A.B.A., B1/1–35.
8 Below, manorial and parochial govt.
9 W.S.R.O., A.B.A., B1/1–2; A.B.A., M5; Eustace, *Arundel*, 142; cf. Tewkesbury: *V.C.H. Glos.* viii. 147.
10 *S.R.S.* xlix. 59. The corp. may have repaired the ch. clock in 1594–5; more surprisingly, it was the mayor who contracted with a carpenter to repair the vicarage at same date: W.S.R.O., A.B.A., F2/1, f. 4; ibid. M3.
11 W.S.R.O., A.B.A., M4.
12 Ibid. A.B.A., A1, f. 68v.
13 Ibid. A.B.A., F3/1.
14 Ibid. A.B.A., A1, ff. 54v., 85v., 261; A.B.A., J1, *passim*; A.B.A., M13.
15 Ibid. A.B.A., M28; cf. above, growth of town.
16 Below, this section.
17 W.S.R.O., A.B.A., F1/37, no. 10; A.B.A., J1, loose sheet between ff. 208v.–209.
18 Ibid. A.B.A., A1, *passim*.
19 Ibid. A.B.A., F1/1, *passim*; Eustace, *Arundel*, 227.
20 A.C.M., MD 1099; W.S.R.O., A.B.A., F1/1, ff. 72–3.
21 W.S.R.O., A.B.A., A1, f. 228.
22 Ibid. A.B.A., F1/1; A.B.A., M48.
23 Ibid. A.B.A., F1/1, f. 90.
24 Ibid. f. 93.
25 Ibid. f. 83.
26 Ibid. ff. 72, 81, 89.
27 Ibid. ff. 66, 72–3, 75, 79.
28 Ibid. ff. 55v., 86, 91–3.
29 Ibid. ff. 81, 90.
30 Ibid. f. 91.
31 B.L. Add. MS. 5687, f. 28; cf. *Arundel Rds.* 28; W.S.R.O., Par. 8/9/1; Par. 8/12/2, f. 8v.
32 *S.A.C.* cxxviii. 166–7; *1st Rep. Com. Mun. Corp.* 673; W.S.R.O., Par. 8/12/2, ff. 44v., 49, 59.
33 W.S.R.O., Par. 8/12/2, f. 19.
34 Ibid. A.B.A., A1, f. 198.
35 Ibid. Par. 8/9/1, f. 69v.
36 Ibid. A.B.A., A1, f. 260v. (his accts. as chwdn. included in corp. bk.); cf. a similar case in 1795: ibid. A.B.A., F1/22, no. 12.

constables.[37] In the later 1640s the corporation may also have controlled the nomination of those parish officers who were not burgesses; at any rate burgesses outnumbered non-burgesses among the names of those signing the notices of election,[38] though the elections continued to be held at the vestry.[39] The description of parish officers in 1655 and later[40] as 'for the borough' seems most likely to be due to an assumption that the areas of the parish and the borough were the same, as they were later. In 1825 the expenses of prosecuting the assailants of a borough constable were ordered to be recouped from the parish.[41]

The mayor was said by the 18th century to act as the lord's deputy in the return and execution of writs within the borough,[42] though the corporation had disclaimed that privilege in 1586.[43] At least twice in the later 16th century and earlier 17th he exercised powers of arrest and imprisonment.[44] The town, however, never had a court of quarter sessions.[45] In 1766 the mayor was said to have the authority of a justice of the peace,[46] though 30 years earlier he never acted as one[47] and *c.* 1800 only very seldom.[48] In the early 19th century mayors arrested and examined offenders, but some persons so committed were forcibly released by others.[49] The mayor had a prison called the dark house or Little ease in 1635,[50] which was presumably also used for offenders coming before quarter sessions. Its site is unknown, as is that of the place of confinement called the Black hole in 1809.[51]

The chief property belonging to the corporation was the burgess brooks, where by *c.* 1539 pasture rights seem already to have been at members' almost exclusive disposal.[52] The justification given in 1648 for what must even then have seemed a usurpation was that it enabled the burgesses more easily to bear the expenses of office and of town government.[53] The corporation spent much money on maintaining the brooks, repairing roads, ditches, and the river wall there,[54] impounding stray animals, catching moles, and improving the pasture by manuring.[55] It also owned other property, chiefly in the town,[56] by the later 16th century,[57] holding some tenements of the earls of Arundel and dukes of Norfolk, including a fulling mill in 1570.[58] Several seem to have been encroachments in the wide area originally open between the foot of High Street and the bridge, including shops near the court house,[59] and land north of the town quay which was later built on.[60] Most of the rest, apart from the 'pest house'[61] and Portreeve's acre on the causeway,[62] was cottage property in the outskirts of the town: in Park Place or Mount Pleasant,[63] King Street,[64] Mill Lane, and elsewhere.[65] Tenements were generally let on leases of between 7 and 120 years, often 21 or 99 years.[66] On three occasions in the later 17th century and earlier 18th the brooks were also let, at a total rent of between £52 10*s.* and £60.[67] From 1758 they were always let, bringing in over £100 a year.[68]

Another chief item of income after the mid 16th century was the fines payable on entry to the corporation. In the 1560s the sum required varied between £5 and £10,[69] but by the early 18th century it had risen to £7 or £12.[70] In the 1560s the money was put into a common fund,[71] but later it went towards the cost of a feast for the corporation.[72] In the 1740s new burgesses had to give £21 or £30 as well as paying for a feast.[73] Fines later rose still higher, to £31 10*s.* by 1760, £63 by 1777, and £105 by 1821;[74] by 1773 the existing burgesses shared the income.[75]

Other regular sources of money were port dues,[76] leases of pasture rights in the brooks to non-burgesses[77] and payments for rights of way there,[78] leases of butchers' shambles,[79] court fines and amercements,[80] and market tolls,[81]

37 Ibid. Par. 8/13/1.
38 *S.A.C.* cxxviii. 166.
39 W.S.R.O., Par. 8/12/2.
40 Ibid. Par. 8/9/1; Par. 8/12/2, f. 8v.; Par. 8/30/12.
41 Ibid. A.B.A., F1/1, f. 83; cf. above, intro.
42 Caraccioli, *Arundel*, 2; cf. *Excursions through Suss.* (1822), 35; Tierney, *Arundel*, ii. 692.
43 Tierney, *Arundel*, ii. 698; cf. *Cal. Pat.* 1553–4, 69.
44 *Acts of P.C.* 1580–1, 26; *Cal. S.P. Dom.* 1635, 49, 203; cf. ibid. 1694–5, 383.
45 The town's inclusion in list of boros. whose quarter sess. were abolished by Municipal Corporations Act, 1835, was in error: *Descriptive Rep. on Quarter Sess., etc., of W. and E. Suss.* (W. and E. Suss. C.C.s, 1954), 4.
46 Caraccioli, *Arundel*, 2; cf. *Excursions through Suss.* (1822), 35.
47 A.C.M., MD 1534, Ric. Holmes to unnamed recipient, 10 Dec. 1735.
48 *Copper Plate Mag.* iv (*c.* 1800), pl. 159; cf. Tierney, *Arundel*, ii. 703 n.
49 *1st Rep. Com. Mun. Corp.* 671; Tierney, *Arundel*, ii. 703.
50 *Cal. S.P. Dom.* 1635, 203.
51 W.S.R.O., A.B.A., J1, f. 224; cf. ibid. f. 242v.
52 Ibid. A.B.A., A1, ff. 8v.–9. For management of brooks, above, agric.
53 W.S.R.O. A.B.A., A1, f. 58v.
54 e.g. ibid. A.B.A., F1/1, *passim*; A.B.A., F1/25, no. 11.
55 e.g. ibid. A.B.A., A1, ff. 48v., 64; A.B.A., F1/1, f. 3; A.B.A., F1/13, no. 1.
56 The exception was in Heene: ibid. A.B.A., P1/13 (TS. cat.); cf. ibid. Par. 8/24/3; Tierney, *Arundel*, ii. 661.
57 W.S.R.O., A.B.A., F2/1, ff. 3–4; cf. ibid. A.B.A., A1, f. 255.
58 A.C.M., A 263, particular of Arundel estate, 1733; 1351, f. [iv.]; ibid. MD 495, f. [64v.]; 535, f. 4 and v.; W.S.R.O., A.B.A., F4/1, nos. 1–2, 6, 10, 13, 16, 18; cf. ibid. A.B.A., F2/3.
59 W.S.R.O., A.B.A., P1/5; A.B.A., P1/8, 11–12, 20, 28, 32, 39 (TS. cat.).
60 P.R.O., C 142/314, no. 150; W.S.R.O., A.B.A., P1/15, 18, 29, 35 (TS. cat.); cf. land in Marygate St. N. of chyd. inclosed shortly before 1712: ibid. A.B.A., P1/27 (TS. cat.).
61 *Arundel Cast. Archives*, iii, p. 58; cf. below, public servs.
62 *Wiston Archives*, i, ed. J. Booker, p. 6.
63 W.S.R.O., A.B.A., P1/30, 45 (TS. cat.); for Whitings dyke, above, growth of town (street names).
64 W.S.R.O., A.B.A., A1, f. 213v.; A.B.A., P1/16 (TS. cat.); cf. above, growth of town (street names).
65 W.S.R.O., A.B.A., A1, ff. 207, 255; A.B.A., P1/17, 19, 22, 24 (TS. cat.); cf. ibid. BO/AR 10/2–3; *S.A.C.* lxxi. 53. For Jury Lane, above, growth of town (street names).
66 W.S.R.O., A.B.A., F2/1, f. 3; A.B.A., P1 (TS. cat.).
67 Ibid. A.B.A., A1, ff. 101v., 121, 136v.
68 Ibid. A.B.A., A1, ff. 194v.–195v., 207v.–209v.; A.B.A., F1/1, *passim*; A.B.A., M25; A.B.A., P1/36 (TS. cat.); above, agric.
69 W.S.R.O., A.B.A., A1, ff. 16v., 17v., 18v. Some elections in later 16th and earlier 17th cents., however, did not require a fine: ibid. A.B.A., A1, *passim*.
70 Ibid. A.B.A., A1, ff. 151, 170.
71 Ibid. f. 18v.
72 Ibid. f. 151.
73 Ibid. ff. 174, 182; cf. *S.A.C.* lxxi. 50. For the feast, *1st Rep. Com. Mun. Corp.* 671.
74 W.S.R.O., A.B.A., A1, ff. 196, 204v., 223v. The last fine, in 1832, was only £63: ibid. f. 234v.
75 *S.A.C.* lxxi. 35, 39, 41–2.
76 Above, port and river traffic (1500–1800).
77 W.S.R.O., A.B.A., F1/1, ff. 3v., 6v.; A.B.A., F3/1, 15.
78 Ibid. A.B.A., A1, ff. 255, 258; A.B.A., F3/1–2, 15.
79 e.g. ibid. A.B.A., A1, ff. 53, 157; A.B.A., F1/1, f. 2v.; A.B.A., F3/2, 15; A.B.A., P1/5.
80 Ibid. A.B.A., F2/3.
81 Ibid. A.B.A., F1/1, f. 88v.; A.B.A., M28.

which in the 1820s amounted to between £13 and £26 a year.[82] In the later 16th century the corporation also engaged in trade, for instance in salt, grain, and hops, hired out a bushel measure, and sold licences to live and trade in the town.[83] Since some income was hypothecated for bridge repair,[84] for the mayor's expenses, or for the sergeants' wages,[85] no general account was made before the reform of 1835.[86]

The only reference to a borough rate is of 1679, for bridge repair.[87] Because that could be represented, however, as falling within the parish's responsibility for the repair of roads, the corporation managed by *c.* 1780 to draw on the poor rate to help meet the cost. In 1835 the parish surveyor of highways did any small necessary repairs to the bridge at the request of the mayor, who paid him and charged the sum to the overseers. By that date the bridge was said to be largely repaired from the poor rate.[88]

When expenditure in any year predominated over income, the difference was supplied by the burgesses in equal shares.[89] In the same way a surplus was divided between them after 1663, the mayor receiving a double share by 1762; the total in question in 1759 was £84 14*s.* 1*d.* and in 1762 £117 9*s.* 2*d.*[90] After 1818 the balance was carried forward instead from year to year and applied to projects of public utility.[91] After 1831 entry fines were so used too,[92] and at the reform of the borough in 1835 the last three fines received were repaid.[93] The total corporation income in 1834 was *c.* £208 a year;[94] in the following year it was said to be capable of reaching £300, even excluding entry fines, if a reasonable rent were taken from the brooks.[95]

IMPROVEMENT COMMISSION. An improvement commission, responsible for paving, lighting, and cleansing the town, and empowered to levy a rate, was set up under an Act of 1785. Though the mayor and burgesses were members *ex officio*, the presence on it to begin with of 46 others visibly diluted the corporation's otherwise virtually exclusive power over the town.[96]

AFTER 1835. Under the Municipal Corporations Act, 1835, borough government was reformed. The new town council was required to meet quarterly, the right of election to it was restored to all ratepayers, entry fines became illegal, and the rents of borough property were raised to a realistic level.[97] Some members of the old corporation refused to pay increased rents on portions of the burgess brooks already leased to them, until required to do so after the town council took them to court.[98] Also under the 1835 Act the council assumed the powers of the improvement commissioners, though the Improvement Act of 1785 was not repealed until 1876.[99] There were 466 burgesses in 1886.[1] Arundel remained a borough until 1974, when it became part of Arun district; the title of mayor, however, was retained by the chairman of the successor parish council.

In 1839 and later the town council consisted of a mayor, four aldermen, and 12 councillors.[2] It had the power to make bylaws.[3] By 1938 meetings were held monthly.[4] There was a deputy mayor by 1910, when committees existed for general purposes, finance, works, and land and allotment gardens.[5] There was a housing committee from 1923.[6]

Officers besides the mayor were a town clerk, a treasurer, and a town crier recorded in the 1830s,[7] and a medical officer, an inspector of nuisances, and a surveyor and collector in 1882.[8] The brookwarden still served in 1902,[9] and the two portreeves in 1882 but apparently not much later.[10] The council's offices were at one time at no. 61 High Street, but in 1994 office space was rented from the legal practice of the then town clerk.[11]

The three-weekly borough court was revived in 1839 for pleas under 40*s.*, the mayor presiding. Twenty-two suits had been begun by 1840, but the court is not recorded after that date.[12]

The town council continued after 1835 to manage the market, to maintain the bridge, and to regulate weights and measures.[13] As successor to the improvement commission it was responsible for paving and cleansing, and under the Public Health Act, 1872, the borough became an urban sanitary district, of which the council was the urban sanitary authority.[14] The council's activities in the fields of sewage disposal, fire fighting, and public lighting, its provision of a cemetery, and its management of the swimming pool are discussed elsewhere.[15] In 1895 it took over the duty of

82 Ibid. A.B.A., F1/1, ff. 75v., 78v., 84v.
83 Ibid. A.B.A., F2/1, ff. 1–2v.; A.B.A., F2/3.
84 Ibid. A.B.A., F2/2.
85 *1st Rep. Com. Mun. Corp.* 674; W.S.R.O., A.B.A., A1, f. 61v.
86 The only general accts. found, of 1732–4, list as income merely property rents, payments for pasture rights, and contribs. from burgesses: W.S.R.O., A.B.A., A1, ff. 157, 160v.
87 W.S.R.O., A.B.A., F2/1, f. 18.
88 *1st Rep. Com. Mun. Corp.* 672; cf. W.S.R.O., A.B.A., F2/2.
89 W.S.R.O., A.B.A., A1, ff. 109, 132v., 157, 160v.; A.B.A., F3/1.
90 Ibid. A.B.A., F1/1, *passim*; A.B.A., M12; *S.A.C.* lxxi. 53.
91 W.S.R.O., A.B.A., F1/1; A.B.A., M48.
92 Ibid. A.B.A., A1, f. 228; *1st Rep. Com. Mun. Corp.* 671.
93 W.S.R.O., A.B.A., A1, ff. 235–6.
94 Tierney, *Arundel*, ii. 705.
95 *1st Rep. Com. Mun. Corp.* 674.
96 Ibid. 672; 25 Geo. III, c. 90.
97 Eustace, *Arundel*, 235.
98 Ibid. 236; *Lond. Gaz.* 27 May 1836, pp. 954–5; 31 May 1836, p. 974; A.C.M., MD 418; W.S.R.O., BO/AR 24/4/1.
99 W.S.R.O., BO/AR 24/4/5; 39 & 40 Vic. c. 13 (Local).
1 W.S.R.O., BO/AR 24/1/1.
2 Pigot, *Nat. Com. Dir.* (1839), 652; *Kelly's Dir. Suss.* (1882, 1938).
3 Eustace, *Arundel*, 236.
4 *Kelly's Dir. Suss.* (1938).
5 Pike, *Bognor Dir.* (1910–11), 179.
6 W.S.R.O., BO/AR 3/4/1.
7 Pigot, *Nat. Com. Dir.* (1839), 653; Eustace, *Arundel*, 236; A.C.M., MD 418, f. [2].
8 *Kelly's Dir. Suss.* (1882).
9 W.S.R.O., BO/AR 24/4/17, f. 8.
10 Ibid. Add. MS. 13353; ibid. BO/AR 24/4/23.
11 *W. Suss. Gaz.* 3 Feb. 1994; local inf.
12 *Cts. of Request*, H.C. 619, pp. 156–7 (1840), xli.
13 W.S.R.O., A.B.A., F2/2; ibid. Add. MS. 13353; ibid. MP 962, notice inviting tenders for renting mkt. tolls, 1855; above, communications (rds.).
14 W.S.R.O., BO/AR 24/4/5.
15 Above, soc. and cultural activities (sport); below, public servs.

appointing overseers for the borough and parish,[16] and in 1903 and later the freehold of the Victoria institute was vested in it.[17]

Besides levying rates, the council took over some of the income of the corporation: two 16th-century rents charge for bridge upkeep, redeemed in the 20th century,[18] and the port dues and market tolls, which together brought in an estimated £10 a year in 1902.[19] The council also took over the corporation's property, including the burgess brooks. At the sale of the brooks to the duke of Norfolk in 1902[20] other borough property included almshouses in Maltravers Street and Mount Pleasant, cottages in Mount Pleasant, the swimming baths in Ford Road, and the reversions of the corn store by the bridge and of Portreeve's acre.[21]

TOWN HALLS. The court house referred to in 1542[22] was perhaps the same as the building mentioned in the 17th and 18th centuries, to which shops were attached.[23] Apparently its lower floor was originally open, for a shop lay below it in 1591.[24] The building stood in the middle of High Street[25] near the entrance to Tarrant Street.[26] An alternative name was the 'town house'.[27] It was used for the holding of the view, the borough court, parliamentary elections,[28] and perhaps sometimes quarter sessions, though part of the former college buildings accommodated the latter in 1635[29] and was presumably the sessions house mentioned in 1638.[30] There was also a 'market house' in the 1690s, evidently separate since reference was made to the pavement between it and the court house.[31] The court house was pulled down in or before 1741,[32] and the remains of the buildings attached to it in or shortly before 1773.[33] Borough business was afterwards transacted in the so-called sacristy of the Fitzalan chapel at the parish church, which was known as the court house apparently in 1793 and certainly later.[34]

A new town hall was built in Maltravers Street by the duke of Norfolk in 1834–5 to the design of Robert Abraham,[35] the use of the 'sacristy' being given up by the town council as a *quid pro quo* in 1848.[36] The building has a flint and sandstone façade with flanking towers in Norman style. A large upstairs room was used in 1847 for balls, concerts, and similar events.[37] The basement had three cells, which from 1844 were used by the county police force;[38] it also housed the town fire engines.[39] The town hall accommodated meetings of the town council and magistrates' courts in 1991.[40]

The borough pound mentioned in 1570[41] perhaps stood in Mill Lane as it did later; the corporation was responsible for its repair in 1709,[42] but it was apparently sold to the duke of Norfolk in 1801.[43] In 1851, when the duke had recently repaired it, it was little used, though it then served Avisford hundred as well as the borough.[44] There were unnamed instruments of punishment at the court house in 1542,[45] but the location of the stocks and whipping post mentioned in the later 18th century is unknown.[46]

The corporation plate includes three maces and three loving cups. The mace in use in the 20th century is silver gilt, and was given in 1676 by Francis Aungier, Viscount Longford, M.P.; the other two, of silver with iron cores, are a pair, probably 15th-century or earlier, but with names or initials and dates respectively of Thomas Bennett, mayor 1594, and two mid 17th-century mayors. Of the three cups one was given in 1677 by a former mayor, one is hallmarked 1725–6, and the third is dated 1830.[47]

SEAL. The seal of the borough was round, and depicted a swallow (*hirondelle*, for Arundel) displayed, on a spiral branch; legend, Roman, SIGILLVM BVRGENSIVM BVRGI DE ARVNDEL.[48] No certain reference has been found to it before 1569;[49] the mayor's seal mentioned in 1438 was probably personal, as was that attached to a deed of 1379.[50] Until 1938 the seal was used as the arms of the borough.[51]

MANORIAL AND PAROCHIAL GOVERNMENT.

There was a court for tenants of the Arundel priory estate in 1272, which in 1280 was said to be three-weekly.[52] The college which succeeded the priory also held a court, in 1408 at Bury.[53] The Great park and the Rewell lay within the jurisdiction of the Arundel forest court of woodplayt, i.e. wood pleas, which in the

16 W.S.R.O., BO/AR 24/4/17, f. 26.
17 *Kelly's Dir. Suss.* (1903, 1938).
18 W.S.R.O., A.B.A., F2/2, ff. 67v., 87v.; cf. above, communications (rds.).
19 Ibid. BO/AR 24/4/17, f. 9; cf. ibid. BO/AR 24/4/23, 30.
20 Ibid. BO/AR 10/5.
21 Ibid. BO/AR 24/4/17, ff. 8–9.
22 Ibid. A.B.A., A1, f. 12v.
23 A.C.M., D 902–25 (MS. cat.); P.R.O., C 142/314, no. 150; W.S.R.O., A.B.A., P1/8, 10, 12 (TS. cat.).
24 W.S.R.O., A.B.A., F2/1, f. 4.
25 Eustace, *Arundel*, 114, 219; A.C.M., D 902–25 (MS. cat.).
26 A.C.M., Hodskinson surv. 1778, f. 4, showing empty site.
27 Eustace, *Arundel*, 214.
28 Ibid.
29 *Camd. Misc.* xvi (Camd. 3rd ser. lii), Hammond, 33.
30 W.S.R.O., Ep. I/55/6 (TS. cat.).
31 A.C.M., A 339, mins. of view, 1696; cf. W.S.R.O., A.B.A., A1, f. 113.
32 Eustace, *Arundel*, 214.
33 Ibid. 219; W.S.R.O., A.B.A., A1, ff. 199v., 201.
34 A.C.M., FA 95, f. 6; ibid. M 900, poll for elec. of mayor, 1767; W.S.R.O., A.B.A., C2, pp. 4, 8; A.B.A., F1/1, f. 91.
35 W.S.R.O., BO/AR 53/1; Horsfield, *Hist. Suss.* ii. 122.
36 A.C.M., FA 59.
37 Hillier, *Arundel* (1847), 29.
38 W.S.R.O., BO/AR 12/1, 8, 11; ibid. QAC/4/W 1, nos. 13–14, 18–19, 21.
39 Below, public servs.
40 Local inf.; cf. *W. Suss. Gaz.* 20 Nov. 1980.
41 A.C.M., MD 535, f. 4; W.S.R.O., A.B.A., F4/1, no. 1; cf. ibid. A.B.A., A1, f. 61v.
42 W.S.R.O., A.B.A., P1/22; ibid. TD/W 5.
43 A.C.M., MD 619, p. 53.
44 *Arundel Rds.* 38. There was a par. pound in the S. marshes in 1905: W.S.R.O., BO/AR 12/18.
45 W.S.R.O., A.B.A., A1, f. 12v.
46 Ibid. A.B.A., J1, ff. 48, 177v.
47 Ibid. A.B.A., A1, f. 96v.; B.L. Add. MS. 5674, f. 13; Eustace, *Arundel*, 193–4, 255–6.
48 Eustace, *Arundel*, 256; illus. at Dallaway, *Hist. W. Suss.* ii (1) (1819), 179.
49 W.S.R.O., A.B.A., A1, f. 19; cf. ibid. f. 185v.
50 *Cal. Close*, 1435–41, 240; A.C.M., D 1158.
51 *Suss. Daily News*, 15 Oct. 1938.
52 *S.R.S.* vii, pp. 87, 118.
53 Hist. MSS. Com. 55, *Var. Coll. I, Bp. of Chich.* p. 184.

1270s was also three-weekly though it had formerly been annual;[54] it survived in 1438[55] but is not heard of later.

Two churchwardens were recorded in 1548[56] and generally later,[57] though in 1624 there were three.[58] Four overseers were usually recorded between 1603 and 1649 and between 1699 and 1737, two between 1650 and 1698, and three between 1738 and 1769. After 1770 there were often five or more, the number rising to 21 in 1811.[59] A woman served the office in 1679.[60] Two surveyors of highways were recorded between 1646 and 1688;[61] in the early 19th century there was sometimes apparently only one and at other times there were three.[62]

The annual vestry was held at the court house in 1675–6, in the church in 1683,[63] and in the 'sacristy' of the Fitzalan chapel at the church in 1779 and 1832.[64] There was never a select vestry.[65]

A rate for church repair and apparently a separate poor rate were mentioned in 1674[66] and a highway rate in 1656.[67] By 1674 the corporation had long been paying half the church rate and perhaps half the poor rate too;[68] in 1729 it defrayed half of all expenditure.[69] The payment was said in 1674 to relate to the burgess brooks[70] and may have been in partial compensation for loss of rights there by non-burgesses. By 1705 it apparently also included what was due from the other property of burgesses.[71] The payment was stopped by the corporation, to protests, in 1822.[72] The levying of a church rate after it ceased to be compulsory in 1868 was contested at the annual vestry meeting by the Roman Catholic priest among others; in 1874 it was refused.[73]

Methods of poor relief used in Arundel in the 17th and 18th centuries were apprenticing, usually to Arundel masters,[74] weekly pay,[75] boarding out,[76] and the provision of clothing[77] and medical care.[78] Between the mid 17th century and the early 19th the overseers also distributed endowed charitable doles.[79] In the 18th century rent, fuel, and food and drink were provided, and a payment was made for schooling in 1772.[80] There was a poorhouse in the north-west part of the town by 1682, when a room with a loft over it was to be built presumably nearby;[81] its site seems to have been on the east side of Park Place, where a possibly 17th-century range survives behind the mid 19th-century workhouse.[82] Expenditure on linen, thread, yarn, and knitting needles in 1678 and later was presumably for work to be done at the poorhouse,[83] and the 'town house' where poor children and apparently widows lived in 1713 was probably the same building.[84] In 1779–80 a new 'workhouse' was built in its garden.[85]

Arundel was a single parish under Gilbert's Act, 1782.[86] The appointment of an assistant overseer by *c.* 1814 had greatly reduced the rise of poor-law expenditure by 1834.[87] Another workhouse, of flint with brick dressings, was built in 1831 on the east side of Park Place,[88] evidently on the site of the earlier building.[89] Clothing was supplied to inmates in the 1830s,[90] when weekly pay was also given.[91] In 1832 between four and twenty labourers a week were out of work in winter and none in summer.[92] Arundel remained separate for poor-law purposes after 1835, the workhouse having 41 inhabitants in 1841, 33 inmates in 1851, and 15 in 1861.[93] A standing committee for the relief of the necessitous poor existed between 1838 and 1842, and included the mayor, the churchwardens, and religious leaders; money was raised from subscriptions and the holding of concerts, and the committee distributed bread weekly in winter at a reduced price.[94] In 1869 Arundel was added to East Preston union,[95] which conveyed the town workhouse to the duke of Norfolk in 1873.[96] During the earlier 20th century it was a club house and in 1985–6 it was converted into flats.[97]

In the 17th century an important part in poor-law administration was played by the corporation, which had already apparently been giving money to the poor in 1579.[98] In the earlier 17th century apprenticeship bonds were sometimes taken out with the mayor or apparently

54 *V.C.H. Suss.* ii. 304.
55 P.R.O., C 139/88, no. 50, m. 19.
56 W.S.R.O., Ep. I/86/20, f. 14v.
57 B.L. Add. MS. 39359, ff. 14–19.
58 *Cal. Assize. Rec. Suss. Jas. I*, p. 141.
59 W.S.R.O., A.B.A., B2; A.B.A., B4 (TS. cat.); ibid. Par. 8/12/2.
60 Ibid. Par. 8/31/1 (1679).
61 Ibid. Par. 8/12/2.
62 Ibid. Par. 8/39/1, f. [1].
63 Ibid. Par. 8/13/1.
64 Ibid. Par. 8/37/22; *S.A.C.* lxxi. 43. For identification cf. below, church [fabric].
65 *Rep. Com. Poor Laws*, H.C. 44, p. 491 (1834), xxxi.
66 W.S.R.O., A.B.A., L3, no. 18, ff. 10–11; cf. Eustace, *Arundel*, 212.
67 W.S.R.O., Par. 8/12/2, f. 9.
68 Ibid. A.B.A., L3, no. 18, ff. 10–11, 32.
69 Ibid. Par. 8/9/1, f. 6.
70 Ibid. A.B.A., L3, no. 18, f. 32.
71 Ibid. Par. 8/11/7, f. 1; cf. *1st Rep. Com. Mun. Corp.* 672.
72 *1st Rep. Com. Mun. Corp.* 672; W.S.R.O., A.B.A., M48.
73 W.S.R.O., Par. 8/12/1, pp. 68–72, 92–3, 98–100; cf. O. Chadwick, *Victorian Ch.* ii. 195.
74 W.S.R.O., A.B.A., B2/1–17; ibid. Par. 8/1/1/1, inside back cover; Par. 8/12/2, ff. 32v.–33; Par. 8/31/1 (1684); Par. 8/31/2 (1708–9); A. Fletcher, *County Community in Peace and War*, 158.
75 W.S.R.O., Par. 8/31/1 (1678); Par. 8/31/2 (1707); Par. 8/31/3 (1771).
76 Ibid. Par. 8/31/1 (1678); Par. 8/31/3 (1771).
77 Ibid. Par. 8/31/1 (1678); Par. 8/31/2 (1707); Par. 8/31/3 (1772).
78 Ibid. Par. 8/31/1 (1678); Par. 8/31/2 (1708–9).
79 Ibid. Par. 8/9/1, ff. 1v., 84v.–85v., 88v., 111v., 113v.; Par. 8/12/2, f. 5v.; Par. 8/31/2, at end.
80 Ibid. Par. 8/31/2 (1707–9, 1713); Par. 8/31/3 (1771–2).
81 Ibid. Par. 8/31/1 (1682); for Whitings dyke, above, growth of town (street names).
82 A.C.M., H 1/3; cf. below, this section.
83 W.S.R.O., Par. 8/31/1 (1678); Par. 8/31/2 (1713). A later proposal of 1779 to organize paupers in sack making was apparently abortive: *S.A.C.* lxxi. 43.
84 W.S.R.O., Par. 8/31/2 (1713), and inv. 1713 at end.
85 Ibid. Par. 8/31/3 (1779–80).
86 *Suss. Poor Law Rec.* 63.
87 *Rep. Com. Poor Laws*, H.C. 44, p. 491 (1834), xxxi.
88 Date on bldg.
89 Cf. A.C.M., H 1/3; W.S.R.O., MP 3041 (photocopy of town plan, 1785).
90 W.S.R.O., Par. 8/9/10, nos. 590, 599, 708.
91 *Rep. Com. Poor Laws*, H.C. 44, p. 547 (1834), xxviii.
92 Ibid. p. 491 (1834), xxxi.
93 *Census*, 1841–61; *Suss. Genealogist and Local Historian*, iii. 50–1.
94 A.C.M., MD 787, 2237.
95 *Suss. Poor Law Rec.* 46.
96 A.C.M., D 3204–6 (MS. cat.).
97 O.S. Map 1/2,500, Suss. LXIII. 1 (1937 edn.); *W. Suss. Gaz.* 31 Oct. 1985.
98 W.S.R.O., A.B.A., F2/3. For the corp.'s administration of char. endowments, above, boro. govt. (activity, property, and income).

the corporation rather than with the parish officers.[99] Surety bonds in the same period, either to secure guardians for minors or orphans or, chiefly, to regulate immigration to the town, were mostly taken out with the mayor,[1] and bastardy bonds in 1618 and 1646 with the mayor or the corporation.[2] By 1600 the corporation held four cottages from the earl of Arundel's representative which were used to house the poor and were later known as the poor cottages.[3] A bequest to the poor of 1615 was to be administered by the mayor, churchwardens, and overseers together.[4] In the 1780s it was the borough court rather than the parish vestry which sought to expel vagrants and beggars.[5]

Before the improvement commission was set up in 1785 the surveyors of highways repaired all the town roads except High Street,[6] and *c.* 1783 they laid out Surrey Street at the west end.[7] In 1652 they had also had responsibility for the repair of a subsidiary quay on the south bank of the river, the town quay being maintained by the corporation.[8] The parish's management of the town well and the 'pest house' are mentioned below.[9]

PARLIAMENTARY REPRESENTATION. The borough returned two members to Parliament from 1295,[10] less apparently for its own importance than for that of the earls of Arundel. One seat was abolished in 1653[11] but restored after 1660. There were over 100 voters in 1661, 138 in 1751,[12] and *c.* 200–300 in the later 18th century.[13] In 1831, when there were 463, the boundary commission proposed increasing the electorate, in order to retain two members, by including Littlehampton and Lyminster in the parliamentary borough.[14] The corporation objected, since the duke of Norfolk's dominance in Littlehampton would bring the borough into his control; if an addition was necessary, the mayor suggested instead Petworth or any parish west of the town.[15] In the event the enlargement of the electorate was achieved by revaluing the town property;[16] one seat, however, was abolished in 1832[17] and the other in 1868.[18] There were only *c.* 340 electors in 1865[19] but, as Disraeli pointed out when disfranchisement was envisaged in 1859, the single Arundel member in effect also represented the 900,000 Roman Catholics in the country.[20] An Arundel division of the county was created in 1974.[21]

There seems to have been no restriction on the parliamentary franchise in the 16th century and early 17th,[22] but from the later 17th century until 1832 it belonged only to those inhabitants who paid scot and lot.[23] The returning officer was the mayor.[24]

In the later 15th century the borough was controlled by the earls of Arundel, and of 17 M.P.s identified in the period 1439–1509 only four were resident.[25] Between 1529 and 1586 all but two of the members known were the earls' nominees. At the attainder of Philip Howard, earl of Arundel, in 1589 patronage passed to Thomas Sackville, Lord Buckhurst, nominees of whom were returned between 1593 and apparently 1601.[26] Another period of Howard influence began in 1614:[27] in 1623 Lord Arundel's protégé Sir George Chaworth was unseated for fraud,[28] but Henry Frederick Howard (d. 1652), later earl of Arundel, Surrey, and Norfolk, was twice M.P. for the town between 1628 and 1640.[29] In 1641 the earl was warned against interfering in the byelection[30] at which Col. John Downes, the future regicide, was returned.[31] In 1658 the inhabitants requested nominations from Henry Howard, the earl of Arundel's brother, later duke of Norfolk,[32] whose son and namesake was said to have the patronage in 1688. The earl of Northumberland, however, had nominated both members in 1661.[33] In the later 17th century and earlier 18th local gentry often sat for the town.[34] In the early 18th century[35] the government had an interest through the Admiralty[36] and the customs service, and both seats were filled between 1715 and 1739 by its supporters, including members of the Lumley family of Stansted House in Stoughton[37] and Sir John Shelley of Michelgrove in Clapham,[38] brother-in-law of the duke of Newcastle.

99 W.S.R.O., A.B.A., B2/1–17.
1 Ibid. A.B.A., B1/1–35.
2 Ibid. A.B.A., B3/1–2 (TS. cat.). Other misc. bonds were sometimes treated similarly: ibid. A.B.A., B4 (TS. cat.). All bonds concerned are among boro. rec.
3 W.S.R.O., A.B.A., F4/1, nos. 1–2, 10, 16.
4 Ibid. A.B.A., M4. The fact that in 1682 an agreement over a poor-law matter was signed by the mayor and 14 others need not be significant; it occurs in overseers' acct. bk., not among boro. rec.: ibid. Par. 8/31/1 (1682).
5 Ibid. A.B.A., J1, ff. 68, 84 and v.
6 A.C.M., D 3210, p. 4.
7 Above, communications (rds.).
8 W.S.R.O., Par. 8/12/2, f. 7; above, port and river traffic (1500–1800).
9 Below, public servs.
10 *S.A.C.* xxx. 161.
11 *Acts & Ords. of Interr.* ed. Firth & Rait, ii. 814.
12 *Hist. Parl., Commons*, 1660–90, i. 418; 1715–54, i. 332.
13 Ibid. 1754–90, i. 388; 1790–1820, ii. 390; *Univ. Brit. Dir.* ii. 57.
14 *Rep. Parl. Bdries.* H.C. 141–V, pp. 63–5 (1831–2), xl; Eustace, *Arundel*, 263.
15 W.S.R.O., Goodwood MS. 639, f. 22; Eustace, *Arundel*, 263–4.
16 W.S.R.O., Goodwood MS. 639, f. 20; Eustace, *Arundel*, 264, citing W.S.R.O., A.B.A., A1, f. 232v.
17 Horsfield, *Hist. Suss.* ii, App. 31.
18 31 & 32 Vic. c. 48.
19 W.S.R.O., MP 962, list of burgesses, 1865.
20 152 *Parl. Deb.* 3rd ser. 1002–3.
21 *Brit. Parl. Elec. Results, 1974–1983*, comp. F. Craig, 55.
22 *Hist. Parl., Commons*, 1558–1603, i. 256; *C.J.* i. 748.
23 Horsfield, *Hist. Suss.* ii, App. 29.
24 W.S.R.O., A.B.A., E1/1–7 (TS. cat.); *S.A.C.* lxxi. 14.
25 *Hist. Parl., Reg. of Members, 1439–1509*, 692–3.
26 *Hist. Parl., Commons*, 1509–58, i. 201; 1558–1603, i. 256; *S.R.S.* lxxiv, p. xxxii; *D.N.B.* s.v. Sir Edw. Stradling.
27 J. K. Gruenfelder, *Infl. in Early Stuart Elecs. 1604–1640*, 132, 172 n.
28 *C.J.* i. 748; *Faction and Parl.* ed. K. Sharpe, 223.
29 *Complete Peerage*, i. 258; ix. 625; *S.A.C.* xxxiii. 85–6.
30 D. Hirst, *The Representative of the People?* 67.
31 *D.N.B.*; cf. W.S.R.O., A.B.A., A1, f. 66.
32 A.C.M., A 262, f. [36]; for identification, above, castle (cast. fabric); woods and parks (Great park).
33 *Hist. Parl., Commons*, 1660–90, i. 418.
34 Ibid. 1660–90, i. 418; 1715–54, i. 332; *Clough and Butler Archives*, ed. J. Booker, p. vi; R. Walcott, *Eng. Politics in Early 18th Cent.* 196. The Lumleys were of Stansted Ho. in Stoughton: below, this section.
35 Rest of para. based mainly on *Hist. Parl., Commons*, 1715–54, i. 332.
36 Walcott, *Eng. Politics*, 38, 196.
37 *V.C.H. Suss.* iv. 122.
38 Ibid. vi (1), 13.

Edward Howard, duke of Norfolk (d. 1777), attempted in 1735 to regain the family interest first by nominating burgesses to the corporation and then by trying to appoint a mayor himself in opposition to the one elected at the annual view of frankpledge.[39] The struggle for Parliamentary control of the borough caused a further dispute over the mayor's election in 1740,[40] and accusations of electoral malpractice were made on other occasions in the 18th century.[41] (Sir) George Colebrooke, chairman of the court of directors of the East India Co. and an associate of the duke of Norfolk, sat for the town 1754–74 and nominated the other member after 1761.[42] Between 1774 and 1820 the duke always had one nomination and sometimes two,[43] the election of the mayor again being an occasion of conflict in 1811.[44] Duke Bernard Edward (d. 1842) gave up his interest after 1820 because of expense,[45] but re-established it after *c.* 1830, espousing the cause of Reform in opposition to the corporation;[46] *c.* 1832 he bought a brewery in the town in order to threaten the livelihood of his rival, the burgess and brewer George Constable.[47]

The Arundel division of the county has always returned Conservative M.P.s with large majorities.[48]

PUBLIC SERVICES. There may have been a common well in the town in 1269.[49] In 1674 Edward Hamper leased to the inhabitants for 1,000 years the well next to his house, which adjoined the court house in High Street. The overseers were to manage the well, each family which used it paying a sum of up to 8*d.* a year, any surplus income going on bread for the poor.[50] The supply was said to be excellent in 1831.[51] In 1834 a pump was presented by Lord Dudley Coutts Stuart, M.P.[52] After 1835 responsibility for water supply was assumed by the new town council.[53] The castle meanwhile had had piped water since 1644 or earlier;[54] in 1731 and presumably before it came from a spring near Swanbourne lake, apparently by way of a cistern in the Little park as later.[55] A new cistern of red brick with stone dressings was constructed there in the mid 19th century.[56] A new pumping house of flint and stone in Norman style was built at Swanbourne shortly before 1846[57] and survived, though roofless, in 1988. By 1874 the duke was providing an additional, free, water supply for the town through standpipes from a separate tank in the Little park. Some private wells nevertheless remained in use in 1883.[58]

The common well in High Street was closed after an outbreak of enteric fever in 1890 was traced to it,[59] and the duke of Norfolk's supply to the town was increased by the sinking of a borehole and the addition of gas engines at Swanbourne, a new reservoir being constructed north of the lake.[60] In 1898 the supply was for domestic use only and each inhabitant could take 30 gallons a day.[61] Part of the rural portion of the parish and parts of Tortington and Lyminster meanwhile also received a supply from the Norfolk estate.[62] The borough water undertaking was acquired in 1965 by Worthing corporation, and the estate undertaking in 1966.[63]

The corporation's responsibility for drainage and rubbish disposal, fitfully exercised,[64] was taken over after 1785 by the improvement commissioners,[65] whose powers passed in 1835 to the town council.[66] Brick sewers were constructed by *c.* 1850 apparently as storm water outlets, but by 1883 they carried into the river nearly all the town's sewage.[67] In 1895–6 a new sewerage system was provided by the council with a loan from the Local Government board, a sewage works being constructed in Tortington.[68] In 1911 the duke of Norfolk granted the town the yearly tenancy of a site for refuse disposal, also in Tortington.[69]

The only police force before 1835 was the two borough constables,[70] the mayor's sergeants *c.* 1650 having the duty of setting a watch.[71] A borough police force whose jurisdiction covered a two-mile radius of the town existed from 1836

39 W.S.R.O., A.B.A., L4, no. 5; A.B.A., M21; Eustace, *Arundel*, 208.

40 *Hist. Parl., Commons*, 1715–54, i. 332–3; A.C.M., MD 1534, Ric. Holmes to Francis Loggin, 30 Oct. 1740; W.S.R.O., A.B.A., L5, bdle. 1, nos. 23, 34.

41 *Hist. Parl., Commons*, 1715–54, i. 332–3; 1754–90, i. 388–9; Hist. MSS. Com. 10, *10th Rep. I, Weston Underwood*, p. 409; Horsfield, *Hist. Suss.* ii, App. 29–30.

42 *D.N.B.* s.v. Hen. Thos. Colebrooke; *Hist. Parl., Commons*, 1754–90, i. 388–9; *S.A.C.* lxxi. 14–15, 30; Horsfield, *Hist. Suss.* ii, App. 30.

43 *Hist. Parl., Commons*, 1754–90, i. 389; 1790–1820, ii. 390–1.

44 *1st Rep. Com. Mun. Corp.* 670.

45 *Peers, Politics and Power: H.L. 1603–1911*, ed. C. Jones and D. L. Jones, 348–9.

46 M. Zimmeck, 'Reform Era Politics in Rye, Arundel, Lewes' (Suss. Univ. M.A. thesis, 1972), 5.

47 Above, other trades and inds. (1800–1945).

48 e.g. *Brit. Parl. Elec. Results, 1974–1983*, comp. F. Craig, 55.

49 B.L. Lansd. Ch. 92.

50 W.S.R.O., A.B.A., P1/10 (orig. lease); ibid. Par. 8/7/27 (20th-cent. copy); cf. ibid. Par. 8/31/1, loose sheet, 1687, in vol. Though orig. lease is among boro. rec. it had been placed in par. chest in 1679: ibid. Par. 8/12/2, f. 27v. John Albery was an overseer in 1674: ibid. Par. 8/12/2 (1674).

51 Lewis, *Topog. Dict. Eng.* (1831).

52 Eustace, *Arundel*, 235.

53 Cf. W.S.R.O., Holmes, Campbell & Co. MS. 595.

54 *S.A.C.* xix. 118.

55 *Plans of Arundel Cast.* 15; A.C.M., A 339, estimate for bldg. pumping engine and engine ho. 1705; ibid. D 6272 (MS. cat.); ibid. K 2/64.

56 A.C.M., MD 2592, plan of cast. grounds; ibid. uncat. archit. drawings, plan of cast. drainage.

57 *Illus. Lond. News*, 5 Dec. 1846, p. 357.

58 *Jnl. of Horticulture and Cottage Gdnr.* 1 Jan. 1874, p. 12; *10th Ann. Rep. on Combined Sanit. Dist. of W. Suss.* (Worthing, 1884), 177 (copy at W.S.R.O., WDC/CL 74/1); cf. Eustace, *Arundel*, 192.

59 *17th Ann. Rep. on Combined Sanit. Dist. of W. Suss.* (Littlehampton, 1891), 87, 89–90, 94.

60 F. H. Edmunds, *Wells and Springs of Suss.* 220–1; *19th Ann. Rep. on Combined Sanit. Dist. of W. Suss.* (Horsham, 1893), 194; A.C.M., H 2/17.

61 W.S.R.O., Holmes, Campbell & Co. MS. 595.

62 Edmunds, *Wells and Springs*, 23; *20th Ann. Rep. on Combined Sanit. Dist. of W. Suss.* (Brighton, 1894), 158.

63 *V.C.H. Suss.* vi (1), 118.

64 e.g. A.C.M., A 339, mins. of view, 1763; W.S.R.O., A.B.A., L5, bdle. 2, nos. 3–21.

65 W.S.R.O., A.B.A., C2, *passim.*

66 Above, boro. govt. (after 1835).

67 *10th Ann. Rep. on Combined Sanit. Dist. of W. Suss.* (Worthing, 1884), 178.

68 W.S.R.O., BO/AR 24/4/17, ff. 4, 9, 11; *23rd Ann. Rep. on Combined Sanit. Dist. of W. Suss.* (Brighton, 1897), 216; O.S. Map 6", Suss. LXIII. NW. (1899 and later edns.).

69 W.S.R.O., BO/AR 12/22.

70 *1st Rep. Com. Mun. Corp.* 672.

71 W.S.R.O., A.B.A., A1, f. 61v.

to 1889, when it was absorbed into the county force. In 1844 there were a 'chief superintendent and high constable', a deputy, and 7 constables, but by 1857 only a superintendent and two constables. The police station in Maltravers Street, of brick and stone in Tudor style, was replaced in 1972 by a new building in the Causeway.[72]

Before the late 18th century the borough view of frankpledge exercised a general oversight of the repair of streets,[73] the surveyors of highways maintaining all except High Street,[74] where occupiers were liable for paving their frontages apparently by the later 17th century[75] and certainly by 1732.[76] Under the improvement Act of 1785 the main streets were newly paved, possibly with Purbeck stone; occupiers thereafter were to sweep their frontages every weekday.[77] High Street was macadamized in 1834[78] and new paving in the market place was laid down *c.* 1895.[79]

Though lighting was one of the tasks which the improvement commissioners were set up to carry out in 1785, there was never enough income for it.[80] It was the corporation which in 1825 paid for 24 lamps, evidently powered by oil.[81] The Arundel Gas Light and Coke Co. was founded in 1838 to supply the town and surroundings. By *c.* 1840 the gasworks was in Ford Road, then in Tortington. In 1897 the company was reincorporated as the Arundel Gas Co., the gasworks was enlarged, and the limit of supply was extended to cover several neighbouring parishes.[82] It is not clear when public gas lighting was first provided, but by 1902 the town council was responsible for it through agreement with the gas company.[83] The gasworks was demolished after 1975.[84]

Electricity was installed temporarily at the castle for Duke Henry's honeymoon in 1877[85] and a permanent supply was laid on there *c.* 1894,[86] an elaborately detailed red brick and timber electricity works in revived vernacular style being built by 1895[87] among the castle outbuildings on London Road. Some estate buildings and the Roman Catholic church were apparently supplied at the same time,[88] but it was only *c.* 1934 that the town in general received a supply from the Bognor Gas and Electricity Co., which had offices in Park Place in 1937.[89] Electric street lighting was introduced *c.* 1964.[90]

A postal service from London began in 1674; by 1752 it was four times weekly[91] and by the mid 1790s daily.[92] There was a daily post to Brighton, Lewes, Portsmouth, and the west of England besides by *c.* 1832.[93] In 1769 there was a salaried postmaster. A post office is recorded in the later 17th century and the later 18th.[94] In the early and mid 19th century it occupied sites in High Street and Tarrant Street,[95] but *c.* 1895 a new red brick and timber building in Tudor style was built in High Street near the bridge.[96]

A 'pest house' or primitive isolation hospital was built by the parish officers *c.* 1759 on land north-west of the Marygate leased from the corporation.[97] After being acquired by the duke of Norfolk it was pulled down shortly before 1832.[98] In 1871 the former workhouse was used as a temporary smallpox hospital.[99] An 'emergency' hospital for the town and surroundings was opened *c.* 1906 in converted Norfolk estate cottages in King Street, its income being provided by voluntary subscriptions and payments from patients. After the withdrawal of support by the duchess of Norfolk in 1917, the hospital was reopened in 1918 as Arundel and district cottage hospital.[1] In 1922 it had seven beds and an operating theatre.[2] A new building, with 14 beds and two cots, was opened in 1931 as Arundel and district hospital, on a site in Chichester Road given by the duke of Norfolk.[3] The buildings were extended in 1964.[4] A clinic was held behind the public library in Maltravers Street in the 1970s[5] and in the old National school building in Surrey Street in the 1980s.

The parish maintained two or more fire engines in 1829–30.[6] After 1836 the borough police force took over responsibility for fire fighting and in the mid 19th century there were three engines, kept in the basement of the town hall, and a voluntary brigade of 24 men.[7] The duke of Norfolk also had a fire engine in 1863 for use on his estate;[8] it was kept in the castle stables by 1938. In 1895 each force was 17 strong.[9] By 1902,

72 N. Poulsom and others, *Suss. Police Forces*, chap. 8; *Brighton Evening Argus*, 22 June 1972.
73 e.g. A.C.M., A 339, mins. of view, 1696, 1763, 1774; W.S.R.O., A.B.A., L5, bdle. 2, nos. 3–21.
74 A.C.M., D 3210, p. 4.
75 Ibid. A 339, mins. of view, 1696; ibid. D 3210, p. 4.
76 W.S.R.O., A.B.A., L5, bdle. 2, no. 13; cf. ibid. A.B.A., M28.
77 25 Geo. III, c. 90; *Univ. Brit. Dir.* ii. 55; A.C.M., D 3211, p. 11. Streets to be paved under the Act were High St. from cast. lodge and chyd. gate to river, Maltravers St., and Tarrant St. (S. side only).
78 W.S.R.O., A.B.A., F1/1, f. 93.
79 Ibid. BO/AR 24/4/17, f. 10.
80 *1st Rep. Com. Mun. Corp.* 672.
81 W.S.R.O., A.B.A., F1/1, f. 83.
82 60 & 61 Vic. c. 88 (Local); W.S.R.O., Holmes, Campbell & Co. MSS., papers relating to gas co. (box 42); ibid. LD II/ZP 2; ibid. TD/W 128; cf. *Arundel Cast. Archives*, iii, p. 59.
83 W.S.R.O., BO/AR 24/4/17, f. 5.
84 *W. Suss. Gaz.* 19 June 1975.
85 J. M. Robinson, *Dukes of Norf.* (1982), 220.
86 Kimpton, *Arundel* (1893), 5.
87 A.C.M., H 2/17.
88 Kimpton, *Arundel* (1893), 5.
89 *Kelly's Dir. Suss.* (1934, 1938); *Arundel, the Gem of Suss.* (Arundel, 1934), 27; ibid. (Arundel, 1937), 13; *Residential Attractions of Bognor Regis, Felpham, Middleton-on-Sea and Dist.* (Gloucester, [1937]), 10 (copy at B.L.).
90 *W. Suss. Gaz.* 20 April 1989.
91 J. Greenwood, *Posts of Suss., Chich. Branch*, 16–17.
92 *Univ. Brit. Dir.* ii. 57.
93 Pigot, *Nat. Com. Dir.* (1832–4), 1003.
94 Greenwood, *Posts of Suss*, 16, 18.
95 Wright, *Arundel* (1818), 7; Pigot, *Nat. Com. Dir.* (1832–4), 1003; A.C.M., uncat. archit. drawings, plan of boro. 1849; O.S. Map 1/2,500, Suss. LXIII. 1 (1877 edn.).
96 A.C.M., uncat. archit. drawings, 1893–4; Kimpton, *Arundel* (1897), 4.
97 A.C.M., HC 222; for site, ibid. H 1/30.
98 W.S.R.O., A.B.A., F1/1, f. 90v.
99 *Census*, 1871.
1 W.S.R.O., HW/AR (TS. cat.); Pike, *Bognor Dir.* (1910–11), 187; A.C.M., uncat. archit. drawings.
2 *Kelly's Dir. Suss.* (1922).
3 Ibid. (1938); *S.C.M.* ix. 672.
4 *W. Suss. Gaz.* 1 Oct. 1964.
5 O.S. Map 1/2,500, TQ 0007–0107 (1971 edn.).
6 W.S.R.O., Par. 8/9/10, no. 631.
7 N. Poulsom and others, *Suss. Police Forces*, chap. 8; Hillier, *Arundel* (1847), 29.
8 *W. Suss. Gaz.* 20 Aug. 1863.
9 *Kelly's Dir. Suss.* (1895, 1938); W.S.R.O., BO/AR 16/1/152.

when the town brigade had only one engine, its management had passed to the town council.[10] In the early 20th century it served surrounding villages too, assisted when necessary by the duke's brigade.[11] The engines were still steam-powered in 1938.[12] By 1944 the town fire station had moved to River Road,[13] and after the service had been taken over by West Sussex county council a new building was built in Ford Road in 1966.[14] The duke's brigade was disbanded *c.* 1948.[15]

Because of the presence of the college buildings south-east of the church the churchyard was small for a place of Arundel's size.[16] An addition on the south side was consecrated in 1848, with a new gateway from London Road.[17] Closure for burials was ordered by the Privy Council in 1854, but was revoked after local opposition later the same year and did not take place until 1883,[18] when a cemetery in Ford Road in Tortington parish was opened[19] under the management of a burial board with the same membership as the town council.[20] Its two chapels were demolished *c.* 1981.[21] A Roman Catholic cemetery was laid out south-west of London Road in 1861 and enlarged before 1903;[22] the lychgate and Gothic stone cross were designed by C. A. Buckler in 1901[23] and the lodge by the estate architect W. Heveningham in 1903.[24]

CHURCH. A minster establishment which existed at Arundel in 1086[25] seems to have been founded before the Conquest, since in 1380 reference was made to the existence at one time of 'twelve secular canons of the English nation'.[26] In the mid 12th century there were ten prebends, including Cocking and Yapton churches; some were in the gift of the chapter of Chichester cathedral.[27] A dean of Arundel was mentioned in 1087.[28] About 1150 the minster was appropriated by Sées abbey (Orne), of which Arundel church became a priory; the existing clerks retained a life interest in their prebends,[29] and Chichester cathedral in compensation for its lost rights received the prebend previously held by William, archdeacon of London, which comprised the churches of Singleton, East Dean, and West Dean.[30] The priory was described as 'utterly desolate' in 1379.[31] In the following year it was suppressed in favour of a college[32] of secular canons dedicated to the Holy Trinity; that in turn was dissolved in 1544.[33]

A vicarage was ordained apparently at the time of the appropriation and certainly by 1158.[34] It was briefly united with Tortington in 1657.[35] From 1897 it was held with Tortington in plurality,[36] and in 1929 Arundel, Tortington, and South Stoke became the united benefice of Arundel with South Stoke and Tortington, the parishes remaining distinct.[37]

The advowson of the vicarage belonged successively to the priory and the college,[38] the Crown presenting in the mid 14th century because of the war with France,[39] and after the Dissolution descended with the rape.[40] The bishop presented in 1570, the Crown in 1585 and 1595, Thomas Sackville, Lord Buckhurst, in 1591, and John Wilson for a turn in 1620. Members of the Howard family or their representatives exercised the advowson between 1663 and 1701, and again in 1811. John Anstis, Garter king of arms, the marquess of Bristol, and the earl of Albemarle, who presented respectively between 1716 and 1732, in 1828, and in 1844, may also have been ducal representatives,[41] as William Williams of Wimbledon, who presented between 1873 and 1887, certainly was.[42] Mary Groome of Sompting presented for a turn in 1780.[43] In 1892 and 1895 Duke Henry (d. 1917) forewent his right of presentation, the Catholic bishop of Southwark having pointed out in 1887 that it would be hard to decide 'whether to put in a religious man who would try to draw people to the Protestant Church, or a respectable man with a very decided taste for field sports'; the University of Oxford therefore presented at those two dates by lapse.[44] In 1896 the duke sold the advowson to W. E. Hubbard of Lower Beeding, who conveyed it in 1897 to the bishop of Chichester.[45] After 1929 two presentations in three to the united benefice of Arundel with South Stoke and Tortington were made by the bishop, and the other by the patron of South Stoke.[46]

10 W.S.R.O., BO/AR 24/4/17, f. 9.
11 *W. Suss. Gaz.* 7 June 1973; Cartland, *Arundel*, p. [ix].
12 *Kelly's Dir. Suss.* (1938).
13 W.S.R.O., BO/AR 16/1/218.
14 Cartland, *Arundel*, 131; inf. from Mr. F. Penfold, Burpham.
15 Inf. from Mr. F. Clifton, Arundel.
16 Cf. Goodliffe, *Littlehampton* (1903), 85.
17 W.S.R.O., Par. 8/1/5/2, flyleaf.
18 Ibid. Par. 8/12/1, pp. 39–40; *Lond. Gaz.* 31 Mar. 1854, pp. 1021–2; 11 Apr. 1854, p. 1128; 29 Aug. 1882, p. 4009.
19 B.L. Add. MS. 39368, f. 52; O.S. Map 6", Suss. LXIII. NW. (1899 edn.).
20 W.S.R.O., BO/AR 25/1; *Kelly's Dir. Suss.* (1887).
21 *W. Suss. Gaz.* 7 Feb. 1980.
22 A. MacCall, *Ch. and Mission of St. Phil.'s, Arundel*, 12 (copy at W.S.R.O. libr.); A.C.M., MD 1927, 1961; below, pl. facing p. 91.
23 A.C.M., MD 22, 2026.
24 W.S.R.O., BO/AR 16/1/22.
25 *V.C.H. Suss.* i. 422.
26 *Cal. Papal Reg.* iv. 239.
27 *S.R.S.* xlvi, pp. 37, 64, 69, 368.
28 *Cal. Doc. France*, ed. Round, p. 233.
29 *S.R.S.* xlvi, p. 14. The date given at *V.C.H. Suss.* ii. 119 is wrong.
30 *S.R.S.* xlvi, pp. 16–17, 26–7, 37, 69.
31 *Cal. Pat.* 1377–81, 402; cf. ibid. 1348–50, 258; *S.R.S.* xlvi, p. 291.
32 *Cal. Pat.* 1377–81, 494.
33 *L. & P. Hen. VIII*, xix (2), pp. 441, 475.
34 W.S.R.O., Par. 8/6/5, f. 3.
35 *Cal. S.P. Dom.* 1657–8, 168.
36 *Chich. Dioc. Kal.* and *Dir.* (1898 and later edns.).
37 *Lond. Gaz.* 8 Nov. 1929, pp. 7197–9.
38 W.S.R.O., Par. 8/6/5, f. 4; B.L. Add. MS. 39327, ff. 162–3; *Reg. Chichele* (Cant. & York Soc.), iii. 457.
39 *Cal. Pat.* 1324–7, 194; 1348–50, 337, 347, 361, 544, 572; 1354–8, 17, 98; 1367–70, 330.
40 e.g. *L. & P. Hen. VIII*, xix (2), p. 475; B.L. Add. MS. 39327, ff. 163v.–168.
41 B.L. Add. MS. 39327, ff. 164–8.
42 Ibid. ff. 168–9; A.C.M., MD 2126, Wm. Williams to duke, 1879; W.S.R.O., Ep. I/22A/1 (1884); cf. *Kelly's Dir. Suss.* (1874).
43 B.L. Add. MS. 39327, f. 167; W.S.R.O., Add. MS. 15637 (TS. cat.).
44 A.C.M., MD 2126, Bp. John Butt to duke, 1887; B.L. Add. MS. 39327, f. 169; cf. F. W. Steer, *Cathedral Ch. of Our Lady and St. Phil., Arundel*, facing p. 26.
45 A.C.M., MD 2176, deed, 1896; *Lond. Gaz.* 6 Aug. 1897, p. 4414.
46 *Lond. Gaz.* 8 Nov. 1929, p. 7198; *Chich. Dioc. Dir.* (1938 and later edns.).

The vicarage was endowed apparently from the first with all small tithes, a third of all hay tithes, and offerings up to 7½*d.* except at Christmas, Candlemas (2 February), and Easter; at those feasts the vicar took two marks as a stipend for an assistant priest. In addition from 1158 he had the great tithes of land called Wynyard (i.e. vineyard), apparently in what was later the Little park, and of two other pieces of land which also seem to have lain north of the town.[47] The vicarage was valued at £5 6*s.* 8*d.* in 1291[48] and at £5 0*s.* 10*d.* net, including a pension of 2*s.* 6*d.* from the college, in 1535;[49] in 1579 it was said to be worth less than £5.[50]

There seems never to have been any glebe.[51] A vicarage house was mentioned in the early 15th century, when the vicar also held of the earl of Arundel two tofts and a garden in the town;[52] the house was still held of the earl between the 16th century and the early 18th.[53] It stood on the south-east side of Mount Pleasant[54] and was of timber.[55] In 1574 it was greatly decayed,[56] and in 1595 it was repaired at the expense of the mayor, a floor or floors apparently being inserted.[57] In 1620 the building had at least seven rooms.[58] It was again repaired *c.* 1663.[59]

By the 17th century the endowment had been augmented by six cow leazes in the burgess brooks and tithes from Cudlow farm in Climping received either in kind or by a money composition.[60] The income was £20 in 1646. In that year the committee of plundered ministers gave a further augmentation of £50 from the former estates of the dean and chapter of Chichester within the rape;[61] the sum was received in 1649[62] but evidently not in 1657 when the vicarage was said to be worth only £30 a year.[63]

In the early 18th century the duke of Norfolk paid £24 a year to the vicar in lieu of the tithes of East Cudlow farm and of land in the parish including the castle and its precincts, the Great and Little parks, and Rewell wood.[64] The real value of the living in 1724 was said to be £38 19*s.* 9*d.*; in addition to the pasture rights mentioned earlier, it then also enjoyed two bullock leazes in the burgess slipes.[65] By 1790 a composition was also received for a third of the hay tithes of the burgess brooks, which had not generally been mown before the mid 18th century.[66] By 1809 all the tithes of the parish were apparently compounded for. The living was then worth £76 12*s.* 2*d.*,[67] but its value was raised to £199 in 1830 with a grant from Queen Anne's Bounty.[68] The vicar's share of tithes was commuted *c.* 1841 at £222 7*s.* 7*d.*[69] In 1887 the outgoing incumbent claimed that the income was just enough to meet necessary expenses and to pay a curate.[70] An extra £18 a year was granted by the ecclesiastical commissioners in 1909.[71]

The vicarage house was in good repair in 1724[72] but was partly blown down 60 years later.[73] By 1796 it had been demolished,[74] the vicar living elsewhere in the town[75] until 1811, when the site of the vicarage was exchanged with the duke of Norfolk for a house on the west side of Parson's Hill.[76] That house was greatly enlarged *c.* 1830[77] but in 1845, when it had become unfit for residence because of poor foundations, it too was demolished.[78] Between 1852 and 1866 the vicar lived in Tower House, London Road, as tenant of the duke.[79] The Parson's Hill site was exchanged with the duke in 1870 for no. 20 Maltravers Street,[80] which was sold before 1946, when no. 26 Maltravers Street was bought as a replacement.[81]

The church had many clergy in the Middle Ages. Ten minster clergy served the parish and neighbouring areas in the later 11th and earlier 12th centuries.[82] The monks who succeeded them may have done some parochial duties, though the vicar was required from 1158 to support an assistant priest.[83] The late medieval college had 12 chaplains, besides the master and other clergy, in 1382, and later there seem usually to have been eight or ten; residence was required.[84] In addition there were private chaplains at the castle[85] and the clergy of the various chantries, chapels, and hospitals, together with the Dominican friars.[86] An anchorite is recorded at the friary *c.* 1402.[87]

Thomas Combe, vicar in 1516, probably held other livings in plurality.[88] Assistant curates are recorded between 1547 and 1582, two at least

47 W.S.R.O., Par. 8/6/5, ff. 2v.–3v.; cf. ibid. Ep. I/25/1 (1615, 1635); ibid. Par. 8/6/8; Tierney, *Arundel*, ii. 654.
48 *Tax. Eccl.* (Rec. Com.), 135.
49 *Valor Eccl.* (Rec. Com.), i. 314, 316.
50 W.S.R.O., Ep. I/23/5, f. 35v.
51 e.g. *S.R.S.* lxxviii. 59; P.R.O., IR 18/10231.
52 *S.R.S.* lxvii. 115–16.
53 A.C.M., A 1240; ibid. MD 535, f. 4.
54 W.S.R.O., Ep. I/25/1 (1615); Tierney, *Arundel*, ii. 654; for Whitings dyke, above, growth of town (street names).
55 W.S.R.O., A.B.A., M3, partly transcr. at Eustace, *Arundel*, 134–5.
56 W.S.R.O., Ep. I/23/4, f. 27v.
57 Ibid. A.B.A., M3; cf. ibid. A.B.A., F2/1, f. 4.
58 Ibid. Ep. I/29/8/11.
59 Ibid. Ep. I/22/1 (1662, *recte* 1663).
60 Ibid. Ep. I/25/1 (1615, 1635); Tierney, *Arundel*, ii. 655; cf. A.C.M., MD 2510; W.S.R.O., A.B.A., A1, ff. 35v., 152; *S.R.S.* lxxviii. 59. In 1663 the endowment also included 'holy breads' said to have been left to priory in 1308; no more is known of them: Tierney, *Arundel*, ii. 655.
61 *S.A.C.* xxxvi. 138.
62 W. A. Shaw, *Hist. Eng. Ch. 1640–1660*, ii. 545.
63 *Cal. S.P. Dom.* 1657–8, 168.
64 W.S.R.O., Par. 8/6/8.
65 *S.R.S.* lxxviii. 59; cf. A.C.M., MD 2510.
66 A.C.M., MD 2469, note of tithes paid to vicar by duke of Norf. 1790; 2510.
67 W.S.R.O., Ep. I/63/10.
68 Hodgson, *Queen Anne's Bounty* (1845), p. cclxii; *Rep. Com. Eccl. Revenues.*
69 W.S.R.O., TD/W 5. Two meadows adjoining the Causeway were then tithe free: ibid.
70 A.C.M., MD 2126, A. S. Thompson to Wm. Williams, [1887].
71 *Lond. Gaz.* 30 Apr. 1909, pp. 3301–2.
72 *S.R.S.* lxxviii. 59.
73 Eustace, *Arundel*, 230, wrongly identifying site of ho.
74 W.S.R.O., Par. 8/1/1/7, flyleaf.
75 Eustace, *Arundel*, 231; A.C.M., A 339, boro. rental, 1784–93; ibid. MD 2469, memo. on site of vicarage ho. 1796.
76 A.C.M., D 610–13, deed of exchange, 1811; W.S.R.O., TD/W 5. For Ibbetsons Lane, above, growth of town (street names).
77 Tierney, *Arundel*, ii. 657; B.L. Add. MS. 39327, f. 168.
78 B.L. Add. MS. 39460, f. 35; W.S.R.O., Ep. I/17/45, f. 149; A.C.M., D 610–13, deed of exchange, 1870.
79 *Kelly's Dir. Suss.* (1852 and later edns.).
80 A.C.M., D 610–13, deed of exchange, 1870; O.S. Map 1/2,500, Suss. LXIII. 1 (1912 edn.); inf. from the vicar, the Revd. M. Weaver.
81 W.S.R.O., Par. 8/6/16; above, pl. facing p. 26.
82 Above, this section.
83 W.S.R.O., Par. 8/6/5, f. 3.
84 Petch, 'Arundel Coll.' 96–7, 99, 114.
85 Above, castle (institutional hist.); *S.R.S.* xli. 47, 51.
86 Above, relig. hos.; below, this section.
87 *Cal. Papal Reg.* iv. 352.
88 W.S.R.O., Par. 86/1/1/1A (TS. cat.).

THE FITZALAN CHAPEL OF ARUNDEL PARISH CHURCH IN THE LATE 19TH CENTURY

succeeding to the living.[89] The incumbent resided in 1563,[90] in 1579,[91] and apparently between 1595 and 1606.[92] In the late 1560s there were still side altars in the church despite the objections of both parishioners and preachers.[93] A later vicar, John German (1585–91), was a Puritan.[94] Thomas Williamson, vicar 1579–84, also held Tortington.[95] Thomas Heyney, domestic chaplain to Lord Arundel, was a licensed preacher and a pluralist.[96] In 1626 he was presented for often omitting services,[97] and in 1643 he was said to preach only rarely and to prevent others from preaching; he was ejected in the same year.[98] In 1639 communion was administered monthly.[99] A curate of Arundel, apparently in Heyney's time, was accused in 1642 of having spoken 'scandalous words against the Protestant religion'.[1] High feelings over ecclesiastical questions are also indicated in 1635 after Dr. Nathaniel Brent's metropolitical visitation, when one of the churchwardens made a 'violent extemporary prayer', audible in the street, that the town might be delivered from the persecution he felt to be imminent.[2]

At least three Puritan ministers served between 1646 and 1662;[3] there may have been a Presbyterian *classis* in the town in 1658.[4]

Between the Restoration and the mid 19th century vicars often held other livings[5] and assistant curates were often recorded.[6] John Carr (1732–79) and William Groome (1780–1811) were generally resident,[7] but after *c.* 1815 William Munsey (1811–28) because of ill health served through a curate who succeeded him as vicar.[8] The curate's stipend in 1839 was £100.[9] Communion was celebrated four times a year in 1680;[10] by 1724, when the frequency was monthly with between 40 and 90 communicants, there were services every day with a sermon on Sunday morning, and a Sunday afternoon lecture supported by contributions from parishioners.[11] Daily services were perhaps still held in 1771.[12] There were 772 candidates at a confirmation in 1811.[13] A volunteer band played in the church[14]

89 *S.R.S.* xli. 47; B.L. Add. MSS. 39327, f. 164; 39359, f. 14 and v.

90 *S.A.C.* lxi. 112.

91 W.S.R.O., Ep. I/23/5, f. 35v.

92 B.L. Add. MS. 39327, f. 164v.

93 *Studies in Suss. Ch. Hist.* ed. M. J. Kitch, 100.

94 R. B. Manning, *Relig. and Soc. in Eliz. Suss.* 200; B.L. Add. MS. 39327, f. 164.

95 B.L. Add. MS. 39327, f. 164.

96 Ibid. f. 165; *Walker Revised*, ed. Matthews, 357.

97 *S.R.S.* xlix. 121.

98 *S.A.C.* xxxvi. 139; *Walker Revised*, ed. Matthews, 357.

99 W.S.R.O., Par. 8/1/1/1, f. 71.

1 Hist. MSS. Com. 4, *5th Rep., H.L.* p. 7.

2 *V.C.H. Suss.* ii. 33.

3 *S.A.C.* xxxvi. 138; W. A. Shaw, *Hist. Eng. Ch. 1640–1660*, ii. 545; *Calamy Revised*, ed. Matthews, 226; *Cal. S.P. Dom.* 1653–4, 416.

4 Shaw, *Hist. Eng. Ch.* ii. 436; Caplan, 'Outline of Nonconf. in Suss.' i. 23–4.

5 B.L. Add. MS. 39327, ff. 166–8.

6 Ibid. 39359, ff. 16–18; W.S.R.O., Par. 8/1/1/5; Par. 8/1/2/1; *S.R.S.* lxxviii. 59.

7 B.L. Add. MS. 39327, ff. 167–8; W.S.R.O., Ep. I/22/1 (1758); ibid. Par. 8/1/1/3–4 (TS. cat.); Par. 8/1/1/5; Par. 8/1/1/7.

8 B.L. Add. MS. 39327, f. 168; W.S.R.O., Par. 8/1/2/1; Par. 8/5/6.

9 W.S.R.O., Par. 8/5/7.

10 Ibid. Par. 8/9/8 (1680).

11 *S.R.S.* lxxviii. 58–9.

12 *S.A.C.* lii. 41.

13 Ibid. lxxi. 54.

14 A.C.M., FA 123, evidence of Wm. Harwood.

before 1817, when an organ was installed, the expense being met by a subscription.[15] The organist had a salary of £26 5*s*. in 1825 and £30 in 1843; a boys' choir existed by 1825 when it practised twice a week.[16]

Communion was held monthly in 1844 and 1865, at the latter date with *c*. 100 communicants.[17] On Census Sunday in 1851 morning service was attended by 448 people besides 221 Sunday schoolchildren, the absence of the duke's household and other families making the totals less than usual.[18] In 1865 congregations were said to number 600 to 800, but the return of the dukes to the Roman Catholic church had led by then to a decline in Anglican baptisms.[19]

The attempt of George Arbuthnot, vicar 1873–9, to clarify the status of the Fitzalan chapel of the church led to an acrimonious lawsuit in which he was defeated,[20] and which caused long-standing ill-feeling between Anglicans and Catholics in the town.[21] A strong character, Arbuthnot had other clashes with parishioners, for instance over free seating.[22] He was also responsible, however, for the introduction of fully choral services including a monthly sung eucharist at which the choir wore cassocks and surplices; two services every weekday; communion on saints' days; and a parish magazine which had a circulation of 430 by 1879.[23] The choir practised daily in 1880.[24]

There were four services on Sundays and two on weekdays in 1882 and 1922,[25] and a regular midweek communion by 1903.[26] By 1912 a choral eucharist was celebrated on two or three Sundays a month.[27] Sunday congregations in 1884 averaged 600 in the morning, 400 in the afternoon, and 700 in the evening, though there were then only *c*. 60 communicants.[28] There was usually a curate from 1879 and there were two in 1903.[29] In 1986 at least two services were held every Sunday.

A chantry was founded in 1441 at the altar of St. Christopher, apparently near the south transept, to commemorate Thomas Salman (d. 1430) and others; the chaplain was to have 1 a. in Arundel for a house and property in Rudgwick.[30] It is not clear if the brotherhood of St. Christopher mentioned in 1487 and 1517[31] was the same. The chantry land lay near the Marygate, where two cottages formerly belonging to it still stood in 1652.[32]

A 'chantry of Bignor' at Arundel was mentioned in 1545, when Urian Aywood of Bignor chose to be buried in its chapel; the latter was said to be in the churchyard,[33] suggesting perhaps that it was attached to the church but accessible from outside.[34]

Eleanor d'Arundel, countess of Arundel (d. 1455), by will founded a chantry in the Lady chapel in memory of her late husband, herself, and others.[35]

There were at least three chapels in the parish outside the church and the castle. In 1343 Richard FitzAlan, earl of Arundel (d. 1376), was licensed to convey to the priory in free alms 30 a. in Arundel to endow a chapel recently founded at the north gate of the town, presumably the Marygate.[36] The chapel was evidently dedicated to St. Mary, for there are later references to a Lady chapel over the gate.[37] Thomas FitzAlan, earl of Arundel (d. 1415), made provision in his will for its rebuilding.[38] The chapel of Our Lady beyond (*outre*) the gate, mentioned in 1375, was perhaps the same as both the chapel of St. Mary 'in the park of Arundel', which was the object of bequests in the 1430s,[39] and the oratory in honour of St. Mary, which earl Richard was licensed to convey to the priory in 1340.[40] A chapel of St. Laurence is recorded between the later 14th century and 1518;[41] its site was north of the town on the west side of the old London road, where the ruins of a chapel still stood in 1636 in a close called Laurence or Chapel croft.[42]

The church of *ST. NICHOLAS*, of which the dedication presumably alludes to Arundel's port, St. Nicholas being the patron saint of sailors,[43] consists of an architectural chancel with north and south chapels and north-east 'sacristy', a low central tower with transepts and short spire, an aisled and clerestoried nave of five bays, a south vestry, and north, south, and west porches. The building, a uniform structure of the later 14th century and earlier 15th, is of knapped and coursed flint with Caen stone and sandstone dressings including some chequerwork; the east walls only are of sandstone ashlar. Only the nave, aisles, and transepts were parochial; the 'chancel', approached by a separate, lower, arch within the east crossing arch, was the chapel of the college of the Holy Trinity founded in 1380,[44] and after the Dissolution passed with the rest of the college's property to

15 W.S.R.O., A.B.A., F1/1, f. 73; ibid. Par. 8/4/16; *Acct. of Ch. and Collegiate Chapel of Holy Trin. at Arundel* (Arundel, 1847), 7 (copy in Chich. Ref. Libr.).

16 W.S.R.O., Par. 8/9/1, *passim*; Par. 8/9/10, no. 936; Par. 8/12/1, p. 3; Par. 8/12/2, f. 130v.

17 Ibid. Ep. I/22A/2 (1844, 1865).

18 *S.R.S.* lxxv, p. 143.

19 W.S.R.O., Ep. I/22A/2 (1865).

20 B.L. Add. MS. 39327, ff. 168–9; below, this section [fabric].

21 e.g. A.C.M., MD 2016; *Suss. Hist.* ii (10), 27; W.S.R.O., Ep. I/22A/1 (1878).

22 *W. Suss. Gaz.* 7 Aug. 1879; *Suss. Hist.* ii (10), 26.

23 A.C.M., MD 2016.

24 P.R.O., ED 7/123.

25 *Kelly's Dir. Suss.* (1882, 1922).

26 W.S.R.O., Ep. I/22A/2 (1903).

27 Pike, *Bognor Dir.* (1912–13), 186.

28 W.S.R.O., Ep. I/22A/1 (1884).

29 Ibid. Par. 8/5/2; A.C.M., MD 2016; *Kelly's Dir. Suss.* (1882 and later edns.).

30 *Cal. Pat.* 1436–41, 525; *S.R.S.* xli. 43, 52; below, this section [fabric]. The chantry had been intended for Lady chapel: *S.R.S.* xli. 52.

31 *S.R.S.* xli. 48; *Archaeologia*, lxi. 82.

32 *Clough and Butler Archives*, ed. J. Booker, p. 24; *S.R.S.* xxxvi. 190.

33 Eustace, *Arundel*, 116.

34 Cf. the Holy Trin. chantry at Horsham: *V.C.H. Suss.* vi (2), 193.

35 *S.R.S.* xli. 52–3; *Complete Peerage*, i. 247; Tierney, *Arundel*, ii. 618.

36 *Cal. Pat.* 1343–5, 120–1.

37 B.L. Add. MS. 39327, f. 170; Tierney, *Arundel*, ii. 676.

38 *S.R.S.* xli. 370.

39 Ibid. 58; *Reg. Chichele* (Cant. & York Soc.), ii. 542.

40 *Cal. Pat.* 1338–40, 531.

41 Petch, 'Arundel Coll.' 151; *S.R.S.* lxvii. 116; Dallaway, *Hist. W. Suss.* ii (1) (1819), 175.

42 A.C.M., MD 505, f. [7v.].

43 Dedic. recorded from 1086: *V.C.H. Suss.* i. 421; W.S.R.O., Par. 8/7/35. Cf. the dedic. of e.g. Brighton ch. and Liverpool chapel: *V.C.H. Lancs.* iv. 43; *V.C.H. Suss.* vii. 259. In 15th and 16th cents. the ch. was usually erroneously described as Holy Trin., the dedic. of the coll.: *Reg. Chichele* (Cant. & York Soc.), iii. 457; *S.R.S.* iv. 134; xli. 41–4.

44 Above, this section.

the earls of Arundel and their successors;[45] since the mid 19th century it has been known as the Fitzalan chapel, the name used here.[46]

Some richly decorated pieces of Caen stone re-used in coffins found in the vault under the Fitzalan chapel may have come from the previous church; one is a fragment of an apparently semicircular window.[47] Twelfth- and 13th-century carved stones re-used in the north and south external walls of the present church are probably also from that building.[48] In 1158 the church had a nave and chancel and evidently a bell tower; the chancel was the priory church, and was separated from the nave by a screen in which there was a 'chancel door of the choir'. The 'chancel of St. Catherine, St. Leonard, and St. Giles', for the repair of whose roof the priory was then responsible, was presumably a series of chapels beside or beyond the chancel.[49] The church was in bad repair in 1349.[50]

The new church, which may have been designed by William Wynford or Henry Yeveley,[51] was probably built from east to west, the Fitzalan chapel being the earliest part. It was in use by 1387, when masses of the Blessed Virgin Mary were to be celebrated at the high altar until a Lady altar could be built.[52] The roof of the chapel, perhaps designed by Hugh Herland,[53] was of groined timber with elaborately decorated bosses.[54] Between the chapel and the crossing is a contemporary iron grille with central folding doors.

Several things suggest that it was originally intended to build the Lady chapel east of the Fitzalan chapel, as in other large medieval churches. The addition of a single side chapel to the Fitzalan chapel spoils the design of the church as a whole, the north wall of the Lady chapel projecting in fact beyond that of the north transept. The north wall of the Fitzalan chapel is pierced, clearly as an afterthought, to create the upper part only of a three-bayed arcade between the two chapels; both the segment-headed clerestory windows of four lights above the arcade and the east window of the Fitzalan chapel are stylistically different from the rest of the church. Had the Lady chapel been built east of the Fitzalan chapel it would have been much easier of access from the college, and the intention to place it there might also explain the existence of the screen wall behind the high altar of the Fitzalan chapel, which otherwise could be expected to stand directly below the east window. The existing low wall replaces the medieval one but retains original north and south doorways; the shallow space behind had a small altar and was perhaps used as an oratory.

The Lady chapel apparently existed by 1421, when John d'Arundel, earl of Arundel (d. 1421), was buried there.[55] Its north side externally is more richly ornamented than any other part of the church, having ogee-arched windows with crowning finials, which were apparently restored in the early 19th century.[56]

It is not clear what the room east of the Lady chapel, known as the sacristy, originally was. A sacristy would more likely have been on the south side of the Fitzalan chapel next to the college buildings. Since it provided access from the castle, it may have been a 'withdrawing room' for the earl's family.

The nave arcade is plainer than that of the Lady chapel. The nave and transept clerestory windows are circular with quatrefoil tracery, and there is a series of original consecration crosses, much repainted.[57] The south transept probably accommodated the parochial altar from the first, as it did between 1511[58] and 1873–4;[59] presumably it was the 'vicar's chancel' mentioned in 1476,[60] the altar being known as the vicar's altar or parish altar.[61] The north transept was evidently the site of a chapel, since a piscina survives on the north side of the north-east crossing pier, and it is not clear why an arch was cut between the transept and the Lady chapel.[62] The rood mentioned between 1487 and 1536[63] stood in front of the arch to the Fitzalan chapel and was reached by stairs in the north-east crossing pier.

The deep flint and stone west porch was clearly the original main entrance to the church, since it once faced a road junction;[64] the south approach to the church postdates the diversion of the London road in the early 19th century.[65] The steeply gabled south porch, also of flint and stone, is a modern rebuilding on old lines;[66] the timber north porch is 16th-century.

In 1511, after a dispute between the college and the parishioners over maintenance of the church, it was resolved that the nave, aisles, and north transept were to be repaired by the parish, while the college would have responsibility not only for the east parts of the building but also, as impropriate rector, for the south transept,

45 Below, this section.

46 A.C.M., MD 2592, plan of cast. grounds; Dallaway, *Hist. W. Suss.* ii (1) (1819), facing p. 169, calls it the Fitzalan sepulchral chapel. Alternative names were Norf. chancel and Norf. chapel: B.L. Add. MS. 5674, ff. 17–22; *S.C.M.* xxviii. 226; Goodliffe, *Littlehampton* (1903), 81. The Lady chapel to N. was called the Arundel chancel in 1780: B.L. Add. MS. 5674, f. 17.

47 *S.A.C.* iii. 79, 83.

48 Cf. *Country Life*, 19 Dec. 1914, p. 819.

49 W.S.R.O., Par. 8/6/5, ff. 3v.–4. The chapel of St. Mary mentioned in 1248 seems less likely to be a Lady chapel in the ch. than an outlying chapel of former minster par.: *Gallia Christiana*, ed. D. de Ste.-Marthe and others, xi (1759), Instrumenta, p. 171; Tierney, *Arundel*, ii. 576.

50 *Cal. Pat.* 1348–50, 258.

51 J. Harvey, *Eng. Medieval Architects*, 355, 366.

52 Petch, 'Arundel Coll.' 221.

53 Harvey, op. cit. 141.

54 Illus. at B.L. Add. MS. 5674, ff. 21–2.

55 Below, this section (mons.); cf. *S.R.S.* xli. 49.

56 Illus. at *Suss. Chs.: the Sharpe Colln.* ed. V. Smith (Lewes, [1979]), no. 12; below, this section.

57 *V.C.H. Suss.* ii. 354.

58 W.S.R.O., Ep. I/1/5, f. 135.

59 e.g. ibid. Par. 8/4/1; *S.A.C.* lxxxiv. 114; cf. below, this section.

60 *Arundel Cast. Archives*, ii, p. 6.

61 *S.R.S.* xli. 43. The high altar was described as that of the coll.: e.g. ibid. viii. 46; xli. 370.

62 *Pace* Dallaway, *Hist. W. Suss.* ii (1) (1819), 175, the chapel seems not to have been that of the Salman chantry, since the chantry's altar of St. Christopher apparently adjoined S. transept: *S.R.S.* xli. 44, locating it near parish altar; cf. above, this section.

63 *S.R.S.* xli. 44.

64 W.S.R.O., MP 3041 (photocopy of town plan, 1785).

65 Above, communications (rds.); public servs. [chyd.].

66 Cf. B.L. Add. MS. 5674, f. 23; *Suss. Chs.: the Sharpe Colln.* ed. V. Smith (Lewes, [1979]), no. 11.

Eastergate:
Barnham Market in the early 20th century

Arundel:
the market in High Street in the late 19th century

The medieval pulpit in the church

Statue of the Virgin and Child on St. Mary's hall, London Road

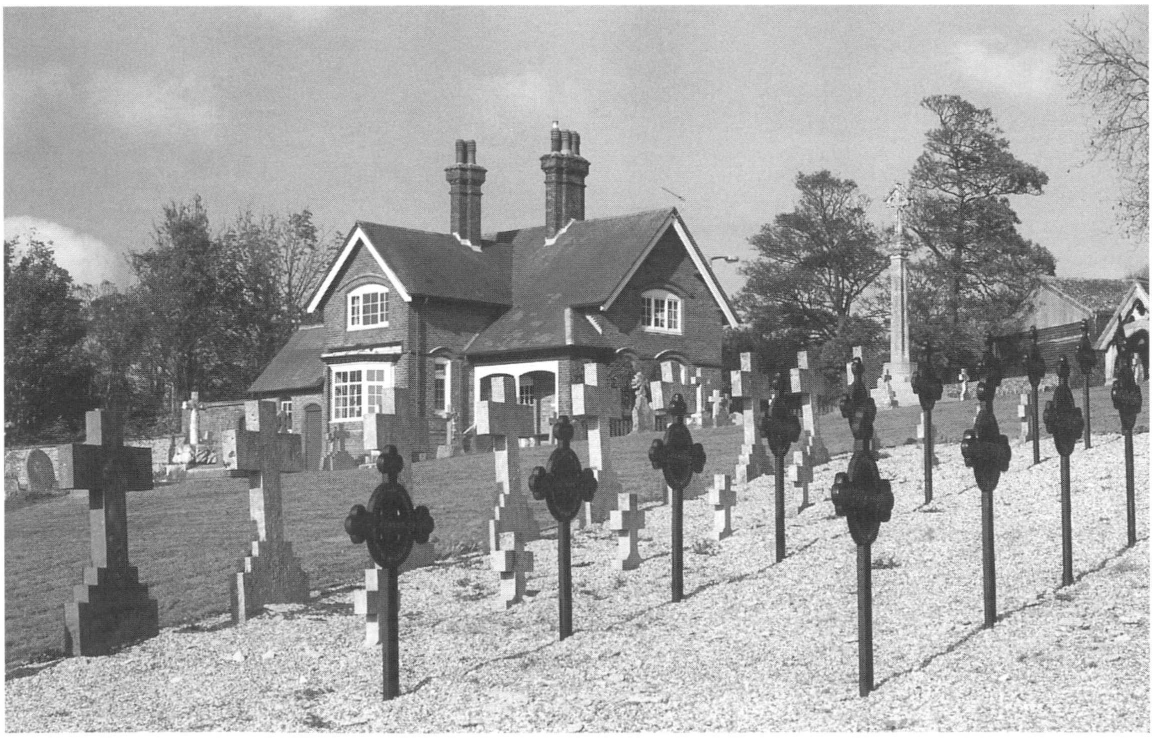

The Roman Catholic cemetery, London Road

ARUNDEL

since that was used as the chancel; the cost of maintaining the tower and crossing was to be shared.[67]

In 1579 the nave and (presumably west) porch were being repaired; the medieval roodloft then partly survived, a clock having been placed in it.[68] In 1603, however, one wall of the tower was 'somewhat decayed'.[69] Thomas Bennet in 1610 devised £5 for church repair, the income to be spent by the mayor and churchwardens with the consent of a majority of the senior burgesses.[70] In 1640 the poor state of the Fitzalan chapel allowed birds to fly into the west parts of the building,[71] and in 1724 two of the cross beams of the nave roof were in poor condition.[72] The east end of the nave was being releaded in 1775 and the south aisle in 1776.[73] At an unknown date lettering, including the ten commandments, was painted on the plaster between the arch of the Fitzalan chapel and the east crossing arch.[74]

The west parts of the church were fully restored during the 1810s. A Gothic altarpiece was erected in 1814.[75] New box pews, replacing a less regular arrangement of pews, were inserted in 1818 to the designs of the duke of Norfolk's surveyor James Teasdale;[76] two large corporation pews, one each for men and women, were next to the west crossing piers.[77] A Gothic-style organ gallery was erected over the arch to the Fitzalan chapel in 1817[78] on the site of the medieval roodloft.[79] Perhaps at the same time the aisle roofs were ceiled and whitewashed.[80] Two large galleries were inserted in the north and south aisles under a faculty of 1823.[81] The result was felt to embody neatness and comfort rather than devotion.[82]

The east parts of the church, meanwhile, passed at the suppression of the college in 1544 to the earls of Arundel, descending afterwards with the rape.[83] The Fitzalan and Lady chapels continued to be the place of burial for members of the FitzAlan and Howard families thereafter, two vaults under the Lady chapel being used at first, and later two further ones under the Fitzalan chapel.[84] In 1589 there was a 'keeper of the church of the college of Arundel' and of the tombs and monuments in it.[85] The two chapels were kept locked in 1635 and later, the Howards and their servants having the keys.[86] Access during the period was presumably generally from the former college courtyard through a door in the south wall,[87] but there were three other points of entry besides. The iron grille between the Fitzalan chapel and the west parts of the church had a keyhole only on its east side;[88] in the earlier 19th century the steward and the Catholic priest each had a key to it.[89] There was access to the Lady chapel by a side door leading from the 'sacristy' to the east, which was used by the 18th century as a schoolroom and a place of meeting for the corporation.[90] At the west end of the Lady chapel the arch to the north transept was filled by a wooden partition with a doorway; in the early 19th century the schoolmistress had a key to that in order to bring schoolchildren from the school in the former college buildings to their pew in the north transept.[91] Only one instance is known when the Howards' exclusive right to the east parts of the church was successfully challenged, when Bishop Hare forced an entry in the 1730s to hold a visitation in the Fitzalan chapel. In 1743 the duke was said to refuse admittance to both the bishop and the vicar.[92]

The windows of the Fitzalan chapel were 'very much broken' in 1603,[93] and in 1640 the timbers of the roof were in poor shape.[94] In 1627 the Arundel estate Act settled £100 a year after the deaths of Thomas Howard, earl of Arundel (d. 1646), and his wife on the repair of the chapel and the castle.[95] The chapel was probably damaged during the siege of the castle in 1643–4, when it may have been used by musketeers as a firing place,[96] and some repairs in glazing and plumbing were carried out in the early 1660s.[97] Despite the Act of 1627, however, the chapels were again in bad condition in the early 18th century, and *c.* 1724, when further repairs were going on, the interior of the Fitzalan chapel remained 'quite indecent and sordid'.[98]

In 1782 the remains of the Fitzalan chapel roof were pulled down together with the parapet above, the falling timbers causing damage to some of the monuments and to the carved wooden stalls.[99] A plain timber roof was put in

67 W.S.R.O., Ep. I/1/5, f. 135. By 1724 S. transept was repaired by par.: *S.R.S.* lxxviii. 59.
68 W.S.R.O., Ep. I/23/5, f. 35v.
69 Ibid. Ep. I/26/1, f. 5v.
70 *S.R.S.* xlix. 59.
71 B.L. Add. MS. 39368, f. 34.
72 *S.R.S.* lxxviii. 58.
73 *S.A.C.* lxxi. 39–40.
74 A.C.M., FA 87; 248, no. 8.
75 W.S.R.O., Par. 8/9/1, f. 91v.; Par. 8/9/10, no. 504.
76 Ibid. Par. 8/4/1; Par. 8/9/1, f. 95v.; A.C.M., FA 246, plans of pews, 1818 and n.d.; Tierney, *Arundel*, ii, facing p. 643; for Teasdale, above, castle (cast. fabric).
77 A.C.M., FA 246, plan of pews, 1818; W.S.R.O., Par. 8/9/1, f. 91v.
78 A.C.M., FA 248, no. 5; Clwyd R.O., Glynne ch. notes, cii. 51; Tierney, *Arundel*, ii, facing p. 643; for date, above, this section.
79 W.S.R.O., Add. MS. 29660; *Country Life*, 19 Dec. 1914, p. 819; cf. B.L. Add. MS. 5674, f. 21.
80 Tierney, *Arundel*, ii. 645.
81 Ibid. 643; W.S.R.O., Ep. I/17/45, f. 8v.; ibid. Par. 8/4/10.
82 Dallaway & Cartwright, *Hist. W. Suss.* ii (1) (1832), 203; Tierney, *Arundel*, ii. 643.
83 *L. & P. Hen. VIII*, xix (2), p. 475; *Camd. Misc.* xvi (Camd. 3rd ser. lii), Hammond, 32; B.L. Add. MS. 39368, f. 43; below, this section.
84 *Camd. Misc.* xvi (Camd. 3rd ser. lii), Hammond, 32–3; *Ven. Phil. Howard, Earl of Arundel* (Cath. Rec. Soc. xxi), 356; *S.A.C.* iii. 78–9; lxxi. 34, 42; Tierney, *Arundel*, ii. 634–5; A.C.M., FA 49–52; B.L. Add. MS. 5699, f. 19.
85 P.R.O., E 178/1906, f. 1v.
86 *V.C.H. Suss.* ii. 33; *Pococke's Travels*, ii (Camd. Soc. 2nd ser. xliv), 107; *S.A.C.* lii. 41; A.C.M., FA 95, ff. 2, 4–6; B.L. Add. MS. 15776, f. 232.
87 A.C.M., FA 95, ff. 2, 7; 246, plan of Fitzalan chapel, 1877; illus. at B.L. Add. MS. 5674, f. 21.
88 *Law Reps., Com. Pleas Div.* iv (1879), 291.
89 A.C.M., FA 95, ff. 2–4.
90 Eustace, *Arundel*, 214; A.C.M., FA 95, f. 6; 113; W.S.R.O., A.B.A., F1/1, f. 91; ibid. Par. 8/13/2.
91 A.C.M., FA 95, ff. 1–2, 4–5.
92 B.L. Add. MS. 15776, f. 232.
93 W.S.R.O., Ep. I/26/1, f. 5v.
94 B.L. Add. MS. 39368, f. 34.
95 3 Chas. I, c. 4 (Priv. Act).
96 W. Freeman, *Arundel Cast. Guide* (c. 1972), 42. Parl. troops were also said to have been billetted in it: Tierney, *Arundel*, ii. 619.
97 A.C.M., A 262, f. [94]; 263, acct. 1664.
98 Ibid. 339, Arundel surv. 1702, f. 3; *S.R.S.* lxxviii. 23, 58–9.
99 Tierney, *Arundel*, ii. 621–2.

its place,[1] and a few years later the chapel was converted into an estate workshop and store for building materials,[2] as it remained in 1835.[3] In the earlier 19th century owls nested in the building,[4] which in 1835 was compared to 'a crumbling and putrid corse chained to a living being'.[5] The upper section of the iron grille to the crossing was covered on its west side in the early 19th century by wooden boarding, the lower section having a curtain to prevent draughts reaching the west parts of the church.[6] The curtain was replaced *c.* 1815 by more boarding with folding doors which could be opened in warm weather for ventilation.[7]

In the late 1830s and early 1840s the two eastern chapels were repaired: much of the south wall of the Fitzalan chapel was rebuilt, four new windows being inserted, while on the north side of the Lady chapel stonework was evidently replaced and a decorated parapet was added.[8] The 'sacristy' east of the Lady chapel was recovered from secular use in 1848.[9] In 1852, as a *quid pro quo* for his installation of warming apparatus under the north transept, the churchwardens allowed Duke Henry Charles (d. 1856) to replace the wooden partition between the transept and the Lady chapel with a permanent wall.[10] A Gothic-style funerary chapel for Duke Henry Granville (d. 1860) and his wife was built *c.* 1864 on the south side of the Fitzalan chapel to the designs of M. E. Hadfield.[11] In 1857 the structure of the east parts of the church was said to be in good order, though a visitor then deplored the 'squalor and desolation' of the interior.[12] The Fitzalan chapel was nevertheless open for public inspection during that period.[13]

A major restoration of the west parts of the church was carried out in 1873–4. A particular impetus was the need to counter the triumphalism expressed in the building of the new Roman Catholic church; in an appeal for funds the work was declared on that account to be of national importance.[14] The two largest contributors to the subscription were the dowager marchioness of Bath and Lord Leconfield; the architect was Sir Gilbert Scott.[15] The pews and galleries were removed; the medieval pulpit, then used as a pew, was restored to its proper purpose; the organ was moved from the east end to the north transept, though part of its loft remained *in situ* until 1977;[16] and a new sanctuary surrounded by a low wall was laid out under the crossing and part of the nave, with an altar and reredos, and choir and clergy stalls.[17]

In 1872, when the restoration was in prospect, the churchwardens wrote to the duke stating their intention to remove the wooden boarding between the crossing and what they regarded as the true chancel, and to replace all or part with plate glass to allow light and air to reach the west parts of the church. In reply the duke's lawyers asserted the chapel as the duke's private property, denying any easement of light and air,[18] and in the following year the duke erected a brick wall across the entire arch east of the iron grille in order to preserve privacy.[19] The new vicar, George Arbuthnot, requested the wall's demolition in 1874;[20] three years later he formally removed a few bricks from it in order to bring the matter to a lawsuit.[21]

The case of the vicar and churchwardens[22] was that the duke's rights in the Fitzalan chapel were only those which any impropriator would have in the chancel of a church;[23] and that the layout of the building as a whole showed it originally to have been in single use, the pulpit and roodloft occupying the normal places for a church with nave and chancel.[24] The evidence for the duke's exclusive ownership, however, was overwhelming. The existence of the lockable iron grille showed a clear intention to separate the two parts of the building from the first.[25] No parochial services could be proved ever to have been held in the east parts of the church.[26] The two chapels had been invariably locked, the earls and dukes as keyholders admitting or excluding whom they chose. Repairs had been carried out without the church authorities being consulted, and vaults had been made and coffins moved without permission asked;[27] conversion to a workshop and lumber room had similarly gone unchallenged. Judgment was given for the duke in 1879 and upheld on appeal in 1880,[28] the point being made that even had the Fitzalan chapel been the parochial chancel in the 14th and 15th centuries, the duke's possession since had been so complete and absolute as to be irrefutable. The vicar's claim to light and air was also turned down.

The two chapels were afterwards conservatively restored *c.* 1886–1902 to the designs of C. A.

1 *Gent. Mag.* lxxiii (1), 131; J. Rouse, *Beauties and Antiq. of Suss.* i. 325; illus. above, p. 88.

2 Tierney, *Arundel*, ii. 622; A.C.M., FA 95, ff. 1–2, 4–5; 118, evidence of Hen. Hartwell.

3 Horsfield, *Hist. Suss.* ii. 130.

4 Wright, *Arundel* (1818), 16; A.C.M., FA 95, f. 1; 115, evidence of Wm. Harwood; 118, evidence of Peter Bridger.

5 Horsfield, *Hist. Suss.* ii. 130.

6 A.C.M., FA 95, f. 3; 121, evidence of Wm. Toogood; 123, evidence of Wm. Harwood.

7 Ibid. FA 87; 95, f. 3; 121, evidence of Wm. Toogood; illus. at ibid. 248, no. 14.

8 Ibid. FA 95, ff. 2, 5–6; 115, evidence of Wm. Harwood; 118, evidence of Hen. Hartwell; ibid. uncat. archit. drawings. The parapet does not appear in Tierney, *Arundel*, ii, frontispiece, or S.A.S. libr., Sharpe colln. no. 12.

9 A.C.M., FA 59. The date 1842 over outer doorway perhaps indicates a previous repair.

10 W.S.R.O., Par. 8/1/2/2, inside back cover.

11 J. M. Robinson, *Dukes of Norf.* (1982), 207; A.C.M., MD 2592, drawings by M. E. Hadfield.

12 *S.A.C.* lxxxiv. 114; cf. *Builder*, 19 Feb. 1876, p. 161.

13 W.S.R.O., Par. 8/12/1, p. 89.

14 Ibid. Par. 8/4/20, subscription appeals, 1873, 1875, and n.d.; A.C.M., FA 97, 99; *Builder*, 17 Oct. 1874, p. 875.

15 W.S.R.O., Par. 8/4/20, subscription appeals, 1873 and n.d.

16 Ibid. Add. MS. 29660; *Builder*, 17 Oct. 1874, p. 875; for pulpit, below, this section (other fittings).

17 W.S.R.O., PH 2559.

18 Ibid. Par. 8/12/1, pp. 81–6.

19 A.C.M., FA 118, evidence of Chas. Gardner.

20 Ibid. 101, corresp. between Revd. G. Arbuthnot and Messrs. Few & Co. 1874.

21 Ibid. 244, Revd. G. Arbuthnot to duke of Norf. 3 July 1877.

22 Para. based mainly on *Law Reps., Com. Pleas Div.* iv (1879), 291–315.

23 W.S.R.O., Par. 8/12/1, p. 82.

24 *The Times*, 27 Mar. 1879, p. 4.

25 Ibid. 8 June 1880, p. 4.

26 Ibid. 4 June 1880, p. 4.

27 Cf. A.C.M., FA 95, f. 7.

28 *The Times*, 8 June 1880, p. 4. The fact that the Anglican burial service had sometimes been used was irrelevant: ibid. 27 Mar. 1879, p. 4; *Law Reps., Com. Pleas Div.* iv (1879), 291; A.C.M., FA 95, f. 6.

Buckler.[29] The medieval groined timber roof of the Fitzalan chapel was reconstructed using 38 of the original bosses, some of which had been found in an outhouse in Poling.[30] The bodies of Duke Henry Granville (d. 1860) and three members of the Hope and Hope Scott families, which had been buried in the castle chapel, were brought to the Fitzalan chapel *c.* 1886, after which burials of members of the Fitzalan-Howard family continued there.[31] In 1906 mass was said occasionally,[32] and in 1989 six times a year in commemoration of deceased members of the Fitzalan-Howard family,[33] thus perpetuating the 'chantry' role of the late medieval college. Access to the chapels was only by special permission in 1903,[34] but in 1907 and generally later they were open for public inspection.[35]

The nave roof was reconstructed in 1893 after damage by woodworm,[36] and *c.* 1902 the south transept was reopened as a Lady chapel for daily services.[37] By 1893 curtains had been placed over the brick wall in front of the Fitzalan chapel,[38] but a scheme proposed in 1895 for the decoration of the wall was not carried out.[39] In the mid 20th century the wall was taken down in two stages, the upper section being replaced by glass in the 1950s and the rest, at the parish's expense, in 1969.[40] The sanctuary under the crossing was reordered in 1976: part of the low wall round it was removed, the altar brought forward, and the choir stalls rearranged diagonally.[41] Not long afterwards meeting rooms and a gallery were constructed in the west bay of the nave, unfortunately further constricting the interior space of the church. The Fitzalan and Lady chapels were again restored after 1976.[42] In 1977 an ecumenical service was held in which both parts of the church were used together for the first time since the Reformation or perhaps ever; similar services have also been held since.[43]

MONUMENTS. An Anglo-Saxon coffin slab perhaps to a priest which probably came from the church was found during rebuilding of the castle in the 19th century.[44] The west parts of the present building have no monuments of importance, but the Fitzalan and Lady chapels have a fine series to members of the FitzAlan and Howard families.[45]

The chief place before the high altar of the Fitzalan chapel is taken by the alabaster tomb chest, originally painted and gilded, of Thomas FitzAlan, earl of Arundel (d. 1415), and his wife Beatrice (d. 1439);[46] its design has been attributed to Thomas Prentys.[47] The recumbent effigies have canopies over their heads, and the tomb chest, which is decorated with figures of 28 ecclesiastics under ogee canopies, partly destroyed, is surrounded by a contemporary iron hearse of which the prickets for ten candles remain.

On the south and north sides of the sanctuary respectively are miniature three-bayed chapels of Sussex marble to William FitzAlan, earl of Arundel (d. 1487), and his wife Joan, and to three successive earls of Arundel of the 16th century. The former[48] has delicate tracery, including ogee arches, filling most of its surfaces both inside and out; on the north side, joined to the main structure like flying buttresses, are four freestanding twisted Cosmati-style columns, with canopies to carry candles. Inside the chapel are two tomb chests, one on top of the other, the west end of the lower one forming an altar. The upper tomb chest is of a different scale from the lower, particularly in its decoration, and seems likely to have been originally part of another monument.[49] The effigies of the earl and countess were lying on top of the upper chest by 1780,[50] but that does not seem to have been their original position since it was too high for them to be seen and since the effigy of the countess had to be mutilated to make it fit the space. Moreover, since the effigies are of limestone,[51] unlike the rest of the monument, they perhaps do not belong to it. They were cleaned between 1980 and 1982 and afterwards resited on a slab lower down.[52] The monument was described as richly gilded in 1635;[53] much colour and gilding on the effigies survived in 1990.[54]

The monument opposite[55] was erected in 1596 by John Lumley, Lord Lumley (d. 1609), as a memorial to his wife's FitzAlan ancestors Thomas, earl of Arundel (d. 1524), William, earl of Arundel (d. 1544), and Henry, earl of Arundel (d. 1580). In design it was intended to echo the monument to William FitzAlan, earl of Arundel (d. 1487), as a conscious piece of antiquarianism, using a bizarre mixture of Gothic and Renaissance details.[56] There are no tomb chests, but only a table on arches along the side wall, perhaps intended as 'a reading desk for the officiating priest'.[57]

In the Lady chapel the chief place before the altar is occupied by the tomb chest[58] of John d'Arundel, earl of Arundel (d. 1421), and his wife Eleanor, again of Sussex marble and deco-

29 A.C.M., FA 254, 259, 261.
30 *S.A.C.* lxxiii. 2; M. Elvins, *Arundel Priory*, 52. Others remained in Poling ch. in 1981: ibid.; cf. *S.A.C.* lx. 86–7; lxxiii. 9; *Country Life*, 19 Dec. 1914, p. 820.
31 *Miscellanea*, xiv (Cath. Rec. Soc. xxvii), 94–6.
32 A. MacCall, *Ch. and Mission of St. Phil.'s, Arundel*, 11 (copy at W.S.R.O. libr.).
33 Inf. from Dr. J. M. Robinson, Arundel Cast.
34 Goodliffe, *Littlehampton* (1903), 81.
35 A.C.M., FA 259; H. R. Mosse, *Mon. Effigies of Suss.* (1933), 13; *Kelly's Dir. Suss.* (1938).
36 *W. Suss. Gaz.* 30 Nov. 1893; W.S.R.O., Par. 8/4/4.
37 W.S.R.O., Ep. I/22A/2 (1903); ibid. Par. 8/12/1 (1901).
38 *W. Suss. Gaz.* 30 Nov. 1893.
39 A.C.M., FA 258, corresp. between Revd. Wal. Crick and duke of Norf. 1895; W.S.R.O., PD 2351.
40 Elvins, *Arundel Priory*, 72; *W. Suss. Gaz.* 13 Mar. 1969; inf. from Mrs. Ian Rodger, Arundel Cast.
41 *Arch. Jnl.* cxlii. 67.
42 J. M. Robinson, *Dukes of Norf.* (1982), 239.
43 A.C.M., FA 262; local inf.
44 *S.A.C.* xlvii. 148–50.
45 Fullest descrip. at F. W. Steer, *Fitzalan Chapel Guide*.
46 Illus. at B.L. Add. MS. 5674, f. 20. Ric. FitzAlan, earl of Arundel (d. 1397), in whose time coll. was founded, was buried at Austin friars ch. in Lond.: *Complete Peerage*, i. 245.
47 J. Harvey, *Eng. Medieval Architects*, 237.
48 Illus. at B.L. Add. MS. 5674, f. 18.
49 Cf. *Gent. Mag.* lxxiii (1), 132.
50 B.L. Add. MS. 5674, f. 18.
51 *Ch. Monuments*, i (2), 65, 67.
52 Ibid. 65–94; *W. Suss. Gaz.* 21 Oct. 1982.
53 *Camd. Misc.* xvi (Camd. 3rd ser. lii), Hammond, 32.
54 Their description in 1635 as 'pure white alabaster' is clearly wrong: ibid.
55 Illus. at B.L. Add. MS. 5674, f. 19.
56 *Country Life*, 27 Jan. 1983, pp. 197–8.
57 Dallaway & Cartwright, *Hist. W. Suss.* ii (1) (1832), 199.
58 Illus. at B.L. Add. MS. 5674, f. 17.

rated by cusped quatrefoils formerly containing shields. Only one of the heraldic panels of enamelled brass inset in its top remained in 1990.[59] The east end of the wall between the two chapels is pierced to accommodate the alabaster monument to John d'Arundel, earl of Arundel (d. 1435), which has an effigy on top and a cadaver in the open tomb chest below. The tomb was originally thought to be a cenotaph, but the earl's remains were found below in 1857.[60]

No monuments were erected to members of the Howard family before the large black marble Gothic tomb chest in the Lady chapel was put up to Lord Henry Howard-Molyneux-Howard (d. 1824) and his family. An appropriately central position in the Fitzalan chapel is given to the Purbeck marble monument to Duke Henry (d. 1917), with coloured heraldic decoration and a bronze effigy by Sir Bertram Mackennal.[61] Duke Henry Granville (d. 1860) and his wife are commemorated by twin Purbeck or Sussex marble tomb chests, with white marble effigies by Matthew Noble,[62] in the chapel built for the purpose on the south side of the Fitzalan chapel; in design the two monuments are based on the medieval tombs nearby. A wall monument to Thomas Howard, earl of Arundel (d. 1646), was put up in the Lady chapel in 1983, with the Latin epitaph he had had composed for himself.[63]

Others buried in the two chapels were priests of the college or servants of the FitzAlan and Howard families; several floor brasses remained in 1990, but some inscriptions which had survived in the later 18th century afterwards disappeared.[64] The pedimented classical wall monument to Robert Spyller (d. 1634), steward of the dowager countess of Arundel, may have been designed by Inigo Jones or Nicholas Stone.[65]

The monuments in the east parts of the church were said in 1728 to be preserved with great care,[66] though another writer in 1735 described them as almost turned to dust.[67] In 1826 a visitor found them 'mouldering to decay' and considered they would soon be irreparable;[68] not until after the lawsuit over the ownership of the chapel were any steps taken to repair them.

OTHER FITTINGS. Many surviving fittings in both sections of the church are contemporary with the present building. The octagonal font of Sussex marble has cusped arcading on both bowl and stem; in 1834 it was painted in stone colour.[69] Before the 1870s it stood in the south transept.[70] The three-sided stone pulpit attached to the south-west pier of the crossing has a carved canopy with ogee-arched decoration;[71] the carved bosses of its vault are gilded. By 1834 it had become a private pew, with curtains like a theatre box.[72] It was restored to its original use *c.* 1874, when the two-stage pulpit that had replaced it[73] was removed. Mural paintings by the north door representing the Seven Deadly Sins and the Seven Acts of Mercy, both in the shape of a wheel, are also late 14th-century; a painting of the Virgin Mary with angels, also on the north wall of the north aisle, seems to be 15th-century.[74] The walls of the Fitzalan chapel are said to have been painted with heraldic decoration.[75]

The iron grille between the Fitzalan chapel and the crossing is also original. It is in three vertical divisions filling the whole height of the arch to the chapel; the lowest division has small cusped and pointed arches, each carrying a spike, while the two upper divisions are plain. Both the Fitzalan chapel and the Lady chapel retain their medieval altars of Sussex marble, the former being *c.* 12 ft. (3.7 metres) wide.[76] The stalls in the Fitzalan chapel, decorated with ogee tracery, were badly damaged by the demolition of the roof in 1782[77] and by later neglect, so that to one visitor in 1857 they seemed 'a hideous collection of *débris*';[78] but they were carefully restored in or after 1887 by C. A. Buckler.[79] The stalls in the Lady chapel, lower and plainer, are largely medieval.

Late medieval stained-glass portraits of earls and countesses of Arundel, together with heraldic decoration, remained in the east window of the Fitzalan chapel in 1634[80] but were perhaps largely destroyed in the Civil War. A fragment showing St. Ambrose and the arms of Thomas Bourgchier, archbishop of Canterbury (d. 1486), remained in one of the south windows of the chapel in 1780[81] but had been removed by 1834.[82] Some late 14th-century glass was said to survive in 1907,[83] but there was none in 1989.

Other fittings in the west parts of the church are chiefly late 19th- or 20th-century, including stained glass of *c.* 1879–86.[84] A new east window was made for the Fitzalan chapel between 1890 and 1893 by Hardman and Co.,[85] showing Christ enthroned above the celebration of a requiem mass in which members of the FitzAlan and Howard families take part. The eastern chapels also contain antique fittings brought from elsewhere, including a large late medieval crucifix on the west wall of the Lady chapel which is probably Spanish.[86]

The ring of eight bells was given in 1855 by

59 Cf. *S.A.C.* lxxvi. 63.
60 Ibid. xii. 232, 236–7, 239; illus. at B.L. Add. MS. 5674, f. 17.
61 F. W. Steer, *Fitzalan Chapel Guide*, 12.
62 A.C.M., A 1975; inf. from Dr. Robinson.
63 Inf. from Dr. Robinson.
64 *S.A.C.* lxxvi. 62–73; B.L. Add. MS. 5699, ff. 14–17.
65 D. Howarth, *Ld. Arundel and his Circle*, 105–6; illus. at J. M. Robinson, *Dukes of Norf.* (1982), 110.
66 *S.A.C.* xi. 182.
67 *S.C.M.* xix. 258.
68 Clwyd R.O., Glynne ch. notes, cii. 51.
69 Tierney, *Arundel*, ii. 644.
70 e.g. ibid.; W.S.R.O., Par. 8/4/1.
71 Above, pl. facing p. 91.
72 Tierney, *Arundel*, ii. 644; cf. *S.A.C.* lxxxiv. 114–15.
73 Tierney, *Arundel*, facing p. 643; *S.A.C.* lxxxiv. 114.
74 *V.C.H. Suss.* ii. 354; A. Caiger-Smith, *Eng. Medieval Mural Paintings*, 53, 176–7; illus. at *Bklet. of Fitzalan Chapel, Arundel* (Arundel, [1931]), pl. 13.
75 Dallaway, *Hist. W. Suss.* ii (1) (1819), 170.
76 *Gent. Mag.* lxxiii (1), 131–2; *S.A.C.* xx. 231; lxxxiv. 114–15; *V.C.H. Suss.* ii. 351. High altar illus. at B.L. Add. MS. 5674, f. 21.
77 Above, this section [fabric].
78 *S.A.C.* lxxxiv. 114; cf. A.C.M., FA 248, no. 7; *Country Life*, 25 Sept. 1986, p. 984.
79 A.C.M., FA 254.
80 Dallaway, *Hist. W. Suss.* ii (1) (1819), 169–70; Tierney, *Arundel*, ii. 619–20.
81 B.L. Add. MS. 5674, f. 22.
82 Tierney, *Arundel*, ii. 620 n.
83 *V.C.H. Suss.* ii. 353.
84 *Chich. Dioc. Kal.* (1882), 158–9; (1883), 161–2; (1887), 148.
85 A.C.M., C 725.
86 Nairn & Pevsner, *Suss.* 88.

the duke and duchess of Norfolk; there were previously six, of which four or five were of 1712 and the sixth had been recast in 1810.[87] The only pre-19th-century plate is a silver paten and flagon of 1735 and a silver paten and a pair of communion cups of 1780.[88]

The registers begin in 1560, but there are gaps in the mid 18th century.[89] In the 1650s there are entries for civil marriages from a wide hinterland.[90]

ROMAN CATHOLICISM. There seems usually to have been a Catholic presence at Arundel since the mid 16th century. Two alien inhabitants reported in 1579 for absence from church were presumably Catholics,[91] and other recusants were recorded from the 1590s;[92] in the later 16th century Arundel served as a port for priests travelling between England and the Continent.[93] Larger congregations are mentioned from the mid 18th century,[94] a huge new church was opened in 1873, and during the 20th century the mission was converted into a parish. At the creation of the diocese of Arundel and Brighton in 1965 the church was raised to the status of a cathedral; the bishop lived at Storrington both then and later, the Arundel priest having the title of administrator.[95]

The dukes of Norfolk encouraged and protected the congregation from the early 18th century,[96] as their predecessors had presumably done. In 1546, when the earl of Arundel appointed a new vicar, he was sworn to recognize the Pope's supremacy.[97] Later earls and dukes, however, were not always Catholics. Thomas Howard, earl of Arundel (d. 1646), publicly professed himself a Protestant in 1615,[98] and Henry Howard, duke of Norfolk (d. 1701), also conformed.[99] Duke Charles (d. 1815) was not a Catholic,[1] and Duke Henry Charles (d. 1856) seceded in 1851 and was reconciled to the Roman church only on his deathbed.[2] Duke Edward (d. 1777) was the first, apparently, to have the role of leader of lay Catholics in England,[3] which was taken up more prominently by Duke Henry (d. 1917) and his successors.[4] Under Duke Henry Granville (1856–60) and especially under his son Henry (d. 1917) Arundel's Catholic character was zealously developed.[5]

Priests recorded in the 18th and earlier 19th centuries were principally private chaplains to the dukes or their families.[6] The dukes' wishes continued to be taken into account later in the appointment of Catholic clergy.[7]

The mission was financed apparently entirely by the duke of Norfolk in the 1790s,[8] but in the 1830s there was also income from what was described as the former 'Paris rents'.[9] Duke Henry's support in the late 19th century and early 20th was particularly munificent:[10] at the latter period the priest had £300 a year and the curates £80 each. After his death in 1917, however, the income greatly declined despite an endowment under his will.[11]

The Catholic priest lived in the castle in the later 18th century,[12] but by 1797 had a house in the restored college buildings next to the then chapel.[13] A presbytery attached to the new church at its south-east corner was built by the duke of Norfolk to the design of J. A. Hansom between 1874 and 1876. Of Bath stone like the church, it is in a more original Gothic style, with dramatic high-pitched roofs and gables.[14]

Recusants were mentioned in the 1590s[15] and the 1620s,[16] four papists in 1676[17] and 1747,[18] and four Catholic families in 1724.[19] Priests were recorded in the 1710s,[20] in 1735,[21] and perhaps continuously from 1748; one served from 1785 to 1824[22] and another, Canon M. A. Tierney, the historian of Arundel, from 1824 to 1862.[23] Eighty-seven Catholics of all ages were listed in the mission area in 1767[24] and 70 in 1781;[25] to the question how many popish families lived in Arundel in 1758 the vicar had replied 'too many'.[26] Confirmations were held in the chapel probably eleven times between 1741 and 1817, on the first occasion with 38 candidates.[27] In the mid 1790s most of the poorer inhabitants of the locality were said to be Catholic.[28] The

87 Elphick, *Bells*, 250–1.
88 *S.A.C.* liii. 232–3.
89 W.S.R.O., Par. 8/1 (TS. cat.); cf. *N. & Q.* 3rd ser. i. 464.
90 Cf. W.S.R.O., Par. 8/1/1/1, ff. 3, 33v.
91 Ibid. Ep. I/23/5, f. 35v.
92 Below, this section.
93 *Studies in Suss. Ch. Hist.* ed. M. J. Kitch, 109; *Cal. S.P. Dom.* 1591–4, 388–9; cf. *Ven. Phil. Howard, Earl of Arundel* (Cath. Rec. Soc. xxi), 51, 71, 73, 75, 254.
94 Below, this section.
95 e.g. *Arundel and Brighton Cath. Dir.* (1970).
96 e.g. *Univ. Brit. Dir.* ii. 55; below, this section.
97 F. W. Steer, *Cathedral Ch. of Our Lady and St. Phil., Arundel*, 9.
98 *Complete Peerage*, i. 255–6.
99 J. M. Robinson, *Dukes of Norf.* (1982), 142.
1 *Univ. Brit. Dir.* ii. 55; *Complete Peerage*, ix. 633. The statement at *S.C.M.* xxv. 573 that Duke Chas. (d. 1786) was a Protestant is presumably an error: cf. Robinson, op. cit. 166–9.
2 Robinson, op. cit. 201–2.
3 *S.C.M.* xxviii. 226.
4 e.g. Robinson, op. cit. 217.
5 Below, this section.
6 G. Anstruther, *Seminary Priests*, iv. 72, 144, 282, 312; *Horace Walpole's Corresp. with Geo. Montagu*, ed. W. S. Lewis and R. S. Brown, i. 96; *S.C.M.* xxviii. 226; *S.A.C.* cxxvi. 251–2.
7 F. W. Steer, *Cathedral Ch.* 16.
8 *Univ. Brit. Dir.* ii. 55.
9 Archives of Dioc. of Arundel and Brighton, Bishop's Ho., Hove, Arundel par. file, corresp. 1831–2.
10 e.g. ibid. Arundel par. file, Southwark dioc. visit. 1912.
11 Ibid. Arundel par. file, Southwark dioc. visits. 1917, 1923, 1950, 1953.
12 e.g. A.C.M., IN 6–7, 42; *Plans of Arundel Cast.* 20.
13 Anstruther, *Seminary Priests*, iv. 312; cf. Tierney, *Arundel*, ii. 613–14.
14 A.C.M., MD 1727; W.S.R.O., PD 832; Steer, *Cathedral Ch.* 16.
15 *Cal. Assize Rec. Suss. Eliz. I*, pp. 253, 268, 361, 375, 382; *Recusant Roll*, i (Cath. Rec. Soc. xviii), 338.
16 *Cal. Assize Rec. Suss. Jas. I*, pp. 123, 131, 141; *S.R.S.* xlix. 6, 14, 23, 42, 48, 56–7, 121.
17 *Compton Census*, ed. Whiteman, 144.
18 W.S.R.O., A.B.A., M22, list of inhabitants, 1747.
19 *S.R.S.* lxxviii. 59.
20 *S.A.C.* cxxvi. 251; Anstruther, *Seminary Priests*, iii. 181.
21 Anstruther, *Seminary Priests*, iv. 282.
22 Ibid. 72, 144, 311–12; *Walpole's Corresp. with Montagu*, ed. Lewis and Brown, i. 96; *S.C.M.* xxviii. 226; *Miscellanea*, vi (Cath. Rec. Soc. vii), 356; xiv (Cath. Rec. Soc. xxvii), 59.
23 *D.N.B.*
24 *Returns of Papists, 1767* (Cath. Rec. Soc.), ii. 145.
25 H.L.R.O., papist return, 1781 (photocopy at W.S.R.O., MP 1271).
26 W.S.R.O., Ep. I/22/1 (1758).
27 Archives of Archdioc. of Westm., vol. A. 40, f. 117 (inf. from Miss M. Kinoulty, Worthing); *Miscellanea*, xiv (Cath. Rec. Soc. xxvii), 53, 87–90.
28 *Univ. Brit. Dir.* ii. 55.

congregation was 78 strong in 1829, when it was one of only seven Catholic congregations in Sussex.[29] On Census Sunday 1851 mass was attended by *c.* 45, the regular congregation then being *c.* 70.[30]

Both Duke Henry Granville (1856–60) and Duke Henry (d. 1917) were strongly influenced by Charles de Montalembert's romantic view of medieval religion and by the Ultramontanism of Fr. Faber and the Oratorians.[31] The Revd. John Butt, assistant curate from 1858 and priest 1862–85, worked hard to build up the congregation using the Oratory's methods of holding popular daily services, setting up schools, and taking a personal interest in the people.[32] An Arundel Catholic magazine was founded in 1880 and flourished until 1891 or later.[33] The new church built between 1869 and 1873 at the expense of the duke was on a scale expressing the triumphalist mood that followed the restoration of the Catholic hierarchy in 1851.[34] There were four priests in 1882.[35] By 1883 the congregation had reached several hundred.[36] Attendance in 1912 was *c.* 600.[37]

After 1838, in an early instance of interdenominational co-operation, Canon Tierney had served with Anglican clergy on a standing committee for poor relief.[38] From the mid 19th century, however, the increasing numbers of Catholics in the town began to cause ill-feeling, exacerbated by the result of the 'Arundel chancel case'.[39] Already by 1865 the vicar was complaining that there were more Catholics than Protestants,[40] and a successor in 1884 alleged that strong pressure was applied to employees of the castle and their families to convert to Rome.[41] A more likely explanation for the increased numbers is that many found it financially beneficial to join the Roman church because of the support given by the duke to Catholic families,[42] a tradition which seems to go back, though on a smaller scale, to the later 18th century.[43]

After 1861 part of the former college buildings accommodated Servite sisters who, besides doing the castle laundry and training girls as domestic servants, taught in the Catholic schools and carried out pastoral visiting.[44] There were 18 sisters in 1871[45] and 15 in 1917.[46] The convent was called St. Wilfrid's priory in 1906 and later. After 1886 a second monastic presence in the area was provided by the closed order of Poor Clares at Crossbush in Lyminster a mile from the town.[47] By 1939 the Servite nuns no longer taught in the Catholic school, though after *c.* 1946 they ran a small private school themselves.[48] The convent was closed in or before 1960.[49]

Duke Henry's Ultramontanist leanings were best expressed in the Corpus Christi celebrations[50] which from *c.* 1877, following Central Italian models, included the decoration of the church with a carpet of flowers and a procession from it to the south bailey of the castle for open-air Benediction. In 1924 and presumably earlier all the Norfolk estate workers were given a holiday.[51] The procession and service continued in the 1980s, when they were held in the evening rather than daytime.[52] By then they had become a major tourist attraction.[53]

Since the pecuniary advantages of adherence to the Catholic church were reduced after 1917 the congregation also then declined,[54] though mass attendances still averaged 400–500 in the 1920s and 30s and there were four priests in 1929 and five in 1939.[55] The Catholic population of the (Catholic) parish was estimated at 750 in 1973.[56]

Other places besides Arundel were served by clergy from the town from the early 18th century. In 1714 the priest said a monthly mass at Michelgrove house in Clapham.[57] The congregation of *c.* 90 at Bishop Challoner's visitation in 1741[58] evidently included outsiders to the town, as later.[59] After *c.* 1793 the priest also served the Catholic community at Slindon.[60] The Revd. John Butt (1862–85) set up missions in neighbouring places on the Norfolk estate, at Littlehampton, Angmering, Houghton, and Amberley.[61] In the 1920s the Arundel clergy also

29 *Studies in Suss. Ch. Hist.* ed. M. J. Kitch, 139.

30 *S.R.S.* lxxv, p. 144.

31 Robinson, *Dukes of Norf.* (1982), 205, 208.

32 *Kelly's Dir. Suss.* (1882 and later edns.); A. MacCall, *Ch. and Mission of St. Phil.'s, Arundel*, 5–7 (copy at W.S.R.O. libr.); cf. ibid. 4; *Miscellanea*, xiv (Cath. Rec. Soc. xxvii), 54. Butt was later bp. of Southwark: MacCall, op. cit. 7.

33 *Arundel Cath. Mag.* (1880–91) (copies in Arundel cathedral archives).

34 Robinson, *Dukes of Norf.* (1982), 214, 216; below, this section.

35 *Kelly's Dir. Suss.* (1882); cf. W.S.R.O., Ep. I/22A/1 (1890). In 1903 and later there were 3: *Kelly's Dir. Suss.* (1903, 1918).

36 Steer, *Cathedral Ch.* 27.

37 Archives of Dioc. of Arundel and Brighton, Bishop's Ho., Hove, Arundel par. file, Southwark dioc. visit. 1912.

38 A.C.M., MD 787.

39 Above, church [fabric].

40 W.S.R.O., Ep. I/22A/2 (1865).

41 Ibid. Ep. I/22A/1 (1884); cf. ibid. Ep. I/22A/1 (1893).

42 *Suss. Hist.* ii (10), 27; Archives of Dioc. of Arundel and Brighton, Bishop's Ho., Hove, Arundel par. file, Southwark dioc. visits. 1948, 1953.

43 *Univ. Brit. Dir.* ii. 55.

44 *Kelly's Dir. Suss.* (1895); MacCall, *St. Phil.'s, Arundel*, 12; Archives of Dioc. of Arundel and Brighton, Bishop's Ho., Hove, Arundel par. file, Southwark dioc. visits. 1917, 1939; cf. *Illus. Lond. News*, 9 April 1887, p. 429.

45 *Census*, 1871.

46 Archives of Dioc. of Arundel and Brighton, Bishop's Ho., Hove, Arundel par. file, Southwark dioc. visit. 1917.

47 Ibid. Arundel par. file, Southwark dioc. visit. 1912, and Lenten returns, 1926; MacCall, *St. Phil.'s, Arundel*, 12.

48 Archives of Dioc. of Arundel and Brighton, Bishop's Ho., Hove, Arundel par. file, Southwark dioc. visits. 1939, 1946, 1959.

49 Ibid. Arundel par. file, corresp. about coll. bldgs. 1960–2.

50 Para. based mainly on A.C.M., MD 1931–2, 1934; Arundel cathedral archives, photos.; *W. Suss. Gaz.* 9 June 1988; Cartland, *Arundel*, 78–9; *Arundel Cathedral Guide* [1989], 24; above, pl. facing p. 42.

51 A. Beckett, *Spirit of the Downs*, 121; T. Edwardes, *Neighbourhood*, 127–31.

52 *Suss. Life*, Jan. 1986, p. 8.

53 *W. Suss. Gaz.* 6 June 1991.

54 Archives of Dioc. of Arundel and Brighton, Bishop's Ho., Hove, Arundel par. file, Southwark dioc. visits. 1929, 1935, 1948, 1953.

55 Ibid. Arundel par. file, Southwark dioc. visit. 1929; A. Dudley to bp. of Southwark, 1939; Lenten returns, 1926, 1939.

56 Ibid. Arundel par. file, par. reg. returns, 1973.

57 *S.A.C.* cxxvi. 252.

58 Archives of Archdioc. of Westm., vol. A. 40, f. 117 (inf. from Miss M. Kinoulty, Worthing).

59 Cf. *S.R.S.* lxxv. 144.

60 *Miscellanea*, vi (Cath. Rec. Soc. vii), 356.

61 MacCall, *St. Phil.'s, Arundel*, 6–7.

served Crossbush in Lyminster, Kingston, East Preston, and Rustington.[62]

Before the later 18th century the medieval castle chapel accommodated both the town congregation and the families of successive dukes.[63] The altarpiece which decorated it in the 18th century and later, representing the Adoration of the Shepherds,[64] survived in an upper storey of the castle in 1987. William Gilpin in 1774 was surprised at the magnificence of both the chapel and its vestments.[65] A sanctuary lamp burnt there in 1785.[66] A new chapel was fitted up apparently in the 1790s in the south-west corner of the former college buildings.[67] In 1818 its altar was raised on steps and had candles and flowers.[68] A west gallery served as a tribune for the duke's family in 1851.[69] The room was lengthened westwards in 1865, and remained in use until the opening of the new church in 1873.[70]

The cathedral church of *OUR LADY AND ST. PHILIP HOWARD*[71] was built, chiefly of Bath stone, in French Gothic style between 1869 and 1873 to the designs of J. A. Hansom.[72] It consists of apsed chancel with ambulatory, flanking chapels, and sacristies capable of accommodating more than 300 clergy,[73] crossing with transepts and crowning flèche, aisled, clerestoried, and stone-vaulted nave, and west narthex with south-west baptistry; a proposed north-west tower and spire *c.* 280 ft. (85 metres) high[74] was not built. The site was former church land, obtained from the vicar by stealth[75] and chosen to allow the building to dominate the town.

The building is much barer internally than other contemporary Catholic churches such as Farm Street church or St. James's, Spanish Place, in London, a fact accentuated by the lack of stained glass in the nave. The confessionals in the south aisle have elaborately crocketed gables, while the south transept altar to St. Philip Neri has a high canopy with a statue of the saint (d. 1595) in French Gothic style. The north transept shrine to St. Philip Howard, i.e. Philip Howard, earl of Arundel (d. 1595), was made in 1971 when the saint's remains were brought from the Fitzalan chapel of the parish church.[76] Most of the stained glass is by Hardman and Co.;[77] some in the chancel is from the destroyed chapel of Derwent Hall (Derbys.).[78] Various designs for a high altar, including two in Gothic style and one in the form of a Cosmatesque baldacchino, were made in the period 1877–1904 by J. S. Hansom, C. A. Buckler, and the estate architect W. Heveningham; some were erected as temporary models, the last of which lasted *c.* 40 years in place.[79] The lack of a stone altar meant that the church could not be consecrated until 1952.[80] The chancel was adapted *c.* 1970 in response to the liturgical requirements of the Second Vatican Council and the elevation to cathedral status.[81]

The magnificent ormolu tabernacle in the Lady chapel was made in 1730 by C. F. Kandler to the design of James Gibbs, and was possibly the first tabernacle made in England since the Reformation.[82] Other antique plate, reliquaries, and vestments were given by Duke Henry.[83]

The church registers begin in 1748. Until the opening of the Catholic cemetery in the mid 19th century most members of the congregation were buried in the parish churchyard.[84]

PROTESTANT NONCONFORMITY.

The schoolmaster reported for saying divine service in the church without licence in 1574[85] may have been a Nonconformist. There were several dissenting groups in Arundel in the mid and later 17th century: in 1676 there were said to be 50 Dissenters in the parish, evidently mostly Presbyterians,[86] and in the 1680s the dissenting faction was still strong enough to put up candidates in parliamentary elections.[87] Dissent declined during the 18th century, but revived at the end of the century and during the 19th.

PRESBYTERIANS AND INDEPENDENTS. There were Presbyterians at Arundel by 1655, including the mayor.[88] In 1669 the congregation was said to number *c.* 40 'mean persons', Samuel Wilmer of

62 *Miscellanea*, xiv (Cath. Rec. Soc. xxvii), 54.

63 *S.C.M.* xxv. 573; *Univ. Brit. Dir.* ii. 55; cf. *Pococke's Travels*, ii (Camd. Soc. 2nd ser. xliv), 108; A.C.M., IN 6, 42.

64 *Univ. Brit. Dir.* ii. 55; Wright, *Arundel* (1818), 25; Hillier, *Arundel* (1847), 59; MacCall, *St. Phil.'s, Arundel*, 3; *Plans of Arundel Cast.* 21.

65 *S.C.M.* xxviii. 226.

66 Ibid. xxv. 573.

67 *Univ. Brit. Dir.* ii. 55; Anstruther, *Seminary Priests*, iv. 312; above, relig. hos. (coll. bldgs.).

68 Wright, *Arundel* (1818), 25.

69 *S.R.S.* lxxv. 144.

70 MacCall, *St. Phil.'s, Arundel*, 3.

71 Above, frontispiece. The original dedic. to St. Phil. Neri was amplified in 1965 to include Our Lady; the modern dedic. dates from 1973: M. Elvins, *Arundel Priory*, 28; A.C.M., MD 2032.

72 F. W. Steer, *Cathedral Ch. of Our Lady and St. Phil., Arundel*, 14, 19, 21 and pls. 2–16; *W. Suss. Gaz.* 6 Jan. 1870.

73 Steer, op. cit. 22.

74 Ibid. pls. 4, 13–14, 17–18; *Builder*, 5 July 1873, p. 529.

75 A.C.M., MD 1931, E. H. Mostyn to duke of Norf. 6 Sept. 1869, transcr. at Steer, *Cathedral Ch.* 16–17.

76 A.C.M., DB 8, programme of consecration of high altar and shrine, 1971; ibid. MD 1688.

77 *Builder*, 5 July 1873, p. 529; cf. Steer, *Cathedral Ch.* 25 and pls. 28–9.

78 Steer, op. cit. 25.

79 Ibid. 23–5, 29, and pls. 20–2; MacCall, *St. Phil.'s, Arundel*, 8; A.C.M., MD 23, 799, 1931; 2232, J. S. Hansom to duke of Norf. 1898; ibid. uncat. archit. drawings, drawings for baldacchino, 1884, 1904; Archives of Dioc. of Arundel and Brighton, Bishop's Ho., Hove, Arundel par. file, Southwark dioc. visit. 1939; N.M.R., photos.; W.S.R.O., PH 2192, 4320.

80 *S.C.M.* xxv. 490; xxvi. 352.

81 A.C.M., DB 8, programme of consecration of high altar and shrine, 1971.

82 T. Friedman, *Jas. Gibbs*, 72, 324; *Arundel Cathedral Guide* [1989], 15; maker's note inside tabernacle (inf. from Mrs. Ian Rodger, Arundel).

83 MacCall, *St. Phil.'s, Arundel*, 9–10; W.S.R.O., MP 3201.

84 *Miscellanea*, xiv (Cath. Rec. Soc. xxvii), 56–93; orig. regs. at Arundel cathedral archives.

85 W.S.R.O., Ep. I/23/4, f. 39.

86 *Compton Census*, ed. Whiteman, 144; below, this section.

87 *Hist. Parl., Commons*, 1660–90, i. 418.

88 W. Albery, *Millennium of Facts in Hist. of Horsham and Suss. 947–1947*, 412, using E.S.R.O., SOF 43/1; cf. W. A. Shaw, *Hist. Eng. Ch. 1640–1660*, ii. 436; Caplan, 'Outline of Nonconf. in Suss.' i. 23–4.

Clapham being their minister.[89] Two Presbyterians were licensed as ministers in 1672,[90] and at the same date the minister of an Independent congregation was licensed to hold meetings at a house in Arundel.[91] In the later 17th century and earlier 18th the Presbyterians and Independents seem to have merged. There was a considerable congregation *c.* 1691, when the minister had £20 or £25 a year as stipend.[92] A house was registered for worship by the Presbyterians in 1712, and the same or another house in 1717. At that period there was a minister, apparently resident.[93] In 1717 the congregation was said to be of Arundel and Midhurst and to be Independent; there were then 90 'hearers'.[94] There were 13 Presbyterian or Independent families in the parish in 1724.[95]

A revived Independent, later Congregationalist, congregation is said to have met from 1780 and to have built a meeting house in Tarrant Street in 1784.[96] There was sometimes a resident minister in the later 18th century, and then and later there were links with the Countess of Huntingdon's Connexion. A Sunday school was founded *c.* 1810 and a chapel choir in 1816. Increased numbers led to the extension of the meeting house in 1822;[97] in 1829 there were 150 members.[98]

A new building adjacent to the old one was erected between 1836 and 1838 of flint with brick dressings and a flint and stone façade; it shares the Norman style of the contemporary town hall by the same architect, Robert Abraham.[99] The new building was known from the first as Trinity chapel.[1] Missionary work was begun at Yapton in the 1840s and at Amberley and Marehill in Pulborough later in the century.[2] The poet and writer George MacDonald was minister 1850–3 with a salary of £150 a year, but had to resign over unorthodox views. The manse at that period was no. 48 Tarrant Street.[3] On Census Sunday 1851 ninety attended in the morning, besides 110 Sunday schoolchildren, and 117 in the evening.[4] Two Sunday services were still held in the later 19th century and earlier 20th. There was a woman minister in 1934.[5] The congregation merged with the Baptists in 1966 as Arundel union church;[6] after the combined congregation split in 1973 services continued to be held in the Tarrant Street building until 1981,[7] but by 1990 it was used as an antiques market.

QUAKERS. Quakers met in Arundel from 1655 or soon afterwards at the house of Nicholas Rickman.[8] They suffered persecution by the borough authorities, then strongly Presbyterian: Rickman and other members of the congregation were imprisoned at Horsham gaol or committed to the house of correction in the later 1650s, one man being sent to Portsmouth for transportation.[9] At that period the meeting served an area between Lurgashall and Petworth in the north, and Sidlesham and Goring in the south.[10] Persecution continued after the Restoration, several Arundel Quakers being gaoled in the years 1662–4.[11] A Quaker burial was recorded in 1661 in a garden in Tarrant Street,[12] and there was a minister, presumably resident, in 1669.[13] In 1675 Edward Hamper leased a building in Tarrant Street to Nicholas Rickman and others for a meeting house, together with adjacent land fronting Tarrant and Arun streets; part was used as a burial ground[14] which survived in 1991.[15]

In 1724 there were four Quaker families in the parish,[16] perhaps including the Hornes, recorded as Quakers at Arundel from 1733 to 1817;[17] Robert Horne (d. 1813) was the miller at Swanbourne mill.[18] Though the congregation was in decline by the later 18th century,[19] there were still 11 Quakers in Arundel in 1801;[20] in the early 19th century members of the Horne and Spencer families were distrained for non-payment of tithes, rates, or taxes.[21] The meeting house was described in 1818 as 'very neat',[22] but the last recorded monthly meeting was held in 1827;[23] the building had perhaps ceased to be used for worship by *c.* 1841[24] and the congregation no longer existed in 1847.[25] The property was later let,[26] and in 1867 the meeting house was pulled down, a Baptist chapel afterwards being built on the site. In the early 20th century the former burial ground was a garden,[27] and both it and the Baptist chapel still belonged to the Quakers in 1922;[28] in 1967 the Quakers continued to own four houses in Arun and Tarrant streets.[29]

BAPTISTS. There were a few Baptists in 1669, with two ministers:[30] one was apparently Robert Fish,

89 *Orig. Rec. of Early Nonconf.* ed. G. L. Turner, i. 28; *V.C.H. Suss.* vi (1), 18.

90 *Orig. Rec. of Early Nonconf.* ed. Turner, i. 390, 510; cf. *Calamy Revised*, ed. Matthews, 210.

91 *Orig. Rec. of Early Nonconf.* ed. Turner, i. 314–15, 467.

92 *Freedom after Ejection*, ed. A. Gordon, 112.

93 W.S.R.O., Ep. I/17/36, ff. 4v., 120v.

94 *S.R.S.* lxxviii. 250–1.

95 Ibid. 59.

96 C. H. Valentine, *Story of Beginnings of Nonconf. in Arundel* (Harpenden, pre 1930), 3, 20 (copy in W.S.R.O. libr.), using hist. notes in W.S.R.O., NC/C 5/1/1–3. There is no record of its registration at P.R.O., RG 31/1, Chich. archdeac.

97 Valentine, *Beginnings of Nonconf.* 20–3; Caplan, 'Outline of Nonconf. in Suss.' iv. 50, 64; cf. Wright, *Arundel* (1818), 25.

98 W.S.R.O., QCR/1/11/W 1.

99 Colvin, *Biog. Dict. Brit. Architects*, 44; W.S.R.O., TD/W 5, wrongly describing the bldg. as Methodist.

1 P.R.O., RG 31/1, Chich. archdeac. no. 207.

2 Valentine, *Beginnings of Nonconf.* 27–8.

3 W. Raeper, *Geo. MacDonald*, 77, 79, 83, 90–1, 94; *S.C.M.* xix. 59.

4 *S.R.S.* lxxv, p. 143.

5 *Kelly's Dir. Suss.* (1882 and later edns.).

6 *Worthing Herald*, 7 Jan. 1966.

7 W.S.R.O., NC/C 5/9/1; below, this section (Baptists).

8 *S.A.C.* lv. 84.

9 Ibid. xvi. 67; *Cal. S.P. Dom.* 1656–7, 229–30; 1658–9, 167; A. Fletcher, *County Community in Peace and War*, 122; Albery, *Millennium of Facts*, 412, using E.S.R.O., SOF 43/1.

10 *S.A.C.* lv. 84.

11 Albery, *Millennium of Facts*, 420–2, 424–5, using E.S.R.O., SOF 43/1; cf. W.S.R.O., Ep. I/22/1 (1662).

12 *S.A.C.* lv. 85.

13 *Orig. Rec. of Early Nonconf.* ed. Turner, i. 28.

14 Cartland, *Arundel*, 46; W.S.R.O., Add. MS. 29769; ibid. TD/W 5.

15 Inf. from Mr. F. Penfold, Burpham.

16 *S.R.S.* lxxviii. 59.

17 W.S.R.O., Add. MSS. 39984–95 (TS. cat.); Hillier, *Arundel* (1847), 17.

18 *S.A.C.* lv. 85.

19 E.S.R.O., SOF 41/3.

20 Ibid. LCG/3/EW 1, f. [42].

21 Ibid. SOF 43/4.

22 Wright, *Arundel* (1818), 25.

23 W.S.R.O., Add. MS. 29745 (19 Oct. 1827).

24 Ibid. TD/W 5.

25 Hillier, *Arundel* (1847), 16.

26 Char. Com. files.

27 *W. Suss. Gaz.* 14 Nov. 1867; *S.A.C.* lv. 85.

28 Eustace, *Arundel*, 182.

29 Char. Com. files.

30 *Orig. Rec. of Early Nonconf.* ed. Turner, i. 28.

rector of Nuthurst, who was licensed as a Presbyterian at Ockley (Surr.) in 1672, and the other apparently William Wilson, vicar of Billingshurst.[31] One Baptist family was mentioned in 1724,[32] but thereafter no more is heard until revival in the mid 19th century.

In 1845 a Providence chapel was erected in Park Place, with a congregation including some from Walberton. Attendances on Census Sunday 1851 were 60 in the afternoon and 100 in the evening; there was also a Sunday school with 30 children.[33] In 1868 the congregation moved to a new chapel in Arun Street, built on the site of the Quaker meeting house,[34] where there were two Sunday services and a weekday evening meeting between 1882 and 1922 or later. The building could seat 150 in 1938. Various ministers served in 1882.[35] For some years the work was overseen by the minister of New Street chapel in Worthing, and after 1901 by the Particular Baptists of Christchurch Road, Worthing.[36] In 1966 the congregation amalgamated with the Congregationalists;[37] the chapel was closed in 1967, a shop front being inserted.[38] When the United Reformed church was created in 1973 a group refused to join and reconstituted the Arundel Baptist church, at first as a joint pastorate with Angmering Baptist church. In 1980 a new building seating 80 was put up off Ford Road.[39] In 1986–7, when there were *c.* 35 members, it was served by a minister from Lancing.[40]

METHODISTS. A former brewhouse in Tarrant Street was registered in 1807 for the worship of Wesleyan Methodists, apparently with a resident minister.[41] There was a Primitive Methodist chapel in Park Place between 1862 and 1874, served by various ministers.[42]

Other Nonconformist places of worship of unknown or uncertain affiliation were recorded in the town in 1705[43] and in the early 19th century,[44] when one minister at least was associated with the Society for Spreading the Light of the Gospel in the Dark Towns and Villages of Sussex.[45] Summer evening services were held in the market place and elsewhere in the town in 1883 in connexion with the Gospel Temperance Society, with speakers from Brighton and Worthing, but were subject to sabotage by 'roughs'.[46]

EDUCATION. In 1269 Master William of Wedon gave property in the town to Arundel priory in return for his maintenance and a house where he could hold a school.[47] Possibly the school had existed before, but no later record of it has been found. In the 15th century the college which succeeded the priory paid for choristers to be taught both singing and grammar; a schoolmaster was mentioned in 1459–60.[48]

Seventeen schoolmasters, not all licensed, were recorded in the later 16th century and earlier 17th, teaching reading, writing, arithmetic, or Latin. One at least was a graduate, another was also the parish clerk, and a third may have been a Nonconformist.[49] In 1651–2 the corporation apparently paid a schoolmaster a regular salary;[50] there is no other evidence for its support of education before the earlier 19th century, but in 1772 the parish overseers were supporting a dame school.[51] The vicar and one other master taught pupils in 1663,[52] and a later vicar in 1721.[53] Two Nonconformists were described as masters of 'Arundel school' in the mid 17th century.[54]

There seems usually to have been at least one school in the town after 1750. John Johnstone, called a writing master in 1756, was still teaching in 1779,[55] while Charles Caraccioli, author of *The Antiquities of Arundel* (1766), described himself as master of the grammar school.[56] By 1767 certainly,[57] and perhaps by 1741,[58] the so-called sacristy of the Fitzalan chapel of the parish church was used as a school, as it continued to be in the early 19th century.[59] Meanwhile the greater frequency of residence of the dukes of Norfolk had led by 1781 to the foundation of a Roman Catholic school, which then also took 20 Church of England children.[60] By the 1790s there were three boarding schools, one kept by a clergyman and the others by ladies.[61] Private schools continued to flourish in the town in the 19th century and early 20th.[62] In 1818 there were 12, with *c.* 240 children; one at least took boarders.[63] By the 1830s there were five boarding schools, besides at least three other private schools, with nearly 200 pupils.[64] Part of the former college

31 *Calamy Revised*, ed. Matthews, 198, 538.
32 *S.R.S.* lxxviii. 59.
33 Ibid. lxxv, p. 144; W.S.R.O., MP 2339.
34 Datestone reset in new ch.; *S.A.C.* lv. 85; O.S. Map 1/2,500, Suss. LXIII. 1 (1877 and later edns.).
35 *Kelly's Dir. Suss.* (1882 and later edns.).
36 W.S.R.O., MP 2339; *Worthing*, ed. F. Migeod, 234; *Baptist Handbk. for 1966*.
37 Above, this section (Presbyterians and Independents).
38 D. R. Elleray, *Victorian Chs. of Suss.* 44.
39 W.S.R.O., NC/B 3 (TS. cat.); datestone on bldg.; *Baptist Union Dir. for 1985–86*.
40 *Suss. Baptist Assoc. Yr. Bk. 1986–7*.
41 W.S.R.O., Ep. I/17/44, f. 44; cf. ibid. Ep. I/41/64.
42 *Kelly's Dir. Suss.* (1862 and later edns.).
43 W.S.R.O., Par. 8/11/7, f. 2.
44 P.R.O., RG 31/1, Chich. archdeac. nos. 59, 84, 190.
45 Caplan, 'Outline of Nonconf. in Suss.' iv. 63; *S.A.C.* cxx. 201.
46 *W. Suss. Gaz.* 30 June 1983.
47 B.L. Lansd. Ch. 92. The acct. in *V.C.H. Suss.* ii. 398 is inaccurate.
48 Petch, 'Arundel Coll.' 155–6.
49 W.S.R.O., Ep. I/17/12, f. 16; Ep. I/17/13, ff. 16v., 42, 46; Ep. I/17/15, f. 49; Ep. I/23/4, ff. 27v., 39; Ep. I/23/5, f. 35v.; Ep. I/23/7, f. 13v.; ibid. STC III/B, ff. 31, 70; STC III/C, ff. 87, 97v.; STC III/E, ff. 79, 104v., 182, 210v.; *Walker Revised*, ed. Matthews, 357.
50 W.S.R.O., A.B.A., F3/1.
51 Ibid. Par. 8/31/3 (1772).
52 Ibid. Ep. I/22/1 (1662, *recte* 1663).
53 B.L. Add. MS. 39356, f. 2.
54 *Calamy Revised*, ed. Matthews, 210, 457.
55 W.S.R.O., Add. MSS. 15795, 15800, 15816 (TS. cat.).
56 Caraccioli, *Arundel*, titlepage.
57 A.C.M., M 900, poll for return of mayor, 1767; cf. *S.A.C.* lxxi. 43.
58 Eustace, *Arundel*, 214.
59 W.S.R.O., Par. 8/13/2; cf. ibid. A.B.A., F1/1, f. 91.
60 H.L.R.O., papist return, 1781 (photocopy at W.S.R.O., MP 1271).
61 *Univ. Brit. Dir.* ii. 56–7.
62 e.g. Wright, *Arundel* (1817), 14; *Kelly's Dir. Suss.* (1845 and later edns.).
63 *Educ. of Poor Digest*, 951.
64 *Educ. Enq. Abstract*, 961–2; Pigot, *Nat. Com. Dir.* (1832–4), 1003; (1839), 653.

buildings was rented from the duke of Norfolk for a school between the early 19th century and 1852.[65]

A British school, sometimes called the free school,[66] was founded in School Lane by the duke of Norfolk in 1814 to accommodate 150 children of each sex; it was supported by voluntary contributions. In 1818 there were 135 girls and 150 boys on the roll.[67] School pence were payable in 1833 and later,[68] and in 1846–7 the school was open to children of all denominations.[69] The buildings were enlarged in 1848 at the duke's expense,[70] and in 1853 the school became a National school with an endowment of £3,600; its catchment area was then defined as the parish and a four-mile radius of the castle.[71] By 1858 the school was known as Arundel Church of England school.[72] An annual grant was received by 1855.[73] Average attendance in 1851 was 130 boys and 85 girls,[74] rising to 286 in 1884–5; in 1913–14 it was 249.[75] Part of the master's house was converted into an infants' schoolroom in 1859 at the expense of the dowager duchess of Norfolk,[76] and there was an infants' mistress by 1874.[77]

Between the 1870s and the 1890s the school's capacity was regularly returned as far in excess of the average attendance, evidently to prevent the setting up of a school board.[78] New buildings on the same site as the old were opened in 1900,[79] and in 1975 the school, by then called Arundel C.E. (Aided) primary school, moved to a new site south of Chichester Road.[80] Average attendance had fallen to 237 in 1921–2 and 218 in 1938,[81] and in 1971 there were 215 children on the roll.[82]

A Sunday school belonging to the Independents was founded *c.* 1810;[83] in 1833 it was attended by 53 boys and 54 girls and had a lending library.[84] An infants' school was begun by the same congregation in 1844 and still flourished in 1859.[85]

St. Philip's Roman Catholic mixed, later girls', school was founded off King Street in 1858,[86] moving to part of the former college buildings before 1875;[87] there was an infants' school too by 1869.[88] A brick and stone boys' school was built by the duke of Norfolk to designs by Hadfield and Goldie in 1860.[89] An annual grant was received by 1865.[90] The combined average attendance of the three schools was 105 in 1871 and 203 in 1878,[91] rising thereafter to 270 in 1900–1 and a peak of 299 in 1905–6.[92] As with the National school, accommodation figures stated in the later 19th century and earlier 20th were vastly in excess of need, the highest total being 824 in 1907.[93]

A new building for the boys' school, designed by J. A. Hansom, was opened on the same site as the old one in 1880;[94] it is of red brick with stone dressings in Tudor style, and includes a prominent statue of the Virgin and Child under a canopy at its south-east corner. New buildings for the girls' and infants' schools, of red and yellow brick, were built nearby *c.* 1898 to designs by Leonard Stokes.[95] The combined average attendance fell after the death of Duke Henry in 1917 to 183 in 1918–19, 133 in 1921–2, 80 in 1931–2, and 51 in 1938; yet at the last date there was still claimed to be accommodation for 525 children.[96]

The girls' and infants' schools were amalgamated in 1922, and in 1936 the boys also moved to the girls' school building,[97] their former school later becoming a parish hall. Proposals made in 1929 and 1931 to amalgamate the Roman Catholic schools with the Anglican ones because of declining numbers were rejected by the bishop of Southwark;[98] a revival of the same idea in 1972, though endorsed by both churches, was successfully opposed by Catholic parents.[99] There were 144 on the roll of the Catholic school in 1950 and 118 in 1965;[1] in 1971, when it was known as St. Philip's R.C. (Aided) primary school, there were 88.[2]

A small private school was started by the Servite sisters in the convent in London Road *c.* 1946 to take Duke Bernard's daughters. In

65 A.C.M., FA 95, ff. 4–5, 7; 123, evidence of Hen. Hartwell; ibid. PM 107; Pigot, *Nat. Com. Dir.* (1839), 653; *Kelly's Dir. Suss.* (1845, 1852).
66 e.g. Tierney, *Arundel*, ii. 715; P.R.O., ED 7/123; W.S.R.O., TD/W 5; inf. from Brit. and Foreign Sch. Soc. Archives Centre, Isleworth (Mdx.).
67 P.R.O., ED 7/123; W.S.R.O., TD/W 5; *Educ. of Poor Digest*, 951.
68 *Educ. Enq. Abstract*, 962; P.R.O., ED 7/123.
69 Nat. Soc. *Inquiry, 1846–7*, Suss. 2–3; cf. P.R.O., ED 7/123.
70 W.S.R.O., Par. 8/1/2/2, end flyleaf.
71 Ibid. Par. 8/25/6 (TS. cat.); P.R.O., ED 7/123.
72 P.R.O., ED 7/123.
73 *Mins. Educ. Cttee. 1854–5*, 228.
74 P.R.O., ED 7/123.
75 *Rep. Educ. Cttee. 1885–6*, 599; *Educ. List 21, 1914*, 521.
76 W.S.R.O., Par. 8/1/2/2, end flyleaf.
77 *Kelly's Dir. Suss.* (1874).
78 *Public Elem. Schs. 1875–6*, 264–5; *Rep. Educ. Cttee. 1885–6*, 599; *1893–4*, 978; cf. W.S.R.O., Ep. I/22A/1 (1887).
79 W.S.R.O., Par. 176/25/27 (TS. cat.); inscr. in bldg.
80 *W. Suss. Gaz.* 4 May 1972; 14 Feb. 1991.
81 *Educ. List 21, 1922*, 340; *1938*, 401.
82 W.S.R.O., WOC/CM 44/2/34.
83 Ibid. NC/C 5/6/1 (TS. cat.); above, protestant nonconf. (Presbyterians and Independents).
84 *Educ. Enq. Abstract*, 962.
85 W.S.R.O., NC/C 5/6/2, 6 (TS. cat.); cf. ibid. Ep. I/47/4.
86 P.R.O., ED 7/123; A. MacCall, *Ch. and Mission of St. Phil.'s, Arundel*, 6 (copy in W.S.R.O. libr.).
87 O.S. Map 1/2,500, Suss. LXIII. 1 (1877 edn.).
88 P.R.O., ED 7/123; cf. A.C.M., uncat. archit. drawings, plan of convent, 1895; W.S.R.O., Ep. I/22A/2 (1865).
89 *Builder*, 4 Aug. 1860, p. 499; P.R.O., ED 7/123.
90 *Rep. Educ. Cttee. 1865–6*, 588.
91 Ibid. *1871–2*, 342; *1878–9*, 1008.
92 *Schs. Parl. Grants, 1900–1*, 243; *Public Elem. Schs. 1907*, 637.
93 *Public Elem. Schs. 1875–6*, 264–5; *1907*, 637; *Rep. Educ. Cttee. 1885–6*, 599; *1893–4*, 978; *Schs. Parl. Grants, 1900–1*, 243; *Educ. List 21, 1922*, 340.
94 MacCall, op. cit. 6; A.C.M., uncat. archit. drawings, plans for sch. 1879; above, pl. facing p. 91; cf. O.S. Map 1/2,500, Suss. LXIII. 1 (1877, 1897 edns.).
95 A.C.M., uncat. archit. drawings, plans for sch. 1898; ibid. MD 1961.
96 *Educ. List 21, 1919*, 341; *1922*, 340; *1932*, 386; *1938*, 401.
97 W.S.R.O., E 8 (TS. cat.).
98 Archives of Dioc. of Arundel and Brighton, Bishop's Ho., Hove, Arundel par. file, Southwark dioc. visits. 1929, 1931.
99 *W. Suss. Gaz.* 4 May 1972.
1 Archives of Dioc. of Arundel and Brighton, Bishop's Ho., Hove, Arundel par. file, Southwark dioc. visit. 1950, and sch. inspection rep. 1965.
2 W.S.R.O., WOC/CM 44/2/34.

1954 it had 32 pupils, 23 of whom were not Catholics. It closed in 1959 or soon afterwards.[3]

A 'middle class' school for older boys called St. Nicholas's school was founded by the vicar George Arbuthnot in 1873 or 1874 to relieve pressure on the National school. In 1879, when run by the assistant curate, it offered both classical and commercial education,[4] but no more is heard of it later. St. Christopher's school for girls, offering a similar education, was founded in or shortly before 1874; in that year it was supported by subscriptions, donations, school pence, and an annual grant.[5] Average attendance was 17 in 1875–6.[6] The school was last mentioned in 1882.[7]

An evening school for older children was founded in 1880.[8] In 1887 the curate and others were teaching boys in the evenings 'with no conspicuous results'.[9] In the 20th century the older children of the parish have been educated at Littlehampton, Worthing, Chichester, and Barnham.[10]

CHARITIES FOR THE POOR. In 1631 George Bland, formerly of Arundel, founded an almshouse on the south side of Maltravers Street for a master, six brothers, and six sisters. There were said to be inmates in 1663, but the income of over £100 a year was then being detained by Bland's executors and others and had not been restored nine years later.[11] The building, of brick, with a chapel, survived in a ruined state in the early 19th century; it was bought by the duke of Norfolk shortly before 1834 and demolished.[12] Two cottages for use as almshouses were built by subscription further west in Maltravers Street in 1887 to commemorate Queen Victoria's Jubilee; since more than half the cost had been defrayed by Duke Henry and other Roman Catholics, every second presentation was to be of a Catholic. The cottages belonged to the town council.[13] Lilian May Holmes by will 1947 left money to provide and maintain houses for old people; eight bungalows were built in Fitzalan Road in 1964[14] and remained in 1986.

Various small rents charge, chiefly on property in Arundel, were received from the mid 16th century for the benefit of the poor and distributed in money or in kind on fixed days.[15] By *c.* 1649 the overseers were making the distribution. The total value then was £3 10*s.*;[16] by 1739 it had risen to £4 15*s.*,[17] by *c.* 1835 to £5 5*s.*,[18] and by *c.* 1860 to £5 18*s.*[19] In the 19th century the payments were known as the widows' doles.[20] They were still received in 1938.[21]

Henry Hilton of Clapham by will proved 1641 left £24 annually for 99 years out of his lands in co. Durham to be distributed among 12 poor inhabitants of the parish, but the money was apparently withheld.[22]

The corporation gave beef doles at Christmas in 1817.[23] Later in the 19th century and in the 20th similar largesse was received from the dukes of Norfolk and their relations in fuel and food.[24]

Mrs. Eliza Rolls by will proved 1911 devised £500, the income to be distributed between six elderly poor people of the parish in cash. At first the distribution was weekly, but in 1977, when the gross income was £49.19, it was annually at Christmas. The Revd. Walter Crick by will 1942 devised £100 for annual distribution to the aged and infirm, also in cash. In the early 1970s the income was £8–£9.[25]

Frank Mustchin (d. 1988) left £700,000 to house old people living within three miles of Arundel.[26]

3 Archives of Dioc. of Arundel and Brighton, Bishop's Ho., Hove, Arundel par. file, Southwark dioc. visits. 1946, 1959, and sch. inspection rep. 1954.

4 *Kelly's Dir. Suss.* (1874); A.C.M., MD 2016; cf. above, church.

5 P.R.O., ED 7/124; A.C.M., MD 2016.

6 *Public Elem. Schs. 1875–6*, 264–5.

7 *Kelly's Dir. Suss.* (1882); cf. A.C.M., D 144–63, sale cat. 1881.

8 P.R.O., ED 7/123.

9 W.S.R.O., Ep. I/22A/1 (1887).

10 Local inf.

11 J. Thorpe, *Reg. Roffense*, 967; *S.R.S.* xxix, p. 10; W.S.R.O., Ep. I/22/1 (1662, *recte* 1663); P.R.O., C 90/20, last item; but cf. ibid. C 91/10, no. 2; Tierney, *Arundel*, ii. 672.

12 Tierney, *Arundel*, ii. 672; W.S.R.O., Add. MS. 20564 (TS. cat.).

13 W.S.R.O., BO/AR 24/1/1, docs. concerning almshos.; BO/AR 24/4/17, f. 8; inscr. on bldg.

14 Char. Com. files; inscr. on bldg.

15 Tierney, *Arundel*, ii. 660–1; W.S.R.O., A.B.A., M4; ibid. Par. 8/31/2, list at end; *S.R.S.* lxxviii. 59; *Char. Don.* H.C. 511, pp. 1260–1 (1816), xvi (2); *30th Rep. Com. Char.* 636–7.

16 W.S.R.O., Par. 8/12/2, f. 5v.

17 Ibid. Par. 8/9/1, f. 1v.

18 *30th Rep. Com. Char.* 636.

19 W.S.R.O., Par. 8/12/1, pp. 54–5. The total of £19 received in 1724 presumably included other income: *S.R.S.* lxxviii. 59.

20 *30th Rep. Com. Char.* 636; cf. W.S.R.O., Par. 8/9/1, ff. 88v., 113v.

21 *Kelly's Dir. Suss.* (1938).

22 P.R.O., C 93/20, no. 29, m. 4; ibid. PROB 11/185 (P.C.C. 36 Evelyn); *V.C.H. Suss.* vi (1), 21.

23 W.S.R.O., A.B.A., F1/1 (1817).

24 Ibid. POL AB/16/1 (23 Dec. 1876); A.C.M., MD 29, 2651; local inf.

25 Char. Com. files; W.S.R.O., Par. 8/24/4–5.

26 *W. Suss. Gaz.* 22 Nov. 1990.

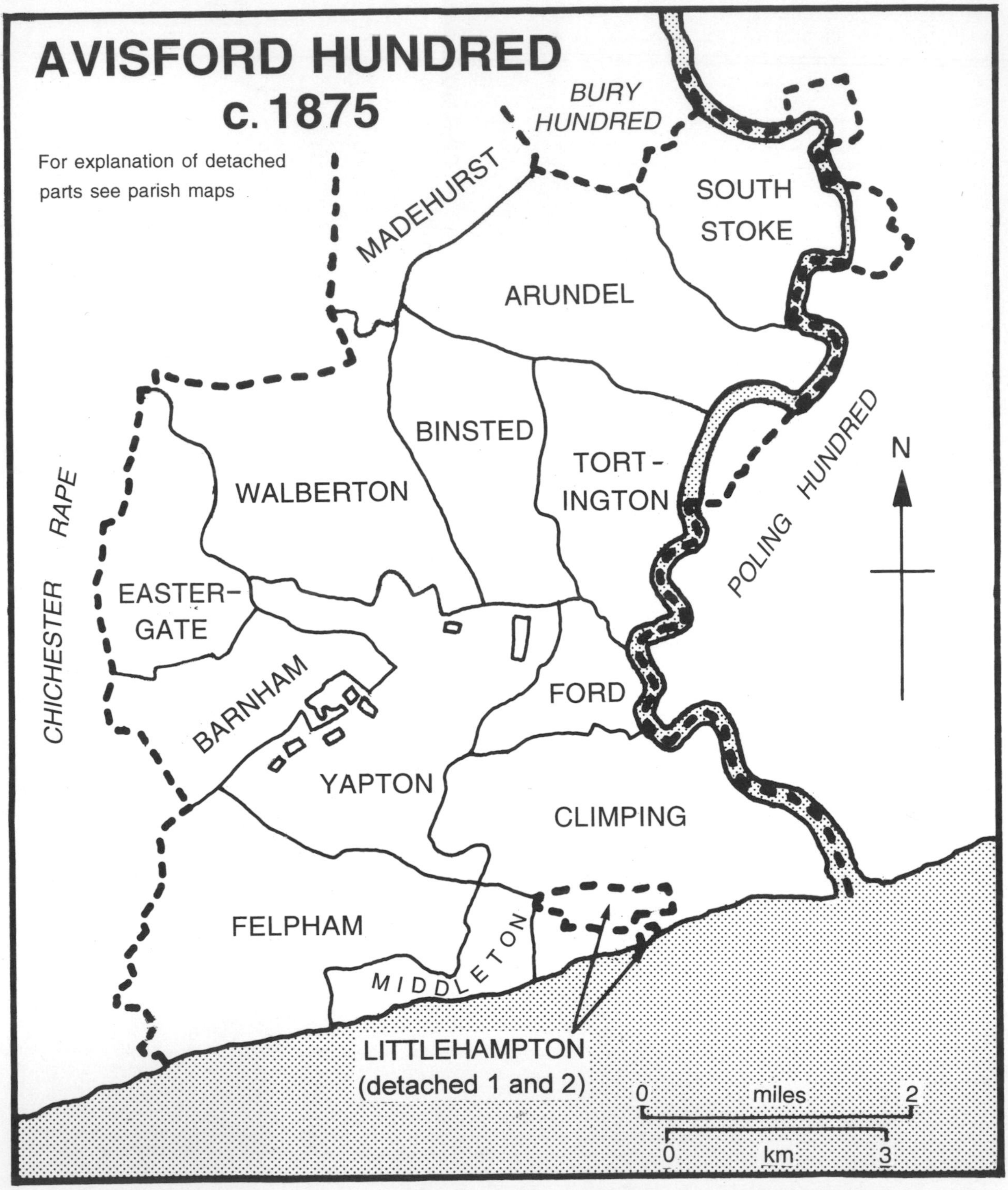
AVISFORD HUNDRED
c. 1875
For explanation of detached parts see parish maps
BURY HUNDRED
MADEHURST
SOUTH STOKE
ARUNDEL
BINSTED
TORT-INGTON
WALBERTON
CHICHESTER RAPE
EASTER-GATE
BARNHAM
POLING HUNDRED
N
FORD
YAPTON
CLIMPING
FELPHAM
MIDDLETON
LITTLEHAMPTON
(detached 1 and 2)
0 miles 2
0 km 3

AVISFORD HUNDRED

(Part)

THE hundred of Avisford descended with Arundel rape.[1] It was called Binsted hundred in 1086 but had its later name by 1166. In 1086 it consisted of the tithings of Barnham, Bilsham (in Yapton), Binsted, Eastergate, Felpham, Middleton, Offham (in South Stoke), Slindon, South Stoke, Tortington, and Walberton.[2] Madehurst was added by 1248,[3] Atherington and Cudlow (both in Climping) and Ford by 1275,[4] and Ilsham (in Climping), Ancton and Flansham (in Felpham), Climping, and Yapton by 1279.[5] Elmer (in Middleton) first appears in 1569.[6] Slindon was not recorded after 1086, later joining the archbishop of Canterbury's Aldwick hundred.[7] Some tithings were paired for fiscal purposes from the late 13th century.[8] In the early 19th century the hundred had upper and lower divisions, also called half-hundreds.[9] Madehurst parish, as geographically extraneous to the hundred, is reserved for treatment elsewhere.

The original meeting place of the hundred was evidently near the crossing of the Binsted brook on the boundary between Binsted and Walberton, where the place name Hundredhouse copse is recorded *c.* 1875.[10] Both the venues later recorded for holding the hundred courts were nearby: Walberton in 1365[11] and the Royal Oak inn in the same parish in the early 19th century.[12]

There are court records for the years 1291–3, 1335–6, 1348–9, 1450–1, 1519, 1536–7, 1548–54, 1569,[13] 1571–3,[14] and 1813–51.[15] Between the late 13th[16] and early 16th centuries the court was held every three or four weeks and a view of frankpledge apparently three times a year, but in the later 16th century the two seem to have been held together twice a year in spring and autumn. In the early 19th century there was an annual view.

The assize of bread and of ale was held between the 14th century and the late 16th, and the view or court oversaw street nuisances and the maintenance of roads, ditches, streams, and fences. Pleas of debt, trespass, detinue, and assault were heard between the late 13th and 15th centuries, and in the 16th cases or presentments involving theft,[17] slander,[18] an affray,[19] right to wreck,[20] the use of common pasture, for instance at the Rewell in Arundel,[21] and coining.[22] By the early 19th century there was very little business at the view.

Arundel borough was extra-hundredal by 1086.[23] Ford, Climping, and Ilsham manor had its own leet jurisdiction by 1279,[24] as did Walberton manor.[25] Right to wreck was claimed at different dates on Atherington and Cudlow manors in

1 e.g. *Feud. Aids*, v. 143; *S.R.S.* xix. 10.
2 *V.C.H. Suss.* i. 395, 431–2; *Pipe R.* 1166 (P.R.S. ix), 92.
3 P.R.O., JUST 1/909A, rot. 23d., as Mellers.
4 *S.A.C.* lxxxiv. 69.
5 P.R.O., JUST 1/917, rot. 21. Climping had been listed in Poling hund. in 1086: *V.C.H. Suss.* i. 430.
6 A.C.M., M 37, rot. 1d.
7 *V.C.H. Suss.* iv. 222.
8 *S.R.S.* x. 79–80, 137, 254–6; lvi. 56–7; *S.A.C.* l. 166–7.
9 W.S.R.O., Holmes, Campbell & Co. MSS., ct. bk. 1813–51; E.S.R.O., QCR/2/1/EW 2 (46–7).
10 O.S. Map 6", Suss. LXII (1880 edn.).
11 *Cal. Inq. p.m.* xii, p. 37.
12 W.S.R.O., Holmes, Campbell & Co. MSS., ct. bk. 1813–51, flyleaf.
13 A.C.M., M 32, rott. 5v.–6; 37, rot. 1d.; 54–7; 268, rot. 5 and d.; 271, ff. [9v., 16v.–18, 19v.]; 835.
14 P.R.O., SC 2/205/55, ff. 2, 11, 23, 42, 46, 55v.
15 W.S.R.O., Holmes, Campbell & Co. MSS., ct. bk. 1813–51.
16 Cf. *Cal. Inq. p.m.* xii, p. 37; xv, p. 80; A.C.M., A 231, rot. 9.
17 P.R.O., SC 2/205/55, ff. 2, 24.
18 A.C.M., M 57, m. 1d.
19 P.R.O., SC 2/205/55, f. 11v.
20 Ibid. f. 2.
21 Ibid. f. 12.
22 Ibid. f. 55v.
23 *V.C.H. Suss.* i. 421; cf. e.g. P.R.O., JUST 1/917, rot. 2; *Pipe R.* 1181 (P.R.S. xxx), 146; *Census*, 1841.
24 Below, Ford, local govt.
25 Below, Walberton, local govt.

Climping and on Felpham manor, on the former two with success, and on the last apparently so.[26]

A bailiff was mentioned from 1406.[27] Two constables were elected from 1569;[28] in 1648 their appointment went by rotation, but on what principle is not clear.[29] In the mid 19th century the constable was chosen by the duke of Norfolk's solicitor.[30] There was a hundred coroner, who was also coroner for Arundel honor, in the early 17th century.[31]

The pound in Arundel served Avisford hundred as well as the borough in the mid 19th century.[32]

26 Below, Climping, local govt.; Felpham, local govt.

27 *S.A.C.* lxxxix. 160.

28 A.C.M., M 37, rot. 1d.; *S.R.S.* liv. 70, 106.

29 *S.R.S.* liv. 149.

30 *Arundel Rds.* 38.

31 *Suss. Coroners' Inquests, 1558–1603*, ed. R. Hunnisett, p. xxv.

32 *Arundel Rds.* 38; W.S.R.O., Par. 76/8/1, f. 79v.

BARNHAM

THE parish of Barnham, well known in the 20th century for its market gardens, lies on the coastal plain north-east of Bognor Regis.[1] The ancient parish was 872 a. in area. Five detached portions to the south-east comprising 31 a. were added to Yapton between 1882 and 1891, so that in 1971 Barnham had 340 ha. (841 a.).[2] The eastern tip of the parish and a salient of Barnham into Yapton in the south-east were transferred to that parish in 1985, and at the same date a block of land comprising parts of Yapton, Walberton, and Eastergate was added to Barnham.[3] The present article deals with the parish as constituted before 1985.

The boundary of the ancient parish partly follows streams. Its configuration seems to show that Barnham once formed part of Eastergate or of a larger area also including Yapton.

The parish lies chiefly on brickearth, with alluvium in the valleys of the streams that separate it from Eastergate and Yapton.[4] The former was called the Walberton brook in 1910[5] but is more usually the Barnham brook; it seems likely to have been tidal in historic times[6] and was probably the site of the 40 a. of arable which lay uncultivated in 1341 because of flooding.[7] There were several ponds in the parish in the 18th and 19th centuries.[8] Land along the Barnham brook in the north part was liable to flooding, sometimes severe, in the later 20th century.[9] Despite the proximity of Barnham station in Eastergate in 1993, only a small part of the parish was then built up, the rest being divided between agriculture and market gardens.

Woodland belonging to the manor yielded three swine in 1086.[10] A grove called 'Chelewardesly', perhaps near the later Choller Farmhouse in Walberton, supplied timber for repairing Barnham manor house and for other purposes in 1253,[11] and closes called the Woodread mead and Middlewood and Littlewood reeds mentioned in the 16th century and early 17th seem from their names to be assarted land; the close of 60 a. called the Great wood in 1558, however, was perhaps then still woodland.[12]

Free warren was granted to the lord of the manor in 1253.[13] The close east of Barnham Court and north of the church was called the Warren *c.* 1762 and later.[14]

The parish is traversed at its north end by an early route from Chichester to Cudlow in Climping, the modern Yapton Road.[15] At the point where it crossed the Barnham brook on the boundary between Barnham and Eastergate there was a bridge by 1317;[16] it was called Barnham bridge in 1649, when the inhabitants of the two parishes shared the cost of its repair.[17] The road's alignment was altered when the railway embankment was built *c.* 1846.[18] Other roads in the parish which linked the various settlements or gave access to the fields included Church, Brook, Leys,[19] and Hill lanes. Parts of Church and Hill lanes are sunk between higher land on either side.[20]

Buses passed through Barnham between Chichester and Littlehampton by 1927 and between Slindon and Bognor Regis by 1934.[21] Both services continued in 1965, though the former then ran only to Yapton.[22] Chichester, Slindon, Bognor Regis, and Arundel were accessible by bus in 1992.

The Portsmouth–Arundel canal was opened through the centre of the parish in 1823,[23] crossing the Barnham brook and the Lidsey rife in the west by embankments, while south and south-east of the village it was crossed itself by two swing bridges, one inscribed 'Stewart Bridge 1820'.[24] After the closure of the canal in the mid 19th century the company's liquidators cut one embankment at the point where it crossed the Barnham brook but the vestry enforced the building of a bridge instead to preserve the right of way.[25]

The Chichester–Brighton railway line crosses the northern tip of the parish. Barnham was served from 1846 by stations at Yapton and at Woodgate in Aldingbourne; at the opening of the Bognor branch railway, which also runs through the parish, in 1864 they were replaced by the station named Barnham in Eastergate.[26]

A hoard of Bronze Age celts was found during the construction of the Bognor railway in the north-west part *c.* 1864.[27] Barnham Court and the parish church lie slightly to the east, towards the centre of the parish and away from the modern main road. There are a few houses or sites of houses nearby, and the close east of Barnham Court and north of the church may show evidence of dwellings otherwise unrecorded.[28] Other houses flanked Church Lane, leading north-east from the church, *c.* 1762,[29]

1 This article was written in 1993–4 and revised in 1996. Topographical details in introduction based mainly on O.S. Maps 1/25,000, SU 80/90 (1981 edn.); 6", Suss. LXII (1880 and later edns.). Map, below, p. 148. For the former Barnham mkt., Barnham rly. sta., and the area of 20th-cent. housing called Barnham or W. Barnham, below, Eastergate.

2 *Census*, 1881–1971; O.S. Map 6", Suss. LXII. SE. (1899 edn.), not showing the detached portions.

3 Arun (Parishes) Order 1985.

4 Geol. Surv. Map 1", drift, sheets 317 (1957 edn.); 332 (1975 edn.).

5 *S.A.C.* liii. 10.

6 Ibid.

7 *Inq. Non.* (Rec. Com.), 368.

8 W.S.R.O., Goodwood MS. E4996; ibid. TD/W 10.

9 Ibid. WDC/SU 19/1/1; *Bognor Regis Observer*, 20 Jan. 1994.

10 *V.C.H. Suss.* i. 431.

11 *Cal. Pat.* 1247–58, 173; O.S. Maps 6", Suss. LXII (1880 edn.); 1/25,000, SU 80/90 (1981 edn.).

12 B.L. Add. MS. 39394, f. 13; P.R.O., C 66/935, m. 1; cf. J. Field, *Eng. Field Names*, s.v. 'reading'.

13 *Cal. Pat.* 1247–58, 245; cf. P.R.O., JUST 1/924, rot. 67.

14 W.S.R.O., Goodwood MS. E4996; ibid. TD/W 10.

15 *S.R.S.* ii, p. 64; lix, p. 76; below, Eastergate, intro. (communications).

16 *Cat. Anct. D.* i, B 723.

17 *S.R.S.* liv. 184.

18 *250 Yrs. of Mapmaking in Suss.* ed. H. Margary, pl. 14; O.S. Map 6", Suss. LXII (1880 edn.); cf. below, this section [rly.].

19 W.S.R.O., QDP/W 34; O.S. Map 1/25,000, SU 90 (1958 edn.).

20 Cf. *Country Life*, 28 Oct. 1916, p. 2.

21 *Kelly's Dir. Suss.* (1927, 1934).

22 W.S.R.O., MP 814, f. [43].

23 P. A. L. Vine, *Lond.'s Lost Route to Sea* (1986), 83.

24 B.L. Maps, O.S.D. 83; *S.N.Q.* xvi. 134.

25 Vine, op. cit. 144–6, 206.

26 *Southern Region Rec.* comp. R. H. Clark, 51, 65, 92.

27 *S.A.C.* xvii. 254–5; lxxii. 46; S.M.R. 1444.

28 Inf. from the late Mr. H. Dart, Barnham, describing footings found in its N. corner.

29 Rest of para. based mainly on W.S.R.O., Goodwood MS. E4996; ibid. TD/W 10.

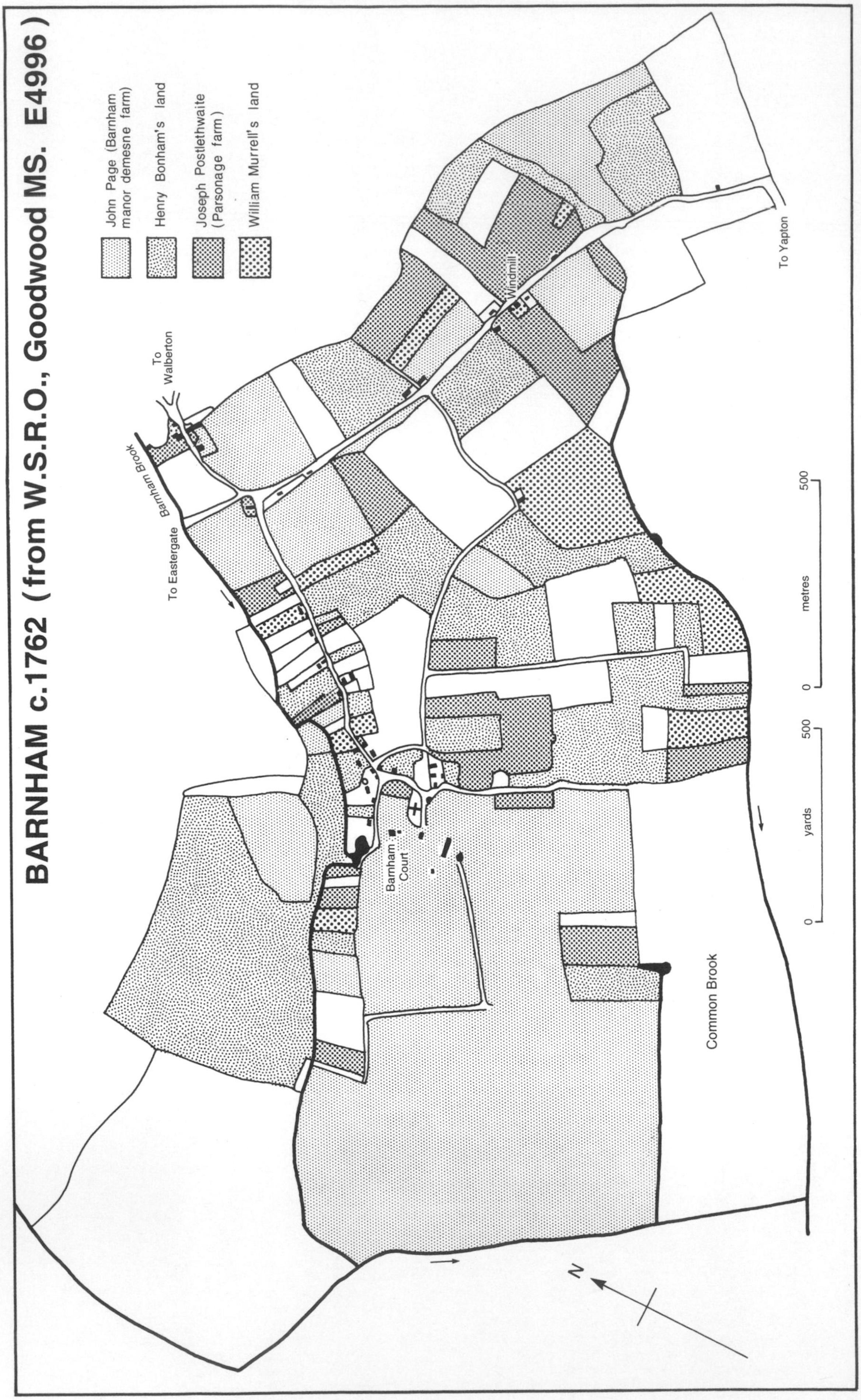

BARNHAM c.1762 (from W.S.R.O., Goodwood MS. E4996)

and since many of them belonged to manorial tenements and occupied parallel plots that pattern was probably medieval.[30] The only pre-19th-century houses in the area described apart from Barnham Court are Manor cottage, north-east of the church, apparently 18th-century and with a red and blue brick front dated W E M/1784 (for William and Elizabeth Murrell),[31] and perhaps the smaller cottage called Curacoa in 1992. About 1762 there had been *c.* 9 others. Two ponds then existed nearby, and later there were as many as seven in the same area.

Parsonage Farmhouse beside the northern boundary of the ancient parish also presumably occupies an early site,[32] but there is no indication of medieval settlement along the Chichester–Cudlow road in the north-east; Luccombe cottage by the junction with Church Lane, of flint with brick dressings, is apparently 18th-century, and the *c.* 8 other buildings shown *c.* 1762 apparently represented recent inclosures from waste land.[33]

From 19 houses in 1801 the total rose to 30 in 1841, 37 in 1871, and 58 in 1901.[34] The opening of the railway station in Eastergate in 1864 caused an immediate increase, five cottages being built by the following year,[35] and a terrace of four flint and brick cottages was put up at the south end of Church Lane in 1890 for the farm labourers of C. F. Field.[36] A few larger houses were built at the north end of Church Lane in the period 1890–1910,[37] and by the early 20th century the junction of Church Lane and Yapton Road, with the inn, school, parish hall, and shop, had become the new focus of the parish. Suggestions for large-scale development to match that in Eastergate, however, were never taken up.[38] After 1918 several pairs of brick houses were erected on new county council smallholdings in Yapton Road and Hill Lane,[39] and in 1948 a small estate of council houses was built at the top of Church Lane.[40] Other individual houses and bungalows were built in the 20th century in both Yapton Road and Church Lane, some farm buildings in the latter also being converted as dwellings; north-west of the church, meanwhile, a few houses were put up beside the nearby orchards. There was further development on either side of Lake Lane north of the railway after 1957,[41] including an area of Arun district council grouped housing for the elderly.[42] In 1994 houses were being built on the site of Barnham Nurseries' 'old nursery' in Yapton Road.[43]

Twelve *villani* and 12 cottars were enumerated on Barnham manor in 1086,[44] but 14th- and 16th-century tax lists do not distinguish Barnham vill from Walberton.[45] Thirty-nine adult males signed the protestation in 1642.[46] There were 16 families in 1724.[47] The population in 1801 was 124, falling to 112 in 1811 and fluctuating thereafter until 1861 between that figure and 173. From 1861, with the opening of Barnham station, there was a steady rise to 255 in 1901, 428 in 1951, 557 in 1971, and 1,222 in the altered area of the parish in 1991.[48]

An inn of unknown site was recorded in 1686[49] and a victualler in 1811.[50] The Murrell Arms at the junction of Church Lane and Yapton Road was opened in 1866.[51]

A men's reading room or club room was opened in or shortly before 1890, when lectures were being held there; it was presumably the same as the corrugated iron building next to the former poorhouse in Yapton Road which was presented to the parish by W. A. Hounsom of Yapton.[52] The parish hall behind it was put up in 1931.[53] A Barnham choral society existed by 1929.[54] In 1965 there were several local groups including a folk dance club,[55] and in 1992 the hall was used by 18 organizations.[56] It belonged by 1965 to the parish council. In the same year the county council managed a library there with voluntary help, which was open twice a week.[57]

A Barnham sports club flourished in 1935,[58] but no sports were played in the parish in 1992.[59]

Mains water was laid on, presumably by the Bognor Water Co., in part of Yapton Road by 1912,[60] and was available in Church Lane in 1933.[61] By 1912 gas mains had been laid by the Bognor Gas Co. in Yapton Road under an Order of 1904.[62] Electricity was supplied at least to Church Lane by 1933[63] and more generally by 1938;[64] the only street lighting in 1965, however, was a single lamp under the railway bridge. Main

30 Cf. *S.A.S. Newsletter*, xliii. 392.

31 F. W. Steer, *Barnham Ch. Guide*, 3; W.S.R.O., Par. 76/1/1/2, f. 4; cf. below, manor.

32 Cf. below, manor.

33 W.S.R.O., Goodwood MS. E4996; ibid. Ep. I/29/13/24; *Goodwood Estate Archives*, i, ed. F. W. Steer and J. Venables, p. 103.

34 *Census*, 1801–1901.

35 W.S.R.O., Ep. I/22A/2 (1865); cf. *Rep. Com. on Children and Women in Agric.* 86.

36 Initials and date on bldgs.; cf. *Kelly's Dir. Suss.* (1895); W.S.R.O., Add. MS. 4575; below, econ. hist. (agric.).

37 O.S. Map 6", Suss. LXII (1880 and later edns.); W.S.R.O., Add. MS. 6096, sale cat. 1904; ibid. MP 2347, ff. 2, 4; cf. *Kelly's Dir. Suss.* (1895 and later edns.).

38 e.g. W.S.R.O., Add. MSS. 4575; 6096, sale cat. 1904; 25532.

39 Ibid. 6096, plan of smallholdings, 1919; O.S. Map 6", Suss. LXII. SE. (1951 edn.).

40 W.S.R.O., MP 2347, f. 12.

41 O.S. Map 1/25,000, SU 90 (1958 edn.); SU 80/90 (1981 edn.).

42 *W. Suss. Gaz.* 30 Dec. 1982.

43 Cf. below, econ. hist. (mkt. gardening).

44 *V.C.H. Suss.* i. 431. A single cottar was listed on the yardland called Borham which may have lain within the par.: ibid. 432; below, manor.

45 *S.R.S.* x. 255; lvi. 57. The lists for 1296 and 1327 omit Barnham: ibid. x. 78–81, 134–8.

46 Ibid. v. 26.

47 *S.R.S.* lxxviii. 60. *Compton Census*, ed. Whiteman, 146, also omits Barnham.

48 *Census*, 1801–1991.

49 P.R.O., WO 30/48, f. 182.

50 *Lavington Estate Archives*, ed. F. W. Steer, p. 82.

51 *W. Suss. Gaz.* 15 Sept. 1966; M. Cutten and V. May, *The Mill and the Murrell* (Barnham, 1992), 38.

52 *W. Suss. Gaz.* 29 Nov. 1990; W.S.R.O., Ep. I/22A/1 (1890); ibid. MP 2347, f. 9; for site, ibid. IR 12, f. 7.

53 *Kelly's Dir. Suss.* (1934); *Bognor Regis Observer*, 17 Nov. 1951.

54 Barnham W.I. scrapbook [1949], p. [33] (copy in possession of Mrs. R. Collins, W. Barnham).

55 W.S.R.O., MP 814, ff. [2, 19].

56 *W. Suss. Gaz.* 10 Dec. 1992.

57 W.S.R.O., MP 814, ff. [2, 19].

58 Ibid. 2788.

59 *W. Suss. Gaz.* 10 Dec. 1992.

60 W.S.R.O., Add. MS. 25532; cf. F. H. Edmunds, *Wells and Springs of Suss.* 25.

61 W.S.R.O., SP 1581.

62 Ibid. Add. MS. 25532; *Suss. Ind. Hist.* xvii. 5.

63 W.S.R.O., SP 1581.

64 *Kelly's Dir. Suss.* (1938).

drainage had been put in by 1965.[65] A sewage treatment works beside the former canal in the west end of the parish existed by 1981.[66]

MANOR AND OTHER ESTATE. Alnoth, a free man, held Barnham in 1066, and William held it of earl Roger in 1086.[67] Perhaps from that date[68] and certainly from 1230, when William de St. John had it,[69] it descended as a member of Halnaker in Boxgrove[70] through Robert de St. John (fl. 1250–3),[71] John de St. John (fl. 1275; d. 1301),[72] and thence in the direct line through John (d. 1329),[73] Hugh (d. 1335),[74] and Edmund (d. 1347).[75] In 1253 it was leased to Master Richard, king's cook, and another for 14 years, and in 1299 to the company of the Bonsignori of Siena for 16 years.[76] It continued to descend with Halnaker[77] until at the death of Thomas Poynings, Lord St. John, in 1429 it passed under a settlement of 1416 to (Sir) John Paulet,[78] husband of his granddaughter Constance. John's son and namesake succeeded his father in 1437, and at his death in 1492[79] was succeeded by his son, Sir John (d. 1525),[80] whose son William Paulet, created in 1539 Lord St. John, exchanged the manor c. 1542 to the Crown.[81]

In 1570 the reversion of Barnham was granted to William Howard, Lord Howard of Effingham.[82] Courts were held in the names of Agnes Browne, widow, and William Browne in 1593 and of William Browne alone in 1596.[83] Sir William Browne of Loseley (Surr.) had the manor in 1608;[84] in 1629 he conveyed it to Sir William Morley[85] (d. 1658 or 1659),[86] after which it once again descended with Halnaker, from 1765 in the Lennox, later Gordon-Lennox, family, dukes of Richmond.[87]

Barnham farm, the manor demesne, then 201 a., was sold in 1700 to the Revd. Thomas Musgrave[88] (d. c. 1725), whose niece and heir Elizabeth married Ogle Riggs.[89] In 1748 they conveyed the farm to John Page, M.P. for Chichester (d. 1779),[90] whose daughter Frances married George White Thomas, M.P.[91] After his death in 1821 it passed to their daughter, also Frances (d. 1835), and her husband Lt.-Genl. John Gustavus Crosbie (d. 1843).[92] About 1848 the estate had 265 a. within the parish.[93] John's son and heir Charles sold it apparently in 1853 to the tenant Richard Cosens,[94] members of whose family had held the lease since 1756 or earlier;[95] the same or another Richard Cosens had himself owned 159 a. in the parish before c. 1848.[96]

After Richard's death in 1871[97] Barnham Court farm was sold apparently to George and Arthur Woodbridge.[98] The land seems to have been divided between Arthur Woodbridge and James Harrison before 1899, and c. 1910 Woodbridge and Joseph Harrison each owned a farm called Church farm, respectively of 166 a. and 187 a. By 1915 Harrison was the only large landowner. In the early 1930s the estate belonged to a Mrs. Kittow;[99] in 1934 she sold it to William Forse, after whose death in 1952 it passed to his son John (d. 1989);[1] John's son William retained it in 1993.

The medieval manor house of Barnham manor mentioned from 1253[2] seems likely to have stood either on the site of its successor Barnham Court or in the close east of it. In 1337 it had a dovecot and two gardens.[3]

Barnham Court[4] is of red brick and has a north-east front of five bays, with two superimposed orders of pilasters and prominent entablatures of cut and moulded brick, above which there are shaped gables surmounted by small pediments alternately segmental and triangular. The pedimented brick doorcase has Doric pilasters against a rusticated surround. The plan is double-pile with four very tall chimneystacks along the side walls

65 W.S.R.O., MP 814, f. [1].

66 O.S. Map 1/25,000, SU 80/90 (1981 edn.).

67 *V.C.H. Suss.* i. 431. The place mentioned in the will of King Alfred (d. 899) was Burnham (Som.), *pace* ibid. 483: P. H. Sawyer, *A.-S. Charters*, p. 422.

68 Cf. *Cal. Doc. France*, ed. Round, pp. 328–9, in which Rob. de Haye grants Barnham ch. to Lessay abbey (Manche); *V.C.H. Suss.* iv. 143. Rest of para. mainly based on ibid.; *Complete Peerage*, s.v. St. John; Winchester.

69 *Cal. Chart. R.* 1226–57, 123.

70 e.g. *S.R.S.* lxvii. 104; *Cal. Inq. p.m.* ii, pp. 83–4; viii, p. 50; ix, pp. 38, 243.

71 *S.R.S.* vii, p. 2; *Cal. Pat.* 1247–58, 245.

72 *Cal. Inq. p.m.* ii, pp. 83–4; iv, pp. 61–2.

73 e.g. *Feud. Aids*, v. 143.

74 *Cal. Inq. p.m.* viii, p. 50.

75 Ibid. ix, pp. 37–9. Wm. Trussel, described as lord in 1341, was Crown lessee during Edm.'s minority: ibid.; *Inq. Non.* (Rec. Com.), 368.

76 *Cal. Pat.* 1247–58, 173; 1292–1301, 482.

77 e.g. *Cal. Inq. p.m.* ix, p. 243; xvii, p. 166; *Blk. Prince's Reg.* iv. 373–4; *Feud. Aids*, v. 155; vi. 524; B.L. Add. MS. 39488, f. 190.

78 B.L. Add. MS. 39495, ff. 24–5.

79 *Cal. Inq. p.m. Hen. VII*, i, pp. 353–4.

80 B.L. Add. Ch. 65771.

81 *L. & P. Hen. VIII*, xvii, p. 99.

82 *Cal. Pat.* 1569–72, pp. 44–5.

83 A.C.M., M 532, ff. [18, 20v. from end]. The Crown licence of 1596 to Chas. Howard, Ld. Howard of Effingham, to alienate the man. to Wm. Browne was presumably retrospective: B.L. Add. MS. 39394, f. 12; cf. *S.R.S.* xix. 22.

84 *S.R.S.* xxix, p. 55; cf. B.L. Add. MS. 39394, f. 13.

85 W.S.R.O., Add. MS. 13256 (TS. cat.).

86 *Goodwood Estate Archives*, i, ed. F. W. Steer and J. Venables, p. 67.

87 Berry, *Suss. Geneal.* annot. Comber, 76; *V.C.H. Suss.* iv. 143–4; *S.R.S.* li, *passim*; W.S.R.O., Goodwood MSS. E1, pp. 11, 86, 222; E2, *passim*; E4, *passim*.

88 *Goodwood Estate Archives*, i, pp. 25–6.

89 *Cowdray Archives*, ed. A. Dibben, i, p. 80; Berry, op. cit. 100; W.S.R.O., Harris MS. 621 (TS. cat.).

90 Berry, op. cit. 141; W.S.R.O., Add. MS. 1807 (TS. cat.); ibid. Harris MSS. 621–2 (TS. cat.); cf. ibid. Goodwood MS. E4996.

91 Berry, op. cit. 141; W.S.R.O., Add. MS. 1808 (TS. cat.); ibid. Raper MSS., leases, 1811, 1819. Frances received the Barnham man. demesne fm. at the partition of John's estate between her and her sister Katharina in 1780: ibid. Add. MS. 999 (TS. cat.).

92 Berry, op. cit. 290–1; W.S.R.O., Add. MS. 4565.

93 W.S.R.O., TD/W 10.

94 Elwes & Robinson, *W. Suss.* 24.

95 *Lavington Estate Archives*, ed. F. W. Steer, p. 60; *Goodwood Estate Archives*, i, p. 102; W.S.R.O., Add. MSS. 999, 1807–8 (TS. cat.); 4553; ibid. Raper MSS., leases of Barnham fm. 1771, 1819.

96 Horsfield, *Hist. Suss.* ii. 115; W.S.R.O., TD/W 10.

97 Mon. in chyd.; cf. W.S.R.O., SP 101.

98 *Kelly's Dir. Suss.* (1887); cf. W.S.R.O., Add. MS. 4575.

99 *Kelly's Dir. Suss.* (1899 and later edns.); W.S.R.O., IR 12, f. 2.

1 Inf. from Mr. W. Forse, Barnham Ct. fm.; mons. in chyd.

2 *Cal. Pat.* 1247–58, 173.

3 P.R.O., C 135/49, no. 25, m. 2.

4 Described and illus. at *Country Life*, 28 Oct. 1916, pp. 2–6.

BARNHAM COURT IN 1876

and a massive oak staircase in the centre of the rear block. The original entrance was probably across the end of the south-eastern room, since divided.

Stylistically the building belongs to the group of 'Artisan Mannerist' houses of the mid 17th century, other examples of which are Albourne Place, Ford Place, and Kew Palace near London;[5] the same bricklayer was perhaps responsible for both Barnham Court and Kew Palace.[6] Since the lord of the manor then lived elsewhere, Barnham Court was clearly built by a lessee, presumably someone with City of London connexions, like the builders of other such houses.[7] Nothing, however, is known of him or of the date of the building.[8] In 1670 it was assessed for 12 hearths.[9]

For most of its history Barnham Court has been a farmhouse rather than a gentleman's house.[10] The interior was remodelled in the early 19th century, and the single-storeyed 17th-century service wing abutting the south-eastern side of the house was extended upwards and south-eastwards in matching style at the same period. The present dining room, formerly the kitchen, was refitted in the 20th century with 17th-century-style panelling and a moulded plaster ceiling.

A possibly 16th-century barn south of the

5 Below, Ford, manor; *V.C.H. Suss.* vi (3), 126; Nairn & Pevsner, *Suss.* 100.

6 Inf. from Mr. N. Cooper, Royal Com. on Hist. Mons. of Eng.

7 *V.C.H. Suss.* vi (3), 126; J. Summerson, *Archit. in Brit. 1530 to 1830* (1969), 89.

8 The link with the Shelley fam. of Michelgrove in Clapham claimed by Elwes & Robinson, *W. Suss.* 24, is unproven; cf. Dallaway, *Hist. W. Suss.* ii (1) (1819), 41; below, church.

9 P.R.O., E 179/191/410, pt. 2, rot. 3: the largest ho. in the par. Cf. W.S.R.O., Ep. I/29/13/36.

10 B.L. Add. MS. 5699, f. 26; *Kelly's Dir. Suss.* (1845 and later edns.).

house, *c.* 150 ft. (46 metres) long with a queen-post roof and two lateral entrances, was demolished in the 1960s.[11]

About 1762 an avenue of trees ran north-eastwards from the entrance front of the house.[12] A small formal garden with crisscrossing paths was laid out behind the building in the 19th century;[13] tall hedges of box and yew survived in 1916[14] but most had gone by 1992. Land to the north between the house and the Barnham brook, including former marlpits,[15] was laid out as a wild garden in the late 1930s, a pond north-west of the house being extended southwards in the 1970s to surround a high island approached by a bridge from the east.[16]

The *RECTORY* estate, which belonged to Boxgrove priory from the late 13th century or earlier,[17] in 1324–5 had a house, two barns, 48 a. of arable, and 3 a. of meadow, besides free tenants.[18] After 1440 it also included all the vicarial tithes and glebe.[19] A portion of tithes descended with Bilsham manor in Yapton between 1568 and 1727.[20] After the Dissolution the reversion of the estate was conveyed in 1537 to Sir William Fitzwilliam,[21] created in the same year earl of Southampton (d. 1542),[22] but by 1566 the rectory had passed to John Standen and Nicholas Knight,[23] then or later Standen's son-in-law.[24] After Nicholas's death in 1584 his son John[25] and others conveyed it in 1587 to John Tilly,[26] apparently the tenant,[27] who died in 1596 or 1597.[28]

Later members of the Tilly family to have the estate were John (fl. 1643),[29] John (fl. 1648–63),[30] Mary (fl. 1673), and the second John's sons George (fl. 1680–4; d. by 1695) and Samuel (fl. 1680–1701), who owned it jointly with Edward Madgwick. In 1695 it was described as a house and 90 a.[31] In 1701 Samuel and Edward conveyed it to William Madgwick.[32] A Mr. Madgwick was described as impropriator in 1724,[33] and William Madgwick in 1758.[34] In 1762 Edward Madgwick conveyed the estate to Joseph Postlethwaite,[35] occupier of Parsonage farm[36] in succession to his father Henry (d. 1730).[37] By 1770 Joseph had been succeeded by his son and namesake,[38] after whose death 1824 × 1827 the farm descended to his daughters Mary Ann, wife of Thomas Tourle, and Susannah, wife of John Rickman, as tenants in common.[39] By 1849, when the farm had only 8 a. in the parish, they had been succeeded by Joseph Legg Postlethwaite and John Joseph Tourle, described as joint owners, who at the commutation of tithes in that year received a rent charge of £302 10*s.*[40] A 'Mr. Rickman', perhaps W. C. Rickman, later patron of the living, was described as lay rector in 1865.[41]

The front range of Parsonage Farmhouse is early 17th-century, with timber-framed walls on a brick plinth; in 1648 the building had a parlour, a hall, and various chambers, and in 1730 there were a study, several chambers, and garrets.[42] A service wing was added to the north-west, probably in the early 18th century.[43] The walls of the older range were largely replaced in brick and flint in the 18th century, the front wall was rebuilt in chequered brick in the early 19th, and the Lutyens-style porch with square wooden piers was added in the 20th.

John Bonham Smith had 225 a. in Barnham in 1747 of which at least 175 a. had passed by *c.* 1762 to his son and heir Henry Bonham. The latter estate, which included Manor cottage in Church Lane, later belonged to John Woods.[44] Joseph Woods (d. 1800) settled it on his granddaughters Elizabeth and Maria James.[45] It was presumably the farm of 146 a. occupied by Joseph Murrell in 1794,[46] and seems to have passed to the dukes of Richmond, who *c.* 1848 had Manor cottage and 123 a. in the parish, divided into two holdings.[47] From 1869 or earlier that land formed a single farm of 168 a.,[48] which in 1919–20 was bought by West Sussex county council for smallholdings.[49]

The yardland called Borham in 1086, which a free man had held in 1066 and which Morin then held of earl Roger,[50] may have been in Barnham; it is not otherwise recorded.

In the mid 18th century and later Shipley and West Dean churches and St. Bartholomew's church, Chichester, had glebe lying within the parish.[51]

ECONOMIC HISTORY. Agriculture.

Arable fields named in the Middle Ages were la

11 S.M.R. 1450; illus. at Barnham W.I. scrapbook [1949], p. [37] (copy in possession of Mrs. R. Collins, W. Barnham).
12 W.S.R.O., Goodwood MS. E4996.
13 Ibid. SP 101.
14 *Country Life*, 28 Oct. 1916, p. 6.
15 W.S.R.O., TD/W 10.
16 Inf. from Mr. Forse.
17 *Tax. Eccl.* (Rec. Com.), 139; cf. *S.R.S.* lix, pp. 45, 143–4, 152, 171.
18 P.R.O., E 106/8/19, rot. 8; cf. *Inq. Non.* (Rec. Com.), 368. A portion of tithes belonged before 1162 to the abbey of La Lucerne (Manche): *Cal. Doc. France*, ed. Round, p. 281.
19 Below, church.
20 *S.R.S.* xix. 77; xx. 508; W.S.R.O., Add. MSS. 8811–12 (TS. cat.).
21 *L. & P. Hen. VIII*, xii (2), p. 352.
22 *Complete Peerage*, s.v. Southampton; P.R.O., C 142/70, no. 28.
23 *S.R.S.* lviii, p. 80.
24 P.R.O., C 2/Eliz. I/T 11/44.
25 *S.R.S.* xxxiii, p. 18, wrongly calling him Ric.
26 Ibid. xix. 22.
27 W.S.R.O., Ep. I/23/4, f. 32v.
28 B.L. Add. MS. 39476, f. 177.
29 *S.R.S.* xix. 23; cf. *S.N.Q.* xvi. 47.
30 W.S.R.O., Ep. I/29/13/27; *S.R.S.* xix. 23.
31 B.L. Add. MS. 39476, ff. 175 and v., 177; W.S.R.O., Harris MSS. 538, 554 (TS. cat.).
32 *S.R.S.* xix. 23.
33 Ibid. lxxviii. 59.
34 W.S.R.O., Ep. I/54/5.
35 *Goodwood Estate Archives*, i, p. 71; cf. W.S.R.O., Goodwood MS. E4996.
36 W.S.R.O., Ep. I/54/5; ibid. Harris MS. 524 (TS. cat.); below, this section.
37 Ibid. Add. MSS. 7711–12 (TS. cat.); ibid. Raper MSS., will of Hen. Postlethwaite, 1730.
38 Ibid. Add. MSS. 321; 1282 (TS. cat.); cf. ibid. 4553.
39 Ibid. 1287 (TS. cat.); *S.R.S.* xix. 23.
40 W.S.R.O., TD/W 10.
41 B.L. Add. MS. 39364, f. 16; cf. below, church.
42 W.S.R.O., Ep. I/29/13/27, 57.
43 Cf. datestone of 1733 with initials JP for Jos. Postlethwaite.
44 W.S.R.O., Goodwood MS. E4996; ibid. MP 3427.
45 Ibid. Add. MS. 5776 (TS. cat.).
46 Ibid. 4553; cf. ibid. 5776 (TS. cat.).
47 W.S.R.O., TD/W 10; cf. Horsfield, *Hist. Suss.* ii. 115; *Kelly's Dir. Suss.* (1845); *Rep. Com. on Children and Women in Agric.* 86.
48 W.S.R.O., Goodwood MSS. E5563–5; ibid. IR 12, f. 1.
49 Ibid. Add. MSS. 6096, deed, 1917, and plan of smallholdings, 1919; 6097, deeds, 1919–20; ibid. Goodwood MS. E21, p. 23; ibid. SP 339.
50 *V.C.H. Suss.* i. 432.
51 W.S.R.O., Goodwood MSS. E4, p. 137; E9, f. 7v.; E4996, E5038; ibid. QDD/6/W 32; ibid. TD/W 10.

Rude,[52] Hayley,[53] and Northfield. The last named perhaps lay east of Church Lane,[54] and from the topography seems likely to be the same as Hill field mentioned in the 17th century.[55] Town and East fields recorded in 1543[56] have not been located. The instruction to all manor tenants to repair fences (*clausur'*) in the arable fields in the same year indicates that at least partial inclosure had taken place.[57]

Crops grown in 1341 included flax and hemp. Arable farming was then the chief land use, the ninth of sheaves being worth nine times those of fleeces and lambs together.[58] In the 17th and 18th centuries wheat was the main crop, others being barley, vetches, peas, oats, and tares.[59] A rotation of wheat, barley, and peas and vetches with or without oats may be indicated in the 17th century.[60] Clover was grown by 1713.[61]

A common meadow called the Long mead was mentioned from 1298,[62] and geese and ducks were prohibited from feeding in the common meadows in 1543.[63] The common brooks mentioned from 1543, perhaps the same, evidently lay in the southern tip of the parish. In that year they were ordered to be protected by a bank on all sides.[64] Tenants of the manor had pasture rights there for small numbers of cattle from the late 16th century.[65]

What was called the 'common brook of meadow or pasture' in 1747 seems likely to have been the same land. The nine tenants who had rights there agreed in that year to mow only part of it in future, and to separate the two sections by a ditch and fences.[66] The section that remained meadow was 72 a. in area *c.* 1762.[67] About 1848 five landowners had between 1½ and 27½ beast leazes, i.e. rights of pasture, in the common brook, then 84 a.[68] The brook was inclosed in 1853 under the General Inclosure Act, Richard Cosens' executors receiving 31 a., Charles Crosbie 21 a., the duke of Richmond 25 a., and the two other commoners smaller areas.[69]

Land along the Barnham brook in the northwest was perhaps always in severalty. The manor demesne farm had 20 a. of meadow in 1086[70] and larger amounts later: 50 a. in 1302,[71] 29 a. in 1337,[72] 40 a. in 1687,[73] and *c.* 100 a. in 1784.[74] Other landowners had smaller pieces in the Middle Ages, for instance the chantry estate and the rectory.[75] At least one estate based outside the parish had meadow within it: the Middleton manor demesne farm, which had 3 a. in 1606.[76] In the 17th century and later meadow on Barnham manor demesne farm included the Tithing and Chantry meads, afterwards called the First and Farthest tithing meadows (8 a.), along the Barnham brook;[77] the first hay crop from each belonged respectively to the rectory estate and another farm by 1783.[78]

Sheep and pigs as well as cattle were widely kept in the parish in the 17th and 18th centuries.[79]

The demesne farm of Barnham manor had 348 a. including 284 a. of arable in 1302,[80] and 319 a. including 290 a. of arable in 1337.[81] That farm was still the largest in the parish in the late 17th and 18th centuries, when it had 190–210 a., divided roughly equally between arable and pasture.[82] About 1762 it included other land, making a total acreage of 263 a.[83] In the mid and later 18th century it was held on leases of 14 or 15 years, and in the early 19th century on a 7-year lease.[84] The two flocks of 200–300 sheep recorded in 1671 and 1776[85] seem to have been on the demesne farm.

There were 12 *villani* and 12 cottars on the manor in 1086.[86] In 1302 there were 12 free tenants; 7 customary tenants holding single yardlands who owed two days' work a week for most of the year, and daily work except on Sundays and holidays during harvest; 11 customary tenants holding half yardlands whose works were assessed at half the rate stated; and 16 cottars who owed two days' work a week during harvest.[87] In the late 16th century there were both freeholders and tenants for life; some holdings were then still described as whole or half yardlands.[88]

Thirteen tenants held land of the manor *c.* 1762, most having a house or what was apparently the site of one along Church Lane. The largest holdings apart from Barnham manor demesne farm were those of Henry Bonham (175 a.), Joseph Postlethwaite of Parsonage farm (76 a.),

52 *S.R.S.* lix, p. 34.
53 W.S.R.O., Add. MS. 12258 (TS. cat.).
54 *S.R.S.* lix, p. 171; cf. ibid. xxxvi. 20.
55 Ibid. xxxvi. 191; *Goodwood Estate Archives*, i, p. 102; W.S.R.O., Add. MSS. 7711, 12425 (TS. cat.); ibid. S.A.S. MS. B 467 (TS. cat.); cf. Hill Lane leading E. from the ch.
56 W.S.R.O., PHA 6683, f. 15v.
57 Ibid. f. 16; cf. P.R.O., C 66/935, m. 1, naming ½ a. and ¼ a. in the 'com. field' of Barnham in 1558.
58 *Inq. Non.* (Rec. Com.), 368; for hemp cf. P.R.O., C 66/935, m. 1; W.S.R.O., Ep. I/29/13/5.
59 W.S.R.O., Ep. I/29/13.
60 Ibid. Ep. I/29/13/32, 42.
61 Ibid. Ep. I/29/13/50, 56–7.
62 Ibid. Add. MSS. 5991, 12425 (TS. cat.); ibid. S.A.S. MS. B 467 (TS. cat.).
63 Ibid. PHA 6683, f. 16v.
64 Ibid.
65 A.C.M., M 532, f. [18v. from end]; W.S.R.O., Add. MSS. 1810, 3027, 12425, 12440 (TS. cat.); ibid. Goodwood MS. E2, p. 27; ibid. S.A.S. MS. B 467 (TS. cat.); *Goodwood Estate Archives*, i, pp. 102–3.
66 W.S.R.O., Add. MS. 21441.
67 Ibid. Goodwood MS. E4996.
68 Ibid. TD/W 10.
69 Ibid. QDD/6/W 17.
70 *V.C.H. Suss.* i. 431.
71 P.R.O., C 133/105, no. 6, m. 2.
72 Ibid. C 135/49, no. 25, m. 2.
73 Ibid. E 134/3 Jas. II East./16, rot. 3.
74 W.S.R.O., Harris MS. 625.
75 *S.R.S.* xxiii, p. 1; xxxvi. 20; *Cal. Pat.* 1321–4, 434; P.R.O., E 106/8/19, rot. 8; for the chantry, below, church.
76 W.S.R.O., Add. MS. 2027, pp. 31, 33.
77 Ibid. Add. MS. 321; ibid. Goodwood MS. E4996; ibid. TD/W 10, giving location; P.R.O., E 134/3 Jas. II East./16, rot. 5.
78 *S.R.S.* xix. 23; P.R.O., E 134/3 Jas. II East./16, rot. 5; W.S.R.O., Add. MS. 321; ibid. Goodwood MS. E4996; ibid. Harris MS. 625; ibid. QDD/6/W 32; ibid. TD/W 10.
79 W.S.R.O., Ep. I/29/13.
80 P.R.O., C 133/105, no. 6, m. 2.
81 Ibid. C 135/49, no. 25, m. 2; cf. *Inq. Non.* (Rec. Com.), 368.
82 P.R.O., E 134/3 Jas. II East./16, rot. 3; W.S.R.O., Add. MS. 1807 (TS. cat.); ibid. Harris MS. 625; ibid. Raper MSS., lease, 1771.
83 W.S.R.O., Goodwood MS. E4996.
84 Ibid. Add. MSS. 1807–8 (TS. cat.); ibid. Raper MSS., leases, 1771, 1811, 1819.
85 Ibid. Ep. I/29/13/36, 64.
86 *V.C.H. Suss.* i. 431. On the yardland called Borham there was 1 cottar: ibid. 432.
87 P.R.O., C 133/105, no. 6, m. 2.
88 A.C.M., M 532, f. [18 and v. from end].

John Hasler (83 a.), and William Murrell (37 a.), and there were then also seven cottages said to be held freehold.[89] By the 18th century some, possibly all, copyholds were held for three lives;[90] they could be sublet.[91] There were still nine freeholds in the early 19th century, when a later Joseph Postlethwaite held the six remaining copyhold tenements and one other tenant held a piece of waste land, the site of a cottage, at the will of the lord.[92] At least two farmers in the 17th and 18th centuries had land in neighbouring parishes too.[93]

Other tenants in the Middle Ages held land of the rectory[94] and chantry[95] estates.

About 1848 the chief holdings were the manor demesne farm, called Barnham farm (265 a.), a farm belonging to Richard Cosens' executors (159 a.), and two belonging to the duke of Richmond (59 a. and 64 a.); all were worked from sites close to the church.[96] The two pairs of farms were amalgamated soon afterwards, and in the 1860s Richard Cosens owned and occupied *c.* 500 a.,[97] while the duke of Richmond's farm, also called Barnham farm (168 a.), was let to C. F. Field on a 14-year lease by 1869.[98] The Cosens farm had been divided into two farms of 187 a. and 166 a., each called Church farm, by *c.* 1910, when the duke of Richmond's farm remained the same size as before.[99] The farm buildings south of Barnham Court already occupied a large area in the mid 19th century,[1] as they still did in 1993. Parsonage farm in 1881 had 60 a.[2]

Most land was still arable in the early 19th century, roughly two thirds of the parish being under crops in 1819;[3] in the late 1840s at least one farm practised a four-course rotation.[4] The very inconvenient intermingling of small closes belonging to different holdings, characteristic of land inclosed at an early date,[5] was redressed in 1862, when *c.* 325 a. were redistributed by agreement into consolidated blocks under the General Inclosure Act.[6] The larger closes that resulted, some over 50 a., allowed cultivation by steam power,[7] and at the same time pipe drains were laid through part of the parish.[8]

From the later 19th century pastoral farming gained in importance. Sheep fattening was apparently practised in 1867,[9] and 1,220 sheep were listed in 1875.[10] One farm specialized in dairying from 1887 or earlier,[11] and by 1909 the proportion of oats to other corn crops grown had greatly increased over what it had been 35 years before.[12]

After 1918 West Sussex county council bought land in the eastern half of the parish as smallholdings for ex-servicemen.[13] About 20–25 were created, each with a house, the tenants disposing of their produce at Barnham market in Eastergate. Most were of 1–3 a. and were used as market gardens[14] or for raising pigs and poultry,[15] but Church farm, which was much larger, had both arable land and grazing for a dairy herd founded in 1921 that still flourished in 1978. The scheme was not as successful as had been hoped, due to lack of experience in the smallholders and the awkward size of holdings; some tenants had bought their land by 1951,[16] other holdings became part-time, and by 1965 much land had been added to adjacent farms. Besides Church farm one other smallholding and one other small farm specialized in dairying in 1965. Two smallholdings then included small retail shops.

The brookland in the south end of the parish was described in 1920 as some of the richest in the neighbourhood.[17] In the later 1930s Barnham Court farm had a prizewinning flock, but it had been dispersed by *c.* 1950.[18] The farm had *c.* 400 a. in 1949[19] and 1965; at the latter date there were both arable land and a herd of Friesians.[20]

In 1985, of 307 ha. (759 a.) returned, three fifths was in owner occupation. Barnham Court farm remained the largest holding and there were 19 others, including market-garden land, of which 13 were less than 2 ha. in area and the rest under 40 ha.; three were specialist dairy holdings and 17 were worked part-time, while the total number of workers in agriculture and market gardening was 79. Land was then equally divided between arable and pasture; the chief crop was wheat (87 ha.) and 439, mostly dairy, cattle were listed.[21] Barnham Court farm in 1993 was a mixed arable and dairy farm, growing wheat, peas, and maize for cattle.[22]

MARKET GARDENING. Cider was made in Barnham in 1341[23] and hops may have been grown in 1637.[24] Orchards were mentioned in 1742[25] and 1839.[26] Three 'gardeners', perhaps market

89 W.S.R.O., Goodwood MS. E4996.
90 Ibid. E2, p. 27; E4996.
91 Ibid. E1, p. 87; E2, p. 61.
92 Ibid. E11, p. 1; E12, p. 1; cf. ibid. E2, p. 27; E9, f. 8.
93 W.S.R.O., Ep. I/29/13/5, 49.
94 *S.R.S.* lix, pp. 193–4; *Inq. Non.* (Rec. Com.), 368; P.R.O., E 106/8/19, rot. 8.
95 *Cal. Pat.* 1321–4, 434.
96 W.S.R.O., TD/W 10.
97 *Rep. Com. on Children and Women in Agric.* 86; cf. P.R.O., HO 107/1652, f. 233v.; W.S.R.O., SP 101.
98 W.S.R.O., Goodwood MS. E5563; cf. ibid. E19, p. 38.
99 W.S.R.O., IR 12, ff. 1–2; cf. above, manor.
1 W.S.R.O., TD/W 10; O.S. Map 6", Suss. LXII (1880 edn.).
2 P.R.O., RG 11/1125, f. 68.
3 Dallaway, *Hist. W. Suss.* ii (1) (1819), 40; cf. W.S.R.O., Add. MS. 4553; ibid. TD/W 10.
4 W.S.R.O., Add. MS. 1810 (TS. cat.).
5 e.g. ibid. Add. MS. 4553; ibid. Goodwood MS. E4996.
6 Ibid. QDD/6/W 32.
7 Ibid. SP 101; *O.S. Area Bk.* (1877).
8 *Rep. Com. on Children and Women in Agric.* 87; W.S.R.O., SP 101.
9 *Rep. Com. on Children and Women in Agric.* 87.
10 P.R.O., MAF 68/433; cf. W.S.R.O., MP 2347, f. 12.
11 *Kelly's Dir. Suss.* (1887 and later edns.).
12 P.R.O., MAF 68/433, 2371.
13 Para. based mainly on W.S.R.O., Add. MS. 6096, plan of smallholdings, 1919; ibid. MP 814, ff. [36, 45]; 2347, f. 10; Jesse, *Agric. of Suss.* 121.
14 Cf. below, this section (mkt. gardening).
15 Cf. *Kelly's Dir. Suss.* (1927 and later edns.).
16 *Bognor Regis Observer*, 17 Nov. 1951.
17 W.S.R.O., LD IV/AO 17A/2.
18 *S.C.M.* xxx. 54.
19 Barnham W.I. scrapbook [1949], p. [36] (copy in possession of Mrs. R. Collins, W. Barnham).
20 W.S.R.O., MP 814, f. [45].
21 M.A.F.F., agric. statistics, 1985.
22 Inf. from Mr. W. Forse, Barnham Ct. fm.
23 *Inq. Non.* (Rec. Com.), 368.
24 W.S.R.O., Ep. I/29/13/20.
25 Ibid. Holmes, Campbell & Co. MS. 953 (TS. cat.).
26 *Goodwood Estate Archives*, i, ed. F. W. Steer and J. Venables, p. 103; cf. W.S.R.O., Goodwood MS. E14, f. 9v.

gardeners, were recorded between 1813 and 1827[27] and two market gardeners in 1845.[28] In the 1870s there were 1¼ a. of orchards on the west side of Church Lane.[29]

The later growth of market gardening in Barnham and Eastergate was due in the first place to the favourable local climate and easy rail transport after 1864 for perishable goods, and secondly to the arrival of the Marshall family *c.* 1880.[30] In 1881 the brothers Harry and Sidney Marshall, though only 21 and 18 respectively, together ran a nursery, employing 13 men and a boy,[31] on two sites: one north of Yapton Road known as the 'old nursery', and the other north-west of the church between the Barnham brook and the railway.[32] The company was known in 1887 as Marshall Bros., but by 1895 it had been divided in two, thereafter trading as S. S. Marshall Ltd. and H. R. Marshall.

The eastern part of the nurseries north of Yapton Road thereafter belonged to H. R. Marshall, and the rest of the land to S. S. Marshall Ltd.,[33] by 1907 Barnham Nurseries Ltd., which also had a large nursery in Eastergate.[34] S. S. Marshall was described as nurseryman, 'market grower', and landscape gardener in 1895 and the firm were also fruit growers in 1899, the fruit farm of 23 a. occupying the land beyond the Barnham brook.[35] H. R. Marshall was a nurseryman, florist, and seedsman in 1895 and also grew fruit in 1903; he had a shop at Brighton in 1895 and one at Southsea (Hants) in 1899.

By 1940 Barnham Nurseries Ltd. had over 300 a. in the Barnham area, growing fruit trees, roses, ornamental trees, and shrubs, and undertaking garden design,[36] as later.[37] The orchards west of the Barnham brook expanded further west across the railway line by 1950.[38] By that date, however, the firm's total acreage had contracted to 230 a. and by 1955 it was 100 a.[39] A 'garden centre' employing *c.* 45 men was opened on the Yapton Road site in 1965[40] but closed in 1981.[41]

The other large firm in the parish, Toynbee's Nurseries,[42] originated in a county council smallholding of *c.* 19 a. further east in Yapton Road held by Frank Toynbee from 1919. At first it grew market-garden produce and soft fruit, but in the 1920s it diversified into landscape gardening, serving especially owners of houses in the new residential estates at Middleton. The firm was later alternatively known as Croftway Nurseries.[43] After 1945 a mail order department supplied both the home and overseas markets, and in 1962 all sorts of plants, trees, and shrubs were sold, besides soft fruit, culinary herbs, grass seed, manure, and peat. In 1965, when the premises extended to *c.* 31 a., 30–40 men were employed. The business survived in different ownership in 1996.

Other market gardeners, including county council smallholders, were mentioned in the 1920s and 30s.[44] In 1992 there were a firm of fruit growers and another specializing in house plants north-west of the Barnham brook, and many small market-garden holdings in the east part of the parish; of the latter some had glasshouses, at least three specialized in flowers,[45] and several had shops on their premises.

MILLS. The mill recorded on the manor in 1086[46] was presumably a water mill on the Barnham brook. A manorial windmill of unknown location was mentioned between 1230 and 1683.[47] Four millers are known by name between 1678 and 1774; one, in 1682, kept stock and had at least 15 a. under crops.[48]

There was a post windmill on the site of the present mill in Yapton Road by *c.* 1762 and perhaps by 1724.[49] After its destruction in 1827 it was replaced before 1830 by the existing four-storeyed tower mill. The woman miller who had it between 1845 and 1862 was also described as a baker.[50] From *c.* 1880[51] until its closure *c.* 1985 the mill was worked by members of the related Baker and Reynolds families. In 1886 Maurice and John Baker were also bakers and dealers in malt and hops, and linseed and cotton cakes, additionally working Aldingbourne mill.[52] From 1905 the business also included that of corn merchant, with retail shops in Littlehampton[53] and Bognor.[54] A steam engine was added to supplement wind power *c.* 1890,[55] a gas engine *c.* 1910, and an electric engine after 1945.[56] Wind ceased to be used in the 1920s or 30s, and the sweeps

27 W.S.R.O., Par. 13/1/2/1.
28 *Kelly's Dir. Suss.* (1845).
29 P.R.O., MAF 68/433; O.S. Map 6", Suss. LXII (1880 edn.).
30 *Barnham and Eastergate Past and Present*, ed. T. Hudson et al. 8–9. Rest of para. based mainly on *Kelly's Dir. Suss.* (1882 and later edns.)
31 P.R.O., RG 11/1125, f. 68v.
32 O.S. Map 6", Suss. LXII. SE., SW. (1899 edn.); W.S.R.O., Add. MS. 24178, undated plan of nurseries.
33 W.S.R.O., Add. MS. 24178, undated plan of nurseries; ibid. IR 12, ff. 5–7; ibid. MP 2347, f. 2. Rest of para. based mainly on *Kelly's Dir. Suss.* (1895 and later edns.).
34 Cf. below, Eastergate, econ. hist. (mkt. gardening).
35 W.S.R.O., IR 12, f. 5; cf. P.R.O., MAF 68/2371. For site, O.S. Map 1/2,500, Suss. LXII. 11 (1912 edn.).
36 *Kelly's Dir. Bognor Regis* (1940), advt. at front.
37 W.S.R.O., Add. MSS. 41253–4.
38 O.S. Map 6", Suss. LXII. SE., SW. (1951 edn.).
39 W.S.R.O., Add. MSS. 41253–4.
40 Ibid. MP 814, f. [29].
41 Ibid. 2793.
42 Para. mainly based on Barnham W.I. scrapbook [1949], p. [25] (copy in possession of Mrs. R. Collins, W. Barnham); W.S.R.O., Add. MS. 41255; ibid. MP 814, f. [29].
43 Cf. *Kelly's Dir. Suss.* (1934).
44 Ibid. (1922 and later edns.); above, this section (agric.).
45 Cf. *W. Suss. Gaz.* 28 Jan. 1993.
46 *V.C.H. Suss.* i. 431.
47 *Cal. Chart. R.* 1226–57, 123; P.R.O., C 133/105, no. 6, m. 2; C 135/49, no. 25, m. 2; W.S.R.O., Raper MSS., deed of windmill and land, 1683. If the highway mentioned in 1247 was Ch. Lane it possibly occupied the later site: *S.R.S.* lix, p. 171.
48 W.S.R.O., Ep. I/29/13/39–40, 58, 63.
49 *250 Yrs. of Mapmaking in Suss.* ed. H. Margary, pls. 5, 14, 19; W.S.R.O., Goodwood MS. E4996; illus. at ibid. PD 2153. Rest of para. based mainly on ibid. MP 2347, f. 6; M. Brunnarius, *Windmills of Suss.* 73–5; *Bognor Regis Observer*, 22 Feb. 1963; cf. M. Cutten and V. May, *The Mill and the Murrell* (Barnham, 1992).
50 *Kelly's Dir. Suss.* (1845 and later edns.).
51 Cf. ibid. (1882).
52 Ibid. (1887); Pike, *Dir. SW. Suss.* (1886–7).
53 *Kelly's Dir. Suss.* (1905 and later edns.); *Suss. Ind. Arch.* (1972), p. 18; W.S.R.O., MP 3152, p. 23.
54 *Kelly's Dir. Suss.* (1922), s.v. Bognor.
55 Cf. ibid. (1895).
56 Cf. ibid. (1934); *W. Suss. Gaz.* 23 Sept. 1976; W.S.R.O., MP 814, f. [21]; ibid. SP 743.

and fan stage were removed from the building in 1958.[57] In 1979 some animal feedstuffs were still processed on site and others bought in for retailing. Six men were employed in 1965.[58]

OTHER TRADES. Trades recorded in the 16th and 17th centuries were those of brewer,[59] butcher, sawyer, shoemaker,[60] and blacksmith.[61] Between 1813 and 1845 tailors, bakers, a grocer, a farrier, and a carpenter were mentioned,[62] but the opening of the canal through the parish in 1823 seems, in the absence of any wharf, to have had no effect on occupations. After 1866 licensees of the Murrell Arms inn successively carried on the trades of carpenter, wheelwright, and blacksmith.[63]

The railway provided employment after 1864; in 1881 two railway porters, a railway clerk, and a ticket collector lived in Barnham.[64] The subsequent growth of population brought further occupations in the later 19th century and early 20th: those of bricklayer,[65] stone mason, patten maker, chimney sweep, and cycle repairer.[66] The three 'agricultural' engine drivers listed in 1881 were probably employees of the firm of Sparks in Yapton.[67]

The smithy at the Murrell Arms ceased working at some time after 1910[68] and the post office stores nearby, which in 1916 dealt in groceries, drapery, boots and shoes, medicines, china and glass, and hardware,[69] closed after 1938.[70] In the early 20th century goods from Chichester were delivered by carrier.[71] A butcher's shop founded by 1962[72] still existed in Yapton Road in 1993, when there was also a large shop selling farm and other produce by Barnham windmill.

A building on the embankment north-east of the railway bridge accommodated at different times a butcher, a fishmonger, a grocer, a hairdresser, and a vet;[73] in 1992 it was a shop dealing in garden machinery. Further north in Lake Lane at the same date were a garage and general stores.

A brickfield on the south side of Yapton Road was worked at least between 1910 and 1913.[74]

By 1965 some residents travelled daily to work in London or other towns,[75] as still happened in 1993.

LOCAL GOVERNMENT. There are court rolls or draft court rolls for Barnham manor for the years 1448 × 1455,[76] 1543, 1548,[77] 1593, 1596,[78] and 1686–1776.[79] A view of frankpledge was held in the 1540s; there is no later record of it though frankpledge jurisdiction was still claimed in 1629.[80] A sheriff's tourn was also held in 1543.[81]

In the 1540s the view and the court held the assize of bread and of ale, heard cases of assault and one plea of land, managed the common lands, saw to the repair of roads, fences, ditches, and houses, and elected a headborough, an aletaster, and two 'curemen'. By the mid 18th century courts were held between six and eight times a decade, but during the years 1761–76 only five times in all. Besides conveyancing they then continued to oversee the common lands and to present buildings in disrepair. Business was dealt with out of court from 1691. A tithingman still served in 1822.[82]

A manor pound was mentioned in 1566.[83] In 1636 it stood beside the vicarage land,[84] perhaps near the church.

Two churchwardens were recorded between 1548 and 1670 and generally after 1862, but there was usually only one between 1674 and 1861.[85] There was a collector for the poor in 1642[86] and there were two overseers in 1826, when 15 parishioners received permanent and 3 casual relief.[87] A parish poorhouse in Yapton Road east of Church Lane had become two cottages by *c.* 1848[88] and was demolished after 1937.[89] The parish clerk received wages in the late 16th century.[90]

Barnham joined Westhampnett union, later Westhampnett rural district, in 1835. From 1933 it was in Chichester rural district[91] and from 1974 in Arun district.

In 1965 the parish council owned the parish hall next to the site of the poorhouse, and five adjacent allotments.[92]

CHURCH. There was a church in 1086.[93] In 1105 the lord of Barnham, Robert de Haye, gave it to Lessay abbey (Manche), together with a measure of wheat called church scot (*cerchet*).[94] It later passed to Lessay's English priory of

57 S.A.S. libr., album of photos. of Suss. windmills, 1958–9, f. 59.

58 W.S.R.O., MP 814, f. [21]. There is no evidence for another mill called Feaver's mill as stated at *S.C.M.* xi. 739. Hen. Fever apparently worked Barnham mill in the 1860s and 70s: *Kelly's Dir. Suss.* (1866 and later edns.); W.S.R.O., Add. MS. 14317 (f).

59 W.S.R.O., PHA 935, f. 80.

60 Ibid. Ep. I/29/13/21, 41, 44.

61 P.R.O., E 179/191/410, pt. 2, rot. 3.

62 W.S.R.O., Par. 13/1/2/1; *Kelly's Dir. Suss.* (1845).

63 *W. Suss. Gaz.* 15 Sept. 1966; *Kelly's Dir. Suss.* (1874 and later edns.); P.R.O., RG 11/1125, f. 69v.; W.S.R.O., MP 2347, f. 6; O.S. Map 6", Suss. LXII. SE. (1899, 1910 edns.).

64 P.R.O., RG 11/1125, ff. 70–71v.

65 Ibid. f. 70v.

66 *Kelly's Dir. Suss.* (1899 and later edns.).

67 P.R.O., RG 11/1125, ff. 70–71v.; below, Yapton, econ. hist. (other trades and inds.).

68 O.S. Map 6", Suss. LXII. SE. (1913 edn.).

69 W.S.R.O., MP 3152, p. 11.

70 *Kelly's Dir. Suss.* (1938).

71 W.S.R.O., MP 2347, f. 8.

72 *Suss. Trade Guide* (1962), 8 (Earleys) (copy at C.I.H.E. libr., GY 155).

73 W.S.R.O., MP 2347, ff. 7–8; cf. *Kelly's Dir. Suss.* (1915 and later edns.).

74 O.S. Map 6", Suss. LXII. SE. (1913 edn.); W.S.R.O., Add. MS. 25509, applic. for certificate concerning estate duty, 1913; ibid. IR 12, f. 8; M. Beswick, *Brickmaking in Suss.* 180.

75 W.S.R.O., MP 814, f. [1].

76 A.C.M., M 530.

77 W.S.R.O., PHA 935, f. 80; 6683, f. 15.

78 A.C.M., M 532, ff. [18, 20v. from end].

79 W.S.R.O., Goodwood MSS. E1, pp. 11, 86, 222, 235; E2, *passim*; E4, pp. 4, 22, 36, 48, 133.

80 Ibid. Add. MS. 13256 (TS. cat.).

81 Ibid. PHA 6683, f. 15.

82 E.S.R.O., QCR/2/1/EW 2 (46); cf. *S.R.S.* liv. 184.

83 A.C.M., MD 2347, m. 2.

84 W.S.R.O., Ep. I/25/1 (1635, *recte* 1636).

85 Ibid. Ep. I/86/20, f. 17v.; B.L. Add. MS. 39359, ff. 26–31.

86 *S.R.S.* v. 26.

87 W.S.R.O., QCR/2/3/W 5.

88 Ibid. TD/W 10, nos. 45, 59, 69.

89 Barnham W.I. scrapbook [1949], pp. [30–1] (copy in possession of Mrs. R. Collins, W. Barnham).

90 W.S.R.O., Ep. I/23/4, f. 32v.

91 Youngs, *Guide to Local Admin. Units of Eng.* i. 502.

92 W.S.R.O., MP 814, f. [2].

93 *V.C.H. Suss.* i. 431.

94 *S.R.S.* lix, pp. 16–17.

Boxgrove. A vicarage was ordained *c.* 1174 × 1180,[95] but as a result of the substitution of an annual pension for the vicarial tithes and glebe in 1440[96] its status came afterwards to seem unclear. Incumbents from the late 16th century were often 'licensed to serve the cure' or granted sequestration of the endowments[97] rather than instituted; they were called at different times minister,[98] curate,[99] or sequestrator[1] as well as vicar, and the benefice was usually described as a perpetual vicarage[2] or curacy.[3] The union of Barnham with Eastergate was suggested in 1881.[4] From 1983 the two parishes were held by a single priest in charge,[5] and in 1985 Aldingbourne, Barnham, and Eastergate became a single benefice, the parishes remaining distinct. In 1992 they were united as the parish of Aldingbourne, Barnham, and Eastergate.[6]

The advowson of the vicarage belonged to Boxgrove priory until the Dissolution, the bishop of Chichester presenting in 1478 and the archbishop of Canterbury in 1464;[7] thereafter it descended with the rectory[8] until 1762, when it was retained by Edward Madgwick at the sale of that estate. By 1776 it had passed to the duke of Richmond.[9] Between *c.* 1830 and 1862 the bishop was patron[10] and in 1859 the Crown presented by lapse.[11] By 1884 the advowson had passed to W. C. Rickman[12] (d. by 1897), whose executors conveyed it *c.* 1915 to the bishop.[13] From 1985 the bishop and the dean and chapter of Chichester were to present jointly.[14]

The vicarage was endowed at its ordination *c.* 1174 × 1180 with offerings and a third of all the tithes of the parish including the rectory estate.[15] There was a house in 1341,[16] which in 1440 had a garden and dovecot.[17] The living was valued in 1291 at £5 6*s.* 8*d.*,[18] but by 1429 it had become so poor that the vicar needed the additional income of the chantry endowment.[19] In 1440 Boxgrove priory substituted an annual pension of £7 6*s.* 8*d.* for the vicar's share of tithes and glebe; though that represented an augmentation[20] the living remained impoverished in the later 15th century and early 16th.[21]

The vicarage house was ruinous in 1573[22] but in good repair in 1665;[23] *c.* 1704, however, it was pulled down by the lay rector and the materials were used to build a house in Yapton.[24] Its site is uncertain but was near the churchyard. The 1 a. previously held with it[25] was being kept from the incumbent in 1724.[26]

The incumbent is said to have received £10 a year from the lay rector in the 17th century.[27] In 1727 the living was augmented with £200 from Queen Anne's Bounty, so that the annual income rose to £24.[28] Four further augmentations, each of £200, were made between 1786 and 1827.[29] There were five closes of glebe in Yapton *c.* 1762[30] and 22½ a. in Barnham and Yapton in 1808;[31] some land in Barnham was exchanged with other land in the parish under a general redistribution of 1862.[32] The average income was £41 16*s.* 4*d.* in 1809[33] and £67 *c.* 1830;[34] in 1875 the stipend was described as 'miserable'.[35] A new vicarage house at the southern end of Church Lane was built shortly before 1903;[36] it was replaced before 1976[37] by a nearby bungalow, which itself ceased to be used in 1983.[38]

The vicar apparently resided in 1440.[39] Between the early 14th century and the early 16th additional spiritual care was presumably provided by the priests of the chantry of St. James,[40] founded in 1324 by ancestors of Sir William Shelley of Michelgrove in Clapham (d. 1549).[41]

In the 1570s sermons were delivered at irregular intervals.[42] At least one early 17th-century vicar was not a licensed preacher, and only three incumbents appointed during the 17th century are known to have been graduates; another was only in deacon's orders.[43] The poverty of the living led to several cases of pluralism between the 17th and early 19th centuries.[44] A Rogationtide procession with perambulation of the parish boundaries, to which occupiers of land brought cakes, was still held in the 17th century.[45]

95 Ibid. pp. 48–50.
96 Below, this section.
97 B.L. Add. MS. 39328, ff. 103–6.
98 Ibid. 39328, ff. 103, 106.
99 Ibid. 39328, ff. 104–6; 39359, ff. 26–9.
1 Ibid. 39328, ff. 106, 111; 39359, ff. 26, 29–30; cf. Dallaway, *Hist. W. Suss.* ii (1) (1819), 41.
2 B.L. Add. MSS. 39328, f. 106; 39368, f. 100.
3 Ibid. Add. MSS. 5699, f. 26; 39328, f. 105; 39368, ff. 96, 98; W.S.R.O., Ep. I/22/1 (1758); *Kelly's Dir. Suss.* (1905).
4 W.S.R.O., Ep. I/22A/1 (1881).
5 *Crockford* (1985–6), s.v. I. Morrison.
6 Inf. from Chich. Dioc. Regy.
7 *S.R.S.* lix, p. 49; B.L. Add. MS. 39328, ff. 100–1.
8 Above, manor (rectory); *L. & P. Hen. VIII*, xii (2), p. 352; *S.R.S.* xix. 22–3; lxxviii. 59.
9 B.L. Add. MS. 5699, f. 26.
10 *Rep. Com. Eccl. Revenues*; *Kelly's Dir. Suss.* (1862).
11 B.L. Add. MS. 39328, f. 107.
12 W.S.R.O., Ep. I/22A/1 (1884).
13 *Chich. Dioc. Kal.* (1897 and later edns.).
14 Inf. from Chich. Dioc. Regy.
15 *S.R.S.* lix, pp. 48–50; cf. ibid. pp. 28–9.
16 *Inq. Non.* (Rec. Com.), 368.
17 B.L. Add. MS. 39328, f. 96.
18 *Tax. Eccl.* (Rec. Com.), 135.
19 *Reg. Chichele* (Cant. & York Soc.), iii. 485.
20 B.L. Add. MS. 39328, f. 96; cf. ibid. 39476, f. 176; W.S.R.O., Ep. I/25/1 (1635).
21 B.L. Add. MS. 39328, f. 97.
22 W.S.R.O., Ep. I/23/2, f. 11; cf. ibid. Ep. I/23/5, f. 35.
23 B.L. Add. MS. 39368, f. 96.
24 *S.R.S.* lxxviii. 60.
25 W.S.R.O., Ep. I/25/1 (1615, 1635).
26 *S.R.S.* lxxviii. 60.
27 Ibid.
28 W.S.R.O., Ep. I/17/37, f. 158.
29 Hodgson, *Queen Anne's Bounty* (1845), p. cclxii.
30 W.S.R.O., Goodwood MS. E4996.
31 Ibid. Ep. I/25/1 (1635), MS. copy, 1801, with addition dated 1808; ibid. note, 1809; cf. W.S.R.O., TD/W 10, 153; *Glebe Lands Return*, H.C. 307, p. 27 (1881), lxiv.
32 W.S.R.O., QDD/6/W 32; cf. above, econ. hist. (agric.).
33 W.S.R.O., Ep. I/63/10.
34 *Rep. Com. Eccl. Revenues.*
35 W.S.R.O., Ep. I/22A/2 (1875).
36 *Kelly's Dir. Suss.* (1903).
37 F. W. Steer, *Barnham Ch. Guide*, 8.
38 Cf. below, this section.
39 B.L. Add. MS. 39328, f. 97.
40 Ibid. ff. 109–10; *Reg. Chichele* (Cant. & York Soc.), iii. 454; *S.R.S.* iv. 120–1.
41 *Cal. Pat.* 1321–4, 434; B.L. Add. MS. 39328, ff. 109–10; P.R.O., C 142/46, no. 15; W.S.R.O., Ep. I/86/20, f. 17v.; cf. *V.C.H. Suss.* vi (1), 13. The chantry of St. Mary mentioned by Dallaway, *Hist. W. Suss.* ii (1) (1819), 42, was apparently the same under a misnomer; cf. *S.A.C.* xii. 84; *S.R.S.* xxxvi, p. xxii; B.L. Add. MS. 39328, f. 109.
42 W.S.R.O., Ep. I/23/1, f. 55; Ep. I/23/4, f. 16; Ep. I/23/5, f. 35.
43 B.L. Add. MS. 39328, f. 104; cf. ibid. 39359, f. 26.
44 Ibid. 39328, f. 105; 39368, f. 95; *Rep. Com. Eccl. Revenues.*
45 *S.R.S.* xlix. 100, 129.

In 1724 services were held only monthly and communion was celebrated three times a year.[46] After the augmentation of 1727 the frequency of services was increased to fortnightly, as apparently continued to be the case in 1758 despite an attempt to enforce weekly holding in 1728 or 1729.[47] In the earlier 19th century the cure was often served by assistant curates or the clergy of neighbouring parishes.[48]

By 1838 services were weekly, alternately in morning and evening;[49] alternation continued in 1851, when *c.* 30 attended in the morning and *c.* 60 in the afternoon.[50] Frequency of communion increased from four times a year in 1838 to eight times in 1844 and later.[51] A. P. Cornwall, vicar 1859–*c.* 1900,[52] lived at Runcton near Chichester in 1884 and perhaps earlier[53] and in Chichester itself from 1887,[54] walking 10 miles each Sunday to take services in 1875. Parish visiting suffered at that period from the lack of any gentleman's family in the parish.[55]

After the building of a new vicarage house shortly before 1903 Barnham had a resident vicar until 1983,[56] but from that date the incumbent lived in Eastergate. Services were no longer held every Sunday in 1995.

The church of *ST. MARY*[57] has a structurally undivided nave and chancel, a north vestry and organ chamber, a south porch, and a west bellcot. The walls are mostly of rubble, much of it plastered, with freestone dressings and areas of later brick. The bellcot is boarded.

The nave is 12th-century and the rear arch of the south doorway and two small windows are of that date. The chancel was built, presumably to replace a smaller unit, early in the 13th century and retains three lancet windows in the east and south walls. At or soon after that time a north aisle and chapel were added, probably accommodating the chantry of St. James founded in 1324.[58] They were linked to the main body of the church by arches cut through the earlier wall. The south doorway, the porch, and a window in the south wall of the nave are 14th-century, as also are reset windows in the north wall. The west doorway and the window above it are 15th- or early 16th-century. The date of demolition of the north aisle and chapel is not known although it must be later than a late medieval graffito on the west respond of the arch to the chapel.[59]

Both nave and chancel were in bad condition in 1579[60] and the nave remained so in 1724.[61] In 1776 the building was described as 'much out of repair'[62] and in 1865 as neither decent nor in proper order.[63] It was restored in the latter year,[64] when the gallery erected shortly before 1844[65] was presumably removed. The arch into the former chapel was reopened *c.* 1930 when the vestry was built.[66]

The square late 12th-century font of Sussex marble has badly rubbed decoration including foliage and arcading; its central supporting pillar is original but the outer four are apparently painted drainpipes.[67] The single bell of *c.* 1348 probably by John Rufford is inscribed 'AFE MA RIA DRA SIA PLE NA' (for 'Ave Maria gratia plena').[68] The top of a four-tiered pyramidal censer in champlevé Limoges enamel was found *c.* 1930 at the east end of the chancel.[69] A French 15th-century painted wooden statue perhaps of St. Genevieve was inserted in the mid 20th century.[70] Box pews had been installed by 1865, when they were described as 5 ft. high and rotten;[71] they were evidently removed in the restoration of that year.

The plate includes a two-handled silver communion cup of 1779.[72] The registers begin in 1676.[73]

ROMAN CATHOLICISM. One parishioner was presented for not receiving Easter communion in 1584[74] and three parishioners were convicted for recusancy in 1668.[75] There were two papists in 1781.[76] Sunday mass was said in Barnham in 1929,[77] and apparently by 1938 a church of timber converted from a workshop stood south-east of the railway bridge;[78] it was served by the priest from Slindon. The church was superseded in 1970 by that at St. Philip Howard school in Eastergate.[79]

PROTESTANT NONCONFORMITY. There was one Baptist in the parish in 1664,[80] and in 1724, presumably because of the infrequency of services at the parish church, four out of the sixteen families living in Barnham were Presbyterian.[81] In 1856 Dissenters attended the Independent chapel in Yapton.[82] The Methodist congregation which flourished in 1992 grew out of Sunday evening meetings held in the market room of Barnham market in Eastergate from

46 Ibid. lxxviii. 60.
47 W.S.R.O., Ep. I/17/37, f. 158; Ep. I/22/1 (1758); cf. *Cowdray Archives*, ed. A. Dibben, i, p. 80.
48 B.L. Add. MS. 39359, f. 30; W.S.R.O., Par. 13/1/2/1; *Rep. Com. Eccl. Revenues.*
49 W.S.R.O., Ep. I/22/2 (1838).
50 *S.R.S.* lxxv, p. 153.
51 W.S.R.O., Ep. I/22/2 (1838); Ep. I/22A/1 (1884); Ep. I/22A/2 (1844).
52 B.L. Add. MS. 39328, f. 107; *Chich. Dioc. Kal.* (1900, 1901).
53 W.S.R.O., Ep. I/22A/1 (1884); Ep. I/22A/2 (1875).
54 *Kelly's Dir. Suss.* (1887 and later edns.).
55 W.S.R.O., Ep. I/22A/2 (1875).
56 *Kelly's Dir. Suss.* (1903); above, this section.
57 Dedic. recorded from 1105: *S.R.S.* lix, p. 16. Ch. fully described at F. W. Steer, *Barnham Ch. Guide.*
58 Above, this section.
59 Illus. at *W. Suss. Gaz.* 11 July 1936.
60 W.S.R.O., Ep. I/23/5, f. 35.
61 *S.R.S.* lxxviii. 59.
62 B.L. Add. MS. 5699, f. 26.
63 W.S.R.O., Ep. I/22A/2 (1865).
64 B.L. Add. MS. 39364, f. 16.
65 W.S.R.O., Ep. I/22A/2 (1844).
66 *S.C.M.* ix. 462.
67 A. K. Walker, *Introd. to Study of Eng. Fonts*, 66.
68 Elphick, *Bells*, 36, 38; Steer, *Ch. Guide*, 6.
69 *Antiq. Jnl.* x. 242.
70 Steer, *Ch. Guide*, 4.
71 W.S.R.O., Ep. I/22A/2 (1865).
72 *S.A.C.* liii. 238–9.
73 W.S.R.O., Par. 13/1.
74 Ibid. Ep. I/23/6, f. 18.
75 *Miscellanea*, v (Cath. Rec. Soc. vi), 318.
76 H.L.R.O., papist return, 1781.
77 Archives of Dioc. of Arundel and Brighton, Bishop's Ho., Hove, Slindon par. file, Southwark dioc. visit. 1929.
78 *Kelly's Dir. Suss.* (1938); W.S.R.O., MP 2347, f. 12; O.S. Map 6", Suss. LXII. SE. (1951 edn.).
79 Below, Eastergate, Rom. Cath.
80 *S.R.S.* xlix. 128–9.
81 Ibid. lxxviii. 60.
82 W.S.R.O., Ep. I/22A/2 (1856).

1923. In 1929 there were 11 church members. The brick chapel south of the railway bridge was opened in 1931;[83] in 1940 it could seat 117.[84] The minister came from Bognor Regis in 1965[85] and from Littlehampton in 1992.[86]

EDUCATION. Licences to teach in the parish were granted in 1580 and 1584, on the second occasion to a reader at the church.[87] In 1818 an old woman kept a school with 10 pupils,[88] but from *c.* 1845 or earlier Barnham children went to school in Eastergate, Walberton, or Yapton.[89] Barnham council school, later Barnham county primary school, was built in Yapton Road in 1906.[90] Average attendance was 85 in 1914, rising to 100 in 1922 and falling to 67 in 1938.[91] A new building was put up in Orchard Way, Eastergate, in 1968[92] and the Yapton Road site was used thereafter by infants.[93] By 1978, as a result of large-scale building in the area, nearly 300 pupils attended on the two sites.[94] There were 278 on the roll in 1993.[95]

A workshop for instruction in carpentry was supported by West Sussex county council in 1895[96] and survived till *c.* 1910 or later.[97] From 1958 many older children from Barnham went to Westergate secondary modern school in Aldingbourne, but after the opening of St. Philip Howard secondary school in Eastergate in 1959 most went there.[98]

CHARITIES FOR THE POOR. None known.

BINSTED

THE small parish of Binsted,[99] still mostly quiet and rural in the 1980s, lies 2½ miles (4 km.) west of Arundel, the Chichester–Arundel road crossing its north end. The ancient parish covered 1,106 a., which were incorporated in Tortington in 1933 and transferred from Tortington to Walberton in 1985.[1] It was regular in shape, *c.* 2¼ miles (3.6 km.) long from north to south and 1 mile (0.6 km.) wide. The ground falls from 150 ft. (45 metres) above sea level in the north to 30 ft. (10 metres) in the south, and lies upon Tertiary gravels and clays. Where the clay meets the Upper Chalk near the northern boundary it is mixed with flinty gravels. The gravels in the north and north-east have been dug commercially. In the east and west the heavier clays of the Reading Beds have yielded material for brick and pottery making.[2]

The southern half of the parish was in 1615 called Lower Binsted,[3] but earlier Hoeland or the Hoes,[4] from an Anglo-Saxon word meaning a heel or projecting ridge of land: it lies between the Binsted brook on the west and a tributary, the streams along much of their courses forming the parish boundary. Both drain south towards the river Arun, and were once subjected to a sewers rate.[5] Springs rise at intervals along the scarp above the Binsted brook. A small stream rising in the centre of the parish flows south-east through Lake copse into the eastern tributary, and two others into the same stream from sources where the clay joins the Upper Chalk further north.

The Chichester–Arundel road was shown on maps in the early 17th century[6] and in 1675 across the north end of the parish.[7] Immediately east of Avisford, the former meeting place of the hundred, it was straightened in 1834.[8] By 1981 it had been rebuilt as a wide dual carriageway.[9] Another east–west route 400 metres to the south may be on the line of the Roman road to Chichester.[10] A broad bridleway between well defined banks, it was mentioned in the 13th or 14th century as the king's highway[11] and shown as a roadway in 1606 and 1715.[12] It was called Arundel highway in 1727,[13] and partly Andrew's Lane and partly Scotland Lane in 1840.[14] The name Old Scotland Lane, used for the whole length in 1899 and later,[15] derives from that of adjoining land,[16] which may have owed a customary payment (or scot). A third east–west road crossing the centre of the parish, mentioned in 1615 as a road between Binsted and Arundel,[17] survived in 1992 as a fairly wide footpath for

83 Ibid. MP 2347, f. 11; Barnham W.I. scrapbook [1949], p. [23] (copy in possession of Mrs. R. Collins, W. Barnham); G. M. M., *A Methodist Tapestry* (Bognor Regis, 1967), 29.
84 *Methodist Ch. Bldg. Return* (1940).
85 W.S.R.O., MP 814, f. [12].
86 Notice at bldg.
87 B.L. Add. MS. 39328, f. 103; W.S.R.O., STC III/C, f. 34.
88 *Educ. of Poor Digest*, 952.
89 W.S.R.O., Ep. I/22A/2 (1865), Eastergate; Ep. I/47/3–4; Nat. Soc. *Inquiry, 1846–7*, Suss. 2–3; *Kelly's Dir. Suss.* (1887 and later edns.).
90 P.R.O., ED 7/123.
91 *Educ. List 21, 1914*, 521; *1922*, 341; *1938*, 401.
92 W.S.R.O., MP 2347, f. 5.
93 *W. Suss. Gaz.* 30 Dec. 1982.
94 W.S.R.O., MP 2347, f. 5.
95 *Dir. of W. Suss. Educ. Service* (1993).
96 *Kelly's Dir. Suss.* (1895).
97 W.S.R.O., IR 12, f. 7.
98 Local inf.; cf. below, Eastergate, educ.
99 This article was written in 1992 and revised in 1996. Maps used include O.S. Maps 1/25,000, SU 80/90 (1981 edn.); 6", Suss. LXII (1880 and later edns.). Map, below, p. 226. Much help was received from Mrs. Emma Tristram, Binsted.
1 *Census*, 1931; 1981. The incorporation into Tortington was strongly resisted: *Southern Wkly. News*, 22 May 1937.
2 Below, econ. hist.
3 W.S.R.O., Ep. I/25/1 (1615).
4 Ibid. Cap. I/28/108.
5 Ibid. LD II/ZP 2.
6 A.C.M., PM 193.
7 Ogilby, *Britannia* (1675), 8.
8 Ibid. Add. MS. 4737.
9 O.S. Map 1/25,000, SU 80/90 (1981 edn.).
10 I. D. Margary, *Rom. Rds. in Brit.* (1967), 75–6; cf. *V.C.H. Suss.* iii. 46 for a nearby Rom. burial.
11 W.S.R.O., Cap. I/15/3–4.
12 Ibid. Add. MSS. 12171, 28767.
13 Ibid. Cap. I/28/103, deed, 1727.
14 Ibid. TD/W 15.
15 Ibid. SP 1621; O.S. Map 6", Suss. LXII. NE. (1899 edn.); SU 90 NE. (1961 edn.).
16 W.S.R.O., TD/W 15, no. 48.
17 Ibid. Ep. I/25/1 (1615).

most of its course within Binsted. West of the church it crosses the Binsted brook by a footbridge called Kenimore bridge in 1727.[18]

A road, mostly metalled, runs in a **U** from the main road round the centre of the parish to link the various settlements but does not cross the parish boundary. It was called Church Lane in 1840[19] and Binsted Lane in 1961.[20] Although by 1990 its section on the east side of the parish had, probably recently, ceased to be used as a through route for vehicles it continued there as an unmetalled trackway, rejoining the Chichester–Arundel road by way of Tortington parish. Another track, leading by 1606 from Binsted Lane into the south-east corner of the parish,[21] was called Hoes Lane in 1840[22] and Hoe Lane in the 20th century. By 1992 it was only a footpath.[23] Footpaths to Ford and Yapton were mentioned in 1728[24] and one leading to Walberton farm in 1729.[25]

Chichester, Bognor Regis, Arundel, and Worthing were accessible by bus in 1992.

Mature woodland covering one third of the parish, mostly in the north, consists of mixed deciduous oak and ash with remnants of coppicing. Its extent has not changed greatly since 1840,[26] and it contains many indications of being ancient.[27] The woodland reaches the parish boundary on the north, which in the Middle Ages was the pale of Arundel Great park. Binsted's woods were evidently part of Arundel forest, which in the early 15th century included Avisford in Walberton.[28] Avisford was the meeting place of the hundred, which was called Binsted hundred in 1086.[29] An earthwork which in 1992 ran south from Avisford through Hundredhouse copse in Binsted[30] was perhaps a forest bank. In the early 15th century the forest included Favarches wood, named after a 14th-century lord of Binsted.[31]

The most northerly woods were demesne woods of Binsted's main estates. In the north-west in the early 17th century Mr. Shelley's wood[32] was presumably the demesne woodland of Binsted manor, until then owned by Sir John Shelley,[33] and in the north-east corner the Queen's wood, so called at the same date[34] and later described as the new inclosure,[35] had probably belonged either to Binsted manor or to Priory farm, Tortington; in 1840 it covered *c.* 50 a.[36] A wood called in 1452 North Lea[37] was apparently that of the later Marsh farm.[38] Goblestubbs copse in the north recalls Alan and Albany Goble, churchwardens 1662–75.[39]

In 1454 a canon of Arundel college hunted with dogs and a bow on the Binsted demesnes, taking pheasants and partridges.[40] Gamekeepers were registered in 1784–5 by Edward Staker of Binsted House and from 1786 to 1861 by the owners of Church farm.[41] About 1910 a gamekeeper to the duke of Norfolk, who had bought some of the Binsted woodland, lived at the north end of the parish.[42]

The demesne woods were apparently separated by Scotland Lane from common woodland and pasture to the south. Further south again, in the centre of the parish, there was evidently an open field before the 17th century, with meadow to the south-east and marshland to the south.[43] In the north-west corner of the parish there was a large assart by 1795;[44] by 1840 that area contained much arable.[45] Field names such as Oak field and Old Furze field indicate their former condition.[46] In the southern half of the parish the only wood to survive in 1992 was the narrow 6-a. Lake copse. The name Oakley, recorded in 1537,[47] suggests the former existence of oak woodland south of the church, and in 1606 Marsh farm included an oak wood of 4 a.[48]

Eight inhabitants were mentioned in 1086.[49] At least 6 of the 22 people taxed in Binsted, Madehurst, and Tortington in 1296 were probably of Binsted,[50] and Binsted may have had up to half of the 15 taxed in Binsted and Tortington in 1327, of the 20 in 1334, and of the 31 in 1524.[51] Forty Binsted men signed the protestation in 1642,[52] 21 adults were reported there in 1676,[53] and the parish had 20 families in 1724.[54] Its population, numbering 100 in 1801 and 111 in 1841, increased to 139 in 1871, but had fallen back to 105 by 1901. It fell further to 87 in 1921 but had risen again to 107 in 1931, the last year for which it was separately recorded.[55]

The south-east corner of the parish has yielded Mesolithic flakes, flints, and axes.[56] In the modern period settlement has been scattered, but the uneven surface of the field north of the church, which now stands isolated, may suggest that there was a village there,[57] linking the church with the former vicarage and the manor house (Church Farm), which are known to be on early sites:[58] a spring near the church makes the site suitable for early occupation. Near the former vicarage what are thought to be the platform for

18 Ibid. LD II/SM 1, p. 14; cf. ibid. TD/W 15, no. 174 (Long canny moor).
19 Ibid. TD/W 15.
20 O.S. Map 6", SU 90 NE. (1961 edn.).
21 W.S.R.O., Add. MSS. 12170–1.
22 Ibid. TD/W 15.
23 O.S. Maps 6", SU 90 NE. (1961 edn.); 1/25,000, SU 80/90 (1981 edn.).
24 W.S.R.O., LD II/SM 1, p. 22.
25 Ibid. LD II/SM 1, p. 31; ibid. TD/W 15.
26 Ibid. TD/W 15; O.S. Map 6", SU 90 NE. (1961 edn.).
27 Inf. from Suss. Wildlife Trust.
28 *S.R.S.* lxvii. 92–3.
29 Above, Avisford Hund.
30 O.S. Nat. Grid 978068.
31 *S.R.S.* lxvii. 92; below, manors (Binsted).
32 A.C.M., PM 193.
33 Below, manors (Binsted).
34 A.C.M., PM 193.
35 *S.R.S.* xxix, p. 11.
36 W.S.R.O., TD/W 15.
37 A.C.M., M 530.
38 Cf. W.S.R.O., Add. MS. 12170.
39 B.L. Add. MS. 39359, ff. 39–40.
40 A.C.M., M 530.
41 *S.R.S.* li. 10–144, *passim.*
42 W.S.R.O., IR 12, f. 11.
43 Below, econ. hist.
44 Gardner, *Suss. Map* (1795).
45 W.S.R.O., TD/W 15.
46 Ibid. nos. 26, 57.
47 P.R.O., SC 6/Hen. VIII/3674, m. 9.
48 W.S.R.O., Add. MS. 2027.
49 *V.C.H. Suss.* i. 431.
50 *S.R.S.* x. 79–80; cf. A.C.M., M 530; P.R.O., SC 6/Hen. VIII/3764, m. 9; *S.A.C.* li. 59; *Inq. Non.* (Rec. Com.), 368.
51 *S.R.S.* x. 137, 256; lvi. 56.
52 Ibid. v. 33.
53 *Compton Census*, ed. Whiteman, 144.
54 *S.R.S.* lxxviii. 60.
55 *Census*, 1801–31.
56 S.M.R. 1342, 1462.
57 M. Beresford, *Lost Villages of Eng.* 204.
58 Below, manors (Binsted); church.

a tithe barn and a medieval bellfounding pit have been excavated.[59] Medieval pottery has been found further north,[60] near the site of a cottage known as Pescod's Croft, at the junction of Binsted Lane and Scotland Lane.[61] The medieval kiln site[62] opposite perhaps included a dwelling. A house standing there in 1601, called All the World, had disappeared by 1715.[63] A house on the site later used for the Black Horse public house beside the lane north-west of Church Farm was apparently built by 1825[64] and scattered houses were built nearby during the 20th century. Marsh Farm, at the south end of the parish, occupies a medieval site, and another small settlement may have stood on the east side of the parish near the later Binsted House[65] and Meadow Lodge. Meadow Lodge, so called by 1867,[66] is a two-storeyed house of red brick, square on plan with a symmetrical front of three bays formerly stuccoed, a modern central porch, and a hipped tiled roof above a modillion eaves cornice. It was built *c.* 1800 apparently for Zacchaeus Staker or his son-in-law William Laker on the site of a cottage which George and Mary Drury leased to Edward Staker in 1682; by 1864 it had passed to H. C. Bones (later Lewis), the rector, whose son owned it in 1936.[67]

North of Marsh Farm a group of dwellings called Oakley cottages was erected on what was probably a medieval assart; the present building is 17th-century in origin, of two bays with a central chimneystack and some moulded beams internally. It housed two families in 1839, three *c.* 1910,[68] and was still inhabited in 1992. Other cottages were new built on the waste in the late 16th and early 17th centuries. Two that stood in 1614 on the common on the east side of the parish,[69] south of the site of Binsted House, had gone by 1876.[70] Morley's Croft a short way south, a timber-framed two-storeyed house of the 17th century, later extended and faced in brick, has an external chimneystack on the east wall towards Binsted Lane. Two cottages with central chimneystacks, shown in 1715 further south on Binsted Lane,[71] were perhaps 17th-century. One had gone by 1840;[72] the other was replaced by two 20th-century cottages. A more substantial house standing in 1715 on the south side of Scotland Lane, with chimneystacks on both end walls, had probably been recently built.[73] A small cottage and garden just west of that house in 1840[74] had disappeared by 1876.[75] Both were clearly built after the common there was inclosed in the 17th century,[76] and both sites were under woodland in 1992. A cottage called Goose Green in the south end of the parish may have been that mentioned in 1669.[77]

There were 19 dwellings in the parish in 1841, 24 in 1881, and 22 in 1911.[78] In 1923 Church Farm and Marsh Farm with their dependent farm cottages accounted for thirteen of those dwellings. The sales of land in that year[79] allowed new houses to be built on scattered sites throughout the parish. By 1950 three new ones had been built in the northern woodland in Wincher's copse and Singer's piece;[80] a mobile home park nearby had *c.* 50 dwellings in 1996.[81]

Alehouse keepers were recorded four times between 1621 and 1650.[82] A vintner was at Binsted in 1691.[83] In a house said to have been built by Edward Staker (d. 1825) for his daughters but used as labourers' cottages, a beerhouse was opened in 1871. It was later rebuilt and was called the Black Horse by 1881,[84] surviving by that name in 1992.

Water was drawn from wells[85] until Bognor Regis urban district council laid a water main beside the Binsted brook shortly before 1939,[86] when electricity was also available.[87]

MANORS AND OTHER ESTATES. Before 1066 three free men held Binsted, and in 1086 Osmelin held it from earl Roger.[88] The overlordship descended to the earl's successors, and Binsted was listed among the manors of the honor of Arundel in 1566.[89] The division among three tenants may have survived, for three lords held Binsted in 1316, Richard Favarche, Henry le Fiste, and William of Bilsham.[90] In 1840 most of the parish lay in three estates, Binsted manor (Church farm), Marsh farm, and the Binsted House estate,[91] but meanwhile two at least of the estates had undergone much change.

In 1314–15 William of Bilsham held land at Bilsham (in Yapton) and Binsted,[92] and in 1345–6 his son John held *BINSTED* manor,[93] later centred on the house called Binsted Farm in the 19th century and *CHURCH FARM* in the 20th.[94] In 1412 John Taverner held land worth £2 in Binsted.[95] Under a settlement of 1444 Edmund Turnant, son of Gillian, daughter and

59 Inf. from Mr. J. Mills, assistant county arch. officer.
60 S.M.R. 1374.
61 Ibid.; W.S.R.O., Add. MS. 12171.
62 Below, econ. hist.
63 P.R.O., C 54/1700, pt. 23; W.S.R.O., Add. MSS. 7742, 12171.
64 Below, this section.
65 Below, manors.
66 W.S.R.O., Par. 22/6/4.
67 Ibid. Add. MS. 10772; ibid. Par. 22/30/1; ibid. TD/W 15; inf. from Mr. J. Barlow, the owner (1990), and abstract of title in his possession.
68 W.S.R.O., IR 12, f. 13; ibid. QDP/W 77.
69 Ibid. Add. MS. 3056.
70 O.S. Map 6", Suss. LXII (1880 edn.).
71 W.S.R.O., Add. MS. 12171.
72 Ibid. TD/W 15.
73 Ibid. Add. MS. 12171.
74 Ibid. TD/W 15.
75 O.S. Map 1/2,500, Suss. LXII. 3 (1880 edn.).
76 Below, econ. hist.
77 *S.R.S.* xxix, p. 11.
78 *Census*, 1841–1911.
79 W.S.R.O., SP 435, 1621.
80 O.S. Map 6", Suss. LXII. NE. (1951 edn.).
81 Inf. from Mrs. E. Tristram, Binsted.
82 *S.R.S.* xlix. 14; liv. 7, 40, 199.
83 E.S.R.O., AMS 1541.
84 *Bognor Regis Post*, 6 June 1936; cf. Pike, *Dir. SW. Suss.* (1886–7); O.S. Map 6", Suss. LXII. NE. (1914 edn.); for Staker, below, manors [Binsted Ho.].
85 e.g. W.S.R.O., Add. MS. 3057; F. H. Edmunds, *Wells and Springs of Suss.* 59.
86 W.S.R.O., Par. 22/4/2; cf. *Southern Wkly. News*, 22 May 1937.
87 *Kelly's Dir. Suss.* (1938).
88 *V.C.H. Suss.* i. 431.
89 *S.R.S.* xix. 9. The rights of Sir Wm. FitzAlan in the man. were allegedly confirmed in 1400: B.L. Add. MS. 5687, f. 56v.; the conf. is not found in *Cal. Pat.*
90 *Feud. Aids*, v. 143.
91 W.S.R.O., TD/W 15.
92 *S.R.S.* xxiii, p. 23.
93 Ibid. p. 113.
94 O.S. Map 6", Suss. LXII. NE. (1880, 1914 edns.).
95 *S.A.C.* x. 136.

coheir of Alice Taverner, perhaps John's widow, had rights in Binsted manor.[96] In 1447 he released Binsted manor to Edmund Nenge, John Michelgrove, and their wives, perhaps the other coheirs.[97] Thereafter the manor descended in the Michelgrove and Shelley families with Michelgrove in Clapham. Following the attainder of William Shelley in 1586–7,[98] the Crown leased much of the demesne in 1595 to Sir Thomas Fludd.[99] In 1612 Fludd or a namesake was claiming under that lease, after the restoration in 1604 of William's nephew (Sir) John Shelley.[1]

In 1615 Sir John Shelley conveyed the manor to Sir Garrett Kempe,[2] and thereafter it passed with the Slindon House estate.[3] In 1840 the Binsted estate of Anne Radclyffe, dowager countess of Newburgh, contained 359 a., chiefly in the west and north-west parts of the parish.[4] Binsted manor remained with the Slindon House estate until *c.* 1908 when it was sold to Lt.-Col. C. P. Henty of Avisford House in Walberton.[5] In 1927 Church farm, of 273 a., was separated from the Avisford House estate by sale to Col. Sir Sidney Wishart (d. 1935), who lived in the farmhouse and worked both Church and Marsh farms through a bailiff.[6] His son E. E. Wishart (d. 1987) inherited the two farms,[7] which belonged in 1992 to Binsted Farms Ltd. run by his son Luke.[8]

Church Farm is largely a brick house of the early 18th century but retains the core of an older house on the east, away from the road.

The estates of Richard Favarche and Henry le Fiste in 1316 have not been traced later, except that Andrew Favarche of Binsted was mentioned in 1331.[9] In 1428 two estates in Binsted paid subsidy as ¼ knight's fee; one was divided between several tenants and the other was held by the prior of Tortington.[10] The priory, which had appropriated Binsted rectory by 1291[11] and acquired further land in 1342,[12] held in 1452 what was called the manor of *MARSH AND BINSTED*,[13] which was evidently the origin of the modern estate called *MARSH FARM*. After the Dissolution the land descended with the rest of Tortington priory's estates[14] until the mid 17th century.[15] In 1606 it comprised 140 a. called Binsted farm, lying chiefly around what was later Marsh Farm.[16]

In 1651 William Thomas sold the land to Thomas Bridger,[17] who was succeeded in or after 1654[18] by his daughter Mary, wife of Richard Shelley. By 1683 it belonged to John Davies and his wife Mary, the Shelleys' daughter.[19] Thomas Fowler of Walberton, the owner in 1738, when Marsh farm had 148 a., was succeeded in 1780 by his son, also Thomas,[20] whose widow Mary was the owner in 1785.[21] Their son Thomas, the next owner, had moved from Felpham to live at Marsh Farm by 1791.[22] His son and heir Thomas remained there until *c.* 1830.[23] Thomas's lands passed to Henry Upton, apparently his son-in-law, who owned Marsh farm by 1840 when it included 268 a. in Binsted.[24] In 1853 he was succeeded by his son Henry,[25] the non-resident owner in the 1880s.[26] In 1903 the estate belonged to Sidney J. Upton (d. by 1909), in 1913 to Sidney H. F. Upton. By 1915[27] Marsh farm, 265 a., was like Church farm part of the Avisford House estate in Walberton,[28] from which it was sold in 1923.[29] By 1936 it had been reunited with Church farm in the ownership of E. E. Wishart,[30] and with Church farm belonged to the Wisharts in 1992.[31]

The earliest part of Marsh Farm is 16th- or early 17th-century, being partly faced with chequered work of knapped flint and stone with red brick dressings. It has a 19th-century wing in flint to the south-east and a modern addition to the west. In 1581–2 it had a barn and a dovehouse.[32] In 1606 the manorial enclosure contained three outbuildings, one near the entrance apparently a gatehouse and two larger ones to the north and west.[33] There was a dovehouse in 1683[34] and 1716.[35] A polygonal horse gin survived in 1969.[36]

The *BINSTED HOUSE* estate, *c.* 1815 called Binsted Ball farm,[37] included former freeholds and copyholds once held of Tortington priory and sold by the Crown as Binsted manor in 1600 to two Londoners. They at once sold that land to William Ottley and Edward Blofield, who in 1601 conveyed it to the Revd. Henry Blaxton, Thomas Knight, and Edward Staker of Yapton.[38] By 1663 Staker or a namesake had acquired other property in Binsted, and Edward Staker (d. 1673) was suceeded by his second son Edward, who bought more land in 1679 and died at Binsted in 1694, apparently without issue.[39] The

96 *Cal. Close*, 1441–7, 458.
97 Ibid. 474.
98 *V.C.H. Suss.* vi (1), 13; cf. e.g. *S.R.S.* xx. 301–2.
99 B.L. Add. Ch. 25671.
1 Ibid. Add. MS. 39488, f. 284.
2 *S.R.S.* xix. 41.
3 *V.C.H. Suss.* iv. 234–5.
4 W.S.R.O., TD/W 15.
5 *Kelly's Dir. Suss.* (1909).
6 Ibid. (1930); *Who Was Who, 1929–40*; W.S.R.O., SP 208.
7 W.S.R.O., Raper MSS., temporary no. 438; *The Times*, 23 Sept. 1987.
8 Inf. from Mr. L. Wishart, Binsted.
9 *Cal. Pat.* 1330–4, 128.
10 *Feud. Aids*, v. 155.
11 Below, church.
12 *Cal. Pat.* 1340–3, 575; *S.A.C.* xxvii. 49.
13 A.C.M., M 530.
14 Below, Tortington, manor (Priory fm.).
15 e.g. P.R.O., SC 6/Hen. VIII/3674, m. 9; SC 6/Eliz. I/2213; *Cal. Pat.* 1580–2, p. 188; *Cal. S.P. Dom.* 1591–4, 498; *S.R.S.* xix. 9; xx. 497; xxix, p. 165.
16 W.S.R.O., Add. MSS. 2027, 12170.
17 Ibid. 7748.
18 *S.R.S.* xx. 305.
19 Ibid. xxix, p. 30.
20 W.S.R.O., Add. MSS. 7774–8.
21 Ibid. Add. MSS. 7779–80.
22 Ibid. Raper MSS., temporary no. 499.
23 Ibid. Par. 22/30/3; cf. B.L. Add. MS. 39359, ff. 41v.–42.
24 W.S.R.O., TD/W 15; cf. Elwes & Robinson, *W. Suss.* 36.
25 W.S.R.O., Par. 22/39/1.
26 Cf. P.R.O., RG 11/1125, f. 76.
27 *Kelly's Dir. Suss.* (1903 and later edns.).
28 Below, Walberton, manor (Avisford Ho.); cf. W.S.R.O., SP 435.
29 W.S.R.O., SP 1621.
30 Ibid. Raper MSS., temporary no. 438.
31 Inf. from Mr. Wishart.
32 P.R.O., C 66/1214, mm. 34–5.
33 W.S.R.O., Add. MSS. 2027, 28767.
34 *S.R.S.* xxix, p. 30.
35 W.S.R.O., Add. MS. 7768.
36 *S.I.A.S. Newsletter*, iii. 1, 8.
37 W.S.R.O., Add. MS. 9248.
38 B.L. Add. MS. 39488, ff. 282–3; P.R.O., C 54/1700, pt. 23.
39 B.L. Add. MS. 39488, f. 285; W.S.R.O., Add. MS. 3058; *S.R.S.* xix. 41.

estate passed in turn to Henry Staker (d. 1726 at Binsted) and to Edward Staker; one or more men called Edward Staker were churchwardens at intervals from 1742 to 1800,[40] and one was a J.P. in 1781.[41] An Edward Staker was buried in Binsted church in 1825.[42] His estate had passed by 1861 to William Henry Read, then occupying Binsted House[43] as in 1882 when he was one of the chief landowners and described as lord of the manor. Edward Staker Read, the owner in 1903 and 1924, had by 1927 been succeeded by C. E. Read.[44] By 1947 the estate had passed to Read's son-in-law Henry Pethers, and most of the land was later bought by E. E. Wishart and added to Binsted Farms Ltd., centred on Church Farm.[45]

Binsted House, standing in 1795 near the parish's eastern boundary,[46] may have incorporated a building of flint of *c.* 1600[47] and have been the house occupied by Henry Staker (d. *c.* 1712) including a hall with a parlour and chamber, a chamber over the hall, and a porch with a room above it.[48] The later house was on an **L**-plan, in classical style and stuccoed. Its south-facing main block had a central porch with a bay window to the east.[49] About 1815 it stood in park-like grounds of 41 a., called the Paddock, with a lake south-west of the house. A north–south road running west of the park had been removed since 1795.[50] The house was demolished *c.* 1940[51] in or following a fire.[52] The park and the site of the house had become woodland by 1992. A small house called Manor House built 330 yd. (300 metres) south of Binsted House by 1927 was occupied in that year by C. E. Read, while his sisters lived in Binsted House.[53] In 1946 Mrs. E. Wishart of Marsh Farm erected near the lake a shrine to the Virgin Mary in memory of her mother.[54]

The dean and chapter of Chichester acquired land in Binsted in 1415,[55] represented in 1536 by two freeholds called Crossbarn and Greycroft.[56] In 1565 the Crown granted other land to the dean and chapter,[57] whose land in Binsted in the early 18th century was part of Burndell or Bundle farm in Yapton.[58] That land, sometimes farmed *c.* 1800 with the Church farm estate,[59] had by 1922 been incorporated into the Avisford House estate in Walberton[60] and by 1936 into Marsh farm.[61]

Tortington or Tortington Cheyneys manor included land in Binsted in 1706 and later.[62] The duke of Norfolk's Binsted property, acquired by 1895 and over 200 a. *c.* 1910, included *c.* 150 a. of woodland in the north end of the parish.[63]

ECONOMIC HISTORY. Binsted was assessed at 4 hides in 1086, relatively high since there was land for only 2 ploughteams, the demesne having 2 teams while 2 *villani* and 6 cottars had ½ team.[64]

The Anglo-Saxon name Binsted signifies a place where beans were grown.[65] In 1341 jurors assessed the value of corn produced in the parish at ten times that of wool and lambs, and placed relatively high values on the tithes paid on cider, on flax and hemp, on piglets and calves, and on milk, honey, and eggs.[66]

Medieval tenants' holdings were not large. Two in 1454 were 12 a. and 10 a.[67] In 1536 three were 15 a., 16 a., and 30 a.[68] A customary yardland called Onlies, which appears to have survived unchanged, was 17 a. in 1701.[69] In 1536 the Tortington priory estate included 13 tenant holdings, of which 6 were freeholds and 7 were copyholds. The freeholds were small, held at rents of *c.* 1*d.* an acre and contributing less than one tenth of the total rental.[70] One of the freeholds had been created in the 13th or 14th century by a grant out of the demesne;[71] the others are likely to have been assarts or enfranchised copyholds. A customary holding was created in 1452 by a grant of demesne pasture and woodland.[72] In 1601 the former priory estate had 10 copyholders.[73]

The glebe of the vicarage, which may give an indication of the pattern of medieval tenant holdings, in 1341 had 10 a. of arable besides meadow and pasture.[74] In 1615[75] and 1840 it lay apparently little changed, with a house, barn, and croft on Binsted Lane north of the church, dispersed arable in the centre and north part of the parish, and a piece of meadow in the far south.[76] A tenant holding with 15 a. in the common field in 1536 indicates open-field agriculture.[77] The field apparently lay in the centre of the parish, east of the church. In 1606 land there belonged to the estates centred on Marsh Farm and Church Farm,[78] and in 1840 all six proprietors of arable land in Binsted had at least one piece there, many of the holdings being intermixed.[79] The land had been inclosed possibly by 1606 and certainly by 1615, when the vicar's

40 B.L. Add. MSS. 5699, f. 36; 39359, ff. 40v.–41v.
41 *S.A.C.* xxxix. 132.
42 Mon. in ch.
43 P.R.O., RG 9/619, f. 83.
44 *Kelly's Dir. Suss.* (1882, 1903, 1924, 1927).
45 Inf. from Mr. Wishart and Mrs. E. Tristram, Binsted.
46 Gardner, *Suss. Map* (1795).
47 Cf. *Chich. Observer*, 13 June 1980.
48 W.S.R.O., Ep. I/29/22/35.
49 C.I.H.E. libr., GY/PH 7277.
50 W.S.R.O., Add. MS. 9248; cf. Gardner, *Suss. Map* (1795).
51 *Chich. Observer*, 13 June 1980; W.S.R.O., Add. MS. 9248.
52 Inf. from Mr. Wishart.
53 *Kelly's Dir. Suss.* (1927); inf. from Mrs. Tristram.
54 *Chich. Observer*, 13 June 1980.
55 *Cal. Pat.* 1413–16, 301.
56 P.R.O., SC 6/Hen. VIII/3674, m. 9.
57 *Cal. Pat.* 1563–6, pp. 206–7.
58 W.S.R.O., Add. MS. 2034; ibid. Cap. I/28/103; cf. *S.R.S.* lii, p. 96.
59 W.S.R.O., Par. 22/30/1.
60 Ibid. SP 435.
61 Ibid. Raper MSS., temporary no. 438.
62 Ibid. Greatham MS. 29; ibid. Raper MSS., temporary no. 357; *S.R.S.* xx. 442.
63 W.S.R.O., IR 12, f. 13; ibid. Par. 22/6/5.
64 *V.C.H. Suss.* i. 431.
65 *P.N. Suss.* (E.P.N.S.), i. 138.
66 *Inq. Non.* (Rec. Com.), 368.
67 A.C.M., M 530.
68 P.R.O., SC 6/Hen. VIII/3674, m. 9.
69 W.S.R.O., Cap. I/28/108.
70 P.R.O., SC 6/Hen. VIII/3674, m. 9.
71 W.S.R.O., Cap. I/15/3–4.
72 A.C.M., M 530.
73 P.R.O., C 54/1700, pt. 23.
74 *Inq. Non.* (Rec. Com.), 368.
75 W.S.R.O., Ep. I/25/1 (1615).
76 Ibid. TD/W 15, nos. 71, 73–4, 76, 138, 170, 178.
77 P.R.O., SC 6/Hen. VIII/3674, m. 9.
78 W.S.R.O., Add. MS. 12170.
79 Ibid. TD/W 15.

glebe lay in severalty,[80] and by 1635 the pieces of glebe had been hedged and ditched.[81] In 1840 the long and narrow shapes of Church croft and of the closes of 3 a. on each side[82] were evidently a survival of former strips in the open field.

The woodland and pasture commons of the parish were divided and inclosed gradually from the late 16th century, and the process may not have been completed until *c.* 1800. In 1581 the Crown leased 9 a. of wood and underwood, described as part of Binsted and Tortington common, to be enclosed and fenced for coppicing;[83] the woodland seems to have been on the south side of Scotland Lane against the boundary with Tortington. A common called Binsted Ball, on the east side of the parish, was mentioned in 1601, but by 1614 at least part of it was in several ownership; later it became the western part of the parkland of Binsted House.[84] Woodland occupying 70 a. immediately north of Binsted Ball was common in 1600 and common was claimed there in 1789, but by *c.* 1815 it was part of the Binsted House estate.[85] West of that woodland there was a tract of common called Binsted heath in 1647,[86] later belonging to Marsh farm and described in part in 1840 as Furze field.[87] Common of pasture was mentioned in 1663 on Binsted's lower common,[88] adjacent to the cottage[89] later called Goose Green, the name of which itself suggests a common.

The marshland in the south end of the parish had been drained by 1572, when Binsted men were ordered to make their portion of the common ditch along the south side of the parish, and in 1573 the meadow land of various tenants was separated by ditches.[90] In 1635, however, there was still common meadow belonging to the parish,[91] perhaps that added to the Church farm estate[92] and called Town mead in 1840.[93]

Copyholders' shares in the meadow, which lay along the three sides of the southern half of the parish, were never large: in 1601 one with 3 crofts and 9 a. of arable had only 1 rood of meadow.[94] Although the smaller estates were mostly bought out, and Marsh farm included the whole south-west corner of the parish as several meadow in 1606,[95] some small holdings of meadow remained in 1838.[96]

After 1600 the three large estates absorbed most of the smaller ones.[97] One of the three was based on Marsh farm, 140 a. in 1606, including 25 a. of meadow and 57 a. of pasture,[98] and 228 a. in 1840.[99] It was said to have kept great flocks of sheep before 1706, when it had a flock of only 40. It also had then a dairy herd of 4 cows, and pigs, geese, ducks, and chickens; it grew wheat and barley in almost equal parts of 51 a. and pease on a further 10 a.[1] In 1797 the farm also produced hops, potatoes, turnips, fruit, pigeons' eggs, honey, and garden herbs.[2] The lessee in 1785 was required to fallow the arable in alternate years or sow it with peas and vetches.[3] Smaller farms grew wheat, barley, peas, and oats in the 17th century. Clover was grown by 1730 and turnips by 1749.[4] The main crops on Binsted's arable in 1840 were wheat, barley, and turnips,[5] as in 1875.[6]

In 1801 the parish had in all 21 draft horses with 8 wagons and 12 carts, 297 sheep with 34 lambs, 43 cattle including 4 fatting oxen, and 107 pigs.[7] During the agricultural unrest of 1830 some ricks in Binsted were burnt.[8] In 1840 Henry Upton, the owner of Marsh farm with 173 a. of arable, also farmed the agricultural land of the Binsted House estate, with a further 73 a. of arable. Church farm, the core of the third main estate, had 135 a. of arable, 38 a. of meadow, and 11 a. of pasture in 1840.[9] About 1880 both Church farm and Marsh farm had considerable acreages of root crops.[10] By 1922 Church farm and Marsh farm, together 710 a. forming two thirds of the parish, both belonged to the Avisford House estate.[11]

Labour had to be imported from adjacent parishes in 1867.[12] In the later 19th century hedges were removed to create larger fields: the largest in 1838 was 14 a.,[13] whereas the big field east of Church Farm was 53 a. in 1903.[14] In 1879 half of Church farm's 94 a. of arable grew turnips and swedes,[15] and in 1889 Marsh farm and the Binsted House land grew 38 a. of turnips and 37 a. of seeds.[16] Wheat, oats, turnips, and tares were the only crops reported in 1909. In 1875 there were 492 sheep and lambs, but none in 1909, when the stock of cattle, at 92, had almost doubled since 1875.[17] In the 1870s a dairyman occupied Meadow Lodge.[18] In 1938 there were a fruit grower and dairy and poultry farms.[19] In the 1990s herbs were grown commercially near the church.

Both the old demesne woods and the former commons that had been taken into the Marsh farm and Binsted House estates were coppiced in the 17th and 18th centuries.[20] Coppices occupied 349 a. of the 378 a. of woodland in the north in 1840, when there were also 13 a. of young

80 Ibid. Ep. I/25/1 (1615).
81 Ibid. Par 22/6/1.
82 Ibid. TD/W 15, nos. 69–71; cf. ibid. Add. MS. 12171.
83 P.R.O., E 309/Box 7/23 Eliz. I/1, no. 6; E 311/24, m. 75.
84 W.S.R.O., Add. MSS. 3053–4, 3056; ibid. MP 1245; ibid. Par. 22/30/2; ibid. TD/W 15.
85 Ibid. Add. MSS. 9248, 17015; ibid. Par. 22/30/2.
86 Ibid. Add. MSS. 7737–8, 7745.
87 Ibid. TD/W 15.
88 Ibid. Add. MS. 3058.
89 Ibid. TD/W 15.
90 P.R.O., SC 2/205/55, ff. 43, 56.
91 W.S.R.O., Par. 22/6/1.
92 Ibid. PHA 3089, p. 107.
93 Ibid. TD/W 15, no. 134.
94 P.R.O., C 54/1700, pt. 23.
95 W.S.R.O., Add. MS. 12170.
96 Ibid. TD/W 15.
97 e.g. ibid. Add. MS. 3058.
98 Ibid. Add. MSS. 2027, 12170.
99 Ibid. TD/W 15.
1 P.R.O., E 126/18, ff. 521, 620v.; E 134/5 Anne East./4.
2 W.S.R.O., Add. MS. 40241.
3 Ibid. Add. MSS. 7779–80.
4 Ibid. Ep. I/29/22.
5 P.R.O., IR 18/10250.
6 Ibid. MAF 68/433.
7 W.S.R.O., MP 2351.
8 W. Albery, *Millennium of Facts in Hist. of Horsham and Suss.* 549.
9 W.S.R.O., TD/W 15.
10 Ibid. Add. MSS. 14316 (t); 14355 (b).
11 Ibid. SP 435.
12 *Rep. Com. on Children and Women in Agric.* 88.
13 W.S.R.O., TD/W 15; O.S. Map 6", Suss. LXII (1880 edn.).
14 W.S.R.O., Slindon MS. NR 97, f. 23v.
15 Ibid. Add. MS. 14316 (t).
16 Ibid. 14355 (b).
17 P.R.O., MAF 68/433, 2371.
18 W.S.R.O., Par. 22/30/3.
19 *Kelly's Dir. Suss.* (1938).
20 W.S.R.O., Add. MSS. 7741, 12171.

Climping:
Climping Mill in the late 19th century

Yapton:
a bridge over the former Portsmouth–Arundel Canal

Walberton: Nos. 1–3 Yapton Lane
of the mid 19th century

Binsted: the former rectory
built *c.* 1865

Climping: the former vicarage
as rebuilt and enlarged *c.* 1833

plantations.[21] The woodland acreage was virtually unchanged in 1875–6.[22] The name Sawpit field recorded in 1838[23] suggests exploitation of the woodland. Sales of timber from Binsted woods were recorded in 1279.[24] A tanner was recorded in 1536,[25] a carpenter in 1559, and a sawyer in 1574.[26] In 1861 two woodmen lived in the parish,[27] and in 1870 a grocer also dealt in timber.[28] A wheelwright in the parish took an apprentice in 1750,[29] and another worked 1861–81 at Marsh farm.[30] A hurdle maker was recorded in 1915.[31]

A mill may once have stood in or near a close called in 1838 Mill Ball, at the head of the valley west of Binsted House.[32]

Pottery was probably made at Binsted in the early 14th century, some inhabitants being surnamed at Potte in 1332[33] and in the early 15th century. Kilns stood on a pocket of Reading Beds clay where Binsted Lane meets the lane from Walberton.[34] The southward slope has been made steeper by digging clay.[35] Two of the kilns and a workshop there, in use in the later 14th century, produced mainly coarse red or sandy cooking pots.[36] Fragments of Binsted ware, with its distinctive decorations and glazes, are distributed widely both ways along the Sussex coast and to a lesser extent inland.[37] The later kiln continued in production until *c.* 1425.[38] One man called Tyler was taxed at Binsted in 1332, and making other pottery may have been subsidiary to making floor tiles and crested ridge tiles.[39] Sherds of green-glazed medieval pottery have been found near the kiln site, at Church farm, and at the former Pescod's Croft.[40] The kiln site, called All the World in the 17th century,[41] was still used in 1715 as a clay pit.[42] In 1738 Thomas Fowler of Marsh farm was concerned with a brickyard.[43] Four 17th-century tile kilns, where lime may also have been burnt, once stood further north, where the Reading Beds join the Upper Chalk, in what were by 1965 the Slindon Gravel Co. pits.[44] The names of Brick Kiln copse and piece recorded in 1838[45] suggest that bricks and tiles may also have been produced from clays in that area. Two of three gravel pits mapped in 1896 were then still in use.[46]

LOCAL GOVERNMENT. In 1536 Binsted was a separate tithing within Avisford hundred and had its own tithingman,[47] but in 1547 and 1593–4 it shared one with Tortington.[48] The only court recorded for Binsted manor was one in 1650 at which only one of three tenants attended.[49] Draft court rolls survive for the years 1452–4 for Tortington priory's manor of Marsh and Binsted,[50] but though it had several copyhold tenants in 1536[51] no courts are known to have been held thereafter.

Between 1604 and 1691 two churchwardens were chosen yearly but thereafter only one:[52] the office was served in the later 18th century mainly by the farmers of the three large estates, who also acted as overseers of the poor, an office mentioned in 1645, and surveyors of highways,[53] occasionally combining two offices.[54] The poor rate, 1*s.* in the £ in 1785, had quadrupled by 1790, meeting resistance,[55] and before 1820 was sometimes 8*s.* in the £. In the years 1813–15 only out-relief was given.[56] In 1829 weekly relief went to 10 people throughout and to 4 others for part of the year. Some people were housed in a parish poorhouse, standing by 1781 on the north side of the churchyard and repaired several times 1809–18.[57] The poorhouse was used as a cottage by 1840 and demolished between 1896 and 1910.[58]

Binsted became part of Westhampnett poor law union in 1835, and was transferred from Westhampnett to Chichester rural district in 1933, when it became part of Tortington civil parish.[59]

CHURCH. Binsted church existed in the mid 12th century.[60] By 1291 it had been appropriated to Tortington priory and a vicarage had been ordained.[61] Between *c.* 1645 and 1689 the lay rector settled the rectorial tithes on the vicarage,[62] so that the incumbents were thereafter rectors.[63] In 1929 Binsted was united with Walberton as the united benefice of Walberton with Binsted, the parishes remaining distinct.[64]

In the Middle Ages Tortington priory presented the vicars, the bishop sometimes collating between 1412 and 1442.[65] The Crown acted as

21 Ibid. TD/W 15.
22 O.S. Map 6", Suss. LXII (1880 edn.).
23 W.S.R.O., TD/W 15, no. 60.
24 *Plac. de Quo Warr.* (Rec. Com.), 903–4.
25 A.C.M., M 271, f. [10].
26 *Cal. Assize Rec. Suss. Eliz. I*, pp. 13, 425.
27 P.R.O., RG 9/619, f. 83.
28 W.S.R.O., Par. 22/39/1.
29 *S.R.S.* xxviii. 214.
30 P.R.O., RG 9/619, f. 83v.; RG 10/1114, f. 84; RG 11/1125, f. 76.
31 *Kelly's Dir. Suss.* (1915).
32 W.S.R.O., MP 1245; ibid. TD/W 15, no. 87.
33 *S.R.S.* x. 256.
34 *S.A.C.* civ, p. xix; cvi. 133; cf. *Medieval Arch.* xi. 316–17; M. R. McCarthy and C. M. Brooks, *Medieval Pottery in Brit.* 298, 439.
35 O.S. Nat. Grid 979066; K. J. Barton, *Medieval Suss. Pottery*, 170–1, 176.
36 McCarthy and Brooks, *Medieval Pottery*, 298, 322, 439.
37 Barton, *Suss. Pottery*, 3, 93–4, 170–9.
38 Ibid. 173.
39 Ibid. 68, 153, 172; *Medieval Arch.* xi. 316–17; *S.R.S.* x. 256.
40 S.M.R. 1343, 1374.
41 P.R.O., C 54/1700, pt. 23; W.S.R.O., Add. MS. 7742.
42 W.S.R.O., Add. MS. 12171.
43 Ibid. Cap. I/22/4, f. 68.
44 S.M.R. 1338 at O.S. Nat. Grid 977073; *S.A.C.* cvi. 137.
45 W.S.R.O., TD/W 15, nos. 4, 28a (O.S. Nat. Grid 985073, 989074).
46 O.S. Map 6", Suss. LXII. NE. (1899 edn.).
47 A.C.M., M 271, f. [10].
48 E.S.R.O., DYK 1123; W.S.R.O., PHA 6677.
49 W.S.R.O., Slindon MSS., bdle. NR 1.
50 A.C.M., M 530.
51 P.R.O., SC 6/Hen. VIII/3674, m. 9.
52 B.L. Add. MS. 39359, ff. 38–43; W.S.R.O., Ep. I/24/13.
53 W.S.R.O., Par. 22/30/1–3; *S.R.S.* liv. 70.
54 e.g. in 1853: B.L. Add. MS. 39359, f. 43v.; W.S.R.O., Par. 22/39/1.
55 W.S.R.O., Par. 22/30/2.
56 *Poor Law Abstract, 1818*, 454–5.
57 W.S.R.O., Par. 22/30/2; ibid. TD/W 15.
58 Ibid. TD/W 15; O.S. Map 6", Suss. LXII. NE. (1899, 1914 edns.).
59 *Suss. Poor Law Rec.* 52; *Census*, 1931 (pt. ii).
60 Below, this section [fabric].
61 *Tax. Eccl.* (Rec. Com.), 135.
62 B.L. Add. MS. 39329, f. 52v.
63 Ibid. 39368, ff. 156–61.
64 *Lond. Gaz.* 5 Mar. 1929, pp. 1554–6.
65 *S.R.S.* iv. 124; B.L. Add. MS. 39329, ff. 48–9.

patron from the Dissolution until 1575, Sir John Caryll and Ralph Hare presented for a turn in 1592, and John Richard in 1605, when the advowson belonged to Jane Shelley, widow.[66] In 1615 Sir John Shelley and his wife Jane sold it to Sir Garrett Kempe of Slindon, with Binsted manor,[67] and it descended until 1862 with the Slindon House estate.[68] The owners, being Roman Catholics,[69] granted turns to present to others: William Neville presented in 1634, Francis Huddleston in 1689, Henry Peckham in 1734, John Dearling in 1737, Sir George Goring in 1753, and John Pannell in 1764. The archbishop of Canterbury presented in 1695, presumably by lapse. In 1765 the next two turns to Binsted and Slindon were assigned to Maurice Smelt, vicar of Donnington, who presented his son John to both livings, and John in turn presented his son Maurice.[70] In 1862 Col. Charles Leslie of Slindon sold the advowson to John Bones, who in 1863 presented his son Henry Christopher.[71] Father and son in 1869 changed their surname to Lewis.[72] The son's executors presented in 1908 and members of the Lewis family in 1927.[73] In 1929 the patronage of the united benefice was agreed to be shared between the patrons of Binsted and the bishop of Chichester in the proportion of one turn to two, but from the mid 1980s the bishop alone was patron.[74]

In 1291 the vicarage was assessed at £4 6*s*. 8*d*.[75] Exempted from taxation in 1414 because of its poverty,[76] the vicarage had in the 15th century an income below 12 marks[77] and in 1579 under 10.[78] The living, as a rectory, was valued at £103 net in 1809 and at £150 on average *c*. 1830.[79] The tithes of land formerly Tortington priory's were disputed in the 18th century.[80] All the tithes were commuted in 1840 for a rent charge of £178 10*s*.[81] The glebe, a house with 10 a. of arable besides grassland in 1341,[82] included in 1615, as in 1840, a house, garden, orchard, barn, 11½ a. of land near the church, and 2 a. of meadow in the south end of the parish.[83] Part of the glebe was sold in the early 20th century and by 1936 only 6 a. remained, including the rectory grounds.[84] The vicarage house mentioned in 1615 occupied the site of the later Glebe House or Glebe cottage 220 yd. (200 metres) north of the church. Though said to be in disrepair in 1682 it was in good repair in 1724.[85] It was burnt down between 1738 and 1746 and rebuilt in 1755 on the same site, and of the same size, to include a hall, parlour, and kitchen, with chambers above, and offices at the back.[86] Usually let thereafter to tenant farmers,[87] it was thought in 1853 unfit for the rector to live in.[88] By 1936 it had been sold.[89] A large new rectory house was built *c*. 1865 for the new rector H. C. Bones (later Lewis)[90] on a piece of glebe south-east of the church. Of red, grey, and yellow brick, it has prominent gables and chimneystacks, and on the entrance front lancet windows and monograms for Bones and his father. It was sold in or after 1943.[91]

A chaplain of Binsted was a witness in a lawsuit *c*. 1200.[92] In 1424 the poverty of the living had led to the neglect of services, but in 1440 a vicar was resident. Possibly then, as between 1478 and 1521, canons of Tortington usually served as vicars. The vicar in 1521 also served Tortington, and in 1528 the prior of Tortington was presented as vicar.[93] A temporary chantry, to be succeeded by an obit, was founded *c*. 1523 and there was 1 a. to provide a lamp in the church in the 1540s.[94] Between the mid 16th century and the early 18th incumbents of Binsted were often pluralists, some living outside the parish.[95] Robert Knight, resident in 1563,[96] was in 1567 in dispute with the churchwardens over the use of vestments and altar cloths.[97] His successor, who also held Madehurst, preached only once a year at Binsted in 1579; neighbouring clergy had provided sermons for the last three years and parishioners also went to hear preachers at Walberton.[98] Francis Heape, vicar 1605–34,[99] initially resident and capable of preaching,[1] was non-resident by 1615, when he let the glebe house.[2] Curates were recorded in 1555[3] and 1662.[4]

William Turner, rector 1696–1701 and a noted author,[5] lived at his other living of Walberton.[6] From 1701 to 1863 Binsted was held in plurality with Slindon,[7] where the incumbents lived at least from 1739,[8] Binsted being served by a resident curate in 1758 and 1769,[9] and again in 1844, when communion was celebrated four times a year.[10] In 1851 services were held morning and afternoon on alternate Sundays.[11] H. C. Bones, rector from 1863, lived at Binsted. By 1884 he was holding communion eight times a year and preached not only in church but in

66 B.L. Add. MS. 39329, ff. 50–2; *Cal. Pat.* 1572–5, p. 422.
67 *S.R.S.* xix. 41; cf. above, manors (Binsted).
68 Cf. *V.C.H. Suss.* iv. 234–5.
69 *Miscellanea*, vi (Cath. Rec. Soc. vii), 353–7.
70 B.L. Add. MS. 39329, ff. 52v.–55; cf. *S.R.S.* xx. 401; *V.C.H. Suss.* iv. 237.
71 B.L. Add. MSS. 39329, ff. 54, 94; 39469, f. 46.
72 Ibid. 39329, f. 54.
73 *Crockford* (1926, 1935).
74 Below, Walberton, church.
75 *Tax. Eccl.* (Rec. Com.), 135.
76 *S.R.S.* viii. 162.
77 B.L. Add. MS. 39329, ff. 46–7.
78 W.S.R.O., Ep. I/23/5, f. 33.
79 Ibid. Ep. I/63/10; *Rep. Com. Eccl. Revenues.*
80 P.R.O., E 126/18, f. 521; E 134/3 Anne Mich./8; W.S.R.O., Add. MS. 40241; ibid. Par. 22/6/3; Par. 22/30/2–3; *S.R.S.* xxix, p. 166.
81 W.S.R.O., TD/W 15.
82 *Inq. Non.* (Rec. Com.), 368.
83 W.S.R.O., Ep. I/25/1 (1615); ibid. Par. 22/6/1; ibid. TD/W 15.
84 Ibid. Raper MSS., temporary no. 438.
85 Ibid. Ep. I/23/10; *S.R.S.* lxxviii. 60.
86 W.S.R.O., Ep. I/40/11.
87 Ibid. Par. 22/30/1–3.
88 Ibid. Ep. I/22/1 (1853).
89 Ibid. Raper MSS., temporary no. 438.
90 Ibid. Par. 22/30/3; above, pl. facing p. 123.
91 Local inf.
92 *Sel. Canterbury Cases* (Selden Soc. xcv), 33.
93 B.L. Add. MS. 39329, ff. 47–49v.
94 *S.R.S.* xvi. 11; xxxvi. 37.
95 e.g. B.L. Add. MS. 39329, f. 50; W.S.R.O., Ep. I/23/5, f. 33.
96 *S.A.C.* lxi. 113; B.L. Add. MS. 39329, f. 50.
97 *Cal. Assize Rec. Suss. Eliz. I*, p. 51.
98 W.S.R.O., Ep. I/23/5, f. 33.
99 Ibid. Ep. I/24/13.
1 B.L. Add. MS. 39329, f. 52.
2 W.S.R.O., Ep. I/25/1 (1615).
3 *S.R.S.* xli. 150.
4 W.S.R.O., Ep. I/22/1 (1662).
5 *D.N.B.*; B.L. Add. MS. 39368, f. 157.
6 *S.N.Q.* xiv. 37–43.
7 B.L. Add. MS. 39329, ff. 53v.–58v.; *S.A.C.* cvi. 14.
8 e.g. W.S.R.O., Ep. I/22/1 (1758); cf. B.L. Add. MS. 5699, f. 35v.
9 W.S.R.O., Ep. I/22/1 (1758, 1769).
10 Ibid. Ep. I/22A/2 (1844).
11 *S.R.S.* lxxv, p. 155.

people's houses. All the children in the parish were said to attend his Sunday school.[12] His successors remained resident until the 1940s.[13]

The church of *ST. MARY*, so named by 1776,[14] is built of flint with stone dressings and consists of chancel and nave with south porch, north vestry, and west tower with low shingled spire. The chancel and nave are divided only by a slight break in the line of the roof, perhaps marking off the separate responsibilities of parish and rector for maintaining the fabric. The main structure is of the earlier or mid 12th century and three windows of that date remain.[15] A low side window may have been put in the chancel *c.* 1250.[16] Other windows and the south doorway were inserted in the 14th century, and the north doorway in the 16th. Parts of the roof are medieval.[17] A major restoration in 1868 to designs by T. G. Jackson,[18] largely at the rector's expense,[19] removed a gallery and ceiling and added the south porch and vestry, along with some external buttresses.[20]

The arcaded circular stone font, projecting slightly over its thick, round pedestal, and the piscina in the south chancel wall are 12th-century.[21] The stumps of a former rood beam, embedded in the north and south walls, have mouldings apparently of the early 14th century. The rood loft was entered by stairs in an external projection on the north side.[22]

Wall paintings apparently covering the whole interior of the church were found at the restoration of 1868.[23] The only painting surviving in 1992 is in the splay of the north chancel window, showing on the west a three-branched tree and on the east a crowned woman, with a star in the apex above them; over the woman a name, lost since 1900, was more probably that of St. Mary than St. Margaret.[24] The lost paintings included Christ in majesty and perhaps Christ's entombment.[25] In the nave floor is a 13th-century glazed and incised tile possibly from the Binsted tile kilns.[26] A bench is possibly medieval. A 17th-century pulpit,[27] later described as triple-deckered, was removed in 1868.[28] Set into the south chancel wall is an apparently post-medieval oak tabernacle.[29]

At or after the restoration of 1868 the church received a multicoloured chancel pavement in the Italian Cosmati manner, a boldly patterned wrought-iron communion rail, and patterned grisaille glass in the east window, designed by T. G. Jackson with Henry Holliday and made by Powell's in 1869.[30] Jackson also designed a new rood screen modelled on the medieval one,[31] but it was removed in 1947.[32]

There were two bells in 1641.[33] The one that survived in 1992 may be of *c.* 1330.[34] The plate includes a cup of 1831 given by the rector Maurice Smelt and a paten of 1806 given by Thomas Fowler.[35] The registers begin in 1638, and in the 17th century and early 18th are extremely confused.[36]

NONCONFORMITY. Although the owners of the Church farm estate were recusants,[37] no Catholics were recorded in Binsted until 1781, when there were 10.[38] Some inhabitants still attended the Catholic chapel at Slindon in the early 19th century.[39]

Quakers were meeting at Binsted in 1655 at the house of Daniel Gittins, who with William Penfold refused to pay tithes and church rate in 1656. Penfold was imprisoned in 1664 for not coming to church and later died in gaol.[40]

EDUCATION. There was no school in Binsted in 1769[41] or in 1818, when a Sunday school in Slindon and day schools in adjoining parishes were thought sufficient for teaching the children of the parish to read.[42] A Sunday school was started in 1830 and taught 25 children in 1833[43] and 24 in 1847, when it had a paid master.[44] The later Oakley cottages were still the school house and Sunday school in 1896.[45] In 1838 and 1844 children from Binsted went to the National school at Slindon.[46] After 1874 Binsted pupils attended Walberton National school,[47] Binsted parish paying a proportionate share of that school's costs.[48] In 1891 H. C. Lewis, rector of Binsted, also assisted that school with his own money.[49] The younger children continued to attend Walberton school in 1992; in 1996 most older children went to school at Westergate in Aldingbourne.[50]

CHARITIES FOR THE POOR. None known.

12 Above, this section; W.S.R.O., Ep. I/22A/2 (1884).
13 e.g. ibid. Ep. I/22/1 (1917); *Crockford* (1940).
14 B.L. Add. MS. 5699, f. 35. It was called St. Mary and St. Peter, perhaps in error, in 1868: *S.A.C.* xx. 233–4.
15 Nairn & Pevsner, *Suss.* 105; *S.A.C.* xliii. 225; Anon. *Binsted Ch. Guide*; *V.C.H. Suss.* ii. 339, 367; the last two state that Tortington priory built the ch., for which there is no doc. evidence.
16 *S.A.C.* xli. 166; xlii. 147 n.
17 *V.C.H. Suss.* ii. 348.
18 *Recollections of T. G. Jackson*, ed. B. H. Jackson, 114.
19 W.S.R.O., Par. 22/12/1.
20 Anon. *Binsted Ch. Guide*, using evidence supplied by the late Miss Charlotte Read of Binsted Ho.
21 *V.C.H. Suss.* ii. 356; Nairn & Pevsner, *Suss.* 105; Anon. *Binsted Ch. Guide.*
22 W.S.R.O., PD 2012, f. 9; *S.A.C.* xxxix. 52.
23 *S.A.C.* xx. 233–4.
24 *Pace* e.g. ibid. xliii. 225–6; below, pl. facing p. 235.
25 Anon. *Binsted Ch. Guide*; *S.A.C.* xxxviii. 5–6; *V.C.H. Suss.* ii. 354.
26 *V.C.H. Suss.* ii. 353; above, econ. hist.
27 W.S.R.O., Ep. 1/22/1 (1662).
28 Anon. *Binsted Ch. Guide*, using evidence from Miss Read.
29 Notwithstanding *V.C.H. Suss.* ii. 351, 367.
30 Nairn & Pevsner, *Suss.* 105.
31 *S.A.C.* xx. 233–4.
32 W.S.R.O., Par. 22/4/3.
33 B.L. Add. MS. 39368, f. 155.
34 Elphick, *Bells*, 36.
35 *S.A.C.* liii. 233.
36 W.S.R.O., Par. 22/1 (TS. cat.).
37 *Miscellanea*, vi (Cath. Rec. Soc. vii), 353–7.
38 W.S.R.O., MP 1271.
39 Ibid. 2415.
40 E.S.R.O., SOF 43/1–2; *S.A.C.* lv. 84; cf. W. Albery, *Millennium of Facts in Hist. of Horsham and Suss.* 426.
41 W.S.R.O., Ep. I/22/1 (1769).
42 *Educ. of Poor Digest*, 953.
43 *Educ. Enq. Abstract*, 963.
44 Nat. Soc. *Inquiry, 1846–7*, Suss. 2–3.
45 O.S. Map 6", Suss. LXII. NE. (1899 edn.); cf. W.S.R.O., Ep. I/22A/1 (1884).
46 W.S.R.O., Ep. I/22/2 (1838); Ep. I/22A/2 (1844).
47 Below, Walberton, educ.; cf. W.S.R.O., Par. 202/25/1–2.
48 W.S.R.O., Par. 22/25/1, loose receipt at ff. 37–8.
49 Ibid. Par. 22/6/5.
50 Local inf.

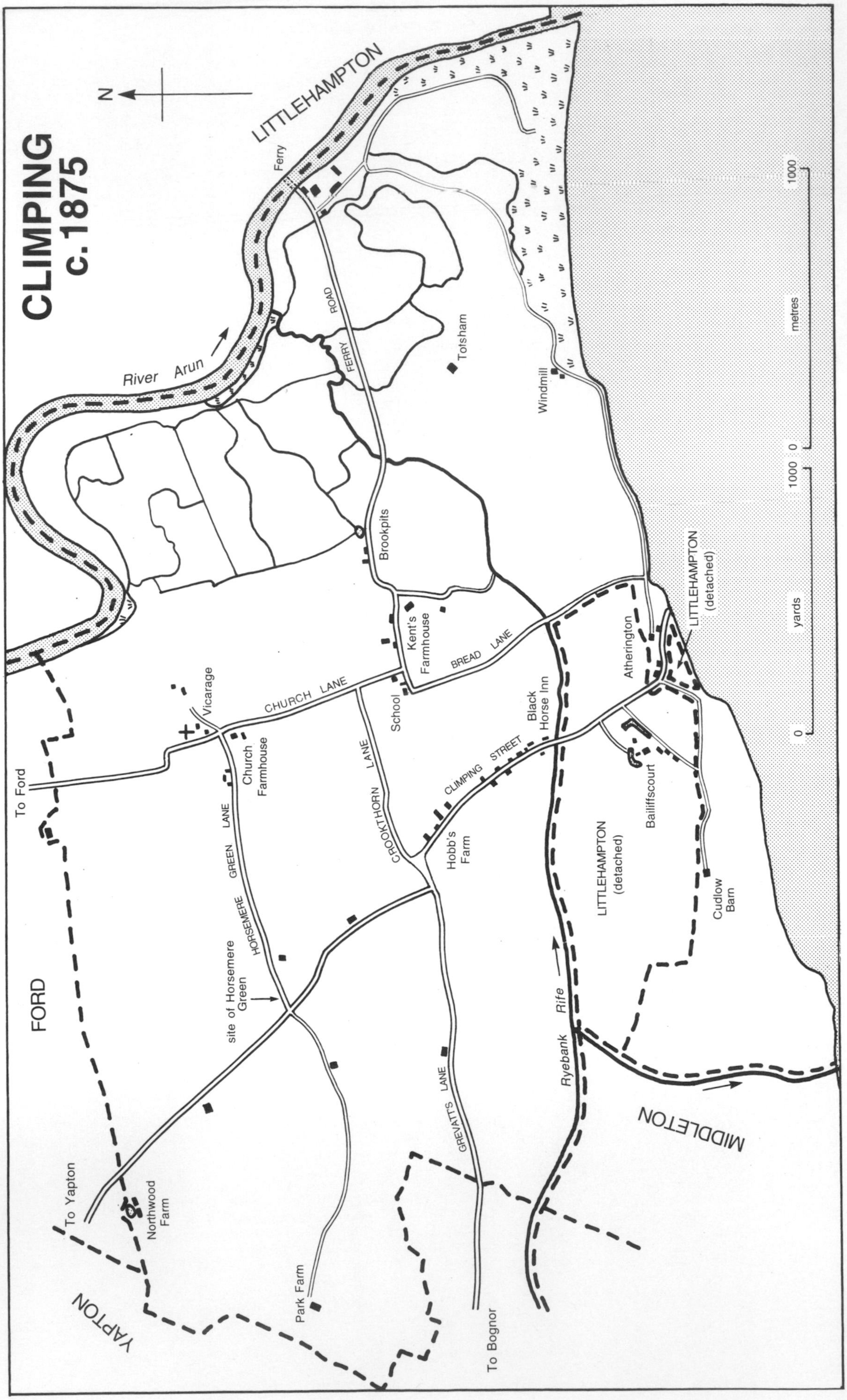
CLIMPING
c.1875
N
LITTLEHAMPTON
Ferry
River Arun
FERRY ROAD
Totsham
Windmill
Brookpits
Kent's Farmhouse
BREAD LANE
CHURCH LANE
Vicarage
School
Black Horse Inn
Atherington
LITTLEHAMPTON (detached)
CLIMPING STREET
Bailiffscourt
Church Farmhouse
To Ford
HORSEMERE GREEN LANE
CROOKTHORN LANE
Hobb's Farm
LITTLEHAMPTON (detached)
Cudlow Barn
FORD
site of Horsemere Green
Ryebank Rife
GREVATT'S LANE
MIDDLETON
To Yapton
Northwood Farm
Park Farm
YAPTON
To Bognor
0 yards 1000
0 metres 1000

CLIMPING

THE parish of Climping, which includes the former parishes of Cudlow and Ilsham, lies along the coast on the west bank of the river Arun.[51] Of Cudlow only the north-western and north-eastern corners remained in 1991, the rest having been lost to the sea;[52] the north-eastern part is represented by Littlehampton golf course and West Beach, while within the north-western part a barn called Cudlow barn existed until 1984.[53] Ilsham, sometimes wrongly said also to have been destroyed by the sea,[54] in fact occupied an east–west strip across the centre of the present parish including the sites of Hobb's Farm, the school, and Brookpits Manor.[55] The area of Climping parish expanded as longshore drift caused the mouth of the river Arun to be deflected eastwards. Construction of a new estuary under an Act of 1733[56] left part of the land beyond the river,[57] but the boundary between Climping and Littlehampton was not adjusted until 1840.[58]

The ancient parish had 1,838 a. *c.* 1875, and was enlarged in 1880 by the addition of two detached parts of Littlehampton (172 a.), the larger of which contained Bailiffscourt house.[59] The link with Littlehampton was tenurial, both the Bailiffscourt otherwise Atherington estate and Littlehampton manor belonging in the Middle Ages to Sées abbey (Orne);[60] but it may not have been established until the 14th century, since though Bailiffscourt was apparently the 2 yardlands in Littlehampton mentioned separately as belonging to Sées in 1341[61] it was claimed to lie in Climping in 1310.[62] The uncertainty continued.[63] One or more occupiers of the Bailiffscourt estate in the 16th century wished to be buried at Littlehampton,[64] where two children of Walter Edmunds were interred *c.* 1590[65] and two sons of later lessees baptized in the 1670s.[66] About 1592, however, Edmunds was presented for non-attendance at Littlehampton church and was disputing his assessment to the church rate.[67] By the mid 17th century the north transept of Climping church was attached to the Bailiffscourt estate, whose inhabitants used it during services.[68] Payment of the Littlehampton church rate was again refused in 1686,[69] and in 1679 the occupier of the farm declined to serve as churchwarden for Littlehampton or to attend church there; it was claimed on his behalf that inhabitants of Bailiffscourt were then invariably buried at Climping and had only rarely served parish offices at Littlehampton, whereas they had often performed highway repair duty in Climping, one man also serving as Avisford hundred constable.[70]

The parish increased in size, evidently through land reclamation, to 2,016 a., including inland water, in 1901 and 2,021 a. in 1921.[71] In 1933 the south-eastern corner (227 a.) was transferred to Littlehampton.[72] In 1971 Climping thus had 1,794 a. (726 ha.).[73] The northern portion of the parish, including Ford prison and the southern part of Ford airfield, was transferred to Ford in 1985.[74]

The present article deals generally with the ancient parish including Cudlow and Ilsham, and with the two detached parts of Littlehampton; after *c.* 1825, however, the date of opening of a chain ferry across the Arun, the south-eastern portion was more closely connected with Littlehampton, and most aspects of its later history are therefore reserved for treatment elsewhere.[75]

The western boundary of Cudlow parish *c.* 1310 was marked by a 'great ditch' ending in a pool called Elmeringpool, i.e. Elmer pool;[76] in 1991 that line remained the Climping–Middleton boundary. One section of the Ryebank rife, which drains the southern part of the parish, was claimed in 1310 as the boundary between Cudlow and Ilsham;[77] what was apparently the same section continued until 1880 to divide Climping from the outlier of Littlehampton containing Bailiffscourt.[78] Since both the 'great ditch' of *c.* 1310 and the Ryebank rife, also called 'the great ditch' in 1606[79] and 'the rife

51 This article was written in 1991 and revised in 1996. Topographical details in introduction based mainly on O.S. Maps 1/25,000, SU 80/90 (1981 edn.); TQ 00/10 (1979 edn.); 6", Suss. LXII–LXIII, LXXIV–LXXV (1879–80 and later edns.). Much help was received from the late Mr. G. Harper, Middleton-on-Sea, and other members of the Clymping local hist. group, and from Miss M. Kendell, Middleton-on-Sea, and Mr. G. Wooldridge, Climping. Much information about the par. is found in TS. cats. of docs. in Eton Coll. Libr., of which copies are in the libr. of the P.R.O.

52 Cf. W.S.R.O., Add. MS. 2031, illus. at *S.A.C.* xliv, facing p. 147, describing them as E. and W. Cudlow; A.C.M., Hodskinson surv. 1778, ff. 42–3.

53 O.S. Map 6", Suss. LXXIV (1879 edn.); inf. from Mr. V. Landymore, Brookpits Man., Climping.

54 *S.N.Q.* xv. 315; P. Brandon, *Suss. Landscape*, 117; *S. Saxons*, ed. P. Brandon, 82.

55 *S.N.Q.* vi. 109–12.

56 6 Geo. II, c. 12.

57 A.C.M., PM 163; *S.N.Q.* xv. 154.

58 P.R.O., IR 18/10401; cf. *Littlehampton Gaz.* 1 Nov. 1946 (perambulation of Littlehampton par. bdry. 1838).

59 *Census*, 1881; O.S. Map 6", Suss. LXII–LXIII, LXXIV–LXXV (1879–80 edn.). The smaller, Shortsmare, was only 4 a. *c.* 1875, but had earlier been larger: below, this section (landscape hist.).

60 e.g. *Cal. Chart. R.* 1257–1300, 180; *Feud. Aids*, v. 142.

61 *Inq. Non.* (Rec. Com.), 393.

62 Eton Coll. Libr. MS. 45/83 (TS. cat.); cf. *Cat. Anct. D.* i, B 177.

63 *S.R.S.* xlii. 26–7; W.S.R.O., Ep. I/29/51/2, 26, describing Atherington as in Climping but perhaps referring to hos. nearby in Climping par.; cf. below, this section (settlement).

64 *S.A.C.* xii. 92–3; *S.R.S.* xliii. 166.

65 B.L. Add. MS. 33410, f. 103.

66 E. Robinson and J. S. Heward, *Reminiscences of Littlehampton* (Arundel, [1933]), 39–40.

67 B.L. Add. MS. 33410, ff. 72, 101–4.

68 W.S.R.O., Ep. I/17/32, f. 93.

69 B.L. Add. MS. 39368, f. 914.

70 W.S.R.O., Ep. I/17/32, ff. 92v.–94.

71 *Census*, 1881–1921.

72 Ibid. 1931 (pt. ii); W.S.R.O., WOC/CC 7/2/9.

73 *Census*, 1971.

74 Arun (Parishes) Order 1985.

75 *V.C.H. Suss.* v (2), Littlehampton (forthcoming).

76 Eton Coll. Libr. MS. 45/83–4 (TS. cat.); below, Middleton-on-Sea, intro. (landscape hist.).

77 Eton Coll. Libr. MS. 45/83 (TS. cat.).

78 O.S. Map 6", Suss. LXXIV–LXXV (1879 edn.).

79 W.S.R.O., Add. MS. 2027, ff. 15–16.

or broad ditch' in 1838,[80] seem to be artificial, they may be pre-medieval estate boundaries.

LANDSCAPE HISTORY. The western part of the ancient parish, including the settlements of Climping, Ilsham, and Atherington,[81] lies on brickearth, of which Climping windmill occupies an outlier further east. The rest of the eastern part lies on alluvium, and once belonged to the wide estuary of the river Arun. Since the alluvium between Atherington and the brickearth outlier to the east can only have been brought by the river, the main channel of the river is likely once to have run there and to have been deflected eastwards later.[82]

The landscape history of the south-eastern corner of the ancient parish is not clear, for two reasons. First, the chronology of the eastward deflection of the lower course of the river Arun is uncertain, the notion of a long lagoon south of the present coastline, sheltered by a spit running from Selsey to a point off Worthing,[83] not being convincing. Secondly, references to incursions by the sea and to sea defences on Atherington manor may sometimes be actually to the river estuary, since the expression 'sea wall' (*murus marinus* or *maritimus*) used there was also employed at Ford, Climping, and Ilsham manor,[84] which fronted only the river.

In the north-eastern part of the parish reclamation from the estuary was apparently going on by the 13th century, when the rectory estate included land east of the village (*villa*) of Climping bounded on three sides by ditches.[85] By the mid 16th century there were defences in that area against the river.[86] Further south some marshland had been reclaimed by the early 16th century on Atherington manor, where a defensive wall, presumably meaning an earth bank, was mentioned in 1511;[87] it may have followed the line of the surviving track running north-east from Climping mill which existed by 1606.[88] By 1540 there were at least 110 a. of demesne marshland pasture at Atherington.[89] The river defences continued to be kept up in the early 18th century; by 1731 Christ's Hospital as landowner had constructed groynes alongside its lands in the north-east, though because of the hindrance to navigation the Littlehampton harbour commissioners ordered them to be abandoned in 1761.[90] Land between the various defences and the river was saltmarsh pasture, known as slipes,[91] which in 1792 were flooded at every spring tide.[92]

The parish of Cudlow, at least in its eastern portion, may represent the early medieval expansion of settlement over reclaimed land in the lower part of the Arun estuary: the manor does not appear in Domesday Book, and the church seems to have originated as a chapelry of Climping.[93] The port which existed there in the 13th and 14th centuries has not been located, but in the 16th century the estuary was said to have two 'havens', Littlehampton and Cudlow, the second of which may have lain in the putative former channel of the river west of Climping mill.[94]

By the 1360s the lord's income from agistment in the Cudlow demesne brooks had been reduced by flooding,[95] which together with erosion continued later to such a degree as to render the living by 1511 a sinecure.[96] By the late 15th century Atherington manor was suffering a decrease in rent income through the incursions of the sea,[97] and in the early 17th strips in the common fields along the coast there were being gradually eaten away.[98] Erosion continued at Atherington in the 18th century, the close called Shortsmare next to the hamlet being reduced from 21 a. in 1606 to 12 a. by 1751 and 9 a. by 1772.[99] A considerable part of the coast was said in 1774 to be swept away each year.[1] The west end of the parish was then apparently the weakest part; despite the building of 12 timber groynes at West Cudlow in the 1770s and 80s the sea was 'daily making fresh encroachments' there *c.* 1790, when the cost of maintaining the defences was greater than the income from the land.[2]

Erosion continued in the 19th century.[3] There were groynes on the coast at five places in the western and central parts of the parish in 1843,[4] and further groynes were constructed there before 1900,[5] which according to one observer had done great damage to the shore east of them.[6] The defences themselves were badly damaged in a gale in 1875,[7] and *c.* 1897 Christ's Hospital acquired the south-west corner of the parish as the only way of protecting its adjacent lands.[8] In 1901 the hospital took a 21-year lease from the Crown of the foreshore of that part of the parish,[9] the sewers commissioners being responsible in 1914 for the rest.[10] New groynes were constructed *c.* 1906.[11] Sea defence at that period

80 *Littlehampton Gaz.* 1 Nov. 1946 (perambulation of Littlehampton par. bdry. 1838).

81 Below, this section (settlement).

82 Geol. Surv. Map 1", drift, sheet 332 (1975 edn.); inf. from Dr. D. Robinson, Univ. of Suss.

83 A. H. Allcroft, *Waters of Arun*, 119.

84 P.R.O., SC 6/Hen. VIII/3659, rot. 3; W.S.R.O., Add. MS. 2027, ff. 20–2; cf. ibid. 2292, rot. 5d.; *Cal. Pat.* 1563–6, p. 364.

85 Eton Coll. Libr. MS. 56/46 (TS. cat.). The land may be the close of vicarial glebe depicted ½ mile (800 metres) SE. of the ch. in 1843: W.S.R.O., TD/W 33, no. 110.

86 W.S.R.O., Add. MS. 2292, rot. 5d.; *Cal. Pat.* 1563–6, p. 364.

87 P.R.O., SC 6/Hen. VIII/3659, rot. 3; cf. W.S.R.O., Add. MS. 2027, ff. 20–2.

88 W.S.R.O., Add. MSS. 2027, f. 21; 2031.

89 P.R.O., SC 6/Hen. VIII/3480, rot. 14d.

90 Guildhall Libr. MSS. 13322, acct. of Ford and Climping, 1731; 13323/2, rep. of view of estates, 1761, p. 2.

91 W.S.R.O., Add. MSS. 1728 (TS. cat.); 2031; cf. ibid. TD/W 33; *250 Yrs. of Mapmaking in Suss.* ed. H. Margary, pl. 19.

92 Guildhall Libr. MS. 13324, rep. of land surveyor, 1792.

93 Below, churches (Cudlow ch.).

94 Leland, *Itin.* ed. Toulmin Smith, iv. 93; below, econ. hist. (other trades and inds.). The suggestion at Allcroft, *Waters of Arun*, 111, 128, is less convincing.

95 A.C.M., A 415.

96 *S.A.C.* cxvi. 281.

97 P.R.O., SC 6/1101/20, rot. 2d.; cf. ibid. SC 6/Hen. VIII/3659, rot. 3.

98 W.S.R.O., Add. MS. 2027, ff. 10, 24.

99 Ibid. Add. MSS. 1727 (TS. cat.); 2027, f. 19; 2031; ibid. MP 2072. It was further reduced later: O.S. Map 6", Suss. LXXV (1879 edn.).

1 Eton Coll. Libr. MS. 45/102 (TS. cat.).

2 A.C.M., Hodskinson surv. 1778, f. 42; ibid. MD 619, p. 12; 773; cf. below, manors (Cudlow).

3 Eton Coll. Libr. MS. 65/240.

4 W.S.R.O., TD/W 33.

5 e.g. O.S. Map 6", Suss. LXXIV–LXXV (1879 edn.).

6 Eton Coll. Libr., Climping corresp. file, 'Clymping Record', 1902–3.

7 Guildhall Libr. MS. 13323/6, rep. of visit to Suss. estate, 1876.

8 Ibid. 12813/14, pp. 46, 71–4, 83.

9 Ibid. 13319, deed, 1914.

10 W.S.R.O., SP 1540, p. 5.

11 *Land Drainage Rec. of W. Suss.* ed. D. Butler, p. 92; cf. *1st Rep. Com. Coast Erosion, Apps. to Evidence* [Cd. 3684], p. 354, H.C. (1907), xxxiv.

was said to be a heavy expense on owners of neighbouring land.[12] In 1991, however, the coast in the centre of the parish was protected by a concrete wall.

The eastward deflection of the mouth of the Arun by 1587 had created a small spit,[13] which grew larger during the 17th century[14] until it was cut by the creation of the present estuary under an Act of 1733.[15] By the mid 17th century the duke of Norfolk was maintaining timber defences both at Cudlow and at Littlehampton to protect the mouth of the river.[16] An embankment roughly parallel with the river existed by *c.* 1736,[17] and by 1772 a westwards extension had been created at its southern end.[18] The embankment was reconstructed on a different alignment after 1778,[19] perhaps before 1785, when a later duke leased to William Bolton land outside the 'sea wall' which Bolton had made at his own expense.[20] It survived as an important landscape feature in 1991. The present embankment beside the river itself throughout the parish was apparently heightened under an Act of 1793.[21]

Meanwhile along the coast in the south-eastern corner of the parish a line of low dunes had been formed, perhaps by the later 17th century[22] and certainly by 1768.[23] The land north of them, known as East Cudlow farm,[24] was largely slipe and sand in 1778,[25] and remained swampy in 1830.[26] Its later history is reserved for treatment elsewhere.[27]

Part of the river bank was breached in a storm in 1913;[28] flooding since then has been less severe, but in 1960 affected the area around the Bognor Regis to Littlehampton road in the centre of the parish.[29]

A feature of the parish in the mid 19th century was its ponds: between four and six at each of the centres of settlement, besides others in the fields.[30] Stakers pond or pool mentioned in 1606[31] was perhaps one of the ponds at Atherington hamlet, the land beside which was registered as common land in 1979.[32] The flat, open landscape was felt in the 1930s to retain 'a stillness that reminds one of the Emilian plains near Ravenna'.[33] Despite much development, something of that atmosphere survived on the remoter parts of Ford airfield in 1990. Climping's coastline then remained largely undeveloped and was subject to National Trust covenants;[34] the beach was a popular goal for summer day visitors from London and elsewhere.[35]

The parish seems generally to have had little woodland, and the woods on the two estates called Climping which supported 40 swine in 1086 may have been in the Weald.[36] The wood at Atherington on the boundary with Middleton mentioned *c.* 1310[37] was probably the same as Southwood depicted in 1606,[38] but in 1378 there was only enough underwood on Atherington manor for fencing.[39] Southwood and two other closes within or beside Bailiffscourt park were described in 1606 as thorny pasture.[40] There were 16 a. of woods in Climping and the detached portion of Littlehampton at Bailiffscourt in the 1840s.[41] The amount was greatly increased in the 1920s and 30s by Lord Moyne, of Bailiffscourt, who planted belts of fully grown trees all over the southern half of the parish, including a wide one along the Middleton boundary.[42] Many of the trees were destroyed in the great storm of 1987.[43]

The park in Climping belonging to Ford, Climping, and Ilsham manor and the successive parks at Bailiffscourt are described below.[44] There may also have been a park at Cudlow, where free warren was granted or confirmed to the earl of Arundel in 1617.[45]

SETTLEMENT. Settlement in the parish has always apparently been scattered. Only a handful of dwellings, including Church Farmhouse and the former vicarage house, remained in 1990 near the church, but earthworks in two closes to south-east and east, yielding finds of medieval and Romano-British date, indicate the existence there of other house sites.[46] A cross may have stood nearby in 1540.[47] There were *c.* 6 houses in 1778.[48] In 1843 three or four flanked a lane along the south-east side of the churchyard.[49]

Other sites of medieval settlement were at Cudlow and Ilsham. Cudlow, which may represent secondary settlement,[50] lay beyond the present

12 Eton Coll. Libr., Climping corresp. file, 'Clymping Record', 1901.

13 *Armada Surv.* ed. Lower.

14 *High Stream of Arundel*, 27; B.L. Sloane MS. 3233, f. 15.

15 6 Geo. II, c. 12.

16 A.C.M., A 262, ff. [24, 38v., 55, 95, 97]; 263, acct. 1661; cf. ibid. 284, p. 6.

17 P.R.O., MR 915, no. 5; cf. ibid. 1111, no. 14 (both illus. at J. Goodwin, *Milit. Defence of W. Suss.* 27, 32).

18 W.S.R.O., MP 2072.

19 *250 Yrs. of Mapmaking in Suss.* pl. 14.

20 W.S.R.O., Holmes, Campbell & Co. MS. 729 (TS. cat.).

21 33 Geo. III, c. 100; cf. Guildhall Libr. MS. 13324, rep. of land surveyor, 1792; *250 Yrs. of Mapmaking in Suss.* pl. 15; B.L. Maps SEC. 1. (13b).

22 Littlehampton Mus. MS. M 037; B.L. Sloane MS. 3233, f. 15; P.R.O., MR 915, no. 5; 1111, no. 24.

23 P.R.O., MR 1111, no. 14.

24 e.g. A.C.M., A 262, f. [55].

25 Ibid. Hodskinson surv. 1778, f. 43; ibid. LM 23.

26 B.L. Maps SEC. 1. (13b).

27 *V.C.H. Suss.* v (2), Littlehampton (forthcoming).

28 *W. Suss. Gaz.* 27 Mar. 1913 (inf. from the late Mr. G. Harper, Middleton-on-Sea).

29 W.S.R.O., WDC/SU 19/1/1.

30 Ibid. TD/W 33.

31 Ibid. Add. MS. 2027, ff. 23, 26–7.

32 W. Suss. C.C. property dept., reg. of com. land.

33 *Chips: The Diaries of Sir Hen. Channon*, ed. R. R. James (1970), 53–4.

34 *W. Suss. Gaz.* 14 Mar. 1974.

35 Cf. *Chich. Observer*, 27 Sept. 1974.

36 *V.C.H. Suss.* i. 430.

37 Eton Coll. Libr. MS. 45/83 (TS. cat.).

38 W.S.R.O., Add. MS. 2031.

39 P.R.O., E 106/11/2, rot. 1.

40 W.S.R.O., Add. MSS. 2027, ff. 16, 19, 24; 2031.

41 Ibid. TD/W 33, 78.

42 Ibid. Add. MS. 35210; *Chich. Observer*, 27 Sept. 1974; O.S. Map 6", Suss. LXII. SE. (1951 edn.); LXIII. SW. (1932 edn.); LXXIV. NE. (1932, 1950 edns.); LXXV. NW. (1932 edn.); below, manors (Atherington).

43 Local inf.

44 Below, manors.

45 B.L. Add. MS. 5687, f. 99. No corroboration has been found for the mention of a park there in 1562 at Dallaway, *Hist. W. Suss.* ii (1) (1819), 16.

46 S.M.R. 2201; *Medieval Village Res. Group Rep.* xix. 8; unpubl. excav. (inf. from the late Mr. Harper).

47 W.S.R.O., Add. MS. 2292, rot. 1.

48 *250 Yrs. of Mapmaking in Suss.* pl. 14.

49 W.S.R.O., TD/W 33. Hos. on copyholds of Ford, Climping, and Ilsham man. at Climping in 1608 are described in detail at Guildhall Libr. MS. 13321, ff. 24–34.

50 Above, this section (landscape hist.).

coastline south or south-east of Atherington;[51] since the second element of its name indicates rising ground,[52] it probably occupied a southwards extension of the brickearth outlier at Climping mill.[53] The reduction of its tax assessment by nearly half in 1450 was probably due to the inroads of the sea,[54] and dwellings were apparently being abandoned in the 1460s.[55] Only two men were listed in Cudlow tithing in the muster roll of 1539.[56] The last record of an inhabitant is of 1620.[57]

The settlement called Ilsham[58] seems to have lain between the present school and Brookpits Manor, to judge from the location of field names including the word Ilsham in 1843.[59] The place called Stroodland,[60] which apparently indicates marshy land overgrown with brushwood,[61] lay at its western end, at the north end of the present village street of Climping.[62] A cross at Ilsham called the king's cross was mentioned in 1533.[63] The place name was used at least until the mid 17th century,[64] Ilsham even sometimes anachronistically being described as a parish.[65]

There were 10 or 12 houses at Ilsham in 1778[66] and 8 or 10 in 1843,[67] some of which survived in 1991. North-east of the school until 1930, when it was destroyed by fire, stood a large late 16th- or early 17th-century timber-framed house with a continuous jetty.[68] Brookpits Manor,[69] which is not related to any manorial estate, is of two storeys with attics; it has a square plan and is built of knapped flint with red brick dressings and brick mullioned windows. The south front has a central projecting brick porch of two storeys, and the east and west fronts have gables. Original panelling and fittings survive, including brick fireplaces with four-centred arches; one on the first floor has the date 1656 moulded in plaster above it, probably indicating the date of building. By 1914 the house was divided into two cottages,[70] as it remained until extensive restoration as a single dwelling between 1972 and 1974.[71]

At the centre of Kent's Farmhouse, south-west of Brookpits, is a long late 17th-century range of flint rubble with brick dressings; it has a large chimneystack at its north-western end, and possibly faced south-east. Additions were made to north-west and south-east in the 18th century, possibly replacing an earlier wing, and in 1731 Edward Kent's farmhouse, evidently the same building, had a hall, parlour, chambers, garrets, and offices.[72] In the early 19th century the south-eastern extension was rebuilt to provide a new main front of four bays facing north-east, and *c.* 1880 a large one-storeyed room was added on the north side by the tenant George Constable. At that period the building was let as a gentleman's house,[73] ornamental grounds being laid out by the 1870s.[74] Kent's Dairy Cottages nearby was originally a timber-framed building, the rear wall of which survives within the present house. Much of the timber framing was later replaced by rubble with brick dressings, and the house was extended southwards in the 17th century. A barn to the south was brought to its present site by Lord Moyne.[75]

It is not clear whether there was settlement at Atherington in the Middle Ages apart from the house of the bailiff of Sées abbey, later known as Bailiffscourt; if there was, it was perhaps removed by the creation of the park in or before the early 17th century.[76] At that date there were *c.* 12 houses at the site of the present hamlet 300 yd. (270 metres) south-east of Bailiffscourt house. The settlement was then called a village (*villa*),[77] and in 1751 was known as Atherington street.[78] Some houses had been destroyed by the sea before 1772.[79] In 1778 there were only *c.* 8 dwellings[80] and by 1843, after further erosion, four or five.[81] Nos. 1 and 2 Atherington Cottages are an early 18th-century building with a later western extension. The disused farm buildings nearby, in poor condition in 1990, include one with stone quoins and windows in medieval style created as a pastiche by Lord Moyne in the 1930s.[82]

By 1606 there were also apparently houses in the present village street to the north[83] which, as the chief road in the parish leading to the sea, later became the main centre of settlement. By the later 18th century it had the largest concentration of dwellings in the parish, *c.* 15 or more.[84] By 1825 it was known as Climping street,[85] and in the 20th century the settlement came to be called Climping village. Buildings there are of various dates between the 18th and 20th centuries, materials including red brick, flint, and beach

51 Below, this section (communications).
52 *P.N. Suss.* (E.P.N.S.), i. 139.
53 W.S.R.O., Add. MSS. 2027, f. 22; 2031, indicating a rd. from Climping mill to Cudlow. Cf. B.L. Sloane MS. 3233, f. 15; O.S. Map 6", Suss. LXXV. NW. (1899 edn.), showing rocks between high- and low-water marks; *S.A.C.* xliv. 148 n.
54 *S.A.C.* xcix. 4.
55 A.C.M., M 531, ff. [83v., 108].
56 *L. & P. Hen. VIII*, xiv (1), p. 296.
57 W.S.R.O., Ep. I/29/51/5.
58 e.g. E.S.R.O., AMS 2667.
59 W.S.R.O., TD/W 33.
60 P.R.O., E 106/8/19, rot. 5; E.S.R.O., AMS 2668–9; *S.R.S.* xlvi, p. 253.
61 Ekwall, *Eng. Place-Names* (1960), 451.
62 W.S.R.O., Add. MS. 2031; cf. *S.R.S.* vii, p. 170.
63 B.L. Add. MS. 39337, f. 108.
64 Ibid. f. 110; W.S.R.O., Ep. I/25/1 (1663); Ep. I/29/51/1, 20; *250 Yrs. of Mapmaking in Suss.* pl. 3; *S.R.S.* xlix. 50; lxxiv, p. 58.
65 B.L. Add. MS. 39337, f. 110; W.S.R.O., Add. MS. 2027, ff. 27–8.
66 *250 Yrs. of Mapmaking in Suss.* pl. 14.
67 W.S.R.O., TD/W 33. Hos. on copyholds of Ford, Climping, and Ilsham man. at Ilsham in 1608 are described in detail at Guildhall Libr. MS. 13321, ff. 12–22.
68 W.S.R.O., PH 9337; for location, inf. from Mr. G. Wooldridge, Climping.
69 Below, pl. facing p. 139.
70 W.S.R.O., SP 1540.
71 Inf. from Mr. V. Landymore, Brookpits Man., Climping.
72 W.S.R.O., Ep. I/29/51/90; cf. Guildhall Libr. MS. 13314, leases, 1712, 1724.
73 Guildhall Libr. MSS. 13315, lease, 1879; 13323/8, rep. of visit to Suss. estate, 1884; W.S.R.O., SP 1540.
74 O.S. Map 6", Suss. LXIII (1879 edn.).
75 Inf. from Mr. Landymore.
76 Below, manors (Atherington).
77 W.S.R.O., Add. MSS. 2027, *passim*; 2031.
78 Ibid. Add. MS. 1727 (TS. cat.).
79 Ibid. MP 2072; cf. O.S. Map 6", Suss. LXXV. NW. (1913 edn.), showing rocks between high- and low-water marks.
80 *250 Yrs. of Mapmaking in Suss.* pl. 14.
81 W.S.R.O., TD/W 33.
82 Ibid. Add. MS. 36625.
83 Ibid. Add. MS. 2031.
84 Ibid. MP 2072; *250 Yrs. of Mapmaking in Suss.* pl. 14.
85 W.S.R.O., Add. MS. 42247.

pebbles, with some rendering. Some houses on the west side of the road were evidently built as encroachments on the roadway.[86]

Another focus of later settlement was Horsemere green in the north, where cottages were beginning to encroach by 1608.[87] Most buildings in that area in 1996, however, were 20th-century, including an estate of large houses built *c.* 1990.

Christ's Hospital built at least seven pairs of labourers' cottages in the later 19th century, some at existing centres of settlement and others elsewhere.[88] Other estate cottages were built in the 1930s by Lord Moyne,[89] for instance in Climping village street.

New building was expected to follow the opening of Littlehampton bridge in 1908.[90] Land in the southern half of the parish was offered for sale for development in 1914 and later,[91] and a light railway from Ford to the west end of the bridge was projected in 1920.[92] In 1924 a syndicate was proposing to develop the parish as a residential seaside resort,[93] and when *c.* 1925 the proprietor of Tortington Park school built Poole Place near the Middleton boundary for her pupils' swimming expeditions, it was apparently in expectation that the area would be developed like neighbouring Middleton.[94] However, as a result of Lord Moyne's purchase of the Bailiffscourt estate in 1927 the southern part of the parish was preserved from building as the largest open area of coast between Bognor Regis and Brighton, known in 1996 as the Climping gap.

There were residential caravans north of the road leading to Littlehampton in 1993. In 1991 the continuing fragmentation of settlement, with the variety of land use, gave the parish a disjointed impression.[95] Many houses were then used by outsiders as second homes, as had already been the case in 1974.[96]

Ten people were taxed at Atherington, 11 at Cudlow, and 12 at Ilsham, in 1327, and 16 at Cudlow in 1332.[97] Figures for Climping tithing were then evidently included in totals for Ford, as in 1524.[98] The protestation of 1642 was signed by 63 adult males,[99] 98 adults were enumerated in the parish in 1676,[1] and there were 20 families in 1724;[2] in each case Bailiffscourt was presumably excluded, as part of Littlehampton. The ancient parish, excluding Bailiffscourt, had 197 inhabitants in 1801, the number rising to 279 in 1841 and, after a fall, to 331 in 1861. The population in 1881 including Bailiffscourt was 270; after falling to 219 in 1901 it rose steadily during the 20th century, despite the transfer of part of the parish to Littlehampton in 1933. The doubling of numbers in the reduced area of the parish between 1931 and 1951 was partly due to the increase of personnel on the enlarged airfield. In 1971 the population was 963, and in 1991 that of the reduced area of the parish was 516.[3]

COMMUNICATIONS. The main approach to Climping by land before the 19th century was from Barnham and Yapton,[4] the road, recorded from the early 13th century, extending apparently by way of the present Climping village street to Cudlow.[5] The Climping–Ford road, later called Ford Lane,[6] was mentioned from 1608,[7] and provided a route to Arundel before the late 18th century and again from *c.* 1846.[8] There was no direct route to Middleton apart from the beach before the 19th century,[9] but a road from Felpham to Madehurst was said to run through Park farm in the north-west corner of the parish in 1564.[10]

Bread Lane, not recorded before the 19th century[11] and only a track in 1991, ran south from the site of the school, beside the field called the Bread,[12] to the coast. The section of the Bognor Regis to Littlehampton road in the centre of the parish was called Crookthorn Lane by 1843.[13] A road to Totsham, i.e. Climping, mill mentioned at an unknown date in the Middle Ages[14] may have been the same as both Mill Street recorded in 1490[15] and Mill Lane which led to the coast in 1780.[16] Stroud Lane recorded in 1558 may be a mistake for Stroodland.[17]

A timber bridge said in 1417 to have crossed the river Arun between Littlehampton and Atherington[18] is not otherwise recorded. The ferry

86 Ibid. TD/W 33.
87 Guildhall Libr. MS. 13321, f. 35.
88 Plaques and dates on bldgs.; cf. W.S.R.O., SP 1540.
89 *John Willmott & Sons (Hitchin) Ltd. 1852–1952* (Hitchin, [1952]), [7] (copy in W.S.R.O. libr.).
90 Eton Coll. Libr., Climping corresp. file, letter from Revd. Hen. Green, 30 Apr. 1908; cf. below, this section (communications).
91 W.S.R.O., SP 315; 1540, p. 3; Eton Coll. Libr., sale cat. 1915.
92 W.S.R.O., QDP/W 256.
93 Eton Coll. Libr., Climping corresp. file, letter from Messrs. Rawlence and Squarey, 25 Apr. 1924.
94 W.S.R.O., MP 2597.
95 Cf. Nairn & Pevsner, *Suss.* 189.
96 *Chich. Observer*, 27 Sept. 1974.
97 *S.R.S.* x. 137–8, 254. In 1296 Atherington was included with Yapton, and Cudlow with Bilsham in Yapton; in 1332 Atherington was included with Eastergate: ibid. 79–80, 255–6.
98 Below, Ford, intro.; *S.R.S.* lvi. 56–7. The surnames (de) Horemer(e) and at Park, possibly relating to places in Climping, occur under Ford in 1327 and 1332: ibid. x. 137, 253; cf. below, manors (Park fm.); econ. hist. (agric.).
99 *S.R.S.* v. 61–2.
1 *Compton Census*, ed. Whiteman, 144.
2 *S.R.S.* lxxviii. 63.
3 *Census*, 1801–1991. The rise of nearly a quarter between 1851 and 1861 was partly due to the building of a fort beside the Arun estuary: cf. *V.C.H. Suss.* v (2), Littlehampton (forthcoming).
4 e.g. Guildhall Libr. MS. 13321, ff. 3–4, 6, 8–9; *250 Yrs. of Mapmaking in Suss.* pls. 14–15.
5 *S.R.S.* lix, p. 76; *Cat. Anct. D.* ii, B 3485.
6 W.S.R.O., TD/W 33.
7 Guildhall Libr. MS. 13321, ff. 4, 10, 40; cf. W.S.R.O., Ep. I/25/1 (1663, *recte* 1664).
8 e.g. *250 Yrs. of Mapmaking in Suss.* pl. 14; below, Ford, intro.
9 *250 Yrs. of Mapmaking in Suss.* pls. 14, 19; inf. from Mr. G. Wooldridge, Climping.
10 A.C.M., MD 2345, rot. 3d.
11 W.S.R.O., SP 1540, map; ibid. TD/W 33; O.S. Map 6", Suss. LXXV. NW. (1899 edn.).
12 Below, econ. hist. (agric.).
13 W.S.R.O., TD/W 33; O.S. Map 6", Suss. LXII. SE. (1899 edn.).
14 *Cat. Anct. D.* ii, B 3485; below, econ. hist. (mills).
15 P.R.O., SC 2/206/44, rot. 2.
16 W.S.R.O., Add. MS. 12630 (TS. cat.).
17 *S.R.S.* xlii. 26; above, this section (settlement).
18 *Cal. Pat.* 1416–22, 143.

at Littlehampton mentioned from the later 13th century[19] evidently plied to Climping, and was reached by a road that ran north-east from Climping mill by 1606.[20] The ferry was for foot passengers only in 1824[21] and perhaps earlier, since in 1788 a Yapton resident rode home from Littlehampton via Arundel.[22]

The river could also be forded near its mouth. The ford was said to be only rarely usable in 1679,[23] but in the early 19th century the shingle bar outside the piers of Littlehampton harbour provided a passage for wagons and carriages several hours a day, though it could be treacherous; it was used, among others, by the millers of Climping, Littlehampton, and Rustington.[24]

A chain ferry across the Arun was set up under an Act of 1824, with a tollgate on the Climping side of the river.[25] The straight road called Ferry Road was made to give access to it, and a new road, later known as West Ground Lane or Grevatt's Lane, was provided at the same time at the west end of the parish to link Climping with Felpham and Bognor.[26] The ferry was replaced in 1908 by a swing bridge, of which the vicar of Climping was a chief promoter;[27] about the same date the two roads cut *c.* 1824 were acquired by Littlehampton urban district council.[28] On both occasions the owner or owners of Bailiffscourt farm were granted exemption from tolls, in 1905 in return for conveying land required.[29] A short section of the Bognor Regis to Littlehampton road east of Church Lane was bypassed *c.* 1934.[30]

The Climping–Yapton road was closed between 1942 and 1959 with the enlargement of Ford airfield.[31] The swing bridge over the Arun was replaced in the early 1970s by a pedestrian bridge of high section, a fixed road bridge with a new access road being built 700 yd. (640 metres) upstream.

In 1992 buses passed through the parish between Portsmouth, Bognor Regis, and Chichester, and Worthing and Brighton.

There was an unlicensed alehouse in 1625.[32] The Black Horse in Climping village street was recorded from 1843[33] and perhaps by 1814.[34]

In the later 19th century and earlier 20th the school was opened one or two evenings a week in winter as a reading room for men attending church, newspapers, games, and free cocoa being provided.[35] Men's clubs were mentioned in 1890[36] and there was a Climping social club in 1922.[37] A village hall near Brookpits Manor was used in the 1920s,[38] and a new one was built *c.* 1936 on a site beside the Bognor Regis to Littlehampton road given by Lord Moyne;[39] the playing field behind it, where cricket, football, and stoolball were played in 1993, was given by the Bailiffscourt estate in 1953.[40] A church hall north of the church was opened in 1991.

The buildings on the part of Ford airfield that lies within the ancient parish[41] were put up soon after the Air Ministry re-acquired the original site in 1937 and extended it to the roads on the south and east. After transfer to the Admiralty in 1939 the airfield was commissioned as H.M.S. *Peregrine*, but for most of the Second World War it served as an R.A.F. night fighter station. By 1945 it had returned to Admiralty control, and in 1947 six squadrons there were concerned with training, trials, and co-operation with ships of the home fleet.[42] Between 1948 and 1951 the runways were extended and relaid in concrete, but the navy left in 1959. From *c.* 1964 to 1971 most of the site was leased to Miles Aviation and Transport (R. & D.) Ltd., which among other things built replicas of historic aircraft for the film industry. Despite fears in the 1970s and 80s that flying would continue on the airfield,[43] by 1996 it had long ceased.

Part of the airfield buildings in Climping were used for Ford open prison, founded in 1960, which straddles the Climping–Ford road. The 184 prisoners there in 1961 provided extra agricultural labour at peak periods on local farms.[44] By 1975, when the prison covered *c.* 100 a., there were over 500 inmates and 82 staff. About 80 a. were then cultivated by the prisoners, especially with trees and shrubs; there was also a light industrial workshop, and some inmates went to work in local towns.[45] A new entrance range, a chapel, and other buildings were put up on the east side of the road in the late 1980s.[46]

Water and electricity were brought to the parish before 1938 by Lord Moyne,[47] but there was no gas supply before *c.* 1990.[48] The Bailiffscourt estate cottages also had main drainage in the

19 *Cal. Inq. p.m.* iv, p. 51; *S.R.S.* lxvii. 115; *Man. of Littlehampton with Toddington, 1633*, ed. F. W. Steer (Littlehampton, 1961), i. 10; W.S.R.O., Add. MS. 1728 (TS. cat.).

20 W.S.R.O., Add. MSS. 2027, f. 21; 2031; cf. ibid. MP 2072, naming 'ferry ho.' on E. bank of river; *250 Yrs. of Mapmaking in Suss.* pl. 14.

21 5 Geo. IV, c. 94 (Local and Personal).

22 *S.C.M.* xx. 129.

23 W.S.R.O., Ep. I/17/32, f. 93.

24 *S.N.Q.* xvii. 198–9; *Suss. Ind. Hist.* v. 31.

25 5 Geo. IV, c. 94 (Local and Personal); W.S.R.O., TD/W 33; *S.N.Q.* xvi. 239–40.

26 W.S.R.O., QDP/W 42; ibid. TD/W 33; O.S. Map 6", Suss. LXII. SE. (1899 edn.); LXIII. SW. (1913 edn.).

27 H. Green, *Clymping Ch. and Par.* (Chich. 1912), 10–11 (copy in S.A.S. libr.).

28 W.S.R.O., QDP/W 226.

29 5 Geo. IV, c. 94 (Local and Personal); 5 Edw. VII, c. 180 (Local).

30 W.S.R.O., Add. MS. 35222; ibid. CC 320.

31 *Bognor Regis Post*, 1 Aug. 1959.

32 *S.R.S.* xlix. 100.

33 W.S.R.O., TD/W 33; *Kelly's Dir. Suss.* (1845 and later edns.).

34 W.S.R.O., Add. MS. 7147 (TS. cat.).

35 Ibid. Ep. I/22A/1 (1884, 1890); Ep. I/22A/2 (1898); Eton Coll. Libr., Climping corresp. file, notebk. 1889; ibid. 'Clymping Record', 1901, 1904–5; Green, *Clymping Ch. and Par.* 12–13.

36 W.S.R.O., Ep. I/22A/1 (1890).

37 *Kelly's Dir. Suss.* (1922); cf. Eton Coll. Libr., Climping corresp. file, Revd. E. F. Leach to bursar, 25 Nov. 1925.

38 Photo. in possession of Mr. V. Landymore, Brookpits Man., Climping.

39 Char. Com. files; local inf.

40 Char. Com. files.

41 Para. based mainly on *Suss. Ind. Hist.* vi. 30–2. For earlier hist. of airfield, below, Ford, intro.

42 *The Aeroplane*, 18 July 1947.

43 *W. Suss. Gaz.* 3 Mar. 1977; 15 Feb. 1979; W.S.R.O., Add. MS. 31576.

44 *Suss. Ind. Hist.* vi. 32; *The Times*, 25 Apr. 1961.

45 *W. Suss. Gaz.* 6 Feb. 1975.

46 Ibid. 15 June 1989; *Bognor Regis Observer*, 14 Jan. 1988.

47 *Kelly's Dir. Suss.* (1938); *Chich. Observer*, 27 Sept. 1974; *Residential Attractions of Bognor Regis, Felpham, Middleton-on-Sea and Dist.* (Gloucester, [1937]), 10 (copy in B.L.).

48 Inf. from Mrs. E. Burn, Climping.

1930s.[49] There was a sewage works east of Climping village street in 1977.[50]

MANORS AND OTHER ESTATES. *CLIMPING* was a member of Ford,[51] which belonged in the Middle Ages to the Bohun family and between 1702 and 1914 to Christ's Hospital. By 1520 the manor was known as Ford, Climping, and Ilsham.[52] It included the northern portion of Climping ancient parish, represented in the 18th century largely by Church, Northwood, and Kent's farms.[53]

Christ's Hospital by 1914 had added other farms,[54] so that most of the parish, except for the south-east corner, then belonged to it.[55] Church and Kent's farms were sold to the Dennis Estates Ltd. of Lincolnshire in 1914,[56] and Northwood farm was bought then or soon afterwards by John Langmead (d. 1950).[57] In 1929 Church farm passed to Thomas Edward Dennis (d. 1940), whose executors sold it in 1941, when it had 154 a., to the tenant W. H. May. After his death in 1982 his nephew K. H. May sold most of the land (118 a.) in 1984 to West Sussex county council.[58] Northwood farm, of 435 a. in Climping and other parishes, belonged in 1991 to the descendants of John Langmead.[59]

Church Farmhouse, the presumed manor house, was said in 1753 to have been newly fronted with brick *c.* 15 years earlier.[60] It was apparently completely rebuilt shortly before 1783,[61] and is a tall **L**-shaped house standing high above the road. An east porch existed in the early 20th century[62] but was later removed. About 1964 the house was divided and internally remodelled.[63] A late 18th-century staircase remained in 1991.

PARK FARM in the north-west represents the medieval park attached to Ford, Climping, and Ilsham manor, which despite being in Climping parish was always called Ford park.[64] John de Bohun was confirmed in free warren in Ford shortly before 1279,[65] and a park had been created by 1297.[66] In 1540 it contained 80 a.,[67] but the acreage was given as 100 a. from 1608.[68] In the 16th century and early 17th it was leased for periods of 21 years,[69] and it seems to have been disparked between 1592 and 1608.[70] The land descended with the manor until some time between 1625 and 1646, when it was sold by Sir Henry Garway to Thomas Bridger.[71] Thomas's sister and heir Margaret Dench was succeeded by her son Ambrose, whose son and namesake conveyed the farm in 1686 to Henry and Grace Hall.[72] Thereafter it perhaps descended with first Middleton manor and then a moiety of that manor[73] until 1803 when a member of the Coote family had it.[74] In 1821 it was settled on Joseph, Ruth, and Richard Coote.[75] The same or another Joseph had it in 1843,[76] and Mary Coote, widow, sold it in 1861 to Christ's Hospital.[77] It later belonged to the Langmead family.[78]

Jordan of Ilsham and others held a fee presumably at *ILSHAM* in 1166.[79] In the later 12th century what was perhaps the same land was divided in two, one moiety being added to Ford manor, of which it was later described as a member.[80] The other moiety, hereafter referred to as Ilsham manor, passed to Reynold Aguillon, who at his death shortly before 1233 held it of the bishop of Chichester.[81] The overlordship of what was presumably the same estate remained with the bishop until 1486[82] or later, fencing service being owed at Aldingbourne park.[83]

Reynold's son Thomas had died without issue probably by 1236[84] and certainly by *c.* 1255. At the latter date the greater part of Ilsham was in four portions belonging to his sisters Cecily, wife of Peter of Gatesden, Godehude, wife of Ralph St. Owen, Alice, wife of Robert Haket, and Mary, wife of William Covert.[85] An alternative name for the manor from the 17th century was *FOURPARTNERS*.[86] Each share comprised a house and 60–80 a.,[87] sometimes described as a hide.[88]

Cecily of Gatesden after her husband's death

49 Inf. from Mr. G. Wooldridge, Climping.
50 O.S. Map 1/25,000, TQ 00/10 (1979 edn.).
51 W.S.R.O., Add. MS. 2293, *passim*.
52 Below, Ford, manor; *Cal. Pat.* 1225–32, 219.
53 Guildhall Libr. MSS. 13307, 13312–15; cf. W.S.R.O., SP 1540, p. 2.
54 Guildhall Libr. MSS. 13323/5, rep. of view of estates, 1860; below, this section.
55 W.S.R.O., SP 1540.
56 Guildhall Libr. MS. 13319, deed, 1914.
57 *W. Suss. Gaz.* 28 May 1981; cf. *Kelly's Dir. Suss.* (1938).
58 W. Suss. C.C. property dept., deeds.
59 Inf. from Mrs. S. Abbot, née Langmead, Hobbs Ct., Yapton.
60 Guildhall Libr. MSS. 13310–13; 13323/2, rep. of view of estates, 1753, p. [5].
61 Ibid. 13313, lease, 1783.
62 W.S.R.O., SP 1540, facing p. 18.
63 Inf. from Mrs. D. Betteridge, Church Fmho.
64 e.g. W.S.R.O., Add. MS. 2292, rot. 3; ibid. Ep. I/29/51/4; *Cal. Pat.* 1578–80, p. 20.
65 *S.A.C.* lxxxiv. 69; *Plac. de Quo Warr.* (Rec. Com.), 756.
66 *Cal. Pat.* 1292–1301, 320; cf. the surname at Park recorded in 1327: *S.R.S.* x. 137.
67 P.R.O., SC 6/Hen. VIII/3480, rot. 16; cf. *Cal. Pat.* 1555–7, 396.
68 Guildhall Libr. MS. 13321, f. 38; W.S.R.O., Add. MS. 11796 (TS. cat.); ibid. S.A.S. MS. WH 270 (TS. cat.).
69 *Cal. Pat.* 1555–7, 396; 1569–72, p. 129; 1578–80, p. 20; Guildhall Libr. MS. 13321, f. 38; cf. W.S.R.O., Ep. I/29/51/4.
70 Guildhall Libr. MS. 13321, f. 38.
71 Ibid.; below, Ford, manor.
72 W.S.R.O., S.A.S. MS. WH 270 (TS. cat.).
73 Below, Middleton-on-Sea, manors (Middleton).
74 Eton Coll. Libr. MS. 65/240; ibid. surv. of Climping rectory, 1803.
75 W.S.R.O., Add. MS. 11796 (TS. cat.).
76 Ibid. TD/W 33.
77 Guildhall Libr. MSS. 13313, leases of Church fm. 1847, 1862; 13323/6, rep. of view of lands at Climping, 1865.
78 Inf. from Mrs. Abbot.
79 *Chich. Acta* (Cant. & York Soc.), p. 97; cf. *Cur. Reg. R.* vii. 263.
80 *S.A.C.* xlvi. 224; xlix. 41; *Cur. Reg. R.* vi. 399; W.S.R.O., Add. MS. 2293, *passim*; below, Ford, manor; cf. *S.R.S.* xix. 171.
81 P.R.O., SC 1/6, no. 94.
82 *S.R.S.* xlvi, pp. 248, 253; *Cal. Inq. p.m.* xviii, p. 217.
83 *S.R.S.* xxxi. 41; xlvi, pp. 261, 264. Two portions of the man., however, were later said to be held in chief: ibid. iii, p. 72; xxxiii, p. 66; P.R.O., C 142/326, no. 21; C 142/454, no. 16.
84 *S.A.C.* lxiii. 229.
85 Ibid.; *S.R.S.* xlvi, p. 167.
86 B.L. Add. MS. 5687, f. 95; W.S.R.O., Ep. I/25/1 (1615, 1663); ibid. TD/W 33; Dallaway, *Hist. W. Suss.* ii (1) (1819), 13; cf. *S.R.S.* xxxi. 41.
87 *Kts. Hospitallers in Eng.* (Camd. Soc. [1st ser.], lxv), 25; *Cal. Pat.* 1391–6, 562; 1422–9, 115; *Cal. Inq. p.m.* xviii, p. 217; *S.R.S.* xxiii, p. 47; xlvi, p. 253; lxvii. 147; B.L. Add. MS. 39394, f. 38.
88 *S.A.C.* lxii. 109; *S.R.S.* xlvi, pp. 253, 261, 264.

1257 × 1279[89] granted her share in or before 1286 to the Knights Hospitaller,[90] with whom it descended until the Dissolution. In 1546 the lands were granted by the Crown to John Edmunds otherwise Baldwin and his son and namesake;[91] by 1571 they were known as the manor of *ILSHAM ST. JOHN*. Between that date and 1688 the estate descended with the demesnes of Yapton manor.[92] Robert Edmunds was dealing with it in 1710,[93] but after his death without issue it again descended with the Yapton manor demesnes until 1800.[94] Before 1819 George White Thomas exchanged a little over half the demesne, described as Stroodland and Ilsham manor farm, for land in Yapton. Other parts of the estate belonged at the last named date to a J. Cutfield, presumably a relative of William Cutfield of Bailiffscourt, and to the only daughter of John Boniface, then a minor. The demesne as a whole was then said to contain 236 a.[95] In 1843 it was 210 a., of which 159 a. belonged to John Boniface and the rest to Mary Boniface and others; it then included what were later Brookpits and Hobb's farms.[96] Those farms were sold to Christ's Hospital shortly before 1860,[97] and passed to the Dennis Estates Ltd. in 1914.[98]

Ralph St. Owen's share of Ilsham manor descended with Clapham until the mid 16th century.[99] It may be the house and 60 a. of land in Climping which John Standen held at his death in 1612 of Ilsham St. John,[1] and of which Thomas Standen, presumably his son, died seised in 1639.[2] If so, it was perhaps absorbed into the Ilsham St. John demesne, since it is not heard of again.

The other two chief shares of Ilsham manor were known as *ILSHAM HAKET* and *ILSHAM PECCHE* or *PECCHY*.[3] Robert Haket was succeeded at an unknown date by John Haket (fl. 1337–47),[4] and a hide at Ilsham formerly John's was conveyed to the earl of Arundel before 1379,[5] perhaps in 1359–60.[6] William Covert had been succeeded by his son Roger before 1279,[7] and the same or another Roger held the Covert land in 1286[8] and *c.* 1300.[9] The share of Robert of Estdean (fl. 1311–20)[10] may be the same. At an unknown date it belonged to John Pecche,[11] but by 1380 it had apparently also passed to the earl of Arundel.[12] About 1414 Thomas FitzAlan, earl of Arundel (d. 1415), granted Ilsham Haket and perhaps also Ilsham Pecche, subject to dower, to Holy Trinity hospital, Arundel;[13] the hospital had both in 1486[14] and retained them until the Dissolution.[15]

In 1546 the hospital's lands in Ilsham were granted by the Crown to Sir Richard Lee, who granted them in the same year to John and Edward Staker in trust for Edward's son John.[16] In the early 17th century the lands were held successively by John Staker (d. 1612), another John, probably his son (fl. 1629; d. 1636), and the latter's son John[17] (d. 1637), whose sister and heir was Jane.[18] They were presumably afterwards absorbed into Ilsham St. John manor.

ATHERINGTON manor may originate in the moiety of Climping which earl Roger gave to Sées abbey (Orne) after *c.* 1082;[19] since it was used by the abbey as a residence for the bailiff of its English lands,[20] it was later alternatively called *BAILIFFSCOURT*. In the mid 14th century the bailiff was the abbey's attorney general or proctor in England.[21] Atherington was described as a manor from 1352.[22] The manor house, park, and part of the demesne occupied the larger of the two detached parts of Littlehampton parish, but the tenants' lands lay in Climping parish.[23] The estate was enlarged in the mid 13th century and later,[24] and seems to be the 2 yardlands in Littlehampton mentioned separately as held by Sées in 1341.[25] After the early 15th century it was held, with the rest of the abbey's English property, by Syon abbey (Mdx.).[26]

At the Dissolution Atherington passed to the Crown.[27] Between *c.* 1532,[28] perhaps earlier,[29] and 1621 or later it was leased to members of the Baldwin otherwise Edmunds family.[30]

89 *S.A.C.* lxiii. 229.
90 Ibid. lxii. 109.
91 *S.R.S.* x. 137; xxxi. 141; *Kts. Hospitallers in Eng.* 25; *L. & P. Hen. VIII*, xxi (2), p. 95.
92 *S.R.S.* iii, pp. 71–3; xxxiii, p. 66; *Wiston Archives*, i, ed. J. Booker, p. 381; B.L. Add. MS. 5687, f. 220; P.R.O., C 142/454, no. 16; W.S.R.O., Add. MS. 12626; below, Yapton, manors (Yapton).
93 *S.R.S.* xx. 509.
94 B.L. Add. MS. 5687, ff. 95, 220; W.S.R.O., Add. MSS. 8811, 12916 (TS. cat.); *S.R.S.* xx. 509; li. 12, 63; below, Yapton, manors (Yapton).
95 Dallaway, *Hist. W. Suss.* ii (1) (1819), 13.
96 W.S.R.O., TD/W 33.
97 Guildhall Libr. MS. 13323/5, rep. of view of estates, 1860.
98 Ibid. 13319, deed, 1914.
99 *S.R.S.* xix. 102; xxxi. 141; xxxiii, p. 2; xlvi, p. 248; *Cal. Inq. p.m.* xviii, p. 217; *Feud. Aids*, vi. 525; cf. *V.C.H. Suss.* vi (1), 11.
1 P.R.O., C 142/326, no. 42; cf. W.S.R.O., S.A.S. MS. B 518 (TS. cat.).
2 P.R.O., C 142/326, no. 42; C 142/578, no. 19.
3 e.g. *Cal. Inq. p.m.* (Rec. Com.), iii. 227; iv. 197–8; *S.R.S.* lxvii. 147.
4 *V.C.H. Suss.* iv. 145; cf. *S.R.S.* xlvi, p. 253; lxvii. 109.
5 *S.R.S.* xlvi, p. 261.
6 Ibid. xxiii, p. 147.
7 *S.A.C.* lxiii. 230.
8 Ibid. lxii. 110.
9 *S.R.S.* xxxi. 136–7.
10 Ibid. xxiii, p. 47; xxxi. 141.
11 Ibid. xlvi, p. 253; lxvii. 109; *S.A.C.* lxiii. 230; cf. John Pecche of Cudlow mentioned 1326: *Cal. Mem. R.* 1326–7, p. 232.
12 *S.R.S.* xlvi, p. 264; cf. *Cal. Inq. p.m.* (Rec. Com.), iii. 227.
13 *Cal. Pat.* 1422–9, 115, 281–2.
14 *S.R.S.* xlvi, p. 253.
15 *Valor Eccl.* (Rec. Com.), i. 315.
16 *L. & P. Hen. VIII*, xxi (1), p. 570; xxi (2), p. 245; cf. *Cal. Pat.* 1560–3, 393.
17 B.L. Add. MS. 39394, f. 38; P.R.O., C 142/326, no. 21; C 142/536, no. 22.
18 *S.R.S.* xiv, p. 214.
19 *Cal. Doc. France*, ed. Round, pp. 233–4, 597; rejecting the idea expressed there and at *P.N. Northants* (E.P.N.S.), 113, that 'Arintona' was Harrington (Northants). Cf. *Cur. Reg. R.* ii. 254; ix. 258.
20 *Cal. Papal Pets.* i. 102.
21 e.g. *Cat. Anct. D.* ii, B 3753; *Cal. Pat.* 1354–8, 249. He was also sometimes wrongly referred to as prior: *Cur. Reg. R.* ix. 258; *Cal. Close*, 1330–3, 591.
22 P.R.O., C 143/302, no. 6 (TS. cat.).
23 e.g. W.S.R.O., Add. MS. 2027, f. 15.
24 *Cal. Pat.* 1281–92, 420; *Cal. Close*, 1333–7, 194–5; *Cat. Anct. D.* iii, B 4182; cf. *Tax. Eccl.* (Rec. Com.), 139.
25 *Inq. Non.* (Rec. Com.), 393.
26 *V.C.H. Suss.* ii. 120; *Valor Eccl.* (Rec. Com.), i. 424–6.
27 e.g. *L. & P. Hen. VIII*, xv, p. 214; A.C.M., M 532, ff. [9, 97v.]; W.S.R.O., PHA 933, f. 69v.; 6677, rot. 1d.
28 *S.R.S.* xvi. 89.
29 Ibid. xliii. 166; lvi. 52–3; *S.A.C.* xii. 92.
30 *S.R.S.* xliii. 166; *Cal. Pat.* 1557–8, 28; 1569–72, p. 124; P.R.O., C 2/Jas. I/E 1/50; W.S.R.O., Add. MS. 2027, f. 16; ibid. S.A.S. MSS. B 489, 646 (TS. cat.). John Baldwin occurred locally *c.* 1310: Eton Coll. Libr. MS. 45/83 (TS. cat.).

Marshland belonging to the manor was let in parcels to various people,[31] but by 1606 all the leases had apparently passed to Walter Edmunds.[32] In 1599 the manor was granted by the Crown to Sir John Spencer,[33] and from 1600 it descended with Priory farm in Tortington[34] until 1633, when Spencer Compton, earl of Northampton, conveyed it to Sir William Morley (d. 1658 or 1659). William's son and heir John (d. 1659) was succeeded by his brother Edward[35] (d. 1667), whose brother Sir William[36] was lord *c.* 1690[37] and died in 1701.[38] A lease for three lives of the manor house and demesne was granted in 1631 to Sir John Chapman.[39] He was living at Bailiffscourt in the mid 17th century[40] and was succeeded before 1664, perhaps before 1651, by his son Abraham.[41]

By 1704 Atherington had passed to the Revd. William Barcroft (d. 1712),[42] whose son and namesake was dealing with it in 1721, was lord *c.* 1735, and died in 1758.[43] The younger William's heir Thomas Townson sold the manor in the following year to Thomas Boniface (d. 1763), whose son and heir John[44] still apparently owned it in 1819.[45] The demesne was again separated from the manor during the later 18th century,[46] and the later history of the manor is not recorded. Before 1796 Laurence Eliot had sold the demesne to John Cutfield,[47] presumably a descendant of the Joseph Cutfield who had leased Bailiffscourt in 1751.[48] At John's death in 1796[49] it passed to his nephew William Cutfield[50] (d. 1842).[51] In 1803 the estate had 367 a.[52] William's sister and heir Charlotte[53] died in 1863,[54] and by 1865 the lands, then 340 a., had been bought by Christ's Hospital.[55] The hospital sold them in 1914 to the Dennis Estates Ltd.[56]

In 1927 the Bailiffscourt estate, *c.* 750 a., was bought by Walter Guinness, created in 1932 Lord Moyne, and during the 17 years until his death in 1944[57] the parish was dominated, as it had never been before, by a single generally resident landowner. The estate had grown to *c.* 1,000 a. by 1974 when Moyne's daughter Grania and her husband Oswald Phipps, marquess of Normanby, sold it to the Post Office staff superannuation fund.[58] In 1982 the fund sold the land to the tenants.[59] John Baird, former tenant of Bailiffscourt farm, *c.* 800 a., resold his land before 1988 to the Wolverhampton borough council pension fund, becoming their tenant instead.[60]

There was a manor house at Atherington, with a dovecot and two gardens, in 1378;[61] by *c.* 1532 it was called Bailiffscourt.[62] In 1606 the building was said to be old and covered with Horsham slates;[63] it was then L-shaped, the main range facing east with a chapel lying east–west at its southern end.[64] The chapel,[65] which survived in 1991, is of flint with stone dressings. It incorporates stonework of the later 11th century or earlier 12th,[66] but is essentially of the later 13th century, with side lancets and a three-light east window of cusped lancets. There are moulded arches to the window splays inside with carved foliage capitals, and a restored double piscina. It seems likely, in view of the presence of windows on the north side of the building, that it was originally freestanding.

The house was remodelled, apparently in the 18th century, with a five-bayed entrance front in classical style, the south wall of the chapel being cased in brick.[67] In 1914 Bailiffscourt was of stone and brick with a slate roof[68] and retained much medieval stonework, especially in its north wall.[69] Rooms listed in 1729 at what may be the house included kitchen, parlour, various chambers, and office buildings, while mention, also apparently there, in the previous year of a chapel chamber[70] perhaps indicates that the chapel was already used for servants' sleeping accommodation, as later;[71] by the late 19th century, however, it had become a dairy and cellar.[72] In 1865 there were three sitting rooms and four bedrooms in the house[73] and by 1914 eight bedrooms and attics,[74] presumably as a result of repairs carried

31 *Cal. Pat.* 1557–8, 406–7.
32 W.S.R.O., Add. MS. 2027, ff. 20–1.
33 P.R.O., C 66/1505, mm. 15, 18.
34 e.g. W.S.R.O., Add. MS. 2031; *S.R.S.* xx. 497; below, Tortington, manor.
35 B.L. Add. MS. 39487, f. 8v.; *Goodwood Estate Archives*, i, ed. F. W. Steer and J. Venables, p. 67.
36 B.L. Add. MS. 39487, f. 10.
37 W.S.R.O., Goodwood MS. E1, ff. 11, 114.
38 *V.C.H. Suss.* iv. 143.
39 *S.R.S.* xix. 14; W.S.R.O., Add. MS. 1726 (TS. cat.).
40 W.S.R.O., Ep. I/17/32, f. 93.
41 Ibid. Add. MS. 1726 (TS. cat.); Eton Coll. Libr. MS. 45/99 (TS. cat.).
42 B.L. Add. MS. 5687, f. 11; Le Neve, *Fasti, 1541–1857, Chich.* 15.
43 B.L. Add. MS. 5687, f. 11; Littlehampton Mus. MS. D 303, f. [7]; N.R.A. Rep. 0517 (rec. of Bailiffscourt Estates, not traceable in 1991); *S.R.S.* xix. 15; Dallaway, *Hist. W. Suss.* ii (1) (1819), 13; *Alum. Cantab. to 1751*, s.v. Barcroft.
44 B.L. Add. MSS. 5687, f. 11, wrongly naming John Boniface; 39487, f. 11; N.R.A. Rep. 0517.
45 Dallaway, *Hist. W. Suss.* ii (1) (1819), 13.
46 B.L. Add. MS. 39487, f. 12v.; W.S.R.O., Add. MS. 1727 (TS. cat.); cf. Add. MSS. 1281, 12440 (TS. cat.).
47 Dallaway, *Hist. W. Suss.* ii (1) (1819), 18; W.S.R.O., S.A.S. MS. OR 202 (TS. cat.).
48 W.S.R.O., Add. MSS. 1727–8 (TS. cat.).
49 F. W. Steer, *Climping Ch. Guide*, 3.
50 W.S.R.O., S.A.S. MS. OR 202 (TS. cat.); cf. ibid. Holmes, Campbell & Co. MSS. 730–3 (TS. cat.).
51 Mon. in ch.
52 Eton Coll. Libr., surv. of Climping rectory, 1803.
53 W.S.R.O., Holmes, Campbell & Co. MS. 142; cf. ibid. TD/W 33.
54 Ibid. Par. 51/1/5/1, p. 29.
55 Guildhall Libr. MS. 13323/6, rep. of view of lands at Climping, 1865; cf. W.S.R.O., IR 19, f. 13.
56 Guildhall Libr. MS. 13319, deed, 1914.
57 G. Young, *Cottage in the Fields*, 218–19; Burke, *Peerage* (1967), 1799–1800.
58 Burke, *Peerage* (1967), 1862; *W. Suss. Gaz.* 14 Mar. 1974.
59 *The Times*, 18 May 1982.
60 *W. Suss. Gaz.* 24 Nov. 1988; cf. *Chich. Observer*, 21 Dec. 1979; inf. from Miss M. Kendell, Middleton-on-Sea.
61 P.R.O., E 106/11/2, rot. 1.
62 *S.R.S.* xvi. 89; cf. *Cal. Assize Rec. Suss. Eliz. I*, p. 91.
63 W.S.R.O., Add. MS. 2027, f. 16.
64 Ibid. 2031.
65 Rest of para. based mainly on *S.A.C.* xliv. 155–61; below, pl. facing p. 138.
66 *V.C.H. Suss.* ii. 366.
67 *S.A.C.* xliv. 155, 161; W.S.R.O., SP 1540, facing p. 30.
68 W.S.R.O., SP 1540, p. 30.
69 *S.A.C.* xliv. 161; *V.C.H. Suss.* ii. 381.
70 W.S.R.O., Ep. I/29/51/86–7.
71 *S.A.C.* xii. 88.
72 *New Illus. Guide to Bognor and Neighbourhood* (Bognor and Lond. post 1888), 39.
73 Guildhall Libr. MS. 13323/6, rep. of view of lands at Climping, 1865.
74 W.S.R.O., SP 1540, p. 30.

out by Christ's Hospital in 1876.[75] In the later 19th century and earlier 20th Bailiffscourt was sometimes let as a gentleman's residence.[76]

A roughly rectangular moat surrounded the house and its outbuildings;[77] the north-western section was dry in 1901[78] but the south-eastern section held water in 1992. The house itself occupied the western part of the enclosure; other buildings which stood within the eastern part[79] were largely removed in the mid 19th century.[80] An octagonal flint and red brick dovecot which remained in 1992 apparently dates from 1816.[81] New outbuildings outside the moat to the south were built between *c.* 1840 and *c.* 1875 and enlarged between 1896 and 1910.[82]

After his purchase of the estate in 1927 Lord Moyne set about an imaginative re-creation of the medieval character of the site.[83] The old house was demolished except for the chapel, which was carefully restored, and a new house in 15th-century style was built to the south-west, beyond the medieval moat, to the designs of Amyas Phillips, a Hitchin antique dealer. The result has been described as an 'astonishing mirage',[84] and is one of the most remarkable creations of its period.

The new house has four irregular ranges of stone round a small courtyard. Part of the materials was found on site, part was original masonry brought from elsewhere, and the rest was new work imitated from medieval examples and 'weathered' to appear old.[85] The large entrance archway, contrasting dramatically with a wall in which windows are few and small, came from Holditch Court in Thorncombe (Dors.),[86] and the new stone is matching honey-coloured Somerset limestone, setting off the Caen stone re-used from the original building.[87] The roof is of Horsham slate. Inside, the building incorporates fittings from other buildings in Somerset, Hertfordshire, and Essex. The rooms were decorated with panelling and tapestries, the furniture being partly genuine antiques and partly fake medieval pieces, even cutlery being designed in medieval style. At least one early guest found the attempt to recreate medieval living conditions ludicrous, the rooms small, badly lit, and uncomfortable, and the guest rooms suggesting nothing so much as 'the cell of a rather "pansy" monk'.[88]

The so-called guest house, also of stone but thatched, which lies detached to the west, is reached by an underground passage. To the north-east various buildings brought from elsewhere were erected, notably a brick and timber gatehouse incorporating both a late medieval building from Loxwood in Wisborough Green and a 17th-century house from Old Basing (Hants), and a one-storeyed timber-framed and thatched cottage from Bignor which was converted to contain the electricity plant. A new thatched garage was built nearby. The sprawling layout of the site combines with the picturesque asymmetry of the buildings to give an illusion of size; the inspiration was presumably the loose layout of buildings as shown on Norden's map of 1606,[89] but the effect is that of an 'open-air' museum of vernacular architecture.

After the Second World War the house was let with all its contents and run as a 'medieval' hotel.[90] After changing hands it remained a hotel in 1994.[91]

Sées abbey was granted free warren on its demesne at Atherington in 1272.[92] There was a park, whose site is indicated by the field names the Plain and perhaps the Parrock north-west of Bailiffscourt house in 1606.[93] A rabbit warren of 13 a. lay north of the house at the same date,[94] but had perhaps ceased to exist by 1664.[95]

Between 1927 and 1932 Lord and Lady Moyne created a new park at Bailiffscourt, extending northwards as far as the Ryebank rife and along the coast in both directions, westwards almost as far as the parish boundary. About 1,500 grown trees, mostly oak and ash, were transported then and later from Slindon, Madehurst, and Arundel to form belts of woodland both within the park and elsewhere on the estate.[96] A new drive to the house was laid out from the north-west, crossing the moat through the re-erected gatehouse.[97] A five-mile route round the estate was known as Lady Moyne's walk.[98]

The manor of *CUDLOW* was held of the honor of Arundel,[99] except that at the division of the d'Aubigny inheritance dower was assigned in 1244 to Isabel d'Aubigny, countess of Arundel.[1] In the early 15th century 40 days' castle guard were said once to have been owed.[2]

Master Alexander the Secular held two fees in Cudlow and Treyford in 1242–3,[3] and Robert de

75 Guildhall Libr. MS. 13323/6, rep. of visit to Suss. estate, 1876.

76 *Kelly's Dir. Suss.* (1895 and later edns.).

77 W.S.R.O., MP 2072; O.S. Map 6", Suss. LXXIV–LXXV (1879 edn.).

78 *S.A.C.* xliv. 154.

79 e.g. W.S.R.O., Add. MS. 2031; ibid. MP 2072.

80 Ibid. TD/W 78; O.S. Map 6", Suss. LXXIV–LXXV (1879 edn.).

81 *S.C.M.* viii. 627–8.

82 W.S.R.O., TD/W 78; O.S. Map 6", Suss. LXXIV–LXXV (1879 and later edns.).

83 Following 3 paras. based mainly on C. Aslet, *Last Country Hos.* 172–81; G. Young, *Cottage in the Fields*, 218–26; *John Willmott & Sons (Hitchin) Ltd. 1852–1952* (Hitchin, [1952]) (copy in W.S.R.O. libr.); C.I.H.E. libr., GY/L 219–22; W.S.R.O., Add. MSS. 35104–35222; O.S. Map 1/2,500, Suss. LXXIV. 4 (1912 and later edns.); below, pls. facing p. 138.

84 Nairn & Pevsner, *Suss.* 41.

85 Inf. from Mr. E. Pratt, Bognor Regis, who worked on the bldgs.

86 Cf. J. Newman and N. Pevsner, *Dorset*, 421.

87 Cf. the same practice in repair of chapel.

88 *Chips, the Diaries of Sir Hen. Channon*, ed. R. R. James (1970), 54, 456–7.

89 W.S.R.O., Add. MS. 2031.

90 Inf. from the first lessee, Mrs. E. Birer, supplied to the late Mr. G. Harper, Middleton-on-Sea; *Chich. Observer*, 27 Sept. 1974.

91 *W. Suss. Gaz.* 9 June 1994.

92 *Cal. Chart. R.* 1257–1300, 180; cf. *S.A.C.* lxxxiv. 69.

93 W.S.R.O., Add. MSS. 2027, f. 19; 2031; cf. ibid. Add. MSS. 1726–7 (TS. cat.); ibid. TD/W 78; O. Rackham, *Trees and Woodland in Brit. Landscape*, 200; *O.E.D.* s.v. parrock.

94 W.S.R.O., Add. MS. 2027, f. 16.

95 Ibid. Add. MS. 1726 (TS. cat.); ibid. TD/W 78.

96 Ibid. Add. MS. 35210; O.S. Map 6", Suss. LXXIV. NE., LXXV. NW. (1932, 1950 edns.); *John Willmott & Sons (Hitchin) Ltd. 1852–1952*, [7]; Young, *Cottage in the Fields*, 224.

97 O.S. Map 6", Suss. LXXIV. NE. (1932 edn.); W.S.R.O., Add. MSS. 35196, 35199.

98 *Chips, the Diaries of Sir Hen. Channon*, 457.

99 e.g. *Bk. of Fees*, ii. 689; *Cal. Inq. p.m.* xv, p. 80.

1 *Close R.* 1242–7, 249–50.

2 *S.R.S.* lxvii. 105.

3 *Bk. of Fees*, ii. 689.

Vilers held Cudlow in 1244.[4] Geoffrey de Fresteng evidently had the manor in 1257,[5] apparently in succession to Humphrey de Fresteng;[6] in 1265 or earlier he granted it to Luke de Vienne[7] (fl. 1275). In 1279–80 the same or another Geoffrey added a grant of 133 a. of marshland.[8] Luke or his namesake still had the manor in 1300,[9] but had been succeeded before 1312 by Peter de Vienne (fl. 1316).[10] Another Luke de Vienne had it between 1325[11] and 1343 or 1344,[12] but had died by 1349–50 when his son John conveyed it, subject to his mother Lettice's life interest, to Richard FitzAlan, earl of Arundel (d. 1376). Lettice and her husband William Cambray[13] had made over their estate to the earl by 1356.[14] At earl Richard's death Cudlow passed to his younger son Sir John d'Arundel, Lord Arundel (d. 1379), who was succeeded in the direct line by John (d. 1390), and John, Lord Maltravers (succ. as earl of Arundel, 1415; d. 1421).[15] Thereafter the manor descended with the rape.[16]

By the early 17th century the surviving land of the manor was in two separate parts.[17] In 1790 John Boniface bought from the duke of Norfolk West Cudlow farm (72 a.),[18] i.e. the south-west corner of the parish. John or a namesake owned 277 a. in that area in 1803[19] and 249 a. in 1843.[20] About 1897, when the land was called Atherington farm, it was bought by Christ's Hospital,[21] passing in 1914 to the Dennis Estates Ltd.[22] East Cudlow farm, i.e. the south-east corner of the parish, remained in the dukes' possession in the 19th century and early 20th.[23] Much of that land in 1863 was shingle.[24] In 1938 it was sold by Duke Bernard (d. 1975) to Walter Guinness, Lord Moyne,[25] thereafter descending with the Bailiffscourt estate until 1982, when it was bought by Littlehampton golf club, the tenants.[26]

A manor house with dovecot was mentioned at Cudlow in 1380.[27]

In 1248 Alménêches abbey (Orne) acquired Climping *RECTORY*,[28] which was later administered by the abbey's English priory of Lyminster.[29] The estate, as that of an alien priory, passed in the 15th century to Eton college.[30] In 1248 it comprised the great tithes of what was then Climping parish, a pension of £5, and land.[31] The pension is not heard of again but the land, then described as 9 a. in the field called 'Horgesleye' at Stroodland in Ilsham,[32] was apparently represented by one of the two parcels which still belonged to the estate in the 20th century:[33] 5 a. east of Climping village street and 3 a. north of Horsemere green.[34] The rectory was valued at £20 in 1291. There were a house and a barn at Stroodland in 1324–5;[35] the house or its successor survived in 1763[36] but had gone by 1774.[37]

The rectory estate was in hand in the mid and later 14th century[38] but was otherwise apparently always leased.[39] John, later Sir John, Chapman, was lessee between 1616 and 1647, and Abraham Chapman between 1649 and 1651;[40] members of the Boniface family had the lease between 1763 and 1849.[41]

After the parishes of Ilsham and Cudlow were amalgamated with Climping in the 15th and 16th centuries, part of the endowment of each benefice was added to Climping rectory. In 1763 the rectory had the great tithes of the medieval Climping parish, of part of the former Ilsham parish, and of the western part of what had been Cudlow parish; in all three places lands called 'holibreads' were, however, exempt.[42] In addition, the great tithes of the lands of Bailiffscourt farm in Littlehampton detached belonged to the rectory by the mid 17th century.[43] At the commutation of tithes in the 1840s Eton college

4 *Close R.* 1242–7, 250. Rob. Vilers, who claimed it in 1351, was presumably a descendant: B.L. Add. MS. 39490, f. 212; cf. Eton Coll. Libr. MS. 45/83 (TS. cat.).
5 Eton Coll. Libr. MS. 56/50 (TS. cat.); cf. below, churches (Cudlow ch.).
6 *S.R.S.* xlvi, p. 90.
7 *Cal. Chart. R.* 1257–1300, 58.
8 *S.R.S.* vii, pp. 83, 118–19; *S.A.C.* lxxxiv. 68, 81 n.
9 *S.R.S.* xlvi, p. 182; cf. ibid. x. 79; *Abbrev. Plac.* (Rec. Com.), 201.
10 Eton Coll. Libr. MS. 63/64 (TS. cat.); *Feud. Aids*, v. 143.
11 *S.R.S.* xlvi, p. 183; cf. ibid. x. 137, 254; xxiii, p. 86; *Cal. Inq. p.m.* vii, p. 230.
12 P.R.O., C 143/265, no. 7 (TS. cat.).
13 *S.R.S.* xxiii, p. 128; B.L. Add. MS. 39490, f. 212.
14 *Cal. Inq. Misc.* iii, pp. 377–8; *Cal. Pat.* 1354–8, 387.
15 *Complete Peerage*, s.v. Arundel; *Cal. Inq. p.m.* xv, p. 80; xviii, p. 251; *Feud. Aids*, vi. 522; P.R.O., C 138/59, no. 51, m. 14; cf. *S.R.S.* xi. 307, 325.
16 e.g. *S.R.S.* xix. 9; xxiii, pp. 261–2; li. 139; *Goodwood Estate Archives*, i, ed. F. W. Steer and J. Venables, p. 142; P.R.O., E 178/1906, f. 2v.
17 W.S.R.O., Add. MS. 2031.
18 A.C.M., MD 619, p. 12.
19 Eton Coll. Libr., surv. of Climping rectory, 1803.
20 W.S.R.O., TD/W 33.
21 Guildhall Libr. MS. 12813/14, pp. 46, 71–4, 83; cf. W.S.R.O., IR 19, f. 9.
22 Guildhall Libr. MS. 13319, deed, 1914.
23 e.g. Dallaway, *Hist. W. Suss.* ii (1) (1819), 16; A.C.M., MD 1626; W.S.R.O., IR 19, f. 15; ibid. TD/W 33.
24 26 & 27 Vic. c. 7 (Private).
25 C. Corfield, 'Cudlow and the Waters', *Rustington Par. Mag.* June 1949–Jan. 1951, p. [35] (copy in W.S.R.O. libr.).
26 G. Seddon, *Littlehampton Golf Club 1889–1989* (Littlehampton, 1989), 11, 22–4.
27 P.R.O., C 136/8, no. 1, m. 18.
28 *S.R.S.* xlvi, pp. 55–6.
29 e.g. *S.A.C.* xlvi. 224.
30 e.g. Eton Coll. Libr. MSS. 45/21–2, 25–81 (TS. cat.).
31 *S.R.S.* xlvi, pp. 55–6; cf. Eton Coll. Libr. MSS. 45/86; 56/7–9 (TS. cat.); below, churches (Climping ch.).
32 *S.R.S.* xlvi, p. 55; P.R.O., E 106/8/19, rot. 5; cf. *S.A.C.* xlvi. 226; W.S.R.O., Ep. VI/1/4, f. 219; Ep. VI/1/5, f. 206v. For Stroodland, above, intro. (settlement).
33 W.S.R.O., IR 19, ff. 8, 11.
34 Ibid. SP 1540, map; ibid. TD/W 33; Eton Coll. Libr. MSS. 45/34, 86 (TS. cat.).
35 *Tax. Eccl.* (Rec. Com.), 135; P.R.O., E 106/8/19, rot. 5; cf. Eton Coll. Libr. MS. 45/34; 56/84 (TS. cat.).
36 Eton Coll. Libr. MS. 45/86 (TS. cat.).
37 Ibid. 45/102 (TS. cat.).
38 *Cal. Close*, 1343–6, 637; *Cal. Fine R.* 1347–56, 235; 1377–83, 170; *S.A.C.* xlvi. 226.
39 *Cal. Fine R.* 1319–27, 318, wrongly naming Sées abbey; 1337–47, 33; *Cal. Close*, 1341–3, 360; *S.A.C.* xlvi. 224; *S.R.S.* lxxviii. 63; B.L. Add. MS. 39332, f. 108; Eton Coll. Libr. MSS. 45/21–2, 25–81; 56/84 (TS. cat.); 61/RR/C/6F; Littlehampton Mus. MS. D 225; W.S.R.O., Ep. I/23/4, f. 28; Ep. I/23/7, f. 13.
40 Eton Coll. Libr. MSS. 45/27–9, 31–2, 34 (TS. cat.).
41 Ibid. 45/41–72 (TS. cat.).
42 Ibid. 45/86 (TS. cat.). For holibreads, below, churches (Climping ch.).
43 W.S.R.O., Ep. I/17/32, f. 93v.; Ep. I/54/42, A. Kelly to J. B. Freeland, 17 Jan. 1840; Eton Coll. Libr. MSS. 45/34, 86, 99 (TS. cat.).

received rents charge of £403 for its tithes in Climping and £56 for those at Bailiffscourt.[44]

Tortington priory had lands in Ilsham and Cudlow in 1535.[45]

ECONOMIC HISTORY. AGRICULTURE. The north part of the parish lay within Ford, Climping, and Ilsham manor, of which the demesne was let in the 16th and early 17th centuries.[46]

The open fields of the manor in Climping adjoined those in Ford,[47] and included Inland or the Inlands,[48] West field,[49] and the Town field,[50] perhaps the same as the 'field of Horgesleye' mentioned in 1248.[51] West field was inclosed by agreement in 1541[52] and the others perhaps about the same time, since most later references to land in the fields are to closes rather than strips.[53]

Common pasture was mentioned at Climping in 1228[54] and a common on the Climping portion of Ford, Climping, and Ilsham manor in 1541.[55] Both references seem likely to be to Horsemere green, recorded from 1608.[56] The green was inclosed before 1843,[57] except for two small pieces on either side of Horsemere Green Lane which were registered as common land in 1971.[58]

Brookland in the parish on Ford, Climping, and Ilsham manor was partly common and partly several. Climping mead was divided into small parcels in 1608.[59] Demesne meadow was recorded in 1086[60] and presumably grew by reclamation from the Arun estuary. In the mid 16th century marshland pasture there was leased in portions, sometimes separately from the demesne farm. By 1564 one holding lying apparently in both Climping and Ford, of which part had been inned recently, totalled over 100 a.[61] In 1608 *c.* 220 a. of marshland in the two parishes were let as a single holding to Sir Edward Caryll and Sir John Morley.[62]

There were 52 *villani* and 48 cottars in all on the two estates called Climping in 1086.[63] Later medieval tenants of Ford, Climping, and Ilsham manor within the parish were not separately listed from those in Ford.[64] In 1540 some copyholders in Climping held whole or half yardlands.[65] Only one freeholder remained in 1608, but there were then many copyholders. Twelve at Climping itself had between 10 and 34 a. each, mostly for three lives, a typical holding consisting of arable, inclosed pasture, and meadow in Climping mead. On the Ilsham section of the manor at the same date eight copyholders held between 19 a. and 50 a. or more with similar ingredients.[66] Encroachments from the waste were also copyholds.[67] Copyholds could be sublet by the 16th century.[68] After the 17th century the tenants' lands were gradually engrossed into the demesne farms.[69]

Across the central east–west strip of the parish the fields of Ilsham manor included 'Prestestrodlond',[70] Hampstead or Littlehampstead,[71] the Bread,[72] which lay east of the present Climping village street,[73] and Westover.[74] Parts at least seem to have been inclosed by the early 17th century.[75] There was common pasture for cattle in the 14th century,[76] and 'Prestebroke' mentioned in 1540 may have been at Ilsham,[77] where North mead and South mead were ordered to be separated by rails in the same year.[78] Demesne meadow and pasture were recorded between the 13th and 15th centuries.[79]

The demesne on at least two of the divisions of Ilsham manor was let in the early 15th century.[80] The manor perhaps never had many tenants.[81]

Arable on Atherington manor in the south part of the parish also lay in open fields, which in 1606 were West field west of the hamlet (23 a.), and various fields and furlongs to south-east, east, and north-east: Mill field (68 a.), divided

44 W.S.R.O., TD/W 33, 78.
45 *Valor Eccl.* (Rec. Com.), i. 312; P.R.O., SC 6/Hen. VIII/3674, rot. 10; cf. below, econ. hist. (agric.).
46 Above, manors (Climping); P.R.O., SC 6/Hen. VIII/3480, rot. 15d.; Guildhall Libr. MS. 13321, ff. 36–42; W.S.R.O., S.A.S. MS. B 665 (TS. cat.); *Cal. Pat.* 1563–6, p. 364.
47 Guildhall Libr. MS. 13321, f. 8; W.S.R.O., Ep. I/25/1 (1663); ibid. TD/W 33, no. 43.
48 Guildhall Libr. MSS. 13296; 13321, f. 29; W.S.R.O., Add. MS. 2292, rot. 2.
49 P.R.O., SC 6/Hen. VIII/3480, rot. 15d.
50 Guildhall Libr. MS. 13321, ff. 25, 39; P.R.O., SC 6/Hen. VIII/3480, rot. 15d.; W.S.R.O., Add. MS. 2293, 12 Apr. 1593; ibid. Ep. I/25/1 (1663).
51 *S.R.S.* xlvi, p. 55; for the name, W.S.R.O., Ep. VI/1/4, f. 219; Ep. VI/1/5, f. 206v.
52 W.S.R.O., Add. MS. 2292, rot. 3d.
53 Ibid. S.A.S. MS. BA 478 (TS. cat.); Guildhall Libr. MS. 13321, ff. 29–30, 32–3.
54 *Cal. Pat.* 1225–32, 219.
55 W.S.R.O., Add. MS. 2292, rot. 3.
56 Guildhall Libr. MS. 13321, ff. 25, 39; cf. Eton Coll. Libr. MS. 45/34 (TS. cat.). The name perhaps derives from a surname recorded in early 14th cent.: *S.R.S.* x. 137, 253; cf. an estate called Hormere or Hormeres: P.R.O., SC 6/Hen. VIII/3480, rot. 15d.; W.S.R.O., PHA 6677, rot. 7d. The name may be related to Horgesleye mentioned above. It was given as Horseman green in 1896: O.S. Map 6", Suss. LXII. SE. (1899 edn.). An alternative name was Climping green: W.S.R.O., Ep. I/25/1 (1615, 1663).
57 W.S.R.O., TD/W 33, implying its former extent.
58 W. Suss. C.C. property dept., reg. of com. land.
59 Guildhall Libr. MS. 13321, ff. 26–7, 29–30, 34; cf. W.S.R.O., Ep. I/25/1 (1615).
60 *V.C.H. Suss.* i. 430.
61 P.R.O., SC 6/Hen. VIII/3480, rot. 16; W.S.R.O., S.A.S. MS. C 172 (TS. cat.); *L. & P. Hen. VIII*, xxi (2), p. 441; *Cal. Pat.* 1563–6, p. 83; cf. ibid. 1572–5, p. 365.
62 Guildhall Libr. MS. 13321, ff. 41–2.
63 *V.C.H. Suss.* i. 430.
64 Above, intro. [popn.].
65 P.R.O., SC 6/Hen. VIII/3480, rot. 15d.
66 Guildhall Libr. MS. 13321, ff. 1–4, 9, 12–35.
67 Ibid. f. 35.
68 W.S.R.O., Add. MSS. 2292, rot. 2; 2293, *passim*.
69 Below, this section.
70 Eton Coll. Libr. MS. 56/17, 43 (TS. cat.).
71 E.S.R.O., AMS 2667–8 (TS. cat.); W.S.R.O., Add. MS. 2027, f. 28.
72 E.S.R.O., AMS 2667 (TS. cat.); P.R.O., SC 12/22/85, f. 1; W.S.R.O., Add. MS. 2027, f. 22; ibid. Ep. I/25/1 (1663).
73 W.S.R.O., MP 2072; ibid. TD/W 33.
74 P.R.O., SC 12/22/85, f. 1; W.S.R.O., Add. MS. 12624 (TS. cat.); ibid. S.A.S. MS. B 517 (TS. cat.).
75 Guildhall Libr. MS. 13321, f. 13; P.R.O., SC 12/22/85, f. 1; W.S.R.O., S.A.S. MS. B 517 (TS. cat.).
76 *Cal. Pat.* 1391–6, 562; cf. Eton Coll. Libr. MS. 56/17 (TS. cat.).
77 P.R.O., SC 6/Hen. VIII/3480, rot. 15d.; cf. 'Prestestrodlond' above.
78 W.S.R.O., Add. MS. 2292, rot. 1d.
79 P.R.O., SC 1/6, no. 94; *Kts. Hospitallers in Eng.* (Camd. Soc. [1st ser.], lxv), 25; *Cal. Pat.* 1391–6, 562; *Cal. Inq. p.m.* xviii, p. 217.
80 *S.R.S.* lxvii. 147; cf. *Kts. Hospitallers in Eng.* 25.
81 e.g. *Cal. Inq. p.m.* xviii, p. 217; *Cal. Pat.* 1391–6, 562; B.L. Add. MS. 5687, f. 219.

The entrance front from the east

The medieval chapel and re-erected buildings in the grounds

CLIMPING: BAILIFFSCOURT HOUSE

FORD: NELSON ROW
on the Ford–Climping road

CLIMPING: BROOKPITS MANOR

into six furlongs including Tatsham or Totsham furlong; Mead field (54 a.), divided into five furlongs; Sheepland field (12 a.); and Wintercroft (10 a.) with its associated Buckherne furlong (11 a.).[82] Mill field in the 14th and 15th centuries was known as Eastfield;[83] Wintercroft was also mentioned in the 14th century.[84] In 1606 land in the fields and furlongs was held in pieces of up to 5 a. Sheepland field was then being eaten away by the sea[85] and had perhaps once been much larger. The fields at Atherington were inclosed before 1772.[86]

There was common pasture for cattle at Atherington in the 14th century,[87] presumably including the Shortsmare, described as Lammas land in 1606.[88] At the same date Atherington mead north-east of Atherington hamlet had 19 a. in pieces of between ¼ a. and 3 a.;[89] it was inclosed at an unknown date. Demesne meadow was recorded in the 14th century[90] and was extended, as presumably on Ford, Climping, and Ilsham manor, by reclamation from the river.[91] In the mid 16th century it was let in portions, sometimes separately from the demesne farm. There were 111 a. of marshland at Atherington in 1540, *c.* 130 a. in 1558,[92] and *c.* 145 a. in 1606, when it was all held with the demesne farm;[93] in the 17th or early 18th century the land was known as Bailiffscourt marshes.[94] Closes of marshland pasture at Atherington were amalgamated from the 17th century.[95]

The Atherington demesne was managed by the bailiff of Sées abbey (Orne) in 1378[96] and presumably generally earlier, but was let in the 15th and early 16th centuries.[97] In 1606 the farm, of 400 a., was held under leases for 21 or 30 years;[98] in 1660 it was of similar size.[99] There were both free and bond tenants between the 14th and 16th centuries,[1] and labour services were still performed on the abbey's demesne, apparently including that in Climping, in 1342.[2] In 1606 only two freeholders remained, but nine copyholders then had up to 50 a. each, typically including open-field arable, inclosed pasture, and rights in Atherington mead.[3] Some land held of Atherington lay in Ilsham.[4] Encroachments from the waste, as on Ford, Climping, and Ilsham manor, were copyholds.[5] Copyholds could be sublet by the 16th century[6] and were heriotable.[7] From the 17th century the tenants' lands were gradually engrossed into the demesne farms;[8] only a few copyholds and one freehold survived in the early 18th century, to disappear after 1758.[9]

Open fields on Cudlow manor included East and West Broadmare; Southfield, Eastfield, and probably Northfield; East garston and presumably West garston and South garston; South street and presumably West street; Westrude and presumably Northrude; and Horsecroft.[10] Since none have been located and there is no evidence of inclosure, all may have been lost to the sea. There was common pasture for cattle in the 14th century[11] and for sheep in the 15th.[12] Demesne meadow is recorded in the 14th and 15th centuries;[13] it may have been relatively poor, since the manor also had 10 a. of meadow at Arundel in 1279–80. There were at least 133 a. of marshland on the demesne farm at the same date,[14] and *c.* 225 a. of meadow and pasture in 1421,[15] much of which was presumably also lost to the sea.

The Cudlow demesne farm was in hand in the 1360s, when there was a sheepfold and income was received from the sale of corn, cider, and stock, and from agistment.[16] It had over 200 a. in 1380,[17] and was claimed to have over 500 a. in 1421.[18] In the mid 15th century it was leased,[19] as its gradually shrinking acreage continued to be later,[20] sometimes after the later 16th century in two portions known as East and West Cudlow.[21] There were both free and bond tenants on the manor in the 14th and 15th centuries.[22]

The four manors of the combined parish were originally self-contained entities; in the early 17th century only one man held of both Ford, Climping, and Ilsham manor and Atherington manor.[23] The rectory estate was leased generally

82 W.S.R.O., Add. MSS. 2027, ff. 10–14; 2031, illus. at *S.A.C.* xliv, facing p. 147.
83 *Cat. Anct. D.* ii, B 3483; P.R.O., SC 6/1101/20, rot. 2d.; cf. *S.A.C.* xliv, facing p. 147.
84 *Cat. Anct. D.* i, B 169.
85 W.S.R.O., Add. MS. 2027, ff. 10–14.
86 Ibid. MP 2072.
87 *Cat. Anct. D.* ii, B 3483; *Cal. Close*, 1333–7, 194.
88 W.S.R.O., Add. MS. 2027, f. 19; cf. *O.E.D.* s.v. Lammas.
89 W.S.R.O., Add. MSS. 2027, ff. 14–15; 2031.
90 P.R.O., E 106/11/2, rot. 1; ibid. SC 2/205/74, rot. [2d.].
91 e.g. W.S.R.O., Ep. I/11/13, ff. 135v., 141, relating to the 1620s.
92 P.R.O., SC 6/Hen. VIII/3480, rot. 14d.; *Cal. Pat.* 1557–8, 406–7.
93 W.S.R.O., Add. MS. 2027, ff. 20–1.
94 Ibid. Add. MS. 1728 (TS. cat.).
95 Ibid. Add. MS. 2031; ibid. TD/W 33.
96 P.R.O., E 106/11/2.
97 Ibid. SC 6/1033/8; SC 6/1037/13; SC 6/Hen. VIII/3480, rot. 14d.; SC 6/Hen. VIII/3658, rot. [3]; *Goodwood Estate Archives*, i, ed. F. W. Steer and J. Venables, p. 141.
98 W.S.R.O., Add. MS. 2027, ff. 16, 19–22.
99 *Goodwood Estate Archives*, i, pp. 141–2; cf. W.S.R.O., Add. MS. 12440 (TS. cat.).
1 P.R.O., E 106/11/2, rot. 1; ibid. SC 2/205/51; SC 2/206/44, rot. 6; SC 6/Hen. VIII/3480, rot. 14d.
2 Ibid. SC 2/205/74, rot. [2d.].
3 W.S.R.O., Add. MS. 2027, ff. 22–8.
4 Ibid. 2027, ff. 9–10; 2031; A.C.M., M 532, f. [27v. from end].
5 W.S.R.O., Add. MS. 2027, ff. 24, 27.
6 Ibid. PHA 6677, rot. 2; cf. ibid. Add. MS. 12628 (TS. cat.); ibid. Goodwood MS. E1, f. 97.
7 Ibid. Add. MS. 2027, f. 10.
8 Below, this section.
9 Littlehampton Mus. MS. D 303; cf. W.S.R.O., MP 2072.
10 A.C.M., A 415; ibid. M 531, f. [108]; Eton Coll. Libr. MSS. 45/83–4 (TS. cat.); 56/50, 62 (TS. cat.).
11 A.C.M., A 415.
12 Ibid. M 531, f. [10v.].
13 Ibid. A 415; P.R.O., C 138/59, no. 51, m. 14.
14 *S.R.S.* vii, pp. 118–19.
15 P.R.O., C 138/59, no. 51, m. 14; cf. A.C.M., M 531, f. [10v.].
16 A.C.M., A 415.
17 P.R.O., C 136/8, no. 1, m. 18.
18 Ibid. C 138/59, no. 51, m. 14.
19 A.C.M., M 531, ff. [10v., 108].
20 Ibid. A 263, rental, 1657, f. [2]; P.R.O., SC 6/Hen. VIII/3480, rot. 15d.; Sandbeck Park, Rotherham, Lumley MS. EMA/1/5.
21 A.C.M., Hodskinson surv. 1778, ff. 42–3; P.R.O., E 178/1906, f. 2v.; ibid. REQ 2/274/46, rott. 6d.–7; W.S.R.O., Add. MS. 2031; *Goodwood Estate Archives*, i, p. 142.
22 A.C.M., M 531, ff. [57v., 72v.]; P.R.O., C 136/8, no. 1, m. 18; C 138/59, no. 51, m. 14.
23 Guildhall Libr. MS. 13321, f. 30; W.S.R.O., Add. MS. 2027, ff. 24–5.

for periods of 10 or 21 years between the 16th century and the 19th,[24] and Tortington priory's land at Ilsham was held by freehold tenants in the early 16th century.[25]

During the 18th century the demesne farms of the parish increased in size through the engrossing of small freeholds and copyholds.[26] On the Christ's Hospital estate in the north and centre there were three chief farms. Northwood farm, perhaps succeeding the grange of the lords of Ford, Climping, and Ilsham on the Ford–Climping boundary recorded in 1310[27] and the copyholds called Northwood in the 17th century,[28] had 189 a. in 1711. Kent's farm was then about the same size, and Church farm had 293 a. in Climping and Ford in 1759; by 1799 those two farms had grown respectively to 250 a. and 338 a.[29] Bailiffscourt farm had 375 a., including 196 a. of brookland, in 1772.[30] Other farms in the 18th century were Cudlow, which had 160 a. in 1778,[31] and Brookpit, of 63 a. in 1760.[32] Leases on all the farms mentioned were of between 11 and 21 years.

Arable farming dominated in the parish in the Middle Ages. The two estates called Climping in 1086 each had the large number of seven tenants' ploughs,[33] and in 1341 the ninth of sheaves was valued at five times that of fleeces and lambs at Cudlow, nearly ten times at Ilsham, and fifteen times at Climping. Other crops grown in 1340 were hemp, flax, and apples, pigs and geese as well as cattle being kept.[34] There were sheep on Cudlow manor in the 14th and 15th centuries.[35] In the 17th and 18th centuries mixed farming was practised. Crops then widely grown were wheat, barley, oats, peas, beans, tares, and vetches, with hemp in the 17th century and clover seed in the early 18th. One farmer *c.* 1633 may have worked a three-course rotation of wheat, barley with vetches, and fallow, and another in 1644 a four-course rotation of wheat, barley, peas with tares, and fallow. Cattle, sheep, and pigs were generally kept. A farmer at Ilsham in 1710 had at least 168 sheep and 59 cattle, and another in 1728 a flock of 312 sheep. Some farmers also had land elsewhere: at Eastergate in 1614 and at Flansham in Felpham in 1729.[36] In 1774 twice as much wheat as barley was grown but there was apparently little meadow.[37] The Christ's Hospital farms were said to be in a good system of husbandry in 1794.[38]

During the 19th and early 20th centuries the parish was divided into large farms, mostly rented. The Christ's Hospital estate was in excellent condition in 1832, with established

OWNERS AND OCCUPIERS OF THE CHIEF FARMS, 1843

Owner	*Occupier*	*Farm*	*Acreage in parish*
John Boniface	in hand	Hobb's	213
"	"	West Cudlow	249
Mary Boniface	Thomas Boniface	[west end of parish]	47
Christ's Hospital	George Boniface	[on Ford boundary]	60
"	John Boniface	Lindfield's barn	72
"	Thomas Boniface	Kent's	223
"	Richard Coote	Church	330
"	Charles White	Northwood	137
Joseph Coote	Richard Coote	Park	73
Charlotte Cutfield	Joseph Coote	East Cudlow	135
"	"	Bailiffscourt	177
Duke of Norfolk	John Boniface	part of East Cudlow	45

(*Sources*: W.S.R.O., TD/W 33, 78; above, manors.)

24 Eton Coll. Libr. MSS. 45/21–2, 25–81 (TS. cat.).
25 P.R.O., SC 6/Hen. VIII/3674, rot. 10; cf. ibid. SC 12/22/85, f. 1.
26 Cf. W.S.R.O., Add. MS. 2027, ff. 22–8; ibid. MP 2072.
27 Eton Coll. Libr. MS. 45/84 (TS. cat.).
28 Guildhall Libr. MS. 13321, ff. 2, 4; cf. W.S.R.O., PHA 6677, rot. 7d.
29 Guildhall Libr. MSS. 13307, 13312–15.
30 W.S.R.O., MP 2072; cf. ibid. Add. MS. 1727 (TS. cat.).
31 A.C.M., Hodskinson surv. 1778, ff. 42–3.
32 E.S.R.O., SAS/BB 7 (TS. cat.).
33 *V.C.H. Suss.* i. 430.
34 *Inq. Non.* (Rec. Com.), 351, 369–70; cf. A.C.M., A 415.
35 A.C.M., A 415; ibid. M 531, f. [10v.].
36 *S.A.C.* xcii. 59; W.S.R.O., Ep. I/29/51/1, 4, 6, 16, 23, 30, 34, 56, 77, 79, 85–7; for hemp cf. ibid. Add. MS. 2027, ff. 16, 25; ibid. Ep. I/25/1 (1663).
37 Eton Coll. Libr. MS. 45/102 (TS. cat.).
38 Guildhall Libr. MS. 13323/3, rep. of John Trumper, 1795.

The entrance front from the east

The medieval chapel and re-erected buildings in the grounds

CLIMPING: BAILIFFSCOURT HOUSE

FORD: NELSON ROW
on the Ford–Climping road

CLIMPING: BROOKPITS MANOR

into six furlongs including Tatsham or Totsham furlong; Mead field (54 a.), divided into five furlongs; Sheepland field (12 a.); and Wintercroft (10 a.) with its associated Buckherne furlong (11 a.).[82] Mill field in the 14th and 15th centuries was known as Eastfield;[83] Wintercroft was also mentioned in the 14th century.[84] In 1606 land in the fields and furlongs was held in pieces of up to 5 a. Sheepland field was then being eaten away by the sea[85] and had perhaps once been much larger. The fields at Atherington were inclosed before 1772.[86]

There was common pasture for cattle at Atherington in the 14th century,[87] presumably including the Shortsmare, described as Lammas land in 1606.[88] At the same date Atherington mead north-east of Atherington hamlet had 19 a. in pieces of between ¼ a. and 3 a.;[89] it was inclosed at an unknown date. Demesne meadow was recorded in the 14th century[90] and was extended, as presumably on Ford, Climping, and Ilsham manor, by reclamation from the river.[91] In the mid 16th century it was let in portions, sometimes separately from the demesne farm. There were 111 a. of marshland at Atherington in 1540, *c.* 130 a. in 1558,[92] and *c.* 145 a. in 1606, when it was all held with the demesne farm;[93] in the 17th or early 18th century the land was known as Bailiffscourt marshes.[94] Closes of marshland pasture at Atherington were amalgamated from the 17th century.[95]

The Atherington demesne was managed by the bailiff of Sées abbey (Orne) in 1378[96] and presumably generally earlier, but was let in the 15th and early 16th centuries.[97] In 1606 the farm, of 400 a., was held under leases for 21 or 30 years;[98] in 1660 it was of similar size.[99] There were both free and bond tenants between the 14th and 16th centuries,[1] and labour services were still performed on the abbey's demesne, apparently including that in Climping, in 1342.[2] In 1606 only two freeholders remained, but nine copyholders then had up to 50 a. each, typically including open-field arable, inclosed pasture, and rights in Atherington mead.[3] Some land held of Atherington lay in Ilsham.[4] Encroachments from the waste, as on Ford, Climping, and Ilsham manor, were copyholds.[5] Copyholds could be sublet by the 16th century[6] and were heriotable.[7] From the 17th century the tenants' lands were gradually engrossed into the demesne farms;[8] only a few copyholds and one freehold survived in the early 18th century, to disappear after 1758.[9]

Open fields on Cudlow manor included East and West Broadmare; Southfield, Eastfield, and probably Northfield; East garston and presumably West garston and South garston; South street and presumably West street; Westrude and presumably Northrude; and Horsecroft.[10] Since none have been located and there is no evidence of inclosure, all may have been lost to the sea. There was common pasture for cattle in the 14th century[11] and for sheep in the 15th.[12] Demesne meadow is recorded in the 14th and 15th centuries;[13] it may have been relatively poor, since the manor also had 10 a. of meadow at Arundel in 1279–80. There were at least 133 a. of marshland on the demesne farm at the same date,[14] and *c.* 225 a. of meadow and pasture in 1421,[15] much of which was presumably also lost to the sea.

The Cudlow demesne farm was in hand in the 1360s, when there was a sheepfold and income was received from the sale of corn, cider, and stock, and from agistment.[16] It had over 200 a. in 1380,[17] and was claimed to have over 500 a. in 1421.[18] In the mid 15th century it was leased,[19] as its gradually shrinking acreage continued to be later,[20] sometimes after the later 16th century in two portions known as East and West Cudlow.[21] There were both free and bond tenants on the manor in the 14th and 15th centuries.[22]

The four manors of the combined parish were originally self-contained entities; in the early 17th century only one man held of both Ford, Climping, and Ilsham manor and Atherington manor.[23] The rectory estate was leased generally

82 W.S.R.O., Add. MSS. 2027, ff. 10–14; 2031, illus. at *S.A.C.* xliv, facing p. 147.
83 *Cat. Anct. D.* ii, B 3483; P.R.O., SC 6/1101/20, rot. 2d.; cf. *S.A.C.* xliv, facing p. 147.
84 *Cat. Anct. D.* i, B 169.
85 W.S.R.O., Add. MS. 2027, ff. 10–14.
86 Ibid. MP 2072.
87 *Cat. Anct. D.* ii, B 3483; *Cal. Close*, 1333–7, 194.
88 W.S.R.O., Add. MS. 2027, f. 19; cf. *O.E.D.* s.v. Lammas.
89 W.S.R.O., Add. MSS. 2027, ff. 14–15; 2031.
90 P.R.O., E 106/11/2, rot. 1; ibid. SC 2/205/74, rot. [2d.].
91 e.g. W.S.R.O., Ep. I/11/13, ff. 135v., 141, relating to the 1620s.
92 P.R.O., SC 6/Hen. VIII/3480, rot. 14d.; *Cal. Pat.* 1557–8, 406–7.
93 W.S.R.O., Add. MS. 2027, ff. 20–1.
94 Ibid. Add. MS. 1728 (TS. cat.).
95 Ibid. Add. MS. 2031; ibid. TD/W 33.
96 P.R.O., E 106/11/2.
97 Ibid. SC 6/1033/8; SC 6/1037/13; SC 6/Hen. VIII/3480, rot. 14d.; SC 6/Hen. VIII/3658, rot. [3]; *Goodwood Estate Archives*, i, ed. F. W. Steer and J. Venables, p. 141.
98 W.S.R.O., Add. MS. 2027, ff. 16, 19–22.
99 *Goodwood Estate Archives*, i, pp. 141–2; cf. W.S.R.O., Add. MS. 12440 (TS. cat.).
1 P.R.O., E 106/11/2, rot. 1; ibid. SC 2/205/51; SC 2/206/44, rot. 6; SC 6/Hen. VIII/3480, rot. 14d.
2 Ibid. SC 2/205/74, rot. [2d.].
3 W.S.R.O., Add. MS. 2027, ff. 22–8.
4 Ibid. 2027, ff. 9–10; 2031; A.C.M., M 532, f. [27v. from end].
5 W.S.R.O., Add. MS. 2027, ff. 24, 27.
6 Ibid. PHA 6677, rot. 2; cf. ibid. Add. MS. 12628 (TS. cat.); ibid. Goodwood MS. E1, f. 97.
7 Ibid. Add. MS. 2027, f. 10.
8 Below, this section.
9 Littlehampton Mus. MS. D 303; cf. W.S.R.O., MP 2072.
10 A.C.M., A 415; ibid. M 531, f. [108]; Eton Coll. Libr. MSS. 45/83–4 (TS. cat.); 56/50, 62 (TS. cat.).
11 A.C.M., A 415.
12 Ibid. M 531, f. [10v.].
13 Ibid. A 415; P.R.O., C 138/59, no. 51, m. 14.
14 *S.R.S.* vii, pp. 118–19.
15 P.R.O., C 138/59, no. 51, m. 14; cf. A.C.M., M 531, f. [10v.].
16 A.C.M., A 415.
17 P.R.O., C 136/8, no. 1, m. 18.
18 Ibid. C 138/59, no. 51, m. 14.
19 A.C.M., M 531, ff. [10v., 108].
20 Ibid. A 263, rental, 1657, f. [2]; P.R.O., SC 6/Hen. VIII/3480, rot. 15d.; Sandbeck Park, Rotherham, Lumley MS. EMA/1/5.
21 A.C.M., Hodskinson surv. 1778, ff. 42–3; P.R.O., E 178/1906, f. 2v.; ibid. REQ 2/274/46, rott. 6d.–7; W.S.R.O., Add. MS. 2031; *Goodwood Estate Archives*, i, p. 142.
22 A.C.M., M 531, ff. [57v., 72v.]; P.R.O., C 136/8, no. 1, m. 18; C 138/59, no. 51, m. 14.
23 Guildhall Libr. MS. 13321, f. 30; W.S.R.O., Add. MS. 2027, ff. 24–5.

for periods of 10 or 21 years between the 16th century and the 19th,[24] and Tortington priory's land at Ilsham was held by freehold tenants in the early 16th century.[25]

During the 18th century the demesne farms of the parish increased in size through the engrossing of small freeholds and copyholds.[26] On the Christ's Hospital estate in the north and centre there were three chief farms. Northwood farm, perhaps succeeding the grange of the lords of Ford, Climping, and Ilsham on the Ford–Climping boundary recorded in 1310[27] and the copyholds called Northwood in the 17th century,[28] had 189 a. in 1711. Kent's farm was then about the same size, and Church farm had 293 a. in Climping and Ford in 1759; by 1799 those two farms had grown respectively to 250 a. and 338 a.[29] Bailiffscourt farm had 375 a., including 196 a. of brookland, in 1772.[30] Other farms in the 18th century were Cudlow, which had 160 a. in 1778,[31] and Brookpit, of 63 a. in 1760.[32] Leases on all the farms mentioned were of between 11 and 21 years.

Arable farming dominated in the parish in the Middle Ages. The two estates called Climping in 1086 each had the large number of seven tenants' ploughs,[33] and in 1341 the ninth of sheaves was valued at five times that of fleeces and lambs at Cudlow, nearly ten times at Ilsham, and fifteen times at Climping. Other crops grown in 1340 were hemp, flax, and apples, pigs and geese as well as cattle being kept.[34] There were sheep on Cudlow manor in the 14th and 15th centuries.[35] In the 17th and 18th centuries mixed farming was practised. Crops then widely grown were wheat, barley, oats, peas, beans, tares, and vetches, with hemp in the 17th century and clover seed in the early 18th. One farmer *c.* 1633 may have worked a three-course rotation of wheat, barley with vetches, and fallow, and another in 1644 a four-course rotation of wheat, barley, peas with tares, and fallow. Cattle, sheep, and pigs were generally kept. A farmer at Ilsham in 1710 had at least 168 sheep and 59 cattle, and another in 1728 a flock of 312 sheep. Some farmers also had land elsewhere: at Eastergate in 1614 and at Flansham in Felpham in 1729.[36] In 1774 twice as much wheat as barley was grown but there was apparently little meadow.[37] The Christ's Hospital farms were said to be in a good system of husbandry in 1794.[38]

During the 19th and early 20th centuries the parish was divided into large farms, mostly rented. The Christ's Hospital estate was in excellent condition in 1832, with established

OWNERS AND OCCUPIERS OF THE CHIEF FARMS, 1843

Owner	*Occupier*	*Farm*	*Acreage in parish*
John Boniface	in hand	Hobb's	213
"	"	West Cudlow	249
Mary Boniface	Thomas Boniface	[west end of parish]	47
Christ's Hospital	George Boniface	[on Ford boundary]	60
"	John Boniface	Lindfield's barn	72
"	Thomas Boniface	Kent's	223
"	Richard Coote	Church	330
"	Charles White	Northwood	137
Joseph Coote	Richard Coote	Park	73
Charlotte Cutfield	Joseph Coote	East Cudlow	135
"	"	Bailiffscourt	177
Duke of Norfolk	John Boniface	part of East Cudlow	45

(*Sources*: W.S.R.O., TD/W 33, 78; above, manors.)

24 Eton Coll. Libr. MSS. 45/21–2, 25–81 (TS. cat.).
25 P.R.O., SC 6/Hen. VIII/3674, rot. 10; cf. ibid. SC 12/22/85, f. 1.
26 Cf. W.S.R.O., Add. MS. 2027, ff. 22–8; ibid. MP 2072.
27 Eton Coll. Libr. MS. 45/84 (TS. cat.).
28 Guildhall Libr. MS. 13321, ff. 2, 4; cf. W.S.R.O., PHA 6677, rot. 7d.
29 Guildhall Libr. MSS. 13307, 13312–15.
30 W.S.R.O., MP 2072; cf. ibid. Add. MS. 1727 (TS. cat.).
31 A.C.M., Hodskinson surv. 1778, ff. 42–3.
32 E.S.R.O., SAS/BB 7 (TS. cat.).
33 *V.C.H. Suss.* i. 430.
34 *Inq. Non.* (Rec. Com.), 351, 369–70; cf. A.C.M., A 415.
35 A.C.M., A 415; ibid. M 531, f. [10v.].
36 *S.A.C.* xcii. 59; W.S.R.O., Ep. I/29/51/1, 4, 6, 16, 23, 30, 34, 56, 77, 79, 85–7; for hemp cf. ibid. Add. MS. 2027, ff. 16, 25; ibid. Ep. I/25/1 (1663).
37 Eton Coll. Libr. MS. 45/102 (TS. cat.).
38 Guildhall Libr. MS. 13323/3, rep. of John Trumper, 1795.

tenants,[39] notably the Cootes, who had been at Church farm since 1759, and the Bonifaces, who had had Kent's farm since 1799.[40] In 1843 the two families dominated the parish (see Table). Leases on the Christ's Hospital estate in the period were of between 10 and 14 years. The Cootes and Bonifaces were still the chief farmers in the 1860s and 70s,[41] but from 1881 they were gradually replaced by the Langmead family, immigrants from Devon. William Langmead (d. 1919) first farmed at Bailiffscourt, and later at Kent's, Brookpit, and Atherington farms; his sons John (d. 1950) and Walter (d. 1971) divided those farms between them, John later adding Northwood farm.[42]

Returns for the parish in the years 1801 and 1803 listed 180–90 cattle, up to *c.* 1,000 sheep, and over 200 pigs.[43] At that period, however, arable was the chief type of farming practised. All but *c.* 300 a. was said to be arable in 1819, though a third of the parish lay on relatively poor soil.[44] In 1843 there were 1,034 a. of arable, and 562 a. of meadow and pasture chiefly in the east, including 426 a. of brookland; the brookland, described as very good, was used chiefly for fattening sheep and cattle.[45] Marshland closes continued to be amalgamated during the 19th century.[46] In 1847 the Christ's Hospital farms, though considered inferior to those at Ford, were well cultivated under a five-course rotation.[47] By 1876 many fences had been removed to create very large closes, for instance that of 78 a. which represented the whole of the former Park farm.[48] Some land was underdrained in the mid 19th century. Stock raising had become more important by 1865[49] and the number of shepherds listed rose from four in 1861 to nine in 1881.[50] In the early 20th century sheep were brought for fattening from West Dean north of Chichester.[51] In 1914 the Langmead farms were specially noted: Kent's with Hobb's for its Southdown flock, and Atherington with Bailiffscourt for sheep, cattle, and prize-winning crops.[52] The Atherington flock was later moved to Northwood farm.[53]

The bigger farms employed large numbers of labourers in the 19th and early 20th centuries. There were 47 in all in the parish in 1831.[54] In 1861 Church farm had 16 men and boys.[55] The parish was well supplied with provident societies from *c.* 1850: a coal club, and later a provident fund and a clothing club.[56] As a result the vicar was able to claim in 1893 that his parishioners were relatively well off: there was overtime work throughout the summer, most of the old people had savings, thrift was generally practised, and there was no begging.[57] Most parishioners remained agricultural labourers in 1923.[58]

The parish continued to be dominated by large farms after the sale of the Christ's Hospital estate in the early 20th century. Church and Bailiffscourt farms were in hand in the 1920s and 30s,[59] when Church farm was claimed to have some of the most fertile land in southern England.[60] Bailiffscourt farm in the 1970s and 80s had 800–860 a., the tenant in 1979 and later also farming at Oving near Chichester;[61] in 1991 the land was worked from buildings at various places in the parish. Northwood farm in 1991 had 435 a. mostly in Climping but, the farmhouse having been sold, was then farmed from Yapton. In the 1950s it had a Friesian dairy herd[62] and pigs were raised on Bailiffscourt farm *c.* 1980,[63] but by *c.* 1990 farming in the parish was again chiefly arable, crops including potatoes, oilseed rape, and linseed.[64] In addition market gardening was practised from the 1950s, chiefly south of Horsemere Green Lane.[65] One holding which flourished between 1960 and 1990 grew cucumbers under glass with a staff of eight.[66] Between 1978[67] and 1990 there was also a mushroom farm belonging to Linfields of Thakeham. Daffodils were grown commercially in 1986.[68]

MILLS. There was a windmill on the Hospitallers' estate at Ilsham in 1338[69] and a mill on Cudlow manor at the same period.[70] A windmill on Atherington manor is mentioned from 1378.[71] In 1485 and later it was called Totsham mill and

39 Ibid. 13323/5, rep. of view of fms. in Surr. and Suss. 1832; rep. of view of estates, 1845.

40 Ibid. 13312–13, 13315.

41 Ibid. 13307, 13313, 13315; 13323/7, partics. of Ford and Climping estate, 1877.

42 *Kelly's Dir. Suss.* (1882 and later edns.), s.v. Climping, Ford; *W. Suss. Gaz.* 28 May 1981; W.S.R.O., IR 19, ff. 9, 11–13; ibid. SP 1540; inf. from Mrs. S. Abbot, née Langmead, Hobbs Ct., Yapton.

43 E.S.R.O., LCG/3/EW 1, ff. [43v.–44, 84v.].

44 Dallaway, *Hist. W. Suss.* ii (1) (1819), 12; cf. Eton Coll. Libr., Climping corresp. file, surv. of Climping rectory, 1803.

45 P.R.O., IR 18/10292; W.S.R.O., TD/W 33.

46 W.S.R.O., TD/W 33; O.S. Map 6", Suss. LXIII, LXXV (1879 edn.).

47 Guildhall Libr. MS. 13323/5, valuation and rep. 1847; rep. on fms. in Ford and Climping, 1853.

48 Ibid. 13323/6, rep. of view of lands at Climping, 1865; O.S. Map 6", Suss. LXII–LXIII, LXXIV–LXXV (1879–80 edn.).

49 Guildhall Libr. MS. 13323/5, valuation and rep. 1847; ibid. 13323/6, rep. of view of lands at Climping, 1865.

50 P.R.O., RG 9/0615, ff. 47v.–49, 51; RG 11/1119, ff. 41v.–43v., 45.

51 W.S.R.O., OH 16. Agric. statistics of later 19th and 20th cents. are not used here because the Ford and Climping totals are intermingled: P.R.O., MAF 68/433, 2371; cf. below, Ford, econ. hist.

52 W.S.R.O., SP 1540.

53 V. Porter, *The Southdown Sheep*, 78; *The Southdown Sheep*, ed. E. Walford-Lloyd, p. xi; *S.C.M.* xxiv. 420; cf. *W. Suss. Gaz.* 28 May 1981.

54 *Census*, 1831.

55 P.R.O., RG 9/615, f. 48.

56 W.S.R.O., Ep. I/22A/2 (1898); ibid. Par. 51/7/17–21 (TS. cat.); Eton Coll. Libr., Climping corresp. file, 'Clymping Record', 1901.

57 W.S.R.O., Ep. I/22A/1 (1893); cf. ibid. SP 1540, p. 1; H. R. Haggard, *Rural Eng.* i. 125–8.

58 Eton Coll. Libr., Climping corresp. file, Revd. E. F. Leach to bursar, 12 Sept. 1923; cf. W.S.R.O., Ep. I/22A/2 (1898).

59 *Kelly's Dir. Suss.* (1922 and later edns.).

60 Littlehampton Mus. MS. D 135.

61 *Chich. Observer*, 21 Dec. 1979; *W. Suss. Gaz.* 14 May 1981; local inf.

62 Inf. from Mrs. Abbot.

63 *W. Suss. Gaz.* 9 Nov. 1978; local inf.

64 D. Robinson and A. Stephens, *Suss. Agric.* (Brighton, 1988), 6–7 (copy in W.S.R.O. libr.); inf. from Mrs. Abbot, and from Mr. G. Wooldridge, Climping.

65 O.S. Maps 1/25,000, SU 90 (1958 edn.); SU 80/90 (1981 edn.); TQ 00/10 (1979 edn.); 6", Suss. LXII. SE. (1951 edn.).

66 Inf. from Mr. P. Bailey, former dir. of Peter Bailey Ltd.

67 *W. Suss. Gaz.* 9 Nov. 1978.

68 Local inf.

69 *Kts. Hospitallers in Eng.* (Camd. Soc. [1st ser.], lxv), 25; cf. *Inq. Non.* (Rec. Com.), 351.

70 *Inq. Non.* (Rec. Com.), 369; A.C.M., A 415.

71 P.R.O., E 106/11/2, rot. 1; W.S.R.O., Add. MSS. 2027, f. 20; 2031; *Cal. Pat.* 1557–8, 28; *250 Yrs. of Map-making in Suss.* ed. H. Margary, pls. 5, 14.

by 1780 alternatively Climping mill.[72] The present octagonal, weatherboarded building of 1799 is an early example of a smock mill.[73] In the 19th century it was kept by members of the Barnard family. A steam engine had been added to supplement wind power by 1895, but the mill ceased to be used soon afterwards.[74] By 1914 it had become two cottages,[75] and in the 1920s it was converted into a single dwelling with the addition of dummy sails.[76] The top storey was removed in 1962. From *c.* 1959 the mill and adjacent buildings were used as a school.[77]

OTHER TRADES AND INDUSTRIES. Surnames between the late 13th century and early 15th suggesting trades included Salter,[78] Isemonger, i.e. ironmonger, and Tailor.[79] At various times between the 16th century and the 18th there were butchers, brewers,[80] smiths,[81] a carpenter,[82] and perhaps a tanner.[83]

The sea provided varied employment. The surname Mariner was apparently recorded at Atherington in 1296 and Shipwright at Cudlow in the early 14th century.[84] Ten coastguards for defence against the French were established *c.* 1295 at Cudlow,[85] which in 1342 sent a ship for the fleet sailing to Brittany, putting it on a par with Seaford and Pevensey.[86] Tithes were paid on saltwater fish in Ilsham parish in 1341, and on both saltwater and freshwater fish in Climping;[87] fish were also landed at Cudlow in 1385,[88] and eels were caught at Elmer pool on the Cudlow–Middleton boundary in 1457.[89] The vicar still apparently received tithe herrings in 1664.[90]

One parishioner at least owned a boat in the 16th century.[91] Seamen were recorded at various times in the 17th, when there were often as many as three;[92] in 1803, however, no boats were listed in the parish, and two years earlier no parishioner was willing to serve as boatman or bargeman in case of invasion.[93] The open coastline and lack of roads made Climping an obvious place for smuggling in the 18th and early 19th centuries. A riding officer had been appointed to combat it by 1730,[94] and one was drowned, possibly nefariously, in the pond opposite his house in 1802.[95] One purpose of the new roads and ferry of *c.* 1824 was the suppression of smuggling.[96] Much oral evidence of the activity in the past was available *c.* 1900.[97]

In the early 19th century one in 11 to 15 families in work was supported chiefly by non-agricultural occupations.[98] Thomas Boniface of Kent's farm was a land surveyor and valuer as well as farmer in 1836.[99] Between the mid 19th century and the earlier 20th there were from time to time shopkeepers,[1] carpenters, smiths,[2] and thatchers. One of the smithies lay south of the church.[3] There were a shoemaker in 1845, a dairyman in 1852, a fishhawker in 1898,[4] and a garage in 1930. Bricks were made north of Horsemere Green Lane in the 1920s.[5]

Bailiffscourt house has been a hotel since the late 1940s,[6] and there were riding stables in the parish from the same period.[7] The holiday industry was also represented by a camping site in 1977;[8] there were two leisure caravan parks in Horsemere Green Lane in 1993,[9] besides other accommodation for visitors there and elsewhere. In 1991 two shops on Bailiffscourt farm sold farm produce.

On the southern part of the former Ford airfield, between Horsemere Green Lane and Ford prison, the Rudford industrial estate was set up after 1969 and greatly expanded in the 1980s.[10] In 1991 there were 80–90 businesses there, some occupying converted hangars and others in small purpose-built units; besides manufacturing firms, especially in engineering, there were representatives of service and transport-related industries.[11] Another part of the former airfield within the parish was used

72 P.R.O., SC 6/1101/20, rot. 2d.; W.S.R.O., Add. MSS. 1281, 12630 (TS. cat.); cf. *Cat. Anct. D.* ii, B 3485; O.S. Map 6", Suss. LXXV (1879 edn.). Cuttleworth mill recorded in 1698 was presumably a mistake for Cudlow: B.L. Sloane MS. 3233, f. 15.

73 M. Brunnarius, *Windmills of Suss.* 112–13 and pl. 121; *S.I.A.S. Newsletter*, iv. 3; date on timber in bldg. (inf. from Clymping local hist. group); above, pl. facing p. 122.

74 Brunnarius, *Windmills*, 112; *Kelly's Dir. Suss.* (1845 and later edns.); W.S.R.O., TD/W 33; cf. O.S. Map 6", Suss. LXXV. NW. (1899, 1913 edns.).

75 W.S.R.O., SP 1540.

76 Brunnarius, *Windmills*, 113; cf. *S.C.M.* iii. 710; xi. 741.

77 *W. Suss. Gaz.* 4 Sept. 1969; 4 July 1985; 31 Dec. 1987; 21 Feb. 1990.

78 *S.R.S.* x. 79, more probably referring to Cudlow than to Bilsham in Yapton; *S.A.C.* lxxxix. 159; *Inq. Non.* (Rec. Com.), 351.

79 *S.R.S.* x. 138; *Inq. Non.* (Rec. Com.), 351.

80 W.S.R.O., Add. MS. 2292, rott. 1, 6; *S.R.S.* xlix. 50.

81 *S.R.S.* xlii. 26; Guildhall Libr. MSS. 13321, f. 44; 13323/2, rep. of view of estates, 1761, p. 7.

82 W.S.R.O., Ep. I/29/51/60.

83 A.C.M., M 271, f. [9v.].

84 *S.R.S.* x. 80, 137, 254.

85 *V.C.H. Suss.* i. 506.

86 Ibid. ii. 138.

87 *Inq. Non.* (Rec. Com.), 351, 370.

88 *Cal. Pat.* 1381–5, 588; cf. A.C.M., A 415.

89 A.C.M., M 531, f. [10v.].

90 W.S.R.O., Ep. I/25/1 (1663, *recte* 1664).

91 *S.R.S.* lxxiv, p. 34.

92 W.S.R.O., Ep. I/55/6, 73, 94, 120, 156–7, 198.

93 E.S.R.O., LCG/3/EW 1, ff. [46, 90v.].

94 *Cal. Treas. Bks. and Papers*, 1729–30, 607; 1735–8, 50, 149; W.S.R.O., Ep. I/29/51/92.

95 W.S.R.O., Par. 51/2/1.

96 Cf. Guildhall Libr. MS. 13326, plan of intended bridge and rds. at Littlehampton, [1821].

97 Goodliffe, *Littlehampton* (1903), 93–4; cf. *W. Suss. Hist.* lii. 10.

98 *Census*, 1811–31. Rest of para. based mainly on W.S.R.O., TD/W 33; *Kelly's Dir. Suss.* (1845 and later edns.).

99 *Rep. Sel. Cttee. on Agric.* H.C. 465, p. 191 (1836), viii (2); Guildhall Libr. MS. 13315; cf. F. W. Steer, *Climping Ch. Guide*, 5.

1 Cf. W.S.R.O., PH 1065, 9317.

2 Cf. Guildhall Libr. MS. 13323/5, rep. of view of fms. in Surr. and Suss. 1832.

3 Cf. O.S. Map 6", Suss. LXIII. SW. (1913 edn.); W.S.R.O., SP 1540.

4 W.S.R.O., Ep. I/22A/2 (1898).

5 M. Beswick, *Brickmaking in Suss.* 193.

6 Above, manors (Atherington).

7 Inf. from Miss M. Kendell, Middleton.

8 O.S. Map 1/25,000, TQ 00/10 (1979 edn.).

9 Inf. from Mr. G. Wooldridge, Climping.

10 *W. Suss. Gaz.* 12 June 1969; 3 Mar. 1983; 2 May, 20 June 1991.

11 W.S.R.O., WNC/CC 14/19.

as a Sunday market, first in the 1970s and again from 1988;[12] in 1991 there were *c.* 200 stalls.[13]

LOCAL GOVERNMENT. Manorial government on the Climping portion of Ford, Climping, and Ilsham manor is discussed below.[14] A reeve of Climping was mentioned *c.* 1310.[15]

There are court rolls or draft court rolls for Atherington manor for the years 1342,[16] 1490–3, 1499,[17] 1547–50,[18] 1594–9,[19] and 1686–1758.[20] That for 1342 also includes entries relating to Sées abbey's lands in Littlehampton, Lyminster, and Eastergate. Only two courts a year were held by 1510,[21] and later in the 16th century sometimes only one.[22] Only six courts in all were held after 1686, the last in 1732, business being transacted out of court from 1692. Besides conveyancing the court dealt with the management of the demesne in 1342, the repair of houses, fences, roads, and ditches, stray beasts,[23] and one case of wreck.[24] A beadle was mentioned in the 15th and 16th centuries.[25] Two 'curemen', perhaps haywards, were elected in the 16th century.[26] A chief pledge served for both Atherington and Eastergate in 1536[27] and there was a tithingman *c.* 1822.[28]

On Cudlow manor three courts a year were held by a bailiff in 1367–8.[29] There are draft court rolls for the years 1457–65, when besides dealing with conveyances the court regulated common pasture, oversaw the repair of tenements, and appointed curemen.[30] Other officers were a headborough in 1275[31] and a chief pledge in 1536.[32] Right of wreck was successfully claimed in 1279.[33]

There is no evidence for separate parochial government at Ilsham or Cudlow. At least two churchwardens served Climping in 1534[34] and apparently usually two between 1548 and 1690. From 1691 to 1872 there was only one, but after 1878 two again.[35] In the later 16th century churchwardens often served two- or three-year terms.[36] There was a single collector for the poor in 1642,[37] and two overseers in the 18th and 19th centuries.[38] A surveyor of highways was recorded in the later 19th century.[39]

A poor rate was levied in 1571[40] and a church rate in the 1620s.[41] Methods of poor relief used in the 18th century and early 19th included weekly pay, the payment of rent, boarding out, and the provision of clothing, fuel, and medical care.[42] A parish poorhouse existed in 1780 next to Climping mill,[43] and was succeeded by another in Horsemere Green Lane[44] which by 1871 had been converted into cottages.[45] It was demolished after 1986.[46] In 1826 thirty-seven parishioners were receiving permanent relief and 16 casual relief.[47] One or more persons received money to emigrate in 1835.[48]

The parish was added to East Preston united parishes (later union, afterwards rural district) in 1799.[49] From 1853 until their transfer to Climping in 1880 the two detached parts of Littlehampton within the parish belonged, perhaps by an oversight, to Littlehampton local health district.[50] Climping was transferred to Chichester rural district in 1933,[51] and from 1974 was in Arun district.

Manorial pounds were mentioned on the Climping part of Ford, Climping, and Ilsham manor[52] and on Atherington manor[53] in the 16th century, but the structure which survived in 1996 on the east side of Climping village street had latterly been parochial.[54]

CHURCHES. CLIMPING. There was a church at Climping by the 1080s,[55] which in 1248 was appropriated to Almenêches abbey (Orne), a vicarage being ordained at the same date.[56] The vicarage, enlarged by parts of the amalgamated rectories of Ilsham and Cudlow, was briefly united with Ford rectory in 1656,[57] and since 1985 has formed part of the united benefice of Climping and Yapton with Ford, the parishes remaining distinct.[58]

Before 1248 the advowson of the church belonged to Almenêches abbey.[59] After that date, though the abbey retained the right of presentation to the vicarage, candidates were to be

12 *W. Suss. Gaz.* 6, 27 Feb. 1975; 27 Apr. 1978; 3 Nov. 1988.
13 Ibid. 4 Apr. 1991.
14 Below, Ford, local govt.
15 Eton Coll. Libr. MS. 45/83 (TS. cat.).
16 P.R.O., SC 2/205/74, rot. [2d.].
17 Ibid. SC 2/206/44, rott. 2, 6; SC 2/206/45, rot. [8].
18 W.S.R.O., PHA 933, ff. 69v.–70v.; 935, ff. 47v.–48v.; 6677, rott. 1d.–2.
19 A.C.M., M 532, ff. [9, 27v., 44, 55v., 72v., 97v. from end].
20 Littlehampton Mus. MS. D 303.
21 P.R.O., SC 6/Hen. VIII/3658, rot. [3].
22 e.g. ibid. SC 6/Hen. VIII/3480, rot. 15; A.C.M., M 532, f. [55v.].
23 P.R.O., SC 2/205/74, rot. [2d.]; SC 2/206/44, rott. 2, 6; Littlehampton Mus. MS. D 303, f. [4]; W.S.R.O., PHA 6677, rot. 2.
24 W.S.R.O., Goodwood MS. E1, f. 30.
25 P.R.O., SC 2/206/44, rot. 2; SC 6/1037/12; SC 6/Hen. VIII/3658, rot. [3].
26 Cf. below, S. Stoke, local govt.; *V.C.H. Suss.* vi (1), 90; vi (3), 153.
27 A.C.M., M 271, f. [9v.].
28 E.S.R.O., QCR/2/1/EW 2 (47).
29 A.C.M., A 415.
30 Ibid. M 278, ff. [14v.–15]; 531, ff. [10v., 40v., 57v., 72v., 83v., 108]; cf. ibid. 532, f. [55v. from end].
31 *S.A.C.* lxxxiv. 69.
32 A.C.M., M 271, f. [9v.].
33 *Plac. de Quo Warr.* (Rec. Com.), 755; cf. *S.A.C.* lxxxiv. 68, 81 n.; *S.R.S.* lxvii. 105.
34 *S.R.S.* xlii. 28.
35 B.L. Add. MS. 39359, ff. 50–5; W.S.R.O., Ep. I/86/20, f. 16v.
36 W.S.R.O., Ep. I/23/5, f. 39v.
37 *S.R.S.* v. 62.
38 W.S.R.O., Par. 51/31/1–2.
39 Ibid. Par. 51/41/1. For disputes over the parochial status of Bailiffscourt, above, intro.
40 W.S.R.O., Ep. I/23/1, f. 57v.
41 *S.R.S.* xlix. 24, 81.
42 W.S.R.O., Par. 51/31/1–2.
43 Ibid. Add. MS. 12630 (TS. cat.).
44 Ibid. TD/W 33.
45 Ibid. SP 1128.
46 Inf. from Mrs. S. Abbot, Hobbs Ct., Yapton.
47 W.S.R.O., QCR/2/3/W 5.
48 Ibid. Par. 51/31/2, f. 113.
49 *Suss. Poor Law Rec.* 32, 46.
50 *Lond. Gaz.* 25 Feb. 1853, pp. 600–1; 43 & 44 Vic. c. 86.
51 *Census*, 1931 (pt. ii).
52 W.S.R.O., Add. MS. 2292, rot. 2.
53 Ibid. PHA 6677, rot. 2.
54 W.S.C.C. property dept., reg. of com. land.
55 *V.C.H. Suss.* i. 430; ii. 121.
56 *S.R.S.* xlvi, pp. 55–6.
57 *S.N.Q.* xv. 118.
58 Inf. from Chich. Dioc. Regy.
59 e.g. *S.A.C.* xlvi. 224; *Chich. Acta* (Cant. & York Soc.), p. 129; Eton Coll. Libr. MS. 56/2–3 (TS. cat.).

nominated by the bishop,[60] presumably as a way of preventing the appointment of foreigners. The Crown presented because of the war with France on three occasions between 1371 and 1415;[61] Lyminster priory, however, was said to hold the advowson of the earl of Arundel in 1391[62] and presented between 1402 and 1411. In 1427 Queen Joan (d. 1437), widow of Henry IV, presented as owner of the priory estates, and the advowson evidently passed with those estates to Eton college, since in 1466 it was exercised by St. George's college, Windsor, to which Eton's estates temporarily belonged.[63] Between 1501 and 1833 Eton presented incumbents, except in 1596 and 1648 when the Crown presented.[64] Since the bishop seems regularly to have exercised his right of nomination, however,[65] the advowson was in effect his.[66] No mention was made of Eton when in 1852 the bishop transferred the advowson to the bishop of Oxford; the latter exchanged it in 1855 with the Crown.[67] Thereafter it was exercised by the Lord Chancellor. After 1985 two presentations in three to the united benefice were to be made by the bishop and the third by the Lord Chancellor.[68]

At its ordination in 1248 the vicarage was endowed with a house, arable and meadow, offerings, and the small tithes of what was then Climping parish.[69] In 1291 it was valued at £5 6*s*. 8*d*.;[70] the figure was still under £8 in 1496[71] but by 1535 had risen to £9 11*s*. net, presumably because of added income from the former rectory of Ilsham.[72]

In the early 17th century[73] there were *c*. 35 a. of glebe scattered round the parish, of which 4 a. were meadow. Some land in the central part represented former glebe of Ilsham parish, notably the plot opposite the present Kent's Farmhouse where Ilsham church had stood.[74] In addition, besides the vicarial tithes of the medieval Climping parish, the vicar had tithe hay from the Ilsham manor demesne; a third of tithe corn from Ilsham manor and from Stroodland in Ilsham, except for 5 a. belonging to Climping rectory; a third of the small tithes of West Cudlow;[75] and tithes of numerous small parcels of land called 'holibreads',[76] which in 1819 totalled *c*. 10 a.[77] Most of the remaining tithes of the former Cudlow parish were enjoyed in the early 17th century and later by the vicars of Arundel.[78]

Further elements in the endowment in 1664 were the tithe of herrings, Good Friday eggs from *c*. 30 named parishioners, and £3 in lieu of the tithe of herbage on *c*. 80 a. of marshland belonging to Bailiffscourt farm.[79] The glebe was calculated as 44 a. in 1724[80] and was 41 a. in the 19th century.[81] In 1656 and 1724 the living was worth £65 or £70 a year,[82] and *c*. 1830 on average £221 net.[83] In 1843 the vicarage endowment remained essentially the same as in the early 17th century,[84] though Bailiffscourt by that date had ceased to pay small tithes either to the vicar of Climping or to the incumbent of Littlehampton.[85] In 1840–1 the vicar received 14*s*. 6*d*. rent charge in lieu of the tithes of one holibread at Bailiffscourt, and in 1843 he received £224 for vicarial tithes in Climping.[86]

The vicarage house in the mid 17th century had a hall, parlour, study, several chambers, and offices;[87] its site was apparently the same as that of the later vicarage house south of the church,[88] of which the rear part is a small building of *c*. 1800 or earlier with a central chimneystack. It was rebuilt and enlarged *c*. 1833 with a three-bayed cement-rendered Gothick façade.[89] It was sold *c*. 1987.[90]

In the late 12th century or early 13th Ralph, archdeacon of Hereford, held Climping church from Alménêches abbey for 4 marks a year, maintaining two nuns there.[91] The only other rector known before the appropriation of the church to Alménêches in 1248 was John of Arundel, chancellor of Chichester cathedral (fl. 1220–48).[92]

The vicar resided in 1440[93] and in 1563.[94] Richard Strong, vicar 1566–87, was a licensed preacher and resided in 1579,[95] but in 1586 the rector of Ford was serving the cure.[96] Church ales were held in 1573.[97] The Puritan Henry Pelter or Pitter, vicar 1587–96, was presented for

60 *S.R.S.* xlvi, pp. 55–6.
61 B.L. Add. MS. 39332, ff. 98–106, on which rest of para. mainly based.
62 *S.A.C.* xlvi. 226.
63 *V.C.H. Bucks.* ii. 167, 170.
64 The presentation of 1648 is described as a Puritan nomination at W. A. Shaw, *Hist. Eng. Ch. 1640–1660*, ii. 358.
65 Cf. *S.R.S.* viii. 12–13; xi. 268 n., 273 n., 317 n.; lxxviii. 63; Dallaway, *Hist. W. Suss.* ii (1) (1819), 13; Eton Coll. Libr. MS. 49/147 (TS. cat.).
66 Cf. *Rep. Com. Eccl. Revenues*, naming bp. as patron.
67 B.L. Add. MS. 39332, f. 105v.; *Lond. Gaz.* 1 June 1855, p. 2105.
68 Inf. from Chich. Dioc. Regy.
69 *S.R.S.* xlvi, p. 55.
70 *Tax. Eccl.* (Rec. Com.), 135.
71 B.L. Add. MS. 39332, f. 94.
72 *Valor Eccl.* (Rec. Com.), i. 317; cf. below, this section (Ilsham ch.).
73 Para. based mainly on W.S.R.O., Ep. I/25/1 (1615).
74 Cf. below, this section (Ilsham ch.).
75 W.S.R.O., Ep. I/11/13, f. 135v.
76 Cf. ibid. Ep. I/25/1 (1663), which adds the small tithes of Ilsham and a third of the great tithes of W. Cudlow; ibid. TD/W 78; Eton Coll. Libr. MSS. 45/86 (TS. cat.); 65/240.
77 Dallaway, *Hist. W. Suss.* ii (1) (1819), 14.
78 W.S.R.O., Ep. I/11/13, f. 135v.; Ep. I/25/1 (1615, 1635, 1663), Arundel; ibid. Par. 8/6/8; cf. Eton Coll. Libr. MS. 45/86 (TS. cat.).
79 W.S.R.O., Ep. I/25/1 (1663, *recte* 1664); cf. ibid. Ep. I/17/32, f. 93 and v.
80 *S.R.S.* lxxviii. 63.
81 *Glebe Lands Return*, p. 28, H.C. 307 (1887), lxiv; W.S.R.O., TD/W 33; cf. ibid. SP 1540, map. The vicar in 1898 wrongly claimed that the holibreads had been part of the glebe: ibid. Ep. I/22A/2 (1898).
82 *S.R.S.* lxxviii. 63; *S.N.Q.* xv. 118.
83 *Rep. Com. Eccl. Revenues*.
84 W.S.R.O., TD/W 33; Dallaway, *Hist. W. Suss.* ii (1) (1819), 13–14.
85 W.S.R.O., Ep. I/54/42, A. Kelly to J. B. Freeland, 17 Jan. 1840; ibid. TD/W 78.
86 Ibid. TD/W 33, 78.
87 Ibid. Ep. I/29/51/34, 62.
88 Ibid. Ep. I/25/1 (1663).
89 Colvin, *Biog. Dict. Brit. Architects*, 650; above, pl. facing p. 123.
90 *W. Suss. Gaz.* 7 May 1987.
91 Eton Coll. Libr. MS. 56/2–3 (TS. cat.).
92 Ibid. 56/8 (TS. cat.); *S.R.S.* xlvi, p. 55.
93 B.L. Add. MS. 39332, f. 94.
94 *S.A.C.* lxi. 112.
95 B.L. Add. MS. 39332, ff. 100v.–102, on which rest of para. mainly based; W.S.R.O., Ep. I/23/5, f. 39v.
96 W.S.R.O., Ep. I/23/7, f. 31; B.L. Add. MS. 39334, f. 133.
97 W.S.R.O., Ep. I/23/2, f. 10v.

baptizing without the sign of the cross in 1590 and afterwards excommunicated, the living being sequestrated for several years before his deprivation. His successor resided between 1596 and 1598 at least and was a preacher.

Between the 17th century and the mid 19th[98] many incumbents held other livings as well, most often Ford. Assistant curates served in the 1610s and sometimes in the 18th century;[99] Christopher Tillier, vicar 1715–46, held Goring and Patching, and by 1733 was living in Arundel where he was buried.[1] In 1724 a curate took Sunday services and celebrated communion three times a year for between 12 and 20 parishioners.[2] John Mansergh, vicar 1788–1833, generally served after 1813 but had several curates[3] and in 1818 was himself curate of Middleton.[4] His successor Owen Marden (d. 1869) lived from *c.* 1838 on his other benefice in Hove,[5] curates[6] occupying the vicarage house which he had rebuilt,[7] among them David Evans who was also rector of Ford.[8] In 1851 morning service was held on alternate Sundays at Climping and Ford, with an average congregation at Climping of 140 including 20 Sunday schoolchildren.[9] Church music in the mid 19th century was provided by a small band.[10]

Under W. H. Jenkins (1869–88) parish life was transformed, with an increase in the frequency of communion from quarterly to monthly,[11] the restoration of the church,[12] the foundation of the National school,[13] and the institution or maintenance of benefit clubs.[14]

Bailiffscourt remained part of Littlehampton ecclesiastical parish until the mid 20th century;[15] evening services were held at the private chapel there in summer in 1952 for the benefit of older parishioners of Climping who could not walk to the church.[16] In the 1980s the moderate 'Prayer book' liturgy used at Climping attracted many non-parishioners to the church, especially from the 'Anglo-Catholic' parish of Felpham with Middleton.[17]

The church of *ST. MARY*, so called by 1524,[18] is partly of ashlar and partly of rubble, in some places plastered; it consists of chancel, nave with transepts, south tower outside the south transept used as a vestry, and south aisle with south porch.[19]

The tower, of the later 12th century, is of massive construction, much of it in fine-jointed Caen stone, and perhaps once served as a lookout in defence of the Arun estuary. Its richly ornamented west doorway, badly weathered below, has a trefoiled head under a semicircular arch with deeply cut chevron and dogtooth ornament, flanked by columns formed of chevrons. On the second stage of each of the three outer faces of the tower is a lancet window with a continuous chevron surround set in a broad shallow pilaster. There is a south-west staircase turret and the parapet is corbelled. The church to which the tower was originally attached seems likely to have been cruciform, since parts of what would have been its transept survive: masonry on the outer east wall which is continuous with that of the tower, the low archway between it and the tower, and the line of its roof on the wall above that archway.

The rest of the church is mid 13th-century, wide, lofty, and of remarkably unified design; it may have been built by John Climping, bishop of Chichester 1253–62.[20] Internally, the chancel and transepts have a continuous string course at sill height except on the south wall of the south transept, and the east wall of the chancel has a three-bayed arcade with stiff-leaf capitals to the columns; it is not clear why its three lancets are of different widths. The north transept has a surviving image bracket on its east wall above what was presumably an altar, and may have been the Lady chapel.[21] Remains of a west porch were depicted in 1782;[22] it had possibly already become ruinous when a south porch with bargeboarded gable was built, perhaps in the 17th century.[23]

In the late 16th century and early 17th sheep were hired out by the parish officers for breeding as a source of income, presumably for church repair.[24] By the mid 17th century the north transept belonged to the Bailiffscourt estate and was known as Bailiffscourt chancel; when Sir John Chapman, lessee of the estate, failed to maintain it the parishioners pulled up the pews there and sold them to pay for repairs.[25] The transept still belonged to Bailiffscourt in the 19th century, when members of the Cutfield family paid for repairs and were buried there;[26] Christ's Hospital seems to have recognized a duty to repair it in 1874,[27] but in 1936 no obligation was

98 Para. based mainly on B.L. Add. MS. 39332, ff. 101v.–106.

99 Ibid. 39359, ff. 51–3; W.S.R.O., Ep. I/22/1 (1742).

1 Cf. B.L. Add. MS. 5699, f. 18v.; W.S.R.O., Ep. I/22/1 (1733), Goring.

2 *S.R.S.* lxxviii. 63.

3 B.L. Add. MS. 39359, f. 54; W.S.R.O., Par. 51/1/2/1; *Rep. Com. Eccl. Revenues.*

4 *Educ. of Poor Digest*, 964.

5 M. Kendell, 'In the Steps of Owen Marden, Vicar of Clymping' (TS. in W.S.R.O. libr.); W.S.R.O., Ep. I/22/2 (1838); Guildhall Libr. MS. 13328, Geo. Boniface to M. S. S. Dipnall, 18 Feb. 1869; *S.R.S.* lxxv, p. 143.

6 B.L. Add. MS. 39359, f. 54; W.S.R.O., Ep. I/22A/2 (1865); ibid. Par. 51/5/1–4.

7 W.S.R.O., TD/W 33; *S.R.S.* lxxv, p. 143.

8 Guildhall Libr. MS. 13328, letter of Revd. David Evans, 28 July 1858; P.R.O., RG 9/615, f. 47v.; *Kelly's Dir. Suss.* (1862, 1866).

9 *S.R.S.* lxxv, p. 143.

10 K. H. Macdermott, *Suss. Ch. Music in the Past*, 27–8.

11 B.L. Add. MS. 39332, f. 106; W.S.R.O., Ep. I/22A/1 (1884); Ep. I/22A/2 (1865).

12 Below, this section.

13 Below, educ.

14 W.S.R.O., Ep. I/22A/1 (1890); ibid. Par. 51/7/17–21 (TS. cat.); above, econ. hist. (agric.).

15 Cf. *Census*, 1901; F. W. Steer, *Climping Ch. Guide*, 7.

16 *W. Suss. Gaz.* 31 July 1952.

17 Personal knowledge.

18 *S.R.S.* xlii. 27.

19 Plan of ch. at *V.C.H. Suss.* ii. 341. The bldg. is fully described at Steer, *Ch. Guide*.

20 Steer, *Ch. Guide*, 1; *S.A.C.* xli. 168.

21 *S.A.C.* xliv. 152; cf. Eton Coll. Libr. MS. 56/66 (TS. cat.).

22 B.L. Add. MS. 5674, f. 36; cf. ibid. 5699, f. 46.

23 Guildhall Libr. MS. 13328, rep. of G. M. Hills, 1869; W.S.R.O., Par. 51/7/7, rep. of P. M. Johnston, 1935; illus. at B.L. Add. MS. 5674, f. 36.

24 W.S.R.O., Ep. I/23/1, f. 57v.; Ep. I/23/5, f. 39v.; *S.R.S.* xlix. 25.

25 W.S.R.O., Ep. I/17/32, f. 93.

26 Dallaway, *Hist. W. Suss.* ii (1) (1819), 14; Guildhall Libr. MS. 13323/6, rep. of view of lands at Climping, 1865; mons. in ch.

27 W.S.R.O., Par. 51/7/7, Clerk, Christ's Hosp., to Revd. W. H. Jenkins, 1874.

said to exist.[28] The chancel, already in a bad state in 1571,[29] was described in 1776 as ruinous, very filthy, and damp for lack of air;[30] by 1804 its roof had been replaced at a lower pitch.[31]

In 1872 the damp, draughts, and decayed seating of the church were clear hindrances to worship.[32] The building was restored in 1874–5 to the designs of G. M. Hills, at the instigation of the Revd. W. H. Jenkins, and with contributions from Eton college as lay rector and Christ's Hospital, both grudgingly given. The chancel roof was raised to its former pitch, the upper part of the tower was rebuilt, the west wall was renewed, keeping the original doorway, windows, and stone coping, and the south porch was rebuilt.[33] Eton college was still responsible for chancel repair in 1937.[34]

Surviving medieval fittings include the 13th-century chest, richly decorated with a trefoil-headed arcade and rosettes, the 15th-century octagonal font, and the late 14th-century stone pulpit, originally attached to the south-west pier of the crossing[35] but moved and altered in 1874–5. Many medieval seats remained in 1842,[36] but in 1992 there were only some panelled bench ends and rails of the early 15th century, incorporated into the late 19th-century pews. The lower portion of the chancel screen survived *ex situ* in 1854, when there were also parclose screens to each transept. All three screens were destroyed in 1870.[37]

Among fittings installed after 1874 are seven framed fresco paintings by Heywood Hardy in the north transept, dating from the 1920s and incorporating local scenes and figures in modern dress.[38]

The plate includes a silver paten of 1661 with an apparently contemporary silver communion cup.[39] There were at least two bells in 1542[40] and four in 1724 and 1776.[41] The two that remained in 1987 were dated 1636 and 1654, both made by Bryan Eldridge the younger; a third, also of 1654, was scrapped in 1874.[42] The registers begin in 1678.[43]

In the churchyard are many monuments to members of the Coote family, and the tomb of Lord and Lady Moyne, whose ashes were originally buried in the chapel at Bailiffscourt.[44]

ILSHAM. There was a church at Ilsham by *c.* 1220.[45] The last known rector was appointed in 1416.[46] The date of demolition of the church is not known, but was perhaps before the early 16th century when Ilsham was described as in Climping parish.[47]

Reynold Aguillon owned the advowson *c.* 1220[48] and it seems to have passed with Ilsham manor, being generally exercised in turn by the descendants or successors of his four daughters;[49] the bishop, however, presented in 1407.[50]

The priest serving the church *c.* 1220 had glebe, small tithes, and offerings, besides a third of the corn tithes of the parish, the other two thirds being settled at that date on Tortington priory.[51] The priory's interest had become a portion worth 13*s.* 4*d.* by 1291,[52] and in 1341 the glebe was 12 a.[53] In 1291 the income of the living was too low to be taxed, and in 1372 the rector was excommunicated for failing to pay the subsidy because of poverty.[54] After the extinction of Ilsham as a parish part of its endowment was added to that of Climping,[55] but Tortington priory's portion, represented by two thirds of the corn tithes from part of the Ilsham St. John manor demesne, descended with Trynebarn rectory in Yapton in the 17th and 18th centuries, passing from Sir George Thomas, Bt., apparently before 1805, to John Boniface of Ford.[56]

The site of the church was a close called Chapel garden on the east side of what in the 17th century was known as Ilsham street, opposite the modern Kent's Farmhouse.[57]

CUDLOW. Apparently before 1257 Humphrey de Fresteng, who seems to have been lord of the manor, agreed with the dean and chapter of Chichester cathedral to nominate a chaplain for Cudlow whom they would present together to the bishop; a house and land including marshland were settled on him then or later, and in 1257 he was described as a rector, though his

28 Ibid. Ld. Moyne to Mr. Maxwell, 2 Nov. 1936.

29 W.S.R.O., Ep. I/23/1, ff. 39, 57v.; cf. ibid. Ep. I/23/4, f. 28; Ep. I/23/5, f. 39v.

30 B.L. Add. MS. 5699, f. 46.

31 *Suss. Chs.: the Sharpe Colln.* ed. V. Smith (Lewes, [1979]); cf. B.L. Add. MS. 36389, f. 144; Guildhall Libr. MS. 13328, rep. of G. M. Hills, 1869.

32 Guildhall Libr. MS. 13328, bp. of Chich. to Revd. W. H. Jenkins, 25 June 1872; cf. ibid. rep. of G. M. Hills, 1869.

33 Ibid. letter of Revd. W. H. Jenkins, 12 Feb. 1873; printed appeal for restor. [1874]; B.L. Add. MS. 39364, f. 101; W.S.R.O., Par. 51/7/7, Clerk, Christ's Hosp., to Revd. W. H. Jenkins, 1874; letter from Eton Coll. 8 Dec. 1874; rep. of P. M. Johnston, 1935.

34 W.S.R.O., Par. 51/7/7, Bursar, Eton Coll., to Revd. J. L. Maxwell, 1937; cf. ibid. Bursar, Eton Coll., to Revd. H. Green, 1909.

35 *V.C.H. Suss.* ii. 341; Clwyd R.O., Glynne ch. notes, lv. 20.

36 Clwyd R.O., Glynne ch. notes, lv. 20.

37 *S.A.C.* xxxix. 50, 53; xliii. 231; cf. Guildhall Libr. MS. 13328, rep. of G. M. Hills, 1869.

38 *Antique Collector*, Aug. 1986, p. 31; Ward, Lock & Co. *Bognor* [1928–9], 35. Three were originally in chancel: W.S.R.O., Par. 51/4/1–4; *S.C.M.* xviii. 32; xxi. 357. Another was in S. aisle in 1991.

39 *S.A.C.* liii. 240.

40 *S.R.S.* xlii. 27.

41 Ibid. lxxviii. 63; B.L. Add. MS. 5699, f. 46.

42 Elphick, *Bells*, 90, 285; W.S.R.O., Par. 51/7/5, bill, 1874.

43 W.S.R.O., Par. 51/1.

44 G. Young, *Cottage in the Fields*, 222–3; *W. Suss. Gaz.* 9 Nov. 1978; inf. from the late Mr. G. Harper, Middleton-on-Sea.

45 B.L. Add. MS. 39337, f. 108.

46 *Reg. Chichele* (Cant. & York Soc.), i. 145.

47 *S.R.S.* xlvi, p. 228.

48 B.L. Add. MS. 39337, f. 108.

49 *S.R.S.* xi. 255, 307; xxiii, pp. 47, 147; *Plac. de Banco, 1327–8* (L. & I. xxxii), ii. 663, 671; *Reg. Chichele* (Cant. & York Soc.), i. 145; cf. above, manors (Ilsham).

50 *S.R.S.* xi. 293.

51 B.L. Add. MS. 39337, f. 108.

52 *Tax. Eccl.* (Rec. Com.), 141.

53 *Inq. Non.* (Rec. Com.), 351.

54 *S.A.C.* lxxxii. 134.

55 Above, this section (Climping ch.).

56 *S.R.S.* xx. 445; xxix, pp. 146, 165–6; Dallaway, *Hist. W. Suss.* ii (1) (1819), 13; Eton Coll. Libr. MS. 45/86 (TS. cat.); W.S.R.O., TD/W 33.

57 W.S.R.O., Ep. I/25/1 (1615, 1663); *S.N.Q.* vi. 111–12, 223–4.

church was called a chapel.[58] A pension of 14*s.* in lieu of tithes was paid to the dean and chapter thereafter.[59] The living was valued at £5 6*s.* 8*d.* in 1291.[60] Perhaps by then, and certainly by 1307, it included some tithes, but the rector's claim in 1307 to the tithes of another 18 yardlands, comprising 288 a., was disputed by Alménêches abbey as rector of Climping. The abbey won the case,[61] and two years later was able to insist that the consecration of Cudlow church and churchyard at that date should in no way prejudice Climping church.[62]

Rectors continued to take the disputed tithes illegally,[63] however, until in 1318 a detailed division of the tithes arising from Cudlow parish was made,[64] which was amended by a judgement of 1346.[65] The rector's glebe was 11 a. in 1341.[66] The parish's status seems to have continued in dispute, since the church was regularly described in the 14th and 15th centuries as the 'church or chapel' of Cudlow.[67] The last incumbent was appointed in 1546 and in 1550 Cudlow was described as within Climping parish. By 1591 Cudlow was said to have been annexed to Arundel vicarage,[68] presumably because Arundel borough and Cudlow manor had then long been in the same lordship.

Incumbents were presented jointly by the lord of the manor and the dean and chapter of Chichester in 1300 and 1325[69] but not apparently afterwards. The advowson thereafter descended with the manor,[70] but John Holand, duke of Exeter, presented for a turn in 1399 and the bishop in 1511.[71]

The depredations of the sea after the mid 14th century reduced the income of the living,[72] which was worth less than £8 in 1485[73] and £1 8*s.* 5*d.* net in 1535.[74] It was presumably on that account that the rector seems often to have been non-resident after 1428.[75] After the amalgamation of the parish with Climping its endowment was split between the rector of Climping, the vicar, and the vicar of Arundel.[76]

The church of *ST. GILES*[77] seems to have stood south of Climping mill; it survived in part in 1698.[78]

NONCONFORMITY. One Baptist family was recorded in 1724.[79] There were two nonconformists in 1898.[80]

EDUCATION. A school was held in Climping in 1808[81] and there were two, with 27 children, in 1818.[82] A small fund for teaching children was mentioned in 1831.[83] A parish school supported by a rate had 40 boys and girls in 1833;[84] it was perhaps the same as the dame school held in a cottage near Kent's Farmhouse in the 1850s, which had between 22 and *c.* 50 pupils.[85] By 1869 the school had moved to a cottage at Atherington.[86]

A National school and master's house were built in 1871 on glebe land roughly in the centre of the parish[87] at the instigation of the Revd. W. H. Jenkins; Christ's Hospital, which had refused earlier requests for help towards school building, was persuaded to contribute.[88] The building was later enlarged. Average attendance was 30 in 1871,[89] rising to 44 in 1884–5[90] and 68 in 1906,[91] and remaining between 40 and 60 thereafter until 1938.[92] In the late 19th century and early 20th Eton college as lay rector gave an annual subscription.[93] Only a few of the 82 pupils on the roll in 1991 were from Climping, the rest coming from a wide hinterland including Yapton, Middleton-on-Sea, and Littlehampton.[94]

Evening classes during winter were held in 1869 in a building in the village[95] and from 1871 at the school or the vicarage;[96] average attendance was 18 in 1890.[97] In 1903 technical subjects were taught.[98] Older pupils went to school in Littlehampton in the early 20th century and in various places in 1993.[99]

CHARITIES FOR THE POOR. None known.

58 *S.R.S.* xlvi, p. 90; Eton Coll. Libr. MS. 56/50 (TS. cat.); above, manors (Cudlow).
59 *S.R.S.* xlvi, pp. 90, 217–18, 375.
60 *Tax. Eccl.* (Rec. Com.), 135.
61 Eton Coll. Libr. MS. 56/56 (TS. cat.).
62 Ibid. 56/58 (TS. cat.).
63 Ibid. 45/83–4; 56/59, 61 (TS. cat.)
64 Ibid. 56/62 (TS. cat.).
65 Ibid. 56/72 (TS. cat.).
66 *Inq. Non.* (Rec. Com.), 369.
67 *S.R.S.* xi. 324; xlvi, pp. 182–3; *Cal. Pat.* 1429–36, 466; Eton Coll. Libr. MS. 56/56 (TS. cat.).
68 B.L. Add. MS. 39332, f. 127v.; *S.R.S.* xlii. 26.
69 *S.R.S.* xlvi, pp. 182–3.
70 Ibid. xi. 307, 325; xxiii, p. 128; *Cal. Pat.* 1429–36, 466; *Cal. Inq. Misc.* iii, p. 378; B.L. Add. MS. 39332, f. 127v.
71 *S.R.S.* xi. 249; B.L. Add. MS. 39332, f. 127.
72 e.g. *S.A.C.* lxxxii. 133–4.
73 B.L. Add. MS. 39332, f. 124.
74 *Valor Eccl.* (Rec. Com.), i. 317.
75 *Feud. Aids*, v. 165; B.L. Add. MS. 39332, f. 124.
76 Above, manors (rectory); this section (Climping ch.).
77 Eton Coll. Libr. MS. 56/50 (TS. cat.).
78 B.L. Sloane MS. 3233, f. 15.
79 *S.R.S.* lxxviii. 63.
80 W.S.R.O., Ep. I/22A/2 (1898).
81 Ibid. Par. 51/31/2, f. 1.
82 *Educ. of Poor Digest*, 955.
83 Lewis, *Topog. Dict. Eng.* (1831).
84 *Educ. Enq. Abstract*, 967; cf. W.S.R.O., Ep. I/22A/2 (1844).
85 W.S.R.O., Ep. I/47/4; Ep. I/47/8/1; Guildhall Libr. MS. 13328, rep. on sch. bldg. 1856; letter of Revd. O. Marden, 28 Feb. 1857.
86 Guildhall Libr. MS. 13328, letter of Revd. W. H. Jenkins, 26 Aug. 1869.
87 P.R.O., ED 7/123; W.S.R.O., Par. 51/25/17.
88 Guildhall Libr. MS. 13328, *passim.*
89 P.R.O., ED 7/123.
90 *Rep. Educ. Cttee. 1885–6*, 600.
91 *Return of Non-Provided Schs.* Suss. 29.
92 *Educ. List 21, 1914*, 522; *1919*, 342; *1922*, 341; *1932*, 386; *1938*, 401.
93 Eton Coll. Libr., Climping corresp. file, letters from Revd. Hen. Green.
94 *W. Suss. Gaz.* 25 Apr. 1991; local inf.
95 Guildhall Libr. MS. 13328, letter of Revd. W. H. Jenkins, 26 Aug. 1869.
96 P.R.O., ED 7/123; W.S.R.O., Ep. I/22A/1 (1878).
97 W.S.R.O., Ep. I/22A/1 (1890); cf. Eton Coll. Libr., Climping corresp. file, notebk. 1889.
98 H. Green, *Clymping Ch. and Par.* (Chichester, 1903), 10 (copy at W.S.R.O. libr.); cf. Eton Coll. Libr., Climping corresp. file, 'Clymping Record', 1901, 1904–5.
99 Local inf.

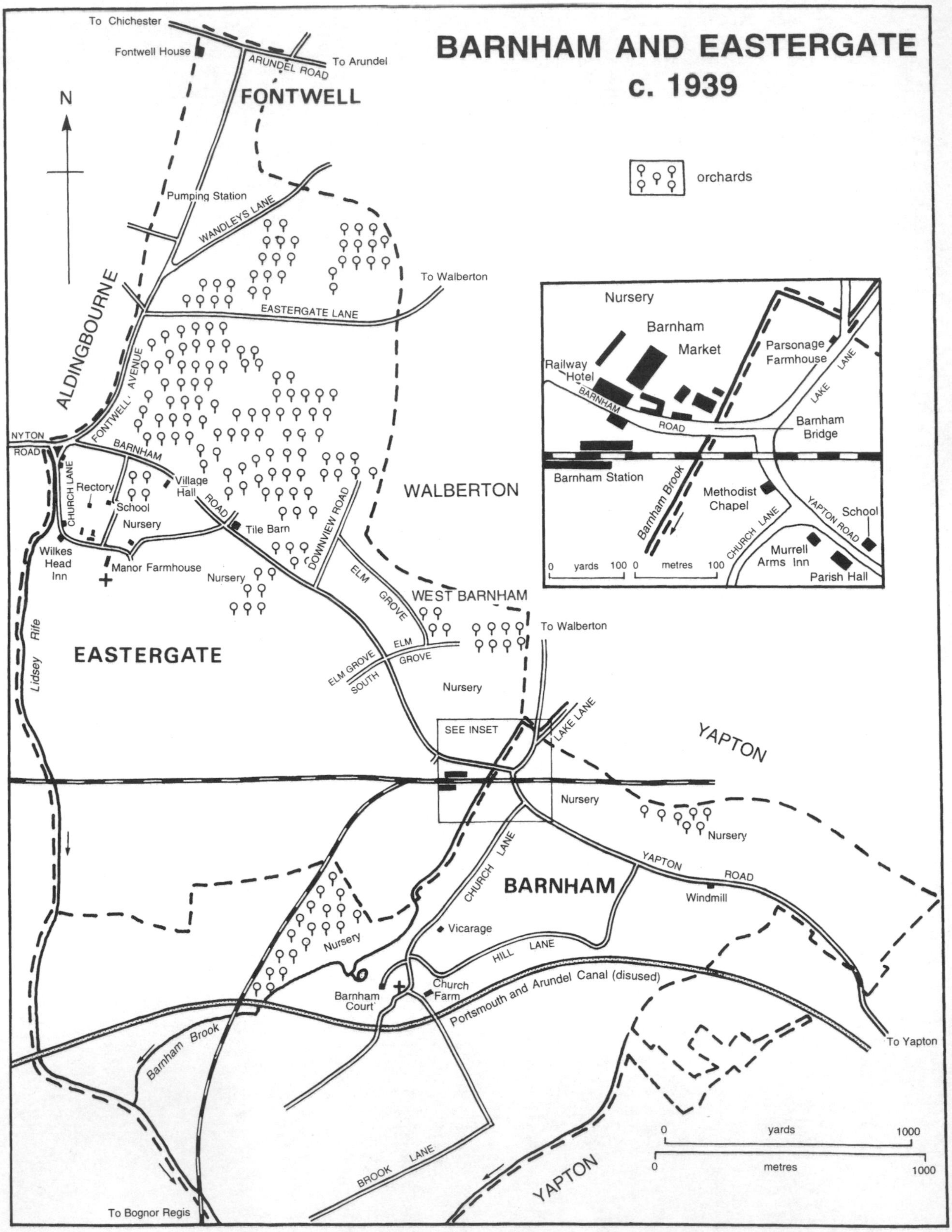
BARNHAM AND EASTERGATE
c. 1939
orchards
To Chichester
Fontwell House
ARUNDEL ROAD
To Arundel
FONTWELL
N
Pumping Station
WANDLEYS LANE
To Walberton
EASTERGATE LANE
ALDINGBOURNE
FONTWELL AVENUE
NYTON ROAD
BARNHAM ROAD
CHURCH LANE
Rectory
School
Village Hall
Nursery
Tile Barn
Wilkes Head Inn
Manor Farmhouse
Nursery
DOWNVIEW ROAD
ELM GROVE
WALBERTON
WEST BARNHAM
To Walberton
Lidsey Rife
EASTERGATE
ELM GROVE
ELM GROVE SOUTH
Nursery
SEE INSET
LAKE LANE
YAPTON
Nursery
Nursery
CHURCH LANE
BARNHAM
YAPTON ROAD
Windmill
Vicarage
HILL LANE
Nursery
Barnham Court
Church Farm
Portsmouth and Arundel Canal (disused)
Barnham Brook
To Yapton
BROOK LANE
YAPTON
To Bognor Regis
0 yards 1000
0 metres 1000
Nursery
Barnham Market
Railway Hotel
BARNHAM ROAD
Parsonage Farmhouse
LAKE LANE
Barnham Bridge
Barnham Station
Barnham Brook
Methodist Chapel
CHURCH LANE
YAPTON ROAD
School
Murrell Arms Inn
Parish Hall
0 yards 100
0 metres 100

EASTERGATE

THE parish of Eastergate,[1] which lies on the coastal plain north-east of Bognor Regis, includes Barnham railway station and most of the built-up area described as Barnham in 1993; the site of the 19th- and 20th-century Barnham market also lay within it. The ancient parish had 918 a. (372 ha.);[2] a small area was transferred to Barnham in 1985.[3] In the Middle Ages both parish and manor were generally called Gate or Gates, but the modern name was in use by the 15th century.[4] The present article deals with the parish as constituted before 1985.

In the south-west and south-east the boundary runs along streams, and in the west and north it partly follows the modern Church Lane, Fontwell Avenue, and Arundel Road. The outline of boundaries suggests that Eastergate and Barnham, perhaps with Yapton too, may once have formed a single administrative area.

The southern part of the parish lies on brickearth and the northern part, including the site of the modern village, on valley gravel; there is alluvium in the valleys of the Barnham brook and Lidsey rife in the south-east and south-west, and a little London clay east and north-east of Barnham station;[5] severe flooding was experienced in the latter area in the later 20th century.[6] A spring in the northern tip of the parish gave its name to the modern settlement of Fontwell.[7] As in other coastal-plain parishes there were several ponds in Eastergate in 1845.[8]

Woodland on the manor yielded five swine in 1086,[9] but in 1558–9 there were only 12 a. of woods, mostly oak; pasture closes then mentioned which included the elements 'wood' or 'rede' were presumably assarts from woodland.[10] Oak, ash, and elm grew in Eastergate in the 18th century,[11] and in 1845 there were 6 a. of woods.[12] The less fertile north end of the parish remained open heathland until 1779.[13] In the late 19th and 20th centuries much land was orchards or market gardens;[14] in 1993 other chief uses were housing and paddocks for horses.

SETTLEMENT. There is evidence for Roman occupation, including possibly a villa site, near the church; the south wall of the chancel incorporates Roman brick. Settlement seems to have continued in the same area in the Middle Ages.[15] Several pre-20th-century buildings are grouped north and north-west of the church, including Manor Farmhouse and its outbuildings.[16] The Old House is 17th-century, timber-framed, with a moulded brick string course on part of the exterior. One gable wall was replaced in brick in the late 17th century and the other rebuilt in flint and brick in the late 18th century or early 19th.[17] Eastergate House further east is late 18th- or early 19th-century, with a three-bayed front of flint with brick dressings.

Another group of older houses[18] stands ¼ mile (400 metres) to the north, at the junction of Church Lane, Fontwell Avenue, and Nyton and Barnham roads. Flint House was apparently a timber-framed building of late medieval origin and had a three-roomed plan with a large chimneystack on the north lateral wall of the main room. During the 17th century and early 18th the outer walls were largely rebuilt in flint and brick and the roof was replaced. In the mid 18th century a wing was added to the north containing principal rooms and a staircase. Malthouse cottages nearby were originally a single house of the early 17th century; its timber framing was largely replaced by flint and brick in the late 17th and 18th centuries, and there are moulded brick mullions and hoodmoulds on the front. The building was converted to cottages *c.* 1800. The island site of Shelley House and its adjacent shop at the top of Church Lane, apparently settled by 1596,[19] presumably represents encroachment on waste land. Shelley House, and the White House to the east of it, are externally 18th-century, of rubble, brick, and flint, partly rendered or painted.

The two settlements remained separate in 1845, when there were *c.* 20 houses there in all, including the new rectory, besides others nearby in Aldingbourne parish forming part of the same group.[20] The area between Barnham Road and the church was further developed with houses and bungalows in the 20th century, part of the rectory grounds being built over, and a market garden and poultry farm being replaced with streets *c.* 1983.[21] In 1993 the church could be approached only through the farmyard of Manor farm, which almost had the character of a village green.[22] The junction of Nyton and Barnham

1 This article was written in 1993–4 and revised in 1996. Topographical details in introduction based mainly on O.S. Maps 1/25,000, SU 90 (1958 edn.); SU 80/90 (1981 edn.); 6", Suss. LXII (1880 and later edns.).
2 *Census* (1881, 1971).
3 Above, Barnham, intro.
4 *Cal. Close*, 1435–41, 388; *S.R.S.* xlvi, p. 256.
5 Geol. Surv. Map 1", drift, sheet 317 (1957 edn.).
6 W.S.R.O., WDC/SU 19/1/1; *Bognor Regis Observer*, 20, 27 Jan. 1994.
7 W.S.R.O., Add. MS. 1802; ibid. Par. 202/7/21; *Suss. in 20th Cent.* 125; cf. R. Coates, *Linguistic Hist. of Early Suss.: the Place-Name Evidence*, 5.
8 W.S.R.O., TD/W 47.
9 *V.C.H. Suss.* i. 432.
10 C.K.S., U 269/E 341, ff. 46–7; cf. J. Field, *Eng. Field Names*, 180.
11 W.S.R.O., Cap. I/4/8/16, 19, 32.
12 Ibid. TD/W 47; cf. O.S. Map 6", Suss. LXII (1880 edn.).
13 Below, econ. hist. (agric.).
14 Below, econ. hist. (mkt. gardening).
15 *S.A.C.* cxvii. 77; S.M.R. 1406–7.
16 Below, manor.
17 Below, pl. facing p. 171.
18 e.g. *250 Yrs. of Mapmaking in Suss.* ed. H. Margary, pl. 14; below, pls. facing p. 171.
19 W.S.R.O., Cap. I/23/1, f. 153.
20 Ibid. TD/W 47. The Long Ho. on the N. side of Nyton Rd. lies in Aldingbourne; it is of the late 18th cent., extended eastwards probably in the early 19th.
21 Personal recollection; cf. *Chich. Observer*, 21 June 1974; *W. Suss. Gaz.* 2 July 1992.
22 Nairn & Pevsner, *Suss.* 214.

roads with Fontwell Avenue retained two open grass islands in the early 20th century; one had a prominent tree,[23] and the village war memorial incorporating a stone lion was constructed on the other *c.* 1920.[24] Road widening had removed part of the grass by 1993.

Several houses were built from the 16th century or earlier on roadside waste along Barnham road.[25] One immediately east of its junction with the modern Fontwell Avenue is probably timber-framed and is faced with flint and brick; it bears a datestone of the 1690s. Buildings opposite the site of the railway station included an inn, the predecessor of the Railway, later Barnham, hotel.[26]

There were said to be many new cottages in 1867,[27] but the opening of Barnham station was not immediately followed by building nearby.[28] A terrace of brick houses east of the Barnham hotel which belonged *c.* 1910 to the London, Brighton, and South Coast Railway[29] had presumably been built by the company: it was apparently the 'railway cottages' mentioned in 1886.[30]

The market gardener E. J. Marshall had apparently begun to put up houses on what he called the Barnham Park estate in 1896,[31] but the development of the area first known as Barnham Junction[32] and later as West Barnham[33] followed immediately on the purchase by the Marshall family of virtually the whole northern half of the parish from the ecclesiastical commissioners in or shortly before 1899. The land was let for 35 years in 1900 to a company called West Barnham Estate[34] and by 1901 building had begun, the land already increasing greatly in value.[35] By 1910 much of Barnham Road, Elm Grove, and Elm Grove South had been developed, while Downview Road had been marked out for building and two houses erected there. The spacious layout of the estate, with large detached houses, shrubberies, and roadside trees and verges,[36] has been compared with London suburbs like Wimbledon,[37] Ealing, and Dulwich.[38] Smaller houses were also put up; some were for nursery workers,[39] but six at the west end of Elm Grove may have been built by the coal merchant Harry Knight.[40]

By 1950 the roads named were almost fully developed.[41] Most of Elm Grove remained private in 1992. There were then more recently built houses among the earlier ones, some of the latter having been converted to flats or nursing homes.

New houses were put up at the end of Elm Grove South by 1965,[42] and between that date and the late 1970s the former Station nursery north of the Barnham hotel was developed as Orchard Way and adjacent roads, with a mixture of houses and bungalows, including some terraces;[43] on the eastern fringe were council houses.

The immediate surroundings of the station were said in 1972 to have an 'impermanent', 'makeshift' character;[44] that was less marked 20 years later, when the recently built shopping centre provided a focus, though the former station yard on the south side of Barnham Road remained ramshackle.

A few buildings had been put up at the south end of Eastergate common by 1778, including what was later the poorhouse in Fontwell Avenue.[45] There seems to have been no settlement in the north end of the parish until the 19th century.[46] Fontwell House is a small 19th-century building of square plan with a three-bayed east front. It was perhaps altered *c.* 1910 by the resident owner A. J. Day, and a large 'luncheon room' was added on the south side in 1923–4 to serve the new racecourse opened at that time; it has a Corinthian colonnade brought from Richmond (Surr.). Stonework from elsewhere, including Arundel castle, was also used in the grounds, for instance in gate piers, in balustrading, and in a circular summerhouse.[47] A small building west of Fontwell House was converted as a post office at the same period using medieval moulded stonework;[48] it survived in 1995. A few houses had been built in the angle between Fontwell Avenue and Wandleys Lane by 1910; more houses and bungalows were put up later in the 20th century, both there, along Wandleys Lane itself, and in Eastergate Lane;[49] in Eastergate Lane is a terrace of nursery workers' cottages.

Twenty-eight tenants of Eastergate manor, perhaps including some in Madehurst, were recorded in 1086[50] and 15 taxpayers were assessed in the vill in 1327.[51] Thirty-seven adult males signed the protestation in 1642[52] and 60 adults were listed in 1676.[53] In 1724 there were 17

23 W.S.R.O., PH 486.
24 *Kelly's Dir. Suss.* (1922).
25 W.S.R.O., Add. MS. 4553; ibid. Cap. I/23/1, f. 153; Cap. I/38/1, ff. 10v., 22v.; ibid. TD/W 47; *S.R.S.* xlvi, p. 203; *250 Yrs. of Mapmaking in Suss.* pls. 14–15; O.S. Map 6", Suss. LXII (1880 edn.); cf. P.R.O., SC 11/653. For the Rough rakes mentioned in 1596 cf. below, econ. hist. (agric.).
26 Below, this section.
27 *Rep. Com. on Children and Women in Agric.* 88.
28 *Census* (1861–81).
29 W.S.R.O., IR 12, f. 28.
30 Pike, *Dir. SW. Suss.* (1886–7), s.v. Barnham.
31 W.S.R.O., Add. MS. 25512; ibid. Ep. I/22A/2 (1898); *Kelly's Dir. Suss.* (1903), s.v. Barnham.
32 e.g. Pike, *Bognor Dir.* (1910–11), 220.
33 O.S. Map 6", Suss. LXII. NE. (1914 edn.).
34 P.R.O., BT 31/16324/64742; W.S.R.O., Add. MS. 24178.
35 W.S.R.O., Add. MS. 25509, Wyatt and Son to T. Read, 25 Sept. 1901; cf. ibid. Ep. I/22A/2 (1903); ibid. MP 2347, f. 1. The co. was wound up in 1930: P.R.O., BT 31/16324/64742.
36 O.S. Map 6", Suss. LXII. NE., SE. (1913–14 edn.); cf. *Kelly's Dir. Suss.* (1905 and later edns.).
37 Nairn & Pevsner, *Suss.* 99.
38 *Chich. Observer*, 4 Aug. 1972.
39 W.S.R.O., MP 2347, f. 2.
40 Ibid. IR 12, ff. 25–6; Pike, *Bognor Dir.* (1910–11), 223; inscrs. on bldgs. 'H.E.K./1901' and 'H.E.K./1906'.
41 O.S. Map 6", Suss. LXII. NE., SE. (1951 edn.).
42 Ibid. 1/25,000, SU 80/90 (1981 edn.); W.S.R.O., MP 814, f. [47].
43 W.S.R.O., MP 814, f. [47]; *Chich. Observer*, 4 Aug. 1972; *W. Suss. Gaz.* 23 Sept. 1976; 30 Dec. 1982; O.S. Map 1/25,000, SU 80/90 (1981 edn.)
44 *Chich. Observer*, 4 Aug. 1972.
45 *250 Yrs. of Mapmaking in Suss.* pls. 14–15; cf. W.S.R.O., TD/W 47; O.S. Map 6", Suss. LXII (1880 edn.).
46 *250 Yrs. of Mapmaking in Suss.* pls. 14, 19; W.S.R.O., TD/W 47.
47 *Suss. in 20th Cent.* 125; C.I.H.E. libr., GY 1796; photo. 1923, at Fontwell Ho.; date on painting in 'luncheon room' at ho.; below, this section (soc. and cultural activities).
48 *W. Suss. Gaz.* 3 Oct. 1968.
49 O.S. Maps 6", Suss. LXII. NE. (1951 edn.); LXII. NW. (1914, 1951 edns.); 1/25,000, SU 80/90 (1981 edn.).
50 *V.C.H. Suss.* i. 432; below, econ. hist. (agric.).
51 *S.R.S.* x. 136. There is no entry in the 1524 subsidy: ibid. lvi.
52 Ibid. v. 76.
53 *Compton Census*, ed. Whiteman, 144.

families.[54] The population in 1801 was 163 and it remained about the same, apart from an unexplained increase in the 1830s, until 1881. It then rose continuously, with especially large increases in the 1900s and 1960s, to 606 in 1911, 943 in 1951, 2,115 in 1971, and 3,018 in 1991.[55]

COMMUNICATIONS. The Roman road from Chichester to Brighton seems to have run through the north part of the parish,[56] and was succeeded by the modern Chichester–Arundel road which formed part of the northern boundary before widening and reconstruction in the 1980s. The parish is bisected by the road from Chichester to Cudlow in Climping recorded from the early 13th century.[57] Barnham bridge, by which it crossed the Barnham brook on the boundary with Barnham, is discussed above.[58] The alignment of the road east of Barnham station was altered when the railway embankment was constructed *c.* 1846.[59]

A road to Walberton, apparently using the lower part of Fontwell Avenue, was mentioned in 1229,[60] and the road to Slindon recorded in 1304[61] was evidently the same. The continuation of the Walberton road, the modern Eastergate Lane, was Stotham Lane in 1596.[62] In 1724 the line of the modern Wandleys Lane formed part of a suggested route between Pagham and Arundel.[63] Fontwell Avenue and Wandleys Lane were given their modern straight courses at the inclosure of Eastergate common in 1779.[64] The trees flanking the northern part of the former road were planted between 1896 and 1910.[65] The 'new lane' and 'the park way street' mentioned in 1596[66] have not been located.

There was a carrier in 1851.[67] Carriers plied to Chichester in 1886[68] and to Bognor Regis and Brighton as well in 1934.[69] Cabs could be hired at the Railway inn from 1874 or earlier,[70] and there was a taxi office at Barnham station in 1992. Motor buses from Bognor to Slindon passed through the parish by 1924[71] and buses from Chichester to Littlehampton by 1927.[72] In 1965 the former service continued but the latter went only to Yapton.[73] In 1992 there were regular buses to Bognor Regis and Yapton and less frequent ones to Chichester, Arundel, and elsewhere.

The Shoreham–Chichester railway was opened through the parish in 1846, with a station at Woodgate in Aldingbourne south of Westergate.[74] At the opening of the Bognor branch line, as a single track, in 1864, a junction station called Barnham was opened in the south-east corner of Eastergate parish.[75] Through trains from London to Bognor began running in 1903[76] and in 1911 the track was doubled.[77] Refreshment rooms were opened on the station by 1895 and a newsagent's by 1909;[78] both remained in 1993. A new station building was put up before 1938,[79] when the lines were electrified.[80] The goods station closed in 1964.[81] In 1996, besides frequent services to London, Brighton, Bognor Regis, Littlehampton, Portsmouth, and Bournemouth, there were occasional trains to Reading (Berks.) and to South Wales via Bristol.

A public house was mentioned in 1606,[82] an inn in 1686,[83] and a victualler from 1799.[84] It is not clear if any can be connected with the Wilkes Head in the village recorded from 1845,[85] the reason for whose name is uncertain. The City Arms inn on Barnham Road in the south-east corner of the parish, recorded between 1809 and 1817,[86] was later called the Barnham Bridge inn[87] and between 1845 and 1862 the Knights of Malta; further changes of name made it the Railway inn by 1866, the Railway hotel by 1895,[88] and the Barnham hotel by 1965.[89] A three-bayed building apparently of the 18th century or earlier 19th[90] was replaced *c.* 1907[91] by the present, much larger, one. In 1861 a bowling alley adjoined it[92] and in 1874 and later the publican was also a cab proprietor and coal merchant.[93] The hotel was a popular venue for wedding receptions, dinners, and dances in 1965[94] and accommodated fortnightly auctions in 1992.[95]

SOCIAL AND CULTURAL ACTIVITIES. In 1623 the vestry agreed that a maypole which had previously been in use should be turned into a ladder for church purposes.[96] A Rogationtide procession, to which occupiers of land brought cakes, was held at the same period.[97]

A village hall in Barnham Road was opened in

54 *S.R.S.* lxxviii. 66.
55 *Census*, 1801–1991.
56 *S.N.Q.* xi. 144, 161.
57 *S.R.S.* ii, p. 64; lix, p. 76; *Cat. Anct. D.* iii, B 3905, 3908.
58 Above, Barnham, intro.
59 Cf. below, this section.
60 *S.R.S.* ii, p. 64.
61 *Cat. Anct. D.* ii, B 3315.
62 W.S.R.O., Cap. I/23/1, ff. 151–2; for Stotham cf. below, econ. hist. (agric.).
63 Budgen, *Suss. Map* (1724).
64 W.S.R.O., QDD/6/W 2.
65 O.S. Map 6", Suss. LXII. NW. (1899, 1914 edns.). The rd. was alternatively Eastergate Lane in 1896 and later: ibid.
66 W.S.R.O., Cap. I/23/1, ff. 151v., 153v.
67 P.R.O., HO 107/1652, f. 240v.
68 Pike, *Dir. SW. Suss.* (1886–7).
69 *Kelly's Dir. Suss.* (1934).
70 Ibid. (1874); (1895), s.v. Barnham.
71 *Chich. Observer*, 21 June 1974; *Kelly's Dir. Suss.* (1927).
72 *Kelly's Dir. Suss.* (1927), s.v. Barnham.
73 W.S.R.O., MP 814, f. [43].
74 *Southern Region Rec.* comp. R. H. Clark, 51, 92.
75 Ibid. 51, 65; G. Young, *Hist. Bognor Regis*, 148–9 and pl. 38.
76 V. Mitchell and K. Smith, *S. Coast Rlys.: Worthing to Chich.* pl. 79.
77 E. Course, *Rlys. of Southern Eng.: the Main Lines*, 189.
78 *Kelly's Dir. Suss.* (1895 and later edns.), s.v. Barnham, Eastergate.
79 O.S. Map 1/2,500, Suss. LXII. 11 (1938 edn.).
80 *Southern Region Rec.* comp. Clark, 62.
81 G. R. Clinker, *Reg. of Closed Stations*, ii, cumulative suppl. 1967, p. 35.
82 A Fletcher, *County Community in Peace and War*, 152.
83 P.R.O., WO 30/48, f. 183.
84 W.S.R.O., Add. MS. 11528 (TS. cat.); ibid. Par. 76/1/2/1.
85 Ibid. TD/W 47.
86 Ibid. Add. MS. 17012.
87 Ibid. TD/W 47; Ch. Commrs., surv. 1861, p. 238, giving both names.
88 *Kelly's Dir. Suss.* (1845 and later edns.), s.v. Barnham, Eastergate.
89 W.S.R.O., MP 814, f. [54].
90 Ibid. PH 1467, f. 80.
91 *Bognor Observer*, 21 Aug. 1907.
92 Ch. Commrs., surv. 1861, p. 238; cf. W.S.R.O., PH 1467, f. 80.
93 *Kelly's Dir. Suss.* (1874 and later edns.), s.v. Barnham, Eastergate.
94 W.S.R.O., MP 814, f. [54].
95 Cf. *W. Suss. Gaz.* 10 Dec. 1992.
96 *S.R.S.* xlix. 74–5.
97 Ibid. 5, 121.

1908; it was provided by A. J. Day of Fontwell House and others, and with two rifle ranges was to serve also as a training centre for the territorial army. The main room is decorated with scenes from Sussex history by the painter Byam Shaw.[98] It was in frequent use in 1993 by local groups including the Eastergate players. The market room of Barnham market also accommodated club meetings and dances in the early 20th century.[99]

Cricket was played on a field south of Wandleys Lane in or before 1845.[1] The recreation ground near the junction of Barnham Road and Fontwell Avenue was presented to the parish by William Collins in the early 20th century;[2] in 1992 both cricket and football were played there. An Eastergate football club and a Barnham and Eastergate cricket club based in Eastergate had existed by 1910.[3] In 1992 there were also clubs for badminton, stoolball, bowls, and table tennis. Fontwell racecourse, straddling the boundary with Aldingbourne, was opened in 1924, and has an oval hurdle course and a figure-of-eight steeplechase course.[4] Fourteen fixtures a year were held in 1974, besides other social events.[5]

The Bognor Water Co. in 1895 constructed a well and pumping station off Fontwell Avenue in the north end of the parish; the village was supplied by 1909[6] and the vicinity of Barnham station by 1912. The Bognor Gas Co. provided gas to the latter area by the same date[7] and more generally by 1938.[8] Electricity was laid on in the 1930s by Chichester corporation[9] and street lighting by the same body in 1946.[10] Main drainage was installed *c.* 1974.[11]

The 'Clubmen' movement of 1645 had a following in Eastergate.[12] Barracks south-east of the village, presumably of the Napoleonic period, were commemorated from 1845 by addresses and a field name.[13]

The composer John Ireland often stayed in the parish in the early 20th century, and named a hymn tune after it.[14]

MANOR. The manor of *GATE*, later *EASTERGATE*, which occupied most of the area of the parish in 1861,[15] was held in 1066 by King Harold and in 1086 by Sées abbey (Orne) of earl Roger, who had given it to them in free alms shortly before.[16] In 1415 it was transferred with the rest of the Sées estates to Syon abbey (Mdx.).[17] After the Dissolution it was retained by the Crown[18] until granted in 1560 to Richard Baker and Sir Richard Sackville.[19] Sackville in 1564–5 exchanged it with the dean and chapter of Chichester,[20] which thereafter had it until the mid 19th century. Between the mid 16th century and the later 18th the demesnes were leased to members of the related Rose, Sheldon, and Dolben families;[21] their successors in 1845 were two members of the Bine family.[22]

In 1860 the manor was made over to the ecclesiastical commissioners,[23] who in 1865 reallotted 404 a. as part of the endowment of Chichester cathedral.[24] That land remained in the hands of the church commissioners, successors to the ecclesiastical commissioners, in 1993.[25] Much of the land was held in 1861 by two tenants, Thomas Wisden with 349 a., mostly leasehold, and James Hamilton, marquess of Abercorn, with 267 a. leasehold and copyhold; in addition the marquess owned 87 a. outside the manor.[26] In or shortly before 1899 the ecclesiastical commissioners sold land including most of the northern half of the parish to the market-gardening firm of S. S. Marshall Ltd., which in 1900 leased 470 a. for 35 years to a development company called West Barnham Estate. After a large area had been developed for housing that company was wound up in 1930.[27]

A manor house on Eastergate manor with a dovecot and garden was recorded in 1379;[28] in 1534 a chapel was alluded to[29] and in 1558–9 the building had a Horsham stone roof.[30] The present Manor Farmhouse is a large and massive timber-framed building of the mid or late 16th century, which has a central range with rooms on two floors and long north and south wings making a **U**-plan with the open side to the west; the north wing contained the kitchen and the south wing the living accommodation. There is close studding on the west face of the building, and the infilling of the timber frame includes brick and flint. The south and west walls contain ashlar blocks presumably either from the previous building or from the church. There are remains of original painted decoration on beams in one

98 *Kelly's Dir. Suss.* (1909); *Barnham and Eastergate Past and Present*, ed. T. Hudson et al. 6; *S.C.M.* xvi. 325.
99 *Barnham and Eastergate Past and Present*, 15.
1 W.S.R.O., TD/W 47.
2 *W. Suss. Gaz.* 2 July 1992; O.S. Map 6", Suss. LXII. NW. (1951 edn.).
3 Pike, *Dir. Bognor* (1910–11), 221; (1912–13), 231.
4 *Bognor Regis Observer*, 12 Aug. 1966; photo. of opening race meeting, 1924, at racecourse.
5 *Bognor Regis Observer*, 22 Nov. 1974.
6 *Kelly's Dir. Suss.* (1895 and later edns.); O.S. Map 6", Suss. LXII. NW. (1899 edn.).
7 *Suss. Ind. Hist.* xvii. 5; W.S.R.O., Add. MS. 25532.
8 *Kelly's Dir. Suss.* (1938).
9 Ibid.; W.S.R.O., QDP/W 304.
10 W.S.R.O., Par. 76/54/4; cf. ibid. MP 814, f. [1].
11 *Chich. Observer*, 21 June 1974.
12 *V.C.H. Suss.* i. 526; cf. below, Walberton, intro.
13 P.R.O., HO 107/1652, f. 237v.; ibid. RG 11/1125, f. 66v.; W.S.R.O., IR 12, f. 15; ibid. TD/W 47; Pike, *Dir. SW. Suss.* (1886–7).
14 *W. Suss. Gaz.* 13 June 1991.
15 Ch. Commrs., surv. 1861, p. 139.
16 *V.C.H. Suss.* i. 432; *Cal. Doc. France*, ed. Round, p. 234.
17 *V.C.H. Mdx.* i. 182–3.
18 *S.R.S.* xlvi, p. 203; *Cal. Pat.* 1554–5, 327; 1557–8, 407–9.
19 *Cal. Pat.* 1558–60, 305–6.
20 Ibid. 1563–6, pp. 206–7; B.L. Add. MS. 39492, f. 57.
21 *S.R.S.* lviii, pp. 48, 139, 171, 187; Berry, *Suss. Geneal.* annot. Comber, 25; *Barnham and Eastergate Past and Present*, 39; W.S.R.O., Add. MS. 32738 (TS. cat.).
22 W.S.R.O., TD/W 47.
23 *Barnham and Eastergate Past and Present*, 37.
24 Ibid.; *Lond. Gaz.* 12 Sept. 1865, pp. 4368–73.
25 e.g. W.S.R.O., IR 12, f. 15; *Chich. Observer*, 21 June 1974.
26 Ch. Commrs., surv. 1861, pp. 139, 141–2, 255; cf. Elwes & Robinson, *W. Suss.* 85; *Kelly's Dir. Suss.* (1874 and later edns.).
27 W.S.R.O., Add. MSS. 24178, copy of resolutions passed 1899, and agreement, 1899; 25520–6; P.R.O., BT 31/16324/64742.
28 P.R.O., E 106/11/2, rot. 2, m. 2. A bull of Innocent IV (1243–54) was found under the ho. in the early 20th cent.: *S.A.C.* xlviii. 100.
29 *S.R.S.* xlii. 121.
30 C.K.S., U 269/E 341, f. 47.

room of the south wing. A fireplace in the same wing has a moulded lintel. The staircase is 18th-century.

Extensive farm buildings to the north and west include a granary on staddle stones and a large barn with a 16th-century roof and 16th-century diapered brickwork in its east wall; it may be the barn roofed with stone mentioned in 1558–9.[31]

Free warren was claimed at Eastergate in the late 13th century,[32] but no park is known.

ECONOMIC HISTORY. AGRICULTURE. The chief open fields and furlongs of the parish in the Middle Ages[33] were Southfield south of Barnham road,[34] Northfield between Barnham road and Fontwell Avenue,[35] the Broomes,[36] the Staines,[37] and Stotham[38] south of Eastergate Lane, and the Rough rakes north of the later railway station.[39] Others were Adderush, also in the east,[40] Garston, south of Barnham Road,[41] and 'Elesstumble'.[42] Mention of a stile in Northfield in 1304[43] indicates partial inclosure by that date, and in the 1460s and 70s tenants of the manor were ordered to repair fences in and between several of the fields.[44] Stotham was apparently being inclosed in 1506, when the tenants' pasture rights on the stubble there were exchanged for rights elsewhere.[45] In 1510, however, the recent inclosure of a rood in 'Elstombyll' was ordered to be undone;[46] pasture rights for sheep in the remaining fields were redefined in 1521;[47] and a term for arable fields (*campis seminal'*) was still in use in 1543.[48] Inclosure seems likely to have been complete by 1596, when much of the area of the fields was in small pasture closes;[49] there is no later indication of communal agricultural practices.

The north end of the parish supplied common heathland.[50] The manor demesne farm in 1378–9 had 16 cow leazes and 200 sheep leazes.[51] In the 17th century each tenant of a yardland claimed 20 sheep leazes on what was by then called Eastergate common and the farmer of the demesne 60; by 1649 part of the common had been inclosed and added to the demesne farm.[52] That the remaining area was not adequate to the tenants' needs is indicated by a presentment at the manor court for overstocking sheep in 1671 and by general restrictions on pasturing cattle and horses and on taking bracken in the 18th century.[53] The tenants' claim to dig marl there was disputed at the later period.[54] The common was inclosed by private agreement in 1779; of the 102 a. which it then comprised 9 tenants received allotments of between 4 a. and 19 a. and 8 others smaller amounts, the total number of plots being 33, mostly small.[55]

The demesne farm had 221 a. of several pasture in 1558–9.[56] In 1778 Manor Farmhouse was adjoined by pasture closes to south, south-west, and south-east.[57]

There were 4 a. of meadow on the demesne farm in 1086,[58] 6 a. in 1378–9,[59] and 21 a. in 1558–9.[60] No common meadow is known.

The demesne farm had 206 a. in 1378–9,[61] 330 a. in 1558–9,[62] and 262 a. in 1649.[63] It was leased from the early 15th century;[64] in the mid 16th leases were for 21 or 30 years but between 1595 and the mid 19th century for three lives.[65]

The 18 *villani* and 10 cottars listed on the manor in 1086[66] are presumably represented by the free tenants and neifs mentioned in the 14th century[67] and the freeholders and copyholders recorded from the later 15th.[68] About 40 persons owed suit to the manor court *c.* 1406.[69] Eight freeholders including the rector were listed in 1473 and 1639.[70] Three freeholds in 1473 consisted of one yardland each, a yardland in 1558–9 being 20 a.; the two which lay in Madehurst were presumably former manorial outliers. The number of copyholders fluctuated between 15 and 22 in the period 1473–1596[71] but by 1639 had fallen to 10. Many copyholds were single or half yardlands in 1473, and by the later 16th century amalgamation had produced one holding of two and a half yardlands (50 a.); others then ranged in size from 5 a. to 27 a. and there were also four copyhold cottages.[72] Copyholds were generally held for three lives from the later 16th century;[73]

31 Ibid.
32 P.R.O., JUST 1/917, rot. 21d.; JUST 1/924, rot. 67.
33 Para. based mainly on *S.R.S.* ii, pp. 64–5; W.S.R.O., Add. MS. 14554 (TS. cat.); ibid. Cap. I/23/1, ff. 151–4; ibid. TD/W 47. For location of Stotham Lane mentioned in 1596, above, intro. (communications).
34 Cf. P.R.O., SC 2/205/75, rot. 2; SC 11/653.
35 Cf. ibid. SC 2/205/75, rot. 2; SC 11/653; *Cat. Anct. D.* ii, B 3315.
36 Cf. P.R.O., SC 2/205/75, rott. 2, 8; SC 2/205/77, rot. 2.
37 Cf. ibid. SC 2/205/75, rot. 8; *Cat. Anct. D.* ii, B 3864.
38 Cf. P.R.O., SC 2/205/77, rot. 2.
39 Cf. *Cat. Anct. D.* iii, B 3905.
40 Cf. ibid.
41 Cf. *Cat. Anct. D.* ii, B 3864.
42 Also called 'Estumble' and 'Elstombyll': P.R.O., SC 2/205/75, rot. 2; SC 2/205/78, rot. 1.
43 *Cat. Anct. D.* ii, B 3315.
44 P.R.O., SC 2/205/75, rott. 2, 8, 13; cf. W.S.R.O., PHA 935, ff. 85v.–86; 6683, f. 18v.
45 P.R.O., SC 2/205/77, rot. 2.
46 Ibid. SC 2/205/78, rot. 1.
47 Ibid. rot. 7.
48 W.S.R.O., PHA 6683, f. 18v.
49 Ibid. Cap. I/23/1, ff. 151–4; cf. ibid. Ep. I/25/1 (1615).
50 C.K.S., U 269/E 341, f. 47.
51 P.R.O., E 106/11/2, rot. 2, m. 2.
52 W.S.R.O., Cap. I/30/3, f. 111; cf. ibid. Ep. I/25/1 (1615).
53 Ibid. Cap. I/32/1, ff. 31v., 78, 92, 102v., 156v.
54 *Barnham and Eastergate Past and Present*, ed. T. Hudson et al. 35.
55 W.S.R.O., QDD/6/W 2; cf. *Barnham and Eastergate Past and Present*, 34–6.
56 C.K.S., U 269/E 341, f. 46.
57 *250 Yrs. of Mapmaking in Suss.* ed. H. Margary, pl. 14.
58 *V.C.H. Suss.* i. 432.
59 P.R.O., E 106/11/2, rot. 2, m. 2.
60 C.K.S., U 269/E 341, f. 46.
61 P.R.O., E 106/11/2, rot. 2, m. 2.
62 C.K.S., U 269/E 341, f. 46.
63 W.S.R.O., Cap. I/30/3, f. 53.
64 P.R.O., SC 6/1033/8; SC 6/1035/11, rot. 2d.; SC 6/Hen. VIII/3480, rot. 18; SC 11/672.
65 *Barnham and Eastergate Past and Present*, 41; *S.R.S.* xlvi, p. 203; lviii, *passim*; C.K.S., U 269/E 341, f. 46; W.S.R.O., Cap. I/30/3, ff. 59–60.
66 *V.C.H. Suss.* i. 432.
67 P.R.O., E 106/11/2, rot. 2, m. 2; *Cat. Anct. D.* ii, B 3754.
68 P.R.O., SC 11/653.
69 Ibid. SC 2/205/51.
70 Ibid. SC 11/653; W.S.R.O., Cap. I/51/14, f. 116; on which rest of para. mainly based; cf. C.K.S., U 269/E 341, f. 46v.
71 Cf. C.K.S., U 269/E 341, ff. 46–7; W.S.R.O., Cap. I/23/1, ff. 151–4; *S.R.S.* xlvi, pp. 202–3.
72 C.K.S., U 269/E 341, f. 46; W.S.R.O., Cap. I/23/1, ff. 151–4; cf. ibid. Cap. I/51/14, f. 116.
73 *Barnham and Eastergate Past and Present*, 38.

they could be sublet by 1515[74] and mortgaged by 1667.[75]

By 1779 there were only 17 tenants in all.[76] Some manorial tenancies were converted to leaseholds in the 17th and 18th centuries,[77] and in 1861 of 748 a. held of the manor 188 a. were copyhold for lives and 561 a. leasehold, mostly also for lives.[78] From the mid 17th century members of the Boniface family were prominent among the tenants,[79] but in 1861 most of the manor land was held by James Hamilton, marquess of Abercorn (267 a.), or Thomas Wisden (349 a.).[80]

In the mid 16th century pastoral farming was apparently dominant, the demesne farm having 221 a. of pasture, including former woodland, to 76 a. of arable.[81] In the 17th and 18th centuries[82] cattle, sheep, pigs, and geese were widely kept; from the later 17th century several flocks of over 100 sheep were mentioned, including two of over 300 in 1679 and 1713. Crops grown in the same period were wheat, clearly the most important, barley,[83] oats, peas, tares, vetches, and hemp.[84] Grasses were introduced by 1728 and turnips by 1770.

Large farms in the 17th and 18th centuries were those of John Spicer (1679), with at least 175 a. of crops, Richard Treagoose (1728), with at least 116 a., and John Boniface (1770), with at least 200 a.[85]

By the 1840s arable land (790 a.) was far more important than meadow and pasture (85 a.).[86] The two largest holdings at that date were centred on Manor Farmhouse (361 a.) and Eastergate House to the north-west (240 a.), the others being much smaller; only Manor farm and a holding of 40 a. worked from Tile barn on Barnham Road were single blocks of land, other holdings being widely scattered.[87] Between the 1840s and *c.* 1875 many closes were amalgamated into larger ones, evidently for arable; the largest had 80 a.[88] In 1861, however, the marquess of Abercorn's land (354 a.), including Wanley's farm (107 a.), was described as a desirable stock farm,[89] and the acreage under grass increased to 194 a. in 1875 and 287 a. in 1909.[90] A shepherd was mentioned in 1881.[91]

In the early 20th century the largest farms were Manor farm (350 a.), what was apparently Tile Barn farm (143 a.), and Wanley's farm in the north (127 a.),[92] and in 1909 there were also 13 holdings under 50 a. in area.[93] A poultry farm existed in 1913, and by 1938 there were four.[94] One remained east of Fontwell Avenue in 1991;[95] another north of Church Lane, which was also a small market garden, had closed before *c.* 1983.[96] Over 500 cattle were kept in 1985, chiefly for meat.[97] By 1995 the only sizeable holding was Manor farm (350 a.), a mixed dairy and arable holding which was farmed with another holding at Tangmere near Chichester.[98] Forty-nine people were employed in agriculture and market gardening in 1985.[99]

MARKET GARDENING. There were 8 a. of orchards in and around the village *c.* 1875.[1] Market gardening and fruit growing on a large scale, however, began after the arrival in the area of the Marshall family *c.* 1880.[2] By 1896 what was later called Station nursery,[3] belonging to Barnham Nurseries Ltd., had been laid out north of the site of Barnham market in Barnham Road.[4] It had grown to 13 a. by 1913[5] and grew further by 1950, when there were glasshouses.[6]

By 1910 there were also market gardens and glasshouses further west, covering much of the land between Station nursery and Eastergate village. South of Barnham Road[7] lay the Brooks nursery of John Poupart and the nursery of J. H. Robinson, both growing fruit.[8] Robinson sold his business to his brother-in-law Jack Langmead in 1952.[9] Another market garden occupied land in the village itself north of the church and manor house.[10] North of Barnham Road some orchards existed by 1910 in the angle of Fontwell Avenue and Eastergate Lane and north of Wandleys Lane.[11] By 1950 virtually the whole area between Fontwell Avenue, Wandleys Lane, and Barnham Road was orchards and glasshouses.[12]

Fruit farming flourished greatly by 1903, supplying the London markets, and by 1913 there were seven firms including those mentioned.[13] In 1909 there were 29 a. under orchards,

74 P.R.O., SC 2/205/78, rot. 3d.; W.S.R.O., Cap. I/5/1, f. 137v.; Cap. I/32/1, ff. 14v., 145v.; Cap. I/38/1, f. 20v.; ibid. PHA 6683, f. 18v.

75 W.S.R.O., Cap. I/32/1, f. 24v.

76 Ibid. QDD/6/W 2.

77 *Barnham and Eastergate Past and Present*, 41.

78 Ch. Commrs., surv. 1861, p. 139.

79 *Barnham and Eastergate Past and Present*, 39; W.S.R.O., Cap. I/4/8/36, rentals, 1806–7; ibid. QDD/6/W 2.

80 Ch. Commrs., surv. 1861, pp. 141–2.

81 C.K.S., U 269/E 341, f. 46.

82 Rest of para. mainly based on W.S.R.O., Ep. I/29/13/5; Ep. I/29/76.

83 Cf. ibid. PHA 6683, f. 18v.

84 Cf. ibid. Cap. I/23/1, ff. 152–4; ibid. Ep. I/25/1 (1615).

85 Ibid. Ep. I/29/76.

86 Ibid. TD/W 47.

87 Ibid.; cf. W.S.R.O., Add. MS. 4628; Ch. Commrs., surv. 1861, p. 254. None of the older bldgs. near the junction of Church La. and Nyton Rd. were then fmhos. with lands: W.S.R.O., TD/W 47.

88 W.S.R.O., TD/W 47; *O.S. Area Bk.* (1877).

89 Ch. Commrs., surv. 1861, pp. 141–2, 255; W.S.R.O., Add. MS. 14572 (TS. cat.).

90 P.R.O., MAF 68/433, 2371.

91 Ibid. RG 11/1125, f. 65.

92 W.S.R.O., Add. MS. 25520; ibid. IR 12, ff. 15, 18.

93 P.R.O., MAF 68/2371.

94 *Kelly's Dir. Suss.* (1913 and later edns.).

95 O.S. Map 1/25,000, SU 80/90 (1991 edn.).

96 *Chich. Observer*, 21 June 1974; *W. Suss. Gaz.* 2 July 1992; above, intro. (settlement).

97 M.A.F.F., agric. statistics, 1985.

98 Inf. from Mr. P. Helyer, Manor fm.

99 M.A.F.F., agric. statistics, 1985.

1 *O.S. Area Bk.* (1877); O.S. Map 6", Suss. LXII (1880 edn.); cf. P.R.O., MAF 68/433.

2 Above, Barnham, econ. hist. (mkt. gardening).

3 W.S.R.O., Add. MS. 41254.

4 O.S. Map 6", Suss. LXII. SE. (1899 edn.).

5 W.S.R.O., Add. MS. 25509, applic. for certificate concerning estate duty, 1913; cf. O.S. Map 6", Suss. LXII. NE., SE. (1913–14 edn.).

6 O.S. Map 6", Suss. LXII. SE. (1951 edn.).

7 Ibid. Suss. LXII. NE., NW. (1914 edn.); W.S.R.O., Add. MS. 25524.

8 W.S.R.O., IR 12, ff. 16, 22; *Kelly's Dir. Suss.* (1903 and later edns.); *W. Suss. Gaz.* 11 Feb. 1982.

9 *Bognor Regis Post*, 21 Nov. 1953.

10 W.S.R.O., IR 12, ff. 15–16; O.S. Map 6", Suss. LXII. NW. (1914 edn.).

11 O.S. Map 6", Suss. LXII. NW. (1914 edn.); cf. W.S.R.O., IR 12, ff. 19, 21.

12 O.S. Map 6", Suss. LXII. NE., NW. (1951 edn.).

13 W.S.R.O., Ep. I/22A/2 (1903); *Kelly's Dir. Suss.* (1903 and later edns.); cf. *Census* (1911).

mostly for apples, and 15 a. growing small fruit.[14] By 1920 peaches were being supplied to large country houses and ocean liners.[15] A market gardener in Elm Grove pioneered the production of cultivated mushrooms in West Sussex in the early 20th century, and there were two mushroom growers in 1934. By 1913 the firm of Phipps and Ireland traded in a wide variety of plants and flowers including alpines and rockery plants,[16] while another business experimented with forcing outdoor daffodils and growing chrysanthemums commercially.[17] One market gardener offered himself as a gardening instructor, presumably for laying out larger gardens, by 1909.[18]

Barnham Nurseries' Station nursery was closed between 1955[19] and 1965 and was later built over. The market-garden site in the village also succumbed to housing development in the early 1980s.[20] In 1985, however, there were still 41 ha. (101 a.) of horticultural crops, notably apples,[21] while one holding in 1982 had previously grown chiefly salad vegetables.[22] Much of the land between the built-up areas of Eastergate and West Barnham remained market gardens and glasshouses in 1993, producing fruit and flowers.[23]

FAIR AND MARKETS. A fair was held in the 1790s,[24] presumably on the close called Ten acre fair field on the east side of Fontwell Avenue recorded in 1845.[25]

In 1882 W. R. Winter of North Bersted began fortnightly Monday auction sales of fatstock alongside Barnham station; by 1885 the frequency was weekly. From 1901 Stride and Son of Chichester were owners of what became known as Barnham market despite being in Eastergate parish.[26] By 1896 an additional site had been acquired north of the Railway hotel in Barnham Road; during the next 14 years it expanded greatly,[27] while the original site ceased to be used.[28] On the new site a large cattle shed was built, and there were pens for sheep, pigs, and poultry.[29] There was a corn exchange by 1903.[30]

An important Christmas fatstock show was held in the early 20th century, at first followed by a dinner at the Railway hotel, and there were special sales, notably for lambs, at Easter and Whitsun.[31]

By 1929 the market had become one of the three or four most important in Sussex; as a fat cattle market it rivalled Lewes, while the trade in sheep was also important. Trade had increased considerably since before 1914, and numbers of stock passing through in a recent typical year were 4,330 cattle, chiefly fat, 3,690 calves, 30,000 sheep and lambs, chiefly fat, and 8,500 pigs, also chiefly fat. The chief customers were butchers from the area between Portsmouth and Eastbourne, others from London and Birmingham occasionally attending to buy pigs. About 20,000 head of poultry a year were sold at the same period, besides eggs, in both cases largely for the coastal towns, while small quantities of fruit and vegetables were dealt with both wholesale and retail. The corn exchange did little business in 1929, but horse sales were then held annually in spring.[32]

By 1945 business had greatly declined, partly because of rail transport's replacement by lorries; the market's hinterland was then apparently only a few miles in radius, small produce mostly being sold.[33] Stride and Son, who also owned Chichester market, therefore closed Barnham market in 1949, later holding the one at Chichester weekly instead of fortnightly.[34]

From 1953 the market-gardening firm of Langmead, Robinson and Co. occupied the site, using the former butter market as offices, the area behind it for retailing fruit, vegetables, and flowers, and the former cattle market for wholesaling.[35] By 1956 the corn merchants Alfred Cortis Ltd. had moved there,[36] and the freehold of the site passed in the following year to a trading society begun by Sussex Associated Farmers Ltd.[37] By 1970 it belonged to the wholesalers Nurdin and Peacock, who replaced the cattle shed with a large 'cash and carry' warehouse.[38]

A market was held illegally on Fontwell racecourse carpark on Sundays between 1975 and 1977[39] and was revived legally on Fridays in 1991.[40]

OTHER TRADES AND INDUSTRIES. Trades mentioned in Eastergate before 1800 included those of smith,[41] brewer,[42] butcher,[43] mariner, tinker,[44] wheelwright,[45] and tailor.[46] A tanner was recorded in the mid 16th century,[47] and a fellmonger in 1662 dealt in wool and various sorts of hides.[48] The house and workshop surrounded by roads

14 P.R.O., MAF 68/2371.
15 *Barnham and Eastergate Past and Present*, ed. T. Hudson et al. 8.
16 W.S.R.O., MP 2347, f. 2; *Kelly's Dir. Suss.* (1913 and later edns.).
17 *Barnham and Eastergate Past and Present*, 8.
18 *Kelly's Dir. Suss.* (1907, 1909).
19 W.S.R.O., Add. MS. 41254.
20 Above, intro. (settlement).
21 M.A.F.F., agric. statistics, 1985.
22 *W. Suss. Gaz.* 18 Mar. 1982.
23 Cf. O.S. Map 1/25,000, SU 80/90 (1991 edn.).
24 *Felpham by the Sea*, ed. T. and A. Hudson, 42–3.
25 W.S.R.O., TD/W 47.
26 *Barnham and Eastergate Past and Present*, 10–11; *Kelly's Dir. Suss.* (1895 and later edns.), s.v. Barnham; W.S.R.O., Par. 13/54/1.
27 O.S. Map 6", Suss. LXII. SE. (1899, 1913 edns.).
28 Ibid. 1/2,500, Suss. LXII. 11 (1912 edn.).
29 W.S.R.O., MP 2347, f. 6; above, pl. facing p. 90.
30 *Barnham and Eastergate Past and Present*, 11.
31 Barnham W.I. scrapbook [1949], pp. [12–13] (copy in possession of Mrs. R. Collins, W. Barnham); *Bognor Regis Post*, 31 Oct. 1970; P. Jerrome and J. Newdick, *Old and New, Teasing and True*, p. 46.
32 *Mkts. and Fairs in Eng. and Wales*, iv (Min. of Agric. and Fisheries, econ. ser. 23), 87, 89, 104, 198, 211.
33 G. Young, *Cottage in the Fields*, 247–58; Barnham W.I. scrapbook [1949], p. [12]; *Barnham and Eastergate Past and Present*, 15.
34 *S.C.M.* xxiii. 38; *Barnham and Eastergate Past and Present*, 15.
35 *Bognor Regis Post*, 21 Nov. 1953.
36 Below, this section (other trades and inds.).
37 *Bognor Regis Post*, 20 Sept. 1957.
38 Ibid. 31 Oct. 1970.
39 *W. Suss. Gaz.* 14 Aug. 1975; *Chich. Observer*, 29 Aug. 1975; *Brighton Evening Argus*, 17 Jan. 1977.
40 *W. Suss. Gaz.* 29 Aug. 1991.
41 *Cat. Anct. D.* i, B 1469; cf. P.R.O., SC 11/653.
42 W.S.R.O., PHA 6683, f. 17v.
43 Ibid. PHA 933, f. 98; *S.R.S.* liv. 106.
44 *Cal. Assize Rec. Suss. Eliz. I*, pp. 124, 230.
45 W.S.R.O., Cap. I/23/1, f. 152.
46 *S.R.S.* xxviii. 192.
47 Ibid. xlii. 116; W.S.R.O., PHA 933, f. 98.
48 W.S.R.O., Ep. I/29/76/13.

on all sides in 1596[49] presumably occupied the island site at the junction of Church Lane and Nyton Road where a grocer's shop flourished from 1845[50] or earlier. An excise officer was mentioned in 1770.[51]

In the early 19th century the trades of butcher, baker, brewer, carpenter, wheelwright, shoemaker, grocer, and draper were represented. A grocer in the early 1850s dealt in corn and coal. There was a music master in 1819.[52] One family out of five or six in work was supported chiefly by activities other than agriculture in 1811 and in 1831.[53] In 1851 there were also a gardener, a basket maker, and two bricklayers.[54]

The grocer's business at the junction of Church Lane and Nyton Road belonged for many years in the 19th and 20th centuries to the Collins family. Between the 1870s and 90s William Collins was also butcher, baker, dairyman, and draper, and kept the post office. In 1878 he farmed land himself, and in 1886 he sold boots and shoes, glass and earthenware.[55]

After 1864 some parishioners worked on the railway, in 1881 at least six.[56] Barnham station also served for the distribution of heavy goods. The landlord of the Railway inn, later hotel, dealt in coal from 1874 or earlier,[57] and there was a 'coal wharf' in the station yard by 1886.[58] A firm of builders' merchants had arrived by 1922.[59] Coal and fuel were still distributed in 1992.

Barnham market, itself owing its existence to the railway, brought ancillary businesses. There was a milk contractor near the station in 1895 and a corn merchant and a horse dealer by 1899.[60] By 1895 the Arundel ironmonger Alfred Pain ran an agency for agricultural implements in the station approach.[61] The corn merchant Alfred Cortis had premises in the station yard by 1907, at first also dealing in coal.[62] By 1956 the firm of Alfred Cortis Ltd. had taken over much of the former market buildings, selling *inter alia* grain, seeds, fertilizers, and animal feed.[63] One branch bank had come to Eastergate by 1905, by 1907 there were two, and by 1913 three, all open on market day only; by 1915 they were open on Fridays as well.[64]

Other trades recorded in the later 19th century were those of dressmaker, firewood dealer,[65] and harness maker.[66] There was a laundry by 1887.[67] No smith is recorded at that period, but besides the smithy in Barnham there were two others just beyond the parish boundary at Westergate in Aldingbourne.[68] In the early 20th century there were a florist, a cycle agent, a saddler,[69] and a firm of engineers.[70] Several retail businesses settled near the station from the early 20th century.[71]

There was a brickfield of unknown location in the mid 19th century.[72] A brickyard was opened in Elm Grove South to serve the development of West Barnham for building after *c.* 1900;[73] clay continued to be dug there until 1950.[74] The firm of West and Dart was responsible for much of that development between *c.* 1905 and 1910;[75] W. H. Dart later continued by himself as builder and contractor, plumber, painter, and house decorator.[76] Another builder and decorator, who was also a hot water and sanitary engineer, had premises at Fontwell.[77] Further builders were recorded in the 1930s[78] and estate agents from the earlier 20th century;[79] there was an architect in the parish in 1903.[80]

Two larger businesses which began near Barnham station expanded far beyond the parish. James L. Penfold[81] set up as an engineer by 1905 in opposition to his family's firm at Arundel. From premises east of the market[82] he at first sold and serviced farm machinery and undertook contract threshing, but the agricultural connexion was gradually relinquished as the firm diversified into haulage, dealing in builders' supplies, and sand and gravel quarrying in Eastergate, Slindon, Eartham, Washington, and the Midhurst area. In the 1930s the business was divided into the Barnham Transport Co. Ltd. and Penfolds Builders Merchants Ltd.; the Penfold Metallising Co. was formed in 1947 and Penfolds Ready Mixed Concrete Ltd. in the 1950s. In 1960 there were a depot at West Worthing and wharves at Littlehampton, Shoreham, and Newhaven, and in 1965 one company within the group operated four ships dredging marine gravel in the Solent.

49 Ibid. Cap. I/23/1, f. 153.
50 Ibid. TD/W 47; *Kelly's Dir. Suss.* (1845).
51 *S.C.M.* ix. 102.
52 W.S.R.O., Add. MS. 17012; ibid. Par. 76/1/2/1; *Kelly's Dir. Suss.* (1845, 1852).
53 *Census* (1811, 1831).
54 P.R.O., HO 107/1652, ff. 238, 240v.–241.
55 *Kelly's Dir. Suss.* (1874 and later edns.); Pike, *Dir. SW. Suss.* (1886–7); *Barnham and Eastergate Past and Present*, pl. [6]; *W. Suss. Gaz.* 2 July 1992; *S.C.M.* iii. 85; W.S.R.O., MP 2347, f. 7.
56 P.R.O., RG 11/1125, ff. 66, 67v.–68.
57 *Kelly's Dir. Suss.* (1874, 1905); ibid. (1895, 1899, 1907), s.v. Barnham.
58 Pike, *Dir. SW. Suss.* (1886–7); cf. *Kelly's Dir. Suss.* (1899).
59 *Kelly's Dir. Suss.* (1922).
60 Ibid. (1895, 1899).
61 Ibid. (1895); cf. ibid. (1934); W.S.R.O., MP 2347, f. 8; *Suss. Trade Guide* (1962), 8 (copy at C.I.H.E. libr., GY 155). A photo. of 1933 at W.S.R.O., MP 2346, however, shows the firm's premises at the mkt.
62 *Kelly's Dir. Suss.* (1907), s.v. Barnham; W.S.R.O., IR 12, f. 29; ibid. MP 2347, f. 8.
63 C.I.H.E. libr., GY 1471; above, this section (fair and mkts.).
64 *Kelly's Dir. Suss.* (1905 and later edns.); cf. W.S.R.O., MP 2347, ff. 8–9.
65 *Kelly's Dir. Suss.* (1878).
66 P.R.O., RG 11/1125, f. 65v.
67 *Kelly's Dir. Suss.* (1887).
68 O.S. Map 6", Suss. LXII (1880 edn.).
69 *Kelly's Dir. Suss.* (1909).
70 Ibid. (1905).
71 Ibid. (1913 and later edns.); W.S.R.O., IR 12, f. 27; ibid. MP 2347, ff. 7–8.
72 M. Beswick, *Brickmaking in Suss.* 191.
73 W.S.R.O., Add. MSS. 24178, accts. of W. Barnham Estate; 25509, Wyatt and Son to T. Read, 25 Sept. 1901; ibid. IR 12, f. 25; O.S. Map 6", Suss. LXII. NE. (1914 edn.); above, intro. (settlement).
74 O.S. Map 6", Suss. LXII. NE. (1951 edn.); W.S.R.O., MP 2347, ff. 1–2.
75 W.S.R.O., MP 2347, ff. 1–2; cf. *Kelly's Dir. Suss.* (1905); ibid. (1909), s.v. Barnham.
76 *Kelly's Dir. Suss.* (1927), s.v. Barnham; *Suss. Trade Guide* (1962), 8; W.S.R.O., MP 3152, p. 43.
77 W.S.R.O., IR 12, f. 20; ibid. MP 3152, p. 36; *Kelly's Dir. Suss.* (1909).
78 *Kelly's Dir. Suss.* (1934, 1938).
79 W.S.R.O., MP 2347, f. 8.
80 *Kelly's Dir. Suss.* (1903).
81 Para. based mainly on [F. Penfold], *Penfolds of Arundel*, 9 (copy at W.S.R.O. libr.); *W. Suss. Gaz.* 11 Feb. 1960; *Kelly's Dir. Suss.* (1905 and later edns.); W.S.R.O., MP 814, f. [38].
82 O.S. Map 1/2,500, Suss. LXII. 11 (1912, 1941 edns.); C.I.H.E. libr., GY/PH 7253.

Nearly 150 people were employed in all in 1960 and *c.* 250 in 1965. The business's connexion with Eastergate ceased after 1967.[83]

Gerald Toynbee after 1918 formed a haulage company called by 1927 F. & G. Toynbee.[84] It later diversified into general civil engineering contracting, and by 1963 was a large organization undertaking construction throughout southern England, including house building, road building, and drainage works. A plant hire subsidiary company was formed in 1962.[85] The firm left the parish in 1971.[86]

The market-gardening business of J. H. Robinson, later Langmead, Robinson and Co., besides the retail shop mentioned above later included a haulage business.[87]

S. S. Marshall of Barnham Nurseries Ltd. also practised as a solicitor in 1905. Two physicians and surgeons were recorded in 1909 and dentists from 1927. There were two insurance agents in 1934.[88]

In 1965 the population of West Barnham was largely retired; some people travelled daily to work in London and other towns, but most workers were employed locally.[89] By 1992, with the growth of population, the 'dormitory' function of the parish had greatly developed.

The railway station in 1976 had a staff of 41.[90] By 1977 there was an engineering works on Barnham Road between West Barnham and Eastergate village and another in the angle between Fontwell Avenue and Wandleys Lane.[91] By 1992 both sites had become small industrial estates[92] with six or seven firms at each. The site formerly occupied by Penfold's and Toynbee's businesses at the same date accommodated several firms particularly representing the leisure industry.

A new shopping centre was built in Barnham Road on former nursery land *c.* 1983.[93] In 1992 it had 13 businesses including a supermarket and an Indian restaurant, and together with other shops in Barnham Road provided a wide variety of retail goods. Besides the grocer's and post office at the corner of Church Lane and Nyton Road mentioned above, there were then also a shop nearby selling game, fish, and smoked foods,[94] and a general store in Fontwell Avenue.

In 1992 there were three banks, two firms of solicitors, and a firm of accountants in the parish, besides two medical practices, two dentists, a vet, and a 'natural health' clinic. At the same date there were two or three riding establishments along and to the east of Fontwell Avenue, and a caravan park beside Wandleys Lane.[95]

In addition to the builder's business at Fontwell in the north end of the parish mentioned above, a post office was opened there in the early 20th century, moving to the part of Fontwell in Walberton parish in 1968.[96]

LOCAL GOVERNMENT. There are court rolls for Eastergate manor for the years 1341–2,[97] various years between 1462 and 1535,[98] and the years 1543, 1548, 1550,[99] 1617–19,[1] and 1660–1874;[2] a view of frankpledge was held between 1543 and 1550 and a sheriff's tourn in 1548, but otherwise the records are of the court baron. In the late 15th century courts were held up to three times a year, in the 16th and 17th centuries often twice yearly in spring and autumn, and between the late 17th and early 19th usually only once a year. After the late 17th century there was sometimes no business, and from 1762 much business was conducted out of court. From 1810 courts were held less regularly, the last in 1855. The place of holding the court in the mid 17th century and presumably at other dates was the hall of Manor Farmhouse.[3]

In the 1340s, when the court's jurisdiction covered Sées abbey's lands in Littlehampton and Atherington in Climping as well as Eastergate, a plea of trespass was heard on at least one occasion. Between the 15th century and the 18th, besides land transactions, the court dealt with the management of the common fields and wastes[4] and the repair of houses,[5] hedges, and ditches.[6] Between 1486 and 1519 it elected two 'curemen',[7] and in 1618 the reeve.[8] The view of frankpledge in the 1540s held the assize of bread and of ale, inspected leather, saw to road repairs, and elected the headborough; a case of assault was heard in 1548. Other officers mentioned were a beadle in the 15th century,[9] and a bailiff between the later 15th and 18th centuries,[10] who in 1535 also served on Syon abbey's manors of Atherington in Climping and Ecclesden in Angmering.[11] The office of reeve had existed by 1229,[12] and in the 1610s was filled by rotation among the tenants of houses in the village street. The headborough in 1536 also represented Atherington.[13] A tithingman still served in 1822.[14]

83 *W. Suss. Gaz.* 16 Feb. 1967; cf. *Suss. Trade Guide* (1962), 8.
84 W.S.R.O., MP 2347, f. 10; *Kelly's Dir. Suss.* (1927), s.v. Barnham.
85 *Bognor Regis Observer*, 22 Feb. 1963.
86 Inf. from Gerald Toynbee (Contractors) Ltd., Bognor Regis.
87 *Bognor Regis Post*, 21 Nov. 1953; *W. Suss. Gaz.* 2 July 1992.
88 *Kelly's Dir. Suss.* (1905 and later edns.).
89 W.S.R.O., MP 814, f. [1].
90 *W. Suss. Gaz.* 23 Sept. 1976.
91 O.S. Map 1/10,000, SU 90 NE., NW. (1979 edn.).
92 Cf. *W. Suss. Gaz.* 9 Feb. 1989.
93 Cf. ibid. 21 Oct. 1982.
94 Cf. ibid. 2 July 1992.
95 Cf. O.S. Map 1/10,000, SU 90 NW. (1979 edn.).
96 *W. Suss. Gaz.* 3 Oct. 1968; C.I.H.E. libr., GY 1796.
97 P.R.O., SC 2/205/74, rott. [1–2].
98 Ibid. SC 2/205/75 (1462–85); SC 2/205/76 (1486–91); SC 2/205/77 (1502–9); SC 2/205/78 (1510–35); SC 2/206/44, rot. 6 (1492–3); SC 2/206/45, rott. [3, 8] (1495, 1499).
99 W.S.R.O., PHA 933, f. 97v.; 935, f. 83v.; 6683, f. 17v.
1 Ibid. Cap. I/38/1, ff. 8, 9, 20v., 21.
2 Ibid. Cap. I/32/1–3.
3 Ibid. Cap. I/30/3, f. 61.
4 e.g. P.R.O., SC 2/205/75, rott. 2, 8, 13; SC 2/205/77, rot. 2; SC 2/205/78, rott. 1, 7; W.S.R.O., Cap. I/32/1, ff. 31v., 78, 102v.; Cap. I/38/1, ff. 10v., 22v.
5 P.R.O., SC 2/205/75, rott. 1, 8d.; SC 2/205/77, rot. 2; SC 2/206/45, rot. [8]; W.S.R.O., Cap. I/32/1, f. 22v.; Cap. I/32/2, f. 34v.; Cap. I/38/1, f. 8 and v.
6 P.R.O., SC 2/205/75, rott. 2, 8, 13; W.S.R.O., Cap. I/38/1, f. 10.
7 P.R.O., SC 2/205/76, rot. 1; SC 2/205/78, rott. 1d., 6; cf. below, S. Stoke, local govt.
8 W.S.R.O., Cap. I/38/1, f. 9v.
9 P.R.O., SC 2/205/75, rot. 4; SC 6/1101/20, rot. 3d.
10 Ibid. SC 2/205/78, rot. 5; SC 2/206/45, rot. [8]; W.S.R.O., Cap. I/32/1, f. 156v.; *Cal. Pat.* 1558–60, 307.
11 *Valor Eccl.* (Rec. Com.), i. 426.
12 *S.R.S.* ii, p. 64.
13 A.C.M., M 271, f. [9v.].
14 E.S.R.O., QCR/2/1/EW 2 (46).

There were apparently always two churchwardens in the period 1548–1662 and from 1883, but from 1664 to 1882 there was usually only one.[15] In 1579 the office rotated by holdings.[16]

Some poor children at least were apprenticed in 1644,[17] and a parish poorhouse existed in the early 19th century in the angle between Fontwell Avenue and Eastergate Lane;[18] by 1845 it was let as cottages[19] and it was later demolished.

The parish joined Westhampnett union, later rural district, in 1835; from 1933 it was in Chichester rural district[20] and from 1974 in Arun district.

CHURCH. There was a church in 1086,[21] which by 1087 belonged to Sées abbey (Orne).[22] It remained a rectory. From 1983 it was held with Barnham by a single priest in charge,[23] and in 1985 Aldingbourne, Barnham, and Eastergate became one benefice, the parishes remaining distinct. In 1992 the three parishes were united as the parish of Aldingbourne, Barnham, and Eastergate.[24]

The advowson descended with the manor,[25] remaining, however, with the dean and chapter of Chichester after 1860.[26] The Crown exercised it between 1348 and 1421 because of the war with France,[27] George Benyon and Henry Blaxton each presented for a turn in the later 16th century, and William Cawley the regicide and Richard Boughton together in 1657.[28] After 1985 the patronage of the united living belonged jointly to the dean and chapter and the bishop.[29]

The living was worth £10 in 1291[30] and £8 or less in 1440; it remained impoverished in 1513[31] and was valued at £6 14*s.* 8*d.* in 1535.[32] By 1473 the rector paid £1 yearly to the lady of the manor,[33] the Crown maintaining the right to the payment after the manor was granted away in 1560.[34] Rent was also paid to the manor for glebe in 1473 and later.[35]

A rectory house of unknown site was mentioned in 1473;[36] in 1635 it had 7 rooms.[37] It may no longer have been used in 1724,[38] and in 1758 had been so much out of repair for many years as not to be habitable.[39] It had been demolished by *c.* 1830.[40] A new house was built in Church Lane in the early 1840s;[41] it is partly of flint and partly rendered, in Tudor style. It was enlarged in 1882–3[42] but was replaced in 1976 by a building in Barnham Road nearer the centre of population.[43]

Between the mid 16th century and the 19th the rector had glebe estimated at between 10 and 20 a.[44] and all the tithes of the parish.[45] Between the 16th century and the 18th he also had common rights for 20 sheep.[46] The glebe was widely scattered in 1615[47] and later;[48] part was sold to redeem land tax in 1803[49] and two outlying plots were exchanged for other land in 1848.[50]

The real value of the living was said to be £50 in 1649[51] and £52 in 1724.[52] By *c.* 1830 it was on average £308 net.[53] At the commutation of tithes in 1845 the rector received a rent charge of £370.[54]

The rector resided apparently in 1440[55] and certainly in 1563.[56] Assistant curates were apparently recorded in the mid 16th century.[57] Between that date and the early 19th century incumbents often held other benefices, usually also in the West Sussex coastal plain,[58] and as dean and chapter appointees they sometimes served as prebendary[59] or vicar choral of Chichester cathedral.[60]

The rector in 1579 was failing to supply the sermons required, either himself or through others, and to instruct children in the catechism,[61] and a successor in 1622 was presented for omission of services;[62] in the following year two parishioners were letting out seats in the church

15 B.L. Add. MS. 39359, ff. 56–61; W.S.R.O., Ep. I/86/20, f. 17v.
16 W.S.R.O., Ep. I/23/5, f. 32.
17 *S.R.S.* liv. 59.
18 *250 Yrs. of Mapmaking in Suss.* ed. H. Margary, pl. 19.
19 W.S.R.O., TD/W 47.
20 Youngs, *Guide to Local Admin. Units of Eng.* i. 509.
21 *V.C.H. Suss.* i. 432.
22 *Cal. Doc. France*, ed. Round, p. 233.
23 *Chich. Dioc. Dir.* (1985–6); local inf.
24 Inf. from Chich. Dioc. Regy.
25 e.g. B.L. Add. MS. 39333, ff. 151–7; *Cal. Pat.* 1563–6, p. 207.
26 e.g. *Chich. Dioc. Kal.* and *Dir. passim.*
27 *Cal. Pat.* 1348–50, 9, 504; B.L. Add. MS. 39333, ff. 150–1.
28 B.L. Add. MS. 39333, ff. 153v.–154.
29 Inf. from Chich. Dioc. Regy.
30 *Tax. Eccl.* (Rec. Com.), 135.
31 B.L. Add. MS. 39333, f. 148.
32 *Valor Eccl.* (Rec. Com.), i. 317.
33 Ibid.; *S.R.S.* xlvi, p. 203; C.K.S., U 269/E 341, f. 46v.; P.R.O., SC 11/653.
34 e.g. B.L. Add. MS. 5699, f. 64; W.S.R.O., Cap. I/30/3, f. 113; Cap. I/51/14, f. 116; Dallaway & Cartwright, *Hist. W. Suss.* ii (1) (1832), 75 n.
35 P.R.O., SC 11/653; W.S.R.O., Cap. I/51/14, f. 116.
36 P.R.O., SC 11/653.
37 W.S.R.O., Ep. I/25/1 (1635).
38 *S.R.S.* lxxviii. 66–7, not mentioning it.
39 W.S.R.O., Ep. I/22/1 (1758).
40 Ibid. Ep. I/22/2 (1838); *Rep. Com. Eccl. Revenues.*
41 W.S.R.O., Ep. I/22A/2 (1844); Ep. I/41/17.
42 *Chich. Dioc. Kal.* (1884), 143.
43 Inscr. on bldg.
44 B.L. Add. MS. 5699, f. 64; C.K.S., U 269/E 341, f. 47; W.S.R.O., Cap. I/30/3, f. 113; ibid. Ep. I/22/2 (1838); Ep. I/25/1 (1615); ibid. TD/W 47; *Glebe Lands Return*, H.C. 307, p. 28 (1887), lxiv; *S.R.S.* lxxviii. 67.
45 C.K.S., U 269/E 341, f. 47; W.S.R.O., TD/W 47.
46 C.K.S., U 269/E 341, f. 46v.; W.S.R.O., Ep. I/25/1 (1615); ibid. QDD/6/W 2.
47 W.S.R.O., Ep. I/25/1 (1615).
48 Ibid. TD/W 47.
49 B.L. Add. MS. 39333, f. 147.
50 Eastergate par. rec., Lovell, Son and Pitfield to Preb. Frazer, 1902.
51 W.S.R.O., Cap. I/30/3, f. 113.
52 *S.R.S.* lxxviii. 66.
53 *Rep. Com. Eccl. Revenues.*
54 W.S.R.O., TD/W 47.
55 B.L. Add. MS. 39333, f. 148.
56 *S.A.C.* lxi. 113.
57 B.L. Add. MS. 39359, f. 56.
58 Ibid. 39333, ff. 153–6; W.S.R.O., Ep. I/23/5, f. 32; *S.A.C.* cvi. 3, 5, 29, 31; *Alum. Cantab. to 1751*, s.v. Baguley, S. Taylor, Wellings; *Alum. Cantab. 1752–1900*, s.v. Toghill; *Alum. Oxon. 1715–1886*, s.v. Pilkington; *Rep. Com. Eccl. Revenues.*
59 B.L. Add. MS. 39333, ff. 153v.–156v.; Le Neve, *Fasti, 1541–1857, Chichester*, 20, 27, 29, 38, 44, 57.
60 B.L. Add. MS. 39333, ff. 155v.–156; *S.A.C.* cvi. 5, 31–2.
61 W.S.R.O., Ep. I/23/5, f. 32.
62 *S.R.S.* xlix. 35; cf. B.L. Add. MS. 39359, f. 57.

for money.[63] Augustine Payne, instituted 1631, was ejected in the 1650s in favour of a 'preacher of the gospel' but restored in 1660.[64]

In 1724 a service with sermon was held each Sunday and communion celebrated three times a year with *c.* 6 communicants.[65] The then rector Thomas Wellings (d. 1736) was buried on his other cure of Aldingbourne, where he had presumably lived.[66] Between the mid 18th century and the mid 19th, for lack of a suitable house, his successors perhaps always resided outside the parish,[67] and in 1758 the incumbent was said not to perform services himself more often than every two months.[68]

Between 1798 and 1849 successive rectors were residentiary canons at Chichester, one serving also as precentor, and had other livings besides.[69] During that period the church was served by assistant curates or the clergy of neighbouring parishes;[70] the curate in 1838 was not resident either,[71] but in 1845 the rector lived in the new rectory house.[72] Two Sunday services were held from *c.* 1832[73] and communion five times a year by 1844, monthly by 1884, and twice monthly by 1898.[74] On Census Sunday 1851 morning service was attended by 95 besides Sunday schoolchildren and afternoon service by 130.[75] A barrel organ had been installed by 1841.[76]

The church's position near the western edge of the parish led some parishioners to use Barnham church at the end of the 19th century, while residents of Westergate in Aldingbourne attended at Eastergate.[77] At the same period the existence of a Salvation Army barracks at Westergate was claimed to foster 'a very irreligious irreverent feeling' among many young parishioners.[78]

The church in 1993 could be approached only through the farmyard of Manor farm; the granary belonging to the farm was used for church purposes from the 1970s.[79] There were both Sunday and weekday services in 1995.

The church of *ST. GEORGE*[80] consists of chancel and nave with north vestry and west bellcot. The walls are mostly pebbledashed over rubble and an exposed part of the south wall of the chancel is of Roman brick laid in herringbone pattern. The bellcot is shingled.

The chancel is late 11th- or early 12th-century, one original window surviving in the north wall.[81] The nave is probably of similar date though with no features earlier than the blocked 14th-century north doorway. There are two much restored 13th-century windows in the south wall of the chancel, and the east window is 14th-century. There are 15th-century windows in the south wall of the nave, and the west window and doorway date from 1534 when money was left to enlarge the church at the west end by 12 ft. (3.7 metres) and to construct a new three-light window.[82] The crown-post nave roof is also 16th-century, and the chancel roof is probably 17th-century.

In 1776 the nave was in good repair though the chancel was 'very ruinous'.[83] A west gallery for the schoolchildren had been inserted by 1856.[84] The chancel was conservatively restored in 1876–7, the roof being raised.[85] In 1883 the nave was restored and reseated, the gallery presumably removed, and the bellcot re-erected at the west end; a vestry was also built[86] but was replaced by new vestries *c.* 1925.[87]

There were remains of 11th-century architectural and figure painting on the north wall of the chancel in 1907,[88] and a window in the south wall of the nave has armorial stained glass datable *c.* 1360 with the FitzAlan arms.[89] Some medieval benches with poppy heads survived in 1776,[90] but by 1847 the church was 'full of hideous high pews'[91] later replaced. The communion rails are 18th-century and there are two early 19th-century Gothic priests' stalls. The east window commemorates Lord Kitchener (d. 1916).[92]

The single bell of 1737 is by Joshua Kipling of Portsmouth.[93] There are a silver communion cup probably of 1568 and a silver paten of 1798.[94] The registers begin in 1564.[95]

ROMAN CATHOLICISM. The dean and chapter of Chichester's lessee William Rose and two other parishioners were indicted for recusancy

63 *S.R.S.* xlix. 74.
64 B.L. Add. MS. 39333, f. 154; Lamb. Pal. Libr., Commonwealth presentation deeds, ii. 250 (TS. cat.); *S.A.C.* xxxiii. 270; *Walker Revised*, ed. Matthews, 360.
65 *S.R.S.* lxxviii. 67.
66 B.L. Add. MS. 39333, f. 155v.; *S.A.C.* cvi. 31.
67 e.g. W.S.R.O., Ep. I/22/1 (1758).
68 Ibid.
69 B.L. Add. MS. 39333, ff. 156–7; *S.A.C.* cvi. 29; Le Neve, *Fasti, 1541–1857, Chichester*, 12, 27, 44, 57, 79–80.
70 B.L. Add. MS. 39359, f. 60; W.S.R.O., Ep. I/22A/2 (1844); ibid. Par. 76/1/2/1; *Rep. Com. Eccl. Revenues.*
71 W.S.R.O., Ep. I/22/2 (1838).
72 Ibid. TD/W 47.
73 Ibid. Ep. I/22/2 (1838); Ep. I/22A/2 (1844); cf. B.L. Add. MS. 39333, f. 156v.
74 W.S.R.O., Ep. I/22A/1 (1884); Ep. I/22A/2 (1844, 1898).
75 *S.R.S.* lxxv, p. 156.
76 W.S.R.O., Par. 76/1/2/1, at end; cf. Clwyd R.O., Glynne ch. notes, lv. 42.
77 W.S.R.O., Ep. I/22A/1 (1887, 1893).
78 Ibid. (1890); cf. *Kelly's Dir. Suss.* (1899), s.v. Aldingbourne.
79 *W. Suss. Gaz.* 7 Dec. 1978; inf. from Mrs. S. Hyland, chwdn.
80 The dedic., not recorded before 1776, replaces the medieval one to St. Mary: *Cal. Doc. France*, ed. Round, p. 233; *S.R.S.* xlii. 116; B.L. Add. MS. 5699, f. 64.
81 Cf. S.A.S. libr., D. T. Powell sketchbook.
82 *S.R.S.* xlii. 116; cf. *Suss. Chs.: the Sharpe Colln.* ed. V. Smith (Lewes, [1979]), showing bellcot not at W. end.
83 B.L. Add. MS. 5699, f. 64.
84 W.S.R.O., Ep. I/22A/1 (1878); Ep. I/22A/2 (1856); Clwyd R.O., Glynne ch. notes, lv. 42.
85 W.S.R.O., Ep. I/22A/1 (1878); *Chich. Dioc. Kal.* (1878), 85.
86 W.S.R.O., Ep. I/22A/1 (1884); *Chich. Dioc. Kal.* (1884), 143; *W. Suss. Gaz.* 17 Nov. 1983.
87 Eastergate par. rec., corresp. about building new vestries, 1925, and faculty, 1925.
88 *V.C.H. Suss.* ii. 354.
89 Nairn & Pevsner, *Suss.* 214.
90 B.L. Add. MS. 5699, f. 64.
91 Clwyd R.O., Glynne ch. notes, lv. 42.
92 *S.A.C.* lxxiii. 113.
93 Elphick, *Bells*, 113, 300.
94 *S.A.C.* liii. 240–1.
95 W.S.R.O., Par. 76/1.

between 1605 and 1615[96] and single recusants on three dates between 1669 and 1767.[97] The church of Blessed (later St.) Philip Howard next to the present St. Philip Howard R.C. school was registered for worship in 1970;[98] it was served at first from Slindon but by 1992 had replaced the church there as the parish church.[99]

PROTESTANT NONCONFORMITY. There were five Dissenters in 1676.[1] In 1903 some parishioners attended Salvation Army services at Westergate in Aldingbourne.[2] Methodist services were held at the market room of Barnham market in the parish from 1923, but later moved to Barnham.[3]

EDUCATION. An unlicensed teacher was recorded in 1600,[4] and in 1758 there was a school in which the catechism was taught;[5] it may have been the same school which was supported by the rector and assistant curate in 1818, when there were 12 pupils.[6]

Eastergate National school was started in 1829 and in 1833 was attended by 15 boys and 18 girls.[7] A new building was built on part of the glebe between 1838 and 1845;[8] of one storey, it was similar in style and materials to the contemporary rectory house nearby. About 1845 there were 98 children on the books from Eastergate, Aldingbourne, and Barnham.[9] The school continued to serve Aldingbourne until at least 1865[10] and Barnham until 1906.[11] In 1855 it was supported by school pence and subscriptions, the shortfall being made up by the rector,[12] and in 1859 it had 46 pupils.[13]

After several years' suspension[14] the school was reopened as Eastergate and Barnham C.E. school in 1873.[15] Average attendance was 43 in 1875–6[16] and 75 in 1905–6;[17] in 1880 there was a lending library.[18] After the opening of Barnham council school average attendance fell to 55 in 1921–2 and 51 in 1937–8.[19] The school was later called Eastergate C.E. (controlled) primary school. A new building near the Wilkes Head inn, the first completely open-plan design in West Sussex, was opened in 1970,[20] the old building becoming first a school of arts and dancing[21] and later a private house.[22] There were 114 children on the roll in 1993.[23]

A private school or 'seminary' existed in the parish between 1855 and 1862.[24]

An evening school for older children was held occasionally in the 1860s,[25] and *c.* 1880 there was another.[26] From 1958 the parish was served by Westergate secondary modern school,[27] but in the following year the Blessed (later St.) Philip Howard R.C. secondary school was opened, originally for senior Roman Catholic boys and girls from the Catholic parishes of Chichester, Arundel, Slindon, Bognor Regis, and Littlehampton;[28] the choice of site was evidently due to easy rail communication, since neither Barnham nor Eastergate had a notable Catholic tradition. The buildings were later extended. In 1982, when the intake was comprehensive, there were 750 on the roll, mostly Catholics; the school was then also used for adult education classes.[29] In 1993 the roll numbered 659.[30]

CHARITIES FOR THE POOR. None known.

FELPHAM

THE former parish of Felpham,[31] which included the hamlets of Flansham and Ancton and which has been noted since the 18th century as a seaside resort, lies on the south coast east of Bognor Regis and within sight of the South Downs. In 1881 the ancient parish had 1,883 a.[32] A small portion of Bersted civil parish (19 a.) was added in 1913.[33] In 1933 the parish was divided in three, 932 a. in the south-west going to Bognor Regis urban district and civil parish,

96 *Cal. Assize Rec. Suss. Jas. I*, pp. 16, 18, 24, 48, 66; *Cal. S.P. Dom.* 1603–10, 383; *S.R.S.* lviii, p. 187.
97 *Miscellanea*, v (Cath. Rec. Soc. vi), 318; *Returns of Papists, 1767* (Cath. Rec. Soc.), ii. 146; *Compton Census*, ed. Whiteman, 144.
98 G.R.O. Worship Reg. no. 72067.
99 *Arundel and Brighton Cath. Dir.* (1976 and later edns.).
1 *Compton Census*, ed. Whiteman, 144.
2 W.S.R.O., Ep. I/22A/2 (1903); above, church.
3 Barnham W.I. scrapbook [1949], p. [23] (copy in possession of Mrs. R. Collins, W. Barnham).
4 W.S.R.O., Ep. I/17/9, f. 250v.
5 Ibid. Ep. I/22/1 (1758).
6 *Educ. of Poor Digest*, 957.
7 *Educ. Enq. Abstract*, 968.
8 *Rep. Educ. Cttee. 1859–60*, 753; W.S.R.O., TD/W 47.
9 W.S.R.O., Ep. I/47/3.
10 Ibid. Ep. I/22A/2 (1865).
11 Ibid.; *Return of Non-Provided Schs.* 29; *Rep. Com. on Children and Women in Agric.* 86. It also served Yapton in 1865: W.S.R.O., Ep. I/22A/2 (1865).
12 W.S.R.O., Ep. I/47/7.
13 Ibid. Ep. I/47/8/1.
14 *Rep. Com. on Children and Women in Agric.* 88; P.R.O., ED 7/123; W.S.R.O., E 76/12/1, p. 2 (TS. cat.).
15 P.R.O., ED 7/123.
16 *Public Elem. Schs. 1875–6*, 266–7.
17 Ibid. *1907*, 638.
18 W.S.R.O., E 76/12/1, p. 128 (TS. cat.).
19 *Educ. List 21, 1922*, 341; *1938*, 402.
20 *Brighton Evening Argus*, 19 Jan. 1970.
21 *Chich. Observer*, 21 June 1974.
22 *Barnham and Eastergate Past and Present*, ed. T. Hudson et al. 55.
23 *Dir. of W. Suss. Educ. Service* (1993). For the sch. in Orchard Way, above, Barnham, educ.
24 *Kelly's Dir. Suss.* (1855, 1862).
25 *Rep. Com. on Children and Women in Agric.* 88.
26 W.S.R.O., Ep. I/22A/1 (1881).
27 *Educ. in W. Suss. 1954–59* (W. Suss. C.C.), 20.
28 Ibid. 7; *W. Suss. Gaz.* 2 June 1960.
29 *W. Suss. Gaz.* 30 Dec. 1982.
30 *Dir. of W. Suss. Educ. Service* (1993).
31 This article was written in 1992 and revised in 1996. Topographical details in introduction based mainly on O.S. Maps 1/25,000, SU 80/90 (1981 edn.); 6", Suss. LXII, LXXIV (1879–80 and later edns.). Much help was received from Mr. R. Iden, Bognor Regis, Dr. E. Thomas, Felpham (on Felpham as a seaside resort), the late Miss H. Gibbs, Mrs. S. Gould, and other members of the Felpham and Middleton local hist. workshop. The correct pronunciation of the par. name is 'Felfam': *S.A.C.* xxxv. 169; *S.C.M.* xxv. 322–3; *P.N. Suss.* (E.P.N.S.), i. 140.
32 *Census*, 1881.
33 Ibid. 1921; W.S.R.O., WOC/CC 7/1/8; cf. below, this section (settlement; soc. and cultural activities).

449 a. in the north including Flansham to Yapton, and 522 a. in the east including Ancton to Middleton.[34] A new civil parish of Felpham was created in 1985, excluding Flansham and Ancton and with other differences from the ancient parish.[35]

The northern and western boundaries of the ancient parish generally followed the Aldingbourne rife and its tributaries the Felpham or Flansham rife[36] and the Ryebank rife; the lower part of the Aldingbourne rife, called *brynes fleot* in 680 and 953, at the latter date bounded the Anglo-Saxon estate of Felpham.[37] Those seem to be early boundaries, whereas the configuration of the eastern boundary with Middleton, which partly follows the modern Middleton and Elmer roads, seems to indicate that Middleton was once part of Felpham.[38]

The present article deals with the area of the ancient parish, except that the part transferred to Middleton in 1933 is treated with the history of Middleton from *c.* 1900.

LANDSCAPE HISTORY. The ancient parish lay chiefly on brickearth with alluvium along the rifes.[39] About 60 a. of arable and 40 a. of pasture succumbed to the sea between 1291 and 1341.[40] The site of that land is unknown, but a small area of alluvium near the east end of the parish presumably once formed part of a larger area now lost, while the offshore ledge nearby may also represent former land.[41]

To prevent the incursion of the sea into the valley of the Aldingbourne rife defences were constructed near its mouth by the early 15th century. A bridge, called Felpham bridge, had been built by 1405,[42] presumably occupying the site of the modern bridge at the point where the estuary is narrowest. The sea wall or bank on the archbishop of Canterbury's land to the west of it, mentioned in 1436,[43] had presumably been built at the same time, and it is likely that there was a similar bank to the east. The two constructions are probably represented by the earthworks which survived in 1992, in Felpham along the north side of Upper Bognor Road, and in Bognor Regis in the grounds of the Chichester Institute of Higher Education.[44] It is not clear whether the sluice mentioned at the bridge from 1454[45] was original to it or had been added later. Flooding during the 15th century damaged the bridge at least twice,[46] and also devastated the archbishop's fishery at the mouth of the rife;[47] in 1455 a road near the bridge, presumably on the sea wall, was also submerged.[48] A commission of walls and ditches for the estuary was formed in 1422 and afterwards renewed.[49]

The sluice mentioned at Felpham in 1535 was perhaps on the same site as the earlier one,[50] but much land had been reclaimed to the south by *c.* 1680 when a lower sluice had been constructed beyond the present coastline;[51] it was evidently of timber[52] and had a double exit.[53]

Four groynes were put up near 'Felpham sluices' before 1721,[54] but thereafter the coast began to be subject to further erosion, as at Bognor to the west.[55] New defences near the sluices were constructed by the sewers commissioners for the western part of Sussex in the early 19th century,[56] while nearby to the east embankments and groynes had been put up by 1828 at the expense of landowners.[57] Parts of the sewers commissioners' groynes were destroyed by heavy seas in 1838;[58] a new sluice and other works were constructed in the same year and further groynes, after more damage, *c.* 1857.[59]

In 1866 the timber sea wall at the mouth of the Aldingbourne rife was badly damaged by storms and a concrete wall was built further inland to replace it. After that too had been damaged in the following winter a third wall with new sluices was constructed still further inland on the present coastline.[60] The coast is reckoned to have receded *c.* 230 yd. (207 metres) in the west part of the parish between 1778 and *c.* 1875,[61] and 3½ a. on Felpham farm was said *c.* 1862 to have been recently washed away.[62] A cottage and land in the south-east corner disappeared between 1824 and *c.* 1840.[63]

Responsibility for the upkeep of defences continued to be divided between the sewers commissioners and landowners, notably the duke of Richmond;[64] and the construction of stronger defences at Bognor, which extended

34 *Census*, 1931 (pt. ii); W.S.R.O., WOC/CC 7/2/8.
35 Arun (Parishes) Order 1985.
36 *S.N.Q.* xvii. 170.
37 *S.A.C.* lxxxvi. 51, 53, 57, wrongly naming it the Ryebank rife; lxxxviii. 72. The Aldingbourne rife was called the Felpham or Shripney rife in 1844: W.S.R.O., Add. MS. 229; cf. ibid. 2073. The course of the rife W. of Felpham village was straightened before 1778: *250 Yrs. of Mapmaking in Suss.* ed. H. Margary, pl. 14.
38 Below, Middleton-on-Sea, intro.
39 Geol. Surv. Map 1", drift, sheet 332 (1975 edn.).
40 *Inq. Non.* (Rec. Com.), 369.
41 *250 Yrs. of Mapmaking in Suss.* pl. 14; Geol. Surv. Map 1", drift, sheet 332 (1975 edn.); O.S. Map 6", Suss. LXXIV. NE. (1913 edn.). It may be the good anchorage ¼ mile (400 metres) off Felpham mentioned in 18th cent.: P.R.O., MR 1111, no. 24.
42 Below, this section (rds.).
43 L. Fleming, *Hist. Pagham*, ii. 378; cf. ibid. 398. For the site of the mill of Pignor, below, econ. hist. (mills).
44 Cf. W.S.R.O., Add. MS. 2060; O.S. Map 6", Suss. LXXIV (1879 and later edns.).
45 Fleming, *Pagham*, ii. 388, 392, 396–7; cf. *O.E.D.* s.v. gote.
46 Fleming, *Pagham*, ii. 380, 390; *S.R.S.* xi. 276–7.
47 Fleming, *Pagham*, ii. 372, 388.
48 Ibid. 285, 369.
49 *Cal. Pat.* 1416–22, 389; 1441–6, 155; 1452–61, 309, 442; 1461–7, 280, 528.
50 *S.A.C.* xcii. 163; cf. e.g. Norden, *Suss. Map* (1595).
51 W.S.R.O., Chich. City Archives AZ 2.
52 *Land Drainage Rec. of W. Suss.* ed. D. Butler, 57.
53 Cf. W.S.R.O., Add. MSS. 2068, 2073; P.R.O., MPHH 218.
54 P.R.O., MPHH 218; Budgen, *Suss. Map* (1724).
55 e.g. W.S.R.O., Add. MSS. 4704, 4708; Fleming, *Pagham*, ii. 548; J. B. Davis, *Origin and Descrip. of Bognor*, 73.
56 *Land Drainage Rec. of W. Suss.* 37; *Suss. Agric. Express*, 3 Mar. 1838; W.S.R.O., Add. MS. 2073; ibid. LD I/ZP 4.
57 W.S.R.O., Add. MS. 2073; ibid. LD I/LL 2/5 (2).
58 *Suss. Agric. Express*, 3 Mar. 1838.
59 *Land Drainage Rec. of W. Suss.* 8, 57; *W. Suss. Gaz.* 23 Oct. 1856.
60 *Land Drainage Rec. of W. Suss.* 58–62; W.S.R.O., LD I/MC 20/27.
61 *S.A.C.* liii. 20, 24–5.
62 W.S.R.O., Goodwood MS. E19, p. 39.
63 Ibid. Add. MS. 2060; ibid. TD/W 54.
64 *Bognor Observer*, 23 Nov. 1898; 2 Dec. 1925; *Rep. Com. Coast Erosion* [Cd. 4461], pp. 19–21, H.C. (1909), xiv; W.S.R.O., Goodwood MSS. 1371; E5615–17.

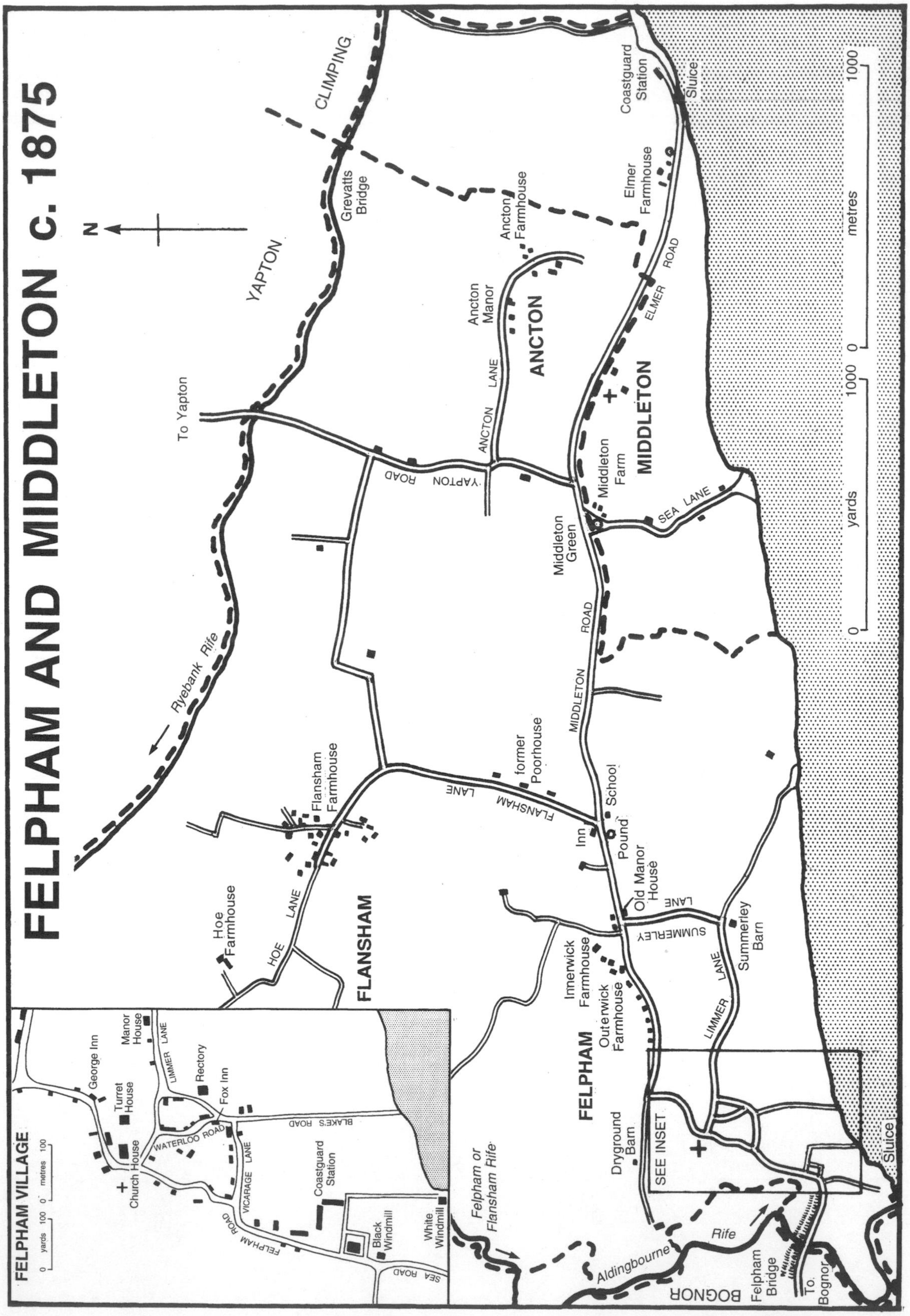
FELPHAM AND MIDDLETON c. 1875
N
CLIMPING
YAPTON
To Yapton
Ryebank Rife
Grevatts Bridge
Ancton Farmhouse
Ancton Manor
ANCTON
ANCTON LANE
YAPTON ROAD
Coastguard Station
Sluice
Elmer Farmhouse
ELMER ROAD
MIDDLETON
Middleton Farm
SEA LANE
Middleton Green
MIDDLETON ROAD
former Poorhouse
FLANSHAM LANE
Flansham Farmhouse
Hoe Farmhouse
HOE LANE
FLANSHAM
School
Pound
Inn
Old Manor House
SUMMERLEY LANE
Summerley Barn
Imerwick Farmhouse
Outerwick Farmhouse
LIMMER LANE
FELPHAM
Dryground Barn
SEE INSET
Felpham or Flansham Rife
Aldingbourne Rife
BOGNOR
Felpham Bridge
To Bognor
Sluice
0 yards 1000
0 metres 1000
FELPHAM VILLAGE
0 yards 100
0 metres 100
Church House
Turret House
George Inn
Manor House
LIMMER LANE
Rectory
Fox Inn
WATERLOO ROAD
BLAKE'S ROAD
VICARAGE LANE
FELPHAM ROAD
Coastguard Station
Black Windmill
White Windmill
SEA ROAD

as far as the parish boundary,[65] seems likely to have added to Felpham's problems. A period of rapid inroads before 1895 destroyed a road near the sluices[66] and caused the White windmill west of Blake's Road to be abandoned;[67] by 1898 several groynes were in disrepair.[68] The sea wall at the Aldingbourne rife was partly renewed *c.* 1912.[69] By the 1930s a short stretch of low sea wall with a promenade extended along part of the coast at least between the Bognor boundary and Blake's Road, the rest of the coastline of the parish then remaining low cliffs of Upper chalk.[70] Defences east of Blake's Road were reconstructed by the army after wartime damage,[71] and a new sea wall and promenade were built between Bognor and Blake's Road in the mid 1950s.[72] The promenade was extended eastwards towards the Middleton boundary in the 1960s.[73] The lower course of the Aldingbourne rife was straightened in 1959 during the construction of Butlin's holiday camp in Bognor Regis.[74] Another new sea wall and promenade were built in the south-west corner of the parish *c.* 1993,[75] and rock groynes were constructed off-shore *c.* 1995.

Apart from breaches of the coastline by the sea, the parish has often experienced flooding in the 19th and 20th centuries as a result of heavy rain in the catchment area of its streams.[76]

Copperas stone was collected from the beach in 1711[77] and sea spinach was gathered in 1828.[78] Eels were caught in the later 19th century or earlier 20th in the Ryebank rife on the Yapton boundary.[79]

As in other parishes on the coastal plain there were several ponds in the 19th century, for instance along the eastern section of Felpham Way.[80] Land use in the late 20th century was mixed. The southern part of the ancient parish was built over, and though the broad meadows backed by trees which had formerly separated Felpham from Bognor Regis had given way to Butlin's holiday camp in 1960,[81] a gap between the two places remained further inland. Much of the north end of the parish was still farmed in 1992, though a large area in the north-west had been converted into a golf course in the 1920s.[82]

There has never apparently been much woodland in the parish; the woods on the manor yielding 30 swine in 1086 may have been in the Weald.[83] Despite the grant of free warren at Felpham to Shaftesbury abbey, owner of the manor, in 1293[84] no park is ever known to have existed.

SETTLEMENT. Settlement before the 18th century seems to have been chiefly nucleated. Felpham village occupies slightly rising ground[85] in the extreme south-west corner of the parish close to the Aldingbourne rife. The road through the village had no importance before the 19th century;[86] hence perhaps the village's hotchpotch street pattern. A 'burnt mound' north-west of the church has revealed Mesolithic and Bronze Age activity,[87] and there may have been Roman settlement at the west end of Limmer Lane.[88]

In the late 18th century and early 19th there were 25–30 dwellings, not all aligned to the roads and with much open land between them;[89] among the larger were Church House, the Old Rectory, Turret House, and the Manor House in Limmer Lane.[90] With the growth of the resort[91] there had been some infilling by the 1870s,[92] including two terraces in Waterloo Road, of which one incorporates a converted farm building faced with beach pebbles. After 1914 a large house, the Forest, later the Gateway school, was built south of the church in grounds of *c.* 2 a. which included specimen trees.[93] Until the 20th century the village was separated from the sea by fields, so that houses on its southern edge had uninterrupted coastal views.[94]

Felpham's rural character, still unspoilt *c.* 1917, when farms continued to abut the main street,[95] was gradually eroded during the next 40 years, as the parish shared in Bognor Regis's growth: already by 1930 one visitor considered that the village had become like other outlying parts of that town,[96] though in 1992 the combination of old buildings, high flint walls, trees, and the picturesque arrangement of roads, retained for it an old-fashioned air. Farm buildings north-east and east of the church were demolished after *c.* 1920[97] and replaced by shops and a garage,

65 *Rep. Com. Coast Erosion*, 20.

66 *W. Suss. Gaz.* 21 Nov. 1895; cf. *Bognor, the Official Guide* (Bognor, [1912]), 6 (copy in C.I.H.E. libr.).

67 O.S. Map 6", Suss. LXXIV (1879 and later edns.); below, econ. hist. (mills).

68 *Bognor Observer*, 23 Nov. 1898.

69 W.S.R.O., Goodwood MS. 1371, printed letter from clerk of sewers com. to duke of Richmond, 1913.

70 *Holiday Hbk. to Bognor Regis and W. Suss.* (Margate, early 1930s), p. viii (copy in C.I.H.E. libr.); Geol. Surv. Map 1", drift, sheet 332 (1975 edn.); W.S.R.O., PH 4624; cf. C.I.H.E. libr., GY/PC 1465, 1486; GY/PH 2155.

71 *Bognor Regis Post*, 12 Oct. 1946.

72 Ibid. 6 Aug. 1955; *Bognor Regis Observer*, 7 Jan. 1955; 13 Apr. 1956; C.I.H.E. libr., GY/PC 1464; GY/PH 2158–9.

73 *Bognor Regis Post*, 2 Oct., 27 Nov. 1965; 14 Sept. 1968.

74 Cf. O.S. Map 1/25,000, SU 90 & SZ 99 (1958 edn.).

75 *Bognor Regis Observer*, 28 Oct. 1993.

76 P.R.O., IR 18/10328; W.S.R.O., Par. 81/12/1, p. [115]; *Land Drainage Rec. of W. Suss.* ed. D. Butler, 20; G. Young, *Come into the Country*, 57; G. Young, *Cottage in the Fields*, 197; G. Beale, *Bognor Regis Golf Club, 1892–1992* (Bognor Regis, 1992), 74; *Bognor Observer*, 11 Nov. 1925; *Bognor Regis Observer*, 22 Dec. 1983; *Bognor Regis Post*, 5 Jan. 1935; 11 Feb. 1950.

77 E.S.R.O., AMS 6185/119.

78 Dally, *Bognor* (1828), 36–7.

79 Young, *Cottage in the Fields*, 197.

80 W.S.R.O., Add. MS. 2073; O.S. Map 6", Suss. LXXIV (1879 edn.).

81 Young, *Cottage in the Fields*, 196; G. Young, *Hist. Bognor Regis*, 253–4 and pl. 88.

82 Below, this section (soc. and cultural activities).

83 *V.C.H. Suss.* i. 395; cf. below, econ. hist. (agric.).

84 *Cal. Chart. R.* 1257–1300, 433.

85 *S.A.C.* liii. 10; O.S. Map 1/2,500, Suss. LXXIV. 2, 6 ([1876] edn.).

86 Below, this section (rds.).

87 *S.A.C.* cxxv. 228–30.

88 Ibid. cxvii. 75.

89 *250 Yrs. of Mapmaking in Suss.* ed. H. Margary, pl. 14; W.S.R.O., TD/W 54.

90 Below, this section [worthies]; manor.

91 Below, this section (Felpham as seaside resort).

92 O.S. Map 6", Suss. LXXIV (1879 edn.).

93 *W. Suss. Gaz.* 30 Mar. 1978; P.R.O., IR 58/22732, no. 125 (inf. from the late Miss H. Gibbs, and Mrs. S. Gould, Felpham); O.S. Map 6", Suss. LXXIV. NW. & SW. (1932 edn.).

94 *Portsmouth Gaz.* 2 Dec. 1799; R. Lister, *Paintings of Wm. Blake*, pl. 25; W.S.R.O., Goodwood MS. E5618.

95 A. H. Anderson, *Bognor and its Neighbourhood* (1st edn. [1917]), 41.

96 *S.C.M.* iv. 32–3.

97 e.g. *Bognor Post*, 28 Jan. 1967.

while a large flat-roofed block of shops with flats above, more appropriate to a London suburb, was built on a prominent site to the south.[98] Turret House was demolished in 1961[99] and the former Gateway school in or after 1978,[1] but the Old Rectory and Church House escaped that fate, and were converted respectively into flats for the elderly and offices.[2] Further houses, shops, and flats, some also for the elderly and some incongruous in architectural style or scale, were built in the same period.[3] Many residents at that time nevertheless strongly wished to preserve the village's separateness from Bognor.[4]

Building materials used in older buildings in the village, as elsewhere in the parish, include timber-framing, brick, flint, sometimes squared and sometimes as cobbles, 'Bognor rock' sandstone rubble, and thatch.

The oldest surviving secular building in the village is Pear Tree cottage in Vicarage Lane, an early 16th-century timber-framed house of three bays with a queen-post roof and internal smoke-hood. A lean-to was afterwards added on the north side, and apparently in the late 16th century or early 17th the house was largely encased in walls of rubble. Two gables were added on the south front in the late 19th or early 20th century. Two demolished buildings north-east and south of the church were also probably 16th- or 17th-century: both apparently had a hall range and parlour cross wing, and the former also a one-storeyed east service end.[5]

Blake's cottage in Blake's Road is apparently 17th-century with later alterations. Other 17th-century buildings, all in Felpham Road, are Lavenham cottage, at right angles to the road, Lavender cottage, and probably the timber-framed house called the Barn next to the George inn.[6] The main range of the timber-framed Fox inn, burnt down in 1946, seems to have been 17th-century to judge from the window shapes, chimneystack, and lobby entrance; its taller cross wing was perhaps slightly later and contained a bay window apparently inserted in the 18th century.[7] The early 19th-century Church cottage in Felpham Road has a 'Gothick' window in the rear wall to light the staircase; the porch of bulbous and uneven flint columns is apparently an addition.

The hamlet of Flansham in the north part of the parish also occupies slightly rising ground, together with Hoe Farmhouse to the north-west;[8] the nearness of brookland suggests that the second element of the name is 'meadow' (*hamm*) rather than 'settlement' (*ham*), as also perhaps at Felpham.[9] A late Bronze Age 'founder's hoard' from Hoe Lane possibly indicates occupation[10] and there is evidence for Roman settlement.[11] About 1844 there were 12 dwellings loosely scattered around a junction of three lanes[12] and in 1898 two farms and 14 cottages.[13] Several new houses and bungalows, some large, were built after *c.* 1910, chiefly at the west end.[14] Though the hamlet's nearness to the Bognor–London road was stressed when Flansham farm was advertised for sale in 1837,[15] by the mid 20th century it was notable for its seclusion and rural aspect despite close proximity to the edge of Bognor's built-up area. Elms grew so thickly in the 1940s as to render part of Hoe Lane virtually a tunnel in summer.[16] Two working farms remained in the hamlet in 1992, though some outbuildings had been converted by then to residential use or offices.[17]

Four older houses survive at Flansham. At Flansham Farmhouse the chimneystack and part of a wall from a late 16th- or early 17th-century house remain. In the 18th century, perhaps *c.* 1764, the date on an adjacent farm building, they were incorporated in a mansard-roofed range running north–south. A second range with a new front was built on the east side in the early 19th century and later extended northwards. At Bonhams a 17th-century house, of which part of the roof remains, was remodelled with walls of knapped flint and brick in the early 18th century, perhaps in 1727, the date inscribed on the east front. The building was extended south and west in the 20th century. Flansham Manor and North Manor were formerly a single house, of which the older southern part retains a cross-passage plan that may be 17th-century. In the 19th century two rear wings were added and the roof of the older range was reconstructed. The interior was remodelled in the early 20th century, when a timber-framed addition was made on the north side using old materials.[18] Chessels is an 18th-century **L**-shaped house in the angle of which substantial half-timbered additions were made soon after 1900.[19]

Ancton hamlet lies close to the Middleton boundary in the east part of the ancient parish. There were only four or five dwellings in the mid 19th century besides two or three houses built on roadside waste in Yapton Road to the west.[20] The 20th-century history of settlement at Ancton is treated below.[21]

The Ancton House hotel, formerly Ancton

98 G. Young, *Cottage in the Fields*, 176.
99 *Bognor Regis Post*, 11 Feb. 1961.
1 *W. Suss. Gaz.* 30 Mar. 1978.
2 *Bognor Regis Post*, 13 Dec. 1958; 29 Jan. 1966.
3 Ibid. 9 Sept. 1961; 7 Nov. 1964; 10 Sept. 1966.
4 *S.C.M.* xxvii. 262; *Bognor Regis Post*, 23 July 1983.
5 W.S.R.O., PD 2012, f. 1; ibid. PH 1418; S.A.S. libr., prints and drawings 1015. The bldg. S. of the ch. was demolished in 1964: *Bognor Regis Post*, 15 Aug. 1964.
6 Illus. at *S.C.M.* iii. 621.
7 *Suss. Daily News*, 14 Oct. 1946; G. Young, *Hist. Bognor Regis*, pl. 14.
8 *S.A.C.* liii. 10; G. Young, *Cottage in the Fields*, 36. The name Hoe indicates a projecting ridge of land: *Eng. P.N. Elements* (E.P.N.S.), i. 256–7.
9 *A.-S. Eng.* ed. P. Clemoes, ii. 25, 44.
10 *S.A.C.* lxxxi. 205–9; S.M.R. 1441.
11 *S.N.Q.* vi. 245.
12 W.S.R.O., TD/W 54; cf. *250 Yrs. of Mapmaking in Suss.* pl. 14.
13 W.S.R.O., Ep. I/22A/2 (1898).
14 O.S. Maps 6", Suss. LXXIV. NE. (1913 and later edns.); 1/25,000, SU 80/90 (1981 edn.); SU 90 & SZ 99 (1958 edn.).
15 W.S.R.O., Slindon MSS., bdle. NR 34, no. 1; cf. below, this section (rds.).
16 G. Young, *Come into the Country*, 81.
17 *W. Suss. Gaz.* 18 June 1992.
18 Young, *Come into the Country*, 136. The datestone reading 1704 is a 20th-cent. addition: inf. from Mr. D. Bingley, North Man., Flansham.
19 G. Young, *Cottage in the Fields*, 37.
20 W.S.R.O., TD/W 54; cf. ibid. Ep. I/22A/2 (1898); O.S. Map 6", Suss. LXXIV (1879 edn.); *250 Yrs. of Mapmaking in Suss.* pl. 14.
21 Below, Middleton-on-Sea, intro. (settlement).

Farmhouse, was built in the 17th century to a **T**-shaped plan, the rear wing having one storey with attics; the tall west cross wing was refronted and remodelled in the early 19th century. Ancton Manor was originally a 17th-century house of three-roomed plan; the central and eastern rooms were probably originally timber-framed and the western room was built or rebuilt in flint with brick dressings in 1677. The eastern section was reconstructed in the same materials in 1751.[22] The whole house was refenestrated in the 19th century, and probably at the same period a staircase was cut through the large 17th-century chimneystack in the centre.

Innerwick and Outerwick, evidently outlying demesne farms of Felpham manor lying between Felpham and Flansham,[23] were the nucleus of Wick tithing recorded from 1543,[24] which in 1803 included the lower part of Flansham Lane.[25] Roman pottery found near Outerwick Farmhouse may indicate earlier settlement in the area,[26] and there was a Romano-British farmstead east of Flansham Lane.[27] The smithy recorded at Wick in 1624[28] perhaps occupied the site of the later one in Felpham Way east of Summerley Lane,[29] and in 1778 there was a cluster of houses near the crossroads formed by those two roads and the modern Firs Avenue. Other houses then existed in Felpham Way to east and west.[30] About 1844 there was a virtually continuous line of houses along the north side only of Felpham Way between the north end of Felpham Road and Outerwick Farmhouse, besides *c.* 16 dwellings east of Outerwick and in Flansham Lane;[31] some in both areas had evidently been built on roadside waste.[32] During the 19th century the junction of Felpham Way, Flansham Lane, and Middleton Road became a focus for the surrounding nucleated settlements in Felpham and Middleton parishes, with the presence of the school, a public house, a pound, and the parish poorhouse.[33]

Innerwick Farmhouse has a three-bayed, two-storeyed, 18th-century front perhaps built in 1734, the date inscribed over the door; the floor heights and fenestration were afterwards altered. Another bay was later added to the east and in the 19th century the house was extended at the back. It was a hotel *c.* 1953.[34] A barn apparently of the 17th century or earlier stood south-west of it in the 1950s[35] but had gone by 1988. The stuccoed Outerwick Farmhouse on Felpham Way was built *c.* 1800 and has two storeys with an attic and an elegant doorcase. In poor condition, it was gutted by fire in 1992.[36] Older houses further west in Felpham Way include the 18th-century Bentinck House of painted red brick, and the grander Wyke House and Richmond House, a single building of the late 18th century or early 19th consisting of a central portion and two recessed wings.

The number of houses in the parish rose from 74 in 1801 to 119 in 1861 and 208 in 1901, with particularly large increases in the 1860s and 80s,[37] largely absorbed within the existing areas of settlement. The history of late 19th- and 20th-century development, on the other hand, is of the gradual spread of houses through the south and central parts of the parish, joining Felpham to Middleton on the east and almost to Bognor on the west, while leaving isolated the hamlets of Flansham and Ancton to the north and north-east. The rapidity of development was often commented on in the 1920s[38] and was matched by large increases in population in the 1920s and 30s.[39] Development was by individual estates, sometimes private, which often did not connect with their neighbours; their picturesque layout, with trees and grass verges[40] that in Limmer Lane formed banks above road level, gave the southern part of the parish the appearance of a 'garden city by the sea'.[41] Several estates remained private in 1992.

Land between the coastguard station south of the village and the sea was offered for sale, as the Felpham Mill building estate, in 1884. The streets east of Sea Road had already been laid out,[42] and during the next 25 years[43] they were built up piecemeal with a mixture of chiefly small brick or rendered terraced and semi-detached houses, many of which were let as apartments in summer.[44] In Canning Road houses were built only on the north side, one terrace having a continuous balcony of seaside character. Directly in front of the sea and along the west side of Sea Road a group of cheaper houses were put up in the 1910s, standing on stilts to avoid flooding; some incorporated railway carriages, and they had outdoor staircases, decorated verandas, and roof gardens.[45] The area was separate

22 Datestones on bldg.
23 *Eng. P.N. Elements* (E.P.N.S.), ii. 259.
24 W.S.R.O., PHA 6683, f. 19. Cf. the surname (at) Wick recorded in 13th and 14th cents.: *S.R.S.* ii, p. 70; x. 135, 254.
25 W.S.R.O., Add. MS. 6973, f. [36v.]; for the poorho. mentioned, below, local govt. Flansham chap. was said in 1593 to lie at Wick, perhaps in error as the two places are far apart: P.R.O., C 142/278, no. 150; for identification, below, church.
26 *S.A.C.* cxvii. 75, 79; S.M.R. 1460.
27 *S.A.C.* cxxxii. 87–100.
28 *30th Rep. Com. Char.* 782.
29 O.S. Map 6", Suss. LXXIV. NE. (1913 edn.); cf. below, econ. hist. (other trades and inds.).
30 *250 Yrs. of Mapmaking in Suss.* pl. 14.
31 W.S.R.O., TD/W 54.
32 e.g. ibid. TD/W 54; ibid. Holmes, Campbell & Co. MSS. 790–4 (TS. cat.).
33 Below, this section [inns]; local govt.; educ.
34 *Bognor Regis, Aldwick and Felpham Official Guide* (*c.* 1953), 67.
35 H.B.M.C. hist. bldgs. list.
36 *Bognor Regis Observer*, 30 Dec. 1992.
37 *Census*, 1801–1901.
38 *Sunny Felpham* [1922], 12 (copy in B.L.); A. H. Anderson, *Bognor and its Neighbourhood* (9th edn. [1925]), 41; Ward, Lock & Co. *Bognor* [1928–9], 23; W.S.R.O., Ep. I/40/Felpham/3169; ibid. Par. 81/54/10; ibid. MP 3121.
39 *Census*, 1921–51.
40 e.g. *Property Reg. to Felpham, Middleton-on-Sea, Aldwick, Pagham and Bognor Regis* (Bognor Regis, [1939]), 10 (copy in B.L.).
41 Anderson, *Bognor and its Neighbourhood* [1925], 41.
42 W.S.R.O., Add. MS. 41293.
43 O.S. Map 6", Suss. LXXIV (1879 and later edns.); P.R.O., IR 58/22732, nos. 158–69, 171–5, 188–98 (inf. from the late Miss H. Gibbs, and Mrs. S. Gould, Felpham), indicating Wm. Tate of Felpham and Alf. Adlington of Bognor as chief developers.
44 Below, this section (Felpham as seaside resort).
45 A. H. Anderson, *Bognor and its Neighbourhood* (1st edn. [1917]), 41; *Bognor Regis Post*, 23 Apr. 1966; *Felpham by the Sea*, ed. T. & A. Hudson, pl. 8; C.I.H.E. libr., GY/PH 252; inf. from Mr. R. Iden, Bognor Regis.

from the village in the 1910s and 20s, when it was known as 'Felpham by the sea'.[46]

East and north-east of the coastguard station the 'Felpham building estate' was marked out for housing by 1904, but development seems not to have begun before *c.* 1910, when Admiralty Road had houses on its north side.[47] There were at least 34 houses in Blake's Road and streets to the east by 1927;[48] the area, described *c.* 1922 as a garden estate,[49] was largely built up by 1934 and fully by 1940.[50]

West of Felpham village, in what until 1913 was part of Bersted parish, the lower part of Links Avenue was built up by the farmer E. F. Sait *c.* 1909–12.[51] By 1934 land to the north, formerly part of Bognor golf course, had also been laid out chiefly with detached houses and bungalows.[52]

After the First World War building development spread along the coast to the east. There were at least four houses on the Felpham Beach estate south of Limmer Lane in 1918[53] and many by 1927.[54] The Summerley estate further east was laid out after *c.* 1922;[55] it was called the chief estate in the parish in 1927[56] and has always retained its exclusivity.[57] Big houses were also built along Limmer Lane itself and in streets to the north.[58] On the Beach estate the streets adopted a rectangular pattern around an oblong green. The western part of the Summerley estate also had straight roads, but the later portion to north and east was on a more picturesque plan with curving roads and a patch of woodland in Crossbush Road.[59] Manor Close north of Limmer Lane has large houses picturesquely arranged around a roughly oval space. By 1934 the area described was largely built up and by 1940 wholly so, except for the eastern part of the Summerley estate which was not finished until after 1945.[60] The remaining land south of Felpham Way and Middleton Road, except for that reserved for recreation, was developed for building in the 1960s and 70s with a mixture of houses and bungalows.[61]

North of the Felpham–Littlehampton road, meanwhile, building had begun around Innerwick Farmhouse *c.* 1923.[62] There were houses in Firs Avenue, Newbarn Lane, and Outerwyke Road by 1927, and more were built in the same area before 1940. On the Roundle estate to the east some houses had been built by 1932 and further roads, including Roundle Square with a central open lawn, marked out, most of the area being built up by 1940. Downview Road further west, leading to the new golf course, was laid out by 1934, when some large houses had been built, others following before 1940.[63] By 1957 there had been further development both east and west of Downview Road, and by 1980 virtually the whole area between the school playing fields on the west and Flansham Lane on the east had been built up with a mixture of detached and semidetached houses and bungalows with some terraced houses.[64]

East of Flansham Lane the Hurstwood private estate was developed during the 1930s.[65] East and north of it Bognor Regis urban district council in 1963 bought 200 a. to be sold off for residential development as needed.[66] The large 'Flansham Park' estate was built there in the 1970s with a mixture of terraced, detached, and semidetached houses, and detached and semidetached bungalows.[67]

Council houses were built in the 1920s and 30s in Felpham Way and Flansham Lane by Westhampnett rural district council[68] and Bognor Regis urban district council; in 1939 the latter had 39.[69]

Besides blocks of flats built in Felpham village[70] three were put up near the sea after the Second World War: one at the south end of Sea Road and two on the promenade further east.

Some of the 67 tenants of Felpham manor recorded in 1086 presumably lived in other parishes.[71] Thirty-nine persons were assessed to the subsidy in Felpham tithing in 1296, 29 in 1327, 35 in 1332,[72] and 73 in 1525.[73] In 1642 the protestation was signed by 89 adult males,[74] and 142 adults were enumerated in 1676.[75] There were 50 families in 1724.[76] From 306 in 1801 the population rose fast to 536 in 1811, perhaps because of the growth of the seaside resort. By 1901 it had reached 744, with an increase of over

46 e.g. A. H. Anderson, *Bognor and its Neighbourhood* (1st edn. [1917]), 41; (*c.* 1930), 29.

47 *Wood's Map of Bognor* (1904); O.S. Map 6", Suss. LXXIV. NW. & SW. (1914 edn.).

48 *Bognor Dir.* (1927); cf. *S.C.M.* iv. 32.

49 *Sunny Felpham* [1922], 7.

50 O.S. Map 6", Suss. LXXIV. NW. & SW. (1932, 1950 edns.).

51 W.S.R.O., Goodwood MS. 1371, Raper, Freeland, and Tyacke to R. H. Freke, 15 Jan. 1909; *Bognor Observer*, 18 Dec. 1912; cf. O.S. Map 6", Suss. LXXIV. NW. & SW. (1914 edn.); above, this section [area]; *Kelly's Dir. Suss.* (1909).

52 O.S. Map 6", Suss. LXXIV. NW. & SW. (1914, 1932 edns.).

53 *Kelly's Dir. Suss.* (1918).

54 *Bognor Dir.* (1927).

55 *Sunny Felpham* [1922], 26; *Bognor Post*, 10 May 1924. Summerley occurs as a field name in the earlier 19th cent.: W.S.R.O., Add. MS. 2060.

56 W.S.R.O., MP 3121.

57 e.g. ibid. SP 926.

58 *Bognor Dir.* (1927); *Bognor Regis Dir.* (1932).

59 O.S. Map 6", Suss. LXXIV. NE. (1950 edn.).

60 *Kelly's Dir. Suss.* (1934); O.S. Map 6", Suss. LXXIV. NE., NW. & SW. (1932, 1950 edns.).

61 O.S. Map 1/25,000, SU 80/90 (1981 edn.); SU 90 & SZ 99 (1958 edn.); *Bognor Regis Post*, 11 Sept. 1965.

62 *Felpham by the Sea*, 32.

63 *Bognor Dir.* (1927); *Bognor Regis Dir.* (1932); *Kelly's Dir. Suss.* (1934); O.S. Map 6", Suss. LXXIV. NE., NW. & SW. (1932, 1950 edns.); W.S.R.O., SP 460.

64 O.S. Map 1/25,000, SU 80/90 (1981 edn.); SU 90 & SZ 99 (1958 edn.); *Bognor Regis Post*, 12 Oct. 1963; 13 May 1967; 20 Feb. 1971.

65 O.S. Map 6", Suss. LXXIV. NE. (1932, 1950 edns.); *Residential Attractions of Bognor Regis, Felpham, Middleton-on-Sea and Dist.* (Gloucester, [1937]), 2, 3, 13 (copy in B.L.); *Property Reg. to Felpham, etc.* 7, 10.

66 G. Young, *Hist. Bognor Regis*, 262.

67 *Bognor Regis Observer*, 26 May 1972; 22 Jun. 1973; 24 May 1974; O.S. Map 1/25,000, SU 80/90 (1981 edn.)

68 *Bognor Observer*, 25 Aug. 1920; *Bognor Regis Dir.* (1932); W.S.R.O., Par. 81/54/7, letters, 15 Jan. 1921; 26 Nov. 1926; *Felpham by the Sea*, 32.

69 *Council Tenants' Hbk.* (Bognor Regis U.D.C. 1950), 7 (copy in W.S.R.O. libr.).

70 Above, this section.

71 *V.C.H. Suss.* i. 395; cf. below, econ. hist. (agric.).

72 *S.R.S.* x. 79, 135, 254–5.

73 Ibid. lvi. 55.

74 Ibid. v. 79–80.

75 *Compton Census*, ed. Whiteman, 144.

76 *S.R.S.* lxxviii. 65.

a quarter in the 1880s, and by 1911 it was 920. Increases of 75 per cent in the 1910s and 20s were put down mainly to summer visitors and residential development respectively. The population in 1931 was 2,827, of whom 2,359 lived in the part of the parish later included in Bognor Regis, 121 in that later included in Yapton, and 347 in that later included in Middleton.[77] In 1991 the new civil parish created in 1985 had 8,896 inhabitants.[78]

ROADS. The chief road access to Felpham before the 19th century was from Yapton.[79] Felpham bridge over the Aldingbourne rife existed by 1405, when after its destruction by flooding contributors to the cost of its repair were granted indulgences.[80] The rebuilt bridge suffered further damage later in the 15th century.[81] In 1807 Arundel and Chichester rapes were to share the expense of building a new bridge,[82] but at its repair in 1850, presumably after flooding, half the cost was paid by the sewers commissioners.[83] In 1878 the bridge had three arches and was of brick; it was replaced in 1924 by a wider bridge faced with stone,[84] which was itself replaced in 1993.[85]

The older roads of the parish linking the various settlements[86] were the eastern part of Felpham Way, Flansham Lane, Yapton Road,[87] and Elmer and Middleton roads. Limmer Lane, called Summer's Lane in the earlier 19th century,[88] perhaps from a surname recorded in the mid 16th,[89] seems to have led to land afterwards lost to the sea[90] and perhaps continued to the former Middleton village. In 1992 its eastern section, on the Summerley estate, was a private road.

In the mid 19th century the main Bognor–London road, which was also the Littlehampton road, ran through Felpham village and along Felpham Way and Flansham Lane; Limmer and Summerley lanes seem to have provided an alternative route in 1883.[91] Sea Road and Blake's Road were laid out in 1840 under the inclosure Act of 1826.[92] With Felpham's rapid growth in the 20th century traffic through the village became very busy[93] until a bypass, the western part of Felpham Way, was opened in 1938.[94] The Bognor Regis to Littlehampton road east of Flansham was straightened at two points before 1966.[95]

A carrier is recorded between 1814 and 1915; in the early 20th century he plied to Chichester three times a week. There were fly and cab proprietors in the earlier 20th century.[96] A daily bus service to Bognor began in 1899;[97] by *c.* 1922 there were frequent services to Littlehampton, Worthing, Brighton, Chichester, and Portsmouth.[98] In 1992 Midhurst and Haslemere (Surr.) could also be reached.

FELPHAM AS A SEASIDE RESORT. Until the mid 18th century Felpham's economy was based on agriculture and maritime activities. After that date it developed a new character as a holiday resort. The poet William Hayley enjoyed sea bathing there as a child in the 1750s,[99] and in 1770 he and others from Chichester visited Felpham for 'a little party of pleasure'.[1] There were bathing machines by 1781;[2] in newspaper advertisements placed between that date and 1799 of houses to let for the season the village, 'at once rural and marine', was extolled as also having a dry and healthy soil, opportunities for sailing, and a 'genteel' clientèle.[3] It was perhaps because of Felpham's evident success as a resort, albeit small, that Sir Richard Hotham chose nearby Bognor *c.* 1785 for his much larger projected undertaking of the same kind.[4]

Hayley bought a furnished cottage at Felpham in 1791 to continue his association with the sea and moved to the village permanently in 1800.[5] The duke of Richmond's sister-in-law, the sculptress Anne Seymour Damer, also visited the place in 1791 and other aristocratic patrons followed, many visiting Hayley.[6] Besides the attractions already indicated, there were great houses nearby to see, while boats could be hired for excursions to the Owers lightship or Selsey Bill.[7] In the early 19th century, in contrast to the grander style represented by Bognor's hotel, subscription room, library, and other visitors' facilities,[8] Felpham remained quiet and informal, while also taking the overflow of Bognor's visitors at busy times. There were several lodging houses in 1807, when in accommodation, views, and

77 *Census*, 1801–1931. The increase in 1821 was attributed to the nearness of Bognor; cf. *Kelly's Dir. Suss.* (1845).
78 *Census*, 1991.
79 e.g. *250 Yrs. of Mapmaking in Suss.* ed. H. Margary, pl. 14.
80 B.L. Add. MS. 39334, f. 32. It existed earlier if it was the bridge of S. Bersted against the sea mentioned in 1275: *S.A.C.* lxxxiv. 61.
81 L. Fleming, *Hist. Pagham*, ii. 380, 388, 390.
82 W.S.R.O., QAB/3/W 1, p. 32.
83 Ibid. QAB/2/W 12, no. 16.
84 S.A.S. libr., prints and drawings 1017; C.I.H.E. libr., GY/PH 2290; G. Young, *Cottage in the Fields*, 196; *Bognor Post*, 11 Oct. 1924.
85 *Bognor Regis Observer*, 23 Sept. 1993.
86 e.g. *250 Yrs. of Mapmaking in Suss.* pl. 14.
87 e.g. *S.R.S.* xxix, p. 33.
88 W.S.R.O., Add. MSS. 2073, 5179.
89 P.R.O., SC 6/Hen. VIII/3480, rot. 17. The modern name is recorded from 1851: *Felpham and Middleton Census Returns 1841–1881*, ed. B. Fletcher, 47.
90 e.g. W.S.R.O., Add. MS. 2060.
91 Ibid. Goodwood MS. E5618; ibid. Par. 81/12/1, p. [115]; ibid. Slindon MSS., bdle. NR 34, no. 1.
92 Ibid. Raper MSS., Felpham inclosure award.
93 G. Young, *Cottage in the Fields*, 176.
94 *W. Suss. Gaz.* 27 Oct. 1988.
95 O.S. Map 6", SU 90 SE. & SZ 99 NE. (1967 edn.).
96 *Felpham and Middleton Census Returns 1841–1881*, 17; *Kelly's Dir. Suss.* (1852 and later edns.); W.S.R.O., Par. 81/1/2/1.
97 *Bognor Observer*, 18 Oct. 1899.
98 *Sunny Felpham* [1922], 44 (copy in B.L.); cf. *Suss. Daily News*, 16 May 1928.
99 *Memoirs of Wm. Hayley*, ed. J. Johnson, i. 156.
1 M. Bishop, *Blake's Hayley*, 44.
2 *Suss. Wkly. Advertiser*, 3 Sept. 1781; cf. *Hants Chron.* 21 July 1783; 29 May 1786; 6 June 1791; J. B. Davis, *Origin and Descrip. of Bognor*, 96; *A New and Complete Guide to Bognor* (Bognor and Chich. 1814), 59.
3 *Hants Chron.* 21 July 1783; 29 May 1786; 6 June 1791; *Portsmouth Gaz.* 2 Dec. 1799; *The Chich. Guide* (Chich. *c.* 1795), 43 (copy in W.S.R.O. libr.).
4 Young, *Bognor Regis*, 10–11.
5 Bishop, *Hayley*, 142, 255, 263; cf. below, this section [worthies].
6 Young, *Bognor Regis*, 30, 59–60; *S.C.M.* iii. 43.
7 Davis, *Bognor*, 57–8; *W. Suss. Hist.* xxiii. 16; cf. *V.C.H. Suss.* ii. 163.
8 e.g. *Beauties of Eng. and Wales, Suss.* 63.

situation Felpham was reckoned far superior to South Bersted.[9]

In the mid 19th century other moneyed or retired people moved into the parish to live permanently,[10] together with at least one artist.[11] Nineteen parishioners besides clergy were listed as private residents in 1887, 30 in 1895, and 47 in 1899.[12] As a seaside resort Felpham retained its lack of formality in 1868 when bathing without machines was allowed there, one secluded place being reserved for women.[13] The resort function developed further thereafter. Two lodging houses were mentioned in 1878 and numbers later increased,[14] though letting lodgings was considered a precarious living in 1898.[15] Fifteen lodging or apartment houses were listed in 1895, 22 in 1899, and 40 in 1905.[16] In 1913 more than half were in Sea Road and streets to the east of it.[17]

From the early 20th century Felpham maintained its dual character of a seaside resort and a place for permanent residence. Both functions were enhanced by its relative seclusion, the mild, sunny, and healthy climate, the nearness of Bognor with its services and entertainments, and easy access from London. Besides the longstanding activities of bathing, fishing, and boating developed new ones like tennis and golf, and *c.* 1922 daily 'charabanc' excursions were on offer. Felpham also retained its lack of conventionality in contrast to larger resorts; unlike at Bognor there were no rules or bylaws about access to the sea, and at least one boarding house *c.* 1922 allowed 'bathing from house'.[18] Bathing huts could also be hired on part of the front.[19] About 1930 Felpham was described as the family resort *par excellence*.[20]

Alongside and gradually in place of apartment houses, holiday homes were built for permanent or occasional occupation or for letting.[21]

A hotel had been said to be a great need in 1884,[22] but none seems to have been built before the 1920s, when there were two: the Beachcroft on the front south of the village and the Southdowns in Felpham Way. By 1934 there were two others in Felpham Way and Flansham Lane.[23] There were several hotels and guest houses in the 1950s and 60s, when many houses were also let furnished;[24] in 1992, however, there were few guest houses and only two hotels in the modern parish.[25] Beach huts at Blake's Road were managed by Bognor Regis urban district council in 1970, when they could be hired daily, weekly, or by the year.[26] Houses by the sea east of Blake's Road retained private access to the beach until the construction of a promenade along that stretch of coast in the 1960s.[27]

SOCIAL AND CULTURAL ACTIVITIES. The annual meeting of a Felpham club or friendly society was celebrated in 1816 with a procession and singing.[28] A regatta and athletic sports were held in 1891.[29] A cricket club is said to have been founded in 1886, at first using a field on the Bognor side of the Aldingbourne rife.[30] By 1945 there was a pitch west of Flansham Lane.[31] Other sports facilities were provided for residents and visitors from the early 20th century. The 9-hole links of the Bognor golf club opened in 1906 lay partly in Felpham after the boundary change of 1913, but were replaced in 1922 by an 18-hole course in the north-west corner of the parish, where existing trees, bushes, and ditches were complemented by new landscaping including the planting of evergreens and flowering shrubs.[32] The club had 600 playing members in 1978.[33] Tennis courts existed by *c.* 1914 in Blake's Road,[34] where a tennis club was founded before *c.* 1922[35] and there was also a putting green in 1928.[36] Further tennis courts were laid down on the Felpham Beach and Summerley estates, the former surviving in 1992.[37] Boating remained popular in the 1920s, when boats could be hired and fishing tackle obtained on the sea front.[38] A boating club which flourished *c.* 1925[39] was succeeded in 1958 by the Felpham sailing club, which had *c.* 100 members, including many from

9 Young, *Bognor Regis*, 54; *Chich. Guide*, 43; Davis, *Bognor*, 51–2, 96–7; cf. Dally, *Bognor* (1828), 64; below, church.

10 Pigot, *Nat. Com. Dir.* (1832–4), 1007; *Kelly's Dir. Suss.* (1845 and later edns.).

11 *Kelly's Dir. Suss.* (1862, 1874); cf. ibid. (1934).

12 Ibid. (1887 and later edns.).

13 W.S.R.O., MP 3188, ff. 37, 61.

14 *Kelly's Dir. Suss.* (1878 and later edns.).

15 W.S.R.O., Ep. I/22A/2 (1898).

16 *Kelly's Dir. Suss.* (1895 and later edns.). Numbers thereafter declined, to 6 in 1934: ibid. (1934).

17 *Kelly's Dir. Suss.* (1913); Pike, *Bognor Dir.* (1912–13).

18 W.S.R.O., Add. MS. 29868, f. 1; *Bognor Observer*, 8 Mar. 1922; *Sunny Felpham* [1922], 7, 12, 24–5, 40, 44 (copy in B.L.); A. H. Anderson, *Bognor and its Neighbourhood* (1st edn. [1917]), 40; (9th edn. [1925]), 41–2; Ward, Lock & Co. *Bognor* [1928–9], 23; *Holiday Hbk. to Bognor Regis and W. Suss.* (Margate, early 1930s), p. viii (copy in C.I.H.E. libr.); *Residential Attractions of Bognor Regis, Felpham, Middleton-on-Sea and Dist.* (Gloucester, [1937]), 9 (copy in B.L.); below, pl. facing p. 170; cf. C.I.H.E. libr., GY 1171. For regulations at Bognor, W.S.R.O., MP 3188, *passim*.

19 *Sunny Felpham* [1922], 9; W.S.R.O., MP 3121.

20 A. H. Anderson, *Bognor Regis and its Neighbourhood* (*c.* 1930), 28.

21 e.g. *Bognor Observer*, 8 Mar. 1922; *Holiday Hbk. to Bognor Regis and W. Suss.* p. viii; *Residential Attractions of Bognor Regis, Felpham, Middleton-on-Sea and Dist.* 22. For later development, above, this section (settlement).

22 W.S.R.O., Add. MS. 41293.

23 *Kelly's Dir. Suss.* (1927, 1934).

24 *Bognor Regis, Aldwick and Felpham Official Guide* (*c.* 1953), 49, 51–2, 60, 67, 69, 71; *Official Guide to Bognor Regis, Aldwick and Felpham* (1962), 52, 60–1, 68, 77–9.

25 Cf. *Bognor Regis Observer*, 2 Jun. 1988.

26 *Official Guide to Bognor Regis, Aldwick and Felpham* (1970), 81.

27 Above, this section (landscape hist.).

28 Henry E. Huntington Libr., San Marino, California, John Marsh's diaries, vol. 31, pp. 47–8 (microfilm at W.S.R.O., MF 1169); cf. M. Bishop, *Blake's Hayley*, 330.

29 C.I.H.E. libr., GY 4165.

30 *Bognor Regis Post*, 23 Sept. 1967; cf. *W. Suss. Gaz.* 21 Nov. 1895; *Kelly's Dir. Suss.* (1927).

31 G. Young, *Cottage in the Fields*, 61–2.

32 G. Beale, *Bognor Regis Golf Club, 1892–1992* (Bognor Regis, 1992), 22, 24–5, 38, 69–70, 74; O.S. Map 6", Suss. LXXIV. NW. & SW. (1914 edn.); above, this section [area].

33 *W. Suss. Gaz.* 30 Mar. 1978.

34 P.R.O., IR 58/22733, no. 266.

35 *Sunny Felpham*, 14, 26.

36 *Felpham by the Sea*, ed. T. & A. Hudson, 41.

37 *Sunny Felpham*, 26; *Bognor Post*, 10 May 1924; inf. from Mrs. S. Hoad, Felpham.

38 *Sunny Felpham*, 12, 31; cf. above, this section (Felpham as seaside resort).

39 A. H. Anderson, *Bognor and its Neighbourhood* (9th edn. [1925]), 42.

Bognor, in 1969 and 400 in 1973, when a club house was opened east of Blake's Road.[40] Sand yachting and horse riding could also be enjoyed in 1928.[41] A sports club was mentioned in 1922,[42] when a football club also existed.[43]

After the incorporation of the west part of the ancient parish into Bognor Regis in 1933, the urban district council *c.* 1935 bought land for recreation south of Felpham Way,[44] where King George's field was opened before 1940. Other sports and recreation grounds in the parish include one by Flansham Lane recorded by the same date.[45] The Arun leisure centre, built jointly by Arun district and West Sussex county councils and managed by the former, was opened at the then Felpham comprehensive school in 1978;[46] in 1992 sports played included squash, basketball, badminton, indoor cricket, and American football. A swimming pool was built there *c.* 1995. In 1992 the district council also owned Old Rectory gardens (2 a.) in Felpham village, which had been conveyed to Bognor Regis urban district council as an open space in 1959.[47]

An outbuilding of the Fox inn was used as a parish room by 1901[48] and in 1914 there was also a club room at the George.[49] A church hall was opened in 1924 in Limmer Lane[50] but in the 1990s was replaced by a community hall nearer the church. Felpham memorial village hall was opened in 1955;[51] a voluntary library run there from 1960 was replaced by a county council mobile library service in 1965.[52] After 1978 the Arun leisure centre offered other meeting places, including a hall to seat 900.[53]

A residents' association was founded as an early environmental pressure group in 1927 and survived in 1979.[54] Other early clubs were an amateur dramatic society, the Falcheham players, started in 1930[55] and still in existence in 1992, and a folk dance club formed in 1933 which had 79 members in 1953.[56] A cottage gardeners', later horticultural, society for Felpham and Middleton existed by 1922 and survived in 1994.[57] The Felpham conservation society, founded in 1980,[58] had 600 members in 1985.[59]

There were two retailers of wine or ale in 1543,[60] one alehouse in 1605, and several in 1613.[61] A victualler was recorded in 1706.[62] Of the two chief inns of the village the Fox existed by 1799[63] and was rebuilt after virtual destruction by fire in 1946,[64] while the George existed, as the George and Dragon, by 1832.[65] There was one other inn there in the mid 19th century[66] and there were two in 1992. The Brewer's Arms in Felpham Way near the junction with Middleton Road also existed by 1839; the landlord carried on a wheelwright's business between that date and 1851, when he also farmed 53 a.[67] The inn was replaced by the Southdowns hotel, a roadhouse, in 1924.[68]

Two coastal beacons had been erected south-east of the church by 1587 in connexion with defence against the Spanish Armada.[69]

An official post to Felpham was set up in 1809.[70]

The Bognor Water Co. was empowered to supply the parish in 1875;[71] some water was still obtained from wells in 1908,[72] but by *c.* 1922 the company was supplying part at least of the parish.[73] There was a main sewer running to the sea by 1883[74] and by 1899 three sewage outfalls, one at Felpham sluice, which also served Bognor, and two further east; many properties in Felpham village, however, then remained without proper drainage.[75] In 1910 a new scheme for the drainage of Bognor and Felpham planned jointly by Bognor urban district council and Westhampnett rural district council was the subject of local opposition,[76] as was a later one of 1928.[77] In 1925 most properties in the parish were still drained by cesspits.[78] The outfall at Felpham sluice remained Bognor's chief means of sewage disposal until a new outfall was opened west of the town centre in 1972.[79]

The Bognor Gas Light and Coke Co. was empowered to supply the parish with gas in

40 *Bognor Regis Post*, 1 Feb. 1969; *Bognor Regis Observer*, 1 Jun. 1973.
41 *Felpham by the Sea*, 41.
42 *Kelly's Dir. Suss.* (1922).
43 *Bognor Dir.* (1922); cf. *Kelly's Dir. Bognor Regis* (1940).
44 *Bognor Regis Observer*, 15 May 1935.
45 O.S. Map 6", Suss. LXXIV. NE. (1950 edn.).
46 *Bognor Regis Observer*, 8 Sept. 1978.
47 Arun D.C., deeds of Old Rectory Gdns.
48 P.R.O., IR 58/22732, no. 112; W.S.R.O., Felpham par. rec., terrier and inv. of ch. 1901 (Acc. 8028); *Bognor Regis Local Hist. Soc. Newsletter*, xxvii. 24.
49 P.R.O., IR 58/22731, no. 69.
50 *Bognor Regis Observer*, 15 Feb. 1974.
51 Ibid. 3 June 1955.
52 *Brighton Evening Argus*, 10 Mar. 1965; *W. Suss. Gaz.* 4 Mar. 1965.
53 *Bognor Regis Observer*, 8 Sept. 1978.
54 Ibid. 6 Apr. 1979.
55 *Felpham Village Coronation Festivities Souvenir Programme* (1953), p. [15] (copy in Worthing Ref. Libr.).
56 Ibid.
57 *Bognor Dir.* (1922, 1929); local inf.
58 *Bognor Regis Observer*, 29 Aug. 1980.
59 *W. Suss. Gaz.* 2 May 1985.
60 W.S.R.O., PHA 6683, f. 19v.
61 *Cal. Assize Rec. Suss. Jas. I*, pp. 18, 54; cf. *S.R.S.* xlix. 4, 33, 43.
62 W.S.R.O., Ep. I/29/81/68.
63 C.I.H.E. libr., GY 322.
64 *Suss. Daily News*, 14 Oct. 1946; 20 Jan. 1950.
65 Pigot, *Nat. Com. Dir.* (1832–4), 1007.
66 *Felpham and Middleton Census Returns 1841–1881*, ed. B. Fletcher, 17, 47.
67 Pigot, *Nat. Com. Dir.* (1839), 659; *Felpham and Middleton Census Returns 1841–1881*, 30; cf. *Kelly's Dir. Suss.* (1852).
68 *Bognor Post*, 29 Nov. 1924.
69 *Armada Surv.* ed. Lower.
70 J. Greenwood, *Posts of Suss.* 21, 38.
71 54 & 55 Vic. c. 188 (Local), reciting Bognor Water Order, 1875.
72 W. Whitaker, *Water Supply of Suss., Suppl.* 151.
73 *Sunny Felpham*, 7; cf. F. H. Edmunds, *Wells and Springs of Suss.* 25, 36.
74 W.S.R.O., Goodwood MS. E5618; cf. ibid. Felpham par. rec., terrier and inv. of ch. 1901 (Acc. 8028).
75 *W. Suss. Gaz.* 9 Feb. 1899; H. C. L. Morris, *Bognor as a Health Resort* (Bognor, 1904), 10; cf. O.S. Map 6", Suss. LXXIV. NW. & SW. (1914 edn.).
76 *Bognor Observer*, 28 Dec. 1910; W.S.R.O., Par. 81/54/5.
77 *Suss. Daily News*, 16 May 1928.
78 W.S.R.O., Par. 81/54/10.
79 *W. Suss. Gaz.* 3 Oct. 1968; *Brighton Evening Argus*, 25 Oct. 1972.

1871[80] and gas street lighting was introduced to the village street in 1923.[81] By 1929 the village was also supplied with electricity,[82] which had reached Flansham hamlet by 1938.[83]

A health centre for Felpham and Middleton was opened at the southern end of Flansham Park in 1979.[84]

The poet William Hayley[85] (d. 1820) built himself a house, the Turret, in Felpham village and moved there permanently in 1800. The two-storeyed building, later known as Turret House, had a lofty turret of square plan over the entrance which carried a circular lookout giving fine coastal views. The upper floor of the three-bayed east front housed a library decorated with busts and pictures. The garden included a covered way for riding exercise.[86] Battlements were added and the building otherwise considerably altered later in the 19th century, and by 1951 the house had been converted into flats. It was demolished in 1961.[87]

Resident in the parish at the same time as Hayley was the Revd. Cyril Jackson, former dean of Christ Church, Oxford (d. 1819), and tutor to the Prince Regent, who leased the Old Rectory from 1807 or earlier; despite the proximity of their houses, however, the two men did not associate.[88]

It was at Hayley's instigation that William Blake spent the years 1800–3 in a cottage close to the Old Rectory, writing, engraving, and painting portraits chiefly of poets for Hayley's library. Though he left Felpham in disillusion Blake was at first happy there, describing it as 'the sweetest spot on earth', 'a dwelling for immortals', and the villagers as 'polite and modest', the men 'the mildest of the human race'.[89]

The Glaswegian artist and printer James Guthrie moved his Pear Tree press to Flansham in 1907 and lived and worked there until his death in 1952. He was visited by his friend the poet Edward Thomas,[90] and in the 1920s by the novelist Evelyn Waugh who proposed himself as his apprentice.[91] Another Edwardian resident of Flansham was the actress Mrs. Lewis Waller (Florence West) (d. 1912), who lived at Chessels house, holding theatrical house parties attended by, among others, Aubrey Beardsley and Mr. and Mrs. Beerbohm Tree.[92]

A Roman Catholic children's home existed in Limmer Lane in the 1880s.[93] Other contemporary institutions were a convalescent home for young women in 1895, a home for convalescent children between *c.* 1910 and 1938, and a nursing home in the 1920s and 30s.[94] In 1992 there were several residential care and nursing homes in the modern parish.

MANOR AND OTHER ESTATES. King Alfred (d. 899) devised an estate at *FELPHAM* to Osferth, a relative,[95] and in 953 King Eadred granted what may have been the same, described as 30 hides, to his mother Eadgifu. From the bounds listed the latter was clearly at least as large as the area of the ancient parish.[96] By 1066 Felpham had passed to Shaftesbury abbey (Dors.),[97] with which it remained until the Dissolution;[98] in 1244 it was apparently two fees.[99] Land held by Shaftesbury in the later Middle Ages in Egdean, Fittleworth, and Kirdford represents Wealden outliers of the Anglo-Saxon estate,[1] but by that period the main part of the manor seems to have been coterminous with Felpham ancient parish.[2] The reduction in hidation between 1066 and 1086 may be due to the creation of Elmer manor.[3] In 1086 Felpham had six haws in Chichester.[4]

In 1574 the Crown granted the manor to Robert Dudley, earl of Leicester;[5] he sold it in 1584 to (Sir) Henry Goring of Burton (d. 1594), who was succeeded in the direct line by Sir William[6] (d. 1601–2) and Sir Henry (d. 1626).[7] The manor house and demesne were excepted from the Crown grant of 1574[8] but also belonged to the Gorings by 1614; they were sold in 1620 and the manor itself in 1623 to pay the second Sir Henry's debts; the purchaser was Nicholas Thompson[9] (d. 1628),[10] whose widow Mary was dealing with the manor in 1630.[11] In 1631, however, Felpham was in the hands of his two daughters and coheirs Elizabeth, wife of John Boys, and Catherine,[12] by 1635 the wife of Robert Anderson.[13] In 1640 the estate was divided

80 8 Edw. VII, c. 70 (Local), reciting Bognor Gas Order, 1871.
81 *Bognor Regis Observer*, 26 Jan. 1973; cf. W.S.R.O., Par. 81/54/9.
82 *Bognor Regis Observer*, 2 Nov. 1979.
83 G. Young, *Chron. of a Country Cottage*, 82.
84 Local inf.
85 Para. based mainly on N. Owens, *Wm. Blake and Felpham* (Bognor Regis, 1986); M. Bishop, *Blake's Hayley*, 200, 204, 212, 255–7, 347, and pls. facing 160–1; *S.C.M.* iii. 41–2; G. C. Williamson and H. Engleheart, *Geo. Engleheart*, facing pp. 12, 14.
86 Dally, *Bognor* (1828), 61.
87 *Bognor Regis Post*, 11 Feb. 1961.
88 *D.N.B.*; J. B. Davis, *Origin and Descrip. of Bognor*, 96; Dally, *Bognor* (1828), 60, 63.
89 *Blake: Complete Writings*, ed. G. Keynes (1969), 803, 808, 810; Owens, *Wm. Blake and Felpham*; [W. Wells], *Wm. Blake's 'Heads of the Poets'* (Manchester City Art Galls. n.d.) (copy in W.S.R.O. libr.).
90 G. Young, *Cottage in the Fields*, 67, 72–6; *S.C.M.* xxvii. 166–7.
91 M. Stannard, *Evelyn Waugh: the Early Years*, 104–5.
92 *D.N.B.* s.v. Waller; Young, op. cit. 37, 159; G. Young, *Come into the Country*, 65.
93 W.S.R.O., Ep. I/22A/1 (1884); *Kelly's Dir. Suss.* (1887); inf. from Mrs. S. Gould, Felpham.
94 *Kelly's Dir. Suss.* (1895 and later edns.); C.I.H.E. libr., GY/PC 1395; W.S.R.O., IR 31, f. 17.
95 *S.A.C.* lxxxvii. 135.
96 Ibid. lxxxviii. 72–3; *brines flert* or *brynes fleot* was the Aldingbourne rife: ibid. lxxxvi. 51, 53, 57; cf. above, intro. [area].
97 *V.C.H. Suss.* i. 395.
98 e.g. *Cal. Chart. R.* 1257–1300, 433; *Feud. Aids*, v. 143; *Valor Eccl.* (Rec. Com.), i. 277.
99 *S.R.S.* lxvii. 104.
1 Ibid. xlvi, p. 326; Hutchins, *Hist. Dorset*, iii (1868), 86–7; *L. & P. Hen. VIII*, xv, p. 214; below, econ. hist. (agric.).
2 e.g. Hutchins, op. cit. 86–7; *L. & P. Hen. VIII*, xv, p. 214; *S.R.S.* ii, p. 44; xix. 162.
3 Below, Middleton-on-Sea, manors (Elmer).
4 *V.C.H. Suss.* i. 395; cf. B.L. Add. MS. 39334, f. 31v., reading 8.
5 *Cal. Pat.* 1572–5, pp. 181, 185.
6 *Goodwood Estate Archives*, i, ed. F. W. Steer and J. Venables, p. 33; *S.R.S.* xxxiii, pp. 35–6.
7 *V.C.H. Suss.* vi (1), 42; cf. W.S.R.O., Add. MS. 41030 (TS. cat.).
8 *Cal. Pat.* 1572–5, p. 185.
9 W.S.R.O., Add. MSS. 41030, 41033–6 (TS. cat.); *Goodwood Estate Archives*, i, p. 34.
10 P.R.O., C 142/452, no. 40.
11 *Cal. S.P. Dom.* 1629–31, 301; A. Fletcher, *County Community in Peace and War*, 173, wrongly reading 1640.
12 P.R.O., C 60/520, no. 28; C 142/452, no. 40.
13 *S.R.S.* xix. 162; cf. *Goodwood Estate Archives*, i, p. 34.

The sea front in the early 20th century looking east

The sea front in 1988 from the south-west

FELPHAM

Eastergate: Malthouse Cottages

Eastergate: Shelley House

Eastergate: The Old House

Yapton: Berri Court from the south

between them, the manor itself, with what were later Innerwick and Outerwick farms and other demesne land, going to Robert and Catherine, and the rest of the demesne in Felpham and Flansham to John and Elizabeth.[14]

Robert Anderson (fl. 1635; d. 1686 × 1688) was succeeded by a namesake (fl. 1697), who was succeeded before 1702 by (Sir) Richard Anderson.[15] He in 1704 sold the manor to Francis Doyley[16] (d. in or after 1711). Francis's son and namesake (fl. 1723–4), was succeeded before 1730 by his son Thomas.[17] At Thomas's death in 1770 the manor passed to his son Matthias,[18] who in 1801 sold it to William Pellett. He and his wife Charlotte sold Felpham in 1821 to John Heather Hussey and William Titchenor, mercers and drapers of Chichester.[19] Hussey died in 1827 and was succeeded by his son William,[20] probably the William Heather Hussey who died *c.* 1862.[21] In 1849 the estate included Hoe farm at Flansham and what was called Manor Farmhouse in Felpham Way. By that date William Titchenor had died,[22] his heirs being his daughters Maria, Elizabeth, and Frances.[23] About 1866 Elizabeth and Frances, with Mary Ann Hussey, evidently William's widow, sold the manor to Charles Thomas Marshall,[24] who conveyed it in 1870 to James Wilson,[25] a civil engineer.[26] Wilson was still lord in 1881.[27] The lordship was later said to belong to W. M. Chinnery (in 1887), Mrs. Auld (1895), James Gibson (1899–1905), and Mrs. J. W. Clayton (1913–38).[28] Manor Farmhouse with 54 a. had meanwhile been exchanged by C. T. Marshall *c.* 1867 to the duke of Richmond.[29]

Elizabeth Thompson's share of the Felpham estate was conveyed by her husband John Boys in 1666 to Roger Sparkes,[30] then vicar of Felpham (d. 1679),[31] from whom it descended in the Sparkes family, apparently through Robert (d. 1698),[32] Thomas (fl. 1703–20), and Thomas's son Robert (d. 1742 or 1743),[33] who devised lands in Felpham to his son, also Thomas.[34] Another Robert Sparkes (perhaps fl. 1792) was one of the chief landowners of the parish in 1819. Robert was succeeded, as tenants in common, by his sons Charles and Francis,[35] who in 1824 had 230 a. in Felpham.[36] In 1827 they conveyed that land to the duke of Richmond,[37] and it afterwards descended with the other estates of the dukedom.[38]

In the mid 19th century the former Sparkes farm was known as Felpham farm.[39] The reunited demesne farm was sold in 1911 to the tenant Robert Sadler,[40] part passing in 1922 to Summerley Estates Ltd.[41]

A manor house, evidently once the residence of Shaftesbury abbey's bailiff, was mentioned from 1530.[42] Its site is unknown, but three buildings were later associated with the manor.

Church House, which descended with the Boys share of the estate,[43] occupies a typical position for a manor house close to the church. It is a three-bayed, two-storeyed building of the early or mid 18th century with a front of red and grey brick and a contemporary staircase.[44] In the 1880s and 90s it was a farmhouse.[45] The building was saved from demolition in 1966[46] and was remodelled internally for office use in 1988.

The Old Manor House in Felpham Way belonged to the Anderson share of the estate[47] and was called Manor Farmhouse in 1849.[48] The main range of the present building is probably 18th-century, with a rendered west front and a later rear extension. In the 1930s it was a hotel[49] and in 1988 it was remodelled as a nursing home.[50]

The Manor House in Limmer Lane owes its name to the fact that successive owners of the manor lived there from 1871; an earlier title was Felpham House.[51] Of the later 18th century,[52] it has a rendered front of five narrow bays and three storeys above a high basement. The interior was extensively refitted in the early 19th century, and later in the century tall bay windows were added to the south front and extensions put up to east and west.[53] Large cellars included the kitchens and servants' hall. The grounds in 1883 covered 2¼ a.,[54] most of which remained garden in 1988.

14 *Goodwood Estate Archives*, i, p. 34.
15 *S.R.S.* xix. 162; W.S.R.O., Add. MSS. 6973, ff. 1–[16]; 47338 (TS. cat.); G.E.C. *Baronetage*, ii. 211–12. He wrongly laid claim to his uncle's baronetcy: ibid. ii. 211.
16 W.S.R.O., Add. MS. 23635.
17 Ibid. Add. MS. 6973, ff. [17–18v.]; ibid. Goodwood MS. E270.
18 Le Neve, *Fasti, 1541–1857, Chich.* 13; *Alum. Cantab. 1752–1900*; cf. W.S.R.O., Add. MS. 6973, ff. [27v., 34v.].
19 W.S.R.O., Add. MS. 23707; ibid. Goodwood MS. E270.
20 Ibid. Add. MSS. 11467 (TS. cat.); 23668; cf. ibid. 6973, f. [37].
21 W.S.R.O., Add. MS. 23709; cf. ibid. 23668; *Goodwood Estate Archives*, i, p. 161.
22 W.S.R.O., Add. MS. 23667.
23 Ibid. 23685, 23697.
24 Ibid. 23704, 23711–12.
25 Elwes & Robinson, *W. Suss.* 89, wrongly reading C. F. Marshall.
26 *Felpham and Middleton Census Returns 1841–1881*, ed. B. Fletcher, 85.
27 W.S.R.O., Add. MS. 6973, f. [39]; cf. *Kelly's Dir. Suss.* (1882).
28 *Kelly's Dir. Suss.* (1887 and later edns.).
29 W.S.R.O., Goodwood MS. E5156; cf. ibid. Add. MS. 29868, f. 1; ibid. IR 31, f. 6.
30 *S.R.S.* xix. 163.
31 B.L. Add. MS. 39334, f. 28.
32 W.S.R.O., Par. 81/1/1/1, f. 91v.
33 *Goodwood Estate Archives*, i, pp. 157, 159; cf. *S.R.S.* iv. 31.
34 W.S.R.O., Slindon MSS., bdle. NR 73, no. 2.
35 Ibid. Goodwood MSS. E2454, E2457; *Goodwood Estate Archives*, i, p. 161; Dallaway, *Hist. W. Suss.* ii (1) (1819), 7.
36 W.S.R.O., Add. MS. 2060.
37 *Goodwood Estate Archives*, i, p. 161.
38 e.g. ibid. p. 242.
39 e.g. W.S.R.O., Goodwood MS. E19, p. 39.
40 Ibid. E21, p. 38.
41 C.I.H.E. libr., GY 665.
42 *Cal. Pat.* 1563–6, p. 356, reciting 1530 lease; 1572–5, p. 185.
43 e.g. W.S.R.O., Add. MS. 2060.
44 A drawing of *c.* 1795 shows a central gable or pediment, probably in error: W.S.R.O., PD 2586B, f. 106.
45 *Felpham and Middleton Census Returns 1841–1881*, 120; *Kelly's Dir. Suss.* (1895).
46 *Bognor Regis Post*, 29 Jan. 1966.
47 e.g. W.S.R.O., Add. MS. 23667; ibid. TD/W 54.
48 Above, this section.
49 *Kelly's Dir. Suss.* (1934, 1938).
50 Cf. *Bognor Regis Observer*, 28 June 1990.
51 *Felpham and Middleton Census Returns 1841–1881*, 85, 116; *Kelly's Dir. Suss.* (1874 and later edns.).
52 Cf. *250 Yrs. of Mapmaking in Suss.* ed. H. Margary, pl. 14. The ho. is apparently that described at *Suss. Wkly. Advertiser*, 3 Sept. 1781; *Hants Chron.* 21 July 1783; 29 May 1786; 6 June 1791 (as 'new built'); *Portsmouth Gaz.* 2 Dec. 1799.
53 Cf. sale poster, 1893, in possession of Mrs. M. Pryce, The Manor Ho., Limmer Lane.
54 W.S.R.O., Goodwood MS. E5618.

INNERWICK FARM[55] was retained by (Sir) Richard Anderson at his sale of the manor in 1704 and sold by him to Richard Gibbs in 1714.[56] Gibbs (d. 1720) was succeeded in turn by his son John (d. 1760) and John's son Richard,[57] from whom the farm passed by 1798 to his mortgagee William Cosens.[58] Meanwhile *OUTERWICK FARM* (183 a.)[59] had been sold in 1791 by Matthias Doyley to Sir Richard Hotham of Bognor, after whose death in 1799 it was acquired by William Cosens. At William's death in 1811 his estate in Felpham was divided between his sons Thomas and Edmund, Thomas receiving Innerwick farm (175 a.) and Edmund Outerwick (134 a.). At Thomas's death in 1864 Innerwick was sold to John Kent, former racehorse trainer to the duke of Richmond,[60] passing also by sale in 1894 to F. J. Neale[61] and in 1919 to P. A. Norman.[62] Outerwick was sold by Edmund Cosens in 1832 to William Allin of Arundel (fl. *c.* 1844),[63] whose daughter and heir Eliza married Henry Hounsom; *c.* 1910 it belonged to Henry's son William A. Hounsom[64] (d. 1934).[65] Between 1899 or earlier and 1912 or later it was let to F. J. Neale.[66] Much of the land of both estates was afterwards built over, but part remained open space in 1992 as a golf course and school playing fields.

Land at Flansham which members of the Wyatt family bought from Robert Dudley, earl of Leicester, 1574 × 1584[67] became the nucleus of the modern *FLANSHAM FARM*. In 1722 Richard Wyatt conveyed 150 a. at Flansham to his son William,[68] presumably the William who died in 1757.[69] Apparently in 1790 the family's estate at Flansham was sold to William Dyer[70] (fl. 1808),[71] who conveyed it in 1823 to George Amoore.[72] Amoore acquired other former Wyatt land at Flansham from Richard Hasler in 1825[73] and in 1840 sold the whole estate, of *c.* 400 a.,[74] to Thomas Sanctuary of Rusper (d. 1876).[75] In 1878 it was enlarged through the purchase by Thomas's son the Ven. Thomas Sanctuary from the heirs of Charles Duke (d. 1860) of Chessels and Chapel farms,[76] which had earlier belonged to the Bridger family.[77] The land comprised *c.* 500 a. in 1879.[78] By 1882 it had passed to C. S. Leslie of Slindon, descending with the Slindon House estate[79] until in 1908 part (242 a.) was sold to John Langmead (d. 1950). From him that part descended in the direct line to Jack (d. 1978) and Donald Langmead (fl. 1988).[80]

An estate at Ancton called Leagores (142 a.), the nucleus of the modern *ANCTON FARM*, was conveyed to Joseph Coote in 1822.[81] Joseph owned 150 a. at Ancton *c.* 1844,[82] which after his death in that year passed to Thomas Coote, who had 149 a. at Ancton in 1858.[83] In 1876 Thomas conveyed the land to (Sir) Frederick Dixon-Hartland, after which it descended with Middleton farm.[84] Another estate at Ancton, farmed from the modern Ancton House hotel,[85] was bought in 1832 from the Bridger family by Richard Coote;[86] *c.* 1844 it had 174 a.[87] After 1852 it too descended with Middleton farm.[88]

The *RECTORY* estate apparently enjoyed all the tithes of the parish before the Dissolution;[89] in 1341 there were besides a house, fixed rents worth 3*s.*, 8a. of land, and some meadow and pasture.[90] The site of the house is likely to have been the same as later;[91] from 1615 there were 6–8 a. of rectorial glebe lying chiefly east of it.[92] In 1351 the estate was managed by a bailiff[93] but from 1521 it seems usually to have been let;[94] between the 17th century and the mid 19th leases were for three lives.[95] In the late 18th

55 Para. largely based on *Felpham by the Sea*, ed. T. & A. Hudson, 26–32.

56 W.S.R.O., Add. MS. 23635–6; ibid. S.A.S. MS. WH 82 (TS. cat.).

57 Ibid. Add. MS. 23654; ibid. Par. 81/1/1/1, f. 94; ibid. S.A.S. MSS. WH 94, 102 (TS. cat.).

58 Ibid. QDE/2/1, Felpham, 1791, 1798 (inf. from the late Miss H. Gibbs, and Mrs. S. Gould, Felpham); ibid. S.A.S. MS. WH 117.

59 Ibid. Add. MS. 45424.

60 Cf. D. Hunn, *Goodwood*, 136–7; *Kelly's Dir. Suss.* (1845 and later edns.).

61 Cf. P.R.O., IR 58/22731, no. 46; W.S.R.O., Add. MS. 20288; *Kelly's Dir. Suss.* (1903).

62 Cf. W.S.R.O., Add. MS. 20288; *Kelly's Dir. Suss.* (1934, 1938).

63 W.S.R.O., TD/W 54.

64 Ibid. IR 31, f. 7; cf. ibid. Add. MS. 14584 (TS. cat.); *Kelly's Dir. Suss.* (1878 and later edns.).

65 Below, Yapton, manors (Yapton Coverts).

66 P.R.O., IR 58/22731, no. 47; W.S.R.O., Add. MS. 14584 (TS. cat.).

67 P.R.O., C 2/Jas. I/W 25/66; C 3/388, no. 38; C 142/278, no. 150; W.S.R.O., S.A.S. MS. B 529 (TS. cat.); above, this section (Felpham man.).

68 W.S.R.O., Slindon MSS., bdle. NR 66, no. 1; cf. *S.R.S.* iv. 31; *S.A.C.* xxiii. 76.

69 W.S.R.O., Add. MS. 34668.

70 Ibid. Slindon MSS., bdle. NR 73, no. 8 (TS. cat.); Elwes & Robinson, *W. Suss.* 89.

71 W.S.R.O., Slindon MSS., bdle. NR 96, no. 1 (TS. cat.).

72 Ibid. Slindon MSS., bdles. NR 34, no. 5; NR 67, no. 2; *S.A.C.* xii. 90 n.

73 W.S.R.O., Slindon MSS., bdle. NR 66, nos. 3, 6–8.

74 Ibid. Slindon MSS., bdles. NR 32, no. 6; NR 34, nos. 1–2, 5; ibid. TD/W 54.

75 Ibid. Slindon MSS., bdles. NR 32, no. 9; NR 34, no. 2; cf. *Kelly's Dir. Suss.* (1852 and later edns.).

76 W.S.R.O., Slindon MSS., bdle. NR 32, nos. 2, 9; ibid. SP 258. The former presumably commemorated a fam. recorded at Flansham in 1683: P.R.O., C 78/1302, no. 9.

77 W.S.R.O., Add. MSS. 514, 11752 (TS. cat.); ibid. Slindon MSS., bdles. NR 32, no. 5; NR 75, nos. 1, 19; NR 95, no. 1; cf. *S.R.S.* iv. 31. In 1819 Thos. Covey Bridger was one of the 2 largest landowners in the par.: Dallaway, *Hist. W. Suss.* ii (1) (1819), 7.

78 W.S.R.O., SP 258.

79 *Kelly's Dir. Suss.* (1882); *V.C.H. Suss.* iv. 235.

80 W.S.R.O., Slindon MSS., NR 97, ff. 32v.–34v.; *Bognor Regis Observer*, 27 Oct. 1978; *W. Suss. Gaz.* 28 May 1981; inf. from Mr. D. Langmead, Flansham.

81 *S.R.S.* xxix, p. 157; W.S.R.O., Add. MSS. 11765 (TS. cat.).

82 W.S.R.O., TD/W 54.

83 Ibid. Add. MS. 11802.

84 Ibid. Add. MS. 11815 (TS. cat.); ibid. IR 31, f. 5; W. Suss. C.C. property dept., terrier.

85 W.S.R.O., Add. MS. 11815.

86 Ibid. Add. MSS. 11772 (TS. cat.); 11813.

87 W.S.R.O., TD/W 54.

88 Ibid. Add. MSS. 11801, 11803, 11805–15 (TS. cat.); ibid. IR 31, f. 5; W. Suss. C.C. property dept., terrier; *Rep. Com. Coast Erosion* [Cd. 4461], p. 19, H.C. (1909), xiv.

89 e.g. *Inq. Non.* (Rec. Com.), 369. Later it had only the great tithes: B.L. Add. MS. 5699, f. 52; W.S.R.O., Ep. I/25/1 (1615); ibid. TD/W 54; Dallaway, *Hist. W. Suss.* ii (1) (1819), 8.

90 *Inq. Non.* (Rec. Com.), 369.

91 W.S.R.O., Ep. I/25/1 (1615): lying N. of S. Town field. Cf. below, econ. hist. (agric.).

92 W.R.S.O., Ep. I/25/1 (1615, 1687); ibid. TD/W 54.

93 B.L. Add. MS. 39334, f. 13.

94 Ibid. Add. MSS. 5699, f. 52; 39334, ff. 18v., 26v.; 39359, f. 68; W.S.R.O., Ep. I/26/1, f. 6; Ep. I/29/81/41; ibid. S.A.S. MS. B 532 (TS. cat.); *S.R.S.* xlii. 145; lviii. 221, 244; lxxviii. 65; Dally, *Bognor* (1828), 56.

95 *S.R.S.* xix. 163; lviii, pp. 221, 244; B.L. Add. MSS. 5699, f. 52; 39334, f. 18v.; W.S.R.O., Ecc. Comm. 3/28 (TS. cat.); ibid. S.A.S. MS. B 532 (TS. cat.); ibid. TD/W 54.

century and early 19th the lease was held by members of the Steele family.[96]

At the commutation of tithes in 1843–4 the rector received £720 2*s.* tithe rent charge;[97] in 1854 that passed to the ecclesiastical commissioners,[98] who in 1865 assigned it as part of the endowment of Chichester cathedral.[99] By 1849 the rectory house was let to the vicar,[1] and from 1861 both it and the 8 a. of glebe were vested in him and his successors.[2]

The long north–south range of the house called the Old Rectory is 17th-century. A taller block with a two-storeyed bay, providing a new entrance and parlour, was added to the south end by the lessee Thomas Steele (d. 1775),[3] the old building becoming the service wing. There is an 18th-century staircase, not *in situ*. A cross wing was added at the north end, probably in the 19th century. The south front was extended westwards after the early 19th century[4] and a colonnade was added to it in the early 20th,[5] when part of the building was used for church purposes.[6] New stables and a coach house were built in 1874.[7] In 1926 the house was bought by F. G. Penny, M.P., created in 1937 Lord Marchwood (d. 1955), whose son and heir Peter sold it in 1958,[8] the interior later being remodelled into 11 flats for old people.[9] At about the same time the exterior was covered in pebbledash.

Tortington priory had 10 a. in Felpham at the Dissolution.[10]

A farm of 80–90 a. at Flansham, with other land and pasture rights, was conveyed in 1624 as part of the founding endowment of Thompson's hospital or almshouse in Petworth. It was later called the Hospital farm.[11] In 1921, when it was 56 a. in area, it was sold by the governors of the almshouse to West Sussex county council.[12]

ECONOMIC HISTORY. AGRICULTURE. The Anglo-Saxon estate called Felpham in 953 had detached land in Egdean or Fittleworth, Kirdford, and Petworth which included both houses and common woodland pasture.[13] Agricultural statistics given for Felpham in Domesday Book seem also to relate to a much larger area than the parish,[14] and the manor still had holdings in Egdean and Fittleworth in 1500.[15] In 1341 the ninth of sheaves was worth nine times as much as those of fleeces and lambs together, indicating predominantly arable farming. Flax, hemp, and apples were grown at that date and cattle and pigs kept, while the rectory estate as well as the manor had tenants.[16] Medieval farms, besides those in the nucleated settlements of Felpham, Flansham, and Ancton, possibly included the outlying demesne holdings of Innerwick and Outerwick,[17] and Hoe farm north-west of Flansham.[18]

Open-field arable is recorded from the 16th century near both Felpham village and Flansham hamlet;[19] it presumably existed earlier as well. At Felpham in the early 19th century Mill, Owlee, Water lane, and Little common fields formed an arc between the south and north-east sides of the village.[20] Punch Gaston common field lay west of Flansham hamlet from the early 17th century,[21] and Wish common field in 1772 was near Flansham brooks.[22] The Hoe and West and North gastons recorded at Flansham in 1638[23] and the Dagmare in the 18th century[24] were apparently other open fields. Only Punch Gaston, of 7 a., remained open there in the earlier 19th century. Woodhill common field, which at the same date lay between Flansham and Outerwick Farmhouse,[25] was perhaps the Wick or Wick common field of 1656. Though land in the latter field was sometimes held with land in the Felpham fields,[26] land in the Flansham fields seems never to have been. No open fields are recorded at Ancton. By 1662 all open-field holdings held of the manor except one of 7 a. had been engrossed or enfranchised.[27]

Apart from Mill brook in the south-west corner of the parish by Felpham bridge, common brookland lay chiefly in the north and north-west along the Ryebank and Felpham rifes, where there were 213 a. in all in 1840;[28] the two

96 B.L. Add. MS. 5699, f. 52; W.S.R.O., Cap. II/5/1, f. 60v.; ibid. Ecc. Comm. 3/4–7 (TS. cat.); Dally, *Bognor* (1828), 56, 58; Dallaway, *Hist. W. Suss.* ii (1) (1819), 8, 363.
97 W.S.R.O., TD/W 54.
98 *Lond. Gaz.* 15 Oct. 1861, pp. 4065, 4069.
99 Ibid. 12 Sept. 1865, pp. 4368–9, 4390.
1 W.S.R.O., Ecc. Comm. 3/29 (TS. cat.); cf. below, church.
2 *Lond. Gaz.* 15 Oct. 1861, pp. 4065, 4069.
3 W.S.R.O., Ecc. Comm. 3/5–6 (TS. cat.); B.L. Add. MS. 5699, f. 52; illus. at ibid. 5674, f. 38.
4 W.S.R.O., PD 1006.
5 It is not shown on ibid. PH 1419, posted before 1910.
6 Inf. from the late Mrs. M. Pain, The Old Rectory, Felpham.
7 W.S.R.O., Felpham par. rec., terrier and inv. of ch. 1901 (Acc. 8028); cf. ibid. Par. 81/6/1 (TS. cat.).
8 Arun D.C., deeds of Old Rectory Gdns.; *Kelly's Dir. Suss.* (1927 and later edns.); Burke, *Peerage* (1967), p. 1653.
9 *Bognor Regis Post*, 13 Dec. 1958.
10 *S.R.S.* xxxvi. 110; P.R.O., SC 6/Hen. VIII/3674, rot. 9d.
11 *30th Rep. Com. Char.* 781–2. The founder, Thos. Thompson, was brother of Nic. Thompson, lord of Felpham man. For the acreage, Dallaway, *Hist. W. Suss.* ii (1) (1819), 7; W.S.R.O., TD/W 54. *30th Rep. Com. Char.* 782, gives *c.* 105 a.
12 W.S.R.O., Add. MS. 6181.
13 *S.A.C.* lxxxviii. 72–3; *P.N. Suss.* (E.P.N.S.), i. 102, 105 n., 117–18, 126.
14 *V.C.H. Suss.* i. 395.
15 Hutchins, *Hist. Dors.* iii (1868), 86–7; cf. *Valor Eccl.* (Rec. Com.), i. 277.
16 *Inq. Non.* (Rec. Com.), 369.
17 *S.R.S.* ii, p. 70; cf. above, manor (Innerwick and Outerwick fms.).
18 *P.N. Suss.* i. 141.
19 P.R.O., SC 6/Hen. VIII/3674, rot. 9d.; W.S.R.O., Add. MS. 12653, 12661 (TS. cat.); *Goodwood Estate Archives*, i, ed. F. W. Steer and J. Venables, pp. 156, 158–9.
20 W.S.R.O., Add. MS. 5179; cf. *Goodwood Estate Archives*, i, p. 159. Alternative names recorded were Great com. field (for Owlee), S. town field (for Mill com. field, since it lay S. of the rectory ho.), and Boiling com. field (for Water lane): W.S.R.O., Ep. I/25/1 (1615); ibid. TD/W 54. Little town, E. town, E., Middle, and Jacobs com. fields have not been located: *Goodwood Estate Archives*, i, pp. 156, 158–60; W.S.R.O., Add. MS. 3293 (TS. cat.).
21 W.S.R.O., Add. MSS. 5179; 11704–74, 12657 (TS. cat.); ibid. Holmes, Campbell & Co. MS. 787 (TS. cat.); ibid. S.A.S. MS. WH 68 (TS. cat.).
22 Ibid. Add. MS. 12661 (TS. cat.); cf. ibid. 11704–74 (TS. cat.).
23 Ibid. Holmes, Campbell & Co. MS. 786 (TS. cat.).
24 Ibid. Add. MS. 12657 (TS. cat.); ibid. S.A.S. MS. WH 109 (TS. cat.).
25 Ibid. Add. MS. 5179.
26 Ibid. Add. MSS. 3293, 12653 (TS. cat.); *Goodwood Estate Archives*, i, p. 158.
27 W.S.R.O., Add. MS. 6973, f. 9.
28 Ibid. Add. MS. 5179; ibid. Raper MSS., Felpham inclosure award, 1840; both wrongly calling Mill brook a com. field.

areas were sometimes known respectively as Felpham[29] and Flansham brooks.[30] There was also common pasture at Wick, of unknown location.[31] A holding of 34 a. at Flansham in 1638 had pasture rights for 6 cattle, 2 horses, and 15 sheep,[32] and on another of 52 a. in 1819 the comparable figures were 3, 3, and 18.[33] Leazes in the brooks were often held with land in the open fields, but there was the same distinction between those at Felpham and those at Flansham.[34] Some common brookland was used as meadow,[35] subject apparently to annual division.[36]

In 1540 five freeholders on Felpham manor had holdings of up to 3 yardlands, while more than 50 copyholders had *c.* 60 tenements between them, some small and others of up to 6 yardlands; none of the land mentioned lay outside the parish.[37] One copyhold at least was held for three lives in 1548,[38] as was common practice later;[39] copyholds could be sublet in the 1540s. The demesne was then leased,[40] as like other monastic demesnes it had been before,[41] and as it continued to be later in the 16th century.[42] Tortington priory had copyhold land in Felpham in 1537,[43] but no other estate outside the parish is ever recorded as having land within it.

During the earl of Leicester's ownership of Felpham 1574–84 much land held of the manor was sold or converted to leasehold, becoming the kernels of later farms, for instance the unnamed holdings of 60 or 80 a. at Ancton in the 17th century.[44] In 1640 there were at least seven farms on the demesne.[45] Only a few small freeholds and copyholds remained at that period and by the late 18th century there were only one or two.[46] Farms generally grew in size between the 17th century and the early 19th; already in 1667 one holding based at Flansham and including a lease of the rectory estate had over 300 a.[47] Outerwick farm in 1791 had 183 a.[48] and Charles and Francis Sparkes' farm in 1824 had 230 a. in the parish besides 77 a. in South Bersted.[49] Closes on the two last named holdings, on Archdeacon Webber's farm in 1834,[50] and on Manor farm, Felpham Way, *c.* 1850,[51] were very scattered, indicating their origin under open-field agriculture.

Mixed farming was practised in the parish between the 16th and 18th centuries. Sheep, cattle, poultry, and pigs were kept, and crops grown were wheat, barley, oats, peas and beans, vetches, and tares with some woad and hemp. A flock of 160 sheep was recorded at one of the Wick farms in 1623, one of 600 besides 110 cattle at Flansham and elsewhere in 1667, and others of between 52 and 131 sheep at other dates;[52] the importance of sheep is indicated by the existence of sheepwashes east of Flansham hamlet and near the Yapton boundary at Bilsham.[53] Parishioners often farmed land in neighbouring parishes as well as in Felpham during the period.[54] Some seeds were being grown by the 1730s, and turnips were mentioned on one farm in 1779.[55]

In the early 19th century twice as much wheat as barley seems to have been grown, with lesser quantities of oats and peas;[56] 117 cattle including draught oxen were listed in 1803, 516 sheep, and the large number of 295 pigs.[57] A three- or four-course rotation is apparently indicated on one farm in 1804,[58] and a six-course rotation, apparently of wheat, turnips, barley, seeds, wheat, and beans with tares, was widely used in 1844.[59] The open fields and common brooks of the parish were inclosed in 1840 under an Act of 1826. At Felpham village the duke of Richmond received 59 a. and five other landowners between 1 and 20 a. each. At Flansham George Amoore received 131 a., the lords of Felpham manor 25 a., Thompson's hospital, Petworth, at least 19 a., and four other landowners between 3 and 22 a. each.[60] Other kinds of agricultural improvement were being practised in 1828,[61] and in 1835 most of the parish was said to be in a high state of cultivation.[62]

About 1844 the two largest holdings were Flansham farm (401 a.), comprising most of the north-west quarter, and Thomas Cosens' farm

29 e.g. ibid. Add. MSS. 3293 (TS. cat.); 6973, f. 1v.; ibid. Ecc. Comm. 3/7 (TS. cat.); *Goodwood Estate Archives*, i, pp. 156, 158–9.

30 e.g. P.R.O., C 3/388, no. 38; W.S.R.O., Add. MS. 12655 (TS. cat.); ibid. Harris MS. 521 (TS. cat.); ibid. S.A.S. MS. WH 67 (TS. cat.).

31 *30th Rep. Com. Char.* 782. The place name Summerley may indicate summer pasture, but it is not recorded before the earlier 19th cent. and the derivation may be from the surname Somer mentioned in 1540: P.R.O., SC 6/Hen. VIII/3480, rot. 17; W.S.R.O., Add. MS. 2060.

32 W.S.R.O., Holmes, Campbell & Co. MS. 786 (TS. cat.).

33 Ibid. Ecc. Comm. 3/7 (TS. cat.). Cf. ibid. Add. MSS. 3293, 12653, 12655 (TS. cat.); ibid. Holmes, Campbell & Co. MSS. 787–9 (TS. cat.); ibid. PHA 6677, rott. 2, 3; ibid. S.A.S. MSS. WH 67–8, 95, 109 (TS. cat.); C.I.H.E. libr., GY 322; *Goodwood Estate Archives*, i, pp. 156, 158–60.

34 e.g. *Goodwood Estate Archives*, i, pp. 156, 158–60; W.S.R.O., Add. MSS. 3293, 12657 (TS. cat.); ibid. Ecc. Comm. 3/7 (TS. cat.); ibid. S.A.S. MS. WH 109 (TS. cat.).

35 B.L. Add. MS. 9459, f. 114v.; W.S.R.O., Add. MSS. 5179; 12657 (TS. cat.); 45424; ibid. Harris MS. 521 (TS. cat.); ibid. Holmes, Campbell & Co. MS. 786 (TS. cat.); ibid. S.A.S. MSS. WH 95, 109 (TS. cat.).

36 W.S.R.O., Add. MS. 33805; ibid. Harris MS. 521 (TS. cat.).

37 P.R.O., SC 6/Hen. VIII/3480, rott. 16d.–17d.

38 W.S.R.O., PHA 6677, rot. 3.

39 Ibid. Add. MS. 6973, ff. 1, [22v.]; *Goodwood Estate Archives*, i, p. 34.

40 W.S.R.O., PHA 6677, rott. 2, 3.

41 *Valor Eccl.* (Rec. Com.), i. 277.

42 *Cal. Pat.* 1572–5, p. 185.

43 P.R.O., SC 6/Hen. VIII/3674, rot. 9d.

44 Ibid. C 2/Jas. I/W 25/66; C 3/388, no. 38; C 142/278, no. 150; W.S.R.O., S.A.S. MS. B 529 (TS. cat.); *S.R.S.* xxix, p. 32; *Goodwood Estate Archives*, i, p. 155; above, manor (Flansham fm.).

45 *Goodwood Estate Archives*, i, p. 34.

46 W.S.R.O., Add. MS. 6973, *passim*.

47 Ibid. Ep. I/29/81/41.

48 Ibid. Add. MS. 45424.

49 Ibid. 2060; above, manor (Felpham).

50 W.S.R.O., Add. MS. 2073.

51 Ibid. SP 750.

52 Ibid. Ep. I/25/1 (1615); Ep. I/29/81; *S.R.S.* xxix, p. 34; xlii. 144–8; cf. *Felpham by the Sea*, ed. T. & A. Hudson, 27. A field name recorded *c.* 1844 suggests flax cultivation at some previous date: W.S.R.O., TD/W 54, no. 209.

53 W.S.R.O., S.A.S. MS. B 529 (TS. cat.); ibid. TD/W 54; *S.R.S.* xxix, p. 35; *Goodwood Estate Archives*, i, p. 154.

54 W.S.R.O., Ep. I/29/81/29, 33, 39, 47, 70; *Felpham by the Sea*, 27.

55 W.S.R.O., Ep. I/29/81/86–7, 91.

56 *L. & I. Soc.* cxcv. 32.

57 E.S.R.O., LCG/3/EW 1, f. [84v.].

58 W.S.R.O., Add. MS. 23666.

59 P.R.O., IR 18/10328.

60 W.S.R.O., Add. MS. 5179; ibid. Raper MSS., inclosure award, 1840, lacking the conclusion.

61 Dally, *Bognor* (1828), 55.

62 Horsfield, *Hist. Suss.* ii. 106; cf. B.L. Add. MS. 9459, f. 117; W.S.R.O., Add. MS. 11809; ibid. Slindon MSS., bdle. NR 34, no. 1.

which included land at Felpham village and at Wick (358 a.);[63] in 1851 they had 17 and 12 labourers respectively.[64] There were six other holdings of between 80 a. and 175 a. *c.* 1844.[65] Ancton farm was held in 1852 with Middleton farm, making *c.* 400 a. in all,[66] while Felpham farm, based at Church House in Felpham village, was held with Barnham manor demesne farm as a combined holding of 389 a. *c.* 1862[67] and 600 a. in 1881.[68] Flansham farm had 512 a. in 1871 and Innerwick farm 522 a. in 1881.[69] Most land was rented between the mid 19th century and earlier 20th[70] and there were said to be no resident landowners in 1867 and 1881.[71] Leases of between 5 and 21 years are recorded between the 1850s and 80s.[72] By *c.* 1910 no farm within the area of the modern parish was more than 250 a. in area.[73]

Felpham participated in the 'Swing' riots of 1830, when a group of 100–150 labourers, later growing to a crowd of 500, forced Thomas Cosens to offer to raise agricultural wages;[74] the introduction of the new Poor Law in 1835 was similarly greeted by a rising.[75] In 1878, on the other hand, work was said to be plentiful and wages reasonable.[76] The predominance of arable in the period 1800–75[77] no longer obtained by the early 20th century: instead of the 856 a. of corn crops, chiefly wheat, and 313 a. of green crops, mostly turnips and swedes, returned in 1875, there was then apparently a smaller total acreage, including a much higher proportion of oats; the corresponding totals for grassland were 463 a. in 1875 and 696 a. in 1909.[78] Many closes were amalgamated between 1844 and *c.* 1875.[79] There were three shepherds in 1871.[80]

Beginning in the late 19th century agricultural land in the south part of the parish succumbed gradually to building development. The chief farmer in the 1920s was P. A. Norman, who besides using his own land at Innerwick farm leased Outerwick and Drygrounds farms.[81] By the 1980s much of that land too had been built over or converted to other uses, notably school playing fields and a golf course. Dairying and poultry farming were practised in the 1920s and 30s[82] and two dairy herds and a poultry farm remained at Flansham in 1992,[83] but by 1995 little dairying was practised.[84] Chessels farm at Flansham was managed in the 1940s and later with a downland farm at Madehurst.[85]

Orchards and market gardens were an alternative land use in the 20th century. Six acres of orchards had been returned in 1875 and there were 2½ a. in the ancient parish, including Ancton, in 1909.[86] A fruit grower was mentioned *c.* 1910[87] and market gardeners and nurserymen from *c.* 1900,[88] notably north of the village[89] and between Flansham and Ancton.[90] Only one market garden remained in the modern parish in 1992, on the east side of Flansham Lane. There were allotments north of the church by 1912, which by 1928 were managed by the parish council.[91]

MILLS. There were two mills in the parish in 1341.[92] One was possibly the predecessor of the windmill recorded on Felpham manor in the 16th century,[93] which since it was said to be in the south-west part of the parish in 1593[94] may have occupied the slight elevation at the corner of Felpham and Upper Bognor roads where later stood what was called the Black windmill.[95] Millers are known by name from the 16th century.[96] The Black windmill was the only mill recorded in the parish in the 17th and 18th centuries.[97] The very tall smock mill called the White windmill, on the sea front west of Blake's Road, was built *c.* 1800[98] but was abandoned because of sea erosion and demolished in 1879.[99] It was presumably Bognor's

63 W.S.R.O., TD/W 54; cf. ibid. Slindon MSS., bdle. NR 34, no. 1.
64 *Felpham and Middleton Census Returns 1841–1881*, ed. B. Fletcher, 27, 32.
65 W.S.R.O., TD/W 54.
66 Ibid. Add. MS. 11801 (TS. cat.).
67 Ibid. Goodwood MS. E19, pp. 38–9.
68 *Felpham and Middleton Census Returns 1841–1881*, 120.
69 Ibid. 107, 126.
70 P.R.O., MAF 68/2371; W.S.R.O., TD/W 54.
71 *Rep. Com. on Children and Women in Agric.* 86; W.S.R.O., Ep. I/22A/1 (1881).
72 W.S.R.O., Add. MSS. 11801, 11807 (TS. cat.); ibid. Goodwood MS. E5089.
73 Ibid. IR 31, ff. 1–2, 7, 10.
74 E. J. Hobsbawm and G. Rudé, *Capt. Swing*, 111; *I am, My Dear Sir*, ed. F. W. Steer, 82–3.
75 *Rep. Sel. Cttee. on Agric.* H.C. 465, p. 193 (1836), viii (2); *W. Suss. Hist.* lvi. 7–9.
76 W.S.R.O., Ep. I/22A/1 (1878).
77 e.g. ibid. Add. MSS. 2060, 23667; ibid. TD/W 54.
78 P.R.O., MAF 68/433, 2371; statistics for Ancton fm. were evidently included under Middleton: below, Middleton-on-Sea, econ. hist. (agric.).
79 W.S.R.O., TD/W 54; O.S. Map 6", Suss. LXII, LXXIV (1879–80 edn.).
80 *Felpham and Middleton Census Returns 1841–1881*, 97–8, 104.
81 *Felpham by the Sea*, ed. T. & A. Hudson, 32; *Kelly's Dir. Suss.* (1934).
82 *Sunny Felpham* [1922], 34, 37 (copy in B.L.); *Kelly's Dir. Suss.* (1922 and later edns.).
83 *W. Suss. Gaz.* 18 June 1992; cf. O.S. Map 1/25,000, SU 80/90 (1991 edn.).
84 Inf. from Mrs. S. Hocking, Yapton.
85 G. Young, *Come into the Country*, 67, 74–5, 80, 125–6; G. Young, *Cottage in the Fields*, 243; *W. Suss. Gaz.* 12 Mar. 1987.
86 P.R.O., MAF 68/433, 2371.
87 *Kelly's Dir. Suss.* (1909, 1913); Pike, *Bognor Dir.* (1910–11).
88 *Kelly's Dir. Suss.* (1899 and later edns.); Pike, *Bognor Dir.* (1910–11); *Bognor Regis Dir.* (1932).
89 O.S. Map 6", Suss. LXXIV. NW. & SW. (1932 edn.).
90 *Kelly's Dir. Suss.* (1905 and later edns.); Pike, *Bognor Dir.* (1910–11); *Kelly's Dir. Bognor Regis* (1962); O.S. Map 1/10,000, SU 90 SE. & SZ 99 NE. (1980 edn.).
91 W.S.R.O., Par. 81/52/3–4; O.S. Map 6", Suss. LXXIV. NW. & SW. (1932 edn.).
92 *Inq. Non.* (Rec. Com.), 369.
93 P.R.O., E 310/25/145, f. 19; E 328/166; ibid. SC 6/Hen. VIII/3480, rot. 17d.; *Cal. Pat.* 1572–5, p. 185.
94 P.R.O., C 142/278, no. 150.
95 e.g. O.S. Map 6", Suss. LXXIV (1879 edn.). The abp. of Cant.'s windmill at 'Pignor' near Felpham bridge recorded in 14th and 15th cents. was in S. Bersted par.: L. Fleming, *Hist. Pagham*, i. 60; ii. 374–5, 377–8, 380–1, 617; W.S.R.O., TD/W 115, no. 490.
96 A.C.M., M 271, f. [9v.]; W.S.R.O., Add. MS. 6973, f. [18v.]; *Cal. Assize Rec. Suss. Eliz. I*, p. 23; *S.R.S.* xlix. 32.
97 e.g. *Goodwood Estate Archives*, i, ed. F. W. Steer and J. Venables, p. 156; *250 Yrs. of Mapmaking in Suss.* ed. H. Margary, pl. 14; P.R.O., MPHH 218.
98 W.S.R.O., LD I/LL 2/13; cf. ibid. Add. MS. 2060; E.S.R.O., LCG/3/EW 1, f. [44]; R. Lister, *Paintings of Wm. Blake*, pl. 25; below, pl. facing p. 187.
99 V. Mills, *Bognor Regis, a Pictorial Hist.* pl. 149; C.I.H.E. libr., GY/PH 5072; sketchbk. of Bognor and dist. by Wm. Colliss, p. [53], in possession of Mr. K. Scutt, Bognor Regis; cf. O.S. Map 6", Suss. LXXIV (1879 edn.); LXXIV. NW. (1899 edn.).

rising population during the 19th century which made two mills viable. About 1844 they were worked together.[1] The Black windmill had also ceased to be used by 1896.[2]

OTHER TRADES AND INDUSTRIES. Felpham's high assessment to tax in Avisford hundred in 1334[3] indicates the presence of other non-agricultural employment. Apart from possibly a chapman at that period[4] and a tailor in 1428,[5] however, occupations for which there is medieval evidence were all associated with the sea. A manorial fishery is recorded in 1086[6] but not later; in the 14th and 15th centuries, however, there was a 'fishery of Felpham' belonging to the archbishop of Canterbury's estate beyond the Aldingbourne rife; it was devastated by the sea in 1426.[7] Fish tithes were paid to the rector in 1341.[8] Several ships or boats were recorded as belonging to Felpham in the 15th and 16th centuries.[9] The estuary of the Aldingbourne rife may have offered a harbour,[10] but in 1587 the only good landing places between Pagham and Littlehampton were on the beach, including one in the east part of the parish and only there around high tide.[11] Most Felpham vessels were in the coastal trade, but one in 1439 plied to the Low Countries; most seem to have been under 50 tons but there were two larger ones in 1572. It was presumably maritime activity which caused the presence in the parish of four aliens, all servants, in 1525.[12] For customs purposes Felpham lay within Chichester port.[13]

Various fishermen were recorded in the 17th and 18th centuries,[14] and other parishioners besides a victualler in 1706[15] probably owned fishing tackle for their own use. Several parishioners were described as seamen in the 17th century, sometimes four at the same date.[16] In 1801 five boats were listed, but no-one was then willing to serve as a boatman in the event of invasion.[17]

Four unmounted coastguards had been established at Felpham *c.* 1295, as one of only three such places in the rape.[18] Riding officers for Felpham were appointed from 1699,[19] and in the 1810s and 20s a coastguard officer, two preventive officers, and many boatmen, presumably stationed at Bognor, were recorded.[20] A coastguard station was built *c.* 1861 midway between Felpham village and the sea, comprising a detached officer's house, a watch house, and two rows of red and yellow brick cottages; the boathouse was east of the modern Blake's Road.[21] In 1887, after the closure of the coastguard station in Bognor, it was described as Bognor coastguard station.[22] There were 46 inmates in all in 1871.[23] The station was closed in the early 1920s,[24] and soon afterwards three large houses were built between the rows of cottages, and a parade of shops in the garden of the officer's house along Felpham Road.[25]

Most other non-agricultural occupations recorded between the 16th and late 18th centuries were those typical of a small village:[26] baker, brewer,[27] butcher,[28] wheelwright, weaver, tailor,[29] shoemaker,[30] carpenter,[31] and blacksmith.[32] Mercers were mentioned from the later 17th century.[33] Most tradesmen presumably lived in the village, but brewers and a butcher were recorded in Ancton and Wick tithings in the 1540s[34] and a smithy was said to lie at Wick in 1624.[35] A butcher of Felpham in 1652 leased a shop and stalls in Arundel high street from the corporation.[36]

In the early 19th century the parish had a very high proportion of tradesmen: more than one in four of those in work in 1831 and as many as one in two in 1811.[37] During the 19th and 20th centuries[38] the number and variety of trades increased in step with Felpham's growth as both

1 W.S.R.O., TD/W 54.
2 O.S. Map 6", Suss. LXXIV. NW. (1899 edn.).
3 Equal with that of Yapton and exceeded only by that of Ford, which included Climping: *S.A.C.* l. 167; below, Ford, econ. hist.
4 *S.R.S.* x. 135; cf. ibid. 79.
5 *Cal. Pat.* 1422–9, 443.
6 *V.C.H. Suss.* i. 395.
7 L. Fleming, *Hist. Pagham*, i. 58; ii. 372.
8 *Inq. Non.* (Rec. Com.), 369.
9 Rest of para. mainly based on *Cal. Pat.* 1436–41, 342; *V.C.H. Suss.* ii. 151; *S.R.S.* lxiv. 73, 143; W.S.R.O., MP 9, ff. 71–2, 114, 118, 122, 128, 159.
10 Cf. Bognor haven mentioned in mid 15th cent.: Fleming, *Hist. Pagham*, ii. 380, 383; *V.C.H. Suss.* iv. 226.
11 *Armada Surv.* ed. Lower.
12 *S.R.S.* lvi. 55.
13 W.S.R.O., Chich. City Archives AZ 2.
14 *Felpham by the Sea*, ed. T. & A. Hudson, 5; W.S.R.O., Ep. I/29/81/16. The 3 men drowned at the 'dragging grounds' in 1589 were presumably also fishing: ibid. Par. 81/1/1/1, f. 64; *O.E.D.* s.v. drag.
15 W.S.R.O., Ep. I/29/81/68.
16 Ibid. Ep. I/55/31, 38, 94, 157, 198, 240; Ep. I/55/6, 73, 120, 156 (TS. cat.).
17 E.S.R.O., LCG/3/EW 1, f. [46].
18 *V.C.H. Suss.* i. 506 and n.
19 *Cal. Treas. Bks.* 1699–1700, 168; *Felpham by the Sea*, 34; *S.R.S.* lxxiii, p. 99; *S.C.M.* xvii. 232, 351; W.S.R.O., Add. MS. 1276 (TS. cat.); ibid. Ep. I/29/81/90.
20 W.S.R.O., Par. 81/1/2/1; for the Bognor coastguard sta. W. of Felpham sluice, ibid. Add. MS. 2060; ibid. TD/W 115, no. 204. The 3 coastguard men recorded at Ancton in 1841 probably belonged to the Elmer coastguard sta.: *Felpham and Middleton Census Returns 1841–1881*, 7–8; below, Middleton-on-Sea, econ. hist. (other trades and inds.).
21 *Felpham by the Sea*, 35; *Kelly's Dir. Suss.* (1866); P.R.O., IR 58/22732, no. 134; IR 58/22733, no. 242; O.S. Map 6", Suss. LXXIV (1879 and later edns.).
22 *Kelly's Dir. Suss.* (1887); inf. from Mr. R. Iden, Bognor Regis.
23 *Census*, 1871.
24 *Kelly's Dir. Suss.* (1922); *Bognor Post*, 20 Mar. 1926.
25 Cf. *Felpham by the Sea*, pl. 6.
26 Rest of para. mainly based on ibid. 5; W.S.R.O., Ep. I/29/81, *passim.*
27 A.C.M., M 271, f. [9v.]; W.S.R.O., PHA 6683, f. 19 and v.
28 Cf. P.R.O., REQ 2/274/46, rot. 5; W.S.R.O., PHA 6677, rot. 2; 6683, f. 19.
29 Cf. *S.R.S.* xlix. 33; *Goodwood Estate Archives*, i, ed. F. W. Steer and J. Venables, p. 158; W.S.R.O., Add. MS. 6973, f. [26v.].
30 Cf. *Cal. Assize Rec. Suss. Jas. I*, p. 73, naming 3 in 1616; W.S.R.O., Add. MS. 6973, ff. [21–2, 34v.].
31 Cf. *Goodwood Estate Archives*, i, p. 160; W.S.R.O., Add. MS. 3296 (TS. cat.).
32 Cf. *S.R.S.* xlix. 33; *Goodwood Estate Archives*, i, pp. 157, 160; W.S.R.O., Raper MSS., deed, 1781 (TS. cat.).
33 *Goodwood Estate Archives*, i, pp. 155, 157–8; one was also a member of the Goldsmiths' Co. of Lond. The grocer and draper of 'Felsham' mentioned in 1743 may have lived at Felsham (Sfk.): *S.R.S.* xxviii. 103.
34 W.S.R.O., PHA 6677, rot. 2; 6683, f. 19 and v.
35 *30th Rep. Com. Char.* 782.
36 W.S.R.O., A.B.A., P 1/8 (TS. cat.).
37 *Census*, 1811–31.
38 Rest of para. based mainly on Pigot, *Nat. Com. Dir.* (1839), 658–9; *Kelly's Dir. Suss.* (1845 and later edns.); *Felpham and Middleton Census Returns 1841–1881*, *passim.*

a seaside resort and a place for residence or retirement. There was usually at least one grocer or shopkeeper in that period.[39] Less usual trades in the mid 19th century were those of cabinet maker,[40] maltster, laundress,[41] marine store dealer,[42] sea defence contractor,[43] and drawing master, while other specialized occupations mentioned later, with dates of first occurrence, were those of florist (1895), greengrocer (1899), stationer (1903), fishmonger (1915), tobacconist, newsagent (1922), and hairdresser (1927). There was a chemist by *c.* 1922[44] and two in 1934, a firm of electrical engineers in 1930, and in the 1930s music sellers, two wine merchants, a landscape gardener, a wireless engineer, a chimney sweep, an upholsterer, and a watchmaker, besides a toy shop. A coal merchant was recorded in the village from 1839;[45] there were two in 1927, one of whom was also a wood merchant and haulage contractor.[46]

Though most tradesmen's premises were in the village in the 19th and 20th centuries, there were two general stores in the Sea Road area in 1910[47] and another in Flansham Lane by 1927.[48] In 1992 the village together with the southern end of Felpham Road retained a wide range of general shops besides more specialized businesses including those of travel agent, antique dealer, jeweller, picture framer, and dealer in business machines, together with a pet shop, a betting shop, and a video film hire business. Other shops in Felpham Way and in Flansham and Summerley lanes then served nearby residential areas. There was also a beach shop on the sea front. In Flansham Lane a former builder's premises[49] were occupied by a firm of heating engineers and another of interior designers.

By 1791 Sir Richard Hotham had started a lime kiln at the seaward end of Limmer Lane to serve his building operations in Bognor.[50] Early 19th-century construction in both Felpham and Bognor presumably gave employment to the bricklayer, masons, and glaziers recorded between 1800 and the 1830s.[51] There was perhaps a brickyard on the south side of Limmer Lane in 1844.[52] In 1862 one builder was listed, but the increased rate of development in the early 20th century brought three firms by 1922, five besides a builders' merchants by 1927, and eight by 1938.[53] Brickfields were worked for short periods in the early 20th century in the area of the modern parish and at Flansham.[54] A house agency at the village post office was mentioned *c.* 1922,[55] and there were three estate agents by 1927, besides estate development companies, and as many as six in 1938, three of whom were also builders. In 1992 there were six in the area of the ancient parish excluding Ancton.

The increasing number of moneyed residents provided work for jobbing gardeners from 1887 or earlier,[56] while the expansion of the seaside resort from the later 19th century, besides giving rise to the lodging houses, guest houses, and hotels mentioned elsewhere,[57] brought cafés and refreshment rooms, of which there were six in 1934 including one on the esplanade. In 1992 there were several restaurants in the area of the ancient parish excluding Ancton, besides two premises selling 'take-away' food. Souvenir 'Felpham arms' china could be bought in the village *c.* 1922.[58]

A wheelwright continued in business until 1905 or later;[59] until *c.* 1900 there were two blacksmiths, one in the village and one in Felpham Way to the east, the latter surviving until the 1930s.[60] With the growth of motor transport two garages had appeared by 1934, both beside what was then still a main route into Bognor Regis. The premises of the Felpham Motor Works south-west of the village, built *c.* 1920, could accommodate 30 cars, some in lock-up garages, and the firm also dealt in cycles.[61] Three garages remained in 1992.

The professional men who resided in the 19th century[62] were presumably non-practising, and at that date Felpham evidently depended on Bognor for professional services, as to a great extent it still did in 1992. There was a vet in 1905, a physician and surgeon by 1927, and a solicitor and a chiropodist by 1934, while an optician attended in 1938. Three branch banks were opened in the early 1930s[63] and remained in 1992. There were then also in the parish two dentists and a solicitor.

Fishing continued in a small way in the 19th and 20th centuries. Two fishermen were mentioned, besides other mariners, in the 1810s,[64] there were four in 1841,[65] and two lived in the Sea Road area in 1905,[66] when they were presumably included in statistics of fishing at Bognor, catching mixed fish including herrings and shellfish.[67] In 1982 both

39 Cf. W.S.R.O., Add. MS. 17007–11; ibid. Par. 81/1/2/1.
40 Ibid. Par. 81/1/2/1.
41 *Felpham and Middleton Census Returns 1841–1881*, 17.
42 Ibid. 45, 90.
43 Ibid. 98.
44 *Sunny Felpham* [1922], 33 (copy in B.L.).
45 Cf. W.S.R.O., TD/W 54, no. 69.
46 *Sunny Felpham*, 34.
47 Pike, *Bognor Dir.* (1910–11).
48 *Kelly's Dir. Suss.* (1927); cf. G. Young, *Come into the Country*, 10.
49 Local inf.
50 W.S.R.O., Add. MS. 2068; *W. Suss. Hist.* xxii. 4.
51 W.S.R.O., Add. MSS. 17007–11; ibid. Par. 81/1/2/1. Rest of para. based mainly on *Kelly's Dir. Suss.* (1862 and later edns.).
52 M. Beswick, *Brickmaking in Suss.* 191.
53 Cf. *Sunny Felpham*, 10, 32.
54 Cf. G. Young, *Come into the Country*, 9; Beswick, op. cit. 191–2; O.S. Map 6", Suss. LXXIV. NE. (1913, 1932 edns.).
55 *Sunny Felpham*, 36.
56 Para. based mainly on *Kelly's Dir. Suss.* (1887 and later edns.). The gdnrs. mentioned 1814×1878 were perhaps more likely market gdnrs.: W.S.R.O., Par. 81/1/2/1; *Felpham and Middleton Census Returns 1841–1881*, 19–20; *Kelly's Dir. Suss.* (1862 and later edns.); cf. above, this section (agric.).
57 Above, intro. (Felpham as seaside resort).
58 *Sunny Felpham*, 38.
59 Pigot, *Nat. Com. Dir.* (1839), 659; *Kelly's Dir. Suss.* (1905). Rest of para. based mainly on ibid. (1887 and later edns.).
60 Cf. W.S.R.O., Add. MSS. 26101 (TS. cat.); 29868, f. 1; ibid. TD/W 54; Pigot, *Nat. Com. Dir.* (1839), 659; O.S. Map 6", Suss. LXXIV (1879 and later edns.).
61 *Bognor Observer*, 1 Sept. 1920; *Sunny Felpham*, 30, 39.
62 W.S.R.O., Par. 81/1/2/1; *Felpham and Middleton Census Returns 1841–1881*, 43.
63 *Kelly's Dir. Suss.* (1905 and later edns.).
64 W.S.R.O., Par. 81/1/2/1; cf. *Land Drainage Rec. of W. Suss.* ed. D. Butler, 37.
65 *Felpham and Middleton Census Returns*, 6, 21.
66 *Kelly's Dir. Suss.* (1905).
67 *V.C.H. Suss.* ii. 269–70.

full- and part-time fishermen operated from the sea front east of Sea Road.[68]

Riding stables existed in the village between the 1930s[69] and 1992.

Many residents in 1996 were retired, and many others worked elsewhere, especially in Chichester.

LOCAL GOVERNMENT. Shaftesbury abbey (Dors.) seems likely by virtue of its status to have had leet jurisdiction on Felpham manor, which enjoyed it in the mid 16th century[70] and apparently in the early 17th.[71] Right of wreck belonged to the lord of the rape in 1209–10[72] but in 1630 was claimed, apparently with success, by the lady of the manor.[73] The abbey had a prison at Felpham in 1248.[74]

There are court rolls or draft court rolls for the view of frankpledge and court baron for various years between 1543 and 1550[75] and for the court alone for the period 1662–1881.[76] Not more than two sessions a year took place in the 1540s, the view in 1543 being followed by a sheriff's tourn. After 1662 courts were held usually once or twice in a decade, the last in 1827; business was treated out of court by 1662. A plea of land and a case of assault were heard in 1543. In the 1540s the view held the assize of bread and of ale, and dealt with stray beasts and the maintenance of streams; the court, besides regulating tenancies, managed the common land and saw to the repair of roads and fences. After 1662 nearly all business was conveyancing, but a house was ordered to be repaired in 1730[77] and a piece of the waste was licensed for inclosure in 1881.[78]

Manor officers were a bailiff in 1535 and 1730,[79] chief pledges for the tithings of Felpham, Ancton, and Wick in the 1540s,[80] and a tithingman *c.* 1822.[81] A manor pound was mentioned in 1547.[82]

Two churchwardens were recorded for many years between 1548 and 1694; there was almost always one only from 1695 to 1850 but afterwards there were usually two.[83] A single overseer served in 1642[84] and two in 1826.[85] A rate for church repair was levied in 1623.[86]

Before Felpham joined the Yapton Gilbert union in the 1780s there was a parish poorhouse in Flansham Lane; afterwards it was rented out by the parish as two cottages[87] and it survived in 1992. Other methods of poor relief employed between 1790 and 1835 included boarding out, apprenticing, the provision of clothing and medical care, and the payment of weekly doles either in lieu of or to supplement wages.[88] Parish work in a gravel pit was said to be organized, not very effectively, in 1835.[89] Ninety-two parishioners were receiving permanent relief in 1826 and 68 casual relief.[90] In 1835, evidently in anticipation of the stricter conditions laid down by the 1834 Poor Law Amendment Act, 43 parishioners joined the Petworth emigration scheme to Canada at the joint expense of the parish and of local landowners. Ten parishioners were still receiving out relief in 1836.[91]

The parish formed part of Westhampnett union, later rural district, after 1835.[92] The development for building of its south-west corner in the late 19th century and early 20th brought suggestions for partial incorporation into Bognor urban district in 1903,[93] for the adoption by the parish of the Lighting and Watching Act, 1833, in 1913–14 and 1922, and for the creation of an urban district of either Felpham or Felpham and Middleton in the mid 1920s.[94] In the event the ancient parish was abolished as a unit in 1933, part going to Bognor Regis and the rest being divided between Middleton and Yapton. A new civil parish was created in 1985.[95]

A parish pound was recorded behind the modern Southdowns hotel *c.* 1844;[96] by the 1870s it had moved to the south side of Felpham Way.[97] There was another pound at the north end of Felpham Road in the 1930s.[98]

CHURCH. There was a church in 1086, which evidently belonged with the manor to Shaftesbury abbey (Dors.).[99] Despite the grant of a licence in 1344[1] the abbey never appropriated the benefice, though it continued until the Dissolution to appoint rectors,[2] the living later becoming a sinecure.[3] A vicarage was ordained by 1386.[4] It was briefly united with Middleton rectory in 1657.[5] In the later 19th century union was often advocated again,[6] and the two benefices were united in 1906, the parishes remaining distinct. The parishes too were united in 1976,

68 *Bognor Regis Post*, 20 Nov. 1982; cf. *W. Suss. Gaz.* 2 May 1985.

69 *Property Reg. to Felpham, Middleton-on-Sea, Aldwick, Pagham and Bognor Regis* (Bognor Regis, [1939]), 8 (copy in B.L.); *Bognor Regis, Aldwick and Felpham: Official Guide* (*c.* 1953), 72.

70 Below, this section.

71 *S.R.S.* xix. 162–3.

72 Ibid. lxvii. 105.

73 *Cal. S.P. Dom.* 1629–31, 301; A. Fletcher, *County Community in Peace and War*, 173, wrongly reading 1640.

74 P.R.O., JUST 1/909A, rot. 23.

75 W.S.R.O., PHA 933, ff. 75, 78, 82; 935, f. 49; 6677, rot. 2; 6683, f. 19.

76 Ibid. Add. MS. 6973.

77 Ibid. f. [19].

78 Ibid. f. [39].

79 Ibid. f. [19]; *Valor Eccl.* (Rec. Com.), i. 277.

80 e.g. W.S.R.O., PHA 6683, f. 19 and v. Flansham was a fourth tithing: ibid. f. 21.

81 E.S.R.O., QCR/2/1/EW 2 (47).

82 W.S.R.O., PHA 6677, rot. 2.

83 Ibid. Ep. I/86/20, f. 17; B.L. Add. MS. 39359, ff. 68–73.

84 *S.R.S.* v. 80.

85 W.S.R.O., QCR/2/3/W 5, no. 16.

86 *S.R.S.* xlix. 81.

87 *Felpham by the Sea*, ed. T. & A. Hudson, 42; W.S.R.O., TD/W 54.

88 *Felpham by the Sea*, 42–7.

89 *1st Rep. Poor Law Com.* H.C. 500, p. 179 (1835), xxxv.

90 W.S.R.O., QCR/2/3/W 5, no. 16.

91 *Rep. Sel. Cttee. on Agric.* H.C. 465, p. 194 (1836), viii (2); *Felpham by the Sea*, 49; *Suss. Fam. Historian*, viii. 282–3.

92 *Suss. Poor Law Rec.* 52.

93 W.S.R.O., UD/BR 3/1/3, pp. 120–1.

94 Ibid. Par. 81/54/7, 9.

95 Above, intro. [area].

96 W.S.R.O., TD/W 54.

97 O.S. Map 6", Suss. LXXIV (1879 edn.).

98 G. Young, *Cottage in the Fields*, 176.

99 *V.C.H. Suss.* i. 395.

1 *Cal. Pat.* 1343–5, 360.

2 Ibid.; B.L. Add. MS. 39334, ff. 14v.–15. It is not clear why the adv. of the rect. was exercised by the Crown in 1392: *Cal. Pat.* 1391–6, 69.

3 e.g. B.L. Add. MS. 5699, f. 52; *Rep. Com. Eccl. Revenues.*

4 B.L. Add. MS. 39334, f. 23v.

5 *S.N.Q.* xv. 118–19.

6 e.g. W.S.R.O., Ep. I/22A/1 (1884, 1893).

when a benefice of Felpham with Middleton was created of which the incumbent was called rector.[7]

The advowson of the vicarage belonged from 1401 or earlier until the mid 19th century to the rector. Two, possibly three, laymen who presented in the later 16th century and earlier 17th were apparently lessees of the rectory estate.[8] Since 1871 the dean and chapter of Chichester have presented to Felpham and later Felpham with Middleton.[9]

The vicar seems to have received a stipend from the rector before the 16th century, since no endowment is known at that period.[10] In 1535 the vicarage was valued at £9 10*s*. 7*d*. net,[11] but in 1579 Felpham and Middleton together were said to be worth well under £5.[12] In the early 17th century there was a vicarage house with two garden plots standing south of the church; the vicar then received all the small tithes including those of hemp, as later.[13] In 1646, when the living was worth £25 a year, an extra £50 was ordered to be paid from the profits of the rectory.[14] Later valuations were £34 in 1724,[15] £36 10*s*. 6*d*. in 1809,[16] and *c*. £166 *c*. 1830.[17]

The vicarage house was said in 1662 to have fallen down many years before,[18] and a replacement was bought before 1687 by the rector and the lord of the manor with contributions from others; it stood north-east of the church and then had a parlour, three chambers, and a study, besides service rooms.[19] In 1724, when some ceilings and parts of the roof and walls were in bad repair, there was also ½ a. of glebe,[20] presumably the close south of the church recorded in 1843.[21] The building was described as unfit for residence *c*. 1830[22] and was later demolished, the vicar in 1843 leasing a house in Limmer Lane. At the commutation of tithes at that date a tithe rent charge of £200 12*s*. was awarded him.[23]

From 1849 or earlier the vicar leased the Old Rectory house,[24] and in 1861 the ecclesiastical commissioners settled it on the living together with 8 a. nearby,[25] afterwards giving an augmentation of £114 a year from 1867.[26] In 1923 a new house for the incumbent in neo-Georgian style was completed on part of the glebe in Limmer Lane to the designs of Adams, Holden, and Pearson.[27]

The spiritual needs of the northern part of the parish were catered for from the mid 14th century or earlier by a chapel of ease at Flansham.[28] By 1547 it had fallen into ruins[29] and in 1640 it was apparently used as a barn,[30] said in 1901 to have been only recently pulled down; foundations then remaining behind Chapel House at the north end of the hamlet indicated a rectangular building similar in scale to Bilsham chapel in Yapton.[31] No chapel is ever recorded at Ancton, whose inhabitants may often have attended Middleton church in the Middle Ages as certainly happened later.[32]

The vicar in 1529 may also have held Barnham. There was apparently an assistant curate in the 1530s, when a brotherhood of St. Christopher was also recorded.[33] Julian Browning, vicar 1556–82, was resident in 1563 and 1579, on the second occasion being described as a preacher; throughout his period of tenure he held Middleton as well.[34] At least two early 17th-century incumbents were also licensed to preach[35] though the second, William Hill, was inhibited in 1635 through suspicion of Nonconformity, having told three parishioners from the pulpit he was certain they would be damned.[36] John Goldwire, minister from 1657, was ejected after the Restoration;[37] his orthodox successor held other benefices including Middleton and in 1662 did not always reside.[38]

In 1724 a service with sermon was held each Sunday by the assistant curate, holy communion being celebrated three times a year with 30–40 communicants.[39] The then vicar may, therefore, have been non-resident, like his predecessor, who was described in his will as of North Mundham.[40] Four other curates are recorded during the 18th century,[41] one of whom was rector of Middleton,[42] and at least two other vicars at that period did not reside though one was said in 1742 to officiate himself.[43] In 1795 the church often accommodated visitors to Bognor who could not find seats in South Bersted church.[44]

J. B. Beed, vicar 1805–47, generally served the

7 Ibid. Par. 81/6/8; Par. 137/6/3.
8 B.L. Add. MS. 39334, ff. 24–29v.
9 Ibid. f. 30; W.S.R.O., Par. 137/6/3; local inf.
10 *S.R.S.* xlvi, pp. 310–11; Dallaway, *Hist. W. Suss.* ii (1) (1819), 8–9, mentioning an endowment of 1506 which has not been corroborated.
11 *Valor Eccl.* (Rec. Com.), i. 317.
12 W.S.R.O., Ep. I/23/5, f. 39v.
13 Ibid. Ep. I/25/1 (1615, 1687); ibid. TD/W 54.
14 *S.A.C.* xxxvi. 142.
15 *S.R.S.* lxxviii. 65.
16 W.S.R.O., Ep. I/63/10.
17 *Rep. Com. Eccl. Revenues.*
18 W.S.R.O., Ep. I/22/1 (1662).
19 Ibid. Ep. I/25/1 (1687).
20 *S.R.S.* lxxviii. 65.
21 W.S.R.O., TD/W 54; cf. above, this section.
22 *Rep. Com. Eccl. Revenues.*
23 W.S.R.O., TD/W 54.
24 Ibid. Ecc. Comm. 3/29, 32 (TS. cat.); ibid. Ep. I/22A/1 (1884); *Felpham and Middleton Census Returns 1841–1881*, ed. B. Fletcher, 46; *Kelly's Dir. Suss.* (1852 and later edns.).
25 *Lond. Gaz.* 15 Oct. 1861, pp. 4065, 4069; W.S.R.O., Felpham par. rec., terrier and inv. of ch. 1901 (Acc. 8028). Part of the vicarial glebe was exchanged for other land in 1867: ibid. deed, 1867 (Acc. 8028).
26 *Lond. Gaz.* 17 July 1868, p. 3997.
27 *Bognor Regis Observer*, 12 Jan. 1973; W.S.R.O., Felpham par. rec., plans of new rectory ho. (Acc. 8028); cf. ibid. TD/W 54, no. 90.
28 *S.R.S.* xlvi, p. 311.
29 W.S.R.O., PHA 6677, rot. 2d.; cf. *Cal. Pat.* 1572–5, p. 185.
30 *Goodwood Estate Archives*, i, ed. F. W. Steer and J. Venables, p. 34.
31 *S.A.C.* xliv. 166; cf. Dallaway, *Hist. W. Suss.* ii (1) (1819), 7; G. Young, *Cottage in the Fields*, 146–50, mentioning pieces of worked stone presumed to be from the chap.
32 W.S.R.O., Ep. I/22A/1 (1878); ibid. Par. 137/1/1/1, p. 39.
33 *S.R.S.* xli. 75; xlii. 147–8.
34 B.L. Add. MS. 39334, f. 26; W.S.R.O., Ep. I/23/5, f. 39v.; *S.A.C.* lxi. 113; below, Middleton-on-Sea, church.
35 B.L. Add. MS. 39334, ff. 26v.–27.
36 *V.C.H. Suss.* ii. 33.
37 *Calamy Revised*, ed. Matthews, 226.
38 B.L. Add. MS. 39334, f. 28; W.S.R.O., Ep. I/22/1 (1662).
39 *S.R.S.* lxxviii. 65.
40 B.L. Add. MS. 39334, f. 28 and v.
41 Ibid. 39359, f. 71 and v.
42 W.S.R.O., Ep. I/22/1 (1782), Middleton.
43 Ibid. Ep. I/22/1 (1742, 1769); B.L. Add. MS. 39334, f. 28v.
44 L. Fleming, *Hist. Pagham*, ii. 557–8. For visitors from Bognor for similar reasons in 19th cent., W.S.R.O., Ep. I/22A/1 (1884, 1890).

cure himself[45] but had assistant curates at various dates.[46] Between the early 19th century and 1868 or later morning and afternoon services were held on successive Sundays alternately with Middleton,[47] though there were two Sunday services in 1838 when Middleton church was not in use. At the latter date communion was celebrated at least five times a year;[48] by 1865 the frequency was monthly and by 1884 weekly.[49] Congregations on Census Sunday 1851 were 220 in the morning and 250 in the afternoon, on each occasion with 30 Sunday schoolchildren besides.[50] In the mid 19th century men and women sat separately in church, and musicians, some playing instruments, at the west end.[51]

In the 1870s and 80s successive vicars served part of the year as canon residentiary of Chichester cathedral;[52] one of them, Edward Tufnell (d. 1896), had previously been bishop of Brisbane (Australia).[53] The assistant curate lived at Richmond House, Felpham Way, in 1895.[54] Weekday cottage services were held at Flansham in winter in 1898, when there were also daily services in the church.[55]

Felpham's Anglo-Catholic tradition, still marked in 1992, began under Donald Manners, vicar 1934–74, who introduced a weekly sung and a daily said eucharist, the first Anglican midnight mass in the area, and reservation of the sacrament in 1937.[56]

The church of *ST. MARY*[57] is faced chiefly with flint and some 'Bognor rock' sandstone and consists of chancel, aisled nave with south porch and north vestry, and west tower also with north vestry.

The nave was apparently built in the 11th or 12th century and the aisles added in the 13th; the north aisle arcade, which is the earlier, was cut through the north wall of the existing building, but the south wall was rebuilt. The north wall has 14th-century clerestory windows. The elegant chancel, long in proportion to the nave, is early 14th-century[58] and the battlemented tower, with some chequerwork decoration, is 15th-century. The altar at the east end of the north aisle was apparently the Lady altar mentioned in 1534, and that in the south aisle perhaps belonged to the brotherhood of St. Christopher recorded in the 1530s.[59] A bequest to the 'town lights' of Felpham, Flansham, and Ancton in 1547[60] may indicate that each tithing of the parish had its own altar. A rood was mentioned in 1535.[61] Rails or a screen still separated chancel and nave in 1776.[62]

The porch mentioned in 1636[63] had perhaps been built recently since the present structure, which was restored or rebuilt *c.* 1800 and in the 20th century, includes 16th- or 17th-century timber work.[64] In 1622 both church and chancel were said to be 'very dark and foul'.[65] The chancel ceiling, windows, and walls were still in poor repair in 1776, when there was a wooden partition behind the communion table, the space between it and the east wall being filled with rubbish.[66] A south gallery had been built in the nave by 1784[67] and was perhaps rebuilt in 1818,[68] but in 1814 accommodation in the church was said to be limited[69] and in 1828 the interior was felt to lack the clean and neat appearance of South Bersted church.[70] In 1845, when the south gallery partly obscured the tower arch, there was also a modern arch of wood in front of the chancel arch and a modern ceiling below the nave roof.[71]

Extensive repairs were carried out *c.* 1851[72] and the tower and the nave roof were restored in 1884. Apparently during the same period most of the chancel window tracery was renewed and its roof replaced. The tower vestry was built in 1899,[73] when the north aisle wall was apparently refaced, and the choir vestry beside the north aisle in 1939.[74]

The much restored Sussex marble font is late 12th-century; it has a shallow square bowl decorated with blank Romanesque arcading in flat strips and rests on five pillars.[75] Its original base lies in the churchyard opposite the south door. The chest is 13th-century, similar to that at Climping but plainer; another medieval chest survived in 1845.[76] At the latter date there were still many medieval open benches, their ends decorated with plain poppyheads;[77] they had mostly been replaced by 1851[78] but one piece survived in the tower gallery in 1992.[79] A medieval stone altar slab, which had perhaps been used as paving in the porch in 1857,[80] also remained in 1992 behind the modern altar,[81] but the altar cloth mentioned in 1845, of velvet

45 B.L. Add. MS. 39334, f. 29v.; W.S.R.O., Ep. I/22/2 (1838); ibid. Par. 81/1/2/1; Pigot, *Nat. Com. Dir.* (1832–4), 1007; *Kelly's Dir. Suss.* (1845).

46 B.L. Add. MS. 39359, f. 72; W.S.R.O., Ep. I/22A/2 (1844); ibid. Par. 81/1/2/1.

47 Below, Middleton-on-Sea, church.

48 W.S.R.O., Ep. I/22/2 (1838).

49 Ibid. Ep. I/22A/1 (1884); Ep. I/22A/2 (1865).

50 *S.R.S.* lxxv, p. 154.

51 S.A.S. libr., MacDermott colln., scrapbook 1, p. 277.

52 W.S.R.O., Ep. I/22A/1 (1881, 1887); Ep. I/22A/2 (1875).

53 B.L. Add. MS. 39334, ff. 39–40.

54 *Kelly's Dir. Suss.* (1895).

55 W.S.R.O., Ep. I/22A/2 (1898); cf. ibid. Ep. I/40/Felpham/3169.

56 Ibid. MP 4001; ibid. Par. 81/3/3; Par. 81/4/5.

57 Dedic. recorded from 1494, when it was in honour of the Assumption: *S.R.S.* xlii. 144.

58 There is no need to link the chancel with the licence granted in 1344 to Shaftesbury abbey to appropriate the ch., since that was not acted on: e.g. W. Page, *Felpham Ch. Guide*, [1], followed by Nairn & Pevsner, *Suss.* 219; cf. above, this section.

59 *S.R.S.* xlii. 144, 148.

60 W.S.R.O., STC I/7, f. 8.

61 *S.R.S.* xlii. 144.

62 B.L. Add. MS. 5699, f. 52.

63 W.S.R.O., Ep. I/26/2, f. 27.

64 Page, *Felpham Ch. Guide*, [5]; cf. B.L. Add. MS. 5674, f. 38.

65 *S.R.S.* xlix. 33.

66 B.L. Add. MS. 5699, f. 52.

67 W.S.R.O., Ep. I/17/43, f. 47.

68 Ibid. Par. 81/12/1, p. [13].

69 Evans, *Worthing* (1814), ii. 206.

70 Dally, *Bognor* (1828), 57.

71 Clwyd R.O., Glynne ch. notes, lv. 28.

72 B.L. Add. MS. 39365, f. 28v.; *Kelly's Dir. Suss.* (1852).

73 W.S.R.O., Ep. I/40/Felpham/5263; ibid. Felpham par. rec., terrier and inv. of ch. 1901 (Acc. 8028).

74 *Bognor Regis Observer*, 17 Aug. 1989.

75 Below, pl. facing p. 235.

76 Clwyd R.O., Glynne ch. notes, lv. 29.

77 Ibid. 28; cf. Dally, *Bognor* (1828), 57.

78 B.L. Add. MS. 39365, f. 28v.

79 Inf. from Mr. J. Hudson, Felpham.

80 *N. & Q.* 2nd ser. iv. 288.

81 Inf. from Mr. Hudson.

embroidered with cloth of gold and made from a medieval cope,[82] had disappeared.

Box pews were built in the church in the later 18th century;[83] one particularly large example near the chancel arch, enclosed entirely on three sides and on the top except for a square hole to admit light, obscured the chancel and darkened the pulpit in 1776, when it was compared to a cabin in a Dutch passage boat.[84]

There were four bells in 1724:[85] one, which survived in 1992, probably of the early 15th century and three dated between 1599 and 1627, one of them made by Bryan Eldridge and one by Henry and Roger Tapsell. The other five bells in place in 1992 were of 1883.[86] The pre-19th-century plate includes a silver-gilt paten cover dated 1580 with a presumably contemporary tazza-shaped cup, and a silver paten of 1724.[87] There are carved royal arms on the north nave wall. A monument in the chancel and a table tomb in the churchyard commemorate Arthur Gore, earl of Arran (d. 1837), and his wife, residents of Bognor.[88] The registers begin in 1554.[89]

NONCONFORMITY. One woman was presented for recusancy in 1626[90] and there was one reputed papist in 1781.[91] In the 19th century some coastguard men and their families were Roman Catholics.[92] In 1934 the former school building in Middleton Road near the junction with Flansham Lane was opened as a chapel, dedicated to St. Peregrine, of the Catholic parish of Bognor Regis. It was extended in 1936[93] and remained in use in 1992.

One Dissenter was listed in 1676[94] and none in 1724.[95] In 1898 most of the nine or ten Nonconformist families of the parish went to church in Bognor but there was also a corrugated iron mission room in Flansham Lane used by Dependants, services being conducted allegedly by either visiting preachers or the local carrier.[96] Dependant services were still held on Wednesdays in the 1930s.[97]

A Methodist Sunday school was started in 1909 in Sea Road, and from 1932 Methodists hired the Dependant chapel for Sunday evening services of what was known as Felpham gospel mission, with an initial average attendance of 16.[98] A red brick Methodist church hall was opened in Felpham Way in 1939 for services and other purposes, seating 200; after 1963 the building was used exclusively for worship[99] and it was enlarged in the 1980s.[1] A resident minister was appointed in 1962 to serve Westergate and Barnham as well as Felpham.[2] In 1967 there were 95 church members[3] and in 1988 *c.* 150.[4]

In 1952 part of a building in the grounds of Turret House in Felpham village was registered for worship by Christians not otherwise designated; services were simple and Evangelical and the premises also accommodated a biblical museum.[5] A Kingdom Hall of Jehovah's Witnesses had been opened by 1988 in Flansham Lane.

EDUCATION. A schoolmaster was licensed to teach English in 1579[6] and another to teach reading and writing in 1584.[7]

There was a girls' school at Felpham by 1818, whose site is unknown. Boys then went to school in South Bersted,[8] but a boys' National school was opened in 1831 near the junction of Flansham Lane and Middleton Road;[9] the position was evidently chosen as central among the various settlements in Felpham and Middleton parishes, since pupils from Middleton had apparently attended school in Felpham in 1818[10] and continued to do so later.[11] There were 30 girls in 1818 and in 1833, and 40 boys at the latter date. The mistress in 1818 received a salary. Finance was then provided by subscriptions and an annual charity sermon, but in 1833 by subscriptions and donations only.[12]

In 1846–7 the school was known as Felpham and Middleton school,[13] though later nomenclature varied.[14] Average attendance was 22 boys and 28 girls in 1855[15] and 60 including infants *c.* 1872. School pence were also received at that period,[16] but a government grant is not recorded before 1874.[17]

A proposal by the vicar to move the school nearer to Felpham village in the early 1870s was prevented by opposition from the rector of Middleton, and instead a new building of red brick was put up on the old site, incorporating the west wall of the old one-storeyed building. In 1888, however, a new school was opened in Felpham Way north of the village, the then

82 Clwyd R.O., Glynne ch. notes, lv. 29.
83 W.S.R.O., Ep. I/17/43, ff. 47, 120; Dally, *Bognor* (1828), 57.
84 B.L. Add. MS. 5699, f. 52.
85 *S.R.S.* lxxviii. 65.
86 Elphick, *Bells*, 52–3, 305–6.
87 *S.A.C.* liii. 241 and facing p. 264.
88 G. Young, *Hist. Bognor Regis*, 122–3.
89 W.S.R.O., Par. 81/1 (TS. cat.); Par. 81/2/1, f. 31.
90 Ibid. Ep. I/37/4; *S.R.S.* xlix. 125.
91 H.L.R.O., papist return, 1781 (inf. from Mr. T. J. McCann, W.S.R.O.).
92 W.S.R.O., Ep. I/22A/2 (1898); ibid. MP 2415, ff. 15–16.
93 *Centenary of Servite Order in G.B. 1864–1964*, 17 (copy at C.I.H.E. libr.).
94 *Compton Census*, ed. Whiteman, 144.
95 *S.R.S.* lxxviii. 65.
96 W.S.R.O., Ep. I/22A/2 (1898); O.S. Map 6", Suss. LXXIV. NE. (1899 and later edns.).
97 W.S.R.O., NC/MIW/2/9/6/20.
98 Ibid. NC/MIW/2/9/6/20, 22.
99 Ibid. NC/MIW/2/9/6/20; *Bognor Regis Post*, 30 Mar. 1963; *Methodist Ch. Bldg. Return* (1940).
1 *Bognor Regis Observer*, 17 Mar. 1988.
2 *Bognor Regis Post*, 30 Mar. 1963.
3 G. M. M., *A Methodist Tapestry* (Bognor Regis, 1967), 30.
4 *Bognor Regis Observer*, 17 Mar. 1988.
5 Ibid. 21 Mar. 1953; *W. Suss. Gaz.* 31 Mar. 1955; G.R.O. Worship Reg. no. 63501.
6 W.S.R.O., Ep. I/23/5, f. 39v.
7 Ibid. STC III/C, f. 94.
8 *Educ. of Poor Digest*, 957.
9 *Educ. Enq. Abstract*, 969; W.S.R.O., TD/W 54.
10 *Educ. of Poor Digest*, 964.
11 Nat. Soc. *Inquiry, 1846–7*, 10; *Public Elem. Schs. 1875–6*, 266–7; W.S.R.O., Ep. I/22/2 (1838), Middleton; Ep. I/47/4; below, this section.
12 *Educ. of Poor Digest*, 957; *Educ. Enq. Abstract*, 969.
13 Nat. Soc. *Inquiry, 1846–7*, Suss. 6–7.
14 *Felpham by the Sea*, ed. T. & A. Hudson, 56.
15 W.S.R.O., Ep. I/47/4.
16 P.R.O., ED 7/123.
17 *Public Elem. Schs. 1875–6*, 266–7.

incumbent, Bishop Tufnell, defraying the cost and the duke of Richmond giving the site. The old school was later used as a house,[18] before being sold to the Roman Catholic church.[19] Average attendance in the period 1893–1922 fluctuated between 95 and 117; by 1932 it had risen to 144 and in 1938 it was 178.[20]

In 1957 new school buildings were opened on a site off Middleton Road close to the original one to house a separate junior department, the infant department also moving there some years later. Both were called in 1957 Felpham C.E. schools and from 1979 Bishop Tufnell C.E. schools.[21] The building of 1888 was afterwards converted first to an arts centre[22] and then to retirement homes. In 1992 there were 308 infants and 252 juniors on the roll.[23]

Downview county primary school in the west part of the parish was opened in 1976.[24] There were 224 on the roll in 1991.[25]

An evening school was held by the vicar and his daughters in the winter of 1878 with satisfactory results; it continued in 1882 but had lapsed by 1884.[26] Older children from Felpham went to school in Bognor after *c.* 1938,[27] but a comprehensive school called at first Felpham comprehensive school and from 1987 Felpham community college was opened in 1974.[28] It had 808 pupils in 1978 and 1,300 in 1985,[29] and there were 898 on the roll in 1991.[30]

Two private schools with 8 boys and 15 girls flourished in 1833.[31] There was a 'seminary' or 'ladies' school' in the 1850s,[32] and a preparatory school with 6–9 pupils occupied the Manor House in Limmer Lane in 1861 and Richmond Villa, Felpham Way, in 1871.[33] In the 20th century there were other private schools,[34] notably the Gateway mixed preparatory school in Felpham village (fl. 1950–78) which at its closure had 185 pupils.[35]

Adult education classes were held at Felpham community college in 1992.

CHARITIES FOR THE POOR. A pair of war memorial cottages for occupation by poor people were built by subscription in Flansham Lane in 1920.[36]

FORD

THE parish of Ford,[37] which in the 20th century gave its name first to an airfield and then to an open prison, lies on the west bank of the river Arun *c.* 2 miles (3.2 km.) from the sea at the point where the river was formerly joined by the Portsmouth to Arundel canal. Until the 12th or 13th century Ford was part of Climping parish, as the layout of parish boundaries corroborates.[38] The parish had 474 a. (192 ha.) in 1881 and in 1971,[39] and was enlarged in 1985 by the addition of portions of Climping, Tortington, and Yapton.[40] This article deals with the area of the ancient parish; the history of the airfield is split between Ford and Climping, while that of the prison is given under Climping.[41]

The parish lies chiefly on brickearth, with alluvium in the valleys of the Arun and of the Binsted brook, the latter forming the northern boundary.[42] The land is virtually flat. There was presumably reclamation from the river estuary in the Middle Ages, as at Climping; a river wall or earthen bank was mentioned from the mid 16th century,[43] when tenants of Ford, Climping, and Ilsham manor had to maintain the section fronting their lands.[44] Outside the river wall lay saltmarshes or slipes, flooded at every spring tide.[45] The groynes in the river mentioned in 1731[46] were evidently a further defence; in 1761, however, the Littlehampton harbour commissioners ordered them to be abandoned and no further ones made, as detrimental to navigation.[47] The river embankment throughout the parish was apparently heightened under an Act of 1793.[48]

Fishing was said to be very good in 1819, when

18 *Felpham by the Sea*, 54, 56; B.L. Add. MS. 39334, f. 30; P.R.O., ED 49/7700; sketchbk. of Bognor and dist. by Wm. Colliss, p. [61], in possession of Mr. K. Scutt, Bognor Regis.

19 Above, nonconf.

20 *Rep. Educ. Cttee. 1893–4*, 980; *Schs. Parl. Grants, 1900–1*, 244; *Public Elem. Schs. 1907*, 638; *Educ. List 21, 1914*, 522; *1922*, 341; *1932*, 387; *1938*, 402.

21 Inf. from Bp. Tufnell C.E. junior sch., and from Mrs. S. Gould, Felpham; *Bognor Regis Observer*, 19 May 1972; 14 Sept. 1979.

22 *Felpham by the Sea*, 56.

23 Inf. from the sch.

24 *Bognor Regis Post*, 14 Feb. 1981.

25 W.S.R.O., WNC/CM 4/1/14.

26 Ibid. Ep. I/22A/1 (1878, 1884).

27 Inf. from Mr. R. Iden, Bognor Regis.

28 *Bognor Regis Observer*, 13 Sept. 1974; inf. from the headmaster, Felpham community coll.

29 *W. Suss. Gaz.* 30 Mar. 1978; 2 May 1985.

30 W.S.R.O., WNC/CM 4/1/14.

31 *Educ. Enq. Abstract*, 969.

32 *Kelly's Dir. Suss.* (1852, 1855).

33 *Felpham and Middleton Census Returns 1841–1881*, ed. B. Fletcher, 56, 96; cf. *Kelly's Dir. Suss.* (1866, 1874); *Felpham by the Sea*, 58.

34 *Felpham by the Sea*, 58; *Kelly's Dir. Suss.* (1927 and later edns.).

35 *W. Suss. Gaz.* 30 Mar. 1978; *Bognor Regis Observer*, 5 May 1978.

36 Char. Com. files; *Bognor Regis Post*, 14 Nov. 1970.

37 This article was written in 1991 and revised in 1996. Topographical details in introduction based mainly on O.S. Maps 1/25,000, SU 80/90 (1981, 1991 edns.), TQ 00/10 (1979 edn.); 6", Suss. LXII–LXIII (1879–80 and later edns.). Map, below, p. 216.

38 O.S. Map 6", Suss. LXII (1880 edn.); below, church; cf. above, Climping, manors (Park fm.).

39 *Census*, 1881, 1971.

40 Arun (Parishes) Order 1985.

41 Below, this section [airfield]; above, Climping, intro.

42 Geol. Surv. Map 1", drift, sheets 317, 332 (1957, 1975 edns.); cf. *250 Yrs. of Mapmaking in Suss.* ed. H. Margary, pls. 14–15, 19.

43 P.R.O., SC 6/Hen. VIII/3480, rot. 15d.; cf. Guildhall Libr. MS. 13321, f. 5.

44 W.S.R.O., Add. MS. 2292, rot. 5d.; cf. *Cal. Pat.* 1563–6, p. 364.

45 Guildhall Libr. MS. 13324, rep. of land surveyor, 1792.

46 Ibid. 13322, acct. of Ford and Climping, 1731; cf. above, Climping, intro. (landscape hist.).

47 Guildhall Libr. MS. 13323/2, rep. of view of estates, 1761, p. 2.

48 33 Geo. III, c. 100; cf. above, Arundel, port and river traffic (1500–1800).

grey mullet were abundant.[49] Mullet were still netted in 1907.[50]

There were 16 a. of woods but no underwood on Ford, Climping, and Ilsham manor in 1284;[51] the woods may have lain in Ford or Climping.[52] There were only 5 a. of woodland in the parish in 1839.[53]

A radial burial of six skeletons in the northern part of the churchyard[54] is perhaps pre-Christian, and there may have been prehistoric settlement south-west of the church.[55] Poorly defined 'humps and bumps', particularly north and west of the church, indicate the sites of the medieval manor house, raised on a mount, the parsonage, and evidently other houses, separated by streets which included Mount Lane and Parsonage Lane in 1608. West of the road to Climping are other putative house sites[56] including one occupied by the later Newhouse Farm. The medieval village, however, was not necessarily large, since population figures for Ford then evidently included Climping tithing.[57]

By 1608 the village was virtually deserted, at least one house having apparently fallen down within the previous 70 years.[58] There were no buildings near the church in the early 19th century,[59] but *c.* 1820 a pair of cottages was built beside the newly constructed canal;[60] it survived as a single dwelling in 1991. By the mid 19th century the road to Yapton was flanked by extensive farm buildings belonging to the two farms of the parish, Ford Place and Newhouse farms.[61] The only remaining pre-19th-century secular buildings nearby are the farmhouses of those two farms. Ford Place is described below.[62] Newhouse Farm was built shortly before 1800[63] of cobbles with red brick dressings, and was extended eastwards apparently in the early 19th century. The Ship and Anchor inn ¼ mile (400 metres) to the north-east[64] is a 17th- or 18th-century building later enlarged on the east side.

There were eight houses in the parish in 1801, but the number had risen to 20 by 1901.[65] In the later 19th century Christ's Hospital as landowner built several pairs of good-quality cottages,[66] of flint or cobbles with brick dressings; there were 14 in all in 1914.[67] In the 1920s the former airfield buildings in the west end of the parish were converted to houses by John Langmead of Northwood Farm in Climping, but they were requisitioned in 1940.[68] The terrace called Nelson Row on the east side of the Ford–Climping road was built *c.* 1938 as the beginning of a large-scale development which was prevented by the Second World War. A crescent of houses was constructed for the navy further north after the war.[69] A housing estate in the west end of the parish, called the Peregrines to commemorate naval use of the airfield,[70] belongs to the eastwards expansion of Yapton village during the late 20th century.

The totals of between 23 and 30 persons taxed in Ford in the late 13th century and early 14th evidently include inhabitants of Climping tithing, which was not listed;[71] Ford and Climping were listed together in 1524.[72] The protestation of 1642 was made by 19 adult males,[73] and 19 adults were enumerated in 1676.[74] In 1724 there were only 5 families.[75] In 1801 the population was 70, rising to 83 in 1821 and, after a fall, to 106 in 1851, later dropping to 102 in 1891. Fourfold expansion in the 1920s from 90 to 360 was mainly due to the conversion of the airfield buildings into dwellings. There were 268 inhabitants in 1961, 456 in 1971, and 1,301 in the enlarged parish including the prison in 1991.[76]

There seems once to have been an important east-west road through the parish, but whether it crossed the river by a ferry or a ford is not clear.[77] Another possible site for the ford from which the parish takes its name is across the Binsted brook in the north, on the road between Ford and Tortington mentioned in 1573.[78] That route had apparently ceased to be used before the late 18th century,[79] but a new road was cut to join the new Arundel road at Ford station *c.* 1846.[80] There was a ferry across the Arun in the early 19th century.[81]

Vicarage Lane recorded in 1608 was presumably a misnomer for Parsonage Lane mentioned above, but Hole Lane and Chalkstreet, Chalkwest, or Chalkcroft Lane named at the same date are unlocated.[82] Roads in the former village had become mere tracks by the late 18th century,[83] so that the church could then be approached only through fields, as still obtained in 1990. The

49 Dallaway, *Hist. W. Suss.* ii (1) (1819), 46.
50 *V.C.H. Suss.* ii. 466.
51 P.R.O., C 133/39, no. 9, m. 3.
52 Cf. below, manor.
53 W.S.R.O., TD/W 59.
54 *S.A.C.* xliii. 106; S.M.R. 2159.
55 *S.A.C.* cvi. 134; S.M.R. 2161.
56 *S.A.C.* xliii. 110–11; cxxvii. 249–51.
57 Below, this section; *pace S.A.C.* cxxvii. 249.
58 *S.A.C.* cxxvii. 249; Guildhall Libr. MS. 13321, ff. 7, 10.
59 *S.A.C.* cxxvii. 249; *250 Yrs. of Mapmaking in Suss.* pl. 19.
60 P. A. L. Vine, *Lond.'s Lost Route to Sea* (1986), 80, 83; cf. W.S.R.O., TD/W 59.
61 W.S.R.O., TD/W 59; O.S. Map 6", Suss. LXII (1879 edn.).
62 Below, manor.
63 Guildhall Libr. MSS. 13301, lease, 1799; 13323/5, rep. of view of fms. in Surr. and Suss. 1832.
64 Below, this section.
65 *Census*, 1801–1901.
66 e.g. dates 1876, 1877 on bldgs.; cf. W.S.R.O., Ep. I/22A/1 (1884).
67 W.S.R.O., SP 1540.
68 Ward, Lock & Co. *Bognor* [1928–9], 33; inf. from Mr. E. Pratt, Bognor Regis, formerly of Yapton.
69 Inf. from Mr. P. Hague, Oving; O.S. Map 6", Suss. LXII. SE. (1951 edn.); above, pl. facing p. 139.
70 Plaque *in situ* commemorating H.M.S. *Peregrine*; cf. above, Climping, intro. [Ford airfield].
71 *S.R.S.* x. 78–9, 137, 253–4.
72 Ibid. lvi. 56–7; cf. *L. & P. Hen. VIII*, xiv (1), p. 296.
73 *S.R.S.* v. 86.
74 *Compton Census*, ed. Whiteman, 144.
75 *S.R.S.* lxxviii. 66.
76 *Census*, 1801–1991; inf. from H.M. Prison, Ford.
77 *S.A.C.* xliii. 105; lxiii. 59; *V.C.H. Suss.* iii. 46; cf. A. H. Allcroft, *Waters of Arun*, 72.
78 P.R.O., SC 2/205/55, f. 46; cf. *250 Yrs. of Mapmaking in Suss.* pl. 14. For field names nearby in Tortington which include the element Ford, W.S.R.O., TD/W 128. Early forms of the par. name were often in the plural: *P.N. Suss.* (E.P.N.S.), i. 141.
79 *250 Yrs. of Mapmaking in Suss.* pls. 14–15; cf. ibid. pls. 19, 26; W.S.R.O., TD/W 59.
80 Guildhall Libr. MS. 13327, plan of land required by rly. co. *c.* 1844; cf. below, Tortington, intro.
81 *250 Yrs. of Mapmaking in Suss.* pls. 19, 26; Dallaway, *Hist. W. Suss.* ii (1) (1819), 46; cf. *Kelly's Dir. Suss.* (1855).
82 Guildhall Libr. MS. 13321, ff. 2–6, 42.
83 *250 Yrs. of Mapmaking in Suss.* pls. 14–15.

Climping–Yapton road in the west part of the parish, an old route, was blocked by the extension of the airfield runways *c.* 1950 but was reopened in 1959.[84] The parish had a bus service in the 1970s.[85]

The Portsmouth to Arundel canal was opened through the parish in 1823, debouching into the river just north-east of the church.[86] There were two locks,[87] one of which survived in 1990, a steam engine nearby for pumping water into the canal,[88] and a pair of cottages, one of them for the engineer[89] or lock keeper.[90] The unusual juxtaposition of canal and church in the landscape was remarked on by a contemporary.[91] Traffic had greatly declined by 1832[92] and the canal fell into disuse not long afterwards;[93] by 1862 the bed was dry.[94] The pumping house was demolished between *c.* 1875 and *c.* 1896.[95]

The Lyminster–Chichester railway was opened through the northern tip of the parish in 1846 with a station, later called Ford station, in Tortington.[96]

An inn existed beside the river in 1813[97] and had its present name the Ship and Anchor by 1817.[98] The publican in 1871 was also a coal merchant.[99] The inn closed *c.* 1918,[1] but after being used as a teahouse was reopened in 1967 with the adjacent marina.[2]

There was a 'village room' in the stables of Ford Place in 1914.[3]

An airfield was opened in the south-west part of the parish in 1918; at first called Ford junction airfield, it was also known as Yapton aerodrome but had its modern name by 1931. Originally a training station, it was briefly occupied by the United States navy later in 1918 and was closed in the following year. The original buildings lay in the western tip of the parish close to Yapton village.[4]

In the 1930s the airfield was used at different times as a flying school, for joy-rides, for building airliners, as the headquarters of Sir Alan Cobham's 'flying circus', and as a base for experimental flying. In 1937, however, it was taken back by the Air Ministry, new buildings being built in Climping parish, while the original buildings continued to be used for experimental purposes. After the closure of the airfield by the Fleet Air Arm in 1959 most of its buildings in Ford were demolished and replaced by housing; part, however, survived in industrial use.[5]

Water in 1928 came from wells,[6] but by 1938 Bognor urban district council had laid on a supply. Gas and electricity were then also available.[7]

MANOR. The estate called Climping held by Earl Godwine (d. 1053) passed after 1066 to earl Roger, who after the death of his wife Mabel *c.* 1082 divided it between Sées and Alménêches abbeys (Orne). Both moieties were called Climping in 1086;[8] Sées abbey's moiety may be the predecessor of Atherington manor in Climping,[9] while that of Alménêches abbey is evidently what from 1520 was called the manor[10] or manors[11] of *FORD, CLIMPING, AND ILSHAM*, which included the northern part of Climping parish.[12] That manor was held of Arundel rape,[13] and was said in the early 15th century once to have owed 40 days' castle guard at Arundel castle.[14]

Savaric son of Cane was granted Alménêches abbey's estate *c.* 1102,[15] and was succeeded in turn by his sons Ralph (d. *c.* 1157) and Savaric (d. *c.* 1187). The younger Savaric's nephew and heir Frank de Bohun (d. 1192) was compelled to yield Ford and Climping to Ralph de Arderne, but Richard I in 1190 declared the transaction void[16] and the land was described as Frank's in 1194.[17] Ralph later renewed his suit, and in 1199 Frank's son Enjuger quitclaimed the manor to him. In 1212 Ralph's son Thomas restored it to Enjuger,[18] and it descended thereafter in the Bohun family[19] as a member of Midhurst.[20] Anthony Bek, bishop of Durham, who died seised of a moiety of Ford, so called, in 1311, was evidently a relative.[21] Ursula, daughter of John de Bohun (d. in or before 1492), and her husband (Sir) Robert Southwell had a moiety of Ford in 1507–8.[22] Sir Henry Owen, son of John's other daughter Mary, was dealing with what was perhaps the other moiety in 1520.[23] By 1534 he

84 Guildhall Libr. MS. 13321, f. 3; above, Climping, intro. (communications).
85 Inf. from Mrs. S. Whitelock, Ford Pla.
86 Vine, *Lond.'s Lost Route to Sea*, 80, 83.
87 Ibid. pl. 59; *Suss. Ind Arch.* (1985), p. 63; O.S. Map 6", Suss. LXIII (1879 edn.).
88 Horsfield, *Hist. Suss.* ii. 114; Lewis, *Topog. Dict. Eng.* (1845); W.S.R.O., TD/W 59; illus. at ibid. PD 1607; Vine, op. cit. pl. 58.
89 W.S.R.O., TD/W 59; Guildhall Libr. MS. 13323/5, rep. of view of fms. in Surr. and Suss. 1832.
90 P.R.O., HO 107/1651, f. 523.
91 Vine, op. cit. 240 n. 167.
92 Guildhall Libr. MS. 13323/5, rep. of view of fms. in Surr. and Suss. 1832.
93 Below, econ. hist.
94 *Kelly's Dir. Suss.* (1862).
95 O.S. Map 6", Suss. LXII–LXIII (1879–80 and later edns.).
96 *Southern Region Rec.* comp. R. H. Clark, 51, 74.
97 B.L. Maps, O.S.D. 83 (E).
98 *S.N.Q.* xi. 30; cf. W.S.R.O., TD/W 59. It was sometimes alternatively the Anchor or the Ship and Lobster: A.C.M., D 6289–90; *Kelly's Dir. Suss.* (1845, 1852).
99 P.R.O., RG 10/1108, f. 38.
1 Allcroft, *Waters of Arun*, 73.
2 Below, econ. hist.; *Yachting and Boating Wkly.* 10 Feb. 1966.
3 W.S.R.O., SP 1540.
4 *Suss. Ind. Hist.* vi. 28, 30, 33.
5 Ibid. 28-32; *Kelly's Dir. Suss.* (1934); cf. below, econ. hist.
6 F. H. Edmunds, *Wells and Springs of Suss.* 29.
7 *Kelly's Dir. Suss.* (1938).
8 *V.C.H. Suss.* i. 430; *Cal. Doc. France*, ed. Round, p. 234.
9 Above, Climping, manors (Atherington).
10 B.L. Add. MS. 39493, f. 141. In 1608 it was described as the man. of Ford and its members: W.S.R.O., Add. MS. 2293, rot. 1.
11 *S.R.S.* xix. 171.
12 For the Ilsham component, above, Climping, manors (Ilsham).
13 e.g. *Cal. Inq. p.m.* ii, p. 28; *Feud. Aids*, v. 143; P.R.O., C 139/58, no. 33.
14 *S.R.S.* lxvii. 105.
15 *Eccl. Hist. of Orderic Vitalis*, ed. Chibnall, vi. 33.
16 *Cal. Pat.* 1358–61, 534–5, reciting 12th-cent. charters; W. H. St. John Hope, *Cowdray and Easebourne Priory*, 1–2 and facing p. 16.
17 *Pipe R.* 1194 (P.R.S. N.S. v), 8.
18 *Cur. Reg. R.* vi. 397–9.
19 St. John Hope, *Cowdray*, 1–12 and facing p. 16, on which rest of para. mainly based; *Bk. of Fees*, ii. 688; *Cal. Inq. p.m.* ii, pp. 27–8, 322; xii, pp. 100–2; *Cal. Pat.* 1358–61, 534; *Cal. Close*, 1447–54, 24; P.R.O., C 139/58, no. 33.
20 *Cal. Inq. p.m.* ii, p. 322.
21 Ibid. ii, p. 322; v, pp. 150–1; Elwes & Robinson, *W. Suss.* 100 n.; cf. *S.R.S.* x. 78.
22 *S.R.S.* xxiii, p. 303.
23 Ibid. xix. 171.

had the whole manor,[24] and in 1538 he conveyed it to John Palmer,[25] who in 1540 sold it to the Crown.[26]

In 1604 the manor was granted to Charles Howard, earl of Nottingham,[27] but it was afterwards resumed by the Crown and granted in 1607 or earlier to Robert Cecil, earl of Salisbury.[28] In 1610 he sold it to George Salter and John Williams of London, who in 1614 sold it to William Garway[29] (d. 1625), from whom it descended in the direct line through Sir Henry, lord mayor of London (d. 1646), to William, M.P. for Chichester and Arundel (d.s.p. 1701).[30] After the successive deaths in 1702 of William's two childless nephews Henry Norris and Sir William Norris, Bt., the estate passed by remainder to Christ's Hospital, London,[31] which owned virtually the entire parish in 1835[32] and *c.* 1,485 a. in Ford and Climping in 1860.[33] In 1914 the hospital's lands in Ford were conveyed to the Dennis Estates Ltd.,[34] but in 1916 they passed to Norman Hague, who was succeeded by his son Reginald.[35] Part of the land was compulsorily purchased by the Air Ministry for the enlargement of Ford airfield in 1937, but after its return in the 1960s Reginald's son Peter still owned much of the parish in 1991.[36]

Before 1273[37] the Bohuns built a substantial house on a raised squarish plot west of the church which was called the court garden in the early 17th century.[38] Foundations were discovered there in 1818 during the building of the canal, and indeterminate earthworks were still visible in the 1980s.[39] A garden or gardens were mentioned in 1284 and later,[40] but although once surrounded by ditches[41] the house is unlikely to have been moated as has been claimed.[42] It had been demolished by 1608.[43] Caen stone seen in 1900 and later at Ford Place and in boundary walls nearby[44] may have come from it.

The brick and flint house called Ford Place, lying ⅓ mile (540 metres) west of the earlier site, belongs to the group of so-called 'Artisan Mannerist' buildings, of City of London connexions.[45] It was built by William Garway apparently before 1670, when he was taxed on two houses in the parish, one with nine hearths and one with three.[46] Garway was living at Ford by 1676.[47] The oldest part of the house, the present southern block, is of two storeys with attics, and has a moulded brick plinth, prominent brick keystones to the windows, a bracketed cornice, and tall chimneys decorated with blind arcading. A wing running northwards from its east end and a single-storeyed extension east of that are almost contemporary. Additions in the angle between the two main ranges were made at two stages in the 18th century, and all the windows were renewed and many of them altered apparently in the mid 19th.[48] In 1753 there were seven rooms on each floor.[49] Original panelling, chimneypieces, and a staircase survived in the early 20th century[50] when the house was let,[51] but were later removed. In 1952 the building was completely remodelled for division into four dwellings.[52]

A large garden east of Ford Place was surrounded by walls of brick, knapped flint, and some worked stone which partly survived in 1991.[53] The house nearby called the Cottage also contains re-used old materials, and includes a dovecot.

ECONOMIC HISTORY. The demesne farm of Ford, Climping, and Ilsham manor in 1311 had 189 a. of arable, *c.* 20 a. of meadow, and at least 11 a. of pasture. Sixteen customers then held 11½ yardlands, owing 1,932 works between Michaelmas and Lammas and an uncertain number during harvest.[54] The ninth of sheaves was valued at 24 times that of fleeces and lambs in 1341, when flax, hemp, and apples were grown, and cattle, pigs, and geese kept.[55] Two inhabitants of Ford or Climping had the surname Shepherd in the late 13th century and early 14th.[56] Oats were raised in 1285.[57] The medieval arable was presumably at least partly in open fields, as later.

In the 16th and 17th centuries the demesne, including marshland, was leased in various parcels, though there seems generally to have been one chief farm.[58] There were a single freehold tenant and several copyhold tenants in the same period, some copyholds being described

24 *Cal. Pat.* 1578–80, p. 53, reciting lease, 1534.
25 *S.R.S.* xix. 171.
26 Guildhall Libr. MS. 13295, deed, 1540.
27 *Cal. S.P. Dom.* 1603–10, 144.
28 Guildhall Libr. MS. 13295, deed, 1607; W.S.R.O., Add. MS. 2293, rot. 4, recording a ct. held in his name, 1605; Hist. MSS. Com. 9, *Salisbury*, xvii, p. 160.
29 Guildhall Libr. MS. 13295, deeds, 1610, 1614.
30 Elwes & Robinson, *W. Suss.* 100 n.; *Hist. Parl., Commons*, 1660–90, ii. 373, 380.
31 W.S.R.O., SP 1540, p. 2; B.L. Add. MS. 39493, f. 141.
32 Horsfield, *Hist. Suss.* ii. 113; cf. W.S.R.O., IR 19, ff. 31–2; ibid. SP 1540; ibid. TD/W 59.
33 Guildhall Libr. MS. 13323/5, rep. of view of estates, 1860.
34 Ibid. 13319, deed, 1914.
35 Inf. from Mrs. S. Whitelock, Ford Pla., and Mr. P. Hague, Oving.
36 Inf. from Mr. Hague; *Suss. Ind. Hist.* vi. 30; *Kelly's Dir. Suss.* (1938).
37 P.R.O., C 133/3, no. 14.
38 *S.A.C.* cxxvii. 249–50; Guildhall Libr. MS. 13321, f. 40; cf. W.S.R.O., Ep. I/25/1 (1635).
39 *S.A.C.* cxxvii. 249. A. H. Allcroft, *Waters of Arun*, 89–90, wrongly locates the site W. of the Arundel–Ford rd.
40 P.R.O., C 133/39, no. 9, m. 3; C 134/21, no. 8, m. 7.
41 B.L. Add. MS. 5699, f. 61.
42 *S.A.C.* cxxvii. 249.
43 Guildhall Libr. MS. 13321, f. 40.
44 *S.A.C.* xliii. 111; personal observation.
45 Nairn & Pevsner, *Suss.* 226; J. Summerson, *Archit. in Brit. 1530 to 1830* (1969), 89.
46 P.R.O., E 179/191/410, pt. 2, rot. 3.
47 Hist. MSS. Com. 5, *6th Rep., Raffles*, 473; cf. ibid. 39, *15th Rep. II, Hodgkin*, p. 70; *Cal. S.P. Dom.* 1687–9, p. 199.
48 Guildhall Libr. MS. 13323/5, rep. of view of estates, 1845.
49 Ibid. 13323/2, rep. of view of estates, 1753.
50 *S.A.C.* xliii. 109; *V.C.H. Suss.* ii. 392; W.S.R.O., SP 1540.
51 e.g. *Kelly's Dir. Suss.* (1909, 1913).
52 Inf. from Mrs. S. Whitelock, Ford Pla.
53 Cf. Guildhall Libr. MS. 13323/2, rep. of view of estates, 1753.
54 P.R.O., C 134/21, no. 8, m. 7. The larger figs. given in 1284 included 30 a. of meadow at Prestbrook, perhaps in Rustington: ibid. C 133/39, no. 9, m. 3; *Cal. Inq. p.m.* ii, p. 322.
55 *Inq. Non.* (Rec. Com.), 369; cf. *S.A.C.* lxxii. 172.
56 *S.R.S.* x. 79, 137, 254.
57 *Cal. Inq. Misc.* i, p. 392.
58 Guildhall Libr. MS. 13321, ff. 38–42; P.R.O., SC 6/Hen. VIII/3480, rott. 15d.–16; *L. & P. Hen. VIII*, xxi (2), p. 441; *Cal. Pat.* 1563–6, pp. 83, 364; 1572–5, pp. 365–6; 1578–80, p. 53.

as single yardlands.[59] Some copyholders held for three lives[60] and their holdings could be sublet.[61] In 1608 eleven copyholders held between three and nine tenements each, making holdings of mostly between 11 a. and 30 a.[62] Open fields mentioned in the period were West field, lying north of the Climping–Yapton road, South field, mentioned from 1540 but described as a new field in 1608,[63] and possibly Town field.[64] By 1608 most holdings in West and South fields were in consolidated closes of between 4 a. and 9 a. in area.[65] Common meadows mentioned then and earlier were the Hose, Hose mead, or Hoslee, and Ford Gore in the west,[66] and the tenants also had common pasture in Walberton.[67] Cattle, sheep, and pigs were kept in the 17th century and early 18th, and wheat, barley, oats, beans, peas, tares, vetches, and hemp were grown. The large farm on which 29 cattle, 221 sheep, 34 pigs, and at least 88 a. of crops were recorded in 1631 was evidently a demesne farm; another, similarly large, in 1647, was held with property at Binsted and Littlehampton.[68]

By the early 18th century[69] most if not all copyholds had been engrossed into the demesne, on which there were two chief farms of 211 a. and 108 a., perhaps the same as the later Ford Place and Newhouse farms; the latter may have originated in the copyhold called Newhouse in 1540.[70] During most of the period of Christ's Hospital's ownership of the Ford estate between the early 18th century and the early 20th the demesne farms were let on leases usually of 14 or 21 years. In the late 18th century Ford Place farm had 368 a. and Newhouse farm nearly 200 a.; each remained much the same in size in the mid 19th. Ford Place farm was held by members of the Staker family between 1744 and the early 19th century, and Newhouse farm by the Bonifaces from 1783 and probably earlier. By 1839 the Bonifaces also had Ford Place farm,[71] and by 1871 the two farms were worked as a single holding of 1,000 a. in Ford and elsewhere, employing 38 men and boys and one woman.[72] The parish later remained within a single holding.[73]

The land was said to be in fine condition in 1794,[74] and in 1853 the two Ford farms were considered the best on Christ Hospital's Sussex estate.[75] Seventy-two cattle, mostly fatting oxen, were listed in 1801, besides 264 sheep and 77 pigs.[76] In 1839 the parish had 270 a. of arable and 189 a. of meadow and pasture. The arable was then worked on a four-course rotation of wheat, turnips, barley, and seeds with beans or peas,[77] and in 1847 on a five-course rotation.[78] By the 1870s consolidation of closes had resulted in some very large fields.[79] There was great unrest in the area in 1830,[80] but in 1884 work was said to be plentiful and wages good.[81] Between 1916 and *c.* 1975 cattle were raised, the land on Ford airfield continuing to be farmed, despite flying activity, in 1969. In 1991 the parish was predominantly arable.[82]

The mill recorded on Ford, Climping, and Ilsham manor in the late 12th century[83] may have been an early windmill, since there is no obvious site for a water mill in Ford or the northern part of Climping. The manorial windmill of 1284[84] and mill of 1542[85] may similarly have been in either Ford or Climping parish.

The surname Smith, perhaps indicating the practice of the trade, was recorded in the late 13th century and early 14th.[86] The high tax assessment levied in 1334[87] evidently applied to Climping tithing too. One alien paid the subsidy in 1524.[88]

The suggestion that Arundel's port once lay at Ford[89] seems unlikely. Some parishioners, nevertheless, earned part or all of their living from the river. The three men of Ford who were to serve in the navy in 1524[90] were presumably mariners, and there were two seamen in 1678.[91] Mention of a dock in the 18th century[92] suggests river trade otherwise unrecorded at that date. Two boats were listed in 1801.[93] A storehouse was depicted at the Ship and Anchor inn in 1813.[94]

The opening of the canal in 1823 seems to have caused an increase in river traffic. There was a wharf with a warehouse at the Ship and Anchor in 1839,[95] though during 1836 only two cargoes were handled there.[96] The site was called Ford quay in the mid 19th century.[97] A railway siding

59 Guildhall Libr. MS. 13321, ff. 1–12; P.R.O., SC 6/Hen. VIII/3480, rot. 15 and d.

60 A.C.M., M 532, f. [68]; Guildhall Libr. MS. 13321, ff. 2–12; W.S.R.O., Add. MS. 2292, rot. 4.

61 W.S.R.O., Add. MS. 2293, 15 Dec. 1608.

62 Guildhall Libr. MS. 13321, ff. 2–12.

63 Ibid. ff. 4, 6; W.S.R.O., Add. MS. 2292, rot. 1d.

64 W.S.R.O., Add. MS. 2293, 12 Apr. 1593; unless it lay in Climping: above, Climping, econ. hist. (agric.).

65 Guildhall Libr. MS. 13321, ff. 2–12, 37.

66 Ibid. ff. 2–4, 6; W.S.R.O., PHA 933, f. 74v.

67 W.S.R.O., Add. MS. 2292, rot. 5; Guildhall Libr. MS. 13321, f. 42.

68 W.S.R.O., Ep. I/29/87/1, 4, 6, 13, 18, 22–3.

69 Para. based mainly on Guildhall Libr. MSS. 13299, 13301, 13303–6.

70 P.R.O., SC 6/Hen. VIII/3480, rot. 15d.

71 W.S.R.O., TD/W 59.

72 P.R.O., RG 10/1108, f. 37; cf. W.S.R.O., Ep. I/22A/1 (1884); ibid. SP 1540.

73 Inf. from Mr. P. Hague, Oving; cf. *Kelly's Dir. Suss.* (1934).

74 Guildhall Libr. MS. 13323/3, rep. of John Trumper, 1795; cf. ibid. 13323/5, val. of estate in Ford and Climping, 1832; rep. of view of estates, 1845.

75 Ibid. 13323/3, rep. on fms. in Ford and Climping, 1853; cf. Dallaway, *Hist. W. Suss.* ii (1) (1819), 46.

76 E.S.R.O., LCG/3/EW 1, f. [43v.]; cf. *S.A.C.* lxxi. 47.

77 P.R.O., IR 18/10334; W.S.R.O., TD/W 59.

78 Guildhall Libr. MS. 13323/5, valuation and rep. 1847.

79 O.S. Map 6", Suss. LXII, LXIII (1879–80 edn.).

80 *I Am, My Dear Sir*, ed. F. W. Steer, 82.

81 W.S.R.O., Ep. I/22A/1 (1884).

82 Inf. from Mr. Hague; *W. Suss. Gaz.* 12 June 1969. Agric. statistics for 1875 and 1909 are not used here because they evidently include land in Climping: P.R.O., MAF 68/433, 2371; cf. above, Climping, econ. hist. (agric.).

83 *S.R.S.* xlvi, p. 87.

84 P.R.O., C 133/39, no. 9, m. 3.

85 W.S.R.O., Add. MS. 2292, rot. 6.

86 *S.R.S.* x. 79, 254.

87 *S.A.C.* l. 166.

88 *S.R.S.* lvi. 57.

89 A. H. Allcroft, *Waters of Arun*, 76–7.

90 *L. & P. Hen. VIII*, iv (1), p. 125.

91 W.S.R.O., Ep. I/55/156 (TS. cat.).

92 *250 Yrs. of Mapmaking in Suss.* ed. H. Margary, pls. 5, 14.

93 E.S.R.O., LCG/3/EW 1, f. [44].

94 B.L. O.S.D. 83 (E).

95 W.S.R.O., TD/W 59.

96 J. H. Farrant, *Mid-Victorian Littlehampton* (Littlehampton, 1972), 2.

97 A.C.M., LM 15; P.R.O., HO 107/1651, f. 522; ibid. RG 10/1108, f. 38.

South Stoke Farmhouse from the south

The Black Rabbit inn on the river Arun in the early 20th century

SOUTH STOKE

Arundel Way on the Elmer Sands estate in the mid 20th century

The old church in the early 19th century shortly before its destruction, showing windmills at Felpham in the background

was constructed apparently in 1850[98] and ships of considerable tonnage were said to discharge their cargoes in 1854;[99] for many years there was a limekiln nearby.[1] The canal was last used commercially in 1847,[2] but there were still a barge owner, a sailor, a shipwright, and a ship's carpenter in the parish in 1871.[3]

Only one or two families in work were supported mostly by non-agricultural pursuits in the early 19th century.[4] There was a carpenter in 1845, a general dealer in 1851, and a shopkeeper in the 1930s.[5]

After the closure of Ford airfield in 1959 its northern part was developed from *c.* 1963 as an industrial estate.[6] By 1973 two large hangars were being used for the manufacture of concrete blocks,[7] the site passing later to Francis Parker PLC, and in 1984 to Tarmac Concrete and Tarmac Topblock; in 1990 the premises, which were very large, included Tarmac's regional office for the south of England.[8] Other construction and engineering firms were nearby in 1985.[9] In 1991 the Ford airfield industrial estate accommodated *c.* 28 firms, mostly small, some in converted hangars and others in new workshops.[10] The former photographic school belonging to the airfield north of the Ford–Yapton road was then occupied by a further six or eight industrial firms.[11] A new brewery called the Arundel brewery began production on the industrial estate in 1992.[12]

A marina and club, with an 8-a. camping and caravan site, were opened at the Ship and Anchor inn in 1967[13] and remained in 1995. In 1975 a hundred boats could be moored and there was accommodation for 125 campers and 35 holiday caravans.[14] There was a forge in Ford Lane in 1990.

LOCAL GOVERNMENT. Ford, Climping, and Ilsham manor had leet jurisdiction by 1279.[15] There are court rolls or draft court rolls for the years 1540–2, 1547–50, and 1593–1609.[16] In the 1540s the view and court were held together twice a year, and the court perhaps twice more. The view held the assize of bread and of ale, elected the constable, and heard cases of theft and once of an affray. The court was responsible for recording tenures and managing common land, elected two 'curemen', perhaps haywards, and held pleas of land. Both courts dealt with nuisances. The jurisdiction of the view, besides Climping, included land in Yapton, Tortington, and Binsted. In the 1590s and 1600s only the court was still held, electing a beadle in 1609. A sheriff's tourn was held in 1542.[17] There was a manor pound in 1566.[18]

Manorial jurisdiction seems to have ceased after the early 17th century, no further courts being recorded. A tithingman still served for Ford and Climping *c.* 1822.[19]

There were apparently two churchwardens between 1548 and 1634, but from 1642 until 1897 or later only one. Members of the Staker family served between 1743 and 1835, and members of the Boniface family in the mid and later 19th century.[20] There was a single overseer in 1642[21] and 1826[22] and a surveyor of highways in the 1880s and 90s.[23]

A church rate was levied in 1621.[24] In 1799 Ford joined East Preston united parishes, later East Preston union,[25] afterwards rural district. Thirty parishioners were receiving permanent relief in 1826, and three casual relief.[26] In 1884 the sole farmer, George Boniface, bore all parish expenses himself.[27] The parish passed to Chichester rural district in 1933[28] and to Arun district in 1974.

CHURCH. Ford church was said to belong to Climping church in the late 12th or early 13th century,[29] and as late as 1284 was described as a chapel.[30] In 1178, however, the pope confirmed Climping and Ford churches, as though they were independent churches, to Alménêches abbey (Orne).[31] When the bishop appropriated Climping to the abbey in 1248 and ordained a vicarage there he reserved his ordinance about Ford, which the abbey had conveyed to him,[32] and Ford retained an incumbent rector. The living was briefly united with Climping vicarage in 1656[33] and in 1875 was united with Yapton vicarage.[34] Since 1985 it has formed part of the united benefice of Climping and Yapton with Ford, the parishes remaining distinct.[35]

Alménêches abbey had the right of presentation *c.* 1200.[36] After 1248 the bishop presumably

98 V. Mitchell and K. Smith, *S. Coast Rlys.: Worthing to Chich.* [65].
99 A.C.M., D 6289.
1 Mitchell and Smith, *S. Coast Rlys.* [65].
2 P. A. L. Vine, *Lond.'s Lost Route to Sea* (1986), 144.
3 P.R.O., RG 10/1108, ff. 37–8.
4 *Census*, 1811–31.
5 *Kelly's Dir. Suss.* (1845 and later edns.); P.R.O., HO 107/1651, f. 522v.
6 *Brighton Evening Argus*, 9 Aug. 1963.
7 *Suss. Ind. Hist.* vi. 32.
8 Inf. from the Managing Dir., Tarmac Topblock Ltd., 1990.
9 *Ind. in W. Suss.* (W. Suss. C.C., 1985).
10 Cf. W.S.R.O., WNC/CC 14/19.
11 Inf. from Mr. P. Hague, Oving; cf. O.S. Map 1/25,000, SU 90 (1958 edn.). For the Rudford ind. estate and for Ford Sunday market, held on the airfield, above, Climping, econ. hist. (other trades and inds.).
12 *W. Suss. Gaz.* 8 Oct. 1992; 4 Nov. 1993.
13 Ibid. 6 Apr. 1967.
14 Ibid. 6 Feb. 1975.
15 *Plac. de Quo Warr.* (Rec. Com.), 756; cf. *Cowdray Archives*, ed. A. Dibben, ii, p. 280.
16 A.C.M., M 532, *passim*; P.R.O., LR 3/115/5, rot. [51]; W.S.R.O., Add. MSS. 2292–3; ibid. PHA 933, ff. 71–4; 935, ff. 44–7; 6677, rot. 7; 6683, ff. 8–14; on which rest of para. mainly based. A copy of ct. roll of 1484 is at Guildhall Libr. MS. 13295/4.
17 W.S.R.O., PHA 6683, ff. 11–14.
18 A.C.M., MD 2347, m. 2; cf. above, Climping, local govt.
19 E.S.R.O., QCR/2/1/EW 2 (47).
20 B.L. Add. MS. 39359, ff. 80–5; W.S.R.O., Ep. I/86/20, f. 16v.; *S.R.S.* v. 86; xlix. 35.
21 *S.R.S.* v. 86.
22 W.S.R.O., QCR/2/3/W 5.
23 Ibid. Par. 87/40/1.
24 *S.R.S.* xlix. 24.
25 *Suss. Poor Law Rec.* 32, 46.
26 W.S.R.O., QCR/2/3/W 5.
27 Ibid. Ep. I/22A/1 (1884); Guildhall Libr. MS. 13301, lease, 1878.
28 *Census* (1931), pt. ii.
29 Eton Coll. Libr. MS. 56/2 (TS. cat.). It is unlikely to be the second ch. mentioned at Climping in 1086, as suggested at *S.A.C.* xliii. 107, since the second estate described there is apparently Atherington in Climping: *V.C.H. Suss.* i. 430; above, Climping, manors (Atherington).
30 P.R.O., C 133/39, no. 9, m. 3.
31 *S.A.C.* xlvi. 224.
32 *S.R.S.* xlvi, pp. 55, 370.
33 *S.N.Q.* xv. 118.
34 *Lond. Gaz.* 10 Aug. 1875, p. 3961.
35 Inf. from Chich. Dioc. Regy.
36 *Chich. Acta* (Cant. & York Soc.), p. 129.

FORD CHURCH *c.* 1900

collated, as he certainly did from 1397.[37] On three occasions between 1429 and 1670 the advowson was exercised by the Crown during vacancy, in 1549 by George Goring for a turn,[38] in 1647 by the House of Lords,[39] and in 1654 by Oliver Cromwell as Lord Protector.[40] The united benefice of Yapton and Ford remained in the bishop's gift,[41] and after 1985 two presentations in three to the new united benefice of Climping and Yapton with Ford were to be made by the bishop and the third by the Lord Chancellor.[42]

The rectory was valued at £5 6*s.* 8*d.* in 1291.[43] Episcopal grants from its endowment to Alménêches abbey (£2 a year from *c.* 1200)[44] and to Wyndham hospital in Shermanbury (£1 from 1262)[45] later lapsed, perhaps before 1341, when the rector had all the tithes as well as a house and land.[46] By the 1480s the value of the living had fallen below £8 because of flooding,[47] but in 1535 it was £9 6*s.* 4*d.* net.[48] The rectory was worth £40 in 1656[49] but only £27 in 1724;[50] in 1662 it was leased.[51] In the early 17th century the glebe was only ¼–½ a. in area.[52] The rectory house north of the church,[53] which had been out of repair in 1573,[54] was burnt down by soldiers

37 *S.R.S.* xi. 241, 259; B.L. Add. MS. 39334, ff. 131–6.
38 *Cal. Pat.* 1429–36, 28; B.L. Add. MS. 39334, ff. 132–4.
39 *L.J.* ix. 522.
40 *S.A.C.* xxxiii. 218.
41 *Lond. Gaz.* 10 Aug. 1875, p. 3961.
42 Inf. from Chich. Dioc. Regy. It is not clear who presented in 1669: B.L. Add. MS. 39334, f. 134. In 1538 the advowson was claimed, evidently in error, to belong to the man.: *S.R.S.* xix. 171.
43 *Tax. Eccl.* (Rec. Com.), 135.
44 *Chich. Acta* (Cant. & York Soc.), p. 129. Eton Coll. Libr. MS. 56/5 (TS. cat.) gives the sum as 2 marks.
45 *S.R.S.* xlvi, p. 299.
46 *Inq. Non.* (Rec. Com.), 369; but cf. *S.R.S.* xix. 77; W.S.R.O., Add. MS. 8811 (TS. cat.).
47 B.L. Add. MS. 39334, f. 126.
48 *Valor Eccl.* (Rec. Com.), i. 316.
49 *S.N.Q.* xv. 118.
50 *S.R.S.* lxxviii. 66.
51 W.S.R.O., Ep. I/29/87/15.
52 Ibid. Ep. I/25/1 (1615, 1635); the rector also leased 22 a. from the demesne: Guildhall Libr. MS. 13321, ff. 10–11.
53 *S.A.C.* cxxvii. 249, 251.
54 W.S.R.O., Ep. I/23/4, f. 4.

during the Civil War[55] and by 1724 its site, together with the glebe, lay intermixed with demesne land,[56] Christ's Hospital or its tenant paying the rector £2 rent between the late 18th century and the late 19th.[57] By *c.* 1830 the net value of the living had risen to *c.* £197.[58] At the commutation of tithes in 1839 the rector was awarded a rent charge of £235 8*s.*[59]

A chantry is recorded in the late 14th century.[60] The incumbent in 1411 was licensed to hold another living,[61] and it was presumably because of the non-residence of his successors that assistant curates were recorded in the 1540s and 60s.[62] The rector in 1579 was a licensed preacher and served the cure himself.[63] Pluralism, however, was the norm between the mid 16th century and the late 18th;[64] non-residence may have been common before the mid 17th century,[65] and after the destruction of the rectory house was presumably continuous. Among the additional livings, chiefly local, held by successive rectors Climping vicarage occurred most often.[66] Many assistant curates were recorded between the later 17th century and the early 19th.[67] Richard Meggot, appointed in 1654, conformed at the Restoration;[68] in 1662 he or his successor was a licensed preacher.[69]

A service with sermon was held every three weeks in 1724, when holy communion was celebrated three times a year with between four and eight communicants.[70] By 1844 communion was quarterly and by 1884 monthly; at the last named date Sunday morning and afternoon services were held alternately with Yapton.[71] The average morning congregation in 1851 was 50 and the afternoon one twice that. The rector was then living at his other cure of Littlehampton.[72] His successor, who was curate of Climping, occupied Climping vicarage.[73] There were still weekly services *c.* 1910,[74] but by 1959 only one a month;[75] in 1990 services were held monthly in summer and on St. Andrew's day (30 November).[76]

The church of *ST. ANDREW*, so called by 1501,[77] is of flint pebble and brick with stone dressings, and consists of chancel and wide nave with north vestry, south porch, and timber bellcot.[78] The nave is probably late 11th-century and has two small windows of that date in the north wall, the eastern one much restored. Over the later medieval north doorway is a reset stone with interlace ornament, perhaps from a freestanding cross.[79] The chancel is early 12th-century and has a plain arch with diaper ornament on the imposts. At that period the floor level, as shown by the basal offset of the chancel arch, was lower. A south aisle was added in the early 13th century, and it was probably at the same time that new windows were put into the north wall of the nave. In the mid 14th century the chancel was lengthened and the present east window put in. By the early 16th century the south aisle had been demolished, perhaps by fire as the surviving west respond of the arcade is reddened; the nave was given a new south wall in which were reset a 14th-century doorway and window. The porch was added at the same time, and the west window and crown-post roof of the nave are probably also contemporary. A steeple was mentioned in 1557.[80]

In 1637[81] the porch was heightened and given a new front of brick surmounted by a shaped gable with segmental pediment. In the earlier 19th century the chancel was shut off from the nave by a screen or doors,[82] and in 1860 the church was in a very bad state, unfit for divine service and almost dangerous for the congregation to be in.[83] It was ruthlessly restored *c.* 1865;[84] the bellcot seems to have been renewed at that time and by 1900 was painted white, evidently to serve as a landmark to shipping.[85] The church was further repaired in 1879 and in 1899–1900, when the north vestry was built.[86] In 1972 it was again in disrepair,[87] but in 1991 it was well kept.

A rood was mentioned in 1539,[88] its loft stair being against the north wall. A recess and piscina south of the chancel arch are evidence of an altar there, perhaps belonging to the chantry mentioned above. Several medieval oak benches with fleur-de-lis poppy heads survived until the mid 19th century.[89] The font has a large plain square limestone bowl of possibly 12th-century date. There are fragments of 15th-century wall paintings, including a Last Judgement over the chancel arch and an Agony in the Garden on the south side of the nave.[90]

One of the two bells was made by Robert Rider (fl. 1351–86) and the other is possibly 17th-century.[91] Before *c.* 1865 the belfry was reached from inside the church by a 'pigeon-house'

55 Ibid. Ep. I/22/1 (1662).
56 *S.R.S.* lxxviii. 66.
57 W.S.R.O., Ep. I/22/2 (1838); ibid. Par. 87/1/1/1, inside back cover; *Glebe Lands Return*, p. 29, H.C. 307 (1887), lxiv.
58 *Rep. Com. Eccl. Revenues.*
59 W.S.R.O., TD/W 59. What was perhaps part of the parsonage or its outbldgs. survived *c.* 1860: *S.A.C.* cxxvii. 249, citing ibid. xliii. 110.
60 *S.R.S.* xlvi, p. 311.
61 *Cal. Papal Reg.* vi. 292.
62 B.L. Add. MS. 39359, f. 80; W.S.R.O., Ep. I/86/20, f. 16v.; *S.R.S.* xlii. 194.
63 W.S.R.O., Ep. I/23/5, f. 38v.
64 B.L. Add. MS. 39334, ff. 132–5; *Alum. Oxon. 1500–1714*, s.v. Chris. Canner, Conyers Richardson, Oliver Whitby; *Alum. Cant. 1752–1900*, s.v. Owen Evans.
65 e.g. *S.R.S.* xlix. 81, 90; cf. ibid. 6, 35; B.L. Add. MS. 39359, f. 81.
66 B.L. Add. MSS. 39334, ff. 132–5; 39461, f. 125.
67 Ibid. 39359, ff. 82–4; W.S.R.O., Ep. I/22/1 (1662); ibid. Par. 87/1/3/1.
68 *S.A.C.* xxxiii. 218.
69 W.S.R.O., Ep. I/22/1 (1662).
70 *S.R.S.* lxxviii. 66.
71 W.S.R.O., Ep. I/22A/1 (1884); Ep. I/22A/2 (1844).
72 *S.R.S.* lxxv, p. 143; B.L. Add. MS. 39334, f. 136.
73 Guildhall Libr. MS. 13328, letter, 28 July 1858; above, Climping, churches (Climping ch.); cf. W.S.R.O., Par. 87/5/1.
74 Pike, *Bognor Dir.* (1910–11), 233.
75 *Brighton Evening Argus*, 4 June 1959.
76 Inf. from the Revd. P. Taylor, Ford; cf. *W. Suss. Gaz.* 6 Feb. 1975.
77 *S.R.S.* xlii. 191.
78 Ch. fully described and illus. at *S.A.C.* xliii. 112–52.
79 Ibid. 119–20.
80 *S.R.S.* xlii. 192.
81 Date on bldg. recorded in 1776: B.L. Add. MS. 5699, f. 61.
82 *S.A.C.* xliii. 148 n.
83 Guildhall Libr. MS. 13323/5, rep. of view of estates, 1860.
84 *S.A.C.* xliii. 113.
85 Ibid. 139.
86 Ibid. 114–15; W.S.R.O., Ep. I/40/Ford/5267.
87 *Chich. Observer*, 4 Feb. 1972.
88 *S.R.S.* xlii. 192.
89 *S.A.C.* xliii. 141; B.L. Add. MS. 5699, f. 61; Guildhall Libr. MS. 13328, application of clergy and chwdns. of Ford for assistance towards ch. repair, June 1858.
90 Cf. *S.A.C.* xliii. 145–51, 154, and facing p. 105.
91 Elphick, *Bells*, 33, 309.

ladder hewn from a tree trunk.[92] The plate includes a silver cup and paten cover of 1567–8, and a silver flagon and paten of 1694–5.[93] The registers begin in 1630 but are confused and incomplete before 1758.[94]

The churchyard is partly bounded by a wall, which was in poor repair in 1991,[95] and otherwise by a bank and ditch. Already by the late 18th century[96] access to the church was only by a footpath through the surrounding field, which could be impassable.[97] Christ's Hospital constructed and maintained the altar tomb in the churchyard, which survived in 1996, of its benefactor William Garway (d. 1701).[98] There are many memorials in the churchyard to members of the Boniface family.[99]

NONCONFORMITY. Three parishioners who did not receive the sacrament in the 1570s and 1580s[1] may have been recusants. There were three female recusants in 1628[2] and another in the later 17th century.[3]

EDUCATION. The rector was licensed to teach in 1585.[4]

In 1818 many children went to school in Arundel.[5] A dame school existed between 1833 and the 1860s with *c.* 15–20 pupils; it was supported by subscriptions and weekly payments,[6] Christ's Hospital paying £5 a year by 1852.[7] After 1871 younger children attended Climping school,[8] but *c.* 1970 many went to Yapton; older children then attended schools in Littlehampton and Chichester.[9]

CHARITIES FOR THE POOR. None known.

MIDDLETON-ON-SEA

THE parish of Middleton-on-Sea,[10] which includes Elmer, lies along the south coast east of Bognor Regis and in the 20th century was a seaside resort. The ancient parish, called Middleton, had 370 a. in 1881[11] but had been reduced in area in previous centuries by sea erosion.[12] The configuration of the western and northern boundaries suggests that the parish was once part of Felpham, and the name Middleton may refer to the manor's central position between Felpham and either Elmer or Cudlow in Climping.[13] Part of the eastern boundary was formed *c.* 1310 by a ditch and part by Elmer pool,[14] while the north-eastern boundary follows the Ryebank rife. The parish was enlarged in 1933 by the addition of Ancton (522 a.) from Felpham parish and in 1971 had 361 ha. (892 a.);[15] its name was extended in 1934 to prevent confusion with other Middletons.[16] The present article deals with the ancient parish until *c.* 1900, after which the history of Ancton is included as well.

LANDSCAPE HISTORY. The ancient parish lies on brickearth, overlain by small areas of coastal alluvium in the centre and at Elmer; the Upper chalk outcrops along the beach.[17] The climate is exceptionally sunny though subject to storms, and before modern development the landscape, to which the South Downs *c.* 6 miles (10 km.) northwards form a backcloth, was windswept with few trees.[18]

Elmer pool, i.e. 'eel pool',[19] mentioned in 953,[20] was presumably fed by the overflow of seawater, as later,[21] and seems naturally to have drained into the Ryebank rife rather than seawards, since the alluvium on which it lay is separated from the coast by a narrow band of brickearth.[22] The land around the pool was evidently marshy since a 'marsh of Elmer' was mentioned in 1318.[23] Eels could be caught in the pool in 1457.[24] Fishing rights there were enjoyed by Elmer manor in 1578[25] and by Felpham manor in the 17th century.[26] The pool survived in 1669[27] but was drained when Elmer sluice was constructed before 1748.[28]

92 *S.A.C.* xliii. 113–14, 139; cf. W.S.R.O., Ep. I/26/2, f. 24v.
93 *S.A.C.* liii. 241–2.
94 W.S.R.O., Par. 87/1 (TS. cat.); cf. B.L. Add. MS. 5699, f. 63.
95 Cf. W.S.R.O., Ep. I/26/2, f. 25; *S.R.S.* lxxviii. 66.
96 Above, intro.
97 Guildhall Libr. MS. 13328, Revd. John Atkyns to Christ's Hosp. 22 Jan. 1853.
98 Ibid. 13323/2, rep. of view of estates, 1761, p. 13; 13323/5, rep. of view of estates, 1845; papers concerning repair of tomb, 1806–7; Goodliffe, *Littlehampton* (1903), 46; illus. at W.S.R.O., F/PD 522.
99 Cf. *S.A.C.* xliii. 112.
1 W.S.R.O., Ep. I/23/2, f. 5; Ep. I/23/6, f. 17v.
2 Ibid. Ep. I/37/4.
3 *Miscellanea*, v (Cath. Rec. Soc. vi), 318.
4 B.L. Add. MS. 39334, f. 132.
5 *Educ. of Poor Digest*, 958.
6 *Educ. Enq. Abstract*, 969; W.S.R.O., Ep. I/22A/2 (1865); Ep. I/47/4; Ep. I/47/8/1.
7 Guildhall Libr. MS. 13328, letter from Revd. John Atkyns, 17 June 1852.
8 Cf. *Kelly's Dir. Suss.* (1887 and later edns.).
9 Local inf.
10 This article was written in 1991 and revised in 1996. Topographical details in introduction based mainly on O.S. Maps 1/25,000, SU 80/90 (1981 edn.); 6", LXXIV (1879 and later edns.). Much help was received from Mr. R. Iden, Bognor Regis, and Miss M. Kendell, Elmer.
11 *Census*, 1881.
12 Below, this section (landscape hist.).
13 The fact that the chief pledge of Middleton appeared at the Felpham view of frankpledge in the 1540s perhaps implies that the *manor* was once part of Felpham: W.S.R.O., PHA 6677, rot. 2.
14 Eton Coll. Libr. MSS. 45/83–4 (TS. cat.); cf. below, this section (landscape hist.).
15 *Census*, 1931 (pt. ii), 1971; W.S.R.O., WOC/CC 7/2/8.
16 W.S.R.O., Par. 137/54/8.
17 Geol. Surv. Map 1", drift, sheet 332 (1975 edn.).
18 W. Page, *Hist. Middleton* (priv. print. 1928), 1 (copy in W.S.R.O. libr.); W.S.R.O., Add. MS. 29868, f. 2.
19 *P.N. Suss.* (E.P.N.S.), i. 142; the name Elmer pool is thus tautological.
20 *S.A.C.* lxxxviii. 72.
21 W.S.R.O., LD I/LL 1/3, f. 5; LD I/LL 1/9.
22 Geol. Surv. Map 1", drift, sheet 332 (1975 edn.); cf. *Armada Surv.* ed. Lower, giving the name Elmer water; W.S.R.O., Add. MS. 2031.
23 Eton Coll. Libr. MS. 56/62 (TS. cat.).
24 A.C.M., M 531, f. [10v.].
25 W.S.R.O., Add. MS. 41028 (TS. cat.).
26 *S.R.S.* xix. 162–3.
27 Ibid. xxix, p. 165.
28 Below, this section.

Erosion along the coast had begun by 1341, when 60 a. of arable were said to have been lost in the last 50 years.[29] Since no open fields have been identified within the parish as it afterwards existed, they may have been among the land destroyed, either then or later. Sea banks had been built by 1570, when the lessee of Middleton farm was required to maintain them;[30] such banks were still kept up in the early 18th century.[31] In 1606 the sea was encroaching 'daily' at several places along the coast in the west, and the process of erosion is indicated by the small size and odd shape of some closes and of a piece of common pasture there at that date.[32] The place name Middleton point was recorded in 1724, perhaps indicating what was later the coastal promontory at the Felpham boundary.[33]

The south wall of the medieval church was only *c.* 60 ft. (18 metres) from high tide mark in 1724,[34] and *c.* 40 years later the building was said to be in danger of being washed away.[35] In 1779 the rector put up a groyne at his own expense to protect the nearby glebe,[36] perhaps the double line of stakes curving to the east which remained on the foreshore in the 1920s.[37] It may have made the problem worse rather than better.[38] By 1789 the sea was within a few feet of the building, many graves in the churchyard had been destroyed, and human remains could be found along the shore.[39]

In the east end of the parish[40] the owner of Elmer farm constructed a sluice before 1748 in order to return the overflow of high tides directly to the sea. An existing ditch between Elmer pool and the Ryebank rife was widened perhaps at the same date and a second channel cut; one of the two was called the Pool ditch in 1848.[41] As a result Elmer pool was drained and became good pasture.[42] Groynes too had been constructed at Elmer by *c.* 1768, but they fell into decay after that date and in 1771 the sluice was destroyed by the sea so that the overflow of seawater once more ran northwards, re-creating a pool of 20–30 a. and causing flooding at Felpham and Ancton.[43] After the sluice was repaired *c.* 1775 the pool was again drained, remaining dry pasture *c.* 1786 except at very high tides.[44] There were two sluices at Elmer in 1910, one on the parish boundary and one 250 yd. (230 metres) west.[45]

Erosion continued in the 19th and 20th centuries.[46] Much land was said to have been lost between *c.* 1800 and 1819,[47] and in 1828 a cottage had recently been swept away.[48] The medieval church itself succumbed to the sea after 1838.[49] Other groynes had meanwhile been put up off Sea Lane by 1838[50] and a new defensive bank was built in 1853, running roughly straight between a point north-west of the site of the old church and the Felpham boundary.[51] At the east end of the parish a road along the coast between a point south-east of Elmer Farmhouse and Elmer sluice was eroded away between 1838 and *c.* 1875.[52] Between 1778 and *c.* 1875 128 yd. (117 metres) are reckoned to have been lost at Middleton and 110 yd. (100 metres) at Elmer.[53]

In 1895 the sea was said to have made great ravages during the previous few years.[54] The lord of Middleton manor spent heavily on banks and groynes at that period, but they often proved ephemeral and most of the surviving glebe east of Sea Lane was removed shortly before 1907.[55] At Elmer embankments were constructed inland south-east of the new Middleton church apparently between 1896 and 1910;[56] but in 1907 the mortgagees of Elmer farm were failing to maintain any defences so that a little land was lost each year.[57] Near the Climping boundary, on the other hand, land was actually gained from the sea between *c.* 1875 and 1896; at the latter date it was rough grass.[58] Remains of two successive sea banks survived there within the modern coastline in 1991.

With the construction of building estates after 1918[59] coast protection acquired new urgency. Capt. Coldicott, the developer of Middleton, at first had no capital to maintain existing defences and much land was lost at the end of Sea Lane in the 1920s and 30s.[60] Individual owners undertook their own defences at that period, some of their concrete constructions causing worse erosion than before. After *c.* 1937 the Middleton-on-Sea Association assumed responsibility, raising money through voluntary contributions.[61] At Elmer a bank erected before 1931 was destroyed in that year, flooding much of the Elmer Sands estate. As a result a similar association was formed to maintain defences there and a timber barricade was built. Between 1937 and 1939 the successor Elmer Sands Association

29 *Inq. Non.* (Rec. Com.), 369. Domesday bk. statistics for the man. presumably allude to this lost land: *V.C.H. Suss.* i. 431.

30 *Cal. Pat.* 1569–72, p. 69.

31 P.R.O., MR 1111, no. 24; W.S.R.O., Add. MS. 508 (TS. cat.).

32 W.S.R.O., Add. MS. 2027, ff. 31, 34, 36, 38, 40.

33 Budgen, *Suss. Map* (1724). In 1896 the name was applied to the headland at the end of Sea Lane: O.S. Map 6", Suss. LXXIV. NE. (1899).

34 Budgen, *Suss. Map* (1724).

35 *S.R.S.* lxxii, p. 86.

36 W.S.R.O., Par. 137/1/1/1, p. 52; perhaps illus. at *Gent. Mag.* lxvi (1), facing p. 369; cf. W.S.R.O., Ep. I/22/1 (1782).

37 Page, *Middleton*, 15.

38 W.S.R.O., Ep. I/22/1 (1782).

39 *Gent. Mag.* lxvi (1), 369 and pl. facing; lxvii (2), 729 and pl. facing; C. Smith, *Elegaic Sonnets* (1789), 79–80; above, pl. facing p. 187; cf. W.S.R.O., Add. MS. 2068.

40 Para. based mainly on W.S.R.O., LD I/LL 1/3, 9.

41 Ibid. TD/W 84.

42 Ibid. LD I/LL 1/10, f. 6.

43 Cf. ibid. LD I/SP 2.

44 Ibid. LD I/LL 1/2, p. [2]; cf. *250 Yrs. of Mapmaking in Suss.* ed. H. Margary, pl. 14.

45 O.S. Map 6", Suss. LXXIV. NE. (1913 edn.).

46 Cf. W.S.R.O., TD/W 84, with later pencil additions noting closes lost to the sea; O.S. Map 6", Suss. LXXIV (1879 and later edns.).

47 Dallaway, *Hist. W. Suss.* ii (1) (1819), 10.

48 Dally, *Bognor* (1828), 67.

49 Below, church [fabric].

50 W.S.R.O., TD/W 84.

51 Ibid. Add. MS. 11799; cf. O.S. Map 6", Suss. LXXIV. NE. (1913 edn.).

52 W.S.R.O., TD/W 84; O.S. Map 6", Suss. LXXIV (1879 edn.).

53 *S.A.C.* liii. 20, 24–5.

54 *Kelly's Dir. Suss.* (1895).

55 *Rep. Com. Coast Erosion* [Cd. 4461], pp. 17–18, 21, H.C. (1909), xiv.

56 O.S. Map 6", Suss. LXXIV. NE. (1899, 1913 edns.).

57 *Rep. Com. Coast Erosion*, pp. 18–19.

58 O.S. Map 6", Suss. LXXIV (1879 and later edns.).

59 Below, this section (settlement).

60 W.S.R.O., Add. MS. 29868, f. 6; O.S. Map 6", Suss. LXXIV. NE. (1932 edn.); but cf. *Bognor Observer*, 14 Feb. 1923; *Bognor Regis Post*, 26 Oct. 1946.

61 W.S.R.O., MP 1257; *Bognor Regis Post*, 22 Apr. 1939; 26 Oct. 1946.

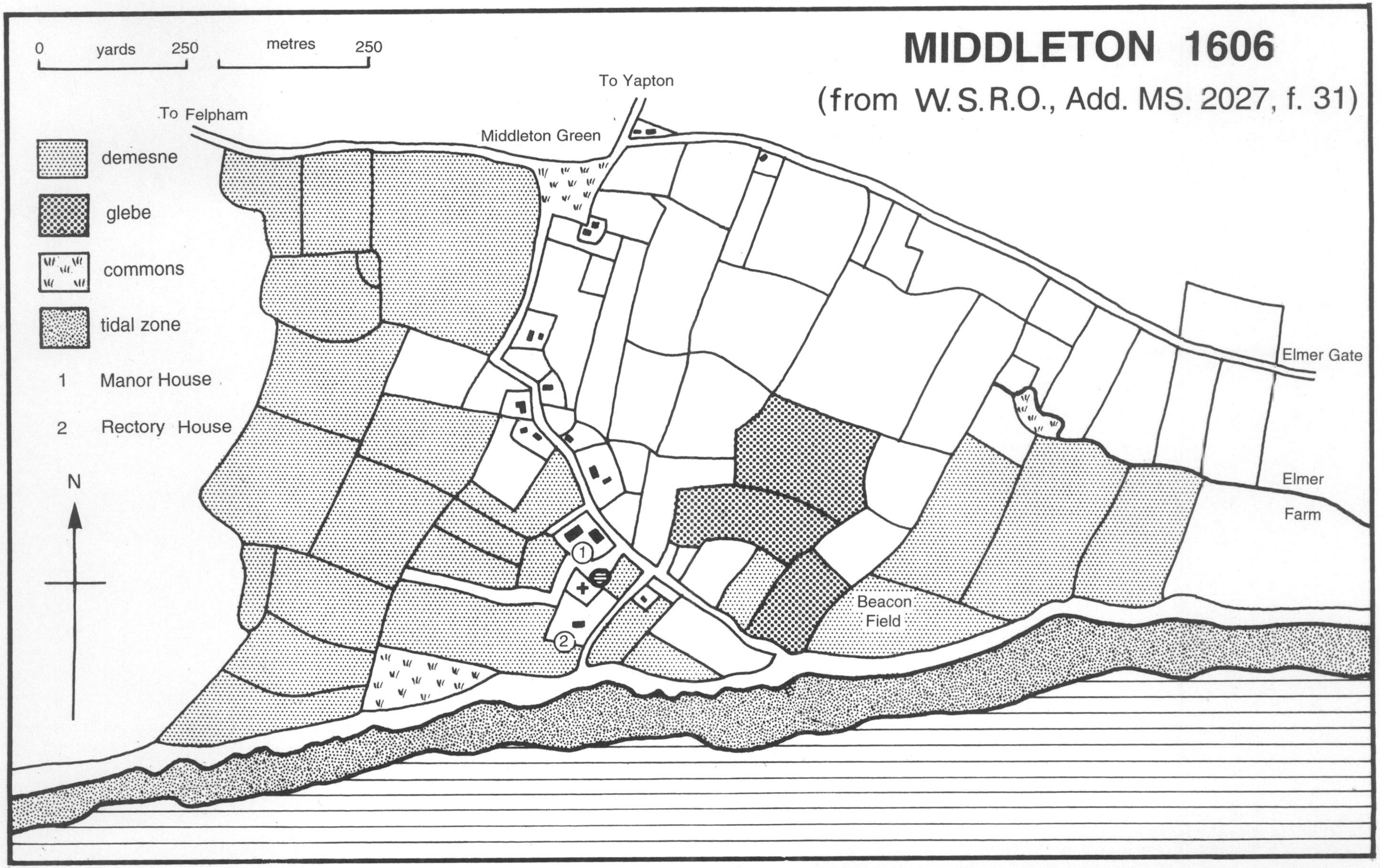

MIDDLETON 1606
(from W.S.R.O., Add. MS. 2027, f. 31)
0 yards 250
metres 250
demesne
glebe
commons
tidal zone
1 Manor House
2 Rectory House
N
To Felpham
Middleton Green
To Yapton
Elmer Gate
Elmer
Farm
Beacon
Field

carried out more permanent works, and further work was done at Elmer in the late 1940s.[62]

New defences were constructed at Middleton in the 1950s, but coastal protection at Elmer remained less adequate,[63] the combination of spring tides with south-westerly gales still causing occasional flooding in the 1970s and later.[64] Between *c.* 1990 and 1993 the National rivers authority and Arun district council built eight rock islands offshore in order to break the force of the sea.[65] By that time most of the coastline of the modern parish was fronted by shingle.[66]

The only woodland recorded in the parish before the 20th century was a copse in the north-east corner,[67] which evidently adjoined the wood of the bailiff of Atherington in Climping mentioned on the Middleton–Climping boundary *c.* 1310.[68] The wood had disappeared by *c.* 1875.[69] Between 1927 and 1932 Walter Guinness, Lord Moyne, planted a thick curtain of trees behind and beside the new estates at Elmer in order to screen them from his property at Bailiffscourt in Climping;[70] the trees survived in 1991.

As in neighbouring parishes there were several ponds in Middleton in the mid 19th century, including one at the north end of Sea Lane which survived in 1991, two near Elmer Farmhouse, and three at the south end of Sea Lane.[71]

SETTLEMENT. Roman pottery and a Roman coin found in the low coastal cliff south of the present Middleton church and elsewhere on the beach suggest settlement nearby.[72] The chief centres of medieval settlement, however, were around the old church beyond the modern coastline off Sea Lane, and apparently at Elmer.

Medieval occupation of the part of Sea Lane since lost to the sea is indicated by remains of wells found there together with 15th- or early 16th-century pottery perhaps from a kiln site.[73] In 1606 there were *c.* 10 dwellings along the lane, including the old Middleton manor house, besides empty crofts which were apparently sites of houses. Two subsidiary lanes flanked the church, with a pond beside one of them.[74] By 1778 there were only *c.* 6 houses there.[75] Before 1838 the old manor house and the southern flanking lane had disappeared,[76] to be followed by the ruins of the church and the northern lane in the mid 19th century.[77] A pair of mid 19th-century flint estate cottages remained in Sea Lane in 1991.

At the junction of Middleton and Elmer roads with Yapton Road in 1606 were two or three dwellings;[78] only one older building remained there in 1996, the one-storeyed, flint and thatched Rose Cottage, which is apparently 17th-century or earlier with 19th-century additions.

The manor house at Elmer may similarly have been a nucleus for settlement: Elmer Road like Sea Lane in Middleton once continued beyond the present coastline and a possibly medieval well has been found on the foreshore south of Sea Way nearby.[79] There seems to have been one other house there in the later 18th century.[80] High Kettle cottage in Elmer Road further west is originally a late 17th- or early 18th-century building of flint with brick dressings and thatch.

In 1801 there were only six houses in the parish; in 1841 there were 19,[81] including the new manor house at Middleton and newly built coastguard cottages at Elmer. Most of the latter remained unoccupied after the departure of the coastguard until demolition between 1910 and 1932.[82] Two larger houses were built during the same period: Middleton Field west of Yapton Road, of 1896 × 1899, home of the owner of the adjacent brickworks,[83] and the half-timbered and pebbledashed Ancton Lodge of 1910 × 1927.[84] Some small brick farmhouses were built in Yapton Road and Ancton Lane after *c.* 1920 for county council smallholders.[85]

After 1918 rapid building development took place along the coast; as in Felpham it progressed piecemeal in individual estates. The west end was the first part to be developed. In 1921 Capt. R. Coldicott began to build detached houses, some large, along Sea Lane, afterwards laying out two branch roads from it roughly parallel to the coast: Sea Way to the west and Old Point to the east. Further houses were put up by him along and to the north of Middleton Road. By 1928 he had erected over 100, at peak output claiming to finish one every ten days.[86] Further east the Southdean estate was also developed after 1921, as an adjunct to the New City holiday resort on the site of a former seaplane factory; *c.* 20 houses had been built there by 1926.[87] East of that was the small Elmer Beach estate, where Central Drive was laid out in or shortly before 1923[88] and *c.* 30

62 W.S.R.O., Add. MS. 47690, p. 35; *Bognor Regis Observer*, 8 Apr. 1936; *Land Drainage Rec. of W. Suss.* ed. D. Butler, p. 117.
63 *Bognor Regis Observer*, 10, 17 Jan. 1958.
64 Ibid. 6 Dec. 1990; W.S.R.O., MP 1425, f. [5].
65 *Bognor Regis Observer*, 4 Apr. 1991; 30 Sept. 1993.
66 *W. Suss. Gaz.* 25 Nov. 1993.
67 *250 Yrs. of Mapmaking in Suss.* pl. 14; Dallaway, *Hist. W. Suss.* ii (1) (1819), 10; W.S.R.O., TD/W 84.
68 Eton Coll. Libr. MS. 45/83 (TS. cat.); above, Climping, intro. (landscape hist.).
69 O.S. Map 6", Suss. LXXIV (1879 edn.).
70 W.S.R.O., Add. MS. 47690, p. 35; O.S. Map 6", Suss. LXXIV. NE. (1932 edn.); above, Climping, manors (Atherington).
71 W.S.R.O., TD/W 84.
72 S.M.R. 1236; *S.A.C.* lxxiii. 204; cxvii. 76; cxxvii. 244.
73 S.M.R. 1235; *S.A.C.* lxvi. 237–8.
74 W.S.R.O., Add. MSS. 2027, f. 31; 2030. On one plot bldgs. had recently been destroyed by fire: ibid. 2027, f. 39.
75 *250 Yrs. of Mapmaking in Suss.* pl. 14.
76 W.S.R.O., TD/W 84; but cf. below, manors (Middleton).
77 O.S. Map 6", Suss. LXXIV (1879 edn.).
78 W.S.R.O., Add. MS. 2027, f. 31.
79 S.M.R. 1465; above, this section (landscape hist.); cf. O.S. Map 6", Suss. LXXIV. NE. (1913 edn.), showing rocks presumably representing the site of former settlement.
80 *250 Yrs. of Mapmaking in Suss.* pl. 14; cf. ibid. pl. 5.
81 *Census*, 1801, 1841.
82 Ibid. 1881–1901; O.S. Map 6", Suss. LXXIV. NE. (1913, 1932 edns.).
83 O.S. Map 6", Suss. LXXIV. NE. (1896, 1913 edns.); *Kelly's Dir. Suss.* (1899).
84 O.S. Map 6", Suss. LXXIV. NE. (1913, 1932 edns.); *Bognor Dir.* (1927).
85 Cf. below, econ. hist. (agric.); O.S. Map 6", Suss. LXXIV. NE. (1932 edn.).
86 W.S.R.O., Add. MS. 29868, ff. 3, 5–6, 8; W. Page, *Hist. Middleton*, 12.
87 *Bognor Post*, 20 Feb. 1926.
88 *Bognor Observer*, 4 Apr. 1923, when it was called Coronado Drive.

houses had been built by 1927.[89] The last two named estates also included houses north of Elmer Road. Much of the area so far described was built up by 1932 and the rest by 1940.[90]

In the south-east corner of the parish a few houses were put up in the 1920s on plots leased from the owner of Elmer farm.[91] Most of the farmland, however, was bought *c.* 1928 and afterwards developed for building, as the Elmer Sands estate, by the surveyor F. C. Stedman, who also laid out estates elsewhere in south-east England.[92] The eastern part around Alleyne Way was largely finished by 1932 and the rest was mostly built up by 1940.[93]

North-west of Middleton church the Harefield estate had been laid out for building by 1929;[94] some houses had been put up by 1932, when there were others to north and west in Yapton Road and along Ancton Lane, and the area was fully developed by 1940, by which date there were also houses to the east between Ancton and Elmer.[95]

The new estates were a mixture of permanent residences and weekend houses and bungalows:[96] both the Elmer Beach and Harefield estates were advertised as suitable for the building of either[97] and at Elmer Sands before 1939 only *c.* 12 houses were permanently occupied.[98] Most estates were private, and some remained so in 1996, with unadopted roads and open spaces managed by residents' associations that either owned or leased them.[99] Many houses had gardens running down to the sea, though in Sea Way Capt. Coldicott instead laid out an open space along the front[1] called the Greensward.

Some visual unity between the different estates was provided by the common elements of open spaces, numerous trees, curving streets, and grass verges and banks.[2] Middleton could thus be described in 1929 as a miniature garden city[3] and in 1937 as a delightful mixture of rural and urban.[4] Another shared feature was the use of romantic, nostalgic, or exotic names for houses.[5]

Houses were varied in design, many adopting neo-vernacular styles. On Capt. Coldicott's estate, perhaps unusually among contemporary seaside developments, the intention was to create an effect of medieval rusticity, the developer designing many of the houses himself, especially in Sea Lane.[6] Rows of shops set back from Middleton Road at the north end of Sea Lane, those on the south side behind a grass bank, were explicitly intended to seem older buildings converted for the purpose; materials used included weatherboarding and lavish 'half-timbering', one pair of premises being an imitation of a 'Wealden' house. The proximity of the manor house and of Middleton green with its pond added to the suggestion of a previously existing settlement.[7]

Elsewhere a few houses were built in the 'International Modern' style, for instance on the Southdean estate, near Ancton, and at Elmer Sands.[8] Others were of more ephemeral construction, with asbestos walls, for instance, on the Southdean estate and at Elmer.[9] Frequent use was made of old railway carriages especially at Elmer, among the grandest examples being three luxury coaches previously used by the Prince of Wales, Princess Mary, and the duke of Sutherland, which were set up as virtually self-sufficient dwellings with their original high-quality fittings, heating and lighting plants, and water cisterns.[10]

New building had removed the gap between Elmer and Ancton by *c.* 1960.[11] The proportion of houses occupied permanently at Elmer Sands greatly increased after 1945 and by 1957 over a third of the *c.* 350 houses there were so used, mostly by retired people. By the 1970s many properties were changing hands, some being enlarged or rebuilt.[12] North-east of the church before 1957 an estate of council houses and old people's bungalows was built by Chichester rural district council in a spacious and varied layout.[13] Cornfields could still be found among the houses in 1965,[14] but the largest remaining open space, Shrubbs field south of Elmer Road, was largely built on after 1964,[15] while two housing developments for retired people were put up in the same area between 1968 and 1974, one of them for members of the National and Local Government Officers Association or their aged dependents.[16] There were other flats for

89 *Bognor Dir.* (1927).
90 O.S. Map 6", Suss. LXXIV. NE. (1932, 1950 edns.); cf. *Bognor Post*, 22 June 1929; *Kelly's Dir. Suss.* (1934); *Kelly's Dir. Bognor Regis* (1940); Ward, Lock & Co. *Bognor* [1928–9], 25.
91 W.S.R.O., Add. MS. 47690, p. 35.
92 Ibid.; D. Hardy and C. Ward, *Arcadia for All*, 138–9.
93 O.S. Map 6", Suss. LXXIV. NE. (1932, 1950 edns.); *Kelly's Dir. Bognor Regis* (1940).
94 *Bognor Post*, 22 June 1929; cf. W.S.R.O., Add. MSS. 23890–1.
95 O.S. Map 6", Suss. LXXIV. NE. (1932, 1950 edns.)
96 e.g. *Bognor Post*, 20 Feb. 1926.
97 W.S.R.O., Add. MS. 23889, p. 5; ibid. MP 3121.
98 Ibid. Add. MS. 47690, p. 35.
99 Ibid. Add. MS. 47690, p. 35; ibid. MP 1257; *Bognor Regis Observer*, 1 Feb. 1974; *W. Suss. Gaz.* 21 Apr. 1977; *S.C.M.* xiii. 500; *Walks around Middleton and Elmer*, ed. S. Gould and H. Gibbs, 17, 19, 22, 26; *Elmer Sands brochure* [1930s], [4] (copy in W.S.R.O. libr.).
1 W.S.R.O., Add. MS. 29868, f. 6.
2 Ibid. 23889, p. 5; *Bognor Post*, 25 Aug. 1928; above, pl. facing p. 187.
3 *Bognor Post*, 22 June 1929.
4 *Bognor Regis Post*, 13 Mar. 1937.
5 e.g. *Bognor Observer*, 4 Apr. 1923; *Bognor Regis Dir.* (1932).
6 W.S.R.O., Add. MS. 29868, ff. 4–5; ibid. MP 3121; *S.C.M.* xiii. 500.
7 For the green, below, econ. hist. (agric.).
8 *Suss.: Environment, Landscape, and Soc.* (Brighton, 1983), 230; *Walks around Middleton and Elmer*, 18, 29; W.S.R.O., SP 1291, 1293.
9 *Suss.: Environment, Landscape, and Soc.* 230; *Walks around Middleton and Elmer*, 20, 22, 26; W.S.R.O., MP 1425, f. [46].
10 *Bognor Observer*, 4 Apr. 1923; *Walks around Middleton and Elmer*, 20–2; W.S.R.O., Add. MS. 47690, p. 35; ibid. MP 1425, ff. [48–9]; illus. at *Archit. Rev.* Dec. 1972, p. 376.
11 O.S. Maps 6", Suss. LXXIV. NE. (1950 edn.); 1/25,000, SU 90 & SZ 99 (1958 edn.); W.S.R.O., MP 1425, f. [51].
12 *Bognor Regis Observer*, 14 Feb. 1975; *Walks around Middleton and Elmer*, 26–7; W.S.R.O., Add. MS. 47690, p. 35; cf. ibid. MP 1425, f. [51].
13 O.S. Map 1/25,000, SU 90 & SZ 99 (1958 edn.); W.S.R.O., MP 1425, f. [51]; *W. Suss. Gaz.* 21 Apr. 1977.
14 Nairn & Pevsner, *Suss.* 270.
15 *Brighton Evening Argus*, 25 Aug. 1964; O.S. Map 1/25,000, SU 80/90 (1981 edn.).
16 *Bognor Regis Observer*, 1 Feb., 26 Apr. 1974; *W. Suss. Gaz.* 3 Oct. 1968; 21 Apr. 1977; W.S.R.O., MP 1425, f. [51].

MIDDLETON ON SEA
Middleton
Ancton
Ancton House
Ancton Lodge
St. Nicholas's Church
Hall
Middleton Manor
Sports Ground
High Barn
Pav.
Middleton Field
Middleton Point
Slipway
Groyne
Slipway
Groynes
High Water Mark of Medium Tides
Low Water Mark of Medium Tides
Hannah's Groyne
Grevatt's Bridge (Foot)
Ryebank Rife
Comet Cottage
Yapton Road
Worms Hovels
Worms Lane
Sheepwash Barn
U.D. By.
Newlands
Club
Tel. Ex.
Medieval Jugs found A.D. 1924

retired people at Elmer in 1991.[17] Meanwhile west of Yapton Road an estate of detached houses had been put up in the early 1970s,[18] to the north and west of which there was further building in the 1990s. Ancton hamlet, however, retained working farms in 1991,[19] when fields separated it from development to the south and there was open country to the north.

Twelve inhabitants of Middleton tithing paid the subsidy in 1327 and 21 in 1332.[20] In 1642 the protestation was signed by 14 adult males.[21] Sixteen parishioners were listed in 1676[22] and there were four families in the mid 18th century.[23] In the early 19th century the population fluctuated between 40 and 50, rising to 100 in 1841 with the opening of the coastguard station at Elmer, and falling after its closure to 35 in 1901. The area of the modern parish had 148 inhabitants in 1921, 918 in 1931, 2,443 in 1951, and 4,197 in 1991.[24]

MIDDLETON AS A SEASIDE RESORT. Visitors to Bognor and Felpham often came to Middleton in the early 19th century to see the ruined church,[25] but the parish's development as a resort in its own right did not begin until after 1920. Safe, sandy beaches were a chief reason for its popularity,[26] and by *c.* 1928 bungalows for renting were in steady demand.[27] Some estates had private beaches,[28] and on the Coldicott estate at Middleton there were beach huts on the Greensward west of Sea Lane.[29] By 1929 Middleton was said to have become a formidable rival to Bognor, than which it was both quieter and cheaper.[30]

The largest attraction was the 'New City' created by Sir Walter Blount, Bt., and opened in 1922 in the former seaplane factory south of the church.[31] It was one of the earliest attempts to provide a self-contained environment for enjoying the seaside. There were *c.* 200 bedrooms, all with central heating and half with private baths, besides a garage for 100 cars; visitors without cars could be met at Barnham station. Almost every form of amusement was claimed to be catered for. One of the hangars accommodated a dance hall and another indoor tennis courts; there were also outdoor tennis courts, a putting green, and rooms for cards and billiards. Sand yacht racing and motor gymkhanas took place on the beach, and children's sports were organized. The New City had its own dairy, farm, ice generating plant, and mineral water factory, besides a laundry, hairdressing rooms, and lending library. By the mid 1920s it was said to be very popular with large numbers of 'distinguished' visitors. A less exclusive alternative, the Elmer Sands holiday resort, existed by the early 1930s, offering similar sporting facilities.[32]

Guest houses and hotels were also opened in the parish in the 1920s and 30s; there was one guest house in 1927[33] and three boarding houses and two hotels in 1934. By the latter date the New City had become the Southdean hotel and sports club,[34] which in 1937 was open to non-residents, and which by then could offer squash courts and a sea-water swimming pool.[35] There were other social and sports clubs in the period. The Middleton sports club in Sea Lane, formed in the early 1920s, was at first merely for cricket but later provided squash, tennis, and hockey as well, together with social activities in winter including lectures and card parties.[36] The Middleton country club on the Harefield estate was opened in 1929, when it had over 70 members who could enjoy cards, billiards, tennis, and dancing.[37] There was a social club at Elmer Sands by 1934.[38]

After the Second World War the renting of furnished property at both Middleton and Elmer continued to be very popular especially for families with children, and both places remained quiet and free from day trippers.[39] The former New City site changed hands several times in the period, being variously known as Southdean holiday camp, the South Coast country club, and the Sussex Coast holiday centre. In 1983 many visitors to it came from the north of England.[40] The Sussex club and holiday centre at Elmer was opened *c.* 1969[41] and in 1974 had a private beach and swimming pool with dancing and entertainment every evening.[42] The Middleton sports club still flourished in 1991 offering bowls and stoolball as well as the sports mentioned earlier.[43] In 1977, when it had 950 members, it was described as the social centre of the village.[44]

17 *Bognor Regis Observer*, 31 Jan. 1991; *Walks around Middleton and Elmer*, 23.

18 Local inf.

19 Inf. from Miss M. Kendell, Elmer.

20 *S.R.S.* x. 135–6, 256, at the first date including Martin of Elmer listed as collector. The return for the 1524 subsidy is largely illegible: ibid. lvi. 57.

21 Ibid. v. 124.

22 *Compton Census*, ed. Whiteman, 144.

23 *S.R.S.* lxxviii. 70; W.S.R.O., Ep. I/22/1 (1758).

24 *Census*, 1801–1991.

25 G. Young, *Hist. Bognor Regis*, 130.

26 *Bognor Regis Post*, 13 Mar. 1937; W.S.R.O., Add. MS. 23889, p. 4.

27 Ward, Lock & Co. *Bognor* [1928–9], 25.

28 e.g. W.S.R.O., MP 3121; *Official Guide to Bognor* (n.d.), 25 (copy at Worthing Ref. Libr.).

29 W.S.R.O., Add. MS. 29868, f. 11.

30 *Bognor Post*, 22 June 1929.

31 Para. based mainly on *Official Guide to Bognor* (n.d.), 25; *Bognor Observer*, 12 July 1922; *Bognor Post*, 20 Feb. 1926; 22 June 1929; Ward, Lock & Co. *Bognor* [1928–9], 25–6; H. Clunn, *Famous S. Coast Pleasure Resorts Past and Present*, 364; *Suss.: Environment, Landscape, and Soc.* (Brighton, 1983), 230; C.I.H.E. libr., GY 1181; GY/PC 1532–42.

32 *Kelly's Dir. Suss.* (1934); *Holiday Hbk. to Bognor Regis and W. Suss.* (Margate, early 1930s), 10–11 (copy in C.I.H.E. libr.); *Elmer Sands brochure* [1930s], [6–7] (copy in W.S.R.O. libr.).

33 W.S.R.O., MP 3121.

34 *Kelly's Dir. Suss.* (1934); cf. *Kelly's Dir. Bognor Regis* (1940).

35 *Bognor Regis Post*, 13 Mar. 1937; *Residential Attractions of Bognor Regis, Felpham, Middleton-on-Sea and Dist.* (Gloucester, [1937]), 19, 24–7 (copy in B.L.).

36 W.S.R.O., Add. MS. 29868, f. 7; ibid. MP 3121.

37 *Bognor Post*, 22 June 1929; cf. W.S.R.O., Add. MS. 23889, p. 4.

38 *Kelly's Dir. Suss.* (1934); cf. *Elmer Sands brochure* [1930s], [6–7] (copy in W.S.R.O. libr.).

39 W.S.R.O., Add. MS. 47690, p. 35; *Official Guide to Bognor Regis, Aldwick and Felpham* (1962), 77–9; personal memory.

40 *Bognor Regis Observer*, 12 Apr. 1947; 13 Dec. 1990; *W. Suss. Gaz.* 21 Apr. 1977; 20 July 1989.

41 *Bognor Regis Observer*, 14 Feb. 1975.

42 *Bognor Regis Official Guide* (1974), [65].

43 *Bognor Regis Observer*, 22 Aug. 1991.

44 *W. Suss. Gaz.* 21 Apr. 1977.

There were five social or sports clubs in 1959; some survived in 1972, when there were also six hotels or public houses, including the former Elmer manor house.[45]

Besides sports and social facilities mentioned above, tennis courts were laid down on the Elmer Beach estate in 1923[46] and a boating and angling club was formed at Elmer after 1936. A putting green was also created there.[47] A community hall stood in Yapton Road in 1927.[48] The church hall built *c.* 1938 accommodated apparently from the 1950s a branch of the county council library service which in 1966 was open one and a half days a week.[49] Playing fields were laid out in Elmer Road *c.* 1970;[50] by 1974 they were managed by the parish council.[51] A village hall, proposed since the 1930s, was opened alongside in 1982.[52] There was another recreation ground west of Yapton road in 1992.

The only roads to Middleton before the 19th century led from Felpham and Yapton;[53] the creation of the Bognor–Littlehampton road *c.* 1824 gave eastwards communication as well.[54] An additional link with Felpham may have been provided by Limmer Lane, which perhaps once connected with Sea Lane beyond the present coastline. In the early 19th century Elmer Road continued eastwards beyond the modern coastline to the sluice west of the Climping boundary.[55] Elmer gate, of unknown significance, stood on it at the division between Middleton and Elmer manors in the 17th century,[56] but is not heard of after 1719.[57] Buses ran from Bognor to Middleton by 1922[58] and to Elmer by 1927,[59] and a carrier continued to ply between Bognor and Middleton in 1938.[60] The road between Bognor and Littlehampton in the north part of the modern parish was straightened in 1963.[61] Portsmouth, Brighton, and Haslemere (Surr.) could be reached by bus from the parish in 1992.

Middleton's water supply in 1928 came from wells, which were sometimes contaminated with seawater.[62] On both the Middleton manor and Elmer Sands building estates cesspits were used for drainage at first and at the former there was a private gas plant.[63] The New City development had its own drainage and sewerage systems and an electricity generator which supplied light to neighbouring houses in 1926.[64] Mains water and electricity reached the parish from Bognor in the later 1920s,[65] but main drainage not until *c.* 10 years later.[66] Street lighting was installed after 1956.[67] A medical centre in Elmer Road was opened by 1991.

A close south-east of Sea Lane called Beacon field in 1606[68] was presumably the site of a beacon for coastal defence. A signal station was set up at the end of Sea Lane in 1794 or 1795 during the threat of a French invasion; after closure in 1802 it was reinstated in the following year and closed finally in 1814.[69]

There was a convalescent home in Yapton Road in 1934.[70]

Twentieth-century residents of Middleton included William Page (d. 1934), antiquary and editor of the *Victoria County History*,[71] the pianist Charlie Kunz (d. 1958),[72] and the music-hall comedian Chesney Allen (d. 1982).[73]

MANORS. The manor of *MIDDLETON* was held in 1066 by five freemen and in 1086 of Roger de Montgomery by William.[74] The overlordship descended with the rape until 1243, when at the division of the d'Aubigny inheritance it passed to Roger de Mohaut,[75] descending then in the direct line to Robert (d. 1275) and Roger, Lord Mohaut (d. 1295 or 1296).[76] After the death of Roger's brother and heir Robert in 1329 it passed to Queen Isabel, wife of Edward II[77] (d. 1358).[78] In 1361 Edward, the Black Prince, had it.[79]

The undertenancy of the manor descended until the mid 15th century with the honor of Halnaker through the St. John and Poynings families.[80] At the

45 *Kelly's Dir. Bognor Regis* (1959, 1972).
46 *Bognor Observer*, 4 Apr. 1923; cf. *Elmer Sands brochure* [1930s], [6–7] (copy in W.S.R.O. libr.).
47 W.S.R.O., Add. MS. 47690, p. 35.
48 *Bognor Dir.* (1927).
49 W.S.R.O., Par. 137/16/1, 5; *Educ. in W. Suss. 1954–59* (W. Suss. C.C.), 119; *Kelly's Dir. Bognor Regis* (1972).
50 Char. Com. files.
51 *Bognor Regis Observer*, 1 Feb. 1974.
52 *W. Suss. Gaz.* 14 Oct. 1982; cf. W.S.R.O., Par. 137/52/1.
53 W.S.R.O., Add. MS. 2027, ff. 31, 35; *250 Yrs. of Mapmaking in Suss.* ed. H. Margary, pl. 14; *S.R.S.* xxix, p. 33.
54 Above, Climping, intro. (communications).
55 W.S.R.O., TD/W 84.
56 Ibid. Add. MS. 2027, f. 31; ibid. S.A.S. MSS. WH 266–7 (TS. cat.); B.L. Add. Ch. 18906 (MS. cal.).
57 W.S.R.O., Add. MS. 41051 (TS. cat.).
58 *Bognor Regis Observer*, 7 Apr. 1972.
59 W.S.R.O., MP 3121.
60 *Kelly's Dir. Suss.* (1938).
61 O.S. Map 1/25,000, SU 90 & SZ 99 (1972 edn.); *Bognor Regis Post*, 17 Aug. 1963; inf. from Mr. R. Iden, Bognor Regis.
62 F. H. Edmunds, *Wells and Springs of Suss.* 36; cf. W.S.R.O., Add. MS. 29868, f. 10.
63 W.S.R.O., Add. MSS. 29868, f. 10; 47690, p. 35.
64 *Bognor Observer*, 12 July 1922; *Bognor Post*, 20 Feb. 1926; *Official Guide to Bognor* (n.d.), 25.
65 *Bognor Post*, 25 Aug. 1928; *Bognor Regis Observer*, 2 Nov. 1979; W.S.R.O., Add. MS. 47690, p. 35; ibid. MP 3121; cf. ibid. Add. MS. 23889, p. 5; *Residential Attractions of Bognor Regis, Felpham, Middleton-on-Sea and Dist.* 10.
66 W.S.R.O., Add. MS. 47690, p. 35; ibid. MP 1425, f. [50]; ibid. Par. 137/54/3.
67 *Bognor Regis Observer*, 29 Mar. 1956.
68 W.S.R.O., Add. MS. 2027, ff. 31, 36.
69 J. Goodwin, *Milit. Defence of W. Suss.* 73; *Gent. Mag.* lxvi (1), 489; *250 Yrs. of Mapmaking in Suss.* pl. 19.
70 *Kelly's Dir. Suss.* (1934).
71 *The Times*, 5 Feb. 1934; *V.C.H. Genl. Intro.* 11–12.
72 *Kelly's Dir. Bognor Regis* (1940); *Bognor Regis Observer*, 21 Mar. 1958.
73 *Bognor Regis Observer*, 18 Nov. 1982.
74 *V.C.H. Suss.* i. 431.
75 *Cal. Pat.* 1232–47, 408.
76 *Cal. Inq. p.m.* ii, pp. 83–4; W. Farrer, *Honors and Kts.' Fees*, ii. 37; *Complete Peerage*, s.v. Mohaut.
77 *Complete Peerage*, s.v. Mohaut; Farrer, *Honors and Kts.' Fees*, ii. 38; W. Page, *Hist. Middleton*, 4; cf. *Cal. Inq. p.m.* ix, p. 38.
78 *Cal. Inq. p.m.* x, p. 356; cf. ibid. xvii, p. 166.
79 *Blk. Prince's Reg.* iv. 373–4.
80 *V.C.H. Suss.* iv. 143; *Cal. Inq. p.m.* ii, p. 84; viii, p. 50; ix, pp. 38–9, 243; xvii, p. 166; *Feud. Aids*, v. 143, 155; vi. 522; *Goodwood Estate Archives*, i, ed. F. W. Steer and J. Venables, p. 35; P.R.O., C 131/50, no. 1. John of Middleton, described as lord in 1276, was presumably John de St. John (fl. 1275; d. 1301): *Cal. Close*, 1272–9, 421; cf. *S.R.S.* vii, p. 125. Wal. de Harpur, however, was said to be lord in 1279, perhaps as mortgagee: *Plac. de Quo Warr.* (Rec. Com.), 752; *Cal. Close*, 1272–9, 421; cf. *S.R.S.* vii, p. 129.

division of the Poynings inheritance in 1458 between the representatives of the three granddaughters of Thomas Poynings, Lord St. John (d. 1429), Middleton passed to Alice's son Thomas Kingston, subject to the life interest of Eleanor, widow of Thomas Poynings' son Hugh, and her husband Godfrey Hilton.[81] At Thomas's death in 1506 he was succeeded in turn by his grandson John Kingston (d. 1514), John's brother Nicholas (d. 1516), Nicholas's sister Mary and her husband Sir Thomas Lisle (d. 1542), and Mary's cousin William Gorfen,[82] who in 1544 sold the manor to the Crown.[83]

In 1599 Middleton was granted to Sir John Spencer,[84] lord mayor of London, descending with Priory farm in Tortington between 1600 and 1640 or later.[85] By 1654 it had apparently passed to Thomas Bridger,[86] who was lord in 1682 and died in the following year.[87] In 1686 Bridger's great-nephew Ambrose Dench conveyed it to Henry Hall and his wife Grace.[88] By 1692 the manor seems to have been divided in two. Members of the Cooper and Peachey families then apparently had a moiety of Middleton farm (200 a.),[89] and in 1699 a moiety of the manor and the portion of the farm west of Sea Lane were settled on Henry Hall and the other moiety with the portion to the east on Thomas Cooper and Thomas Lewknor.[90]

In 1710 Hall's son Thomas mortgaged his share of the farm (99 a.) to Thomas Sparkes (d. in or after 1734). Henry Sparkes, apparently Thomas's son,[91] had that land in 1762 and 1771,[92] and in 1775 his nephew and heir Thomas sold it to Richard Coote[93] (d. 1803).[94] Henry Peckham of Chichester at his death in 1764 had some interest in a moiety of the manor with lands in Middleton, which he devised, after Thomas Ludgater's life interest, to his cousin Harry Peckham.[95] In 1776 those two conveyed their interest in what was evidently the Hall share of the manor farm to Thomas Palmer and Richard Coote.[96] Richard was succeeded by his nephew Joseph Coote[97] (d. 1814),[98] who devised his lands in Middleton to his sons Joseph and Richard as tenants in common.[99] Joseph was dealing with a moiety of the manor in 1821,[1] and had Middleton farm in 1828.[2]

The second moiety of the manor descended in the Cooper family. Thomas Cooper was described as lord in 1712,[3] and in 1732 his daughter Mary Johnson conveyed the moiety, together with 88 a., to her nephew, another Thomas Cooper.[4] It was evidently later re-united with the first moiety but by the early 19th century, with manor courts no longer held and with the extinction of common grazing rights, the lordship of the manor had become only notional.

Joseph Coote (d. 1844) was succeeded by Richard Coote. At that date Middleton farm had 137 a.,[5] roughly the same acreage as in the early 20th century.[6] In 1852 Richard leased the farm to his son Middleton Richard Coote, who surrendered the lease in 1866. After Richard's death in 1873[7] it was sold by his executors *c.* 1875 to Frederick Dixon-Hartland, M.P. (created Bt. 1892; d. 1909).[8] In 1911 Sir Frederick's executors sold both manor and farm to George Stay;[9] he in 1919 sold 396 a. at Middleton and Ancton in Felpham to West Sussex county council for smallholdings, and most of the rest shortly before to Capt. R. Coldicott, who developed his land after 1921 for building.[10]

A manor house at Middleton was mentioned in the later 16th century, when it was evidently the residence of successive Crown lessees.[11] Standing north of the old church at the south end of Sea Lane beyond the present coastline, it may have consisted of a central range with two cross wings;[12] in 1683 it had a hall, parlour, and office rooms, with chambers above.[13] Part may still have been standing *c.* 1875.[14] A new three-bayed, two-storeyed, stuccoed building was built before 1828[15] to replace it on the corner of Sea Lane and Middleton Road, where it occupies a slight elevation. The Doric porch is a copy made in the 1920s or 30s of one in Chichester,[16] and the high-quality joinery inside the house may also belong to the modernization carried out at that time.

A park west of the manor house may be indicated by field names, the Parks and the Coney ground or Coney field, recorded in 1683 and later.[17]

The reputed manor of *ELMER*, which was not apparently called a manor before 1590,[18] perhaps originated in the four hides and five yardlands which three Frenchmen held of Middleton in

81 *Complete Peerage*, s.v. St. John; *Cal. Close*, 1454–61, 374–5; B.L. Add. MS. 39495, ff. 24–5; cf. ibid. 39340, f. 111v.
82 *V.C.H. Hants*, iii. 269; *L. & P. Hen. VIII*, i (1), p. 465; i (2), p. 1329; B.L. Add. MS. 39340, f. 112 and v.
83 *L. & P. Hen. VIII*, xx (1), p. 208.
84 P.R.O., C 66/1505, mm. 4–10.
85 Below, Tortington, manor (Priory fm.); W.S.R.O., Add. MS. 2027, f. 33; *S.R.S.* xiv, p. 224; xx. 497; xxix, p. 165.
86 *S.R.S.* xx. 305.
87 W.S.R.O., Par. 137/1/1/1, p. 39.
88 Ibid. S.A.S. MS. WH 270 (TS. cat.).
89 Ibid. 271 (TS. cat.); cf. ibid. 273 (TS. cat.).
90 Ibid. 297; cf. *S.R.S.* xx. 305.
91 W.S.R.O., Add. MS. 11783 (TS. cat.); ibid. S.A.S. MSS. WH 283, 293 (TS. cat.).
92 Ibid. Add. MS. 11786–7 (TS. cat.).
93 Ibid. Add. MS. 11788 (TS. cat.); cf. ibid. Ep. I/22/1 (1782).
94 Ibid. Par. 51/1/1/1, f. 82v.
95 B.L. Add. MS. 39498, f. 136.
96 W.S.R.O., Add. MS. 11790 (TS. cat.).
97 Ibid. Holmes, Campbell & Co. MS. 82.
98 Ibid. Par. 51/1/5/1, p. 2.
99 Ibid. Holmes, Campbell & Co. MS. 107.
1 *S.R.S.* xx. 305; cf. Dallaway, *Hist. W. Suss.* ii (1) (1819), 10.
2 Dally, *Bognor* (1828), 68.
3 W.S.R.O., Add. MS. 11784 (TS. cat.).
4 Ibid. S.A.S. MS. WH 292 (TS. cat.).
5 Ibid. Par. 51/1/5/1, p. 19; ibid. TD/W 84.
6 Ibid. IR 31, f. 27.
7 Ibid. Add. MSS. 11801, 11805, 11811 (TS. cat.).
8 *Kelly's Dir. Suss.* (1874 and later edns.); Burke, *Peerage* (1915), 990–1; Page, *Middleton*, 11; W.S.R.O., Add. MS. 11809.
9 Page, *Middleton*, 11; cf. *Kelly's Dir. Suss.* (1913).
10 W. Suss. C.C. property dept., terrier, deed, 1919; W.S.R.O., Add. MS. 29868, ff. 3, 8; above, intro. (settlement).
11 *Cal. Pat.* 1569–72, p. 69; 1572–5, p. 532.
12 W.S.R.O., Add. MS. 2027, f. 31.
13 Ibid. Ep. I/29/137/8.
14 O.S. Map 6", Suss. LXXIV (1879 edn.).
15 Dally, *Bognor* (1828), 68.
16 W.S.R.O., Add. MS. 29868, f. 9.
17 Ibid. Ep. I/29/137/8; ibid. TD/W 84.
18 P.R.O., C 2/Eliz. I/C 11/20.

1086;[19] since Felpham manor's hidation had been reduced by about the same amount since 1066[20] the estate may have been detached from that. At the division of the d'Aubigny inheritance in 1243 the overlordship passed with the share of Robert Tattershall.[21] William de Montfort held five fees in Elmer and elsewhere between 1303 and his death in 1310,[22] and William Elmer at his death *c.* 1325 held a house and six yardlands there of Barpham manor in Angmering; his heir was his son, also William.[23]

An estate called the manor of Elmer and comprising a house and *c.* 100 a. was said to have passed from John Standbridge (d. *c.* 1520) to his daughter Joan, wife of John Cowper, whose son John (d. *c.* 1540) was succeeded in the direct line by Robert, Ralph (d. *c.* 1578), and Edward (fl. 1590). In 1590, however, it was also claimed by Richard Cooke, who alleged that he had bought it from Henry Greene, son and heir of Nicholas.[24]

Cooke evidently made good his claim, for in 1603 the manor passed from him to Sir Henry Goring,[25] who with his wife Elizabeth conveyed it in 1614 to Sir Allen Apsley and Henry Bartellot.[26] Apsley evidently made over his share in 1620 to Sir Nicholas Jordan,[27] who with Bartellot sold the manor in the same year to Nicholas Thompson (d. 1628).[28] In 1640 Nicholas's two daughters and coheirs Elizabeth, wife of John Boys, and Catherine, wife of Robert Anderson, conveyed it to Robert and John Spence,[29] and in 1685 it was settled on John's son and namesake on his marriage. The manor farm then contained 183 a.[30] From the younger John (d. 1713) it passed to his son Robert (d. 1750), whose great-nephew Thomas Powys, later Lord Lilford,[31] apparently sold it *c.* 1768 to Thomas Palmer. Palmer still owned it *c.* 1790[32] and a namesake was living there in 1841, though by 1851 he had become a pauper.[33]

In 1848 Elmer farm, of 180 a., belonged to the executors of Edward Bowden Puttock,[34] and by 1874 it had passed to members of the Redford family.[35] In 1907 it was in the hands of mortgagees.[36] Between *c.* 1910 and 1913 both manor and farm were bought by Ralph Brown,[37] who *c.* 1928 sold the land to F. C. Stedman (d. 1963), who disposed of it in three portions: two were soon afterwards developed for building, but Walter Guinness, later Lord Moyne, bought *c.* 120 a. in the north-east corner of the parish as a buffer between those new estates and his land at Bailiffscourt in Climping.[38]

The former Elmer manor house, perhaps of the later 17th century, is of flint with brick dressings and has two stories divided by a plat band and an attic storey with dormer windows of 'eyebrow' form; the pedimented front doorcase is probably 18th-century. Agricultural labourers lived in the house in the later 19th century.[39] By 1962 it had become a hotel[40] and in 1991 it was used as a club.

Before 1176 William d'Aubigny, earl of Arundel, gave land in Middleton, apparently ½ hide, to Boxgrove priory to maintain a lamp in the chapter house.[41] Tortington priory had land at Elmer in 1535.[42]

ECONOMIC HISTORY. AGRICULTURE. Two *villani* were recorded on Middleton manor in 1086 and ten *villani* and four cottars on what may have been Elmer manor.[43] No tenants of Elmer are recorded later, but there were both free and copyhold tenants of Middleton in the early 17th century,[44] and at least one remained in the later 17th.[45] Copyholds seem generally to have been held for lives[46] and in the 1590s could be sublet.[47] In 1606 two freehold estates totalled 26 a. but there were 98 a. of copyholds, of which 56 a. were held by Thomas Lende. Most of the tenants' land was scattered around the manor, each estate having a house or a plot on the village street. Some cottages were then also held at copyhold.[48]

The parish was later divided between the two demesne farms, which were generally leased.[49] Middleton farm already had 133 a. in 1606[50] and Elmer farm 183 a. in 1682.[51] They remained about the same size in the 1840s;[52] in 1831 the population consisted chiefly of landless labourers.[53] Later in the 19th century Middleton farm was held together with Ancton farm in Felpham with a combined acreage of 300 a. in 1861[54] and 326 a. by the 1910s, when Elmer farm had 217 a.[55]

19 *V.C.H. Suss.* i. 431.
20 Ibid. 395.
21 *S.R.S.* lxvii. 103; cf. *V.C.H. Suss.* iv. 41; *Cal. Inq. p.m.* iv, pp. 103, 107, 257, 260; *Feud. Aids*, vi. 639.
22 *V.C.H. Suss.* iv. 41; *Cal. Inq. p.m.* iv, pp. 107, 260.
23 *Cal. Inq. p.m.* vi, p. 410.
24 P.R.O., C 2/Eliz. I/C 11/20; cf. W.S.R.O., Add. MS. 41028 (TS. cat.).
25 Conveyance of man. 1603, formerly in possession of Mr. F. Marcham (V.C.H. slip).
26 W.S.R.O., Add. MS. 41030 (TS. cat.).
27 Ibid. 41033 (TS. cat.).
28 Ibid. 41035 (TS. cat.); *S.R.S.* xiv, p. 226.
29 W.S.R.O., Add. MS. 41038 (TS. cat.).
30 Ibid. S.A.S. MS. WH 269 (TS. cat.); *S.R.S.* xix. 151.
31 B.L. Add. MS. 5687, f. 138; Dallaway, *Hist. W. Suss.* ii (1) (1819), 10; Berry, *Suss. Geneal.* annot. Comber, 26–7; *Complete Peerage*, s.v. Lilford; cf. W.S.R.O., LD I/LL 1/3, f. 1.
32 W.S.R.O., LD I/LL 1/9.
33 *Felpham and Middleton Census Returns 1841–1881*, ed. B. Fletcher, 137, 142.
34 W.S.R.O., TD/W 84.
35 *Kelly's Dir. Suss.* (1874); cf. *Rep. Com. on Children and Women in Agric.* 86; Elwes & Robinson, *W. Suss.* 150.
36 *Rep. Com. Coast Erosion* [Cd. 4461], pp. 18–19, H.C. (1909), xiv.
37 W.S.R.O., IR 31, f. 27; *Kelly's Dir. Suss.* (1913).
38 D. Hardy and C. Ward, *Arcadia for All*, 138; W.S.R.O., Add. MS. 47690, p. 35; ibid. RD/WH 34/1, Middleton, f. 13.
39 *Felpham and Middleton Census Returns 1841–1881*, 153, 155.
40 *Official Guide to Bognor Regis, Aldwick and Felpham* (1962), 67; cf. *Brighton Evening Argus*, 26 Jan. 1979.
41 *S.R.S.* lix, pp. 13, 49; cf. *Close R.* 1247–51, 561–2.
42 *Valor Eccl.* (Rec. Com.), i. 312; cf. P.R.O., SC 6/Hen. VIII/3674, rot. 9d.
43 *V.C.H. Suss.* i. 431.
44 W.S.R.O., Add. MS. 2027, ff. 33–4, 37–40; ibid. S.A.S. MS. WH 264.
45 Ibid. S.A.S. MSS. WH 266–7 (TS. cat.).
46 Ibid. Add. MS. 2027, f. 33; ibid. PHA 6677, rot. 2.
47 A.C.M., M 532, ff. [27, 87v. from end].
48 W.S.R.O., Add. MS. 2027, ff. 31, 33–4, 37–40, assuming 4 a. near Elmer to be copyhold.
49 Ibid. Add. MS. 11809; ibid. Ep. I/29/198/4; ibid. TD/W 84; P.R.O., MAF 68/433, 2371; cf. W.S.R.O., Add. MS. 2027, ff. 34–6; ibid. S.A.S. MS. WH 264.
50 W.S.R.O., Add. MS. 2027, f. 36.
51 *Wiston Archives*, i, ed. J. Booker, p. 383.
52 W.S.R.O., TD/W 84.
53 *Census*, 1831.
54 *Felpham and Middleton Census Returns 1841–1881*, 149.
55 P.R.O., IR 58/22731, no. 31; W.S.R.O., IR 31, f. 27; cf. ibid. Add. MS. 11809.

The ninth of sheaves was worth eleven times those of fleeces and lambs in 1341, though 60 a. of arable had been lost to the sea since 1291. Apples, flax, and hemp were also then grown, and cattle and pigs kept, the parishioners being said to live by great labour.[56] Middleton manor in 1606[57] lay in small closes and no open fields are known in the parish, though they may have lain in the part lost to the sea before that date. At that period the land west of Sea Lane was mostly several pasture. Three pieces of common pasture then also remained: Middleton green at the junction of Middleton Road and Sea Lane (3 a.), a meadow east of the village divided between three copyholders, and a piece of land by the sea south-west of the old church (6 a.). North Horn mead south-west of the modern manor house had apparently once been commonable too, since one freeholder then had rights there and in 1699 another had the cut of ½ a. of grass from it.[58] A small inclosure was made from Middleton green *c.* 1700.[59]

In the 17th century cattle, sheep, and pigs continued to be kept, and wheat, barley, peas, vetches, hemp, beans, oats, and tares were grown. One of the two manor farms in 1664 had 180 or more sheep, at least 100 a. of crops, chiefly wheat and barley, and 22 a. of summer fallow. In 1683 the farmer of Middleton farm also leased land at Bilsham in Yapton.[60]

In the mid 19th century there was five or six times as much arable as meadow and pasture.[61] Large crops of wheat had been taken in 1796,[62] and in 1801 and 1803 only small numbers of stock were listed.[63] During the late 19th century and early 20th the acreage of pasture in the area of the modern parish increased, while more fodder crops were grown than earlier. A shepherd was recorded in 1881, and by 1909 the large total of 1,231 sheep were listed;[64] there were *c.* 500 head of Southdown sheep on Middleton and Ancton farms in 1912,[65] though in the previous year the Middleton part of the combined farm had been mostly arable.[66] Most closes in Middleton were amalgamated into larger ones during the mid 19th century; *c.* 1875 the two largest were of 67 a. and 95 a.[67]

After 1919 much of the area of the modern parish was divided up by West Sussex county council into smallholdings.[68] There were eight or ten in the 1930s run chiefly from premises in Yapton Road or Ancton Lane;[69] one specialized in milk production,[70] four or five in poultry, and one or two others in fruit or market-garden produce.[71] There were still several holdings in 1960,[72] but by 1992 they had been amalgamated into three. One then remained a poultry farm; another, Elms farm, had 76 a. of which 66 a. were grazed by Hereford cattle and 10 a. were a nursery for fruit and ornamental trees; while Guernsey farm, of 106 a., had mostly vegetables and soft fruit besides 1,500 free-range chickens, and included a farm shop in Yapton Road opened in 1988.[73]

OTHER TRADES AND INDUSTRIES. The mill mentioned at Middleton in the 1190s[74] may later have been lost to the sea, since the only other indication of a mill is field names recorded near Grevatts bridge north of Elmer in the mid 19th century.[75]

The surnames Taylor and Thatcher, perhaps indicating the practice of trades, were recorded in 1332.[76] Pottery found in a well belonging to a house in the lost section of Sea Lane may indicate the existence of a medieval kiln nearby.[77]

A 'stade' or landing place on the beach between Middleton and Elmer was accessible only around high tide in 1587.[78] In the 17th century two or three seamen were sometimes recorded at a single date.[79] The appointment of a riding officer by 1730[80] suggests that smuggling was already common, as it continued to be later in the 18th century, notably at Elmer sluice.[81] A coastguard station accommodating 10 men was built beside the sluice *c.* 1831[82] and was closed in 1881.[83]

No other non-agricultural occupations are recorded in the 19th century.[84] In 1910 the engineer Norman Thompson,[85] attracted to the area by the large expanse of firm sand and the constant winds along the shore, founded an aircraft works which after the removal of much of the sand in a storm in 1913 turned to making seaplanes. The firm was later called the Norman Thompson Flight Co. During the First World War it supplied aircraft to the navy, the workforce growing from ten at the beginning

56 *Inq. Non.* (Rec. Com.), 369.
57 Rest of para. mainly based on W.S.R.O., Add. MSS. 2027, ff. 31, 35, 37–40; 2030.
58 Ibid. Add. MS. 11778 (TS. cat.).
59 Ibid. S.A.S. MS. WH 276 (TS. cat.).
60 Ibid. Ep. I/29/137; cf. ibid. Add. MS. 2027, f. 36.
61 Ibid. TD/W 84.
62 *Gent. Mag.* lxvi (1), 369; cf. *Kelly's Dir. Suss.* (1845).
63 E.S.R.O., LCG/3/EW 1, ff. [43v.–44, 84v.].
64 P.R.O., MAF 68/433, 2371, the statistics evidently including Ancton fm. in Felpham; *Felpham and Middleton Census Returns 1841–1881*, 154.
65 *W. Suss. Gaz.* 12 Sept. 1912.
66 P.R.O., IR 58/22733, no. 220.
67 W.S.R.O., TD/W 84; O.S. Map 6", Suss. LXXIV (1879); *O.S. Area Bk.* (1879).
68 W. Page, *Hist. Middleton*, 12; O.S. Map 6", Suss. LXXIV. NE. (1932 edn.).
69 *Kelly's Dir. Suss.* (1934); *Kelly's Dir. Bognor Regis* (1940).
70 Cf. *Bognor Regis Dir.* (1932).
71 *Sunny Felpham* [1922], 35 (copy in B.L.); *Kelly's Dir. Suss.* (1922), s.v. Felpham; *Bognor Regis Dir.* (1932).
72 Jesse, *Agric. of Suss.* 121; *Kelly's Dir. Bognor Regis* (1959).
73 Inf. from Mr. I. R. Gibbs, Guernsey Fm., Middleton, and Mr. T. A. Redman, Elms Fm., Middleton.
74 *Pipe R.* 1194 (P.R.S. N.S. v), 8; *Chanc. R.* 1196 (P.R.S. N.S. vii), 200.
75 W.S.R.O., TD/W 84.
76 *S.R.S.* x. 256.
77 *S.A.C.* lxvi. 237–8; above, intro. (settlement).
78 *Armada Surv.* ed. Lower.
79 W.S.R.O., Ep. I/55/31, 94, 157; ibid. Ep. I/55/6, 73, 120 (TS. cat.).
80 *Cal. Treas. Bks. and Papers*, 1729–30, 607.
81 W.S.R.O., Goodwood MS. 154, ff. J1–2; *S.A.C.* lii. 59, reading 'Elweys'; *S.C.M.* xx. 284; *W. Suss. Hist.* lii. 11.
82 *Census*, 1831–71; W.S.R.O., Par. 137/1/2/1; cf. ibid. MP 2415, ff. 15–16; ibid. TD/W 84.
83 W.S.R.O., Ep. I/22A/1 (1878); *W. Suss. Hist.* lii. 15; *Census*, 1871–81.
84 *Census*, 1811–31; *Felpham and Middleton Census Returns 1841–1881.*
85 Rest of para. based mainly on *Bognor Regis Local Hist. Soc. Newsletter*, xiv. 20–3; xv. 24–6; xvi. 32–6; W.S.R.O., MP 2004.

to between 700 and 900. Workers were brought by bus or lorry from Bognor and elsewhere,[86] a request to put up workers' cottages at Middleton being turned down by Westhampnett rural district council in 1916.[87] About 250 aircraft in all were built, some by sub-contractors, but with the cancellation of orders at the end of the war the firm went into liquidation.

Building development from *c.* 1920 brought new work in the building trades and in brickmaking. A brickfield which existed north of Sea Lane by 1899[88] was closed in the 1930s.[89] Capt. R. Coldicott founded a building firm to develop his land at Middleton, which later became Middleton Builders (fl. 1993).[90] There were two other builders in 1927, besides two house or estate agents, an architect, and a landscape gardener.[91] In 1940 there were four or five building firms.[92]

Retail businesses grew up to cater for the new estates. In 1927 there were said to be ample shopping facilities in the west end, including an exhaustive general stores at the New City,[93] and with the construction of further shops in the 1930s at both Middleton and Elmer[94] it was claimed in 1937 that residents of both places had no need to go elsewhere to shop.[95] Sait's dairies, recorded from 1930,[96] survived in 1970 as one of the few private dairies then remaining on the south coast.[97] By 1940 there were also three branch banks, three or more doctors, an insurance agent, and a firm of solicitors.[98] There was a motor engineer in the parish in 1922[99] and garages at both Middleton and Elmer by 1937,[1] one of them built *c.* 1929 as an adjunct to the Harefield estate.[2] The New City resort employed nearly 80 staff at the height of the season in 1926[3] and other work was provided by hotels, guest houses, and refreshment rooms mentioned from 1927.[4] The Elmer Sands estate in 1957 employed several workmen continuously on maintenance.[5] In 1991 four separate groups of shops in Middleton and Elmer roads included wine merchants, car showrooms, a bathroom and kitchen centre, a television and electrical shop, and a computer firm. There were then also banks, two building society branches, an insurance office, and a solicitor at Middleton, and estate agents at both places, besides various restaurants and take-away food shops.

One workshop had been built at the junction of Yapton Road and Ancton Lane before 1980;[6] by 1992 at least one other firm had arrived at what was then called the Middleton business park, while nearby were a joinery firm and a gardening and landscape contractor.

Three riding stables were recorded in the 1930s, at Elmer, at Southdean, and in Yapton Road.[7] A caravan park laid out north-east of Ancton Lane by 1978[8] still existed in 1992.

In the 1980s and 90s many inhabitants were retired or worked in other places, especially neighbouring towns.

LOCAL GOVERNMENT. There are court rolls or draft court rolls for Middleton manor for the years 1547 and 1595–9, when the court was held up to twice a year.[9] The last recorded court baron took place in 1606.[10] Besides land transactions the court dealt in the 1590s with the repair of tenements. The assize of bread and of ale was claimed for the manor in 1288,[11] and strays, felons' goods, the profits of wrecks, and other franchises in 1606;[12] none are known ever to have been enjoyed.[13] A chief pledge was mentioned in the mid 16th century[14] and a tithingman *c.* 1822.[15]

Elmer manor seems never to have had courts. There was a tithingman *c.* 1822.[16] Right to wreck was apparently asserted in 1571.[17]

There were two churchwardens apparently between 1548 and 1634 but thereafter only one before the 20th century.[18] A single overseer served in 1642[19] and 1826[20] and there was a waywarden in the later 19th century.[21] Three parishioners were receiving permanent relief and one casual relief in 1826.[22]

The parish joined Westhampnett union in 1835, and was later first in Westhampnett and

86 *Bognor Regis Local Hist. Soc. Newsletter*, xxvii. 23.
87 *Bognor Observer*, 12 Apr., 7 June 1916.
88 *Kelly's Dir. Suss.* (1899).
89 O.S. Map 6", Suss. LXXIV. NE. (1913 and later edns.); *Bognor Dir.* (1924).
90 W.S.R.O., Add. MS. 29868, ff. 3, 7, 9.
91 *Kelly's Dir. Suss.* (1927).
92 *Kelly's Dir. Bognor Regis* (1940).
93 W.S.R.O., MP 3121; *Bognor Observer*, 12 July 1922; *Bognor Post*, 22 June 1929; *Kelly's Dir. Suss.* (1927).
94 W.S.R.O., Add. MSS. 23896; 29868, ff. 9–11; ibid. MP 1425, f. [50].
95 *Bognor Regis Post*, 13 Mar. 1937.
96 *Kelly's Dir. Suss.* (1930).
97 *Official Guide to Bognor Regis, Aldwick and Felpham* (1970), 77.
98 *Kelly's Dir. Bognor Regis* (1940).
99 *Kelly's Dir. Suss.* (1922).
1 *Bognor Regis Post*, 13 Mar. 1937; *Bognor Dir.* (1927); cf. *Elmer Sands brochure* [1930s], [6–7] (copy in W.S.R.O. libr.).
2 *Bognor Post*, 22 June 1929; W.S.R.O., Add. MS. 23889, p. 4; cf. ibid. 23891. 3 *Bognor Post*, 20 Feb. 1926.
4 *Kelly's Dir. Suss.* (1927 and later edns.); *Kelly's Dir. Bognor Regis* (1940, 1959).
5 W.S.R.O., Add. MS. 47690, p. 35.
6 O.S. Map 1/25,000, SU 80/90 (1981 edn.).
7 W.S.R.O., Add. MS. 47690, p. 35; *Holiday Hbk. to Bognor Regis and W. Suss.* (Margate, early 1930s), 34 (copy in C.I.H.E. libr.); *Residential Attractions of Bognor Regis, Felpham, Middleton-on-Sea and Dist.* (Gloucester, [1937]), 19–20 and back cover; *Kelly's Dir. Bognor Regis* (1940); cf. *Elmer Sands brochure* [1930s], [6–7].
8 O.S. Map 1/10,000, SU 90 SE. & SZ 99 NE. (1980 edn.).
9 W.S.R.O., PHA 6677, rot. 2; A.C.M., M 532, ff. [26, 42v., 55, 80, 87v., 98v. from end].
10 W.S.R.O., Add. MS. 2027, f. 33.
11 P.R.O., JUST 1/924, rot. 67.
12 W.S.R.O., Add. MS. 2027, f. 34.
13 Cf. *S.R.S.* lxvii. 105; *Plac. de Quo Warr.* (Rec. Com.), 752–3; A.C.M., A 1675.
14 A.C.M., M 271, f. [10]; W.S.R.O., PHA 6677, rot. 2.
15 E.S.R.O., QCR/2/1/EW 2 (47).
16 Ibid.
17 P.R.O., SC 2/205/55, f. 2.
18 B.L. Add. MS. 39359, ff. 110–15; W.S.R.O., Ep. I/86/20, f. 17.
19 *S.R.S.* v. 124.
20 W.S.R.O., QCR/2/3/W 5, no. 17.
21 Ibid. Par. 137/9/2 (TS. cat.).
22 Ibid. QCR/2/3/W 5, no. 17.

after 1933 in Chichester rural district.[23] From 1974 it was in Arun district.

CHURCH. There was a church at Middleton in 1086.[24] The living remained a rectory. It was briefly united with Felpham in 1657[25] and again in 1906. The parishes, which had remained distinct, were also united in 1976, creating a benefice of Felpham with Middleton of which the incumbent was called rector.[26]

The advowson descended with the manor until 1599, when it was retained by the Crown; in 1546 John Knight and others presented for a turn.[27] Presentations after 1720 were often made by the Lord Chancellor.[28] In 1865 the Crown sold it to George Hartwell Roe (d. 1874), whose widow Eliza (d. 1889) devised it to the rector, the Revd. Alfred Conder, apparently her son-in-law (d. 1895).[29] It afterwards passed from his executors to W. H. B. Fletcher of Bognor, who gave it in 1901 to the dean and chapter of Chichester,[30] the patrons of Felpham vicarage.

The living was worth £8 in 1291[31] and the same or less in the 15th century. In 1513 it was said to have been impoverished by floods[32] and its value declined to £5 10*s*. 6*d*. net by 1535[33] and less than £5 in 1579.[34] In 1341 there were a house and 24 a. of arable, besides a tenant or tenants who paid 4*s*. rent.[35] The house stood south of the old church in 1606, and at the same period the glebe, by then only 16 a., lay together in three closes east of Sea Lane.[36] In 1617 the house was said to be very decayed and so near the sea that it was likely to be soon destroyed.[37] The building in fact fell down some years before 1663,[38] perhaps through the action of the sea which afterwards, despite the construction of a groyne in the later 18th century,[39] reduced the glebe to *c*. 5 a. by 1819,[40] 3 a. by 1887,[41] and 1½ a. by 1926 when it was sold.[42] The rectory barn still stood in 1758[43] but afterwards disappeared.

The value of the living increased to £35 by 1657,[44] nearly £41 by 1724,[45] £95 by 1782,[46] and £118 15*s*. 3*d*. by 1809.[47] Some tithes at Elmer, defined in 1848 as half the corn tithes arising from Elmer farm[48] and presumably representing Tortington priory's portion of 1291,[49] descended with Trynebarn rectory in Yapton in the later 17th century[50] and in 1848 belonged to George Puttock. At the commutation of tithes in that year he received a rent charge of £27 and the rector one of £128.[51]

Medieval rectors included one killed in an insurrection at Winchelsea in the mid 13th century,[52] another deprived for incest,[53] and Geoffrey Spede, registrar to the bishop of Chichester in 1382.[54] Rectors resided in 1440,[55] 1563,[56] 1579,[57] 1615,[58] and 1622,[59] but John Lewes (1616–19) neither resided nor always provided a substitute to serve in his absence,[60] as also happened in the early 1660s when holy communion was sometimes not held at the appointed times.[61] Julian Browning (1546–82) was a licensed preacher,[62] as was Adam Page (inst. 1619; fl. 1642), but Browning's successor was not a graduate.[63] Assistant curates served in the 1610s.[64] From the mid 16th century or earlier rectors often held other local benefices as well, especially Felpham,[65] and after the destruction of the glebe house in the mid 17th century they presumably always lived outside the parish.[66]

By 1724 services were held fortnightly, as they continued to be in 1782. Communion was celebrated three times a year in 1724 but with only three communicants.[67] Thomas Durnford, rector 1768–99, held Kirdford besides and was curate of South Bersted and Felpham though he served Middleton himself.[68]

James Douglas (1799–1819)[69] served the church for a time while incumbent of Chiddingfold (Surr.), but from 1803 he lived at Kenton (Suff.) and from *c*. 1810 at Preston near Brighton where he was a chaplain to the Prince Regent. By the early 19th century morning and afternoon services were held on successive Sundays alternately with Felpham,

23 *Suss. Poor Law Rec.* 52; *Census*, 1931 (pt. ii).
24 *V.C.H. Suss.* i. 431.
25 *S.N.Q.* xv. 118–19.
26 W.S.R.O., Par. 81/6/8; Par. 137/6/3.
27 *Cal. Close*, 1272–9, 421; 1454–61, 375; *Cal. Inq. p.m.* ix, p. 41; xvii, p. 166; *L. & P. Hen. VIII*, xx (1), p. 208; *S.R.S.* vii, p. 125; B.L. Add. MS. 39340, ff. 111–14; W.S.R.O., Ep. I/23/5, f. 32v.; cf. above, manors (Middleton).
28 B.L. Add. MSS. 5699, f. 89; 39340, ff. 116v.–117; *S.R.S.* lxxviii. 69.
29 B.L. Add. MS. 39469, ff. 217–18; cf. below, this section.
30 W. Page, *Hist. Middleton*, 20; *Lond. Gaz.* 26 July 1901, p. 4945.
31 *Tax. Eccl.* (Rec. Com.), 135.
32 B.L. Add. MS. 39340, f. 109.
33 *Valor Eccl.* (Rec. Com.), i. 316.
34 W.S.R.O., Ep. I/23/5, f. 32v.
35 *Inq. Non.* (Rec. Com.), 369.
36 W.S.R.O., Add. MS. 2027, f. 31; ibid. Ep. I/25/1 (1615).
37 B.L. Add. MS. 39340, ff. 108, 114v.
38 W.S.R.O., Ep. I/22/1 (1662, *recte* 1663).
39 Ibid. Par. 137/1/1/1, p. 52.
40 Dallaway, *Hist. W. Suss.* ii (1) (1819), 11; cf. W.S.R.O., TD/W 84.
41 *Glebe Lands Return*, H.C. 307, p. 30 (1887), lxiv.
42 W.S.R.O., Par. 81/6/6; cf. *Rep. Com. Coast Erosion* [Cd. 4461], p. 18, H.C. (1909), xiv.
43 W.S.R.O., Ep. I/22/1 (1758); *S.R.S.* lxxviii. 70.
44 *S.N.Q.* xv. 118.
45 *S.R.S.* lxxviii. 70.
46 W.S.R.O., Ep. I/22/1 (1782).
47 Ibid. Ep. I/63/10.
48 Ibid. TD/W 84.
49 *Tax. Eccl.* (Rec. Com.), 141.
50 *S.R.S.* xxix, pp. 165–6; cf. ibid. xx. 445; Dallaway, *Hist. W. Suss.* ii (1) (1819), 11.
51 W.S.R.O., TD/W 84.
52 *Cal. Pat.* 1258–66, 579.
53 B.L. Add. MS. 39340, f. 111v.
54 *S.R.S.* xliii. 215.
55 B.L. Add. MS. 39340, f. 109.
56 *S.A.C.* lxi. 112.
57 W.S.R.O., Ep. I/23/5, f. 32v.
58 Ibid. Ep. I/25/1 (1615).
59 *S.R.S.* xlix. 33, 42.
60 B.L. Add. MS. 39340, f. 114v.
61 W.S.R.O., Ep. I/22/1 (1662).
62 Ibid. Ep. I/23/5, f. 32v.; B.L. Add. MS. 39340, f. 113.
63 B.L. Add. MS. 39340, f. 114 and v.; *S.R.S.* v. 124.
64 B.L. Add. MS. 39359, f. 111; W.S.R.O., Par. 137/2/1, f. 1.
65 B.L. Add. MS. 39340, ff. 113, 114v., 115v.; *S.A.C.* xxxv. 184 n.; *Alum. Cantab. to 1751*, s.v. John Turner.
66 No corroboration has been found for the statement that two 17th-cent. rectors lived at Ancton in Felpham: Page, *Middleton*, 15.
67 W.S.R.O., Ep. I/22/1 (1742, 1758, 1782); *S.R.S.* lxxviii. 70.
68 B.L. Add. MS. 39340, f. 116v.; W.S.R.O., Ep. I/22/1 (1782); *S.A.C.* xxiv. 176 n.
69 Para. based mainly on B.L. Add. MS. 39340, f. 116v.; W.S.R.O., Ep. I/22/1 (1806); ibid. PHA 101, partly transcr. at R. Jessup, *Man of Many Talents*, 243–50; M. A. Lower, *Worthies of Suss.* 302–3; *D.N.B.*

a practice which continued until 1868 or later[70] despite the bishop's stipulation of weekly duty in 1803. The vicar of Felpham, J. B. Beed,[71] served as curate with a stipend of £20 in 1803, but in 1806 he was presented by the churchwarden for drinking in church during services, for not doing regular duty, and for reading the services too fast. Later in the same year the lack of a curate sometimes meant that no service was held. Other local clergy served the church in the 1810s.[72] There were seldom more than six or seven in the congregation in 1804.

Douglas's successor lived in Bognor in the 1820s but died in 1832 in Horsham gaol, where he had been imprisoned for debt; thereafter until 1847 the living was held in plurality with Felpham. Assistant curates continued to serve in the 1820s and 30s but the virtual destruction of the church in 1838 put an end to the holding of services[73] until the new building was opened in 1849. The construction of the coastguard station at Elmer, meanwhile, had doubled the potential congregation and on Census Sunday 1851 morning service was attended by 50 people.[74] Communion was celebrated six times a year in 1856 for *c.* 8 communicants, monthly by 1878, and fortnightly by 1903.[75]

In 1851 and 1861 the rector lived in Felpham,[76] and his successor Alfred Conder (1866–95) in Bognor, where he ran a successful private school and took a leading role in the town's affairs.[77] Average congregations in 1868 were said to be 70 in the morning and 120 in the evening, evidently including children from the rector's school.[78] Between the 1870s and 90s, on the other hand, services were sometimes abandoned for lack of a congregation. In 1887 most churchgoers were non-parishioners.[79]

With the beginning of building development after *c.* 1920 an assistant priest was appointed to the united benefice in 1923 to serve Middleton.[80] The practice continued until the 1980s, when the parochial work for Felpham and Middleton was shared instead between the clergy.[81] A house for the curate was built near the church *c.* 1930[82] but was replaced in the 1980s by one on the Flansham Park estate in Felpham. A building in Elmer Road was bought instead *c.* 1992.[83]

The old church of *ST. NICHOLAS*[84] consisted of chancel, nave with south aisle and north porch,[85] and west tower.[86] It may have incorporated part of the building mentioned in 1086,[87] but the window forms and the four-bayed south aisle arcade depicted shortly before its destruction were 13th-century.[88]

A light to the Virgin Mary was mentioned *c.* 1535 and a rood in 1538;[89] the latter had gone by 1602 when the building was in poor condition. The porch was evidently built afterwards since there was none at that date.[90] In 1663 the chancel was in danger of falling down through neglect[91] but it was repaired before 1724 when, however, the nave had become 'a common burial place',[92] perhaps because part of the churchyard had already been eroded away.[93] By the late 18th century most of the chancel had been destroyed, the south aisle demolished and its arcade filled in, and part of the west end including the tower removed.[94] Repairs were carried out in 1803.[95] Meanwhile, the sea had reached to within a few feet of the building by 1789, breaking up many of the graves so that human remains were washed onto the beach.[96] A very high tide early in 1838 virtually destroyed what was left of the building, rendering it unusable;[97] the ruins survived in 1847[98] but had disappeared by *c.* 1849.[99] A small portion of the north part of the churchyard remained in 1860.[1]

The new church, with the same dedication, consists of apsed chancel and nave without structural division, and west porch and vestry. There is a bellcot. Of flint with stone dressings and some brick and in 13th-century style, the building was consecrated in 1849 on a site given by Richard Coote, lord of Middleton manor.[2] Originally it was small and rectangular;[3] the one-storeyed western extension was added in 1949[4] and the apse in 1978.[5] A west gallery was built *c.* 1928 to house an organ.[6]

70 W.S.R.O., Ep. I/22/2 (1838); Ep. I/22A/2 (1868).
71 Above, Felpham, church.
72 W.S.R.O., Par. 137/1/2/1; *Educ. of Poor Digest*, 955, 964.
73 B.L. Add. MS. 39340, f. 117; W.S.R.O., Ep. I/22/2 (1838); ibid. Par. 137/1/2/1.
74 *S.R.S.* lxxv, p. 154; cf. above, econ. hist. (other trades and inds.).
75 W.S.R.O., Ep. I/22A/1 (1878); Ep. I/22A/2 (1856, 1903).
76 *Felpham and Middleton Census Returns 1841–1881*, ed. B. Fletcher, pp. 47, 69.
77 *Bognor - the First Resort?*, ed. A. Foster and others, 40–50; *Kelly's Dir. Suss.* (1882); W.S.R.O., Ep. I/22A/1 (1878); Ep. I/22A/2 (1875).
78 W.S.R.O., Ep. I/22A/2 (1868); Page, *Middleton*, 20.
79 W.S.R.O., Ep. I/22A/1 (1887, 1893); Ep. I/22A/2 (1875).
80 Page, *Middleton*, 21; *Kelly's Dir. Suss.* (1927).
81 Local inf.
82 W.S.R.O., Par. 137/6/5 (TS. cat.); *Bognor Regis Post*, 10 Feb. 1934.
83 Local inf.
84 Above, pl. facing p. 187. Dedic. recorded from 1276 and presumably chosen for its maritime connexion: *Cal. Close*, 1272–9, 421; *S.R.S.* xliii. 213; cf. above, Arundel, church [fabric].
85 *Gent. Mag.* lxvi (1), 369 and pl. facing; lxxv (2), facing p. 801.
86 W.S.R.O., Add. MS. 2027, f. 31; ibid. Ep. I/26/1, f. 6v.
87 *V.C.H. Suss.* i. 431.
88 G. Reynolds, *Later Paintings and Drawings of John Constable*, ii, pl. 1010; *Gent. Mag.* lxxv (2), facing p. 801.
89 *S.R.S.* xliii. 214.
90 W.S.R.O., Ep. I/26/1, f. 6v.
91 Ibid. Ep. I/22/1 (1662, *recte* 1663).
92 *S.R.S.* lxxviii. 70.
93 Cf. above, intro. (landscape hist.).
94 B.L. Add. MS. 5699, f. 89; *Gent. Mag.* lxvi (1), 369 and pl. facing; lxxv (2), facing p. 801.
95 W.S.R.O., PHA 101, acct. 1803.
96 *Gent. Mag.* lxvii (2), 729; C. Smith, *Elegaic Sonnets* (1789), 79–80; cf. G. Reynolds, *Cat. of Constable Colln.* pl. 281.
97 *Suss. Agric. Express*, 3 Mar. 1838; W.S.R.O., Ep. I/22/2 (1838); ibid. TD/W 84; cf. above, this section. A drawing of 1841 by W. E. Partridge at Worthing Ref. Libr. shows only part of the bldg. standing.
98 P.R.O., IR 18/10413, f. 1.
99 *Gent. Mag.* cxxv. 82; O.S. Map 6", Suss. LXXIV (1879 edn.).
1 *S.A.C.* xii. 95 n.
2 Ibid.; *Gent. Mag.* cxxv. 82.
3 e.g. W.S.R.O., PH 5689–90.
4 *Architect and Bldg. News*, 10 Mar. 1950, p. 267.
5 *W. Suss. Gaz.* 9 Feb. 1978.
6 W.S.R.O., Ep. I/40/Middleton/2573.

There was one bell in 1724[7] and more than one in 1664,[8] but the present bell is of 1840.[9] Some 'old and rotten' seats survived in 1724[10] and the medieval font in the late 18th century;[11] all were afterwards destroyed. There are a silver communion cup and paten cover of 1576.[12] The registers begin in 1553.[13] Remains of at least one tombstone from the old churchyard, found on the beach, could be seen in the new churchyard in 1992.[14]

NONCONFORMITY. The lack of resident Anglican clergy in the 19th century encouraged other denominations. Two coastguard families in the 1830s attended Slindon Roman Catholic church,[15] and others in 1868 occasional services held in a private house by an itinerant Congregational preacher. In 1878 there was a family of 'Bible Christians', and in 1887 a congregation of Brethren met in an outbuilding at Middleton farm. There were said to be 10 Nonconformists in 1898.[16]

EDUCATION. The history of Felpham and Middleton National, later C.E., school is treated under Felpham. Some children attended Yapton school in 1867.[17] In 1940 there were four private schools in the modern parish including an 'open air' school in Sea Way; one at least remained in 1972.[18] In 1992 most younger children went to school in Felpham or Climping and most older ones to Felpham or Chichester.[19]

CHARITIES FOR THE POOR. None known.

SOUTH STOKE

THE parish of South Stoke,[20] roughly half of which lies within Arundel park, had 1,279 a. including water in 1881 and 521 ha. (1,287 a.) in 1981.[21] Its boundaries may perpetuate those of the estate called Stoke in 975;[22] part of the northern boundary follows what may be a Roman road,[23] and the entire eastern boundary, except for a small part opposite Burpham village, runs along either the modern or the former course of the river Arun.[24]

The parish lies mostly on the Upper chalk,[25] which rises to 400 ft. (122 metres) in the north-west, with fine views of the Arun valley and the coastal plain. 'Redehill', mentioned in 1527, was perhaps near Red Lane, the road from Arundel to Whiteways in Houghton.[26] Before the later 18th century much of the Chalk land was open sheepwalk.[27] Two steep-sided dry valleys meet in the south-west; the more westerly, called Pughdean or Pughdean bottom,[28] contains Swanbourne lake, a former mill pond said in 1595 to be too cold for fish in summer but never to freeze in winter.[29] On the edge of the higher ground two small areas of valley gravel carry the settlements of South Stoke and Offham, and there is alluvium along the river valley.

The river channel seems to have been much wider in Roman times than in the 20th century,[30] but later made pronounced meanders. Some land had presumably been reclaimed by 1086, when there were 48 a. of meadow at Offham manor.[31] Pasture and meadow belonging to Boxgrove priory was flooded *c.* 1525,[32] and it may have been as a result that river defences were created or renewed soon afterwards.[33] The tenants of Offham manor were responsible for repairing the southern section in 1553 and later,[34] and probably those of South Stoke manor the northern section. Further flooding has been experienced since the early 19th century.[35] In 1840 the sewers commissioners cut a new shorter channel near South Stoke church,[36] and *c.* 1863 the London, Brighton, and South Coast Railway Co. made a longer cut to avoid the expense of building two swing bridges over the meander at Offham.[37] The first cut was claimed to have reduced flooding.[38] Land outside the river defences was in osier beds *c.* 1840 and apparently at other dates.[39] Two successive banks were depicted in the north-east corner of the parish in the mid 19th century.[40] After further floods in the mid 20th the river banks were heightened in 1966 and later.[41]

7 *S.R.S.* lxxviii. 70.
8 B.L. Add. MS. 39368, f. 985.
9 Elphick, *Bells*, 351.
10 *S.R.S.* lxxviii. 70.
11 B.L. Add. MS. 5699, f. 89.
12 *S.A.C.* liii. 242–3 and facing p. 264.
13 W.S.R.O., Par. 137/1.
14 Cf. Page, *Middleton*, 20.
15 W.S.R.O., MP 2415, ff. 15–16.
16 Ibid. Ep. I/22A/1 (1878, 1887); Ep. I/22A/2 (1868, 1898).
17 *Rep. Com. on Children and Women in Agric.* 86.
18 *Kelly's Dir. Bognor Regis* (1940, 1972).
19 Local inf.
20 This article was written in 1991 and revised in 1995. Topographical details in introduction based mainly on O.S. Maps 1/25,000, TQ 00/10, 01/11 (1979, 1984 edns.); 6", Suss. L, LXIII (1879 and later edns.). Map, above, p. 10. Much help was received from Mrs. J. Haydon, S. Stoke Fmho., and Mrs. P. Dyson, Offham.
21 *Census*, 1881, 1981.
22 Below, manors.
23 S.M.R. 2449; A. H. Allcroft, *Waters of Arun*, 3.
24 For changes in course of river, below.
25 Para. based mainly on Geol. Surv. Map 1", drift, sheet 317 (1957 edn.).
26 *S.R.S.* lxxiv, p. 17; above, Arundel, communications (rds.).
27 A.C.M., Hodskinson surv. 1778, f. 6; ibid. MD 2489.
28 e.g. ibid. Hodskinson surv. 1778, f. 22; *Arundel Rds.* facing p. [3].
29 W.S.R.O., MP 1768, s.v. Arundel.
30 Above, Arundel, intro.
31 *V.C.H. Suss.* i. 432.
32 A.C.M., A 241, rot. 2.
33 Cf. *S.R.S.* lii, p. 88.
34 A.C.M., M 31, rot. 5; 299, f. [14].
35 e.g. *Arundel Rds.* 46, 50, 54, 58; *S.A.C.* lxiii. 59.
36 *Land Drainage Rec. W. Suss.* ed. D. Butler, p. xxxiii.
37 P. A. L. Vine, *Lond.'s Lost Route to Sea* (1986), 155; for the date, below, this section [communications].
38 *Arundel Rds.* 26, 50.
39 W.S.R.O., TD/W 116; cf. ibid. Add. MS. 29772 (TS. cat.); A.C.M., A 262, f. [2v.]; 1347, ff. [1v.–2]; ibid. D 799–811 (MS. cat.); O.S. Map 6", Suss. L (1879 and later edns.).
40 A.C.M., MD 2139; O.S. Map 6", Suss. L (1879 edn.).
41 Inf. from Mrs. Haydon and Mrs. Dyson; *W. Suss. Gaz.* 10 Nov. 1988.

A fishery at Offham manor yielded *2s.* in 1086,[42] and there was another at South Stoke manor in 1276–7.[43] Later they were generally farmed, sometimes with the demesne lands of their respective manors;[44] in the early 15th century they were held together.[45] Fishing continued to be carried on in the parish later,[46] and from the mid 19th century there was good angling at the Black Rabbit inn below Offham.[47]

The woodland yielding three swine at Offham manor in 1086[48] presumably lay in the Weald, where the manor later had outlying lands.[49] A demesne wood on South Stoke manor mentioned in 1325–6[50] and the woods from which both manors received income in the early 15th century[51] may also have been wealden. Stoke wood or common was depicted in the parish in the early 17th,[52] but has not been located. The 100 a. of wood at Offham acquired by Arundel priory in the mid 13th century[53] were probably also within the parish, and may have included Offham hanger north-east of Swanbourne lake. In 1431, however, the master of Arundel college, the priory's successor, was cutting trees at 'Offham wood' without licence.[54] In 1722 beech and oak in Offham hanger were said to belong to the lord, the copyholders claiming underwood.[55] The wood was a noted feature of the scenery of the parish from the early 19th century,[56] but was severely damaged in the great storm of 1987. Heron wood nearby was a breeding place for herons in 1570.[57] Mill hanger west of Swanbourne lake was mentioned from 1636.[58]

A rabbit warren called Pughdean warren existed between the 1490s and 1787, when it occupied 27 a.[59] on the east side of Pughdean bottom;[60] the many earthworks visible there in the 1830s, including that called Bevis's grave,[61] seem more likely to be pillow mounds of the warren than prehistoric remains. The lodge mentioned from the early 17th century[62] lay in the valley.[63] A warrener was recorded in 1660 and later.[64] In 1760 the warren was encroaching on the common downs,[65] but in 1787 the land was bought by the duke of Norfolk and incorporated into the new Arundel park,[66] the lodge being destroyed.

The new park was inclosed between 1787 and 1789, when it had fences and gates; besides Pughdean warren it included the former South Stoke and Offham common downs.[67] The site of Dry lodge, a castellated structure in the north part of the parish later destroyed, represents the former northern limit of the park,[68] but by 1813 the park extended beyond the parish boundary into Houghton. It was further enlarged to the north-east between that date[69] and 1834.[70] A stone wall was built to enclose it.[71] Blue Doors lodge on the park's north-eastern boundary apparently existed by 1843,[72] and the lodges at Offham and Swanbourne, the latter in Jacobean style, were designed by William Burn in 1850 and 1852 respectively.[73] Prominent figures of a lion and a horse crown the gatepiers at the Offham entrance. Most of the park's area in the 19th century and later was open grassland diversified by plantations.[74] There were deer by 1791,[75] and preserves for pheasants in the south-east part by the 1870s.[76]

The chief feature of the new park was the lake at Swanbourne, enlarged and landscaped after the 1780s from the existing mill pond. Two islands depicted at the south-east end in 1778 were later reduced in size.[77] Herons nested there in the earlier 19th century,[78] and in the later 19th and earlier 20th there were various sorts of waterfowl including swans, with peacocks on shore nearby.[79] Pleasure boats were for hire by *c.* 1940,[80] and in 1989, when the lakeside was a popular place for walks, the Swanbourne lodge was converted into a tea shop.[81]

There was prehistoric settlement over much of the upland area of the parish, traces of a

42 *V.C.H. Suss.* i. 432.
43 P.R.O., SC 6/1029/22.
44 A.C.M., A 432, 1805, 1845; B.L. Add. MS. 5701, f. 19; P.R.O., SC 6/Eliz. I/2214, rot. 31; Petch, 'Arundel Coll.' 307; *Valor Eccl.* (Rec. Com.), i. 313.
45 *S.R.S.* lxvii. 130–1.
46 e.g. W.S.R.O., Ep. I/29/185/10.
47 *Breads's Guide Worthing* (1865), 67; *V.C.H. Suss.* ii. 466.
48 *V.C.H. Suss.* i. 432.
49 Below, econ. hist.
50 P.R.O., DL 25/1658 (TS. cat.).
51 *S.R.S.* lxvii. 130–1.
52 A.C.M., PM 193; cf. W.S.R.O., Ep. I/25/1 (1615, *recte* 1616).
53 *Cal. Close*, 1330–3, 261–2; cf. P.R.O., E 106/8/19, rot. 18.
54 A.C.M., M 834.
55 Ibid. MD 719, ff. [2v.–3].
56 e.g. Tierney, *Arundel*, i. 8.
57 A.C.M., MD 535, f. 15v.; cf. ibid. MD 719, f. [2v.]; ibid. PM 193.
58 Ibid. A 339, Arundel surv. 1702, f. 2; ibid. MD 505, f. [6]; 719, f. [2v.]; ibid. Hodskinson surv. 1778, f. 6.
59 Ibid. A 231, rot. 3; 241, rot. 1d.; ibid. D 6342–66 (MS. cat.); P.R.O., SC 6/Eliz. I/2214, rot. 4; W.S.R.O., Ep. I/25/1 (1635), Arundel; *Valor Eccl.* (Rec. Com.), i. 313; Petch, 'Arundel Coll.' 308.
60 Gardner, *Suss. Map* (1778–83).
61 Tierney, *Arundel*, i. 39 n.; *S.N.Q.* xvii. 38–40; cf. S.M.R. 1975.
62 A.C.M., PM 193; W.S.R.O., Ep. I/29/185/14.
63 A.C.M., MD 2534; *250 Yrs. of Mapmaking in Suss.* ed. H. Margary, pl. 19.
64 W.S.R.O., Ep. I/29/185/14, 26; ibid. Slindon MSS., ct. bk. 1739–72, f. 129; *Returns of Papists, 1767* (Cath. Rec. Soc.), ii. 146; cf. *Miscellanea*, xiv (Cath. Rec. Soc. xxvii), 57–8; *S.R.S.* xxviii. 44.
65 W.S.R.O., Slindon MSS., ct. bk. 1739–72, f. 129.
66 A.C.M., MD 619, p. 9.
67 Ibid. A 1347, ff. [1v.–2]; ibid. MD 619, pp. 9, 117; 2489, 2534.
68 Ibid. LM 18; O.S. Map 6", Suss. L (1879 edn.); cf. Gardner, *Suss. Map* (1795).
69 *250 Yrs. of Mapmaking in Suss.* pl. 19.
70 W.S.R.O., TD/W 116.
71 Tierney, *Arundel*, i. 97.
72 W.S.R.O., TD/W 116, no. 78a; illus. at *Chich. Observer*, 23 May 1996.
73 Date on bldg.; *Connoisseur*, Mar. 1978, p. 172; A.C.M., uncat. archit. drawings.
74 *250 Yrs. of Mapmaking in Suss.* pls. 19, 26; W.S.R.O., TD/W 116; O.S. Map 6", Suss. L (1879 and later edns.).
75 A.C.M., MD 2489; cf. Tierney, *Arundel*, i. 97.
76 O.S. Map 6", Suss. L (1879 and later edns.).
77 *250 Yrs. of Mapmaking in Suss.* pls. 14–15, 19, 26; A.C.M., Hodskinson surv. 1778, ff. 6, 22; ibid. LM 18; W.S.R.O., TD/W 116; O.S. Map 6", Suss. L, LXIII (1879 and later edns.); *S.A.C.* cxviii. 378.
78 *S.A.C.* xxv. 4; cf. *S.C.M.* ix. 731.
79 Kimpton, *Arundel* (1897), 6; *Gardeners' Mag.* 24 Mar. 1900, suppl. p. vi; *Arundel, the Gem of Suss.* (Arundel, 1934), 28; *W. Suss. Gaz.* 19 June 1975.
80 *W. Suss. Gaz.* 24 Aug. 1989.
81 Ibid. 4 May 1989.

large field system surviving in the 20th century.[82] At Shepherd's Garden north-north-west of Swanbourne lake an early Roman villa seems to have succeeded previous occupation,[83] while Nanny's croft in the extreme north apparently had a Roman settlement with a cemetery.[84]

The two chief settlements in later centuries were at South Stoke and Offham, each occupying a spur of higher ground which projected into the Arun valley. Mention in 1570 of 'the toft of a tenement' and 'the toft of a cottage' at Offham may indicate the contraction of settlement there.[85] By 1795 only a few houses remained at each place,[86] as was still the case in 1991. Other houses in the parish then were the Black Rabbit inn and associated cottages in the south part, and the various lodges of the park. There had been 19 houses in all in 1801 and 24 in 1901.[87]

Most buildings in the parish are of flint or brick. At nos. 38–9 South Stoke beside the churchyard a flint rubble and brick range probably replaces timber framing; the massive chimneystack at the north end of the building has decorative brickshafts of the early 17th century resting on a base of clunch in large blocks. A house beside the old road from Offham to South Stoke, later rebuilt, incorporates a datestone for 1661.[88] There are several Norfolk estate cottages of the 19th and 20th centuries.[89]

Thirteen taxpayers were assessed in 1327 and 1332[90] and *c.* 18 in 1524.[91] The protestation in 1642 was signed by 28 adult males[92] and 33 adults were enumerated in the Compton census of 1676.[93] In 1724 there were 13 families.[94] From 106 in 1801 the population fluctuated between 99 and 115 until 1871, rising to 133 in 1881 and falling to 65 in 1961. It was 67 in 1981.[95] South Stoke village had 15 residents in 1966.[96]

The river Arun was the chief artery of transport in the past, several inhabitants owning a boat in the 17th century.[97] Only one boat and one barge, however, were recorded in 1801 and none in 1803.[98]

A putative Roman road along part of the northern boundary is mentioned above, and the site of a possibly Roman ford above South Stoke village was traceable in 1991.[99] There was a ferry in 1778 at the site of the Black Rabbit inn[1] and another later between Offham and Peppering in Burpham.[2] An iron footbridge dated 1843 gives access to the land beyond the cut of 1840 near South Stoke village, and a similar bridge was constructed *c.* 1860 to link Offham to its meadows.[3] The suspension footbridge between South Stoke and North Stoke existed by 1876.[4]

There was also land communication, across low spurs of the chalk, between South Stoke, Offham, and Arundel, and in 1778 downland tracks led to Bury and Madehurst.[5] The path along the river bank to Houghton existed by 1809.[6] The South Stoke to Offham road ran ⅛ mile (200 metres) east of the modern road in 1778;[7] its line was followed by a footpath in 1995. The gradient of the Arundel road south-west of Offham seems to have been artificially reduced by a cutting. When the duke of Norfolk created Arundel new park in the 1780s local opposition prevented him from closing the roads from Arundel via Pughdean bottom to South Stoke and Houghton,[8] but the Pughdean bottom to South Stoke road and some other downland roads were closed under the inclosure Award of 1809, the rector of South Stoke retaining a right of way for himself or his curate across the park to Whiteways in Houghton.[9] The duke made another unsuccessful attempt to close the track from Swanbourne mill to Pughdean bottom along the west side of Swanbourne lake in or before 1809,[10] and his successor in 1850 tried abortively to close both that and the road between Swanbourne and the Black Rabbit.[11]

The Mid Sussex railway was opened through the parish in 1863.[12]

The keeper of Pughdean warren is said to have kept a public house there before 1791.[13] The Black Rabbit inn nearby, whose name alludes to the warren, was recorded, at first as the Black Coney, from the 1780s.[14] Before the mid 20th century it largely served riverside traffic: first presumably boatmen, and later excursionists from Arundel and Littlehampton, who came in large numbers by 1829 to enjoy various recreations and the view of Arundel castle.[15] In the 1890s there were dancing, bowls, and croquet,[16] and about the same time rowing boats were hired

82 S.M.R. 1996, 2491.
83 Ibid. 1975; *S.A.C.* lxxvii. 223–43.
84 S.M.R. 2449. 85 A.C.M., MD 535, ff. 14v.–15.
86 Gardner, *Suss. Map* (1795); cf. W.S.R.O., TD/W 116.
87 *Census*, 1801, 1901.
88 Cf. W.S.R.O., Par. 185/1/1/1, f. 10; for the old rd., below, this section. 89 For rectory ho., below, church.
90 *S.R.S.* x. 136–7, 254, evidently indicating S. Stoke since N. Stoke is given separately: ibid. 144, 267.
91 Ibid. lvi. 57.
92 Ibid. v. 168, taking the 2 Edw. Pipers to be the same.
93 *Compton Census*, ed. Whiteman, 144.
94 *S.R.S.* lxxviii. 72.
95 *Census*, 1801–1981.
96 *Brighton Evening Argus*, 24 Feb. 1966.
97 W.S.R.O., Ep. I/29/185/1, 7, 10, 22; Ep. I/55/234.
98 E.S.R.O., LCG/3/EW 1, ff. [44, 90v.].
99 Allcroft, *Waters of Arun*, 3; inf. from Mrs. Haydon.
1 A.C.M., Hodskinson surv. 1778, f. 21.
2 Inf. from Mrs. Dyson. The ferryman's cottage, since demolished, is illus. at T. Edwardes, *Neighbourhood*, facing p. 280: inf. from Mrs. Dyson.
3 *S.N.Q.* xvii. 211–12.
4 O.S. Map 6", Suss. L (1879 edn.).
5 A.C.M., Hodskinson surv. 1778, f. 21; Gardner, *Suss. Map* (1778–83).
6 W.S.R.O., Add. MS. 5161.
7 A.C.M., Hodskinson surv. 1778, f. 21; cf. O.S. Map 6", Suss. L (1879 edn.).
8 A.C.M., MD 2489, 2534.
9 W.S.R.O., Add. MS. 5161; cf. A.C.M., LM 18.
10 *S.A.C.* lxxi. 53.
11 E.S.R.O., FIG 527; W.S.R.O., Par. 8/12/1, pp. 19–25; cf. above, Arundel, communications (rds.).
12 *Southern Region Rec.* comp. R. H. Clark, 52.
13 A.C.M., MD 2489.
14 Ibid. A 339, Offham man. rental, 1784–93; *Kelly's Dir. Suss.* (1845 and later edns.); *250 Yrs. of Mapmaking in Suss.* ed. H. Margary, pl. 15. The inn had its modern name by 1813: ibid. pl. 19.
15 A.C.M., FC 435; cf. Pike, *Dir. SW. Suss.* (1886–7).
16 *Ellis's Popular Guide Arundel* (Arundel, pre 1893), 29–30 (copy in C.I.H.E. libr.); Kimpton, *Arundel* (1893), p. vii.

out.[17] Tea gardens were mentioned in 1895.[18] The inn was enlarged *c.* 1900[19] and again in 1990.

There was a volunteer rifle range at Pughdean bottom from the 1870s.[20]

A reservoir to supply Arundel with water was built north-east of Swanbourne lake by 1896.[21] A water tower attached to 'Chapel barn' at South Stoke farm supplied the village before its connexion to the mains in 1960,[22] while Offham hamlet formerly received water from a reservoir a little uphill on its west side.[23] Mains electricity reached the parish *c.* 1950.[24]

A reserve of the Wildfowl Trust, from 1989 the Wildfowl and Wetlands Trust, was opened in 1976 on 55 a. leased from the duke of Norfolk between Swanbourne lake and the river. It had 700 duck, geese, and swans of 90 species from all over the world besides native birds, and was partly open to the public then and later. A visitors' centre was opened in 1980.[25]

MANORS AND OTHER ESTATES. King Edgar in 975 granted to his kinsman Osweard land at Stoke which from the description of bounds seems likely to represent the later South Stoke and Offham manors.[26] Wulfnoth, a free man, held four hides at *SOUTH STOKE* in 1066, and Ernald held the same of earl Roger in 1086.[27] The manor was later generally held of the rape when not resumed into the earl's demesne. At the division of the d'Aubigny inheritance it was assigned in 1244 to the share of Roger de Somery and his wife.[28]

Since Robert de Caux was dealing with South Stoke in the early 13th century, members of the same family mentioned locally in the 12th may also have held it: Robert (fl. 1139–40), Hugh, who held three fees of Arundel rape in 1166, and Godfrey (fl. 1180).[29] Robert (fl. 1205)[30] in 1207 accepted Hugh de Nevill as mesne tenant between himself and the earl of Arundel,[31] the agreement being ratified by the next earl in 1222.[32] Hugh seems in fact to have displaced Robert, since in 1227 he was licensed to lease the manor for ten years to the bishop of Chichester.[33] He died *c.* 1234.[34] His widow Beatrice de Fay had the manor as dower and was still alive in 1241;[35] in 1242–3, however, three fees in South Stoke and Warningcamp were held by John de Nevill.[36] John (d. 1246) was succeeded by his son Hugh (d. 1269), whose brother and heir John[37] (d. *c.* 1282) was succeeded by his son, another Hugh,[38] during whose minority Albin de Bevery had the keeping.[39] The second Hugh came of age in 1298,[40] settled the manor on his son, also Hugh, in 1323–4,[41] and had died by 1336.[42] It is not clear whether Master Thomas de Nevill, who held land in the parish in 1341–2,[43] was lord of South Stoke, but in 1357–8 Sir John de Nevill sold the manor to Richard FitzAlan, earl of Arundel (d. 1376).[44]

Thereafter the manor descended for a time with the rape,[45] though the gift of it to Arundel college by earl Thomas (d. 1415) could only take effect after the death of Margaret, widow of Roland Lenthall, in 1423;[46] the college already had rents in the parish.[47] After the Dissolution South Stoke was granted by the Crown in 1544 to Henry FitzAlan, earl of Arundel (d. 1580),[48] after which it again descended with the rape until the forfeiture of earl Philip in 1589.[49] The advowson, which descended with the manor, was exercised by the Crown in that year,[50] but the manor was sold by earl Philip's trustees William Dix and Richard Cutte in or before 1591 to Thomas Sackville, Lord Buckhurst.[51]

By 1593 South Stoke had passed to Sir Thomas Palmer and his wife Alice, who conveyed it in that year to Anthony Kempe of Slindon[52] (d. 1597). Anthony's son and heir (Sir) Garrett[53] was succeeded by his son and namesake; one or other leased it in 1649 for 21 years to John Caryll and others,[54] in whose names courts were held in 1650 and 1653.[55] In 1664 it seems to have been settled on the younger Garrett's son Anthony,[56] recorded as lord between 1669 and 1710,[57] who died in 1715. His son and heir, another Anthony, died in 1753, having settled the manor on his

17 W.S.R.O., PH 1467, f. 93; *Kelly's Dir. Suss.* (1905); Goodliffe, *Littlehampton* (1903), pp. xxiii, 57–8; above, pl. facing p. 186.

18 *Kelly's Dir. Suss.* (1895).

19 Cartland, *Arundel*, 119–20.

20 Ibid. 83; O.S. Map 6", Suss. L (1879 and later edns.).

21 O.S. Map 6", Suss. L. SW. (1899 edn.).

22 Inf. from Mr. R. Haydon, S. Stoke Fmho.

23 Inf. from Mrs. Dyson.

24 Inf. from Mrs. Haydon.

25 *W. Suss. Gaz.* 18 Nov. 1976; 29 June 1989; *Country Life*, 3 July 1980, p. 8.

26 *Cart. Sax.* ed. Birch, iii, pp. 648–9; R. Forsberg, *Contribution to a Dict. of Old Eng. P.N.s* (Uppsala, 1950), 92–3, 214–15; inf. from Prof. R. Coates, Univ. of Suss. *Maerce cumb* seems to be Pughdean bottom, *hogebura mearce* the bdry. with Houghton, and *tha ea* the river Arun. That the 2 mans. were originally 1 is suggested by the similarity of their Domesday bk. entries: *V.C.H. Suss.* i. 431–2.

27 *V.C.H. Suss.* i. 431.

28 *S.A.C.* lix. 15.

29 Ibid. 11–12.

30 *Cur. Reg. R.* iii. 276.

31 *S.R.S.* ii, pp. 27–8; *S.A.C.* lix. 11.

32 *Cur. Reg. R.* x. 349.

33 *Cal. Chart. R.* 1226–57, 87.

34 *Ex. e Rot. Fin.* (Rec. Com.), i. 260.

35 *Cur. Reg. R.* xv, p. 257; *Close R.* 1237–42, 272.

36 *Bk. of Fees*, ii. 689.

37 W. Farrer, *Honors and Kts.' Fees*, iii. 49.

38 *Cal. Inq. p.m.* ii, p. 256; *Cal. Pat.* 1281–92, 105.

39 *Cal. Pat.* 1281–92, 57; 1292–1301, 68.

40 *Cal. Close*, 1296–1302, 162.

41 *S.R.S.* xxiii, p. 55. It is not clear why Thos. Praeres was said to be lord in 1316: *Feud. Aids*, v. 143.

42 B.L. Add. MS. 39502, f. 283.

43 *Abbrev. Rot. Orig.* (Rec. Com.), ii. 149.

44 *S.R.S.* xxiii, p. 143; *35th Dep. Kpr's. Rep.* App. p. 26.

45 e.g. *Cal. Inq. Misc.* vi, pp. 220–3; *Cal. Pat.* 1396–9, 360.

46 *Cal. Pat.* 1422–9, 116; P.R.O., C 139/5, no. 35; cf. *Feud. Aids*, vi. 521. Marg. exercised the advowson, which descended with the man., in 1403, and Roland between 1407 and 1410: *S.R.S.* xi. 273, 293, 303, 311.

47 *Cal. Pat.* 1377–81, 151. It had perhaps also succeeded to the 100 a. woodland at Offham belonging to its predecessor Arundel priory: *Cal. Close*, 1330–3, 261; above, intro.

48 *L. & P. Hen. VIII*, xix (2), p. 475.

49 *S.R.S.* xix. 9; P.R.O., E 178/1906, ff. 3v., 6.

50 B.L. Add. MS. 39347, f. 165; below, church.

51 Dallaway, *Hist. W. Suss.* ii (1) (1819), 192; Elwes & Robinson, *W. Suss.* 216–17; A.C.M., M 532, ff. [1, 4v. from end].

52 *S.R.S.* xx. 289. Rest of para. based mainly on *V.C.H. Suss.* iv. 234–5; Berry, *Suss. Geneal.* annot. Comber, 75; *Complete Peerage*, s.v. Newburgh.

53 P.R.O., C 142/252, no. 28.

54 *S.R.S.* xx. 401–2.

55 W.S.R.O., Slindon MSS., ct. bk. 1650–60, pp. 38, 158.

56 Ibid. Add. MS. 37517.

57 Ibid. Slindon MSS., ct. bks. 1662–97, f. 30v.; 1699–1738, f. 30v.

daughter Barbara and her husband James Radclyffe, Viscount Kynnaird[58] (succ. as earl of Newburgh 1755; d. 1786). James's son and heir Anthony (d.s.p. 1814) conveyed to the duke of Norfolk first in 1787 a portion of South Stoke down[59] and later in 1798 the manor and demesne lands,[60] which thereafter descended again with the rape,[61] passing after 1975 to the family of Duke Miles (fl. 1995).[62] By the mid 19th century virtually the whole parish belonged to the Norfolk estate.[63] The lordship of the wealden portion of the manor, sometimes called South Stoke in the Weald, meanwhile passed from Anthony Radclyffe, earl of Newburgh (d. 1814), first to his widow Anne (d. 1861) and then to her cousin Col. Charles Leslie of Slindon (d. 1870);[64] it presumably continued to descend with Slindon.

South Stoke Farmhouse is a large early 19th-century house of two storeys and five bays, built of brick and flint with a cemented entrance front.[65] The sloping site accommodates a spacious basement at the rear facing the river. The medieval manor house mentioned in 1386[66] seems unlikely to have had such an exposed position and may have lain nearer the church. The elaborately detailed 19th-century Gothic 'Chapel barn' near the house is of two storeys in brick and stone with a fine timber roof.

Alwine, a free man, held *OFFHAM,* containing four hides, in 1066, and Azo held it of earl Roger in 1086.[67] The overlordship thereafter descended with that of South Stoke.

Henry II while in possession of Arundel rape granted Hugh Esturmi ⅔ fee in Offham, which was confirmed to him successively by William d'Aubigny, earl of Arundel (d. 1193), and by William's son and namesake.[68] Hugh still had the land in 1203,[69] and in 1212, as earlier at South Stoke, Hugh de Nevill intruded himself as mesne tenant.[70] Richard of Thorney and later Reynold Aguillon also had an interest in the manor at the same period.[71] Hugh Esturmi was still apparently tenant in 1249,[72] but mention of a namesake in 1263 and *c.* 1282[73] may be retrospective. Before 1303 William Sturmy made over his interest in Offham to Peter de Champvent and his wife Agnes, Peter being succeeded in that year by his son John.[74] John de Champvent and Richard de Heghes were said to be lords in 1316.[75] John held a fee in Offham in 1322,[76] while Richard de Heghes, who was dealing with land there in 1324–5,[77] was taxed in the parish in 1327 and 1332.[78]

In 1345 Offham was settled on Richard FitzAlan, earl of Arundel (d. 1376),[79] after which it descended with the rape, generally remaining in demesne.[80] Margaret Lenthall had a life interest in 1412,[81] and after her death in 1423 Sir John Cornwall, later Lord Fanhope, and William Ryman had the keeping.[82] In the later 16th century the demesnes were leased successively to Richard Pellatt (d. 1567)[83] and Sir Thomas Palmer (fl. 1570).[84] After the forfeiture of Philip Howard, earl of Arundel, in 1589, courts were held in the name of Queen Elizabeth between 1591 and 1594,[85] but the manor had evidently been restored to Philip's widow Anne by 1596.[86] Arthur Onslow had a 60-year lease of it in 1673.[87]

The medieval manor house at Offham was in disrepair in 1431[88] and had been demolished by 1570;[89] it may have occupied a close west of the hamlet called Court field or Court garden, where remains of a large building are said to have been found in the late 19th century or early 20th.[90] The present Offham House is of flint, with brick dressings and a datestone, now reset, for 1717. The south front was refenestrated and hung with mathematical tiles in the early 19th century, and the house was remodelled and enlarged in the early 20th in brick and sandstone. Some rooms have 18th-century proportions, but most decoration is late 19th- or 20th-century. Between 1970 and 1982 the building was leased as a Catholic children's home[91] and in 1993 it was a guest house.

The Knights Hospitaller had lands at Offham by the mid 13th century,[92] which may have been the same as the ¼ fee which they held of South Stoke in the early 15th.[93] They were presumably the lands in the parish held of Poling St. John manor in 1737.[94]

The dean and chapter of Chichester were granted land at Offham in the mid 13th century;[95] in 1532 and later it was said once to have been three tenements, and in 1595 it comprised

58 B.L. Add. MS. 5688, f. 121.
59 A.C.M., MD 619, p. 9.
60 Ibid. D 2779–89.
61 e.g. *S.R.S.* li. 85, 104, 139.
62 Local inf.
63 A.C.M., LM 16; W.S.R.O., TD/W 116; cf. ibid. IR 45, ff. [10–13].
64 W.S.R.O., Slindon MSS., ct. bk. 1807–99, *passim*; *S.R.S.* li. 144.
65 Above, pl. facing p. 186.
66 *Cal. Inq. Misc.* vi, p. 221.
67 *V.C.H. Suss.* i. 432.
68 W. Farrer, *Honors and Kts.' Fees*, iii. 42.
69 *Cur. Reg. R.* ii. 277.
70 *S.R.S.* ii, pp. 32–3.
71 Ibid. p. 45; *Cur. Reg. R.* v. 88–9; viii. 185; ix. 161, 355; *Rot. Litt. Claus.* (Rec. Com.), ii. 149–50; *Bruton and Montacute Cartularies* (Som. Rec. Soc. viii), pp. 86–7; *Bracton's Note Bk.* ed. Maitland, ii, p. 155.
72 *S.R.S.* xlvi, p. 59.
73 *Bruton and Montacute Cartularies*, p. 87; *Cal. Inq. p.m.* ii, p. 256.
74 *Cal. Inq. p.m.* iv, p. 94.
75 *Feud. Aids*, v. 143.
76 Ibid. vi. 639.
77 *S.R.S.* xxiii, p. 56.
78 Ibid. x. 136, 254.
79 *Cal. Close*, 1346–9, 243–4, enrolling an earlier deed.
80 *Cal. Inq. Misc.* vi, pp. 220–3; *Feud. Aids*, v. 155; *Cal. Pat.* 1553–4, 315–16; *S.R.S.* li. 27, 139.
81 *Feud. Aids*, vi. 521.
82 *Cal. Fine R.* 1422–30, 63; *Complete Peerage*, s.v. Fanhope; above, this section.
83 *S.A.C.* xxxviii. 111–12.
84 A.C.M., MD 535, f. 15.
85 Ibid. M 532, ff. [13, 38, 49, 60].
86 Ibid. 286, rot. 9d.
87 *Arundel Cast. Archives*, ed. F. W. Steer, iv. 85, misreading as Cuslow.
88 A.C.M., M 834; cf. *Cal. Inq. Misc.* vi, p. 221.
89 A.C.M., MD 535, f. 15v.
90 W.S.R.O., TD/W 116; A. H. Allcroft, *Waters of Arun*, 41.
91 *Arundel and Brighton Cath. Dir.* (1970 and later edns.); *W. Suss. Gaz.* 8 July 1982.
92 *Cal. Inq. Misc.* ii, p. 46.
93 *S.R.S.* lxvii. 130.
94 Ibid. xx. 356; cf. *Cal. Pat.* 1547–8, 223; P.R.O., C 142/259, no. 80.
95 *S.R.S.* xlvi, p. 37; cf. W.S.R.O., Cap. I/17/52 (TS. cat.).

75 a. Before 1789 it had 120 sheep leazes on Offham down.[96] In 1853 the estate, then 46 a., was conveyed by the dean and chapter to the duke of Norfolk,[97] afterwards descending with South Stoke.

Other religious houses with lands in the parish were Boxgrove priory, which held 1 a. of meadow of South Stoke manor from the early 13th century,[98] and Maiden Bradley priory (Wilts.) and St. Mary's hospital, Chichester, which each held 4 a. of meadow of Offham manor by the early 15th.[99] The hospital's land was sold to the duke of Norfolk in 1900.[1] Pynham priory in Lyminster had presumably had the land belonging to Calceto manor which was settled on Cardinal Wolsey's college at Oxford in 1526,[2] and which later descended in the Browne family, viscounts Montague.[3] Other land in the parish was said in 1622–3 once to have belonged to Tortington priory.[4]

ECONOMIC HISTORY. The estate called Stoke in 975, besides land in the parish, had three wealden outliers called *Siblinc hyrst*, *Trowing sceaddas*, and *Rocisfald*,[5] apparently represented by lands later held of South Stoke and Offham manors at Wisborough Green and elsewhere.[6]

In the Middle Ages there were demesne farms belonging to the two manors of the parish, that at South Stoke in 1294 having apparently 133 a. under crops.[7] After both manors passed to the earls of Arundel in the mid 14th century, the farms served in the late 14th and early 15th as home farms to Arundel castle.[8] At an unknown date in the early 15th century each was considered able to support 2 farm horses, 9 oxen, 20 cows, and a bull, with 250 wether sheep at South Stoke and 300 at Offham.[9] By 1413–14, however, the Offham demesnes were at farm,[10] and from 1436 those of South Stoke as well,[11] South Stoke manor having passed to Arundel college. There was a flock of 230 sheep on the Offham farm at an unknown date in the later Middle Ages.[12]

The demesne arable lay next to the settlements of South Stoke and Offham, presumably partly in open fields, though no reference to open-field agriculture has been found before the mid 16th century.[13] The South Stoke demesne farm had 70 a. of arable and the Offham farm 60 a. in the early 15th century, the latter being more valuable.[14]

There was demesne meadow and brookland pasture in the Arun valley, lying in the meanders of the river near the two settlements; in the south end of the parish was other demesne meadow which descended with Arundel castle.[15] In 1086 South Stoke manor had 24 a. and Offham 48 a.,[16] and in 1386 there were 40 a. on each manor.[17] Besides that belonging to the demesne farms, small pieces of meadow were held by tenants of both manors in the early 15th century.[18] Because of the high quality of the land other pieces were granted to landowners outside the parish, notably religious houses.[19]

There was also demesne upland pasture on the downs. The 200 a. and 100 a. of pasture at South Stoke and Offham manors respectively in the early 15th century[20] were probably chiefly there. A demesne sheepfold was mentioned at South Stoke in 1276–7.[21]

Common meadow apparently also existed from the 13th century,[22] and common downland was mentioned at Offham from 1386;[23] in 1431 the lord of South Stoke was pasturing sheep there illegally.[24]

Medieval tenants of the two manors presumably held strips in any open fields that existed, and had common pasture rights. Ten *villani* and 4 cottars were recorded on South Stoke manor in 1086, and 8 *villani*, 5 cottars, and 5 *servi* on Offham manor.[25] Fixed rents at South Stoke brought in £11 in 1386 and £8 in the early 15th century, and at Offham £6 and £7 13*s*. at the same two dates.[26] In the early 15th century free and customary tenants at South Stoke had estates mostly between 4 a. and 20 a. or described as one or two yardlands; a much larger estate of 100 a. was Lowfold farm in Wisborough Green. At Offham at the same date freehold estates were mostly of less than 10 a. Rents were in money or in kind. Some labour services remained on both manors in the early 15th century.[27] In 1372 female neifs could only marry by licence.[28] In the 15th century tenements of Offham could be sublet.[29]

Arable predominated over pasture in the Middle Ages to judge from the fact that the ninth of sheaves in 1340 brought in four times as much as those of fleeces and lambs.[30] Wheat, barley, oats, peas, beans, and vetch were grown in the late 13th[31] and the 14th century.[32] Other crops mentioned at the same period were apples, flax,

96 *S.R.S.* lii, pp. 87–8; lviii, pp. 61, 211, 233; W.S.R.O., Cap. I/28/75, lease, 1789; Cap. I/51/14, f. 88.

97 W.S.R.O., Cap. I/28/75, deed, 1853; *Arundel Cast. Archives*, iii. 64.

98 *S.R.S.* lix, p. 89; lxvii. 130; *Valor Eccl.* (Rec. Com.), i. 306; cf. P.R.O., C 142/233, no. 99.

99 *S.R.S.* lxvii. 131; cf. *Cal. Pat.* 1580–2, p. 171; P.R.O., E 178/4655; W.S.R.O., Cap. IV/6/46, leases, 1715, 1806.

1 A.C.M., uncat. deed, 1900.

2 *S.R.S.* xix. 87.

3 Ibid. xxxiii, p. 34; *Cowdray Archives*, ed. A. Dibben, i, p. 19.

4 P.R.O., SC 12/22/85, ff. 1–2.

5 *Cart. Sax.* ed. Birch, iii, p. 649.

6 Below, this section.

7 P. F. Brandon, 'Com. Lands and Wastes of Suss.' (Lond. Univ. Ph.D. thesis, 1963), 281, citing P.R.O., SC 6/1030/3.

8 *Cal. Inq. Misc.* vi, p. 221; A.C.M., A 1805–6, 1808, 1812.

9 *S.R.S.* lxvii. 130–1.

10 A.C.M., A 1845; cf. ibid. A 231, rot. 3; ibid. M 834.

11 Ibid. A 432, rot. 4; Petch, 'Arundel Coll.' 307–8.

12 A.C.M., M 316.

13 Below, this section.

14 *S.R.S.* lxvii. 130–1.

15 Cf. A.C.M., MD 505, f. [10v.].

16 *V.C.H. Suss.* i. 431–2.

17 *Cal. Inq. Misc.* vi, p. 221.

18 *S.R.S.* lxvii. 130–1.

19 Ibid. lix, p. 89, naming one early 13th-cent. tenant as Osbert of Graffham; lxvii. 130–1; above, manors; W.S.R.O., Add. MS. 32841 (TS. cat.), naming meadow apparently belonging to Halnaker man. in Boxgrove; cf. ibid. Cap. IV/6/46, lease, 1715; P.R.O., C 142/341, no. 49; *S.R.S.* lxxviii. 69.

20 *S.R.S.* lxvii. 130–1.

21 P.R.O., SC 6/1029/22.

22 Ibid.; W.S.R.O., Add. MS. 32841 (TS. cat.).

23 *Cal. Inq. Misc.* vi, p. 221; A.C.M., M 282, rot. 2.

24 A.C.M., M 834.

25 *V.C.H. Suss.* i. 431–2.

26 *Cal. Inq. Misc.* vi, p. 221; *S.R.S.* lxvii. 130–1.

27 *S.R.S.* lxvii. 130–2; W.S.R.O., Add. MS. 6777 (TS. cat.); Dallaway, *Hist. W. Suss.* ii (1) (1819), 191.

28 A.C.M., M 825, rot. 2d.

29 Ibid. 834.

30 *Inq. Non.* (Rec. Com.), 367.

31 Brandon, 'Com. Lands and Wastes of Suss.' 281; P.R.O., SC 6/1029/22.

32 *Cal. Inq. Misc.* vi, p. 221.

and hemp. Geese, doves, and pigs were kept in 1340.[33]

Between the 16th century and the 18th the two demesne farms were apparently always let,[34] Offham manor farm in the mid 17th century and perhaps earlier to members of the Sowton family.[35] Offham farm in 1570 included 160 a. of pasture and rough ground and 28 a. of meadow,[36] and in 1778 had 314 a.;[37] South Stoke manor farm had 298 a. in 1797.[38] Twenty-one-year leases were mentioned in 1539, 1570, and 1778.[39] Other demesne land was leased in small parcels by 1589.[40]

Both manors had free and copyhold[41] tenements between the 16th century and the 18th, some copyholders holding for three lives.[42] Besides land in the parish, there were tenements of South Stoke in Wisborough Green,[43] Madehurst,[44] Rudgwick, and Fittleworth,[45] and of Offham in Burpham,[46] Kirdford,[47] Wisborough Green,[48] Billingshurst,[49] and 'the Manwood', evidently Manhood hundred south of Chichester.[50] Holdings on Offham manor lying within the parish were generally of less than 10 a. in 1570,[51] but by the 18th century tenants of South Stoke manor in the parish and in Madehurst had amassed composite estates of between 22 a. and 80 a.[52] Copyholds could be sublet on both manors,[53] and widow's bench obtained at Offham in 1527.[54] By 1650 there were only 6 free tenants at South Stoke and 8 customary tenants, 5 of whom were in Wisborough Green;[55] in 1696 Offham manor had 7 free and 6 or 8 customary tenants.[56] The rectory estate had tenants as well in 1553.[57] From the late 18th century the smaller holdings of the parish were being vigorously engrossed by the duke of Norfolk.[58]

Middle field was mentioned in 1548.[59] In 1553 the demesne farmer and tenants of Offham manor decided to inclose the open fields there,[60] but their wish was evidently frustrated since several open fields and furlongs remained in the early 17th century, including Stony furlong and Bury furlong, and East, Townsend, Milne, and Wall fields. Milne field presumably lay near the probable windmill site on the downs in Arundel parish, and Wall field may have been reclaimed land by the river embankment. One copyhold tenement in 1614 comprised land in six fields or furlongs.[61] There was perhaps an open field called South laine at South Stoke at the same period.[62] Hilland or Highland field south-west of Offham hamlet, mentioned from 1674, was still in strips belonging to different owners in 1778,[63] at least one of which survived until 1808.[64] The fields had all been inclosed, by engrossing or by agreement between owners, before *c.* 1840.[65]

Small parcels of several meadow continued to be held of Offham manor in 1605[66] and a Poling farmer may have been leasing meadow in South Stoke in 1566.[67] In 1636 the 64 a. of several pasture belonging to Arundel castle in the south part of the parish was let, mostly in small parcels but two larger amounts of 14 a. and 24 a. to John and Thomas Sowton respectively.[68]

Much pasture and meadow continued to be commonable in the same period. North mead at Offham was at least partly inclosed *c.* 1520 by John Sowton,[69] perhaps the demesne farmer.[70] In 1553 the farmer and tenants decided to inclose various brooks and meads,[71] but as with the open fields clearly abortively. Various common meadows or brooks are recorded later both there[72] and at South Stoke,[73] subject to rights of

33 P.R.O., SC 6/1029/22; *Inq. Non.* (Rec. Com.), 367.

34 A.C.M., A 241, rot. IV.; 281, honor acct. [1702–3], f. 2; ibid. MD 535, f. 15; P.R.O., SC 6/Eliz. I/2214, rott. 4, 31; W.S.R.O., Slindon MSS., ct. bk. 1650–60, p. 39; *Valor Eccl.* (Rec. Com.), i. 313.

35 A.C.M., A 262, f. [2v.]; 1351, f. 2; cf. *Valor Eccl.* (Rec. Com.), i. 296; *S.R.S.* xlv. 173; *Lavington Estate Archives*, ed. F. W. Steer, p. 46; *Goodwood Estate Archives*, i, ed. F. W. Steer and J. Venables, p. 2; W.S.R.O., Ep. I/29/185/18; ibid. Slindon MSS., ct. bk. 1662–97, f. 120.

36 A.C.M., MD 535, f. 15.

37 Ibid. Hodskinson surv. 1778, f. 25.

38 37 Geo. III, c. 39 (Priv. Act).

39 A.C.M., D 6259 (MS. cat.); ibid. Hodskinson surv. 1778, f. 23; ibid. MD 535, f. 15.

40 P.R.O., E 178/1906, ff. 2, 3v.; W.S.R.O., Slindon MSS., ct. bk. 1650–60, pp. 38, 158.

41 *Valor Eccl.* (Rec. Com.), i, p. 313; A.C.M., A 262, f. [2v.]; 1351, f. 2; ibid. M 282, rot. 2; ibid. MD 495, f. [3 and v.]; 535, ff. 14v.–15v.; P.R.O., E 178/1906, ff. 2, 3v.; W.S.R.O., Slindon MSS., ct. bk. 1699–1738, f. 9; quit rent bk. 1745–1807.

42 A.C.M., M 31, rot. 5; 283, rot. 1; 301, p. [21]; ibid. MD 535, ff. 14v.–15; W.S.R.O., Slindon MSS., quit rent bk. 1745–1807, rental of S. Stoke man. *c.* 1807.

43 A.C.M., M 283, rot. 2d.; W.S.R.O., Add. MSS. 8653, 10125 (TS. cat.); ibid. Slindon MSS., ct. bks. 1650–60, pp. 38, 158; 1739–72, *passim*; quit rent bk. 1745–1807, rental of S. Stoke man. *c.* 1807.

44 W.S.R.O., Slindon MSS., ct. bks. 1662–97, f. 72v.; 1699–1738, f. 71; 1773–1809, pp. 18–19; cf. *S.R.S.* lxvii. 130.

45 B.L. Add. MS. 5688, f. 120; W.S.R.O., Slindon MSS., ct. bk. 1807–99, *passim*.

46 A.C.M., A 339, Offham man. rental, 1784–93; ibid. M 282, rot. 2; 301, pp. [113, 307]; ibid. MD 495, f. [3v.]; 535, f. 15 and v.

47 P.R.O., SC 2/205/53, rot. 6; A.C.M., M 299, f. [14]; ibid. MD 535, f. 15; cf. ibid. A 231, rot. 3; ibid. M 834.

48 A.C.M., A 339, Offham man. rental, 1784–93; ibid. M 299, f. [15v.]; ibid. MD 535, f. 15.

49 Ibid. A 339, Offham man. rental, 1784–93; ibid. MD 535, f. 15; cf. ibid. M 834.

50 Ibid. M 299, f. [14v.]; ibid. MD 535, f. 15; cf. P.R.O., SC 6/1029/22; *S.R.S.* lxvii. 131; *V.C.H. Suss.* iv. 198.

51 A.C.M., MD 535, ff. 14v.–15v.

52 W.S.R.O., Slindon MSS., ct. bk. 1699–1738, ff. 9, 66v., 71.

53 A.C.M., M 299, f. [15]; ibid. MD 535, f. 15v.; P.R.O., SC 2/205/53, rot. 6; W.S.R.O., Slindon MSS., ct. bk. 1739–72, f. 69.

54 A.C.M., M 314, rot. 1.

55 W.S.R.O., Slindon MSS., ct. bk. 1650–60, pp. 38, 158.

56 A.C.M., M 580, p. 92.

57 Ibid. M 31, rot. 8.

58 Ibid. D 6025–77, 6342–66 (MS. cat.); ibid. MD 619, pp. 5–127, *passim*; cf. ibid. Hodskinson surv. 1778, f. 22.

59 W.S.R.O., Ep. I/86/20, f. 18.

60 A.C.M., M 31, rot. 8.

61 Ibid. MD 495, f. [3 and v.]; W.S.R.O., Ep. I/25/1 (1615); cf. above, Arundel, mills. It is not clear whether Overfurlong, mentioned at same date, was a field or a meadow: P.R.O., E 315/414, f. 51; ibid. SC 12/22/85, f. 2.

62 W.S.R.O., Ep. I/25/1 (1615).

63 A.C.M., M 301, p. [67]; ibid. Hodskinson surv. 1778, f. 24.

64 Ibid. D 6025–77 (MS. cat.).

65 W.S.R.O., TD/W 116.

66 P.R.O., C 142/289, no. 66.

67 *Cal. Assize Rec. Suss. Eliz. I*, p. 48.

68 A.C.M., MD 505, f. [10v.].

69 Ibid. A 241, rot. IV.

70 Cf. above, this section.

71 A.C.M., M 31, rot. 8.

72 Ibid. D 1086–1123, 6155–74 (MS. cat.); ibid. M 301, p. [169]; ibid. MD 495, f. [3v.]; 535, f. 15v.; W.S.R.O., Cap. IV/6/46, lease, 1715; ibid. Ep. I/25/1 (1615).

73 W.S.R.O., Ep. I/25/1 (1615); ibid. Slindon MSS., ct. bk. 1662–97, f. 120.

pasture for cattle, horses, sheep, and pigs;[74] in the early 17th century the season was from May to September.[75] One piece of brookland was apparently intercommonable between Offham and Burpham manors.[76]

In 1778 Offham common mead comprised strips of between ¼ a. and 5 a. belonging to *c.* 8 landowners, including the lord of the manor. On Offham cow pasture of 50 a. at the same date the duke of Norfolk as lord had 35 leazes and four tenants between 2 and 12.[77] The dukes thereafter acquired further leazes with the estates to which they belonged.[78] The remaining mowing rights, including those of the rector and the vicar of Madehurst, were extinguished in 1809 under an inclosure Act of 1799.[79]

On South Stoke manor down in 1650 the demesne farmer had 480 sheep leazes, various tenants 60 or 120, and the rector 60.[80] On Offham manor down in 1570 the farmer and the tenants each had 300 leazes.[81] By the mid 18th century the farmer's entitlement at Offham had been reduced to 200 leazes and some tenants had as few as 10;[82] in 1789 the dean and chapter of Chichester had 120.[83] Offham down comprised 168 a. in 1778.[84] Presentments for overstocking the common downs in 1617,[85] and an order of 1598 for the South Stoke manor flock to cease trespassing on the Offham downland,[86] may indicate pressure on a scarce resource. Fences erected on the downs were ordered to be removed in 1617[87] and later.[88] After 1787 the duke of Norfolk began to engross pasture rights with the tenements to which they belonged,[89] and in 1787 he bought the freehold of part of South Stoke down, of 172 a., from the earl of Newburgh.[90] All pasture rights on the downs had been extinguished by 1809.[91]

Barley, wheat, oats, peas, rye, and tares were grown in the 17th and 18th centuries. Flocks of between 137 and 237 sheep were recorded at the same period, presumably on the demesne farms, and cattle and pigs were widely kept. In 1776 what was evidently South Stoke farm had 371 sheep, 40 cattle, and 35 pigs.[92]

During the 19th century and most of the 20th the parish continued to have two large tenanted farms.[93] Between *c.* 1840 and *c.* 1910 South Stoke farm had *c.* 250 a. and Offham farm 150–200 a.[94] but from 1980 or earlier the two farms were held as a single holding of *c.* 500 a.[95] The chief occupation in the parish in the 19th century and earlier 20th was that of agricultural labourer on the Norfolk estate.[96]

Pasture was more important than arable during the same period. In 1843 there were 173 a. of arable and 911 a. of grass including 527 a. within the deer park.[97] Five hundred and sixty-five sheep had been kept in 1801, besides 99 cattle and 67 pigs; comparable numbers in 1803 were 656, 85, and 79.[98] In 1819 the meadows of the Arun valley were described as very luxuriant as a result of their occasional inundation.[99] Some closes in the brooks were amalgamated between the 1830s and 1870s.[1] About 1840 part of the duke of Norfolk's meadow land was let to three farmers, two of whom apparently resided outside the parish, in parcels of 28 a., 38 a., and 50 a.[2] Four hundred and sixty-two acres of wheat were returned in 1875, 102 a. of oats, 30 a. of barley, and small acreages of turnips and swedes and other crops. Permanent grassland then totalled 819 a., 265 sheep, 131 cattle, and 22 pigs being listed.[3]

By 1909 the acreage of arable had declined to *c.* 130 a. as against 36 a. of rotation grass and 839 a. of permanent grass.[4] Watercress was grown in beds east of Swanbourne lake between 1896 and the 1930s.[5] In 1980 the chief farm of the parish practised mixed farming, with arable, dairying, and beef raising.[6] In 1990, when the dairy unit was at Offham, the lack of upland pasture caused by the creation of the new Arundel park was compensated for by the tenant's keeping a 300-ewe flock in Wales for folding on the land at South Stoke.[7]

It is not clear whether the two mills mentioned after the Offham entry in Domesday Book were in the parish.[8] A female miller was recorded in South Stoke tithing in 1536.[9]

A tinker of Pughdean bottom was accused of coining money in 1573.[10] Tradesmen recorded in the early 17th century were a bricklayer and a basket maker.[11] A chalk pit at Offham was

74 Ibid. Slindon MSS., ct. bk. 1662–97, f. 120; A.C.M., M 119, p. 296; 147; 299, f. [14v.]; 301, p. [169]; ibid. MD 535, f. 15v.

75 A.C.M., M 299, f. [14v.]; cf. ibid. 147.

76 Ibid. M 32, rot. 9; 299, f. [14]; cf. ibid. K 2/62, pp. 46–7.

77 Ibid. Hodskinson surv. 1778, ff. 21, 23, 26.

78 e.g. ibid. D 6342–66 (MS. cat.); ibid. MD 619, p. 9.

79 W.S.R.O., Add. MS. 5161; 39 Geo. III, c. 84 (Private).

80 W.S.R.O., Slindon MSS., ct. bk. 1650–60, pp. 39–40; cf. ibid. ct. bk. 1699–1738, f. 66v.

81 A.C.M., MD 535, f. 15v.

82 Ibid. Hodskinson surv. 1778, f. 26; ibid. M 119, pp. 294, 296.

83 W.S.R.O., Cap. I/28/75, lease, 1789.

84 A.C.M., Hodskinson surv. 1778, f. 26.

85 Ibid. M 299, f. [15], assuming downs to be implied.

86 Ibid. 147.

87 Ibid. 299, f. [14v.].

88 Ibid. 301, p. [171].

89 A.C.M., D 6025–77, 6342–66 (MS. cat.); ibid. MD 619, pp. 5, 7, 9, 29; W.S.R.O., Add. MS. 5161.

90 A.C.M., D 6342–66 (MS. cat.); ibid. MD 619, p. 9.

91 W.S.R.O., Add. MS. 5161; cf. ibid. Slindon MSS., ct. bk. 1773–1809, p. [151]; A.C.M., MD 619, pp. 115, 117.

92 W.S.R.O., Ep. I/29/185/1, 10, 18, 28–30; 37 Geo. III, c. 39 (Priv. Act): Thos. Parlett, lessee of the fm. in 1797, was the son of Jos. Parlett (d. *c.* 1776).

93 W.S.R.O., TD/W 116; ibid. IR 45, ff. [10–11]; *Kelly's Dir. Suss.* (1852 and later edns.).

94 A.C.M., MD 2046–52, sketch map of Offham fm. 1856; 2139; W.S.R.O., IR 45, ff. [10–11]; ibid. TD/W 116.

95 Inf. from Mrs. J. Haydon, S. Stoke Fmho.; *W. Suss. Gaz.* 17 Jan. 1980.

96 *Census*, 1831; W.S.R.O., IR 45, ff. [11–13]; ibid. Par. 185/41/2.

97 P.R.O., IR 18/10479, f. 1; W.S.R.O., TD/W 116; cf. A.C.M., A 1347, f. [iv.].

98 E.S.R.O., LCG/3/EW 1, ff. [43v., 84v.].

99 Dallaway, *Hist. W. Suss.* ii (1) (1819), 191.

1 W.S.R.O., TD/W 116; O.S. Map 6", Suss. L (1879 edn.).

2 W.S.R.O., TD/W 116; the third, Jas. Olliver, was tenant of the Black Rabbit inn. Cf. A.C.M., MD 2046–52, sketch map of Offham fm. 1856; 2139.

3 P.R.O., MAF 68/433.

4 Ibid. MAF 68/2371.

5 O.S. Map 6", Suss. LXIII. NW. (1899 and later edns.); W.S.R.O., IR 45, f. [13].

6 *W. Suss. Gaz.* 17 Jan. 1980.

7 Inf. from Mrs. Haydon.

8 *V.C.H. Suss.* i. 432.

9 A.C.M., M 271, f. [10].

10 P.R.O., SC 2/205/55, f. 55v.

11 W.S.R.O., Ep. I/29/185/2, 7.

worked from 1724 or earlier until some time in the 20th century,[12] the river being used for transport.[13] Only between one and three families in the parish lived predominantly by non-agricultural occupations in the early 19th century.[14] There were charcoal burners in Arundel park by Swanbourne lake in the early 20th.[15]

LOCAL GOVERNMENT. A court at South Stoke manor is referred to from the later 13th century.[16] There are court rolls or draft court rolls for the years 1371–2, 1448–55, 1572, 1578, 1591,[17] 1650–3, 1663–82, and 1701–1899.[18] In 1578 courts were possibly being held every three weeks,[19] but later seldom more than annually: in the later 17th century and mid 18th the frequency was between twice and five times a decade, and thereafter usually less. Business was transacted out of court from 1724 and the last court was held in 1889. In later times business consisted entirely of conveyancing and monitoring the common pastures, but courts of 1371–2, held jointly for South Stoke and Offham, heard a plea of detinue and another concerning land.[20] After 1807 the only transactions recorded concerned outlying holdings of the manor in the Weald. There was a reeve in 1276–7,[21] a tithingman in 1536 and later,[22] and a bailiff in 1889.[23]

A separate court for Offham manor is recorded from the early 15th century;[24] there are court rolls or draft court rolls for the years 1431, 1457–65, 1526–7, various years between 1542 and 1605,[25] and the years 1614–18 and 1672–1844.[26] Three courts a year were held in 1413–14[27] and up to three in the 16th and early 17th centuries, but the frequency was less after 1672: *c.* 10 times a decade at first, falling to between three and five times by the late 18th century. Only three courts were held in the 19th century, the last in 1844. Business was transacted out of court from 1728. In 1542 one court was held at Poling.[28] The business dealt with was the recording of changes in tenure, the regulation of common pasture, oversight of the repair of houses, roads, fences, and ditches, and of the maintenance of river defences.[29] There was a reeve in 1372 and 1599.[30] Two officers later called curemen[31] were elected from 1596 to oversee the common brooks;[32] the hayward elected from 1602 may have had the same office under another name.[33]

Two churchwardens were recorded between 1560 and the mid 17th century but between 1681 and 1897 there was generally only one.[34] In 1884 no parishioner was eligible for the office.[35] There were two churchwardens again by 1917.[36] A single overseer was recorded in 1642[37] and a surveyor of highways in the 19th century.[38] There was a paid parish clerk in 1662.[39]

A parish pest house at Pughdean bottom is recorded *c.* 1800.[40] In the mid 1820s 15 parishioners were receiving relief.[41] The parish remained independent for poor-law purposes until 1869, when it was included in East Preston union. From East Preston rural district it passed in 1933 to Worthing rural district[42] and in 1974 to Arun district.

CHURCH. There was a church in 1086.[43] It was always a rectory.[44] In 1929 the living was united with those of Arundel and Tortington as the united benefice of Arundel with South Stoke and Tortington, the parishes remaining distinct.[45]

The advowson seems always to have descended with the manor before the mid 18th century.[46] The Crown presented during forfeiture in 1397.[47] Sir Thomas Palmer presented for a turn in 1563, John Lumley, Lord Lumley, in 1566, Arundel corporation in 1615, and Charles Elstob in 1706.[48] A Mr. Aylward of Chichester was said to be patron in 1724.[49] Anthony Kempe (d. 1753) sold the advowson in 1731 to Daniel Gittins (d. by 1743), whose son and namesake was rector 1733–61; in 1761 it was exercised by the latter's executors Susanna and Anne Dawtrey. In the same year Robert Drewitt of Houghton sold it to William Fitzwilliam, Earl Fitzwilliam,[50] from whom it passed to the family's tutor, Thomas Carter, then rector of South Stoke.[51] In 1768 Carter sold it to Thomas Lear of Angmering, who sold it in 1783 to Charles Howard, earl of Surrey, later duke of Norfolk.[52] William Keppel, earl of Albemarle, presented because of recusancy in

12 Budgen, *Suss. Map* (1724); A.C.M., Hodskinson surv. 1778, f. 21; O.S. Maps 1/25,000, TQ 00 (1959 edn.); 6", Suss. L (1879 and later edns.).

13 W.S.R.O., A.B.A., F1/12, no. 7.

14 *Census*, 1811–31.

15 Cartland, *Arundel*, 122.

16 *Cal. Inq. p.m.* ii, p. 256.

17 A.C.M., M 283, rott. 1, 2d.; 530; 532, ff. [1, 4v. from end]; 564, rot. 2; 825.

18 W.S.R.O., Slindon MSS., ct. bks. 1650–60, pp. 38, 158; 1662–97, ff. 13, 30v., 49v., 67v., 72v., 120; 1699–1738, 1739–72, 1773–1809, 1807–99, *passim*.

19 A.C.M., M 283, rott. 1, 2d.

20 Ibid. 825, mm. 2–3.

21 P.R.O., SC 6/1029/22.

22 A.C.M., M 271, f. [10]; E.S.R.O., QCR/2/1/EW 2 (46); W.S.R.O., Par. 8/7/39.

23 W.S.R.O., Slindon MSS., ct. bk. 1807–99, p. 154.

24 A.C.M., A 1845; *S.R.S.* lxvii. 131.

25 A.C.M., M 31, rott. 5, 8; 32, rot. 9; 147–8; 277, rot. 1d.; 278, f. [15]; 282, rot. 2; 284, rot. 2; 286, rot. 9d.; 314, rot. 1; 315, rot. 1; 531, ff. [3, 18, 32v., 51, 64, 100v., 107v.]; 532, ff. [13, 25v., 32, 38, 49, 52, 59v., 60] and f. [33 from end]; 565, rot. 4d.; 834; 859, rot. 8; P.R.O., SC 2/205/53, rot. 6.

26 A.C.M., M 119, *passim*; 299, ff. [14–15]; 301, 310–12, 580, *passim*.

27 Ibid. A 1845.

28 Ibid. M 859, rot. 8d.

29 Ibid. 31, rot. 5; 299, f. [14].

30 Ibid. 315, rot. 1d.; 825, m. 3.

31 Ibid. 299, ff. [14v.–15v.].

32 Ibid. 286, rot. 9d.

33 Ibid. 148.

34 B.L. Add. MS. 39359, ff. 134–9; *S.R.S.* v. 168.

35 W.S.R.O., Ep. I/22A/1 (1884).

36 Ibid. Ep. I/22/2 (1917).

37 *S.R.S.* v. 168.

38 W.S.R.O., Par. 185/39/1.

39 Ibid. Ep. I/22/1 (1662).

40 *Arundel Rds.* 47–8.

41 W.S.R.O., QCR/2/3/W 5.

42 *Suss. Poor Law Rec.* 46; Youngs, *Guide to Local Admin. Units of Eng.* i. 523.

43 *V.C.H. Suss.* i. 431.

44 The vicarage mentioned in 1291 was a mistake: *Tax. Eccl.* (Rec. Com.), 135.

45 *Lond. Gaz.* 8 Nov. 1929, pp. 7197–8.

46 *Cal. Inq. p.m.* ii, p. 256; *S.R.S.* xx. 289; xxiii, pp. 55, 143; B.L. Add. MS. 39347, ff. 163–166v.

47 *Cal. Pat.* 1396–9, 222.

48 B.L. Add. MS. 39347, ff. 164v.–166v.

49 *S.R.S.* lxxviii. 72.

50 B.L. Add. MS. 39347, ff. 166v., 168–9, wrongly describing Wm. as Ric.; *Complete Peerage*, s.v. Fitzwilliam.

51 B.L. Add. MSS. 5699, f. 117; 39347, f. 166v.

52 Ibid. 39347, f. 169.

1832, and the University of Oxford in 1856 and 1893.[53] From the union of benefices in 1929 the duke of Norfolk was to have one presentation in three.[54]

The rectory was valued at £5 in 1291,[55] and was worth £8 or less in 1440[56] and £11 15*s.* 10*d.* net in 1535.[57] It was at farm between 1560 and *c.* 1570.[58] Meanwhile the demesne tithes of Offham had been granted by Aseio, apparently the Domesday tenant Azo, to the abbey of Troarn (Calvados); in a confirmation of 1233 an exception was made for the small tithes of land formerly of Reynold Aguillon. In 1263, when the portion belonged to the abbey's English priory of Bruton (Som.), it was defined as the great tithes only of the demesnes of Hugh Sturmi and others and of their tenants, the rector paying the priory 2*s.* a year for the small tithes.[59] The priory retained the portion evidently until the Dissolution,[60] after which it was granted by the Crown in 1544 to Thomas Bowyer and his wife Joan.[61] Later members of the Bowyer family had lands in the parish,[62] and *c.* 1640 the rector is said to have paid Sir Thomas Bowyer £1 12*s.* a year.[63] By the mid 19th century, however, the rector owned all the tithes.[64]

In 1616 the rectory estate included a house, an orchard, 8 a. of arable, 15 a. of meadow and pasture, and a piece of woodland.[65] The real value of the living in 1724 was said to be £50.[66] The old timber-framed rectory house was demolished in 1737, a new one being built on roughly the same site *c.* 1742;[67] it is an **L**-shaped building in flint with brick dressings, of two storeys with attics. Original fittings include a fine staircase and panelling in one room. The building was repaired *c.* 1800.[68] The angle between the wings was filled in and a bay window was added to the east front in the mid 19th century, and a porch was built and the attic storey added in the 20th. The rector's mowing rights in the common meadows were exchanged for 4 a. of land under the inclosure Award of 1809,[69] and after the sale of part of the glebe to redeem land tax before 1819[70] there were 17 a. in all in different parts of the parish.[71] The average net income of the living was £162 *c.* 1830.[72] At the commutation of tithes in 1843 the rector was awarded a tithe rent charge of £223.[73] The income was claimed in 1917 to be insufficient to meet expenses.[74] After the union of benefices the rectory house was sold to the duke of Norfolk in 1931; it was later leased.[75]

The rector resided in 1440,[76] and a successor in 1483 was licensed to hold two benefices.[77] Occasional assistant curates are recorded in the mid 16th century, two of whom were also called reader.[78] In the 1570s sermons were preached by neighbouring clergy at least four times a year, the rector, though resident, not being licensed to preach.[79] Henry Staples, minister by 1653, was ejected in 1662 for Nonconformity.[80] Between the mid 17th century and the early 19th rectors were often pluralists and sometimes non-resident,[81] serving through curates,[82] two of whom in the early 19th century had stipends of £25 and £50.[83] In 1761 the incumbent lived at Arundel.[84] There was a weekly service with sermon in 1724, and holy communion three times a year.[85]

Between 1799 and 1803 the living was held by James Dallaway, the duke of Norfolk's secretary and historian of Sussex.[86] His successor William Wilton, rector 1804–9, was an Evangelical preacher who drew Congregationalists from Arundel to hear him.[87] Attendances on Census Sunday 1851 were 30 in the morning and 32 in the afternoon besides Sunday schoolchildren.[88] Meanwhile the frequency of communion increased from eight times a year in 1844 to *c.* 10 times in 1884 and weekly in 1898. In the later 19th century the strong Roman Catholic influence of the duke of Norfolk was felt by successive rectors as a great hindrance.[89] The last incumbent of the separate benefice also held North Stoke,[90] and there were alternate morning and evening Sunday services at the two churches in 1922.[91] By 1963 services at South Stoke were only monthly.[92] In 1990 there were two services a month and an annual summer ecumenical service to which many came from Arundel by boat.[93]

The church of *ST. LEONARD*[94] consists of chancel and nave with south porch and slim west

53 Ibid. f. 167v.
54 *Lond. Gaz.* 8 Nov. 1929, p. 7198.
55 *Tax. Eccl.* (Rec. Com.), 135, mistakenly reading vicarage: cf. above.
56 B.L. Add. MS. 39347, f. 161.
57 *Valor Eccl.* (Rec. Com.), i. 317.
58 B.L. Add. MS. 39359, f. 134; W.S.R.O., Ep. I/23/2, f. 23.
59 *Cal. Doc. France*, ed. Round, pp. 167, 170; *Bruton and Montacute Cartularies* (Som. Rec. Soc. viii), pp. 79–81, 85–7; cf. *V.C.H. Suss.* i. 432.
60 *Tax. Eccl.* (Rec. Com.), 141; *Cal. Pat.* 1385–9, 373; B.L. Add. MS. 39347, f. 163.
61 *L. & P. Hen. VIII*, xix (1), p. 281.
62 *S.R.S.* xx. 376; W.S.R.O., S.A.S. MS. BA 472 (TS. cat.).
63 P.R.O., E 134/22 Chas. II Mich./8, m. 3.
64 W.S.R.O., TD/W 116.
65 Ibid. Ep. I/25/1 (1615, *recte* 1616).
66 *S.R.S.* lxxviii. 72.
67 B.L. Add. MS. 39368, f. 1305; W.S.R.O., Ep. I/40/3; ibid. Par. 185/1/1/2, titlepage.
68 W.S.R.O., Par. 185/1/1/2, titlepage.
69 Ibid. Add. MS. 5161.
70 Dallaway, *Hist. W. Suss.* ii (1) (1819), 193.
71 W.S.R.O., TD/W 116; cf. A.C.M., LM 16; ibid. MD 2139.
72 *Rep. Com. Eccl. Revenues.*
73 W.S.R.O., TD/W 116.
74 Ibid. Ep. I/22/2 (1917).
75 Ibid. Add. MS. 18085 (TS. cat.); A.C.M., MD 802, 2183.
76 B.L. Add. MS. 39347, f. 161.
77 *Cal. Papal Reg.* xiii (2), 831.
78 B.L. Add. MS. 39359, f. 134; *S.R.S.* xxxvi. 141; xlv. 175; lviii, p. 67.
79 W.S.R.O., Ep. I/23/5, f. 34.
80 *Calamy Revised*, ed. A. G. Matthews, 459; Caplan, 'Outline of Nonconf. in Suss.' i. 40, 63.
81 B.L. Add. MS. 39347, f. 166v.; W.S.R.O., Ep. I/22/1 (1662); *S.A.C.* lviii. 122; cvi. 11, 13; *Alum. Oxon. 1500–1714*, s.v. John Fortrie; *1715–1886*, s.v. Wm. Wilton; *Educ. of Poor Digest*, 954, 970.
82 B.L. Add. MS. 39359, ff. 135v.–138.
83 W.S.R.O., Ep. I/68/1/9; Ep. I/68/3/10.
84 *S.A.C.* cvi. 13.
85 *S.R.S.* lxxviii. 72.
86 *D.N.B.*; *S.N.Q.* iii. 23.
87 B.L. Add. MS. 39347, f. 167; C. H. Valentine, *Story of Beginnings of Nonconf. in Arundel* (Harpenden, pre 1930), 22 (copy in W.S.R.O. libr.).
88 *S.R.S.* lxxv, p. 144.
89 W.S.R.O., Ep. I/22A/1 (1884); Ep. I/22A/2 (1844, 1898).
90 *Chich. Dioc. Kal.* and *Dir.* (1892 and later edns.).
91 W.S.R.O., Par. 185/7/3.
92 *Brighton Evening Argus*, 21 May 1963.
93 Local inf.
94 The dedic. was assumed in the mid 19th cent. from the mention of a picture of St. Leonard in the ch. in 1539: *S.R.S.* xlv. 174; lxxv, p. 144; O.S. Map 6", Suss. L (1879 edn.). Par. expenditure between 1708 and 1718 'for a St. James's bill', always apparently shortly before St. James's day (25 July) suggests a different orig. dedic.: W.S.R.O., Par. 185/9/1 (TS. cat.).

tower. Though much renewed in the mid 19th century, it retains its spacious late 11th- or 12th-century proportions, with an original lancet and external rendering in the north wall, and plain north and south doorways, the former blocked. The west wall was rebuilt to include the tower in the 13th century; the tower is flanked by two lancets, which make a striking composition on the inner west wall of the nave.[95] The stone-vaulted porch, lavish for so small a building, is 14th-century, and the crown-post roof of the nave is late medieval. At the thorough mid 19th-century restoration[96] the former weatherboarded cap of the tower[97] was replaced by a tall shingled spire, the chancel was refenestrated in 13th-century style and given a new crown-post roof, and the chancel arch and the windows in the south wall of the nave were renewed.

The single bell was made by Bryan Eldridge in 1657.[98] There is no pre-19th-century plate,[99] and there seem never to have been any monuments of importance.[1] A medieval altar slab was said to survive in 1907.[2]

The registers begin in 1553 and are apparently defective for three periods between the 16th and 18th centuries.[3]

NONCONFORMITY. Three Dissenters were listed in 1676[4] and one recusant family between 1724 and 1767.[5] There were Catholics again in the parish in the later 19th century; in 1898, when there were four Catholic families, one of the two farmers was Catholic and the other a Scottish Presbyterian.[6]

EDUCATION. A Sunday school held in the church in 1846–7 was attended by 12 boys and 14 girls; it was supported by subscriptions and had a paid assistant mistress.[7] In the later 19th and 20th centuries younger children have gone to school in Arundel, and by the 1960s older children went to Littlehampton.[8]

CHARITIES FOR THE POOR. None known.

TORTINGTON

THE parish of Tortington, site of a medieval Augustinian priory, lies on the west bank of the river Arun south of Arundel town.[9] The ancient parish had 1,116 a., but in 1902 the north-east corner (*c.* 85 a.) was added to Arundel parish and borough, together with a strip of waste land on the north side of the Chichester–Arundel road including the White Swan public house;[10] part of the former land was already built up, and most of the rest of it was developed later.[11] In 1933 Tortington acquired the whole of Binsted, making a total of 2,136 a. (864 ha.),[12] but in 1985 the enlarged parish was divided up, portions being added to Arundel, Ford, Slindon, and Walberton.[13] The present article deals with the ancient parish except that some aspects of the history of the north-east quarter before 1902 are treated under Arundel.[14]

The ancient parish was roughly triangular in shape, with the apex in the south. The land slopes gently from north to south, and towards the valleys of the river Arun and of a tributary stream in the east and west respectively. Most of the parish lies on brickearth, with clay and gravels in the north-east and north-west corners and alluvium in the valleys.[15]

The valley land since its inning from the river estuary has generally been pasture and meadow.[16] In the mid 16th century the lord of the manor built a bank to defend part at least of the common brook from the river,[17] and in 1606 riverside land belonging to the Priory estate had defensive banks to north and south as well as east.[18] Land outside the banks, called slipes, was used as saltmarsh pasture.[19] By the late 18th century the river was embanked throughout the parish.[20] There were occasional floods in the mid 19th century[21] and later until the banks were heightened in the 1960s.[22]

A duck decoy in the south-west was recorded apparently from 1666.[23]

The north-east corner of the parish lay within Arundel Great park in the Middle Ages,[24] and in 1331 was described as a park called the

95 Illus. at *S.A.C.* ciii, facing p. 32.
96 Cf. Clwyd R.O., Glynne ch. notes, ci. 66–7.
97 *Suss. Chs.: the Sharpe Colln.* ed. V. Smith (Lewes, [1979]); W.S.R.O., PD 2012, f. 55.
98 Elphick, *Bells*, 388.
99 *S.A.C.* liii. 237.
1 Cf. B.L. Add. MS. 5699, f. 116.
2 *V.C.H. Suss.* ii. 351.
3 W.S.R.O., Par. 185/1 (TS. cat.).
4 *Compton Census*, ed. Whiteman, 144.
5 W.S.R.O., Ep. I/22/1 (1758); *S.R.S.* lxxviii. 72; *Miscellanea*, xiv (Cath. Rec. Soc. xxvii), 57–8; *Returns of Papists, 1767* (Cath. Rec. Soc.), ii. 146.
6 W.S.R.O., Ep. I/22A/1 (1884); Ep. I/22A/2 (1898).
7 Nat. Soc. *Inquiry, 1846–7*, Suss. 14–15.
8 W.S.R.O., Ep. I/22A/2 (1865); *Educ. in W. Suss. 1959–64* (W. Suss. C.C.), 51.
9 This article was written in 1991 and revised in 1995. Topographical details in introduction based mainly on O.S. Maps 1/25,000, SU 80/90 (1991 edn.); TQ 00/10 (1979 edn.); 6", Suss. LXII, LXIII (1879–80 and later edns.).
10 *Census*, 1881, 1911; W.S.R.O., WOC/CC 8/6.
11 Above, Arundel, growth of town.
12 *Census*, 1931 (pt. ii), 1971.
13 Arun (Parishes) Order 1985.
14 Above, Arundel, growth of town; soc. and cultural activities (sport); other trades and inds. (1800–1945); public servs. The modern hist. of the White Swan public ho. is treated here: below, this section.
15 Geol. Surv. Map 1", drift, sheet 317 (1957 edn.).
16 *250 Yrs. of Mapmaking in Suss.* ed. H. Margary, pls. 14, 19; below, econ. hist. (agric.).
17 A.C.M., M 32, rot. 8d.
18 W.S.R.O., Add. MS. 2027, ff. 42, 45; cf. *S.A.C.* xxv. 60; *S.R.S.* xxix, p. 165.
19 *Cal. Inq. p.m.* vii, p. 150; *S.A.C.* xxv. 60; *S.R.S.* xxix, p. 165; A.C.M., MD 505, f. [5]; W.S.R.O., Add. MSS. 2027, ff. 42, 45; 11215 (TS. cat.); 47691; ibid. TD/W 128.
20 *250 Yrs. of Mapmaking in Suss.* pl. 15.
21 P.R.O., IR 18/10496.
22 Inf. from Mr. T. Luckin, Manor Fm.
23 W.S.R.O., Add. MS. 11215 (TS. cat.); ibid. Ep. I/29/198/20; O.S. Map 6", Suss. LXII. SE. (1899 and later edns.).
24 *V.C.H. Suss.* i. 431; A.C.M., MD 505, f. [5]; P.R.O., E 134/17 Chas. II Trin./3, rot. 5; cf. below, manors.

Rooks.[25] In the 1660s Rooks wood of *c.* 160 a. was said to lie three quarters in Tortington and a quarter in Arundel; most was underwood and bushes where cattle and horses were pastured in summer, but the lessee after 1663 cut much wood and timber and divided the land into closes.[26] By the early 18th century only 40–60 a. remained woods,[27] the rest having been converted to agriculture.[28] There was a large pond beside the boundary with Arundel in the early 19th century.[29]

The north-west part of the parish was common heathland apparently by 1468,[30] with a gate called Heathgate[31] or Knowles gate on its south side. The lord of the manor had been inclosing land there before 1606.[32] The land was called Tortington common by 1581.[33] By 1706 it was woodland,[34] as it continued to be in 1990; by *c.* 1840 it was coppiced, together with the remains of Rooks wood.[35] At the latter date there were 232 a. of woodland in the parish, including 221 a. at Tortington common.[36] In 1852 the woods of the parish were well stocked with game.[37] The southern portion of Tortington common in the 1980s was chiefly old deciduous woodland and the northern part mixed deciduous with conifers.[38] In 1990, like the neighbouring part of Binsted, Tortington common felt surprisingly remote, considering its nearness to Arundel and to the Chichester–Arundel road.

Roman pottery and tiles have been found in a close south of the priory[39] and a medieval moated site further south-east.[40] Other medieval settlement perhaps lay chiefly near the priory or the church and manor house.[41] Subsidiary settlement in the west part, including Knowles farm,[42] apparently represents assarts from Tortington common.[43] There were only nine houses in 1801, 14 in 1831, 20 in 1851, and 29 in 1871.[44] A pair of cottages dated 1846 by Ford station in the southern tip of the parish were evidently built by the railway company,[45] and there are many Norfolk estate cottages of the late 19th century and early 20th. A caravan site near the station had both permanent and temporary residences in 1991.[46]

Medieval and early 16th-century population figures for Tortington are subsumed in those for Binsted.[47] Nineteen adult males signed the protestation in 1642[48] and in 1676 thirty inhabitants were listed in the Compton census.[49] There were nine families in 1724.[50] In 1801 the population was 68, rising to 88 in 1821 and, after a fall, to 452 in 1901. The reduced area of the parish excluding the partly urban north-east corner had 132 inhabitants in 1901 and 152 in 1931, and the enlarged area including Binsted had 259 in 1931, rising to 294 in 1951, 617 in 1961, and 945 in 1981.[51]

A route across the north end of the parish south of the modern Chichester–Arundel road apparently existed in Roman times[52] and was still used in the 17th and 18th centuries.[53] In 1990 it survived as a track. Priory Road represents what was presumably the first part of the medieval road from Arundel, which originally continued to the priory and thence to the church and manor house.[54] Its northern section had ceased to be used by 1795,[55] when another road to Tortington, first noted in 1778, led south from the Chichester–Arundel road near the site of the White Swan public house. The section of road between the priory and the church was diverted westwards in the early 19th century to give privacy to the grounds of Tortington House.[56] A southwards continuation of the road from Tortington church to Ford was mentioned in 1573,[57] apparently fording the Binsted brook.[58] It ceased to be used apparently by the late 18th century and certainly by 1847.[59] The modern north–south road through the parish was made in 1846 by the railway company to link Arundel with what was then its station.[60] Until the road was taken over by the county council in 1937[61] a toll was levied at the level crossing by the station to pay for upkeep.[62] Other roads in the parish were various paths leading towards the river depicted in 1778,[63] and a road from the site of the White Swan public house to Binsted.

The railway line from Lyminster to Chichester was opened through the parish in 1846 with a station in the south corner to serve Arundel; at

25 *Cal. Inq. p.m.* vii, p. 227; the name includes the element 'oak': *P.N. Suss.* (E.P.N.S.), i. 137.
26 A.C.M., PM 87; P.R.O., E 134/17 Chas. II Trin./3, rott. 3, 5.
27 A.C.M., A 339, Arundel surv. 1702, f. 3; ibid. MD 719, f. [1v.].
28 W.S.R.O., Par. 198/31/1, f. 12; *250 Yrs. of Mapmaking in Suss.* pl. 15.
29 A.C.M., K 2/64, f. [15v.]; W.S.R.O., LD II/ZP 2; ibid. TD/W 128.
30 A.C.M., M 828.
31 Ibid. M 271, f. [9v.].
32 Ibid. PM 193; W.S.R.O., Add. MS. 2027, ff. 43, 46; cf. below, econ. hist.
33 P.R.O., E 311/24, m. 75; cf. A.C.M., PM 193; Gardner, *Suss. Map* (1778–83).
34 W.S.R.O., Add. MS. 11215 (TS. cat.); cf. *250 Yrs. of Mapmaking in Suss.* pls. 5, 14–15, 19, 26.
35 W.S.R.O., TD/W 128; cf. ibid. IR 19, f. 64; ibid. Par. 8/6/8; A.C.M., MD 719, f. [1v.].
36 W.S.R.O., TD/W 128.
37 E.S.R.O., SAY 2828; cf. A.C.M., D 6282.
38 Suss. Wildlife Trust, *A 27 Arundel Bypass: an Ecological Assessment* (n.d., late 1980s).
39 S.M.R. 4434.
40 Ibid. 2006.
41 e.g. W.S.R.O., Add. MS. 47691; cf. Norden, *Suss. Map* (1595), which names Torton in the N. and Tortington in the S. as if indicating separate settlements at priory and ch. For manor ho., below, manors.
42 Cf. Gardner, *Suss. Map* (1778–83); below, econ. hist.
43 Cf. Bodl. MS. Rawl. B. 318, p. 172.
44 *Census*, 1801–71.
45 Cf. W.S.R.O., IR 19, f. 66.
46 *W. Suss. Gaz.* 26 Sept. 1991; cf. O.S. Map 1/25,000, TQ 00/10 (1979 edn.).
47 *S.R.S.* x. 79, 137, 256; lvi. 54, 56; cf. *L. & P. Hen. VIII*, xiv (1), p. 296.
48 *S.R.S.* v. 181.
49 *Compton Census*, ed. Whiteman, 144.
50 *S.R.S.* lxxviii. 73.
51 *Census*, 1801–1981.
52 I. D. Margary, *Rom. Rds. in Brit.* (1967), 75–6; *S.N.Q.* xi. 163. Rest of para. based mainly on *250 Yrs. of Mapmaking in Suss.* pls. 14–15, 19, 26.
53 A.C.M., FC 399, map of Tortington, 1724; ibid. PM 193.
54 Cf. W.S.R.O., Add. MS. 11215 (TS. cat.); ibid. QAB/3/W 1, p. 6.
55 Cf. A.C.M., K 2/64, f. [15v.]; W.S.R.O., TD/W 128.
56 Cf. W.S.R.O., TD/W 128. The grounds then lay N. and NE. of the ho.: below, manors.
57 P.R.O., SC 2/205/55, f. 46.
58 Above, Ford, intro.
59 A.C.M., LM 15; cf. W.S.R.O., TD/W 128.
60 A.C.M., D 6280–1 (MS. cat.); ibid. LM 15; cf. below.
61 *S.N.Q.* xi. 28; cf. W.S.R.O., IR 19, f. 66.
62 P. Jerrome and J. Newdick, *Not Submitted Elsewhere*, 92.
63 Cf. W.S.R.O., Add. MS. 2027, f. 45.

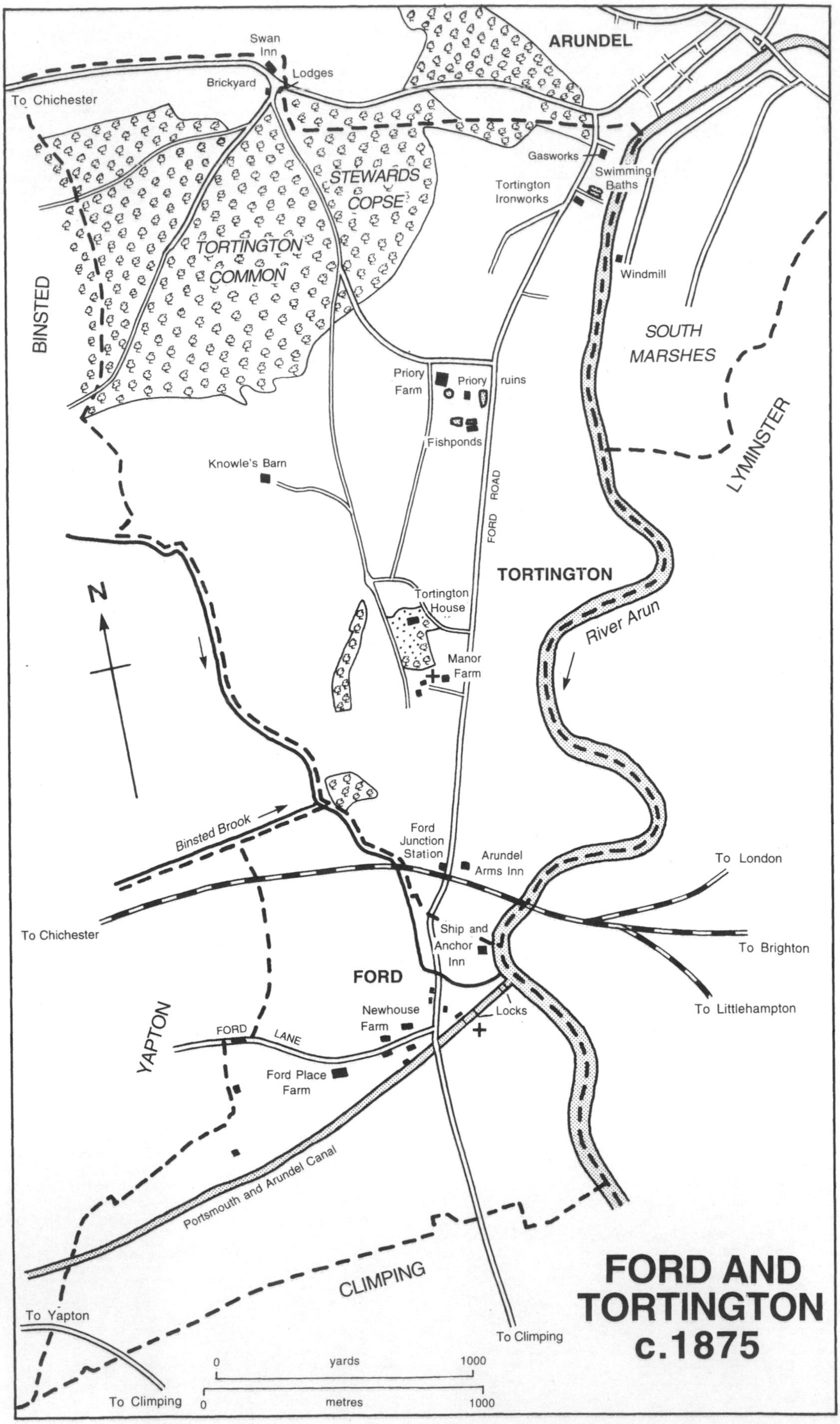

ARUNDEL
Swan Inn
Lodges
Brickyard
To Chichester
STEWARDS COPSE
TORTINGTON COMMON
BINSTED
Gasworks
Swimming Baths
Tortington Ironworks
Windmill
SOUTH MARSHES
LYMINSTER
Priory Farm
Priory
ruins
Fishponds
Knowle's Barn
FORD ROAD
TORTINGTON
N
Tortington House
River Arun
Manor Farm
Binsted Brook
Ford Junction Station
Arundel Arms Inn
To London
To Chichester
Ship and Anchor Inn
To Brighton
FORD
Locks
To Littlehampton
YAPTON
Newhouse Farm
FORD LANE
Ford Place Farm
Portsmouth and Arundel Canal
CLIMPING
FORD AND TORTINGTON c.1875
To Yapton
To Climping
0 yards 1000
0 metres 1000
To Climping

first called Arundel, it was renamed Ford Junction after the opening of the lines to Littlehampton and Arundel in 1863, and was later known simply as Ford.[64] Because of the need for ships to reach the port at Arundel, the railway crossed the river by what was described as 'a drawbridge on the telescopic principle', originally of wood, and carrying only one track. It was replaced in 1862 by a double-track bridge of iron, also of 'telescopic' construction, which could accommodate heavier traffic. A fixed bridge was built when the line was electrified in 1938.[65] The station was closed to goods traffic in 1962.[66]

In spite of the parish's long river frontage there were no barges, boats, or boatmen in 1801,[67] but after the opening of the railway a wharf south-east of the station, accessible by a siding, was leased to the railway company for 99 years from 1850.[68] There was a landing stage on the river further north opposite the church in 1896.[69]

A building on the site of the White Swan beside the Chichester–Arundel road existed in 1724,[70] and was a public house by 1772 when it was known as the Mile house.[71] That name continued to be used in the 20th century[72] though the inn was the Swan by the 1840s[73] and the White Swan between the 1880s[74] and the 1980s. Members of the Jupp family were publicans for over 75 years, farming land nearby in the later 19th century.[75] The building was greatly enlarged after 1964,[76] and in 1991 was the Arundel Resort hotel. The tall, barge-boarded Arundel Arms inn, built beside Ford station to serve rail travellers, existed by 1847;[77] in 1852, when it was also called the hotel or the Railway inn, it had pleasure grounds including a bowling green,[78] and in the 1880s, when horses and carriages could be hired there, the publican was also a wine and spirit merchant.[79]

Part of the rural portion of the parish was apparently supplied with mains water from Arundel by 1928.[80] Gas and electricity were available there in 1938.[81]

MANOR AND OTHER ESTATES. The manor of *TORTINGTON*, then four hides, was held in 1066 by Leofwine, a free man, and in 1086 of earl Roger by Ernucion.[82] The overlordship descended with the rape, passing at the division of the d'Aubigny inheritance in 1243 to Robert Tattershall,[83] but being resumed by 1454.[84]

Pharamus de Tracy had land in Tortington in 1216,[85] and his son Roger was described as lord of Tortington in 1234–5.[86] John de Tracy conveyed the manor in 1279 to William of Bracklesham, dean of Chichester,[87] who gave it in 1295 to Ellis de Cheyney;[88] John's widow Margery claimed dower in 1297.[89] The manor was later generally known as *TORTINGTON CHEYNEYS*. Ellis de Cheyney was assessed at the highest tax payment in Tortington, Binsted, and Madehurst in 1296;[90] he held a fee there in 1316 and perhaps in 1322[91] but had apparently died by 1327,[92] and his son William was succeeded before 1341–2 by his own son, also William[93] (d. by 1363). Ellis's widow Joan had dower in 1346–7[94] and was still alive in 1351, when she made over her interest to Eleanor FitzAlan, countess of Arundel.[95]

In 1373 Ralph de Restwold quitclaimed the manor to Richard FitzAlan, earl of Arundel (d. 1376),[96] his son William making over his interest in 1373–4.[97] Thereafter the manor remained in demesne[98] until it passed, under the will of Thomas FitzAlan, earl of Arundel (d. 1415), and subject to the life interest of his widow Beatrice (d. 1439), to Holy Trinity hospital at Arundel,[99] which held it until the Dissolution.[1]

In 1546 the Crown granted the manor to Sir Richard Lee;[2] he and his wife Margaret conveyed it in 1547 to Henry FitzAlan, earl of Arundel,[3] who together with John Lumley, Lord Lumley, sold it in 1567 to John Apsley.[4] A court was held in the name of Ann, widow of Henry's son Henry FitzAlan, Lord Maltravers (d. 1556), in 1574,[5] but John Apsley had the estate in 1573 and 1574,[6] in 1583 John Browne was said to be lord of the manor,[7] and

64 *Southern Region Rec.* comp. R. H. Clark, 51–2, 74; O.S. Map 6", Suss. LXIII (1879 edn.).
65 *Southern Region Rec.* 62; P. A. L. Vine, *Lond.'s Lost Route to Sea* (1986), 142–4; V. Mitchell and K. Smith, *S. Coast Rlys.: Worthing to Chich.* pls. 59, 62; *Illus. Lond. News*, 14 Nov. 1846, p. 320; *W. Suss. Gaz.* 31 July 1862.
66 C. R. Clinker, *Reg. of Closed Stations*, ii (1964), 41.
67 E.S.R.O., LCG/3/EW 1, ff. [44, 46].
68 A.C.M., D 6289–90; W.S.R.O., IR 19, f. 66; O.S. Map 6", Suss. LXIII (1879 and later edns.).
69 O.S. Map 6", Suss. LXIII. NW. (1899 edn.).
70 A.C.M., FC 399, map of Tortington, 1724.
71 Ibid. H 1/3; cf. ibid. FC 148; *S.A.C.* lxxi. 53.
72 A.C.M., MD 733; *Kelly's Dir. Suss.* (1907 and later edns.), s.v. Arundel.
73 W.S.R.O., TD/W 128; *Kelly's Dir. Suss.* (1845 and later edns.).
74 Pike, *Dir. SW. Suss.* (1886–7).
75 A.C.M., MD 733; ibid. uncat. deed of Tortington estate, 1879; *Kelly's Dir. Suss.* (1887 and later edns.), s.v. Arundel and Tortington; cf. below, econ. hist. [brickmaking].
76 Cf. A.C.M., MD 733.
77 Ibid. LM 15.
78 E.S.R.O., SAY 2828; *Kelly's Dir. Suss.* (1852), s.v. Ford.
79 Pike, *Dir. SW. Suss.* (1886–7), s.v. Ford.
80 F. H. Edmunds, *Wells and Springs of Suss.* 23.
81 *Kelly's Dir. Suss.* (1938).
82 *V.C.H. Suss.* i. 431.
83 *Cal. Pat.* 1232–47, 408; *S.R.S.* lxvii. 103; cf. *Cal. Inq. p.m.* iv, pp. 107, 260; viii, pp. 164, 230; *Cal. Close*, 1307–13, 100–1; *Feud. Aids*, vi. 639.
84 *Cal. Pat.* 1452–61, 203. In 1428 it was said to be held of the hon. of Tregoze: *Feud. Aids*, v. 155.
85 *S.R.S.* lix, p. 69.
86 P.R.O., E 210/8279 (TS. cat.).
87 *S.R.S.* vii, p. 105; W.S.R.O., W. D. Peckham card index of Chich. cathedral clergy.
88 *S.R.S.* vii, p. 165; *Year Bk.* 16 Edw. III (i) (Rolls Ser.), 121.
89 B.L. Add. MS. 39503, f. 122.
90 *S.R.S.* x. 79.
91 *Feud. Aids*, v. 143; vi. 639.
92 *S.R.S.* x. 137.
93 *Year Bk.* 16 Edw. III (i) (Rolls Ser.), 121.
94 *S.R.S.* xxiii, p. 155.
95 P.R.O., E 210/9411; *Complete Peerage*, s.v. Arundel.
96 *Cal. Close*, 1369–74, 572.
97 *S.R.S.* xxiii, p. 175.
98 e.g. *Cal. Pat.* 1381–5, 66.
99 Ibid. 1422–9, 114–15; P.R.O., C 139/98, mm. 19–21.
1 e.g. A.C.M., M 828; *S.R.S.* xvi. 87; *Cal. Close*, 1435–41, 402.
2 *L. & P. Hen. VIII*, xxi (1), p. 570.
3 *S.R.S.* xx. 444; *Cal. Pat.* 1547–8, 213.
4 *Cal. Pat.* 1566–9, p. 101; P.R.O., C 3/5/34, m. 1.
5 Bodl. MS. Rawl. B. 318, p. 172; *Complete Peerage*, s.v. Arundel; cf. *S.R.S.* xx. 441; *Clough and Butler Archives*, ed. J. Booker, p. 21.
6 P.R.O., C 2/Eliz. I/A 5/6; C 3/5/34, m. 1.
7 B.L. Add. MS. 39348, f. 255.

in 1587 he and John Apsley conveyed it to Roger Gratwicke.[8] At Roger's death without issue in 1596 the manor passed to his cousin (Sir) William Gratwicke of East Malling (Kent)[9] (d. 1613), whose son William[10] (d. in or after 1651)[11] was succeeded in turn by his sons William (d.s.p. 1666) and Francis (d.s.p. 1670),[12] Francis's heir being his nephew Oliver Weekes (d. 1689).[13] Oliver's son Carew Weekes, M.P. for Arundel,[14] and his wife Catherine sold the manor in 1706 to William Leeves of Arundel.[15] At William's death in 1710[16] the lordship passed to his eldest son Robert (d. 1743), who was succeeded by his son, also Robert (d.s.p. 1744). In 1790 the younger Robert's brothers-in-law and heirs Robert Edwards, Robert Lamport, and Henry Johnson conveyed Tortington to the duke of Norfolk,[17] after which it again descended with the rape.[18]

The demesne lands of the manor were separated from the lordship in 1710, passing successively to William Leeves's younger sons William (d. 1717 × 1724) and Richard (d. 1738), Richard's son and heir William (d. 1764) being succeeded by his son William Mill Leeves (d. 1788).[19] In 1738 there were *c.* 400 a. in Tortington besides land in Binsted.[20] After the death of William Mill Leeves's widow Elizabeth in 1809 the estate passed to his cousin William Fowler, who took the surname Leeves and died in 1837.[21] By 1819 it comprised 1,054 a.[22] William Leeves's son and heir William sold it in 1839 to the banker John Smith of Dale Park in Madehurst (d. by 1842), whose son John Abel Smith, with James Hamilton, marquess of Abercorn, and others conveyed it in 1853 to Joseph M. Montefiore.[23] He and the duke of Norfolk were the two chief landowners in the parish in 1870.[24] After the duke's purchase of the Tortington estate, then comprising 965 a., in 1879, virtually all the parish belonged to the Norfolk estate[25] except for 30 a. in the south-west which, however, were acquired from the Slindon estate in 1907.[26] The trustees of the late Bernard, duke of Norfolk, retained woodland in the north and north-west in 1995, but most of the agricultural land had been sold by then to the Luckin family, previously tenants.[27]

The original manor house, called Manor Farm in 1990, is a substantial 17th-century building of red brick incorporating parts of a 16th-century house, notably the windows with hoodmoulds on the north façade. Behind the modern porch on the south façade is an 18th-century-style Portland stone pilastered door surround. Adjacent freestanding walls have diaper brickwork and a depressed-arched opening of 16th-century character, and a stone with the inscription RG/1590 for Roger Gratwicke. Another stone reading 1659 G/WM, for William Gratwicke and his wife, was recorded in the later 18th century when the building had become a farmhouse.[28] Several fragments of medieval stonework evidently from the priory survive both in the house and in its outbuildings. In 1666 the building had a hall, kitchen, great and little parlours, and at least 10 chambers, besides extensive outbuildings.[29] The house has been altered at various later dates, notably in the early 19th century. The walled garden to the north is apparently 18th-century.[30]

A new house, later called Tortington House,[31] was built shortly before 1699.[32] It is presumably represented by the lower range with attic dormers depicted in 1782 behind a grander two-storeyed north-facing range of five bays with a central pediment, which was perhaps built in 1739.[33] The north range survived in 1988, but the south range was replaced in the early 19th century;[34] at the same time the interior was remodelled and extensively refitted. Either then or a little later a service block was added to the west, and further remodelling of the ground floor, partly in Gothic style, and of the staircase took place in the later 19th century.[35] In 1921 there were 19 bedrooms.[36] After having various occupiers in the 19th century and early 20th,[37] the house was converted into a Catholic girls' boarding school called Tortington Park school in 1922; in the mid 1960s before closure in 1969 there were *c.* 200 pupils.[38] Extensive additions were made for the school in the 1920s and 30s.[39] Since 1971 the building has been used as the English campus of New England College at Henniker (New Hampshire), with *c.* 200–270 students.[40]

North-west of the house were late 18th-century stables round three sides of a courtyard, which was entered through a tall archway;[41] much of the block survived in 1988 though converted to other uses.

8 *S.R.S.* xx. 441.
9 B.L. Add. MS. 39394, f. 187; P.R.O., C 142/247, no. 77; *S.A.C.* lx. 44; cf. mon. in ch.
10 P.R.O., C 142/342, no. 115; *S.A.C.* lx. 39.
11 W.S.R.O., Raper MSS., deed, 1651.
12 *S.A.C.* lx. 39–40; cxxxii. 139; W.S.R.O., Ep. I/29/198/20.
13 *S.A.C.* lx. 39; cxxxii. 140; cf. *S.R.S.* xx. 442.
14 *S.A.C.* lx. 39.
15 W.S.R.O., Add. MS. 11215 (TS. cat.).
16 *S.A.C.* lxxiii. 115.
17 B.L. Add. MS. 5688, ff. 146v., 156.
18 e.g. *S.R.S.* li. 102, 139; *Kelly's Dir. Suss.* (1887).
19 Dallaway, *Hist. W. Suss.* ii (1) (1819), 78–9; *S.A.C.* lxxiii. 115; *Greatham Archives*, ed. A. Dibben, p. 3; A.C.M., FC 399, map of Tortington, 1724; B.L. Add. MS. 5688, f. 146v.; W.S.R.O., S.A.S. MS. WH 92 (TS. cat.).
20 W.S.R.O., Raper MSS., deed, 1738.
21 Dallaway, *Hist. W. Suss.* ii (1) (1819), 78–9; *S.A.C.* lxxiii. 115; W.S.R.O., Par. 198/7/5, p. 8.
22 Dallaway, op. cit. 77 n.
23 A.C.M., uncat. deeds, 1832, 1839, 1853; ibid. D 6279 (MS. cat.); W.S.R.O., Par. 198/7/5, pp. 8–9; *D.N.B.* s.v. J. A. Smith; cf. E.S.R.O., SAY 2828–30.
24 Lower, *Hist. Suss.* ii. 206; for the duke's lands, below.
25 A.C.M., uncat. deed, 1879; ibid. D 6292–4; ibid. P 5/37, nos. 1, 11.
26 Ibid. uncat. deed, 1907.
27 Inf. from Messrs. Cluttons, Arundel; below, econ. hist. (agric.).
28 B.L. Add. MS. 5688, f. 147.
29 W.S.R.O., Ep. I/29/198/20.
30 The bldg. as in 1782 is apparently shown in B.L. Add. MS. 5674, f. 35.
31 e.g. *250 Yrs. of Mapmaking in Suss.* ed. H. Margary, pl. 19; O.S. Map 6", Suss. LXIII (1879 edn.).
32 W.S.R.O., Raper MSS., deeds, 1699.
33 B.L. Add. MS. 5674, f. 35; date on bldg. (inf. from Mr. B. Banister, Arun D.C.).
34 Cf. Dallaway, *Hist. W. Suss.* ii (1) (1819), 78; W.S.R.O., Add. MS. 47083.
35 Cf. O.S. Map 6", Suss. LXIII (1879 and later edns.).
36 W.S.R.O., SP 1225.
37 Hillier, *Arundel* (1847), 11; *Kelly's Dir. Suss.* (1855 and later edns.).
38 *W. Suss. Gaz.* 20 Mar. 1969.
39 *Tortington Pk., Arundel, Suss.* (n.d.) (copy in W.S.R.O. libr.).
40 *W. Suss. Gaz.* 28 Oct. 1971; 22 Feb. 1979.
41 B.L. Add. MS. 5674, f. 35.

Pleasure grounds north and north-east of the house had been laid out by 1813, the road between Priory Farm and the church being afterwards diverted to the west. They were replaced by a new layout on the south side, including a pond, before 1840. Two other ornamental ponds existed further west by the same date;[42] they survived in 1852[43] but had been filled in by the 1870s.[44] In the early 19th century the house was approached from the north by way of a pair of flint-and-brick lodges on the Chichester–Arundel road that survived in 1991.[45] An alternative, eastern, approach, which by 1876[46] had become the main one, was provided after the construction of Ford Road in 1846.[47] A nine-hole golf course was laid out in the grounds after 1922.[48]

The Tortington priory estate, called a manor in 1380,[49] was the later *PRIORY FARM*. In the early 16th century it comprised 160 a. of demesne besides tenants' lands.[50] At the Dissolution it was granted in tail male to the priory's last lessee Henry FitzAlan, Lord Maltravers (d. 1556),[51] but before 1582 it was resumed by the Crown, being leased in that year to Philip Howard, earl of Arundel.[52] After his attainder in 1589 it was leased successively by the Crown to Thomas Sackville, Lord Buckhurst, in 1590,[53] and to George, John, and Francis Holmden for three lives in 1594.[54] In 1600 it was granted to Sir John Spencer, lord mayor of London (d. 1610), passing to his daughter Elizabeth and her husband William Compton, earl of Northampton (d. 1630).[55] In 1606 the estate was reckoned at 284 a. including common land,[56] and in 1669 it had 193 a.[57] William's son and heir Spencer sold it in 1633 to William Thomas of Westdean near Seaford[58] (d. 1640), from whose son and heir William it passed *c.* 1654 to his son Francis.[59] Sir William Thomas, Bt. (d. 1706), had it in 1669[60] and conveyed it in 1698 to Richard Scrase. After Scrase's sale of it in 1714 or 1715 to William Leeves[61] it descended with the demesne lands of Tortington manor.[62]

The house called Tortington Priory House[63] had an east–west range with a cross wing at the east end. It apparently included part of the medieval priory buildings, since an outbuilding depicted in 1606 at its south-east corner[64] is presumably represented by the barn which survived in 1995,[65] containing remains of the mid 13th-century church: part of the north wall of the nave, including two wall-shafts and a section of the vault with traces of windows; part of the west wall of the nave; and the west wall of the north transept. In 1656 the house had a hall, three ground-floor rooms, and four chambers with garrets,[66] and in 1707 there were a parlour, a kitchen, and offices, with chambers above.[67] The house had evidently been demolished by 1782,[68] perhaps as a result of the amalgamation of the manor and priory estates.

A building including ashlar masonry depicted to the south in 1782[69] may also have been part of the priory. Many pieces of worked stone, including fragments of columns, survived in farm buildings nearby in 1909.[70] The monastic fishponds east, south, and north-west of the priory site remained in 1990.[71]

The modern Priory Farm is a brick-and-tile building of *c.* 1900 in revived vernacular style. In the 1930s it was a school for abnormal boys.[72]

Land in the north-east corner of the parish which descended with the rape in demesne[73] evidently included the hide of Tortington manor which earl Roger took for his new park at Arundel between 1067 and 1086.[74] In the mid 14th century the earl of Arundel acquired other land in the area from Tortington priory.[75] In 1661 the duke of Norfolk had Rooks wood (147 a.) and other land,[76] and in 1819 the ducal estate comprised 208 a. in all.[77] Arundel town council acquired 44 a. as building land in 1902.[78]

Boxgrove priory had 3½ a. of meadow at Tortington from *c.* 1216.[79] Land granted to Arundel priory in the early 13th century[80] and in 1353[81] perhaps passed to its successor Arundel college, which also acquired other land in the parish.[82]

42 *250 Yrs. of Mapmaking in Suss.* pls. 19, 26; W.S.R.O., TD/W 128.
43 E.S.R.O., SAY 2829.
44 O.S. Map 6", Suss. LXIII (1879 edn.).
45 *250 Yrs. of Mapmaking in Suss.* pl. 19; W.S.R.O., TD/W 128.
46 O.S. Map 6", Suss. LXIII (1879 edn.); cf. W.S.R.O., SP 1225.
47 W.S.R.O., Add. MS. 4544; cf. A.C.M., D 6281 (MS. cat.).
48 *W. Suss. Gaz.* 20 Mar. 1969.
49 *S.A.C.* v. 239. For the priory's hist., *V.C.H. Suss.* ii. 82–3.
50 *Valor Eccl.* (Rec. Com.), i. 312.
51 *L. & P. Hen. VIII*, xiii (1), p. 247; *Complete Peerage*, s.v. Arundel.
52 *Cal. Pat.* 1580–2, p. 188.
53 P.R.O., E 310/25/144, f. 8.
54 *Cal. S.P. Dom.* 1591–4, 498.
55 B.L. Add. MS. 6344, f. 178v.; *Complete Peerage*, s.v. Northampton.
56 W.S.R.O., Add. MS. 2027, ff. 45–6.
57 *S.R.S.* xxix, p. 165.
58 *Complete Peerage*, s.v. Northampton; *S.R.S.* xxix, p. 165.
59 B.L. Add. MS. 39503, f. 124.
60 *S.R.S.* xxix, p. 165; G. E. C., *Baronetage*, iii. 95–6. It is not clear why the estate was said in 1656 to have belonged to Chas. I: *S.A.C.* xxv. 60.
61 Dallaway, *Hist. W. Suss.* ii (1) (1819), 80; *S.R.S.* xx. 442; W.S.R.O., Raper MSS., deed, 1698.
62 e.g. Caraccioli, *Arundel*, 268; *Gent. Mag.* lxiv (2), 785; W.S.R.O., IR 19, f. 64; ibid. TD/W 128.
63 *S.A.C.* xxv. 60.
64 W.S.R.O., Add. MS. 2027, f. 42.
65 Above, pl. facing p. 74.
66 *S.A.C.* xxv. 60.
67 W.S.R.O., Ep. I/29/198/25.
68 B.L. Add. MS. 5674, f. 37.
69 Ibid.; cf. J. Rouse, *Beauties and Antiq. of Suss.* ii, pl. 113.
70 *S.A.C.* lii. 165 n.; *S.N.Q.* xi. 46; cf. *S.C.M.* xiv. 436; above, this section [Manor fm.].
71 Cf. A.C.M., LM 15. The plan of the monastic ch. and of bldgs. to the S. was revealed by excavation in 1909: *S.N.Q.* xi. 45–6.
72 *Kelly's Dir. Suss.* (1938).
73 *Cal. Inq. p.m.* vii, p. 227; A.C.M., A 339, Arundel surv. 1702, f. 3; ibid. H 1/30; ibid. Hodskinson surv. 1778, f. 12; ibid. MD 719, f. [iv.]; 775; ibid. PM 112; Sandbeck Park, Rotherham, Lumley MS. EMA/1/5; W.S.R.O., IR 19, f. 64; ibid. TD/W 128; 26 & 27 Vic. c. 7 (Private); cf. above, intro. [woods].
74 *V.C.H. Suss.* i. 431; cf. above, Arundel Rape.
75 *Cal. Close*, 1419–22, 33, naming land at 'Rokes', i.e. Rooks wood; cf. above, intro.
76 A.C.M., PM 87; cf. ibid. MD 505, f. [5].
77 Dallaway, *Hist. W. Suss.* ii (1) (1819), 77 n., 81.
78 W.S.R.O., BO/AR 24/4/17; 24/2/1, statement to L.G.B. enquiry by J. J. Robinson, 1913.
79 *S.R.S.* lix, p. 69.
80 P.R.O., E 210/8279 (TS. cat.).
81 *Cal. Pat.* 1350–4, 399.
82 Ibid. 1381–5, 66; cf. *L. & P. Hen. VIII*, xix (2), p. 475.

The dean and chapter of Chichester had 2 a. in the west part from 1566;[83] in 1876, apparently, they passed to the tenant J. M. Montefiore.[84]

ECONOMIC HISTORY. AGRICULTURE. The demesne farm of Tortington manor had two ploughs in 1086, when 6 *villani* and 2 cottars were recorded there.[85] In the early 15th century there were 135 a. of arable, 52 a. of meadow, and 100 a. of pasture on the demesne farm, which could support 2 farm horses, a bull, 18 oxen, 24 cows, and 300 wether sheep.[86] Fixed rents of tenants of the manor then brought in £3 12*s*.; there were 14 tenants, most with holdings of between 1 a. and 10 a.[87] The demesne was let by 1430.[88] The other chief estate at the same period was that belonging to the priory.

Arable farming was more important than pastoral in the Middle Ages, to judge from the fact that in 1340 the ninth of sheaves was valued at more than eight times those of fleeces and lambs together.[89] Wheat, barley, peas, and vetch were grown in the late 14th century.[90] An open field was mentioned in 1470, when cattle and sheep could be put on the stubble between harvest and All Saints' day (1 November).[91] Other crops grown in 1340 were apples, flax, and hemp.[92]

The 30 a. of meadow mentioned on Tortington manor in 1086[93] apparently lay in the Arun valley, where Boxgrove priory had 3½ a. of meadow from *c.* 1216.[94] Arundel priory was confirmed in 19½ a. of pasture in Summer leaze in Tortington, perhaps in the river valley, in 1234–5.[95] There was much less meadow in the parish, however, than in other riverside parishes nearby. Common meadow evidently existed as well as several.[96] Common pasture on the heath, evidently what was later Tortington common in the north-west, was mentioned in 1470, when sheep could be put there after All Saints' day.[97]

Between the 16th and 18th centuries there were tenants of Tortington manor, of the priory estate, of the dean and chapter of Chichester, and of various manors outside the parish: Yapton Coverts in Yapton,[98] Wick in Lyminster,[99] Binsted,[1] and Oldbury and Seabeach in Boxgrove.[2] Copyholds of Tortington paid heriots in kind in the 1550s, when some were held for lives;[3] there were tenements of the manor in other parishes as well as in Tortington.[4] The priory estate had copyhold and apparently freehold tenements of up to 8 a. in 1536–7,[5] but by 1608 all its lands within the parish had evidently been subsumed into the demesne farm, the many freehold, copyhold, and leasehold tenements then all lying in other parishes.[6] A tenement of the dean and chapter of Chichester was held for three lives.[7] By the end of the 18th century no manor tenants remained.[8]

The manorial demesnes were leased in 1532 for 70 years.[9] Those of the priory were in hand in the early 16th century[10] but later were apparently usually leased.[11] Priory farm had 160 a. in the early 16th century[12] and 197 a. in 1606,[13] but in 1656 the land was let in two parcels, that including the farmhouse to Thomas Sowton, perhaps of South Stoke.[14] In 1754 the two chief farms in the parish besides Manor and Priory farms were Knowles farm in the west and Rooks farm in the north-east corner.[15]

Plural open fields were mentioned in the mid 16th century.[16] The close called East field, surrounded in 1606 by demesne land of Tortington manor,[17] was perhaps part of a former open field. Since no later references to open fields have been found others may also have been inclosed by the same date. Closes were combined into larger units on Priory farm by 1606[18] and on Manor farm by 1706.[19] Most of Rooks wood was converted to agriculture between the 1660s and the early 18th century.[20] Crops grown between the 16th and 18th centuries were wheat, barley, oats, and beans.[21] Manor farm had an orchard in 1706,[22] and hops were grown in the north-west corner of the parish in or before 1724.[23]

Common brookland was being inclosed *c.* 1550,[24] and no later reference to common meadow or brookland has been found, though Priory farm in 1606 had the first cut of 5 a. of meadow called Trendle mead belonging to Manor farm.[25] The

83 *S.R.S.* lviii, pp. 52, 133, 195, 253; W.S.R.O., Cap. I/28/108; for the site, ibid. TD/W 128.
84 A.C.M., uncat. conveyance of reversion, 1858; ibid. D 6287–8 (MS. cat.).
85 *V.C.H. Suss.* i. 431.
86 *S.R.S.* lxvii. 146; cf. A.C.M., M 316.
87 *S.R.S.* lxvii. 146.
88 A.C.M., A 1848.
89 *Inq. Non.* (Rec. Com.), 368.
90 *Cal. Inq. Misc.* vi, p. 222.
91 A.C.M., M 828.
92 *Inq. Non.* (Rec. Com.), 368.
93 *V.C.H. Suss.* i. 431.
94 *S.R.S.* lix, p. 69.
95 P.R.O., E 210/8279 (TS. cat.).
96 Cf. below.
97 A.C.M., M 828.
98 *S.R.S.* xx. 508.
99 Ibid. xix. 150; xx. 488.
1 Ibid. xix. 41.
2 *Goodwood Estate Archives*, i, ed. F. W. Steer and J. Venables, p. 50.
3 A.C.M., M 32, rot. 8d.; 829.
4 Ibid. 829; Bodl. MS. Rawl. B. 318, p. 174; W.S.R.O., Add. MSS. 3054–5 (TS. cat.); ibid. S.A.S. MS. B 660 (TS. cat.); *S.R.S.* iii, pp. 98–9.
5 P.R.O., SC 6/Hen. VIII/3674, rot. 9.
6 Ibid. LR 2/197, ff. 80–2; W.S.R.O., Add. MS. 2027, ff. 45–6.
7 *S.R.S.* lviii, pp. 133, 195.
8 B.L. Add. MS. 5688, f. 156; cf. A.C.M., FC 494.
9 A.C.M., D 6277 (MS. cat.).
10 *Valor Eccl.* (Rec. Com.), i. 312.
11 e.g. Sandbeck Park, Rotherham, Lumley MS. EMA/1/5; W.S.R.O., Add. MS. 2027, f. 45; ibid. Ep. I/29/198/4.
12 *Valor Eccl.* (Rec. Com.), i. 312.
13 W.S.R.O., Add. MS. 2027, ff. 45–6.
14 *S.A.C.* xxv. 60; above, S. Stoke, econ. hist.
15 W.S.R.O., Par. 198/31/1, f. 12; for the site, ibid. Add. MS. 2027, f. 43; Bodl. MS. Rawl. B. 318, p. 172; O.S. Map 6", Suss. LXII. NE. (1899 edn.); cf. A.C.M., H 1/30; ibid. PM 112.
16 A.C.M., M 32, rot. 8d.; Bodl. MS. Rawl. B. 318, p. 174.
17 W.S.R.O., Add. MS. 2027, ff. 42, 46.
18 Ibid. ff. 45–6.
19 W.S.R.O., Add. MS. 11215 (TS. cat.).
20 Above, intro.
21 Sandbeck Park, Rotherham, Lumley MS. EMA/1/5; W.S.R.O., Ep. I/29/198/2, 6, 12, 17, 27.
22 W.S.R.O., Add. MS. 11215 (TS. cat.).
23 A.C.M., FC 399, map of Tortington, 1724. For another hop gdn., W.S.R.O., TD/W 128.
24 A.C.M., M 32, rot. 8d.
25 W.S.R.O., Add. MS. 2027, ff. 42, 46.

owner of an estate of two yardlands held of the priory in 1537 probably exercised his pasture rights, viz. 300 sheep leazes and pannage for 13 pigs,[26] on Tortington common, the heathland in the north-west. In 1606, when the common comprised 174 a., Tortington manor and the Priory estate each claimed half.[27] Part was then apparently still commonable, but the southern end had already been inclosed by the lord of the manor.[28] The whole common was woodland, apparently in severalty, by 1706.[29]

Marshland in the Arun valley was held severally in 1606 by the earl of Arundel, the lord of Tortington manor, and the Priory estate.[30] The earl had 66 a. of several meadow and pasture in 1570, all let to one tenant,[31] and 20–23 a. of meadow in 1636;[32] Priory farm had 53 a. of meadow in 1606.[33] In 1706 Manor farm was said to have over 200 a. of meadow and pasture including saltmarsh outside the river defences.[34] The tenants of Tortington manor additionally claimed common pasture for pigs in the Rewell in Arundel in 1571.[35] Pasture in the parish was apparently used for overnight grazing before Arundel fair in 1625.[36] Flocks of between 66 and 173 sheep were recorded between 1644 and 1755; Priory farm had 142 in 1707.[37]

Between the early 19th century and the early 20th Manor and Priory farms remained the two chief farms in the parish; Manor farm had 380–405 a. and Priory farm between 214 and 265 a.[38] Sixteen other occupiers were listed in 1875 and seven in 1909; all the latter had less than 50 a.[39] Since *c.* 1910 the two chief farms have been held together, from *c.* 1930 by members of the Luckin family, who later bought the land from the duke of Norfolk.[40] In 1956 the united holding had *c.* 700 a.[41] and in 1988, when the area was roughly the same, it extended from the river Arun to Binsted, with the railway as its southern boundary.[42]

Corn crops were said to be abundant in 1801, when wheat (62 a.), barley (33 a.), oats (29 a.), peas (7 a.), and turnips or rape (11 a.) were named.[43] Two closes of former saltmarsh had been converted to arable by 1842,[44] but the area of arable remained small between the mid 19th century and the earlier 20th: 247 a. in 1841, 252 in 1875, and 182 a. in 1909, as against totals of meadow and pasture at the same dates of 524 a., 492 a., and 505 a.[45] Besides the crops mentioned, beans and mangolds were listed in 1875 and vetches or tares in 1909.[46] There was a withy bed south-west of Tortington House *c.* 1840.[47] Totals of livestock listed in the parish were 122 cattle, predominantly fatting oxen, 160 sheep, and 18 pigs in 1801,[48] 270 cattle, 475 sheep, and 75 pigs in 1875, and 200 cattle, 426 sheep, and 63 pigs in 1909.[49] Meadow was described as very rich in 1852.[50] In 1934 there was a dairy farm supplying Dare's dairy in Arundel.[51] Mixed farming was practised in 1956.[52]

TRADE AND INDUSTRY. A miller of Tortington was recorded *c.* 1262.[53] Other parishioners in non-agricultural occupations before 1800 were a smith in 1248,[54] a brewer and a mariner in the 16th century,[55] and a tailor in 1625.[56] No other examples of river-based trades are recorded. In 1821 and 1831 two families out of 13 were supported chiefly by trade or manufacture.[57]

The chief non-agricultural activity before the 19th century was brickmaking. A bricklayer, i.e. brickmaker, was recorded in 1620,[58] and other brickmakers in 1665[59] and 1711.[60] There was a brick kiln in the north-west corner of the parish by 1724;[61] later the site was a little to the east. Between *c.* 1840 and 1852 the farmer of Priory farm worked it;[62] in the latter year a considerable trade was said to be carried on, the bricks being claimed as the best in the county.[63] Between 1855 and 1879 the brickyard was held with the Swan inn nearby, and between 1895 and *c.* 1910 by the builder Arthur Burrell of Arundel.[64]

The site later occupied by the firm of Penfolds in Ford Road in the north-east corner of the parish was already in industrial use in 1808, when a freestanding horse gin stood there.[65] About 1840 it was occupied as sawpits[66] and by 1852 the firm of George Lashmar and Co., seed crushers, had it, using part of the premises as an oil mill.[67] After Lashmar's business closed in 1856[68] two other firms of seed crushers suc-

26 *S.R.S.* xlv. 253.
27 W.S.R.O., Add. MS. 2027, ff. 43, 46; cf. *L. & P. Hen. VIII*, xi, p. 591.
28 W.S.R.O., Add. MS. 2027, ff. 43, 46.
29 Ibid. 11215 (TS. cat.).
30 Ibid. 2027, ff. 42, 45.
31 A.C.M., MD 535, f. 4v.
32 Ibid. 505, ff. [5, 16v.].
33 W.S.R.O., Add. MS. 2027, f. 46.
34 Ibid. 11215 (TS. cat.).
35 P.R.O., SC 2/205/55, f. 12.
36 *S.R.S.* xlix. 101.
37 W.S.R.O., Ep. I/29/198/17, 25, 27.
38 Ibid. IR 19, f. 64; ibid. TD/W 128; A.C.M., MD 531, 2003; ibid. uncat. deed of Tortington estate, 1879; E.S.R.O., SAY 2828.
39 P.R.O., MAF 68/433, 2371.
40 W.S.R.O., IR 19, f. 64; *Kelly's Dir. Suss.* (1913 and later edns.); inf. from Mr. T. Luckin, Manor Fm.
41 *W. Suss. Gaz.* 12 Apr. 1956.
42 Inf. from Mr. Luckin.
43 *L. & I. Soc.* cxcv. 36, 49.
44 A.C.M., LM 15.
45 W.S.R.O., TD/W 128; P.R.O., MAF 68/433, 2371.
46 P.R.O., MAF 68/433, 2371.
47 W.S.R.O., TD/W 128; cf. O.S. Map 6", Suss. LXII. NE. (1914 edn.).
48 E.S.R.O., LCG/3/EW 1, f. [43v.].
49 P.R.O., MAF 68/433, 2371.
50 E.S.R.O., SAY 2828.
51 *Arundel, the Gem of Suss.* (Arundel, 1934), 3.
52 *W. Suss. Gaz.* 12 Apr. 1956.
53 P.R.O., JUST 1/912A, rot. 44d.
54 Ibid. JUST 1/909A, rot. 23d.
55 *S.R.S.* xvi. 89; A.C.M., M 271, f. [9v.].
56 W.S.R.O., A.B.A., B1/28 (TS. cat.).
57 *Census*, 1821–31.
58 W.S.R.O., A.B.A., B1/22 (TS. cat.).
59 P.R.O., E 134/17 Chas. II Trin./3, rot. 5.
60 W.S.R.O., Ep. I/29/198/26.
61 A.C.M., FC 399, map of Tortington, 1724.
62 Ibid. H 1/3; W.S.R.O., TD/W 128; *250 Yrs. of Mapmaking in Suss.* ed. H. Margary, pls. 14–15; *Kelly's Dir. Suss.* (1845, 1852); M. Beswick, *Brickmaking in Suss.* 220.
63 E.S.R.O., SAY 2828.
64 *Kelly's Dir. Suss.* (1855 and later edns.); A.C.M., uncat. deed of Tortington estate, 1879; W.S.R.O., IR 19, f. 65; above, Arundel, other trades and inds. (1800–1945).
65 A.C.M., PM 112; cf. *Suss. Ind. Arch.* (1972), p. 27. The gin was moved *c.* 1990 to the Amberley Chalkpits Mus.
66 W.S.R.O., TD/W 128.
67 Ibid. LD II/ZP 2; *Kelly's Dir. Suss.* (1852).
68 [F. Penfold], *Penfolds of Arundel*, 7 (copy at W.S.R.O. libr.).

ceeded it before 1866.[69] The later history of the site is given elsewhere.[70]

A corn store was built north of Ford railway station in the south end of the parish *c.* 1890.[71] Two successive firms of corn merchants had it between 1895 and 1930.[72] A coal merchant's premises were nearby in 1895.[73] In 1990 a small industrial estate occupied the site.

There was a gamekeeper at Tortington House in 1895[74] and pheasants were reared in the woods of Tortington common in the 20th century.[75] Riding stables existed at Tortington House in the 1930s[76] and there was an 'equine centre' in 1990. An arboretum in the north-west corner which also flourished in 1990 had been founded *c.* 1965.[77]

LOCAL GOVERNMENT. There are court rolls or draft court rolls of Tortington manor for the years 1362, 1448 × 1455, 1468–72, 1551, 1553,[78] and 1574.[79] At least two courts a year were held in 1362.[80] In 1470 the court regulated common pasture.[81] Courts had ceased to be held by 1776,[82] but a tithingman still served in 1822.[83] The priory also had a court for its tenants in 1535.[84]

Churchwardens are recorded from 1524.[85] There seem usually to have been two before 1642,[86] but between 1662 and 1890 there was only one.[87] A church rate was levied in 1625–6[88] and from 1785.[89]

A single overseer was recorded in 1642[90] and between 1746 and 1789. Between 1746 and the 1830s methods of poor relief included weekly pay, the payment of rent, apprenticing, and the provision of clothing and medical care. Parish work in spinning was carried on in 1787.[91] Seven persons were receiving permanent relief in 1826.[92]

Between 1795 and 1832 a member of the Newland family served in most years as the single surveyor of highways.[93]

The parish joined East Preston united parishes (later East Preston union, afterwards rural district) in 1799.[94] In 1933 it passed to Chichester rural district[95] and in 1974 to Arun district.

CHURCH. The living was a rectory by *c.* 1150[96] and had passed by 1380 to Tortington priory.[97] A vicarage was ordained before 1291[98] but was resumed by the priory in 1400; thereafter the prior could appoint or remove clergy at will.[99] After the Dissolution the benefice became a perpetual curacy. The incumbent was described as a chaplain in 1551,[1] and two early 17th-century successors were deacons licensed to serve the parish.[2] Most incumbents at that period, however, were loosely called vicars, and the benefice was often referred to as a vicarage.[3] In 1657 it was briefly united with Arundel vicarage.[4] From 1897 it was held in plurality with Arundel,[5] and in 1929 South Stoke was added, to form the united benefice of Arundel with South Stoke and Tortington, the parishes remaining distinct.[6] The church was declared redundant in 1978.[7]

The advowson of the rectory was apparently conveyed in 1214 by Pharamus de Tracy to William d'Aubigny, earl of Arundel.[8] By 1389 the advowson of the vicarage belonged to Tortington priory.[9] After the Dissolution the right to present clergy descended with Tortington manor at least between 1547 and 1596,[10] in 1605, and apparently continuously from 1661.[11] In 1579, however, the earl of Arundel was said to be patron.[12] There were other anomalies: the presentation in 1583 was made by 'letters of donation',[13] and incumbents presented by the lord of the manor in 1605 and 1661 were afterwards presented again by the Crown. The Crown also exercised the advowson in 1611 and 1614, and Oliver Cromwell as Lord Protector in 1655.[14]

Sir William Morley of Halnaker in Boxgrove presented for a turn in 1676, and between 1747 and 1767 the advowson was exercised by Samuel Leeves, a relative of the lords of the manor.[15] During the recusancy of Bernard Edward, duke of Norfolk (d. 1842), Francis Lovel presented in 1817 and William Keppel, earl of Albemarle, in 1833.[16] The advowson was bought in 1896 for transfer to the bishop of Chichester in 1897.[17] After 1929 the bishop made two appointments in three to the new united benefice.[18]

The vicarage was valued at £4 6*s.* 8*d.* in 1291[19] and at less than five marks (£3 6*s.* 8*d.*) by 1400.[20] In 1341 the vicar had a corrody in the priory for

69 *Kelly's Dir. Suss.* (1862, 1866).
70 Above, Arundel, other trades and inds. (1800–1945).
71 W.S.R.O., SP 1249.
72 *Kelly's Dir. Suss.* (1895 and later edns.).
73 Ibid. (1895), s.v. Ford.
74 Ibid. (1895).
75 O.S. Map 6", Suss. LXII. NE. (1914, 1951 edns.).
76 *Kelly's Dir. Suss.* (1934, 1938), s.v. Arundel.
77 Inf. from the proprietor, Arundel Arboretum.
78 A.C.M., M 32, rot. 8d.; 221, 530, 828–9.
79 Bodl. MS. Rawl. B. 318, pp. 172, 174.
80 A.C.M., M 221.
81 Ibid. 828.
82 B.L. Add. MS. 5688, f. 147.
83 E.S.R.O., QCR/2/1/EW 2 (46).
84 *Valor Eccl.* (Rec. Com.), i. 312.
85 *S.R.S.* xlv. 251.
86 Ibid. v. 181; W.S.R.O., Ep. I/86/20, f. 18v.; B.L. Add. MS. 39359, ff. 140–1.
87 B.L. Add. MS. 39359, ff. 141v.–145.
88 *S.R.S.* xlix. 110, 125.
89 W.S.R.O., Par. 198/9/1.
90 *S.R.S.* v. 181.
91 W.S.R.O., Par. 198/31/1–2.
92 E.S.R.O., QCR/2/3/W 5.
93 W.S.R.O., Par. 198/40/1.
94 *Suss. Poor Law Rec.* 32, 46.
95 *Census* (1931), pt. ii.
96 *S.R.S.* xl. 65.
97 *S.A.C.* v. 233.
98 *Tax. Eccl.* (Rec. Com.), 135.
99 *Cal. Papal Reg.* v. 304.
1 Dallaway, *Hist. W. Suss.* ii (1) (1819), 82 n., citing an unknown source.
2 B.L. Add. MS. 39348, f. 255.
3 Ibid.; P.R.O., E 134/17 Chas. II Trin./3, rot. 3; W.S.R.O., Ep. I/22/1 (1662); Ep. I/23/5, f. 33v.; *S.R.S.* v. 181; cf. Dallaway, *Hist. W. Suss.* ii (1) (1819), 81.
4 *Cal. S.P. Dom.* 1657–8, 168, 293.
5 *Chich. Dioc. Kal.* and *Dir.* (1898 and later edns.).
6 *Lond. Gaz.* 8 Nov. 1929, pp. 7197–9.
7 *W. Suss. Gaz.* 15 Mar. 1979.
8 *S.R.S.* ii, p. 33.
9 B.L. Add. MS. 39348, f. 251v.
10 Ibid. f. 255; *S.R.S.* xx. 444; *S.A.C.* lxxx. 121.
11 B.L. Add. MSS. 5688, ff. 146v., 156; 39348, ff. 255–60; *S.R.S.* xx. 442; lxxviii. 72; Horsfield, *Hist. Suss.* ii. 119.
12 W.S.R.O., Ep. I/23/5, f. 33v.
13 B.L. Add. MS. 39348, f. 255.
14 Ibid. ff. 255–7.
15 B.L. Add. MSS. 5688, f. 146v.; 39348, ff. 257–9.
16 Ibid. 39348, f. 260.
17 Ibid. f. 267; *Lond. Gaz.* 6 Aug. 1897, p. 4414.
18 *Lond. Gaz.* 8 Nov. 1929, p. 7198.
19 *Tax. Eccl.* (Rec. Com.), 135.
20 *Cal. Papal Reg.* v. 304.

himself and a servant.[21] In the later 15th century and early 16th the living was worth less than £8.[22] After the Dissolution the incumbent had neither a permanent endowment nor a house,[23] but he seems instead always to have enjoyed the rectory estate, including all the tithes of the parish except those of Priory farm.[24] That estate, sometimes loosely described as the vicarage, was sublet in the 1610s and the 1660s.[25] Besides Priory farm, Rooks wood was claimed to be tithe free in 1722,[26] and all the woods of the parish were tithe free in 1819.[27] Tithe-free land *c.* 1840 totalled 409 a., including parts of Manor farm (73 a.) and Priory farm (114 a.), besides woodland (224 a.).[28] The living was worth £30 in 1657[29] and *c.* £40 in 1724;[30] in the late 18th century tithe compositions brought in £117,[31] and average net income was £158 *c.* 1830.[32] At the commutation of tithes in 1841 the vicar received £175 tithe rent charge.[33] The owner of the manor demesnes had been responsible for chancel repair in 1724,[34] but by 1844 that duty had devolved on the vicar as a condition of his lease of the rectory estate.[35]

The vicar in 1521 also held Binsted.[36] There was a chantry in the church in the mid 16th century.[37] Curates mentioned between 1545 and 1581[38] may have been serving the benefice in lieu of an incumbent, since the only incumbent known to have been appointed at the time was the vicar of Arundel, who served 1576–9.[39] Adam Page, incumbent 1614–43, also held Middleton,[40] and may have lived there since assistant curates were recorded in 1625 and later.[41] One parishioner at least attended Yapton church in 1622.[42]

The vicar in 1662 resided constantly despite having other benefices and was licensed to preach.[43] Three 18th-century incumbents held other cures, but one of them, Nicholas Lester (1709–46),[44] was claimed never to have missed either his Sunday services or his parochial duties, and always to have lived in great harmony with his parishioners.[45] In 1724 communion was celebrated four times a year, with 6–10 communicants.[46] Two assistant curates served successively the years 1753–80,[47] presumably in the absence of the incumbent, but a third succeeded as vicar in 1794.[48] There was more non-residence in the early 19th century,[49] the curate licensed in 1829 having a stipend of £50 and living in Arundel.[50]

The frequency of communion increased between 1844 and 1865 to seven times a year, and by 1884 to monthly.[51] In 1851 there were alternate morning and afternoon services on successive Sundays with average congregations of 25–45.[52] Vicars lived in Arundel from 1866.[53] About 1890 it was proposed to enlarge the church because of increasing population,[54] and the churchyard was extended in 1894.[55] Alternate morning and afternoon services were still held in 1897, and weekly services in 1915.[56] Summer visitors from Arundel and elsewhere often attended in the early 20th century.[57] After becoming redundant in 1978 the church was used only for festivals.[58]

The church of *ST. MARY MAGDALENE*,[59] of flint and chalk rubble with stone dressings, consists of chancel with north vestry and nave with south aisle, vestigial south porch, and timber bellcot. The chancel and nave are 12th-century, surviving features including deep-splayed windows and the striking chancel arch and reset south doorway, with rich chevron work and beakhead ornament.[60] The nave crown-post roof is medieval. A south aisle was constructed in the 13th century, the Norman doorway evidently being moved outwards; when the aisle was destroyed, at some time before the 1780s, the doorway was moved back and the two-bayed aisle arcade blocked up.[61] A recess at the east end of the south external wall of the chancel was evidently once internal, indicating the presence of a chapel there, perhaps the Lady chapel

21 *Inq. Non.* (Rec. Com.), 368.
22 B.L. Add. MS. 39348, f. 250. There is no entry for the par. in *Valor Eccl.* (Rec. Com.).
23 Dallaway, *Hist. W. Suss.* ii (1) (1819), 82; *Rep. Com. Eccl. Revenues*; *S.R.S.* lxxviii. 73; A.C.M., MD 2469, wrongly calling the benefice a rectory; W.S.R.O., Ep. I/22/1 (1662, 1742); Ep. I/22/2 (1838); Ep. I/25/1 (1663).
24 Dallaway, *Hist. W. Suss.* ii (1) (1819), 81–2; *Rep. Com. Eccl. Revenues*; W.S.R.O., Ep. I/25/1 (1663). No land was then attached to the rectory estate, though it had been in 1341: *Inq. Non.* (Rec. Com.), 368.
25 P.R.O., C 2/Jas. I/G 12/28; ibid. E 134/17 Chas. II Trin./3, rot. 3.
26 A.C.M., MD 719, f. [2].
27 Dallaway, *Hist. W. Suss.* ii (1) (1819), 81.
28 W.S.R.O., TD/W 128.
29 *Cal. S.P. Dom.* 1657–8, 168.
30 *S.R.S.* lxxviii. 73.
31 A.C.M., MD 2469.
32 *Rep. Com. Eccl. Revenues.*
33 W.S.R.O., TD/W 128.
34 *S.R.S.* lxxviii. 73.
35 W.S.R.O., Ep. I/22A/2 (1844).
36 B.L. Add. MS. 39348, f. 253.
37 *S.R.S.* xxxvi. 118.
38 Ibid. xlv. 251; B.L. Add. MS. 39359, f. 140 and v.
39 B.L. Add. MS. 39348, f. 255; W.S.R.O., Ep. I/23/5, f. 33v.
40 B.L. Add. MS. 39348, f. 255v.; P.R.O., E 134/17 Chas. II Trin./3, rot. 3; *S.A.C.* xxxv. 184 n. 23.
41 B.L. Add. MS. 39359, f. 141; P.R.O., E 134/17 Chas. II Trin./3, rot. 3.
42 *S.R.S.* xlix. 48.
43 W.S.R.O., Ep. I/22/1 (1662).
44 B.L. Add. MS. 39348, ff. 258–9; *Alum. Cantab. to 1751*, s.v. Wm. Byass.
45 W.S.R.O., Par. 198/1/1/2, f. 3v.; cf. ibid. Ep. I/22/1 (1742).
46 *S.R.S.* lxxviii. 73.
47 B.L. Add. MS. 39359, f. 143.
48 Ibid. 39348, f. 259; 39359, f. 143v.
49 Ibid. 39359, f. 144 and v.; cf. *D.N.B.* s.v. John Duncumb; *Alum. Cantab. 1752–1900*, s.v. T. B. Morris.
50 W.S.R.O., Par. 198/5/1.
51 Ibid. Ep. I/22A/1 (1884); Ep. I/22A/2 (1844, 1865).
52 *S.R.S.* lxxv, p. 144.
53 *Kelly's Dir. Suss.* (1874 and later edns.); (1866), s.v. Arundel.
54 A.C.M., PM 138; *Chich. Dioc. Kal.* (1893), 148.
55 B.L. Add. MS. 39348, f. 266.
56 W.S.R.O., Par. 198/3/1–2.
57 *S.A.C.* lii. 163.
58 *W. Suss. Gaz.* 22 Feb. 1979; local inf.
59 *S.R.S.* ii, p. 33. The priory had the same dedic.: ibid. lix, p. 121. *Chich. Dioc. Kal.* (1877 and later edns.), followed by Nairn & Pevsner, *Suss.* 353, alternatively gives St. Thos. For descrips. of the ch., *S.A.C.* lii. 163–77; F. W. Steer, *Tortington Ch. Guide.*
60 Below, pl. facing p. 235.
61 B.L. Add. MS. 5674, f. 35; S.A.S. libr., undated newspaper cutting in copy of P. M. Johnston, *Tortington Ch. and Priory* (priv. print. 1904); cf. *Suss. Chs.: the Sharpe Colln.* ed. V. Smith (Lewes, [1979]). The fact that the aisle's decay was not mentioned in late 16th- and 17th-cent. presentments may imply that it was destroyed soon after the Dissolution: B.L. Add. MS. 39368, ff. 1413–14; W.S.R.O., Ep. I/23/5, f. 33v.; Ep. I/26/1, f. 7v.; Ep. I/26/2, f. 24v.; *S.R.S.* xlix. 66, 101.

mentioned in 1500.[62] A porch existed in 1546[63] and there was also a lead-covered steeple.[64]

The chancel arch was reconstructed in 1750, a dropped keystone being put in;[65] it was perhaps about that time that the chancel was ceiled, the result being described in 1776 as very neat.[66] It is not clear if the timber south porch depicted in the 1780s[67] was that of 1546. The bellcot existed by the 1780s,[68] and was later painted white like that of Ford church, presumably to serve as a landmark for river traffic.[69] A general restoration was carried out in 1867, when a new south aisle was built, the 13th-century arcade being uncovered and re-used, and the south doorway being again moved outwards.[70] The vestry was added in 1892[71] and the bellcot reconstructed in 1904.[72]

The circular Caen stone font, of the 12th century, is richly decorated with a cable moulding and arcading with foliage.[73] A single late medieval bench remained in the south aisle in 1990. There were two bells in 1724;[74] one, possibly of the mid 16th century, survived in 1936, when the second was of 1873.[75] The pulpit is early 17th-century. The plate includes a silver communion cup of 1635.[76] There are monuments to successive lords of the manor: Roger Gratwicke (d. 1596), and members of the Leeves family. The registers begin in 1560 and are apparently incomplete for much of the 17th century.[77]

NONCONFORMITY. Three Roman Catholics were recorded in the 1620s, including the lord of the manor William Gratwicke.[78] A single Catholic family was listed in 1742.[79] A Catholic chapel consecrated at Tortington Park school in 1948 was also used by local people until 1958 or later.[80]

Some parishioners in the mid 17th century belonged to the Arundel Quaker meeting, two at least refusing to attend Tortington church.[81]

EDUCATION. There was apparently a school at Tortington priory in 1501.[82] The vicar was licensed to teach boys in 1606,[83] and a 'school chamber' was mentioned at Manor Farm in 1666.[84]

Since the early 19th century children from the parish have gone to school in Arundel, Madehurst, or Littlehampton.[85]

CHARITIES FOR THE POOR. None known.

WALBERTON

THE parish of Walberton,[86] including most of the settlement called Fontwell, lies on the coastal plain 3 miles (5 km.) west-south-west of Arundel. In 1881 it contained 1,752 a. Two detached portions in Yapton (20 a.) were transferred to that parish 1882 × 1891, and in 1971 there were 701 ha. (1,732 a.).[87] In 1985 a small area in the south-west was transferred to Barnham and a larger area in the north-east to Slindon, while Walberton was extended eastwards to include the former parish of Binsted latterly in Tortington.[88] The present article treats the history of the parish as it existed before the last mentioned changes.

The ancient parish was roughly square in shape, the eastern boundary partly following a stream and the northern and southern ones partly roads or tracks. The northern and central parts chiefly occupy valley gravel, reaching *c.* 125 ft. (38 metres) north of the Chichester–Arundel road, while the southern end, partly overlaid by brickearth, is flat. On the eastern boundary the virtually straight Binsted brook forms a steep valley; in the west another stream passes east of Fontwell and alongside Walberton green at the western end of the village on its way to Barnham. Both valleys carry deposits of Eocene clays.[89] Ponds were depicted at and below Walberton green in 1846.[90] The one at the green, which had existed by 1756,[91] remained in 1994; an island was constructed after 1951,[92] and 54 mallard flocked there in 1988.[93]

The parish lay on the south-western edge of the medieval Arundel Great park, and retains woodland in its northern part. In 1086 the manor woods, possibly including land outside the parish, yielded four swine.[94] Woodland called Hiefalde was given by the lord of Walberton to Boxgrove

62 *S.R.S.* xlv. 250; cf. *L. & P. Hen. VIII*, i (1), p. 326.
63 *S.R.S.* xlv. 250.
64 Ibid. xlix. 101.
65 Inscr. *in situ.*
66 B.L. Add. MS. 5699, f. 126.
67 Ibid. 5674, f. 35.
68 Ibid.
69 *S.A.C.* xliii. 139.
70 S.A.S. libr., undated newspaper cutting in copy of Johnston, *Tortington Ch. and Priory*.
71 *Chich. Dioc. Kal.* (1893), 148.
72 P. M. Johnston, *Tortington Ch. and Priory* (priv. print. 1904), 13 (copies at W.S.R.O. and S.A.S. librs.).
73 Below, pl. facing p. 235.
74 *S.R.S.* lxxviii. 73.
75 Elphick, *Bells*, 69–70, 395.
76 *S.A.C.* liii. 237.
77 W.S.R.O., Par. 198/1 (TS. cat.).
78 Ibid. Ep. I/37/4; *S.A.C.* lxix. 119.
79 W.S.R.O., Ep. I/22/1 (1742).
80 Archives of Dioc. of Arundel and Brighton, Bishop's Ho., Hove, Arundel par. file, corresp. about the sch.; Lenten returns, 1958.
81 *S.A.C.* lv. 84; W.S.R.O., Ep. I/22/1 (1662).
82 *S.R.S.* xlv. 252.
83 B.L. Add. MS. 39348, f. 255.
84 W.S.R.O., Ep. I/29/198/20.
85 *Educ. of Poor Digest*, 971; Nat. Soc. *Inquiry, 1846–7*, Suss. 14–15; *Kelly's Dir. Suss.* (1882 and later edns.).
86 This article was written in 1995 and revised in 1996. Topographical details in introduction based mainly on O.S. Maps 1/25,000, SU 80/90 (1991 edn.); 6", Suss. LXII (1880 and later edns.). Much help was received from Mr. J. Eyre, Walberton Park.
87 *Census*, 1881–1971.
88 Arun (Parishes) Order 1985.
89 Geol. Surv. Map 1", drift, sheet 317 (1957 edn.).
90 W.S.R.O., TD/W 133.
91 Ibid. Add. MS. 1802.
92 *Par. of Walberton* (Walberton par. council, 1994), [31] (copy in W.S.R.O. libr.).
93 Ibid. [31–2]; *W. Suss. Gaz.* 14 Jan. 1988.
94 *V.C.H. Suss.* i. 431.

priory *c.* 1180–7.[95] Coppicing was mentioned from 1362,[96] Potwell copse was named from 1586,[97] and Wandleys copse from 1756.[98] Shellbridge wood in the north-east corner commemorated Shulbrede priory in Linchmere, which had owned land in Walberton in the Middle Ages.[99] In the same area lay woodland called Sawyers Dean belonging to Ford, Climping, and Ilsham manor,[1] represented by the modern Danes wood.[2] In 1847 there were 161 a. of coppice, chiefly in the north.[3]

Most of the northern end of the parish was open common land in the early 17th century.[4] It was inclosed in 1769.[5] Walberton green at the west end of the village existed by 1585.[6] In 1918 it belonged to the Walberton House estate,[7] and in 1951 it was bought by the parish council.[8] The wooden 'jubilee arch', originally put up in 1935, was re-erected in 1982 after removal for safety reasons.[9] The green is often waterlogged in wet weather.[10]

Land in the south-east corner of the parish may have been marshy in the Middle Ages and later.[11]

PARKS. Parkland has been important in recent centuries. Nothing is known of a medieval park at Walberton manor though free warren was granted in 1253[12] and in the mid 16th century there were keepers of Walberton chase, one of whom was the earl of Arundel.[13] A close called the Grove south-west of the manor house and church in 1630, and other large closes further east at the same date,[14] may have been parkland. In 1776 Richard Nash was said recently to have 'laid open' the grounds of Walberton House and 'planted round' the churchyard,[15] and two years later a park was shown as an oblong area south of the house extending eastwards as far as Yapton Lane.[16] A footpath running from the church to parcels of glebe in the south-east corner of the parish was diverted to the south-west in 1820–1 to give more privacy to the house.[17] The park was enlarged westwards between *c.* 1875 and 1896.[18] By the 1840s the main approach to the house was from Yapton Lane to the east;[19] in 1902 it had an avenue of trees. A secondary drive from the village, which was flanked by lawns and flowerbeds in 1902,[20] became the only access after 1945, the western section of the old main drive being removed. The lodge on Yapton Lane was demolished in 1995. Much of the park had been converted to agriculture by 1993, though some battered parkland trees and a ha-ha then remained near the house.

A park existed at Avisford by 1756.[21] By *c.* 1875 it included much of the land between the Chichester–Arundel road, Yapton Lane on the east, and Tye Lane on the west,[22] and during the next 20 years it was extended southwards almost to the village street.[23] It was described as 'tastefully adorned with sylvan beauty' in 1835[24] and as 'grandly timbered' in 1883.[25] The entrance lodge which stood on Yapton Lane in 1756[26] was rebuilt in the mid 19th century in Italianate style. A second carriage drive was constructed from the village street *c.* 1897, with a lodge of red brick.[27] The park had 129 a. in 1922, when it was divided into enclosures with iron fencing,[28] but after the sale of the house *c.* 1928[29] its area was much reduced.[30] Some holm oaks and a cedar of Lebanon still remained from the early 19th-century park in 1988.[31] A 9-hole golf course was opened south-west of the house before 1985[32] and was extended east of Yapton Lane in 1996.

In 1994, besides woods and parkland, land use was divided between agriculture, market gardening, and housing. Parts of the north-east and north-west corners of the parish were worked for gravel and bricks in the late 19th and early 20th centuries.[33]

SETTLEMENT. Walberton village lies near the centre of the parish away from any important route. Re-use of Roman tile in the church fabric[34] suggests Roman settlement nearby, and excavation in the churchyard has revealed evidence of Anglo-Saxon occupation.[35] Later settlement was chiefly along the serpentine course of the Street a little to the north.

The earliest known secular building is probably the timber-framed Old Hall cottage, containing a two-bayed late medieval hall into which an upper floor and a chimneystack were inserted in the 17th century; a cellar at the east end under the

95 *S.R.S.* lix, p. 26.
96 P.R.O., C 135/174, no. 14, m. 2; cf. W.S.R.O., Par. 202/7/21 (19th-cent. copy of lost map of 1630).
97 P.R.O., E 310/25/145, f. 49.
98 W.S.R.O., Add. MS. 1802; cf. ibid. Par. 202/7/21; *250 Yrs. of Mapmaking in Suss.* ed. H. Margary, pl. 14.
99 W.S.R.O., Add. MSS. 1802, naming Shulbred wood; 5156, f. [7]; below, manor.
1 Guildhall Libr. MS. 13321, ff. 42–3; P.R.O., SC 6/Hen. VIII/3480, rot. 16.
2 *250 Yrs. of Mapmaking in Suss.* pl. 14; W.S.R.O., Add. MSS. 7569a, 7778 (TS. cat.); ibid. SP 317.
3 W.S.R.O., TD/W 133.
4 A.C.M., PM 193; Guildhall Libr. MS. 13321, f. 42.
5 Below, econ. hist. (agric.).
6 P.R.O., E 310/25/145, f. 50.
7 W.S.R.O., SP 303.
8 Ibid. Par. 202/52/4.
9 *Par. of Walberton* (Walberton par. council, 1994), [27].
10 B. Dixon, *Unknown to Hist. and Fame* (Arundel, 1992), 5.
11 W.S.R.O., Add. MSS. 4322, 37986 (TS. cat.).
12 *Cal. Pat.* 1247–58, 245; cf. *S.A.C.* lxxxiv. 69.
13 *L. & P. Hen. VIII*, xix (1), p. 643; xxi (2), p. 435.
14 W.S.R.O., Par. 202/7/21.
15 B.L. Add. MS. 5699, f. 131.
16 *250 Yrs. of Mapmaking in Suss.* pls. 14–15; the evidence for a park in a map of 1756 is equivocal: W.S.R.O., Add. MS. 1802.
17 W.S.R.O., QR/W 717, f. 109; 719, f. 118.
18 O.S. Map 6", Suss. LXII (1880 edn.); LXII. NE. (1899 edn.).
19 Ibid. LXII. NE. (1914 edn.); W.S.R.O., TD/W 133.
20 W.S.R.O., SP 1264.
21 Ibid. Add. MS. 1802.
22 O.S. Map 6", Suss. LXII (1880 edn.); cf. W.S.R.O., SP 1263.
23 O.S. Map 6", Suss. LXII. NE. (1899 edn.). The southwards diversion of a footpath in the added area in 1813–14 perhaps indicates an earlier unfinished plan for enlargement: W.S.R.O., QR/W 691, ff. 106–9.
24 Horsfield, *Hist. Suss.* ii. 117.
25 W.S.R.O., SP 1263.
26 Ibid. Add. MS. 1802.
27 B. Dixon, *Unknown to Hist. and Fame*, 22, 80.
28 W.S.R.O., SP 435.
29 Below, manor (Avisford Ho.).
30 *W. Suss. Gaz.* 15 Mar. 1973.
31 Ibid. 14 Jan. 1988.
32 Ibid. 19 Dec. 1985.
33 O.S. Maps 6", Suss. LXII. NW. (1899 edn.); 1/25,000, SU 80/90 (1991 edn.); W.S.R.O., SP 317.
34 Below, church [fabric].
35 *S.A.C.* cxxxii. 194.

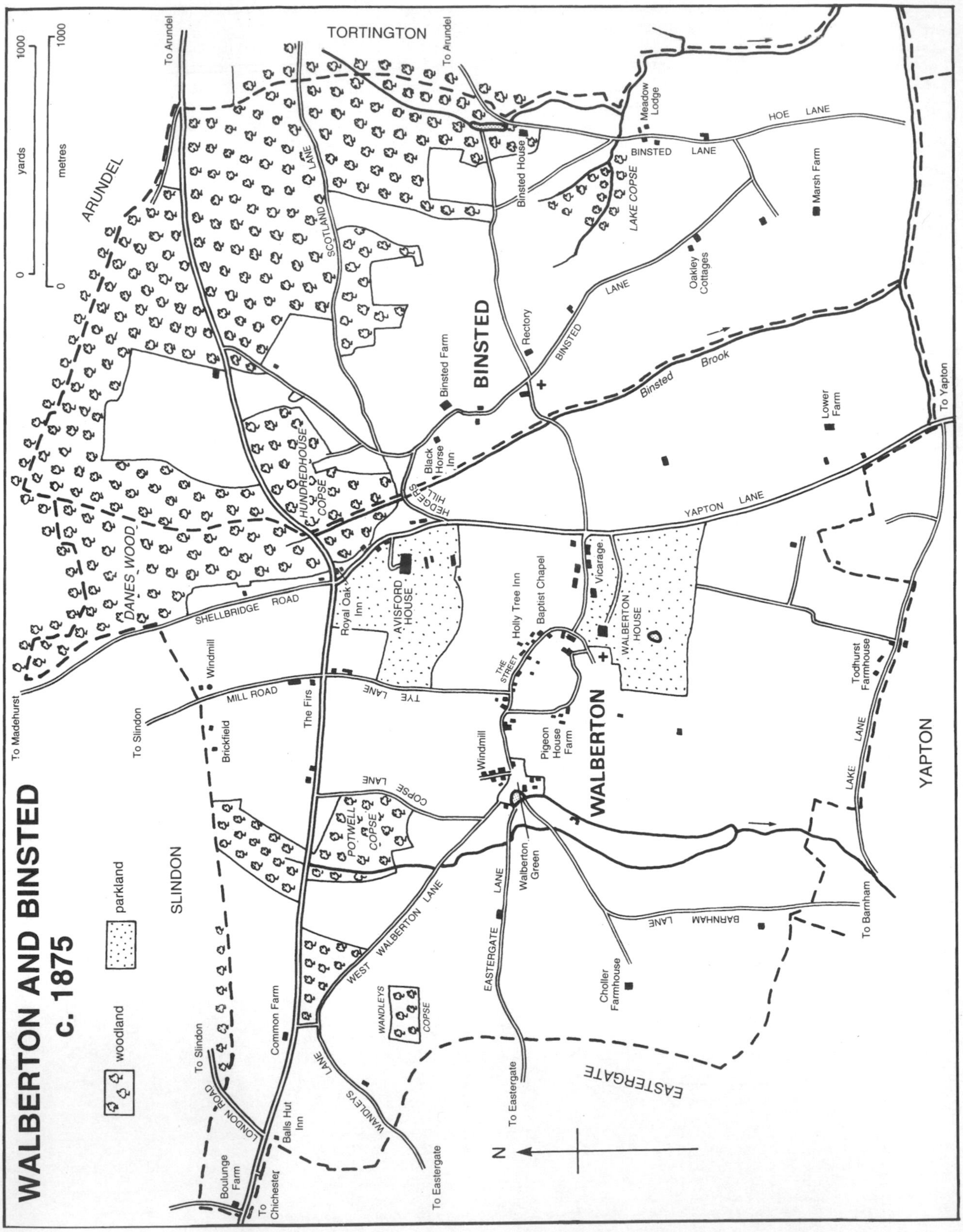
WALBERTON AND BINSTED
c. 1875
woodland
parkland
yards
metres
0
1000
TORTINGTON
ARUNDEL
BINSTED
WALBERTON
SLINDON
YAPTON
EASTERGATE
To Arundel
To Madehurst
To Slindon
To Chichester
To Eastergate
To Barnham
To Yapton
HOE LANE
BINSTED LANE
Meadow Lodge
Binsted House
LAKE COPSE
Marsh Farm
Oakley Cottages
BINSTED LANE
Rectory
Binsted Farm
Binsted Brook
Black Horse Inn
HEDGERS HILL
HUNDREDHOUSE COPSE
SCOTLAND LANE
DANES WOOD
SHELLBRIDGE ROAD
Royal Oak Inn
AVISFORD HOUSE
YAPTON LANE
Lower Farm
Vicarage
WALBERTON HOUSE
Holly Tree Inn
Baptist Chapel
THE STREET
Windmill
MILL ROAD
TYE LANE
The Firs
Brickfield
Pigeon House Farm
COPSE LANE
POTWELL COPSE
Walberton Green
Todhurst Farmhouse
LAKE LANE
BARNHAM LANE
EASTERGATE LANE
WEST WALBERTON LANE
WANDLEYS COPSE
WANDLEYS LANE
Choller Farmhouse
Common Farm
Balls Hut Inn
LONDON ROAD
Boulunge Farm
N

probable site of the medieval service quarters was perhaps dug in the early 18th century.[36] The building is faced in flint and brick. The west end of Pear Tree cottage on the corner of Tye Lane, also timber-framed and similarly faced, is late 16th- or 17th-century, and originally had a projecting eastern chimneystack; it was enlarged eastwards *c.* 1700. On one wall of the western downstairs room is a mural painting of a ship. At Magnolia cottage near the church a central stack is similarly flanked by a probably 17th-century southern section and a later, possibly 18th-century, northern one. Smugglers Steps at the east end of the village, one-storeyed with dormers, is late 17th-century with later extensions.

In 1630 the centre of the modern village was partly settled, but most houses and crofts lay at the eastern end and in a back road running west from a point near the church[37] which survived in 1994 as a footpath. In 1756 there were *c.* 9 houses in the eastern section of the Street, including the vicarage, and *c.* 17 in the central section between the church and the modern Dairy Lane, where close spacing in adjacent narrow plots may indicate a planned layout. The back road then had 10 or 11 buildings.[38]

Among several 18th-century buildings is the so-called Dower House, formerly Park House,[39] a double-pile structure of *c.* 1750 perhaps including parts of an earlier building[40] and with 19th-century and later additions. At Pigeon House farm is a probably 18th-century round dovecot of flint with brick dressings.[41] Early 19th-century houses in the Street include the stuccoed Myrtle cottage and Jessamine cottage of grey and red brick.

In the 1840s there were 35–40 dwellings between Dairy and Yapton lanes, but by then the back road had ceased to be of much importance.[42]

At the western end of the modern village street Walberton green was a separate focus of settlement until the early 20th century. The surnames Westeton and Westcote recorded in 1327[43] may refer to dwellers in that area, which may also be the West Walberton mentioned in 1740.[44] The thatched Friars Oak and Friars Oak cottage south-east of the green comprise a 17th-century timber-framed building enlarged on the west in the 19th century and faced with painted brick. Another possibly timber-framed house on the north side of the green once had 17th-century mullioned windows;[45] it was refaced in brick and flint apparently in 1763[46] and was derelict in 1995. Adjacent to the last named was formerly a building with a five- or six-bayed brick front also in 17th-century style with a plat band between the storeys.[47] Six houses were depicted at the eastern end of the green in 1756.[48] Barrack Row to the east is a brick terrace whose name, recorded from 1851, apparently does not allude to military use.[49] In the 1840s there were *c.* 7 houses around the green besides others, including a windmill, in Mill Lane to the east.[50]

Some gaps along the village street were filled by new buildings in the mid 19th century, notably an imposing brick house near Tye Lane dated 1865 which perhaps belonged to the farmer and maltster Richard Suter.[51]

In the 1880s and 90s several terraces of flint, brick, and stone, including re-used medieval ashlar, were put up on the south side of the central part of the street by the builder and dairy farmer W. E. Booker.[52] Two incorporate older buildings, one with a datestone for 1681; another, which includes the post office, has Norman-style arched windows and a terracotta portrait medallion commemorating Queen Victoria's jubilee of 1887. Booker also built pairs of semidetached houses on the east side of Dairy Lane after 1896.[53] The artisan character of the new terraces contrasted strongly with the seigneurial eastern end of the village lying between the enlarged parks belonging to Walberton House and Avisford House. The Dower House at the same date was a gentleman's house, with well laid out grounds that included a tennis lawn.[54]

Infilling continued during the 20th century.[55] Council houses were built from 1920[56] and by the mid 20th century formed a large estate west of Dairy Lane.[57] Two working farms remained in the village in the early 20th century, Pigeon House farm and Street farm near Walberton green.[58] By 1950 a road of detached houses had been built at the east end;[59] a close of houses and bungalows was put up nearby before 1963,[60] and a street of luxury dwellings north-west of the church *c.* 1974[61] on land first offered for building in 1918.[62] North-east of the church a bend in the Street was straightened in 1957 and a shopping parade constructed.[63]

New dwellings were also provided in the 20th century by converting former business

36 Cf. datestone for 1705 in cellar.
37 W.S.R.O., Par. 202/7/21.
38 Ibid. Add. MS. 1802; cf. *250 Yrs. of Mapmaking in Suss.* pl. 14.
39 O.S. Map 6", Suss. LXII. NE. (1914 edn.).
40 Cf. W.S.R.O., SP 303.
41 Below, pl. facing p. 251.
42 W.S.R.O., TD/W 133. For the increase in nos. since later 18th cent. cf. *250 Yrs. of Mapmaking in Suss.* pl. 14; *Census*, 1821–31.
43 *S.R.S.* x. 134.
44 W.S.R.O., Add. MS. 8522 (TS. cat.).
45 Dixon, *Unknown to Hist. and Fame*, 6.
46 Datestone on bldg.
47 Dixon, *Unknown to Hist. and Fame*, 90; C.I.H.E. libr., GY/PC 2619, 2623.
48 W.S.R.O., Add. MS. 1802.
49 P.R.O., HO 107/1652, f. 310v., naming Barrack Ho.; cf. *O.E.D.* s.v. barrack.
50 W.S.R.O., TD/W 133. The name Walberton green was apparently applied also to the W. end of the Street in 1896: O.S. Map 6", Suss. LXII. NE. (1899 edn.); cf. Pike, *Dir. SW. Suss.* (1886–7).
51 Inscr. R.C.S./1865 on bldg.; *Kelly's Dir. Suss.* (1862, 1866).
52 O.S. Map 6", Suss. LXII. NE. (1899 edn.); inscrs. on bldgs.; below, econ. hist. (other trades and inds.).
53 O.S. Map 6", Suss. LXII. NE. (1899, 1914 edns.); inf. from Mr. J. Booker, Walberton.
54 W.S.R.O., SP 1264; cf. *Kelly's Dir. Suss.* (1905 and later edns.).
55 O.S. Map 6", Suss. LXII. NE. (1914, 1951 edns.).
56 N. Wyatt, *An Ever-Rolling Stream* (Pulborough, 1993), 14; *Par. of Walberton* (Walberton par. council, 1994), [15]; W.S.R.O., Par. 202/54/14, p. 9.
57 O.S. Map 6", SU 90 NE. (1963 edn.).
58 Wyatt, op. cit. 13–14, 31; W.S.R.O., SP 303, 1264. For location of Street fm. cf. ibid. IR 12, f. 38.
59 O.S. Map 6", Suss. LXII. NE. (1951 edn.).
60 Ibid. SU 90 NE. (1963 edn.).
61 W.S.R.O., MP 1220, f. 20; *W. Suss. Gaz.* 18 Sept. 1975.
62 W.S.R.O., SP 303.
63 Ibid. Par. 202/54/14, p. 16.

premises,[64] the manor house, its outbuildings, and the old National school.[65] Some older houses latterly divided into cottages were restored for single occupation. A copy of a medieval 'Wealden' house was put up in 1987.[66]

Already in 1972 too much new building was felt to have occurred too fast, giving Walberton a partially suburban character.[67] By 1990 incomers, many of whom did not stay long, were the dominant group.[68]

Building land was offered for sale near Walberton green from 1902,[69] and the settlement there was linked with the rest of the village by new building during the 20th century. There are three 20th-century houses north of the green, and a close of new houses at the south-east corner. By the mid 20th century 20–25 houses had been constructed beyond the green along the road to Barnham.[70]

A second centre of settlement in the parish was at Avisford in the north-east corner. The name evidently refers to a crossing of the Binsted brook on the Walberton–Binsted boundary. Roman finds north of the Chichester–Arundel road and west of Shellbridge Road, including glass and earthenware vessels, suggest occupation there in the 1st century A.D.[71] In the Middle Ages Avisford was important as the centre of the hundred.[72] It was mentioned as a place *c.* 1217, when a windmill was to be built there.[73] The name Avisford Hill described the steep incline from the Binsted brook to the site of the present Royal Oak inn;[74] an alternative name for the high ground in that area was Beacon Hill.[75]

There were at least two cottages on waste land at Avisford in 1609,[76] though nothing was depicted in 1630.[77] By 1778 there were *c.* 6 houses between the Royal Oak and the junction of Yapton Lane and Hedgers Hill leading to Binsted, some apparently on sites reclaimed from roadside waste;[78] beside Hedgers Hill itself stands Beam Ends, a small, probably 17th-century, timber-framed building originally only two rooms wide, which seems also to have been built on waste land. Similar in scale and probably in date was a cottage on the east side of Yapton Lane opposite Avisford House demolished in the late 19th or early 20th century.[79] The elaborate nos. 1–3 Yapton Lane is an **L**-shaped mid 19th-century building of varied materials, with scalloped bargeboards and gabled dormers; in 1883 it belonged to the Avisford House estate.[80]

West of Avisford where Tye Lane reached Walberton common lay a cluster of houses[81] which may be Tye Lane End mentioned in 1769.[82] After the inclosure of the common and the realignment of the Chichester–Arundel road in the latter year,[83] large houses could be built nearby to take advantage of the fine coastal views available from the high ground. Besides Avisford House mentioned below, Hill cottage at the north end of Tye Lane and Firgrove on the corner of Mill Road, formerly the Firs, existed by 1778;[84] the latter is an **L**-shaped 18th-century house with a three-bayed south front and 19th-century or later additions and alterations including a ballroom at the east end.[85] Woodlands to the west was built before 1813.[86]

More dwellings were put up nearby from the late 19th century; for instance, building land was offered for sale in 1883 between Mill and Shellbridge roads,[87] along both of which stand big 20th-century houses.[88] In 1994 the north-eastern part of the parish, with its woods, straight roads, and predominantly recent buildings, and with the open Slindon common beyond, suggested wildness only lately tamed.

In the north-west corner, on the border with Eastergate, lies the hamlet of Fontwell. The place name is recorded in 1630,[89] and the cottage built on the manor waste 'near the west woods end' before 1598 may have been there.[90] A house called Common Farm[91] near the junction of the Chichester–Arundel road with West Walberton Lane existed by 1778,[92] but the present building, afterwards renamed Goodacres, is of the early 19th century and stuccoed. The three-bayed house called Days, formerly Boulunge Farm and intermediately the Hermitage,[93] was apparently built in 1778[94] and is faced with Roman cement. There are one-storeyed extensions at both ends, that on the west of brick with a reset early 16th-century stone doorcase, and that on the east rendered like the house but with windows in Gothick style. Pieces of medieval to 18th-century stonework, some moulded, are used as kerbstones along the north–south track which follows

64 e.g. ibid. Add. MS. 35871 (TS. cat.); *Bognor Regis Observer*, 12 Nov. 1987.
65 Below, manor (Walberton); educ.
66 *W. Suss. Gaz.* 14 Jan. 1988.
67 *Bognor Regis Observer*, 7 July 1972; cf. Nairn & Pevsner, *Suss.* 362.
68 *W. Suss. Gaz.* 15 Nov. 1990.
69 W.S.R.O., SP 303, 1264.
70 O.S. Map 6", Suss. LXII. NE. (1914, 1951 edns.).
71 *S.A.C.* cxvii. 77, 79; *V.C.H. Suss.* iii. 49, 67; Dallaway, *Hist. W. Suss.* ii (1) (1819), 367–9; S.M.R. 1325.
72 Above, Avisford Hund.; cf. the adjacent Hundred-house copse in Binsted: O.S. Map 6", Suss. LXII (1880 edn.). The local pronunciation in 1864 was said to be 'hare's foot': *S.A.C.* xvi. 258.
73 *S.R.S.* lix, p. 77. Members of the Stockman fam. were described as of Avisford in the 14th cent.: *Cat. Anct. D.* i, B 125, 1462; ii, B 3753; *Cal. Pat.* 1330–4, 128.
74 W.S.R.O., Add. MSS. 1802; 5156, f. [13]; Ogilby, *Britannia* (1675), 8.
75 W.S.R.O., Par. 202/7/21; cf. below, this section.
76 P.R.O., SP 14/47, no. 75, ff. 153, 156.
77 W.S.R.O., Par. 202/7/21.
78 *250 Yrs. of Mapmaking in Suss.* ed. H. Margary, pl. 14; cf. W.S.R.O., TD/W 133.
79 B. Dixon, *Unknown to Hist. and Fame*, 23.
80 W.S.R.O., SP 1263; above, pl. facing p. 123.
81 *250 Yrs. of Mapmaking in Suss.* pl. 5.
82 W.S.R.O., Add. MS. 5156, f. [8]. The 'mean cottage' mentioned on one of the Heath crofts in 1630 may have been in the same area: ibid. 2301, m. 1; cf. below, econ. hist. (agric.).
83 Below, this section (communications); econ. hist. (agric.).
84 *250 Yrs. of Mapmaking in Suss.* pl. 14; below, manor (Avisford Ho.).
85 Illus. at *Suss. in 20th Cent.* 149.
86 *250 Yrs. of Mapmaking in Suss.* pl. 19.
87 W.S.R.O., SP 1263.
88 Cf. O.S. Map 6", Suss. LXII. NE. (1951 edn.).
89 W.S.R.O., Par. 202/7/21; cf. ibid. Add. MS. 1802.
90 A.C.M., M 532, f. [85v.] from end.
91 e.g. O.S. Map 6", Suss. LXII (1880 edn.).
92 *250 Yrs. of Mapmaking in Suss.* pl. 14.
93 e.g. O.S. Map 6", Suss. LXII. NW. (1899 edn.).
94 Datestone on front.

the parish boundary immediately to the west. All were presumably brought to the site by the owner A. J. Day.[95]

Merryvale cottage, off Arundel Road, of three bays, was 18th- or 19th-century; it survived in 1962[96] but was later demolished. Park cottage in London Road, of flint and brick, was derelict in 1992.

There were *c.* 6 dwellings in all at Fontwell in the 1840s.[97] Land was offered for building between the Chichester–Arundel road and Wandleys Lane in 1893.[98] By 1910 the name Fontwell was used to describe the area around the Hermitage,[99] but as new houses were built further east in the 1920s and 30s, both along the Chichester–Arundel road and north of it[1] the name was extended to include those. A bypass road was constructed in 1988.[2]

The remainder of the parish had scattered dwellings before the mid 19th century.[3] The former Choller Farmhouse off the road to Barnham, embodying a medieval open-field name,[4] is an 18th- or early 19th-century building faced with Roman cement. Todhurst Farmhouse on the southern border, probably contemporary, also commemorates an open-field name.[5] It was called Southwood Farm in 1813.[6] There were two or three more houses nearby in Lake Lane in 1778, as well as others along West Walberton Lane and three in the southern part of Yapton Lane which evidently occupied land reclaimed from roadside waste.[7] Walberton Farmhouse east of Yapton Lane is apparently a 19th-century building with Edwardian additions, and Wanley House near Fontwell is of *c.* 1900.

Several older houses besides the two great mansions of the parish were occupied by gentry families in the late 19th and early 20th centuries, including Choller and Todhurst Farmhouses.[8]

Land near Barnham station in the south-west was offered for building in 1902[9] but not then developed. During the 20th century there has been much building along rural roads, notably Yapton Lane east of the village, Lake Lane in the south, and West Walberton, Wandleys, and Copse lanes north-west of the village;[10] in the latter area detached houses and bungalows, some large, occupy a woodland setting. In Eastergate Lane are houses constructed for nursery workers. Much building dates from the 1920s when Walberton's population almost doubled;[11] the pace of development increased again after *c.* 1950.

Thirty-nine people were assessed to subsidy in Walberton in 1327 and 46 in Walberton and Barnham together in 1332[12] and in 1524.[13] Twenty-one 'inhabitants' and 14 servants and other residents were recorded on the manor in 1624.[14] In 1642 the protestation was signed by 61 parishioners,[15] and in 1670 the number assessed to the hearth tax was 47 with 5 discharged.[16] Fifty-five people were listed in the Compton census in 1676[17] and there were 49 families in 1724.[18] From 502 in 1801 the population rose to 687 in 1821, but then fell to 561 by 1841, partly through temporary absence but mainly through emigration or transfer to the workhouse.[19] Thereafter it remained between 578 and 628 until 1911. In the 1920s it almost doubled because of residential development, and it continued to increase thereafter to 1,485 in 1951, 1,792 in 1971, and 1,916 in 1991.[20]

COMMUNICATIONS. The Roman road from Chichester to Brighton crossed the north end of the parish roughly on the line of the modern Chichester–Arundel road.[21] Avisford bridge, evidently on the Binsted boundary, was mentioned in 1553[22] and Mackrells bridge near Potwell copse in 1630.[23] Before 1769 the road ran further south between Potwell copse and the Royal Oak inn at Avisford,[24] its present straighter course being fixed at inclosure in that year.[25] The section in the east end of the parish became a dual carriageway in the late 1960s, when the steep descent from the Royal Oak was embanked and made more level.[26] The rest of the road within the parish was made a dual carriageway, and a bypass for Fontwell was constructed, in 1988.[27]

Walberton village itself is the focus of roads and tracks from several directions.[28] The road to Eastergate existed by 1229;[29] it was called Eastergate Lane in 1756, when Barnham and West Walberton lanes were also named.[30] Tye Lane, i.e. the road leading to the common, was called Tyle Lane in 1635 and later;[31] it was the Arundel road in 1615.[32] Yapton Lane existed by 1608;[33] the section north of Walberton village street was known as Hole Lane in 1756 and later.[34] The road formed part of the Arundel–Bognor road in 1849.[35] Lake Lane

95 *Kelly's Dir. Suss.* (1895); cf. above, Eastergate, intro. (settlement).
96 *Bognor Regis Post*, 9 Feb. 1962.
97 W.S.R.O., TD/W 133.
98 Ibid. SP 1227.
99 O.S. Map 6", Suss. LXII. NW. (1914 edn.).
1 Ibid. LXII. NE. (1951 edn.); *Par. of Walberton* (Walberton par. council, 1994), [22–3].
2 Below, this section (communications).
3 e.g. W.S.R.O., TD/W 133.
4 *S.R.S.* lix, p. 193; cf. below, econ. hist. (agric.).
5 Below, econ. hist. (agric.).
6 *250 Yrs. of Mapmaking in Suss.* pl. 19.
7 Ibid. pl. 14.
8 *Kelly's Dir. Suss.* (1845 and later edns.); W.S.R.O., SP 1263–4.
9 W.S.R.O., SP 1264, pp. 10, 12.
10 e.g. O.S. Map 6", Suss. LXII. NE. (1951 edn.).
11 Below, this section.
12 *S.R.S.* x. 134–5, 255.
13 Ibid. lvi. 57.
14 W.S.R.O., Add. MS. 2299, p. 4.
15 *S.R.S.* v. 185.
16 P.R.O., E 179/191/410, pt. 2, rot. 2d.
17 *Compton Census*, ed. Whiteman, 144.
18 *S.A.C.* lxxviii. 73.
19 *Census*, 1801–41; below, local govt.
20 *Census*, 1851–1991.
21 *S.N.Q.* xi. 144.
22 A.C.M., M 32, rot. 5d.
23 W.S.R.O., Add. MS. 2301, m. 2; cf. Ogilby, *Britannia* (1675), 8.
24 W.S.R.O., Add. MS. 1802.
25 Ibid. 5156.
26 *Bognor Regis Observer*, 25 July 1967.
27 Local inf.; O.S. Map 1/25,000, SU 80/90 (1981, 1991 edns.).
28 e.g. W.S.R.O., Par. 202/7/21.
29 *S.R.S.* ii, p. 64.
30 W.S.R.O., Add. MS. 1802.
31 Ibid. Add. MS. 1802; ibid. Ep. I/25/1 (1635); for 'tye' meaning common, *P.N. Suss.* (E.P.N.S.), i. 144.
32 W.S.R.O., Ep. I/25/1 (1615); for location of glebe described, below, church.
33 Guildhall Libr. MS. 13321, ff. 42–3; cf. *S.R.S.* xxix, p. 145.
34 P.R.O., HO 107/1652, f. 302v.; W.S.R.O., Add. MS. 1802.
35 Lewis, *Topog. Dict. Eng.* (1849).

along the southern boundary of the parish was called Shipley Lane from 1756[36] but had its present name by 1819.[37] The road to Binsted was called Hedgers Hill by 1851,[38] evidently from a surname recorded a century earlier.[39]

Other roads south of the Chichester–Arundel road were Todworth or Todder Lane in the south-east mentioned in 1615,[40] Choller Lane in the south-west mentioned from 1635,[41] Wandleys Lane near Fontwell recorded by 1724[42] and called Wandlass Lane in 1756,[43] and Copse and Puck lanes recorded from 1756, the latter running south from Pigeon House Farm.[44]

Tracks across Walberton common in the north to Slindon and Madehurst[45] became the straight London, Mill, and Shellbridge roads at inclosure in 1769.[46] London Road was part of the Balls hut to Storrington turnpike road between 1812 and 1880;[47] from 1988 it formed part of the Fontwell bypass road.

There were several carriers[48] in Walberton between the mid 19th century and the early 20th. For most of that period the Burches and the Bowleys successively offered a carrying service from the Holly Tree inn in the village; in 1886 Allan Bowley plied twice weekly to Chichester and another carrier daily to Arundel and Barnham.[49] Arundel was still served in 1915, Chichester in 1922, and Barnham in 1938. The firm of C. W. Burch were haulage contractors from 1938 or earlier.[50]

The Bowleys also provided horse-drawn passenger transport to Barnham and Arundel stations by 1886.[51] In 1927 motor buses went to Arundel, Bognor, Littlehampton, and Worthing, and by 1934 to Chichester.[52] The parish was unusually well connected by bus services in 1992, when Storrington and Guildford could also be reached.

Between 1846 and 1864 Walberton was served by Yapton station at its south-eastern corner.[53]

An alehouse keeper was recorded in 1596[54] and an unlicensed tavern in 1641.[55] The Anchor alehouse, adjacent to or including a smithy in 1677,[56] has not been located but may have been the inn with one guest bed and stabling for one horse recorded in 1686.[57] Two inns outside the village were recorded from the mid 18th century. Balls hut at Fontwell had that name from 1756.[58] There was a smithy there *c.* 1832[59] and the publican in 1852 was a wheelwright.[60] Badger baiting was an attraction during the 19th century.[61] In the early 20th the inn was popular with cyclists[62] and in the mid 20th with coaches and day trippers.[63] It was renamed the Fontwell in the 1980s but was demolished in 1992 after the building of the Fontwell bypass. The Royal Oak at Avisford existed by 1756[64] but its name is not recorded until 1808;[65] the building has two stories and three bays and is apparently early 19th-century. The Avisford hundred view was generally held there in the earlier 19th century[66] and in 1861 an annual New Year's eve ball.[67] In 1886 there was a large room where over 100 could dine, picnics and beanfeasts as well as teas and dinners being hosted.[68] The Holly Tree inn in the village street was recorded from 1845[69] and so called in 1867. The building was refurbished in the later 19th century.[70] In 1886 it offered accommodation for visitors, including families.[71] Both the last named inns survived in 1994.

SOCIAL AND CULTURAL ACTIVITIES. An unusual variety of social and cultural facilities was available in Walberton in the 19th century and early 20th, mostly provided or supported by resident landowners and clergy. A parish library for Walberton and Yapton was formed *c.* 1810 with subscriptions from local gentry; the books were to be chosen by the vicar and kept at Walberton vicarage.[72] In the second half of the 19th century there were two libraries, one at the vicarage and the other, founded by Mrs. Reynell Pack, at Avisford House.[73] Thomas Vogan, vicar from 1843, started the annual Walberton and Yapton flower, fruit, and vegetable show in 1856; it was still held in 1867.[74] His wife meanwhile ran a clothing club,[75] and in the early 20th century there was a coal club, also apparently founded by the incumbent.[76]

A club and reading room, with books, magazines, and games, was started in 1883; it occupied part of the former tithe barn of the vicarage, and in 1888 was open six nights a week in winter with a good attendance.[77] A new village hall of timber

36 W.S.R.O., Add. MS. 1802; cf. ibid. 11828 (TS. cat.).
37 Ibid. 8531 (TS. cat.).
38 P.R.O., HO 107/1652, ff. 302v.–303.
39 W.S.R.O., Add. MSS. 1802; 4322 (TS. cat.).
40 Ibid. Add. MS. 1802; ibid. Ep. I/25/1 (1615).
41 Ibid. Add. MSS. 1802; 2299, p. [29].
42 *250 Yrs. of Mapmaking in Suss.* ed. H. Margary, pl. 5.
43 W.S.R.O., Add. MS. 1802.
44 Ibid.; cf. *250 Yrs. of Mapmaking in Suss.* pls. 14–15.
45 *250 Yrs. of Mapmaking in Suss.* pl. 5; W.S.R.O., Add. MS. 1802.
46 W.S.R.O., Add. MS. 5156.
47 52 Geo. III, c. 92 (Local and Personal); 38 & 39 Vic. c. 194 (Local).
48 Para. based mainly on P.R.O., HO 107/1090, f. 12v.; HO 107/1652, f. 313v.; *Kelly's Dir. Suss.* (1852 and later edns.); B. Dixon, *Unknown to Hist. and Fame*, 63, 78–9.
49 Pike, *Dir. SW. Suss.* (1886–7).
50 Cf. *W. Suss. Gaz.* 18 Sept. 1975.
51 Pike, *Dir. SW. Suss.* (1886–7); *Kelly's Dir. Suss.* (1895 and later edns.).
52 *Kelly's Dir. Suss.* (1927 and later edns.).
53 Below, Yapton, intro. (communications).
54 A.C.M., M 532, f. [54] from end.
55 W.S.R.O., Add. MS. 2299, p. [44].
56 Ibid. 4296 (TS. cat.).
57 P.R.O., WO 30/48, f. 185.
58 W.S.R.O., Add. MS. 1802.
59 Pigot, *Nat. Com. Dir.* (1832–4), 1051.
60 *Kelly's Dir. Suss.* (1852).
61 Dixon, *Unknown to Hist. and Fame*, 65.
62 *W. Suss. Gaz.* 13 July 1995.
63 *Par. of Walberton* (Walberton par. council, 1994), [23].
64 W.S.R.O., Add. MS. 1802.
65 Ibid. 47459 (TS. cat.).
66 W.S.R.O., Holmes, Campbell & Co. MSS., Avisford hund. ct. bk. 1813–51, flyleaf.
67 Dixon, *Unknown to Hist. and Fame*, 67.
68 Pike, *Dir. SW. Suss.* (1886–7).
69 *Kelly's Dir. Suss.* (1845 and later edns.).
70 Dixon, *Unknown to Hist. and Fame*, 63–4.
71 Pike, *Dir. SW. Suss.* (1886–7).
72 W.S.R.O., Par. 202/7/1, pamphlet relating to libr. 1811.
73 Dixon, *Unknown to Hist. and Fame*, 44–5; Pike, *Dir. SW. Suss.* (1886–7).
74 Dixon, *Unknown to Hist. and Fame*, 104–5; B.L. Add. MS. 39350, f. 237.
75 Dixon, *Unknown to Hist. and Fame*, 54.
76 Diary of Revd. W. P. Crawley, vicar 1899–1907, in possession of Mrs. M. G. Maloney, Chich.
77 Dixon, *Unknown to Hist. and Fame*, 44–5; below, church.

was erected in 1909 towards the eastern end of the Street at the expense of Mrs. Long of the Firs; though intended for general village use it always belonged to the church. There was a rifle range there,[78] and a Walberton miniature rifle club flourished between 1913 and 1920.[79]

The name Maypole field attached in 1847 to a close east of the Holly Tree inn[80] presumably alludes to past revelries. There was a cricket club by 1869, which used part of the field in 1889; a pavilion was erected in the following year.[81] In 1922 and presumably earlier the field belonged to the Avisford House estate.[82] A 6-a. close north of the cricket ground was sold to the parish council in 1928 for recreation.[83] Walberton green was also used for recreation including cricket and boxing by the late 19th century.[84]

A short-lived Walberton bonfire society was mentioned in 1905.[85]

W. G. Hunter, vicar 1915–37, patronized the village hall, the flower show, the boys' club, and the cricket and football clubs.[86] Since the 1970s, with the influx to the village of many outsiders, social organizations have proliferated, including clubs for badminton, stoolball, and table tennis, an operatic society, and a decorative and fine arts society. The Walberton horticultural society had 419 members in 1994.[87] The village hall was replaced in the 1980s by a building of brick and flint near the recreation ground.

The mission room at Fontwell was used for dances, youth club meetings, and other social events after 1930.[88] A community centre called Fontwell hall was opened in Arundel Road in 1989.[89]

PUBLIC SERVICES. Water in the past was provided by wells, which in dry weather in the late 19th century could be supplemented from the pond at Walberton green.[90] The Bognor Water Company constructed a reservoir in the north-west corner of the parish at Fontwell before 1910, and under an agreement of that year laid mains and supplied Walberton village street throughout its length.[91] Main drainage was installed from 1960.[92] Gas reached the village in 1903.[93] Avisford House had its own electricity supply in 1922,[94] and by *c.* 1937 the Bognor Gas and Electricity Company provided electricity more generally.[95] There was street lighting in the village from *c.* 1948.[96]

The high ground near Avisford was apparently a beacon site in the early 17th century or before.[97] An encampment of 'Clubmen' at Walberton in 1645 was dispersed by *c.* 50 horse and foot sent from Arundel castle, two 'malignant ministers' being captured and one person killed.[98]

The Prince Regent and Mrs. Fitzherbert visited Gen. John Whyte at Walberton House in the early 19th century.[99] Walberton was affected by the Swing riots of 1830, which Richard Prime of Walberton House had a hand in quelling.[1]

In 1988 a CARE community for the mentally handicapped moved from Petworth to a 20-a. site in Eastergate Lane. In 1989 there were 27 residents, each with a cottage.[2] A nursing home off Yapton Lane accepted both long- and short-stay patients in 1991.

MANOR AND OTHER ESTATES. The manor of *WALBERTON* was held in 1066 by three free men, and William held it of earl Roger in 1086.[3] Perhaps from that date and certainly from 1200, when Olive de St. John was dealing with it,[4] it descended as a member of Halnaker in Boxgrove[5] in the St. John and Poynings families, generally passing with Barnham[6] or Middleton,[7] other members of Halnaker, until 1429.[8] After the death in that year of Thomas Poynings, Lord St. John,[9] Walberton passed, like Halnaker, successively to his widow Maud (d. 1453) for her life,[10] to John Bonville, son of their granddaughter Joan[11] (d. 1494), and then to John's son-in-law Thomas West,[12] later Lord de la Warr, who with his wife Elizabeth gave both manors in 1540 to the Crown as part of an exchange.[13]

Members of the Racton family leased the Walberton demesnes between 1526[14] and 1609[15] or later. In 1611 the manor was granted by the Crown to Simon Stone,[16] after whose death in 1615[17] his executors sold it in 1616 to Thomas

78 W.S.R.O., Par. 202/43/1, f. [1]; *W. Suss. Gaz.* 13, 27 Jan. 1983; *Kelly's Dir. Suss.* (1913); illus. at J. Godfrey, *Arundel and Arun Valley in Old Photos.* 103.
79 W.S.R.O., Add. MSS. 16658–65 (TS. cat.).
80 Ibid. TD/W 133.
81 Dixon, *Unknown to Hist. and Fame*, 102–4; O.S. Map 6", Suss. LXII. NE. (1899 edn.).
82 W.S.R.O., SP 435.
83 Ibid. Par. 202/52/3.
84 Dixon, *Unknown to Hist. and Fame*, 4; cf. W.S.R.O., SP 490.
85 W.S.R.O., Par. 202/43/2.
86 Ibid. Par. 202/7/12; *Crockford* (1932).
87 *Bognor Regis Observer*, 10 Feb. 1994.
88 *Par. of Walberton* (Walberton par. council, 1994), [22].
89 *W. Suss. Gaz.* 16 Feb. 1989. For sports facilities available at Avisford Ho. after 1976, above, this section (parks); below, econ. hist. (other trades and inds.).
90 Dixon, *Unknown to Hist. and Fame*, 5.
91 W.S.R.O., Par. 202/54/1; Par. 202/54/14, p. 8; O.S. Map 6", Suss. LXII. NW. (1914 edn.); cf. F. H. Edmunds, *Wells and Springs of Suss.* 25.
92 *W. Suss. Gaz.* 15 Nov. 1990.
93 W.S.R.O., Par. 202/54/14, p. 7; cf. ibid. SP 303.
94 Ibid. SP 435.
95 *Residential Attractions of Bognor Regis, Felpham, Middleton-on-Sea and Dist.* (Gloucester, [1937]), 10 (copy in B.L.).
96 W.S.R.O., Par. 202/54/14, p. 13; cf. ibid. MP 814, f. [1].
97 Ibid. Par. 202/7/21.
98 C. Thomas-Stanford, *Suss. in Great Civil War*, 168–71; cf. W.S.R.O., Par. 202/1/1/1, f. 73v.
99 Dixon, *Unknown to Hist. and Fame*, 9.
1 Ibid. 12; *I am, My Dear Sir*, ed. F. W. Steer, 82–4.
2 *Bognor Regis Observer*, 27 Apr. 1989.
3 *V.C.H. Suss.* i. 431.
4 *Cur. Reg. R.* i. 214; cf. *S.R.S.* ii, p. 29.
5 *Cal. Inq. p.m.* iv, p. 62.
6 e.g. ibid. ii, p. 84; *Feud. Aids*, v. 143, 155; *S.R.S.* vii, p. 2.
7 e.g. *S.R.S.* xxiii, p. 157; P.R.O., C 131/50, no. 1.
8 Gerard de Lisle, who apparently held it in 1332, was the husband of Eliz., widow of Edmund St. John: *S.R.S.* x. 255; *Cal. Inq. p.m.* x, p. 472.
9 Above, Barnham, manor.
10 *Goodwood Estate Archives*, i, ed. F. W. Steer and J. Venables, p. 36; P.R.O., C 139/150, no. 28.
11 B.L. Add. MS. 39495, ff. 24–5.
12 *Cal. Inq. p.m. Hen. VII*, i, p. 455.
13 *L. & P. Hen. VIII*, xv, p. 176.
14 Ibid. xxi (2), p. 438; *Cal. Pat.* 1563–6, p. 169; 1578–80, p. 196.
15 P.R.O., SP 14/47, no. 75, f. 159.
16 W.S.R.O., Add. MS. 4272 (TS. cat.).
17 B.L. Add. MS. 39504, ff. 24, 25v.

Bennet[18] (created Bt. 1660; d. 1667). Bennet's son Levinus[19] with his wife Judith sold it in 1677 to Richard Nash,[20] a member of a family recorded in the parish since 1630,[21] who had perhaps been living in the manor house in 1670.[22] Richard was succeeded in 1680 or 1681 by his son John[23] (d. 1732), whose heir was his nephew Richard.[24] At Richard's death 1790[25] × 1794 he was succeeded by his son Gawen Richard,[26] who in 1801 conveyed Walberton to Gen. John Whyte.[27] After Whyte's death in 1816[28] his son and heir Alexander sold it in 1817 to Richard Prime;[29] by that date the estate comprised over 1,400 a.,[30] remaining about the same size in the mid 19th century.[31]

Richard Prime, a strong Tory (d. 1866), was M.P. for the western division of Sussex 1847–54 and the dominant figure in Walberton in his day. His son and heir (Capt.) Arthur (d. 1883) devised the reversion of the estate to his five illegitimate children.[32] Thereafter the manor house was let or unoccupied until in 1903 the estate was sold by Prime's trustees to Joseph Liddle, who lived at Walberton[33] until his death in 1930.[34] Part of the land was sold to the Avisford House estate in the early 20th century or before: Walberton farm in the south-east part of the parish (250 a.) by *c.* 1910,[35] Lower farm (72 a.) by 1917,[36] and Todhurst and Pigeon House farms (313 a.) between 1918 and 1922.[37]

By 1938 Walberton House and perhaps the remaining estate had passed to Liddle's son-in-law Percy G. Heywood.[38] In 1954 the house and *c.* 160 a. were bought by Frederick James Marquis, Viscount and later earl of Woolton (d. 1964), who resumed the Primes' role of squire;[39] after the death of his son and successor Roger in 1969 the house was again sold.[40]

There was a manor house at Walberton by 1302.[41] It or its successor was presumably either the house with nine hearths where Capt. Richard Nash lived in 1670, or that with seven where Thomas Nash lived at the same date.[42] The building which existed before the modern one stood north of the site of that and faced the lane to the church; it had a main front of late 17th-century character with seven bays, the central three recessed. Its south front as depicted in 1790 had a central Venetian window and flanking two-storeyed canted bays all apparently belonging to a mid 18th-century refacing. A lower range to the east shown in 1790, presumably accommodating service uses, may have incorporated earlier work.[43] The house in 1756 was approached through a walled forecourt entered from the lane to the church.[44]

Walberton House was rebuilt and greatly enlarged *c.* 1803 by Gen. Whyte, apparently to his own designs. Partly because of faulty construction,[45] it was replaced in 1817–18 by Richard Prime with a larger building on a new site designed in plain Greek Revival style by Sir Robert Smirke.[46] Of asymmetrical plan, it consisted of a main south-facing range of seven bays and an east-facing one of three bays. A one-storeyed Doric colonnade ran along the south and west fronts, and an octagonal entrance hall also of one storey was recessed in the south-east angle between the two main ranges. Two service ranges running north[47] were curtailed between 1910 and 1950.[48] The western section of the colonnade and the eastern bay of its southern section were removed *c.* 1960,[49] and at some point the entrance hall was replaced by a smaller lobby. In the early 1980s the house, renamed Walberton Park, was split into five apartments, the grand staircase hall, library, and dining room remaining undivided. At the same time a north-west wing containing eight more apartments was added in matching style.[50]

A garden was mentioned in 1362.[51] In 1756 large formal gardens adjoined the then manor house to south and south-east, including two square-plan areas each with diagonal paths and a round pond; there were then also shrubberies and a kitchen garden.[52] In 1902 the new house had two walled kitchen gardens, with a cucumber house, mushroom house, and vinery.[53] The former stables to the north were reconstructed for domestic use *c.* 1930 and from *c.* 1970 formed two dwellings called in 1993 Manor Lodge and West Manor Lodge. A new house called Walberton House was built in 1983 in the kitchen gardens; of low profile, it is topped by an 18th-century cupola brought from Farnham (Surr.).[54]

The hide less a yardland held of Walberton manor by Rolland in 1086 has not been identified, but if within the parish presumably lay

18 W.S.R.O., Add. MS. 4274 (TS. cat.); cf. ibid. 2299, pp. 2–[66], [68–9].
19 G.E.C. *Baronetage*, iii. 130.
20 W.S.R.O., Add. MS. 33376 (TS. cat.).
21 B.L. Add. MS. 5699, f. 131; cf. W.S.R.O., Add. MS. 4282 (TS. cat.); *Wiston Archives*, i, ed. J. Booker, p. 254.
22 Below, this section.
23 B.L. Add. MS. 39504, f. 23; W.S.R.O., Add. MS. 1013 (TS. cat.).
24 W.S.R.O., Add. MS. 4317.
25 *S.R.S.* xx. 457; cf. *Univ. Brit. Dir.* ii. 56.
26 *S.R.S.* li. 43; W.S.R.O., Add. MS. 11827 (TS. cat.).
27 *S.R.S.* xx. 457; Dallaway, *Hist. W. Suss.* ii (1) (1819), 73.
28 Mon. in ch.
29 Dallaway, op. cit. 73, 367.
30 W.S.R.O., Add. MS. 4354.
31 Ibid. TD/W 133; *Extracts from Inf. received by H.M. Com. as to Admin. and Operation of Poor Laws* (1833), 72 (B.L. class mark B.S. 68/2); each giving acreage in the par. only.
32 B. Dixon, *Unknown to Hist. and Fame*, 13–15; mons. in ch. and chyd.
33 *Kelly's Dir. Suss.* (1887 and later edns.); diary of Revd. W. P. Crawley, vicar 1899–1907, in possession of Mrs. M. G. Maloney, Chich.
34 Mon. in chyd.
35 W.S.R.O., IR 12, f. 34.
36 Ibid. SP 434.
37 Ibid. 303, 435.
38 *Kelly's Dir. Suss.* (1938); inf. from Mr. J. Eyre, Walberton Park.
39 *The Times*, 15 Dec. 1964; inf. from Mr. Eyre.
40 *The Times*, 8 Jan. 1969; *Daily Telegraph*, 7 Jan. 1970.
41 P.R.O., C 133/105, no. 6, m. 2.
42 Ibid. E 179/191/410, pt. 2, rot. 2d.
43 B.L. Add. MS. 5678, f. 28.
44 W.S.R.O., Add. MS. 1802.
45 Dallaway, *Hist. W. Suss.* ii (1) (1819), 73, 367.
46 Dallaway & Cartwright, *Hist. W. Suss.* ii (1) (1832), 78.
47 Horsfield, *Hist. Suss.* ii, facing p. 117; W.S.R.O., SP 1264, facing p. 4.
48 O.S. Map 6", Suss. LXII. NE. (1914, 1951 edns.).
49 Colvin, *Biog. Dict. Brit. Architects*, 745.
50 Sale cats. 1981, 1983 (copies at N.M.R.); *W. Suss. Gaz.* 27 May 1982.
51 P.R.O., C 135/174, no. 14, m. 2.
52 W.S.R.O., Add. MS. 1802.
53 Ibid. SP 1264.
54 *W. Suss. Gaz.* 14 Jan. 1988; inf. from Mr. J. Eyre, Walberton Park.

in the north-east since the yardland had been incorporated since 1066 in Arundel Great park.[55]

Thomas Fowler (d. 1772)[56] had manorial freeholds totalling 88 a. in 1747[57] on which before 1756 he built what became *AVISFORD HOUSE*;[58] his son and namesake sold the house and 80 a. in 1780 to William Halsted,[59] from whom it had passed by 1787 to Adm. (Sir) George Montagu, later commander-in-chief at Portsmouth.[60] In 1811 Montagu sold the estate to Gen. Sir William Houston, and by 1819 it had grown to *c.* 120 a.[61] Apparently in 1834 and certainly before 1838 it passed to (Lt.-Gen.) Sir Thomas Reynell, Bt. (d. 1848),[62] and in 1847 it comprised 142 a.[63] Thomas's widow Lady Elizabeth Reynell and their son-in-law Sir John Anson, Bt., were living at the house in 1851–2, but at Elizabeth's death in 1856 the estate passed to her son Lt.-Col. Arthur John Pack, who added the surname Reynell in 1857 and died in 1860. His widow and heir Frederica Reynell Pack and their son Arthur D. H. H. Reynell Pack[64] sold it in 1883 to William H. Boswall Preston,[65] whose heir Thomas H. Boswall Preston conveyed it in 1892 to (Lt.-Col.) C. P. Henty.[66] He enlarged the estate by buying Walberton farm in the south-east corner of the parish (250 a.) before *c.* 1910[67] and the adjacent Lower farm (72 a.) by 1917.[68]

In 1917 or 1918 Henty sold the estate, by then *c.* 650 a. in Walberton and Eastergate, to Edgar C. Fairweather.[69] He further enlarged it before 1922 to 1,385 a., for instance by the purchase of Todhurst and Pigeon House farms (313 a.),[70] and was still one of two chief landowners in the parish in 1927.[71] From 1928 until 1973 Avisford House was used as a Roman Catholic boys' preparatory school which had 60–90 pupils.[72] In 1976 it was bought with *c.* 40 a. by Mr. Tony Pagett-Fynn for conversion to a hotel and country club;[73] he sold it in 1994 with 62 a. to Stakis PLC.[74]

A house at Avisford existed by 1756.[75] Its appearance then seems likely to be represented by a drawing of 1790 showing a main north-facing block of nine bays and two storeys with a hipped roof, and service outbuildings to the east.[76] The site had been chosen for its wide view of the coastal plain including the Isle of Wight. The house was enlarged in the mid 19th century, notably on the south-west.[77] Much interior redecoration is probably of that date; it includes a one-storeyed billiard room on the south front and the stone main staircase with cast-iron balustrading. In 1883 the ground floor also had a domed entrance porch, a conservatory, a library, and a dining room with French windows to a paved colonnade; on a mezzanine floor were two communicating drawing rooms facing south and west, the latter with a domed ceiling.[78] Extensive additions were made for the hotel after 1976, raising the number of bedrooms by 1994 to 126 and incorporating large facilities for leisure activities and conferences.[79]

There were pleasure grounds, a kitchen garden, and a shrubbery in 1756.[80] The kitchen garden lay south of the house in 1847,[81] and in 1883 there were two vineries, besides rhododendrons and evergreen shrubs around the house.[82] By 1922, when the pleasure grounds were described as fully mature, there were glasshouses and a bamboo garden.[83] The walled kitchen garden and one vinery survived in 1995.

The *RECTORY* estate, including woodland called Hiefalde, two thirds of the great tithes, and rents from free and villein tenants, belonged to Boxgrove priory between the 12th century and the Dissolution;[84] it was valued at £12 in 1291[85] and leased in the 1530s[86] and presumably before. It was granted by the Crown in 1561 to the bishop of Chichester[87] and regularly leased thereafter, for 21 years in 1570[88] and for three lives after that, the lease descending between 1760 and the mid 19th century with the manor.[89] By 1839 the estate comprised only tithes, including some from Yapton.[90]

Small areas of land in Walberton belonged in the Middle Ages to the dean and chapter of Chichester cathedral,[91] Tortington[92] and Shulbrede priories,[93] and apparently Barnham chantry.[94]

In 1847 the only estates in Walberton more than 40 a. in area which did not belong to the two chief landowners were in the north: 101 a.

55 *V.C.H. Suss.* i. 431.
56 52 Geo. III, c. 123 (Private).
57 W.S.R.O., Add. MS. 2299, p. [106].
58 Ibid. Add. MS. 1802.
59 Ibid. Raper MSS., deed, 1780.
60 Ibid. QDE/2/1, Walberton, 1787; *D.N.B.*; cf. B.L. Add. MS. 5674, f. 39; 52 Geo. III, c. 123 (Private).
61 *S.A.C.* lxxi. 54; Dallaway, *Hist. W. Suss.* ii (1) (1819), 74.
62 W.S.R.O., SP 1263, p. [11]; Burke, *Land. Gent.* (1914), 1444; *Bognor Guide* (Petworth, 1838), 77 (copy in Chich. Ref. Libr.).
63 W.S.R.O., TD/W 133.
64 Burke, *Land. Gent.* (1914), 1444; *Kelly's Dir. Suss.* (1852); P.R.O., HO 107/1652, f. 303v.
65 Lincs. Archives, BRA 10287/1, sale cat. 1883, including contract for purchase.
66 W.S.R.O., Raper MSS., schedule of Avisford Ho. estate documents handed over, 1892; *Kelly's Dir. Suss.* (1895, 1905).
67 W.S.R.O., IR 12, f. 34.
68 Ibid. SP 434.
69 Ibid.; *Kelly's Dir. Suss.* (1915, 1918).
70 W.S.R.O., SP 303, 435.
71 *Kelly's Dir. Suss.* (1927).
72 *W. Suss. Gaz.* 15 Mar. 1973; Archives of Dioc. of Arundel and Brighton, Bishop's Ho., Hove, Arundel and Slindon par. files.
73 *W. Suss. Gaz.* 14 Apr. 1977; 11 Apr. 1990.
74 *Bognor Regis Observer*, 19 May 1994.
75 W.S.R.O., Add. MS. 1802.
76 B.L. Add. MS. 5674, f. 39, illus. below, pl. facing p. 234.
77 W.S.R.O., TD/W 133; O.S. Map 6", Suss. LXII (1880 edn.).
78 W.S.R.O., SP 1263; B. Dixon, *Unknown to Hist. and Fame*, 20.
79 *W. Suss. Gaz.* 19 Dec. 1985; 9 Apr. 1987; *Bognor Regis Observer*, 19 May 1994; below, econ. hist. (other trades and inds.).
80 W.S.R.O., Add. MS. 1802.
81 Ibid. TD/W 133.
82 Ibid. SP 1263.
83 Ibid. 435.
84 *S.R.S.* lix, pp. 17, 25–6; *V.C.H. Suss.* i. 431; P.R.O., E 106/8/19, rot. 8.
85 *Tax. Eccl.* (Rec. Com.), 135.
86 *Valor Eccl.* (Rec. Com.), i. 306.
87 *Cal. Pat.* 1560–3, 33.
88 *S.R.S.* lviii, p. 74.
89 Ibid. xx. 457; B.L. Add. MS. 5699, f. 131; W.S.R.O., Add. MS. 4353; ibid. Ep. VI/56/18.
90 W.S.R.O., Ep. VI/57/6.
91 *Cal. Pat.* 1413–16, 301; *S.R.S.* xlvi, p. 86; lii, p. 96.
92 *Cal. Pat.* 1340–3, 575; cf. P.R.O., C 142/269, no. 100.
93 *Inq. Non.* (Rec. Com.), 375; *S.A.C.* lxxxix. 159.
94 *Cal. Pat.* 1321–4, 434.

owned by William, George, and John Halsted[95] and 84 a., chiefly woods, belonging to John Abel Smith of Dale Park in Madehurst. The Dale Park estate continued to own land in the north part in 1883.[96]

ECONOMIC HISTORY. AGRICULTURE. Walberton manor demesne farm had three ploughs in 1086, and six *servi*.[97] It continued to be the chief farm in the parish until the 17th century. In 1302 there were 341 a. of arable and 5 a. of meadow,[98] and in 1362 there were 318 a. of arable and 10 a. of meadow besides pasture for cows, sheep, and apparently horses;[99] in the mid 15th century the arable was expressed as four ploughlands.[1] In 1543 the farm was leased for 21 years[2] and in 1580 for three lives; in 1609 it had 309 a.[3] and in 1630 it had 351 a.[4] Already by 1543 there were at least 163 a. of demesne land besides, leased to others;[5] by 1630, evidently through engrossing, the total was nearly 300 a.[6]

In 1756 the manor demesnes seem to have included three chief farms worked from houses in or near the village street, the two largest belonging to the buildings later called Park House (the modern Dower House) (363 a.) and Friars Oak (186 a.) at Walberton green.[7] About 1817 the Walberton House estate included Home or Pigeon House farm (289 a.), Choller farm (261 a.), 'East farm' (188 a.), Common farm at Fontwell (186 a.), Todhurst farm (125 a.), 'Walberton Street farm' (79 a.), and an unnamed holding (151 a.); Home and East farms were held together, as were Choller and Common farms.[8] In 1847 there were five chief holdings: Pigeon House or Dairy farm (187 a.), Choller and Common farms (429 a.), Todhurst farm (140 a.), the modern Walberton and Lower farms (248 a.), and an unnamed farm attached to a house near the Holly Tree inn (67 a.).[9] Other farms of 142 a. and 97 a. were worked at the same date from Avisford House and Woodlands in Arundel Road respectively.[10]

There were 19 *villani* and 13 cottars on Walberton manor in 1086,[11] and in 1302 there were 10 free tenants, 23 customary tenants, all but one holding a single yardland, and 19 cottars. Each customary tenant then rendered 1½*d.* at Michaelmas and a hen or hens, and owed work service every day except Sundays and feast days at harvest time, and five days a month during the rest of the year.[12]

The cottars' lands were apparently later regarded as copyholds.[13] By 1609 eight freeholders had estates of up to 38 a., totalling perhaps less than 100 a. in all; of the 32 copyhold tenants many had a single yardland (14–16 a.) and some one and a half or two yardlands. All copyholds in 1609 were held for lives.[14] There had been some rationalization by 1630, when six freeholders had estates of between 5 a. and 46 a. and 17 copyholders estates of between 6 a. and 37 a.; at that date there were also 10 cottagers.[15] Some freehold and copyhold tenements lay in Yapton in 1543.[16] By 1555 at least one tenant was a non-parishioner.[17] Copyholds could be sublet by 1594.[18]

By the mid 18th century, evidently after much enfranchisement, there were *c.* 20 freeholders and *c.* 8 copyholders besides other tenants of uncertain status; four freeholds were over 40 a. in area but copyholds were smaller.[19] In the absence of manorial records after the later 18th century the further process of enfranchisement is unclear.

On the hide less a yardland held of Walberton manor by Rolland in 1086 there were two *villani* and four cottars,[20] while Boxgrove priory's rectory estate had two or more villeins in the 1180s.[21] By 1204 at least one freeholder held of the priory,[22] and there were more freeholders later.[23] In 1630 the former Boxgrove lands lay in two holdings of 47 a. and 65 a. which were considered as freeholds of Walberton manor.[24] Sawyers Dean, comprising 60–80 a. including woodland in the north-east, belonged to Ford, Climping, and Ilsham manor.[25]

Open fields lay scattered around the central and southern parts of the parish in the Middle Ages:[26] the Hempshard,[27] the Gaston or Garston,[28] and the Sinder or Sinders north and north-east of the village centre; Stone Lee and Pendall or the Pendolls east of Yapton Lane; the Todder, Tedworth, or Todhurst in the south; Puthurst

95 W.S.R.O., TD/W 133.
96 Ibid. SP 1263, plan.
97 *V.C.H. Suss.* i. 431.
98 P.R.O., C 133/105, no. 6, m. 2.
99 Ibid. C 135/174, no. 14, m. 2.
1 Ibid. C 139/150, no. 28.
2 Ibid. SC 6/Hen. VIII/3483, rot. 35d.
3 Ibid. SP 14/47, no. 75, ff. 159–160v.
4 W.S.R.O., Add. MS. 2301, m. 1.
5 P.R.O., SC 6/Hen. VIII/3483, rot. 35d.
6 W.S.R.O., Add. MS. 2301, mm. 1–2.
7 Ibid. 1802; cf. ibid. 2299, pp. [106–10], apparently showing those fms. as neither freehold nor copyhold in 1747.
8 W.S.R.O., Add. MS. 4354.
9 Ibid. TD/W 133. The last was apparently called Church fm. in 1851: P.R.O., HO 107/1652, f. 311v.; cf. *Kelly's Dir. Suss.* (1862, 1866). Shipleys fm. mentioned in 1840 was probably Todhurst fm. since Lake Lane on which it stood was alternatively Shipley Lane: W.S.R.O., Add. MS. 4356 (TS. cat.); above, intro. (communications).
10 W.S.R.O., TD/W 133.
11 *V.C.H. Suss.* i. 431.
12 P.R.O., C 133/105, no. 6, m. 2; cf. ibid. C 135/174, no. 14, m. 2.
13 e.g. ibid. SP 14/47, no. 75, ff. 150–7; W.S.R.O., Add. MSS. 1802; 2301, m. 3.
14 P.R.O., SP 14/47, no. 75, ff. 127–57; cf. W.S.R.O., Add. MS. 12841 (TS. cat.). The copyhold yardland of 39 a. mentioned must be a mistake: P.R.O., SP 14/47, no. 75, f. 132.
15 W.S.R.O., Add. MS. 2301, mm. 2–4, not including vicarage and 2 former Boxgrove priory holdings listed among freeholds; for latter cf. below, this section.
16 P.R.O., SC 6/Hen. VIII/3483, rot. 35 and d.; cf. ibid. SC 12/15, no. 54.
17 *S.A.C.* xii. 103.
18 A.C.M., M 532, f. [9] from end; cf. W.S.R.O., Add. MS. 2299, f. 6.
19 W.S.R.O., Add. MSS. 1802; 2299, pp. [106–10]; cf. ibid. 5156.
20 *V.C.H. Suss.* i. 431.
21 *S.R.S.* lix, p. 26; cf. P.R.O., E 106/8/19, rot. 8.
22 *S.R.S.* lix, p. 155.
23 *Inq. Non.* (Rec. Com.), 375; *L. & P. Hen. VIII*, xii (1), p. 1.
24 W.S.R.O., Add. MS. 2301, m. 4.
25 e.g. P.R.O., SC 6/Hen. VIII/3480, rot. 16; Guildhall Libr. MS. 13321, ff. 42–3.
26 Para. based mainly on P.R.O., SC 6/Hen. VIII/3483, rot. 35d.; W.S.R.O., Add. MSS. 1802; 2301, mm. 1–4; ibid. Par. 202/7/21; ibid. TD/W 133; evidently representing the pre-16th-cent. situation. The 'com. fields' of Walberton were mentioned in 1356: *S.R.S.* lix, p. 16.
27 Cf. P.R.O., SP 14/47, no. 75, ff. 137, 141.
28 Ibid. f. 128; W.S.R.O., Add. MS. 284 (TS. cat.).

WALBERTON:
AVISFORD HOUSE FROM THE NORTH IN 1790

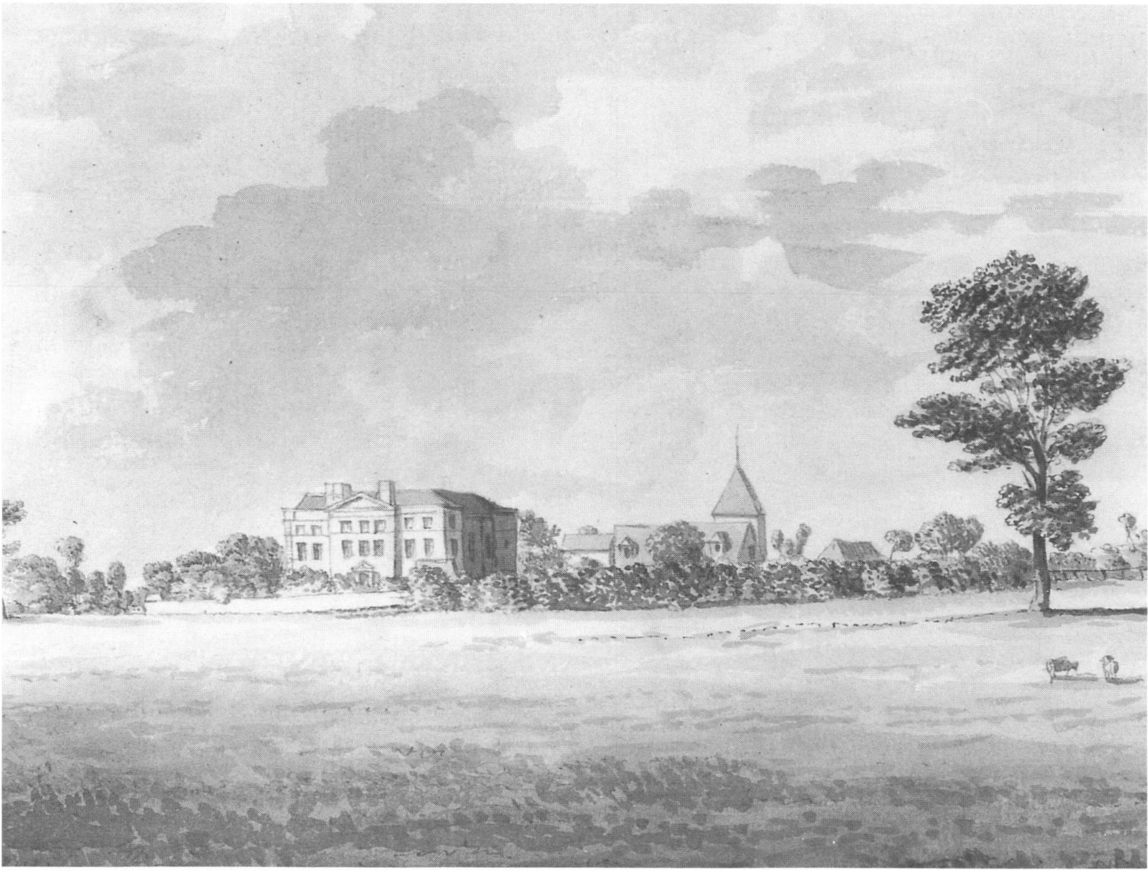

YAPTON:
YAPTON PLACE AND THE CHURCH FROM THE NORTH-WEST IN 1782

Tortington:
THE 12TH-CENTURY FONT IN THE CHURCH

Felpham:
THE 12TH-CENTURY FONT IN THE CHURCH

Binsted:
MEDIEVAL WALL PAINTING IN THE CHURCH

Tortington:
THE 12TH-CENTURY SOUTH DOORWAY OF THE CHURCH,
in its fourth location

east of Barnham Lane; and the Chollers, Chalder, or Choleworth,[29] and the Breach, Beech, or Birch[30] west of it; the name of the latter suggests reclamation from waste land.[31] Prestcroft, described as near Avisford in the early 13th century, may have lain along Mill Road,[32] while the Tye, mentioned in the Middle Ages and later, presumably lay beside the common.[33] Northeldfield recorded in 1404[34] and the Rye hammes mentioned in the early 17th century[35] are unlocated, though the latter presumably lay on poorer soil suitable for rye. It is not clear whether the Furze field mentioned in 1556 was an open field.[36]

Parts at least of the fields had been inclosed by 1543, when closes of between 5 a. and 25 a. were mentioned in four of them.[37] By the early 17th century most of the fields lay in parcels of between 2 a. and 8 a. which were either long and narrow or roughly square, each manorial tenement continuing to have land in various areas of the parish.[38] Some land formerly open arable had by then been converted to pasture, a trend that continued later.[39]

There was common meadow in the lower-lying south-west and south-east parts of the parish. Eastmead or the East meads east of Barnham Lane was mentioned *c.* 1291[40] and Westmead or the West meads west of the same road in 1609.[41] Broadmead[42] and Little meads[43] mentioned from the 16th and early 17th century respectively have not been located, but the former may be partly represented by the Pendolls mead and Withy mead in the south-east mentioned in 1630.[44] In the early 17th century the home farm, copyholds, and freeholds all had parcels in those common meadows, mostly under 2 a. in area.[45]

The chief common pasture was Walberton common in the north, which abutted Eastergate and Slindon commons. It is not clear whether it offered the grazing for oxen, cows, and pigs to which Boxgrove priory was entitled in the mid 12th century.[46] In 1609 it was divided into East heath and West heath, each of 80 a.,[47] the division apparently being made by the land called Mackrells brooks, the modern Ashbeds wood, which existed as a demesne inclosure apparently by 1585.[48] Two other inclosures had been made by 1630 at the western end:[49] pasture and woodland called the Wenlasse or Wandlass between the modern Wandleys and West Walberton lanes recorded from 1543[50] and land west of Wandleys Lane called the new inclosure. The 18 demesne closes called the Heath crofts totalling 32 a. apparently represent intakes along the southern edge of the common.[51] In 1630 and in 1756 two areas in the west and north-east respectively were disputed with Eastergate and Slindon manors; judgment in each case was evidently given against Walberton, since the areas concerned remained outside the parish. Shellbridge common in the north-east corner named in 1630 had presumably been commonable in the Middle Ages by tenants of Shulbrede priory.[52]

In 1609 tenants of Walberton manor could put all sorts of cattle on the East heath, while sharing the West heath with tenants of other lords.[53] Overstocking and illegal encroachments were presented in the 1590s; in 1598 grazing rights were fixed at three beasts, two horses, and 20 sheep for each yardland.[54] Encroachments were still controlled in the 17th and 18th centuries.[55] In 1769 the common comprised 256 a. The lord of the manor was then entitled to at least four fifths of the grazing either as lord or as owner of former manorial tenements; others who had rights included Thomas Fowler of Avisford House and the vicar. Since, however, those rights had apparently been very little exercised for a long time and the common was of little advantage to any of the commoners it was inclosed in that year, the lord receiving 120 a. at the west end, the vicar 7 a. on the Slindon boundary, and 23 other parties allotments of between 1 a. and 20 a.[56]

Walberton green at the west end of the village where roads diverged to Barnham, Eastergate, and Fontwell is recorded from 1585.[57] In the 17th century it extended further south-east than later.[58] Nothing is known of grazing rights before the late 19th century when villagers seem to have had free use of it. Fences were erected *c.* 1890 to prevent access by gypsies, and the

29 *S.R.S.* lix, pp. 16, 193.
30 P.R.O., SP 14/47, no. 75, f. 141.
31 J. Field, *Eng. Field Names*, 27.
32 *S.R.S.* lix, p. 77; below, this section (mills).
33 *S.R.S.* lix, p. 193; *P.N. Suss.* (E.P.N.S.), i. 144; P.R.O., SP 14/47, no. 75, ff. 129, 132; W.S.R.O., Add. MSS. 8525, 33378 (TS. cat.).
34 *S.A.C.* lxxxix. 159.
35 P.R.O., SP 14/47, no. 75, ff. 130, 132–3; W.S.R.O., Add. MS. 2301, mm. 1–2.
36 *S.R.S.* lxxiv, p. 58.
37 P.R.O., SC 6/Hen. VIII/3483, rot. 35d.
38 Ibid. SP 14/47, no. 75, ff. 128–51, 159–60; W.S.R.O., Add. MS. 2301, mm. 1–4; ibid. Par. 202/7/21.
39 P. Brandon, 'Com. Lands and Wastes of Suss.' (Lond. Univ. Ph.D. thesis, 1963), 312–13; W.S.R.O., Add. MS. 1802.
40 A.C.M., M 54, m. 2; W.S.R.O., Add. MS. 2301, m. 1; ibid. Par. 202/7/21.
41 P.R.O., SP 14/47, no. 75, ff. 133, 135, 139; W.S.R.O., Add. MS. 1802.
42 P.R.O., SP 14/47, no. 75, ff. 129, 132–3, 160; W.S.R.O., Add. MSS. 12841, 33378 (TS. cat.); ibid. S.A.S. MS. B 645 (TS. cat.).
43 W.S.R.O., Add. MS. 2301, m. 3.
44 Ibid. Add. MSS. 1802; 2301, m. 1; ibid. Par. 202/7/21; cf. P.R.O., SC 6/Hen. VIII/3483, rot. 35d. Marshland pasture for cattle apparently in Walberton was mentioned in 1431: W.S.R.O., Add. MS. 37986 (TS. cat.).
45 P.R.O., SP 14/47, no. 75, ff. 129–60, *passim*; W.S.R.O., Add. MS. 2301, mm. 1–4; cf. ibid. Ep. I/25/1 (1615).
46 *S.R.S.* lix, p. 48.
47 P.R.O., SP 14/47, no. 75, f. 164.
48 Ibid. E 310/25/145, f. 50; W.S.R.O., Add. MS. 2301, m. 1; ibid. Par. 202/7/21.
49 W.S.R.O., Par. 202/7/21.
50 Ibid.; P.R.O., SC 6/Hen. VIII/3483, rot. 35d.; cf. ibid. E 310/15/65, f. 30; ibid. SP 14/47, no. 75, f. 162.
51 W.S.R.O., Add. MS. 2301, m. 1; ibid. Par. 202/7/21; cf. ibid. Add. MS. 1802, recording field name Com. croft there; ibid. Ep. I/25/1 (1615).
52 Ibid. Add. MS. 1802; ibid. Par. 202/7/21; above, manor.
53 P.R.O., SP 14/47, no. 75, f. 164.
54 A.C.M., M 532, ff. [67 and v., 86v.–87] from end.
55 W.S.R.O., Add. MS. 2299, pp. 19, 21, [105].
56 Ibid. Add. MSS. 2299, *passim*, for disuse of com. rights; 5156; 9 Geo. III, c. 20 (Priv. Act).
57 P.R.O., E 310/25/145, f. 50; cf. W.S.R.O., Add. MS. 8236 (TS. cat.).
58 W.S.R.O., Par. 202/7/21; O.S. Map 6", Suss. LXII (1880 edn.).

grazing was let by the manor estate at a nominal rent; grazing continued until the mid 20th century and most of the fencing remained in 1994.[59] Sheep were washed in the pond on the green in the 19th and early 20th centuries.[60] The green was registered as a village green in 1967, the registration becoming final in 1971.[61]

Walberton manor in 1086 had 14 a. of several meadow,[62] but the 100 a. of pasture mentioned in the 15th century[63] may describe Walberton common. Several meadow in later centuries included the demesne close called the Tithing mead (3 a.), the first cut from which was usually awarded to the vicar *c.* 1630 in lieu of tithe hay.[64] Several demesne pasture included the Best pasture (18 a.) north of Lake Lane.[65]

Crops grown in 1341 included hemp, flax, apples, and pears; sheep, cows, pigs, and geese were then raised.[66] In the 17th and 18th centuries wheat was the most common crop, others regularly recorded being barley, oats, peas, beans, hemp, tares, and vetch.[67] Hops were apparently grown in 1644. Buckwheat was mentioned in 1687, clover seed in 1748,[68] and turnips in 1776.[69] Cattle, sheep, and pigs were widely kept in the same period; at least three farmers before 1700 had flocks of over 100 sheep, and one in 1726 had 476. Geese, hens, ducks, and a turkey were mentioned on one holding in 1670.[70] All the copyholds recorded in 1609 had much more arable than several pasture, presumably because tenants then still used the common wastes.[71]

In the first half of the 19th century arable remained dominant: in 1819 most of the parish was said to be under crops[72] and in 1847 there were over 1,100 a. of arable to 325 a. of meadow and pasture.[73] Wheat was still the chief crop in 1801,[74] when there were no fatting oxen, apparently 784 sheep, and 235 pigs.[75] Steam cultivation was possibly introduced *c.* 1860, and in 1881 for the first time most corn was cut by machinery.[76] In the mid 19th century many parishioners worked as labourers for the seven or eight landowners, of whom the most important were resident; some in 1867, however, worked in Madehurst.[77] A shepherd, a cowherd, and a cow keeper were recorded in 1851.[78]

By 1875, though arable remained important, with returns of 624 a. of wheat, barley, oats, and peas and 294 a. of other crops, the area of grassland had increased to *c.* 500 a., 1,218 sheep and lambs being listed.[79] The Avisford House home farm in 1883 had a small area of arable, and grazing meadow and park pasture highly suitable for both fattening cattle and dairying.[80] There was one dairy farmer by 1887, two in the early 20th century, and a pig dealer in 1895.[81] Arable acreage returned had dropped to 721 a. by 1909, when that of grassland had risen to 670 a. and the largest corn crop was oats. At the latter date there was seven times as much rented as owner-occupied land, five holdings having between 50 a. and 300 a. and one more than 300 a.[82] On the Walberton House estate in the early 20th century were Pigeon House and Todhurst farms, held together as 313 a. in 1918, and Choller farm, of 173 a. in 1902,[83] while the Avisford House estate included Walberton and Lower farms in the south-east corner and Wandleys farm in the north-west in the 1910s.[84] In 1922, when there were a dairy farm and a stud farm on the Avisford House estate, much of its agricultural land was in hand.[85] Most farms in the early 20th century practised mixed agriculture. Todhurst and Pigeon House farms in 1918 were claimed to produce very heavy corn crops, and the Avisford House estate ran a successful sheep flock and Shorthorn herd in 1922. After 1923 Pigeon House farm was centred on its dairy herd, which increased beyond the carrying capacity of the farm so that cattle were driven up to 20 miles afield for summer grazing. Sheep, pigs, and poultry were also kept there at that time.[86]

Allotment land west of Walberton green was let to the parish council by the owners of Choller farm in 1917.[87] After *c.* 1918 the county council as landowner let 205 a. in the south-west corner of the parish as smallholdings; in 1920 seven were of 5 a. or less and six others between 10 a. and 49 a.[88] There were eight smallholders in 1938[89] and some remained in 1995.[90] There was a poultry breeder in 1922 and there were two in the 1930s.[91]

In 1985 holdings listed in the parish emphasized pasture farming rather than arable, among stock returned being 551 cattle kept chiefly for milking and 3,794 head of poultry, mostly hens for laying. Of the non-horticultural enterprises

59 W.S.R.O., Par. 202/7/5, Revd. W. H. Irvine to Ric. Holmes, 9 Jan. 1891, and reply, 12 Jan. 1891; B. Dixon, *Unknown to Hist. and Fame*, 5–6; *Par. of Walberton* (Walberton par. council, 1994), [26–7].

60 *Par. of Walberton*, [30]; Dixon, *Unknown to Hist. and Fame*, 4; W.S.R.O., Add. MS. 836 (TS. cat.).

61 W. Suss. C.C. property dept., reg. of village greens.

62 *V.C.H. Suss.* i. 431; cf. P.R.O., C 133/105, no. 6, m. 2; C 139/150, no. 28.

63 P.R.O., C 139/39, no. 34; C 139/150, no. 28.

64 Ibid. SC 6/Hen. VIII/3483, rot. 35d.; ibid. SP 14/47, no. 75, f. 159; W.S.R.O., Add. MS. 2301, m. 1.

65 W.S.R.O., Add. MS. 1802; ibid. Par. 202/7/21; ibid. TD/W 133.

66 *Inq. Non.* (Rec. Com.), 375.

67 P.R.O., E 134/13 Wm. III Mich./20; W.S.R.O., Ep. I/29/202; *S.R.S.* xlix. 81; cf. Young, *Agric. of Suss.* 100–1.

68 W.S.R.O., Ep. I/29/202/24, 52, 78.

69 Dallaway, *Hist. W. Suss.* ii (1) (1819), 74 n.

70 W.S.R.O., Ep. I/29/202.

71 P.R.O., SP 14/47, no. 75, ff. 132–49, excluding copyhold cottages.

72 Dallaway, *Hist. W. Suss.* ii (1) (1819), 72.

73 W.S.R.O., TD/W 133.

74 *L. & I. Soc.* cxcv. 36.

75 E.S.R.O., LCG/3/EW 1, f. [43v.]; cf. ibid. f. [84v.].

76 Dixon, *Unknown to Hist. and Fame*, 94.

77 *Census*, 1831; *Rep. Com. on Children and Women in Agric.* 87–8.

78 P.R.O., HO 107/1652, ff. 302 and v., 317v.

79 Ibid. MAF 68/433.

80 W.S.R.O., SP 1263.

81 *Kelly's Dir. Suss.* (1887 and later edns.); Pigeon Ho. fm. had been called Dairy fm. in 1847: W.S.R.O., TD/W 133.

82 P.R.O., MAF 68/2371.

83 W.S.R.O., IR 12, ff. 33–4; ibid. SP 303, 1264.

84 Ibid. IR 12, ff. 34, 47; ibid. SP 434.

85 Ibid. SP 435.

86 Ibid. 303, 434–5, 1264; N. Wyatt, *An Ever-Rolling Stream* (Pulborough, 1993), 13, 31–2.

87 W.S.R.O., Par. 202/52/1–2; cf. ibid. Par. 202/49/1, pp. 231–2.

88 Ibid. Add. MS. 6097, plan of smallholdings, 1920; ibid. SP 303; cf. Wyatt, op. cit. 14.

89 *Kelly's Dir. Suss.* (1938).

90 Inf. from Mr. J. Eyre, Walberton Park; cf. *Southern Wkly. News*, 2 Dec. 1955.

91 *Kelly's Dir. Suss.* (1922 and later edns.); cf. *Par. of Walberton* (Walberton par. council, 1994), [22].

analysed two were specialist dairy holdings and one mainly so. Most land was evidently worked from farms outside the parish.[92] Pigeon House farm in 1995 had 160 a., chiefly arable with some grassland used by dairy cattle from Barnham Court farm.[93] Choller farm at the same date kept both dairy and beef cattle together with milking ewes; it comprised 76 a. with another 90 a. of grazing in other places.[94]

MARKET GARDENING. A market gardener was recorded in 1851 at Fontwell, and parishioners described as gardeners at the same date may have been involved in the same activity.[95] Half an acre of orchard was listed in 1875.[96] The baker Harry Hartley was a fruit grower too by 1895; his nursery was at the east end of the village street and had seven glasshouses on its 1½ a. in 1904, but it seems to have ceased to exist soon afterwards.[97] John Goodacre founded a market-gardening business at Fontwell by 1899,[98] also growing fruit by 1910.[99]

In 1909 there were 2 a. of small fruit and *c.* 3 a. of orchards in the parish.[1] The industry expanded greatly in the 1930s, and in 1938, besides Goodacres, there were a fruit grower, four nurserymen, and a firm called Todhurst nurseries, occupying land along Eastergate Lane in the west and Barnham and Yapton lanes in the south.[2] The site of Goodacres nursery was later largely built over.[3]

There was further expansion after the mid 20th century. The 26 ha. (64 a.) of horticultural crops listed in 1985 included 17 ha. of vegetables grown under glass and 2 ha. of orchards and small fruit. Eight general horticultural holdings and one chiefly involved in fruit growing were returned in that year, when market gardening evidently accounted for most of the 374 people listed as working on the land. In 1993 market gardens and glasshouses, some producing flowers, continued to occupy much land between Yapton and Lake lanes in the south and around Eastergate and Barnham lanes in the west.[4]

MILLS. Mill tithes from Walberton were taken by Tortington priory in the Middle Ages.[5] There seems to have been a water mill in the south-west corner of the parish, where a field name Mill mead is recorded in 1630 and later;[6] that may have been the ruined water mill mentioned in 1609.[7] About 1217 Boxgrove priory was granted land in a field called Prestcroft near Avisford to build a windmill;[8] the site may be that of the later mill in Mill Road. The other later windmill site east of Walberton green may also have been in use by 1565 when the surname Westmill was recorded.[9] There were two mills during the 19th century,[10] a post mill at Avisford[11] and a smock mill at Walberton green.[12] The occupiers of both were also bakers *c.* 1832[13] and often later.[14] Charles Gardiner of the mill in Mill Road farmed 25 a. in 1851.[15] That mill had gone by 1896; the other had then apparently ceased to be used[16] and was demolished, except for part of its base, soon afterwards.[17]

FAIR. In the later 19th century a 'gypsy fair' was held on 29 May at the Royal Oak inn and there were horse sales on Sunday afternoons at Walberton green.[18]

OTHER TRADES AND INDUSTRIES. Trades specifically mentioned or suggested by surnames in the Middle Ages were those of carpenter,[19] wheelwright, and smith.[20] Additional occupations recorded between the 16th century and the late 18th were mostly connected with food,[21] clothing,[22] and building or construction.[23] The site of the forge mentioned in 1537[24] is not known, but may have been at the junction of the village street with Yapton Lane where there was a smithy by 1635.[25] In 1677 a forge stood next to an alehouse which may have been on the site of the Royal Oak inn at Avisford or Balls hut at Fontwell.[26] A shovel maker was mentioned in 1671. A wheelwright in 1753 had a shop in Slindon as well as one in Walberton.[27] There was a weaver in 1674[28] and a maltster from

92 M.A.F.F., agric. statistics, 1985, covering only 197 ha. (487 a.).
93 Inf. from Mr. W. Forse, Barnham Ct. fm.
94 Inf. from Mr. K. C. Brundle, Choller fm.
95 P.R.O., HO 107/1652, ff. 303 and v., 307, 311v., 313, 314v., 316v., 317v.
96 Ibid. MAF 68/433.
97 *Kelly's Dir. Suss.* (1895 and later edns.); W.S.R.O., SP 1231.
98 *Kelly's Dir. Suss.* (1899 and later edns.).
99 Ibid. (1913 and later edns.); O.S. Map 6", Suss. LXII. NE. (1914 edn.); *Par. of Walberton* (Walberton par. council, 1994), [22].
1 P.R.O., MAF 68/2371.
2 *Kelly's Dir. Suss.* (1934, 1938); O.S. Map 6", Suss. LXII. NE. (1951 edn.).
3 O.S. Maps 6", Suss. LXII. NE. (1914 and later edns.); 1/25,000, SU 80/90 (1991 edn.).
4 M.A.F.F., agric. statistics, 1985; O.S. Map 1/25,000, SU 80/90 (1991 edn.); inf. from nurseries; personal observation.
5 *S.R.S.* lix, p. 188.
6 W.S.R.O., Add. MS. 1802; ibid. Par. 202/7/21; ibid. TD/W 133.
7 P.R.O., SP 14/47, no. 75, f. 160.
8 *S.R.S.* lix, p. 77.
9 *Cal. Assize Rec. Suss. Eliz. I*, p. 36.
10 *250 Yrs. of Mapmaking in Suss.* ed. H. Margary, pl. 19; E.S.R.O., LCG/3/EW 1, ff. [44, 88v.]; W.S.R.O., Par. 202/1/2/1; ibid. TD/W 133; O.S. Map 6", Suss. LXII (1880 edn.).
11 W.S.R.O., SP 1263.
12 M. Brunnarius, *Windmills of Suss.* 169.
13 Pigot, *Nat. Com. Dir.* (1832–4), 1051.
14 P.R.O., HO 107/1652, f. 309; Pike, *Dir. SW. Suss.* (1886–7); B. Dixon, *Unknown to Hist. and Fame*, 92. Both mills are illus. at ibid. 83.
15 P.R.O., HO 107/1652, f. 305.
16 O.S. Map 6", Suss. LXII. NE. (1899 edn.); cf. *Kelly's Dir. Suss.* (1895, 1899).
17 Brunnarius, *Windmills*, 169; *S.C.M.* xi. 807.
18 Dixon, *Unknown to Hist. and Fame*, 5, 35.
19 *S.R.S.* lix, pp. 17, 53.
20 Ibid. x. 135; W.S.R.O., Add. MS. 284 (TS. cat.).
21 A.C.M., M 532, ff. [8, 70v.] from end; P.R.O., E 134/13 Wm. III Mich./20, rot. 3; W.S.R.O., Add. MS. 4335 (TS. cat.); ibid. Ep. I/29/202/72.
22 *Cal. Assize Rec. Suss. Eliz. I*, p. 36; *Goodwood Estate Archives*, i, ed. F. W. Steer and J. Venables, p. 102; *S.R.S.* xxviii. 96; P.R.O., E 134/13 Wm. III Mich./20, rot. 3; W.S.R.O., Add. MSS. 7569c, 8305 (TS. cat.).
23 W.S.R.O., Ep. I/29/202/47, 71; P.R.O., E 134/13 Wm. III Mich./20, rot. 3; *Cal. Assize Rec. Suss. Eliz. I*, p. 243; *S.R.S.* xxviii. 43, 147.
24 *L. & P. Hen. VIII*, xiii (1), p. 287; cf. P.R.O., SC 6/Hen. VIII/3483, rot. 35d.
25 W.S.R.O., Ep. I/25/1 (1635); cf. ibid. Add. MSS. 1802; 2301, m. 2.
26 Above, intro. [inns]; W.S.R.O., Add. MS. 4296 (TS. cat.); cf. ibid. Ep. I/29/202/44.
27 W.S.R.O., Ep. I/29/202/39, 79.
28 Ibid. Add. MS. 8236 (TS. cat.).

1713.[29] A mason who died *c.* 1676 did business with people in Barnham, Felpham, and Slindon, and made loans to inhabitants of Arundel, Barnham, Madehurst, and Yapton.[30] Two parishioners were charged with coining in 1597.[31]

Three bricklayers were recorded between 1642 and 1727[32] and a brickmaker in 1751.[33] A close called Brick kiln field in 1756 lay east of Walberton House,[34] but the chief later brickmaking site was in the north, west of Mill Road.[35] Five parishioners worked in brickmaking in 1851[36] and many in 1867.[37] The site near Mill Road was still active in 1874 but was disused by 1896.[38] Clay and gravel have been dug elsewhere in the north part of the parish in the 19th and 20th centuries, notably in Danes wood.[39]

In the 19th and early 20th centuries there was an unusually high proportion of people in the parish earning their living otherwise than by agriculture: between 1811 and 1831 roughly one in three of those in work.[40] The smithy at the junction of the Street and Yapton Lane was active throughout the period,[41] and there was another in the village centre in 1847[42] and in the early 20th century.[43] Wheelwrights and carpenters included members of the Lintott family at Walberton green,[44] the Suters, one of whom repaired threshing machines in the 1850s,[45] and the Sergants, who were also builders.[46] Some parishioners worked in the woods in 1867[47] and the licensee of the Holly Tree inn was a wood merchant in 1886.[48] There was a cabinet maker from 1918.[49]

There were also generally at least two grocers or drapers in the same period.[50] John Humphrey began his grocery business in 1861; in 1898 he was described besides as draper, butcher, tea and provision merchant, and dealer in china, glass, earthenware, ironmongery, boots and shoes, and patent medicines. By then his premises had three separate units for the grocery, drapery, and butcher's operations.[51] Humphrey's stores were still run by members of the family in 1965,[52] but afterwards closed.

A brewery existed at the east end of the village by 1800;[53] it belonged to Messrs. Ellis and Farnden *c.* 1832[54] but from 1845 to the Ellis family alone.[55] It was closed in the 1920s.[56] The buildings were extensive, with a tall brick chimney.[57]

William Booker (d. 1900)[58] began his career as a bricklayer's labourer, but after taking over the stock in trade of Thomas Caiger in 1858 became a stonemason[59] and later a builder and contractor and dairy farmer. The building business was continued in the family until the 1990s[60] and was responsible for construction at Barnham market, Fontwell waterworks, and Bognor isolation hospital.[61] About 1890 up to 27 men were employed. By the late 19th century the firm also dealt in funerals and house decoration, and in 1913 they were hire carters, and gas, water, and sanitary engineers.[62]

Other less common trades recorded in the parish during the 19th and early 20th centuries were those of glazier, painter,[63] plumber,[64] tinplate worker,[65] photographer,[66] coal merchant,[67] corn merchant,[68] horse and cattle dealer, stationer, and fishmonger.[69] Several dressmakers and a female tailor lived in Walberton in 1851.[70] There was an artist in 1862, a firm of engineers and machinists in 1874, a cycle agent in 1918, a motor engineer in 1927, and a garage in 1934.[71]

29 Ibid. Add. MSS. 1802; 8295–7 (TS. cat.); ibid. Ep. I/29/202/63.
30 Ibid. Ep. I/29/202/42.
31 *Cal. Assize Rec. Suss. Eliz. I*, p. 336.
32 W.S.R.O., Add. MS. 4304 (TS. cat.); ibid. Ep.I/29/202/22; ibid. Harris MS. 587 (TS. cat.).
33 Ibid. Add. MS. 4322 (TS. cat.).
34 Ibid. Add. MS. 1802; ibid. TD/W 133; M. Beswick, *Brickmaking in Suss.* 221.
35 W.S.R.O., Raper MSS., deed, 1780, apparently locating site near Sawyers Dean in NE.; ibid. TD/W 133. For Sawyers Dean, above, intro.
36 P.R.O., HO 107/1652, ff. 308, 311 and v., 312v.–313, 315.
37 *Rep. Com. on Children and Women in Agric.* 87.
38 W.S.R.O., Add. MS. 14286g; O.S. Map 6", Suss. LXII (1880 edn.); LXII. NE. (1899 edn.).
39 O.S. Map 6", Suss. LXII. NE. (1899 and later edns.); W.S.R.O., SP 317.
40 *Census*, 1811–31.
41 Dixon, *Unknown to Hist. and Fame*, 90–1; *Kelly's Dir. Suss.* (1845 and later edns.); W.S.R.O., TD/W 133; O.S. Map 6", Suss. LXII. NE. (1914, 1951 edns.).
42 W.S.R.O., TD/W 133.
43 *Kelly's Dir. Suss.* (1922, 1927); for Booker's premises, below, this section.
44 W.S.R.O., Add. MS. 29687 (TS. cat.); ibid. TD/W 133; Pigot, *Nat. Com. Dir.* (1832–4), 1051.
45 W.S.R.O., Add. MSS. 8301, 30254 (TS. cat.); ibid. Par. 202/1/2/1; Pigot, *Nat. Com. Dir.* (1832–4), 1051.
46 Dixon, *Unknown to Hist. and Fame*, 86–8; Pike, *Dir. SW. Suss.* (1886–7).
47 *Rep. Com. on Children and Women in Agric.* 87.
48 Pike, *Dir. SW. Suss.* (1886–7).
49 *Kelly's Dir. Suss.* (1918 and later edns.)
50 Ibid. (1845 and later edns.); Pigot, *Nat. Com. Dir.* (1832–4), 1051; Pike, *Dir. SW. Suss.* (1886–7); Dixon, *Unknown to Hist. and Fame*, 78, 92; W.S.R.O., Add. MS. 7569j (TS. cat.); ibid. SP 1263.
51 Dixon, *Unknown to Hist. and Fame*, 75–7; cf. W.S.R.O., Holmes, Campbell & Co. MS. 840 (TS. cat.); ibid. MP 3152, p. 12.
52 *W. Suss. Gaz.* 21 Oct. 1965; cf. *Bognor Regis Observer*, 12 Apr. 1957; N. Wyatt, *An Ever-Rolling Stream*, 43–4.
53 Dixon, *Unknown to Hist. and Fame*, 68; Pike, *Dir. SW. Suss.* (1886–7), advt.; O.S. Map 6", Suss. LXII (1880 and later edns.); W.S.R.O., Par. 202/1/2/1; ibid. TD/W 133. It may have originated in cottage and maltho. occupied by Mary Ellis in 1757: ibid. Add. MS. 8296 (TS. cat.).
54 Pigot, *Nat. Com. Dir.* (1832–4), 1051.
55 *Kelly's Dir. Suss.* (1845 and later edns.); W.S.R.O., IR 12, f. 44; ibid. TD/W 133.
56 W.S.R.O., Add. MS. 35871 (TS. cat.); *Kelly's Dir. Suss.* (1922 and later edns.); F. H. Edmunds, *Wells and Springs of Suss.* 203.
57 Dixon, *Unknown to Hist. and Fame*, 62, 69.
58 C.I.H.E. libr., GY 1866. Rest of para. based mainly on Dixon, *Unknown to Hist. and Fame*, 79–80, 82.
59 Cf. *Kelly's Dir. Suss.* (1866); Pike, *Dir. SW. Suss.* (1886–7).
60 *Southern Wkly. News*, 2 Dec. 1955; *W. Suss. Gaz.* 15 Nov. 1990; inf. from Mr. J. Booker, Walberton.
61 C.I.H.E. libr., GY 1866.
62 *Kelly's Dir. Suss.* (1913), advt. suppl. p. 108. At rear of firm's premises in 1995 were 4 walls largely composed of re-used masonry, including a possibly 10th-cent. coffin slab apparently of a priest, much medieval and later moulded work, and an inscr. dated 1796. The source of some of it may be the former coll. bldgs. at Arundel: S.M.R. 1337; *S.A.C.* xlvii. 148–50; inf. from Dr. J. M. Robinson, Arundel Cast.
63 P.R.O., HO 107/1090, ff. 13v., 15; W.S.R.O., Par. 202/1/2/1.
64 Pigot, *Nat. Com. Dir.* (1832–4), 1051.
65 P.R.O., HO 107/1090, f. 17.
66 *Kelly's Dir. Suss.* (1862).
67 Pike, *Dir. SW. Suss.* (1886–7).
68 *Kelly's Dir. Suss.* (1887).
69 Ibid. (1903 and later edns.).
70 P.R.O., HO 107/1652, ff. 302–15, *passim*.
71 *Kelly's Dir. Suss.* (1862 and later edns.).

Domestic service employed many throughout the same period; in 1851, for instance, the household at Avisford House totalled 19. One gamekeeper was recorded in 1841 and two in 1851. There were eight laundresses in 1851.[72]

The growth of motoring after the First World War led to the opening of refreshment rooms by 1922. The timber-framed Beam Ends in Hedgers Hill was a tea garden by 1938[73] and after reopening *c.* 1990 also offered bed and breakfast.[74] There were two other guest houses in Walberton in 1993. In addition, the Avisford Park hotel and country club, opened in 1976, expanded greatly thereafter: by 1985 it served the conference and management training markets as well as tourism and had two squash courts, a swimming pool, and a 9-hole golf course.[75] In 1990 it employed 90 staff.[76] In 1991 a self-contained hotel and business centre under the same ownership, with a banqueting hall seating 350, was opened to the south.[77] In 1994 the hotel, renamed Stakis Arundel, had 126 beds.[78]

A riding school flourished in 1938.[79]

There were an accountant and a physician and surgeon in 1927, and a midwife in 1934. An estate agent practised in 1938.[80]

Already by 1955 many residents worked outside the parish, some at Ford naval air station and others in London.[81] The number increased greatly after that date.

In 1993 shops and other businesses in the village street included two general stores and newsagents, a hardware and garden shop, a shop selling curtains, a hairdresser, a launderette, and a garage. There were also a solicitor, an estate agent, and a doctor's surgery.

At Fontwell the Dean family ran a construction firm from 1935 which was responsible for much building in the parish, though by 1974 it did most of its business in Arundel.[82] A shopping parade was opened in 1939.[83] At first there were a butcher, a grocer, a haberdasher, and a newsagent,[84] and the post office moved there from its previous site near Fontwell racecourse in 1968.[85] The wine merchant, the saddler, and the business selling guns and fishing tackle which flourished in 1992, however, chiefly served passing traffic. Fontwell's roadside location also brought successive cafés and garages or petrol stations.[86] Two small factories had arrived north of the settlement by 1957,[87] and by 1991 the Orchard Way industrial estate had 21 units, mostly accommodating firms in building or related industries.[88] The construction of the bypass road in 1988 reduced custom for Fontwell's businesses,[89] but by 1993 a new restaurant, motel, and garage had been built beside it. There was also a medical centre in 1992.

Outside the village and Fontwell hamlet in 1993 there were two small business estates in Tye Lane and Lake Lane; a firm of horticultural engineers, a timber yard,[90] and a mixed industrial site in Arundel Road; and a garage and a garden machinery business in Yapton Lane.

LOCAL GOVERNMENT. Leet jurisdiction was successfully claimed for Walberton manor in 1279,[91] but in the early 16th century was the subject of controversy between Lord de la Warr as lord of the manor and the earl of Arundel as lord of the rape. After arbitration in 1520 the Walberton view of frankpledge was defined as inferior to the hundred courts, the earl retaining 'the suit royal of the headboroughs and their tithings'.[92] There was a headborough for Walberton and Barnham together in 1293;[93] in 1536–7 he attended the hundred court but apparently only as a formality.[94] A bailiff served in 1543;[95] the earl of Arundel held the office in 1546.[96]

There are court records for the years 1594–9[97] and 1623–1772.[98] In the 1590s a view of frankpledge was held usually once a year and a court baron usually twice. Besides the standard business of regulating land transactions, managing common land, and controlling nuisances, the view held the assize of bread and of ale, oversaw highway repair, and heard at least one case of assault and another of trespass. Sometimes business normal to the view was done at the court instead. A pound was mentioned in 1596;[99] it was perhaps the one in the Street still apparently used to store roadmen's materials in 1964,[1] which was restored as a garden *c.* 1982.[2]

Between 1623 and 1641 a view and court were held annually in autumn;[3] the pattern continued less regularly during the rest of the 17th century, the last view being held in 1686. In 1685 and 1747 the tenants and their holdings were listed in full. In the 18th century there were never

72 P.R.O., HO 107/1090, ff. 13v., 17; HO 107/1652, ff. 303–18, *passim*; Dixon, *Unknown to Hist. and Fame*, 18.
73 *Kelly's Dir. Suss.* (1922, 1938).
74 Inf. from Mr. R. Botteley, Beam Ends tearoom.
75 *W. Suss. Gaz.* 19 Dec. 1985; above, manor (Avisford Ho.).
76 *W. Suss. Gaz.* 11 Apr. 1990.
77 *Chich. Observer*, 14 Nov. 1991.
78 *Bognor Regis Observer*, 19 May 1994.
79 *Kelly's Dir. Suss.* (1938).
80 Ibid. (1927 and later edns.).
81 *Southern Wkly. News*, 2 Dec. 1955.
82 *Bognor Regis Observer*, 22 Nov. 1974; W.S.R.O., Par. 202/52/4; *Par. of Walberton* (Walberton par. council, 1994), [23, 27].
83 *Bognor Regis Observer*, 22 Nov. 1974.
84 *Par. of Walberton*, [23]; cf. *Bognor Regis Observer*, 21 June 1957.
85 *W. Suss. Gaz.* 3 Oct. 1968; cf. above, Eastergate, econ. hist. (other trades and inds.).
86 *Par. of Walberton*, [22–3]; *Bognor Regis Observer*, 21 June 1957.
87 *Bognor Regis Observer*, 21 June 1957; 22 Feb. 1963.
88 W.S.R.O., WNC/CC 14/19, pp. 44–5.
89 *Bognor Regis Observer*, 2 Apr. 1992.
90 Cf. O.S. Map 1/25,000, SU 80/90 (1991 edn.).
91 *Plac. de Quo Warr.* (Rec. Com.), 755; *S.R.S.* xlvi, p. 271.
92 *Goodwood Estate Archives*, i, ed. F. W. Steer and J. Venables, p. 38.
93 A.C.M., M 54, m. 6d.
94 Ibid. M 271, ff. [10v., 19v.].
95 P.R.O., SC 6/Hen. VIII/3483, rot. 35.
96 *L. & P. Hen. VIII*, xxi (2), p. 435.
97 A.C.M., M 532, ff. [8, 25, 47v., 54, 62, 67, 69v., 76, 85v., 96, 106] from end.
98 W.S.R.O., Add. MSS. 2299; 2300, pp. 1–5.
99 A.C.M., M 532, f. [54] from end; cf. W.S.R.O., Add. MS. 2299, p. 1.
1 *W. Suss. Gaz.* 20 Feb. 1964.
2 Ibid. 27 May 1982.
3 W.S.R.O., Add. MS. 2299, pp. 1–[45], assuming the view on p. [36] is for 1638 not 1640. Rest of para. based mainly on ibid. 2299, *passim*.

more than two courts in a decade, business being treated out of court by 1755. Fines for committing nuisances were still collected in the late 1640s, but at the last view the only business was the election of a headborough. A bailiff still served in 1623 and there was an under-constable in 1633.

Two churchwardens were recorded generally between 1548 and 1681 and from 1774, but in the intervening period there was almost always one only.[4] There were two overseers by 1642.[5] Waywardens served in the 19th century[6] and presumably earlier. The parish clerk received £3 a year in 1817.[7]

In 1643 payments were made to widows for keeping their own or others' children and to one old man who was bedridden.[8] Other methods of poor relief used during the 18th century and early 19th included weekly pay; apprenticing; the provision of clothing, flour, fuel, and medical care; and help with rent, burial expenses, and in time of illness.[9] The parish owned and apparently let out bedding in 1720.[10] From the 1780s it had a share in the Gilbert union workhouse at Yapton. By 1832 there were also four parish cottages for the use of poor people;[11] they stood at Walberton green[12] and were sold *c.* 1839.[13]

A hundred and forty-seven parishioners were receiving permanent relief in 1825–6, and 86 casual relief.[14] In 1832 a doctor received £16 a year to attend the poor. During the years around 1830 the occupiers of land agreed to employ all the parish labourers in numbers proportionate to their land-tax assessments.[15] In the early 1830s at least 29 paupers were helped to emigrate, chiefly to Canada under Lord Egremont's scheme; a third of the expense was defrayed by landowners, with the rest to be paid from the rates within four years.[16]

In 1835 Walberton joined Westhampnett union, later rural district, and from 1933 it was in Chichester rural district.[17] After 1974 it was in Arun district.

The parish council looked after the pond on Walberton green from 1894 and after 1951 was owner of the green.[18] From 1917 it leased 1 a. west of the green from the owners of Choller farm for allotments.[19] In 1928 C. E. Stern sold to the council 6 a. east of the Holly Tree inn for a recreation ground.[20]

CHURCH. There was a church in 1086.[21] In 1105 Robert de Haye, lord of Walberton, gave it to Lessay abbey (Manche),[22] from which it passed to the abbey's priory of Boxgrove. A vicarage was ordained *c.* 1174–80.[23] The living was united to Yapton between 1753 and 1875.[24] In 1929 Walberton was united with Binsted as the united benefice of Walberton with Binsted, the parishes remaining distinct.[25]

The advowson of the vicarage belonged to Boxgrove priory from *c.* 1174–80[26] until the Dissolution, the Crown presenting in the 14th century during the war with France and the bishop of Chichester for a turn in 1505.[27] In 1558 the Crown granted the advowson to the bishop,[28] who presented until the early 20th century, except in 1709 when the Crown presented[29] and 1802 when the archbishop collated.[30] In 1929 the patronage of the united benefice was agreed to be shared between the bishop and the patrons of Binsted in the proportion of two turns to one, but from the mid 1980s the bishop alone was patron.[31]

The church had been endowed before 1086 with two yardlands,[32] and *c.* 1160 Boxgrove priory was confirmed in possession of William de St. John's gift of 11 yardlands at Walberton with grazing for 12 oxen, 12 cows, and pigs.[33] At its ordination *c.* 1174–80 the vicarage was endowed with offerings and a third of all tithes.[34] In 1291 it was valued at £10.[35] In 1440 the living was augmented with the rest of the tithes of the parish in return for a yearly payment to Boxgrove priory of 10*s*.;[36] the pension was still paid in 1535,[37] but the arrangement was evidently later rescinded, since in 1635 and later the vicar was entitled to only a third of the corn tithes, and hay tithes only from certain closes; however, in 1635 he also received all the tithes of 39 closes called holibreads and a third of corn tithes from *c.* 150 a. in Yapton.[38] Tithes from Walberton which had been granted by the St. John family to the abbey of La Lucerne (Manche) were resumed in

4 B.L. Add. MS. 39359, ff. 146–51; W.S.R.O., Ep. I/86/20, f. 17.
5 *S.R.S.* v. 185; liv. 39; cf. W.S.R.O., Par. 202/8/1 (TS. cat.).
6 W.S.R.O., Par. 202/12/1 (TS. cat.).
7 Ibid. Ep. I/41/65.
8 *S.R.S.* liv. 39.
9 W.S.R.O., Par. 202/8/1, ff. 12v.–13, 17–19, 28v.–29v.; Par. 202/30/1, ff. 2 and v., 16, 26v.–27v., 131; B. Dixon, *Unknown to Hist. and Fame*, 27–8; *Extracts from Inf. received by H.M. Com. as to Admin. and Operation of Poor Laws* (1833), 72 (B.L. class mark B.S. 68/2).
10 W.S.R.O., Par. 202/8/1, f. 11v.
11 Ibid. Par. 202/30/1, ff. 2, 26v.; *Extracts as to Admin. and Operation of Poor Laws*, 72; below, Yapton, local govt.
12 P.R.O., HO 107/1652, ff. 309v.–310; *Par. of Walberton* (Walberton par. council, 1994), [5].
13 W.S.R.O., Par. 202/8/1, f. 91.
14 Ibid. QCR/2/3/W 5, no. 13.
15 *Extracts as to Admin. and Operation of Poor Laws*, 72.
16 Ibid. 73; Dixon, *Unknown to Hist. and Fame*, 12, 28–30, 113–14; *Suss. Family Historian*, viii. 283; W.S.R.O., Par. 202/8/1, f. 90 and v.
17 *Suss. Poor Law Rec.* 53; Youngs, *Guide to Local Admin. Units of Eng.* i. 524.
18 *Par. of Walberton*, [31–2].
19 W.S.R.O., Par. 202/52/1–2.
20 Ibid. Par. 202/52/3.
21 *V.C.H. Suss.* i. 431.
22 *S.R.S.* lix, p. 16.
23 Ibid. pp. 48–50.
24 *Lond. Gaz.* 14 May 1875, pp. 2570–1.
25 Ibid. 5 Mar. 1929, pp. 1554–6. The 2 detached pts. of Walberton within Yapton, already transferred to the civil par., were to become part of Yapton ecclesiastical par.: ibid.; W.S.R.O., Par. 225/6/14, letter, 1928; above, intro.
26 *S.R.S.* lix, p. 49.
27 B.L. Add. MS. 39349, ff. 5–7v.
28 *Cal. Pat.* 1557–8, 438.
29 B.L. Add. MS. 39349, ff. 8v.–11; *Chich. Dioc. Kal.* (1920).
30 B.L. Add. MS. 39350, f. 237.
31 *Lond. Gaz.* 5 Mar. 1929, p. 1555; *Chich. Dioc. Dir.* (1931 and later edns.).
32 *V.C.H. Suss.* i. 431.
33 *S.R.S.* lix, pp. 47–8. For later hist. of estate, above, manor (rectory).
34 *S.R.S.* lix, pp. 48–50.
35 *Tax. Eccl.* (Rec. Com.), 135.
36 B.L. Add. MS. 39349, f. 2.
37 *Valor Eccl.* (Rec. Com.), i. 306.
38 B.L. Add. MS. 5699, f. 131; W.S.R.O., Ep. I/25/1 (1635); Ep. VI/57/6.

1162,[39] and mill tithes paid to Tortington priory in the Middle Ages are not heard of again,[40] but a portion of Walberton tithes descended with Bilsham manor in Yapton in the 16th and 17th centuries.[41] Both the rectorial and vicarial tithes were let in 1700.[42]

The living was worth £8 or less in 1440,[43] and its net value in 1535 was £10 18*s.* 10*d.*[44] In 1573–4 the income seems to have been enjoyed by the farmer or farmers of the rectory estate,[45] but by 1579 the vicar had it again.[46] The living was valued at £49 5*s.*10*d.* in 1724[47] and at £80 in 1750;[48] *c.* 1830 the average net income of the united benefice of Walberton and Yapton was £468.[49]

The glebe was originally scattered closes. In the early 17th century there were an orchard and 1 a. south of the vicarage house, 3 a. in the Todder open field, 5–8 a. called Heath croft lying west of Tye lane, and 1–3 a. of meadow in Westmead next to Barnham lane,[50] besides a 3-a. close called the Tithing mead in the south-east corner of the parish granted by the manor tenants in lieu of tithe hay.[51] In 1724 there were 14 a. of arable and 5 a. of meadow or pasture.[52] In 1743 Heath croft, then reckoned as 10 a., was exchanged with Thomas Fowler and his trustees for 6 a. in the Todder and 4 a. in Westmead.[53] At the inclosure of Walberton common in 1769 the vicar was awarded 7 a. on the Slindon boundary.[54] In 1849 the outlying portions in the south-east and south-west (21 a.) were exchanged with the lord of the manor for a compact block west of Tye Lane, and the close in the north with members of the Halsted family for 4 a. east of Potwell copse; the vicar also received ¼ a. north-west of the vicarage house for giving up a right of way across the manorial demesne.[55]

A vicarage house was mentioned in 1411[56] and was in poor condition in 1573.[57] It presumably occupied the same site as the later vicarage house on the south side of the village street, which in 1615 had two outhouses and a carthouse.[58] Rooms mentioned in 1644 were hall, parlour, kitchen, and three chambers.[59] The building called in 1995 the Old Vicarage has at its core a possibly 18th-century two-storeyed section of brick including the present entrance hall and a single-storeyed wing to the east. In 1757–8 after the union of the livings of Walberton and Yapton the vicarage house at Yapton was demolished and that at Walberton rebuilt;[60] the two-storeyed range on the west side perhaps belongs to that date. Robert Hardy, vicar from 1802,[61] spent over £1,000 on improving the building before 1812. It remained too small, however, and apparently in that year he added a drawing room along the south side with a bowed western end[62] and perhaps the staircase as well; as a result the house was said in 1819 to have been nearly rebuilt.[63] In 1862 one end of the former tithe barn was converted into a coach house and stable and the other into a large room for parish purposes.[64] Further additions and alterations were made to the house *c.* 1875;[65] the present drawing room with south-facing canted bay seems to be of that period. The house was sold before *c.* 1980[66] but remained in single ownership in 1995; meanwhile a new brick building was put up to replace it on the north side of the village street.

At the commutation of tithes in 1847 Richard Prime as lessee of the rectory estate received £313 3*s.* tithe rent charge besides £4 15*s.* payable from the glebe when not occupied by the vicar. The vicar received £362 7*s.* 6*d.* together with £1 9*s.* 2*d.* in lieu of vicarial tithes from the glebe close (7 a.) in the north part of the parish.[67]

The vicar in 1411 was excommunicated for the partial castration of a chaplain of Slindon.[68] His successor resided in 1440.[69] A later vicar was reported in 1538 for speaking against the Crown's expropriation of Church funds.[70]

The vicar resided in 1563,[71] but a successor in 1574 was often absent.[72] From the early 17th century several vicars held other local livings,[73] though they generally seem to have resided.[74] Curates were mentioned on occasion in the early 17th century and in the 18th and mid 19th centuries; one at least succeeded as vicar.[75] The curate in 1706 apparently lived in the vicarage house.[76]

Henry Jordan, minister in 1661, was ejected in the following year.[77] In 1724 the incumbent himself held morning and evening services with sermon on alternate Sundays; at that date communion was celebrated four times yearly to 30 or 40 communicants.[78]

Michael Dorset, the first incumbent of the

39 *Cal. Doc. France*, ed. Round, p. 281.
40 *S.R.S.* lix, p. 188.
41 Ibid. xix. 77; xx. 508.
42 P.R.O., E 134/13 Wm. III Mich./20, rot. 3.
43 B.L. Add. MS. 39349, f. 3.
44 *Valor Eccl.* (Rec. Com.), i. 317.
45 W.S.R.O., Ep. I/23/2, f. 10v.; Ep. I/23/4, f. 31; cf. B.L. Add. MS. 39359, f. 146.
46 W.S.R.O., Ep. I/23/5, f. 39.
47 *S.R.S.* lxxviii. 74.
48 Ibid. lxxiii, p. 300.
49 *Rep. Com. Eccl. Revenues.*
50 W.S.R.O., Ep. I/25/1 (1615, 1635); ibid. Par. 202/6/2.
51 Ibid. Add. MS. 2301, m. 4; ibid. TD/W 133.
52 *S.R.S.* lxxviii. 74.
53 W.S.R.O., Par. 202/6/2.
54 Ibid. Add. MS. 5156.
55 Ibid. Par. 202/21/4–5. The land exchanged with lord of man. was already occupied by vicar in 1847: ibid. TD/W 133.
56 *S.R.S.* viii. 190.
57 W.S.R.O., Ep. I/23/2, f. 23.
58 Ibid. Ep. I/25/1 (1615).
59 Ibid. Ep. I/29/202/24.
60 Ibid. Ep. I/22/1 (1758); ibid. Par. 202/1/1/1, f. 73v.; below, Yapton, church.
61 B.L. Add. MS. 39350, f. 237.
62 W.S.R.O., Ep. I/40/49; ibid. Par. 202/4/1; Par. 202/6/4.
63 Dallaway, *Hist. W. Suss.* ii (1) (1819), 74.
64 W.S.R.O., Par. 202/4/3.
65 *Lond. Gaz.* 18 May 1894, p. 2927.
66 Local inf.
67 W.S.R.O., TD/W 133.
68 *S.R.S.* viii. 135, 190–3.
69 B.L. Add. MS. 39349, f. 3.
70 *L. & P. Hen. VIII*, xiii (1), pp. 286–7.
71 *S.A.C.* lxi. 113.
72 W.S.R.O., Ep. I/23/3, f. 23v.
73 *D.N.B.* s.v. Wm. Turner; *Rep. Com. Eccl. Revenues*; B.L. Add. MSS. 5699, f. 131; 39349, ff. 9–10v. Jas. Crowe (d. 1554 or 1555) also held S. Stoke: ibid. 39347, f. 164.
74 B.L. Add. MSS. 5699, f. 131 and v.; 39349, f. 9; W.S.R.O., Ep. I/22/1 (1733, 1742); Ep. I/29/202/24, 31; *D.N.B.* s.v. Wm. Turner; *S.A.C.* cvi. 11; *S.R.S.* lxxviii. 74.
75 B.L. Add. MS. 39359, ff. 147–50; W.S.R.O., Ep. I/22/1 (1758).
76 W.S.R.O., Par. 202/1/1/1, f. 73v.
77 B.L. Add. MS. 39349, f. 9v.; *Calamy Revised*, ed. A. G. Matthews, 302.
78 *S.R.S.* lxxviii. 74.

united benefice of Walberton and Yapton, served for 52 years and also held three other livings.[79] Robert Hardy, vicar 1802–43, a chaplain to the Prince Regent,[80] addressed earnest pamphlets to his parishioners and founded a parish library.[81] His successor Thomas Vogan[82] increased the number of Sunday services to two and introduced monthly communion;[83] in 1845 he incurred local disapproval because of High Church practices.[84] Attendances on Census Sunday in 1851 were 150 in the morning and 140 in the afternoon, in each case with 24 Sunday schoolchildren besides.[85] A parish orchestra was abandoned in or before 1857,[86] but by 1865 there was a choir instead.[87] Communion services were held *c.* 30 times a year by 1884 and weekly by 1903.[88] In 1995 there were two or three Sunday services and holy communion on Fridays.

A mission room at Fontwell was built in 1930 on a site given by the Goodacre family. Services were held at least weekly[89] but the room was closed at some time after 1957.[90]

The church of *ST. MARY*[91] consists of chancel and aisled nave with north porch. The walls are of flint rubble, including some Roman tile, with ashlar and brick dressings. A timber bell turret is surmounted by a shingled spire. The early history of the building has been obscured by extensive restoration and rebuilding in the 18th, 19th, and early 20th centuries.

During the later 12th century two-bayed north and south arcades were cut into the eastern end of the possibly pre-Conquest nave; a gable cross which may have been pre-Conquest was discovered in the west wall *c.* 1903.[92] The chancel was built early in the 13th century to a width greater than that of the nave and was given lancet windows; the chancel arch was rebuilt in the 14th century. The stone north porch with trefoil-headed windows was added late in the 13th century, by which time, if not originally, the aisles were as long as the nave. Probably in the 15th century the nave and aisles were re-roofed with a single roof and the bell turret was added. At the same period some refenestration took place, of which only one window in the north aisle and the three-light west window survived into the 20th century.[93]

The church was in poor condition in 1603;[94] in 1724 one of the cross beams of the nave roof was said to be ready to fall,[95] and in 1742 the bell turret, though recently repaired, was threatening collapse.[96] A west gallery[97] was erected before 1790, when it was lit by dormer windows on both sides of the church.[98] In the later 18th century or earlier 19th the south aisle was nearly all taken down and rebuilt with thinner walls of brick and flint rubble, and windows with wooden casements were inserted in the walls of both aisles.[99] It was perhaps at that time that the large round-headed western arches of the nave arcades were inserted or rebuilt.[1] Further alterations were made in the 1850s and 60s: the west door was stopped up; the remains of the gallery were removed, apparently together with part of the support to the belfry; and the north porch was restored with new outer and inner archways and apparently shortened.[2] The west end of the nave was used as a vestry by the late 19th century.[3]

The chancel was carefully restored *c.* 1894.[4] By 1903 the nave was in a dangerous state, probably as a result of the removal of the sub-frame to the belfry and the insertion of the large arches in the nave walls. The architect Richard Creed carried out a drastic restoration in 1903–4, paid for by subscription. Both aisles and much of the nave were taken down and rebuilt,[5] with new windows to the aisles and external buttresses to the west wall, the belfry support was reconstructed, and both roofs were renewed.

New vestries and a meeting room were constructed within the west end of the church in 1992–3.[6]

The font in 1776 was square, supported on four columns;[7] it was replaced in 1843.[8] The present tub-shaped font was inserted at the 1903–4 restoration after being found in a farmyard.[9] In 1636 the position of the minister's seat in the chancel rather than the nave made him largely inaudible.[10] The pews were described as 'very bad' in 1776[11] and too high in 1844.[12] Most fittings in 1994 were late 19th-century or 20th-century, but a 17th-century communion table then stood at the west end of the north aisle.

Plural bells were mentioned in 1542.[13] In 1724 there were three dating from between 1572 and 1712; they were recast in 1903, when three more were added.[14]

The flagon for communion wine was said to

79 *S.A.C.* cvi. 11.
80 Ibid. xxii. 114; B.L. Add. MS. 39350, f. 237.
81 W.S.R.O., Par. 202/7/1; above, intro. (soc. and cultural activities).
82 B.L. Add. MS. 39350, f. 237.
83 W.S.R.O., Ep. I/22A/2 (1844).
84 B. Dixon, *Unknown to Hist. and Fame*, 49.
85 *S.R.S.* lxxv. 155.
86 Dixon, op. cit. 55.
87 W.S.R.O., Par. 202/7/7.
88 Ibid. Ep. I/22A/1 (1884); Ep. I/22A/2 (1903).
89 Ibid. Par. 202/3/4; O.S. Map 6", Suss. LXII. NE. (1951 edn.).
90 *Bognor Regis Observer*, 21 June 1957.
91 Dedic. recorded from mid 12th cent.: *S.R.S.* lix, p. 48. Ch. fully described at F. W. Steer, *Walberton Ch. Guide*.
92 *V.C.H. Suss.* ii. 349, 365. The cross was in vicarage gdn. in 1920 but had disappeared by 1976: F. Harrison, *Notes on Suss. Chs.* (1920), 204; Steer, *Ch. Guide*, 1.
93 Clwyd R.O., Glynne ch. notes, ci. 65; W.S.R.O., PH 6091.
94 W.S.R.O., Ep. I/26/1, f. 6v.
95 *S.R.S.* lxxviii. 73.
96 W.S.R.O., Ep. I/22/1 (1742).
97 Ibid. Par. 202/7/20.
98 B.L. Add. MS. 5674, f. 39, illus. at *Suss. Views* (S.R.S.), 170; Steer, *Ch. Guide*, pl. 1.
99 W.S.R.O., Par. 202/7/20.
1 Ibid.; Dallaway, *Hist. W. Suss.* ii (1) (1819), 74.
2 W.S.R.O., Par. 202/7/20; Par. 202/12/1, ff. 20v., 24, 26v., 28 and v., 42; Clwyd R.O., Glynne ch. notes, ci. 65; cf. *Suss. Views* (S.R.S.), 170.
3 W.S.R.O., Par. 202/7/20.
4 Goodliffe, *Littlehampton* (1903), 51; W.S.R.O., Par. 202/4/6, R. Creed's bill. Rest of para. based mainly on ibid. Ep. I/40/Walberton/4444; ibid. Par. 202/4/5–6, 10–14; Par. 202/7/27. The vicar began the work before a faculty had been issued: ibid. Ep. I/40/Walberton/4444.
5 *Chich. Dioc. Gazette* (1904), 86.
6 *Par. of Walberton* (Walberton par. council, 1994), [42].
7 B.L. Add. MS. 5699, f. 131v.
8 W.S.R.O., Par. 202/7/4, f. 2; Par. 202/8/1, f. 92.
9 *Chich. Dioc. Gazette* (1904), 86.
10 W.S.R.O., Ep. I/26/2, f. 26v.
11 B.L. Add. MS. 5699, f. 131.
12 W.S.R.O., Ep. I/22A/2 (1844).
13 *S.R.S.* xlv. 278.
14 Ibid. lxxviii. 73; Elphick, *Bells*, 400–1.

resemble an alehouse pot in 1636.[15] The existing cup, flagon, and patens, all of silver, date from 1718–19.[16]

A possibly pre-Conquest stone coffin was discovered in 1834 lying across the doorway of the north porch,[17] and was preserved under the west window in 1976.[18] The memorial tablet to the Revd. Philip Blakeway (d. 1915) is by Eric Gill.[19] In the churchyard are three headstones of the later 18th century and earlier 19th with low-relief carvings depicting the fatal accidents of the deceased.[20]

The registers begin in 1556.[21] A registrar for Walberton was appointed in 1654.[22]

NONCONFORMITY. The shoemaker who stole the pyx and chalice in 1565[23] may have been a Catholic sympathizer. One Catholic family was mentioned between 1724 and 1742.[24] In 1781 there were 10 Catholics, who heard mass at the neighbouring Slindon chapel.[25]

The Dissenter mentioned in 1676[26] was perhaps a Baptist since a Baptist meeting was recorded in 1710, when it belonged to the Kent association of general Baptist churches.[27] In 1714, when a chapel was registered for worship, it was served from Chichester.[28] In 1724 there were two general Baptist families and one Presbyterian.[29]

A Methodist congregation met in a rented room from 1810[30] until 1846, when one of the outbuildings of the windmill near Walberton green was registered for worship by the Wesleyan minister at Chichester; the congregation remained part of the Chichester district circuit thereafter.[31] Attendance was *c.* 25 in 1851[32] and *c.* 12 in 1884;[33] services were held in the afternoon at the earlier date and fortnightly in 1891.[34] The congregation was said to be sustained in 1865 by the influence of one shopkeeper,[35] and ceased to exist *c.* 1916,[36] Walberton Methodists thereafter going to Barnham or Westergate in Aldingbourne.[37]

Another Nonconformist chapel was founded in 1846 by *c.* 13 parishioners offended by the High Church practices of the vicar. Under the direction of a minister in Worthing, they met at first in a cottage in the centre of the village, but in 1847 a brick and flint chapel was opened next door. By that date there were *c.* 22 communicants.[38] In 1851 there were morning and evening services each attended by 50 people,[39] and in 1884, when the minister was still non-resident and the congregation described itself as Baptist, half came from other parishes.[40]

In 1886[41] an imposing new chapel was opened, of red and yellow brick, flint, and hung tiles; like the Methodist chapel, it stood at the west end of the village away from the parish church. A baptistry for total immersion was inaugurated in 1900 and in 1905 the building could seat 100.[42] The former chapel meanwhile was used as the Sunday school until the mid 20th century[43] but by 1993 had become a garage. In 1903 a local grocer, evidently Henry Humphrey, acted as minister.[44]

A brick church hall was put up in 1953[45] on the opposite side of the street. The congregation, which had 25 members in 1966,[46] was affiliated to the Fellowship of independent evangelical churches in 1973.[47] A resident pastor was appointed in 1992[48] and in 1993 there were two Sunday services and weekday meetings.

In the late 19th century Salvation Army services were held on Sunday afternoons at Walberton green.[49] At least one family adhered to the sect in 1903.[50]

EDUCATION. A 'poor man' kept an unlicensed school in 1622.[51]

John Nash, lord of the manor, by will dated 1732 left a schoolhouse and £12 a year for teaching 18 poor children; since the occupier of the schoolhouse was to continue as master the school had evidently existed before.[52] In 1742 the only subject was reading.[53] The schoolhouse was demolished *c.* 1780 and replaced by another building which stood west of the Holly Tree inn. In 1816 both the use of the house and the master's income were being withheld by Gen. Whyte, but the status quo was resumed after his death later that year. The building belonged to the parish by 1847.[54]

15 W.S.R.O., Ep. I/26/2, f. 26v.
16 Ibid. Par. 202/8/1, f. 55v.; *S.A.C.* liii. 237–8; *S.R.S.* lxxviii. 74.
17 W.S.R.O., Par. 202/8/1, f. 75 and v.; Dixon, *Unknown to Hist. and Fame*, 54.
18 Steer, *Ch. Guide*, 2.
19 W.S.R.O., Ep. I/40/Walberton/3756.
20 Cf. Dixon, *Unknown to Hist. and Fame*, 56–7; Steer, *Ch. Guide*, 6.
21 W.S.R.O., Par. 202/1/1/1 (TS. cat.).
22 Ibid. f. 18.
23 *Cal. Assize Rec. Suss. Eliz. I*, p. 36.
24 *S.R.S.* lxxviii. 73; W.S.R.O., Ep. I/22/1 (1733, 1742). The alleged early 17th-cent. recusant mentioned at *V.C.H. Suss.* iv. 109 n. was of Warblington (Hants).
25 W.S.R.O., MP 1271; *Miscellanea*, vi (Cath. Rec. Soc. vii), 360–1.
26 *Compton Census*, ed. Whiteman, 144.
27 F. Buffard, *Kent and Suss. Baptist Assocs.* 31.
28 Caplan, 'Outline of Nonconf. in Suss.' ii. 16.
29 *S.R.S.* lxxviii. 73.
30 G. M. M., *A Methodist Tapestry* (Bognor Regis, 1967), 28.
31 P.R.O., RG 31/1, Chich. archdeac. no. 248; Dixon, *Unknown to Hist. and Fame*, 51.
32 *S.R.S.* lxxv, p. 156.
33 W.S.R.O., Ep. I/22A/1 (1884).
34 Dixon, op. cit. 76.
35 W.S.R.O., Ep. I/22A/2 (1865).
36 G. M. M., *Methodist Tapestry*, 29.
37 Dixon, op. cit. 51.
38 Ibid. 49; P.R.O., HO 129/91/3/7/10, evidently reading Geo. Robard Paul; cf. ibid. HO 129/90/1/3/9.
39 *S.R.S.* lxxv, p. 156.
40 W.S.R.O., Ep. I/22A/1 (1884).
41 Para. based mainly on Dixon, *Unknown to Hist. and Fame*, 50–1.
42 *Kelly's Dir. Suss.* (1905).
43 O.S. Map 6", Suss. LXII. NE. (1899 and later edns.).
44 W.S.R.O., Ep. I/22A/2 (1903); *Par. of Walberton* (Walberton par. council, 1994), [47]; N. Wyatt, *An Ever-Rolling Stream*, 42–3.
45 *Southern Wkly. News*, 2 Dec. 1955; date on bldg.
46 *Baptist Handbk.* (1966).
47 D. R. Elleray, *Victorian Chs. of Suss.* 82.
48 *W. Suss. Gaz.* 6 Feb. 1992.
49 Dixon, *Unknown to Hist. and Fame*, 6.
50 W.S.R.O., Ep. I/22A/2 (1903).
51 *S.R.S.* xlix. 55.
52 W.S.R.O., Par. 202/24/1; *Char. Don.* H.C. 511, pp. 1260–1 (1816), xvi (2).
53 W.S.R.O., Ep. I/22/1 (1742).
54 *V.C.H. Suss.* ii. 439; *Educ. of Poor Digest*, 972; W.S.R.O., Par. 202/7/4, ff. 4–5; ibid. TD/W 133; illus. at Dixon, *Unknown to Hist. and Fame*, 36; above, manor (Walberton).

From 1824 the school was a National school. There were 44 boys and 20 girls in 1833[55] and 39 boys and 52 girls in 1846–7.[56] In 1867 there were 59 on the roll, with an average attendance of 45.[57] Eighteen children were still taught free in 1833[58] and in the mid 19th century some pupils came from Yapton and Barnham.[59] In 1833 the master received £18 5*s*. a year[60] and in 1846–7 there was also a paid mistress. In the latter year additional income was received from subscriptions;[61] 20 years later the lord of the manor Arthur Prime was making up the shortfall, then £40–50,[62] and using his resulting influence to choose the teachers.[63]

A new school building of red brick was put up as Walberton and Binsted National school in 1874[64] apparently at the expense of Arthur Prime;[65] it consisted of a schoolroom and a classroom. Average attendance was under 40 until *c*. 1880,[66] rising to 76 in 1884–5, 86 in 1893–4, and 113 in 1905–6.[67] After a decrease in the 1910s and 20s it was between 128 and 151 in the 1930s.[68] The rent charge of £12 was redeemed in 1903.[69] A new infants' classroom was built in 1927.[70]

The school continued to take pupils of all ages until Westergate secondary modern school was opened in 1958.[71] A new building for Walberton and Binsted C.E. primary school was built in 1964 north-east of the old one, which was converted into houses.[72] There were 172 on the roll in 1993.[73]

Other, fee-paying, schools flourished in the 19th century. Three in 1819 had 25 pupils between them,[74] and two in 1833 had 53.[75] In 1851 Mary White kept a small school behind her grocer's shop.[76] In 1850–1 Miss Pack of Avisford House built a girls' school and school cottage of flint with brick dressings in Gothic style on the north side of the village street near its east end.[77] In 1867 infants also attended there, the roll totalling 68 with an average attendance of 50.[78] The school ceased *c*. 1875, the building becoming a private house.[79] A private adventure dame school of unknown location was attended by 32 children paying 3*d*. a week in 1867.[80] Both the last two schools mentioned, like the National school, took pupils from other parishes, but the vicar nevertheless reckoned that at least 100 Walberton children were being educated.[81] In 1883 one school catered for children of Dissenters.[82] Boarding pupils were taken at the vicarage in 1891.[83]

A night school was held three times a week in winter in 1875.[84] In the 1890s classes were held in the parish room at the vicarage under the patronage of Lady Anson: girls could learn cooking, laundry work, nursing, and home health, and boys drawing, gardening, and horticulture.[85]

CHARITIES FOR THE POOR. John Moorey and John Wyatt in 1625 gave ½ a. beside Lake Lane for the benefit of the poor; it was known as the Poor croft. By 1724 half its income was for church uses;[86] *c*. 1835 the total was 10*s*. a year[87] and by 1882 £1 distributed in money.[88] The land was sold in 1925 and the proceeds invested.[89]

Mrs. Elizabeth Nash in 1716 granted land in Sidlesham, the income to be spent on the poor of various parishes, Walberton receiving £1. The same sum was still received in 1962, but under a Scheme of 1982 the net income from the endowment was re-apportioned, three tenths to go to Walberton which by 1990 received £540.[90]

The Walberton, Binsted, and West Barnham sick poor fund, succeeding a nursing association for the same places, was set up in 1954, with a nurse's cottage in West Walberton Lane. Its income in the 1990s subsumed those from the two charities mentioned and was spent, among other things, on a ramp for the village hall and in assistance for school journeys.[91]

William Johnson in 1934 left £300, the income to be devoted to Walberton's sick and poor.[92]

55 *Educ. Enq. Abstract*, 983.
56 Nat. Soc. *Inquiry, 1846–7*, Suss. 14–15.
57 *Rep. Com. on Children and Women in Agric.* 87.
58 *Educ. Enq. Abstract*, 983.
59 W.S.R.O., Ep. I/47/3.
60 *Educ. Enq. Abstract*, 983.
61 Nat. Soc. *Inquiry, 1846–7*, Suss. 14–15.
62 *Rep. Com. on Children and Women in Agric.* 87.
63 *Schs. Inquiry Com.* 296–7.
64 P.R.O., ED 7/123; *Kelly's Dir. Suss.* (1874).
65 Char. Com. files, Scheme, 1875.
66 P.R.O., ED 7/123; *Rep. Educ. Cttee. 1878–9*, 1012.
67 *Rep. Educ. Cttee. 1885–6*, 602–3; *1893–4*, 984; *Public Elem. Schs. 1907*, 641.
68 *Educ. List 21, 1914*, 252; *1919*, 344; *1922*, 343; *1932*, 389; *1938*, 404.
69 W.S.R.O., Par. 202/25/1.
70 Ibid. Par. 202/25/2; *Par. of Walberton* (Walberton par. council, 1994), [35].
71 *Par. of Walberton*, [35].
72 *W. Suss. Gaz.* 27 May 1982; *Educ. in W. Suss. 1959–64* (W. Suss. C.C.), 160.
73 *Dir. of W. Suss. Educ. Service* (1993).
74 *Educ. of Poor Digest*, 972.
75 *Educ. Enq. Abstract*, 983.
76 Dixon, *Unknown to Hist. and Fame*, 42; P.R.O., HO 107/1652, f. 313v.
77 *Cat. of Drawings Colln. of R.I.B.A., L–N*, pp. 45–6; Dixon, *Unknown to Hist. and Fame*, 43–4; cf. *Kelly's Dir. Suss.* (1862); W.S.R.O., SP 1263.
78 *Rep. Com. on Children and Women in Agric.* 87.
79 *Cat. of Drawings Colln. of R.I.B.A., L–N*, p. 46.
80 *Rep. Com. on Children and Women in Agric.* 87. It may have occupied angle between Yapton Lane and Hedgers Hill, where a bldg. called Old Sch. Laundry Ho. stood in 1993.
81 *Rep. Com. on Children and Women in Agric.* 87.
82 *W. Suss. Gaz.* 14 July 1983.
83 P.R.O., RG 12/843, f. 27v.
84 Ibid. ED 7/123.
85 Dixon, *Unknown to Hist. and Fame*, 45, 76; cf. diary of Revd. W. P. Crawley, vicar 1899–1907, in possession of Mrs. M. G. Maloney, Chich.
86 *Char. Don.* H.C. 511, pp. 1260–1 (1816), xvi (2); *S.R.S.* lxxviii. 73; W.S.R.O., Add. MS. 1802; cf. ibid. Par. 202/8/1, f. 17.
87 *30th Rep. Com. Char.* 639.
88 *Kelly's Dir. Suss.* (1882).
89 F. W. Steer, *Walberton Ch. Guide*, 2 n.
90 *2nd Rep. Com. Char.* 185–6; *S.R.S.* lxxviii. 73–4; *W. Suss. Gaz.* 3 Dec. 1981; Char. Com. files.
91 Char. Com. files.
92 Steer, *Ch. Guide*, 2.

YAPTON

THE parish of Yapton[93] lies on the coastal plain south-west of Arundel and *c.* 2 miles (3 km.) from the sea. In 1881 it had 1,740 a. and was irregular in shape.[94] Between 1882 and 1891 it was enlarged by the addition of two detached parts of Walberton in the north (20 a.) and five detached parts of Barnham in the west (31 a.),[95] the latter representing parts of estates formerly centred in Barnham.[96] In 1933 a further 449 a. including Flansham hamlet was added from Felpham, so that in 1971 the area was 906 ha. (2,239 a.).[97] In 1985 two salients of Barnham within Yapton, one of which had also once partly belonged to an estate centred in Barnham, were added to Yapton, while the north-western tip of Yapton was transferred to Barnham and a larger area in the north-east, including Wicks Farmhouse, to Ford.[98] The present article treats the history of the parish as constituted before 1985.

The southern boundary follows the Ryebank rife and parts of the northern boundary a stream and roads, but the configuration of the old western boundary with Barnham and Eastergate suggests that the three parishes may once have formed a single area.

Most of the parish lies on brickearth, with alluvium in the valleys of streams in the north-east and south.[99] Flooding was common in the Middle Ages[1] and still occurred in the mid 20th century.[2] The deep Ryebank rife which marks the southern boundary is apparently an artificial channel linking two streams which once flowed west and east.[3] A pond called the great pond[4] and later Greens pond formerly lay across the Yapton–Barnham boundary west of Yapton village.[5]

There was woodland yielding six swine on what was apparently Yapton manor in 1086,[6] and a wood of the lord of Bilsham, much of it oak, was mentioned in the 16th century.[7] In the 19th and 20th centuries, however, there was virtually no woodland.[8]

William of Etchingham had free warren in his demesne lands in Yapton in 1316.[9] There is no evidence for a park in the parish before *c.* 1813, when parkland extended south of Yapton Place as far as the line of the future Portsmouth–Arundel canal, and northwards and westwards to Ford Lane and North End Road.[10] After the demolition of Yapton Place in the 1830s[11] the land was returned to agriculture[12] except for a small area around the remains of the house.[13]

SETTLEMENT. There is scattered evidence for occupation between the Bronze Age and Romano-British periods in the southern half of the parish.[14] The best agricultural land in the parish, however, lies around the village.[15] Medieval settlement there may have centred on the church, south of which earthworks define roughly rectangular areas perhaps representing house plots.[16] In later centuries dwellings were loosely scattered along Main and North End roads and along the two streets linking them to the church, Church Road and Church Lane;[17] there were *c.* 45 dwellings in that area *c.* 1840.[18]

The earliest known secular building in the village is Coachman's cottage in Church Lane, a probably 16th-century timber-framed house with a later west wing lying north–south. The Old Malthouse and Laburnum cottages at the west end of the village are apparently 17th-century. Apart from houses in the village associated with three manors,[19] other buildings put up before 1800 are chiefly small, materials usually being flint and brick, with roofs of thatch, tile, or slate; one house near the school in North End Road and another at the west end of Main Road have datestones for 1734.

Stakers Farmhouse in North End Road, apparently 18th-century, and Yew Tree House which faces it have similar stuccoed façades of mid 19th-century character, while Park Lodge in Church Lane is early 19th-century with a Doric porch between two later projecting bay windows. Church House opposite the church is a small, stuccoed, double-pile house of 1831 which was extended to the south in the later 20th century. Reset beams in the cellar and a datestone apparently for 1692 may survive from an earlier building on the site. Two ball finials in the garden which once decorated the gate piers had come from the demolished Yapton Place.[20]

From the mid 19th century wealthy families

93 This article was written in 1995 and revised in 1996. Topographical details in introduction based mainly on O.S. Maps 1/25,000, SU 80/90 (1991 edn.); 6", Suss. LXII, LXXIV (1879–80 and later edns.).

94 *Census*, 1881.

95 Ibid. 1891; O.S. Map 6", Suss. LXII (1880 edn.).

96 W.S.R.O., Add. MS. 4553.

97 Ibid. WOC/CC 7/2/8; *Census*, 1931 (pt. ii), 1971.

98 Arun (Parishes) Order 1985; W.S.R.O., Add. MS. 4553.

99 Geol. Surv. Map 1", drift, sheets 317 (1957 edn.); 332 (1975 edn.).

1 P.R.O., C 135/94, no. 2; cf. A.C.M., M 32, rot. 6.

2 W.S.R.O., WDC/SU 19/1/1.

3 Ibid. LD I/LL 1/8, p. [1]; cf. the pattern of alluvium shown at Geol. Surv. Map 1", drift, sheet 332 (1975 edn.).

4 W.S.R.O., Add. MS. 28591.

5 Ibid. TD/W 153; Pike, *Dir. SW. Suss.* (1886–7).

6 *V.C.H. Suss.* i. 433; below, manors (Yapton).

7 A.C.M., M 31, rot. 6d.; 819.

8 Dallaway, *Hist. W. Suss.* ii (1) (1819), 42; W.S.R.O., TD/W 153; O.S. Map 6", Suss. LXII (1880 and later edns.).

9 *Cal. Pat.* 1313–17, 430.

10 *250 Yrs. of Mapmaking in Suss.* ed. H. Margary, pl. 19; cf. ibid. pl. 26; W.S.R.O., Add. MS. 12925 (TS. cat.). For Yapton Pla., below, manors (Yapton).

11 Below, manors (Yapton).

12 W.S.R.O., TD/W 153.

13 Ibid. IR 12, f. 64.

14 S.M.R. 1445–6, 1451, 1459, 1467–70, 1473; *S.A.C.* xcviii. 16–18; cxvii. 77; cxxi. 198; cxxv. 51–67.

15 P.R.O., IR 18/10533.

16 S.M.R. 1458.

17 e.g. *250 Yrs. of Mapmaking in Suss.* pls. 14–15, 19.

18 W.S.R.O., TD/W 153.

19 Below, manors (Yapton, Yapton Coverts, Bercourt and Wildbridge).

20 G. Young, *Cottage in the Fields*, 168.

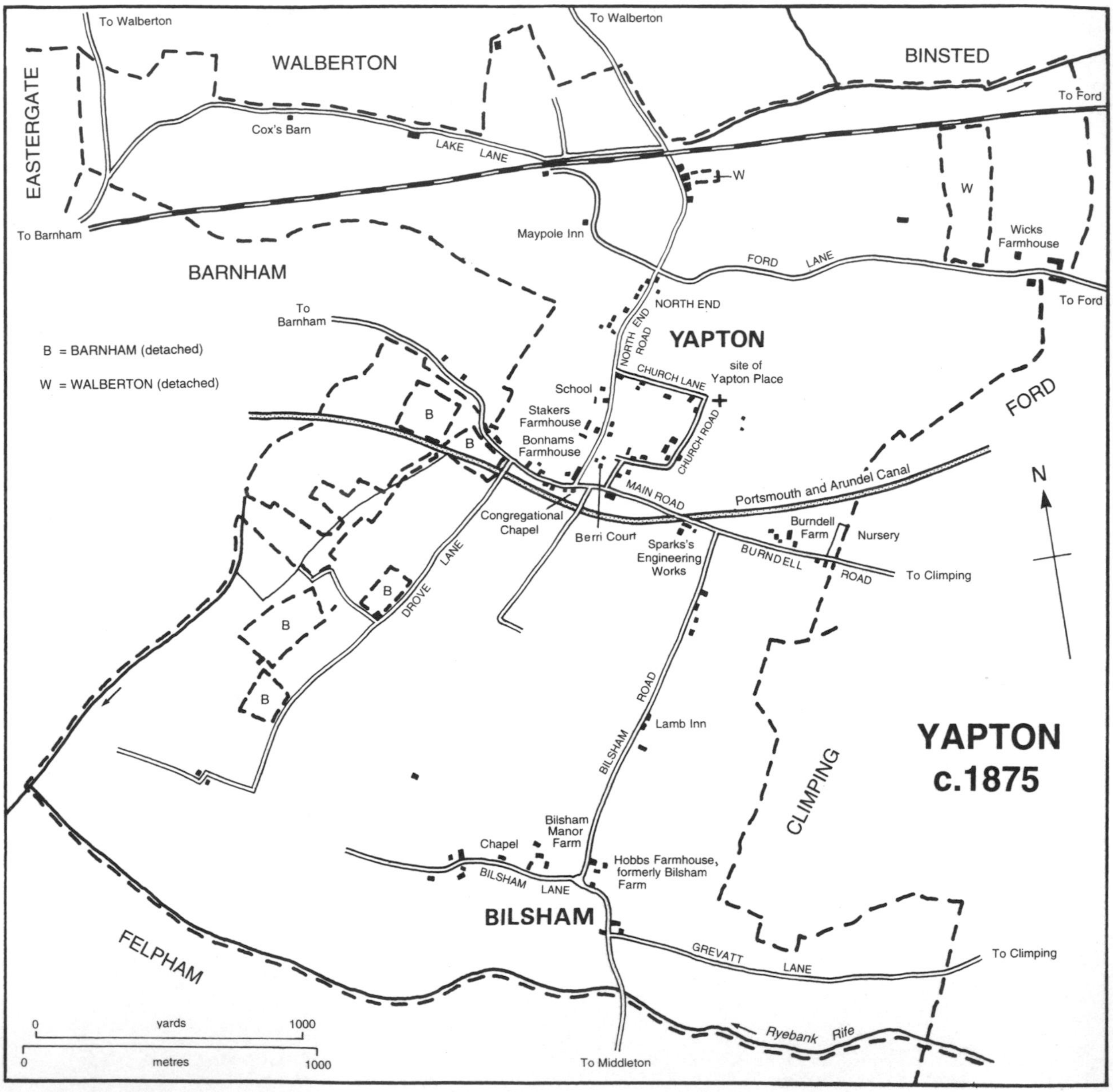
YAPTON
c.1875
To Walberton
To Walberton
WALBERTON
BINSTED
EASTERGATE
To Ford
Cox's Barn
LAKE LANE
W
W
To Barnham
Maypole Inn
Wicks Farmhouse
FORD LANE
BARNHAM
To Ford
NORTH END
To Barnham
YAPTON
NORTH END ROAD
B = BARNHAM (detached)
W = WALBERTON (detached)
CHURCH LANE
site of Yapton Place
School
CHURCH ROAD
Stakers Farmhouse
FORD
Bonhams Farmhouse
B
B
MAIN ROAD
Portsmouth and Arundel Canal
N
Congregational Chapel
Berri Court
Burndell Farm
Nursery
Sparks's Engineering Works
BURNDELL ROAD
To Climping
B
DROVE LANE
B
B
BILSHAM ROAD
Lamb Inn
CLIMPING
Bilsham Manor Farm
Chapel
Hobbs Farmhouse, formerly Bilsham Farm
BILSHAM LANE
BILSHAM
FELPHAM
GREVATT LANE
To Climping
Ryebank Rife
0
yards
1000
0
metres
1000
To Middleton

lived in the larger houses of the village.[21] Park Lodge, Yapton Lodge, Yew Tree House, and Stakers Farmhouse each had a tennis lawn in the early 20th century.[22] Members of the Sparks family, owners of an engineering works, lived at Church House, Yapton Lodge, Grove Lodge, and the large red-brick Sunnyside in Church Road in the late 19th and 20th centuries.[23] Smaller houses were also built in the village in the late 19th century and early 20th,[24] including three terraces of cottages in Bilsham and Burndell roads for employees of the engineering works.[25]

In the mid 20th century several roads were laid out south of the village on either side of Bilsham Road; they contain both houses and bungalows, including many council houses.[26] North of Burndell Road other closes, chiefly of terraced and semidetached houses, were built in the later 20th century.[27] One larger house of the 1930s was the Arts-and-Crafts style Dyers Croft in Main Road. In 1991, despite recent infilling by new houses and closes,[28] the older part of the village was still characterized by large houses in walled gardens with much greenery. There was an estate of mobile homes south of Main Road in 1994. The modern centre of the village, with the church, the village hall, and tall trees round the edges of the playing field, suggests, quite unhistorically, a long-established green.

At Bilsham late Anglo-Saxon finds around the medieval chapel may suggest a nucleus of settlement there at that date.[29] The second element of the place name is apparently *hamm*, alluding to low-lying land beside the Ryebank rife.[30] Buildings in the hamlet dating from before *c.* 1800 besides those mentioned elsewhere[31] include Bilsham Croft and Old Bilsham Farmhouse, both of flint with brick dressings; the former has 16th-century timbers, and the latter may be partly 17th-century. There were *c.* 10 dwellings in all at Bilsham *c.* 1840.[32] In the mid 20th century elm trees since cut down made of Bilsham Lane virtually a narrow tunnel.[33]

North of Yapton village along the road to Walberton is a scattering of buildings of the 18th century or earlier, some perhaps built on roadside waste.[34] The name North End described the area by *c.* 1813.[35] Four cottages near the railway were built by the railway company.[36] More houses were put up there in the 20th century including some council houses,[37] and a mobile home park lay to the west in 1994.

On the south side of Burndell Road eight dwellings which existed *c.* 1840 were evidently built on roadside waste since their plots have a continuous southern boundary. There was also ribbon development before 1900 along Bilsham Road between Yapton village and Bilsham;[38] there too some houses occupy former waste land, a terrace on the east side facing south.[39] Many detached houses and bungalows were built in Lake Lane in the north-west corner of the parish in the 20th century, besides some cottages for nursery workers.[40] There are 19th- or 20th-century cottages near Wicks Farmhouse on the Ford boundary.

The place called Wildbridge, mentioned from the early 13th century and called a vill *c.* 1237,[41] seems to have lain near the Walberton boundary,[42] the first element of the name perhaps alluding to an exposed situation.[43]

Fifteen persons were assessed to subsidy in Yapton vill in 1327 and 9 at Bilsham;[44] in 1332 the figure for Yapton was 32, but Bilsham was then included with Madehurst,[45] and in 1524 Yapton's total was 24 and Bilsham's apparently 8.[46] Eighty-four parishioners signed the protestation in 1642,[47] and 122 inhabitants were listed in the Compton census in 1676.[48] There were 48 families in 1724.[49] From 543 in 1801 the population fell to 512 in 1811, then rose and fell alternately during the 19th century and early 20th, reaching 712 in 1921; thereafter the increase was continuous, to 1,505 in the enlarged parish including Flansham in 1951, and 3,742 in 1981. Rates of increase in the three decades 1951–81 were 33, 25, and 50 per cent respectively. In 1991 the altered area of the parish had 3,377 inhabitants.[50]

COMMUNICATIONS. The parish is bisected by the road from Chichester to Climping, mentioned

21 *Kelly's Dir. Suss.* (1862 and later edns.); W.S.R.O., SP 1240–2, 1244–6.

22 W.S.R.O., SP 326, 1245, 1247; inf. from Mr. A. R. M. White, Stakers Fmho.

23 W.S.R.O., IR 12, f. 64; ibid. MP 3541, pp. 5, 7–9; ibid. SP 326; below, econ. hist. (other trades and inds.).

24 e.g. O.S. Map 6", Suss. LXII (1880 and later edns.).

25 W.S.R.O., MP 3541, p. 4; ibid. SP 326; Pike, *Bognor Dir.* (1910–11). Holkham cottages were named for John Sparks's native village: below, econ. hist. (other trades and inds.).

26 O.S. Map 6", Suss. LXII. SE. (1913 and later edns.); SU 90 SE. (1980 edn.); *Bognor Regis Observer*, 22 Feb. 1963; *Residential Attractions of Bognor Regis, Felpham, Middleton-on-Sea and Dist.* (Gloucester, [1937]), 3, 13 (copy in B.L.).

27 O.S. Map 6", Suss. LXII. SE. (1951 edn.); SU 90 SE. (1980 edn.).

28 e.g. ibid. SU 90 SE. (1980 edn.); *W. Suss. Gaz.* 19 Sept. 1991.

29 P. Drewett, D. Rudling, and M. Gardiner, *SE. to AD 1000*, 340; S.M.R. 1472.

30 *S. Saxons*, ed. P. Brandon, 82.

31 Below, manors (Bilsham); church [Bilsham chapel].

32 W.S.R.O., TD/W 153.

33 Young, *Cottage in the Fields*, 169; inf. from Mr. A. Misselbrook, Bilsham.

34 *250 Yrs. of Mapmaking in Suss.* pls. 14–15, 19, 26; W.S.R.O., TD/W 153.

35 W.S.R.O., PM 280; cf. O.S. Map 6", Suss. LXII (1880 edn.); W.S.R.O., IR 12, f. 67.

36 W.S.R.O., IR 12, f. 50.

37 O.S. Map 6", Suss. LXII. SE. (1913, 1951 edns.).

38 W.S.R.O., TD/W 153; *250 Yrs. of Mapmaking in Suss.* pls. 14–15, 19, 26.

39 W.S.R.O., Add. MSS. 12922 (TS. cat.); 13888, p. 118; ibid. TD/W 153.

40 O.S. Map 6", Suss. LXII. NE., SE. (1951 edn.); SU 90 SE. (1980 edn.).

41 *S.R.S.* xlvi, p. 91; lix, pp. 68, 125, 163–4; cf. below, church.

42 W.S.R.O., Add. MS. 12263 (TS. cat.), describing it as in Walberton.

43 *P.N. Suss.* (E.P.N.S.), i. 145.

44 *S.R.S.* x. 135–6. Wm. of Bilsham, however, was listed under Binsted with Tortington: ibid. 137.

45 Ibid. 254, 256.

46 *S.R.S.* lvi. 56, 58.

47 Ibid. v. 201–2.

48 *Compton Census*, ed. Whiteman, 144.

49 *S.R.S.* lxxviii. 74.

50 *Census*, 1801–1991.

from *c.* 1212;[51] the enlargement of Ford airfield south-east of the village caused its closure at that point between 1942 and 1959.[52] Bilsham Road leading to Felpham and Middleton is recorded from 1646,[53] and North End Road leading to Walberton and Arundel from 1678;[54] by 1835 they formed part of the route from London to Bognor.[55] The corner of Main and Bilsham roads was called Bognor bridge by 1886.[56]

Drove Lane mentioned from 1542[57] was presumably the Flansham road recorded in 1641.[58] The road from Bilsham to Climping was called Grevatt Lane in the 1820s, when it became part of a new road between Bognor and Littlehampton;[59] it remained private until acquired by Littlehampton urban district council, together with the Arun ferry to which it led, in the early 1900s.[60] A new section of road to replace part of Grevatt Lane was cut to the south before 1967.[61]

Both Lake Lane and Ford Lane in the north were named in 1778.[62] They originally formed a continuous route,[63] whose central section in the parish is sunk between the land on either side, indicating a long period of use.

Cab or fly proprietors were listed between 1895 and 1905.[64] There were bus services in 1992 to Bognor Regis, Littlehampton, Chichester, and Arundel.

The Portsmouth–Arundel canal was constructed through the centre of the parish *c.* 1821[65] and opened in 1823,[66] but it had little effect on Yapton as there was no wharf.[67] By the mid 19th century it had ceased to be used.[68] It crossed Main Road on the site of the modern recreation ground; earthworks were still apparently visible there in 1945[69] but were later levelled. The route remained traceable west of the village in 1995; one brick bridge survived there and another near the Ford boundary in the east.[70]

The Worthing–Chichester railway was opened through the north end of the parish in 1846;[71] to avoid the need for two level crossings the eastern section of Lake Lane was diverted to run north of the line.[72] There was a station on the road to Walberton from 1846 to 1847 and from 1849 to 1864;[73] the building survived in 1995.

An inn in 1686 had three guest beds and stabling for two horses[74] and an innholder was mentioned in 1725.[75] The site referred to seems likely to be that later occupied by the Shoulder of Mutton, afterwards the Shoulder of Mutton and Cucumber, which was recorded from *c.* 1832, when the publican was also a wheelwright.[76] The Black Dog, also in Main Road, and two outlying inns, the Maypole and the Lamb, are recorded from the 1870s or 80s.[77] All four remained in 1995.

Bowls was played in the parish in 1553,[78] and in 1623 a fiddler from Boxgrove was presented for leading dancing on Sundays.[79] The parish bounds were still beaten at Rogationtide in the 1620s; refreshments had previously been provided by landholders, the occupier of the Yapton manor demesnes giving a dinner to most parishioners.[80]

The owner of Stakers farm in 1896 allowed the vicar to put up an iron recreation room on land next to the school in North End Road at the rent of 1*s.* a year.[81] In 1932 part of the former Sparks's engineering works south of Main Road was conveyed to trustees as a village hall for Yapton and Ford.[82] It was replaced *c.* 1988 by a purpose-built building of brick on the other side of the road,[83] next to which there was a county council youth centre in 1991. In 1955 the old hall was used by 14 clubs and societies and served also as a cinema at weekends and as a library staffed by voluntary helpers two days a week;[84] the new hall was even more popular as a venue in 1995. A Yapton and district cottage gardeners' society, founded *c.* 1905, still flourished in 1991.[85]

From the early 20th century a field north-east of the church and Church Farmhouse was used as a recreation ground by permission of the owner Walter Langmead.[86] In 1948 West Sussex county council bought 8 a. north of Main Road which was thereafter known as King George's field; in 1980 it was conveyed to the parish council.[87] A football club flourished by 1928,[88] and in 1992 there were clubs for football, cricket, stoolball, badminton, and short mat bowls.

A Yapton and Ford festival, with dancing, sports, and a car rally, was held in 1962.[89]

Gas was supplied from Bognor by 1912.[90]

51 *S.R.S.* lix, p. 76; cf. *Goodwood Estate Archives*, i, ed. F. W. Steer and J. Venables, p. 103; W.S.R.O., Cap. I/28/103, deed, 1727; above, Barnham, intro.
52 *Bognor Regis Post*, 1 Aug. 1959.
53 *S.R.S.* xxix, p. 33.
54 Ibid. pp. 145–6; cf. W.S.R.O., Add. MS. 12889 (TS. cat.).
55 Horsfield, *Hist. Suss.* ii. 114, wrongly calling it a turnpike; Lewis, *Topog. Dict. Eng.* (1849).
56 Pike, *Dir. SW. Suss.* (1886–7); cf. W.S.R.O., IR 12, f. 58.
57 A.C.M., M 859, rot. 11; cf. W.S.R.O., Add. MSS. 2034, 4553; ibid. S.A.S. MS. B 658 (TS. cat.).
58 W.S.R.O., S.A.S. MS. WH 68 (TS. cat.).
59 5 Geo. IV, c. 94 (Local and Personal); W.S.R.O., QDP/W 42; cf. ibid. TD/W 153.
60 5 Edw. VII, c. 180 (Local); W.S.R.O., QDP/W 226.
61 O.S. Map 6", SU 90 SE. (1967 edn.).
62 W.S.R.O., Add. MS. 1806, pp. 2, 5.
63 Ibid. TD/W 153.
64 *Kelly's Dir. Suss.* (1895 and later edns.).
65 *Census*, 1831.
66 P. A. L. Vine, *Lond.'s Lost Route to Sea* (1986), 83.
67 Pigot, *Nat. Com. Dir.* (1832–4), 1051.
68 Above, Ford, intro.; cf. *Kelly's Dir. Suss.* (1862).
69 Young, *Cottage in the Fields*, 116; O.S. Map 6", Suss. LXII. SE. (1951 edn.).
70 Above, pl. facing p. 122.
71 *Southern Region Rec.* comp. R. H. Clark, 51.
72 W.S.R.O., TD/W 153; O.S. Map 6", Suss. LXII (1880 edn.).
73 *Southern Region Rec.* comp. Clark, 92.
74 P.R.O., WO 30/48, f. 185.
75 W.S.R.O., Ep. I/29/225/82.
76 Pigot, *Nat. Com. Dir.* (1832–4), 1051.
77 O.S. Map 6", Suss. LXII (1880 edn.); Pike, *Dir. SW. Suss.* (1886–7).
78 A.C.M., M 32, rot. 5d.
79 *S.R.S.* xlix. 66, 75.
80 Ibid. 16, 122.
81 W.S.R.O., Par. 225/25/5, memo. concerning recreation rm.
82 Ibid. Par. 225/16/1.
83 *Bognor Regis Observer*, 21 July 1988.
84 *Southern Wkly. News*, 30 Sept. 1955.
85 *W. Suss. Gaz.* 15 Aug. 1991.
86 Ibid. 23 Feb. 1995; O.S. Map 6", Suss. LXII. SE. (1951 edn.); cf. below, manors (Yapton).
87 Char. Com. files.
88 *Bognor Regis Observer*, 15 Mar. 1957.
89 C.I.H.E. libr., GY 1509.
90 W.S.R.O., SP 1247; cf. ibid. 326; *Residential Attractions of Bognor Regis, Felpham, Middleton-on-Sea and Dist.* (Gloucester, [1937]), 10.

Yapton Lodge had its own electric lighting plant in 1924,[91] and electricity was available more generally by *c.* 1937.[92] There was street lighting by 1965.[93] The Bognor water company supplied parts of the parish in 1928.[94]

Some Yapton labourers took part in the agricultural riots of 1830.[95] Ford airfield, at one time named after Yapton, is described above; the noise of aeroplanes was a constant background in 1955.[96]

There was a nursing home in North End Road from *c.* 1982.[97]

The poet Andrew Young (d. 1971) retired to Park Lodge in or before 1967.[98]

MANORS AND OTHER ESTATES. The 2½ hide held by Ansgot of earl Godwine (d. 1053) and by Acard of earl Roger in 1086 seem likely to be what was later *YAPTON* manor.[99] The 'land of Yapton' which Humphrey Visdeleu demised to Simon of Norwich and his assigns for four years in 1231[1] was perhaps the same. The manors of *YAPTON SHULBREDE*, *YAPTON COVERTS*, and *BERCOURT* and *WILDBRIDGE*, originating in the 13th and 14th centuries,[2] seem once to have been part of Yapton manor, since all like Yapton itself were later held of the lord of River in Tillington as mesne lord.[3]

Undertenants of Yapton manor were William of Etchingham (fl. 1295–1316),[4] his relative William le Moyne (fl. 1326),[5] and Edward de St. John 'the nephew' (fl. 1341–6).[6] The descent is then lost until 1568, when Henry FitzAlan, earl of Arundel, with John Lumley, Lord Lumley, and his wife Jane, granted Yapton to John Edmunds.[7] The title Yapton manor is not recorded after 1621, when in any case it may have referred to one of the other manors of the parish;[8] what were presumably the demesnes, however, with the probable manor house adjacent to the church,[9] thereafter passed in the direct line[10] from John Edmunds (d. 1571) to Walter[11] (d. 1612), William (d. 1630), William[12] (d. 1658), and Henry (d. 1675), whose heir was his brother John. The latter at his death without issue in 1688 was succeeded by his sister Charity and her husband Laurence Eliot, who at his death in 1726 settled the estate on Samuel and John Marsh. Courts were held in the name of Samuel between 1729 and 1739 for manors that descended with the Yapton manor demesnes,[13] and after his death, at Yapton, in 1740 or 1741 his surviving executors sold the estate in 1749 to George Thomas.

Thomas (created Bt. 1766), former Governor of Pennsylvania and of the Leeward Islands,[14] was living at Yapton Place by 1750.[15] He was succeeded at his death in 1774 by his son Sir William (d. 1777), whose nephew and heir George White also resided; he took the surname Thomas in or before 1781 and was M.P. for Chichester. At his death in 1821[16] his heir was Inigo Thomas (d. 1847), who was succeeded in the direct line by Freeman (d. in or after 1853), Freeman Frederick (d. 1868), and Freeman, who took the surname Freeman-Thomas in 1892 and was created Lord Willingdon in 1910.[17] About 1840 the estate comprised 563 a. including Wicks farm (260. a.) in the east part of the parish.[18] By *c.* 1910 most of the land had passed to John Metters, who owned Wicks Farmhouse and 320 a.,[19] and who was called lord of the manor in 1913.[20] Wicks farm was bought by the tenant Walter Langmead *c.* 1916, descending to his grandson Andrew (fl. 1995).[21] Church Farmhouse, on the other hand, and the former park (27 a.) remained the property of Lord Willingdon *c.* 1910,[22] and by 1924 had passed to the Sparks family.[23]

Yapton House[24] or Place,[25] the presumed manor house, was evidently the 'great farm' where William Edmunds lived in 1621.[26] As depicted in 1782 it was a large building with a seven-bayed north front of 18th-century character, the central three bays projecting with a pediment and a pedimented doorcase or porch, and the ends marked by stone quoins. The irregularity of the west front suggests that older work was incorporated at the rear.[27] In the 1790s the house was said to have recently been 'improved'.[28] The

91 W.S.R.O., SP 326.
92 *Residential Attractions of Bognor Regis, etc.* 10.
93 W.S.R.O., MP 814, f. [1].
94 F. H. Edmunds, *Wells and Springs of Suss.* 25.
95 E. J. Hobsbawm and G. Rudé, *Capt. Swing*, 111.
96 Above, Climping, intro.; Ford, intro.; *Southern Wkly. News*, 30 Sept. 1955.
97 Inf. from Mrs. S. Hocking, Yapton.
98 *Suss. Life*, Jan. 1967, p. 27; *The Times*, 29 Nov. 1971; B. Smith and P. Haas, *Writers in Suss.* 96–8.
99 *V.C.H. Suss.* i. 432–3.
1 *Cal. Chart. R.* 1226–57, 151.
2 Below, this section.
3 e.g. *Cal. Inq. p.m.* v, p. 315; viii, pp. 484–5; B.L. Add. MS. 5702, f. 58; cf. *S.R.S.* x. 136, 256 (Yapton); ii, p. 94 (Yapton Shulbrede); xxxiii, p. 66; *Cal. Pat.* 1553, 367 (Yapton Coverts); *Cal. Inq. p.m.* iv, p. 107; xvi, p. 158; xviii, p. 23; *Percy Chartulary* (Surtees Soc. cxvii), 407 (Bercourt and Wildbridge).
4 *Cal. Chart. R.* 1257–1300, 461; *Cal. Pat.* 1313–17, 430; *Feud. Aids*, v. 143.
5 B.L. Add. MS. 5702, f. 58.
6 *S.R.S.* xxiii, p. 95; *Cal. Inq. p.m.* viii, pp. 484–5.
7 *Cal. Pat.* 1566–9, p. 301.
8 P.R.O., C 2/Jas. I/E 2/66; below, econ. hist. (agric.).
9 Below, this section.
10 Rest of para. based mainly on B.L. Add. MS. 39504, ff. 462–84.
11 *S.R.S.* iii, p. 71.
12 Ibid. xiv, pp. 77–8; cf. ibid. v. 201.
13 W.S.R.O., Add. MS. 13888, pp. 3–9; below, this section.
14 G.E.C. *Baronetage*, v. 141.
15 W.S.R.O., Par. 225/6/4.
16 Berry, *Suss. Geneal.* annot. Comber, 290–1; Dallaway, *Hist. W. Suss.* ii (1) (1819), 43; *Univ. Brit. Dir.* ii. 56; W.S.R.O., Par. 202/7/13.
17 Dallaway, op. cit. 366; Burke, *Peerage* (1935), 2500–1; W.S.R.O., Add. MS. 13888, pp. 71–end.
18 W.S.R.O., TD/W 153; cf. Wickhouse and land called the Weekes in 17th cent.: ibid. Add. MS. 37194 (TS. cat.); *S.R.S.* xxxiii, p. 66.
19 W.S.R.O., IR 12, f. 53.
20 *Kelly's Dir. Suss.* (1913).
21 Inf. from Mr. P. Hague, Oving; *W. Suss. Gaz.* 28 May 1981; cf. *Kelly's Dir. Suss.* (1918 and later edns.); W.S.R.O., SP 326.
22 W.S.R.O., IR 12, f. 64; cf. below, this section.
23 W.S.R.O., MP 3541, p. 6; ibid. SP 326.
24 B.L. Add. MSS. 5674, f. 37; 39504, f. 471; *250 Yrs. of Mapmaking in Suss.* ed. H. Margary, pls. 19, 26.
25 *250 Yrs. of Mapmaking in Suss.* pl. 5; W.S.R.O., Add. MS. 8811.
26 *S.R.S.* xlix. 16. The 'mansion ho.' in Yapton divided at arbitration in 1608 evidently belonged to another estate: W.S.R.O., Add. MS. 12880 (TS. cat.); cf. *S.R.S.* xiv, p. 144.
27 B.L. Add. MS. 5674, f. 37, illus. above, pl. facing p. 234.
28 *Univ. Brit. Dir.* ii. 56.

Thomas trustees were empowered to demolish it in 1829;[29] it was still inhabited by a tenant *c.* 1832[30] but by *c.* 1840 had disappeared.[31] The site of the house is shown by a raised area in the garden north of the building called Church Farmhouse in 1995, perhaps representing rubble from the demolished building. Church Farmhouse itself was at first apparently a 17th-century timber-framed service range of one storey running south from the west front of the manor house. After *c.* 1835 it was heightened and converted into two cottages, later becoming one house which was enlarged to the north. The walled garden of the manor house survives on the west and north-west, and a possibly 18th-century dovecot to the south-east.

The manor of *YAPTON SHULBREDE*, first so called in 1544,[32] evidently originated in the land which Shulbrede priory had from 1239 or earlier until the Dissolution.[33] In 1544 the Crown granted it to John Pope,[34] who conveyed it in the same year to John Edmunds and his son John;[35] after 1568 it descended almost continuously with the Yapton manor demesnes.[36]

The manor or reputed manor of *YAPTON COVERTS*, of which neither courts nor tenants are known, was first so named in 1505,[37] but presumably derived from land with which John le Covert was dealing in 1346–7;[38] he or a namesake had been a taxpayer in the parish in 1332.[39] By 1477 it had perhaps passed to Thomas Bellingham,[40] who died seised of a 'manor of Yapton' in 1490. His son and heir Ralph[41] had the manor in 1505[42] and was succeeded in 1532 by his son John (d. 1542), whose son Ralph[43] had it in 1551.[44] Ralph's brother-in-law Richard Boys[45] was dealing with it in 1559,[46] but in 1592 with his son Samuel conveyed it to Walter Edmunds.[47] After Walter's death in 1612 it diverged from the descent of the Yapton manor demesnes through other members of the Edmunds family.[48]

In 1693[49] Yapton Coverts was settled, together with 135 a., the future Bonhams farm, on John Tippetts and his wife Mary, cousin and heir of Robert Edmunds. After Tippetts's death in or before 1709, it was sold in 1713 by his heirs to John Smith and his son John; the latter's brother and heir William, succeeding in or before 1735, devised it in 1736 to his nephew John Bonham, who took the surname Smith. John's son Henry Bonham, who succeeded 1747 × 1787, sold both manor and land in 1790 to Charles Billinghurst and Joseph Long. In 1818 Charles conveyed them to his sons Charles and Thomas, who in 1840 sold them to Thomas Duke. After Duke's death in 1853 his executors sold them in 1860 to Richard Redford (fl. 1871).[50] Apparently in 1876 the estate was bought by Henry Hounsom.[51] His son William A. Hounsom[52] had it by 1903; he was described as the chief landowner in Yapton between 1909 and 1915[53] and died in 1934.

Bonhams Farmhouse has a stuccoed front apparently of the early 19th century with earlier work behind; the main range is of two storeys with attics and there is a late 19th-century one-storeyed extension on the west.

The manors, later manor, of *BERCOURT* or *BERECOURT* and *WILDBRIDGE* were first so called in the mid 14th century,[54] but presumably derived from fees or parts of fees mentioned at those places from *c.* 1243.[55] The undertenancy of the two manors was settled in 1364–5 on Edward de St. John and his wife Joan.[56] Edward died 1379 × 1386, and after Joan's death in 1386 the manors passed under the 1364–5 settlement to Sir John d'Arundel (d. 1390).[57] His son John, Lord Maltravers, was lord in 1412, and after his succession as earl of Arundel in 1415[58] the manors descended with the rape.[59] They were considered a single manor by the early 15th century.[60]

In 1568 Henry FitzAlan, earl of Arundel, granted Bercourt and Wildbridge to John Edmunds.[61] Thereafter it descended with the Yapton manor demesnes[62] until at the death of Walter Edmunds in 1612 it passed to his son Christopher (d. 1620),[63] whose widow Mary married George Oglander in 1620 or 1621. In 1633 they conveyed the manor to William Madgwick;[64]

29 Elwes & Robinson, *W. Suss.* 277.
30 Pigot, *Nat. Com. Dir.* (1832–4), 1051.
31 W.S.R.O., TD/W 153.
32 *L. & P. Hen. VIII*, xix (2), p. 190.
33 *S.R.S.* ii, p. 94; *Inq. Non.* (Rec. Com.), 368; *Valor Eccl.* (Rec. Com.), i. 322; cf. *Cal. Inq. Misc.* ii, p. 266.
34 *L. & P. Hen. VIII*, xix (2), p. 190.
35 W.S.R.O., Add. MS. 4529.
36 e.g. *S.R.S.* xiv, pp. 77–8; xx. 509; li. 12, 63; but cf. B.L. Add. MS. 5687, f. 220; W.S.R.O., Add. MS. 12900 (TS. cat.).
37 *Cal. Pat.* 1547–8, 303, reciting earlier deeds.
38 *S.R.S.* xxiii, p. 117.
39 Ibid. x. 256; cf. *Inq. Non.* (Rec. Com.), 368. Rob. le Covert was assessed to subsidy in Yapton in 1327 and 1332: *S.R.S.* x. 136, 257.
40 E.S.R.O., SAS/D 19 (TS. cat.); cf. *S.R.S.* xxiii, p. 281.
41 *Cal. Inq. p.m. Hen. VII*, i, p. 262; cf. below, this section [other relig. hos.' lands].
42 *Cal. Pat.* 1547–8, 303.
43 Berry, *Suss. Geneal.* annot. Comber, 190; *S.R.S.* xiv, pp. 21–2.
44 *Cal. Pat.* 1553, 367; cf. ibid. 1547–8, 303–4.
45 Berry, op. cit. 190.
46 *S.R.S.* xx. 436; cf. W.S.R.O., Add. MS. 32845 (TS. cat.).
47 Berry, op. cit. 190; *S.R.S.* xx. 508.
48 B.L. Add. MS. 39488, ff. 186–7; W.S.R.O., Add. MSS. 12884, 12887 (TS. cat.); above, this section (Yapton).
49 W.S.R.O., Add. MS. 12902 (TS. cat.). Rest of para. based mostly on W.S.R.O., MP 3427 (cal. of deeds of Bonhams fm., Yapton, in possession of Mr. A. Broughton, Bonhams Fmho.); abstract of title to Bonhams fm. and man. of Yapton Coverts, 1876, in possession of Mr. Broughton.
50 *Jnl. of Bath and W. of Eng. Soc.* 3rd ser. iii. 39; cf. *Kelly's Dir. Suss.* (1874).
51 W.S.R.O., Add. MS. 14307 (o) (TS. cat.); sale cat. of Bonhams fm. 1876, in possession of Mr. Broughton.
52 Above, Felpham, manor (Innerwick fm.).
53 *Kelly's Dir. Suss.* (1903 and later edns.); cf. W.S.R.O., IR 12, f. 52; ibid. SP 326.
54 *S.R.S.* xxiii, p. 157.
55 Ibid. lxvii. 103; *Cal. Inq. p.m.* iv, p. 107; W.S.R.O., Add. MS. 12263 (TS. cat.).
56 *S.R.S.* xxiii, p. 157.
57 *Cal. Fine R.* 1377–83, 138; *Complete Peerage*, s.v. Arundel barony; *Cal. Inq. p.m.* xvi, pp. 156–8; cf. ibid. xviii, p. 23.
58 *Complete Peerage*, s.v. Arundel barony; *Feud. Aids*, vi. 522.
59 P.R.O., C 139/71, no. 37, m. 32; *S.R.S.* xix. 56; xxiii, p. 261; *Lavington Estate Archives*, ed. F. W. Steer, p. 24.
60 P.R.O., C 138/59, no. 51, m. 14; C 139/71, no. 37, m. 32.
61 *S.R.S.* xx. 508.
62 e.g. ibid. iii, pp. 71–2; W.S.R.O., Add. MS. 37609 (TS. cat.).
63 B.L. Add. MSS. 39488, f. 187; 39504, f. 463.
64 *S.R.S.* xix. 34; xlix. 16.

The Congregational chapel of 1861

The medieval chapel at Bilsham in 1996

Walberton:
Dovecot at Pigeon House farm

Yapton:
Glasshouses at Pollards Nurseries

he or a namesake was dealing with it in 1662 and 1674[65] and Edward Madgwick in 1694.[66] Another William owned land in Yapton in 1705.[67] In 1771 William Madgwick sold manor and lands to Ann Billinghurst, whose relative John Billinghurst[68] had been lessee in 1752.[69] After Ann's death 1798 × 1807 they were sold to James Penfold; at that date the lands totalled 131 a.[70] About 1840 John Boniface was owner of the farm[71] and in 1877 Ann Boniface.[72] The manor house, variously called Bury, Berea, and Berri Court in the 19th and 20th centuries, seems often to have been let from the 1880s.[73]

A manor house at Bercourt was mentioned in 1460.[74] Its successor was called Berri Court in 1995.[75] It is L-shaped, its outer walls and some re-used ceiling beams probably being 17th-century. Parts of the staircase and one door surround on the first floor suggest a late 18th-century remodelling, and there was a much more thorough one in the early 19th century, when a new wing was added between the existing ranges. At some date the south front was given a parapet, later removed, and in the late 19th century or early 20th a conservatory was built along it; after its removal a pedimented doorcase was added. The building materials include flint, brick, stucco, and Bognor rock sandstone.

In 1946 there were well matured grounds containing fine specimen trees, a walled garden, a tennis lawn, and a tea lawn with lily pool.[76] They remained notable in 1995, making ingenious use of the small site.

A manor at *BILSHAM* was held by Godwine, a free man, in 1066, and by Hugh of earl Roger in 1086; there was also a sub-manor containing three hides which was held by three free men in 1066 and by Warin in 1086.[77] At the division of the d'Aubigny inheritance after 1243 one fee at Bilsham formed part of Robert Tattersall's portion.[78] Members of the Avenell family held land at Bilsham between 1197 and 1244.[79]

Lettice of Bilsham, who was dealing with ½ yardland at Bilsham in 1241,[80] was perhaps related to William of Bilsham who held ¼ fee there in 1303.[81] It was called Bilsham manor in 1345, when William of Bilsham (fl. 1327) died seised of it; his son and heir John[82] (d. 1349) was succeeded by his brother Roger,[83] but the lands have not been identified later.

Another ¼ fee which Philip de Croft held in 1242[84] had passed by 1303 to Hugh de Croft,[85] who in 1307 granted a life interest to Andrew of Medstead in the manor of Bilsham, so called.[86] The reversion was conveyed by Hugh son of Hugh de Croft to Richard FitzAlan, earl of Arundel, in 1337–8,[87] after which it presumably passed with the rape.

By 1291 Arundel priory had an estate in Yapton.[88] By 1325, when there were two barns, at least 197 a., and both free and customary tenants, it was described as a manor,[89] also later called Bilsham.

In 1316 the vill of Bilsham was said to be divided between William of Bilsham and Andrew of Medstead, while the prior of Arundel's estate was described as part of Yapton vill.[90] It is not clear which estate was the land at Bilsham owned by John Taverner in 1412.[91]

Arundel priory's estate passed with the other priory endowments in 1380 to Arundel college. A further 108 a. were granted by the earl of Arundel in 1386. From 1394–5 until the Dissolution the lands were at farm.[92] The manor was described as ¼ fee in 1428.[93] In 1544 the Crown granted it to the earl of Arundel.[94]

After the Dissolution there were two estates at Bilsham, whose relationship to the estates mentioned is not clear. One, called *BILSHAM* manor and having a court and tenants,[95] evidently incorporated either or both of the former Croft and Arundel college estates. It was conveyed in 1568 by Henry FitzAlan, earl of Arundel, John Lumley, Lord Lumley, and his wife Jane to John Edmunds,[96] and thereafter descended with the Yapton manor demesnes.[97] The attached farm had 75 a. in 1667[98] and 100 a. in 1699,[99] and corresponded to the later Hobbs farm east of Bilsham Road.[1] By *c.* 1910 that farm belonged to G. and S. Sparks[2] and in 1929, when it was 76 a., to Miss S. E. Sparks.[3]

The second estate belonged by 1608 to Sir Garrett Kempe, lord of Slindon manor,[4] and though never a manor was the later Bilsham Manor farm west of Bilsham Road. Garrett and Anthony Kempe were dealing with Bilsham

65 Ibid. xix. 34; cf. ibid. v. 201.
66 W.S.R.O., Harris MS. 509 (TS. cat.).
67 *S.R.S.* iv. 30.
68 Deed, 1771, in possession of Mr. Broughton.
69 W.S.R.O., Par. 225/2/6.
70 Ibid. MP 3427, f. [2]; ibid. SP 249.
71 Ibid. TD/W 153; cf. *30th Rep. Com. Char.* 639.
72 W.S.R.O., Par. 225/7/3.
73 Ibid. SP 249, 1243; Pike, *Dir. SW. Suss.* (1886–7); *Kelly's Dir. Suss.* (1895 and later edns.)
74 A.C.M., M 531, f. [58v.].
75 Above, pl. facing p. 171. 76 E.S.R.O., SAS/PS 86.
77 *V.C.H. Suss.* i. 431–2.
78 *S.R.S.* lxvii. 103; cf. *Cal. Inq. p.m.* iv, p. 260; xii, pp. 431, 433.
79 *Close R.* 1242–7, 249; *S.R.S.* ii, pp. 3–4, 43, 91–3; cf. ibid. xxiii, p. 89; *Yr. Bk.* 14 Edw. II (Selden Soc.), 100–1.
80 *S.R.S.* ii, p. 102.
81 *Cal. Inq. p.m.* iv, p. 107; cf. *S.R.S.* x. 80.
82 *Cal. Inq. p.m.* viii, p. 421; *S.R.S.* x. 135, 137; xxiii, p. 113; *Inq. Non.* (Rec. Com.), 368.
83 *Cal. Inq. p.m.* ix, p. 142.
84 *Bk. of Fees*, ii. 689; cf. *S.R.S.* ii, p. 91.
85 *Cal. Inq. p.m.* iv, p. 107.
86 *S.R.S.* vii, pp. 197–8.
87 Ibid. xxiii, p. 89.
88 *Tax. Eccl.* (Rec. Com.), 139; *Inq. Non.* (Rec. Com.), 368.
89 P.R.O., E 106/8/19, rot. 16.
90 *Feud. Aids*, v. 143.
91 Ibid. vi. 522–3.
92 Petch, 'Arundel Coll.' 304–5; *Cal. Pat.* 1385–9, 104.
93 *Feud. Aids*, v. 154.
94 *L. & P. Hen. VIII*, xix (2), p. 475.
95 Below, econ. hist. (agric.); local govt.
96 *Cal. Pat.* 1566–9, p. 301.
97 *S.R.S.* iii, pp. 71–2; xiv, pp. 77–8; xix. 77; li. 12, 63; B.L. Add. MS. 5687, f. 220; N.R.A. Man. Doc. Reg.
98 W.S.R.O., Add. MS. 37194 (TS. cat.).
99 Ibid. Add. MS. 12905 (TS. cat.).
1 e.g. ibid. TD/W 153.
2 Ibid. IR 12, f. 54; cf. ibid. SP 326.
3 Ibid. SP 326, loose TS. draft sale cat. of part of Hobbs fm. 1929.
4 B.L. Add. Ch. 18906 (MS. cal.); *V.C.H. Suss.* iv. 234; cf. W.S.R.O., Ep. I/25/1 (1615).

farm, so called, in 1664,[5] and the same or another Anthony Kempe in 1685.[6] Thereafter it evidently descended with Slindon[7] until in 1908 it was sold to the tenant John C. Loveys (d. 1931).[8] The farm comprised *c.* 190 a. in 1819,[9] 216 a. *c.* 1840,[10] and 381 a. *c.* 1910.[11] Loveys' son Walter succeeded him in it before 1924, and was succeeded by his son John.[12]

There was a manor house on the land belonging to the Bilsham family in the 1340s.[13] Hobbs Farmhouse, called Bilsham Farm *c.* 1875[14] and evidently the true manor house of Bilsham manor, was erected in or shortly before 1718.[15] It is of two storeys and rendered, with a tiled roof. The farmhouse which belonged to the Slindon House estate is in two parts. The north end is a 17th-century timber-framed house called in 1995 Manor cottage; it has north and south rooms separated by a chimneystack, with another chimneystack, perhaps originally that of the kitchen, at the south end. It was encased in brick in the late 18th or early 19th century. In the early 19th century a taller block of three bays, called Bilsham Manor in 1995, was added at the south end, stuccoed and with a projecting porch; the older range became its service end.

Elizabeth Shelley, née Michelgrove, had property at Bilsham before 1474,[16] which then descended with Clapham until the later 16th century.[17] The estate was called a manor in 1581,[18] but it has not been identified.

Yapton *RECTORY* belonged to Arundel priory before 1380, and passed with the priory's other estates to Arundel college.[19] It was at farm to the former bailiff with the college's manor at Bilsham in 1394–5, and presumably continued to be farmed with that until the Dissolution.[20] It was then granted to the earl of Arundel,[21] descending thereafter usually with the Yapton manor demesnes.[22] It remained a manor, with courts and tenants.[23] Members of the Standen family leased it in the later 16th century.[24]

There was a rectory house in the 1560s,[25] but its site is unknown.

Tithes valued at 13*s.* 4*d.* were payable to Tortington priory in 1291;[26] by 1535 they were valued at £5 6*s.* 8*d.*[27] From that date the estate was sometimes referred to as the *RECTORY* of *TRYNEBARN* or *TRINEBARN*;[28] it included a tithe barn south-west of the Yapton–Climping road with 1 a. opposite it.[29] Between 1568 and 1571 at least the estate descended with the Yapton manor demesnes,[30] but by 1589 it belonged to the Crown.[31] Thereafter the lordship apparently followed the descent of Priory farm, Tortington,[32] until in 1693 Sir William Thomas, Bt., conveyed it to John Dobell.[33] Sir John Miller, Bt., was dealing with it in 1709,[34] and after his death in 1721 it passed to his son John (d. 1735), whose son Challen[35] sold it in 1756 to Walter Sydserfe.[36] He settled it in 1759 on his daughter Margaret at her marriage with William Thomas, and after 1774 it again descended with the Yapton manor demesnes.[37]

The house and land which Urse of Linch gave to Chichester cathedral in 1199 became the nucleus of Burndell or Bundle farm east of the village.[38] In 1595 it was held for three lives,[39] but in the early 16th century and from the late 17th to the mid 19th it was leased for 21-year periods.[40] In 1862, when the cathedral's estate was for sale, it comprised *c.* 130 a. in Yapton and Binsted.[41] Burndell farm belonged to William Wareham *c.* 1910.[42]

Tortington priory was granted land in Yapton from 1235[43] which included a mill[44] and by 1537 totalled at least 78 a. The estate, which then had 13 tenants,[45] was still called a manor in 1602, when Thomas Knight was dealing with it.[46]

Other religious houses which owned land in Yapton included Boxgrove priory (from the later 12th century),[47] Durford abbey in Rogate (from the late 12th or early 13th century),[48] Waverley abbey near Farnham (Surr.) (from 1220 or

5 W.S.R.O., Add. MS. 37517; cf. *S.R.S.* xx. 401–2.
6 *Goodwood Estate Archives*, i, ed. F. W. Steer and J. Venables, i, p. 92.
7 *V.C.H. Suss.* iv. 234–5; Dallaway, *Hist. W. Suss.* ii (1) (1819), 45; *S.R.S.* li. 144; W.S.R.O., Par. 202/7/13; ibid. Slindon MSS., bdle. NR 30, nos. 6, 16; ibid. TD/W 153.
8 W.S.R.O., Slindon MS. NR 97, f. 30; mon. in chyd.
9 Dallaway, op. cit. 45.
10 W.S.R.O., TD/W 153.
11 Ibid. IR 12, f. 51.
12 Ibid. SP 326; fam. tree in possession of Mrs. S. Abbot, Bilsham.
13 *Cal. Inq. p.m.* viii, p. 421; P.R.O., C 135/94, no. 2.
14 O.S. Map 6", Suss. LXII (1880 edn.).
15 W.S.R.O., Add. MS. 12916.
16 P.R.O., C 142/46, no. 15; *V.C.H. Suss.* vi (1), 13.
17 *S.R.S.* xxxiii, p. 2; P.R.O., E 310/25/143, f. 2; E 310/25/144, f. 42.
18 *S.R.S.* xx. 301–2.
19 Above, this section (Bilsham); below, church.
20 Petch, 'Arundel Coll.' 304–5; *Valor Eccl.* (Rec. Com.), i. 313.
21 *S.R.S.* xix. 56.
22 e.g. ibid. iii, p. 71; xiv, p. 77; xx. 509; li. 12, 63; *Cal. Pat.* 1566–9, p. 301; B.L. Add. MS. 5687, f. 220; W.S.R.O., Add. MSS. 12916, 12921 (TS. cat.).
23 Below, econ. hist. (agric.); local govt.
24 P.R.O., C 2/Eliz. I/S 23/59.
25 Ibid.
26 *Tax. Eccl.* (Rec. Com.), 141; cf. *S.R.S.* ii, p. 83, apparently mentioning the priory's barn at Yapton.
27 *Valor Eccl.* (Rec. Com.), i. 312.
28 Ibid.; *S.R.S.* xx. 445. The name, also recorded as Tyne barn, is unexplained unless indicating a wooden bldg. in distinction from other barns of stone: ibid. xxix, pp. 165–6; W.S.R.O., Add. MS. 28534 (TS. cat.); *O.E.D.* s.v. treen.
29 W.S.R.O., Add. MSS. 2027, p. 53; 2031.
30 B.L. Add. MS. 39394, f. 206; *S.R.S.* iii, pp. 71–2.
31 P.R.O., E 310/25/144, f. 8.
32 W.S.R.O., Add. MSS. 2027, p. 53; 2031; *S.R.S.* xxix, pp. 165–6; above, Tortington, manor (Priory fm.).
33 *S.R.S.* xxix, p. 166.
34 W.S.R.O., Add. MS. 28534 (TS. cat.).
35 G.E.C. *Baronetage*, iv. 194; Berry, *Suss. Geneal.* annot. Comber, 292–3; *S.R.S.* xx. 445.
36 W.S.R.O., Add. MS. 28552 (TS. cat.).
37 4 Geo. IV, c. 16 (Private).
38 *S.R.S.* xlvi, p. 86; cf. ibid. p. 91; *Cal. Pat.* 1413–16, 301.
39 W.S.R.O., Cap. I/51/14, f. 89.
40 Ibid. Add. MS. 4534 (TS. cat.); ibid. Cap. I/28/103; Ch. Commrs., surv. 1861, p. 291; *S.R.S.* lii, p. 82. Another early 16th-cent. lease was for 60 yrs.: ibid. p. 96.
41 W.S.R.O., Add. MSS. 28642–3.
42 Ibid. IR 12, f. 51.
43 *S.R.S.* ii, pp. 83–4; *Cal. Pat.* 1340–3, 575; *Inq. Non.* (Rec. Com.), 368.
44 *Tax. Eccl.* (Rec. Com.), 139.
45 P.R.O., SC 6/Hen. VIII/3674, rot. 9d.
46 W.S.R.O., Add. MS. 33380 (TS. cat.); cf. *S.R.S.* xiv, pp. 136–7.
47 *S.R.S.* lix, pp. 18, 49, 53, 68, 77, 123–4, 135–6, 155; *Cal. Inq. Misc.* ii, p. 64; *Valor Eccl.* (Rec. Com.), i. 306.
48 *Chich. Acta* (Cant. & York Soc.), p. 166; *Valor Eccl.* (Rec. Com.), i. 321.

earlier),[49] Hardham priory (by 1534),[50] and the Hospital of St. John (from before 1290).[51]

Chichester corporation held land of Tortington priory in 1537.[52] In 1582 its estate comprised 74 a., including 35 a. at Bilsham,[53] and there were 60 a. *c.* 1806–7, lying in scattered parcels chiefly along Bilsham and Drove lanes.[54] Between the late 17th century and the mid 19th leases were for 21 years.[55]

STAKERS FARM west of the village was held of Laurence and Charity Eliot in 1699 by Thomas Staker.[56] Benjamin Staker was occupier in 1781[57] and was succeeded by his son Zaccheus (d. 1795 × 1797), whose heir was his son Benjamin. Benjamin acquired the freehold of the farm in 1808[58] and sold it in 1824 to John Browning Staker, apparently his brother.[59] After John's death in 1836 his executors sold the farm in 1837 to the Revd. Thomas Penny White[60] (d. 1845 × 1860), and after the death of Thomas's widow Charlotte *c.* 1861 it passed to their son Arthur,[61] who at his death in 1899 left it to his nephew (Sir) Herbert White. He in 1929 conveyed it to Anthony P. White,[62] from whom it passed to A. R. M. White (fl. 1995). The farm had 271 a. in Yapton and elsewhere in 1699,[63] 128 a. *c.* 1840,[64] and 234 a. in Yapton and Barnham in 1929.[65]

The Yapton manor with which members of the Venables family were dealing between 1597 and 1610[66] has not been identified.

ECONOMIC HISTORY. AGRICULTURE. Six *villani* and six cottars held land in 1086 of what was later apparently Yapton manor.[67] References to a freeholder with 7 a. in 1551[68] and a copyholder with 18 a. *c.* 1614[69] may be to one of the other manors of the parish, since the title Yapton manor was used loosely to describe other manors and estates at different times, and since the main manor cannot be traced after 1621.[70] Tenants of Yapton Shulbrede are recorded from 1544.[71] Several copyholds remained in the 18th and early 19th centuries; they could be sublet by 1772.[72] On Bercourt and Wildbridge manor in the 15th and 16th centuries there were both free and copyhold tenants.[73] Some demesne land was being leased out in small parcels in 1460.[74] Copyholds could be sublet by 1535[75] and were being enfranchised by the mid 17th century.[76]

Fourteen *villani* were listed on Bilsham manor in 1086, and 5 *villani* and 5 cottars on its sub-manor.[77] There were both free and customary tenants on the Arundel priory[78] and Bilsham family[79] manors in the earlier 14th century, but all the latter died during the Black Death, their lands remaining unoccupied in 1349.[80] There were still free and copyhold tenants at Bilsham in the 16th century.[81] Copyholds could be sublet by 1549.[82] Two copyholds of 22 a., each described as a yardland, and one cottage tenement remained in the 18th century.[83]

The rectory manor had both free and copyhold tenants in 1621.[84] Only copyholds survived by the 18th century,[85] when one of 17½ a. was called a yardland and there was another of 17 a. Copyholds could be sublet by 1730.[86]

Waverley abbey's estate had tenants in the 14th century,[87] and 4 freeholders, 7 copyholders, and 2 leaseholders held land of Tortington priory in 1537.[88] Land was also held of manors outside the parish: Walberton,[89] Ilsham St. John in Climping,[90] Tortington,[91] Avenells or East Angmering in Angmering,[92] and Barnham.[93]

The demesne farm belonging to the Bilsham family's manor at Bilsham had 126 a. in 1345[94] and at least 160 a. in 1349,[95] and that belonging to Arundel priory's manor in the same place had *c.* 200 a. at the same period, labour services still apparently being exacted in the 1320s.[96] After 1394 the Arundel priory land, which by then had passed to Arundel college, was let, the first farmer being the former bailiff.[97] The Bercourt and Wildbridge manor demesne farm had 200 a. of arable, apparently 80 a. of several pasture, and 12 a. of several meadow in 1421; labour services were mentioned then but it is not clear whether they were still performed.[98] The Bercourt and Wildbridge demesnes were let by 1460.[99]

Open arable fields seem to have ringed Yapton

49 *Cur. Reg. R.* viii. 286–7; *S.R.S.* xlvi, p. 327; *Valor Eccl.* (Rec. Com.), ii. 35.
50 *S.R.S.* xix. 201–2.
51 *Cal. Inq. Misc.* ii, p. 46; *Cal. Inq. p.m. Hen. VII*, i, p. 262.
52 P.R.O., SC 6/Hen. VIII/3674, rot. 9d.
53 Dallaway, *Hist. W. Suss.* i (1), 161 n.
54 W.S.R.O., Chich. city archives, AS/1, pp. 10–11.
55 Ibid. Slindon MSS., bdle. NR 48, nos. 2, 5–9; P.R.O., PROB 5/2808.
56 W.S.R.O., Add. MS. 12905 (TS. cat.); cf. ibid. 12911 (TS. cat.).
57 Ibid. Par. 202/7/13.
58 Ibid. Add. MSS. 10772, 28567 (TS. cat.); 30481.
59 Ibid. 10772, 28570 (TS. cat.).
60 Ibid. 28573, 28576 (TS. cat.).
61 Ibid. 28580–3 (TS. cat.).
62 Ibid. Par. 225/25/1/12.
63 Ibid. Add. MS. 12905 (TS. cat.).
64 Ibid. TD/W 153.
65 Ibid. Par. 225/25/1/12.
66 *S.R.S.* xx. 456.
67 *V.C.H. Suss.* i. 432–3.
68 A.C.M., M 829.
69 P.R.O., C 2/Jas. I/E 2/66; cf. ibid. C 2/Eliz. I/M 15/54.
70 Above, manors (Yapton); *S.R.S.* xiv, pp. 21 (Yapton Coverts), 137 (Tortington priory's land); xx. 508 (Bercourt and Wildbridge); P.R.O., E 106/8/19, rot. 16 (Bilsham).
71 *L. & P. Hen. VIII*, xix (2), p. 190.
72 W.S.R.O., Add. MS. 13888, pp. 3, 5, 32, 129, 178.
73 A.C.M., M 28, rot. 6; 31, rot. 6; 278, f. [14]; P.R.O., C 138/59, no. 51, m. 14.
74 A.C.M., M 531, f. [58].
75 Ibid. 28, rot. 6.
76 W.S.R.O., Add. MS. 12889 (TS. cat.).
77 *V.C.H. Suss.* i. 431–2.
78 P.R.O., E 106/8/19, rot. 16.
79 Ibid. C 135/77, no. 1.
80 *Cal. Inq. p.m.* ix, p. 142.
81 A.C.M., M 819, 829.
82 Ibid. 553, m. 4.
83 W.S.R.O., Add. MS. 13888, pp. 1, 27, 39.
84 P.R.O., C 2/Jas. I/E 2/65; cf. A.C.M., M 553, m. 4.
85 W.S.R.O., Add. MS. 13888, *passim.*
86 Ibid. p. 4.
87 *S.R.S.* xlvi, p. 327.
88 P.R.O., SC 6/Hen. VIII/3674, rot. 9d.
89 Ibid. SC 6/Hen. VIII/3483, rot. 35 and d.
90 W.S.R.O., Add. MSS. 7083; 12626 (TS. cat.).
91 Ibid. 12895 (TS. cat.).
92 Ibid. 12882 (TS. cat.).
93 Ibid. 13256 (TS. cat.).
94 P.R.O., C 135/77, no. 1.
95 Ibid. C 135/94, no. 2.
96 Ibid. E 106/8/19, rot. 16; *Inq. Non.* (Rec. Com.), 368.
97 Petch, 'Arundel Coll.' 304.
98 P.R.O., C 138/59, no. 51, m. 14.
99 A.C.M., M 531, ff. [58, 73v.]; cf. ibid. A 1870; ibid. M 859, rot. 5.

village on three sides in the Middle Ages: East Town field north of Ford Lane,[1] the Cinders east of Bilsham Road,[2] and Tacklee or South Street field south-west of the village.[3] The Warmare or Warnmere north of Main Road on the site of the modern recreation ground may also have been an open field.[4] Several other open fields mentioned from the early 13th century are unlocated.[5] A three-course rotation of the fields at Bilsham was apparently practised in the 1340s.[6]

The open fields were apparently inclosed piecemeal by agreement through exchanges like that evidenced in 1553 at Bilsham between the farmer of the manor demesnes and the tenants.[7] By 1460 land on Bercourt and Wildbridge manor in a field called Woodcroft already formed small closes.[8] In the mid 16th century, though some land remained commonable,[9] there were closes in individual open fields of up to 19 a.[10] The trend to consolidation continued later.[11]

Crops grown in the Middle Ages included wheat, barley,[12] flax, hemp, and apples, while cattle, sheep, pigs, and geese were raised.[13]

A tenants' pasture on Bercourt and Wildbridge manor was mentioned in 1542,[14] but no other common pasture is known in the parish except possibly for marshland in the north-east[15] and roadside waste along Main and Bilsham roads including Berri Court green in the centre of the village,[16] the location of which is not clear. Common meadow called East Town mead or meads[17] presumably lay in the north-east, and there was other common meadow at Bilsham.[18] Pasture and meadow were also held severally;[19] it was presumably for its quality that meadow in the parish was granted to landowners in other places.[20] Tenants of one of the Bilsham manors could common on the demesne meadow outside the hay season in the mid 14th century.[21]

In the 17th and 18th centuries demesne farms remained prominent. That centred on Yapton Place was known as 'the great farm' in 1621 and 1718.[22] The future Hobbs farm had 75 a. in 1667[23] and 100 a. in 1699,[24] and Bury Court farm, the Bercourt and Wildbridge manor farm, 131 a. in 1807.[25] The demesne farm of Yapton Coverts manor, later Bonhams farm, had 135 a. in 1693,[26] and Burndell farm 106 a. in 1595 and 93 a. in 1727, on each occasion including land in neighbouring parishes.[27] Stakers farm had 271 a. in Yapton and elsewhere in 1699.[28]

Crops grown in the 17th and 18th centuries[29] were wheat, barley, oats, peas, vetch, and tares, with clover seed by 1731; wheat seems usually to have had the highest acreage. Hemp[30] was also grown. Animals raised at that period were chiefly sheep, cattle, and pigs, with some poultry. Inhabitants by the later 17th and early 18th centuries sometimes farmed in neighbouring parishes as well as in Yapton, and one farmer at Bilsham in 1671 had stock in the Weald at Kirdford. Sheep were washed by the mid 18th century where Bilsham Road crossed the Ryebank rife.[31]

Some farms in the earlier 19th century remained in scattered closes.[32] About 1840 there were five chief farms in the parish: Wicks, representing the Yapton manor demesnes (260 a.), Bonhams (131 a.), and Stakers (128 a.) in the north half; and in the south the future Bilsham Manor and Hobbs farms of 216 a. and 138 a. respectively.[33] Those remained the chief farms *c.* 1910, when Wicks farm had 320 a. and Bilsham Manor farm 381 a.;[34] most land in the parish was then rented.[35] Only one of the larger landowners was resident in 1867.[36]

Arable farming predominated in the earlier 19th century; there were reckoned to be only 100 a. of pasture in 1819,[37] and *c.* 1840 there was nearly four times as much arable as meadow and pasture, wheat remaining the chief crop.[38] There were numerous field barns, especially in the south-west part of the parish, *c.* 1813.[39] The land in the centre was said to be very productive in 1841. A six-course rotation was then widely practised, viz. turnips; barley or oats; seeds; wheat; peas, beans, or tares; and wheat.[40] Much of Bonhams farm was pipe-drained by 1871.[41]

In the mid 19th century Yapton supplied

1 W.S.R.O., Ep. I/86/20, f. 16v.; ibid. S.A.S. MS. B 652 (TS. cat.); ibid. TD/W 153.
2 Ibid. TD/W 153.
3 Ibid. Add. MSS. 2034; 8762, 12889 (TS. cat.); ibid. S.A.S. MSS. B 651, 658 (TS. cat.); ibid. TD/W 153; *S.R.S.* xxix, p. 146; xlvi, p. 86; lix, pp. 75–6.
4 *S.R.S.* lix, pp. 78, 88; W.S.R.O., SP 326; ibid. TD/W 153.
5 e.g. *S.R.S.* ii, p. 84; lix, pp. 121–2, 193; *S.A.C.* lxxxix. 162; W.S.R.O., Add. MS. 28561 (TS. cat.).
6 P.R.O., C 135/77, no. 1; C 135/94, no. 2.
7 A.C.M., M 31, rot. 6d.
8 Ibid. 531, f. [58].
9 Ibid. 282, rot. 1d.; 314, rot. 7; 859, rot. 5d.
10 P.R.O., SC 6/Hen. VIII/3674, rot. 9d.; W.S.R.O., S.A.S. MS. B 645 (TS. cat.).
11 W.S.R.O., Add. MSS. 2034; 8762, 12880, 12924 (TS. cat.); ibid. S.A.S. MS. B 651 (TS. cat.).
12 *S.R.S.* xxiii. 79.
13 *Inq. Non.* (Rec. Com.), 368; P.R.O., E 106/8/19, rot. 16.
14 A.C.M., M 859, rot. 11.
15 W.S.R.O., S.A.S. MS. C 315 (TS. cat.).
16 Ibid. Add. MSS. 7076, 12897, 12919, 12922 (TS. cat.); A.C.M., M 553, m. 4; above, intro. (settlement).
17 W.S.R.O., Add. MS. 8762 (TS. cat.); ibid. S.A.S. MS. B 652 (TS. cat.); *S.R.S.* xxix, p. 146.
18 W.S.R.O., Add. MS. 2068; ibid. S.A.S. MS. B 645 (TS. cat.); ibid. TD/W 153.
19 *V.C.H. Suss.* i. 431–2; P.R.O., C 138/59, no. 51, m. 14; ibid. E 106/8/19, rot. 16.
20 *S.R.S.* lix, p. 122; W.S.R.O., Add. MS. 1802.
21 P.R.O., C 135/77, no. 1.
22 *S.R.S.* xlix. 16; W.S.R.O., Add. MS. 12916 (TS. cat.).
23 W.S.R.O., Add. MS. 37194 (TS. cat.).
24 Ibid. Add. MS. 12905 (TS. cat.).
25 Ibid. SP 249.
26 Ibid. Add. MS. 12902 (TS. cat.).
27 Ibid. Cap. I/28/103, deed, 1727; Cap. I/51/14, ff. 89–90; cf. ibid. Par. 202/7/6, ff. 75–6.
28 Ibid. Add. MSS. 12905, 12911 (TS. cat.).
29 Para. mainly based on ibid. Ep. I/29/225.
30 Ibid. S.A.S. MS. B 655 (TS. cat.).
31 Ibid. Add. MSS. 2068, 2194; ibid. Slindon MSS., bdle. NR 65, no. 12.
32 Ibid. Chich. city archives, AS/1, pp. 10–11.
33 Ibid. TD/W 153.
34 Ibid. IR 12, ff. 50–4; cf. ibid. Slindon MSS., bdle. NR 30, no. 6.
35 P.R.O., MAF 68/2371.
36 *Rep. Com. on Children and Women in Agric.* 86.
37 Dallaway, *Hist. W. Suss.* ii (1) (1819), 42.
38 P.R.O., IR 18/10533; W.S.R.O., TD/W 153; cf. *L. & I. Soc.* cxcv. 37.
39 W.S.R.O., PM 280.
40 P.R.O., IR 18/10533.
41 *Jnl. of Bath and W. of Eng. Soc.* 3rd ser. iii. 39–41, describing contemporary operations on the fm. in detail; cf. *Rep. Com. on Children and Women in Agric.* 87.

agricultural labour to other parishes and was a popular place of residence for lodgers. About 3 a. of glebe were let as allotments in 1867.[42]

In 1875 arable crops returned totalled c. 1,000 a., the chief being wheat, oats, and turnips and swedes; there were then 533 a. of grass, with 193 cattle, 720 sheep, and 85 pigs. The proportion of pasture to arable was slightly higher in 1909; oats were then the largest crop and numbers of cattle and pigs were greater, though there were fewer sheep.[43] The Loveys family from Devon bred cattle at Bilsham during the later 19th century and early 20th.[44] There was also a dairy herd at Cox's farm in the north-west in the early 20th century.[45] Church farm was described as a dairy farm in 1924[46] and Hobbs farm had pedigree Jerseys in 1957.[47] Wicks farm in 1924 had a Southdown flock as well as pedigree shorthorn cattle and a small Guernsey herd.[48]

In 1985 the 10 holdings listed in the parish included three of 100–200 ha. in area; two and a half times as much land was rented as was in owner occupation. Wheat remained the chief crop and stock kept were 133 beef cattle, 759 pigs, 278 sheep and lambs, and 165 poultry, chiefly hens for laying.[49] In 1991 Northwood farm of 435 a. based at Bilsham, which included much land in Climping, was almost all arable, including some oilseed rape and linseed. Wicks farm was then c. 400 a.[50] By 1996 those two farms were worked with a holding in Ford as a co-operative of c. 1,200 a. The parish was then 95 per cent arable, growing cereals, pulses, and oilseed rape. In the south-west part Drove Lane farm (250 a.) fattened continental breeds of beef cattle on 39 a. of permanent grassland, while some land near Bilsham was farmed from Flansham. There were then very few agricultural workers in the parish.[51]

MARKET GARDENING. Henry Kennett had a nursery in Burndell Road on the eastern boundary c. 1840;[52] it still flourished in 1882. Another nurseryman was listed in Yapton in the 1850s.[53] In 1909 Barnham Nurseries Ltd. worked 2 a. of small fruit and 1 a. of orchards in the north-west corner;[54] the firm acquired more land nearby after 1918.[55] Pollards Nurseries Ltd., originally from Cheshunt (Herts.), moved to a site on the south side of Lake Lane c. 1960; in 1965, when there were 4½ a. under glass, two thirds cucumbers and the rest roses, the workforce included several Italian families.[56] By 1978 glasshouses on the site totalled 29,[57] but the scale of operations had been greatly reduced by 1994.

Southdown Flowers beside Yapton Lane north of the railway line was set up in 1960, selling mixed flowers to supermarkets. In 1991 it had 30 a. and employed 132 workers there and in a site further west on Lake Lane; after bankruptcy in that year the main site was bought by a Dutch firm[58] which in 1995 had 12 a. and employed c. 50. It then grew both seasonal and round-the-year crops and imported cut flowers, supplying cut flowers and pot plants to multiple stores, garden centres, and the wholesale trade.[59]

Frampton's Nurseries, with 6 a. in Lake Lane, had revolutionized flower-growing techniques in the 1950s and 60s but went bankrupt in 1992.[60] Another nursery north of Church Lane flourished between 1978[61] or earlier and 1994. A nursery in Bilsham Road offered a landscaping service in 1991.

In 1985 45 ha. of horticultural crops were listed in the parish including 37 ha. of peas, 2 ha. of strawberries, and 3 ha. of bulbs.[62]

MILLS. John of Polingford erected a windmill in Yapton without licence in the 1270s.[63] It is not clear if that was Tortington priory's mill at Yapton recorded in 1291.[64] The mill of Bilsham mentioned in 1293[65] was perhaps the same as the windmill belonging to Arundel college, which had a manor there, in the 1390s; a century later it was vacant and by 1500 it was derelict.[66] There was a water mill on Bercourt and Wildbridge manor in 1460.[67] No later mill is recorded, presumably latterly because of the nearness of Barnham windmill.

OTHER TRADES AND INDUSTRIES. There was a butcher at Bilsham in 1335[68] and apparently a shoemaker in the parish in 1327;[69] a butcher mentioned in 1655 had c. 75 animals and at least 20 a. of land.[70] Brewers were recorded on three occasions between 1450 and 1542, including two members of the Dammer family.[71] Other trades recorded before 1800 were those of tailor,[72]

42 P.R.O., HO 107/1652, ff. 265–84, *passim*; ibid. RG 9/619, ff. 1–16, *passim*; both recording more agric. labourers living in par. than working there; *Rep. Com. on Children and Women in Agric.* 86.

43 P.R.O., MAF 68/433, 2371.

44 *Bognor Regis Post*, 5 Nov. 1966; *W. Suss. Gaz.* 10 Nov. 1966.

45 W.S.R.O., MP 2347, f. 7; *Kelly's Dir. Suss.* (1927), s.v. Barnham; cf. ibid. (1895 and later edns.).

46 W.S.R.O., SP 326.

47 *Bognor Regis Observer*, 15 Mar. 1957.

48 *The Southdown Sheep*, ed. E. Walford-Lloyd (Chich. 1924), p. xii.

49 M.A.F.F., agric. statistics, 1985.

50 Inf. from Mrs. S. Abbot, Northwood fm.; Mrs. S. Whitelock, Ford Pla.; *Bognor Regis Observer*, 15 July 1993.

51 Inf. from Mrs. S. Hocking, Drove Lane fm., and Mr. A. R. M. White, Stakers fm.

52 W.S.R.O., TD/W 153.

53 *Kelly's Dir. Suss.* (1845 and later edns.).

54 P.R.O., MAF 68/433; W.S.R.O., Add. MSS. 24178, undated plan of nurseries; 25509, applic. for certificate concerning estate duty, 1913; ibid. IR 12, f. 68; O.S. Map 6", Suss. LXII. NE., SE. (1913–14 edn.).

55 *Barnham and Eastergate Past and Present*, ed. T. Hudson et al. 9; W.S.R.O., Add. MS. 41254, facing p. 81.

56 W.S.R.O., MP 814, ff. [35–6].

57 O.S. Map 6", SU 90 SE. (1980 edn.); cf. above, pl. facing p. 251.

58 O.S. Map 6", SU 90 SE. (1980 edn.); *W. Suss. Gaz.* 20 June 1991; *Bognor Regis Observer*, 10 Oct. 1991.

59 *W. Suss. Gaz.* 16 Sept. 1993; inf. from the Director, Southdown Flowers.

60 *Bognor Regis Observer*, 9 Apr. 1992.

61 O.S. Map 6", SU 90 SE. (1980 edn.).

62 M.A.F.F., agric. statistics, 1985.

63 *Plac. de Quo Warr.* (Rec. Com.), 752; cf. P.R.O., JUST 1/917, rot. 21d.

64 *Tax. Eccl.* (Rec. Com.), 139.

65 A.C.M., M 54, m. 5; cf. *S.R.S.* x. 136.

66 Petch, 'Arundel Coll.' 306.

67 A.C.M., M 531, f. [58v.].

68 Ibid. 55, m. 1.

69 *S.R.S.* x. 136.

70 W.S.R.O., Ep. I/29/225/38.

71 Ibid. Add. MS. 2292, rot. 6; A.C.M., M 56, m. 2; 271, f. [10].

72 W.S.R.O., Add. MS. 37820 (TS. cat.); ibid. Ep. I/29/225/27, 30, 86; ibid. S.A.S. MSS. B 646 (TS. cat.); WH 267 (TS. cat.); *S.R.S.* xxviii. 114.

weaver,[73] blacksmith,[74] carpenter,[75] wheelwright,[76] mercer,[77] thatcher,[78] and wig maker.[79] A smithy erected near Berri Court in the centre of the village *c.* 1549[80] survived as a business into the 20th century.[81] Some parishioners were said to practise physic and surgery without licence in 1742.[82]

Thirty-six families out of 92 in work in 1811 were supported chiefly by non-agricultural pursuits,[83] and many different trades continued to be practised in the 19th and early 20th centuries. Others occupying sites in the village itself besides the smithy mentioned included a wheelwright's or carpenter's also near Berri Court[84] and a general store in Main Road.[85] By the early 20th century there were two bakers, two butchers, two shoemakers, and five grocers, among others, in the parish; one of the grocers was at Bilsham.[86]

Less common occupations recorded in the 19th and early 20th centuries[87] were those of wood dealer and coal and manure merchant, tea dealer, station master, signalman,[88] watch repairer, harness maker,[89] upholsterer, cycle repairer, fruiterer, and piano teacher. After 1922 Albert James ran a business making toy motor cars.[90]

There was a builder in 1845 and another from 1887, latterly in Burndell Road, who did business over a wide area:[91] in 1912 the firm also acted as decorators, contractors, and undertakers.[92] A firm of builders' merchants flourished in 1934.[93]

The chief employer in Yapton in the later 19th and earlier 20th century, however, was Sparks's engineering works.[94] John Sparks (d. 1880) from Holkham (Norf.) began an agricultural machinery business in the parish in 1856. By 1864[95] he was established on the western corner of Main and Bilsham roads, which came to be called Sparks corner, the site containing various workshops and stores.[96] By 1861 twelve men and four boys were employed, and by 1871 there were 30 men and 7 boys; many like their employer had come from Norfolk.[97] Six threshing machines were hired out in 1867[98] and ploughing machines, steam wagons, and other traction engines in the later 19th century and early 20th. By *c.* 1900 the firm also hired out steam rollers, especially to local councils in Sussex and elsewhere; in 1903–4 it dug and hauled stones for new roads laid out at Goodwood racecourse. In 1916 a repair service for all kinds of machinery was offered and pumping, irrigation, and dredging were undertaken. In addition, small implements were manufactured for farm and garden.

Part of the works site was used as brickfields by 1895[99] and Church and Hobbs farms were bought to provide further land for the same purpose.[1] At the peak of operations *c.* 800,000 bricks a year were produced. The brickyard covered 3 a. north of Burndell Road in 1924, when bricks were in great demand.[2]

After John Sparks's death in 1880 the firm was carried on by his widow Sarah (d. 1914), but disputes between their children George and Eliza led to a lawsuit in 1924 which resulted in the sale at auction of the whole concern. Thereafter the agricultural machinery business continued under Eliza's control until closure in 1931.[3] About 1932 the main engine shed was converted into the village hall;[4] by 1991 it had become a general store.

Another brickyard flourished briefly in the 1930s to serve the construction of new estates in the parish.[5]

A surgeon practised in Yapton from 1862; his successor described himself as also a physician and in 1938 there was another besides.[6] There were two doctor's and one dentist's surgeries in 1991, besides a firm of solicitors and an estate agent.

The growth of motoring and tourism from *c.* 1920 brought a motor garage and two tearooms by 1934.[7] Wicks Farmhouse was a guest house in 1993.

There were a haulage contractor and a dog-breeding business in the 1930s.[8] In the 1960s and 70s a baker in Lake Lane in the north-west corner of the parish delivered in nearby villages.[9] A full-time thatcher worked at Bilsham in 1983.[10] In 1991 a variety of shops and businesses in Main, North End, Burndell, and Bilsham roads included a second-hand tool firm, a scrap metal merchant's founded in 1953, and a joinery works. There was a small industrial estate near the Lamb inn in Bilsham Road in 1994.

In 1958 many inhabitants worked at Ford

73 W.S.R.O., Ep. I/29/225/44; *S.R.S.* xxviii. 67.
74 W.S.R.O., Add. MSS. 7076, 12886 (TS. cat.); ibid. Ep. I/29/225/33, 70, 87; *S.R.S.* xxviii. 21, 59, 180.
75 W.S.R.O., Add. MS. 7081 (TS. cat.); ibid. Ep. I/29/225/93; *S.R.S.* xxviii. 138.
76 W.S.R.O., Add. MSS. 7083–4 (TS. cat.).
77 Ibid. 7078 (TS. cat.); *S.R.S.* xlix. 48.
78 P.R.O., E 134/3 Jas. II East./16, rot. 3.
79 *S.R.S.* xxviii. 210.
80 A.C.M., M 553, m. 4; cf. W.S.R.O., Add. MS. 12919 (TS. cat.).
81 W.S.R.O., IR 12, f. 61; ibid. TD/W 153; O.S. Map 6", Suss. LXII (1880 and later edns.).
82 W.S.R.O., Ep. I/22/1 (1742).
83 *Census*, 1811.
84 W.S.R.O., Add. MSS. 7089, 7094 (TS. cat.); 13888, p. 87; ibid. IR 12, f. 62; ibid. TD/W 153.
85 *Bognor Regis Post*, 21 Mar. 1958; *Southern Wkly. News*, 30 Sept. 1955.
86 *Kelly's Dir. Suss.* (1903 and later edns.).
87 Para. based mainly on ibid. (1845 and later edns.).
88 Pike, *Bognor Dir.* (1910–11).
89 Cf. W.S.R.O., IR 12, f. 58.
90 *Bognor Regis Observer*, 22 Feb. 1963.
91 *Kelly's Dir. Suss.* (1845 and later edns.); Pike, *Dir. SW. Suss.* (1886–7); W.S.R.O., MP 2347, f. 1.
92 H. Green, *Clymping Ch. and Par.* (Chich. 1912), [24] (copy in S.A.S. libr.).
93 *Kelly's Dir. Suss.* (1934).
94 Para. based mainly on W.S.R.O., MP 3152, p. 44; 3541.
95 Ibid. Par. 225/16/1.
96 Ibid. SP 326.
97 P.R.O., RG 9/619, f. 6; RG 10/1114, f. 5v.; cf. *Rep. Com. on Children and Women in Agric.* 86.
98 *Rep. Com. on Children and Women in Agric.* 86.
99 *Kelly's Dir. Suss.* (1895 and later edns.); M. Beswick, *Brickmaking in Suss.* 226; O.S. Map 6", Suss. LXII. SE. (1899 and later edns.); W.S.R.O., IR 12, f. 58.
1 Above, manors (Yapton, Bilsham).
2 Beswick, op. cit. 226–7; W.S.R.O., MP 3541, p. 6; ibid. SP 326; cf. O.S. Map 6", Suss. LXII. SE. (1913 edn.).
3 W.S.R.O., MP 3541, pp. 5–9; ibid. SP 326.
4 Ibid. MP 3541, p. 4; ibid. Par. 225/16/1.
5 Beswick, op. cit. 227.
6 *Kelly's Dir. Suss.* (1862 and later edns.); W.S.R.O., SP 1245.
7 *Kelly's Dir. Suss.* (1934).
8 Ibid. (1934, 1938).
9 *Suss. Trade Guide* (1962), 7 (copy at C.I.H.E. libr., GY 155); personal memory.
10 *W. Suss. Gaz.* 27 Jan. 1983.

naval air station or further afield. The coastal towns also provided seasonal work in the 20th century.[11]

LOCAL GOVERNMENT. There are court rolls for Yapton manor for 1517,[12] 1545,[13] and 1551,[14] in each case for a single court. In 1551 the court was held at Arundel castle. Tenants were presented for non-repair of their houses in 1517. The court held in 1545 was also for Bercourt and Wildbridge.

Court rolls for Yapton Shulbrede manor survive for the years 1726, 1731, and 1772–1853. After 1772 there were generally one or two courts in a decade but most business was treated out of court. Only conveyancing was dealt with.[15]

Court rolls or draft court rolls survive for Bercourt and Wildbridge manor for various years between 1460 and 1553.[16] Two courts were held three weeks apart in 1460[17] but thereafter no more than one is recorded in any year. Besides conveyancing the court dealt with encroachments on the common lands, stray animals, and the repair of houses, ditches, and fences. There was a pound in the 16th century.[18]

There are court rolls for a manor or manors at Bilsham relating to four courts held between 1517 and 1553, on the last occasion at Bercourt,[19] another four between 1722 and 1790, and seven between 1810 and 1851.[20] Presentments were made in the 16th century for cutting down trees and for non-repair of a gate, but only conveyancing was dealt with after 1722 when most business was treated out of court.

There are court rolls for Yapton Rectory manor for the years 1549,[21] 1553,[22] and 1723–1846.[23] In 1553 the court was held at Bercourt. Five courts were held between 1723 and 1739; after 1770 the frequency of holding was up to seven or eight times a decade. Pound breach was presented in 1549 and the non-repair of houses in 1553 but after 1723, when most business was treated out of court, only land transactions are recorded.

Tithingmen served for 'Yapton' and Bilsham *c.* 1822.[24]

There seem always to have been two churchwardens between 1548[25] and 1672. From 1681 to 1860 there was only one but from 1861 two again served.[26] Two overseers were named in 1642[27] but only one in the 1740s. At the latter period it was common to serve as overseer and churchwarden in successive years.[28] The parish clerk in 1817 was paid a salary of £3.[29]

The parish agreed in 1746 to buy a building for use as a workhouse;[30] it presumably occupied the same site as the 19th-century workhouse near the Black Dog inn.[31] Other paupers were boarded out in 1754.[32] A Gilbert union for Yapton, Felpham, and Walberton was founded in the 1780s.[33]

In the early 1830s nearly all able-bodied labourers received an allowance or regular relief during part of the year and many the whole year.[34] Parish work on the roads, however, was not productive.[35] In 1835–6 more than 30 parishioners were helped by the vestry to emigrate to New York and Canada.[36] The workhouse ceased to be used by 1839[37] and was later let as cottages.[38]

A parish pound was constructed *c.* 1842 and was moved to a new site in 1852.[39]

After 1894 the parish council managed successive playing fields in Yapton.[40]

From 1835 Yapton was in Westhampnett union,[41] later rural district; in 1933 it was transferred to Chichester rural district[42] and in 1974 to Arun district.

CHURCH. There was apparently a church at Yapton in 1086,[43] which before 1255 was a prebend of Arundel's minster church. In 1255 it was appropriated to Sées abbey (Orne),[44] passing to its English priory of Arundel and in 1380, with the priory's other possessions, to Arundel college.[45] A vicarage was ordained in 1255.[46] The living was united to Walberton between 1753 and 1875[47] and to Ford from 1875.[48] In 1985 Climping was added to make the benefice of Climping and Yapton with Ford, the parishes remaining distinct.[49]

At the ordination of the vicarage in 1255 the bishop reserved the right of collation.[50] The Crown and the dean and chapter of Chichester presented during vacancy in 1415 and 1430

11 'Our Village within Living Memory' (TS. 1958, in possession of Mrs. S. Hocking, Yapton).
12 A.C.M., M 819. A ct. bk. of 1448 × 1455 was too fragile to be used: ibid. 530.
13 P.R.O., SC 2/205/53, rot. 5.
14 A.C.M., M 829.
15 W.S.R.O., Add. MS. 13888, *passim.*
16 A.C.M., M 28, rot. 6; 31, rot. 6; 278, f. [14]; 282, rot. 1d.; 314, rot. 7; 531, ff. [58 and v., 73v.]; 553, m. 4; 859, rott. 4d., 11; cf. above, this section.
17 A.C.M., M 531, f. [58 and v.].
18 Ibid. 282, rot. 1d.; 859, rot. 11.
19 Ibid. 31, rot. 6d.; 553, m. 4; 819; 829. A ct. bk. of 1448 × 1455 was too fragile to be used: ibid. 530.
20 W.S.R.O., Add. MS. 13888, *passim.*
21 A.C.M., M 553, m. 4.
22 Ibid. 31, rot. 6d.
23 W.S.R.O., Add. MS. 13888, *passim*; cf. P.R.O., C 2/Jas. I/E 2/65.
24 E.S.R.O., QCR/2/1/EW 2 (47).
25 W.S.R.O., Ep. I/86/20, f. 16v.
26 B.L. Add. MS. 39359, ff. 152–7.
27 *S.R.S.* v. 202.
28 W.S.R.O., Par. 225/2/6, pp. 2–4.
29 Ibid. Ep. I/41/65.
30 Ibid. Par. 225/2/6, p. 5.
31 Ibid. MP 3427, f. [3]; ibid. NC/C/SCU/WD 20; sketchbk. of Bognor and dist. by Wm. Colliss, p. [12], in possession of Mr. K. Scutt, Bognor Regis.
32 W.S.R.O., Par. 225/2/6, p. 77.
33 *Suss. Poor Law Rec.* p. xx; *Felpham by the Sea*, ed. T. & A. Hudson, 42.
34 *Rep. Com. Poor Laws*, H.C. 44, p. 536 (1834), xxviii.
35 *1st Rep. Poor Law Com.* H.C. 500, p. 179 (1835), xxxv.
36 *Sel. Cttee. on Agric.* H.C. 465, p. 194 (1836), viii (2); *Suss. Family Historian*, viii. 283; W.S.R.O., Par. 225/12/1, ff. 2–3 (TS. cat.); Par. 225/38/1.
37 W.S.R.O., Par. 202/54/3.
38 e.g. Pike, *Dir. SW. Suss.* (1886–7).
39 W.S.R.O., Par. 225/12/1, ff. 7, 21v. (TS. cat.).
40 *W. Suss. Gaz.* 23 Feb. 1995.
41 *Suss. Poor Law Rec.* 53.
42 Youngs, *Guide to Local Admin. Units of Eng.* i. 526.
43 *V.C.H. Suss.* i. 433; cf. above, manors (Yapton).
44 *S.R.S.* xlvi, p. 368; cf. above, Arundel, church.
45 *V.C.H. Suss.* ii. 108–9.
46 *S.R.S.* xlvi, p. 368.
47 *Lond. Gaz.* 14 May 1875, pp. 2570–1.
48 Ibid. 10 Aug. 1875, pp. 3960–1.
49 Inf. from Chich. Dioc. Regy.
50 *S.R.S.* xlvi, p. 368.

respectively,[51] and from 1501 the bishop always collated except during vacancy and on two occasions when the archbishop of Canterbury exercised the patronage.[52] After the union of livings in 1985 the bishop (as former patron of both Yapton and Ford) was to collate on two occasions in three and the Lord Chancellor (as former patron of Climping) to present on the third.[53]

The vicarage was valued at £5 6*s*. 8*d*. in 1291[54] and at £7 11*s*. in 1535.[55] In the 1570s the living was let.[56] By 1724 the real value was £43 16*s*. 1*d*.[57] and in 1750 it was £60;[58] the average net income of Yapton and Walberton together, however, was £468 *c*. 1830.[59]

A vicarage house existed in 1255,[60] perhaps standing south or south-west of the church as apparently later.[61] In 1573 it was in decay for lack of thatching,[62] and by 1662 most of the building had collapsed through neglect[63] so that a new vicarage house was built *c*. 1664.[64] After the union of the living with Walberton it was pulled down in 1757–8.[65] Incumbents of Yapton with Ford from 1875 at first lived in rented housing[66] but *c*. 1905 a new vicarage was provided through alterations and additions to a house in North End Road.[67] That was later sold, and a new house south of Church Lane was bought in 1990 for the incumbent of the benefice of Climping and Yapton with Ford.[68]

There were 21 a. of glebe divided between four locations in 1255.[69] In the early 17th century there were 22 a. in all: an orchard next to the house, 12 a. called Simpoles in the eastern angle of Burndell and Bilsham roads, and 9 a. unlocated.[70] The last named land was exchanged in 1750 for 11 a. elsewhere,[71] and the site of the demolished vicarage house with its garden and a croft was exchanged before 1822 for 3 a. in Yapton Lane, Walberton.[72] Other land had been exchanged for land in Walberton by 1838[73] so that only 12 a. remained in Yapton *c*. 1840: the close called Simpoles, now reckoned as 9 a., and 3 a. by the Walberton boundary.[74] There were 22½ a. in all belonging to the living of Yapton in the two parishes in 1887.[75]

At the ordination of the vicarage in 1255 most of Yapton's tithes were settled on the vicar except for those of corn and pulses.[76] Some corn tithes were payable to the vicar in 1615.[77] By 1841, however, the vicar's entitlement was all the small tithes, hay tithes from part of the parish, and half the hay tithes from the rest, besides all the tithes of 'holibreads', i.e. small portions of various fields around the parish.[78]

Tithe portions also belonged to others from the Middle Ages. The tithes at Wildbridge and elsewhere which Boxgrove priory had in 1253[79] seem to be represented by those later payable to Walberton rectory and vicarage, since Walberton rectory had belonged to Boxgrove.[80] Similarly, Syon abbey (Mdx.) as successor to Sées abbey (Orne) had both great and small tithes from land at Wildbridge in 1473,[81] which descended with Eastergate manor farm;[82] in 1649 the portion was said to comprise corn tithes from 20 a.[83] 'Trynebarn rectory', representing tithes belonging to Tortington priory from 1291 or earlier, is discussed above.[84]

At commutation in 1841 the vicar received £188 6*s*. 9*d*. as vicar of Yapton and £5 2*s*. 6*d*. as vicar of Walberton; the bishop £10 5*s*.; Inigo Thomas £396 for corn tithes from 774 a., presumably including those of Trynebarn rectory, besides £6 for corn tithes from the vicarial glebe; and the dean and chapter of Chichester and various individuals £232 13*s*. 11*d*. in all for corn tithes from their own or others' lands.[85]

In the later Middle Ages the pastoral needs of the southern part of the parish were served by a chapel at Bilsham.[86] The vicar of Yapton resided in 1440[87] and 1563[88] and the vicar from 1558 was a former chantry priest.[89] A successor in 1571 was presented for negligence in saying services.[90] John Curtis, vicar from 1575, also held Eastergate;[91] he was a licensed preacher, though the bishop and others preached at Yapton too in his time.[92] Hugh Roberts, who succeeded him in 1596, was also a preacher[93] and clearly had Puritan sympathies, eschewing a surplice for the celebration of communion, which could be received standing or sitting rather than kneeling, and which he refused in 1622 to two parishioners who knew none of the commandments.[94] Many outsiders, evidently sympathizers, attended Yapton church at that period.[95] In 1623

51 B.L. Add. MS. 39350, f. 230 and v.; cf. *S.R.S.* xlvi, p. 368.
52 B.L. Add. MS. 39350, ff. 232–7.
53 Inf. from Chich. Dioc. Regy.
54 *Tax. Eccl.* (Rec. Com.), 135.
55 *Valor Eccl.* (Rec. Com.), i. 316.
56 W.S.R.O., Ep. I/23/2, f. 11; Ep. I/23/4, f. 31.
57 *S.R.S.* lxxviii. 74.
58 Ibid. lxxiii. 300.
59 *Rep. Com. Eccl. Revenues*.
60 *S.R.S.* xlvi, p. 368; cf. *Inq. Non.* (Rec. Com.), 368.
61 W.S.R.O., Par. 202/7/16; Par. 225/6/5.
62 Ibid. Ep. I/23/2, f. 10v.
63 Ibid. Ep. I/22/1 (1662).
64 B.L. Add. MS. 39368, f. 1589.
65 W.S.R.O., Ep. I/22/1 (1758); Ep. I/40/12.
66 Ibid. Ep. I/22A/1 (1884).
67 Ibid. Par. 225/6/9–10.
68 *W. Suss. Gaz.* 23 May 1990.
69 *S.R.S.* xlvi, p. 368; cf. *Inq. Non.* (Rec. Com.), 368.
70 W.S.R.O., Ep. I/25/1 (1615, 1635).
71 Ibid. Par. 225/6/4.
72 Ibid. Par. 225/6/5; cf. ibid. Ep. I/40/49.
73 Ibid. Ep. I/22/2 (1838).
74 Ibid. TD/W 153.
75 *Glebe Lands Return*, H.C. 307, p. 32 (1887), lxiv.
76 *S.R.S.* xlvi, p. 368, mentioning all the tithes except those of corn and pulses; but cf. below, this section.
77 W.S.R.O., Ep. I/25/1 (1615).
78 P.R.O., IR 18/10533. For holibreads cf. *V.C.H. Suss.* vi (1), 62.
79 *S.R.S.* lix, p. 188.
80 W.S.R.O., Ep. I/25/1 (1635), Walberton; ibid. TD/W 153; *S.R.S.* xx. 457; above, Walberton, manor (rectory).
81 P.R.O., SC 11/653; above, Eastergate, manor.
82 *S.R.S.* xlvi, p. 203; lviii, pp. 48, 139, 226; W.S.R.O., Add. MS. 46667 (TS. cat.); ibid. Cap. I/28/59–60, lease, 1830.
83 Dallaway & Cartwright, *Hist. W. Suss.* ii (1) (1832), 74 n.
84 Above, manors (Trynebarn rectory).
85 W.S.R.O., TD/W 153; cf. ibid. Add. MS. 11796; ibid. Slindon MSS., bdles. NR 49, no. 2; NR 63, no. 5; *S.R.S.* xx. 305. The rector of Burton near Petworth received £13 15*s*. for corn tithes from 30 a., for what reason is not clear.
86 *S.R.S.* xlvi, p. 311; below, this section.
87 B.L. Add. MS. 39350, f. 227.
88 *S.A.C.* lxi. 112.
89 Ibid. cxvi. 284; B.L. Add. MS. 39350, f. 233.
90 W.S.R.O., Ep. I/23/1, f. 56v.
91 B.L. Add. MS. 39350, f. 233v.
92 W.S.R.O., Ep. I/23/5, f. 35.
93 B.L. Add. MS. 39350, f. 234.
94 *S.R.S.* xlix. 34, 57.
95 Ibid. 48.

a parishioner was reported as saying that church attendance on Sundays was no longer important since 'every day ... is a Christian's Sabbath'.[96] A Puritan conventicle was recorded in the parish in 1603.[97]

The vicar in 1662 was said to come only to collect his tithes; there was then a curate with a stipend of £30. His successor but one, however, served for 50 years from 1669. Two other vicars in the earlier 18th century held Walberton, the second being also the bishop's chaplain.[98] In 1724 a Sunday service with sermon was held alternately in morning and evening and communion was celebrated four times a year with 40–50 communicants.[99]

During the period of the union with Walberton, 1753–1875, Yapton was often served by curates.[1] In 1838 morning and afternoon services were on alternate Sundays in the two parishes,[2] but by 1844 the new vicar T. S. L. Vogan had introduced two Sunday services at Yapton with monthly communion.[3] Attendances on Census Sunday in 1851 were 100 in the morning and 150 in the afternoon, on each occasion with 64 Sunday schoolchildren besides.[4] A string band had played in the church in the 1780s[5] and then or later also a bassoon.[6] By 1872 an organ had been installed and there was a paid choir.[7]

In 1884, when services were held alternately at Yapton and Ford, congregations were *c.* 150 in the morning and 180–200 in the afternoon. Communion was then celebrated *c.* 33 times a year with an average of 16–18 communicants[8] and by 1903 it was weekly.[9] About 1910, when there was an assistant curate, choral evensong was held on Wednesdays in winter.[10] Two or more services were held on Sundays in 1994 after the union with Climping.

The church of *ST. MARY* (the dedication is implied by 1555)[11] consists of chancel, aisled nave, south-west tower in continuation of the south aisle, and west porch; the nave and aisles are covered by a single roof which comes down to little more than 3 ft. (1 metre) above the level of the churchyard. The building is chiefly of flint rubble and brick with ashlar dressings and the tower, which leans markedly, is shingled.[12]

The tower and the arcades are of *c.* 1200; the north arcade has four bays and the south arcade only three, the four octagonal piers and one circular one, which are of different heights, having capitals of varied design. Masonry at the base of the tower, however, may be earlier,[13] and the tower's position in the angle between nave and aisle suggests that it may be a fragment of an older building. A window of *c.* 1100 at the east end of the south aisle may also be from that earlier church. The spacious chancel was built in the earlier 13th century and has lancet windows and a contemporary priest's door. The chancel arch with fluted corbels of a kind also found at Climping was enlarged a little later. The quatrefoil windows in the south aisle appear to be 14th-century, and the west window, the timber-framed west porch, and the crown-post roof of the nave are 15th-century.

In 1617, when the tower was already beginning to lean dangerously, it was recommended to build buttresses to support it;[14] they are of brick and re-used Caen stone, some of it moulded. Large dormer windows were inserted *c.* 1670,[15] perhaps to light a gallery, and the roof was ceiled in 1726.[16] The chancel was rebuilt apparently in the later 18th century[17] and was restored between 1902 and 1905, when the east window dating from the time of that rebuilding was replaced with lancets and the east gable reconstructed;[18] the work on the second occasion was done by the vicar and churchwardens, not the rector.[19] The rest of the church was restored in 1870–1, a west gallery being removed and a new west window put in.[20] An altar was installed at the east end of the south aisle in 1905.[21] Fire damaged the tower in 1909.[22]

The font, on a circular base, is 11th- or 12th-century; its cylindrical bowl of Sussex marble has continuous arcading with a sword-shaped cross in each opening, and a chevron frieze above. There are traces of medieval painting, clearest on the north wall of the nave. Monuments include a 13th-century coffin slab and a memorial to Stephen Roe, founder of the village school. Of the four bells one was mid 14th-century, another of 1617, and two of 1712; all were recast after the fire of 1909,[23] the rim of the medieval one being converted into a candelabrum. The plate includes a communion cup, two patens, and a flagon, all of silver and of various dates between 1657 and 1716.[24] A new pulpit and high pews were inserted in 1765[25] and replaced in 1871.[26] The existing pulpit is of 1905.[27]

The registers begin in 1538.[28] Registrars were appointed in 1656 and 1659.[29]

96 Ibid. 66.
97 S. B. Babbage, *Puritanism and Ric. Bancroft*, 192.
98 B.L. Add. MS. 39350, ff. 235–7; W.S.R.O., Ep. I/22/1 (1662, 1742, 1758).
99 *S.R.S.* lxxviii. 74.
1 B.L. Add. MS. 39359, ff. 155–6; W.S.R.O., Ep. I/22/1 (1758); Ep. I/22A/2 (1844, 1865).
2 W.S.R.O., Ep. I/22/2 (1838).
3 Ibid. Ep. I/22A/2 (1844); B.L. Add. MS. 39350, f. 237.
4 *S.R.S.* lxxv, p. 154.
5 W.S.R.O., Par. 225/2/6, pp. 46, 52.
6 *S.A.C.* lx. 33.
7 W.S.R.O., Par. 225/12/2, f. 15v.
8 Ibid. Ep. I/22A/1 (1884); above, Ford, church.
9 W.S.R.O., Ep. I/22A/2 (1903).
10 Pike, *Bognor Dir.* (1910–11).
11 *S.R.S.* xlv. 423. For the bldg. in general, Anon., *Yapton and its Ch.* (Littlehampton, 1964).
12 Cf. W.S.R.O., Ep. I/41/65.
13 Ibid. Par. 225/4/3.
14 B.L. Add. MS. 39350, f. 238.
15 Ibid. Add. MSS. 5674, f. 37, illus. above, pl. facing p. 234; 39350, f. 239; *Suss. Chs.: the Sharpe Colln.* ed. V. Smith (Lewes, [1979]).
16 B.L. Add. MS. 5699, f. 136v.
17 Dallaway, *Hist. W. Suss.* ii (1) (1819), 45; *Suss. Chs.: the Sharpe Colln.*; cf. W.S.R.O., Par. 225/2/6, pp. 68–9.
18 *Chich. Dioc. Gaz.* (1903), 60–1; B.L. Add. MS. 39350, f. 239; W.S.R.O., Ep. I/22A/2 (1903); ibid. Par. 225/4/6.
19 Cf. W.S.R.O., Par. 225/12/2, f. 78v.
20 Ibid. Par. 225/4/2; B.L. Add. MS. 39364, f. 317.
21 W.S.R.O., Par. 225/4/7.
22 Ibid. Par. 225/12/2, f. 77; *Suss. Daily News*, 15 Mar. 1909.
23 Elphick, *Bells*, 38, 418; *S.A.C.* xcv. 149.
24 *S.A.C.* liii. 238.
25 W.S.R.O., Ep. I/22A/2 (1844); ibid. Par. 225/2/6, p. 26.
26 B.L. Add. MS. 39364, f. 317.
27 *Chich. Dioc. Gaz.* (1906), 68.
28 W.S.R.O., Par. 225/1 (TS. cat.).
29 Ibid. Par. 225/1/1/2, f. 1 (TS. cat.).

The chapel at Bilsham consisted of a single undivided space and was originally of flint with sandstone dressings.[30] It was built in the 14th century, windows of that date remaining in the north and east walls as well as a north doorway. It seems to have fallen out of use by 1551.[31] By *c.* 1840 it was used as cottages, the south wall having been rebuilt in brick.[32] About 1878 it was restored: post-medieval windows on the south side were replaced by plain two-light ones with brick surrounds, the south doorway was rebuilt, also in brick, and a new tiebeam roof was inserted to replace the lost medieval one.[33] Thereafter the building was used for storage[34] until conversion as a house after 1972.[35]

NONCONFORMITY. John Trunell the elder, who was detaining the cope, chalice lid, and silver pyx in 1571,[36] may have been a Catholic sympathizer.

Puritan leanings in the parish in the early 17th century are discussed above.[37] The Lutter or Luttard family were Baptists in the 1660s;[38] in 1669 John Lutter was described as a Presbyterian and there were *c.* 6 members of that sect.[39] Six Nonconformists were listed in 1676[40] and one Quaker family in 1724.[41]

An Independent, later Congregational,[42] congregation existed from the mid 19th century and perhaps from 1830.[43] A first-floor room in the former workhouse was registered for worship in 1846[44] and another room on a different site in 1850; the registering minister on the second occasion was George MacDonald of Arundel.[45] On Census Sunday in 1851 the evening congregation totalled 24, and 42 children attended Sunday school in the afternoon.[46] Some Dissenters from Barnham attended in 1856.[47] In 1865 the chief shopkeeper of the village led the congregation and the minister apparently came from Littlehampton.[48]

A purpose-built chapel of flint, brick, and stone was erected in 1861 at the expense of Henry Bateman.[49] In 1884 it was said to be attended by two well-to-do families, a few poor parishioners, and a fair number of outsiders. The minister then did not reside[50] but in 1886 and *c.* 1910 he occupied the house attached to the chapel.[51] At the latter date two Sunday services and a Sunday school were held.[52]

In 1991 the congregation was known as Yapton Evangelical free church.[53] The manse had been demolished at some time after 1972 and meetings were then held in the village hall as the chapel was too small.[54]

EDUCATION. Three licensed teachers were recorded between 1579 and 1606.[55] The vicar Edward Burnand (d. 1719) was said to have taught in the church during the whole of his 50-year ministry.[56] There were other unlicensed teachers in the mid 18th century.[57]

In 1766 Stephen Roe, a native of Yapton buried in Islington (Mdx.), devised £20 for teaching poor boys and girls.[58] By 1833, when his school had become a National school, 20 pupils were taught free and another 14 paid fees,[59] but in 1846–7 there were only 20 in all, other Yapton children going to school in Walberton.[60] The schoolmaster was appointed by the vicar and parish officers in 1838.[61]

A new school was built in North End Road, partly through subscriptions, in 1864[62] and was enlarged in the 1880s when a separate infant class was started.[63] By then there were three teachers.[64] In 1872 as well as the income from the Roe charity and voluntary subscriptions finance was received from school pence, the vicar making up the shortfall.[65] By 1874–5 there was also a government grant.[66] In 1867 pupils included children from adjacent parishes.[67] Average attendance was 61 in 1873[68] and 84 in 1884–5.[69] Thereafter it continued to rise, to 129 in 1893–4,[70] 152 in 1900–1,[71] and 181 including 62 infants in 1905–6;[72] after falling in

30 Ibid. PD 1700; *S.A.C.* xliv. 165–6.
31 Dallaway, *Hist. W. Suss.* ii (1) (1819), 45, citing an untraced source.
32 W.S.R.O., TD/W 153; cf. *S.A.C.* xii. 104; xxviii. 200; Lower, *Hist. Suss.* ii. 278.
33 *S.A.C.* xxviii. 200; W.S.R.O., PD 1700.
34 W.S.R.O., IR 12, f. 51; ibid. PH 5117; G. Young, *Cottage in the Fields*, 173 and facing p. 216; Nairn & Pevsner, *Suss.* 104.
35 Sale cat. 1972 (copy at N.M.R.); W.S.R.O., PH 4579–80; 13150, ff. 41–3; above, pl. facing p. 250.
36 W.S.R.O., Ep. I/23/1, ff. 26v., 57.
37 Above, church.
38 W.S.R.O., Ep. I/22/1 (1662); *S.R.S.* xlix. 129.
39 *Orig. Rec. of Early Nonconf.* ed. G. L. Turner, i. 28; ii. 1026. He is wrongly identified as a Catholic recusant at *Miscellanea*, v (Cath. Rec. Soc. vi), 319.
40 *Compton Census*, ed. Whiteman, 144.
41 *S.R.S.* lxxviii. 74.
42 *Kelly's Dir. Suss.* (1862); O.S. Map 6", Suss. LXII (1880 edn.).
43 P.R.O., RG 31/1, Chich. archdeac. no. 159.
44 Ibid. no. 249; W.S.R.O., MP 2593.
45 P.R.O., RG 31/1, Chich. archdeac. no. 259; *S.R.S.* lxxv, p. 155; cf. above, Arundel, protestant nonconf. (Presbyterians and Independents).
46 *S.R.S.* lxxv, p. 155.
47 W.S.R.O., Ep. I/22A/2 (1856), Barnham.
48 Ibid. Ep. I/22A/2 (1865).
49 *Pioneers Still: Suss. Cong. Union and Home Missionary Soc. 1849–1949*, 14; *Kelly's Dir. Suss.* (1862); date on bldg.; above, pl. facing p. 250.
50 W.S.R.O., Ep. I/22A/1 (1884).
51 Pike, *Dir. SW. Suss.* (1886–7); W.S.R.O., IR 12, f. 56; cf. ibid. Ep. I/22A/2 (1903).
52 Pike, *Bognor Dir.* (1910–11).
53 Cf. D. R. Elleray, *Victorian Chs. of Suss.* 85.
54 Local inf.
55 *S.N.Q.* xiv. 271; W.S.R.O., STC III/C, f. 23; STC III/E, ff. 25v., 103v.; cf. ibid. Ep. I/23/5, f. 35.
56 B.L. Add. MSS. 5699, f. 136; 39350, f. 236.
57 W.S.R.O., Ep. I/22/1 (1742, 1758).
58 Mon. in ch.; *2nd Rep. Com. Char.* 188.
59 *Educ. Enq. Abstract*, 985.
60 Nat Soc. *Inquiry, 1846–7*, Suss. 16–17.
61 W.S.R.O., Ep. I/22/2 (1838).
62 Ibid. Par. 225/25/1/10 (TS. cat.); Par. 225/25/2, statement of accts. of Yapton National sch. 1863; accts. of Yapton National sch. 1864; P.R.O., ED 7/123.
63 W.S.R.O., Par. 225/25/2, list of subs. towards cost of bldg. infants' sch.
64 *Kelly's Dir. Suss.* (1882).
65 P.R.O., ED 7/123.
66 *Public Elem. Schs. 1875–6*, 270–1.
67 *Rep. Com. on Children and Women in Agric.* 86.
68 P.R.O., ED 7/123.
69 *Rep. Educ. Cttee. 1885–6*, 602–3.
70 Ibid. *1893–4*, 985.
71 *Schs. Parl. Grants, 1900–1*, 246.
72 *Public Elem. Schs. 1907*, 642.

the 1910s and 20s it rose again to 162 in 1931–2 and 201 in 1937–8.[73]

The school was remodelled in 1960–1[74] and extended in 1974.[75] It was called Yapton C.E. controlled school in 1959.[76] The Roe charity produced £18.48 for educational purposes in 1990.[77] There were 273 children on the roll in 1993.[78]

Two other day schools with 20 children existed in 1819[79] and in 1833 there were four: one with 16 pupils of both sexes and three infant schools with 25 pupils in all.[80] A boys' boarding school was recorded *c.* 1832,[81] a private girls' school at Yapton Lodge in 1882, and a boys and girls' preparatory school apparently at the same building in 1938.[82] A school attached to the Congregational chapel was apparently well attended in 1856[83] and had 90–100 pupils, two thirds of whom came from other parishes, in 1884.[84] On the same site later was the Kingsway school, of Evangelical Christian character, which had *c.* 30 pupils in 1991[85] but had gone by 1994.

An evening school in the 1860s had *c.* 20 pupils;[86] another was held occasionally *c.* 1880.[87] In 1958 older children went to school at Westergate in Aldingbourne or elsewhere.[88]

CHARITIES FOR THE POOR. Before 1724 Mrs. Madgwick, lady of Bercourt manor, gave 13*s.* 4*d.* a year, half for the poor and half for a Good Friday sermon.[89]

Stephen Roe by will dated 1766 left £16 a year to support seven householders or ex-householders not receiving alms. About 1835 £15 was distributed[90] and in 1867–8 £17 15*s.* 11*d.* in money.[91] The income was £14.68 in 1990.[92] By the last date the parish council administered the fund.[93]

73 *Educ. List 21, 1914*, 526; *1922*, 344; *1932*, 389; *1938*, 404.
74 *Educ. in W. Suss. 1959–64* (W. Suss. C.C.), 162.
75 *Chich. Observer*, 13 Sept. 1974.
76 W.S.R.O., Par. 225/25/9, plans for sch. 1959.
77 Char. Com. files.
78 *Dir. of W. Suss. Educ. Service* (1993).
79 *Educ. of Poor Digest*, 974.
80 *Educ. Enq. Abstract*, 985.
81 Pigot, *Nat. Com. Dir.* (1832–4), 1051.
82 *Kelly's Dir. Suss.* (1882, 1938).
83 W.S.R.O., Ep. I/22A/2 (1856), Barnham.
84 Ibid. Ep. I/22A/1 (1884).
85 Local inf.
86 *Rep. Com. on Children and Women in Agric.* 86.
87 W.S.R.O., Ep. I/22A/1 (1884).
88 'Our Village within Living Memory' (TS. 1958, in possession of Mrs. S. Hocking, Yapton).
89 *S.R.S.* lxxviii. 74; *30th Rep. Com. Char.* 639.
90 *30th Rep. Com. Char.* 639.
91 *Char. Digest Suss.* H.C. 433 (20), p. 31 (1867–8), lii (2).
92 Char. Com. files.
93 Local inf.

INDEX

NOTE. A page number in italic denotes an illustration on that page or a plate facing that page. The pages containing the substantive history of a parish are set in bold type. A page number followed by *n* is a reference only to the footnotes on that page.

CORRIGENDA TO VOLUMES VI (PARTS 1–3) AND VII

Earlier lists of corrigenda will be found in Volume VI (3), 222, and *Index to Volumes I–IV, VII, and IX*, 141–4

Vol. VI (1),	page	187*b*,	line 12, *omit* 'which'
Vol. VI (3),	page	141*b*,	lines 8–7 from end, *omit* ', Secretary of State to Queen Elizabeth,'
,,	,,	156*b*,	lines 5–4 from end, *for* ', despite his official position, was' *read* 'harboured'
,,	,,	209*a*,	line 2 from end, *add* 135
,,	,,	209*a*,	last line, *delete* 151
Vol. VII,	page	177*a*,	line 25, *for* '1872' *read* '1862'
,,	,,	177,	note 90, *add* 'The date of the botanist's death is wrongly given; cf. *D.N.B.*'